OSW

OFFICIAL SCRABBLE® WORDS

OSW

OFFICIAL SCRABBLE® WORDS

GUILD PUBLISHING

LONDON · NEW YORK · SYDNEY · TORONTO

Typeset by Waddie & Co. Ltd., Edinburgh.

Printed in Great Britain by Richard Clay Ltd, Bungay, Suffolk.

Preface

At last we have the book which Scrabble® players have been wanting for many years. *Official Scrabble® Words (OSW)* is the definitive work which will save family arguments in social games and enable challenges to be dealt with quickly and efficiently in Scrabble Clubs and tournaments.

J W Spear & Sons and Chambers have had a close relationship going back to when the UK Scrabble Club movement adopted *Chambers 20th Century Dictionary* as its reference work. *Chambers* (now published as *Chambers English Dictionary*) is loved by Scrabble players throughout most of the English-speaking world because of the rich fund of useful Scrabble words it contains.

Official Scrabble Words uses this source so it almost certainly contains your pet Scrabble words and thousands of others. *OSW* is complementary to *Chambers English Dictionary* which remains the reference work when you want to check a definition.

The task of adjudicating on well over 150,000 words was a mammoth one. I would like to thank the main adjudicating committee, the groups of volunteer Scrabble players who acted as the initial adjudicators (all named on p. vi) and, of course, Catherine Schwarz and her colleagues at Chambers for the dedicated way they handled the many problems. I also thank the members of the Australian Scrabble Players' Association who have made their contribution in helping Chambers' editorial team.

I am sure that the work they all have done will add to the enjoyment and satisfaction that you obtain from playing Scrabble.

Francis A Spear
Chairman and Chief Executive
J W Spear & Sons PLC

Main Committee:
Darryl Francis, *London Scrabble League*
Leonard Hodge, *Scrabble Club Co-ordinator and Chairman*
Angus Macdonald, *Mapperley Scrabble Club*
Philip Nelkon, *London Scrabble League*
Allan Simmons, *Postal Scrabble Club*

Initial Adjudicating Committee:
Steve Ablitt-Jones *Croydon SC*
Olive Behan *Glenthorn SC*
Jackie Fallows *Isle of Wight SC*
Raye Green *Leicester SC*
Mary Grylls *Grantham SC*
Ian Gucklhorn *London Scrabble League*
Dorothy Harrison *Plymouth SC*
Josef Kollar *Hythe SC*
Kevin Morris *Bristol SC*
Jane McLeman *Frodsham SC*
Norman Smith *Edinburgh SC*
Roy Upton *Derby SC*
Mike Willis *Milton Keynes SC*

The publishers wish to acknowledge the computing help of
Peter Schwarz in the compilation of *Official Scrabble® Words*.

The book was prepared on a Sirius microcomputer using
programs run under the UCSD-p system and the large-file
editor ASE. The final text was sorted on the Edinburgh
University Multi-Access System (EMAS).

Introduction

Official Scrabble® Words is the final authority on allowed Scrabble® words. It is based on the 1988 edition of *Chambers English Dictionary*. All words listed in that dictionary are permitted in Scrabble except:

> those only spelt with an initial capital letter;
> abbreviations;
> prefixes and suffixes;
> those requiring apostrophes and hyphens.

Official Scrabble Words fully takes account of the 1988 revision of the rules used for the National Scrabble Championship and other official Scrabble events. The differences between the new, revised rules and the earlier rules can be summarised here:

> foreign words are now allowed;
> names of letters and letter sounds are now allowed;
> obsolete words and words from the works of Shakespeare, Spenser and Milton are now allowed;
> adverbs are only allowed if in *Chambers*.

Let us look at these differences in slightly more detail, as well as at the approaches that have been taken towards certain groups of words.

Foreign words

Foreign words appearing in *Chambers English Dictionary* have been included in *Official Scrabble Words*. Where a specific plural form appears in *Chambers*, we have included only that form, but where no plural is shown in the dictionary, we have used our judgment, and the appropriate plural form has been included. In some instances, this will be a foreign plural; in others, it will be an English plural (usually the addition of an -S); occasionally both types of plural will be included. Do be aware that not all plural forms in *OSW* are explicitly shown in *Chambers*.

Letters and letter sounds

Names of letters and letter sounds appearing in *Chambers English Dictionary* are included in *Official Scrabble Words*. The reasons for barring these from the National Scrabble Championship and other official events were never clear, and these words are now welcomed back into the realm of valid Scrabble words. This allows the inclusion here of a flurry of words such as MU, NU and XI, as well as AITCH, VAU and YPSILON. Their plural forms are also included.

Obsolete words

Obsolete words are included in *Official Scrabble Words*, along with many of their relevant inflected forms (such as plurals and verb inflections). We have included plurals of most obsolete nouns. We have included verb inflections of many, but certainly not all, obsolete verbs. We have not included comparative and superlative forms of obsolete adjectives. We have not included derivatives of obsolete words, unless explicitly shown in *Chambers*. (For example, BROACH and BROACHER are both allowable words, and BROCH is in the dictionary as an obsolete spelling of BROACH – so BROACH, BROACHER and BROCH are all allowable, but we have not included the assumed BROCHER.)

Words marked in *Chambers* as being from the works of Shakespeare, Spenser and Milton have been treated in the same way as obsolete words.

Adverbs

Adverbs have only been included in *Official Scrabble Words* if they are included in *Chambers*. No attempt has been made to include adverbial forms which are not explicitly shown in the dictionary.

Users of *OSW* may find it helpful if we outline our thinking on certain other groups of words, as well as on the word lengths included in the book.

Plurals

With very few exceptions, we have included in *Official Scrabble Words* the plurals of all nouns. Plural forms have been shown for all nouns ending in -ISM, -ITY and -NESS. While these plurals may be little used in regular English, all are available for use if needed in the English language. We have also included the plural forms of chemicals, chemical elements, minerals, man-made materials, natural materials, fibres, drugs, gases, rocks, oils, vitamins, enzymes, diseases, illnesses, and the like.

Comparatives and superlatives

We have included a wide range of comparatives and superlatives in *Official Scrabble Words*. We have considered the possible comparative and superlative forms of all adjectives in *OSW*, and we have based our final selection on a range of criteria. These have included commonness or familiarity of the adjective, number of syllables, meaning, and whether the adjective is dialect, obsolete or foreign. We also took into account the euphony of the -ER and -EST forms, current usage, and listings in other dictionaries. We cannot say that we have applied a mechanical formula in deciding which comparatives and superlatives to include. We have allowed the -IER and -IEST forms of many adjectives ending in -Y, but by no means all. We have not excluded the comparatives and superlatives of all adjectives of three syllables or more – some have been included. We have not excluded the comparatives and superlatives of all adjectives ending with certain specific groups of letters, such as -ATE, -ENT, -ETE and -ID. We have certainly included some of these comparatives and superlatives. Overall we think you will find our selection of comparatives and superlatives more than adequate for Scrabble games, whether played at a cosy social level or a cut-throat championship level.

Interjections

Interjections are treated not as nouns, but as parts of speech which do not permit plurals. In *Official Scrabble Words*, an interjection has no inflected forms, unless explicitly indicated in *Chambers*. A plural is only allowed if an interjection is also shown to be a noun; and verb forms are only allowed if an interjection is shown to be a verb. Some examples:

> AH, QUOTHA and UM are interjections only,
> so no inflected forms are allowed;

EH is an interjection and a verb, so the inflected verb forms **EHS, EHED** and **EHING** are allowed;

OOH is an interjection, verb and noun, so the verb forms **OOHS, OOHED** and **OOHING** are allowed; **OOHS** is also the plural form of the noun.

If *Chambers* quite clearly lists a plural form of an interjection (for example, as at **LO**), then that is allowable.

Accents

Accented letters have been retained in *Official Scrabble Words*, even though there are no accents in English-language Scrabble sets. Accents are to be ignored. Occasionally, two forms of an allowable Scrabble word are given in *OSW*, one accented, one not. An example is **PATE** and **PÂTÉ**. Retention of accents has been considered desirable because we have anticipated that *OSW* may well be used as the authority for other word-games which do *not* allow accented words. Inclusion of the accents will enable the players of those other games to discard accented words if they wish to.

Word lengths

Official Scrabble Words users may well want to understand what criteria have been employed in considering word lengths. In compiling *OSW* we began by listing all the valid but uninflected words of length up to (and including) 9 letters. We then allowed the relevant inflections of these (namely plurals, verb forms, and comparatives and superlatives), resulting in words up to 13 letters long. (It is possible for a 9-letter verb to double a final consonant before adding -ING, giving 13 letters in all!) Here are some examples:

the 9-letter noun **CACODEMON** gives rise to the 10-letter plural **CACODEMONS**;

the 9-letter noun **CACOPHONY** gives rise to the 11-letter plural **CACOPHONIES**;

the 9-letter noun **CANTHARIS** gives rise to the 11-letter plural **CANTHARIDES**;

the 9-letter verb **CALCULATE** gives rise to
these verb inflections: **CALCULATED,**
CALCULATES and **CALCULATING,** having
10 or 11 letters;

the 8-letter verb **CARBURET** gives rise to
these verb inflections: **CARBURETS,**
CARBURETTED and **CARBURETTING,** having
9, 11 or 12 letters.

If any inflected form of 9 letters is also a singular noun in its
own right, then a plural form of that noun is also included. For
example:

the 9-letter verb **CATERWAUL** gives rise to
these verb inflections: **CATERWAULS,**
CATERWAULED and **CATERWAULING;** but
since **CATERWAULING** is also shown in
Chambers as a noun, the plural form
CATERWAULINGS has been included here;

the 8-letter verb **CROSSCUT** gives rise to
these verb inflections: **CROSSCUTS** and
CROSSCUTTING; but since **CROSSCUTTING** is
also shown in *Chambers* as a noun, the plural
form **CROSSCUTTINGS** has been included
here.

There are a few instances of 9-letter adjectives which add an -**S**
to become 10-letter nouns. For example, **CANONICAL** is an
adjective only, yet **CANONICALS** is a noun. In such cases, we
have included the -**S** form. After all, if **CANONICAL** was a noun
rather than an adjective, we would have included its plural
form **CANONICALS.** There are instances of singular nouns
having more than 9 letters, but with plurals of 9 letters or less.
The singulars have not been included here, but the plurals
have. For example, the singular **CYNOMOLGUS** has 10 letters,
so hasn't been included, but its plural **CYNOMOLGI** has 9 letters,
so is included.

Order of words

All the words in *Official Scrabble Words* are listed in strict
alphabetical sequence regardless of length. It is important to

bear this in mind, particularly when checking the validity of plurals. For example:

> the plural of **FAD** is not listed immediately after **FAD** but is shown at its correct alphabetical place between **FADOS** and **FADY**;
>
> to determine whether **FAB** has a plural or not, it is necessary to check between the entries **FABRICS** and **FABULAR**. It is not listed there, so **FABS** is not allowed.

Official Scrabble Words does not list the definitions of any words. If you wish to discover the meaning of a word included, then it is necessary to consult *Chambers English Dictionary*.

Apparent misspellings

There are some instances where it may appear that a word has been misspelt. This can occur when the normal spelling is greater than 9 letters and therefore excluded, but an older or obsolete spelling of the same word qualifies for inclusion. For example:

> **SENSUALTY** and its plural form **SENSUALTIES** both appear in *Official Scrabble Words* because **SENSUALTY** is a 9-letter noun. The regular spelling **SENSUALITY** and its plural form **SENSUALITIES** are not listed because **SENSUALITY** is longer than 9 letters.

Official Scrabble Words will not answer every possible enquiry regarding the validity of words. For uninflected words longer than 9 letters, you will have to turn to *Chambers* itself. For example, **CYNOMOLGUS**, mentioned above, is perfectly valid for use in Scrabble; it's just that it isn't included here. There are plenty of other 10-15 letter words which could be played on a Scrabble board and are in *Chambers*. However, we felt that such words fell outside the scope of *OSW*.

If after considering the guidelines here you believe you have found an error, either of inclusion or omission, then please write to Catherine Schwarz at W and R Chambers, Edinburgh.

Darryl Francis, Leonard Hodge,
Angus Macdonald, Philip Nelkon,
Allan Simmons
UK *Official Scrabble® Words Committee*

A

AA
AARDVARK
AARDVARKS
AARDWOLF
AARDWOLVES
AAS
AASVOGEL
AASVOGELS
ABA
ABAC
ABACA
ABACAS
ABACI
ABACK
ABACS
ABACTINAL
ABACTOR
ABACTORS
ABACUS
ABACUSES
ABAFT
ABALONE
ABALONES
ABAMPERE
ABAMPERES
ABAND
ABANDED
ABANDING
ABANDON
ABANDONED
ABANDONEE
ABANDONEES
ABANDONING
ABANDONS
ABANDS
ABAS
ABASE
ABASED
ABASEMENT
ABASEMENTS
ABASES
ABASH
ABASHED
ABASHES
ABASHING
ABASHLESS
ABASHMENT
ABASHMENTS
ABASING
ABASK
ABATABLE
ABATE
ABATED
ABATEMENT
ABATEMENTS
ABATES
ABATING
ABATIS
ABATOR
ABATORS
ABATTIS
ABATTOIR
ABATTOIRS
ABATTU

ABATURE
ABATURES
ABAXIAL
ABAYA
ABAYAS
ABB
ABBA
ABBACIES
ABBACY
ABBAS
ABBATIAL
ABBÉ
ABBÉS
ABBESS
ABBESSES
ABBEY
ABBEYS
ABBOT
ABBOTS
ABBOTSHIP
ABBOTSHIPS
ABBS
ABCEE
ABCEES
ABDABS
ABDICABLE
ABDICANT
ABDICATE
ABDICATED
ABDICATES
ABDICATING
ABDOMEN
ABDOMENS
ABDOMINAL
ABDUCE
ABDUCED
ABDUCENT
ABDUCES
ABDUCING
ABDUCT
ABDUCTED
ABDUCTEE
ABDUCTEES
ABDUCTING
ABDUCTION
ABDUCTIONS
ABDUCTOR
ABDUCTORS
ABDUCTS
ABEAM
ABEAR
ABEARING
ABEARS
ABED
ABEIGH
ABELE
ABELES
ABELIA
ABELIAS
ABERRANCE
ABERRANCES
ABERRANCIES
ABERRANCY
ABERRANT

ABERRATE
ABERRATED
ABERRATES
ABERRATING
ABESSIVE
ABESSIVES
ABET
ABETMENT
ABETMENTS
ABETS
ABETTED
ABETTER
ABETTERS
ABETTING
ABETTOR
ABETTORS
ABEYANCE
ABEYANCES
ABEYANCIES
ABEYANCY
ABEYANT
ABHOR
ABHORRED
ABHORRENT
ABHORRER
ABHORRERS
ABHORRING
ABHORRINGS
ABHORS
ABID
ABIDANCE
ABIDANCES
ABIDDEN
ABIDE
ABIDED
ABIDES
ABIDING
ABIDINGLY
ABIDINGS
ABIES
ABIGAIL
ABIGAILS
ABILITIES
ABILITY
ABIOSES
ABIOSIS
ABIOTIC
ABJECT
ABJECTED
ABJECTING
ABJECTION
ABJECTIONS
ABJECTLY
ABJECTS
ABJOINT
ABJOINTED
ABJOINTING
ABJOINTS
ABJURE
ABJURED
ABJURER
ABJURERS
ABJURES
ABJURING

ABLATE
ABLATED
ABLATES
ABLATING
ABLATION
ABLATIONS
ABLATIVAL
ABLATIVE
ABLATIVES
ABLATOR
ABLATORS
ABLAUT
ABLAUTS
ABLAZE
ABLE
ABLED
ABLER
ABLES
ABLEST
ABLET
ABLETS
ABLING
ABLINS
ABLOOM
ABLOW
ABLUSH
ABLUTION
ABLUTIONS
ABLY
ABNEGATE
ABNEGATED
ABNEGATES
ABNEGATING
ABNEGATOR
ABNEGATORS
ABNORMAL
ABNORMITIES
ABNORMITY
ABNORMOUS
ABOARD
ABODE
ABODED
ABODEMENT
ABODEMENTS
ABODES
ABODING
ABOIDEAU
ABOIDEAUS
ABOIL
ABOITEAU
ABOITEAUS
ABOLISH
ABOLISHED
ABOLISHES
ABOLISHING
ABOLITION
ABOLITIONS
ABOLLA
ABOLLAE
ABOLLAS
ABOMASA
ABOMASUM
ABOMASUS
ABOMASUSES

ABOMINATE
ABOMINATED
ABOMINATES
ABOMINATING
ABONDANCE
ABONDANCES
ABORAL
ABORD
ABORDED
ABORDING
ABORDS
ABORE
ABORIGEN
ABORIGENS
ABORIGIN
ABORIGINE
ABORIGINES
ABORIGINS
ABORNE
ABORT
ABORTED
ABORTING
ABORTION
ABORTIONS
ABORTIVE
ABORTS
ABOUGHT
ABOULIA
ABOULIAS
ABOUND
ABOUNDED
ABOUNDING
ABOUNDS
ABOUT
ABOUTS
ABOVE
ABRADANT
ABRADANTS
ABRADE
ABRADED
ABRADES
ABRADING
ABRAID
ABRAIDED
ABRAIDING
ABRAIDS
ABRAM
ABRASION
ABRASIONS
ABRASIVE
ABRASIVES
ABRAXAS
ABRAXASES
ABRAY
ABRAYED
ABRAYING
ABRAYS
ABRAZO
ABRAZOS
ABREACT
ABREACTED
ABREACTING
ABREACTS
ABREAST

ABRÉGÉ
ABRÉGÉS
ABRICOCK
ABRICOCKS
ABRIDGE
ABRIDGED
ABRIDGER
ABRIDGERS
ABRIDGES
ABRIDGING
ABRIM
ABRIN
ABRINS
ABROACH
ABROAD
ABROGATE
ABROGATED
ABROGATES
ABROGATING
ABROGATOR
ABROGATORS
ABROOKE
ABROOKED
ABROOKES
ABROOKING
ABRUPT
ABRUPTER
ABRUPTEST
ABRUPTION
ABRUPTIONS
ABRUPTLY
ABRUPTS
ABSCESS
ABSCESSES
ABSCIND
ABSCINDED
ABSCINDING
ABSCINDS
ABSCISE
ABSCISED
ABSCISES
ABSCISIN
ABSCISING
ABSCISINS
ABSCISS
ABSCISSA
ABSCISSAE
ABSCISSAS
ABSCISSE
ABSCISSES
ABSCISSIN
ABSCISSINS
ABSCOND
ABSCONDED
ABSCONDER
ABSCONDERS
ABSCONDING
ABSCONDS
ABSEIL
ABSEILED
ABSEILING
ABSEILINGS
ABSEILS
ABSENCE
ABSENCES
ABSENT
ABSENTED
ABSENTEE
ABSENTEES
ABSENTING

ABSENTLY
ABSENTS
ABSEY
ABSEYS
ABSINTH
ABSINTHE
ABSINTHES
ABSINTHS
ABSIT
ABSITS
ABSOLUTE
ABSOLUTES
ABSOLVE
ABSOLVED
ABSOLVER
ABSOLVERS
ABSOLVES
ABSOLVING
ABSONANT
ABSORB
ABSORBATE
ABSORBATES
ABSORBED
ABSORBENT
ABSORBENTS
ABSORBER
ABSORBERS
ABSORBING
ABSORBS
ABSTAIN
ABSTAINED
ABSTAINER
ABSTAINERS
ABSTAINING
ABSTAINS
ABSTERGE
ABSTERGED
ABSTERGES
ABSTERGING
ABSTINENT
ABSTRACT
ABSTRACTED
ABSTRACTER
ABSTRACTEST
ABSTRACTING
ABSTRACTS
ABSTRICT
ABSTRICTED
ABSTRICTING
ABSTRICTS
ABSTRUSE
ABSTRUSER
ABSTRUSEST
ABSURD
ABSURDER
ABSURDEST
ABSURDITIES
ABSURDITY
ABSURDLY
ABTHANE
ABTHANES
ABULIA
ABULIAS
ABUNA
ABUNAS
ABUNDANCE
ABUNDANCES
ABUNDANCIES
ABUNDANCY
ABUNDANT

ABUNE
ABURST
ABUSAGE
ABUSAGES
ABUSE
ABUSED
ABUSER
ABUSERS
ABUSES
ABUSING
ABUSION
ABUSIONS
ABUSIVE
ABUSIVELY
ABUT
ABUTILON
ABUTILONS
ABUTMENT
ABUTMENTS
ABUTS
ABUTTAL
ABUTTALS
ABUTTED
ABUTTER
ABUTTERS
ABUTTING
ABUZZ
ABVOLT
ABVOLTS
ABY
ABYE
ABYEING
ABYES
ABYING
ABYSM
ABYSMAL
ABYSMALLY
ABYSMS
ABYSS
ABYSSAL
ABYSSES
ACACIA
ACACIAS
ACADEME
ACADEMES
ACADEMIA
ACADEMIAS
ACADEMIC
ACADEMICS
ACADEMIES
ACADEMIST
ACADEMISTS
ACADEMY
ACAJOU
ACAJOUS
ACALEPH
ACALEPHA
ACALEPHAN
ACALEPHANS
ACALEPHAS
ACALEPHE
ACALEPHES
ACALEPHS
ACANTH
ACANTHA
ACANTHAS
ACANTHIN
ACANTHINE
ACANTHINS
ACANTHOID

ACANTHOUS
ACANTHS
ACANTHUS
ACANTHUSES
ACAPNIA
ACAPNIAS
ACARI
ACARIAN
ACARIASES
ACARIASIS
ACARICIDE
ACARICIDES
ACARID
ACARIDAN
ACARIDANS
ACARIDEAN
ACARIDEANS
ACARIDIAN
ACARIDIANS
ACARIDS
ACARINE
ACAROID
ACAROLOGIES
ACAROLOGY
ACARPOUS
ACARUS
ACATER
ACATERS
ACATES
ACATOUR
ACATOURS
ACAUDAL
ACAUDATE
ACAULINE
ACAULOSE
ACCABLÉ
ACCEDE
ACCEDED
ACCEDENCE
ACCEDENCES
ACCEDER
ACCEDERS
ACCEDES
ACCEDING
ACCEND
ACCENDED
ACCENDING
ACCENDS
ACCENSION
ACCENSIONS
ACCENT
ACCENTED
ACCENTING
ACCENTOR
ACCENTORS
ACCENTS
ACCENTUAL
ACCEPT
ACCEPTANT
ACCEPTANTS
ACCEPTED
ACCEPTER
ACCEPTERS
ACCEPTING
ACCEPTIVE
ACCEPTOR
ACCEPTORS
ACCEPTS
ACCESS
ACCESSARIES

ACCESSARY
ACCESSED
ACCESSES
ACCESSING
ACCESSION
ACCESSIONS
ACCESSORIES
ACCESSORY
ACCIDENCE
ACCIDENCES
ACCIDENT
ACCIDENTS
ACCIDIE
ACCIDIES
ACCINGE
ACCINGED
ACCINGES
ACCINGING
ACCITE
ACCITED
ACCITES
ACCITING
ACCLAIM
ACCLAIMED
ACCLAIMING
ACCLAIMS
ACCLIMATE
ACCLIMATED
ACCLIMATES
ACCLIMATING
ACCLIVITIES
ACCLIVITY
ACCLIVOUS
ACCLOY
ACCLOYED
ACCLOYING
ACCLOYS
ACCOAST
ACCOASTED
ACCOASTING
ACCOASTS
ACCOIED
ACCOIL
ACCOILS
ACCOLADE
ACCOLADES
ACCOMPANIED
ACCOMPANIES
ACCOMPANY
ACCOMPANYING
ACCOMPT
ACCOMPTED
ACCOMPTING
ACCOMPTS
ACCORAGE
ACCORAGED
ACCORAGES
ACCORAGING
ACCORD
ACCORDANT
ACCORDED
ACCORDER
ACCORDERS
ACCORDING
ACCORDION
ACCORDIONS
ACCORDS
ACCOST
ACCOSTED
ACCOSTING

ACCOSTS
ACCOUNT
ACCOUNTED
ACCOUNTING
ACCOUNTINGS
ACCOUNTS
ACCOURAGE
ACCOURAGED
ACCOURAGES
ACCOURAGING
ACCOURT
ACCOURTED
ACCOURTING
ACCOURTS
ACCOUTRE
ACCOUTRED
ACCOUTRES
ACCOUTRING
ACCOY
ACCOYED
ACCOYING
ACCOYLD
ACCOYS
ACCREDIT
ACCREDITED
ACCREDITING
ACCREDITS
ACCRETE
ACCRETED
ACCRETES
ACCRETING
ACCRETION
ACCRETIONS
ACCRETIVE
ACCREW
ACCREWED
ACCREWING
ACCREWS
ACCRUAL
ACCRUALS
ACCRUE
ACCRUED
ACCRUES
ACCRUING
ACCUMBENT
ACCURACIES
ACCURACY
ACCURATE
ACCURSE
ACCURSED
ACCURSES
ACCURSING
ACCURST
ACCUSABLE
ACCUSAL
ACCUSALS
ACCUSE
ACCUSED
ACCUSER
ACCUSERS
ACCUSES
ACCUSING
ACCUSTOM
ACCUSTOMED
ACCUSTOMING
ACCUSTOMS
ACE
ACED
ACEDIA
ACEDIAS

ACELLULAR
ACERB
ACERBATE
ACERBATED
ACERBATES
ACERBATING
ACERBER
ACERBEST
ACERBIC
ACERBITIES
ACERBITY
ACEROSE
ACEROUS
ACERVATE
ACES
ACESCENCE
ACESCENCES
ACESCENCIES
ACESCENCY
ACESCENT
ACETABULA
ACETAL
ACETALS
ACETAMIDE
ACETAMIDES
ACETATE
ACETATES
ACETIC
ACETIFIED
ACETIFIES
ACETIFY
ACETIFYING
ACETONE
ACETONES
ACETOSE
ACETOUS
ACETYL
ACETYLENE
ACETYLENES
ACETYLS
ACHAENIUM
ACHAENIUMS
ACHAGE
ACHAGES
ACHARNÉ
ACHARYA
ACHARYAS
ACHATES
ACHE
ACHED
ACHENE
ACHENES
ACHENIAL
ACHENIUM
ACHENIUMS
ACHES
ACHIER
ACHIEST
ACHIEVE
ACHIEVED
ACHIEVER
ACHIEVERS
ACHIEVES
ACHIEVING
ACHIMENES
ACHING
ACHINGS
ACHKAN
ACHKANS
ACHROMAT

ACHROMATS
ACHY
ACICULAR
ACICULATE
ACID
ACIDER
ACIDEST
ACIDFREAK
ACIDFREAKS
ACIDIC
ACIDIFIED
ACIDIFIES
ACIDIFY
ACIDIFYING
ACIDITIES
ACIDITY
ACIDOSES
ACIDOSIS
ACIDS
ACIDULATE
ACIDULATED
ACIDULATES
ACIDULATING
ACIDULOUS
ACIERAGE
ACIERAGES
ACIERATE
ACIERATED
ACIERATES
ACIERATING
ACIFORM
ACING
ACINI
ACINIFORM
ACINOSE
ACINOUS
ACINUS
ACKEE
ACKEES
ACKERS
ACKNEW
ACKNOW
ACKNOWING
ACKNOWN
ACKNOWNE
ACKNOWS
ACLINIC
ACME
ACMES
ACMITE
ACMITES
ACNE
ACNES
ACOCK
ACOEMETI
ACOLD
ACOLUTHIC
ACOLYTE
ACOLYTES
ACOLYTH
ACOLYTHS
ACONITE
ACONITES
ACONITIC
ACONITINE
ACONITINES
ACONITUM
ACONITUMS
ACORN
ACORNED

ACORNS
ACOSMISM
ACOSMISMS
ACOSMIST
ACOSMISTS
ACOUCHIES
ACOUCHY
ACOUSTIC
ACOUSTICS
ACQUAINT
ACQUAINTED
ACQUAINTING
ACQUAINTS
ACQUEST
ACQUESTS
ACQUIESCE
ACQUIESCED
ACQUIESCES
ACQUIESCING
ACQUIGHT
ACQUIGHTED
ACQUIGHTING
ACQUIGHTS
ACQUIRAL
ACQUIRALS
ACQUIRE
ACQUIRED
ACQUIRES
ACQUIRING
ACQUIST
ACQUISTS
ACQUIT
ACQUITE
ACQUITED
ACQUITES
ACQUITING
ACQUITS
ACQUITTAL
ACQUITTALS
ACQUITTED
ACQUITTING
ACRAWL
ACRE
ACREAGE
ACREAGES
ACRED
ACRES
ACRID
ACRIDER
ACRIDEST
ACRIDIN
ACRIDINE
ACRIDINES
ACRIDINS
ACRIDITIES
ACRIDITY
ACRIMONIES
ACRIMONY
ACROBAT
ACROBATIC
ACROBATICS
ACROBATS
ACROGEN
ACROGENS
ACROLEIN
ACROLEINS
ACROLITH
ACROLITHS
ACROMIAL
ACROMION

ACROMIONS
ACRONYM
ACRONYMIC
ACRONYMS
ACROPETAL
ACROPHONIES
ACROPHONY
ACROPOLIS
ACROPOLISES
ACROSPIRE
ACROSPIRES
ACROSS
ACROSTIC
ACROSTICS
ACROTER
ACROTERIA
ACROTERS
ACROTISM
ACROTISMS
ACRYLIC
ACRYLICS
ACT
ACTA
ACTED
ACTIN
ACTINAL
ACTING
ACTINGS
ACTINIA
ACTINIAE
ACTINIAN
ACTINIANS
ACTINIAS
ACTINIC
ACTINIDE
ACTINIDES
ACTINISM
ACTINISMS
ACTINIUM
ACTINIUMS
ACTINOID
ACTINOIDS
ACTINON
ACTINONS
ACTINS
ACTION
ACTIONIST
ACTIONISTS
ACTIONS
ACTIVATE
ACTIVATED
ACTIVATES
ACTIVATING
ACTIVATOR
ACTIVATORS
ACTIVE
ACTIVELY
ACTIVISM
ACTIVISMS
ACTIVIST
ACTIVISTS
ACTIVITIES
ACTIVITY
ACTON
ACTONS
ACTOR
ACTORS
ACTRESS
ACTRESSES
ACTS

ACTUAL	ADAPTORS	ADDUCTED	ADIT	ADMISSIVE
ACTUALISE	ADAPTS	ADDUCTING	ADITS	ADMIT
ACTUALISED	ADAW	ADDUCTION	ADJACENCIES	ADMITS
ACTUALISES	ADAWED	ADDUCTIONS	ADJACENCY	ADMITTED
ACTUALISING	ADAWING	ADDUCTIVE	ADJACENT	ADMITTING
ACTUALIST	ADAWS	ADDUCTOR	ADJECTIVE	ADMIX
ACTUALISTS	ADAXIAL	ADDUCTORS	ADJECTIVES	ADMIXED
ACTUALITIES	ADAYS	ADDUCTS	ADJOIN	ADMIXES
ACTUALITY	ADD	ADEEM	ADJOINED	ADMIXING
ACTUALIZE	ADDAX	ADEEMED	ADJOINING	ADMIXTURE
ACTUALIZED	ADDAXES	ADEEMING	ADJOINS	ADMIXTURES
ACTUALIZES	ADDED	ADEEMS	ADJOINT	ADMONISH
ACTUALIZING	ADDEEM	ADEMPTION	ADJOINTS	ADMONISHED
ACTUALLY	ADDEEMED	ADEMPTIONS	ADJOURN	ADMONISHES
ACTUARIAL	ADDEEMING	ADENINE	ADJOURNED	ADMONISHING
ACTUARIES	ADDEEMS	ADENINES	ADJOURNING	ADMONITOR
ACTUARY	ADDEND	ADENITIS	ADJOURNS	ADMONITORS
ACTUATE	ADDENDA	ADENITISES	ADJUDGE	ADNASCENT
ACTUATED	ADDENDS	ADENOID	ADJUDGED	ADNATE
ACTUATES	ADDENDUM	ADENOIDAL	ADJUDGES	ADNATION
ACTUATING	ADDER	ADENOIDS	ADJUDGING	ADNATIONS
ACTUATION	ADDERS	ADENOMA	ADJUNCT	ADO
ACTUATIONS	ADDERWORT	ADENOMAS	ADJUNCTLY	ADOBE
ACTUATOR	ADDERWORTS	ADENOMATA	ADJUNCTS	ADOBES
ACTUATORS	ADDICT	ADENOSINE	ADJURE	ADONISE
ACTURE	ADDICTED	ADENOSINES	ADJURED	ADONISED
ACTURES	ADDICTING	ADEPT	ADJURES	ADONISES
ACUITIES	ADDICTION	ADEPTER	ADJURING	ADONISING
ACUITY	ADDICTIONS	ADEPTEST	ADJUST	ADONIZE
ACULEATE	ADDICTIVE	ADEPTS	ADJUSTED	ADONIZED
ACULEATED	ADDICTS	ADEQUACIES	ADJUSTER	ADONIZES
ACUMEN	ADDING	ADEQUACY	ADJUSTERS	ADONIZING
ACUMENS	ADDIO	ADEQUATE	ADJUSTING	ADOORS
ACUMINATE	ADDIOS	ADERMIN	ADJUSTOR	ADOPT
ACUMINATED	ADDITION	ADERMINS	ADJUSTORS	ADOPTED
ACUMINATES	ADDITIONS	ADESPOTA	ADJUSTS	ADOPTER
ACUMINATING	ADDITIVE	ADESSIVE	ADJUTAGE	ADOPTERS
ACUPOINT	ADDITIVES	ADESSIVES	ADJUTAGES	ADOPTING
ACUPOINTS	ADDLE	ADHARMA	ADJUTANCIES	ADOPTION
ACUSHLA	ADDLED	ADHARMAS	ADJUTANCY	ADOPTIONS
ACUSHLAS	ADDLEMENT	ADHERE	ADJUTANT	ADOPTIOUS
ACUTE	ADDLEMENTS	ADHERED	ADJUTANTS	ADOPTIVE
ACUTELY	ADDLES	ADHERENCE	ADJUVANCIES	ADOPTS
ACUTENESS	ADDLING	ADHERENCES	ADJUVANCY	ADORABLE
ACUTENESSES	ADDOOM	ADHERENT	ADJUVANT	ADORABLY
ACUTER	ADDOOMED	ADHERENTS	ADJUVANTS	ADORATION
ACUTES	ADDOOMING	ADHERER	ADMASS	ADORATIONS
ACUTEST	ADDOOMS	ADHERERS	ADMASSES	ADORE
ACYCLIC	ADDORSED	ADHERES	ADMEASURE	ADORED
ACYCLOVIR	ADDRESS	ADHERING	ADMEASURED	ADORER
ACYCLOVIRS	ADDRESSED	ADHESION	ADMEASURES	ADORERS
ACYL	ADDRESSEE	ADHESIONS	ADMEASURING	ADORES
ACYLS	ADDRESSEES	ADHESIVE	ADMIN	ADORING
AD	ADDRESSER	ADHESIVES	ADMINICLE	ADORINGLY
ADAGE	ADDRESSERS	ADHIBIT	ADMINICLES	ADORN
ADAGES	ADDRESSES	ADHIBITED	ADMINS	ADORNED
ADAGIO	ADDRESSING	ADHIBITING	ADMIRABLE	ADORNING
ADAGIOS	ADDRESSOR	ADHIBITS	ADMIRABLY	ADORNMENT
ADAMANT	ADDRESSORS	ADIABATIC	ADMIRAL	ADORNMENTS
ADAMANTS	ADDREST	ADIAPHORA	ADMIRALS	ADORNS
ADAPT	ADDS	ADIEU	ADMIRANCE	ADOS
ADAPTABLE	ADDUCE	ADIEUS	ADMIRANCES	ADOWN
ADAPTED	ADDUCED	ADIEUX	ADMIRE	ADPRESS
ADAPTER	ADDUCENT	ADIOS	ADMIRED	ADPRESSED
ADAPTERS	ADDUCER	ADIPIC	ADMIRER	ADPRESSES
ADAPTING	ADDUCERS	ADIPOCERE	ADMIRERS	ADPRESSING
ADAPTION	ADDUCES	ADIPOCERES	ADMIRES	ADRAD
ADAPTIONS	ADDUCIBLE	ADIPOSE	ADMIRING	ADREAD
ADAPTIVE	ADDUCING	ADIPOSITIES	ADMISSION	ADREADED
ADAPTOR	ADDUCT	ADIPOSITY	ADMISSIONS	ADREADING

ADREADS
ADRED
ADRENAL
ADRENALS
ADRIFT
ADROIT
ADROITER
ADROITEST
ADROITLY
ADRY
ADS
ADSCRIPT
ADSCRIPTS
ADSORB
ADSORBATE
ADSORBATES
ADSORBED
ADSORBENT
ADSORBENTS
ADSORBING
ADSORBS
ADSUM
ADULARIA
ADULARIAS
ADULATE
ADULATED
ADULATES
ADULATING
ADULATION
ADULATIONS
ADULATOR
ADULATORS
ADULATORY
ADULT
ADULTERER
ADULTERERS
ADULTERIES
ADULTERY
ADULTHOOD
ADULTHOODS
ADULTS
ADUMBRATE
ADUMBRATED
ADUMBRATES
ADUMBRATING
ADUNC
ADUNCATE
ADUNCATED
ADUNCITIES
ADUNCITY
ADUNCOUS
ADUST
ADUSTED
ADUSTING
ADUSTS
ADVANCE
ADVANCED
ADVANCES
ADVANCING
ADVANTAGE
ADVANTAGED
ADVANTAGES
ADVANTAGING
ADVECTION
ADVECTIONS
ADVENE
ADVENED
ADVENES
ADVENING
ADVENT

ADVENTIVE
ADVENTIVES
ADVENTS
ADVENTURE
ADVENTURED
ADVENTURES
ADVENTURING
ADVERB
ADVERBIAL
ADVERBS
ADVERSARIES
ADVERSARY
ADVERSE
ADVERSELY
ADVERSER
ADVERSEST
ADVERSITIES
ADVERSITY
ADVERT
ADVERTED
ADVERTENT
ADVERTING
ADVERTISE
ADVERTISED
ADVERTISES
ADVERTISING
ADVERTISINGS
ADVERTS
ADVEW
ADVEWED
ADVEWING
ADVEWS
ADVICE
ADVICEFUL
ADVICES
ADVISABLE
ADVISABLY
ADVISE
ADVISED
ADVISEDLY
ADVISER
ADVISERS
ADVISES
ADVISING
ADVISINGS
ADVISOR
ADVISORS
ADVISORY
ADVOCAAT
ADVOCAATS
ADVOCACIES
ADVOCACY
ADVOCATE
ADVOCATED
ADVOCATES
ADVOCATING
ADVOCATOR
ADVOCATORS
ADVOUTRER
ADVOUTRERS
ADVOUTRIES
ADVOUTRY
ADVOWSON
ADVOWSONS
ADWARD
ADWARDED
ADWARDING
ADWARDS
ADYNAMIA
ADYNAMIAS

ADYNAMIC
ADYTA
ADYTUM
ADZE
ADZES
AE
AECIA
AECIDIA
AECIDIUM
AECIUM
AEDILE
AEDILES
AEFALD
AEFAULD
AEFAWLD
AEGIRINE
AEGIRINES
AEGIRITE
AEGIRITES
AEGIS
AEGISES
AEGLOGUE
AEGLOGUES
AEGROTAT
AEGROTATS
AEMULE
AEMULED
AEMULES
AEMULING
AEOLIAN
AEOLIPILE
AEOLIPILES
AEOLIPYLE
AEOLIPYLES
AEON
AEONIAN
AEONS
AERATE
AERATED
AERATES
AERATING
AERATION
AERATIONS
AERATOR
AERATORS
AERIAL
AERIALIST
AERIALISTS
AERIALITIES
AERIALITY
AERIALLY
AERIALS
AERIE
AERIER
AERIES
AERIEST
AERIFORM
AEROBE
AEROBES
AEROBIC
AEROBICS
AEROBIONT
AEROBIONTS
AEROBOMB
AEROBOMBS
AEROBUS
AEROBUSES
AERODART
AERODARTS
AERODROME

AERODROMES
AERODYNE
AERODYNES
AEROFOIL
AEROFOILS
AEROGRAM
AEROGRAMS
AEROGRAPH
AEROGRAPHS
AEROLITE
AEROLITES
AEROLITH
AEROLITHS
AEROLITIC
AEROLOGIES
AEROLOGY
AEROMANCIES
AEROMANCY
AEROMETER
AEROMETERS
AEROMETRIES
AEROMETRY
AEROMOTOR
AEROMOTORS
AERONAUT
AERONAUTS
AERONOMIES
AERONOMY
AEROPHONE
AEROPHONES
AEROPHYTE
AEROPHYTES
AEROPLANE
AEROPLANES
AEROSHELL
AEROSHELLS
AEROSOL
AEROSOLS
AEROSPACE
AEROSPACES
AEROSTAT
AEROSTATS
AEROTAXES
AEROTAXIS
AEROTRAIN
AEROTRAINS
AERY
AESC
AESCES
AESCULIN
AESCULINS
AESIR
AESTHESES
AESTHESIA
AESTHESIAS
AESTHESIS
AESTHETE
AESTHETES
AESTHETIC
AESTHETICS
AESTIVAL
AESTIVATE
AESTIVATED
AESTIVATES
AESTIVATING
AETHER
AETHERS
AETIOLOGIES
AETIOLOGY
AFALD

AFAR
AFARA
AFARAS
AFAWLD
AFEAR
AFEARD
AFEARED
AFEARING
AFEARS
AFFABLE
AFFABLY
AFFAIR
AFFAIRE
AFFAIRES
AFFAIRS
AFFEAR
AFFEARD
AFFEARE
AFFEARED
AFFEARES
AFFEARING
AFFEARS
AFFECT
AFFECTED
AFFECTER
AFFECTERS
AFFECTING
AFFECTION
AFFECTIONED
AFFECTIONING
AFFECTIONS
AFFECTIVE
AFFECTS
AFFEER
AFFEERED
AFFEERING
AFFEERS
AFFERENT
AFFIANCE
AFFIANCED
AFFIANCES
AFFIANCING
AFFICHE
AFFICHES
AFFIDAVIT
AFFIDAVITS
AFFIED
AFFIES
AFFILIATE
AFFILIATED
AFFILIATES
AFFILIATING
AFFINE
AFFINED
AFFINES
AFFINITIES
AFFINITY
AFFIRM
AFFIRMANT
AFFIRMANTS
AFFIRMED
AFFIRMER
AFFIRMERS
AFFIRMING
AFFIRMS
AFFIX
AFFIXED
AFFIXES
AFFIXING
AFFLATED

AFFLATION
AFFLATIONS
AFFLATUS
AFFLATUSES
AFFLICT
AFFLICTED
AFFLICTING
AFFLICTS
AFFLUENCE
AFFLUENCES
AFFLUENT
AFFLUENTS
AFFLUX
AFFLUXES
AFFLUXION
AFFLUXIONS
AFFOORD
AFFOORDED
AFFOORDING
AFFOORDS
AFFORCE
AFFORCED
AFFORCES
AFFORCING
AFFORD
AFFORDED
AFFORDING
AFFORDS
AFFOREST
AFFORESTED
AFFORESTING
AFFORESTS
AFFRAP
AFFRAPPED
AFFRAPPING
AFFRAPS
AFFRAY
AFFRAYED
AFFRAYING
AFFRAYS
AFFRENDED
AFFRET
AFFRETS
AFFRICATE
AFFRICATED
AFFRICATES
AFFRIGHT
AFFRIGHTED
AFFRIGHTING
AFFRIGHTS
AFFRONT
AFFRONTÉ
AFFRONTED
AFFRONTÉE
AFFRONTEE
AFFRONTING
AFFRONTINGS
AFFRONTS
AFFUSION
AFFUSIONS
AFFY
AFFYDE
AFFYING
AFGHAN
AFGHANS
AFIELD
AFIRE
AFLAJ
AFLAME
AFLATOXIN

AFLATOXINS
AFLOAT
AFOOT
AFORE
AFOREHAND
AFORESAID
AFORETIME
AFOUL
AFRAID
AFREET
AFREETS
AFRESH
AFRIT
AFRITS
AFRO
AFRONT
AFROS
AFT
AFTER
AFTERCARE
AFTERCARES
AFTEREYE
AFTEREYED
AFTEREYES
AFTEREYING
AFTERGAME
AFTERGAMES
AFTERGLOW
AFTERGLOWS
AFTERINGS
AFTERMATH
AFTERMATHS
AFTERMOST
AFTERNOON
AFTERNOONS
AFTERS
AFTERTIME
AFTERTIMES
AFTERWARD
AFTERWARDS
AFTERWORD
AFTERWORDS
AFTMOST
AGA
AGAÇANT
AGAÇANTE
AGACERIE
AGACERIES
AGAIN
AGAINST
AGALACTIA
AGALACTIAS
AGALLOCH
AGALLOCHS
AGAMI
AGAMIC
AGAMID
AGAMIDS
AGAMIS
AGAMOID
AGAMOIDS
AGAMOUS
AGAPAE
AGAPE
AGAR
AGARIC
AGARICS
AGARS
AGAS
AGAST

AGATE
AGATES
AGAVE
AGAVES
AGAZE
AGAZED
AGE
AGED
AGEDNESS
AGEDNESSES
AGEE
AGEING
AGEINGS
AGEISM
AGEISMS
AGEIST
AGEISTS
AGELAST
AGELASTIC
AGELASTS
AGELESS
AGELONG
AGEN
AGENCIES
AGENCY
AGENDA
AGENDAS
AGENE
AGENES
AGENT
AGENTED
AGENTIAL
AGENTING
AGENTS
AGES
AGGER
AGGERS
AGGRACE
AGGRACED
AGGRACES
AGGRACING
AGGRADE
AGGRADED
AGGRADES
AGGRADING
AGGRATE
AGGRATED
AGGRATES
AGGRATING
AGGRAVATE
AGGRAVATED
AGGRAVATES
AGGRAVATING
AGGREGATE
AGGREGATED
AGGREGATES
AGGREGATING
AGGRESS
AGGRESSED
AGGRESSES
AGGRESSING
AGGRESSOR
AGGRESSORS
AGGRI
AGGRIEVE
AGGRIEVED
AGGRIEVES
AGGRIEVING
AGGRO
AGGROS

AGGRY
AGHA
AGHAS
AGHAST
AGILA
AGILAS
AGILE
AGILELY
AGILER
AGILEST
AGILITIES
AGILITY
AGIN
AGING
AGINGS
AGINIZE
AGINIZED
AGINIZES
AGINIZING
AGINNER
AGINNERS
AGIO
AGIOS
AGIOTAGE
AGIOTAGES
AGIST
AGISTED
AGISTER
AGISTERS
AGISTING
AGISTMENT
AGISTMENTS
AGISTOR
AGISTORS
AGISTS
AGITATE
AGITATED
AGITATES
AGITATING
AGITATION
AGITATIONS
AGITATIVE
AGITATO
AGITATOR
AGITATORS
AGITPROP
AGITPROPS
AGLEE
AGLET
AGLETS
AGLEY
AGLIMMER
AGLITTER
AGLOW
AGMA
AGMAS
AGNAIL
AGNAILS
AGNAME
AGNAMED
AGNAMES
AGNATE
AGNATES
AGNATIC
AGNATICAL
AGNATION
AGNATIONS
AGNISE
AGNISED
AGNISES

AGNISING
AGNIZE
AGNIZED
AGNIZES
AGNIZING
AGNOMEN
AGNOMENS
AGNOMINA
AGNOSTIC
AGNOSTICS
AGO
AGOG
AGOGE
AGOGES
AGOGIC
AGOGICS
AGOING
AGON
AGONE
AGONIC
AGONIES
AGONISE
AGONISED
AGONISES
AGONISING
AGONIST
AGONISTES
AGONISTIC
AGONISTICS
AGONISTS
AGONIZE
AGONIZED
AGONIZES
AGONIZING
AGONS
AGONY
AGOOD
AGORA
AGORAS
AGOROT
AGOUTA
AGOUTAS
AGOUTI
AGOUTIES
AGOUTIS
AGOUTY
AGRAFFE
AGRAFFES
AGRAPHA
AGRAPHIA
AGRAPHIAS
AGRAPHIC
AGRAPHON
AGRARIAN
AGRASTE
AGRAVIC
AGREE
AGREEABLE
AGREEABLY
AGREED
AGREEING
AGREEMENT
AGREEMENTS
AGREES
AGRÉGÉ
AGRÉGÉS
AGRÉMENS
AGRÉMENT
AGRÉMENTS
AGRESTAL

AGRESTIAL
AGRESTIC
AGRIMONIES
AGRIMONY
AGRIN
AGRIOLOGIES
AGRIOLOGY
AGRISE
AGRISED
AGRISES
AGRISING
AGRIZE
AGRIZED
AGRIZES
AGRIZING
AGROLOGIES
AGROLOGY
AGRONOMIC
AGRONOMICS
AGRONOMIES
AGRONOMY
AGROUND
AGRYZE
AGRYZED
AGRYZES
AGRYZING
AGUACATE
AGUACATES
AGUE
AGUED
AGUES
AGUISE
AGUISED
AGUISES
AGUISH
AGUISHLY
AGUISING
AGUIZE
AGUIZED
AGUIZES
AGUIZING
AGUTI
AGUTIS
AH
AHA
AHEAD
AHEAP
AHEIGHT
AHEM
AHIGH
AHIMSA
AHIMSAS
AHIND
AHINT
AHOLD
AHORSE
AHOY
AHULL
AHUNGERED
AHUNGRY
AI
AIA
AIAS
AIBLINS
AID
AIDANCE
AIDANCES
AIDANT
AIDE
AIDED

AIDER
AIDERS
AIDES
AIDFUL
AIDING
AIDLESS
AIDOI
AIDOS
AIDS
AIERIES
AIERY
AIGLET
AIGLETS
AIGRETTE
AIGRETTES
AIGUILLE
AIGUILLES
AIKIDO
AIKIDOS
AIKONA
AIL
AILANTHUS
AILANTHUSES
AILANTO
AILANTOS
AILED
AILERON
AILERONS
AILETTE
AILETTES
AILING
AILMENT
AILMENTS
AILS
AIM
AIMED
AIMING
AIMLESS
AIMLESSLY
AIMS
AIN
AÎNÉ
AÎNÉE
AIOLI
AIOLIS
AIR
AIRBORNE
AIRBURST
AIRBURSTS
AIRCRAFT
AIRDRAWN
AIRDROME
AIRDROMES
AIRED
AIRER
AIRERS
AIRFIELD
AIRFIELDS
AIRFRAME
AIRFRAMES
AIRGAP
AIRGAPS
AIRGRAPH
AIRGRAPHS
AIRHOLE
AIRHOLES
AIRIER
AIRIEST
AIRILY
AIRINESS

AIRINESSES
AIRING
AIRINGS
AIRLESS
AIRLIFT
AIRLIFTED
AIRLIFTING
AIRLIFTS
AIRLINE
AIRLINER
AIRLINERS
AIRLINES
AIRMAIL
AIRMAILED
AIRMAILING
AIRMAILS
AIRMAN
AIRMEN
AIRN
AIRNED
AIRNING
AIRNS
AIRPLANE
AIRPLANES
AIRPORT
AIRPORTS
AIRS
AIRSCREW
AIRSCREWS
AIRSHAFT
AIRSHAFTS
AIRSHIP
AIRSHIPS
AIRSICK
AIRSPACE
AIRSPACES
AIRSTOP
AIRSTOPS
AIRSTREAM
AIRSTREAMS
AIRSTRIP
AIRSTRIPS
AIRT
AIRTED
AIRTIGHT
AIRTIME
AIRTIMES
AIRTING
AIRTS
AIRWARD
AIRWARDS
AIRWAVE
AIRWAVES
AIRWAY
AIRWAYS
AIRWOMAN
AIRWOMEN
AIRWORTHY
AIRY
AIS
AISLE
AISLED
AISLES
AISLING
AISLINGS
AIT
AITCH
AITCHBONE
AITCHBONES
AITCHES

AITS
AITU
AITUS
AIZLE
AIZLES
AJAR
AJEE
AJOWAN
AJOWANS
AJUTAGE
AJUTAGES
AJWAN
AJWANS
AKE
AKED
AKEE
AKEES
AKENE
AKENES
AKES
AKIMBO
AKIN
AKINESES
AKINESIA
AKINESIAS
AKINESIS
AKING
AKKAS
AKOLUTHOS
AKOLUTHOSES
AKVAVIT
AKVAVITS
ALA
ALAAP
ALAAPS
ALABAMINE
ALABAMINES
ALABASTER
ALABASTERS
ALACK
ALACRITIES
ALACRITY
ALAE
ALAIMENT
ALAIMENTS
ALALAGMOI
ALALAGMOS
ALALIA
ALALIAS
ALAMEDA
ALAMEDAS
ALAMODE
ALAMODES
ALAMORT
ALAND
ALANG
ALANGS
ALANNAH
ALANNAHS
ALAP
ALAPA
ALAPAS
ALAPS
ALAR
ALARM
ALARMED
ALARMEDLY
ALARMING
ALARMISM
ALARMISMS

ALARMIST
ALARMISTS
ALARMS
ALARUM
ALARUMED
ALARUMING
ALARUMS
ALARY
ALAS
ALASTRIM
ALASTRIMS
ALATE
ALATED
ALAY
ALAYED
ALAYING
ALAYS
ALB
ALBACORE
ALBACORES
ALBARELLI
ALBARELLO
ALBARELLOS
ALBATA
ALBATAS
ALBATROSS
ALBATROSSES
ALBE
ALBEDO
ALBEDOS
ALBEE
ALBEIT
ALBERGI
ALBERGO
ALBERT
ALBERTITE
ALBERTITES
ALBERTS
ALBESCENT
ALBESPINE
ALBESPINES
ALBESPYNE
ALBESPYNES
ALBICORE
ALBICORES
ALBINESS
ALBINESSES
ALBINISM
ALBINISMS
ALBINO
ALBINOISM
ALBINOISMS
ALBINOS
ALBINOTIC
ALBITE
ALBITES
ALBITISE
ALBITISED
ALBITISES
ALBITISING
ALBITIZE
ALBITIZED
ALBITIZES
ALBITIZING
ALBRICIAS
ALBS
ALBUGO
ALBUGOS
ALBUM
ALBUMEN

ALBUMENS
ALBUMIN
ALBUMINS
ALBUMS
ALBURNOUS
ALBURNUM
ALBURNUMS
ALCAHEST
ALCAHESTS
ALCAIDE
ALCAIDES
ALCALDE
ALCALDES
ALCARRAZA
ALCARRAZAS
ALCATRAS
ALCATRASES
ALCAYDE
ALCAYDES
ALCÁZAR
ALCÁZARS
ALCHEMIC
ALCHEMIES
ALCHEMIST
ALCHEMISTS
ALCHEMY
ALCHERA
ALCHERAS
ALCHYMIES
ALCHYMY
ALCOHOL
ALCOHOLIC
ALCOHOLICS
ALCOHOLS
ALCORZA
ALCORZAS
ALCOVE
ALCOVES
ALDEA
ALDEAS
ALDEHYDE
ALDEHYDES
ALDER
ALDERMAN
ALDERMEN
ALDERN
ALDERS
ALDOSE
ALDOSES
ALDRIN
ALDRINS
ALE
ALEATORIC
ALEATORIES
ALEATORY
ALEBENCH
ALEBENCHES
ALECOST
ALECOSTS
ALECTRYON
ALECTRYONS
ALEE
ALEFT
ALEGAR
ALEGARS
ALEGGE
ALEGGED
ALEGGES
ALEGGING
ALEMBIC

ALEMBICS
ALEMBROTH
ALEMBROTHS
ALENGTH
ALEPH
ALEPHS
ALEPINE
ALEPINES
ALERCE
ALERCES
ALERION
ALERIONS
ALERT
ALERTED
ALERTER
ALERTEST
ALERTING
ALERTLY
ALERTNESS
ALERTNESSES
ALERTS
ALES
ALEURON
ALEURONE
ALEURONES
ALEURONS
ALEVIN
ALEVINS
ALEW
ALEWASHED
ALEWIFE
ALEWIVES
ALEWS
ALEXIA
ALEXIAS
ALEXIC
ALEXIN
ALEXINS
ALEYE
ALEYED
ALEYES
ALEYING
ALFA
ALFALFA
ALFALFAS
ALFAQUÍ
ALFAQUÍS
ALFAS
ALFÉRECES
ALFÉREZ
ALFORJA
ALFORJAS
ALFRESCO
ALGA
ALGAE
ALGAL
ALGAROBA
ALGAROBAS
ALGARROBA
ALGARROBAS
ALGARROBO
ALGARROBOS
ALGATE
ALGATES
ALGEBRA
ALGEBRAIC
ALGEBRAS
ALGERINE
ALGERINES
ALGESES

ALGESIA
ALGESIAS
ALGESIS
ALGICIDE
ALGICIDES
ALGID
ALGIDITIES
ALGIDITY
ALGIN
ALGINATE
ALGINATES
ALGINIC
ALGINS
ALGOID
ALGOLOGIES
ALGOLOGY
ALGORISM
ALGORISMS
ALGORITHM
ALGORITHMS
ALGUACIL
ALGUACILS
ALGUAZIL
ALGUAZILS
ALGUM
ALGUMS
ALIAS
ALIASES
ALIBI
ALIBIS
ALICANT
ALICANTS
ALICYCLIC
ALIDAD
ALIDADE
ALIDADES
ALIDADS
ALIEN
ALIENABLE
ALIENAGE
ALIENAGES
ALIENATE
ALIENATED
ALIENATES
ALIENATING
ALIENATOR
ALIENATORS
ALIENED
ALIENEE
ALIENEES
ALIENING
ALIENISM
ALIENISMS
ALIENIST
ALIENISTS
ALIENOR
ALIENORS
ALIENS
ALIFORM
ALIGARTA
ALIGARTAS
ALIGHT
ALIGHTED
ALIGHTING
ALIGHTS
ALIGN
ALIGNED
ALIGNING
ALIGNMENT
ALIGNMENTS

ALIGNS
ALIKE
ALIMENT
ALIMENTAL
ALIMENTED
ALIMENTING
ALIMENTS
ALIMONIES
ALIMONY
ALINE
ALINED
ALINEMENT
ALINEMENTS
ALINES
ALINING
ALIPED
ALIPEDS
ALIPHATIC
ALIQUANT
ALIQUOT
ALISMA
ALISMAS
ALIT
ALIUNDE
ALIVE
ALIZARE
ALIZARES
ALIZARIN
ALIZARINE
ALIZARINES
ALIZARINS
ALKAHEST
ALKAHESTS
ALKALI
ALKALIES
ALKALIFIED
ALKALIFIES
ALKALIFY
ALKALIFYING
ALKALINE
ALKALIS
ALKALISE
ALKALISED
ALKALISES
ALKALISING
ALKALIZE
ALKALIZED
ALKALIZES
ALKALIZING
ALKALOID
ALKALOIDS
ALKALOSES
ALKALOSIS
ALKANE
ALKANES
ALKANET
ALKANETS
ALKENE
ALKENES
ALKYD
ALKYDS
ALKYL
ALKYLS
ALKYNE
ALKYNES
ALL
ALLANTOIC
ALLANTOID
ALLANTOIDS
ALLANTOIS

ALLANTOISES
ALLATIVE
ALLATIVES
ALLAY
ALLAYED
ALLAYER
ALLAYERS
ALLAYING
ALLAYINGS
ALLAYMENT
ALLAYMENTS
ALLAYS
ALLEDGE
ALLEDGED
ALLEDGES
ALLEDGING
ALLÉE
ALLÉES
ALLEGE
ALLEGED
ALLEGEDLY
ALLEGER
ALLEGERS
ALLEGES
ALLEGGE
ALLEGGED
ALLEGGES
ALLEGGING
ALLEGIANT
ALLEGING
ALLEGORIC
ALLEGORIES
ALLEGORY
ALLEGRO
ALLEGROS
ALLEL
ALLELE
ALLELES
ALLELS
ALLELUIA
ALLELUIAH
ALLELUIAHS
ALLELUIAS
ALLEMANDE
ALLEMANDES
ALLENARLY
ALLERGEN
ALLERGENS
ALLERGIC
ALLERGIES
ALLERGY
ALLERION
ALLERIONS
ALLEVIATE
ALLEVIATED
ALLEVIATES
ALLEVIATING
ALLEY
ALLEYED
ALLEYS
ALLEYWAY
ALLEYWAYS
ALLHEAL
ALLHEALS
ALLIANCE
ALLIANCES
ALLICE
ALLICES
ALLICHOLIES
ALLICHOLY

ALLIED	ALLOWANCES	ALNAGERS	ALTAR	ALUMINIZED
ALLIES	ALLOWED	ALNAGES	ALTARAGE	ALUMINIZES
ALLIGARTA	ALLOWEDLY	ALOD	ALTARAGES	ALUMINIZING
ALLIGARTAS	ALLOWING	ALODIAL	ALTARS	ALUMINOUS
ALLIGATE	ALLOWS	ALODIUM	ALTARWISE	ALUMINUM
ALLIGATED	ALLOY	ALODIUMS	ALTER	ALUMINUMS
ALLIGATES	ALLOYED	ALODS	ALTERABLE	ALUMISH
ALLIGATING	ALLOYING	ALOE	ALTERANT	ALUMIUM
ALLIGATOR	ALLOYS	ALOED	ALTERANTS	ALUMIUMS
ALLIGATORS	ALLS	ALOES	ALTERCATE	ALUMNA
ALLIS	ALLSEED	ALOETIC	ALTERCATED	ALUMNAE
ALLISES	ALLSEEDS	ALOETICS	ALTERCATES	ALUMNI
ALLNESS	ALLSPICE	ALOFT	ALTERCATING	ALUMNUS
ALLNESSES	ALLSPICES	ALOGIA	ALTERED	ALUMS
ALLNIGHT	ALLUDE	ALOGIAS	ALTERING	ALUNITE
ALLOCABLE	ALLUDED	ALOGICAL	ALTERITIES	ALUNITES
ALLOCARPIES	ALLUDES	ALOHA	ALTERITY	ALURE
ALLOCARPY	ALLUDING	ALOHAS	ALTERN	ALURES
ALLOCATE	ALLURE	ALONE	ALTERNANT	ALVEARIES
ALLOCATED	ALLURED	ALONELY	ALTERNANTS	ALVEARY
ALLOCATES	ALLURER	ALONENESS	ALTERNAT	ALVEATED
ALLOCATING	ALLURERS	ALONENESSES	ALTERNATE	ALVEOLAR
ALLOD	ALLURES	ALONG	ALTERNATED	ALVEOLATE
ALLODIAL	ALLURING	ALONGSIDE	ALTERNATES	ALVEOLE
ALLODIUM	ALLUSION	ALONGST	ALTERNATING	ALVEOLES
ALLODIUMS	ALLUSIONS	ALOOF	ALTERNATS	ALVEOLI
ALLODS	ALLUSIVE	ALOOFLY	ALTERNE	ALVEOLUS
ALLOGAMIES	ALLUVIA	ALOOFNESS	ALTERNES	ALVINE
ALLOGAMY	ALLUVIAL	ALOOFNESSES	ALTERS	ALWAY
ALLOGRAPH	ALLUVION	ALOPECIA	ALTESSE	ALWAYS
ALLOGRAPHS	ALLUVIONS	ALOPECIAS	ALTESSES	ALYSSUM
ALLOMETRIES	ALLUVIUM	ALOPECOID	ALTEZA	ALYSSUMS
ALLOMETRY	ALLY	ALOUD	ALTEZAS	AM
ALLOMORPH	ALLYCHOLIES	ALOW	ALTEZZA	AMABILE
ALLOMORPHS	ALLYCHOLY	ALOWE	ALTEZZAS	AMADAVAT
ALLONGE	ALLYING	ALP	ALTHAEA	AMADAVATS
ALLONGES	ALLYL	ALPACA	ALTHAEAS	AMADOU
ALLONS	ALLYLS	ALPACAS	ALTHORN	AMADOUS
ALLONYM	ALMA	ALPARGATA	ALTHORNS	AMAH
ALLONYMS	ALMAH	ALPARGATAS	ALTHOUGH	AMAHS
ALLOPATH	ALMAHS	ALPEEN	ALTIMETER	AMAIN
ALLOPATHIES	ALMAIN	ALPEENS	ALTIMETERS	AMALGAM
ALLOPATHS	ALMAINS	ALPENHORN	ALTISSIMO	AMALGAMS
ALLOPATHY	ALMANAC	ALPENHORNS	ALTITUDE	AMANDINE
ALLOPHONE	ALMANACS	ALPHA	ALTITUDES	AMANDINES
ALLOPHONES	ALMANDINE	ALPHABET	ALTO	AMANITA
ALLOPLASM	ALMANDINES	ALPHABETS	ALTOS	AMANITAS
ALLOPLASMS	ALMAS	ALPHAS	ALTRICES	AMARACUS
ALLOSAUR	ALME	ALPHASORT	ALTRICIAL	AMARACUSES
ALLOSAURS	ALMEH	ALPHASORTED	ALTRUISM	AMARANT
ALLOSTERIES	ALMEHS	ALPHASORTING	ALTRUISMS	AMARANTH
ALLOSTERY	ALMERIES	ALPHASORTS	ALTRUIST	AMARANTHS
ALLOT	ALMERY	ALPHORN	ALTRUISTS	AMARANTIN
ALLOTMENT	ALMES	ALPHORNS	ALTS	AMARANTS
ALLOTMENTS	ALMIGHTY	ALPINE	ALUDEL	AMARYLLID
ALLOTROPE	ALMIRAH	ALPINES	ALUDELS	AMARYLLIDS
ALLOTROPES	ALMIRAHS	ALPINISM	ALULA	AMARYLLIS
ALLOTROPIES	ALMOND	ALPINISMS	ALULAS	AMARYLLISES
ALLOTROPY	ALMONDS	ALPINIST	ALUM	AMASS
ALLOTS	ALMONER	ALPINISTS	ALUMINA	AMASSABLE
ALLOTTED	ALMONERS	ALPS	ALUMINAS	AMASSED
ALLOTTEE	ALMONRIES	ALREADY	ALUMINATE	AMASSES
ALLOTTEES	ALMONRY	ALRIGHT	ALUMINATES	AMASSING
ALLOTTERIES	ALMOST	ALS	ALUMINISE	AMASSMENT
ALLOTTERY	ALMOUS	ALSIKE	ALUMINISED	AMASSMENTS
ALLOTTING	ALMS	ALSIKES	ALUMINISES	AMATE
ALLOW	ALMUG	ALSO	ALUMINISING	AMATED
ALLOWABLE	ALMUGS	ALSOON	ALUMINIUM	AMATES
ALLOWABLY	ALNAGE	ALSOONE	ALUMINIUMS	AMATEUR
ALLOWANCE	ALNAGER	ALT	ALUMINIZE	AMATEURS

AMATING
AMATION
AMATIONS
AMATIVE
AMATOL
AMATOLS
AMATORIAL
AMATORIAN
AMATORY
AMAUROSES
AMAUROSIS
AMAUROTIC
AMAZE
AMAZED
AMAZEDLY
AMAZEMENT
AMAZEMENTS
AMAZES
AMAZING
AMAZINGLY
AMAZON
AMAZONIAN
AMAZONITE
AMAZONITES
AMAZONS
AMBAGE
AMBAGES
AMBAGIOUS
AMBAN
AMBANS
AMBASSAGE
AMBASSAGES
AMBASSIES
AMBASSY
AMBATCH
AMBATCHES
AMBER
AMBERED
AMBERGRIS
AMBERGRISES
AMBERITE
AMBERITES
AMBERJACK
AMBERJACKS
AMBEROID
AMBEROIDS
AMBEROUS
AMBERS
AMBERY
AMBIANCE
AMBIANCES
AMBIENCE
AMBIENCES
AMBIENT
AMBIENTS
AMBIGUITIES
AMBIGUITY
AMBIGUOUS
AMBIT
AMBITION
AMBITIONS
AMBITIOUS
AMBITS
AMBITTY
AMBIVERT
AMBIVERTS
AMBLE
AMBLED
AMBLER
AMBLERS

AMBLES
AMBLING
AMBLINGS
AMBLYOPIA
AMBLYOPIAS
AMBO
AMBONES
AMBOS
AMBRIES
AMBROID
AMBROIDS
AMBROSIA
AMBROSIAL
AMBROSIAN
AMBROSIAS
AMBROTYPE
AMBROTYPES
AMBRY
AMBULACRA
AMBULANCE
AMBULANCES
AMBULANT
AMBULANTS
AMBULATE
AMBULATED
AMBULATES
AMBULATING
AMBULATOR
AMBULATORS
AMBUSCADE
AMBUSCADED
AMBUSCADES
AMBUSCADING
AMBUSCADO
AMBUSCADOES
AMBUSCADOS
AMBUSH
AMBUSHED
AMBUSHES
AMBUSHING
AMEARST
AMEBA
AMEBAS
AMEBIC
AMEER
AMEERS
AMELCORN
AMELCORNS
AMELIA
AMELIAS
AMEN
AMENABLE
AMENABLY
AMENAGE
AMENAGED
AMENAGES
AMENAGING
AMENAUNCE
AMENAUNCES
AMEND
AMENDABLE
AMENDE
AMENDED
AMENDER
AMENDERS
AMENDES
AMENDING
AMENDMENT
AMENDMENTS
AMENDS

AMENE
AMENED
AMENING
AMENITIES
AMENITY
AMENS
AMENT
AMENTA
AMENTAL
AMENTIA
AMENTIAS
AMENTS
AMENTUM
AMERCE
AMERCED
AMERCES
AMERCING
AMERICIUM
AMERICIUMS
AMETHYST
AMETHYSTS
AMI
AMIABLE
AMIABLY
AMIANTHUS
AMIANTHUSES
AMIANTUS
AMIANTUSES
AMICABLE
AMICABLY
AMICE
AMICES
AMID
AMIDE
AMIDES
AMIDMOST
AMIDSHIPS
AMIDST
AMIE
AMIES
AMIGO
AMIGOS
AMILDAR
AMILDARS
AMINE
AMINES
AMIR
AMIRS
AMIS
AMISES
AMISS
AMISSES
AMISSIBLE
AMISSING
AMITIES
AMITOSES
AMITOSIS
AMITOTIC
AMITY
AMLA
AMLAS
AMMAN
AMMANS
AMMETER
AMMETERS
AMMIRAL
AMMIRALS
AMMO
AMMON
AMMONAL

AMMONALS
AMMONIA
AMMONIAC
AMMONIAS
AMMONITE
AMMONITES
AMMONIUM
AMMONIUMS
AMMONOID
AMMONOIDS
AMMONS
AMMOS
AMNESIA
AMNESIAC
AMNESIACS
AMNESIAS
AMNESIC
AMNESICS
AMNESTIED
AMNESTIES
AMNESTY
AMNESTYING
AMNIA
AMNION
AMNIOTIC
AMOEBA
AMOEBAE
AMOEBAEAN
AMOEBIC
AMOEBOID
AMOK
AMOMUM
AMOMUMS
AMONG
AMONGST
AMOOVE
AMOOVED
AMOOVES
AMOOVING
AMORAL
AMORALISM
AMORALISMS
AMORALIST
AMORALISTS
AMORCE
AMORCES
AMORET
AMORETS
AMORETTI
AMORETTO
AMORINI
AMORINO
AMORISM
AMORISMS
AMORIST
AMORISTS
AMORNINGS
AMOROSA
AMOROSAS
AMOROSITIES
AMOROSITY
AMOROSO
AMOROSOS
AMOROUS
AMOROUSLY
AMORPHISM
AMORPHISMS
AMORPHOUS
AMORT
AMORTISE

AMORTISED
AMORTISES
AMORTISING
AMORTIZE
AMORTIZED
AMORTIZES
AMORTIZING
AMOSITE
AMOSITES
AMOUNT
AMOUNTED
AMOUNTING
AMOUNTS
AMOUR
AMOURETTE
AMOURETTES
AMOURS
AMOVE
AMOVED
AMOVES
AMOVING
AMP
AMPASSIES
AMPASSY
AMPERAGE
AMPERAGES
AMPERE
AMPERES
AMPERSAND
AMPERSANDS
AMPERZAND
AMPERZANDS
AMPHIBIAN
AMPHIBIANS
AMPHIBOLE
AMPHIBOLES
AMPHIBOLIES
AMPHIBOLY
AMPHIGORIES
AMPHIGORY
AMPHIOXUS
AMPHIOXUSES
AMPHIPOD
AMPHIPODS
AMPHOLYTE
AMPHOLYTES
AMPHORA
AMPHORAE
AMPHORIC
AMPLE
AMPLENESS
AMPLENESSES
AMPLER
AMPLEST
AMPLIFIED
AMPLIFIER
AMPLIFIERS
AMPLIFIES
AMPLIFY
AMPLIFYING
AMPLITUDE
AMPLITUDES
AMPLOSOME
AMPLOSOMES
AMPLY
AMPOULE
AMPOULES
AMPS
AMPUL
AMPULE

AMPULES
AMPULLA
AMPULLAE
AMPULS
AMPUTATE
AMPUTATED
AMPUTATES
AMPUTATING
AMPUTATOR
AMPUTATORS
AMPUTEE
AMPUTEES
AMRIT
AMRITA
AMRITAS
AMRITS
AMTMAN
AMTMANS
AMTRACK
AMTRACKS
AMUCK
AMULET
AMULETIC
AMULETS
AMUSABLE
AMUSE
AMUSED
AMUSEDLY
AMUSEMENT
AMUSEMENTS
AMUSER
AMUSERS
AMUSES
AMUSETTE
AMUSETTES
AMUSING
AMUSINGLY
AMUSIVE
AMYGDAL
AMYGDALA
AMYGDALAS
AMYGDALE
AMYGDALES
AMYGDALIN
AMYGDALINS
AMYGDALS
AMYGDULE
AMYGDULES
AMYL
AMYLASE
AMYLASES
AMYLENE
AMYLENES
AMYLOID
AMYLOIDAL
AMYLOPSIN
AMYLOPSINS
AMYLS
AMYLUM
AMYLUMS
AN
ANA
ANABAS
ANABASES
ANABASIS
ANABATIC
ANABIOSES
ANABIOSIS
ANABIOTIC
ANABLEPS

ANABLEPSES
ANABOLIC
ANABOLISM
ANABOL!SMS
ANABRANCH
ANABRANCHES
ANACHARIS
ANACHARISES
ANACONDA
ANACONDAS
ANACRUSES
ANACRUSIS
ANADEM
ANADEMS
ANAEMIA
ANAEMIAS
ANAEMIC
ANAEROBE
ANAEROBES
ANAEROBIC
ANAGLYPH
ANAGLYPHS
ANAGLYPTA
ANAGLYPTAS
ANAGOGE
ANAGOGES
ANAGOGIC
ANAGOGIES
ANAGOGY
ANAGRAM
ANAGRAMMED
ANAGRAMMING
ANAGRAMS
ANAL
ANALCIME
ANALCIMES
ANALCITE
ANALCITES
ANALECTA
ANALECTIC
ANALECTS
ANALEPTIC
ANALGESIA
ANALGESIAS
ANALGESIC
ANALGESICS
ANALLY
ANALOG
ANALOGIC
ANALOGIES
ANALOGISE
ANALOGISED
ANALOGISES
ANALOGISING
ANALOGIST
ANALOGISTS
ANALOGIZE
ANALOGIZED
ANALOGIZES
ANALOGIZING
ANALOGON
ANALOGONS
ANALOGOUS
ANALOGS
ANALOGUE
ANALOGUES
ANALOGY
ANALYSAND
ANALYSANDS
ANALYSE

ANALYSED
ANALYSER
ANALYSERS
ANALYSES
ANALYSING
ANALYSIS
ANALYST
ANALYSTS
ANALYTIC
ANALYTICS
ANALYZE
ANALYZED
ANALYZER
ANALYZERS
ANALYZES
ANALYZING
ANAMNESES
ANAMNESIS
ANAN
ANANA
ANANAS
ANANASES
ANANDROUS
ANANKE
ANANKES
ANANTHOUS
ANAPAEST
ANAPAESTS
ANAPEST
ANAPESTS
ANAPHASE
ANAPHASES
ANAPHORA
ANAPHORAS
ANAPHORIC
ANAPLASTIES
ANAPLASTY
ANAPTYXES
ANAPTYXIS
ANARAK
ANARAKS
ANARCH
ANARCHAL
ANARCHIAL
ANARCHIC
ANARCHIES
ANARCHISE
ANARCHISED
ANARCHISES
ANARCHISING
ANARCHISM
ANARCHISMS
ANARCHIST
ANARCHISTS
ANARCHIZE
ANARCHIZED
ANARCHIZES
ANARCHIZING
ANARCHS
ANARCHY
ANAS
ANASARCA
ANASARCAS
ANASTASES
ANASTASIS
ANASTATIC
ANATASE
ANATASES
ANATHEMA
ANATHEMAS

ANATOMIC
ANATOMIES
ANATOMISE
ANATOMISED
ANATOMISES
ANATOMISING
ANATOMIST
ANATOMISTS
ANATOMIZE
ANATOMIZED
ANATOMIZES
ANATOMIZING
ANATOMY
ANATROPIES
ANATROPY
ANATTA
ANATTAS
ANATTO
ANATTOS
ANBURIES
ANBURY
ANCE
ANCESTOR
ANCESTORS
ANCESTRAL
ANCESTRIES
ANCESTRY
ANCHOR
ANCHORAGE
ANCHORAGES
ANCHORED
ANCHORESS
ANCHORESSES
ANCHORET
ANCHORETS
ANCHORING
ANCHORITE
ANCHORITES
ANCHORS
ANCHOVETA
ANCHOVETAS
ANCHOVIES
ANCHOVY
ANCHYLOSE
ANCHYLOSED
ANCHYLOSES
ANCHYLOSING
ANCHYLOSIS
ANCIENT
ANCIENTLY
ANCIENTRIES
ANCIENTRY
ANCIENTS
ANCILE
ANCILES
ANCILLARIES
ANCILLARY
ANCIPITAL
ANCLE
ANCLES
ANCOME
ANCOMES
ANCON
ANCONES
ANCORA
ANCRESS
ANCRESSES
AND
ANDANTE
ANDANTES

ANDANTINO
ANDANTINOS
ANDESINE
ANDESINES
ANDESITE
ANDESITES
ANDESITIC
ANDIRON
ANDIRONS
ANDROGEN
ANDROGENS
ANDROGYNE
ANDROGYNES
ANDROGYNIES
ANDROGYNY
ANDROID
ANDROIDS
ANDROLOGIES
ANDROLOGY
ANDROMEDA
ANDROMEDAS
ANDS
ANDVILE
ANDVILES
ANE
ANEAR
ANEARED
ANEARING
ANEARS
ANEATH
ANECDOTAL
ANECDOTE
ANECDOTES
ANECHOIC
ANELACE
ANELACES
ANELE
ANELED
ANELES
ANELING
ANEMIA
ANEMIAS
ANEMIC
ANEMOGRAM
ANEMOGRAMS
ANEMOLOGIES
ANEMOLOGY
ANEMONE
ANEMONES
ANENT
ANERLY
ANEROID
ANEROIDS
ANES
ANESTRA
ANESTRI
ANESTROUS
ANESTRUM
ANESTRUS
ANETIC
ANEURIN
ANEURINS
ANEURISM
ANEURISMS
ANEURYSM
ANEURYSMS
ANEW
ANGARIES
ANGARY
ANGEKKOK

ANGEKKOKS	ANGSTROM	ANIMÉS	ANNEALS	ANODAL
ANGEKOK	ANGSTROMS	ANIMES	ANNECTENT	ANODE
ANGEKOKS	ANGSTS	ANIMISM	ANNELID	ANODES
ANGEL	ANGUIFORM	ANIMISMS	ANNELIDS	ANODIC
ANGELHOOD	ANGUINE	ANIMIST	ANNEX	ANODISE
ANGELHOODS	ANGUIPED	ANIMISTIC	ANNEXE	ANODISED
ANGELIC	ANGUIPEDE	ANIMISTS	ANNEXED	ANODISES
ANGELICA	ANGUISH	ANIMOSITIES	ANNEXES	ANODISING
ANGELICAL	ANGUISHED	ANIMOSITY	ANNEXING	ANODIZE
ANGELICAS	ANGUISHES	ANIMUS	ANNEXION	ANODIZED
ANGELS	ANGUISHING	ANIMUSES	ANNEXIONS	ANODIZES
ANGELUS	ANGULAR	ANION	ANNEXMENT	ANODIZING
ANGELUSES	ANGULATED	ANIONIC	ANNEXMENTS	ANODYNE
ANGER	ANHEDONIA	ANIONS	ANNEXURE	ANODYNES
ANGERED	ANHEDONIAS	ANISE	ANNEXURES	ANOESES
ANGERING	ANHEDRAL	ANISEED	ANNICUT	ANOESIS
ANGERLESS	ANHUNGRED	ANISEEDS	ANNICUTS	ANOESTRA
ANGERLY	ANHYDRIDE	ANISES	ANNO	ANOESTRI
ANGERS	ANHYDRIDES	ANISETTE	ANNOTATE	ANOESTRUM
ANGICO	ANHYDRITE	ANISETTES	ANNOTATED	ANOESTRUS
ANGICOS	ANHYDRITES	ANKER	ANNOTATES	ANOETIC
ANGINA	ANHYDROUS	ANKERITE	ANNOTATING	ANOINT
ANGINAL	ANICONIC	ANKERITES	ANNOTATOR	ANOINTED
ANGINAS	ANICONISM	ANKERS	ANNOTATORS	ANOINTING
ANGIOGRAM	ANICONISMS	ANKH	ANNOUNCE	ANOINTS
ANGIOGRAMS	ANICONIST	ANKHS	ANNOUNCED	ANOMALIES
ANGIOMA	ANICONISTS	ANKLE	ANNOUNCER	ANOMALOUS
ANGIOMAS	ANICUT	ANKLED	ANNOUNCERS	ANOMALY
ANGIOMATA	ANICUTS	ANKLES	ANNOUNCES	ANOMIC
ANGLE	ANIGH	ANKLET	ANNOUNCING	ANOMIE
ANGLED	ANIGHT	ANKLETS	ANNOY	ANOMIES
ANGLER	ANIL	ANKUS	ANNOYANCE	ANOMY
ANGLERS	ANILE	ANKUSES	ANNOYANCES	ANON
ANGLES	ANILINE	ANKYLOSE	ANNOYED	ANONYM
ANGLESITE	ANILINES	ANKYLOSED	ANNOYING	ANONYMA
ANGLESITES	ANILITIES	ANKYLOSES	ANNOYS	ANONYMAS
ANGLEWISE	ANILITY	ANKYLOSING	ANNS	ANONYMITIES
ANGLICE	ANILS	ANKYLOSIS	ANNUAL	ANONYMITY
ANGLICISE	ANIMA	ANLACE	ANNUALISE	ANONYMOUS
ANGLICISED	ANIMAL	ANLACES	ANNUALISED	ANONYMS
ANGLICISES	ANIMALIC	ANLAGE	ANNUALISES	ANOPHELES
ANGLICISING	ANIMALISE	ANLAGES	ANNUALISING	ANORAK
ANGLICISM	ANIMALISED	ANN	ANNUALIZE	ANORAKS
ANGLICISMS	ANIMALISES	ANNA	ANNUALIZED	ANORECTIC
ANGLICIST	ANIMALISING	ANNAL	ANNUALIZES	ANORECTICS
ANGLICISTS	ANIMALISM	ANNALISE	ANNUALIZING	ANORETIC
ANGLICIZE	ANIMALISMS	ANNALISED	ANNUALLY	ANORETICS
ANGLICIZED	ANIMALIST	ANNALISES	ANNUALS	ANOREXIA
ANGLICIZES	ANIMALISTS	ANNALISING	ANNUITANT	ANOREXIAS
ANGLICIZING	ANIMALITIES	ANNALIST	ANNUITANTS	ANOREXIC
ANGLIFIED	ANIMALITY	ANNALISTS	ANNUITIES	ANOREXICS
ANGLIFIES	ANIMALIZE	ANNALIZE	ANNUITY	ANOREXIES
ANGLIFY	ANIMALIZED	ANNALIZED	ANNUL	ANOREXY
ANGLIFYING	ANIMALIZES	ANNALIZES	ANNULAR	ANORTHIC
ANGLING	ANIMALIZING	ANNALIZING	ANNULARS	ANORTHITE
ANGLINGS	ANIMALLY	ANNALS	ANNULATE	ANORTHITES
ANGLIST	ANIMALS	ANNAS	ANNULATED	ANOSMIA
ANGLISTS	ANIMAS	ANNAT	ANNULATES	ANOSMIAS
ANGLOPHIL	ANIMATE	ANNATES	ANNULET	ANOTHER
ANGLOPHILS	ANIMATED	ANNATS	ANNULETS	ANOUGH
ANGORA	ANIMATES	ANNATTA	ANNULI	ANOUROUS
ANGORAS	ANIMATING	ANNATTAS	ANNULLED	ANOW
ANGRIER	ANIMATION	ANNATTO	ANNULLING	ANOXIA
ANGRIES	ANIMATIONS	ANNATTOS	ANNULMENT	ANOXIAS
ANGRIEST	ANIMATISM	ANNEAL	ANNULMENTS	ANOXIC
ANGRILY	ANIMATISMS	ANNEALED	ANNULOSE	ANSATE
ANGRINESS	ANIMATOR	ANNEALER	ANNULS	ANSATED
ANGRINESSES	ANIMATORS	ANNEALERS	ANNULUS	ANSERINE
ANGRY	ANIMÉ	ANNEALING	ANOA	ANSWER
ANGST	ANIME	ANNEALINGS	ANOAS	ANSWERED

ANSWERER ANTHOID ANTIPODAL ANXIETIES APEMEN
ANSWERERS ANTHOLOGIES ANTIPODE ANXIETY APEPSIA
ANSWERING ANTHOLOGY ANTIPODES ANXIOUS APEPSIAS
ANSWERS ANTHRACIC ANTIPOLE ANXIOUSLY APEPSIES
ANT ANTHRAX ANTIPOLES ANY APEPSY
ANTA ANTHRAXES ANTIPOPE ANYBODIES APERÇU
ANTACID ANTHROPIC ANTIPOPES ANYBODY APERÇUS
ANTACIDS ANTHURIUM ANTIQUARIES ANYHOW APERIENT
ANTAE ANTHURIUMS ANTIQUARK ANYONE APERIENTS
ANTAR ANTI ANTIQUARKS ANYONES APERIES
ANTARS ANTIAR ANTIQUARY ANYROAD APERIODIC
ANTBEAR ANTIARS ANTIQUATE ANYTHING APÉRITIF
ANTBEARS ANTIBODIES ANTIQUATED ANYTHINGS APÉRITIFS
ANTE ANTIBODY ANTIQUATES ANYTIME APERITIVE
ANTECEDE ANTIC ANTIQUATING ANYWAY APERITIVES
ANTECEDED ANTICHLOR ANTIQUE ANYWAYS APERT
ANTECEDES ANTICHLORS ANTIQUED ANYWHEN APERTNESS
ANTECEDING ANTICIVIC ANTIQUELY ANYWHERE APERTNESSES
ANTECHOIR ANTICIZE ANTIQUES ANYWISE APERTURE
ANTECHOIRS ANTICIZED ANTIQUING ANZIANI APERTURES
ANTED ANTICIZES ANTIQUITIES AORIST APERY
ANTEDATE ANTICIZING ANTIQUITY AORISTIC APES
ANTEDATED ANTICK ANTIS AORISTS APETALIES
ANTEDATES ANTICKE ANTISCIAN AORTA APETALOUS
ANTEDATING ANTICKED ANTISCIANS AORTAL APETALY
ANTEFIX ANTICKES ANTISERA AORTAS APEX
ANTEFIXA ANTICKING ANTISERUM AORTIC APEXES
ANTEFIXAL ANTICKS ANTISERUMS AORTITIS APHAGIA
ANTEFIXES ANTICLINE ANTISHIP AORTITISES APHAGIAS
ANTEING ANTICLINES ANTISPAST AOUDAD APHANITE
ANTELOPE ANTICOUS ANTISPASTS AOUDADS APHANITES
ANTELOPES ANTICS ANTISTAT APACE APHASIA
ANTELUCAN ANTIDOTAL ANTISTATS APACHE APHASIAC
ANTENATAL ANTIDOTE ANTITHET APACHES APHASIACS
ANTENATI ANTIDOTES ANTITHETS APAGE APHASIAS
ANTENNA ANTIENT ANTITOXIC APAGOGE APHASIC
ANTENNAE ANTIENTS ANTITOXIN APAGOGES APHELIA
ANTENNAL ANTIGEN ANTITOXINS APAGOGIC APHELIAN
ANTENNARY ANTIGENIC ANTITRADE APAID APHELIC
ANTENNAS ANTIGENS ANTITRADES APANAGE APHELION
ANTENNULE ANTIHELICES ANTITYPAL APANAGED APHERESES
ANTENNULES ANTIHELIX ANTITYPE APANAGES APHERESIS
ANTEPAST ANT!KNOCK ANTITYPES APART APHESES
ANTEPASTS ANTIKNOCKS ANTITYPIC APARTHEID APHESIS
ANTERIOR ANTILOG ANTIVENIN APARTHEIDS APHETIC
ANTEROOM ANTILOGIES ANTIVENINS APARTMENT APHETISE
ANTEROOMS ANTILOGS ANTIVIRAL APARTMENTS APHETISED
ANTES ANTILOGY ANTLER APARTNESS APHETISES
ANTEVERT ANTIMASK ANTLERED APARTNESSES APHETISING
ANTEVERTED ANTIMASKS ANTLERS APATETIC APHETIZE
ANTEVERTING ANTIMONIC ANTLIA APATHATON APHETIZED
ANTEVERTS ANTIMONIES ANTLIAE APATHATONS APHETIZES
ANTHELIA ANTIMONY ANTLIATE APATHETIC APHETIZING
ANTHELICES ANTING ANTONYM APATHIES APHICIDE
ANTHELION ANTINGS ANTONYMS APATHY APHICIDES
ANTHELIX ANTINODAL ANTRE APATITE APHID
ANTHEM ANTINODE ANTRES APATITES APHIDES
ANTHEMED ANTINODES ANTRORSE APAY APHIDIAN
ANTHEMIA ANTINOMIC ANTRUM APAYD APHIDIANS
ANTHEMING ANTINOMIES ANTRUMS APAYING APHIDICAL
ANTHEMION ANTINOMY ANTS APAYS APHIDS
ANTHEMS ANTIPAPAL ANUCLEATE APE APHIS
ANTHER ANTIPASTO ANUCLEATED APEAK APHONIA
ANTHERS ANTIPASTOS ANURIA APED APHONIAS
ANTHESES ANTIPATHIES ANURIAS APEDOM APHONIC
ANTHESIS ANTIPATHY ANUROUS APEDOMS APHONIES
ANTHOCARP ANTIPHON ANUS APEEK APHONOUS
ANTHOCARPS ANTIPHONIES ANUSES APEHOOD APHONY
ANTHOCYAN ANTIPHONS ANVIL APEHOODS APHORISE
ANTHOCYANS ANTIPHONY ANVILS APEMAN APHORISED

APHORISER	APODES	APOTHEGM	APPERIL	APPOSES
APHORISERS	APODICTIC	APOTHEGMS	APPERILL	APPOSING
APHORISES	APODOSES	APOTHEM	APPERILLS	APPOSITE
APHORISING	APODOSIS	APOTHEMS	APPERILS	APPRAISAL
APHORISM	APODOUS	APOZEM	APPERTAIN	APPRAISALS
APHORISMS	APODS	APOZEMS	APPERTAINED	APPRAISE
APHORIST	APOENZYME	APPAID	APPERTAINING	APPRAISED
APHORISTS	APOENZYMES	APPAIR	APPERTAINS	APPRAISER
APHORIZE	APOGAEIC	APPAIRED	APPESTAT	APPRAISERS
APHORIZED	APOGAMIES	APPAIRING	APPESTATS	APPRAISES
APHORIZER	APOGAMOUS	APPAIRS	APPETENCE	APPRAISING
APHORIZERS	APOGAMY	APPAL	APPETENCES	APPREHEND
APHORIZES	APOGEAL	APPALLED	APPETENCIES	APPREHENDED
APHORIZING	APOGEAN	APPALLING	APPETENCY	APPREHENDING
APHOTIC	APOGEE	APPALS	APPETENT	APPREHENDS
APHTHA	APOGEES	APPALTI	APPETIBLE	APPRESS
APHTHAE	APOGRAPH	APPALTO	APPETISE	APPRESSED
APHTHOUS	APOGRAPHS	APPANAGE	APPETISED	APPRESSES
APHYLLIES	APOLLINE	APPANAGED	APPETISER	APPRESSING
APHYLLOUS	APOLLO	APPANAGES	APPETISERS	APPRISE
APHYLLY	APOLLOS	APPARAT	APPETISES	APPRISED
APIAN	APOLOGIA	APPARATS	APPETISING	APPRISES
APIARIAN	APOLOGIAS	APPARATUS	APPETITE	APPRISING
APIARIES	APOLOGIES	APPARATUSES	APPETITES	APPRIZE
APIARIST	APOLOGISE	APPAREL	APPETIZE	APPRIZED
APIARISTS	APOLOGISED	APPARELLED	APPETIZED	APPRIZER
APIARY	APOLOGISES	APPARELLING	APPETIZER	APPRIZERS
APICAL	APOLOGISING	APPARELS	APPETIZERS	APPRIZES
APICALLY	APOLOGIST	APPARENCIES	APPETIZES	APPRIZING
APICES	APOLOGISTS	APPARENCY	APPETIZING	APPRIZINGS
APICULATE	APOLOGIZE	APPARENT	APPLAUD	APPRO
APIECE	APOLOGIZED	APPARENTS	APPLAUDED	APPROACH
APING	APOLOGIZES	APPARITOR	APPLAUDER	APPROACHED
APIOL	APOLOGIZING	APPARITORS	APPLAUDERS	APPROACHES
APIOLS	APOLOGUE	APPAY	APPLAUDING	APPROACHING
APISH	APOLOGUES	APPAYD	APPLAUDS	APPROBATE
APISHLY	APOLOGY	APPAYING	APPLAUSE	APPROBATED
APISHNESS	APOMICTIC	APPAYS	APPLAUSES	APPROBATES
APISHNESSES	APOMIXES	APPEACH	APPLE	APPROBATING
APISM	APOMIXIS	APPEACHED	APPLES	APPROOF
APISMS	APOOP	APPEACHES	APPLIABLE	APPROOFS
APIVOROUS	APOPHATIC	APPEACHING	APPLIANCE	APPROS
APLANAT	APOPHYGE	APPEAL	APPLIANCES	APPROVAL
APLANATIC	APOPHYGES	APPEALED	APPLICANT	APPROVALS
APLANATS	APOPHYSES	APPEALING	APPLICANTS	APPROVE
APLASIA	APOPHYSIS	APPEALS	APPLICATE	APPROVED
APLASIAS	APOPLEX	APPEAR	APPLIED	APPROVER
APLASTIC	APOPLEXES	APPEARED	APPLIES	APPROVERS
APLENTY	APOPLEXIES	APPEARER	APPLIQUÉ	APPROVES
APLITE	APOPLEXY	APPEARERS	APPLIQUÉS	APPROVING
APLITES	APORIA	APPEARING	APPLY	APPUI
APLOMB	APORIAS	APPEARS	APPLYING	APPUIED
APLOMBS	APORT	APPEASE	APPOINT	APPUIS
APLUSTRE	APOSITIA	APPEASED	APPOINTED	APPULSE
APLUSTRES	APOSITIAS	APPEASES	APPOINTEE	APPULSES
APNEA	APOSPORIES	APPEASING	APPOINTEES	APPUY
APNEAS	APOSPORY	APPELLANT	APPOINTING	APPUYED
APNOEA	APOSTASIES	APPELLANTS	APPOINTOR	APPUYING
APNOEAS	APOSTASY	APPELLATE	APPOINTORS	APPUYS
APOCOPATE	APOSTATE	APPEND	APPOINTS	APRAXIA
APOCOPATED	APOSTATES	APPENDAGE	APPORT	APRAXIAS
APOCOPATES	APOSTATIC	APPENDAGES	APPORTION	APRÈS
APOCOPATING	APOSTIL	APPENDANT	APPORTIONED	APRICATE
APOCOPE	APOSTILLE	APPENDANTS	APPORTIONING	APRICATED
APOCOPES	APOSTILLES	APPENDED	APPORTIONS	APRICATES
APOCRINE	APOSTILS	APPENDICES	APPORTS	APRICATING
APOCRYPHA	APOSTLE	APPENDING	APPOSE	APRICOCK
APOD	APOSTLES	APPENDIX	APPOSED	APRICOCKS
APODAL	APOSTOLIC	APPENDIXES	APPOSER	APRICOT
APODE	APOTHECIA	APPENDS	APPOSERS	APRICOTS

APRIORISM	AQUARIUM	ARAPUNGA	ARCCOS	ARCHON
APRIORISMS	AQUARIUMS	ARAPUNGAS	ARCCOSES	ARCHONS
APRIORIST	AQUAS	ARAR	ARCED	ARCHONTIC
APRIORISTS	AQUATIC	ARAROBA	ARCH	ARCHWAY
APRIORITIES	AQUATICS	ARAROBAS	ARCHAEI	ARCHWAYS
APRIORITY	AQUATINT	ARARS	ARCHAEUS	ARCHWISE
APRON	AQUATINTA	ARAUCARIA	ARCHAIC	ARCING
APRONED	AQUATINTAS	ARAUCARIAS	ARCHAISE	ARCINGS
APRONFUL	AQUATINTED	ARAYSE	ARCHAISED	ARCKED
APRONFULS	AQUATINTING	ARAYSED	ARCHAISER	ARCKING
APRONING	AQUATINTS	ARAYSES	ARCHAISERS	ARCKINGS
APRONS	AQUAVIT	ARAYSING	ARCHAISES	ARCO
APROPOS	AQUAVITS	ARBA	ARCHAISING	ARCS
APSE	AQUEDUCT	ARBALEST	ARCHAISM	ARCSECOND
APSES	AQUEDUCTS	ARBALESTS	ARCHAISMS	ARCSECONDS
APSIDAL	AQUEOUS	ARBALIST	ARCHAIST	ARCSINS
APSIDES	AQUIFER	ARBALISTS	ARCHAISTS	ARCSINS
APSIDIOLE	AQUIFERS	ARBAS	ARCHAIZE	ARCTAN
APSIDIOLES	AQUILEGIA	ARBITER	ARCHAIZED	ARCTANS
APSIS	AQUILEGIAS	ARBITERS	ARCHAIZER	ARCTIC
APT	AQUILINE	ARBITRAGE	ARCHAIZERS	ARCTICS
APTED	AQUIVER	ARBITRAGED	ARCHAIZES	ARCTOID
APTER	AR	ARBITRAGES	ARCHAIZING	ARCTOPHIL
APTERAL	ARABA	ARBITRAGING	ARCHANGEL	ARCTOPHILS
APTERIA	ARABAS	ARBITRAL	ARCHANGELS	ARCUATE
APTERIUM	ARABESQUE	ARBITRARY	ARCHDUCAL	ARCUATED
APTEROUS	ARABESQUED	ARBITRATE	ARCHDUCHIES	ARCUATION
APTERYX	ARABESQUES	ARBITRATED	ARCHDUCHY	ARCUATIONS
APTERYXES	ARABICA	ARBITRATES	ARCHDUKE	ARCUS
APTEST	ARABICAS	ARBITRATING	ARCHDUKES	ARCUSES
APTING	ARABIN	ARBITRESS	ARCHED	ARDEB
APTITUDE	ARABINOSE	ARBITRESSES	ARCHEI	ARDEBS
APTITUDES	ARABINOSES	ARBITRIUM	ARCHER	ARDENCIES
APTLY	ARABINS	ARBITRIUMS	ARCHERESS	ARDENCY
APTNESS	ARABISE	ARBLAST	ARCHERESSES	ARDENT
APTNESSES	ARABISED	ARBLASTER	ARCHERIES	ARDENTLY
APTOTE	ARABISES	ARBLASTERS	ARCHERS	ARDOUR
APTOTES	ARABISING	ARBLASTS	ARCHERY	ARDOURS
APTOTIC	ARABIZE	ARBOR	ARCHES	ARDRI
APTS	ARABIZED	ARBOREAL	ARCHEST	ARDRIGH
APYRETIC	ARABIZES	ARBOREOUS	ARCHETYPE	ARDRIGHS
APYREXIA	ARABIZING	ARBORET	ARCHETYPES	ARDRIS
APYREXIAS	ARABLE	ARBORETA	ARCHEUS	ARDUOUS
AQUA	ARACEAE	ARBORETS	ARCHIL	ARDUOUSLY
AQUABATIC	ARACEOUS	ARBORETUM	ARCHILOWE	ARE
AQUABATICS	ARACHIS	ARBORIST	ARCHILOWES	AREA
AQUABOARD	ARACHISES	ARBORISTS	ARCHILS	AREACH
AQUABOARDS	ARACHNID	ARBOROUS	ARCHIMAGE	AREACHED
AQUACADE	ARACHNIDS	ARBORS	ARCHIMAGES	AREACHES
AQUACADES	ARACHNOID	ARBOUR	ARCHING	AREACHING
AQUADROME	ARACHNOIDS	ARBOURED	ARCHITECT	AREAD
AQUADROMES	ARAGONITE	ARBOURS	ARCHITECTED	AREADING
AQUAE	ARAGONITES	ARBUTE	ARCHITECTING	AREADS
AQUAFER	ARAISE	ARBUTES	ARCHITECTS	AREAL
AQUAFERS	ARAISED	ARBUTUS	ARCHIVAL	AREAR
AQUALUNG	ARAISES	ARBUTUSES	ARCHIVE	AREAS
AQUALUNGS	ARAISING	ARC	ARCHIVES	ARECA
AQUANAUT	ARAK	ARCADE	ARCHIVIST	ARECAS
AQUANAUTS	ARAKS	ARCADED	ARCHIVISTS	ARED
AQUAPLANE	ARALIA	ARCADES	ARCHIVOLT	AREDD
AQUAPLANES	ARALIAS	ARCADING	ARCHIVOLTS	AREDE
AQUARELLE	ARAME	ARCADINGS	ARCHLET	AREDES
AQUARELLES	ARAMES	ARCANA	ARCHLETS	AREDING
AQUARIA	ARANEID	ARCANE	ARCHLUTE	AREFIED
AQUARIAN	ARANEIDS	ARCANELY	ARCHLUTES	AREFIES
AQUARIANS	ARANEOUS	ARCANER	ARCHLY	AREFY
AQUARIIST	ARAPAIMA	ARCANEST	ARCHNESS	AREFYING
AQUARIISTS	ARAPAIMAS	ARCANIST	ARCHNESSES	ARENA
AQUARIST	ARAPONGA	ARCANISTS	ARCHOLOGIES	ARENAS
AQUARISTS	ARAPONGAS	ARCANUM	ARCHOLOGY	ARENATION

ARENATIONS
AREOLA
AREOLAE
AREOLAR
AREOLATE
AREOLATED
AREOLE
AREOLES
AREOMETER
AREOMETERS
AREOSTYLE
AREOSTYLES
ARERE
ARES
ARET
ARÊTE
ARÊTES
ARETS
ARETT
ARETTED
ARETTING
ARETTS
AREW
ARGAL
ARGALA
ARGALAS
ARGALI
ARGALIS
ARGAN
ARGAND
ARGANDS
ARGANS
ARGEMONE
ARGEMONES
ARGENT
ARGENTINE
ARGENTINES
ARGENTITE
ARGENTITES
ARGENTS
ARGHAN
ARGHANS
ARGIL
ARGILLITE
ARGILLITES
ARGILS
ARGININE
ARGININES
ARGOL
ARGOLS
ARGON
ARGONAUT
ARGONAUTS
ARGONS
ARGOSIES
ARGOSY
ARGOT
ARGOTS
ARGUABLE
ARGUABLY
ARGUE
ARGUED
ARGUER
ARGUERS
ARGUES
ARGUFIED
ARGUFIES
ARGUFY
ARGUFYING
ARGUING

ARGULI
ARGULUS
ARGUMENT
ARGUMENTS
ARGUS
ARGUSES
ARGUTE
ARGUTELY
ARGYLE
ARGYLES
ARGYRIA
ARGYRIAS
ARGYRITE
ARGYRITES
ARHYTHMIA
ARHYTHMIAS
ARHYTHMIC
ARIA
ARIAS
ARID
ARIDER
ARIDEST
ARIDITIES
ARIDITY
ARIDLY
ARIDNESS
ARIDNESSES
ARIEL
ARIELS
ARIETTA
ARIETTAS
ARIETTE
ARIETTES
ARIGHT
ARIL
ARILLARY
ARILLATE
ARILLATED
ARILLI
ARILLODE
ARILLODES
ARILLUS
ARILS
ARIOSI
ARIOSO
ARIOSOS
ARIOT
ARIPPLE
ARIS
ARISE
ARISEN
ARISES
ARISH
ARISHES
ARISING
ARISTA
ARISTAE
ARISTAS
ARISTATE
ARISTO
ARISTOS
ARK
ARKED
ARKING
ARKITE
ARKITES
ARKOSE
ARKOSES
ARKS
ARLES

ARLESED
ARLESES
ARLESING
ARM
ARMADA
ARMADAS
ARMADILLO
ARMADILLOS
ARMAMENT
ARMAMENTS
ARMATURE
ARMATURES
ARMBAND
ARMBANDS
ARMCHAIR
ARMCHAIRS
ARMED
ARMET
ARMETS
ARMFUL
ARMFULS
ARMGAUNT
ARMHOLE
ARMHOLES
ARMIES
ARMIGER
ARMIGERAL
ARMIGERO
ARMIGEROS
ARMIGERS
ARMIL
ARMILLA
ARMILLAE
ARMILLARY
ARMILLAS
ARMILS
ARMING
ARMISTICE
ARMISTICES
ARMLESS
ARMLET
ARMLETS
ARMLOCK
ARMLOCKS
ARMOIRE
ARMOIRES
ARMOR
ARMORIAL
ARMORIES
ARMORIST
ARMORISTS
ARMORS
ARMORY
ARMOUR
ARMOURED
ARMOURER
ARMOURERS
ARMOURIES
ARMOURS
ARMOURY
ARMOZEEN
ARMOZEENS
ARMOZINE
ARMOZINES
ARMPIT
ARMPITS
ARMS
ARMURE
ARMURES
ARMY

ARNA
ARNAS
ARNICA
ARNICAS
ARNOTTO
ARNOTTOS
ARNUT
ARNUTS
AROBA
AROBAS
AROID
AROIDS
AROINT
AROINTED
AROINTING
AROINTS
AROLLA
AROLLAS
AROMA
AROMAS
AROMATIC
AROMATICS
AROMATISE
AROMATISED
AROMATISES
AROMATISING
AROMATIZE
AROMATIZED
AROMATIZES
AROMATIZING
AROSE
AROUND
AROUSAL
AROUSALS
AROUSE
AROUSED
AROUSER
AROUSERS
AROUSES
AROUSING
AROW
AROYNT
AROYNTED
AROYNTING
AROYNTS
ARPEGGIO
ARPEGGIOS
ARPENT
ARPENTS
ARQUEBUS
ARQUEBUSE
ARQUEBUSES
ARRACACHA
ARRACACHAS
ARRACK
ARRACKS
ARRAH
ARRAIGN
ARRAIGNED
ARRAIGNER
ARRAIGNERS
ARRAIGNING
ARRAIGNINGS
ARRAIGNS
ARRANGE
ARRANGED
ARRANGER
ARRANGERS
ARRANGES
ARRANGING

ARRANT
ARRANTLY
ARRAS
ARRASED
ARRASENE
ARRASENES
ARRASES
ARRAUGHT
ARRAY
ARRAYED
ARRAYING
ARRAYMENT
ARRAYMENTS
ARRAYS
ARREAR
ARREARAGE
ARREARAGES
ARREARS
ARRECT
ARREDD
ARREEDE
ARREEDES
ARREEDING
ARREST
ARRESTED
ARRESTEE
ARRESTEES
ARRESTER
ARRESTERS
ARRESTING
ARRESTIVE
ARRESTOR
ARRESTORS
ARRESTS
ARRÊT
ARRÊTS
ARRIAGE
ARRIAGES
ARRIDE
ARRIDED
ARRIDES
ARRIDING
ARRIÉRÉ
ARRIERO
ARRIEROS
ARRIS
ARRISES
ARRISH
ARRISHES
ARRIVAL
ARRIVALS
ARRIVANCE
ARRIVANCES
ARRIVANCIES
ARRIVANCY
ARRIVE
ARRIVED
ARRIVES
ARRIVING
ARRIVISME
ARRIVISMES
ARRIVISTE
ARRIVISTES
ARROBA
ARROBAS
ARROGANCE
ARROGANCES
ARROGANCIES
ARROGANCY
ARROGANT

ARROGATE	ARTHROPOD	ASCARIDES	ASHAMEDLY	ASPARTAMES
ARROGATED	ARTHROPODS	ASCARIDS	ASHAMES	ASPECT
ARROGATES	ARTHROSES	ASCARIS	ASHAMING	ASPECTED
ARROGATING	ARTHROSIS	ASCAUNT	ASHEN	ASPECTING
ARROW	ARTIC	ASCEND	ASHERIES	ASPECTS
ARROWED	ARTICHOKE	ASCENDANT	ASHERY	ASPECTUAL
ARROWING	ARTICHOKES	ASCENDANTS	ASHES	ASPEN
ARROWROOT	ARTICLE	ASCENDED	ASHET	ASPENS
ARROWROOTS	ARTICLED	ASCENDENT	ASHETS	ASPER
ARROWS	ARTICLES	ASCENDENTS	ASHIER	ASPERATE
ARROWWOOD	ARTICLING	ASCENDER	ASHIEST	ASPERATED
ARROWWOODS	ARTICS	ASCENDERS	ASHINE	ASPERATES
ARROWY	ARTICULAR	ASCENDING	ASHIVER	ASPERATING
ARROYO	ARTIER	ASCENDS	ASHLAR	ASPERGE
ARROYOS	ARTIEST	ASCENSION	ASHLARED	ASPERGED
ARS	ARTIFACT	ASCENSIONS	ASHLARING	ASPERGER
ARSE	ARTIFACTS	ASCENSIVE	ASHLARINGS	ASPERGERS
ARSEHOLE	ARTIFICE	ASCENT	ASHLARS	ASPERGES
ARSEHOLES	ARTIFICER	ASCENTS	ASHLER	ASPERGILL
ARSENAL	ARTIFICERS	ASCERTAIN	ASHLERED	ASPERGILLS
ARSENALS	ARTIFICES	ASCERTAINED	ASHLERING	ASPERGING
ARSENATE	ARTILLERIES	ASCERTAINING	ASHLERINGS	ASPERITIES
ARSENATES	ARTILLERY	ASCERTAINS	ASHLERS	ASPERITY
ARSENIATE	ARTISAN	ASCESES	ASHORE	ASPEROUS
ARSENIATES	ARTISANAL	ASCESIS	ASHRAM	ASPERS
ARSENIC	ARTISANS	ASCETIC	ASHRAMA	ASPERSE
ARSENICAL	ARTIST	ASCETICAL	ASHRAMAS	ASPERSED
ARSENICS	ARTISTE	ASCETICS	ASHRAMS	ASPERSES
ARSENIDE	ARTISTES	ASCI	ASHY	ASPERSING
ARSENIDES	ARTISTIC	ASCIAN	ASIDE	ASPERSION
ARSENIOUS	ARTISTRIES	ASCIANS	ASIDES	ASPERSIONS
ARSENITE	ARTISTRY	ASCIDIA	ASINICO	ASPERSIVE
ARSENITES	ARTISTS	ASCIDIAN	ASINICOS	ASPERSOIR
ARSES	ARTLESS	ASCIDIANS	ASININE	ASPERSOIRS
ARSHEEN	ARTLESSLY	ASCIDIUM	ASININITIES	ASPERSORY
ARSHEENS	ARTS	ASCITES	ASININITY	ASPHALT
ARSHIN	ARTSIER	ASCITIC	ASK	ASPHALTED
ARSHINE	ARTSIEST	ASCITICAL	ASKANCE	ASPHALTIC
ARSHINES	ARTSMAN	ASCLEPIAD	ASKANCED	ASPHALTING
ARSHINS	ARTSMEN	ASCLEPIADS	ASKANCES	ASPHALTS
ARSINE	ARTSY	ASCLEPIAS	ASKANCING	ASPHALTUM
ARSINES	ARTWORK	ASCLEPIASES	ASKANT	ASPHALTUMS
ARSIS	ARTWORKS	ASCONCE	ASKANTED	ASPHODEL
ARSON	ARTY	ASCORBATE	ASKANTING	ASPHODELS
ARSONIST	ARUM	ASCORBATES	ASKANTS	ASPHYXIA
ARSONISTS	ARUMS	ASCORBIC	ASKARI	ASPHYXIAS
ARSONITE	ARVAL	ASCOSPORE	ASKARIS	ASPHYXIES
ARSONITES	ARVO	ASCOSPORES	ASKED	ASPHYXY
ARSONS	ARVOS	ASCOT	ASKER	ASPIC
ART	ARY	ASCOTS	ASKERS	ASPICK
ARTAL	ARYBALLOS	ASCRIBE	ASKESES	ASPICKS
ARTEFACT	ARYBALLOSES	ASCRIBED	ASKESIS	ASPICS
ARTEFACTS	ARYL	ASCRIBES	ASKEW	ASPIDIA
ARTEL	ARYLS	ASCRIBING	ASKING	ASPIDIOID
ARTELS	ARYTENOID	ASCUS	ASKLENT	ASPIDIUM
ARTEMISIA	ARYTENOIDS	ASEISMIC	ASKS	ASPINE
ARTEMISIAS	AS	ASEITIES	ASLAKE	ASPINES
ARTERIAL	ASAFETIDA	ASEITY	ASLAKED	ASPIRANT
ARTERIES	ASAFETIDAS	ASEPALOUS	ASLAKES	ASPIRANTS
ARTERIOLE	ASANA	ASEPSES	ASLAKING	ASPIRATE
ARTERIOLES	ASANAS	ASEPSIS	ASLANT	ASPIRATED
ARTERITIS	ASAR	ASEPTATE	ASLEEP	ASPIRATES
ARTERITISES	ASARUM	ASEPTIC	ASLOPE	ASPIRATING
ARTERY	ASARUMS	ASEPTICS	ASMEAR	ASPIRATOR
ARTESIAN	ASBESTIC	ASEXUAL	ASMOULDER	ASPIRATORS
ARTFUL	ASBESTINE	ASEXUALLY	ASOCIAL	ASPIRE
ARTFULLY	ASBESTOS	ASH	ASP	ASPIRED
ARTHRITIC	ASBESTOSES	ASHAKE	ASPARAGUS	ASPIRES
ARTHRITICS	ASBESTOUS	ASHAME	ASPARAGUSES	ASPIRIN
ARTHRITIS	ASCARID	ASHAMED	ASPARTAME	ASPIRING

ASPIRINS	ASSENTS	ASSONANCE	ASTERID	ASTRODOMES
ASPORT	ASSERT	ASSONANCES	ASTERIDS	ASTROFELL
ASPORTED	ASSERTED	ASSONANT	ASTERISK	ASTROFELLS
ASPORTING	ASSERTER	ASSONATE	ASTERISKED	ASTROID
ASPORTS	ASSERTERS	ASSONATED	ASTERISKING	ASTROIDS
ASPOUT	ASSERTING	ASSONATES	ASTERISKS	ASTROLABE
ASPRAWL	ASSERTION	ASSONATING	ASTERISM	ASTROLABES
ASPREAD	ASSERTIONS	ASSORT	ASTERISMS	ASTROLOGIES
ASPROUT	ASSERTIVE	ASSORTED	ASTERN	ASTROLOGY
ASPS	ASSERTOR	ASSORTER	ASTEROID	ASTRONAUT
ASQUAT	ASSERTORS	ASSORTERS	ASTEROIDS	ASTRONAUTS
ASQUINT	ASSERTORY	ASSORTING	ASTERS	ASTRONOMIES
ASS	ASSERTS	ASSORTS	ASTERT	ASTRONOMY
ASSAGAI	ASSES	ASSOT	ASTERTED	ASTROPHEL
ASSAGAIED	ASSESS	ASSOTS	ASTERTING	ASTROPHELS
ASSAGAIING	ASSESSED	ASSOTT	ASTERTS	ASTRUT
ASSAGAIS	ASSESSES	ASSOTTED	ASTHENIA	ASTUCIOUS
ASSAI	ASSESSING	ASSOTTING	ASTHENIAS	ASTUCITIES
ASSAIL	ASSESSOR	ASSUAGE	ASTHENIC	ASTUCITY
ASSAILANT	ASSESSORS	ASSUAGED	ASTHENICS	ASTUN
ASSAILANTS	ASSET	ASSUAGES	ASTHMA	ASTUNNED
ASSAILED	ASSETS	ASSUAGING	ASTHMAS	ASTUNNING
ASSAILING	ASSEVER	ASSUAGINGS	ASTHMATIC	ASTUNS
ASSAILS	ASSEVERED	ASSUASIVE	ASTHORE	ASTUTE
ASSAIS	ASSEVERING	ASSUETUDE	ASTHORES	ASTUTELY
ASSART	ASSEVERS	ASSUETUDES	ASTICHOUS	ASTUTER
ASSARTED	ASSHOLE	ASSUMABLE	ASTIGMIA	ASTUTEST
ASSARTING	ASSHOLES	ASSUMABLY	ASTIGMIAS	ASTYLAR
ASSARTS	ASSIDUITIES	ASSUME	ASTILBE	ASUDDEN
ASSASSIN	ASSIDUITY	ASSUMED	ASTILBES	ASUNDER
ASSASSINS	ASSIDUOUS	ASSUMEDLY	ASTIR	ASWARM
ASSAULT	ASSIEGE	ASSUMES	ASTOMOUS	ASWAY
ASSAULTED	ASSIEGED	ASSUMING	ASTONE	ASWIM
ASSAULTER	ASSIEGES	ASSUMINGS	ASTONED	ASWING
ASSAULTERS	ASSIEGING	ASSUMPSIT	ASTONES	ASWIRL
ASSAULTING	ASSIENTO	ASSUMPSITS	ASTONIED	ASWOON
ASSAULTS	ASSIENTOS	ASSURABLE	ASTONIES	ASYLUM
ASSAY	ASSIGN	ASSURANCE	ASTONING	ASYLUMS
ASSAYABLE	ASSIGNAT	ASSURANCES	ASTONISH	ASYMMETRIES
ASSAYED	ASSIGNATS	ASSURE	ASTONISHED	ASYMMETRY
ASSAYER	ASSIGNED	ASSURED	ASTONISHES	ASYMPTOTE
ASSAYERS	ASSIGNEE	ASSUREDLY	ASTONISHING	ASYMPTOTES
ASSAYING	ASSIGNEES	ASSUREDS	ASTONY	ASYNDETIC
ASSAYINGS	ASSIGNING	ASSURER	ASTONYING	ASYNDETON
ASSAYS	ASSIGNOR	ASSURERS	ASTOOP	ASYNDETONS
ASSEGAAI	ASSIGNORS	ASSURES	ASTOUND	ASYNERGIA
ASSEGAAIED	ASSIGNS	ASSURGENT	ASTOUNDED	ASYNERGIAS
ASSEGAAIING	ASSIST	ASSURING	ASTOUNDING	ASYSTOLE
ASSEGAAIS	ASSISTANT	ASSWAGE	ASTOUNDS	ASYSTOLES
ASSEGAI	ASSISTANTS	ASSWAGED	ASTRADDLE	AT
ASSEGAIED	ASSISTED	ASSWAGES	ASTRAGAL	ATABAL
ASSEGAIING	ASSISTING	ASSWAGING	ASTRAGALS	ATABALS
ASSEGAIS	ASSISTS	ASTABLE	ASTRAKHAN	ATABEG
ASSEMBLE	ASSIZE	ASTARE	ASTRAKHANS	ATABEGS
ASSEMBLÉ	ASSIZED	ASTART	ASTRAL	ATABEK
ASSEMBLED	ASSIZER	ASTARTED	ASTRAND	ATABEKS
ASSEMBLER	ASSIZERS	ASTARTING	ASTRAY	ATABRIN
ASSEMBLERS	ASSIZES	ASTARTS	ASTREX	ATABRINS
ASSEMBLES	ASSIZING	ASTATIC	ASTREXES	ATACAMITE
ASSEMBLÉS	ASSOCIATE	ASTATINE	ASTRICT	ATACAMITES
ASSEMBLIES	ASSOCIATED	ASTATINES	ASTRICTED	ATACTIC
ASSEMBLING	ASSOCIATES	ASTATKI	ASTRICTING	ATAGHAN
ASSEMBLY	ASSOCIATING	ASTATKIS	ASTRICTS	ATAGHANS
ASSENT	ASSOIL	ASTEISM	ASTRIDE	ATALAYA
ASSENTED	ASSOILED	ASTEISMS	ASTRINGE	ATALAYAS
ASSENTER	ASSOILING	ASTELIC	ASTRINGED	ATAMAN
ASSENTERS	ASSOILS	ASTELIES	ASTRINGER	ATAMANS
ASSENTING	ASSOILZIE	ASTELY	ASTRINGERS	ATAP
ASSENTIVE	ASSOILZIED	ASTER	ASTRINGES	ATAPS
ASSENTOR	ASSOILZIEING	ASTERIA	ASTRINGING	ATARACTIC
ASSENTORS	ASSOILZIES	ASTERIAS	ASTRODOME	ATARACTICS

ATARAXIA	ATHRILL	ATONEMENTS	ATTEMPERING	ATTRAP
ATARAXIAS	ATHROB	ATONER	ATTEMPERS	ATTRAPPED
ATARAXIC	ATHROCYTE	ATONERS	ATTEMPT	ATTRAPPING
ATARAXICS	ATHROCYTES	ATONES	ATTEMPTED	ATTRAPS
ATARAXIES	ATHWART	ATONIC	ATTEMPTER	ATTRIBUTE
ATARAXY	ATILT	ATONICITIES	ATTEMPTERS	ATTRIBUTED
ATAVISM	ATIMIES	ATONICITY	ATTEMPTING	ATTRIBUTES
ATAVISMS	ATIMY	ATONIES	ATTEMPTS	ATTRIBUTING
ATAVISTIC	ATINGLE	ATONING	ATTEND	ATTRIST
ATAXIA	ATLAS	ATONINGLY	ATTENDANT	ATTRISTED
ATAXIAS	ATLASES	ATONY	ATTENDANTS	ATTRISTING
ATAXIC	ATMAN	ATOP	ATTENDED	ATTRISTS
ATAXIES	ATMANS	ATOPIC	ATTENDEE	ATTRITE
ATAXY	ATMOLOGIES	ATOPIES	ATTENDEES	ATTRITION
ATCHIEVE	ATMOLOGY	ATOPY	ATTENDER	ATTRITIONS
ATCHIEVED	ATMOLYSE	ATRAMENT	ATTENDERS	ATTUENT
ATCHIEVES	ATMOLYSED	ATRAMENTS	ATTENDING	ATTUITE
ATCHIEVING	ATMOLYSES	ATREMBLE	ATTENDS	ATTUITED
ATE	ATMOLYSING	ATRESIA	ATTENT	ATTUITES
ATEBRIN	ATMOLYSIS	ATRESIAS	ATTENTAT	ATTUITING
ATEBRINS	ATMOLYZE	ATRIA	ATTENTATS	ATTUITION
ATELIER	ATMOLYZED	ATRIAL	ATTENTION	ATTUITIONS
ATELIERS	ATMOLYZES	ATRIP	ATTENTIONS	ATTUITIVE
ATHANASIES	ATMOLYZING	ATRIUM	ATTENTIVE	ATTUNE
ATHANASY	ATMOMETER	ATROCIOUS	ATTENTS	ATTUNED
ATHANOR	ATMOMETERS	ATROCITIES	ATTENUANT	ATTUNES
ATHANORS	ATOC	ATROCITY	ATTENUANTS	ATTUNING
ATHEISE	ATOCIA	ATROPHIED	ATTENUATE	ATWAIN
ATHEISED	ATOCIAS	ATROPHIES	ATTENUATED	ATWEEL
ATHEISES	ATOCS	ATROPHY	ATTENUATES	ATWEEN
ATHEISING	ATOK	ATROPHYING	ATTENUATING	ATWIXT
ATHEISM	ATOKAL	ATROPIA	ATTERCOP	ATYPICAL
ATHEISMS	ATOKE	ATROPIAS	ATTERCOPS	AUBADE
ATHEIST	ATOKES	ATROPIN	ATTEST	AUBADES
ATHEISTIC	ATOKOUS	ATROPINE	ATTESTED	AUBERGE
ATHEISTS	ATOKS	ATROPINES	ATTESTER	AUBERGES
ATHEIZE	ATOLL	ATROPINS	ATTESTERS	AUBERGINE
ATHEIZED	ATOLLS	ATROPISM	ATTESTING	AUBERGINES
ATHEIZES	ATOM	ATROPISMS	ATTESTOR	AUBRIETIA
ATHEIZING	ATOMIC	ATROPOUS	ATTESTORS	AUBRIETIAS
ATHELING	ATOMICAL	ATTABOY	ATTESTS	AUBURN
ATHELINGS	ATOMICITIES	ATTACH	ATTIC	AUCEPS
ATHEMATIC	ATOMICITY	ATTACHÉ	ATTICS	AUCESPSES
ATHEOLOGIES	ATOMIES	ATTACHED	ATTIRE	AUCTION
ATHEOLOGY	ATOMISE	ATTACHES	ATTIRED	AUCTIONED
ATHEOUS	ATOMISED	ATTACHÉS	ATTIRES	AUCTIONING
ATHERINE	ATOMISER	ATTACHING	ATTIRING	AUCTIONS
ATHERINES	ATOMISERS	ATTACK	ATTIRINGS	AUCTORIAL
ATHEROMA	ATOMISES	ATTACKED	ATTITUDE	AUCUBA
ATHEROMAS	ATOMISING	ATTACKER	ATTITUDES	AUCUBAS
ATHETESES	ATOMISM	ATTACKERS	ATTOLLENT	AUDACIOUS
ATHETESIS	ATOMISMS	ATTACKING	ATTOLLENTS	AUDACITIES
ATHETISE	ATOMIST	ATTACKS	ATTONCE	AUDACITY
ATHETISED	ATOMISTIC	ATTAIN	ATTONE	AUDIBLE
ATHETISES	ATOMISTS	ATTAINDER	ATTONED	AUDIBLY
ATHETISING	ATOMIZE	ATTAINDERS	ATTONES	AUDIENCE
ATHETIZE	ATOMIZED	ATTAINED	ATTONING	AUDIENCES
ATHETIZED	ATOMIZER	ATTAINING	ATTORN	AUDIENT
ATHETIZES	ATOMIZERS	ATTAINS	ATTORNED	AUDIENTS
ATHETIZING	ATOMIZES	ATTAINT	ATTORNEY	AUDILE
ATHETOID	ATOMIZING	ATTAINTED	ATTORNEYS	AUDILES
ATHETOIDS	ATOMS	ATTAINTING	ATTORNING	AUDIO
ATHETOSES	ATOMY	ATTAINTS	ATTORNS	AUDIOGRAM
ATHETOSIS	ATONAL	ATTAP	ATTRACT	AUDIOGRAMS
ATHIRST	ATONALISM	ATTAPS	ATTRACTED	AUDIOLOGIES
ATHLETA	ATONALISMS	ATTAR	ATTRACTING	AUDIOLOGY
ATHLETAS	ATONALITIES	ATTARS	ATTRACTOR	AUDIOPHIL
ATHLETE	ATONALITY	ATTASK	ATTRACTORS	AUDIOPHILS
ATHLETES	ATONE	ATTASKT	ATTRACTS	AUDIOS
ATHLETIC	ATONED	ATTEMPER	ATTRAHENT	AUDIPHONE
ATHLETICS	ATONEMENT	ATTEMPERED	ATTRAHENTS	AUDIPHONES

AUDIT
AUDITED
AUDITING
AUDITION
AUDITIONED
AUDITIONING
AUDITIONS
AUDITIVE
AUDITOR
AUDITORIA
AUDITORIES
AUDITORS
AUDITORY
AUDITRESS
AUDITRESSES
AUDITS
AUF
AUFGABE
AUFGABES
AUFS
AUGER
AUGERS
AUGHT
AUGHTS
AUGITE
AUGITES
AUGITIC
AUGMENT
AUGMENTED
AUGMENTER
AUGMENTERS
AUGMENTING
AUGMENTOR
AUGMENTORS
AUGMENTS
AUGUR
AUGURAL
AUGURED
AUGURER
AUGURERS
AUGURIES
AUGURING
AUGURS
AUGURSHIP
AUGURSHIPS
AUGURY
AUGUST
AUGUSTE
AUGUSTER
AUGUSTES
AUGUSTEST
AUGUSTLY
AUGUSTS
AUK
AUKLET
AUKLETS
AUKS
AULA
AULARIAN
AULARIANS
AULAS
AULD
AULDER
AULDEST
AULIC
AULOI
AULOS
AUMAIL
AUMAILED
AUMAILING
AUMAILS

AUMBRIES
AUMBRY
AUMIL
AUMILS
AUNT
AUNTER
AUNTERS
AUNTIE
AUNTIES
AUNTS
AUNTY
AURA
AURAE
AURAL
AURALLY
AURAS
AURATE
AURATED
AURATES
AUREATE
AUREI
AUREITIES
AUREITY
AURELIA
AURELIAN
AURELIANS
AURELIAS
AUREOLA
AUREOLAS
AUREOLE
AUREOLED
AUREOLES
AUREUS
AURIC
AURICLE
AURICLED
AURICLES
AURICULA
AURICULAR
AURICULAS
AURIFIED
AURIFIES
AURIFORM
AURIFY
AURIFYING
AURISCOPE
AURISCOPES
AURIST
AURISTS
AUROCHS
AUROCHSES
AURORA
AURORAE
AURORAL
AURORALLY
AURORAS
AUROREAN
AUROUS
AUSPICATE
AUSPICATED
AUSPICATES
AUSPICATING
AUSPICE
AUSPICES
AUSTENITE
AUSTENITES
AUSTERE
AUSTERELY
AUSTERER
AUSTEREST
AUSTERITIES

AUSTERITY
AUTACOID
AUTACOIDS
AUTARCHIC
AUTARCHIES
AUTARCHY
AUTARKIC
AUTARKIES
AUTARKIST
AUTARKISTS
AUTARKY
AUTEUR
AUTEURS
AUTHENTIC
AUTHOR
AUTHORED
AUTHORESS
AUTHORESSES
AUTHORIAL
AUTHORING
AUTHORINGS
AUTHORISE
AUTHORISED
AUTHORISES
AUTHORISH
AUTHORISING
AUTHORISM
AUTHORISMS
AUTHORITIES
AUTHORITY
AUTHORIZE
AUTHORIZED
AUTHORIZES
AUTHORIZING
AUTHORS
AUTISM
AUTISMS
AUTISTIC
AUTO
AUTOBUS
AUTOBUSES
AUTOCADE
AUTOCADES
AUTOCAR
AUTOCARP
AUTOCARPS
AUTOCARS
AUTOCLAVE
AUTOCLAVES
AUTOCRACIES
AUTOCRACY
AUTOCRAT
AUTOCRATS
AUTOCROSS
AUTOCROSSES
AUTOCUE
AUTOCUES
AUTOCYCLE
AUTOCYCLES
AUTODYNE
AUTOFLARE
AUTOFLARES
AUTOGAMIC
AUTOGAMIES
AUTOGAMY
AUTOGENIC
AUTOGENIES
AUTOGENY
AUTOGIRO
AUTOGIROS
AUTOGRAFT

AUTOGRAFTED
AUTOGRAFTING
AUTOGRAFTS
AUTOGRAPH
AUTOGRAPHED
AUTOGRAPHING
AUTOGRAPHS
AUTOGYRO
AUTOGYROS
AUTOHARP
AUTOHARPS
AUTOLATRIES
AUTOLATRY
AUTOLOGIES
AUTOLOGY
AUTOLYSE
AUTOLYSED
AUTOLYSES
AUTOLYSING
AUTOLYSIS
AUTOLYTIC
AUTOLYZE
AUTOLYZED
AUTOLYZES
AUTOLYZING
AUTOMAT
AUTOMATA
AUTOMATE
AUTOMATED
AUTOMATES
AUTOMATIC
AUTOMATICS
AUTOMATING
AUTOMATON
AUTOMATONS
AUTOMATS
AUTONOMIC
AUTONOMICS
AUTONOMIES
AUTONOMY
AUTONYM
AUTONYMS
AUTOPHAGIES
AUTOPHAGY
AUTOPHOBIES
AUTOPHOBY
AUTOPHONIES
AUTOPHONY
AUTOPILOT
AUTOPILOTS
AUTOPISTA
AUTOPISTAS
AUTOPOINT
AUTOPOINTS
AUTOPSIA
AUTOPSIAS
AUTOPSIED
AUTOPSIES
AUTOPSY
AUTOPSYING
AUTOPTIC
AUTOROUTE
AUTOROUTES
AUTOS
AUTOSCOPIES
AUTOSCOPY
AUTOSOMAL
AUTOSOME
AUTOSOMES
AUTOTELIC
AUTOTIMER

AUTOTIMERS
AUTOTOMIES
AUTOTOMY
AUTOTOXIN
AUTOTOXINS
AUTOTROPH
AUTOTROPHS
AUTOTYPE
AUTOTYPED
AUTOTYPES
AUTOTYPING
AUTOVAC
AUTOVACS
AUTUMN
AUTUMNAL
AUTUMNS
AUTUMNY
AUTUNITE
AUTUNITES
AUXESES
AUXESIS
AUXETIC
AUXETICS
AUXILIAR
AUXILIARIES
AUXILIARS
AUXILIARY
AUXIN
AUXINS
AUXOMETER
AUXOMETERS
AVA
AVADAVAT
AVADAVATS
AVAIL
AVAILABLE
AVAILABLY
AVAILE
AVAILED
AVAILES
AVAILFUL
AVAILING
AVAILS
AVAL
AVALANCHE
AVALANCHED
AVALANCHES
AVALANCHING
AVALE
AVALED
AVALES
AVALING
AVANT
AVANTI
AVARICE
AVARICES
AVAS
AVAST
AVATAR
AVATARS
AVAUNT
AVAUNTED
AVAUNTING
AVAUNTS
AVE
AVENGE
AVENGED
AVENGEFUL
AVENGEING
AVENGER
AVENGERS

AVENGES
AVENGING
AVENIR
AVENIRS
AVENS
AVENSES
AVENTAIL
AVENTAILE
AVENTAILES
AVENTAILS
AVENTRE
AVENTRED
AVENTRES
AVENTRING
AVENTURE
AVENTURES
AVENUE
AVENUES
AVER
AVERAGE
AVERAGED
AVERAGES
AVERAGING
AVERMENT
AVERMENTS
AVERRED
AVERRING
AVERS
AVERSE
AVERSELY
AVERSION
AVERSIONS
AVERSIVE
AVERT
AVERTABLE
AVERTED
AVERTEDLY
AVERTIBLE
AVERTING
AVERTS
AVES
AVGAS
AVGASES
AVIAN
AVIARIES
AVIARIST
AVIARISTS
AVIARY
AVIATE
AVIATED
AVIATES
AVIATING
AVIATION
AVIATIONS
AVIATOR
AVIATORS
AVIATRIX
AVIATRIXES
AVID
AVIDER
AVIDEST
AVIDITIES
AVIDITY
AVIDLY
AVIETTE
AVIETTES
AVIFAUNA
AVIFAUNAS
AVIFORM
AVINE
AVION

AVIONIC
AVIONICS
AVIONS
AVISANDUM
AVISANDUMS
AVISE
AVISED
AVISEMENT
AVISEMENTS
AVISES
AVISING
AVISO
AVISOS
AVITAL
AVIZANDUM
AVIZANDUMS
AVIZE
AVIZED
AVIZEFULL
AVIZES
AVIZING
AVOCADO
AVOCADOS
AVOCATION
AVOCATIONS
AVOCET
AVOCETS
AVOID
AVOIDABLE
AVOIDANCE
AVOIDANCES
AVOIDED
AVOIDING
AVOIDS
AVOISION
AVOISIONS
AVOSET
AVOSETS
AVOUCH
AVOUCHED
AVOUCHES
AVOUCHING
AVOUÉ
AVOUÉS
AVOURE
AVOURES
AVOUTERER
AVOUTERERS
AVOUTRER
AVOUTRERS
AVOUTRIES
AVOUTRY
AVOW
AVOWABLE
AVOWAL
AVOWALS
AVOWED
AVOWEDLY
AVOWING
AVOWRIES
AVOWRY
AVOWS
AVOYER
AVOYERS
AVULSE
AVULSED
AVULSES
AVULSING
AVULSION
AVULSIONS
AVUNCULAR

AVYZE
AVYZED
AVYZES
AVYZING
AW
AWA
AWAIT
AWAITED
AWAITING
AWAITS
AWAKE
AWAKED
AWAKEN
AWAKENED
AWAKENING
AWAKENINGS
AWAKENS
AWAKES
AWAKING
AWAKINGS
AWANTING
AWARD
AWARDED
AWARDING
AWARDS
AWARE
AWARENESS
AWARENESSES
AWARER
AWAREST
AWARN
AWARNED
AWARNING
AWARNS
AWASH
AWATCH
AWAVE
AWAY
AWAYES
AWAYS
AWDL
AWDLS
AWE
AWEARIED
AWEARY
AWED
AWEEL
AWELESS
AWES
AWESOME
AWESOMELY
AWESTRIKE
AWESTRIKES
AWESTRIKING
AWESTRUCK
AWETO
AWETOS
AWFUL
AWFULLY
AWFULNESS
AWFULNESSES
AWHAPE
AWHAPED
AWHAPES
AWHAPING
AWHEEL
AWHEELS
AWHILE
AWING
AWKWARD
AWKWARDER

AWKWARDEST
AWKWARDLY
AWL
AWLBIRD
AWLBIRDS
AWLS
AWMOUS
AWMRIE
AWMRIES
AWMRY
AWN
AWNED
AWNER
AWNERS
AWNIER
AWNIEST
AWNING
AWNINGS
AWNLESS
AWNS
AWNY
AWOKE
AWOKEN
AWORK
AWRACK
AWRONG
AWRY
AWSOME
AX
AXE
AXED
AXEL
AXELS
AXES
AXIAL
AXIALLY
AXIL
AXILE
AXILLA
AXILLAE
AXILLAR
AXILLARY
AXILS
AXING
AXINITE
AXINITES
AXIOLOGIES
AXIOLOGY
AXIOM
AXIOMATIC
AXIOMATICS
AXIOMS
AXIS
AXISES
AXLE
AXLES
AXOID
AXOIDS
AXOLOTL
AXOLOTLS
AXON
AXONS
AXOPLASM
AXOPLASMS
AY
AYAH
AYAHS
AYAHUASCO
AYAHUASCOS
AYATOLLAH
AYATOLLAHS

AYE
AYELP
AYENBITE
AYENBITES
AYES
AYGRE
AYONT
AYRE
AYRES
AYRIE
AYRIES
AYU
AYURVEDIC
AYUS
AYWORD
AYWORDS
AZALEA
AZALEAS
AZAN
AZANS
AZEOTROPE
AZEOTROPES
AZIDE
AZIDES
AZIMUTH
AZIMUTHAL
AZIMUTHS
AZIONE
AZIONES
AZOIC
AZOLLA
AZOLLAS
AZONAL
AZONIC
AZOTE
AZOTES
AZOTH
AZOTHS
AZOTIC
AZOTISE
AZOTISED
AZOTISES
AZOTISING
AZOTIZE
AZOTIZED
AZOTIZES
AZOTIZING
AZOTOUS
AZULEJO
AZULEJOS
AZURE
AZUREAN
AZURES
AZURINE
AZURINES
AZURITE
AZURITES
AZURN
AZURY
AZYGIES
AZYGOUS
AZYGY
AZYM
AZYME
AZYMES
AZYMITE
AZYMITES
AZYMOUS
AZYMS

B

BA
BAA
BAAED
BAAING
BAAINGS
BAAS
BAASES
BAASSKAP
BAASSKAPS
BABA
BABACOOTE
BABACOOTES
BABAS
BABASSU
BABASSUS
BABBIT
BABBITS
BABBITTED
BABBITTING
BABBLE
BABBLED
BABBLER
BABBLERS
BABBLES
BABBLIER
BABBLIEST
BABBLING
BABBLINGS
BABBLY
BABE
BABELDOM
BABELDOMS
BABELISH
BABELISM
BABELISMS
BABES
BABICHE
BABICHES
BABIED
BABIER
BABIES
BABIEST
BABIRUSSA
BABIRUSSAS
BABLAH
BABLAHS
BABOO
BABOON
BABOONERIES
BABOONERY
BABOONISH
BABOONS
BABOOS
BABOOSH
BABOOSHES
BABOUCHE
BABOUCHES
BABU
BABUCHE
BABUCHES
BABUDOM
BABUDOMS
BABUISM
BABUISMS

BABUL
BABULS
BABUS
BABUSHKA
BABUSHKAS
BABY
BABYFOOD
BABYFOODS
BABYHOOD
BABYHOODS
BABYING
BABYISH
BACCA
BACCAE
BACCARA
BACCARAS
BACCARAT
BACCARATS
BACCARE
BACCAS
BACCATE
BACCHANAL
BACCHANALS
BACCHANT
BACCHANTE
BACCHANTES
BACCHANTS
BACCHIAC
BACCHII
BACCHIUS
BACCIES
BACCIFORM
BACCO
BACCOES
BACCOS
BACCY
BACH
BACHARACH
BACHARACHS
BACHED
BACHELOR
BACHELORS
BACHES
BACHING
BACHS
BACILLAR
BACILLARY
BACILLI
BACILLUS
BACK
BACKACHE
BACKACHES
BACKARE
BACKBAND
BACKBANDS
BACKBIT
BACKBITE
BACKBITER
BACKBITERS
BACKBITES
BACKBITING
BACKBITTEN
BACKBOND
BACKBONDS

BACKBONE
BACKBONED
BACKBONES
BACKCHAT
BACKCHATS
BACKCHATTED
BACKCHATTING
BACKCOURT
BACKCOURTS
BACKDOWN
BACKDOWNS
BACKDROP
BACKDROPS
BACKED
BACKER
BACKERS
BACKET
BACKETS
BACKFALL
BACKFALLS
BACKFILL
BACKFILLED
BACKFILLING
BACKFILLS
BACKFIRE
BACKFIRED
BACKFIRES
BACKFIRING
BACKFISCH
BACKFISCHES
BACKHAND
BACKHANDS
BACKHOE
BACKHOES
BACKING
BACKINGS
BACKLASH
BACKLASHES
BACKLIST
BACKLISTS
BACKLOG
BACKLOGS
BACKMOST
BACKPACK
BACKPACKED
BACKPACKING
BACKPACKINGS
BACKPACKS
BACKPAY
BACKPAYS
BACKPIECE
BACKPIECES
BACKROOM
BACKS
BACKSAW
BACKSAWS
BACKSET
BACKSETS
BACKSEY
BACKSEYS
BACKSHISH
BACKSHISHES
BACKSIDE
BACKSIDES

BACKSIGHT
BACKSIGHTS
BACKSLID
BACKSLIDE
BACKSLIDES
BACKSLIDING
BACKSPACE
BACKSPACED
BACKSPACES
BACKSPACING
BACKSPEER
BACKSPEERED
BACKSPEERING
BACKSPEERS
BACKSPEIR
BACKSPEIRED
BACKSPEIRING
BACKSPEIRS
BACKSPIN
BACKSPINS
BACKSTAGE
BACKSTALL
BACKSTALLS
BACKSTAYS
BACKSTOP
BACKSTOPS
BACKSWORD
BACKSWORDS
BACKTRACK
BACKTRACKED
BACKTRACKING
BACKTRACKS
BACKVELD
BACKVELDS
BACKWARD
BACKWARDS
BACKWASH
BACKWASHED
BACKWASHES
BACKWASHING
BACKWATER
BACKWATERS
BACKWOODS
BACKWORD
BACKWORDS
BACKWORK
BACKWORKS
BACKYARD
BACKYARDS
BACLAVA
BACLAVAS
BACON
BACONS
BACTERIA
BACTERIAL
BACTERIAN
BACTERIC
BACTERISE
BACTERISED
BACTERISES
BACTERISING
BACTERIUM
BACTERIZE
BACTERIZED

BACTERIZES
BACTERIZING
BACTEROID
BACTEROIDS
BACULINE
BACULITE
BACULITES
BAD
BADDIE
BADDIES
BADDISH
BADDY
BADE
BADGE
BADGER
BADGERED
BADGERING
BADGERLY
BADGERS
BADGES
BADINAGE
BADINAGES
BADIOUS
BADLANDS
BADLY
BADMAN
BADMASH
BADMASHES
BADMEN
BADMINTON
BADMINTONS
BADMOUTH
BADMOUTHED
BADMOUTHING
BADMOUTHS
BADNESS
BADNESSES
BAEL
BAELS
BAETYL
BAETYLS
BAFF
BAFFED
BAFFIES
BAFFING
BAFFLE
BAFFLED
BAFFLEGAB
BAFFLEGABS
BAFFLER
BAFFLERS
BAFFLES
BAFFLING
BAFFS
BAFFY
BAFT
BAFTS
BAG
BAGARRE
BAGARRES
BAGASSE
BAGASSES
BAGATELLE
BAGATELLES

BAGEL	BAILORS	BALANCED	BALKING	BALLOTING
BAGELS	BAILS	BALANCER	BALKINGLY	BALLOTS
BAGFUL	BAILSMAN	BALANCERS	BALKINGS	BALLOW
BAGFULS	BAILSMEN	BALANCES	BALKLINE	BALLOWS
BAGGAGE	BAININ	BALANCING	BALKLINES	BALLPARK
BAGGAGES	BAININS	BALANITIS	BALKS	BALLS
BAGGED	BAIRN	BALANITISES	BALKY	BALLY
BAGGIER	BAIRNLIKE	BALAS	BALL	BALLYHOO
BAGGIEST	BAIRNLY	BALASES	BALLABILE	BALLYHOOS
BAGGILY	BAIRNS	BALATA	BALLABILES	BALLYRAG
BAGGING	BAISEMAIN	BALATAS	BALLABILI	BALLYRAGGED
BAGGINGS	BAISEMAINS	BALBOA	BALLAD	BALLYRAGGING
BAGGIT	BAIT	BALBOAS	BALLADE	BALLYRAGS
BAGGITS	BAITED	BALCONET	BALLADED	BALM
BAGGY	BAITER	BALCONETS	BALLADEER	BALMED
BAGMAN	BAITERS	BALCONIED	BALLADEERED	BALMIER
BAGMEN	BAITFISH	BALCONIES	BALLADEERING	BALMIEST
BAGNIO	BAITFISHES	BALCONY	BALLADEERS	BALMILY
BAGNIOS	BAITING	BALD	BALLADES	BALMINESS
BAGPIPE	BAITINGS	BALDACHIN	BALLADING	BALMINESSES
BAGPIPER	BAITS	BALDACHINS	BALLADIST	BALMING
BAGPIPERS	BAIZE	BALDAQUIN	BALLADISTS	BALMORAL
BAGPIPES	BAIZED	BALDAQUINS	BALLADRIES	BALMORALS
BAGPIPING	BAIZES	BALDER	BALLADRY	BALMS
BAGPIPINGS	BAIZING	BALDEST	BALLADS	BALMY
BAGS	BAJADA	BALDING	BALLAN	BALNEAL
BAGUETTE	BAJADAS	BALDISH	BALLANS	BALNEARIES
BAGUETTES	BAJAN	BALDLY	BALLANT	BALNEARY
BAGUIO	BAJANS	BALDMONEY	BALLANTS	BALONEY
BAGUIOS	BAJRA	BALDMONEYS	BALLAST	BALONEYS
BAGWASH	BAJRAS	BALDNESS	BALLASTED	BALOO
BAGWASHES	BAJREE	BALDNESSES	BALLASTING	BALOOS
BAGWIG	BAJREES	BALDPATE	BALLASTS	BALSA
BAGWIGS	BAJRI	BALDPATED	BALLAT	BALSAM
BAH	BAJRIS	BALDPATES	BALLATS	BALSAMED
BAHADA	BAKE	BALDRIC	BALLCOCK	BALSAMIC
BAHADAS	BAKEAPPLE	BALDRICK	BALLCOCKS	BALSAMING
BAHT	BAKEAPPLES	BALDRICKS	BALLED	BALSAMS
BAHTS	BAKEBOARD	BALDRICS	BALLERINA	BALSAMY
BAHUVRIHI	BAKEBOARDS	BALE	BALLERINAS	BALSAS
BAHUVRIHIS	BAKED	BALECTION	BALLERINE	BALTHASAR
BAIGNOIRE	BAKEHOUSE	BALECTIONS	BALLET	BALTHASARS
BAIGNOIRES	BAKEHOUSES	BALED	BALLETIC	BALTHAZAR
BAIL	BAKEMEAT	BALEEN	BALLETS	BALTHAZARS
BAILABLE	BAKEMEATS	BALEENS	BALLING	BALU
BAILBOND	BAKEN	BALEFUL	BALLINGS	BALUS
BAILBONDS	BAKER	BALEFULLY	BALLISTA	BALUSTER
BAILED	BAKERIES	BALER	BALLISTAE	BALUSTERS
BAILEE	BAKERS	BALERS	BALLISTAS	BALZARINE
BAILEES	BAKERY	BALES	BALLISTIC	BALZARINES
BAILER	BAKES	BALING	BALLISTICS	BAM
BAILERS	BAKESTONE	BALISTA	BALLIUM	BAMBINI
BAILEY	BAKESTONES	BALISTAE	BALLIUMS	BAMBINO
BAILEYS	BAKEWARE	BALISTAS	BALLOCKS	BAMBINOS
BAILIE	BAKEWARES	BALK	BALLOCKSED	BAMBOO
BAILIES	BAKHSHISH	BALKANISE	BALLOCKSES	BAMBOOS
BAILIFF	BAKHSHISHES	BALKANISED	BALLOCKSING	BAMBOOZLE
BAILIFFS	BAKING	BALKANISES	BALLON	BAMBOOZLED
BAILING	BAKINGS	BALKANISING	BALLONET	BAMBOOZLES
BAILIWICK	BAKLAVA	BALKANIZE	BALLONETS	BAMBOOZLING
BAILIWICKS	BAKLAVAS	BALKANIZED	BALLONS	BAMMED
BAILLI	BAKSHEESH	BALKANIZES	BALLOON	BAMMER
BAILLIAGE	BAKSHEESHES	BALKANIZING	BALLOONED	BAMMERS
BAILLIAGES	BALADIN	BALKED	BALLOONING	BAMMING
BAILLIE	BALADINE	BALKER	BALLOONINGS	BAMPOT
BAILLIES	BALADINES	BALKERS	BALLOONS	BAMPOTS
BAILLIS	BALADINS	BALKIER	BALLOT	BAMS
BAILMENT	BALALAIKA	BALKIEST	BALLOTED	BAN
BAILMENTS	BALALAIKAS	BALKINESS	BALLOTEE	BANAL
BAILOR	BALANCE	BALKINESSES	BALLOTEES	BANALER

BANALEST
BANALITIES
BANALITY
BANALLY
BANANA
BANANAS
BANAUSIAN
BANAUSIC
BANC
BANCO
BANCOS
BANCS
BAND
BANDAGE
BANDAGED
BANDAGES
BANDAGING
BANDALORE
BANDALORES
BANDANA
BANDANAS
BANDANNA
BANDANNAS
BANDAR
BANDARS
BANDBRAKE
BANDBRAKES
BANDEAU
BANDEAUX
BANDED
BANDELET
BANDELETS
BANDELIER
BANDELIERS
BANDEROL
BANDEROLE
BANDEROLES
BANDEROLS
BANDH
BANDHED
BANDHING
BANDHS
BANDICOOT
BANDICOOTED
BANDICOOTING
BANDICOOTS
BANDIED
BANDIER
BANDIES
BANDIEST
BANDING
BANDINGS
BANDIT
BANDITRIES
BANDITRY
BANDITS
BANDITTI
BANDITTIS
BANDOBAST
BANDOBASTS
BANDOG
BANDOGS
BANDOLEER
BANDOLEERS
BANDOLERO
BANDOLEROS
BANDOLIER
BANDOLIERS
BANDOLINE
BANDOLINES

BANDOOK
BANDOOKS
BANDORA
BANDORAS
BANDORE
BANDORES
BANDROL
BANDROLS
BANDS
BANDSMAN
BANDSMEN
BANDSTAND
BANDSTANDS
BANDSTER
BANDSTERS
BANDURA
BANDURAS
BANDWAGON
BANDWAGONS
BANDWIDTH
BANDWIDTHS
BANDY
BANDYING
BANDYINGS
BANDYMAN
BANDYMEN
BANE
BANEBERRIES
BANEBERRY
BANED
BANEFUL
BANEFULLY
BANES
BANG
BANGED
BANGER
BANGERS
BANGING
BANGLE
BANGLED
BANGLES
BANGS
BANGSRING
BANGSRINGS
BANGSTER
BANGSTERS
BANI
BANIA
BANIAN
BANIANS
BANIAS
BANING
BANISH
BANISHED
BANISHES
BANISHING
BANISTER
BANISTERS
BANJAX
BANJAXED
BANJAXES
BANJAXING
BANJO
BANJOES
BANJOIST
BANJOISTS
BANJOS
BANJULELE
BANJULELES
BANK

BANKABLE
BANKED
BANKER
BANKERS
BANKET
BANKETS
BANKING
BANKINGS
BANKROLL
BANKROLLS
BANKRUPT
BANKRUPTED
BANKRUPTING
BANKRUPTS
BANKS
BANKSIA
BANKSIAS
BANKSMAN
BANKSMEN
BANLIEUE
BANLIEUES
BANNED
BANNER
BANNERALL
BANNERALLS
BANNERED
BANNERET
BANNERETS
BANNEROL
BANNEROLS
BANNERS
BANNING
BANNOCK
BANNOCKS
BANNS
BANQUET
BANQUETED
BANQUETER
BANQUETERS
BANQUETING
BANQUETINGS
BANQUETS
BANQUETTE
BANQUETTES
BANS
BANSHEE
BANSHEES
BANT
BANTAM
BANTAMS
BANTED
BANTENG
BANTENGS
BANTER
BANTERED
BANTERER
BANTERERS
BANTERING
BANTERINGS
BANTERS
BANTING
BANTINGS
BANTLING
BANTLINGS
BANTS
BANXRING
BANXRINGS
BANYAN
BANYANS
BANZAI

BAOBAB
BAOBABS
BAP
BAPS
BAPTISE
BAPTISED
BAPTISES
BAPTISING
BAPTISM
BAPTISMAL
BAPTISMS
BAPTIST
BAPTISTRIES
BAPTISTRY
BAPTISTS
BAPTIZE
BAPTIZED
BAPTIZES
BAPTIZING
BAPU
BAPUS
BAR
BARACAN
BARACANS
BARAGOUIN
BARAGOUINS
BARATHEA
BARATHEAS
BARATHRUM
BARATHRUMS
BARB
BARBARIAN
BARBARIANS
BARBARIC
BARBARISE
BARBARISED
BARBARISES
BARBARISING
BARBARISM
BARBARISMS
BARBARITIES
BARBARITY
BARBARIZE
BARBARIZED
BARBARIZES
BARBARIZING
BARBAROUS
BARBASCO
BARBASCOS
BARBASTEL
BARBASTELS
BARBATE
BARBATED
BARBE
BARBECUE
BARBECUED
BARBECUES
BARBECUING
BARBED
BARBEL
BARBELS
BARBER
BARBERED
BARBERING
BARBERRIES
BARBERRY
BARBERS
BARBES
BARBET
BARBETS

BARBETTE
BARBETTES
BARBICAN
BARBICANS
BARBICEL
BARBICELS
BARBING
BARBITAL
BARBITALS
BARBITONE
BARBITONES
BARBOLA
BARBOLAS
BARBOTINE
BARBOTINES
BARBS
BARBULE
BARBULES
BARCA
BARCAROLE
BARCAROLES
BARCAS
BARCHAN
BARCHANE
BARCHANES
BARCHANS
BARD
BARDED
BARDIC
BARDING
BARDLING
BARDLINGS
BARDS
BARDSHIP
BARDSHIPS
BARDY
BARE
BAREBACK
BAREBOAT
BAREBONE
BAREBONES
BARED
BAREFACED
BAREFOOT
BAREGE
BAREGES
BAREGINE
BAREGINES
BARELY
BARENESS
BARENESSES
BARER
BARES
BARESARK
BARESARKS
BAREST
BARF
BARFED
BARFING
BARFLIES
BARFLY
BARFS
BARFUL
BARGAIN
BARGAINED
BARGAINER
BARGAINERS
BARGAINING
BARGAINS
BARGAIST

BARGAISTS
BARGANDER
BARGANDERS
BARGE
BARGED
BARGEE
BARGEES
BARGEESE
BARGELLO
BARGELLOS
BARGEMAN
BARGEMEN
BARGEPOLE
BARGEPOLES
BARGES
BARGEST
BARGESTS
BARGHEST
BARGHESTS
BARGING
BARGOOSE
BARIC
BARILLA
BARILLAS
BARING
BARISH
BARITE
BARITES
BARITONE
BARITONES
BARIUM
BARIUMS
BARK
BARKAN
BARKANS
BARKED
BARKEEPER
BARKEEPERS
BARKEN
BARKENED
BARKENING
BARKENS
BARKER
BARKERS
BARKHAN
BARKHANS
BARKIER
BARKIEST
BARKING
BARKLESS
BARKS
BARKY
BARLEY
BARLEYS
BARM
BARMAID
BARMAIDS
BARMAN
BARMBRACK
BARMBRACKS
BARMEN
BARMIER
BARMIEST
BARMINESS
BARMINESSES
BARMIZVAH
BARMIZVAHS
BARMKIN
BARMKINS
BARMS

BARMY
BARN
BARNACLE
BARNACLED
BARNACLES
BARNED
BARNEY
BARNEYS
BARNING
BARNS
BARNSTORM
BARNSTORMED
BARNSTORMING
BARNSTORMS
BARNYARD
BARNYARDS
BAROCCO
BAROCCOS
BAROCK
BAROCKS
BAROGRAM
BAROGRAMS
BAROGRAPH
BAROGRAPHS
BAROMETER
BAROMETERS
BAROMETRIES
BAROMETRY
BAROMETZ
BAROMETZES
BARON
BARONAGE
BARONAGES
BARONESS
BARONESSES
BARONET
BARONETCIES
BARONETCY
BARONETS
BARONIAL
BARONIES
BARONNE
BARONNES
BARONS
BARONY
BAROQUE
BAROQUES
BAROSCOPE
BAROSCOPES
BAROSTAT
BAROSTATS
BAROUCHE
BAROUCHES
BARP
BARPERSON
BARPERSONS
BARPS
BARQUE
BARQUES
BARRACAN
BARRACANS
BARRACE
BARRACES
BARRACK
BARRACKED
BARRACKER
BARRACKERS
BARRACKING
BARRACKINGS
BARRACKS

BARRACOON
BARRACOONS
BARRACUDA
BARRACUDAS
BARRAGE
BARRAGES
BARRANCA
BARRANCAS
BARRANCO
BARRANCOS
BARRAT
BARRATOR
BARRATORS
BARRATRIES
BARRATRY
BARRATS
BARRÉ
BARRE
BARRED
BARREFULL
BARREL
BARRELAGE
BARRELAGES
BARRELFUL
BARRELFULS
BARRELLED
BARRELLING
BARRELS
BARREN
BARRENER
BARRENEST
BARRES
BARRET
BARRETS
BARRETTE
BARRETTES
BARRICADE
BARRICADED
BARRICADES
BARRICADING
BARRICADO
BARRICADOED
BARRICADOES
BARRICADOING
BARRICADOS
BARRICO
BARRICOES
BARRICOS
BARRIER
BARRIERED
BARRIERING
BARRIERS
BARRING
BARRINGS
BARRIO
BARRIOS
BARRISTER
BARRISTERS
BARROW
BARROWS
BARRULET
BARRULETS
BARS
BARTENDER
BARTENDERS
BARTER
BARTERED
BARTERER
BARTERERS
BARTERING

BARTERS
BARTISAN
BARTISANED
BARTISANS
BARTIZAN
BARTIZANS
BARTON
BARTONS
BARWOOD
BARWOODS
BARYE
BARYES
BARYON
BARYONS
BARYTA
BARYTAS
BARYTES
BARYTIC
BARYTON
BARYTONE
BARYTONES
BARYTONS
BAS
BASAL
BASALT
BASALTIC
BASALTS
BASAN
BASANITE
BASANITES
BASANS
BASBLEU
BASBLEUS
BASCULE
BASCULES
BASE
BASEBALL
BASEBALLS
BASEBOARD
BASEBOARDS
BASECOURT
BASECOURTS
BASED
BASELARD
BASELARDS
BASELESS
BASELY
BASEMAN
BASEMEN
BASEMENT
BASEMENTS
BASENESS
BASENESSES
BASENJI
BASENJIS
BASEPLATE
BASEPLATES
BASER
BASES
BASEST
BASH
BASHAW
BASHAWISM
BASHAWISMS
BASHAWS
BASHED
BASHER
BASHERS
BASHES
BASHFUL

BASHFULLY
BASHING
BASHINGS
BASHLESS
BASHLYK
BASHLYKS
BASIC
BASICALLY
BASICITIES
BASICITY
BASICS
BASIDIA
BASIDIAL
BASIDIUM
BASIFIXED
BASIFUGAL
BASIL
BASILAR
BASILICA
BASILICAL
BASILICAN
BASILICAS
BASILICON
BASILICONS
BASILISK
BASILISKS
BASILS
BASIN
BASINET
BASINETS
BASINFUL
BASINFULS
BASING
BASINS
BASIPETAL
BASIS
BASK
BASKED
BASKET
BASKETFUL
BASKETFULS
BASKETRIES
BASKETRY
BASKETS
BASKING
BASKS
BASMIZVAH
BASMIZVAHS
BASNET
BASNETS
BASOCHE
BASOCHES
BASON
BASONS
BASQUE
BASQUED
BASQUES
BASQUINE
BASQUINES
BASS
BASSE
BASSED
BASSER
BASSES
BASSEST
BASSET
BASSETED
BASSETING
BASSETS
BASSI

BASSIER	BATHE	BATTED	BAUKING	BAYT
BASSIEST	BATHED	BATTEL	BAUKS	BAYTED
BASSINET	BATHER	BATTELED	BAULK	BAYTING
BASSINETS	BATHERS	BATTELER	BAULKED	BAYTS
BASSING	BATHES	BATTELERS	BAULKING	BAZAAR
BASSIST	BATHETIC	BATTELING	BAULKS	BAZAARS
BASSISTS	BATHHOUSE	BATTELS	BAUR	BAZAR
BASSO	BATHHOUSES	BATTEMENT	BAURS	BAZARS
BASSOON	BATHING	BATTEMENTS	BAUSOND	BAZAZZ
BASSOONS	BATHMIC	BATTEN	BAUXITE	BAZAZZES
BASSOS	BATHMISM	BATTENED	BAUXITES	BAZOOKA
BASSWOOD	BATHMISMS	BATTENING	BAUXITIC	BAZOOKAS
BASSWOODS	BATHOLITE	BATTENINGS	BAVARDAGE	BDELLIUM
BASSY	BATHOLITES	BATTENS	BAVARDAGES	BDELLIUMS
BAST	BATHOLITH	BATTER	BAVIN	BE
BASTA	BATHOLITHS	BATTERED	BAVINS	BEACH
BASTARD	BATHORSE	BATTERIE	BAWBEE	BEACHED
BASTARDIES	BATHORSES	BATTERIES	BAWBEES	BEACHES
BASTARDLY	BATHOS	BATTERING	BAWBLE	BEACHHEAD
BASTARDS	BATHOSES	BATTERO	BAWBLES	BEACHHEADS
BASTARDY	BATHROBE	BATTEROS	BAWCOCK	BEACHIER
BASTE	BATHROBES	BATTERS	BAWCOCKS	BEACHIEST
BASTED	BATHROOM	BATTERY	BAWD	BEACHING
BASTER	BATHROOMS	BATTIER	BAWDIER	BEACHY
BASTERS	BATHS	BATTIEST	BAWDIES	BEACON
BASTES	BATHTUB	BATTILL	BAWDIEST	BEACONED
BASTIDE	BATHTUBS	BATTILLED	BAWDILY	BEACONING
BASTIDES	BATHYAL	BATTILLING	BAWDINESS	BEACONS
BASTILLE	BATHYBIUS	BATTILLS	BAWDINESSES	BEAD
BASTILLES	BATHYBIUSES	BATTING	BAWDKIN	BEADED
BASTINADE	BATHYLITE	BATTINGS	BAWDKINS	BEADIER
BASTINADED	BATHYLITES	BATTLE	BAWDRIES	BEADIEST
BASTINADES	BATHYLITH	BATTLED	BAWDRY	BEADING
BASTINADING	BATHYLITHS	BATTLER	BAWDS	BEADINGS
BASTINADO	BATIK	BATTLERS	BAWDY	BEADLE
BASTINADOED	BATIKS	BATTLES	BAWL	BEADLEDOM
BASTINADOES	BATING	BATTLING	BAWLED	BEADLEDOMS
BASTINADOING	BATISTE	BATTOLOGIES	BAWLER	BEADLES
BASTINADOS	BATISTES	BATTOLOGY	BAWLERS	BEADMAN
BASTING	BATLER	BATTS	BAWLEY	BEADMEN
BASTINGS	BATLERS	BATTUE	BAWLEYS	BEADS
BASTION	BATLET	BATTUES	BAWLING	BEADSMAN
BASTIONED	BATLETS	BATTUTA	BAWLINGS	BEADSMEN
BASTIONS	BATMAN	BATTUTAS	BAWLS	BEADY
BASTLE	BATMEN	BATTY	BAWN	BEAGLE
BASTLES	BATMIZVAH	BATWOMAN	BAWNS	BEAGLED
BASTO	BATMIZVAHS	BATWOMEN	BAWR	BEAGLER
BASTOS	BATOLOGIES	BAUBLE	BAWRS	BEAGLERS
BASTS	BATOLOGY	BAUBLES	BAXTER	BEAGLES
BAT	BATON	BAUBLING	BAXTERS	BEAGLING
BATABLE	BATONED	BAUCHLE	BAY	BEAGLINGS
BATATA	BATONING	BAUCHLED	BAYADÈRE	BEAK
BATATAS	BATONS	BAUCHLES	BAYADÈRES	BEAKED
BATCH	BATOON	BAUCHLING	BAYARD	BEAKER
BATCHED	BATOONED	BAUD	BAYARDS	BEAKERS
BATCHES	BATOONING	BAUDEKIN	BAYBERRIES	BEAKS
BATCHING	BATOONS	BAUDEKINS	BAYBERRY	BEAM
BATE	BATRACHIA	BAUDRIC	BAYE	BEAMED
BATEAU	BATS	BAUDRICK	BAYED	BEAMER
BATEAUX	BATSMAN	BAUDRICKE	BAYES	BEAMERS
BATED	BATSMEN	BAUDRICKES	BAYING	BEAMIER
BATELESS	BATSWING	BAUDRICKS	BAYLE	BEAMIEST
BATELEUR	BATSWINGS	BAUDRICS	BAYLES	BEAMILY
BATELEURS	BATT	BAUDS	BAYONET	BEAMINESS
BATEMENT	BATTA	BAUERA	BAYONETED	BEAMINESSES
BATEMENTS	BATTALIA	BAUERAS	BAYONETING	BEAMING
BATES	BATTALIAS	BAUHINIA	BAYONETS	BEAMINGLY
BATH	BATTALION	BAUHINIAS	BAYOU	BEAMINGS
BATHCUBE	BATTALIONS	BAUK	BAYOUS	BEAMISH
BATHCUBES.	BATTAS	BAUKED	BAYS	BEAMLESS

BEAMS	BEATINGS	BECK	BEDEAFENING	BEDRIDDEN
BEAMY	BEATITUDE	BECKE	BEDEAFENS	BEDRIGHT
BEAN	BEATITUDES	BECKED	BEDECK	BEDRIGHTS
BEANED	BEATNIK	BECKES	BEDECKED	BEDRITE
BEANFEAST	BEATNIKS	BECKET	BEDECKING	BEDRITES
BEANFEASTS	BEATS	BECKETS	BEDECKS	BEDROCK
BEANIE	BEAU	BECKING	BEDEGUAR	BEDROCKS
BEANIES	BEAUFET	BECKON	BEDEGUARS	BEDROOM
BEANING	BEAUFETS	BECKONED	BEDEL	BEDROOMS
BEANO	BEAUFFET	BECKONING	BEDELL	BEDROP
BEANOS	BEAUFFETS	BECKONS	BEDELLS	BEDROPPED
BEANPOLE	BEAUFIN	BECKS	BEDELS	BEDROPPING
BEANPOLES	BEAUFINS	BECLOUD	BEDELSHIP	BEDROPS
BEANS	BEAUISH	BECLOUDED	BEDELSHIPS	BEDROPT
BEANSTALK	BEAUT	BECLOUDING	BEDEMAN	BEDS
BEANSTALKS	BEAUTEOUS	BECLOUDS	BEDEMEN	BEDSIDE
BEAR	BEAUTIED	BECOME	BEDERAL	BEDSIDES
BEARABLE	BEAUTIES	BECOMES	BEDERALS	BEDSOCKS
BEARABLY	BEAUTIFIED	BECOMING	BEDES	BEDSORE
BEARBINE	BEAUTIFIES	BECQUEREL	BEDESMAN	BEDSORES
BEARBINES	BEAUTIFUL	BECQUERELS	BEDESMEN	BEDSPREAD
BEARD	BEAUTIFY	BECURL	BEDEVIL	BEDSPREADS
BEARDED	BEAUTIFYING	BECURLED	BEDEVILLED	BEDSTEAD
BEARDIE	BEAUTS	BECURLING	BEDEVILLING	BEDSTEADS
BEARDIES	BEAUTY	BECURLS	BEDEVILS	BEDSTRAW
BEARDING	BEAUTYING	BED	BEDEW	BEDSTRAWS
BEARDLESS	BEAUX	BEDABBLE	BEDEWED	BEDTICK
BEARDS	BEAUXITE	BEDABBLED	BEDEWING	BEDTICKS
BEARE	BEAUXITES	BEDABBLES	BEDEWS	BEDTIME
BEARED	BEAVER	BEDABBLING	BEDFAST	BEDTIMES
BEARER	BEAVERED	BEDAD	BEDFELLOW	BEDUCK
BEARERS	BEAVERIES	BEDAGGLE	BEDFELLOWS	BEDUCKED
BEARES	BEAVERS	BEDAGGLED	BEDIDE	BEDUCKING
BEARING	BEAVERY	BEDAGGLES	BEDIGHT	BEDUCKS
BEARINGS	BEBEERINE	BEDAGGLING	BEDIGHTING	BEDUIN
BEARISH	BEBEERINES	BEDARKEN	BEDIGHTS	BEDUINS
BÉARNAISE	BEBEERU	BEDARKENED	BEDIM	BEDUNG
BÉARNAISES	BEBEERUS	BEDARKENING	BEDIMMED	BEDUNGED
BEARS	BEBOP	BEDARKENS	BEDIMMING	BEDUNGING
BEARSKIN	BEBOPPED	BEDASH	BEDIMMINGS	BEDUNGS
BEARSKINS	BEBOPPING	BEDASHED	BEDIMS	BEDUST
BEARWARD	BEBOPS	BEDASHES	BEDIZEN	BEDUSTED
BEARWARDS	BEBUNG	BEDASHING	BEDIZENED	BEDUSTING
BEAST	BEBUNGS	BEDAUB	BEDIZENING	BEDUSTS
BEASTHOOD	BECALL	BEDAUBED	BEDIZENS	BEDWARD
BEASTHOODS	BECALLED	BEDAUBING	BEDLAM	BEDWARDS
BEASTIE	BECALLING	BEDAUBS	BEDLAMISM	BEDWARF
BEASTIES	BECALLS	BEDAWIN	BEDLAMISMS	BEDWARFED
BEASTILY	BECALM	BEDAWINS	BEDLAMITE	BEDWARFING
BEASTINGS	BECALMED	BEDAZE	BEDLAMITES	BEDWARFS
BEASTLIER	BECALMING	BEDAZED	BEDLAMS	BEDYDE
BEASTLIEST	BECALMS	BEDAZES	BEDMAKER	BEDYE
BEASTLIKE	BECAME	BEDAZING	BEDMAKERS	BEDYED
BEASTLY	BÉCASSE	BEDAZZLE	BEDOUIN	BEDYEING
BEASTS	BÉCASSES	BEDAZZLED	BEDOUINS	BEDYES
BEAT	BECAUSE	BEDAZZLES	BEDPAN	BEE
BEATABLE	BECCACCIA	BEDAZZLING	BEDPANS	BEECH
BEATEN	BECCACCIAS	BEDBUG	BEDPOST	BEECHEN
BEATER	BECCAFICO	BEDBUGS	BEDPOSTS	BEECHES
BEATERS	BECCAFICOS	BEDCOVER	BEDRAGGLE	BEEF
BEATH	BÉCHAMEL	BEDCOVERS	BEDRAGGLED	BEEFALO
BEATHED	BÉCHAMELS	BEDDABLE	BEDRAGGLES	BEEFALOES
BEATHING	BECHANCE	BEDDED	BEDRAGGLING	BEEFALOS
BEATHS	BECHANCED	BEDDER	BEDRAL	BEEFCAKE
BEATIFIC	BECHANCES	BEDDERS	BEDRALS	BEEFCAKES
BEATIFIED	BECHANCING	BEDDING	BEDRENCH	BEEFEATER
BEATIFIES	BECHARM	BEDDINGS	BEDRENCHED	BEEFEATERS
BEATIFY	BECHARMED	BEDE	BEDRENCHES	BEEFED
BEATIFYING	BECHARMING	BEDEAFEN	BEDRENCHING	BEEFIER
BEATING	BECHARMS	BEDEAFENED	BEDRID	BEEFIEST

BEEFING	BEFLUM	BEGIFTS	BEGUNKS	BEINGS
BEEFS	BEFLUMMED	BEGILD	BEHALF	BEINKED
BEEFSTEAK	BEFLUMMING	BEGILDED	BEHALVES	BEINNESS
BEEFSTEAKS	BEFLUMS	BEGILDING	BEHAPPEN	BEINNESSES
BEEFTEA	BEFOAM	BEGILDS	BEHAPPENED	BEJABERS
BEEFTEAS	BEFOAMED	BEGIN	BEHAPPENING	BEJADE
BEEFY	BEFOAMING	BEGINNE	BEHAPPENS	BEJADED
BEEGAH	BEFOAMS	BEGINNER	BEHATTED	BEJADES
BEEGAHS	BEFOG	BEGINNERS	BEHAVE	BEJADING
BEEHIVE	BEFOGGED	BEGINNES	BEHAVED	BEJANT
BEEHIVES	BEFOGGING	BEGINNING	BEHAVES	BEJANTS
BEEKEEPER	BEFOGS	BEGINNINGS	BEHAVING	BEJESUIT
BEEKEEPERS	BEFOOL	BEGINS	BEHAVIOR	BEJESUITED
BEEN	BEFOOLED	BEGIRD	BEHAVIORS	BEJESUITING
BEENAH	BEFOOLING	BEGIRDED	BEHAVIOUR	BEJESUITS
BEENAHS	BEFOOLS	BEGIRDING	BEHAVIOURS	BEJEWEL
BEEP	BEFORE	BEGIRDS	BEHEAD	BEJEWELLED
BEEPED	BEFORTUNE	BEGIRT	BEHEADAL	BEJEWELLING
BEEPER	BEFORTUNED	BEGLAMOUR	BEHEADALS	BEJEWELS
BEEPERS	BEFORTUNES	BEGLAMOURED	BEHEADED	BEKAH
BEEPING	BEFORTUNING	BEGLAMOURING	BEHEADING	BEKAHS
BEEPS	BEFOUL	BEGLAMOURS	BEHEADINGS	BEKISS
BEER	BEFOULED	BEGLERBEG	BEHEADS	BEKISSED
BEERHALL	BEFOULING	BEGLERBEGS	BEHELD	BEKISSES
BEERHALLS	BEFOULS	BEGLOOM	BEHEMOTH	BEKISSING
BEERIER	BEFRIEND	BEGLOOMED	BEHEMOTHS	BEKNAVE
BEERIEST	BEFRIENDED	BEGLOOMING	BEHEST	BEKNAVED
BEERINESS	BEFRIENDING	BEGLOOMS	BEHESTS	BEKNAVES
BEERINESSES	BEFRIENDS	BEGNAW	BEHIGHT	BEKNAVING
BEERS	BEFRINGE	BEGNAWED	BEHIGHTING	BEKNOWN
BEERY	BEFRINGED	BEGNAWING	BEHIGHTS	BEL
BEES	BEFRINGES	BEGNAWS	BEHIND	BELABOUR
BEESOME	BEFRINGING	BEGO	BEHINDS	BELABOURED
BEESTINGS	BEFUDDLE	BEGOES	BEHOLD	BELABOURING
BEESWAX	BEFUDDLED	BEGOING	BEHOLDEN	BELABOURS
BEESWAXED	BEFUDDLES	BEGONE	BEHOLDER	BELACE
BEESWAXES	BEFUDDLING	BEGONIA	BEHOLDERS	BELACED
BEESWAXING	BEG	BEGONIAS	BEHOLDING	BELACES
BEESWING	BEGAD	BEGORED	BEHOLDINGS	BELACING
BEESWINGED	BEGAN	BEGORRA	BEHOLDS	BELAH
BEESWINGS	BEGAR	BEGORRAH	BEHOOF	BELAHS
BEET	BEGARS	BEGOT	BEHOOFS	BELAID
BEETED	BEGAT	BEGOTTEN	BEHOOVE	BELAMIES
BEETING	BEGEM	BEGRIME	BEHOOVED	BELAMOURE
BEETLE	BEGEMMED	BEGRIMED	BEHOOVES	BELAMOURES
BEETLED	BEGEMMING	BEGRIMES	BEHOOVING	BELAMY
BEETLES	BEGEMS	BEGRIMING	BEHOTE	BELATE
BEETLING	BEGET	BEGRUDGE	BEHOTES	BELATED
BEETROOT	BEGETS	BEGRUDGED	BEHOTING	BELATES
BEETROOTS	BEGETTER	BEGRUDGES	BEHOVE	BELATING
BEETS	BEGETTERS	BEGRUDGING	BEHOVED	BELAUD
BEEVES	BEGETTING	BEGS	BEHOVEFUL	BELAUDED
BEFALL	BEGGAR	BEGUILE	BEHOVELY	BELAUDING
BEFALLEN	BEGGARDOM	BEGUILED	BEHOVES	BELAUDS
BEFALLING	BEGGARDOMS	BEGUILER	BEHOVING	BELAY
BEFALLS	BEGGARED	BEGUILERS	BEHOWL	BELAYING
BEFANA	BEGGARIES	BEGUILES	BEHOWLED	BELAYS
BEFANAS	BEGGARING	BEGUILING	BEHOWLING	BELCH
BEFELD	BEGGARLY	BEGUIN	BEHOWLS	BELCHED
BEFELL	BEGGARS	BEGUINAGE	BEIGE	BELCHER
BEFFANA	BEGGARY	BEGUINAGES	BEIGEL	BELCHERS
BEFFANAS	BEGGED	BEGUINE	BEIGELS	BELCHES
BEFIT	BEGGING	BEGUINES	BEIGES	BELCHING
BEFITS	BEGGINGLY	BEGUINS	BEIGNET	BELDAM
BEFITTED	BEGGINGS	BEGUM	BEIGNETS	BELDAME
BEFITTING	BEGHARD	BEGUMS	BEIN	BELDAMES
BEFLOWER	BEGHARDS	BEGUN	BEING	BELDAMS
BEFLOWERED	BEGIFT	BEGUNK	BEINGLESS	BELEAGUER
BEFLOWERING	BEGIFTED	BEGUNKED	BEINGNESS	BELEAGUERED
BEFLOWERS	BEGIFTING	BEGUNKING	BEINGNESSES	BELEAGUERING

29

BELEAGUERS
BELEE
BELEED
BELEEING
BELEES
BELEMNITE
BELEMNITES
BELFRIED
BELFRIES
BELFRY
BELGA
BELGARD
BELGARDS
BELGAS
BELIE
BELIED
BELIEF
BELIEFS
BELIER
BELIERS
BELIES
BELIEVE
BELIEVED
BELIEVER
BELIEVERS
BELIEVES
BELIEVING
BELIKE
BELITTLE
BELITTLED
BELITTLES
BELITTLING
BELIVE
BELL
BELLBIND
BELLBINDS
BELLCOTE
BELLCOTES
BELLE
BELLED
BELLES
BELLETER
BELLETERS
BELLHOP
BELLHOPS
BELLIBONE
BELLIBONES
BELLICOSE
BELLIED
BELLIES
BELLING
BELLMAN
BELLMEN
BELLOW
BELLOWED
BELLOWER
BELLOWERS
BELLOWING
BELLOWS
BELLPUSH
BELLPUSHES
BELLS
BELLWORT
BELLWORTS
BELLY
BELLYFUL
BELLYFULS
BELLYING
BELLYINGS
BELOMANCIES

BELOMANCY
BELONG
BELONGED
BELONGER
BELONGERS
BELONGING
BELONGINGS
BELONGS
BELOVE
BELOVED
BELOVEDS
BELOVES
BELOVING
BELOW
BELS
BELT
BELTED
BELTER
BELTERS
BELTING
BELTINGS
BELTS
BELTWAY
BELTWAYS
BELUGA
BELUGAS
BELVEDERE
BELVEDERES
BELYING
BEMA
BEMAD
BEMADDED
BEMADDING
BEMADS
BEMAS
BEMATA
BEMAUL
BEMAULED
BEMAULING
BEMAULS
BEMAZED
BEMEAN
BEMEANED
BEMEANING
BEMEANS
BEMEDAL
BEMEDALLED
BEMEDALLING
BEMEDALS
BEMETE
BEMETED
BEMETES
BEMETING
BEMIRE
BEMIRED
BEMIRES
BEMIRING
BEMOAN
BEMOANED
BEMOANER
BEMOANERS
BEMOANING
BEMOANINGS
BEMOANS
BEMOCK
BEMOCKED
BEMOCKING
BEMOCKS
BEMOIL
BEMOILED

BEMOILING
BEMOILS
BEMONSTER
BEMONSTERED
BEMONSTERING
BEMONSTERS
BEMOUTH
BEMOUTHED
BEMOUTHING
BEMOUTHS
BEMUD
BEMUDDED
BEMUDDING
BEMUDDLE
BEMUDDLED
BEMUDDLES
BEMUDDLING
BEMUDS
BEMUFFLE
BEMUFFLED
BEMUFFLES
BEMUFFLING
BEMUSE
BEMUSED
BEMUSES
BEMUSING
BEN
BENAME
BENAMED
BENAMES
BENAMING
BENCH
BENCHED
BENCHER
BENCHERS
BENCHES
BENCHING
BEND
BENDED
BENDER
BENDERS
BENDING
BENDINGLY
BENDINGS
BENDLET
BENDLETS
BENDS
BENDWISE
BENDY
BENE
BENEATH
BENEDICT
BENEDIGHT
BENEFACT
BENEFACTED
BENEFACTING
BENEFACTS
BENEFIC
BENEFICE
BENEFICED
BENEFICES
BENEFIT
BENEFITED
BENEFITING
BENEFITS
BENEMPT
BENES
BENET
BENETS
BENETTED

BENETTING
BENGALINE
BENGALINES
BENI
BENIGHT
BENIGHTED
BENIGHTEN
BENIGHTENED
BENIGHTENING
BENIGHTENINGS
BENIGHTENS
BENIGHTER
BENIGHTERS
BENIGHTING
BENIGHTINGS
BENIGHTS
BENIGN
BENIGNACIES
BENIGNACY
BENIGNANT
BENIGNER
BENIGNEST
BENIGNITIES
BENIGNITY
BENIGNLY
BENIS
BENISEED
BENISEEDS
BENISON
BENISONS
BÉNITIER
BÉNITIERS
BENJ
BENJAMIN
BENJAMINS
BENJES
BENNE
BENNES
BENNET
BENNETS
BENNI
BENNIES
BENNIS
BENNY
BENS
BENT
BENTHIC
BENTHOAL
BENTHONIC
BENTHOS
BENTHOSES
BENTIER
BENTIEST
BENTONITE
BENTONITES
BENTS
BENTWOOD
BENTWOODS
BENTY
BENUMB
BENUMBED
BENUMBING
BENUMBS
BENZAL
BENZALS
BENZENE
BENZENES
BENZIDINE
BENZIDINES
BENZIL

BENZILS
BENZINE
BENZINES
BENZOATE
BENZOATES
BENZOIC
BENZOIN
BENZOINS
BENZOL
BENZOLE
BENZOLES
BENZOLINE
BENZOLINES
BENZOLS
BENZOYL
BENZOYLS
BENZYL
BENZYLS
BEPAINT
BEPAINTED
BEPAINTING
BEPAINTS
BEPAT
BEPATCHED
BEPATS
BEPATTED
BEPATTING
BEPEARL
BEPEARLED
BEPEARLING
BEPEARLS
BEPELT
BEPELTED
BEPELTING
BEPELTS
BEPEPPER
BEPEPPERED
BEPEPPERING
BEPEPPERS
BEPESTER
BEPESTERED
BEPESTERING
BEPESTERS
BEPITIED
BEPITIES
BEPITY
BEPITYING
BEPLASTER
BEPLASTERED
BEPLASTERING
BEPLASTERS
BEPLUMED
BEPOMMEL
BEPOMMELED
BEPOMMELING
BEPOMMELLED
BEPOMMELLING
BEPOMMELS
BEPOWDER
BEPOWDERED
BEPOWDERING
BEPOWDERS
BEPRAISE
BEPRAISED
BEPRAISES
BEPRAISING
BEPROSE
BEPROSED
BEPROSES
BEPROSING

BEPUFF	BERLINE	BESEEKES	BESMEARING	BESPOUTED
BEPUFFED	BERLINES	BESEEKING	BESMEARS	BESPOUTING
BEPUFFING	BERLINS	BESEEM	BESMIRCH	BESPOUTS
BEPUFFS	BERM	BESEEMED	BESMIRCHED	BESPREAD
BEQUEATH	BERMS	BESEEMING	BESMIRCHES	BESPREADING
BEQUEATHED	BEROB	BESEEMINGS	BESMIRCHING	BESPREADS
BEQUEATHING	BEROBBED	BESEEMLY	BESMUT	BESPRENT
BEQUEATHS	BEROBBING	BESEEMS	BESMUTCH	BEST
BEQUEST	BEROBS	BESEEN	BESMUTCHED	BESTAD
BEQUESTS	BERRET	BESEES	BESMUTCHES	BESTADDE
BERATE	BERRETS	BESET	BESMUTCHING	BESTAIN
BERATED	BERRIED	BESETMENT	BESMUTS	BESTAINED
BERATES	BERRIES	BESETMENTS	BESMUTTED	BESTAINING
BERATING	BERRY	BESETS	BESMUTTING	BESTAINS
BERAY	BERRYING	BESETTER	BESOGNIO	BESTAR
BERAYED	BERRYINGS	BESETTERS	BESOGNIOS	BESTARRED
BERAYING	BERSERK	BESETTING	BESOIN	BESTARRING
BERAYS	BERSERKER	BESHADOW	BESOINS	BESTARS
BERBERINE	BERSERKERS	BESHADOWED	BESOM	BESTEAD
BERBERINES	BERSERKEST	BESHADOWING	BESOMS	BESTEADED
BERBERIS	BERSERKLY	BESHADOWS	BESORT	BESTEADING
BERBERISES	BERSERKS	BESHAME	BESORTED	BESTEADS
BERCEAU	BERTH	BESHAMED	BESORTING	BESTED
BERCEAUX	BERTHA	BESHAMES	BESORTS	BESTIAL
BERCEUSE	BERTHAGE	BESHAMING	BESOT	BESTIALS
BERCEUSES	BERTHAGES	BESHINE	BESOTS	BESTIARIES
BERDACHE	BERTHAS	BESHINES	BESOTTED	BESTIARY
BERDACHES	BERTHE	BESHINING	BESOTTING	BESTICK
BERE	BERTHED	BESHONE	BESOUGHT	BESTICKING
BEREAVE	BERTHES	BESHREW	BESOULED	BESTICKS
BEREAVED	BERTHING	BESHREWED	BESPAKE	BESTILL
BEREAVEN	BERTHS	BESHREWING	BESPANGLE	BESTILLED
BEREAVES	BERYL	BESHREWS	BESPANGLED	BESTILLING
BEREAVING	BERYLLIA	BESIDE	BESPANGLES	BESTILLS
BEREFT	BERYLLIAS	BESIDES	BESPANGLING	BESTING
BERES	BERYLLIUM	BESIEGE	BESPAT	BESTIR
BERET	BERYLLIUMS	BESIEGED	BESPATE	BESTIRRED
BERETS	BERYLS	BESIEGER	BESPATTER	BESTIRRING
BERG	BESAINT	BESIEGERS	BESPATTERED	BESTIRS
BERGAMA	BESAINTED	BESIEGES	BESPATTERING	BESTORM
BERGAMAS	BESAINTING	BESIEGING	BESPATTERS	BESTORMED
BERGAMASK	BESAINTS	BESIEGINGS	BESPEAK	BESTORMING
BERGAMASKS	BESANG	BESIGH	BESPEAKING	BESTORMS
BERGAMOT	BESAT	BESIGHED	BESPEAKS	BESTOW
BERGAMOTS	BESAW	BESIGHING	BESPECKLE	BESTOWAL
BERGANDER	BESCATTER	BESIGHS	BESPECKLED	BESTOWALS
BERGANDERS	BESCATTERED	BESING	BESPECKLES	BESTOWED
BERGENIA	BESCATTERING	BESINGING	BESPECKLING	BESTOWER
BERGENIAS	BESCATTERS	BESINGS	BESPED	BESTOWERS
BERGÈRE	BESCRAWL	BESIT	BESPEED	BESTOWING
BERGFALL	BESCRAWLED	BESITS	BESPEEDING	BESTOWS
BERGFALLS	BESCRAWLING	BESITTING	BESPEEDS	BESTREAK
BERGHAAN	BESCRAWLS	BESLAVE	BESPICE	BESTREAKED
BERGHAANS	BESCREEN	BESLAVED	BESPICED	BESTREAKING
BERGMEHL	BESCREENED	BESLAVER	BESPICES	BESTREAKS
BERGMEHLS	BESCREENING	BESLAVERED	BESPICING	BESTREW
BERGOMASK	BESCREENS	BESLAVERING	BESPIT	BESTREWED
BERGOMASKS	BESCRIBBLE	BESLAVERS	BESPITS	BESTREWING
BERGS	BESCRIBBLED	BESLAVES	BESPITTING	BESTREWN
BERGYLT	BESCRIBBLES	BESLAVING	BESPOKE	BESTREWS
BERGYLTS	BESCRIBBLING	BESLOBBER	BESPOKEN	BESTRID
BERIBERI	BESEE	BESLOBBERED	BESPORT	BESTRIDDEN
BERIBERIS	BESEECH	BESLOBBERING	BESPORTED	BESTRIDE
BERK	BESEECHED	BESLOBBERS	BESPORTING	BESTRIDES
BERKELIUM	BESEECHER	BESLUBBER	BESPORTS	BESTRIDING
BERKELIUMS	BESEECHERS	BESLUBBERED	BESPOT	BESTRODE
BERKS	BESEECHES	BESLUBBERING	BESPOTS	BESTROWN
BERLEY	BESEECHING	BESLUBBERS	BESPOTTED	BESTS
BERLEYS	BESEEING	BESMEAR	BESPOTTING	BESTSELL
BERLIN	BESEEKE	BESMEARED	BESPOUT	BESTSELLING

BESTSELLS	BETIMING	BEVATRON	BEZES	BICAMERAL
BESTSOLD	BETING	BEVATRONS	BEZIQUE	BICARB
BESTUCK	BÊTISE	BEVEL	BEZIQUES	BICARBS
BESTUD	BÊTISES	BEVELLED	BEZOAR	BICE
BESTUDDED	BETITLE	BEVELLER	BEZOARDIC	BICEPS
BESTUDDING	BETITLED	BEVELLERS	BEZOARS	BICEPSES
BESTUDS	BETITLES	BEVELLING	BEZONIAN	BICES
BESUNG	BETITLING	BEVELLINGS	BEZONIANS	BICHORD
BET	BETOIL	BEVELMENT	BEZZES	BICIPITAL
BETA	BETOILED	BEVELMENTS	BEZZLE	BICKER
BETACISM	BETOILING	BEVELS	BEZZLED	BICKERED
BETACISMS	BETOILS	BEVER	BEZZLES	BICKERING
BETAINE	BETOKEN	BEVERAGE	BEZZLING	BICKERS
BETAINES	BETOKENED	BEVERAGES	BHAJAN	BICONCAVE
BETAKE	BETOKENING	BEVERS	BHAJANS	BICONVEX
BETAKEN	BETOKENS	BEVIES	BHAKTI	BICUSPID
BETAKES	BÉTON	BEVUE	BHAKTIS	BICUSPIDS
BETAKING	BETONIES	BEVUES	BHANG	BICYCLE
BETAS	BÉTONS	BEVVIED	BHANGS	BICYCLED
BETATRON	BETONY	BEVVIES	BHARAL	BICYCLES
BETATRONS	BETOOK	BEVVY	BHARALS	BICYCLING
BÊTE	BETOSS	BEVY	BHEESTIE	BICYCLIST
BETE	BETOSSED	BEWAIL	BHEESTIES	BICYCLISTS
BETED	BETOSSES	BEWAILED	BHEESTY	BID
BETEEM	BETOSSING	BEWAILING	BHEL	BIDDABLE
BETEEME	BETRAY	BEWAILINGS	BHELS	BIDDEN
BETEEMED	BETRAYAL	BEWAILS	BHINDI	BIDDER
BETEEMES	BETRAYALS	BEWARE	BHINDIS	BIDDERS
BETEEMING	BETRAYED	BEWARED	BHISTEE	BIDDIES
BETEEMS	BETRAYER	BEWARES	BHISTEES	BIDDING
BETEL	BETRAYERS	BEWARING	BHISTI	BIDDINGS
BETELS	BETRAYING	BEWEEP	BHISTIS	BIDDY
BÊTES	BETRAYS	BEWEEPING	BIANNUAL	BIDE
BETES	BETREAD	BEWEEPS	BIAS	BIDED
BETH	BETREADING	BEWEPT	BIASED	BIDENT
BETHANKIT	BETREADS	BEWET	BIASES	BIDENTAL
BETHEL	BETRIM	BEWETS	BIASING	BIDENTALS
BETHELS	BETRIMMED	BEWETTED	BIASINGS	BIDENTATE
BETHESDA	BETRIMMING	BEWETTING	BIASSED	BIDENTS
BETHESDAS	BETRIMS	BEWHORE	BIASSES	BIDES
BETHINK	BETROD	BEWHORED	BIASSING	BIDET
BETHINKING	BETRODDEN	BEWHORES	BIATHLON	BIDETS
BETHINKS	BETROTH	BEWHORING	BIATHLONS	BIDING
BETHOUGHT	BETROTHAL	BEWIG	BIAXAL	BIDINGS
BETHRALL	BETROTHALS	BEWIGGED	BIAXIAL	BIDON
BETHRALLED	BETROTHED	BEWIGGING	BIB	BIDONS
BETHRALLING	BETROTHEDS	BEWIGS	BIBACIOUS	BIDS
BETHRALLS	BETROTHING	BEWILDER	BIBATION	BIELD
BETHS	BETROTHS	BEWILDERED	BIBATIONS	BIELDIER
BETHUMB	BETS	BEWILDERING	BIBBED	BIELDIEST
BETHUMBED	BETTED	BEWILDERS	BIBBER	BIELDS
BETHUMBING	BETTER	BEWITCH	BIBBERS	BIELDY
BETHUMBS	BETTERED	BEWITCHED	BIBBING	BIEN
BETHUMP	BETTERING	BEWITCHES	BIBCOCK	BIENNIAL
BETHUMPED	BETTERINGS	BEWITCHING	BIBCOCKS	BIENNIALS
BETHUMPING	BETTERS	BEWRAY	BIBELOT	BIER
BETHUMPS	BETTIES	BEWRAYED	BIBELOTS	BIERS
BETHWACK	BETTING	BEWRAYING	BIBFUL	BIESTINGS
BETHWACKED	BETTINGS	BEWRAYS	BIBFULS	BIFACIAL
BETHWACKING	BETTOR	BEY	BIBLE	BIFARIOUS
BETHWACKS	BETTORS	BEYOND	BIBLES	BIFF
BETID	BETTY	BEYONDS	BIBLICAL	BIFFED
BETIDE	BETUMBLED	BEYS	BIBLICISM	BIFFIN
BETIDED	BETWEEN	BEZ	BIBLICISMS	BIFFING
BETIDES	BETWEENS	BEZANT	BIBLICIST	BIFFINS
BETIDING	BETWIXT	BEZANTS	BIBLICISTS	BIFFS
BETIGHT	BEURRÉ	BEZAZZ	BIBLIST	BIFID
BETIME	BEURRE	BEZAZZES	BIBLISTS	BIFILAR
BETIMED	BEURRÉS	BEZEL	BIBS	BIFOCAL
BETIMES	BEURRES	BEZELS	BIBULOUS	BIFOCALS

BIFOLD	BILBO	BILLOWY	BINTURONG	BIOTAS
BIFOLIATE	BILBOES	BILLS	BINTURONGS	BIOTIC
BIFORM	BILBOS	BILLY	BIO	BIOTIN
BIFURCATE	BILE	BILLYBOY	BIOASSAY	BIOTINS
BIFURCATED	BILES	BILLYBOYS	BIOASSAYS	BIOTITE
BIFURCATES	BILGE	BILLYCOCK	BIOBLAST	BIOTITES
BIFURCATING	BILGED	BILLYCOCKS	BIOBLASTS	BIOTYPE
BIG	BILGES	BILOBAR	BIOCIDAL	BIOTYPES
BIGA	BILGIER	BILOBATE	BIOCIDE	BIPAROUS
BIGAE	BILGIEST	BILOBED	BIOCIDES	BIPARTITE
BIGAMIES	BILGING	BILOBULAR	BIODATA	BIPED
BIGAMIST	BILGY	BILOCULAR	BIOETHICS	BIPEDAL
BIGAMISTS	BILHARZIA	BILTONG	BIOG	BIPEDS
BIGAMOUS	BILHARZIAS	BILTONGS	BIOGAS	BIPHENYL
BIGAMY	BILIAN	BIMANAL	BIOGASES	BIPHENYLS
BIGENER	BILIANS	BIMANOUS	BIOGEN	BIPINNATE
BIGENERIC	BILIARIES	BIMBASHI	BIOGENIC	BIPLANE
BIGENERS	BILIARY	BIMBASHIS	BIOGENIES	BIPLANES
BIGG	BILIMBI	BIMBO	BIOGENOUS	BIPOD
BIGGED	BILIMBING	BIMBOS	BIOGENS	BIPODS
BIGGER	BILIMBINGS	BIMONTHLY	BIOGENY	BIPOLAR
BIGGEST	BILIMBIS	BIN	BIOGRAPH	BIPYRAMID
BIGGIE	BILINGUAL	BINARIES	BIOGRAPHIES	BIPYRAMIDS
BIGGIES	BILIOUS	BINARY	BIOGRAPHS	BIRCH
BIGGIN	BILIOUSLY	BINATE	BIOGRAPHY	BIRCHED
BIGGING	BILIRUBIN	BINAURAL	BIOGS	BIRCHEN
BIGGINS	BILIRUBINS	BIND	BIOHAZARD	BIRCHES
BIGGISH	BILITERAL	BINDER	BIOHAZARDS	BIRCHING
BIGGS	BILK	BINDERIES	BIOLOGIES	BIRD
BIGGY	BILKED	BINDERS	BIOLOGIST	BIRDBATH
BIGHA	BILKER	BINDERY	BIOLOGISTS	BIRDBATHS
BIGHAS	BILKERS	BINDING	BIOLOGY	BIRDCAGE
BIGHEADED	BILKING	BINDINGS	BIOMASS	BIRDCAGES
BIGHORN	BILKS	BINDS	BIOMASSES	BIRDCALL
BIGHORNS	BILL	BINDWEED	BIOME	BIRDCALLS
BIGHT	BILLABONG	BINDWEEDS	BIOMES	BIRDED
BIGHTS	BILLABONGS	BINE	BIOMETRIC	BIRDER
BIGNESS	BILLBOARD	BINERVATE	BIOMETRICS	BIRDERS
BIGNESSES	BILLBOARDS	BINES	BIOMETRIES	BIRDIE
BIGOT	BILLBOOK	BING	BIOMETRY	BIRDIED
BIGOTED	BILLBOOKS	BINGE	BIOMORPH	BIRDIEING
BIGOTRIES	BILLED	BINGED	BIOMORPHS	BIRDIES
BIGOTRY	BILLET	BINGEING	BIONIC	BIRDING
BIGOTS	BILLETED	BINGER	BIONICS	BIRDINGS
BIGS	BILLETING	BINGERS	BIONOMIC	BIRDMAN
BIGWIG	BILLETS	BINGES	BIONOMICS	BIRDMEN
BIGWIGS	BILLHEAD	BINGING	BIONT	BIRDS
BIJOU	BILLHEADS	BINGLE	BIONTIC	BIRDSEED
BIJOUX	BILLHOOK	BINGLED	BIONTS	BIRDSEEDS
BIJWONER	BILLHOOKS	BINGLES	BIOPARENT	BIRDSHOT
BIJWONERS	BILLIARD	BINGLING	BIOPARENTS	BIRDSHOTS
BIKE	BILLIARDS	BINGO	BIOPHOR	BIRDWING
BIKED	BILLIE	BINGOS	BIOPHORE	BIRDWINGS
BIKER	BILLIES	BINGS	BIOPHORES	BIREME
BIKERS	BILLING	BINK	BIOPHORS	BIREMES
BIKES	BILLINGS	BINKS	BIOPIC	BIRETTA
BIKIE	BILLION	BINNACLE	BIOPICS	BIRETTAS
BIKIES	BILLIONS	BINNACLES	BIOPLASM	BIRIYANI
BIKING	BILLIONTH	BINNED	BIOPLASMS	BIRIYANIS
BIKINGS	BILLIONTHS	BINNING	BIOPLAST	BIRK
BIKINI	BILLMAN	BINOCLE	BIOPLASTS	BIRKEN
BIKINIS	BILLMEN	BINOCLES	BIOPSIES	BIRKIE
BILABIAL	BILLON	BINOCULAR	BIOPSY	BIRKIES
BILABIALS	BILLONS	BINOCULARS	BIOS	BIRKS
BILABIATE	BILLOW	BINOMIAL	BIOSCOPE	BIRL
BILANDER	BILLOWED	BINOMIALS	BIOSCOPES	BIRLE
BILANDERS	BILLOWIER	BINOMINAL	BIOSPHERE	BIRLED
BILATERAL	BILLOWIEST	BINS	BIOSPHERES	BIRLER
BILBERRIES	BILLOWING	BINT	BIOSTABLE	BIRLERS
BILBERRY	BILLOWS	BINTS	BIOTA	BIRLES

BIRLIEMAN
BIRLIEMEN
BIRLING
BIRLINGS
BIRLINN
BIRLINNS
BIRLS
BIRR
BIRRS
BIRSE
BIRSES
BIRSLE
BIRSLED
BIRSLES
BIRSLING
BIRSY
BIRTH
BIRTHDAY
BIRTHDAYS
BIRTHDOM
BIRTHDOMS
BIRTHMARK
BIRTHMARKS
BIRTHS
BIRTHWORT
BIRTHWORTS
BIRYANI
BIRYANIS
BIS
BISCACHA
BISCACHAS
BISCUIT
BISCUITS
BISCUITY
BISE
BISECT
BISECTED
BISECTING
BISECTION
BISECTIONS
BISECTOR
BISECTORS
BISECTS
BISERIAL
BISERRATE
BISES
BISEXUAL
BISH
BISHES
BISHOP
BISHOPDOM
BISHOPDOMS
BISHOPED
BISHOPESS
BISHOPESSES
BISHOPING
BISHOPRIC
BISHOPRICS
BISHOPS
BISK
BISKS
BISMAR
BISMARS
BISMILLAH
BISMUTH
BISMUTHS
BISON
BISONS
BISQUE
BISQUES

BISSON
BISTABLE
BISTER
BISTERS
BISTORT
BISTORTS
BISTOURIES
BISTOURY
BISTRE
BISTRED
BISTRES
BISTRO
BISTROS
BISULCATE
BIT
BITCH
BITCHED
BITCHERIES
BITCHERY
BITCHES
BITCHIER
BITCHIEST
BITCHILY
BITCHING
BITCHY
BITE
BITER
BITERS
BITES
BITING
BITINGS
BITO
BITONAL
BITOS
BITS
BITSIER
BITSIEST
BITSY
BITT
BITTACLE
BITTACLES
BITTE
BITTED
BITTEN
BITTER
BITTERER
BITTEREST
BITTERISH
BITTERLY
BITTERN
BITTERNS
BITTERS
BITTIE
BITTIER
BITTIES
BITTIEST
BITTING
BITTOCK
BITTOCKS
BITTOR
BITTORS
BITTOUR
BITTOURS
BITTS
BITTUR
BITTURS
BITTY
BITUMED
BITUMEN
BITUMENS

BIVALENCE
BIVALENCES
BIVALENCIES
BIVALENCY
BIVALENT
BIVALENTS
BIVALVE
BIVALVES
BIVARIANT
BIVARIANTS
BIVARIATE
BIVARIATES
BIVIOUS
BIVIUM
BIVIUMS
BIVOUAC
BIVOUACKED
BIVOUACKING
BIVOUACS
BIVVIED
BIVVIES
BIVVY
BIVVYING
BIZ
BIZARRE
BIZAZZ
BIZAZZES
BIZCACHA
BIZCACHAS
BIZONAL
BIZONE
BIZONES
BIZZES
BLAB
BLABBED
BLABBER
BLABBERS
BLABBING
BLABBINGS
BLABS
BLACK
BLACKBALL
BLACKBALLED
BLACKBALLING
BLACKBALLINGS
BLACKBALLS
BLACKBAND
BLACKBANDS
BLACKBIRD
BLACKBIRDS
BLACKBOY
BLACKBOYS
BLACKBUCK
BLACKBUCKS
BLACKCAP
BLACKCAPS
BLACKCOCK
BLACKCOCKS
BLACKED
BLACKEN
BLACKENED
BLACKENING
BLACKENS
BLACKER
BLACKEST
BLACKFISH
BLACKFISHES
BLACKGAME
BLACKGAMES
BLACKHEAD

BLACKHEADS
BLACKING
BLACKINGS
BLACKISH
BLACKJACK
BLACKJACKS
BLACKLEAD
BLACKLEADS
BLACKLEG
BLACKLEGGED
BLACKLEGGING
BLACKLEGS
BLACKLIST
BLACKLISTED
BLACKLISTING
BLACKLISTINGS
BLACKLISTS
BLACKMAIL
BLACKMAILED
BLACKMAILING
BLACKMAILS
BLACKNESS
BLACKNESSES
BLACKOUT
BLACKOUTS
BLACKS
BLACKTOP
BLACKTOPS
BLACKWASH
BLACKWASHES
BLACKWOOD
BLACKWOODS
BLAD
BLADDED
BLADDER
BLADDERED
BLADDERS
BLADDERY
BLADDING
BLADE
BLADED
BLADES
BLADS
BLAE
BLAEBERRIES
BLAEBERRY
BLAER
BLAES
BLAEST
BLAG
BLAGGED
BLAGGING
BLAGS
BLAGUE
BLAGUES
BLAGUEUR
BLAGUEURS
BLAH
BLAHED
BLAHING
BLAHS
BLAIN
BLAINS
BLAISE
BLAIZE
BLAMABLE
BLAMABLY
BLAME
BLAMEABLE
BLAMEABLY

BLAMED
BLAMEFUL
BLAMELESS
BLAMES
BLAMING
BLANCH
BLANCHED
BLANCHES
BLANCHING
BLANCO
BLANCOED
BLANCOES
BLANCOING
BLAND
BLANDER
BLANDEST
BLANDISH
BLANDISHED
BLANDISHES
BLANDISHING
BLANDLY
BLANDNESS
BLANDNESSES
BLANDS
BLANK
BLANKED
BLANKER
BLANKEST
BLANKET
BLANKETED
BLANKETIES
BLANKETING
BLANKETINGS
BLANKETS
BLANKETY
BLANKIES
BLANKING
BLANKLY
BLANKNESS
BLANKNESSES
BLANKS
BLANKY
BLANQUET
BLANQUETS
BLARE
BLARED
BLARES
BLARING
BLARNEY
BLARNEYED
BLARNEYING
BLARNEYS
BLASÉ
BLASH
BLASHES
BLASHY
BLASPHEME
BLASPHEMED
BLASPHEMES
BLASPHEMIES
BLASPHEMING
BLASPHEMY
BLAST
BLASTED
BLASTEMA
BLASTEMAS
BLASTER
BLASTERS
BLASTING
BLASTINGS

BLASTMENT
BLASTMENTS
BLASTOID
BLASTOIDS
BLASTS
BLASTULA
BLASTULAE
BLASTULAR
BLASTULAS
BLAT
BLATANT
BLATANTER
BLATANTEST
BLATANTLY
BLATE
BLATER
BLATEST
BLATHER
BLATHERED
BLATHERING
BLATHERS
BLATS
BLATT
BLATTANT
BLATTED
BLATTER
BLATTERED
BLATTERING
BLATTERS
BLATTING
BLATTS
BLAUBOK
BLAUBOKS
BLAUD
BLAUDED
BLAUDING
BLAUDS
BLAWORT
BLAWORTS
BLAY
BLAYS
BLAZE
BLAZED
BLAZER
BLAZERS
BLAZES
BLAZING
BLAZON
BLAZONED
BLAZONER
BLAZONERS
BLAZONING
BLAZONRIES
BLAZONRY
BLAZONS
BLEACH
BLEACHED
BLEACHER
BLEACHERIES
BLEACHERS
BLEACHERY
BLEACHES
BLEACHING
BLEACHINGS
BLEAK
BLEAKER
BLEAKEST
BLEAKIER
BLEAKIEST
BLEAKLY

BLEAKNESS
BLEAKNESSES
BLEAKS
BLEAKY
BLEAR
BLEARED
BLEARER
BLEAREST
BLEAREYED
BLEARIER
BLEARIEST
BLEARING
BLEARS
BLEARY
BLEAT
BLEATED
BLEATER
BLEATERS
BLEATING
BLEATINGS
BLEATS
BLEB
BLEBS
BLED
BLEE
BLEED
BLEEDER
BLEEDERS
BLEEDING
BLEEDINGS
BLEEDS
BLEEP
BLEEPED
BLEEPER
BLEEPERS
BLEEPING
BLEEPS
BLEES
BLEMISH
BLEMISHED
BLEMISHES
BLEMISHING
BLENCH
BLENCHED
BLENCHES
BLENCHING
BLEND
BLENDE
BLENDED
BLENDER
BLENDERS
BLENDES
BLENDING
BLENDINGS
BLENDS
BLENNIES
BLENNY
BLENT
BLESBOK
BLESBOKS
BLESS
BLESSED
BLESSEDER
BLESSEDEST
BLESSEDLY
BLESSES
BLESSING
BLESSINGS
BLEST
BLET

BLETHER
BLETHERED
BLETHERING
BLETHERINGS
BLETHERS
BLETS
BLETTED
BLETTING
BLEUÂTRE
BLEW
BLEWART
BLEWARTS
BLEWITS
BLEWITSES
BLEWS
BLEY
BLEYS
BLIGHT
BLIGHTED
BLIGHTER
BLIGHTERS
BLIGHTIES
BLIGHTING
BLIGHTINGS
BLIGHTS
BLIGHTY
BLIMBING
BLIMBINGS
BLIMEY
BLIMP
BLIMPISH
BLIMPS
BLIMY
BLIN
BLIND
BLINDAGE
BLINDAGES
BLINDED
BLINDER
BLINDERS
BLINDEST
BLINDFISH
BLINDFISHES
BLINDFOLD
BLINDFOLDED
BLINDFOLDING
BLINDFOLDS
BLINDING
BLINDINGS
BLINDLESS
BLINDLY
BLINDNESS
BLINDNESSES
BLINDS
BLINDWORM
BLINDWORMS
BLINI
BLINIS
BLINK
BLINKARD
BLINKARDS
BLINKED
BLINKER
BLINKERED
BLINKERING
BLINKERS
BLINKING
BLINKS
BLINNED
BLINNING

BLINS
BLINTZ
BLINTZE
BLINTZES
BLIP
BLIPPED
BLIPPING
BLIPS
BLISS
BLISSES
BLISSFUL
BLISSLESS
BLIST
BLISTER
BLISTERED
BLISTERING
BLISTERS
BLISTERY
BLITE
BLITES
BLITHE
BLITHELY
BLITHER
BLITHERED
BLITHERING
BLITHERS
BLITHEST
BLITZ
BLITZED
BLITZES
BLITZING
BLIVE
BLIZZARD
BLIZZARDS
BLOAT
BLOATED
BLOATER
BLOATERS
BLOATING
BLOATINGS
BLOATS
BLOB
BLOBBED
BLOBBING
BLOBS
BLOC
BLOCK
BLOCKADE
BLOCKADED
BLOCKADES
BLOCKADING
BLOCKAGE
BLOCKAGES
BLOCKED
BLOCKER
BLOCKERS
BLOCKHEAD
BLOCKHEADS
BLOCKHOLE
BLOCKHOLES
BLOCKIER
BLOCKIEST
BLOCKING
BLOCKINGS
BLOCKISH
BLOCKS
BLOCKWORK
BLOCKWORKS
BLOCKY
BLOCS

BLOKE
BLOKES
BLONCKET
BLOND
BLONDE
BLONDER
BLONDES
BLONDEST
BLONDS
BLOOD
BLOODED
BLOODHEAT
BLOODHEATS
BLOODIED
BLOODIER
BLOODIES
BLOODIEST
BLOODILY
BLOODING
BLOODLESS
BLOODLUST
BLOODLUSTS
BLOODROOT
BLOODROOTS
BLOODS
BLOODSHED
BLOODSHEDS
BLOODSHOT
BLOODWOOD
BLOODWOODS
BLOODY
BLOODYING
BLOOM
BLOOMED
BLOOMER
BLOOMERIES
BLOOMERS
BLOOMERY
BLOOMIER
BLOOMIEST
BLOOMING
BLOOMLESS
BLOOMS
BLOOMY
BLOOP
BLOOPED
BLOOPER
BLOOPERS
BLOOPING
BLOOPS
BLOOSME
BLOOSMED
BLOOSMES
BLOOSMING
BLORE
BLORES
BLOSSOM
BLOSSOMED
BLOSSOMING
BLOSSOMINGS
BLOSSOMS
BLOSSOMY
BLOT
BLOTCH
BLOTCHED
BLOTCHES
BLOTCHIER
BLOTCHIEST
BLOTCHING
BLOTCHINGS

BLOTCHY	BLUDES	BLUFFING	BLUSTERIEST	BOBBINET
BLOTS	BLUDGE	BLUFFLY	BLUSTERING	BOBBINETS
BLOTTED	BLUDGED	BLUFFNESS	BLUSTERS	BOBBING
BLOTTER	BLUDGEON	BLUFFNESSES	BLUSTERY	BOBBINS
BLOTTERS	BLUDGEONED	BLUFFS	BLUSTROUS	BOBBISH
BLOTTIER	BLUDGEONING	BLUGGY	BLUTWURST	BOBBLE
BLOTTIEST	BLUDGEONS	BLUID	BLUTWURSTS	BOBBLED
BLOTTING	BLUDGER	BLUIDIER	BO	BOBBLES
BLOTTINGS	BLUDGERS	BLUIDIEST	BOA	BOBBLING
BLOTTO	BLUDGES	BLUIDS	BOAR	BOBBY
BLOTTY	BLUDGING	BLUIDY	BOARD	BOBBYSOCK
BLOUBOK	BLUDIE	BLUING	BOARDED	BOBBYSOCKS
BLOUBOKS	BLUDIER	BLUINGS	BOARDER	BOBCAT
BLOUSE	BLUDIEST	BLUISH	BOARDERS	BOBCATS
BLOUSED	BLUDY	BLUNDER	BOARDING	BOBOLINK
BLOUSES	BLUE	BLUNDERED	BOARDINGS	BOBOLINKS
BLOUSING	BLUEBACK	BLUNDERER	BOARDROOM	BOBS
BLOUSON	BLUEBACKS	BLUNDERERS	BOARDROOMS	BOBSLED
BLOUSONS	BLUEBEARD	BLUNDERING	BOARDS	BOBSLEDS
BLOW	BLUEBEARDS	BLUNDERINGS	BOARDWALK	BOBSLEIGH
BLOWBALL	BLUEBELL	BLUNDERS	BOARDWALKS	BOBSLEIGHS
BLOWBALLS	BLUEBELLS	BLUNGE	BOARFISH	BOBSTAYS
BLOWDOWN	BLUEBERRIES	BLUNGED	BOARFISHES	BOBTAIL
BLOWDOWNS	BLUEBERRY	BLUNGER	BOARISH	BOBTAILED
BLOWED	BLUEBIRD	BLUNGERS	BOARS	BOBTAILING
BLOWER	BLUEBIRDS	BLUNGES	BOART	BOBTAILS
BLOWERS	BLUEBUCK	BLUNGING	BOARTS	BOBWHEEL
BLOWFLIES	BLUEBUCKS	BLUNK	BOAS	BOBWHEELS
BLOWFLY	BLUECAP	BLUNKED	BOAST	BOBWIG
BLOWGUN	BLUECAPS	BLUNKER	BOASTED	BOBWIGS
BLOWGUNS	BLUECOAT	BLUNKERS	BOASTER	BOCAGE
BLOWHARD	BLUECOATS	BLUNKING	BOASTERS	BOCAGES
BLOWHARDS	BLUED	BLUNKS	BOASTFUL	BOCCA
BLOWHOLE	BLUEFISH	BLUNT	BOASTING	BOCCAS
BLOWHOLES	BLUEFISHES	BLUNTED	BOASTINGS	BOCHE
BLOWIER	BLUEGOWN	BLUNTER	BOASTLESS	BOCHES
BLOWIEST	BLUEGOWNS	BLUNTEST	BOASTS	BOCK
BLOWING	BLUEGRASS	BLUNTING	BOAT	BOCKED
BLOWLAMP	BLUEGRASSES	BLUNTISH	BOATBILL	BOCKING
BLOWLAMPS	BLUEING	BLUNTLY	BOATBILLS	BOCKS
BLOWN	BLUEINGS	BLUNTNESS	BOATED	BOD
BLOWPIPE	BLUENESS	BLUNTNESSES	BOATEL	BODACH
BLOWPIPES	BLUENESSES	BLUNTS	BOATELS	BODACHS
BLOWS	BLUENOSE	BLUR	BOATER	BODDLE
BLOWSE	BLUENOSES	BLURB	BOATERS	BODDLES
BLOWSED	BLUEPRINT	BLURBS	BOATHOUSE	BODE
BLOWSES	BLUEPRINTED	BLURRED	BOATHOUSES	BODED
BLOWSIER	BLUEPRINTING	BLURRING	BOATING	BODEFUL
BLOWSIEST	BLUEPRINTS	BLURS	BOATINGS	BODEGA
BLOWSY	BLUER	BLURT	BOATMAN	BODEGAS
BLOWTORCH	BLUES	BLURTED	BOATMEN	BODEGUERO
BLOWTORCHES	BLUESIER	BLURTING	BOATRACE	BODEGUEROS
BLOWY	BLUESIEST	BLURTINGS	BOATRACES	BODEMENT
BLOWZE	BLUEST	BLURTS	BOATS	BODEMENTS
BLOWZED	BLUESTONE	BLUSH	BOATSWAIN	BODES
BLOWZES	BLUESTONES	BLUSHED	BOATSWAINS	BODGE
BLOWZIER	BLUESY	BLUSHER	BOATTAIL	BODGED
BLOWZIEST	BLUETTE	BLUSHERS	BOATTAILS	BODGER
BLOWZY	BLUETTES	BLUSHES	BOB	BODGERS
BLUB	BLUEWEED	BLUSHET	BOBA	BODGES
BLUBBED	BLUEWEEDS	BLUSHETS	BOBAC	BODGIE
BLUBBER	BLUEWING	BLUSHFUL	BOBACS	BODGIES
BLUBBERED	BLUEWINGS	BLUSHING	BOBAK	BODGING
BLUBBERING	BLUEY	BLUSHINGS	BOBAKS	BODICE
BLUBBERS	BLUEYS	BLUSHLESS	BOBAS	BODICES
BLUBBING	BLUFF	BLUSTER	BOBBED	BODIED
BLUBS	BLUFFED	BLUSTERED	BOBBERIES	BODIES
BLUCHER	BLUFFER	BLUSTERER	BOBBERY	BODIKIN
BLUCHERS	BLUFFERS	BLUSTERERS	BOBBIES	BODIKINS
BLUDE	BLUFFEST	BLUSTERIER	BOBBIN	BODILESS

BODILY
BODING
BODINGS
BODKIN
BODKINS
BODLE
BODLES
BODRAG
BODRAGS
BODS
BODY
BODYGUARD
BODYGUARDS
BODYING
BODYSHELL
BODYSHELLS
BODYWORK
BODYWORKS
BOEREWORS
BOFF
BOFFED
BOFFIN
BOFFING
BOFFINS
BOFFS
BOG
BOGAN
BOGANS
BOGBEAN
BOGBEANS
BOGEY
BOGEYISM
BOGEYISMS
BOGEYS
BOGGARD
BOGGARDS
BOGGART
BOGGARTS
BOGGED
BOGGIER
BOGGIEST
BOGGINESS
BOGGINESSES
BOGGING
BOGGLE
BOGGLED
BOGGLER
BOGGLERS
BOGGLES
BOGGLING
BOGGY
BOGIE
BOGIES
BOGLAND
BOGLANDS
BOGLE
BOGLES
BOGOAK
BOGOAKS
BOGONG
BOGONGS
BOGS
BOGUS
BOGY
BOGYISM
BOGYISMS
BOH
BOHEA
BOHEAS
BOHUNK

BOHUNKS
BOIL
BOILED
BOILER
BOILERIES
BOILERS
BOILERY
BOILING
BOILINGS
BOILS
BOING
BOINGED
BOINGING
BOINGS
BOINK
BOINKED
BOINKING
BOINKS
BOK
BOKE
BOKED
BOKES
BOKING
BOKO
BOKOS
BOKS
BOLAS
BOLD
BOLDEN
BOLDENED
BOLDENING
BOLDENS
BOLDER
BOLDEST
BOLDLY
BOLDNESS
BOLDNESSES
BOLE
BOLECTION
BOLECTIONS
BOLERO
BOLEROS
BOLES
BOLETI
BOLETUS
BOLETUSES
BOLIDE
BOLIDES
BOLIVAR
BOLIVARES
BOLIVARS
BOLIVIANO
BOLIVIANOS
BOLIX
BOLIXED
BOLIXES
BOLIXING
BOLL
BOLLARD
BOLLARDS
BOLLED
BOLLEN
BOLLETRIE
BOLLETRIES
BOLLING
BOLLIX
BOLLIXED
BOLLIXES
BOLLIXING
BOLLOCK

BOLLOCKED
BOLLOCKING
BOLLOCKINGS
BOLLOCKS
BOLLOCKSED
BOLLOCKSES
BOLLOCKSING
BOLLS
BOLO
BOLOMETER
BOLOMETERS
BOLOMETRIES
BOLOMETRY
BOLONEY
BOLONEYS
BOLOS
BOLSHEVIK
BOLSHEVIKS
BOLSHIE
BOLSHIER
BOLSHIES
BOLSHIEST
BOLSHY
BOLSTER
BOLSTERED
BOLSTERING
BOLSTERINGS
BOLSTERS
BOLT
BOLTED
BOLTER
BOLTERS
BOLTHEAD
BOLTHEADS
BOLTHOLE
BOLTHOLES
BOLTING
BOLTINGS
BOLTS
BOLUS
BOLUSES
BOMA
BOMAS
BOMB
BOMBARD
BOMBARDED
BOMBARDING
BOMBARDON
BOMBARDONS
BOMBARDS
BOMBASINE
BOMBASINES
BOMBAST
BOMBASTED
BOMBASTIC
BOMBASTING
BOMBASTS
BOMBAX
BOMBAXES
BOMBAZINE
BOMBAZINES
BOMBE
BOMBÉ
BOMBED
BOMBER
BOMBERS
BOMBES
BOMBILATE
BOMBILATED
BOMBILATES

BOMBILATING
BOMBINATE
BOMBINATED
BOMBINATES
BOMBINATING
BOMBING
BOMBO
BOMBORA
BOMBORAS
BOMBOS
BOMBPROOF
BOMBS
BOMBSHELL
BOMBSHELLS
BOMBSITE
BOMBSITES
BOMBYCID
BOMBYCIDS
BON
BONA
BONAMANI
BONAMANO
BONANZA
BONANZAS
BONASSUS
BONASSUSES
BONASUS
BONASUSES
BONBON
BONBONS
BONCE
BONCES
BOND
BONDAGE
BONDAGER
BONDAGERS
BONDAGES
BONDED
BONDER
BONDERS
BONDING
BONDINGS
BONDMAID
BONDMAIDS
BONDMAN
BONDMEN
BONDS
BONDSMAN
BONDSMEN
BONDSTONE
BONDSTONES
BONDUC
BONDUCS
BONE
BONED
BONEHEAD
BONEHEADS
BONELESS
BONER
BONERS
BONES
BONESET
BONESETS
BONEYARD
BONEYARDS
BONFIRE
BONFIRES
BONG
BONGED
BONGING

BONGO
BONGOS
BONGRACE
BONGRACES
BONGS
BONHOMIE
BONHOMIES
BONHOMMIE
BONHOMMIES
BONHOMOUS
BONIBELL
BONIBELLS
BONIE
BONIER
BONIEST
BONIFACE
BONIFACES
BONILASSE
BONILASSES
BONINESS
BONINESSES
BONING
BONINGS
BONISM
BONISMS
BONIST
BONISTS
BONITO
BONITOS
BONJOUR
BONK
BONKED
BONKERS
BONKING
BONKS
BONNE
BONNES
BONNET
BONNETED
BONNETING
BONNETS
BONNIBELL
BONNIBELLS
BONNIE
BONNIER
BONNIES
BONNIEST
BONNILY
BONNINESS
BONNINESSES
BONNY
BONSAI
BONSOIR
BONSPIEL
BONSPIELS
BONTEBOK
BONTEBOKS
BONUS
BONUSES
BONXIE
BONXIES
BONY
BONZE
BONZER
BONZES
BOO
BOOB
BOOBED
BOOBIES
BOOBING

BOOBOO
BOOBOOK
BOOBOOKS
BOOBOOS
BOOBS
BOOBY
BOOBYISH
BOOBYISM
BOOBYISMS
BOODIE
BOODIED
BOODIES
BOODLE
BOODLES
BOODY
BOODYING
BOOED
BOOGIE
BOOGIES
BOOH
BOOHED
BOOHING
BOOHS
BOOING
BOOK
BOOKABLE
BOOKCASE
BOOKCASES
BOOKED
BOOKFUL
BOOKIE
BOOKIER
BOOKIES
BOOKIEST
BOOKING
BOOKINGS
BOOKISH
BOOKLAND
BOOKLANDS
BOOKLESS
BOOKLET
BOOKLETS
BOOKLICE
BOOKLORE
BOOKLORES
BOOKLOUSE
BOOKMAKER
BOOKMAKERS
BOOKMAN
BOOKMARK
BOOKMARKS
BOOKMEN
BOOKPLATE
BOOKPLATES
BOOKREST
BOOKRESTS
BOOKS
BOOKSHELF
BOOKSHELVES
BOOKSHOP
BOOKSHOPS
BOOKSIE
BOOKSIER
BOOKSIEST
BOOKSTALL
BOOKSTALLS
BOOKSTAND
BOOKSTANDS
BOOKSTORE
BOOKSTORES

BOOKSY
BOOKWORK
BOOKWORKS
BOOKWORM
BOOKWORMS
BOOKY
BOOM
BOOMED
BOOMER
BOOMERANG
BOOMERANGED
BOOMERANGING
BOOMERANGS
BOOMERS
BOOMING
BOOMINGS
BOOMS
BOOMSLANG
BOOMSLANGS
BOON
BOONDOCKS
BOONG
BOONGS
BOONS
BOOR
BOORD
BOORDE
BOORDES
BOORDS
BOORISH
BOORISHLY
BOORS
BOOS
BOOSE
BOOSED
BOOSES
BOOSING
BOOST
BOOSTED
BOOSTER
BOOSTERS
BOOSTING
BOOSTS
BOOT
BOOTBLACK
BOOTBLACKS
BOOTED
BOOTEE
BOOTEES
BOOTH
BOOTHOSE
BOOTHS
BOOTIES
BOOTIKIN
BOOTIKINS
BOOTING
BOOTLACE
BOOTLACES
BOOTLAST
BOOTLASTS
BOOTLEG
BOOTLEGGED
BOOTLEGGING
BOOTLEGGINGS
BOOTLEGS
BOOTLESS
BOOTLICK
BOOTLICKED
BOOTLICKING
BOOTLICKINGS

BOOTLICKS
BOOTMAKER
BOOTMAKERS
BOOTS
BOOTTREE
BOOTTREES
BOOTY
BOOZE
BOOZED
BOOZER
BOOZERS
BOOZES
BOOZEY
BOOZIER
BOOZIEST
BOOZILY
BOOZING
BOOZY
BOP
BOPPED
BOPPER
BOPPERS
BOPPING
BOPS
BOR
BORA
BORACHIO
BORACHIOS
BORACIC
BORACITE
BORACITES
BORAGE
BORAGES
BORANE
BORANES
BORAS
BORATE
BORATES
BORAX
BORAXES
BORAZON
BORAZONS
BORD
BORDAR
BORDARS
BORDE
BORDEL
BORDELLO
BORDELLOS
BORDELS
BORDER
BORDEREAU
BORDEREAUX
BORDERED
BORDERER
BORDERERS
BORDERING
BORDERS
BORDES
BORDS
BORDURE
BORDURES
BORE
BOREAL
BORECOLE
BORECOLES
BORED
BOREDOM
BOREDOMS
BOREE

BOREEN
BOREENS
BOREES
BOREHOLE
BOREHOLES
BOREL
BORER
BORERS
BORES
BORGHETTO
BORGHETTOS
BORGO
BORGOS
BORIC
BORIDE
BORIDES
BORING
BORINGS
BORN
BORNE
BORNÉ
BORNITE
BORNITES
BORON
BORONIA
BORONIAS
BORONS
BOROUGH
BOROUGHS
BORREL
BORRELL
BORROW
BORROWED
BORROWER
BORROWERS
BORROWING
BORROWINGS
BORROWS
BORS
BORSCH
BORSCHES
BORSCHT
BORSCHTS
BORSTAL
BORSTALL
BORSTALLS
BORSTALS
BORT
BORTS
BORTSCH
BORTSCHES
BORTSCHT
BORTSCHTS
BORZOI
BORZOIS
BOS
BOSBOK
BOSBOKS
BOSCAGE
BOSCAGES
BOSCHBOK
BOSCHBOKS
BOSCHE
BOSCHES
BOSCHVELD
BOSCHVELDS
BOSH
BOSHES
BOSHTA
BOSHTER

BOSK
BOSKER
BOSKET
BOSKETS
BOSKIER
BOSKIEST
BOSKINESS
BOSKINESSES
BOSKS
BOSKY
BOSOM
BOSOMED
BOSOMING
BOSOMS
BOSOMY
BOSON
BOSONS
BOSS
BOSSED
BOSSER
BOSSES
BOSSEST
BOSSIER
BOSSIEST
BOSSILY
BOSSINESS
BOSSINESSES
BOSSING
BOSSY
BOSTANGI
BOSTANGIS
BOSTON
BOSTONS
BOSTRYX
BOSTRYXES
BOSUN
BOSUNS
BOT
BOTANIC
BOTANICAL
BOTANIES
BOTANISE
BOTANISED
BOTANISES
BOTANISING
BOTANIST
BOTANISTS
BOTANIZE
BOTANIZED
BOTANIZES
BOTANIZING
BOTANY
BOTARGO
BOTARGOES
BOTARGOS
BOTCH
BOTCHED
BOTCHER
BOTCHERIES
BOTCHERS
BOTCHERY
BOTCHES
BOTCHIER
BOTCHIEST
BOTCHING
BOTCHINGS
BOTCHY
BOTEL
BOTELS
BOTFLIES

BOTFLY	BOUILLI	BOURGEONS	BOWLED	BOYCOTT
BOTH	BOUILLIS	BOURGS	BOWLER	BOYCOTTED
BOTHAN	BOUILLON	BOURKHA	BOWLERED	BOYCOTTING
BOTHANS	BOUILLONS	BOURKHAS	BOWLERING	BOYCOTTS
BOTHER	BOUK	BOURLAW	BOWLERS	BOYED
BOTHERED	BOUKS	BOURLAWS	BOWLINE	BOYFRIEND
BOTHERING	BOULDER	BOURN	BOWLINES	BOYFRIENDS
BOTHERS	BOULDERS	BOURNE	BOWLING	BOYG
BOTHIE	BOULE	BOURNES	BOWLINGS	BOYGS
BOTHIES	BOULES	BOURNS	BOWLS	BOYHOOD
BOTHOLE	BOULEVARD	BOURREE	BOWMAN	BOYHOODS
BOTHOLES	BOULEVARDS	BOURREES	BOWMEN	BOYING
BOTHY	BOULLE	BOURSE	BOWNE	BOYISH
BOTHYMAN	BOULLES	BOURSES	BOWNED	BOYISHLY
BOTHYMEN	BOULT	BOURSIER	BOWNES	BOYO
BOTONÉ	BOULTED	BOURSIERS	BOWNING	BOYOS
BOTRYOID	BOULTER	BOURTREE	BOWPOT	BOYS
BOTRYOSE	BOULTERS	BOURTREES	BOWPOTS	BOZZETTI
BOTS	BOULTING	BOUSE	BOWR	BOZZETTO
BOTT	BOULTINGS	BOUSED	BOWRS	BRA
BOTTE	BOULTS	BOUSES	BOWS	BRABBLE
BOTTEGA	BOUN	BOUSIER	BOWSE	BRABBLED
BOTTEGAS	BOUNCE	BOUSIEST	BOWSED	BRABBLES
BOTTES	BOUNCED	BOUSING	BOWSER	BRABBLING
BOTTIES	BOUNCER	BOUSY	BOWSERS	BRACCATE
BOTTINE	BOUNCERS	BOUT	BOWSES	BRACCIA
BOTTINES	BOUNCES	BOUTADE	BOWSHOT	BRACCIO
BOTTLE	BOUNCIER	BOUTADES	BOWSHOTS	BRACE
BOTTLED	BOUNCIEST	BOUTIQUE	BOWSING	BRACED
BOTTLEFUL	BOUNCILY	BOUTIQUES	BOWSPRIT	BRACELET
BOTTLEFULS	BOUNCING	BOUTON	BOWSPRITS	BRACELETS
BOTTLER	BOUNCY	BOUTONNÉ	BOWSTRING	BRACER
BOTTLERS	BOUND	BOUTONNÉE	BOWSTRINGED	BRACERS
BOTTLES	BOUNDARIES	BOUTONS	BOWSTRINGING	BRACES
BOTTLING	BOUNDARY	BOUTS	BOWSTRINGS	BRACH
BOTTOM	BOUNDED	BOUZOUKI	BOWSTRUNG	BRACHES
BOTTOMED	BOUNDEN	BOUZOUKIS	BOWWOW	BRACHET
BOTTOMING	BOUNDER	BOVATE	BOWWOWS	BRACHETS
BOTTOMS	BOUNDERS	BOVATES	BOWYER	BRACHIAL
BOTTONY	BOUNDING	BOVINE	BOWYERS	BRACING
BOTTS	BOUNDLESS	BOVVER	BOX	BRACK
BOTTY	BOUNDS	BOVVERS	BOXCAR	BRACKEN
BOTULISM	BOUNED	BOW	BOXCARS	BRACKENS
BOTULISMS	BOUNING	BOWAT	BOXED	BRACKET
BOUCHE	BOUNS	BOWATS	BOXEN	BRACKETED
BOUCHÉ	BOUNTEOUS	BOWBENT	BOXER	BRACKETING
BOUCHES	BOUNTIES	BOWED	BOXERS	BRACKETS
BOUCHÉS	BOUNTIFUL	BOWEL	BOXES	BRACKISH
BOUCLÉ	BOUNTREE	BOWELLED	BOXFUL	BRACKS
BOUCLÉS	BOUNTREES	BOWELLING	BOXFULS	BRACT
BOUDERIE	BOUNTY	BOWELS	BOXIER	BRACTEAL
BOUDERIES	BOUNTYHED	BOWER	BOXIEST	BRACTEATE
BOUDOIR	BOUNTYHEDS	BOWERED	BOXINESS	BRACTEATES
BOUDOIRS	BOUQUET	BOWERIES	BOXINESSES	BRACTEOLE
BOUFFANT	BOUQUETS	BOWERING	BOXING	BRACTEOLES
BOUGE	BOURASQUE	BOWERS	BOXINGS	BRACTLESS
BOUGED	BOURASQUES	BOWERY	BOXKEEPER	BRACTLET
BOUGES	BOURBON	BOWES	BOXKEEPERS	BRACTLETS
BOUGET	BOURBONS	BOWET	BOXROOM	BRACTS
BOUGETS	BOURD	BOWETS	BOXROOMS	BRAD
BOUGH	BOURDER	BOWFIN	BOXWALLAH	BRADAWL
BOUGHPOT	BOURDERS	BOWFINS	BOXWALLAHS	BRADAWLS
BOUGHPOTS	BOURDON	BOWGET	BOXWOOD	BRADS
BOUGHS	BOURDONS	BOWGETS	BOXWOODS	BRAE
BOUGHT	BOURDS	BOWHEAD	BOXY	BRAES
BOUGHTEN	BOURG	BOWHEADS	BOY	BRAG
BOUGHTS	BOURGEOIS	BOWING	BOYAR	BRAGGART
BOUGIE	BOURGEON	BOWL	BOYARS	BRAGGARTS
BOUGIES	BOURGEONED	BOWLDER	BOYAU	BRAGGED
BOUGING	BOURGEONING	BOWLDERS	BOYAUX	BRAGGING

BRAGLY	BRANCHERS	BRASHY	BRAVI	BREADTHS
BRAGS	BRANCHERY	BRASIER	BRAVING	BREAK
BRAID	BRANCHES	BRASIERS	BRAVO	BREAKABLE
BRAIDE	BRANCHIA	BRASS	BRAVOES	BREAKABLES
BRAIDED	BRANCHIAE	BRASSARD	BRAVOS	BREAKAGE
BRAIDER	BRANCHIAL	BRASSARDS	BRAVURA	BREAKAGES
BRAIDEST	BRANCHIER	BRASSART	BRAVURAS	BREAKAWAY
BRAIDING	BRANCHIEST	BRASSARTS	BRAW	BREAKAWAYS
BRAIDINGS	BRANCHING	BRASSERIE	BRAWER	BREAKBACK
BRAIDS	BRANCHINGS	BRASSERIES	BRAWEST	BREAKDOWN
BRAIL	BRANCHLET	BRASSES	BRAWL	BREAKDOWNS
BRAILED	BRANCHLETS	BRASSET	BRAWLED	BREAKER
BRAILING	BRANCHY	BRASSETS	BRAWLER	BREAKERS
BRAILS	BRAND	BRASSICA	BRAWLERS	BREAKFAST
BRAIN	BRANDADE	BRASSICAS	BRAWLIER	BREAKFASTED
BRAINCASE	BRANDADES	BRASSIE	BRAWLIEST	BREAKFASTING
BRAINCASES	BRANDED	BRASSIER	BRAWLING	BREAKFASTS
BRAINED	BRANDER	BRASSIÈRE	BRAWLINGS	BREAKING
BRAINIER	BRANDERED	BRASSIÈRES	BRAWLS	BREAKINGS
BRAINIEST	BRANDERING	BRASSIES	BRAWLY	BREAKNECK
BRAINING	BRANDERS	BRASSIEST	BRAWN	BREAKS
BRAINISH	BRANDIED	BRASSILY	BRAWNED	BREAM
BRAINLESS	BRANDIES	BRASSY	BRAWNIER	BREAMED
BRAINPAN	BRANDING	BRAST	BRAWNIEST	BREAMING
BRAINPANS	BRANDISE	BRASTING	BRAWNS	BREAMS
BRAINS	BRANDISES	BRASTS	BRAWNY	BREARE
BRAINSICK	BRANDISH	BRAT	BRAWS	BREARES
BRAINWASH	BRANDISHED	BRATCHET	BRAXIES	BREASKIT
BRAINWASHED	BRANDISHES	BRATCHETS	BRAXY	BREASKITS
BRAINWASHES	BRANDISHING	BRATLING	BRAY	BREAST
BRAINWASHING	BRANDLING	BRATLINGS	BRAYED	BREASTED
BRAINWASHINGS	BRANDLINGS	BRATS	BRAYER	BREASTING
BRAINY	BRANDRETH	BRATTICE	BRAYERS	BREASTPIN
BRAIRD	BRANDRETHS	BRATTICED	BRAYING	BREASTPINS
BRAIRDED	BRANDS	BRATTICES	BRAYS	BREASTS
BRAIRDING	BRANDY	BRATTICING	BRAZE	BREATH
BRAIRDS	BRANGLE	BRATTICINGS	BRAZED	BREATHE
BRAISE	BRANGLED	BRATTIER	BRAZELESS	BREATHED
BRAISED	BRANGLES	BRATTIEST	BRAZEN	BREATHER
BRAISES	BRANGLING	BRATTISH	BRAZENED	BREATHERS
BRAISING	BRANGLINGS	BRATTISHED	BRAZENING	BREATHES
BRAIZE	BRANK	BRATTISHES	BRAZENLY	BREATHFUL
BRAIZES	BRANKED	BRATTISHING	BRAZENRIES	BREATHIER
BRAKE	BRANKIER	BRATTISHINGS	BRAZENRY	BREATHIEST
BRAKED	BRANKIEST	BRATTLE	BRAZENS	BREATHILY
BRAKELESS	BRANKING	BRATTLED	BRAZES	BREATHING
BRAKEMAN	BRANKS	BRATTLES	BRAZIER	BREATHINGS
BRAKEMEN	BRANKY	BRATTLING	BRAZIERS	BREATHS
BRAKES	BRANLE	BRATTLINGS	BRAZIL	BREATHY
BRAKIER	BRANLES	BRATTY	BRAZILS	BRECCIA
BRAKIEST	BRANNIER	BRATWURST	BRAZING	BRECCIAS
BRAKING	BRANNIEST	BRATWURSTS	BREACH	BRECHAM
BRAKY	BRANNY	BRAUNCH	BREACHED	BRECHAMS
BRALESS	BRANS	BRAUNCHED	BREACHES	BRED
BRAMBLE	BRANSLE	BRAUNCHING	BREACHING	BREDE
BRAMBLES	BRANSLES	BRAUNCHS	BREAD	BREDED
BRAMBLIER	BRANTLE	BRAVA	BREADED	BREDES
BRAMBLIEST	BRANTLES	BRAVADO	BREADHEAD	BREDING
BRAMBLING	BRAS	BRAVADOED	BREADHEADS	BREE
BRAMBLINGS	BRASERO	BRAVADOES	BREADING	BREECH
BRAMBLY	BRASEROS	BRAVADOING	BREADLINE	BREECHED
BRAME	BRASES	BRAVADOS	BREADLINES	BREECHES
BRAMES	BRASH	BRAVE	BREADNUT	BREECHING
BRAN	BRASHED	BRAVED	BREADNUTS	BREECHINGS
BRANCARD	BRASHER	BRAVELY	BREADROOM	BREED
BRANCARDS	BRASHES	BRAVER	BREADROOMS	BREEDER
BRANCH	BRASHEST	BRAVERIES	BREADROOT	BREEDERS
BRANCHED	BRASHIER	BRAVERY	BREADROOTS	BREEDING
BRANCHER	BRASHIEST	BRAVES	BREADS	BREEDINGS
BRANCHERIES	BRASHING	BRAVEST	BREADTH	BREEDS

BREEKS	BREWERIES	BRIDIES	BRINDISI	BRITCHES
BREEM	BREWERS	BRIDING	BRINDISIS	BRITS
BREER	BREWERY	BRIDLE	BRINDLE	BRITSCHKA
BREERED	BREWING	BRIDLED	BRINDLED	BRITSCHKAS
BREERING	BREWINGS	BRIDLER	BRINDLES	BRITSKA
BREERS	BREWIS	BRIDLERS	BRINE	BRITSKAS
BREES	BREWISES	BRIDLES	BRINED	BRITTLE
BREESE	BREWS	BRIDLING	BRINES	BRITTLER
BREESES	BREWSTER	BRIDOON	BRING	BRITTLEST
BREEZE	BREWSTERS	BRIDOONS	BRINGER	BRITZKA
BREEZED	BRIAR	BRIEF	BRINGERS	BRITZKAS
BREEZES	BRIARED	BRIEFED	BRINGING	BRITZSKA
BREEZIER	BRIARS	BRIEFER	BRINGINGS	BRITZSKAS
BREEZIEST	BRIBE	BRIEFEST	BRINGS	BRIZE
BREEZILY	BRIBED	BRIEFING	BRINIER	BRIZES
BREEZING	BRIBER	BRIEFINGS	BRINIES	BRO
BREEZY	BRIBERIES	BRIEFLESS	BRINIEST	BROACH
BREGMA	BRIBERS	BRIEFLY	BRINING	BROACHED
BREGMATA	BRIBERY	BRIEFNESS	BRINISH	BROACHER
BREGMATIC	BRIBES	BRIEFNESSES	BRINJAL	BROACHERS
BREHON	BRIBING	BRIEFS	BRINJALS	BROACHES
BREHONS	BRICABRAC	BRIER	BRINJARRIES	BROACHING
BRELOQUE	BRICABRACS	BRIERED	BRINJARRY	BROAD
BRELOQUES	BRICK	BRIERS	BRINK	BROADBAND
BREME	BRICKBAT	BRIERY	BRINKMAN	BROADCAST
BREN	BRICKBATS	BRIG	BRINKMEN	BROADCASTED
BRENNE	BRICKCLAY	BRIGADE	BRINKS	BROADCASTING
BRENNES	BRICKCLAYS	BRIGADED	BRINY	BROADCASTS
BRENNING	BRICKED	BRIGADES	BRIO	BROADEN
BRENS	BRICKEN	BRIGADIER	BRIOCHE	BROADENED
BRENT	BRICKIE	BRIGADIERS	BRIOCHES	BROADENING
BRENTER	BRICKIER	BRIGADING	BRIONIES	BROADENS
BRENTEST	BRICKIES	BRIGAND	BRIONY	BROADER
BRER	BRICKIEST	BRIGANDRIES	BRIOS	BROADEST
BRERE	BRICKING	BRIGANDRY	BRIQUET	BROADISH
BRERES	BRICKINGS	BRIGANDS	BRIQUETS	BROADLOOM
BRERS	BRICKLE	BRIGHT	BRIQUETTE	BROADLY
BRETASCHE	BRICKLER	BRIGHTEN	BRIQUETTES	BROADNESS
BRETASCHES	BRICKLEST	BRIGHTENED	BRISÉ	BROADNESSES
BRETESSE	BRICKS	BRIGHTENING	BRISÉS	BROADS
BRETESSES	BRICKWALL	BRIGHTENS	BRISK	BROADSIDE
BRETHREN	BRICKWALLS	BRIGHTER	BRISKED	BROADSIDES
BRETON	BRICKWORK	BRIGHTEST	BRISKEN	BROADTAIL
BRETONS	BRICKWORKS	BRIGHTLY	BRISKENED	BROADTAILS
BRETTICE	BRICKY	BRIGS	BRISKENING	BROADWAY
BRETTICED	BRICKYARD	BRIGUE	BRISKENS	BROADWAYS
BRETTICES	BRICKYARDS	BRIGUED	BRISKER	BROADWISE
BRETTICING	BRICOLE	BRIGUES	BRISKEST	BROCADE
BREVE	BRICOLES	BRIGUING	BRISKET	BROCADED
BREVES	BRIDAL	BRIGUINGS	BRISKETS	BROCADES
BREVET	BRIDALS	BRILL	BRISKING	BROCAGE
BREVETÉ	BRIDE	BRILLIANT	BRISKISH	BROCAGES
BREVETED	BRIDECAKE	BRILLIANTED	BRISKLY	BROCARD
BREVETING	BRIDECAKES	BRILLIANTING	BRISKNESS	BROCARDS
BREVETS	BRIDED	BRILLIANTS	BRISKNESSES	BROCATEL
BREVETTED	BRIDEMAID	BRILLS	BRISKS	BROCATELS
BREVETTING	BRIDEMAIDS	BRIM	BRISKY	BROCCOLI
BREVIARIES	BRIDEMAN	BRIMFUL	BRISLING	BROCCOLIS
BREVIARY	BRIDEMEN	BRIMING	BRISLINGS	BROCH
BREVIATE	BRIDES	BRIMINGS	BRISTLE	BROCHAN
BREVIATES	BRIDESMAN	BRIMLESS	BRISTLED	BROCHANS
BREVIER	BRIDESMEN	BRIMMED	BRISTLES	BROCHÉ
BREVIERS	BRIDEWELL	BRIMMER	BRISTLIER	BROCHÉS
BREVITIES	BRIDEWELLS	BRIMMERS	BRISTLIEST	BROCHS
BREVITY	BRIDGE	BRIMMING	BRISTLING	BROCHURE
BREW	BRIDGED	BRIMS	BRISTLY	BROCHURES
BREWAGE	BRIDGES	BRIMSTONE	BRISTOLS	BROCK
BREWAGES	BRIDGING	BRIMSTONES	BRISURE	BROCKAGE
BREWED	BRIDGINGS	BRIMSTONY	BRISURES	BROCKAGES
BREWER	BRIDIE	BRINDED	BRIT	BROCKED

BROCKET
BROCKETS
BROCKIT
BROCKRAM
BROCKRAMS
BROCKS
BROD
BRODDED
BRODDING
BRODEKIN
BRODEKINS
BRODKIN
BRODKINS
BRODS
BROG
BROGAN
BROGANS
BROGGED
BROGGING
BROGH
BROGHS
BROGS
BROGUE
BROGUES
BROIDER
BROIDERED
BROIDERER
BROIDERERS
BROIDERIES
BROIDERING
BROIDERINGS
BROIDERS
BROIDERY
BROIL
BROILED
BROILER
BROILERS
BROILING
BROILS
BROKAGE
BROKAGES
BROKE
BROKED
BROKEN
BROKENLY
BROKER
BROKERAGE
BROKERAGES
BROKERIES
BROKERS
BROKERY
BROKES
BROKING
BROLGA
BROLGAS
BROLLIES
BROLLY
BROMATE
BROMATES
BROMELIA
BROMELIAD
BROMELIADS
BROMELIAS
BROMIC
BROMIDE
BROMIDES
BROMIDIC
BROMINE
BROMINES
BROMMER

BROMMERS
BROMOFORM
BROMOFORMS
BRONCHI
BRONCHIA
BRONCHIAL
BRONCHO
BRONCHOS
BRONCHUS
BRONCO
BRONCOS
BROND
BRONDS
BRONDYRON
BRONDYRONS
BRONZE
BRONZED
BRONZEN
BRONZES
BRONZIER
BRONZIEST
BRONZIFIED
BRONZIFIES
BRONZIFY
BRONZIFYING
BRONZING
BRONZINGS
BRONZITE
BRONZITES
BRONZY
BROO
BROOCH
BROOCHED
BROOCHES
BROOCHING
BROOD
BROODED
BROODER
BROODERS
BROODIER
BROODIEST
BROODING
BROODMARE
BROODMARES
BROODS
BROODY
BROOK
BROOKED
BROOKING
BROOKITE
BROOKITES
BROOKLET
BROOKLETS
BROOKLIME
BROOKLIMES
BROOKS
BROOKWEED
BROOKWEEDS
BROOL
BROOLS
BROOM
BROOMBALL
BROOMBALLS
BROOMED
BROOMIER
BROOMIEST
BROOMING
BROOMRAPE
BROOMRAPES
BROOMS

BROOMY
BROOS
BROOSE
BROOSES
BROS
BROSE
BROSES
BROTH
BROTHEL
BROTHELS
BROTHER
BROTHERLY
BROTHERS
BROTHS
BROUGH
BROUGHAM
BROUGHAMS
BROUGHS
BROUGHT
BROUHAHA
BROUHAHAS
BROUZE
BROUZES
BROW
BROWBEAT
BROWBEATEN
BROWBEATING
BROWBEATS
BROWLESS
BROWN
BROWNED
BROWNER
BROWNEST
BROWNIE
BROWNIER
BROWNIES
BROWNIEST
BROWNING
BROWNINGS
BROWNISH
BROWNNESS
BROWNNESSES
BROWNOUT
BROWNOUTS
BROWNS
BROWNY
BROWS
BROWSE
BROWSED
BROWSES
BROWSING
BROWSINGS
BROWST
BROWSTS
BRUCHID
BRUCHIDS
BRUCINE
BRUCINES
BRUCITE
BRUCITES
BRUCKLE
BRUHAHA
BRUHAHAS
BRUILZIE
BRUILZIES
BRUISE
BRUISED
BRUISER
BRUISERS
BRUISES

BRUISING
BRUISINGS
BRUIT
BRUITED
BRUITING
BRUITS
BRÛLÉ
BRULYIE
BRULYIES
BRULZIE
BRULZIES
BRUMAL
BRUMBIES
BRUMBY
BRUME
BRUMES
BRUMMER
BRUMMERS
BRUMOUS
BRUNCH
BRUNCHES
BRUNET
BRUNETS
BRUNETTE
BRUNETTES
BRUNT
BRUNTED
BRUNTING
BRUNTS
BRUSH
BRUSHED
BRUSHER
BRUSHERS
BRUSHES
BRUSHIER
BRUSHIEST
BRUSHING
BRUSHINGS
BRUSHWOOD
BRUSHWOODS
BRUSHWORK
BRUSHWORKS
BRUSHY
BRUSQUE
BRUSQUELY
BRUSQUER
BRUSQUEST
BRUST
BRUSTED
BRUSTING
BRUSTS
BRUT
BRUTAL
BRUTALISE
BRUTALISED
BRUTALISES
BRUTALISING
BRUTALISM
BRUTALISMS
BRUTALIST
BRUTALISTS
BRUTALITIES
BRUTALITY
BRUTALIZE
BRUTALIZED
BRUTALIZES
BRUTALIZING
BRUTALLY
BRUTE
BRUTED

BRUTENESS
BRUTENESSES
BRUTES
BRUTIFIED
BRUTIFIES
BRUTIFY
BRUTIFYING
BRUTING
BRUTISH
BRUTISHLY
BRUXISM
BRUXISMS
BRYOLOGIES
BRYOLOGY
BRYONIES
BRYONY
BRYOPHYTE
BRYOPHYTES
BUAT
BUATS
BUAZE
BUAZES
BUB
BUBA
BUBAL
BUBALINE
BUBALIS
BUBALISES
BUBALS
BUBAS
BUBBIES
BUBBLE
BUBBLED
BUBBLES
BUBBLIER
BUBBLIES
BUBBLIEST
BUBBLING
BUBBLY
BUBBY
BUBINGA
BUBINGAS
BUBO
BUBOES
BUBONIC
BUBS
BUBUKLE
BUBUKLES
BUCCAL
BUCCANEER
BUCCANEERED
BUCCANEERING
BUCCANEERINGS
BUCCANEERS
BUCCANIER
BUCCANIERED
BUCCANIERING
BUCCANIERS
BUCCINA
BUCCINAS
BUCELLAS
BUCELLASES
BUCHU
BUCHUS
BUCK
BUCKAROO
BUCKAROOS
BUCKAYRO
BUCKAYROS
BUCKBEAN

BUCKBEANS
BUCKBOARD
BUCKBOARDS
BUCKCART
BUCKCARTS
BUCKED
BUCKEEN
BUCKEENS
BUCKER
BUCKEROO
BUCKEROOS
BUCKERS
BUCKET
BUCKETED
BUCKETFUL
BUCKETFULS
BUCKETING
BUCKETINGS
BUCKETS
BUCKHORN
BUCKHORNS
BUCKHOUND
BUCKHOUNDS
BUCKIE
BUCKIES
BUCKING
BUCKINGS
BUCKISH
BUCKLE
BUCKLED
BUCKLER
BUCKLERS
BUCKLES
BUCKLING
BUCKLINGS
BUCKO
BUCKOES
BUCKRA
BUCKRAM
BUCKRAMED
BUCKRAMING
BUCKRAMS
BUCKRAS
BUCKS
BUCKSAW
BUCKSAWS
BUCKSHEE
BUCKSHEES
BUCKSHISH
BUCKSHISHES
BUCKSHOT
BUCKSHOTS
BUCKSKIN
BUCKSKINS
BUCKSOM
BUCKTEETH
BUCKTHORN
BUCKTHORNS
BUCKTOOTH
BUCKU
BUCKUS
BUCKWHEAT
BUCKWHEATS
BUCOLIC
BUCOLICAL
BUCOLICS
BUD
BUDDED
BUDDIER
BUDDIES

BUDDIEST
BUDDING
BUDDINGS
BUDDLE
BUDDLED
BUDDLEIA
BUDDLEIAS
BUDDLES
BUDDLING
BUDDY
BUDGE
BUDGED
BUDGER
BUDGEREE
BUDGERO
BUDGEROS
BUDGEROW
BUDGEROWS
BUDGERS
BUDGES
BUDGET
BUDGETARY
BUDGETED
BUDGETING
BUDGETS
BUDGIE
BUDGIES
BUDGING
BUDLESS
BUDMASH
BUDMASHES
BUDO
BUDOS
BUDS
BUFF
BUFFA
BUFFALO
BUFFALOED
BUFFALOES
BUFFALOING
BUFFE
BUFFED
BUFFER
BUFFERED
BUFFERING
BUFFERS
BUFFET
BUFFETED
BUFFETING
BUFFETINGS
BUFFETS
BUFFI
BUFFING
BUFFO
BUFFOON
BUFFOONS
BUFFS
BUFO
BUFOS
BUG
BUGABOO
BUGABOOS
BUGBANE
BUGBANES
BUGBEAR
BUGBEARS
BUGGAN
BUGGANE
BUGGANES
BUGGANS

BUGGED
BUGGER
BUGGERED
BUGGERIES
BUGGERING
BUGGERS
BUGGERY
BUGGIES
BUGGIN
BUGGING
BUGGINGS
BUGGINS
BUGGY
BUGHOUSE
BUGHOUSES
BUGLE
BUGLED
BUGLER
BUGLERS
BUGLES
BUGLET
BUGLETS
BUGLING
BUGLOSS
BUGLOSSES
BUGONG
BUGONGS
BUGS
BUGWORT
BUGWORTS
BUHL
BUHLS
BUHRSTONE
BUHRSTONES
BUIK
BUIKS
BUILD
BUILDED
BUILDER
BUILDERS
BUILDING
BUILDINGS
BUILDS
BUILT
BUIRDLIER
BUIRDLIEST
BUIRDLY
BUIST
BUISTED
BUISTING
BUISTS
BUKE
BUKES
BUKSHEE
BUKSHEES
BUKSHI
BUKSHIS
BULB
BULBAR
BULBED
BULBIL
BULBILS
BULBING
BULBOUS
BULBS
BULBUL
BULBULS
BULGE
BULGED
BULGER

BULGERS
BULGES
BULGIER
BULGIEST
BULGINE
BULGINES
BULGINESS
BULGINESSES
BULGING
BULGY
BULIMIA
BULIMIAS
BULIMIC
BULIMICS
BULIMIES
BULIMUS
BULIMUSES
BULIMY
BULK
BULKED
BULKER
BULKERS
BULKHEAD
BULKHEADS
BULKIER
BULKIEST
BULKILY
BULKINESS
BULKINESSES
BULKING
BULKS
BULKY
BULL
BULLA
BULLACE
BULLACES
BULLAE
BULLARIES
BULLARY
BULLAS
BULLATE
BULLBAT
BULLBATS
BULLDOG
BULLDOGGED
BULLDOGGING
BULLDOGS
BULLDOZE
BULLDOZED
BULLDOZER
BULLDOZERS
BULLDOZES
BULLDOZING
BULLDUST
BULLDUSTS
BULLED
BULLER
BULLERED
BULLERING
BULLERS
BULLET
BULLETIN
BULLETINS
BULLETRIE
BULLETRIES
BULLETS
BULLFIGHT
BULLFIGHTS
BULLFINCH
BULLFINCHES

BULLFROG
BULLFROGS
BULLGINE
BULLGINES
BULLHEAD
BULLHEADS
BULLIED
BULLIES
BULLING
BULLION
BULLIONS
BULLISH
BULLISHLY
BULLOCK
BULLOCKS
BULLS
BULLSHIT
BULLSHITS
BULLSHITTED
BULLSHITTING
BULLWHACK
BULLWHACKED
BULLWHACKING
BULLWHACKS
BULLY
BULLYING
BULLYISM
BULLYISMS
BULLYRAG
BULLYRAGGED
BULLYRAGGING
BULLYRAGS
BULRUSH
BULRUSHES
BULRUSHY
BULSE
BULSES
BULWARK
BULWARKED
BULWARKING
BULWARKS
BUM
BUMALO
BUMBAZE
BUMBAZED
BUMBAZES
BUMBAZING
BUMBLE
BUMBLED
BUMBLES
BUMBLING
BUMBO
BUMBOS
BUMF
BUMFS
BUMKIN
BUMKINS
BUMMALO
BUMMALOTI
BUMMALOTIS
BUMMAREE
BUMMAREES
BUMMED
BUMMEL
BUMMELS
BUMMER
BUMMERS
BUMMING
BUMMLE
BUMMLED

BUMMLES	BUNGIES	BUOYANCY	BURGRAVES	BUROOS
BUMMLING	BUNGING	BUOYANT	BURGS	BURP
BUMMOCK	BUNGLE	BUOYED	BURGUNDIES	BURPED
BUMMOCKS	BUNGLED	BUOYING	BURGUNDY	BURPING
BUMP	BUNGLER	BUOYS	BURHEL	BURPS
BUMPED	BUNGLERS	BUPLEVER	BURHELS	BURQA
BUMPER	BUNGLES	BUPLEVERS	BURIAL	BURQAS
BUMPERED	BUNGLING	BUR	BURIALS	BURR
BUMPERING	BUNGLINGS	BURAN	BURIED	BURRED
BUMPERS	BUNGS	BURANS	BURIES	BURREL
BUMPH	BUNGY	BURBLE	BURIN	BURRELL
BUMPHS	BUNIA	BURBLED	BURINIST	BURRELLS
BUMPIER	BUNIAS	BURBLES	BURINISTS	BURRELS
BUMPIEST	BUNION	BURBLING	BURINS	BURRHEL
BUMPINESS	BUNIONS	BURBLINGS	BURITI	BURRHELS
BUMPINESSES	BUNJE	BURBOT	BURITIS	BURRIER
BUMPING	BUNJEE	BURBOTS	BURK	BURRIEST
BUMPKIN	BUNJEES	BURD	BURKA	BURRING
BUMPKINS	BUNJES	BURDASH	BURKAS	BURRO
BUMPOLOGIES	BUNJIE	BURDASHES	BURKE	BURROS
BUMPOLOGY	BUNJIES	BURDEN	BURKED	BURROW
BUMPS	BUNJY	BURDENED	BURKES	BURROWED
BUMPTIOUS	BUNK	BURDENING	BURKHA	BURROWING
BUMPY	BUNKED	BURDENOUS	BURKHAS	BURROWS
BUMS	BUNKER	BURDENS	BURKING	BURRS
BUN	BUNKERED	BURDIE	BURKS	BURRSTONE
BUNA	BUNKERING	BURDIES	BURL	BURRSTONES
BUNAS	BUNKERS	BURDOCK	BURLAP	BURRY
BUNCE	BUNKHOUSE	BURDOCKS	BURLAPS	BURS
BUNCED	BUNKHOUSES	BURDS	BURLED	BURSA
BUNCES	BUNKING	BUREAU	BURLER	BURSAE
BUNCH	BUNKO	BUREAUS	BURLERS	BURSAL
BUNCHED	BUNKOED	BUREAUX	BURLESQUE	BURSAR
BUNCHES	BUNKOING	BURETTE	BURLESQUED	BURSARIAL
BUNCHIER	BUNKOS	BURETTES	BURLESQUES	BURSARIES
BUNCHIEST	BUNKS	BURG	BURLESQUING	BURSARS
BUNCHING	BUNKUM	BURGAGE	BURLETTA	BURSARY
BUNCHINGS	BUNKUMS	BURGAGES	BURLETTAS	BURSE
BUNCHY	BUNNIA	BURGANET	BURLEY	BURSES
BUNCING	BUNNIAS	BURGANETS	BURLEYS	BURSIFORM
BUNCO	BUNNIES	BURGEE	BURLIER	BURSITIS
BUNCOED	BUNNY	BURGEES	BURLIEST	BURSITISES
BUNCOING	BUNODONT	BURGEON	BURLINESS	BURST
BUNCOMBE	BUNRAKU	BURGEONED	BURLINESSES	BURSTED
BUNCOMBES	BUNRAKUS	BURGEONING	BURLING	BURSTEN
BUNCOS	BUNS	BURGEONS	BURLS	BURSTER
BUND	BUNT	BURGER	BURLY	BURSTERS
BUNDED	BUNTED	BURGERS	BURN	BURSTING
BUNDING	BUNTER	BURGESS	BURNED	BURSTS
BUNDLE	BUNTERS	BURGESSES	BURNER	BURTHEN
BUNDLED	BUNTIER	BURGH	BURNERS	BURTHENED
BUNDLES	BUNTIEST	BURGHAL	BURNET	BURTHENING
BUNDLING	BUNTING	BURGHER	BURNETS	BURTHENS
BUNDLINGS	BUNTINGS	BURGHERS	BURNING	BURTON
BUNDOBUST	BUNTLINE	BURGHS	BURNINGS	BURTONS
BUNDOBUSTS	BUNTLINES	BURGLAR	BURNISH	BURWEED
BUNDOOK	BUNTS	BURGLARED	BURNISHED	BURWEEDS
BUNDOOKS	BUNTY	BURGLARIES	BURNISHER	BURY
BUNDS	BUNYA	BURGLARING	BURNISHERS	BURYING
BUNDU	BUNYAS	BURGLARS	BURNISHES	BUS
BUNDUS	BUNYIP	BURGLARY	BURNISHING	BUSBIES
BUNG	BUNYIPS	BURGLE	BURNISHINGS	BUSBOY
BUNGALOID	BUONAMANI	BURGLED	BURNOUS	BUSBOYS
BUNGALOIDS	BUONAMANO	BURGLES	BURNOUSE	BUSBY
BUNGALOW	BUOY	BURGLING	BURNOUSES	BUSED
BUNGALOWS	BUOYAGE	BURGONET	BURNS	BUSES
BUNGED	BUOYAGES	BURGONETS	BURNSIDE	BUSGIRL
BUNGEE	BUOYANCE	BURGOO	BURNSIDES	BUSGIRLS
BUNGEES	BUOYANCES	BURGOOS	BURNT	BUSH
BUNGIE	BUOYANCIES	BURGRAVE	BUROO	BUSHCRAFT

BUSHCRAFTS
BUSHED
BUSHEL
BUSHELLED
BUSHELLER
BUSHELLERS
BUSHELLING
BUSHELLINGS
BUSHELS
BUSHES
BUSHFIRE
BUSHFIRES
BUSHIDO
BUSHIDOS
BUSHIER
BUSHIES
BUSHIEST
BUSHINESS
BUSHINESSES
BUSHING
BUSHMAN
BUSHMEN
BUSHVELD
BUSHVELDS
BUSHWALK
BUSHWALKED
BUSHWALKING
BUSHWALKINGS
BUSHWALKS
BUSHWHACK
BUSHWHACKED
BUSHWHACKING
BUSHWHACKINGS
BUSHWHACKS
BUSHY
BUSIED
BUSIER
BUSIES
BUSIEST
BUSILY
BUSINESS
BUSINESSES
BUSING
BUSINGS
BUSK
BUSKED
BUSKER
BUSKERS
BUSKET
BUSKETS
BUSKIN
BUSKINED
BUSKING
BUSKINGS
BUSKINS
BUSKS

BUSKY
BUSMAN
BUSMEN
BUSS
BUSSED
BUSSES
BUSSING
BUSSINGS
BUSSU
BUSSUS
BUST
BUSTARD
BUSTARDS
BUSTED
BUSTEE
BUSTEES
BUSTER
BUSTERS
BUSTIER
BUSTIERS
BUSTIEST
BUSTING
BUSTLE
BUSTLED
BUSTLER
BUSTLERS
BUSTLES
BUSTLING
BUSTS
BUSTY
BUSY
BUSYBODIES
BUSYBODY
BUSYING
BUSYNESS
BUSYNESSES
BUT
BUTADIENE
BUTADIENES
BUTANE
BUTANES
BUTANOL
BUTANOLS
BUTCH
BUTCHER
BUTCHERED
BUTCHERIES
BUTCHERING
BUTCHERINGS
BUTCHERLY
BUTCHERS
BUTCHERY
BUTCHES
BUTCHEST
BUTCHING
BUTCHINGS

BUTE
BUTENE
BUTENES
BUTES
BUTLER
BUTLERAGE
BUTLERAGES
BUTLERED
BUTLERIES
BUTLERING
BUTLERS
BUTLERY
BUTMENT
BUTMENTS
BUTS
BUTT
BUTTE
BUTTED
BUTTER
BUTTERBUR
BUTTERBURS
BUTTERCUP
BUTTERCUPS
BUTTERED
BUTTERFLIES
BUTTERFLY
BUTTERIER
BUTTERIES
BUTTERIEST
BUTTERINE
BUTTERINES
BUTTERING
BUTTERNUT
BUTTERNUTS
BUTTERS
BUTTERY
BUTTES
BUTTIES
BUTTING
BUTTLE
BUTTLED
BUTTLES
BUTTLING
BUTTOCK
BUTTOCKED
BUTTOCKING
BUTTOCKS
BUTTON
BUTTONED
BUTTONING
BUTTONS
BUTTONSES
BUTTONY
BUTTRESS
BUTTRESSED
BUTTRESSES

BUTTRESSING
BUTTS
BUTTY
BUTTYMAN
BUTTYMEN
BUTYL
BUTYLENE
BUTYLENES
BUTYLS
BUTYRATE
BUTYRATES
BUTYRIC
BUVETTE
BUVETTES
BUXOM
BUXOMER
BUXOMEST
BUXOMNESS
BUXOMNESSES
BUY
BUYABLE
BUYABLES
BUYER
BUYERS
BUYING
BUYS
BUZZ
BUZZARD
BUZZARDS
BUZZED
BUZZER
BUZZERS
BUZZES
BUZZIER
BUZZIEST
BUZZING
BUZZINGLY
BUZZINGS
BUZZY
BWANA
BWANAS
BWAZI
BWAZIS
BY
BYCATCH
BYCATCHES
BYCOKET
BYCOKETS
BYE
BYES
BYGOING
BYGOINGS
BYGONE
BYGONES
BYKE
BYKED

BYKES
BYKING
BYLANDER
BYLANDERS
BYLAW
BYLAWS
BYLINE
BYLINES
BYLIVE
BYNEMPT
BYPASS
BYPASSED
BYPASSES
BYPASSING
BYPATH
BYPATHS
BYPLACE
BYPLACES
BYRE
BYREMAN
BYREMEN
BYRES
BYREWOMAN
BYREWOMEN
BYRLADY
BYRLAKIN
BYRLAW
BYRLAWS
BYRNIE
BYRNIES
BYROAD
BYROADS
BYROOM
BYROOMS
BYS
BYSSAL
BYSSINE
BYSSOID
BYSSUS
BYSSUSES
BYSTANDER
BYSTANDERS
BYTE
BYTES
BYTOWNITE
BYTOWNITES
BYWAY
BYWAYS
BYWONER
BYWONERS
BYWORD
BYWORDS
BYWORK
BYWORKS
BYZANT
BYZANTS

C

CAATINGA
CAATINGAS
CAB
CABA
CABAL
CABALA
CABALAS
CABALETTA
CABALETTAS
CABALETTE
CABALISM
CABALISMS
CABALIST
CABALISTS
CABALLED
CABALLER
CABALLERO
CABALLEROS
CABALLERS
CABALLINE
CABALLING
CABALS
CABANA
CABANAS
CABARET
CABARETS
CABAS
CABASES
CABBAGE
CABBAGED
CABBAGES
CABBAGING
CABBAGY
CABBALA
CABBALAS
CABBALISM
CABBALISMS
CABBALIST
CABBALISTS
CABBIE
CABBIES
CABBY
CABER
CABERS
CABIN
CABINED
CABINET
CABINETS
CABINING
CABINS
CABLE
CABLED
CABLEGRAM
CABLEGRAMS
CABLES
CABLEWAY
CABLEWAYS
CABLING
CABLINGS
CABMAN
CABMEN
CABOB
CABOBS
CABOC

CABOCEER
CABOCEERS
CABOCHED
CABOCHON
CABOCHONS
CABOCS
CABOODLE
CABOODLES
CABOOSE
CABOOSES
CABOSHED
CABOTAGE
CABOTAGES
CABRÉ
CABRIE
CABRIES
CABRIOLE
CABRIOLES
CABRIOLET
CABRIOLETS
CABRIT
CABRITS
CABS
CACAFOGO
CACAFOGOS
CACAFUEGO
CACAFUEGOS
CACAO
CACAOS
CACHAEMIA
CACHAEMIAS
CACHAEMIC
CACHALOT
CACHALOTS
CACHE
CACHECTIC
CACHED
CACHES
CACHET
CACHETS
CACHEXIA
CACHEXIAS
CACHEXIES
CACHEXY
CACHING
CACHOLONG
CACHOLONGS
CACHOLOT
CACHOLOTS
CACHOU
CACHOUS
CACHUCHA
CACHUCHAS
CACIQUE
CACIQUES
CACIQUISM
CACIQUISMS
CACKLE
CACKLED
CACKLER
CACKLERS
CACKLES
CACKLING
CACODEMON

CACODEMONS
CACODOXIES
CACODOXY
CACODYL
CACODYLIC
CACODYLS
CACOEPIES
CACOEPY
CACOETHES
CACOLET
CACOLETS
CACOLOGIES
CACOLOGY
CACOMIXL
CACOMIXLS
CACOON
CACOONS
CACOPHONIES
CACOPHONY
CACOTOPIA
CACOTOPIAS
CACTI
CACTIFORM
CACTUS
CACTUSES
CACUMEN
CACUMENS
CACUMINAL
CAD
CADASTRAL
CADASTRE
CADASTRES
CADAVER
CADAVERIC
CADAVERS
CADDICE
CADDICES
CADDIE
CADDIED
CADDIES
CADDIS
CADDISES
CADDISH
CADDY
CADDYING
CADDYSS
CADDYSSES
CADE
CADEAU
CADEAUX
CADENCE
CADENCED
CADENCES
CADENCIES
CADENCY
CADENT
CADENTIAL
CADENZA
CADENZAS
CADES
CADET
CADETS
CADETSHIP
CADETSHIPS

CADGE
CADGED
CADGER
CADGERS
CADGES
CADGING
CADGY
CADI
CADIE
CADIES
CADIS
CADMIUM
CADMIUMS
CADRANS
CADRANSES
CADRE
CADRES
CADS
CADUAC
CADUACS
CADUCEAN
CADUCEI
CADUCEUS
CADUCITIES
CADUCITY
CADUCOUS
CAECA
CAECAL
CAECILIAN
CAECILIANS
CAECUM
CAERULE
CAERULEAN
CAESAR
CAESARS
CAESE
CAESIOUS
CAESIUM
CAESIUMS
CAESTUS
CAESTUSES
CAESURA
CAESURAL
CAESURAS
CAFARD
CAFARDS
CAFÉ
CAFÉS
CAFETERIA
CAFETERIAS
CAFF
CAFFEINE
CAFFEINES
CAFFEISM
CAFFEISMS
CAFFILA
CAFFILAS
CAFFS
CAFILA
CAFILAS
CAFTAN
CAFTANS
CAGE
CAGEBIRD

CAGEBIRDS
CAGED
CAGELING
CAGELINGS
CAGES
CAGEWORK
CAGEWORKS
CAGEY
CAGEYNESS
CAGEYNESSES
CAGIER
CAGIEST
CAGILY
CAGINESS
CAGINESSES
CAGING
CAGOT
CAGOTS
CAGOUL
CAGOULE
CAGOULES
CAGOULS
CAGY
CAGYNESS
CAGYNESSES
CAHIER
CAHIERS
CAHOOT
CAHOOTS
CAILLACH
CAILLACHS
CAILLEACH
CAILLEACHS
CAILLIACH
CAILLIACHS
CAIMAC
CAIMACAM
CAIMACAMS
CAIMACS
CAIMAN
CAIMANS
CAIN
CAINS
CAÏQUE
CAIQUE
CAÏQUES
CAIQUES
CAIRD
CAIRDS
CAIRN
CAIRNED
CAIRNGORM
CAIRNGORMS
CAIRNS
CAISSON
CAISSONS
CAITIFF
CAITIFFS
CAITIVE
CAITIVES
CAJEPUT
CAJEPUTS
CAJOLE
CAJOLED

CAJOLER	CALCIFIES	CALIBRED	CALLOWEST	CALVES
CAJOLERIES	CALCIFUGE	CALIBRES	CALLOWS	CALVING
CAJOLERS	CALCIFY	CALICES	CALLS	CALVITIES
CAJOLERY	CALCIFYING	CALICHE	CALLUS	CALX
CAJOLES	CALCINE	CALICHES	CALLUSES	CALXES
CAJOLING	CALCINED	CALICO	CALM	CALYCES
CAJUN	CALCINES	CALICOES	CALMANT	CALYCINAL
CAJUPUT	CALCINING	CALICOS	CALMANTS	CALYCINE
CAJUPUTS	CALCITE	CALID	CALMATIVE	CALYCLE
CAKE	CALCITES	CALIDITIES	CALMATIVES	CALYCLED
CAKED	CALCIUM	CALIDITY	CALMED	CALYCLES
CAKES	CALCIUMS	CALIF	CALMER	CALYCOID
CAKEWALK	CALCSPAR	CALIFS	CALMEST	CALYCULE
CAKEWALKED	CALCSPARS	CALIGO	CALMING	CALYCULES
CAKEWALKING	CALCULAR	CALIGOES	CALMLY	CALYPSO
CAKEWALKS	CALCULARY	CALIGOS	CALMNESS	CALYPSOS
CAKIER	CALCULATE	CALIOLOGIES	CALMNESSES	CALYPTRA
CAKIEST	CALCULATED	CALIOLOGY	CALMS	CALYPTRAS
CAKING	CALCULATES	CALIPASH	CALMSTANE	CALYX
CAKINGS	CALCULATING	CALIPASHES	CALMSTANES	CALYXES
CAKY	CALCULI	CALIPEE	CALMSTONE	CALZONE
CALABASH	CALCULOSE	CALIPEES	CALMSTONES	CALZONES
CALABASHES	CALCULOUS	CALIPERS	CALMY	CALZONI
CALABOOSE	CALCULUS	CALIPH	CALOMEL	CAM
CALABOOSES	CALCULUSES	CALIPHAL	CALOMELS	CAMAIEU
CALABRESE	CALDARIUM	CALIPHATE	CALORIC	CAMAIEUS
CALABRESES	CALDARIUMS	CALIPHATES	CALORICS	CAMAIEUX
CALAMANCO	CALDERA	CALIPHS	CALORIE	CAMAN
CALAMANCOS	CALDERAS	CALISAYA	CALORIES	CAMANACHD
CALAMARIES	CALDRON	CALISAYAS	CALORIFIC	CAMANACHDS
CALAMARY	CALDRONS	CALIVER	CALORIST	CAMANS
CALAMI	CALEFIED	CALIVERS	CALORISTS	CAMARILLA
CALAMINE	CALEFIES	CALIX	CALOTTE	CAMARILLAS
CALAMINES	CALEFY	CALK	CALOTTES	CAMARON
CALAMINT	CALEFYING	CALKED	CALOTYPE	CAMARONS
CALAMINTS	CALEMBOUR	CALKER	CALOTYPES	CAMAS
CALAMITE	CALEMBOURS	CALKERS	CALOYER	CAMASES
CALAMITES	CALENDAR	CALKIN	CALOYERS	CAMASH
CALAMITIES	CALENDARED	CALKING	CALP	CAMASHES
CALAMITY	CALENDARING	CALKINS	CALPA	CAMASS
CALAMUS	CALENDARS	CALKS	CALPAC	CAMASSES
CALANDO	CALENDER	CALL	CALPACK	CAMBER
CALANDRIA	CALENDERED	CALLA	CALPACKS	CAMBERED
CALANDRIAS	CALENDERING	CALLANT	CALPACS	CAMBERING
CALANTHE	CALENDERS	CALLANTS	CALPAS	CAMBERS
CALANTHES	CALENDRER	CALLAS	CALPS	CAMBIAL
CALASH	CALENDRERS	CALLED	CALQUE	CAMBIFORM
CALASHES	CALENDRIES	CALLER	CALQUED	CAMBISM
CALAVANCE	CALENDRY	CALLERS	CALQUES	CAMBISMS
CALAVANCES	CALENDS	CALLET	CALQUING	CAMBIST
CALCANEAL	CALENDULA	CALLETS	CALTHA	CAMBISTRIES
CALCANEAN	CALENDULAS	CALLID	CALTHAS	CAMBISTRY
CALCANEUM	CALENTURE	CALLIDITIES	CALTHROP	CAMBISTS
CALCANEUMS	CALENTURES	CALLIDITY	CALTHROPS	CAMBIUM
CALCAR	CALF	CALLIGRAM	CALTRAP	CAMBIUMS
CALCARATE	CALFDOZER	CALLIGRAMS	CALTRAPS	CAMBOGE
CALCARINE	CALFDOZERS	CALLING	CALTROP	CAMBOGES
CALCARS	CALFLESS	CALLINGS	CALTROPS	CAMBREL
CALCEATE	CALFSKIN	CALLIOPE	CALUMBA	CAMBRELS
CALCEATED	CALFSKINS	CALLIOPES	CALUMBAS	CAMBRIC
CALCEATES	CALIATOUR	CALLIPER	CALUMET	CAMBRICS
CALCEATING	CALIATOURS	CALLIPERED	CALUMETS	CAMCORDER
CALCED	CALIBER	CALLIPERING	CALUMNIES	CAMCORDERS
CALCEDONIES	CALIBERED	CALLIPERS	CALUMNY	CAME
CALCEDONY	CALIBERS	CALLOSITIES	CALVE	CAMEL
CALCES	CALIBRATE	CALLOSITY	CALVED	CAMELBACK
CALCIC	CALIBRATED	CALLOUS	CALVER	CAMELBACKS
CALCICOLE	CALIBRATES	CALLOUSLY	CALVERED	CAMELEER
CALCIFIC	CALIBRATING	CALLOW	CALVERING	CAMELEERS
CALCIFIED	CALIBRE	CALLOWER	CALVERS	CAMELEON

CAMELEONS	CAMPEST	CANASTER	CANEPHORS	CANNONADES
CAMELID	CAMPHANE	CANASTERS	CANES	CANNONADING
CAMELIDS	CAMPHANES	CANCAN	CANESCENT	CANNONED
CAMELINE	CAMPHENE	CANCANS	CANFUL	CANNONEER
CAMELINES	CAMPHENES	CANCEL	CANFULS	CANNONEERS
CAMELISH	CAMPHINE	CANCELEER	CANG	CANNONIER
CAMELLIA	CAMPHINES	CANCELEERED	CANGLE	CANNONIERS
CAMELLIAS	CAMPHIRE	CANCELEERING	CANGLED	CANNONING
CAMELOID	CAMPHIRES	CANCELEERS	CANGLES	CANNONRIES
CAMELOIDS	CAMPHOR	CANCELIER	CANGLING	CANNONRY
CAMELOT	CAMPHORIC	CANCELIERED	CANGS	CANNONS
CAMELOTS	CAMPHORS	CANCELIERING	CANGUE	CANNOT
CAMELRIES	CAMPIER	CANCELIERS	CANGUES	CANNS
CAMELRY	CAMPIEST	CANCELLED	CANICULAR	CANNULA
CAMELS	CAMPING	CANCELLI	CANID	CANNULAE
CAMEO	CAMPION	CANCELLING	CANIDS	CANNULAS
CAMEOS	CAMPIONS	CANCELS	CANIER	CANNULATE
CAMERA	CAMPLE	CANCER	CANIEST	CANNY
CAMERAL	CAMPLED	CANCERATE	CANIKIN	CANOE
CAMERAMAN	CAMPLES	CANCERATED	CANIKINS	CANOED
CAMERAMEN	CAMPLING	CANCERATES	CANINE	CANOEING
CAMERAS	CAMPS	CANCERATING	CANINES	CANOEINGS
CAMERATED	CAMPSITE	CANCEROUS	CANING	CANOEIST
CAMES	CAMPSITES	CANCERS	CANINGS	CANOEISTS
CAMESE	CAMPUS	CANCRINE	CANINITIES	CANOES
CAMESES	CAMPUSES	CANCROID	CANINITY	CANON
CAMION	CAMPY	CANCROIDS	CANISTER	CAÑON
CAMIONS	CAMS	CANDELA	CANISTERED	CANONESS
CAMIS	CAMSHAFT	CANDELAS	CANISTERING	CANONESSES
CAMISADE	CAMSHAFTS	CANDENT	CANISTERS	CANONIC
CAMISADES	CAMSHEUGH	CANDID	CANITIES	CANONICAL
CAMISADO	CAMSHO	CANDIDA	CANKER	CANONICALS
CAMISADOS	CAMSHOCH	CANDIDACIES	CANKERED	CANONISE
CAMISARD	CAMSTAIRY	CANDIDACY	CANKERING	CANONISED
CAMISARDS	CAMSTANE	CANDIDAS	CANKEROUS	CANONISES
CAMISE	CAMSTANES	CANDIDATE	CANKERS	CANONISING
CAMISES	CAMSTEARY	CANDIDATES	CANKERY	CANONIST
CAMISOLE	CAMSTONE	CANDIDER	CANN	CANONISTS
CAMISOLES	CAMSTONES	CANDIDEST	CANNA	CANONIZE
CAMLET	CAMUS	CANDIDLY	CANNABIC	CANONIZED
CAMLETS	CAMUSES	CANDIE	CANNABIN	CANONIZES
CAMMED	CAN	CANDIED	CANNABINS	CANONIZING
CAMMING	CAÑADA	CANDIES	CANNABIS	CANONRIES
CAMOMILE	CAÑADAS	CANDLE	CANNABISES	CANONRY
CAMOMILES	CANAIGRE	CANDLED	CANNACH	CANONS
CAMOUFLET	CANAIGRES	CANDLES	CANNACHS	CAÑONS
CAMOUFLETS	CANAILLE	CANDLING	CANNAE	CANOODLE
CAMP	CANAILLES	CANDOCK	CANNAS	CANOODLED
CAMPAGNA	CANAKIN	CANDOCKS	CANNED	CANOODLES
CAMPAGNAS	CANAKINS	CANDOR	CANNEL	CANOODLING
CAMPAIGN	CANAL	CANDORS	CANNELS	CANOPIED
CAMPAIGNED	CANALISE	CANDOUR	CANNELURE	CANOPIES
CAMPAIGNING	CANALISED	CANDOURS	CANNELURES	CANOPY
CAMPAIGNS	CANALISES	CANDY	CANNER	CANOPYING
CAMPANA	CANALISING	CANDYING	CANNERIES	CANOROUS
CAMPANAS	CANALIZE	CANDYTUFT	CANNERS	CANS
CAMPANERO	CANALIZED	CANDYTUFTS	CANNERY	CANST
CAMPANEROS	CANALIZES	CANE	CANNIBAL	CANSTICK
CAMPANILE	CANALIZING	CANED	CANNIBALS	CANSTICKS
CAMPANILES	CANALS	CANEFRUIT	CANNIER	CANT
CAMPANILI	CANAPÉ	CANEFRUITS	CANNIEST	CANTABANK
CAMPANIST	CANAPÉS	CANEH	CANNIKIN	CANTABANKS
CAMPANISTS	CANARD	CANEHS	CANNIKINS	CANTABILE
CAMPEADOR	CANARDS	CANELLA	CANNILY	CANTABILES
CAMPEADORS	CANARIED	CANELLAS	CANNINESS	CANTALOUP
CAMPED	CANARIES	CANEPHOR	CANNINESSES	CANTALOUPS
CAMPER	CANARY	CANEPHORA	CANNING	CANTAR
CAMPERS	CANARYING	CANEPHORAS	CANNON	CANTARS
CAMPESINO	CANASTA	CANEPHORE	CANNONADE	CANTATA
CAMPESINOS	CANASTAS	CANEPHORES	CANNONADED	CANTATAS

CANTATE
CANTATES
CANTDOG
CANTDOGS
CANTED
CANTEEN
CANTEENS
CANTER
CANTERED
CANTERING
CANTERS
CANTEST
CANTHARI
CANTHARID
CANTHARIDES
CANTHARIDS
CANTHARIS
CANTHARUS
CANTHI
CANTHOOK
CANTHOOKS
CANTHUS
CANTICLE
CANTICLES
CANTICO
CANTICOED
CANTICOING
CANTICOS
CANTICOY
CANTICOYED
CANTICOYING
CANTICOYS
CANTICUM
CANTICUMS
CANTIER
CANTIEST
CANTILENA
CANTILENAS
CANTINA
CANTINAS
CANTINESS
CANTINESSES
CANTING
CANTINGS
CANTION
CANTIONS
CANTLE
CANTLED
CANTLES
CANTLET
CANTLETS
CANTLING
CANTO
CANTON
CANTONAL
CANTONED
CANTONING
CANTONS
CANTOR
CANTORIAL
CANTORIS
CANTORS
CANTOS
CANTRED
CANTREDS
CANTREF
CANTREFS
CANTRIP
CANTRIPS
CANTS

CANTUS
CANTY
CANUCK
CANUCKS
CANVAS
CANVASED
CANVASES
CANVASING
CANVASS
CANVASSED
CANVASSER
CANVASSERS
CANVASSES
CANVASSING
CANY
CANYON
CANYONS
CANZONA
CANZONAS
CANZONE
CANZONET
CANZONETS
CANZONI
CAP
CAPA
CAPABLE
CAPABLER
CAPABLEST
CAPACIOUS
CAPACITIES
CAPACITOR
CAPACITORS
CAPACITY
CAPARISON
CAPARISONED
CAPARISONING
CAPARISONS
CAPAS
CAPE
CAPED
CAPELET
CAPELETS
CAPELIN
CAPELINE
CAPELINES
CAPELINS
CAPELLET
CAPELLETS
CAPELLINE
CAPELLINES
CAPER
CAPERED
CAPERER
CAPERERS
CAPERING
CAPERS
CAPES
CAPIAS
CAPIASES
CAPILLARIES
CAPILLARY
CAPING
CAPITA
CAPITAL
CAPITALLY
CAPITALS
CAPITAN
CAPITANI
CAPITANO
CAPITANOS

CAPITANS
CAPITATE
CAPITAYN
CAPITAYNS
CAPITELLA
CAPITULA
CAPITULAR
CAPITULARS
CAPITULUM
CAPLE
CAPLES
CAPLIN
CAPLINS
CAPO
CAPOCCHIA
CAPOCCHIAS
CAPON
CAPONIER
CAPONIERE
CAPONIERES
CAPONIERS
CAPONISE
CAPONISED
CAPONISES
CAPONISING
CAPONIZE
CAPONIZED
CAPONIZES
CAPONIZING
CAPONS
CAPORAL
CAPORALS
CAPOS
CAPOT
CAPOTAINE
CAPOTASTO
CAPOTASTOS
CAPOTE
CAPOTED
CAPOTES
CAPOTING
CAPOTS
CAPPED
CAPPER
CAPPERS
CAPPING
CAPPINGS
CAPRATE
CAPRATES
CAPRIC
CAPRICCI
CAPRICCIO
CAPRICCIOS
CAPRICE
CAPRICES
CAPRID
CAPRIDS
CAPRIFIED
CAPRIFIES
CAPRIFIG
CAPRIFIGS
CAPRIFOIL
CAPRIFOILS
CAPRIFOLE
CAPRIFOLES
CAPRIFORM
CAPRIFY
CAPRIFYING
CAPRINE
CAPRIOLE

CAPRIOLED
CAPRIOLES
CAPRIOLING
CAPROATE
CAPROATES
CAPROIC
CAPRYLATE
CAPRYLATES
CAPRYLIC
CAPS
CAPSAICIN
CAPSAICINS
CAPSICUM
CAPSICUMS
CAPSID
CAPSIDS
CAPSIZAL
CAPSIZALS
CAPSIZE
CAPSIZED
CAPSIZES
CAPSIZING
CAPSTAN
CAPSTANS
CAPSTONE
CAPSTONES
CAPSULAR
CAPSULARY
CAPSULATE
CAPSULE
CAPSULES
CAPSULISE
CAPSULISED
CAPSULISES
CAPSULISING
CAPSULIZE
CAPSULIZED
CAPSULIZES
CAPSULIZING
CAPTAIN
CAPTAINCIES
CAPTAINCY
CAPTAINED
CAPTAINING
CAPTAINRIES
CAPTAINRY
CAPTAINS
CAPTAN
CAPTANS
CAPTION
CAPTIONED
CAPTIONING
CAPTIONS
CAPTIOUS
CAPTIVATE
CAPTIVATED
CAPTIVATES
CAPTIVATING
CAPTIVE
CAPTIVED
CAPTIVES
CAPTIVING
CAPTIVITIES
CAPTIVITY
CAPTOR
CAPTORS
CAPTURE
CAPTURED
CAPTURES
CAPTURING

CAPUCCIO
CAPUCCIOS
CAPUCHE
CAPUCHES
CAPUCHIN
CAPUCHINS
CAPUL
CAPULS
CAPUT
CAPYBARA
CAPYBARAS
CAR
CARABIN
CARABINE
CARABINES
CARABINS
CARACAL
CARACALS
CARACARA
CARACARAS
CARACK
CARACKS
CARACOL
CARACOLE
CARACOLED
CARACOLES
CARACOLING
CARACOLLED
CARACOLLING
CARACOLS
CARACT
CARACTS
CARACUL
CARACULS
CARAFE
CARAFES
CARAMBA
CARAMBOLA
CARAMBOLAS
CARAMBOLE
CARAMBOLED
CARAMBOLES
CARAMBOLING
CARAMEL
CARAMELLED
CARAMELLING
CARAMELS
CARANGID
CARANGIDS
CARANGOID
CARANNA
CARANNAS
CARANX
CARAP
CARAPACE
CARAPACES
CARAPS
CARAT
CARATS
CARAUNA
CARAUNAS
CARAVAN
CARAVANCE
CARAVANCES
CARAVANED
CARAVANER
CARAVANERS
CARAVANING
CARAVANNED
CARAVANNING

CARAVANS	CARCAJOUS	CAREERISM	CARJACOUS	CARNOTITES
CARAVEL	CARCAKE	CAREERISMS	CARK	CARNY
CARAVELS	CARCAKES	CAREERIST	CARKED	CARNYING
CARAWAY	CARCANET	CAREERISTS	CARKING	CAROB
CARAWAYS	CARCANETS	CAREERS	CARKS	CAROBS
CARB	CARCASE	CAREFREE	CARL	CAROCHE
CARBAMATE	CARCASED	CAREFUL	CARLINE	CAROCHES
CARBAMATES	CARCASES	CAREFULLY	CARLINES	CAROL
CARBAMIDE	CARCASING	CARELESS	CARLISH	CAROLLED
CARBAMIDES	CARCASS	CARÈME	CARLOAD	CAROLLER
CARBARYL	CARCASSED	CARÈMES	CARLOADS	CAROLLERS
CARBARYLS	CARCASSES	CARER	CARLOCK	CAROLLING
CARBIDE	CARCASSING	CARERS	CARLOCKS	CAROLS
CARBIDES	CARCINOMA	CARES	CARLOT	CAROM
CARBINE	CARCINOMAS	CARESS	CARLOTS	CAROMED
CARBINEER	CARCINOMATA	CARESSED	CARLS	CAROMEL
CARBINEERS	CARD	CARESSES	CARMAN	CAROMELLED
CARBINES	CARDAMINE	CARESSING	CARMELITE	CAROMELLING
CARBINIER	CARDAMINES	CARESSINGS	CARMELITES	CAROMELS
CARBINIERS	CARDAMOM	CARET	CARMEN	CAROMING
CARBOLIC	CARDAMOMS	CARETAKE	CARMINE	CAROMS
CARBOLICS	CARDAMON	CARETAKER	CARMINES	CAROTENE
CARBON	CARDAMONS	CARETAKERS	CARNAGE	CAROTENES
CARBONADE	CARDAMUM	CARETAKES	CARNAGES	CAROTID
CARBONADES	CARDAMUMS	CARETAKING	CARNAHUBA	CAROTIN
CARBONADO	CARDBOARD	CARETOOK	CARNAHUBAS	CAROTINS
CARBONADOED	CARDBOARDS	CARETS	CARNAL	CAROUSAL
CARBONADOES	CARDECU	CAREWORN	CARNALISE	CAROUSALS
CARBONADOING	CARDECUE	CAREX	CARNALISED	CAROUSE
CARBONADOS	CARDECUES	CARFAX	CARNALISES	CAROUSED
CARBONATE	CARDECUS	CARFAXES	CARNALISING	CAROUSEL
CARBONATED	CARDED	CARFOX	CARNALISM	CAROUSELS
CARBONATES	CARDER	CARFOXES	CARNALISMS	CAROUSER
CARBONATING	CARDERS	CARFUFFLE	CARNALIST	CAROUSERS
CARBONIC	CARDI	CARFUFFLED	CARNALISTS	CAROUSES
CARBONISE	CARDIAC	CARFUFFLES	CARNALITIES	CAROUSING
CARBONISED	CARDIACAL	CARFUFFLING	CARNALITY	CARP
CARBONISES	CARDIACS	CARGEESE	CARNALIZE	CARPAL
CARBONISING	CARDIALGIES	CARGO	CARNALIZED	CARPALS
CARBONIZE	CARDIALGY	CARGOED	CARNALIZES	CARPARK
CARBONIZED	CARDIES	CARGOES	CARNALIZING	CARPARKS
CARBONIZES	CARDIGAN	CARGOING	CARNALLED	CARPED
CARBONIZING	CARDIGANS	CARGOOSE	CARNALLING	CARPEL
CARBONS	CARDINAL	CARIACOU	CARNALLY	CARPELS
CARBONYL	CARDINALS	CARIACOUS	CARNALS	CARPENTER
CARBONYLS	CARDING	CARIAMA	CARNATION	CARPENTERED
CARBOXYL	CARDIOID	CARIAMAS	CARNATIONS	CARPENTERING
CARBOXYLS	CARDIOIDS	CARIBE	CARNAUBA	CARPENTERS
CARBOY	CARDIS	CARIBES	CARNAUBAS	CARPENTRIES
CARBOYS	CARDITIS	CARIBOU	CARNELIAN	CARPENTRY
CARBS	CARDITISES	CARIBOUS	CARNELIANS	CARPER
CARBUNCLE	CARDOON	CARICES	CARNEOUS	CARPERS
CARBUNCLES	CARDOONS	CARIERE	CARNET	CARPET
CARBURATE	CARDPUNCH	CARIERES	CARNETS	CARPETED
CARBURATED	CARDPUNCHES	CARIES	CARNEY	CARPETING
CARBURATES	CARDS	CARILLON	CARNEYED	CARPETINGS
CARBURATING	CARDUUS	CARILLONNED	CARNEYING	CARPETS
CARBURET	CARDUUSES	CARILLONNING	CARNEYS	CARPING
CARBURETS	CARDY	CARILLONS	CARNIED	CARPINGLY
CARBURETTED	CARE	CARINA	CARNIES	CARPINGS
CARBURETTING	CARED	CARINAS	CARNIFEX	CARPORT
CARBURISE	CAREEN	CARINATE	CARNIFEXES	CARPORTS
CARBURISED	CAREENAGE	CARING	CARNIVAL	CARPS
CARBURISES	CAREENAGES	CARIOCA	CARNIVALS	CARPUS
CARBURISING	CAREENED	CARIOCAS	CARNIVORE	CARPUSES
CARBURIZE	CAREENING	CARIOLE	CARNIVORES	CARR
CARBURIZED	CAREENS	CARIOLES	CARNOSE	CARRACK
CARBURIZES	CAREER	CARIOUS	CARNOSITIES	CARRACKS
CARBURIZING	CAREERED	CARITAS	CARNOSITY	CARRACT
CARCAJOU	CAREERING	CARJACOU	CARNOTITE	CARRACTS

CARRAGEEN
CARRAGEENS
CARRAT
CARRATS
CARRAWAY
CARRAWAYS
CARRECT
CARRECTS
CARREL
CARRELL
CARRELLS
CARRELS
CARRIAGE
CARRIAGES
CARRIED
CARRIER
CARRIERS
CARRIES
CARRIOLE
CARRIOLES
CARRION
CARRIONS
CARRITCH
CARRITCHES
CARRONADE
CARRONADES
CARROT
CARROTS
CARROTY
CARROUSEL
CARROUSELS
CARRS
CARRY
CARRYCOT
CARRYCOTS
CARRYING
CARRYTALE
CARRYTALES
CARS
CARSE
CARSES
CART
CARTA
CARTAGE
CARTAGES
CARTAS
CARTE
CARTED
CARTEL
CARTELISE
CARTELISED
CARTELISES
CARTELISING
CARTELIZE
CARTELIZED
CARTELIZES
CARTELIZING
CARTELS
CARTER
CARTERS
CARTES
CARTILAGE
CARTILAGES
CARTING
CARTLOAD
CARTLOADS
CARTOGRAM
CARTOGRAMS
CARTOLOGIES
CARTOLOGY

CARTON
CARTONAGE
CARTONAGES
CARTONED
CARTONING
CARTONS
CARTOON
CARTOONED
CARTOONING
CARTOONS
CARTOUCH
CARTOUCHE
CARTOUCHES
CARTRIDGE
CARTRIDGES
CARTROAD
CARTROADS
CARTS
CARTULARIES
CARTULARY
CARTWAY
CARTWAYS
CARTWHEEL
CARTWHEELED
CARTWHEELING
CARTWHEELS
CARUCAGE
CARUCAGES
CARUCATE
CARUCATES
CARUNCLE
CARUNCLES
CARVACROL
CARVACROLS
CARVE
CARVED
CARVEL
CARVELS
CARVEN
CARVER
CARVERS
CARVES
CARVIES
CARVING
CARVINGS
CARVY
CARYATIC
CARYATID
CARYATIDES
CARYATIDS
CARYOPSES
CARYOPSIDES
CARYOPSIS
CASA
CASAS
CASBAH
CASBAHS
CASCABEL
CASCABELS
CASCADE
CASCADED
CASCADES
CASCADING
CASCARA
CASCARAS
CASCHROM
CASCHROMS
CASCO
CASCOS
CASE

CASEATION
CASEATIONS
CASEBOOK
CASEBOOKS
CASED
CASEIN
CASEINS
CASEMAKER
CASEMAKERS
CASEMAN
CASEMATE
CASEMATED
CASEMATES
CASEMEN
CASEMENT
CASEMENTS
CASEOUS
CASERN
CASERNE
CASERNES
CASERNS
CASES
CASH
CASHAW
CASHAWS
CASHED
CASHES
CASHEW
CASHEWS
CASHIER
CASHIERED
CASHIERER
CASHIERERS
CASHIERING
CASHIERINGS
CASHIERS
CASHING
CASHLESS
CASHMERE
CASHMERES
CASING
CASINGS
CASINO
CASINOS
CASK
CASKED
CASKET
CASKETS
CASKING
CASKS
CASQUE
CASQUES
CASSAREEP
CASSAREEPS
CASSARIPE
CASSARIPES
CASSATA
CASSATAS
CASSATION
CASSATIONS
CASSAVA
CASSAVAS
CASSEROLE
CASSEROLED
CASSEROLES
CASSEROLING
CASSETTE
CASSETTES
CASSIA
CASSIAS

CASSIMERE
CASSIMERES
CASSINO
CASSINOS
CASSIS
CASSISES
CASSOCK
CASSOCKED
CASSOCKS
CASSONADE
CASSONADES
CASSONE
CASSONES
CASSOULET
CASSOULETS
CASSOWARIES
CASSOWARY
CAST
CASTANETS
CASTAWAY
CASTAWAYS
CASTE
CASTED
CASTELESS
CASTELLAN
CASTELLANS
CASTELLUM
CASTELLUMS
CASTER
CASTERS
CASTES
CASTIGATE
CASTIGATED
CASTIGATES
CASTIGATING
CASTING
CASTINGS
CASTLE
CASTLED
CASTLES
CASTLING
CASTOCK
CASTOCKS
CASTOR
CASTOREUM
CASTOREUMS
CASTORIES
CASTORS
CASTORY
CASTRAL
CASTRATE
CASTRATED
CASTRATES
CASTRATI
CASTRATING
CASTRATO
CASTS
CASUAL
CASUALISE
CASUALISED
CASUALISES
CASUALISING
CASUALISM
CASUALISMS
CASUALIZE
CASUALIZED
CASUALIZES
CASUALIZING
CASUALLY
CASUALS

CASUALTIES
CASUALTY
CASUARINA
CASUARINAS
CASUIST
CASUISTIC
CASUISTRIES
CASUISTRY
CASUISTS
CAT
CATACLASM
CATACLASMS
CATACLYSM
CATACLYSMS
CATACOMB
CATACOMBS
CATAFALCO
CATAFALCOES
CATALASE
CATALASES
CATALEPSIES
CATALEPSY
CATALEXES
CATALEXIS
CATALO
CATALOES
CATALOG
CATALOGED
CATALOGER
CATALOGERS
CATALOGING
CATALOGS
CATALOGUE
CATALOGUED
CATALOGUES
CATALOGUING
CATALOS
CATALPA
CATALPAS
CATALYSE
CATALYSED
CATALYSER
CATALYSERS
CATALYSES
CATALYSING
CATALYSIS
CATALYST
CATALYSTS
CATALYTIC
CATALYZE
CATALYZED
CATALYZER
CATALYZERS
CATALYZES
CATALYZING
CATAMARAN
CATAMARANS
CATAMENIA
CATAMITE
CATAMITES
CATAMOUNT
CATAMOUNTS
CATAPAN
CATAPANS
CATAPHYLL
CATAPHYLLS
CATAPLASM
CATAPLASMS
CATAPLEXIES
CATAPLEXY

CATAPULT
CATAPULTED
CATAPULTING
CATAPULTS
CATARACT
CATARACTS
CATARHINE
CATARRH
CATARRHAL
CATARRHS
CATASTA
CATASTAS
CATATONIA
CATATONIAS
CATATONIC
CATATONICS
CATATONIES
CATATONY
CATAWBA
CATAWBAS
CATBIRD
CATBIRDS
CATBOAT
CATBOATS
CATCALL
CATCALLED
CATCALLING
CATCALLS
CATCH
CATCHABLE
CATCHED
CATCHEN
CATCHER
CATCHERS
CATCHES
CATCHFLIES
CATCHFLY
CATCHIER
CATCHIEST
CATCHING
CATCHINGS
CATCHMENT
CATCHMENTS
CATCHPOLE
CATCHPOLES
CATCHPOLL
CATCHPOLLS
CATCHT
CATCHUP
CATCHUPS
CATCHWEED
CATCHWEEDS
CATCHWORD
CATCHWORDS
CATCHY
CATE
CATECHISE
CATECHISED
CATECHISES
CATECHISING
CATECHISINGS
CATECHISM
CATECHISMS
CATECHIST
CATECHISTS
CATECHIZE
CATECHIZED
CATECHIZES
CATECHIZING
CATECHIZINGS

CATECHOL
CATECHOLS
CATECHU
CATECHUS
CATEGORIES
CATEGORY
CATELOG
CATELOGS
CATENA
CATENAE
CATENARIES
CATENARY
CATENAS
CATENATE
CATENATED
CATENATES
CATENATING
CATER
CATERAN
CATERANS
CATERED
CATERER
CATERERS
CATERESS
CATERESSES
CATERING
CATERINGS
CATERS
CATERWAUL
CATERWAULED
CATERWAULING
CATERWAULINGS
CATERWAULS
CATES
CATFISH
CATFISHES
CATGUT
CATGUTS
CATHARISE
CATHARISED
CATHARISES
CATHARISING
CATHARIZE
CATHARIZED
CATHARIZES
CATHARIZING
CATHARSES
CATHARSIS
CATHARTIC
CATHARTICS
CATHEAD
CATHEADS
CATHECTIC
CATHEDRA
CATHEDRAL
CATHEDRALS
CATHEDRAS
CATHETER
CATHETERS
CATHETUS
CATHETUSES
CATHEXES
CATHEXIS
CATHISMA
CATHISMAS
CATHODAL
CATHODE
CATHODES
CATHODIC
CATHOLIC

CATHOOD
CATHOODS
CATHOUSE
CATHOUSES
CATION
CATIONS
CATKIN
CATKINS
CATLING
CATLINGS
CATMINT
CATMINTS
CATNAP
CATNAPS
CATNEP
CATNEPS
CATNIP
CATNIPS
CATOPTRIC
CATOPTRICS
CATS
CATSKIN
CATSKINS
CATSUIT
CATSUITS
CATSUP
CATSUPS
CATTABU
CATTABUS
CATTALO
CATTALOES
CATTALOS
CATTED
CATTERIES
CATTERY
CATTIER
CATTIES
CATTIEST
CATTILY
CATTINESS
CATTINESSES
CATTING
CATTISH
CATTISHLY
CATTLE
CATTLEMAN
CATTLEMEN
CATTY
CAUCHEMAR
CAUCHEMARS
CAUCUS
CAUCUSED
CAUCUSES
CAUCUSING
CAUDAD
CAUDAL
CAUDATE
CAUDATED
CAUDEX
CAUDEXES
CAUDICES
CAUDICLE
CAUDICLES
CAUDILLO
CAUDILLOS
CAUDLE
CAUDLED
CAUDLES
CAUDLING
CAUDRON

CAUDRONS
CAUF
CAUGHT
CAUK
CAUKER
CAUKERS
CAUKS
CAUL
CAULD
CAULDER
CAULDEST
CAULDRIFE
CAULDRON
CAULDRONS
CAULDS
CAULES
CAULICLE
CAULICLES
CAULIFORM
CAULINARY
CAULINE
CAULIS
CAULK
CAULKED
CAULKER
CAULKERS
CAULKING
CAULKINGS
CAULKS
CAULOME
CAULOMES
CAULS
CAUM
CAUMED
CAUMING
CAUMS
CAUMSTANE
CAUMSTANES
CAUMSTONE
CAUMSTONES
CAUP
CAUPS
CAUSAL
CAUSALITIES
CAUSALITY
CAUSALLY
CAUSATION
CAUSATIONS
CAUSATIVE
CAUSATIVES
CAUSE
CAUSED
CAUSELESS
CAUSEN
CAUSER
CAUSERIE
CAUSERIES
CAUSERS
CAUSES
CAUSEWAY
CAUSEWAYED
CAUSEWAYING
CAUSEWAYS
CAUSEY
CAUSEYED
CAUSEYING
CAUSEYS
CAUSING
CAUSTIC
CAUSTICS

CAUTEL
CAUTELOUS
CAUTELS
CAUTER
CAUTERANT
CAUTERANTS
CAUTERIES
CAUTERISE
CAUTERISED
CAUTERISES
CAUTERISING
CAUTERISM
CAUTERISMS
CAUTERIZE
CAUTERIZED
CAUTERIZES
CAUTERIZING
CAUTERS
CAUTERY
CAUTION
CAUTIONED
CAUTIONER
CAUTIONERS
CAUTIONING
CAUTIONRIES
CAUTIONRY
CAUTIONS
CAUTIOUS
CAUVES
CAVALCADE
CAVALCADED
CAVALCADES
CAVALCADING
CAVALIER
CAVALIERED
CAVALIERING
CAVALIERO
CAVALIEROS
CAVALIERS
CAVALLA
CAVALLAS
CAVALLIES
CAVALLY
CAVALRIES
CAVALRY
CAVASS
CAVASSES
CAVATINA
CAVATINAS
CAVE
CAVEAT
CAVEATS
CAVED
CAVEL
CAVELS
CAVEMAN
CAVEMEN
CAVENDISH
CAVENDISHES
CAVER
CAVERN
CAVERNED
CAVERNING
CAVERNOUS
CAVERNS
CAVERS
CAVES
CAVESSON
CAVESSONS
CAVETTI

CAVETTO
CAVIAR
CAVIARE
CAVIARES
CAVIARIE
CAVIARIES
CAVIARS
CAVICORN
CAVICORNS
CAVIE
CAVIER
CAVIERS
CAVIES
CAVIL
CAVILLED
CAVILLER
CAVILLERS
CAVILLING
CAVILLINGS
CAVILS
CAVING
CAVINGS
CAVITATE
CAVITATED
CAVITATES
CAVITATING
CAVITIED
CAVITIES
CAVITY
CAVORT
CAVORTED
CAVORTING
CAVORTS
CAVY
CAW
CAWED
CAWING
CAWINGS
CAWK
CAWKER
CAWKERS
CAWKS
CAWS
CAXON
CAXONS
CAY
CAYENNE
CAYENNED
CAYENNES
CAYMAN
CAYMANS
CAYS
CAYUSE
CAYUSES
CAZIQUE
CAZIQUES
CEAS
CEASE
CEASED
CEASELESS
CEASES
CEASING
CEASINGS
CEAZE
CEAZED
CEAZES
CEAZING
CEBADILLA
CEBADILLAS
CECA

CECILS
CECITIES
CECITY
CECUM
CEDAR
CEDARED
CEDARN
CEDARS
CEDARWOOD
CEDARWOODS
CEDE
CEDED
CEDES
CEDI
CEDILLA
CEDILLAS
CEDING
CEDIS
CEDRATE
CEDRATES
CEDRINE
CEDULA
CEDULAS
CEE
CEES
CEIL
CEILED
CEILI
CEILIDH
CEILIDHS
CEILING
CEILINGED
CEILINGS
CEILIS
CEILS
CEINTURE
CEINTURES
CEL
CELADON
CELADONS
CELANDINE
CELANDINES
CELEBRANT
CELEBRANTS
CELEBRATE
CELEBRATED
CELEBRATES
CELEBRATING
CELEBRITIES
CELEBRITY
CELERIAC
CELERIACS
CELERIES
CELERITIES
CELERITY
CELERY
CELESTA
CELESTAS
CELESTE
CELESTES
CELESTIAL
CELESTIALS
CELESTINE
CELESTINES
CELIAC
CELIBACIES
CELIBACY
CELIBATE
CELIBATES
CELL

CELLA
CELLAE
CELLAR
CELLARAGE
CELLARAGES
CELLARED
CELLARER
CELLARERS
CELLARET
CELLARETS
CELLARING
CELLARIST
CELLARISTS
CELLARMAN
CELLARMEN
CELLAROUS
CELLARS
CELLED
CELLIST
CELLISTS
CELLO
CELLOS
CELLPHONE
CELLPHONES
CELLS
CELLULAR
CELLULE
CELLULES
CELLULITE
CELLULITES
CELLULOID
CELLULOIDS
CELLULOSE
CELLULOSES
CELOM
CELOMS
CELS
CELSITUDE
CELSITUDES
CELT
CELTS
CEMBALIST
CEMBALISTS
CEMBALO
CEMBALOS
CEMBRA
CEMBRAS
CEMENT
CEMENTA
CEMENTED
CEMENTING
CEMENTITE
CEMENTITES
CEMENTS
CEMENTUM
CEMETERIES
CEMETERY
CEMITARE
CEMITARES
CENACLE
CENACLES
CENDRÉ
CENOBITE
CENOBITES
CENOTAPH
CENOTAPHS
CENOTE
CENOTES
CENSE
CENSED

CENSER
CENSERS
CENSES
CENSING
CENSOR
CENSORED
CENSORIAL
CENSORIAN
CENSORING
CENSORS
CENSUAL
CENSURE
CENSURED
CENSURES
CENSURING
CENSUS
CENSUSED
CENSUSES
CENSUSING
CENT
CENTAGE
CENTAGES
CENTAL
CENTALS
CENTAUR
CENTAURIES
CENTAURS
CENTAURY
CENTAVO
CENTAVOS
CENTENARIES
CENTENARY
CENTENIER
CENTENIERS
CENTER
CENTERED
CENTERING
CENTERINGS
CENTERS
CENTESES
CENTESIS
CENTIARE
CENTIARES
CENTIGRAM
CENTIGRAMS
CENTIME
CENTIMES
CENTINEL
CENTINELL
CENTINELLS
CENTINELS
CENTIPEDE
CENTIPEDES
CENTNER
CENTNERS
CENTO
CENTOIST
CENTOISTS
CENTONATE
CENTONEL
CENTONELL
CENTONELLS
CENTONELS
CENTONIST
CENTONISTS
CENTOS
CENTRAL
CENTRALLY
CENTRE
CENTRED

CENTREING
CENTREINGS
CENTRES
CENTRIC
CENTRICAL
CENTRIES
CENTRING
CENTRINGS
CENTRISM
CENTRISMS
CENTRIST
CENTRISTS
CENTRODE
CENTRODES
CENTROID
CENTROIDS
CENTRUM
CENTRUMS
CENTRY
CENTS
CENTUM
CENTUMS
CENTUMVIR
CENTUMVIRI
CENTUPLE
CENTUPLED
CENTUPLES
CENTUPLING
CENTURIAL
CENTURIES
CENTURION
CENTURIONS
CENTURY
CEORL
CEORLS
CEP
CEPHALAD
CEPHALATE
CEPHALIC
CEPHALICS
CEPHALOUS
CEPHEID
CEPHEIDS
CEPS
CERACEOUS
CERAMET
CERAMETS
CERAMIC
CERAMICS
CERAMIST
CERAMISTS
CERASIN
CERASINS
CERASTES
CERATE
CERATED
CERATES
CERATITIS
CERATITISES
CERATODUS
CERATODUSES
CERATOID
CERBERIAN
CERCAL
CERCARIA
CERCARIAE
CERCARIAN
CERCARIAS
CERCI
CERCUS

CERCUSES	CERULEAN	CEYLONITES	CHAGRINS	CHALS
CERE	CERULEIN	CH	CHAI	CHALUMEAU
CEREAL	CERULEINS	CHA	CHAIN	CHALUMEAUX
CEREALIST	CERULEOUS	CHABAZITE	CHAINED	CHALYBITE
CEREALISTS	CERUMEN	CHABAZITES	CHAINING	CHALYBITES
CEREALS	CERUMENS	CHABOUK	CHAINLESS	CHAM
CEREBELLA	CERUSE	CHABOUKS	CHAINLET	CHAMADE
CEREBRAL	CERUSES	CHACE	CHAINLETS	CHAMADES
CEREBRATE	CERUSITE	CHACED	CHAINS	CHAMBER
CEREBRATED	CERUSITES	CHACES	CHAINSAW	CHAMBERED
CEREBRATES	CERUSSITE	CHACING	CHAINSAWS	CHAMBERER
CEREBRATING	CERUSSITES	CHACK	CHAINWORK	CHAMBERERS
CEREBRIC	CERVELAT	CHACKED	CHAINWORKS	CHAMBERING
CEREBRUM	CERVELATS	CHACKING	CHAIR	CHAMBERINGS
CEREBRUMS	CERVICAL	CHACKS	CHAIRDAYS	CHAMBERS
CERED	CERVINE	CHACMA	CHAIRED	CHAMBRÉ
CEREMENT	CERVIX	CHACMAS	CHAIRING	CHAMELEON
CEREMENTS	CERVIXES	CHACO	CHAIRLIFT	CHAMELEONS
CEREMONIES	CESAREVNA	CHACOES	CHAIRLIFTS	CHAMELOT
CEREMONY	CESAREVNAS	CHACONNE	CHAIRMAN	CHAMELOTS
CEREOUS	CESIUM	CHACONNES	CHAIRMEN	CHAMFER
CERES	CESIUMS	CHACOS	CHAIRS	CHAMFERED
CERESIN	CESPITOSE	CHAD	CHAIS	CHAMFERING
CERESINE	CESS	CHADAR	CHAISE	CHAMFERS
CERESINES	CESSATION	CHADARS	CHAISES	CHAMFRAIN
CERESINS	CESSATIONS	CHADDAR	CHAKRA	CHAMFRAINS
CERGE	CESSE	CHADDARS	CHAKRAS	CHAMFRON
CERGES	CESSED	CHADOR	CHAL	CHAMFRONS
CERIA	CESSER	CHADORS	CHALAN	CHAMISAL
CERIAS	CESSERS	CHADS	CHALANED	CHAMISALS
CERING	CESSES	CHAETA	CHALANING	CHAMISE
CERIPH	CESSING	CHAETAE	CHALANS	CHAMISES
CERIPHS	CESSION	CHAETODON	CHALAZA	CHAMISO
CERISE	CESSIONS	CHAETODONS	CHALAZAE	CHAMISOS
CERISES	CESSPIT	CHAETOPOD	CHALAZAS	CHAMLET
CERITE	CESSPITS	CHAETOPODS	CHALDAISM	CHAMLETS
CERITES	CESSPOOL	CHAFE	CHALDAISMS	CHAMOIS
CERIUM	CESSPOOLS	CHAFED	CHALDER	CHAMOMILE
CERIUMS	CESTODE	CHAFER	CHALDERS	CHAMOMILES
CERMET	CESTODES	CHAFERS	CHALDRON	CHAMP
CERMETS	CESTOID	CHAFES	CHALDRONS	CHAMPAC
CERNE	CESTOIDS	CHAFF	CHALET	CHAMPACS
CERNED	CESTUI	CHAFFED	CHALETS	CHAMPAGNE
CERNES	CESTUIS	CHAFFER	CHALICE	CHAMPAGNES
CERNING	CESTUS	CHAFFERED	CHALICED	CHAMPAIGN
CERNUOUS	CESTUSES	CHAFFERER	CHALICES	CHAMPAIGNS
CEROGRAPH	CESURA	CHAFFERERS	CHALK	CHAMPAK
CEROGRAPHS	CESURAS	CHAFFERIES	CHALKED	CHAMPAKS
CEROMANCIES	CESURE	CHAFFERING	CHALKFACE	CHAMPART
CEROMANCY	CESURES	CHAFFERS	CHALKFACES	CHAMPARTS
CEROON	CETACEAN	CHAFFERY	CHALKIER	CHAMPED
CEROONS	CETACEANS	CHAFFIER	CHALKIEST	CHAMPERS
CERRIAL	CETACEOUS	CHAFFIEST	CHALKING	CHAMPERTIES
CERRIS	CETANE	CHAFFINCH	CHALKPIT	CHAMPERTY
CERRISES	CETANES	CHAFFINCHES	CHALKPITS	CHAMPING
CERT	CETE	CHAFFING	CHALKS	CHAMPION
CERTAIN	CETERACH	CHAFFINGS	CHALKY	CHAMPIONED
CERTAINLY	CETERACHS	CHAFFLESS	CHALLAN	CHAMPIONING
CERTAINTIES	CETES	CHAFFRON	CHALLANED	CHAMPIONS
CERTAINTY	CETOLOGIES	CHAFFRONS	CHALLANING	CHAMPLEVÉ
CERTES	CETOLOGY	CHAFFS	CHALLANS	CHAMPLEVÉS
CERTIFIED	CETYL	CHAFFY	CHALLENGE	CHAMPS
CERTIFIER	CETYLS	CHAFING	CHALLENGED	CHAMS
CERTIFIERS	CETYWALL	CHAFT	CHALLENGES	CHANCE
CERTIFIES	CETYWALLS	CHAFTS	CHALLENGING	CHANCED
CERTIFY	CEVADILLA	CHAGAN	CHALLIS	CHANCEFUL
CERTIFYING	CEVADILLAS	CHAGANS	CHALLISES	CHANCEL
CERTITUDE	CEYLANITE	CHAGRIN	CHALONE	CHANCELS
CERTITUDES	CEYLANITES	CHAGRINED	CHALONES	CHANCER
CERTS	CEYLONITE	CHAGRINING	CHALONIC	CHANCERS

CHANCES	CHAPELRY	CHARGERS	CHARTED	CHATTED
CHANCIER	CHAPELS	CHARGES	CHARTER	CHATTEL
CHANCIEST	CHAPERON	CHARGING	CHARTERED	CHATTELS
CHANCING	CHAPERONE	CHARIER	CHARTERER	CHATTER
CHANCRE	CHAPERONED	CHARIEST	CHARTERERS	CHATTERED
CHANCRES	CHAPERONES	CHARILY	CHARTERING	CHATTERER
CHANCROID	CHAPERONING	CHARINESS	CHARTERS	CHATTERERS
CHANCROIDS	CHAPERONS	CHARINESSES	CHARTING	CHATTERING
CHANCROUS	CHAPES	CHARING	CHARTISM	CHATTERINGS
CHANCY	CHAPESS	CHARIOT	CHARTISMS	CHATTERS
CHANDLER	CHAPESSES	CHARIOTED	CHARTIST	CHATTIER
CHANDLERIES	CHAPITER	CHARIOTING	CHARTISTS	CHATTIES
CHANDLERS	CHAPITERS	CHARIOTS	CHARTLESS	CHATTIEST
CHANDLERY	CHAPKA	CHARISM	CHARTS	CHATTING
CHANGE	CHAPKAS	CHARISMA	CHARWOMAN	CHATTY
CHANGED	CHAPLAIN	CHARISMAS	CHARWOMEN	CHAUFE
CHANGEFUL	CHAPLAINS	CHARISMS	CHARY	CHAUFED
CHANGER	CHAPLESS	CHARITIES	CHAS	CHAUFES
CHANGERS	CHAPLET	CHARITY	CHASE	CHAUFF
CHANGES	CHAPLETED	CHARIVARI	CHASED	CHAUFFED
CHANGING	CHAPLETS	CHARIVARIS	CHASER	CHAUFFER
CHANK	CHAPMAN	CHARK	CHASERS	CHAUFFERS
CHANKS	CHAPMEN	CHARKED	CHASES	CHAUFFEUR
CHANNEL	CHAPPED	CHARKING	CHASING	CHAUFFEURED
CHANNELLED	CHAPPESS	CHARKS	CHASINGS	CHAUFFEURING
CHANNELLING	CHAPPESSES	CHARLADIES	CHASM	CHAUFFEURS
CHANNELS	CHAPPIE	CHARLADY	CHASMED	CHAUFFING
CHANOYU	CHAPPIER	CHARLATAN	CHASMIC	CHAUFFS
CHANOYUS	CHAPPIES	CHARLATANS	CHASMIER	CHAUFING
CHANSON	CHAPPIEST	CHARLEY	CHASMIEST	CHAUMER
CHANSONS	CHAPPING	CHARLEYS	CHASMS	CHAUMERS
CHANT	CHAPPY	CHARLIE	CHASMY	CHAUNCE
CHANTAGE	CHAPRASSI	CHARLIES	CHASSÉ	CHAUNCED
CHANTAGES	CHAPRASSIS	CHARLOCK	CHASSE	CHAUNCES
CHANTED	CHAPS	CHARLOCKS	CHASSÉED	CHAUNCING
CHANTER	CHAPTER	CHARLOTTE	CHASSÉING	CHAUNGE
CHANTERS	CHAPTERED	CHARLOTTES	CHASSÉS	CHAUNGED
CHANTEUSE	CHAPTERING	CHARM	CHASSES	CHAUNGES
CHANTEUSES	CHAPTERS	CHARMED	CHASSEUR	CHAUNGING
CHANTEY	CHAPTREL	CHARMER	CHASSEURS	CHAUNT
CHANTEYS	CHAPTRELS	CHARMERS	CHASSIS	CHAUNTED
CHANTIE	CHAR	CHARMEUSE	CHASTE	CHAUNTER
CHANTIES	CHARA	CHARMEUSES	CHASTELY	CHAUNTERS
CHANTING	CHARABANC	CHARMFUL	CHASTEN	CHAUNTING
CHANTOR	CHARABANCS	CHARMING	CHASTENED	CHAUNTRIES
CHANTORS	CHARACIN	CHARMLESS	CHASTENER	CHAUNTRY
CHANTRESS	CHARACINS	CHARMS	CHASTENERS	CHAUNTS
CHANTRESSES	CHARACT	CHARNECO	CHASTENING	CHAUSSES
CHANTRIES	CHARACTER	CHARNECOS	CHASTENS	CHAUSSURE
CHANTRY	CHARACTERED	CHARNEL	CHASTER	CHAUSSURES
CHANTS	CHARACTERING	CHARNELS	CHASTEST	CHAUVIN
CHANTY	CHARACTERS	CHAROSET	CHASTISE	CHAUVINS
CHAOS	CHARACTS	CHAROSETH	CHASTISED	CHAVE
CHAOSES	CHARADE	CHAROSETHS	CHASTISES	CHAVENDER
CHAOTIC	CHARADES	CHAROSETS	CHASTISING	CHAVENDERS
CHAP	CHARAS	CHARPIE	CHASTITIES	CHAW
CHAPARRAL	CHARASES	CHARPIES	CHASTITY	CHAWDRON
CHAPARRALS	CHARCOAL	CHARPOY	CHASUBLE	CHAWDRONS
CHAPATI	CHARCOALS	CHARPOYS	CHASUBLES	CHAWED
CHAPATIS	CHARD	CHARQUI	CHAT	CHAWING
CHAPATTI	CHARDS	CHARQUIS	CHÂTEAU	CHAWS
CHAPATTIS	CHARE	CHARR	CHÂTEAUX	CHAY
CHAPBOOK	CHARED	CHARRED	CHÂTELAIN	CHAYA
CHAPBOOKS	CHARES	CHARRING	CHÂTELAINS	CHAYAS
CHAPE	CHARET	CHARRS	CHATON	CHAYOTE
CHAPEAU	CHARETS	CHARRY	CHATONS	CHAYOTES
CHAPEAUS	CHARGE	CHARS	CHATOYANT	CHAYS
CHAPEL	CHARGED	CHART	CHATS	CHE
CHAPELESS	CHARGEFUL	CHARTA	CHATTA	CHEAP
CHAPELRIES	CHARGER	CHARTAS	CHATTAS	CHEAPEN

CHEAPENED	CHEERERS	CHEMITYPES	CHESSEL	CHIASTIC
CHEAPENER	CHEERFUL	CHEMITYPIES	CHESSELS	CHIAUS
CHEAPENERS	CHEERFULLER	CHEMITYPY	CHESSES	CHIAUSED
CHEAPENING	CHEERFULLEST	CHEMMIES	CHESSMAN	CHIAUSES
CHEAPENS	CHEERIER	CHEMMY	CHESSMEN	CHIAUSING
CHEAPER	CHEERIEST	CHEMOSTAT	CHEST	CHIBOL
CHEAPEST	CHEERILY	CHEMOSTATS	CHESTED	CHIBOLS
CHEAPIE	CHEERING	CHEMURGIC	CHESTFUL	CHIBOUK
CHEAPIES	CHEERIO	CHEMURGIES	CHESTFULS	CHIBOUKS
CHEAPLY	CHEERIOS	CHEMURGY	CHESTIER	CHIBOUQUE
CHEAPNESS	CHEERLESS	CHENAR	CHESTIEST	CHIBOUQUES
CHEAPNESSES	CHEERLY	CHENARS	CHESTNUT	CHIC
CHEAPO	CHEERO	CHENET	CHESTNUTS	CHICA
CHEAPS	CHEEROS	CHENETS	CHESTS	CHICANE
CHEAPY	CHEERS	CHENILLE	CHESTY	CHICANED
CHEAT	CHEERY	CHENILLES	CHEVALET	CHICANER
CHEATED	CHEESE	CHENIX	CHEVALETS	CHICANERIES
CHEATER	CHEESED	CHENIXES	CHEVALIER	CHICANERS
CHEATERIES	CHEESES	CHEQUE	CHEVALIERS	CHICANERY
CHEATERS	CHEESIER	CHEQUER	CHEVELURE	CHICANES
CHEATERY	CHEESIEST	CHEQUERED	CHEVELURES	CHICANING
CHEATING	CHEESING	CHEQUERING	CHEVEN	CHICANINGS
CHEATS	CHEESY	CHEQUERS	CHEVENS	CHICANO
CHECHAKO	CHEETAH	CHEQUES	CHEVEREL	CHICANOS
CHECHAKOES	CHEETAHS	CHEQUIER	CHEVERELS	CHICAS
CHECHAKOS	CHEEWINK	CHEQUIEST	CHEVERIL	CHICCORIES
CHECHAQUA	CHEEWINKS	CHEQUY	CHEVERILS	CHICCORY
CHECHAQUAS	CHEF	CHER	CHEVERON	CHICER
CHECHAQUO	CHEFS	CHERALITE	CHEVERONS	CHICEST
CHECHAQUOS	CHEKA	CHERALITES	CHEVERYE	CHICH
CHÉCHIA	CHEKAS	CHÈRE	CHEVERYES	CHICHA
CHÉCHIAS	CHEKIST	CHERIMOYA	CHEVIED	CHICHAS
CHECK	CHEKISTS	CHERIMOYAS	CHEVIES	CHICHES
CHECKED	CHELA	CHERISH	CHEVILLE	CHICHI
CHECKER	CHELAE	CHERISHED	CHEVILLES	CHICHIS
CHECKERED	CHELAS	CHERISHES	CHEVIN	CHICK
CHECKERS	CHELASHIP	CHERISHING	CHEVINS	CHICKADEE
CHECKIER	CHELASHIPS	CHERNOZEM	CHEVRETTE	CHICKADEES
CHECKIEST	CHELATE	CHERNOZEMS	CHEVRETTES	CHICKAREE
CHECKING	CHELATED	CHEROOT	CHEVRON	CHICKAREES
CHECKLIST	CHELATES	CHEROOTS	CHEVRONED	CHICKEN
CHECKLISTS	CHELATING	CHERRIED	CHEVRONS	CHICKENED
CHECKMATE	CHELATION	CHERRIER	CHEVRONY	CHICKENING
CHECKMATED	CHELATIONS	CHERRIES	CHEVY	CHICKENS
CHECKMATES	CHELATOR	CHERRIEST	CHEVYING	CHICKLING
CHECKMATING	CHELATORS	CHERRY	CHEW	CHICKLINGS
CHECKROOM	CHELICERA	CHERRYING	CHEWED	CHICKS
CHECKROOMS	CHELICERAE	CHERT	CHEWET	CHICKWEED
CHECKS	CHELIPED	CHERTIER	CHEWETS	CHICKWEEDS
CHECKY	CHELIPEDS	CHERTIEST	CHEWIER	CHICLE
CHEECHAKO	CHELOID	CHERTS	CHEWIEST	CHICLES
CHEECHAKOES	CHELOIDAL	CHERTY	CHEWING	CHICLY
CHEECHAKOS	CHELOIDS	CHERUB	CHEWINK	CHICON
CHEEK	CHELONIAN	CHERUBIC	CHEWINKS	CHICONS
CHEEKED	CHELONIANS	CHERUBIM	CHEWS	CHICORIES
CHEEKIER	CHEMIC	CHERUBIMS	CHEWY	CHICORY
CHEEKIEST	CHEMICAL	CHERUBIN	CHEZ	CHICS
CHEEKILY	CHEMICALS	CHERUBINS	CHI	CHID
CHEEKING	CHEMICKED	CHERUBS	CHIACK	CHIDDEN
CHEEKS	CHEMICKING	CHERUP	CHIACKED	CHIDE
CHEEKY	CHEMICS	CHERUPED	CHIACKING	CHIDED
CHEEP	CHEMISE	CHERUPING	CHIACKINGS	CHIDER
CHEEPED	CHEMISES	CHERUPS	CHIACKS	CHIDERS
CHEEPER	CHEMISM	CHERVIL	CHIAO	CHIDES
CHEEPERS	CHEMISMS	CHERVILS	CHIASM	CHIDING
CHEEPING	CHEMIST	CHESIL	CHIASMA	CHIDINGS
CHEEPS	CHEMISTRIES	CHESILS	CHIASMAS	CHIDLINGS
CHEER	CHEMISTRY	CHESNUT	CHIASMS	CHIEF
CHEERED	CHEMISTS	CHESNUTS	CHIASMUS	CHIEFDOM
CHEERER	CHEMITYPE	CHESS	CHIASMUSES	CHIEFDOMS

CHIEFER
CHIEFERIES
CHIEFERY
CHIEFESS
CHIEFESSES
CHIEFEST
CHIEFLESS
CHIEFLING
CHIEFLINGS
CHIEFLY
CHIEFRIES
CHIEFRY
CHIEFS
CHIEFSHIP
CHIEFSHIPS
CHIEFTAIN
CHIEFTAINS
CHIEL
CHIELD
CHIELDS
CHIELS
CHIFFON
CHIFFONS
CHIGGER
CHIGGERS
CHIGNON
CHIGNONS
CHIGOE
CHIGOES
CHIGRE
CHIGRES
CHIHUAHUA
CHIHUAHUAS
CHIK
CHIKARA
CHIKARAS
CHIKHOR
CHIKHORS
CHIKOR
CHIKORS
CHIKS
CHILBLAIN
CHILBLAINS
CHILD
CHILDBED
CHILDBEDS
CHILDE
CHILDED
CHILDER
CHILDHOOD
CHILDHOODS
CHILDING
CHILDISH
CHILDLESS
CHILDLIKE
CHILDLY
CHILDNESS
CHILDNESSES
CHILDREN
CHILDS
CHILE
CHILES
CHILI
CHILIAD
CHILIADS
CHILIAGON
CHILIAGONS
CHILIARCH
CHILIARCHS
CHILIASM

CHILIASMS
CHILIAST
CHILIASTS
CHILIS
CHILL
CHILLED
CHILLER
CHILLERS
CHILLEST
CHILLI
CHILLIER
CHILLIES
CHILLIEST
CHILLILY
CHILLING
CHILLINGS
CHILLIS
CHILLNESS
CHILLNESSES
CHILLS
CHILLUM
CHILLUMS
CHILLY
CHIMAERA
CHIMAERAS
CHIMAERID
CHIMAERIDS
CHIMB
CHIMBS
CHIME
CHIMED
CHIMER
CHIMERA
CHIMERAS
CHIMERE
CHIMERES
CHIMERIC
CHIMERS
CHIMES
CHIMING
CHIMLEY
CHIMLEYED
CHIMLEYING
CHIMLEYS
CHIMNEY
CHIMNEYED
CHIMNEYING
CHIMNEYS
CHIMP
CHIMPS
CHIN
CHINA
CHINAMPA
CHINAMPAS
CHINAR
CHINAROOT
CHINAROOTS
CHINARS
CHINAS
CHINCAPIN
CHINCAPINS
CHINCH
CHINCHES
CHINCOUGH
CHINCOUGHS
CHINDIT
CHINDITS
CHINÉ
CHINE
CHINED

CHINES
CHINING
CHINK
CHINKAPIN
CHINKAPINS
CHINKARA
CHINKARAS
CHINKED
CHINKIER
CHINKIEST
CHINKING
CHINKS
CHINKY
CHINLESS
CHINO
CHINOOK
CHINOOKS
CHINOS
CHINOVNIK
CHINOVNIKS
CHINS
CHINSTRAP
CHINSTRAPS
CHINTZ
CHINTZES
CHINTZIER
CHINTZIEST
CHINTZY
CHINWAG
CHINWAGGED
CHINWAGGING
CHINWAGS
CHIP
CHIPBOARD
CHIPBOARDS
CHIPMUCK
CHIPMUCKS
CHIPMUNK
CHIPMUNKS
CHIPOCHIA
CHIPOCHIAS
CHIPOLATA
CHIPOLATAS
CHIPPED
CHIPPER
CHIPPIE
CHIPPIER
CHIPPIES
CHIPPIEST
CHIPPING
CHIPPINGS
CHIPPY
CHIPS
CHIRAGRA
CHIRAGRAS
CHIRAGRIC
CHIRAL
CHIRALITIES
CHIRALITY
CHIRIMOYA
CHIRIMOYAS
CHIRK
CHIRKED
CHIRKING
CHIRKS
CHIRL
CHIRLED
CHIRLING
CHIRLS
CHIRM

CHIRMED
CHIRMING
CHIRMS
CHIROLOGIES
CHIROLOGY
CHIRONOMIES
CHIRONOMY
CHIROPODIES
CHIROPODY
CHIRP
CHIRPED
CHIRPER
CHIRPERS
CHIRPIER
CHIRPIEST
CHIRPILY
CHIRPING
CHIRPS
CHIRPY
CHIRR
CHIRRED
CHIRRING
CHIRRS
CHIRRUP
CHIRRUPED
CHIRRUPING
CHIRRUPS
CHIRRUPY
CHIRT
CHIRTED
CHIRTING
CHIRTS
CHIS
CHISEL
CHISELLED
CHISELLING
CHISELLINGS
CHISELS
CHIT
CHITAL
CHITALS
CHITCHAT
CHITCHATS
CHITCHATTED
CHITCHATTING
CHITIN
CHITINOUS
CHITINS
CHITLINGS
CHITON
CHITONS
CHITS
CHITTED
CHITTER
CHITTERED
CHITTERING
CHITTERINGS
CHITTERS
CHITTIER
CHITTIES
CHITTIEST
CHITTING
CHITTY
CHIV
CHIVALRIC
CHIVALRIES
CHIVALRY
CHIVE
CHIVED
CHIVES

CHIVIED
CHIVIES
CHIVING
CHIVS
CHIVVED
CHIVVIED
CHIVVIES
CHIVVING
CHIVVY
CHIVVYING
CHIVY
CHIVYING
CHLAMYDES
CHLAMYDIA
CHLAMYDIAS
CHLAMYS
CHLOASMA
CHLOASMAS
CHLORACNE
CHLORACNES
CHLORAL
CHLORALS
CHLORATE
CHLORATES
CHLORDAN
CHLORDANE
CHLORDANES
CHLORDANS
CHLORIC
CHLORIDE
CHLORIDES
CHLORINE
CHLORINES
CHLORITE
CHLORITES
CHLORITIC
CHLOROSES
CHLOROSIS
CHLOROTIC
CHLOROUS
CHOBDAR
CHOBDARS
CHOC
CHOCHO
CHOCHOS
CHOCK
CHOCKED
CHOCKER
CHOCKING
CHOCKS
CHOCOLATE
CHOCOLATES
CHOCS
CHOCTAW
CHOCTAWS
CHODE
CHOENIX
CHOENIXES
CHOICE
CHOICEFUL
CHOICELY
CHOICER
CHOICES
CHOICEST
CHOIR
CHOIRBOY
CHOIRBOYS
CHOIRED
CHOIRING
CHOIRMAN

CHOIRMEN
CHOIRS
CHOKE
CHOKEBORE
CHOKEBORES
CHOKED
CHOKEDAMP
CHOKEDAMPS
CHOKER
CHOKERS
CHOKES
CHOKEY
CHOKEYS
CHOKIDAR
CHOKIDARS
CHOKIER
CHOKIES
CHOKIEST
CHOKING
CHOKY
CHOLAEMIA
CHOLAEMIAS
CHOLAEMIC
CHOLECYST
CHOLECYSTS
CHOLELITH
CHOLELITHS
CHOLER
CHOLERA
CHOLERAIC
CHOLERAS
CHOLERIC
CHOLERS
CHOLI
CHOLIAMB
CHOLIAMBS
CHOLIC
CHOLINE
CHOLINES
CHOLIS
CHOLTRIES
CHOLTRY
CHOMP
CHOMPED
CHOMPING
CHOMPS
CHONDRAL
CHONDRE
CHONDRES
CHONDRI
CHONDRIFIED
CHONDRIFIES
CHONDRIFY
CHONDRIFYING
CHONDRIN
CHONDRINS
CHONDRITE
CHONDRITES
CHONDROID
CHONDRULE
CHONDRULES
CHONDRUS
CHOOK
CHOOKIE
CHOOKIES
CHOOKS
CHOOM
CHOOMS
CHOOSE
CHOOSER

CHOOSERS
CHOOSES
CHOOSEY
CHOOSIER
CHOOSIEST
CHOOSING
CHOOSY
CHOP
CHOPIN
CHOPINE
CHOPINES
CHOPINS
CHOPPED
CHOPPER
CHOPPERS
CHOPPIER
CHOPPIEST
CHOPPING
CHOPPINGS
CHOPPY
CHOPS
CHORAGI
CHORAGIC
CHORAGUS
CHORAGUSES
CHORAL
CHORALE
CHORALES
CHORALLY
CHORALS
CHORD
CHORDAL
CHORDATE
CHORDATES
CHORDS
CHORE
CHOREA
CHOREAS
CHOREE
CHOREES
CHOREGI
CHOREGIC
CHOREGUS
CHOREGUSES
CHORES
CHOREUS
CHOREUSES
CHORIA
CHORIAMB
CHORIAMBS
CHORIC
CHORINE
CHORINES
CHORIOID
CHORIOIDS
CHORION
CHORIONIC
CHORISES
CHORISIS
CHORIST
CHORISTER
CHORISTERS
CHORISTS
CHORIZO
CHORIZONT
CHORIZONTS
CHORIZOS
CHOROID
CHOROIDS
CHOROLOGIES

CHOROLOGY
CHORTLE
CHORTLED
CHORTLES
CHORTLING
CHORUS
CHORUSED
CHORUSES
CHORUSING
CHOSE
CHOSEN
CHOSES
CHOU
CHOUGH
CHOUGHS
CHOULTRIES
CHOULTRY
CHOUNTER
CHOUNTERED
CHOUNTERING
CHOUNTERS
CHOUSE
CHOUSED
CHOUSES
CHOUSING
CHOUT
CHOUTS
CHOUX
CHOW
CHOWDER
CHOWDERS
CHOWKIDAR
CHOWKIDARS
CHOWRI
CHOWRIES
CHOWRIS
CHOWRY
CHOWS
CHRISM
CHRISMAL
CHRISMALS
CHRISMS
CHRISOM
CHRISOMS
CHRISTEN
CHRISTENED
CHRISTENING
CHRISTENINGS
CHRISTENS
CHRISTIE
CHRISTIES
CHRISTOM
CHRISTOMS
CHRISTY
CHROMA
CHROMAKEY
CHROMAKEYS
CHROMAS
CHROMATE
CHROMATES
CHROMATIC
CHROMATICS
CHROMATIN
CHROMATINS
CHROME
CHROMED
CHROMES
CHROMIC
CHROMIDIA
CHROMING

CHROMITE
CHROMITES
CHROMIUM
CHROMIUMS
CHROMO
CHROMOS
CHRONIC
CHRONICAL
CHRONICLE
CHRONICLED
CHRONICLES
CHRONICLING
CHRONICS
CHRONON
CHRONONS
CHRYSALID
CHRYSALIDES
CHRYSALIDS
CHRYSALIS
CHRYSALISES
CHRYSANTH
CHRYSANTHS
CHTHONIAN
CHTHONIC
CHUB
CHUBBED
CHUBBIER
CHUBBIEST
CHUBBY
CHUBS
CHUCK
CHUCKED
CHUCKIE
CHUCKIES
CHUCKING
CHUCKLE
CHUCKLED
CHUCKLES
CHUCKLING
CHUCKLINGS
CHUCKS
CHUDDAH
CHUDDAHS
CHUDDAR
CHUDDARS
CHUFA
CHUFAS
CHUFF
CHUFFED
CHUFFIER
CHUFFIEST
CHUFFS
CHUFFY
CHUG
CHUGGED
CHUGGING
CHUGS
CHUKAR
CHUKARS
CHUKKA
CHUKKAS
CHUKKER
CHUKKERS
CHUKOR
CHUKORS
CHUM
CHUMLEY
CHUMLEYED
CHUMLEYING
CHUMLEYS

CHUMMAGE
CHUMMAGES
CHUMMED
CHUMMIER
CHUMMIES
CHUMMIEST
CHUMMING
CHUMMY
CHUMP
CHUMPS
CHUMS
CHUNDER
CHUNDERED
CHUNDERING
CHUNDERS
CHUNK
CHUNKIER
CHUNKIEST
CHUNKS
CHUNKY
CHUNNEL
CHUNNELS
CHUNNER
CHUNNERED
CHUNNERING
CHUNNERS
CHUNTER
CHUNTERED
CHUNTERING
CHUNTERS
CHUPATI
CHUPATIS
CHUPATTI
CHUPATTIS
CHUPRASSIES
CHUPRASSY
CHURCH
CHURCHED
CHURCHES
CHURCHIER
CHURCHIEST
CHURCHING
CHURCHINGS
CHURCHISM
CHURCHISMS
CHURCHLY
CHURCHMAN
CHURCHMEN
CHURCHWAY
CHURCHWAYS
CHURCHY
CHURINGA
CHURINGAS
CHURL
CHURLISH
CHURLS
CHURN
CHURNED
CHURNING
CHURNINGS
CHURNS
CHURR
CHURRED
CHURRING
CHURRS
CHURRUS
CHURRUSES
CHUSE
CHUSES
CHUSING

CHUT
CHUTE
CHUTES
CHUTIST
CHUTISTS
CHUTNEY
CHUTNEYS
CHUTZPAH
CHUTZPAHS
CHYACK
CHYACKED
CHYACKING
CHYACKS
CHYLDE
CHYLE
CHYLES
CHYLURIA
CHYLURIAS
CHYME
CHYMES
CHYMIFIED
CHYMIFIES
CHYMIFY
CHYMIFYING
CHYMISTRIES
CHYMISTRY
CHYMOUS
CHYND
CHYPRE
CHYPRES
CIAO
CIAOS
CIBATION
CIBATIONS
CIBOL
CIBOLS
CIBORIA
CIBORIUM
CICADA
CICADAS
CICALA
CICALAS
CICATRICE
CICATRICES
CICATRISE
CICATRISED
CICATRISES
CICATRISING
CICATRIX
CICATRIXES
CICATRIZE
CICATRIZED
CICATRIZES
CICATRIZING
CICELIES
CICELY
CICERO
CICERONE
CICERONED
CICERONES
CICERONI
CICERONING
CICEROS
CICHLID
CICHLIDS
CICHLOID
CICINNUS
CICINNUSES
CICISBEI
CICISBEO

CICLATON
CICLATONS
CICLATOUN
CICLATOUNS
CICUTA
CICUTAS
CIDARIS
CIDARISES
CIDE
CIDED
CIDER
CIDERKIN
CIDERKINS
CIDERS
CIDERY
CIDES
CIDING
CIEL
CIELED
CIELING
CIELINGS
CIELS
CIERGE
CIERGES
CIG
CIGAR
CIGARETTE
CIGARETTES
CIGARILLO
CIGARILLOS
CIGARS
CIGGIE
CIGGIES
CIGGY
CIGS
CILIA
CILIARY
CILIATE
CILIATED
CILICE
CILICES
CILICIOUS
CILIOLATE
CILIUM
CILL
CILLS
CIMAR
CIMARS
CIMELIA
CIMEX
CIMICES
CIMIER
CIMIERS
CIMINITE
CIMINITES
CIMOLITE
CIMOLITES
CINCH
CINCHED
CINCHES
CINCHING
CINCHONA
CINCHONAS
CINCHONIC
CINCINNUS
CINCINNUSES
CINCT
CINCTURE
CINCTURED
CINCTURES

CINCTURING
CINDER
CINDERS
CINDERY
CINEAST
CINEASTE
CINÉASTE
CINEASTES
CINÉASTES
CINEASTS
CINEMA
CINEMAS
CINEMATIC
CINEOL
CINEOLE
CINEOLES
CINEOLS
CINERAMIC
CINERARIA
CINERARIAS
CINERARY
CINERATOR
CINERATORS
CINEREA
CINEREAL
CINEREAS
CINEREOUS
CINGULUM
CINGULUMS
CINNABAR
CINNABARS
CINNAMIC
CINNAMON
CINNAMONS
CINQUAIN
CINQUAINS
CINQUE
CINQUES
CION
CIONS
CIPHER
CIPHERED
CIPHERING
CIPHERINGS
CIPHERS
CIPOLIN
CIPOLINS
CIPOLLINO
CIPOLLINOS
CIPPI
CIPPUS
CIRCA
CIRCADIAN
CIRCAR
CIRCARS
CIRCINATE
CIRCITER
CIRCLE
CIRCLED
CIRCLER
CIRCLERS
CIRCLES
CIRCLET
CIRCLETS
CIRCLING
CIRCLINGS
CIRCS
CIRCUIT
CIRCUITED
CIRCUITIES

CIRCUITING
CIRCUITRIES
CIRCUITRY
CIRCUITS
CIRCUITY
CIRCULAR
CIRCULARS
CIRCULATE
CIRCULATED
CIRCULATES
CIRCULATING
CIRCULATINGS
CIRCUS
CIRCUSES
CIRCUSSY
CIRCUSY
CIRÉ
CIRÉS
CIRL
CIRLS
CIRQUE
CIRQUES
CIRRATE
CIRRHOPOD
CIRRHOPODS
CIRRHOSES
CIRRHOSIS
CIRRHOTIC
CIRRI
CIRRIFORM
CIRRIPED
CIRRIPEDE
CIRRIPEDES
CIRRIPEDS
CIRROSE
CIRROUS
CIRRUS
CISCO
CISCOES
CISCOS
CISELEUR
CISELEURS
CISELURE
CISELURES
CISLUNAR
CISSIER
CISSIES
CISSIEST
CISSOID
CISSOIDS
CISSY
CIST
CISTED
CISTERN
CISTERNS
CISTIC
CISTRON
CISTRONS
CISTS
CISTUS
CISTUSES
CISTVAEN
CISTVAENS
CIT
CITABLE
CITADEL
CITADELS
CITAL
CITALS
CITATION

CITATIONS
CITATORY
CITE
CITED
CITER
CITERS
CITES
CITESS
CITESSES
CITHARA
CITHARAS
CITHARIST
CITHARISTS
CITHER
CITHERN
CITHERNS
CITHERS
CITIES
CITIFIED
CITIFIES
CITIFY
CITIFYING
CITIGRADE
CITING
CITIZEN
CITIZENRIES
CITIZENRY
CITIZENS
CITO
CITOLE
CITOLES
CITRANGE
CITRANGES
CITRATE
CITRATES
CITREOUS
CITRIC
CITRIN
CITRINE
CITRINES
CITRINS
CITRON
CITRONS
CITROUS
CITRUS
CITRUSES
CITS
CITTERN
CITTERNS
CITY
CITYSCAPE
CITYSCAPES
CIVE
CIVES
CIVET
CIVETS
CIVIC
CIVICALLY
CIVICS
CIVIL
CIVILIAN
CIVILIANS
CIVILISE
CIVILISED
CIVILISER
CIVILISERS
CIVILISES
CIVILISING
CIVILIST
CIVILISTS

CIVILITIES
CIVILITY
CIVILIZE
CIVILIZED
CIVILIZER
CIVILIZERS
CIVILIZES
CIVILIZING
CIVILLER
CIVILLEST
CIVILLY
CIVISM
CIVISMS
CIVVIES
CIVVY
CIZERS
CLABBER
CLABBERS
CLACHAN
CLACHANS
CLACK
CLACKBOX
CLACKBOXES
CLACKDISH
CLACKDISHES
CLACKED
CLACKER
CLACKERS
CLACKING
CLACKS
CLAD
CLADDED
CLADDING
CLADDINGS
CLADE
CLADES
CLADISM
CLADISMS
CLADIST
CLADISTIC
CLADISTICS
CLADISTS
CLADODE
CLADODES
CLADOGRAM
CLADOGRAMS
CLADS
CLAES
CLAG
CLAGGED
CLAGGING
CLAGGY
CLAGS
CLAIM
CLAIMABLE
CLAIMANT
CLAIMANTS
CLAIMED
CLAIMER
CLAIMERS
CLAIMING
CLAIMS
CLAM
CLAMANCIES
CLAMANCY
CLAMANT
CLAMANTLY
CLAMBAKE
CLAMBAKES
CLAMBE

CLAMBER
CLAMBERED
CLAMBERING
CLAMBERS
CLAME
CLAMED
CLAMES
CLAMING
CLAMMED
CLAMMIER
CLAMMIEST
CLAMMILY
CLAMMING
CLAMMY
CLAMOR
CLAMORED
CLAMORING
CLAMOROUS
CLAMORS
CLAMOUR
CLAMOURED
CLAMOURER
CLAMOURERS
CLAMOURING
CLAMOURS
CLAMP
CLAMPDOWN
CLAMPDOWNS
CLAMPED
CLAMPER
CLAMPERED
CLAMPERING
CLAMPERS
CLAMPING
CLAMPS
CLAMS
CLAN
CLANG
CLANGED
CLANGER
CLANGERS
CLANGING
CLANGINGS
CLANGOR
CLANGORED
CLANGORING
CLANGORS
CLANGOUR
CLANGOURED
CLANGOURING
CLANGOURS
CLANGS
CLANK
CLANKED
CLANKING
CLANKINGS
CLANKLESS
CLANKS
CLANNISH
CLANS
CLANSHIP
CLANSHIPS
CLANSMAN
CLANSMEN
CLAP
CLAPBOARD
CLAPBOARDS
CLAPBREAD
CLAPBREADS
CLAPDISH

CLAPDISHES
CLAPNET
CLAPNETS
CLAPPED
CLAPPER
CLAPPERED
CLAPPERING
CLAPPERINGS
CLAPPERS
CLAPPING
CLAPPINGS
CLAPS
CLAPTRAP
CLAPTRAPS
CLAQUE
CLAQUES
CLAQUEUR
CLAQUEURS
CLARENCE
CLARENCES
CLARENDON
CLARENDONS
CLARET
CLARETED
CLARETING
CLARETS
CLARIES
CLARIFIED
CLARIFIER
CLARIFIERS
CLARIFIES
CLARIFY
CLARIFYING
CLARINET
CLARINETS
CLARINI
CLARINO
CLARINOS
CLARION
CLARIONET
CLARIONETS
CLARIONS
CLARITIES
CLARITY
CLARKIA
CLARKIAS
CLARSACH
CLARSACHS
CLART
CLARTED
CLARTIER
CLARTIEST
CLARTING
CLARTS
CLARTY
CLARY
CLASH
CLASHED
CLASHES
CLASHING
CLASHINGS
CLASP
CLASPED
CLASPER
CLASPERS
CLASPING
CLASPINGS
CLASPS
CLASS
CLASSABLE

CLASSED
CLASSES
CLASSIBLE
CLASSIC
CLASSICAL
CLASSICS
CLASSIER
CLASSIEST
CLASSIFIC
CLASSIFIED
CLASSIFIES
CLASSIFY
CLASSIFYING
CLASSING
CLASSIS
CLASSLESS
CLASSMAN
CLASSMATE
CLASSMATES
CLASSMEN
CLASSROOM
CLASSROOMS
CLASSY
CLASTIC
CLAT
CLATCH
CLATCHED
CLATCHES
CLATCHING
CLATHRATE
CLATS
CLATTED
CLATTER
CLATTERED
CLATTERER
CLATTERERS
CLATTERING
CLATTERS
CLATTING
CLAUCHT
CLAUCHTED
CLAUCHTING
CLAUCHTS
CLAUGHT
CLAUGHTED
CLAUGHTING
CLAUGHTS
CLAUSAL
CLAUSE
CLAUSES
CLAUSTRA
CLAUSTRAL
CLAUSTRUM
CLAUSULA
CLAUSULAE
CLAUSULAR
CLAUT
CLAUTED
CLAUTING
CLAUTS
CLAVATE
CLAVATED
CLAVATION
CLAVATIONS
CLAVE
CLAVECIN
CLAVECINS
CLAVER
CLAVERED
CLAVERING

CLAVERS
CLAVES
CLAVICLE
CLAVICLES
CLAVICORN
CLAVICORNS
CLAVICULA
CLAVICULAS
CLAVIE
CLAVIER
CLAVIERS
CLAVIES
CLAVIFORM
CLAVIGER
CLAVIGERS
CLAVIS
CLAVULATE
CLAW
CLAWBACK
CLAWBACKS
CLAWED
CLAWING
CLAWLESS
CLAWS
CLAY
CLAYED
CLAYEY
CLAYIER
CLAYIEST
CLAYING
CLAYISH
CLAYMORE
CLAYMORES
CLAYS
CLEAN
CLEANED
CLEANER
CLEANERS
CLEANEST
CLEANING
CLEANINGS
CLEANLIER
CLEANLIEST
CLEANLY
CLEANNESS
CLEANNESSES
CLEANS
CLEANSE
CLEANSED
CLEANSER
CLEANSERS
CLEANSES
CLEANSING
CLEANSINGS
CLEAR
CLEARAGE
CLEARAGES
CLEARANCE
CLEARANCES
CLEARCOLE
CLEARCOLES
CLEARED
CLEARER
CLEARERS
CLEAREST
CLEARING
CLEARINGS
CLEARLY
CLEARNESS
CLEARNESSES

CLEARS
CLEARWAY
CLEARWAYS
CLEARWING
CLEARWINGS
CLEAT
CLEATED
CLEATING
CLEATS
CLEAVABLE
CLEAVAGE
CLEAVAGES
CLEAVE
CLEAVED
CLEAVER
CLEAVERS
CLEAVES
CLEAVING
CLEAVINGS
CLECHÉ
CLECK
CLECKED
CLECKING
CLECKINGS
CLECKS
CLEEK
CLEEKED
CLEEKING
CLEEKIT
CLEEKS
CLEEP
CLEEPING
CLEEPS
CLEEVE
CLEEVES
CLEF
CLEFS
CLEFT
CLEFTS
CLEG
CLEGS
CLEITHRAL
CLEM
CLEMATIS
CLEMATISES
CLEMENCE
CLEMENCES
CLEMENCIES
CLEMENCY
CLEMENT
CLEMENTLY
CLEMMED
CLEMMING
CLEMS
CLENCH
CLENCHED
CLENCHES
CLENCHING
CLEPE
CLEPES
CLEPING
CLEPSYDRA
CLEPSYDRAS
CLERECOLE
CLERECOLES
CLERGIES
CLERGY
CLERGYMAN
CLERGYMEN
CLERIC

CLERICAL
CLERICALS
CLERICATE
CLERICATES
CLERICITIES
CLERICITY
CLERICS
CLERIHEW
CLERIHEWS
CLERISIES
CLERISY
CLERK
CLERKDOM
CLERKDOMS
CLERKED
CLERKESS
CLERKESSES
CLERKING
CLERKISH
CLERKLESS
CLERKLIER
CLERKLIEST
CLERKLING
CLERKLINGS
CLERKLY
CLERKS
CLERKSHIP
CLERKSHIPS
CLERUCH
CLERUCHIA
CLERUCHIAS
CLERUCHIES
CLERUCHS
CLERUCHY
CLEUCH
GLEUCHS
CLEUGH
CLEUGHS
CLEVE
CLEVEITE
CLEVEITES
CLEVER
CLEVERER
CLEVEREST
CLEVERISH
CLEVERLY
CLEVES
CLEVIS
CLEVISES
CLEW
CLEWED
CLEWING
CLEWS
CLIANTHUS
CLIANTHUSES
CLICHÉ
CLICHÉD
CLICHÉS
CLICK
CLICKED
CLICKER
CLICKERS
CLICKET
CLICKETED
CLICKETING
CLICKETS
CLICKING
CLICKINGS
CLICKS
CLIED

CLIENT
CLIENTAGE
CLIENTAGES
CLIENTAL
CLIENTÈLE
CLIENTÈLES
CLIENTS
CLIES
CLIFF
CLIFFED
CLIFFHANG
CLIFFHANGING
CLIFFHANGS
CLIFFHUNG
CLIFFIER
CLIFFIEST
CLIFFS
CLIFFY
CLIFT
CLIFTED
CLIFTS
CLIFTY
CLIMACTIC
CLIMATAL
CLIMATE
CLIMATED
CLIMATES
CLIMATIC
CLIMATING
CLIMATISE
CLIMATISED
CLIMATISES
CLIMATISING
CLIMATIZE
CLIMATIZED
CLIMATIZES
CLIMATIZING
CLIMATURE
CLIMATURES
CLIMAX
CLIMAXED
CLIMAXES
CLIMAXING
CLIMB
CLIMBABLE
CLIMBED
CLIMBER
CLIMBERS
CLIMBING
CLIMBINGS
CLIMBS
CLIME
CLIMES
CLINAMEN
CLINAMENS
CLINCH
CLINCHED
CLINCHER
CLINCHERS
CLINCHES
CLINCHING
CLINE
CLINES
CLING
CLINGER
CLINGERS
CLINGIER
CLINGIEST
CLINGING
CLINGS

CLINGY
CLINIC
CLINICAL
CLINICIAN
CLINICIANS
CLINICS
CLINIQUE
CLINIQUES
CLINK
CLINKED
CLINKER
CLINKERS
CLINKING
CLINKS
CLINOAXES
CLINOAXIS
CLINQUANT
CLINQUANTS
CLINT
CLINTS
CLIP
CLIPBOARD
CLIPBOARDS
CLIPE
CLIPED
CLIPES
CLIPING
CLIPPED
CLIPPER
CLIPPERS
CLIPPIE
CLIPPIES
CLIPPING
CLIPPINGS
CLIPS
CLIPT
CLIQUE
CLIQUES
CLIQUEY
CLIQUIER
CLIQUIEST
CLIQUISH
CLIQUISM
CLIQUISMS
CLIQUY
CLITELLA
CLITELLAR
CLITELLUM
CLITHRAL
CLITIC
CLITICS
CLITORAL
CLITORIS
CLITORISES
CLITTER
CLITTERED
CLITTERING
CLITTERS
CLIVERS
CLOACA
CLOACAE
CLOACAL
CLOACALIN
CLOACINAL
CLOAK
CLOAKED
CLOAKING
CLOAKROOM
CLOAKROOMS
CLOAKS

CLOAM
CLOAMS
CLOBBER
CLOBBERED
CLOBBERING
CLOBBERS
CLOCHARD
CLOCHARDS
CLOCHE
CLOCHES
CLOCK
CLOCKED
CLOCKER
CLOCKERS
CLOCKING
CLOCKS
CLOCKWISE
CLOCKWORK
CLOCKWORKS
CLOD
CLODDED
CLODDIER
CLODDIEST
CLODDING
CLODDISH
CLODDY
CLODLY
CLODPATE
CLODPATED
CLODPATES
CLODPOLE
CLODPOLES
CLODPOLL
CLODPOLLS
CLODS
CLOFF
CLOFFS
CLOG
CLOGDANCE
CLOGDANCES
CLOGGED
CLOGGER
CLOGGERS
CLOGGIER
CLOGGIEST
CLOGGING
CLOGGY
CLOGS
CLOISON
CLOISONNÉ
CLOISONNÉS
CLOISONS
CLOISTER
CLOISTERED
CLOISTERING
CLOISTERS
CLOISTRAL
CLOKE
CLOKED
CLOKES
CLOKING
CLOMB
CLONAL
CLONE
CLONED
CLONES
CLONIC
CLONING
CLONK
CLONKED

CLONKING
CLONKS
CLONUS
CLONUSES
CLOOP
CLOOPS
CLOOT
CLOOTS
CLOP
CLOPPED
CLOPPING
CLOPS
CLOQUÉ
CLOQUÉS
CLOSE
CLOSED
CLOSELY
CLOSENESS
CLOSENESSES
CLOSER
CLOSERS
CLOSES
CLOSEST
CLOSET
CLOSETED
CLOSETING
CLOSETS
CLOSING
CLOSINGS
CLOSURE
CLOSURED
CLOSURES
CLOSURING
CLOT
CLOTBUR
CLOTBURS
CLOTE
CLOTEBUR
CLOTEBURS
CLOTES
CLOTH
CLOTHE
CLOTHED
CLOTHES
CLOTHIER
CLOTHIERS
CLOTHING
CLOTHINGS
CLOTHS
CLOTPOLL
CLOTPOLLS
CLOTS
CLOTTED
CLOTTER
CLOTTERED
CLOTTERING
CLOTTERS
CLOTTIER
CLOTTIEST
CLOTTING
CLOTTINGS
CLOTTY
CLOTURE
CLOTURED
CLOTURES
CLOTURING
CLOU
CLOUD
CLOUDAGE
CLOUDAGES

CLOUDED
CLOUDIER
CLOUDIEST
CLOUDILY
CLOUDING
CLOUDINGS
CLOUDLAND
CLOUDLANDS
CLOUDLESS
CLOUDLET
CLOUDLETS
CLOUDS
CLOUDY
CLOUGH
CLOUGHS
CLOUR
CLOURED
CLOURING
CLOURS
CLOUS
CLOUT
CLOUTED
CLOUTERLY
CLOUTING
CLOUTS
CLOVE
CLOVEN
CLOVER
CLOVERED
CLOVERS
CLOVERY
CLOVES
CLOW
CLOWDER
CLOWDERS
CLOWN
CLOWNED
CLOWNERIES
CLOWNERY
CLOWNING
CLOWNINGS
CLOWNISH
CLOWNS
CLOWNSHIP
CLOWNSHIPS
CLOWS
CLOY
CLOYE
CLOYED
CLOYES
CLOYING
CLOYLESS
CLOYMENT
CLOYMENTS
CLOYS
CLOYSOME
CLOZE
CLUB
CLUBABLE
CLUBBABLE
CLUBBED
CLUBBING
CLUBBINGS
CLUBBISH
CLUBBISM
CLUBBISMS
CLUBBIST
CLUBBISTS
CLUBHOUSE
CLUBHOUSES

CLUBLAND
CLUBLANDS
CLUBMAN
CLUBMEN
CLUBROOM
CLUBROOMS
CLUBROOT
CLUBROOTS
CLUBS
CLUBWOMAN
CLUBWOMEN
CLUCK
CLUCKED
CLUCKING
CLUCKS
CLUCKY
CLUDGIE
CLUDGIES
CLUE
CLUED
CLUEING
CLUELESS
CLUES
CLUMBER
CLUMBERS
CLUMP
CLUMPED
CLUMPIER
CLUMPIEST
CLUMPING
CLUMPS
CLUMPY
CLUMSIER
CLUMSIEST
CLUMSILY
CLUMSY
CLUNCH
CLUNCHES
CLUNG
CLUNK
CLUNKED
CLUNKING
CLUNKS
CLUPEID
CLUPEIDS
CLUPEOID
CLUPEOIDS
CLUSIA
CLUSIAS
CLUSTER
CLUSTERED
CLUSTERING
CLUSTERS
CLUSTERY
CLUTCH
CLUTCHED
CLUTCHES
CLUTCHING
CLUTTER
CLUTTERED
CLUTTERING
CLUTTERS
CLY
CLYING
CLYPE
CLYPEAL
CLYPEATE
CLYPED
CLYPEI
CLYPES

CLYPEUS
CLYPING
CLYSTER
CLYSTERS
CNIDA
CNIDAE
CNIDARIA
COACH
COACHDOG
COACHDOGS
COACHED
COACHEE
COACHEES
COACHER
COACHERS
COACHES
COACHIES
COACHING
COACHINGS
COACHMAN
COACHMEN
COACHWHIP
COACHWHIPS
COACHWORK
COACHWORKS
COACHY
COACT
COACTED
COACTING
COACTION
COACTIONS
COACTIVE
COACTS
COADJUTOR
COADJUTORS
COADUNATE
COADUNATED
COADUNATES
COADUNATING
COAGULANT
COAGULANTS
COAGULATE
COAGULATED
COAGULATES
COAGULATING
COAGULUM
COAGULUMS
COAITA
COAITAS
COAL
COALBALL
COALBALLS
COALED
COALER
COALERS
COALESCE
COALESCED
COALESCES
COALESCING
COALFIELD
COALFIELDS
COALFISH
COALFISHES
COALIER
COALIEST
COALING
COALISE
COALISED
COALISES
COALISING

COALITION
COALITIONS
COALIZE
COALIZED
COALIZES
COALIZING
COALMAN
COALMEN
COALS
COALY
COAMING
COAMINGS
COAPT
COAPTED
COAPTING
COAPTS
COARB
COARBS
COARCTATE
COARSE
COARSELY
COARSEN
COARSENED
COARSENING
COARSENS
COARSER
COARSEST
COARSISH
COAST
COASTAL
COASTED
COASTER
COASTERS
COASTING
COASTINGS
COASTLINE
COASTLINES
COASTS
COASTWARD
COASTWARDS
COASTWISE
COAT
COATE
COATED
COATEE
COATEES
COATER
COATERS
COATES
COATI
COATING
COATINGS
COATIS
COATLESS
COATRACK
COATRACKS
COATS
COATSTAND
COATSTANDS
COAX
COAXED
COAXER
COAXERS
COAXES
COAXIAL
COAXIALLY
COAXING
COAXINGLY
COB
COBALT

COBALTIC	COCCOLITH	COCKNEYFYING	CODFISH	COFFERED
COBALTITE	COCCOLITHS	COCKNEYS	CODFISHES	COFFERING
COBALTITES	COCCOS	COCKPIT	CODGER	COFFERS
COBALTS	COCCUS	COCKPITS	CODGERS	COFFIN
COBB	COCCYGEAL	COCKROACH	CODICES	COFFINED
COBBED	COCCYGES	COCKROACHES	CODICIL	COFFING
COBBER	COCCYGIAN	COCKS	CODICILS	COFFINING
COBBERS	COCCYX	COCKSCOMB	CODIFIED	COFFINITE
COBBIER	COCH	COCKSCOMBS	CODIFIER	COFFINITES
COBBIEST	COCHES	COCKSFOOT	CODIFIERS	COFFINS
COBBING	COCHINEAL	COCKSFOOTS	CODIFIES	COFFLE
COBBLE	COCHINEALS	COCKSHIES	CODIFY	COFFLES
COBBLED	COCHLEA	COCKSHOOT	CODIFYING	COFFRET
COBBLER	COCHLEAE	COCKSHOOTS	CODILLA	COFFRETS
COBBLERIES	COCHLEAR	COCKSHOT	CODILLAS	COFFS
COBBLERS	COCHLEARE	COCKSHOTS	CODILLE	COFT
COBBLERY	COCHLEARES	COCKSHUT	CODILLES	COG
COBBLES	COCHLEARS	COCKSHUTS	CODING	COGENCE
COBBLING	COCHLEAS	COCKSHY	CODINGS	COGENCES
COBBLINGS	COCHLEATE	COCKSIER	CODIST	COGENCIES
COBBS	COCK	COCKSIEST	CODISTS	COGENCY
COBBY	COCKADE	COCKSPUR	CODLIN	COGENER
COBIA	COCKADES	COCKSPURS	CODLING	COGENERS
COBIAS	COCKATEEL	COCKSURE	CODLINGS	COGENT
COBLE	COCKATEELS	COCKSWAIN	CODLINS	COGENTER
COBLES	COCKATIEL	COCKSWAINED	CODON	COGENTEST
COBLOAF	COCKATIELS	COCKSWAINING	CODONS	COGENTLY
COBLOAVES	COCKATOO	COCKSWAINS	CODS	COGGED
COBNUT	COCKATOOS	COCKSY	COED	COGGER
COBNUTS	COCKBIRD	COCKTAIL	COEDS	COGGERS
COBRA	COCKBIRDS	COCKTAILS	COEHORN	COGGIE
COBRAS	COCKBOAT	COCKY	COEHORNS	COGGIES
COBRIC	COCKBOATS	COCKYOLLIES	COELIAC	COGGING
COBRIFORM	COCKED	COCKYOLLY	COELOM	COGGLE
COBS	COCKER	COCO	COELOMATE	COGGLED
COBURG	COCKERED	COCOA	COELOMATES	COGGLES
COBURGS	COCKEREL	COCOANUT	COELOME	COGGLIER
COBWEB	COCKERELS	COCOANUTS	COELOMES	COGGLIEST
COBWEBBED	COCKERING	COCOAS	COELOMIC	COGGLING
COBWEBBIER	COCKERS	COCONUT	COELOMS	COGGLY
COBWEBBIEST	COCKET	COCONUTS	COELOSTAT	COGIE
COBWEBBING	COCKETS	COCOON	COELOSTATS	COGIES
COBWEBBY	COCKEYE	COCOONED	COEMPTION	COGITABLE
COBWEBS	COCKEYED	COCOONERIES	COEMPTIONS	COGITATE
COCA	COCKEYES	COCOONERY	COENOBIA	COGITATED
COCAINE	COCKFIGHT	COCOONING	COENOBITE	COGITATES
COCAINES	COCKFIGHTS	COCOONS	COENOBITES	COGITATING
COCAINISE	COCKHORSE	COCOPLUM	COENOBIUM	COGNATE
COCAINISED	COCKHORSES	COCOPLUMS	COENOSARC	COGNATES
COCAINISES	COCKIER	COCOS	COENOSARCS	COGNATION
COCAINISING	COCKIES	COCOTTE	COENZYME	COGNATIONS
COCAINISM	COCKIEST	COCOTTES	COENZYMES	COGNISANT
COCAINISMS	COCKILY	COCTILE	COEQUAL	COGNISE
COCAINIST	COCKINESS	COCTION	COEQUALLY	COGNISED
COCAINISTS	COCKINESSES	COCTIONS	COEQUALS	COGNISES
COCAINIZE	COCKING	COD	COERCE	COGNISING
COCAINIZED	COCKLAIRD	CODA	COERCED	COGNITION
COCAINIZES	COCKLAIRDS	CODAS	COERCES	COGNITIONS
COCAINIZING	COCKLE	CODDED	COERCIBLE	COGNITIVE
COCAS	COCKLED	CODDING	COERCIBLY	COGNIZANT
COCCAL	COCKLES	CODDLE	COERCING	COGNIZE
COCCI	COCKLING	CODDLED	COERCION	COGNIZED
COCCID	COCKLOFT	CODDLES	COERCIONS	COGNIZES
COCCIDIA	COCKLOFTS	CODDLING	COERCIVE	COGNIZING
COCCIDIUM	COCKMATCH	CODE	COEVAL	COGNOMEN
COCCIDS	COCKMATCHES	CODED	COEVALS	COGNOMENS
COCCO	COCKNEY	CODEINE	COFF	COGNOMINA
COCCOID	COCKNEYFIED	CODEINES	COFFEE	COGNOSCE
COCCOLITE	COCKNEYFIES	CODES	COFFEES	COGNOSCED
COCCOLITES	COCKNEYFY	CODEX	COFFER	COGNOSCES

COGNOSCING	COINCIDE	COLIC	COLLIERIES	COLONIAL
COGNOVIT	COINCIDED	COLICKY	COLLIERS	COLONIALS
COGNOVITS	COINCIDES	COLICS	COLLIERY	COLONIC
COGS	COINCIDING	COLIFORM	COLLIES	COLONICS
COGUE	COINED	COLIFORMS	COLLIGATE	COLONIES
COGUES	COINER	COLIN	COLLIGATED	COLONISE
COHABIT	COINERS	COLINS	COLLIGATES	COLONISED
COHABITED	COINING	COLISEUM	COLLIGATING	COLONISES
COHABITEE	COININGS	COLISEUMS	COLLIMATE	COLONISING
COHABITEES	COINS	COLITIS	COLLIMATED	COLONIST
COHABITING	COIR	COLITISES	COLLIMATES	COLONISTS
COHABITS	COIRS	COLL	COLLIMATING	COLONIZE
COHERE	COISTREL	COLLAGE	COLLINEAR	COLONIZED
COHERED	COISTRELS	COLLAGEN	COLLING	COLONIZES
COHERENCE	COISTRIL	COLLAGENS	COLLINGS	COLONIZING
COHERENCES	COISTRILS	COLLAGES	COLLISION	COLONNADE
COHERENCIES	COITAL	COLLAGIST	COLLISIONS	COLONNADES
COHERENCY	COITION	COLLAGISTS	COLLOCATE	COLONS
COHERENT	COITIONS	COLLAPSE	COLLOCATED	COLONY
COHERER	COITUS	COLLAPSED	COLLOCATES	COLOPHON
COHERERS	COITUSES	COLLAPSES	COLLOCATING	COLOPHONIES
COHERES	COJOIN	COLLAPSING	COLLODION	COLOPHONS
COHERING	COJOINED	COLLAR	COLLODIONS	COLOPHONY
COHERITOR	COJOINING	COLLARD	COLLOGUE	COLOR
COHERITORS	COJOINS	COLLARDS	COLLOGUED	COLORANT
COHESIBLE	COKE	COLLARED	COLLOGUES	COLORANTS
COHESION	COKED	COLLARING	COLLOGUING	COLORED
COHESIONS	COKERNUT	COLLARS	COLLOID	COLORIFIC
COHESIVE	COKERNUTS	COLLATE	COLLOIDAL	COLORING
COHIBIT	COKES	COLLATED	COLLOIDS	COLORS
COHIBITED	COKIER	COLLATES	COLLOP	COLOSSAL
COHIBITING	COKIEST	COLLATING	COLLOPS	COLOSSEUM
COHIBITS	COKING	COLLATION	COLLOQUE	COLOSSEUMS
COHO	COKY	COLLATIONS	COLLOQUED	COLOSSI
COHOE	COL	COLLATIVE	COLLOQUES	COLOSSUS
COHOES	COLA	COLLATOR	COLLOQUIA	COLOSSUSES
COHOG	COLANDER	COLLATORS	COLLOQUIED	COLOSTOMIES
COHOGS	COLANDERS	COLLEAGUE	COLLOQUIES	COLOSTOMY
COHORN	COLAS	COLLEAGUED	COLLOQUING	COLOSTRIC
COHORNS	COLATION	COLLEAGUES	COLLOQUY	COLOSTRUM
COHORT	COLATIONS	COLLEAGUING	COLLOQUYING	COLOSTRUMS
COHORTS	COLATURE	COLLECT	COLLOTYPE	COLOTOMIES
COHOS	COLATURES	COLLECTED	COLLOTYPES	COLOTOMY
COHUNE	COLCANNON	COLLECTING	COLLS	COLOUR
COHUNES	COLCANNONS	COLLECTINGS	COLLUDE	COLOURANT
COIF	COLCHICA	COLLECTOR	COLLUDED	COLOURANTS
COIFED	COLCHICUM	COLLECTORS	COLLUDER	COLOURED
COIFFEUR	COLCHICUMS	COLLECTS	COLLUDERS	COLOUREDS
COIFFEURS	COLCOTHAR	COLLED	COLLUDES	COLOURFUL
COIFFEUSE	COLCOTHARS	COLLEEN	COLLUDING	COLOURING
COIFFEUSES	COLD	COLLEENS	COLLUSION	COLOURINGS
COIFFURE	COLDBLOOD	COLLEGE	COLLUSIONS	COLOURIST
COIFFURED	COLDBLOODS	COLLEGER	COLLUSIVE	COLOURISTS
COIFFURES	COLDER	COLLEGERS	COLLUVIES	COLOURMAN
COIFFURING	COLDEST	COLLEGES	COLLY	COLOURMEN
COIFING	COLDHOUSE	COLLEGIA	COLLYING	COLOURS
COIFS	COLDHOUSES	COLLEGIAL	COLLYRIA	COLOURY
COIGN	COLDISH	COLLEGIAN	COLLYRIUM	COLS
COIGNE	COLDLY	COLLEGIANS	COLLYRIUMS	COLT
COIGNED	COLDNESS	COLLEGIUM	COLOBI	COLTED
COIGNES	COLDNESSES	COLLEGIUMS	COLOBUS	COLTER
COIGNING	COLDS	COLLET	COLOBUSES	COLTERS
COIGNS	COLE	COLLETS	COLOCYNTH	COLTING
COIL	COLES	COLLIDE	COLOCYNTHS	COLTISH
COILED	COLEUS	COLLIDED	COLON	COLTS
COILING	COLEUSES	COLLIDES	COLONEL	COLTSFOOT
COILS	COLEY	COLLIDING	COLONELCIES	COLTSFOOTS
COIN	COLEYS	COLLIE	COLONELCY	COLTWOOD
COINAGE	COLIBRI	COLLIED	COLONELS	COLTWOODS
COINAGES	COLIBRIS	COLLIER	COLONES	COLUBER

COLUBERS	COMBRETUM	COMMANDS	COMMON	COMPACTORS
COLUBRIAD	COMBRETUMS	COMMAS	COMMONAGE	COMPACTS
COLUBRIADS	COMBS	COMMENCE	COMMONAGES	COMPAGE
COLUBRINE	COMBUST	COMMENCED	COMMONED	COMPAGES
COLUGO	COMBUSTED	COMMENCES	COMMONER	COMPANDER
COLUGOS	COMBUSTING	COMMENCING	COMMONERS	COMPANDERS
COLUMBARIES	COMBUSTS	COMMEND	COMMONEST	COMPANDOR
COLUMBARY	COMBWISE	COMMENDAM	COMMONEY	COMPANDORS
COLUMBATE	COMBY	COMMENDAMS	COMMONEYS	COMPANIED
COLUMBATES	COME	COMMENDED	COMMONING	COMPANIES
COLUMBIC	COMEDIAN	COMMENDING	COMMONLY	COMPANING
COLUMBINE	COMEDIANS	COMMENDS	COMMONS	COMPANION
COLUMBINES	COMEDIC	COMMENSAL	COMMORANT	COMPANIONED
COLUMBITE	COMEDIES	COMMENSALS	COMMORANTS	COMPANIONING
COLUMBITES	COMEDO	COMMENT	COMMOS	COMPANIONS
COLUMBIUM	COMEDOS	COMMENTED	COMMOT	COMPANY
COLUMBIUMS	COMEDOWN	COMMENTER	COMMOTE	COMPANYING
COLUMEL	COMEDOWNS	COMMENTERS	COMMOTES	COMPARE
COLUMELLA	COMEDY	COMMENTING	COMMOTION	COMPARED
COLUMELLAE	COMELIER	COMMENTOR	COMMOTIONS	COMPARES
COLUMELS	COMELIEST	COMMENTORS	COMMOTS	COMPARING
COLUMN	COMELY	COMMENTS	COMMOVE	COMPART
COLUMNAL	COMER	COMMER	COMMOVED	COMPARTED
COLUMNAR	COMERS	COMMERCE	COMMOVES	COMPARTING
COLUMNED	COMES	COMMERCED	COMMOVING	COMPARTS
COLUMNIST	COMET	COMMERCES	COMMUNAL	COMPASS
COLUMNISTS	COMETARY	COMMERCING	COMMUNARD	COMPASSED
COLUMNS	COMETHER	COMMÈRE	COMMUNARDS	COMPASSES
COLURE	COMETHERS	COMMÈRES	COMMUNE	COMPASSING
COLURES	COMETIC	COMMERGE	COMMUNED	COMPASSINGS
COLZA	COMETS	COMMERGED	COMMUNES	COMPAST
COLZAS	COMFIER	COMMERGES	COMMUNING	COMPEAR
COMA	COMFIEST	COMMERGING	COMMUNINGS	COMPEARED
COMAE	COMFIT	COMMERS	COMMUNION	COMPEARING
COMAL	COMFITS	COMMIE	COMMUNIONS	COMPEARS
COMARB	COMFITURE	COMMIES	COMMUNISE	COMPEER
COMARBS	COMFITURES	COMMINATE	COMMUNISED	COMPEERED
COMART	COMFORT	COMMINATED	COMMUNISES	COMPEERING
COMARTS	COMFORTED	COMMINATES	COMMUNISING	COMPEERS
COMAS	COMFORTER	COMMINATING	COMMUNISM	COMPEL
COMATE	COMFORTERS	COMMINGLE	COMMUNISMS	COMPELLED
COMATES	COMFORTING	COMMINGLED	COMMUNIST	COMPELLING
COMATOSE	COMFORTS	COMMINGLES	COMMUNISTS	COMPELS
COMB	COMFREY	COMMINGLING	COMMUNITIES	COMPEND
COMBAT	COMFREYS	COMMINUTE	COMMUNITY	COMPENDIA
COMBATANT	COMFY	COMMINUTED	COMMUNIZE	COMPENDS
COMBATANTS	COMIC	COMMINUTES	COMMUNIZED	COMPERE
COMBATED	COMICAL	COMMINUTING	COMMUNIZES	COMPERED
COMBATING	COMICALLY	COMMIS	COMMUNIZING	COMPERES
COMBATIVE	COMICS	COMMISSAR	COMMUTATE	COMPERING
COMBATS	COMING	COMMISSARS	COMMUTATED	COMPESCE
COMBE	COMINGS	COMMIT	COMMUTATES	COMPESCED
COMBED	COMIQUE	COMMITS	COMMUTATING	COMPESCES
COMBER	COMIQUES	COMMITTAL	COMMUTE	COMPESCING
COMBERS	COMITADJI	COMMITTALS	COMMUTED	COMPETE
COMBES	COMITADJIS	COMMITTED	COMMUTER	COMPETED
COMBIER	COMITAL	COMMITTEE	COMMUTERS	COMPETENT
COMBIEST	COMITATUS	COMMITTEES	COMMUTES	COMPETES
COMBINATE	COMITATUSES	COMMITTING	COMMUTING	COMPETING
COMBINE	COMITIA	COMMIX	COMMUTUAL	COMPILE
COMBINED	COMITIES	COMMIXED	COMOSE	COMPILED
COMBINES	COMITY	COMMIXES	COMOUS	COMPILER
COMBING	COMMA	COMMIXING	COMP	COMPILERS
COMBINGS	COMMAND	COMMO	COMPACT	COMPILES
COMBINING	COMMANDED	COMMODE	COMPACTED	COMPILING
COMBLE	COMMANDER	COMMODES	COMPACTER	COMPITAL
COMBLES	COMMANDERS	COMMODITIES	COMPACTEST	COMPLAIN
COMBLESS	COMMANDING	COMMODITY	COMPACTING	COMPLAINED
COMBO	COMMANDO	COMMODORE	COMPACTLY	COMPLAINING
COMBOS	COMMANDOS	COMMODORES	COMPACTOR	COMPLAININGS

COMPLAINS
COMPLAINT
COMPLAINTS
COMPLEAT
COMPLECT
COMPLECTED
COMPLECTING
COMPLECTS
COMPLETE
COMPLETED
COMPLETER
COMPLETES
COMPLETEST
COMPLETING
COMPLEX
COMPLEXED
COMPLEXER
COMPLEXES
COMPLEXEST
COMPLEXING
COMPLEXLY
COMPLEXUS
COMPLEXUSES
COMPLIANT
COMPLICE
COMPLICES
COMPLIED
COMPLIER
COMPLIERS
COMPLIES
COMPLIN
COMPLINE
COMPLINES
COMPLINS
COMPLISH
COMPLISHED
COMPLISHES
COMPLISHING
COMPLOT
COMPLOTS
COMPLOTTED
COMPLOTTING
COMPLY
COMPLYING
COMPO
COMPONÉ
COMPONENT
COMPONENTS
COMPONY
COMPORT
COMPORTED
COMPORTING
COMPORTS
COMPOS
COMPOSE
COMPOSED
COMPOSER
COMPOSERS
COMPOSES
COMPOSING
COMPOSITE
COMPOSITED
COMPOSITES
COMPOSITING
COMPOST
COMPOSTED
COMPOSTER
COMPOSTERS
COMPOSTING
COMPOSTS

COMPOSURE
COMPOSURES
COMPOT
COMPOTE
COMPOTES
COMPOTIER
COMPOTIERS
COMPOTS
COMPOUND
COMPOUNDED
COMPOUNDING
COMPOUNDS
COMPRADOR
COMPRADORS
COMPRESS
COMPRESSED
COMPRESSES
COMPRESSING
COMPRINT
COMPRINTED
COMPRINTING
COMPRINTS
COMPRISAL
COMPRISALS
COMPRISE
COMPRISED
COMPRISES
COMPRISING
COMPS
COMPT
COMPTABLE
COMPTED
COMPTER
COMPTERS
COMPTIBLE
COMPTING
COMPTROLL
COMPTROLLED
COMPTROLLING
COMPTROLLS
COMPTS
COMPULSE
COMPULSED
COMPULSES
COMPULSING
COMPUTANT
COMPUTANTS
COMPUTE
COMPUTED
COMPUTER
COMPUTERS
COMPUTES
COMPUTING
COMPUTIST
COMPUTISTS
COMRADE
COMRADELY
COMRADES
COMS
COMUS
COMUSES
CON
CONACRE
CONACRED
CONACRES
CONACRING
CONARIA
CONARIAL
CONARIUM
CONATION

CONATIONS
CONATIVE
CONATUS
CONCAUSE
CONCAUSES
CONCAVE
CONCAVED
CONCAVELY
CONCAVES
CONCAVING
CONCAVITIES
CONCAVITY
CONCEAL
CONCEALED
CONCEALING
CONCEALS
CONCEDE
CONCEDED
CONCEDER
CONCEDERS
CONCEDES
CONCEDING
CONCEIT
CONCEITED
CONCEITING
CONCEITS
CONCEITY
CONCEIVE
CONCEIVED
CONCEIVES
CONCEIVING
CONCENT
CONCENTED
CONCENTER
CONCENTERED
CONCENTERING
CONCENTERS
CONCENTING
CONCENTRE
CONCENTRED
CONCENTRES
CONCENTRING
CONCENTS
CONCEPT
CONCEPTI
CONCEPTS
CONCEPTUS
CONCEPTUSES
CONCERN
CONCERNED
CONCERNING
CONCERNS
CONCERT
CONCERTED
CONCERTING
CONCERTO
CONCERTOS
CONCERTS
CONCETTI
CONCETTO
CONCH
CONCHA
CONCHAE
CONCHATE
CONCHE
CONCHED
CONCHES
CONCHIE
CONCHIES
CONCHING

CONCHITIS
CONCHITISES
CONCHOID
CONCHOIDS
CONCHS
CONCHY
CONCIERGE
CONCIERGES
CONCILIAR
CONCISE
CONCISED
CONCISELY
CONCISER
CONCISES
CONCISEST
CONCISING
CONCISION
CONCISIONS
CONCLAVE
CONCLAVES
CONCLUDE
CONCLUDED
CONCLUDES
CONCLUDING
CONCOCT
CONCOCTED
CONCOCTER
CONCOCTERS
CONCOCTING
CONCOCTOR
CONCOCTORS
CONCOCTS
CONCOLOR
CONCORD
CONCORDAT
CONCORDATS
CONCORDED
CONCORDING
CONCORDS
CONCOURS
CONCOURSE
CONCOURSES
CONCREATE
CONCREATED
CONCREATES
CONCREATING
CONCRETE
CONCRETED
CONCRETER
CONCRETES
CONCRETEST
CONCRETING
CONCREW
CONCREWED
CONCREWING
CONCREWS
CONCUBINE
CONCUBINES
CONCUPIES
CONCUPY
CONCUR
CONCURRED
CONCURRING
CONCURS
CONCUSS
CONCUSSED
CONCUSSES
CONCUSSING
CONCYCLIC
COND

CONDEMN
CONDEMNED
CONDEMNING
CONDEMNS
CONDENSE
CONDENSED
CONDENSER
CONDENSERS
CONDENSES
CONDENSING
CONDER
CONDERS
CONDIDDLE
CONDIDDLED
CONDIDDLES
CONDIDDLING
CONDIGN
CONDIGNLY
CONDIMENT
CONDIMENTED
CONDIMENTING
CONDIMENTS
CONDITION
CONDITIONED
CONDITIONING
CONDITIONINGS
CONDITIONS
CONDOLE
CONDOLED
CONDOLENT
CONDOLES
CONDOLING
CONDOM
CONDOMS
CONDONE
CONDONED
CONDONES
CONDONING
CONDOR
CONDORS
CONDUCE
CONDUCED
CONDUCES
CONDUCING
CONDUCIVE
CONDUCT
CONDUCTED
CONDUCTI
CONDUCTING
CONDUCTOR
CONDUCTORS
CONDUCTS
CONDUCTUS
CONDUIT
CONDUITS
CONDYLAR
CONDYLE
CONDYLES
CONDYLOID
CONDYLOMA
CONDYLOMATA
CONE
CONED
CONES
CONEY
CONEYS
CONFAB
CONFABBED
CONFABBING
CONFABS

CONFECT	CONFLICT	CONGLOBING	CONJURER	CONQUERS
CONFECTED	CONFLICTED	CONGO	CONJURERS	CONQUEST
CONFECTING	CONFLICTING	CONGOS	CONJURES	CONQUESTS
CONFECTS	CONFLICTS	CONGOU	CONJURIES	CONS
CONFER	CONFLUENT	CONGOUS	CONJURING	CONSCIENT
CONFEREE	CONFLUENTS	CONGREE	CONJURINGS	CONSCIOUS
CONFEREES	CONFLUX	CONGREED	CONJUROR	CONSCIOUSES
CONFERRED	CONFLUXES	CONGREEING	CONJURORS	CONSCRIBE
CONFERRER	CONFORM	CONGREES	CONJURY	CONSCRIBED
CONFERRERS	CONFORMAL	CONGREET	CONK	CONSCRIBES
CONFERRING	CONFORMED	CONGREETED	CONKED	CONSCRIBING
CONFERS	CONFORMER	CONGREETING	CONKER	CONSCRIPT
CONFERVA	CONFORMERS	CONGREETS	CONKERS	CONSCRIPTED
CONFERVAE	CONFORMING	CONGRESS	CONKIES	CONSCRIPTING
CONFESS	CONFORMS	CONGRESSED	CONKING	CONSCRIPTS
CONFESSED	CONFOUND	CONGRESSES	CONKS	CONSEIL
CONFESSES	CONFOUNDED	CONGRESSING	CONKY	CONSEILS
CONFESSING	CONFOUNDING	CONGRUE	CONN	CONSENSUS
CONFESSOR	CONFOUNDS	CONGRUED	CONNATE	CONSENSUSES
CONFESSORS	CONFRÈRE	CONGRUENT	CONNATION	CONSENT
CONFEST	CONFRÈRES	CONGRUES	CONNATIONS	CONSENTED
CONFESTLY	CONFRÉRIE	CONGRUING	CONNATURE	CONSENTING
CONFETTI	CONFRÉRIES	CONGRUITIES	CONNATURES	CONSENTS
CONFIDANT	CONFRONT	CONGRUITY	CONNE	CONSERVE
CONFIDANTS	CONFRONTÉ	CONGRUOUS	CONNECT	CONSERVED
CONFIDE	CONFRONTED	CONIA	CONNECTED	CONSERVER
CONFIDED	CONFRONTING	CONIAS	CONNECTER	CONSERVERS
CONFIDENT	CONFRONTS	CONIC	CONNECTERS	CONSERVES
CONFIDENTS	CONFUSE	CONICAL	CONNECTING	CONSERVING
CONFIDER	CONFUSED	CONICALLY	CONNECTOR	CONSIDER
CONFIDERS	CONFUSES	CONICALS	CONNECTORS	CONSIDERED
CONFIDES	CONFUSING	CONICS	CONNECTS	CONSIDERING
CONFIDING	CONFUSION	CONIDIA	CONNED	CONSIDERINGS
CONFIGURE	CONFUSIONS	CONIDIAL	CONNER	CONSIDERS
CONFIGURED	CONFUTE	CONIDIUM	CONNERS	CONSIGN
CONFIGURES	CONFUTED	CONIES	CONNES	CONSIGNED
CONFIGURING	CONFUTES	CONIFER	CONNEXION	CONSIGNEE
CONFINE	CONFUTING	CONIFERS	CONNEXIONS	CONSIGNEES
CONFINED	CONGA	CONIFORM	CONNEXIVE	CONSIGNER
CONFINER	CONGAED	CONIINE	CONNING	CONSIGNERS
CONFINERS	CONGAING	CONIINES	CONNINGS	CONSIGNING
CONFINES	CONGAS	CONIMA	CONNIVE	CONSIGNOR
CONFINING	CONGÉ	CONIMAS	CONNIVED	CONSIGNORS
CONFIRM	CONGEAL	CONINE	CONNIVENT	CONSIGNS
CONFIRMED	CONGEALED	CONINES	CONNIVER	CONSIST
CONFIRMEE	CONGEALING	CONING	CONNIVERS	CONSISTED
CONFIRMEES	CONGEALS	CONJECT	CONNIVES	CONSISTING
CONFIRMER	CONGÉD	CONJECTED	CONNIVING	CONSISTS
CONFIRMERS	CONGEE	CONJECTING	CONNOTATE	CONSOLATE
CONFIRMING	CONGEED	CONJECTS	CONNOTATED	CONSOLATED
CONFIRMINGS	CONGEEING	CONJEE	CONNOTATES	CONSOLATES
CONFIRMOR	CONGEES	CONJEED	CONNOTATING	CONSOLATING
CONFIRMORS	CONGÉING	CONJEEING	CONNOTE	CONSOLE
CONFIRMS	CONGENER	CONJEES	CONNOTED	CONSOLED
CONFISEUR	CONGENERS	CONJOIN	CONNOTES	CONSOLER
CONFISEURS	CONGENIAL	CONJOINED	CONNOTING	CONSOLERS
CONFIT	CONGER	CONJOINING	CONNOTIVE	CONSOLES
CONFITEOR	CONGERIES	CONJOINS	CONNS	CONSOLING
CONFITEORS	CONGERS	CONJOINT	CONNUBIAL	CONSOLS
CONFITS	CONGERY	CONJUGAL	CONODONT	CONSOMMÉ
CONFITURE	CONGÉS	CONJUGANT	CONODONTS	CONSOMMÉS
CONFITURES	CONGEST	CONJUGANTS	CONOID	CONSONANT
CONFIX	CONGESTED	CONJUGATE	CONOIDAL	CONSONANTS
CONFIXED	CONGESTING	CONJUGATED	CONOIDIC	CONSONOUS
CONFIXES	CONGESTS	CONJUGATES	CONOIDS	CONSORT
CONFIXING	CONGIARIES	CONJUGATING	CONQUER	CONSORTED
CONFLATE	CONGIARY	CONJUGATINGS	CONQUERED	CONSORTER
CONFLATED	CONGLOBE	CONJUNCT	CONQUERING	CONSORTERS
CONFLATES	CONGLOBED	CONJURE	CONQUEROR	CONSORTIA
CONFLATING	CONGLOBES	CONJURED	CONQUERORS	CONSORTING

CONSORTS
CONSPIRE
CONSPIRED
CONSPIRER
CONSPIRERS
CONSPIRES
CONSPIRING
CONSTABLE
CONSTABLES
CONSTANCIES
CONSTANCY
CONSTANT
CONSTANTS
CONSTATE
CONSTATED
CONSTATES
CONSTATING
CONSTER
CONSTERED
CONSTERING
CONSTERS
CONSTRAIN
CONSTRAINED
CONSTRAINING
CONSTRAINS
CONSTRICT
CONSTRICTED
CONSTRICTING
CONSTRICTS
CONSTRUCT
CONSTRUCTED
CONSTRUCTING
CONSTRUCTS
CONSTRUE
CONSTRUED
CONSTRUER
CONSTRUERS
CONSTRUES
CONSTRUING
CONSUL
CONSULAGE
CONSULAGES
CONSULAR
CONSULARS
CONSULATE
CONSULATES
CONSULS
CONSULT
CONSULTA
CONSULTAS
CONSULTED
CONSULTEE
CONSULTEES
CONSULTER
CONSULTERS
CONSULTING
CONSULTOR
CONSULTORS
CONSULTS
CONSUME
CONSUMED
CONSUMER
CONSUMERS
CONSUMES
CONSUMING
CONSUMINGS
CONSUMPT
CONSUMPTS
CONTACT
CONTACTED

CONTACTING
CONTACTOR
CONTACTORS
CONTACTS
CONTADINA
CONTADINAS
CONTADINE
CONTADINI
CONTADINO
CONTAGION
CONTAGIONS
CONTAGIUM
CONTAGIUMS
CONTAIN
CONTAINED
CONTAINER
CONTAINERS
CONTAINING
CONTAINS
CONTANGO
CONTANGOED
CONTANGOING
CONTANGOS
CONTE
CONTECK
CONTECKS
CONTEMN
CONTEMNED
CONTEMNER
CONTEMNERS
CONTEMNING
CONTEMNOR
CONTEMNORS
CONTEMNS
CONTEMPER
CONTEMPERED
CONTEMPERING
CONTEMPERS
CONTEMPT
CONTEMPTS
CONTEND
CONTENDED
CONTENDER
CONTENDERS
CONTENDING
CONTENDINGS
CONTENDS
CONTENT
CONTENTED
CONTENTING
CONTENTS
CONTES
CONTEST
CONTESTED
CONTESTER
CONTESTERS
CONTESTING
CONTESTS
CONTEXT
CONTEXTS
CONTICENT
CONTINENT
CONTINENTS
CONTINUA
CONTINUAL
CONTINUE
CONTINUED
CONTINUER
CONTINUERS
CONTINUES

CONTINUING
CONTINUO
CONTINUOS
CONTINUUM
CONTLINE
CONTLINES
CONTO
CONTORNO
CONTORNOS
CONTORT
CONTORTED
CONTORTING
CONTORTS
CONTOS
CONTOUR
CONTOURED
CONTOURING
CONTOURS
CONTRA
CONTRACT
CONTRACTED
CONTRACTING
CONTRACTS
CONTRAIL
CONTRAILS
CONTRAIR
CONTRALTI
CONTRALTO
CONTRALTOS
CONTRARIED
CONTRARIES
CONTRARY
CONTRARYING
CONTRAS
CONTRAST
CONTRASTED
CONTRASTING
CONTRASTS
CONTRASTY
CONTRATE
CONTRIST
CONTRISTED
CONTRISTING
CONTRISTS
CONTRITE
CONTRIVE
CONTRIVED
CONTRIVER
CONTRIVERS
CONTRIVES
CONTRIVING
CONTROL
CONTROLLED
CONTROLLING
CONTROLS
CONTROUL
CONTROULED
CONTROULING
CONTROULS
CONTUMACIES
CONTUMACY
CONTUMELIES
CONTUMELY
CONTUND
CONTUNDED
CONTUNDING
CONTUNDS
CONTUSE
CONTUSED
CONTUSES

CONTUSING
CONTUSION
CONTUSIONS
CONTUSIVE
CONUNDRUM
CONUNDRUMS
CONURBAN
CONURBIA
CONURBIAS
CONVECTOR
CONVECTORS
CONVENE
CONVENED
CONVENER
CONVENERS
CONVENES
CONVENING
CONVENOR
CONVENORS
CONVENT
CONVENTED
CONVENTING
CONVENTS
CONVERGE
CONVERGED
CONVERGES
CONVERGING
CONVERSE
CONVERSED
CONVERSES
CONVERSING
CONVERT
CONVERTED
CONVERTER
CONVERTERS
CONVERTING
CONVERTOR
CONVERTORS
CONVERTS
CONVEX
CONVEXED
CONVEXES
CONVEXITIES
CONVEXITY
CONVEXLY
CONVEY
CONVEYAL
CONVEYALS
CONVEYED
CONVEYER
CONVEYERS
CONVEYING
CONVEYOR
CONVEYORS
CONVEYS
CONVICT
CONVICTED
CONVICTING
CONVICTS
CONVINCE
CONVINCED
CONVINCES
CONVINCING
CONVIVE
CONVIVED
CONVIVES
CONVIVIAL
CONVIVING
CONVOCATE
CONVOCATED

CONVOCATES
CONVOCATING
CONVOKE
CONVOKED
CONVOKES
CONVOKING
CONVOLUTE
CONVOLUTED
CONVOLVE
CONVOLVED
CONVOLVES
CONVOLVING
CONVOY
CONVOYED
CONVOYING
CONVOYS
CONVULSE
CONVULSED
CONVULSES
CONVULSING
CONY
COO
COOED
COOEE
COOEED
COOEEING
COOEES
COOEY
COOEYED
COOEYING
COOEYS
COOF
COOFS
COOING
COOINGLY
COOINGS
COOK
COOKABLE
COOKED
COOKER
COOKERIES
COOKERS
COOKERY
COOKHOUSE
COOKHOUSES
COOKIE
COOKIES
COOKING
COOKMAID
COOKMAIDS
COOKOUT
COOKOUTS
COOKROOM
COOKROOMS
COOKS
COOKSHOP
COOKSHOPS
COOKWARE
COOKWARES
COOKY
COOL
COOLABAH
COOLABAHS
COOLAMON
COOLAMONS
COOLANT
COOLANTS
COOLED
COOLER
COOLERS

COOLEST	COPARTNER	COPULATE	CORBIE	CORKS
COOLIBAH	COPARTNERS	COPULATED	CORBIES	CORKWING
COOLIBAHS	COPATAINE	COPULATES	CORCASS	CORKWINGS
COOLIBAR	COPATRIOT	COPULATING	CORCASSES	CORKWOOD
COOLIBARS	COPATRIOTS	COPY	CORD	CORKWOODS
COOLIE	COPE	COPYBOOK	CORDAGE	CORKY
COOLIES	COPECK	COPYBOOKS	CORDAGES	CORM
COOLING	COPECKS	COPYHOLD	CORDATE	CORMORANT
COOLISH	COPED	COPYHOLDS	CORDED	CORMORANTS
COOLLY	COPEPOD	COPYING	CORDIAL	CORMOUS
COOLNESS	COPEPODS	COPYISM	CORDIALLY	CORMS
COOLNESSES	COPER	COPYISMS	CORDIALS	CORMUS
COOLS	COPERED	COPYIST	CORDIFORM	CORMUSES
COOLTH	COPERING	COPYISTS	CORDINER	CORN
COOLTHS	COPERS	COPYRIGHT	CORDINERS	CORNACRE
COOLY	COPES	COPYRIGHTED	CORDING	CORNACRED
COOM	COPIED	COPYRIGHTING	CORDINGS	CORNACRES
COOMB	COPIER	COPYRIGHTS	CORDITE	CORNACRING
COOMBS	COPIERS	COQUET	CORDITES	CORNAGE
COOMED	COPIES	COQUETRIES	CORDLESS	CORNAGES
COOMIER	COPILOT	COQUETRY	CÓRDOBA	CORNBRASH
COOMIEST	COPILOTS	COQUETS	CÓRDOBAS	CORNBRASHES
COOMING	COPING	COQUETTE	CORDON	CORNCRAKE
COOMS	COPINGS	COQUETTED	CORDONED	CORNCRAKES
COOMY	COPIOUS	COQUETTES	CORDONING	CORNEA
COON	COPIOUSLY	COQUETTING	CORDONS	CORNEAL
COONS	COPITA	COQUILLA	CORDOTOMIES	CORNEAS
COONTIE	COPITAS	COQUILLAS	CORDOTOMY	CORNED
COONTIES	COPPED	COQUILLE	CORDOVAN	CORNEL
COONTY	COPPER	COQUILLES	CORDOVANS	CORNELIAN
COOP	COPPERAS	COQUITO	CORDS	CORNELIANS
COOPED	COPPERASES	COQUITOS	CORDUROY	CORNELS
COOPER	COPPERED	COR	CORDUROYS	CORNEMUSE
COOPERAGE	COPPERING	CORACLE	CORDWAIN	CORNEMUSES
COOPERAGES	COPPERINGS	CORACLES	CORDWAINS	CORNEOUS
COOPERANT	COPPERISH	CORACOID	CORDYLINE	CORNER
COOPERATE	COPPERS	CORACOIDS	CORDYLINES	CORNERED
COOPERATED	COPPERY	CORAGGIO	CORE	CORNERING
COOPERATES	COPPICE	CORAGGIOS	CORED	CORNERS
COOPERATING	COPPICED	CORAL	CORELESS	CORNET
COOPERED	COPPICES	CORALLA	CORELLA	CORNETCIES
COOPERIES	COPPICING	CORALLINE	CORELLAS	CORNETCY
COOPERING	COPPICINGS	CORALLINES	COREOPSIS	CORNETIST
COOPERINGS	COPPIES	CORALLITE	COREOPSISES	CORNETISTS
COOPERS	COPPIN	CORALLITES	CORER	CORNETS
COOPERY	COPPING	CORALLOID	CORERS	CORNETT
COOPING	COPPINS	CORALLUM	CORES	CORNETTI
COOPS	COPPLE	CORALS	CORF	CORNETTO
COOS	COPPLES	CORAMINE	CORGI	CORNETTS
COOSEN	COPPY	CORAMINES	CORGIS	CORNFIELD
COOSENS	COPRA	CORANACH	CORIA	CORNFIELDS
COOSER	COPRAS	CORANACHS	CORIANDER	CORNFLIES
COOSERS	COPRESENT	CORANTO	CORIANDERS	CORNFLOUR
COOSIN	COPROLITE	CORANTOES	CORING	CORNFLOURS
COOSINED	COPROLITES	CORANTOS	CORIOUS	CORNFLY
COOSINING	COPROLOGIES	CORBAN	CORIUM	CORNHUSK
COOSINS	COPROLOGY	CORBANS	CORIUMS	CORNHUSKS
COOST	COPS	CORBE	CORK	CORNI
COOT	COPSE	CORBEAU	CORKAGE	CORNICE
COOTIKIN	COPSED	CORBEAUS	CORKAGES	CORNICED
COOTIKINS	COPSES	CORBEIL	CORKED	CORNICES
COOTS	COPSEWOOD	CORBEILLE	CORKER	CORNICHE
COP	COPSEWOODS	CORBEILLES	CORKERS	CORNICHES
COPACETIC	COPSIER	CORBEILS	CORKIER	CORNICING
COPAIBA	COPSIEST	CORBEL	CORKIEST	CORNICLE
COPAIBAS	COPSING	CORBELLED	CORKINESS	CORNICLES
COPAIVA	COPSY	CORBELS	CORKINESSES	CORNIER
COPAIVAS	COPULA	CORBES	CORKING	CORNIEST
COPAL	COPULAR	CORBICULA	CORKIR	CORNIFIC
COPALS	COPULAS	CORBICULAE	CORKIRS	CORNIFORM

CORNING
CORNIST
CORNISTS
CORNLAND
CORNLANDS
CORNLOFT
CORNLOFTS
CORNO
CORNOPEAN
CORNOPEANS
CORNPIPE
CORNPIPES
CORNS
CORNSTALK
CORNSTALKS
CORNSTONE
CORNSTONES
CORNU
CORNUA
CORNUAL
CORNUTE
CORNUTED
CORNUTES
CORNUTING
CORNUTO
CORNUTOS
CORNWORM
CORNWORMS
CORNY
COROCORE
COROCORES
COROCORO
COROCOROS
CORODIES
CORODY
COROLLA
COROLLARIES
COROLLARY
COROLLAS
COROLLINE
CORONA
CORONACH
CORONACHS
CORONAE
CORONAL
CORONALS
CORONARIES
CORONARY
CORONAS
CORONATE
CORONATED
CORONER
CORONERS
CORONET
CORONETED
CORONETS
CORONIS
CORONISES
CORONIUM
CORONIUMS
CORONOID
COROZO
COROZOS
CORPORA
CORPORAL
CORPORALS
CORPORAS
CORPORASES
CORPORATE
CORPOREAL

CORPORIFIED
CORPORIFIES
CORPORIFY
CORPORIFYING
CORPOSANT
CORPOSANTS
CORPS
CORPSE
CORPSED
CORPSES
CORPSING
CORPULENT
CORPUS
CORPUSCLE
CORPUSCLES
CORRADE
CORRADED
CORRADES
CORRADING
CORRAL
CORRALLED
CORRALLING
CORRALS
CORRASION
CORRASIONS
CORRECT
CORRECTED
CORRECTER
CORRECTEST
CORRECTING
CORRECTLY
CORRECTOR
CORRECTORS
CORRECTS
CORRELATE
CORRELATED
CORRELATES
CORRELATING
CORRIDA
CORRIDAS
CORRIDOR
CORRIDORS
CORRIE
CORRIES
CORRIGENT
CORRIGENTS
CORRIVAL
CORRIVALLED
CORRIVALLING
CORRIVALS
CORRODE
CORRODED
CORRODENT
CORRODENTS
CORRODES
CORRODIES
CORRODING
CORRODY
CORROSION
CORROSIONS
CORROSIVE
CORROSIVES
CORRUGATE
CORRUGATED
CORRUGATES
CORRUGATING
CORRUPT
CORRUPTED
CORRUPTER
CORRUPTERS

CORRUPTEST
CORRUPTING
CORRUPTLY
CORRUPTS
CORS
CORSAGE
CORSAGES
CORSAIR
CORSAIRS
CORSE
CORSELET
CORSELETS
CORSES
CORSET
CORSETED
CORSETIER
CORSETIERS
CORSETING
CORSETRIES
CORSETRY
CORSETS
CORSIVE
CORSIVES
CORSLET
CORSLETED
CORSLETS
CORSNED
CORSNEDS
CORSO
CORSOS
CORTÈGE
CORTÈGES
CORTEX
CORTEXES
CORTICAL
CORTICATE
CORTICES
CORTICOID
CORTICOIDS
CORTILE
CORTILES
CORTISOL
CORTISOLS
CORTISONE
CORTISONES
CORUNDUM
CORUNDUMS
CORUSCANT
CORUSCATE
CORUSCATED
CORUSCATES
CORUSCATING
CORVÉE
CORVÉES
CORVES
CORVET
CORVETED
CORVETING
CORVETS
CORVETTE
CORVETTED
CORVETTES
CORVETTING
CORVID
CORVIDS
CORVINE
CORVUS
CORVUSES
CORYBANT
CORYBANTES

CORYBANTS
CORYMB
CORYMBOSE
CORYMBS
CORYPHAEI
CORYPHE
CORYPHEE
CORYPHEES
CORYPHENE
CORYPHENES
CORYPHES
CORYZA
CORYZAS
COS
COSE
COSECANT
COSECANTS
COSECH
COSECHS
COSED
COSEISMAL
COSEISMIC
COSES
COSH
COSHED
COSHER
COSHERED
COSHERER
COSHERERS
COSHERIES
COSHERING
COSHERINGS
COSHERS
COSHERY
COSHES
COSHING
COSIER
COSIERS
COSIES
COSIEST
COSILY
COSINE
COSINES
COSINESS
COSINESSES
COSING
COSMEA
COSMEAS
COSMESES
COSMESIS
COSMETIC
COSMETICS
COSMIC
COSMICAL
COSMISM
COSMISMS
COSMIST
COSMISTS
COSMOCRAT
COSMOCRATS
COSMOGENIES
COSMOGENY
COSMOGONIES
COSMOGONY
COSMOLOGIES
COSMOLOGY
COSMONAUT
COSMONAUTS
COSMORAMA
COSMORAMAS

COSMOS
COSMOSES
COSMOTRON
COSMOTRONS
COSPONSOR
COSPONSORED
COSPONSORING
COSPONSORS
COSS
COSSES
COSSET
COSSETED
COSSETING
COSSETS
COSSIE
COSSIES
COST
COSTA
COSTAE
COSTAL
COSTALS
COSTARD
COSTARDS
COSTATE
COSTATED
COSTE
COSTEAN
COSTEANED
COSTEANING
COSTEANINGS
COSTEANS
COSTED
COSTER
COSTERS
COSTES
COSTING
COSTIVE
COSTIVELY
COSTLIER
COSTLIEST
COSTLY
COSTMARIES
COSTMARY
COSTREL
COSTRELS
COSTS
COSTUME
COSTUMED
COSTUMER
COSTUMERS
COSTUMES
COSTUMIER
COSTUMIERS
COSTUMING
COSTUS
COSTUSES
COSY
COT
COTANGENT
COTANGENTS
COTE
COTEAU
COTEAUX
COTED
CÔTELETTE
CÔTELETTES
COTELINE
COTELINES
COTERIE
COTERIES

COTES	COUCHÉ	COUPÉ	COURTING	COVER
COTH	COUCHED	COUPED	COURTINGS	COVERAGE
COTHS	COUCHEE	COUPEE	COURTLET	COVERAGES
COTHURN	COUCHÉE	COUPEES	COURTLETS	COVERALL
COTHURNI	COUCHEES	COUPER	COURTLIER	COVERALLS
COTHURNS	COUCHÉES	COUPERS	COURTLIEST	COVERED
COTHURNUS	COUCHÉS	COUPES	COURTLIKE	COVERING
COTICULAR	COUCHES	COUPÉS	COURTLING	COVERINGS
COTILLION	COUCHETTE	COUPING	COURTLINGS	COVERLET
COTILLIONS	COUCHETTES	COUPLE	COURTLY	COVERLETS
COTILLON	COUCHING	COUPLED	COURTROOM	COVERLID
COTILLONS	COUCHINGS	COUPLER	COURTROOMS	COVERLIDS
COTING	COUDÉ	COUPLERS	COURTS	COVERS
COTINGA	COUGAR	COUPLES	COURTSHIP	COVERSLIP
COTINGAS	COUGARS	COUPLET	COURTSHIPS	COVERSLIPS
COTISE	COUGH	COUPLETS	COURTYARD	COVERT
COTISED	COUGHED	COUPLING	COURTYARDS	COVERTLY
COTISES	COUGHER	COUPLINGS	COUSCOUS	COVERTS
COTISING	COUGHERS	COUPON	COUSCOUSES	COVERTURE
COTLAND	COUGHING	COUPONS	COUSIN	COVERTURES
COTLANDS	COUGHINGS	COUPS	COUSINAGE	COVES
COTQUEAN	COUGHS	COUPURE	COUSINAGES	COVET
COTQUEANS	COUGUAR	COUPURES	COUSINLY	COVETABLE
COTS	COUGUARS	COUR	COUSINRIES	COVETED
COTT	COULD	COURAGE	COUSINRY	COVETING
COTTA	COULÉE	COURAGES	COUSINS	COVETISE
COTTABUS	COULÉES	COURANT	COUTER	COVETISES
COTTABUSES	COULIS	COURANTE	COUTERS	COVETOUS
COTTAGE	COULISSE	COURANTES	COUTH	COVETS
COTTAGED	COULISSES	COURANTS	COUTHER	COVEY
COTTAGER	COULOIR	COURB	COUTHEST	COVEYS
COTTAGERS	COULOIRS	COURBARIL	COUTHIE	COVIN
COTTAGES	COULOMB	COURBARILS	COUTHIER	COVING
COTTAGEY	COULOMBS	COURBED	COUTHIEST	COVINGS
COTTAR	COULTER	COURBETTE	COUTHY	COVINOUS
COTTARS	COULTERS	COURBETTES	COUTIL	COVINS
COTTAS	COUMARIC	COURBING	COUTILLE	COVYNE
COTTED	COUMARIN	COURBS	COUTILLES	COVYNES
COTTER	COUMARINS	COURD	COUTILS	COW
COTTERS	COUNCIL	COURE	COUTURE	COWAGE
COTTIER	COUNCILOR	COURED	COUTURES	COWAGES
COTTIERS	COUNCILORS	COURES	COUTURIER	COWAN
COTTISE	COUNCILS	COURGETTE	COUTURIERS	COWANS
COTTISED	COUNSEL	COURGETTES	COUVADE	COWARD
COTTISES	COUNSELLED	COURIER	COUVADES	COWARDED
COTTISING	COUNSELLING	COURIERS	COUVERT	COWARDICE
COTTOID	COUNSELLINGS	COURING	COUVERTS	COWARDICES
COTTOIDS	COUNSELS	COURLAN	COVALENCIES	COWARDING
COTTON	COUNT	COURLANS	COVALENCY	COWARDLY
COTTONADE	COUNTABLE	COURS	COVALENT	COWARDREE
COTTONADES	COUNTED	COURSE	COVARIANT	COWARDREES
COTTONED	COUNTER	COURSED	COVARIANTS	COWARDRIES
COTTONING	COUNTERED	COURSER	COVARIED	COWARDRY
COTTONS	COUNTERING	COURSERS	COVARIES	COWARDS
COTTONY	COUNTERS	COURSES	COVARY	COWBANE
COTTOWN	COUNTESS	COURSING	COVARYING	COWBANES
COTTOWNS	COUNTESSES	COURSINGS	COVE	COWBELL
COTTS	COUNTIES	COURT	COVED	COWBELLS
COTWAL	COUNTING	COURTED	COVELET	COWBERRIES
COTWALS	COUNTLESS	COURTEOUS	COVELETS	COWBERRY
COTYLAE	COUNTRIES	COURTESAN	COVELLITE	COWBIRD
COTYLE	COUNTROL	COURTESANS	COVELLITES	COWBIRDS
COTYLEDON	COUNTROLS	COURTESIED	COVEN	COWBOY
COTYLEDONS	COUNTRY	COURTESIES	COVENANT	COWBOYS
COTYLES	COUNTS	COURTESY	COVENANTED	COWED
COTYLOID	COUNTSHIP	COURTESYING	COVENANTING	COWER
COUCAL	COUNTSHIPS	COURTEZAN	COVENANTS	COWERED
COUCALS	COUNTY	COURTEZANS	COVENS	COWERING
COUCH	COUP	COURTIER	COVENT	COWERS
COUCHANT	COUPE	COURTIERS	COVENTS	COWFEEDER

COWFEEDERS
COWFISH
COWFISHES
COWGIRL
COWGIRLS
COWGRASS
COWGRASSES
COWHAGE
COWHAGES
COWHAND
COWHANDS
COWHEARD
COWHEARDS
COWHEEL
COWHEELS
COWHERD
COWHERDS
COWHIDE
COWHIDED
COWHIDES
COWHIDING
COWHOUSE
COWHOUSES
COWING
COWISH
COWITCH
COWITCHES
COWL
COWLED
COWLICK
COWLICKS
COWLING
COWLINGS
COWLS
COWMAN
COWMEN
COWP
COWPAT
COWPATS
COWPED
COWPING
COWPOKE
COWPOKES
COWPOX
COWPOXES
COWPS
COWRIE
COWRIES
COWRY
COWS
COWSHED
COWSHEDS
COWSLIP
COWSLIPS
COX
COXA
COXAE
COXAL
COXALGIA
COXALGIAS
COXCOMB
COXCOMBIC
COXCOMBRIES
COXCOMBRY
COXCOMBS
COXED
COXES
COXIER
COXIEST
COXINESS

COXINESSES
COXING
COXSWAIN
COXSWAINED
COXSWAINING
COXSWAINS
COXY
COY
COYED
COYER
COYEST
COYING
COYISH
COYISHLY
COYLY
COYNESS
COYNESSES
COYOTE
COYOTES
COYPU
COYPUS
COYS
COYSTREL
COYSTRELS
COYSTRIL
COYSTRILS
COZ
COZE
COZED
COZEN
COZENAGE
COZENAGES
COZENED
COZENER
COZENERS
COZENING
COZENS
COZES
COZIER
COZIERS
COZIES
COZIEST
COZING
COZY
COZZES
CRAB
CRABBED
CRABBEDLY
CRABBIER
CRABBIEST
CRABBILY
CRABBING
CRABBY
CRABLIKE
CRABS
CRABSTICK
CRABSTICKS
CRABWISE
CRACK
CRACKDOWN
CRACKDOWNS
CRACKED
CRACKER
CRACKERS
CRACKING
CRACKJAW
CRACKLE
CRACKLED
CRACKLES
CRACKLIER

CRACKLIEST
CRACKLING
CRACKLINGS
CRACKLY
CRACKNEL
CRACKNELS
CRACKPOT
CRACKPOTS
CRACKS
CRACKSMAN
CRACKSMEN
CRACOWE
CRACOWES
CRADLE
CRADLED
CRADLES
CRADLING
CRADLINGS
CRAFT
CRAFTED
CRAFTIER
CRAFTIEST
CRAFTILY
CRAFTING
CRAFTLESS
CRAFTS
CRAFTSMAN
CRAFTSMEN
CRAFTWORK
CRAFTWORKS
CRAFTY
CRAG
CRAGFAST
CRAGGED
CRAGGIER
CRAGGIEST
CRAGGY
CRAGS
CRAGSMAN
CRAGSMEN
CRAIG
CRAIGS
CRAKE
CRAKED
CRAKES
CRAKING
CRAM
CRAMBO
CRAMBOES
CRAME
CRAMES
CRAMESIES
CRAMESY
CRAMMABLE
CRAMMED
CRAMMER
CRAMMERS
CRAMMING
CRAMOISIES
CRAMOISY
CRAMP
CRAMPED
CRAMPET
CRAMPETS
CRAMPIER
CRAMPIEST
CRAMPING
CRAMPIT
CRAMPITS
CRAMPON

CRAMPONS
CRAMPS
CRAMPY
CRAMS
CRAN
CRANAGE
CRANAGES
CRANBERRIES
CRANBERRY
CRANCH
CRANCHED
CRANCHES
CRANCHING
CRANE
CRANED
CRANES
CRANIA
CRANIAL
CRANING
CRANIUM
CRANIUMS
CRANK
CRANKCASE
CRANKCASES
CRANKED
CRANKER
CRANKEST
CRANKIER
CRANKIEST
CRANKILY
CRANKING
CRANKLE
CRANKLED
CRANKLES
CRANKLING
CRANKNESS
CRANKNESSES
CRANKS
CRANKY
CRANNIED
CRANNIES
CRANNOG
CRANNOGS
CRANNY
CRANNYING
CRANREUCH
CRANREUCHS
CRANS
CRANTS
CRANTSES
CRAP
CRAPE
CRAPED
CRAPES
CRAPIER
CRAPIEST
CRAPING
CRAPLE
CRAPLES
CRAPPED
CRAPPING
CRAPS
CRAPULENT
CRAPULOUS
CRAPY
CRARE
CRARES
CRASES
CRASH
CRASHED

CRASHES
CRASHING
CRASHPAD
CRASHPADS
CRASIS
CRASS
CRASSER
CRASSEST
CRASSLY
CRASSNESS
CRASSNESSES
CRATCH
CRATCHES
CRATE
CRATED
CRATER
CRATEROUS
CRATERS
CRATES
CRATING
CRATON
CRATONS
CRATUR
CRATURS
CRAUNCH
CRAUNCHED
CRAUNCHES
CRAUNCHING
CRAVAT
CRAVATS
CRAVATTED
CRAVATTING
CRAVE
CRAVED
CRAVEN
CRAVENLY
CRAVENS
CRAVER
CRAVERS
CRAVES
CRAVING
CRAVINGS
CRAW
CRAWFISH
CRAWFISHES
CRAWL
CRAWLED
CRAWLER
CRAWLERS
CRAWLIER
CRAWLIEST
CRAWLING
CRAWLINGS
CRAWLS
CRAWLY
CRAWS
CRAYER
CRAYERS
CRAYFISH
CRAYFISHES
CRAYON
CRAYONED
CRAYONING
CRAYONS
CRAZE
CRAZED
CRAZES
CRAZIER
CRAZIES
CRAZIEST

CRAZILY
CRAZINESS
CRAZINESSES
CRAZING
CRAZY
CREACH
CREACHS
CREAGH
CREAGHS
CREAK
CREAKED
CREAKIER
CREAKIEST
CREAKILY
CREAKING
CREAKS
CREAKY
CREAM
CREAMED
CREAMER
CREAMERIES
CREAMERS
CREAMERY
CREAMIER
CREAMIEST
CREAMING
CREAMS
CREAMY
CREANCE
CREANCES
CREANT
CREASE
CREASED
CREASES
CREASIER
CREASIEST
CREASING
CREASOTE
CREASOTED
CREASOTES
CREASOTING
CREASY
CREATABLE
CREATE
CREATED
CREATES
CREATIC
CREATINE
CREATINES
CREATING
CREATION
CREATIONS
CREATIVE
CREATOR
CREATORS
CREATRESS
CREATRESSES
CREATRIX
CREATRIXES
CREATURAL
CREATURE
CREATURES
CRÈCHE
CRÈCHES
CREDAL
CREDENCE
CREDENCES
CREDENDA
CREDENDUM
CREDENT

CREDENZA
CREDENZAS
CREDIBLE
CREDIBLY
CREDIT
CREDITED
CREDITING
CREDITOR
CREDITORS
CREDITS
CREDO
CREDOS
CREDULITIES
CREDULITY
CREDULOUS
CREE
CREED
CREEDAL
CREEDS
CREEING
CREEK
CREEKIER
CREEKIEST
CREEKS
CREEKY
CREEL
CREELS
CREEP
CREEPER
CREEPERED
CREEPERS
CREEPIE
CREEPIER
CREEPIES
CREEPIEST
CREEPING
CREEPS
CREEPY
CREES
CREESE
CREESED
CREESES
CREESH
CREESHED
CREESHES
CREESHING
CREESHY
CREESING
CREMASTER
CREMASTERS
CREMATE
CREMATED
CREMATES
CREMATING
CREMATION
CREMATIONS
CREMATOR
CREMATORIES
CREMATORS
CREMATORY
CRÈME
CRÊME
CRÈMES
CRÊMES
CREMOCARP
CREMOCARPS
CREMONA
CREMONAS
CREMOR
CREMORNE

CREMORNES
CREMORS
CREMOSIN
CREMSIN
CRENA
CRENAS
CRENATE
CRENATED
CRENATION
CRENATIONS
CRENATURE
CRENATURES
CRENEL
CRENELATE
CRENELATED
CRENELATES
CRENELATING
CRENELLED
CRENELLING
CRENELS
CRENULATE
CRENULATED
CREODONT
CREODONTS
CREOLE
CREOLES
CREOLIAN
CREOLIANS
CREOLIST
CREOLISTS
CREOSOTE
CREOSOTED
CREOSOTES
CREOSOTING
CREPANCE
CREPANCES
CRÊPE
CRÊPED
CRÊPES
CRÊPING
CREPITANT
CREPITATE
CREPITATED
CREPITATES
CREPITATING
CREPITUS
CREPITUSES
CREPOLINE
CREPOLINES
CREPON
CREPONS
CREPT
CREPUSCLE
CREPUSCLES
CRÊPY
CRESCENDO
CRESCENDOED
CRESCENDOING
CRESCENDOS
CRESCENT
CRESCENTS
CRESCIVE
CRESOL
CRESOLS
CRESS
CRESSES
CRESSET
CRESSETS
CRESSIER
CRESSIEST

CRESSY
CREST
CRESTED
CRESTING
CRESTLESS
CRESTS
CRETIC
CRETICS
CRETIN
CRETINISM
CRETINISMS
CRETINOID
CRETINOUS
CRETINS
CRETISM
CRETISMS
CRETONNE
CRETONNES
CREUTZER
CREUTZERS
CREVASSE
CREVASSED
CREVASSES
CREVASSING
CREVICE
CREVICES
CREW
CREWE
CREWED
CREWEL
CREWELIST
CREWELISTS
CREWELLED
CREWELLING
CREWELS
CREWES
CREWING
CREWS
CRIANT
CRIB
CRIBBAGE
CRIBBAGES
CRIBBED
CRIBBING
CRIBBLE
CRIBBLED
CRIBBLES
CRIBBLING
CRIBELLA
CRIBELLAR
CRIBELLUM
CRIBLÉ
CRIBRATE
CRIBROSE
CRIBS
CRIBWORK
CRIBWORKS
CRICK
CRICKED
CRICKET
CRICKETED
CRICKETER
CRICKETERS
CRICKETING
CRICKETINGS
CRICKETS
CRICKEY
CRICKING
CRICKS
CRICKY

CRICOID
CRICOIDS
CRIED
CRIER
CRIERS
CRIES
CRIKEY
CRIME
CRIMED
CRIMEFUL
CRIMELESS
CRIMES
CRIMINAL
CRIMINALS
CRIMINATE
CRIMINATED
CRIMINATES
CRIMINATING
CRIMINE
CRIMING
CRIMINI
CRIMINOUS
CRIMMER
CRIMMERS
CRIMP
CRIMPED
CRIMPER
CRIMPERS
CRIMPIER
CRIMPIEST
CRIMPING
CRIMPLE
CRIMPLED
CRIMPLES
CRIMPLING
CRIMPS
CRIMPY
CRIMSON
CRIMSONED
CRIMSONING
CRIMSONS
CRINAL
CRINATE
CRINATED
CRINE
CRINED
CRINES
CRINGE
CRINGED
CRINGER
CRINGERS
CRINGES
CRINGING
CRINGINGS
CRINGLE
CRINGLES
CRINING
CRINITE
CRINITES
CRINKLE
CRINKLED
CRINKLES
CRINKLIER
CRINKLIES
CRINKLIEST
CRINKLING
CRINKLY
CRINOID
CRINOIDAL
CRINOIDS

CRINOLINE	CROAKIEST	CROOK	CROSSER	CROUPIEST
CRINOLINES	CROAKILY	CROOKBACK	CROSSES	CROUPING
CRINOSE	CROAKING	CROOKBACKED	CROSSEST	CROUPON
CRINUM	CROAKINGS	CROOKBACKS	CROSSETTE	CROUPONS
CRINUMS	CROAKS	CROOKED	CROSSETTES	CROUPOUS
CRIOLLO	CROAKY	CROOKEDER	CROSSFALL	CROUPS
CRIOLLOS	CROC	CROOKEDEST	CROSSFALLS	CROUPY
CRIPES	CROCEATE	CROOKEDLY	CROSSFIRE	CROUSE
CRIPPLE	CROCEOUS	CROOKER	CROSSFIRES	CROUSELY
CRIPPLED	CROCHE	CROOKEST	CROSSFISH	CROUSTADE
CRIPPLES	CROCHES	CROOKING	CROSSFISHES	CROUSTADES
CRIPPLING	CROCHET	CROOKS	CROSSING	CROUT
CRIPPLINGS	CROCHETED	CROON	CROSSINGS	CROÛTE
CRISE	CROCHETING	CROONED	CROSSISH	CROÛTES
CRISES	CROCHETINGS	CROONER	CROSSJACK	CROÛTON
CRISIS	CROCHETS	CROONERS	CROSSJACKS	CROÛTONS
CRISP	CROCK	CROONING	CROSSLET	CROUTS
CRISPATE	CROCKED	CROONINGS	CROSSLETS	CROW
CRISPATED	CROCKERIES	CROONS	CROSSLY	CROWD
CRISPED	CROCKERY	CROP	CROSSNESS	CROWDED
CRISPER	CROCKET	CROPBOUND	CROSSNESSES	CROWDER
CRISPERS	CROCKETS	CROPFUL	CROSSOVER	CROWDERS
CRISPEST	CROCKING	CROPFULL	CROSSOVERS	CROWDIE
CRISPIER	CROCKS	CROPFULS	CROSSROAD	CROWDIES
CRISPIEST	CROCODILE	CROPLAND	CROSSROADS	CROWDING
CRISPIN	CROCODILES	CROPLANDS	CROSSTREE	CROWDS
CRISPING	CROCOITE	CROPPED	CROSSTREES	CROWED
CRISPINS	CROCOITES	CROPPER	CROSSWALK	CROWFOOT
CRISPLY	CROCS	CROPPERS	CROSSWALKS	CROWFOOTS
CRISPNESS	CROCUS	CROPPIES	CROSSWAY	CROWING
CRISPNESSES	CROCUSES	CROPPING	CROSSWAYS	CROWN
CRISPS	CROFT	CROPPINGS	CROSSWIND	CROWNED
CRISPY	CROFTER	CROPPY	CROSSWINDS	CROWNER
CRISSA	CROFTERS	CROPS	CROSSWISE	CROWNERS
CRISSUM	CROFTING	CROPSICK	CROSSWORD	CROWNET
CRISTA	CROFTINGS	CROQUET	CROSSWORDS	CROWNETS
CRISTAE	CROFTS	CROQUETED	CROSSWORT	CROWNING
CRISTATE	CROISSANT	CROQUETING	CROSSWORTS	CROWNINGS
CRIT	CROISSANTS	CROQUETS	CROST	CROWNLESS
CRITERIA	CROMACK	CROQUETTE	CROTAL	CROWNLET
CRITERION	CROMACKS	CROQUETTES	CROTALA	CROWNLETS
CRITH	CROMB	CROQUIS	CROTALINE	CROWNS
CRITHS	CROMBED	CRORE	CROTALISM	CROWNWORK
CRITIC	CROMBING	CRORES	CROTALISMS	CROWNWORKS
CRITICAL	CROMBS	CROSIER	CROTALS	CROWS
CRITICISE	CROME	CROSIERED	CROTALUM	CROZE
CRITICISED	CROMED	CROSIERS	CROTCH	CROZES
CRITICISES	CROMES	CROSS	CROTCHED	CROZIER
CRITICISING	CROMING	CROSSBAND	CROTCHES	CROZIERS
CRITICISM	CROMLECH	CROSSBANDS	CROTCHET	CRU
CRITICISMS	CROMLECHS	CROSSBAR	CROTCHETS	CRUBEEN
CRITICIZE	CROMORNA	CROSSBARS	CROTCHETY	CRUBEENS
CRITICIZED	CROMORNAS	CROSSBEAM	CROTON	CRUCES
CRITICIZES	CROMORNE	CROSSBEAMS	CROTONS	CRUCIAL
CRITICIZING	CROMORNES	CROSSBILL	CROTTLE	CRUCIAN
CRITICS	CRONE	CROSSBILLS	CROTTLES	CRUCIANS
CRITIQUE	CRONES	CROSSBIT	CROUCH	CRUCIATE
CRITIQUES	CRONET	CROSSBITE	CROUCHED	CRUCIATED
CRITS	CRONETS	CROSSBITES	CROUCHES	CRUCIATES
CRITTER	CRONIES	CROSSBITING	CROUCHING	CRUCIATING
CRITTERS	CRONK	CROSSBITTEN	CROUP	CRUCIBLE
CRITTUR	CRONKER	CROSSBOW	CROUPADE	CRUCIBLES
CRITTURS	CRONKEST	CROSSBOWS	CROUPADES	CRUCIFER
CRIVENS	CRONY	CROSSBRED	CROUPE	CRUCIFERS
CRIVVENS	CRONYISM	CROSSCUT	CROUPED	CRUCIFIED
CROAK	CRONYISMS	CROSSCUTS	CROUPER	CRUCIFIER
CROAKED	CROODLE	CROSSCUTTING	CROUPERS	CRUCIFIERS
CROAKER	CROODLED	CROSSCUTTINGS	CROUPES	CRUCIFIES
CROAKERS	CROODLES	CROSSE	CROUPIER	CRUCIFIX
CROAKIER	CROODLING	CROSSED	CROUPIERS	CRUCIFIXES

CRUCIFORM
CRUCIFY
CRUCIFYING
CRUCK
CRUCKS
CRUD
CRUDDIER
CRUDDIEST
CRUDDLE
CRUDDLED
CRUDDLES
CRUDDLING
CRUDDY
CRUDE
CRUDELY
CRUDENESS
CRUDENESSES
CRUDER
CRUDES
CRUDEST
CRUDITÉS
CRUDITIES
CRUDITY
CRUDS
CRUDY
CRUE
CRUEL
CRUELLER
CRUELLEST
CRUELLS
CRUELLY
CRUELNESS
CRUELNESSES
CRUELS
CRUELTIES
CRUELTY
CRUES
CRUET
CRUETS
CRUISE
CRUISED
CRUISER
CRUISERS
CRUISES
CRUISEWAY
CRUISEWAYS
CRUISIE
CRUISIES
CRUISING
CRUIVE
CRUIVES
CRULLER
CRULLERS
CRUMB
CRUMBED
CRUMBIER
CRUMBIEST
CRUMBING
CRUMBLE
CRUMBLED
CRUMBLES
CRUMBLIER
CRUMBLIES
CRUMBLIEST
CRUMBLING
CRUMBLY
CRUMBS
CRUMBY
CRUMEN
CRUMENAL

CRUMENALS
CRUMENS
CRUMHORN
CRUMHORNS
CRUMMACK
CRUMMACKS
CRUMMIER
CRUMMIES
CRUMMIEST
CRUMMOCK
CRUMMOCKS
CRUMMY
CRUMP
CRUMPED
CRUMPER
CRUMPEST
CRUMPET
CRUMPETS
CRUMPING
CRUMPLE
CRUMPLED
CRUMPLES
CRUMPLING
CRUMPLINGS
CRUMPS
CRUMPY
CRUNCH
CRUNCHED
CRUNCHES
CRUNCHIER
CRUNCHIEST
CRUNCHING
CRUNCHY
CRUNKLE
CRUNKLED
CRUNKLES
CRUNKLING
CRUOR
CRUORS
CRUPPER
CRUPPERS
CRURAL
CRUS
CRUSADE
CRUSADED
CRUSADER
CRUSADERS
CRUSADES
CRUSADING
CRUSADO
CRUSADOS
CRUSE
CRUSES
CRUSET
CRUSETS
CRUSH
CRUSHABLE
CRUSHED
CRUSHER
CRUSHERS
CRUSHES
CRUSHING
CRUSIAN
CRUSIANS
CRUSIE
CRUSIES
CRUST
CRUSTA
CRUSTAE
CRUSTAL

CRUSTATE
CRUSTATED
CRUSTED
CRUSTIER
CRUSTIEST
CRUSTILY
CRUSTING
CRUSTLESS
CRUSTS
CRUSTY
CRUSY
CRUTCH
CRUTCHED
CRUTCHES
CRUTCHING
CRUVE
CRUVES
CRUX
CRUXES
CRUZEIRO
CRUZEIROS
CRWTH
CRWTHS
CRY
CRYING
CRYINGS
CRYOGEN
CRYOGENIC
CRYOGENICS
CRYOGENIES
CRYOGENS
CRYOGENY
CRYOLITE
CRYOLITES
CRYOMETER
CRYOMETERS
CRYONIC
CRYONICS
CRYOPROBE
CRYOPROBES
CRYOSCOPE
CRYOSCOPES
CRYOSCOPIES
CRYOSCOPY
CRYOSTAT
CRYOSTATS
CRYOTRON
CRYOTRONS
CRYPT
CRYPTADIA
CRYPTAL
CRYPTIC
CRYPTICAL
CRYPTO
CRYPTOGAM
CRYPTOGAMS
CRYPTON
CRYPTONS
CRYPTONYM
CRYPTONYMS
CRYPTOS
CRYPTS
CRYSTAL
CRYSTALS
CSÁRDÁS
CSÁRDÁSES
CTENE
CTENES
CTENIFORM
CTENOID

CUB
CUBAGE
CUBAGES
CUBATURE
CUBATURES
CUBBED
CUBBIES
CUBBING
CUBBINGS
CUBBISH
CUBBY
CUBE
CUBEB
CUBEBS
CUBED
CUBES
CUBHOOD
CUBHOODS
CUBIC
CUBICA
CUBICAL
CUBICALLY
CUBICAS
CUBICLE
CUBICLES
CUBIFORM
CUBING
CUBISM
CUBISMS
CUBIST
CUBISTS
CUBIT
CUBITAL
CUBITS
CUBITUS
CUBITUSES
CUBLESS
CUBOID
CUBOIDAL
CUBOIDS
CUBS
CUCKOLD
CUCKOLDED
CUCKOLDING
CUCKOLDLY
CUCKOLDOM
CUCKOLDOMS
CUCKOLDRIES
CUCKOLDRY
CUCKOLDS
CUCKOLDY
CUCKOO
CUCKOOS
CUCULLATE
CUCUMBER
CUCUMBERS
CUCURBIT
CUCURBITS
CUD
CUDBEAR
CUDBEARS
CUDDEEHIH
CUDDEEHIHS
CUDDEN
CUDDENS
CUDDIE
CUDDIES
CUDDIN
CUDDINS
CUDDLE

CUDDLED
CUDDLES
CUDDLIER
CUDDLIEST
CUDDLING
CUDDLY
CUDDY
CUDGEL
CUDGELLED
CUDGELLER
CUDGELLERS
CUDGELLING
CUDGELLINGS
CUDGELS
CUDS
CUDWEED
CUDWEEDS
CUE
CUED
CUEING
CUEIST
CUEISTS
CUES
CUESTA
CUESTAS
CUFF
CUFFED
CUFFIN
CUFFING
CUFFINS
CUFFLE
CUFFLED
CUFFLES
CUFFLING
CUFFO
CUFFS
CUIF
CUIFS
CUING
CUIRASS
CUIRASSED
CUIRASSES
CUIRASSING
CUISH
CUISHES
CUISINE
CUISINES
CUISINIER
CUISINIERS
CUISSE
CUISSER
CUISSERS
CUISSES
CUIT
CUITER
CUITERED
CUITERING
CUITERS
CUITIKIN
CUITIKINS
CUITS
CUITTLE
CUITTLED
CUITTLES
CUITTLING
CULCH
CULCHES
CULET
CULETS
CULEX

CULICES
CULICID
CULICIDS
CULICINE
CULINARY
CULL
CULLED
CULLENDER
CULLENDERS
CULLER
CULLERS
CULLET
CULLETS
CULLIED
CULLIES
CULLING
CULLINGS
CULLION
CULLIONLY
CULLIONS
CULLIS
CULLISES
CULLS
CULLY
CULLYING
CULLYISM
CULLYISMS
CULM
CULMED
CULMEN
CULMENS
CULMINANT
CULMINATE
CULMINATED
CULMINATES
CULMINATING
CULMING
CULMS
CULOTTE
CULOTTES
CULPABLE
CULPABLY
CULPATORY
CULPRIT
CULPRITS
CULT
CULTCH
CULTCHES
CULTER
CULTERS
CULTIC
CULTIGEN
CULTIGENS
CULTISH
CULTISM
CULTISMS
CULTIST
CULTISTS
CULTIVAR
CULTIVARS
CULTIVATE
CULTIVATED
CULTIVATES
CULTIVATING
CULTORIST
CULTORISTS
CULTRATE
CULTRATED
CULTS
CULTURAL

CULTURE
CULTURED
CULTURES
CULTURING
CULTURIST
CULTURISTS
CULTUS
CULTUSES
CULVER
CULVERIN
CULVERINS
CULVERS
CULVERT
CULVERTS
CUM
CUMARIN
CUMARINS
CUMBENT
CUMBER
CUMBERED
CUMBERER
CUMBERERS
CUMBERING
CUMBERS
CUMBRANCE
CUMBRANCES
CUMBROUS
CUMEC
CUMECS
CUMIN
CUMINS
CUMMER
CUMMERS
CUMMIN
CUMMINS
CUMQUAT
CUMQUATS
CUMSHAW
CUMSHAWS
CUMULATE
CUMULATED
CUMULATES
CUMULATING
CUMULI
CUMULOSE
CUMULUS
CUNABULA
CUNCTATOR
CUNCTATORS
CUNEAL
CUNEATE
CUNEATIC
CUNEIFORM
CUNEIFORMS
CUNETTE
CUNETTES
CUNJEVOI
CUNJEVOIS
CUNNER
CUNNERS
CUNNING
CUNNINGLY
CUNNINGS
CUNT
CUNTS
CUP
CUPBEARER
CUPBEARERS
CUPBOARD
CUPBOARDED

CUPBOARDING
CUPBOARDS
CUPEL
CUPELLED
CUPELLING
CUPELS
CUPFUL
CUPFULS
CUPGALL
CUPGALLS
CUPHEAD
CUPHEADS
CUPID
CUPIDITIES
CUPIDITY
CUPIDS
CUPMAN
CUPMEN
CUPOLA
CUPOLAED
CUPOLAING
CUPOLAR
CUPOLAS
CUPOLATED
CUPPA
CUPPAS
CUPPED
CUPPER
CUPPERS
CUPPING
CUPPINGS
CUPREOUS
CUPRIC
CUPRITE
CUPRITES
CUPROUS
CUPS
CUPULAR
CUPULATE
CUPULE
CUPULES
CUR
CURABLE
CURAÇAO
CURAÇAOS
CURACIES
CURAÇOA
CURAÇOAS
CURACY
CURARA
CURARAS
CURARE
CURARES
CURARI
CURARINE
CURARINES
CURARIS
CURARISE
CURARISED
CURARISES
CURARISING
CURARIZE
CURARIZED
CURARIZES
CURARIZING
CURASSOW
CURASSOWS
CURAT
CURATE
CURATES

CURATIVE
CURATOR
CURATORS
CURATORY
CURATRIX
CURATRIXES
CURATS
CURB
CURBABLE
CURBED
CURBING
CURBLESS
CURBS
CURCH
CURCHES
CURCULIO
CURCULIOS
CURCUMA
CURCUMAS
CURCUMINE
CURCUMINES
CURD
CURDED
CURDIER
CURDIEST
CURDINESS
CURDINESSES
CURDING
CURDLE
CURDLED
CURDLES
CURDLING
CURDS
CURDY
CURE
CURÉ
CURED
CURELESS
CURER
CURERS
CURES
CURÉS
CURETTAGE
CURETTAGES
CURETTE
CURETTED
CURETTES
CURETTING
CURFEW
CURFEWS
CURFUFFLE
CURFUFFLED
CURFUFFLES
CURFUFFLING
CURIA
CURIAE
CURIALISM
CURIALISMS
CURIALIST
CURIALISTS
CURIAS
CURIE
CURIES
CURIET
CURIETS
CURING
CURIO
CURIOS
CURIOSA
CURIOSITIES

CURIOSITY
CURIOUS
CURIOUSER
CURIOUSLY
CURIUM
CURIUMS
CURL
CURLED
CURLER
CURLERS
CURLEW
CURLEWS
CURLICUE
CURLICUES
CURLIER
CURLIEST
CURLINESS
CURLINESSES
CURLING
CURLINGS
CURLS
CURLY
CURN
CURNEY
CURNIER
CURNIEST
CURNS
CURNY
CURPEL
CURPELS
CURR
CURRACH
CURRACHS
CURRAGH
CURRAGHS
CURRAJONG
CURRAJONGS
CURRANT
CURRANTS
CURRANTY
CURRAWONG
CURRAWONGS
CURRED
CURRENCIES
CURRENCY
CURRENT
CURRENTLY
CURRENTS
CURRICLE
CURRICLES
CURRICULA
CURRIE
CURRIED
CURRIER
CURRIERS
CURRIES
CURRING
CURRISH
CURRISHLY
CURRS
CURRY
CURRYING
CURRYINGS
CURS
CURSAL
CURSE
CURSED
CURSEDLY
CURSENARY
CURSER

CURSERS
CURSES
CURSING
CURSINGS
CURSITOR
CURSITORS
CURSITORY
CURSIVE
CURSIVELY
CURSOR
CURSORARY
CURSORES
CURSORIAL
CURSORILY
CURSORS
CURSORY
CURST
CURSTNESS
CURSTNESSES
CURSUS
CURSUSES
CURT
CURTAIL
CURTAILED
CURTAILING
CURTAILS
CURTAIN
CURTAINED
CURTAINING
CURTAINS
CURTAL
CURTALS
CURTANA
CURTANAS
CURTATE
CURTATION
CURTATIONS
CURTAXE
CURTAXES
CURTER
CURTEST
CURTILAGE
CURTILAGES
CURTLY
CURTNESS
CURTNESSES
CURTSEY
CURTSEYED
CURTSEYING
CURTSEYS
CURTSIED
CURTSIES
CURTSY
CURTSYING
CURULE
CURVATE
CURVATED
CURVATION
CURVATIONS
CURVATIVE
CURVATURE
CURVATURES
CURVE
CURVED
CURVES
CURVESOME
CURVET
CURVETED
CURVETING
CURVETS

CURVETTED
CURVETTING
CURVIER
CURVIEST
CURVIFORM
CURVING
CURVITAL
CURVITIES
CURVITY
CURVY
CUSCUS
CUSCUSES
CUSEC
CUSECS
CUSH
CUSHAT
CUSHATS
CUSHES
CUSHIER
CUSHIEST
CUSHION
CUSHIONED
CUSHIONET
CUSHIONETS
CUSHIONING
CUSHIONS
CUSHIONY
CUSHY
CUSK
CUSKS
CUSP
CUSPATE
CUSPED
CUSPID
CUSPIDAL
CUSPIDATE
CUSPIDOR
CUSPIDORE
CUSPIDORES
CUSPIDORS
CUSPS
CUSS
CUSSED
CUSSER
CUSSERS
CUSSES
CUSSING
CUSTARD
CUSTARDS
CUSTOCK
CUSTOCKS
CUSTODE
CUSTODES
CUSTODIAL
CUSTODIAN
CUSTODIANS
CUSTODIER
CUSTODIERS
CUSTODIES
CUSTODY
CUSTOM
CUSTOMARIES
CUSTOMARY
CUSTOMED
CUSTOMER
CUSTOMERS
CUSTOMISE
CUSTOMISED
CUSTOMISES
CUSTOMISING

CUSTOMIZE
CUSTOMIZED
CUSTOMIZES
CUSTOMIZING
CUSTOMS
CUSTOS
CUSTREL
CUSTRELS
CUSTUMARIES
CUSTUMARY
CUT
CUTANEOUS
CUTAWAY
CUTAWAYS
CUTBACK
CUTBACKS
CUTCH
CUTCHA
CUTCHERIES
CUTCHERRIES
CUTCHERRY
CUTCHERY
CUTCHES
CUTE
CUTER
CUTES
CUTESIER
CUTESIEST
CUTEST
CUTESY
CUTEY
CUTEYS
CUTICLE
CUTICLES
CUTICULAR
CUTIE
CUTIES
CUTIKIN
CUTIKINS
CUTIN
CUTINISE
CUTINISED
CUTINISES
CUTINISING
CUTINIZE
CUTINIZED
CUTINIZES
CUTINIZING
CUTINS
CUTIS
CUTISES
CUTLASS
CUTLASSES
CUTLER
CUTLERIES
CUTLERS
CUTLERY
CUTLET
CUTLETS
CUTLINE
CUTLINES
CUTPURSE
CUTPURSES
CUTS
CUTTER
CUTTERS
CUTTIER
CUTTIES
CUTTIEST
CUTTING

CUTTINGS
CUTTLE
CUTTLES
CUTTO
CUTTOE
CUTTOES
CUTTY
CUTWORM
CUTWORMS
CUVÉE
CUVÉES
CUVETTE
CUVETTES
CUZ
CUZZES
CWM
CWMS
CYAN
CYANAMIDE
CYANAMIDES
CYANATE
CYANATES
CYANIC
CYANIDE
CYANIDED
CYANIDES
CYANIDING
CYANIDINGS
CYANIN
CYANINE
CYANINES
CYANINS
CYANISE
CYANISED
CYANISES
CYANISING
CYANITE
CYANITES
CYANIZE
CYANIZED
CYANIZES
CYANIZING
CYANOGEN
CYANOGENS
CYANOSED
CYANOSES
CYANOSIS
CYANOTIC
CYANOTYPE
CYANOTYPES
CYANS
CYANURET
CYANURETS
CYATHI
CYATHIA
CYATHIUM
CYATHUS
CYATHUSES
CYCAD
CYCADS
CYCLAMATE
CYCLAMATES
CYCLAMEN
CYCLAMENS
CYCLE
CYCLED
CYCLER
CYCLERS
CYCLES
CYCLEWAY

CYCLEWAYS
CYCLIC
CYCLICAL
CYCLICISM
CYCLICISMS
CYCLICITIES
CYCLICITY
CYCLING
CYCLINGS
CYCLIST
CYCLISTS
CYCLO
CYCLOID
CYCLOIDAL
CYCLOIDS
CYCLOLITH
CYCLOLITHS
CYCLONE
CYCLONES
CYCLONIC
CYCLOPEAN
CYCLOPES
CYCLOPIAN
CYCLOPIC
CYCLOPS
CYCLORAMA
CYCLORAMAS
CYCLOS
CYCLOSES
CYCLOSIS
CYCLOTRON
CYCLOTRONS
CYCLUS
CYCLUSES
CYDER
CYDERS
CYESES
CYESIS
CYGNET
CYGNETS
CYLICES
CYLINDER
CYLINDERS
CYLINDRIC
CYLIX
CYMA
CYMAGRAPH
CYMAGRAPHS
CYMAR
CYMARS
CYMAS
CYMATIUM
CYMATIUMS
CYMBAL
CYMBALIST
CYMBALISTS
CYMBALO
CYMBALOES
CYMBALOS
CYMBALS
CYMBIDIA
CYMBIDIUM
CYMBIDIUMS
CYMBIFORM
CYME
CYMES
CYMOGRAPH
CYMOGRAPHS
CYMOID
CYMOPHANE

CYMOPHANES
CYMOSE
CYMOUS
CYNANCHE
CYNANCHES
CYNEGETIC
CYNIC
CYNICAL
CYNICALLY
CYNICISM
CYNICISMS
CYNICS
CYNOMOLGI
CYNOSURE
CYNOSURES
CYPHER
CYPHERED
CYPHERING
CYPHERS
CYPRESS

CYPRESSES
CYPRIAN
CYPRIANS
CYPRID
CYPRIDES
CYPRIDS
CYPRINE
CYPRINOID
CYPRIS
CYPRUS
CYPRUSES
CYST
CYSTIC
CYSTID
CYSTIDEAN
CYSTIDEANS
CYSTIDS
CYSTIFORM
CYSTITIS
CYSTITISES

CYSTOCARP
CYSTOCARPS
CYSTOCELE
CYSTOCELES
CYSTOID
CYSTOIDS
CYSTOLITH
CYSTOLITHS
CYSTOTOMIES
CYSTOTOMY
CYSTS
CYTASE
CYTASES
CYTE
CYTES
CYTISI
CYTISINE
CYTISINES
CYTISUS
CYTODE

CYTODES
CYTOID
CYTOKININ
CYTOKININS
CYTOLOGIES
CYTOLOGY
CYTOLYSES
CYTOLYSIS
CYTON
CYTONS
CYTOPLASM
CYTOPLASMS
CYTOSINE
CYTOSINES
CYTOTOXIC
CYTOTOXIN
CYTOTOXINS
CZAPKA
CZAPKAS
CZAR

CZARDAS
CZARDASES
CZARDOM
CZARDOMS
CZAREVICH
CZAREVICHES
CZAREVNA
CZAREVNAS
CZARINA
CZARINAS
CZARISM
CZARISMS
CZARIST
CZARISTS
CZARITZA
CZARITZAS
CZARS

D

DA
DAB
DABBED
DABBER
DABBERS
DABBING
DABBITIES
DABBITY
DABBLE
DABBLED
DABBLER
DABBLERS
DABBLES
DABBLING
DABBLINGS
DABCHICK
DABCHICKS
DABS
DABSTER
DABSTERS
DACE
DACES
DACHA
DACHAS
DACHSHUND
DACHSHUNDS
DACITE
DACITES
DACKER
DACKERED
DACKERING
DACKERS
DACOIT
DACOITAGE
DACOITAGES
DACOITIES
DACOITS
DACOITY
DACTYL
DACTYLAR
DACTYLIC
DACTYLIST
DACTYLISTS
DACTYLS
DAD
DADDED
DADDIES
DADDING
DADDLE
DADDLED
DADDLES
DADDLING
DADDOCK
DADDOCKS
DADDY
DADO
DADOED
DADOES
DADOING
DADOS
DADS
DAEDAL
DAEDALE
DAEDALIC

DAEMON
DAEMONIC
DAEMONS
DAFF
DAFFED
DAFFIER
DAFFIES
DAFFIEST
DAFFING
DAFFINGS
DAFFODIL
DAFFODILS
DAFFS
DAFFY
DAFT
DAFTAR
DAFTARS
DAFTER
DAFTEST
DAFTIE
DAFTIES
DAFTLY
DAFTNESS
DAFTNESSES
DAG
DAGABA
DAGABAS
DAGGA
DAGGAS
DAGGED
DAGGER
DAGGERS
DAGGING
DAGGLE
DAGGLED
DAGGLES
DAGGLING
DAGLOCK
DAGLOCKS
DAGO
DAGOBA
DAGOBAS
DAGOES
DAGS
DAGWOOD
DAGWOODS
DAH
DAHABEEAH
DAHABEEAHS
DAHABIEH
DAHABIEHS
DAHABIYAH
DAHABIYAHS
DAHABIYEH
DAHABIYEHS
DAHL
DAHLIA
DAHLIAS
DAHLS
DAHS
DAIDLE
DAIDLED
DAIDLES
DAIDLING

DAIKER
DAIKERED
DAIKERING
DAIKERS
DAIKON
DAIKONS
DAILIES
DAILY
DAIMEN
DAIMIO
DAIMIOS
DAIMON
DAIMONIC
DAIMONS
DAINE
DAINED
DAINES
DAINING
DAINT
DAINTIER
DAINTIES
DAINTIEST
DAINTILY
DAINTY
DAIQUIRI
DAIQUIRIS
DAIRIES
DAIRY
DAIRYING
DAIRYINGS
DAIRYMAID
DAIRYMAIDS
DAIRYMAN
DAIRYMEN
DAIS
DAISES
DAISIED
DAISIES
DAISY
DAK
DAKER
DAKERED
DAKERING
DAKERS
DAKOIT
DAKOITI
DAKOITIS
DAKOITS
DAKS
DAL
DALE
DALES
DALESMAN
DALESMEN
DALI
DALIS
DALLE
DALLES
DALLIANCE
DALLIANCES
DALLIED
DALLIER
DALLIERS
DALLIES

DALLOP
DALLOPS
DALLY
DALLYING
DALMAHOY
DALMAHOYS
DALMATIC
DALMATICS
DALS
DALT
DALTON
DALTONS
DALTS
DAM
DAMAGE
DAMAGED
DAMAGES
DAMAGING
DAMAN
DAMANS
DAMAR
DAMARS
DAMASCENE
DAMASCENED
DAMASCENES
DAMASCENING
DAMASCENINGS
DAMASK
DAMASKED
DAMASKEEN
DAMASKEENED
DAMASKEENING
DAMASKEENS
DAMASKIN
DAMASKINED
DAMASKING
DAMASKINING
DAMASKINS
DAMASKS
DAMASQUIN
DAMASQUINED
DAMASQUINING
DAMASQUINS
DAMASSIN
DAMASSINS
DAMBOARD
DAMBOARDS
DAMBROD
DAMBRODS
DAME
DAMES
DAMFOOL
DAMMAR
DAMMARS
DAMME
DAMMED
DAMMER
DAMMERS
DAMMING
DAMMIT
DAMN
DAMNABLE
DAMNABLY
DAMNATION

DAMNATIONS
DAMNATORY
DAMNED
DAMNEDER
DAMNEDEST
DAMNIFIED
DAMNIFIES
DAMNIFY
DAMNIFYING
DAMNING
DAMNS
DAMOISEL
DAMOISELS
DAMOSEL
DAMOSELS
DAMOZEL
DAMOZELS
DAMP
DAMPED
DAMPEN
DAMPENED
DAMPENING
DAMPENS
DAMPER
DAMPERS
DAMPEST
DAMPIER
DAMPIEST
DAMPING
DAMPINGS
DAMPISH
DAMPLY
DAMPNESS
DAMPNESSES
DAMPS
DAMPY
DAMS
DAMSEL
DAMSELFLIES
DAMSELFLY
DAMSELS
DAMSON
DAMSONS
DAN
DANCE
DANCEABLE
DANCED
DANCER
DANCERS
DANCES
DANCETTE
DANCETTÉ
DANCETTEE
DANCETTES
DANCETTY
DANCING
DANCINGS
DANDELION
DANDELIONS
DANDER
DANDERED
DANDERING
DANDERS
DANDIACAL

DANDIER
DANDIES
DANDIEST
DANDIFIED
DANDIFIES
DANDIFY
DANDIFYING
DANDILY
DANDIPRAT
DANDIPRATS
DANDLE
DANDLED
DANDLER
DANDLERS
DANDLES
DANDLING
DANDRIFF
DANDRIFFS
DANDRUFF
DANDRUFFS
DANDY
DANDYFUNK
DANDYFUNKS
DANDYISH
DANDYISM
DANDYISMS
DANDYPRAT
DANDYPRATS
DANEGELD
DANEGELDS
DANEGELT
DANEGELTS
DANELAGH
DANELAGHS
DANELAW
DANELAWS
DANG
DANGED
DANGER
DANGERED
DANGERING
DANGEROUS
DANGERS
DANGING
DANGLE
DANGLED
DANGLER
DANGLERS
DANGLES
DANGLING
DANGLINGS
DANGS
DANIO
DANIOS
DANK
DANKER
DANKEST
DANKISH
DANKNESS
DANKNESSES
DANKS
DANNEBROG
DANNEBROGS
DANS
DANSEUR
DANSEURS
DANSEUSE
DANSEUSES
DANT
DANTED

DANTING
DANTON
DANTONED
DANTONING
DANTONS
DANTS
DAP
DAPHNE
DAPHNES
DAPHNID
DAPHNIDS
DAPPED
DAPPER
DAPPERER
DAPPEREST
DAPPERLY
DAPPERS
DAPPING
DAPPLE
DAPPLED
DAPPLES
DAPPLING
DAPS
DAPSONE
DAPSONES
DARAF
DARAFS
DARBIES
DARE
DARED
DAREFUL
DARES
DARG
DARGA
DARGAS
DARGLE
DARGLES
DARGS
DARI
DARIC
DARICS
DARING
DARINGLY
DARINGS
DARIOLE
DARIOLES
DARIS
DARK
DARKEN
DARKENED
DARKENING
DARKENS
DARKER
DARKEST
DARKEY
DARKEYS
DARKIE
DARKIES
DARKISH
DARKLE
DARKLED
DARKLES
DARKLING
DARKLINGS
DARKLY
DARKMANS
DARKNESS
DARKNESSES
DARKROOM
DARKROOMS

DARKS
DARKSOME
DARKY
DARLING
DARLINGS
DARN
DARNED
DARNEDER
DARNEDEST
DARNEL
DARNELS
DARNER
DARNERS
DARNING
DARNINGS
DARNS
DARRAIGN
DARRAIGNE
DARRAIGNED
DARRAIGNES
DARRAIGNING
DARRAIGNS
DARRAIN
DARRAINE
DARRAINED
DARRAINES
DARRAINING
DARRAINS
DARRAYN
DARRAYNED
DARRAYNING
DARRAYNS
DARRE
DARRED
DARRES
DARRING
DARSHAN
DARSHANS
DART
DARTED
DARTER
DARTERS
DARTING
DARTINGLY
DARTLE
DARTLED
DARTLES
DARTLING
DARTRE
DARTRES
DARTROUS
DARTS
DARZI
DARZIS
DAS
DASH
DASHBOARD
DASHBOARDS
DASHED
DASHEEN
DASHEENS
DASHEKI
DASHEKIS
DASHER
DASHERS
DASHES
DASHIKI
DASHIKIS
DASHING
DASHINGLY

DASSIE
DASSIES
DASTARD
DASTARDIES
DASTARDLY
DASTARDS
DASTARDY
DASYPOD
DASYPODS
DASYURE
DASYURES
DATA
DATABANK
DATABANKS
DATABASE
DATABASES
DATABLE
DATABUS
DATABUSES
DATABUSSES
DATAL
DATALLER
DATALLERS
DATARIA
DATARIAS
DATARIES
DATARY
DATE
DATEABLE
DATED
DATELESS
DATER
DATERS
DATES
DATING
DATINGS
DATIVAL
DATIVE
DATIVES
DATOLITE
DATOLITES
DATUM
DATURA
DATURAS
DATURINE
DATURINES
DAUB
DAUBE
DAUBED
DAUBER
DAUBERIES
DAUBERS
DAUBERY
DAUBES
DAUBIER
DAUBIEST
DAUBING
DAUBINGS
DAUBS
DAUBY
DAUD
DAUDED
DAUDING
DAUDS
DAUGHTER
DAUGHTERS
DAULT
DAULTS
DAUNDER
DAUNDERED

DAUNDERING
DAUNDERS
DAUNER
DAUNERED
DAUNERING
DAUNERS
DAUNT
DAUNTED
DAUNTER
DAUNTERS
DAUNTING
DAUNTLESS
DAUNTON
DAUNTONED
DAUNTONING
DAUNTONS
DAUNTS
DAUPHIN
DAUPHINE
DAUPHINES
DAUPHINS
DAUR
DAURED
DAURING
DAURS
DAUT
DAUTED
DAUTIE
DAUTIES
DAUTING
DAUTS
DAVENPORT
DAVENPORTS
DAVIT
DAVITS
DAW
DAWBRIES
DAWBRY
DAWCOCK
DAWCOCKS
DAWD
DAWDED
DAWDING
DAWDLE
DAWDLED
DAWDLER
DAWDLERS
DAWDLES
DAWDLING
DAWDS
DAWED
DAWING
DAWISH
DAWK
DAWKS
DAWN
DAWNED
DAWNER
DAWNERED
DAWNERING
DAWNERS
DAWNING
DAWNINGS
DAWNS
DAWS
DAWT
DAWTED
DAWTIE
DAWTIES
DAWTING

DAWTS
DAY
DAYBREAK
DAYBREAKS
DAYDREAM
DAYDREAMED
DAYDREAMING
DAYDREAMS
DAYDREAMT
DAYGLO
DAYLIGHT
DAYLIGHTS
DAYLONG
DAYMARK
DAYMARKS
DAYNT
DAYS
DAYSMAN
DAYSMEN
DAYSPRING
DAYSPRINGS
DAYSTAR
DAYSTARS
DAYTALE
DAYTALER
DAYTALERS
DAYTALES
DAYTIME
DAYTIMES
DAZE
DAZED
DAZEDLY
DAZES
DAZING
DAZZLE
DAZZLED
DAZZLER
DAZZLERS
DAZZLES
DAZZLING
DAZZLINGS
DEACON
DEACONESS
DEACONESSES
DEACONRIES
DEACONRY
DEACONS
DEAD
DEADED
DEADEN
DEADENED
DEADENER
DEADENERS
DEADENING
DEADENINGS
DEADENS
DEADER
DEADERS
DEADEST
DEADHOUSE
DEADHOUSES
DEADING
DEADLIER
DEADLIEST
DEADLINE
DEADLINES
DEADLOCK
DEADLOCKED
DEADLOCKING
DEADLOCKS

DEADLY
DEADNESS
DEADNESSES
DEADPAN
DEADPANS
DEADS
DEAF
DEAFEN
DEAFENED
DEAFENING
DEAFENINGS
DEAFENS
DEAFER
DEAFEST
DEAFLY
DEAFNESS
DEAFNESSES
DEAL
DEALBATE
DEALER
DEALERS
DEALFISH
DEALFISHES
DEALING
DEALINGS
DEALS
DEALT
DEAN
DEANER
DEANERIES
DEANERS
DEANERY
DEANS
DEANSHIP
DEANSHIPS
DEAR
DEARE
DEARED
DEARER
DEARES
DEAREST
DEARIE
DEARIES
DEARING
DEARLING
DEARLINGS
DEARLY
DEARN
DEARNESS
DEARNESSES
DEARNFUL
DEARNLY
DEARNS
DEARS
DEARTH
DEARTHS
DEARY
DEASIL
DEASILS
DEASIUL
DEASIULS
DEASOIL
DEASOILS
DEATH
DEATHFUL
DEATHLESS
DEATHLIER
DEATHLIEST
DEATHLIKE
DEATHLY

DEATHS
DEATHSMAN
DEATHSMEN
DEATHWARD
DEATHWARDS
DEATHY
DEAVE
DEAVED
DEAVES
DEAVING
DEAW
DEAWIE
DEAWS
DEAWY
DEB
DEBACLE
DÉBÂCLE
DEBACLES
DÉBÂCLES
DEBAG
DEBAGGED
DEBAGGING
DEBAGGINGS
DEBAGS
DEBAR
DEBARK
DEBARKED
DEBARKING
DEBARKS
DEBARMENT
DEBARMENTS
DEBARRASS
DEBARRASSED
DEBARRASSES
DEBARRASSING
DEBARRED
DEBARRING
DEBARS
DEBASE
DEBASED
DEBASER
DEBASERS
DEBASES
DEBASING
DEBATABLE
DEBATE
DEBATED
DEBATEFUL
DEBATER
DEBATERS
DEBATES
DEBATING
DEBAUCH
DEBAUCHED
DEBAUCHEE
DEBAUCHEES
DEBAUCHER
DEBAUCHERS
DEBAUCHES
DEBAUCHING
DEBBIES
DEBBY
DEBEL
DEBELLED
DEBELLING
DEBELS
DEBENTURE
DEBENTURES
DEBILE
DEBILITIES

DEBILITY
DEBIT
DEBITED
DEBITING
DEBITOR
DEBITORS
DEBITS
DEBONAIR
DEBOSH
DEBOSHED
DEBOSHES
DEBOSHING
DEBOUCH
DÉBOUCHÉ
DEBOUCHED
DÉBOUCHÉS
DEBOUCHES
DEBOUCHING
DEBRIDE
DEBRIDED
DEBRIDES
DEBRIDING
DEBRIEF
DEBRIEFED
DEBRIEFING
DEBRIEFS
DEBRIS
DEBRUISED
DEBS
DEBT
DEBTED
DEBTEE
DEBTEES
DEBTOR
DEBTORS
DEBTS
DEBUG
DEBUGGED
DEBUGGING
DEBUGS
DEBUNK
DEBUNKED
DEBUNKING
DEBUNKS
DEBUS
DEBUSES
DEBUSSED
DEBUSSES
DEBUSSING
DÉBUT
DÉBUTANT
DEBUTANTE
DEBUTANTES
DÉBUTANTS
DÉBUTS
DECACHORD
DECACHORDS
DECAD
DECADAL
DECADE
DECADENCE
DECADENCES
DECADENCIES
DECADENCY
DECADENT
DECADENTS
DECADES
DECADS
DECAGON
DECAGONAL

DECAGONS
DECAGRAM
DECAGRAMS
DECAL
DECALCIFIED
DECALCIFIES
DECALCIFY
DECALCIFYING
DECALITRE
DECALITRES
DECALOGUE
DECALOGUES
DECALS
DECAMETRE
DECAMETRES
DECAMP
DECAMPED
DECAMPING
DECAMPS
DECANAL
DECANE
DECANES
DECANI
DECANT
DECANTATE
DECANTATED
DECANTATES
DECANTATING
DECANTED
DECANTER
DECANTERS
DECANTING
DECANTS
DECAPOD
DECAPODAL
DECAPODAN
DECAPODS
DECARB
DECARBED
DECARBING
DECARBS
DECARE
DECARES
DECASTERE
DECASTERES
DECASTICH
DECASTICHS
DECASTYLE
DECASTYLES
DECATHLON
DECATHLONS
DECAUDATE
DECAUDATED
DECAUDATES
DECAUDATING
DECAY
DECAYED
DECAYING
DECAYS
DECCIE
DECCIES
DECEASE
DECEASED
DECEASES
DECEASING
DECEDENT
DECEDENTS
DECEIT
DECEITFUL
DECEITS

DECEIVE
DECEIVED
DECEIVER
DECEIVERS
DECEIVES
DECEIVING
DECEMVIR
DECEMVIRI
DECEMVIRS
DECENCIES
DECENCY
DECENNARIES
DECENNARY
DECENNIA
DECENNIAL
DECENNIUM
DECENNIUMS
DECENT
DECENTLY
DECEPTION
DECEPTIONS
DECEPTIVE
DECEPTORY
DECERN
DECERNED
DECERNING
DECERNS
DECESSION
DECESSIONS
DÉCHÉANCE
DÉCHÉANCES
DECIARE
DECIARES
DECIBEL
DECIBELS
DECIDABLE
DECIDE
DECIDED
DECIDEDLY
DECIDER
DECIDERS
DECIDES
DECIDING
DECIDUA
DECIDUAL
DECIDUAS
DECIDUATE
DECIDUOUS
DECIGRAM
DECIGRAMS
DECILITRE
DECILITRES
DECILLION
DECILLIONS
DECIMAL
DECIMALLY
DECIMALS
DECIMATE
DECIMATED
DECIMATES
DECIMATING
DECIMATOR
DECIMATORS
DÉCIME
DÉCIMES
DECIMETRE
DECIMETRES
DECIPHER
DECIPHERED
DECIPHERING

DECIPHERS
DECISION
DECISIONS
DECISIVE
DECISORY
DECISTERE
DECISTERES
DECK
DECKCHAIR
DECKCHAIRS
DECKED
DECKER
DECKERS
DECKING
DECKINGS
DECKLE
DECKLED
DECKLES
DECKO
DECKOED
DECKOING
DECKOS
DECKS
DECLAIM
DECLAIMED
DECLAIMER
DECLAIMERS
DECLAIMING
DECLAIMS
DECLARANT
DECLARANTS
DECLARE
DECLARED
DECLARER
DECLARERS
DECLARES
DECLARING
DECLASS
DÉCLASSÉ
DECLASSED
DÉCLASSÉE
DECLASSES
DECLASSING
DECLINAL
DECLINANT
DECLINATE
DECLINE
DECLINED
DECLINES
DECLINING
DECLIVITIES
DECLIVITY
DECLIVOUS
DECLUTCH
DECLUTCHED
DECLUTCHES
DECLUTCHING
DECO
DECOCT
DECOCTED
DECOCTING
DECOCTION
DECOCTIONS
DECOCTIVE
DECOCTS
DECOCTURE
DECOCTURES
DECODE
DECODED
DECODER

DECODERS
DECODES
DECODING
DECOHERER
DECOHERERS
DECOKE
DECOKED
DECOKES
DECOKING
DECOLLATE
DECOLLATED
DECOLLATES
DECOLLATING
DÉCOLLETÉ
DECOLOR
DECOLORED
DECOLORING
DECOLORS
DECOLOUR
DECOLOURED
DECOLOURING
DECOLOURS
DECOMPLEX
DECOMPOSE
DECOMPOSED
DECOMPOSES
DECOMPOSING
DECONGEST
DECONGESTED
DECONGESTING
DECONGESTS
DECONTROL
DECONTROLLED
DECONTROLLING
DECONTROLS
DÉCOR
DECORATE
DECORATED
DECORATES
DECORATING
DECORATOR
DECORATORS
DECOROUS
DÉCORS
DECORUM
DECORUMS
DECOUPAGE
DECOUPAGES
DECOUPLE
DECOUPLED
DECOUPLES
DECOUPLING
DECOUPLINGS
DECOY
DECOYED
DECOYING
DECOYS
DECREASE
DECREASED
DECREASES
DECREASING
DECREE
DECREED
DECREEING
DECREES
DECREET
DECREETS
DECREMENT
DECREMENTED
DECREMENTING

DECREMENTS
DECODES
DECREPIT
DECRETAL
DECRETALS
DECRETIST
DECRETISTS
DECRETIVE
DECRETORY
DECREW
DECREWED
DECREWING
DECREWS
DECRIAL
DECRIALS
DECRIED
DECRIER
DECRIERS
DECRIES
DECROWN
DECROWNED
DECROWNING
DECROWNS
DECRY
DECRYING
DECRYPT
DECRYPTED
DECRYPTING
DECRYPTS
DECTET
DECTETS
DECUBITI
DECUBITUS
DECUMAN
DECUMANS
DECUMBENT
DECUPLE
DECUPLED
DECUPLES
DECUPLING
DECURIA
DECURIAS
DECURIES
DECURION
DECURIONS
DECURRENT
DECURSION
DECURSIONS
DECURSIVE
DECURVE
DECURVED
DECURVES
DECURVING
DECURY
DECUSSATE
DECUSSATED
DECUSSATES
DECUSSATING
DEDAL
DEDALIAN
DEDANS
DEDICANT
DEDICANTS
DEDICATE
DEDICATED
DEDICATEE
DEDICATEES
DEDICATES
DEDICATING
DEDICATOR
DEDICATORS

DEDIMUS
DEDIMUSES
DEDUCE
DEDUCED
DEDUCES
DEDUCIBLE
DEDUCING
DEDUCT
DEDUCTED
DEDUCTING
DEDUCTION
DEDUCTIONS
DEDUCTIVE
DEDUCTS
DEE
DEED
DEEDED
DEEDER
DEEDEST
DEEDFUL
DEEDIER
DEEDIEST
DEEDILY
DEEDING
DEEDLESS
DEEDS
DEEDY
DEEING
DEEJAY
DEEJAYED
DEEJAYING
DEEJAYS
DEEM
DEEMED
DEEMING
DEEMS
DEEMSTER
DEEMSTERS
DEEN
DEENS
DEEP
DEEPEN
DEEPENED
DEEPENING
DEEPENS
DEEPER
DEEPEST
DEEPFELT
DEEPIE
DEEPIES
DEEPLY
DEEPMOST
DEEPNESS
DEEPNESSES
DEEPS
DEER
DEERBERRIES
DEERBERRY
DEERE
DEERHORN
DEERHORNS
DEERLET
DEERLETS
DEERSKIN
DEERSKINS
DEES
DEEV
DEEVE
DEEVED
DEEVES

DEEVING
DEEVS
DEFACE
DEFACED
DEFACER
DEFACERS
DEFACES
DEFACING
DEFAECATE
DEFAECATED
DEFAECATES
DEFAECATING
DEFALCATE
DEFALCATED
DEFALCATES
DEFALCATING
DEFAME
DEFAMED
DEFAMES
DEFAMING
DEFAMINGS
DEFAST
DEFASTE
DEFAT
DEFATS
DEFATTED
DEFATTING
DEFAULT
DEFAULTED
DEFAULTER
DEFAULTERS
DEFAULTING
DEFAULTS
DEFEAT
DEFEATED
DEFEATING
DEFEATISM
DEFEATISMS
DEFEATIST
DEFEATISTS
DEFEATS
DEFEATURE
DEFEATURES
DEFECATE
DEFECATED
DEFECATES
DEFECATING
DEFECATOR
DEFECATORS
DEFECT
DEFECTED
DEFECTING
DEFECTION
DEFECTIONS
DEFECTIVE
DEFECTIVES
DEFECTOR
DEFECTORS
DEFECTS
DEFENCE
DEFENCED
DEFENCES
DEFEND
DEFENDANT
DEFENDANTS
DEFENDED
DEFENDER
DEFENDERS
DEFENDING
DEFENDS

DEFENSE
DEFENSES
DEFENSIVE
DEFENSIVES
DEFER
DEFERABLE
DEFERENCE
DEFERENCES
DEFERENT
DEFERENTS
DEFERMENT
DEFERMENTS
DEFERRAL
DEFERRALS
DEFERRED
DEFERRER
DEFERRERS
DEFERRING
DEFERS
DEFFLY
DEFIANCE
DEFIANCES
DEFIANT
DEFIANTLY
DEFICIENT
DEFICIENTS
DEFICIT
DEFICITS
DEFIED
DEFIER
DEFIERS
DEFIES
DEFILADE
DEFILADED
DEFILADES
DEFILADING
DEFILE
DEFILED
DEFILER
DEFILERS
DEFILES
DEFILING
DEFINABLE
DEFINABLY
DEFINE
DEFINED
DEFINER
DEFINERS
DEFINES
DEFINING
DEFINITE
DEFLATE
DEFLATED
DEFLATER
DEFLATERS
DEFLATES
DEFLATING
DEFLATION
DEFLATIONS
DEFLATOR
DEFLATORS
DEFLECT
DEFLECTED
DEFLECTING
DEFLECTOR
DEFLECTORS
DEFLECTS
DEFLEX
DEFLEXED
DEFLEXES

DEFLEXING
DEFLEXION
DEFLEXIONS
DEFLEXURE
DEFLEXURES
DEFLORATE
DEFLORATED
DEFLORATES
DEFLORATING
DEFLOWER
DEFLOWERED
DEFLOWERING
DEFLOWERS
DEFLUENT
DEFLUXION
DEFLUXIONS
DEFOLIANT
DEFOLIANTS
DEFOLIATE
DEFOLIATED
DEFOLIATES
DEFOLIATING
DEFORCE
DEFORCED
DEFORCES
DEFORCING
DEFOREST
DEFORESTED
DEFORESTING
DEFORESTS
DEFORM
DEFORMED
DEFORMER
DEFORMERS
DEFORMING
DEFORMITIES
DEFORMITY
DEFORMS
DEFOUL
DEFOULED
DEFOULING
DEFOULS
DEFRAUD
DEFRAUDED
DEFRAUDER
DEFRAUDERS
DEFRAUDING
DEFRAUDS
DEFRAY
DEFRAYAL
DEFRAYALS
DEFRAYED
DEFRAYER
DEFRAYERS
DEFRAYING
DEFRAYS
DEFREEZE
DEFREEZES
DEFREEZING
DEFROCK
DEFROCKED
DEFROCKING
DEFROCKS
DEFROST
DEFROSTED
DEFROSTER
DEFROSTERS
DEFROSTING
DEFROSTS
DEFROZE

DEFROZEN
DEFT
DEFTER
DEFTEST
DEFTLY
DEFTNESS
DEFTNESSES
DEFUNCT
DEFUNCTS
DEFUSE
DEFUSED
DEFUSES
DEFUSING
DEFUZE
DEFUZED
DEFUZES
DEFUZING
DEFY
DEFYING
DÉGAGÉ
DEGARNISH
DEGARNISHED
DEGARNISHES
DEGARNISHING
DEGAS
DEGASES
DEGASSED
DEGASSING
DEGAUSS
DEGAUSSED
DEGAUSSES
DEGAUSSING
DEGENDER
DEGENDERED
DEGENDERING
DEGENDERS
DÉGOÛT
DÉGOÛTS
DEGRADE
DEGRADED
DEGRADES
DEGRADING
DEGRAS
DEGREASE
DEGREASED
DEGREASES
DEGREASING
DEGREE
DEGREES
DEGUM
DEGUMMED
DEGUMMING
DEGUMS
DEGUST
DEGUSTATE
DEGUSTATED
DEGUSTATES
DEGUSTATING
DEGUSTED
DEGUSTING
DEGUSTS
DEHISCE
DEHISCED
DEHISCENT
DEHISCES
DEHISCING
DEHORN
DEHORNED
DEHORNER
DEHORNERS

DEHORNING
DEHORNS
DEHORT
DEHORTED
DEHORTER
DEHORTERS
DEHORTING
DEHORTS
DEHYDRATE
DEHYDRATED
DEHYDRATES
DEHYDRATING
DEI
DEICIDAL
DEICIDE
DEICIDES
DEICTIC
DEICTICS
DEID
DEIDER
DEIDEST
DEIDS
DEIFIC
DEIFICAL
DEIFIED
DEIFIER
DEIFIERS
DEIFIES
DEIFORM
DEIFY
DEIFYING
DEIGN
DEIGNED
DEIGNING
DEIGNS
DEIL
DEILED
DEILING
DEILS
DEINOSAUR
DEINOSAURS
DEIPAROUS
DEISEAL
DEISEALS
DEISHEAL
DEISHEALS
DEISM
DEISMS
DEIST
DEISTIC
DEISTICAL
DEISTS
DEITIES
DEITY
DEIXES
DEIXIS
DEJECT
DEJECTA
DEJECTED
DEJECTING
DEJECTION
DEJECTIONS
DEJECTORY
DEJECTS
DEJEUNE
DÉJEUNER
DÉJEUNERS
DEJEUNES
DEKALOGIES
DEKALOGY

DEKKO
DEKKOED
DEKKOING
DEKKOS
DEL
DELAINE
DELAINES
DELAPSE
DELAPSED
DELAPSES
DELAPSING
DELAPSION
DELAPSIONS
DELATE
DELATED
DELATES
DELATING
DELATION
DELATIONS
DELATOR
DELATORS
DELAY
DELAYED
DELAYER
DELAYERS
DELAYING
DELAYS
DELE
DELEBLE
DELED
DELEGABLE
DELEGACIES
DELEGACY
DELEGATE
DELEGATED
DELEGATES
DELEGATING
DELEING
DELENDA
DELES
DELETE
DELETED
DELETES
DELETING
DELETION
DELETIONS
DELETIVE
DELETORY
DELF
DELFS
DELFT
DELFTS
DELI
DELIBATE
DELIBATED
DELIBATES
DELIBATING
DELIBLE
DELICACIES
DELICACY
DELICATE
DELICATES
DELICE
DELICES
DELICIOUS
DELICT
DELICTS
DELIGHT
DELIGHTED
DELIGHTING
DELIGHTS

DELIMIT
DELIMITED
DELIMITING
DELIMITS
DELINEATE
DELINEATED
DELINEATES
DELINEATING
DELIQUIUM
DELIQUIUMS
DELIRIA
DELIRIANT
DELIRIANTS
DELIRIOUS
DELIRIUM
DELIRIUMS
DELIS
DELIVER
DELIVERED
DELIVERER
DELIVERERS
DELIVERIES
DELIVERING
DELIVERLY
DELIVERS
DELIVERY
DELL
DELLS
DELOUSE
DELOUSED
DELOUSES
DELOUSING
DELPH
DELPHIAN
DELPHIC
DELPHIN
DELPHINIA
DELPHS
DELS
DELTA
DELTAIC
DELTAS
DELTOID
DELUBRUM
DELUBRUMS
DELUDABLE
DELUDE
DELUDED
DELUDER
DELUDERS
DELUDES
DELUDING
DELUGE
DELUGED
DELUGES
DELUGING
DELUNDUNG
DELUNDUNGS
DELUSION
DELUSIONS
DELUSIVE
DELUSORY
DELVE
DELVED
DELVER
DELVERS
DELVES
DELVING
DEMAGOGIC
DEMAGOGIES
DEMAGOGUE

DEMAGOGUES
DEMAGOGY
DEMAIN
DEMAINE
DEMAINES
DEMAINS
DEMAN
DEMAND
DEMANDANT
DEMANDANTS
DEMANDED
DEMANDER
DEMANDERS
DEMANDING
DEMANDS
DEMANNED
DEMANNING
DEMANNINGS
DEMANS
DEMARCATE
DEMARCATED
DEMARCATES
DEMARCATING
DÉMARCHE
DÉMARCHES
DEMARK
DEMARKED
DEMARKING
DEMARKS
DEMAYNE
DEMAYNES
DEME
DEMEAN
DEMEANE
DEMEANED
DEMEANES
DEMEANING
DEMEANOR
DEMEANORS
DEMEANOUR
DEMEANOURS
DEMEANS
DEMENT
DEMENTATE
DEMENTATED
DEMENTATES
DEMENTATING
DEMENTED
DÉMENTI
DEMENTIA
DEMENTIAS
DEMENTING
DÉMENTIS
DEMENTS
DEMERARA
DEMERARAS
DEMERGE
DEMERGED
DEMERGER
DEMERGERS
DEMERGES
DEMERGING
DEMERIT
DEMERITS
DEMERSAL
DEMERSE
DEMERSED
DEMERSES
DEMERSING
DEMERSION

DEMERSIONS
DEMES
DEMESNE
DEMESNES
DEMIC
DEMIES
DEMIGOD
DEMIGODS
DEMIJOHN
DEMIJOHNS
DEMIPIQUE
DEMIPIQUES
DEMIREP
DEMIREPS
DEMISABLE
DEMISE
DEMISED
DEMISES
DEMISING
DEMISS
DEMISSION
DEMISSIONS
DEMISSIVE
DEMISSLY
DEMIST
DEMISTED
DEMISTER
DEMISTERS
DEMISTING
DEMISTS
DEMIT
DEMITASSE
DEMITASSES
DEMITS
DEMITTED
DEMITTING
DEMIURGE
DEMIURGES
DEMIURGIC
DEMIURGUS
DEMIURGUSES
DEMO
DEMOB
DEMOBBED
DEMOBBING
DEMOBS
DEMOCRACIES
DEMOCRACY
DEMOCRAT
DEMOCRATIES
DEMOCRATS
DEMOCRATY
DÉMODÉ
DEMODED
DEMOLISH
DEMOLISHED
DEMOLISHES
DEMOLISHING
DEMOLOGIES
DEMOLOGY
DEMON
DEMONESS
DEMONESSES
DEMONIAC
DEMONIACS
DEMONIAN
DEMONIC
DEMONISE
DEMONISED
DEMONISES

DEMONISING
DEMONISM
DEMONISMS
DEMONIST
DEMONISTS
DEMONIZE
DEMONIZED
DEMONIZES
DEMONIZING
DEMONRIES
DEMONRY
DEMONS
DEMOS
DEMOSES
DEMOTE
DEMOTED
DEMOTES
DEMOTIC
DEMOTING
DEMOTION
DEMOTIONS
DEMOTIST
DEMOTISTS
DEMOUNT
DEMOUNTED
DEMOUNTING
DEMOUNTS
DEMPSTER
DEMPSTERS
DEMPT
DEMULCENT
DEMULCENTS
DEMULSIFIED
DEMULSIFIES
DEMULSIFY
DEMULSIFYING
DEMUR
DEMURE
DEMURED
DEMURELY
DEMURER
DEMURES
DEMUREST
DEMURING
DEMURRAGE
DEMURRAGES
DEMURRAL
DEMURRALS
DEMURRED
DEMURRER
DEMURRERS
DEMURRING
DEMURS
DEMY
DEMYSHIP
DEMYSHIPS
DEMYSTIFIED
DEMYSTIFIES
DEMYSTIFY
DEMYSTIFYING
DEN
DENARIES
DENARII
DENARIUS
DENARY
DENATURE
DENATURED
DENATURES
DENATURING
DENAY

DENAYED	DENSIFIER	DEODORISING	DEPILATORS	DEPREHENDING
DENAYING	DENSIFIERS	DEODORIZE	DEPLANE	DEPREHENDS
DENAYS	DENSIFIES	DEODORIZED	DEPLANED	DEPRESS
DENAZIFIED	DENSIFY	DEODORIZES	DEPLANES	DEPRESSED
DENAZIFIES	DENSIFYING	DEODORIZING	DEPLANING	DEPRESSES
DENAZIFY	DENSITIES	DEONTIC	DEPLETE	DEPRESSING
DENAZIFYING	DENSITY	DEONTICS	DEPLETED	DEPRESSOR
DENDRITE	DENT	DEOXIDATE	DEPLETES	DEPRESSORS
DENDRITES	DENTAL	DEOXIDATED	DEPLETING	DEPRIVAL
DENDRITIC	DENTALIA	DEOXIDATES	DEPLETION	DEPRIVALS
DENDROID	DENTALIUM	DEOXIDATING	DEPLETIONS	DEPRIVE
DENDRON	DENTALIUMS	DEOXIDISE	DEPLETIVE	DEPRIVED
DENDRONS	DENTALS	DEOXIDISED	DEPLETORY	DEPRIVES
DENE	DENTARIA	DEOXIDISES	DEPLORE	DEPRIVING
DENES	DENTARIAS	DEOXIDISING	DEPLORED	DEPROGRAM
DENGUE	DENTARIES	DEOXIDIZE	DEPLORES	DEPROGRAMMED
DENGUES	DENTARY	DEOXIDIZED	DEPLORING	DEPROGRAMMING
DENIABLE	DENTATE	DEOXIDIZES	DEPLOY	DEPROGRAMS
DENIABLY	DENTATED	DEOXIDIZING	DEPLOYED	DEPSIDE
DENIAL	DENTATION	DEPAINT	DEPLOYING	DEPSIDES
DENIALS	DENTATIONS	DEPAINTED	DEPLOYS	DEPTH
DENIED	DENTED	DEPAINTING	DEPLUME	DEPTHLESS
DENIER	DENTEL	DEPAINTS	DEPLUMED	DEPTHS
DENIERS	DENTELLE	DEPART	DEPLUMES	DEPURANT
DENIES	DENTELLES	DEPARTED	DEPLUMING	DEPURANTS
DENIGRATE	DENTELS	DEPARTER	DEPONE	DEPURATE
DENIGRATED	DENTEX	DEPARTERS	DEPONED	DEPURATED
DENIGRATES	DENTEXES	DEPARTING	DEPONENT	DEPURATES
DENIGRATING	DENTICLE	DEPARTINGS	DEPONENTS	DEPURATING
DENIM	DENTICLES	DEPARTS	DEPONES	DEPURATOR
DENIMS	DENTIFORM	DEPARTURE	DEPONING	DEPURATORS
DENITRATE	DENTIL	DEPARTURES	DEPORT	DEPUTE
DENITRATED	DENTILS	DEPASTURE	DEPORTED	DEPUTED
DENITRATES	DENTIN	DEPASTURED	DEPORTEE	DEPUTES
DENITRATING	DENTINE	DEPASTURES	DEPORTEES	DEPUTIES
DENITRIFIED	DENTINES	DEPASTURING	DEPORTING	DEPUTING
DENITRIFIES	DENTING	DÉPÊCHE	DEPORTS	DEPUTISE
DENITRIFY	DENTINS	DÉPÊCHES	DEPOSABLE	DEPUTISED
DENITRIFYING	DENTIST	DEPEINCT	DEPOSAL	DEPUTISES
DENIZEN	DENTISTRIES	DEPEINCTED	DEPOSALS	DEPUTISING
DENIZENED	DENTISTRY	DEPEINCTING	DEPOSE	DEPUTIZE
DENIZENING	DENTISTS	DEPEINCTS	DEPOSED	DEPUTIZED
DENIZENS	DENTITION	DEPEND	DEPOSER	DEPUTIZES
DENNED	DENTITIONS	DEPENDANT	DEPOSERS	DEPUTIZING
DENNET	DENTOID	DEPENDANTS	DEPOSES	DEPUTY
DENNETS	DENTS	DEPENDED	DEPOSING	DÉRACINÉ
DENNING	DENTURE	DEPENDENT	DEPOSIT	DERAIGN
DENOTABLE	DENTURES	DEPENDENTS	DEPOSITED	DERAIGNED
DENOTATE	DENUDATE	DEPENDING	DEPOSITING	DERAIGNING
DENOTATED	DENUDATED	DEPENDS	DEPOSITOR	DERAIGNS
DENOTATES	DENUDATES	DEPICT	DEPOSITORS	DERAIL
DENOTATING	DENUDATING	DEPICTED	DEPOSITS	DERAILED
DENOTE	DENUDE	DEPICTER	DEPOT	DERAILER
DENOTED	DENUDED	DEPICTERS	DEPOTS	DERAILERS
DENOTES	DENUDES	DEPICTING	DEPRAVE	DERAILING
DENOTING	DENUDING	DEPICTION	DEPRAVED	DERAILS
DENOUNCE	DENY	DEPICTIONS	DEPRAVES	DERANGE
DENOUNCED	DENYING	DEPICTIVE	DEPRAVING	DERANGED
DENOUNCER	DENYINGLY	DEPICTOR	DEPRAVITIES	DERANGES
DENOUNCERS	DEODAND	DEPICTORS	DEPRAVITY	DERANGING
DENOUNCES	DEODANDS	DEPICTS	DEPRECATE	DERATE
DENOUNCING	DEODAR	DEPICTURE	DEPRECATED	DERATED
DENS	DEODARS	DEPICTURED	DEPRECATES	DERATES
DENSE	DEODATE	DEPICTURES	DEPRECATING	DERATING
DENSELY	DEODATES	DEPICTURING	DEPREDATE	DERATINGS
DENSENESS	DEODORANT	DEPILATE	DEPREDATED	DERATION
DENSENESSES	DEODORANTS	DEPILATED	DEPREDATES	DERATIONED
DENSER	DEODORISE	DEPILATES	DEPREDATING	DERATIONING
DENSEST	DEODORISED	DEPILATING	DEPREHEND	DERATIONS
DENSIFIED	DEODORISES	DEPILATOR	DEPREHENDED	DERAY

DERAYED
DERAYING
DERAYS
DERBIES
DERBY
DERE
DERED
DERELICT
DERELICTS
DERES
DERHAM
DERHAMS
DERIDE
DERIDED
DERIDER
DERIDERS
DERIDES
DERIDING
DERING
DERISIBLE
DERISION
DERISIONS
DERISIVE
DERISORY
DERIVABLE
DERIVABLY
DERIVATE
DERIVATES
DERIVE
DERIVED
DERIVES
DERIVING
DERM
DERMA
DERMAL
DERMAS
DERMATIC
DERMATOID
DERMATOME
DERMATOMES
DERMIC
DERMIS
DERMISES
DERMOID
DERMOIDS
DERMS
DERN
DERNFUL
DERNIER
DERNLY
DERNS
DEROGATE
DEROGATED
DEROGATES
DEROGATING
DERRICK
DERRICKED
DERRICKING
DERRICKS
DERRIÈRE
DERRIÈRES
DERRIES
DERRINGER
DERRINGERS
DERRIS
DERRISES
DERRY
DERTH
DERTHS
DERV

DERVISH
DERVISHES
DERVS
DESALT
DESALTED
DESALTING
DESALTINGS
DESALTS
DESCALE
DESCALED
DESCALES
DESCALING
DESCANT
DESCANTED
DESCANTING
DESCANTS
DESCEND
DESCENDED
DESCENDER
DESCENDERS
DESCENDING
DESCENDINGS
DESCENDS
DESCENT
DESCENTS
DESCHOOL
DESCHOOLED
DESCHOOLING
DESCHOOLINGS
DESCHOOLS
DESCRIBE
DESCRIBED
DESCRIBER
DESCRIBERS
DESCRIBES
DESCRIBING
DESCRIED
DESCRIES
DESCRIVE
DESCRIVED
DESCRIVES
DESCRIVING
DESCRY
DESCRYING
DESECRATE
DESECRATED
DESECRATES
DESECRATING
DESELECT
DESELECTED
DESELECTING
DESELECTS
DESERT
DESERTED
DESERTER
DESERTERS
DESERTING
DESERTION
DESERTIONS
DESERTS
DESERVE
DESERVED
DESERVER
DESERVERS
DESERVES
DESERVING
DESEX
DESEXED
DESEXES
DESEXING

DESICCANT
DESICCANTS
DESICCATE
DESICCATED
DESICCATES
DESICCATING
DESIGN
DESIGNATE
DESIGNATED
DESIGNATES
DESIGNATING
DESIGNED
DESIGNER
DESIGNERS
DESIGNFUL
DESIGNING
DESIGNINGS
DESIGNS
DESILVER
DESILVERED
DESILVERING
DESILVERS
DESINE
DESINED
DESINENCE
DESINENCES
DESINENT
DESINES
DESINING
DESIPIENT
DESIRABLE
DESIRABLES
DESIRABLY
DESIRE
DESIRED
DESIRER
DESIRERS
DESIRES
DESIRING
DESIROUS
DESIST
DESISTED
DESISTING
DESISTS
DESK
DESKBOUND
DESKILL
DESKILLED
DESKILLING
DESKILLS
DESKS
DESKTOP
DESMAN
DESMANS
DESMID
DESMIDS
DESMINE
DESMINES
DESMODIUM
DESMODIUMS
DESMOID
DESMOSOME
DESMOSOMES
DÉSOEUVRÉ
DESOLATE
DESOLATED
DESOLATER
DESOLATERS
DESOLATES
DESOLATING

DESOLATOR
DESOLATORS
DESORB
DESORBED
DESORBING
DESORBS
DESPAIR
DESPAIRED
DESPAIRING
DESPAIRS
DESPATCH
DESPATCHED
DESPATCHES
DESPATCHING
DESPERADO
DESPERADOES
DESPERADOS
DESPERATE
DESPIGHT
DESPIGHTS
DESPISAL
DESPISALS
DESPISE
DESPISED
DESPISER
DESPISERS
DESPISES
DESPISING
DESPITE
DESPITES
DESPOIL
DESPOILED
DESPOILER
DESPOILERS
DESPOILING
DESPOILS
DESPOND
DESPONDED
DESPONDING
DESPONDINGS
DESPONDS
DESPOT
DESPOTAT
DESPOTATE
DESPOTATES
DESPOTATS
DESPOTIC
DESPOTISM
DESPOTISMS
DESPOTS
DESPUMATE
DESPUMATED
DESPUMATES
DESPUMATING
DESSE
DESSERT
DESSERTS
DESSES
DESTEMPER
DESTEMPERED
DESTEMPERING
DESTEMPERS
DESTINATE
DESTINATED
DESTINATES
DESTINATING
DESTINE
DESTINED
DESTINES
DESTINIES

DESTINING
DESTINY
DESTITUTE
DESTITUTED
DESTITUTES
DESTITUTING
DESTRIER
DESTRIERS
DESTROY
DESTROYED
DESTROYER
DESTROYERS
DESTROYING
DESTROYS
DESTRUCT
DESTRUCTED
DESTRUCTING
DESTRUCTS
DESUETUDE
DESUETUDES
DESULPHUR
DESULPHURED
DESULPHURING
DESULPHURS
DESULTORY
DESYATIN
DESYATINS
DESYNE
DESYNED
DESYNES
DESYNING
DETACH
DETACHED
DETACHES
DETACHING
DETAIL
DETAILED
DETAILING
DETAILS
DETAIN
DETAINED
DETAINEE
DETAINEES
DETAINER
DETAINERS
DETAINING
DETAINS
DETECT
DETECTED
DETECTING
DETECTION
DETECTIONS
DETECTIVE
DETECTIVES
DETECTOR
DETECTORS
DETECTS
DETENT
DÉTENTE
DÉTENTES
DETENTION
DETENTIONS
DETENTS
DÉTENU
DÉTENUE
DÉTENUES
DÉTENUS
DETER
DETERGE
DETERGED

DETERGENT	DETRIMENTS	DEVIATE	DEVONPORTS	DEXTRORSE
DETERGENTS	DETRITAL	DEVIATED	DÉVOT	DEXTROSE
DETERGES	DETRITION	DEVIATES	DEVOTE	DEXTROSES
DETERGING	DETRITIONS	DEVIATING	DEVOTED	DEXTROUS
DETERMENT	DETRITUS	DEVIATION	DEVOTEDLY	DEY
DETERMENTS	DETRUDE	DEVIATIONS	DEVOTEE	DEYS
DETERMINE	DETRUDED	DEVIATOR	DEVOTEES	DHAK
DETERMINED	DETRUDES	DEVIATORS	DEVOTES	DHAKS
DETERMINES	DETRUDING	DEVIATORY	DEVOTING	DHAL
DETERMINING	DETRUSION	DEVICE	DEVOTION	DHALS
DETERRED	DETRUSIONS	DEVICEFUL	DEVOTIONS	DHARMA
DETERRENT	DEUCE	DEVICES	DÉVOTS	DHARMAS
DETERRENTS	DEUCED	DEVIL	DEVOUR	DHARMSALA
DETERRING	DEUCEDLY	DEVILDOM	DEVOURED	DHARMSALAS
DETERS	DEUCES	DEVILDOMS	DEVOURER	DHARNA
DETERSION	DEUDDARN	DEVILESS	DEVOURERS	DHARNAS
DETERSIONS	DEUDDARNS	DEVILESSES	DEVOURING	DHOBI
DETERSIVE	DEUS	DEVILET	DEVOURS	DHOBIS
DETERSIVES	DEUTERATE	DEVILETS	DEVOUT	DHOLE
DETEST	DEUTERATED	DEVILING	DEVOUTER	DHOLES
DETESTED	DEUTERATES	DEVILINGS	DEVOUTEST	DHOLL
DETESTING	DEUTERATING	DEVILISH	DEVOUTLY	DHOLLS
DETESTS	DEUTERIDE	DEVILISM	DEVVEL	DHOOLIES
DETHRONE	DEUTERIDES	DEVILISMS	DEVVELLED	DHOOLY
DETHRONED	DEUTERIUM	DEVILKIN	DEVVELLING	DHOOTI
DETHRONER	DEUTERIUMS	DEVILKINS	DEVVELS	DHOOTIS
DETHRONERS	DEUTERON	DEVILLED	DEW	DHOTI
DETHRONES	DEUTERONS	DEVILLING	DEWAN	DHOTIS
DETHRONING	DEUTON	DEVILMENT	DEWANI	DHOW
DETHRONINGS	DEUTONS	DEVILMENTS	DEWANIS	DHOWS
DETINUE	DEVA	DEVILRIES	DEWANNIES	DHURRA
DETINUES	DEVALL	DEVILRY	DEWANNY	DHURRAS
DETONATE	DEVALLED	DEVILS	DEWANS	DHURRIE
DETONATED	DEVALLING	DEVILSHIP	DEWATER	DHURRIES
DETONATES	DEVALLS	DEVILSHIPS	DEWATERED	DI
DETONATING	DEVALUATE	DEVILTRIES	DEWATERING	DIABASE
DETONATOR	DEVALUATED	DEVILTRY	DEWATERS	DIABASES
DETONATORS	DEVALUATES	DEVIOUS	DEWED	DIABASIC
DETORSION	DEVALUATING	DEVIOUSLY	DEWFULL	DIABETES
DETORSIONS	DEVALUE	DEVISABLE	DEWIER	DIABETIC
DETORT	DEVALUED	DEVISAL	DEWIEST	DIABETICS
DETORTED	DEVALUES	DEVISALS	DEWILY	DIABLERIE
DETORTING	DEVALUING	DEVISE	DEWINESS	DIABLERIES
DETORTION	DEVAS	DEVISED	DEWINESSES	DIABLERY
DETORTIONS	DEVASTATE	DEVISEE	DEWING	DIABOLIC
DETORTS	DEVASTATED	DEVISEES	DEWITT	DIABOLISE
DETOUR	DEVASTATES	DEVISER	DEWITTED	DIABOLISED
DETOURED	DEVASTATING	DEVISERS	DEWITTING	DIABOLISES
DETOURING	DEVEL	DEVISES	DEWITTS	DIABOLISING
DETOURS	DEVELLED	DEVISING	DEWLAP	DIABOLISM
DETOXIFIED	DEVELLING	DEVISOR	DEWLAPPED	DIABOLISMS
DETOXIFIES	DEVELOP	DEVISORS	DEWLAPS	DIABOLIZE
DETOXIFY	DEVELOPE	DEVITRIFIED	DEWLAPT	DIABOLIZED
DETOXIFYING	DEVELOPED	DEVITRIFIES	DEWPOINT	DIABOLIZES
DETRACT	DEVELOPER	DEVITRIFY	DEWPOINTS	DIABOLIZING
DETRACTED	DEVELOPERS	DEVITRIFYING	DEWS	DIABOLO
DETRACTING	DEVELOPES	DEVLING	DEWY	DIABOLOGIES
DETRACTINGS	DEVELOPING	DEVLINGS	DEXTER	DIABOLOGY
DETRACTOR	DEVELOPS	DEVOICE	DEXTERITIES	DIABOLOS
DETRACTORS	DEVELS	DEVOICED	DEXTERITY	DIACHYLON
DETRACTS	DEVEST	DEVOICES	DEXTEROUS	DIACHYLONS
DETRAIN	DEVESTED	DEVOICING	DEXTERS	DIACHYLUM
DETRAINED	DEVESTING	DEVOID	DEXTRAL	DIACHYLUMS
DETRAINING	DEVESTS	DEVOIR	DEXTRALLY	DIACID
DETRAINS	DEVIANCE	DEVOIRS	DEXTRAN	DIACODION
DÉTRAQUÉ	DEVIANCES	DEVOLVE	DEXTRANS	DIACODIONS
DÉTRAQUÉE	DEVIANCIES	DEVOLVED	DEXTRIN	DIACODIUM
DÉTRAQUÉES	DEVIANCY	DEVOLVES	DEXTRINE	DIACODIUMS
DÉTRAQUÉS	DEVIANT	DEVOLVING	DEXTRINES	DIACONAL
DETRIMENT	DEVIANTS	DEVONPORT	DEXTRINS	DIACONATE

DIACONATES
DIACRITIC
DIACRITICS
DIACT
DIACTINAL
DIACTINE
DIACTINIC
DIADEM
DIADEMED
DIADEMS
DIADOCHI
DIADROM
DIADROMS
DIAERESES
DIAERESIS
DIAGLYPH
DIAGLYPHS
DIAGNOSE
DIAGNOSED
DIAGNOSES
DIAGNOSING
DIAGNOSIS
DIAGONAL
DIAGONALS
DIAGRAM
DIAGRAMS
DIAGRAPH
DIAGRAPHS
DIAGRID
DIAGRIDS
DIAL
DIALECT
DIALECTAL
DIALECTIC
DIALECTICS
DIALECTS
DIALIST
DIALISTS
DIALLAGE
DIALLAGES
DIALLAGIC
DIALLED
DIALLER
DIALLERS
DIALLING
DIALLINGS
DIALOG
DIALOGIC
DIALOGISE
DIALOGISED
DIALOGISES
DIALOGISING
DIALOGIST
DIALOGISTS
DIALOGITE
DIALOGITES
DIALOGIZE
DIALOGIZED
DIALOGIZES
DIALOGIZING
DIALOGS
DIALOGUE
DIALOGUED
DIALOGUES
DIALOGUING
DIALS
DIALYSE
DIALYSED
DIALYSER
DIALYSERS

DIALYSES
DIALYSING
DIALYSIS
DIALYTIC
DIALYZE
DIALYZED
DIALYZER
DIALYZERS
DIALYZES
DIALYZING
DIAMAGNET
DIAMAGNETS
DIAMANTÉ
DIAMANTÉS
DIAMETER
DIAMETERS
DIAMETRAL
DIAMETRIC
DIAMOND
DIAMONDED
DIAMONDS
DIAMYL
DIANDRIES
DIANDROUS
DIANDRY
DIANETICS℠
DIANODAL
DIANOETIC
DIANTHUS
DIANTHUSES
DIAPASE
DIAPASES
DIAPASON
DIAPASONS
DIAPAUSE
DIAPAUSES
DIAPENTE
DIAPENTES
DIAPER
DIAPERED
DIAPERING
DIAPERINGS
DIAPERS
DIAPHONE
DIAPHONES
DIAPHRAGM
DIAPHRAGMS
DIAPHYSES
DIAPHYSIS
DIAPIR
DIAPIRIC
DIAPIRISM
DIAPIRISMS
DIAPIRS
DIAPYESES
DIAPYESIS
DIAPYETIC
DIAPYETICS
DIARCH
DIARCHAL
DIARCHIC
DIARCHIES
DIARCHY
DIARIAL
DIARIAN
DIARIES
DIARISE
DIARISED
DIARISES
DIARISING

DIARIST
DIARISTS
DIARIZE
DIARIZED
DIARIZES
DIARIZING
DIARRHEA
DIARRHEAL
DIARRHEAS
DIARRHEIC
DIARRHOEA
DIARRHOEAS
DIARY
DIASCOPE
DIASCOPES
DIASPORA
DIASPORAS
DIASPORE
DIASPORES
DIASTASE
DIASTASES
DIASTASIC
DIASTASIS
DIASTATIC
DIASTEMA
DIASTEMATA
DIASTER
DIASTERS
DIASTOLE
DIASTOLES
DIASTOLIC
DIASTYLE
DIASTYLES
DIATHERMIES
DIATHERMY
DIATHESES
DIATHESIS
DIATHETIC
DIATOM
DIATOMIC
DIATOMIST
DIATOMISTS
DIATOMITE
DIATOMITES
DIATOMS
DIATONIC
DIATRETUM
DIATRETUMS
DIATRIBE
DIATRIBES
DIATROPIC
DIAXON
DIAXONS
DIAZEPAM
DIAZEPAMS
DIAZEUXES
DIAZEUXIS
DIAZO
DIAZOES
DIAZOS
DIB
DIBASIC
DIBBED
DIBBER
DIBBERS
DIBBING
DIBBLE
DIBBLED
DIBBLER
DIBBLERS

DIBBLES
DIBBLING
DIBBS
DIBS
DIBUTYL
DICACIOUS
DICACITIES
DICACITY
DICAST
DICASTERIES
DICASTERY
DICASTIC
DICASTS
DICE
DICED
DICENTRA
DICENTRAS
DICER
DICERS
DICES
DICEY
DICH
DICHASIA
DICHASIAL
DICHASIUM
DICHOGAMIES
DICHOGAMY
DICHORD
DICHORDS
DICHOTOMIES
DICHOTOMY
DICHROIC
DICHROISM
DICHROISMS
DICHROITE
DICHROITES
DICHROMAT
DICHROMATS
DICHROMIC
DICHT
DICHTED
DICHTING
DICHTS
DICIER
DICIEST
DICING
DICINGS
DICK
DICKENS
DICKENSES
DICKER
DICKERED
DICKERING
DICKERS
DICKEY
DICKEYS
DICKIE
DICKIER
DICKIES
DICKIEST
DICKS
DICKTY
DICKY
DICLINISM
DICLINISMS
DICLINOUS
DICOT
DICOTS
DICROTIC
DICROTISM

DICROTISMS
DICROTOUS
DICT
DICTA
DICTATE
DICTATED
DICTATES
DICTATING
DICTATION
DICTATIONS
DICTATOR
DICTATORS
DICTATORY
DICTATRIX
DICTATRIXES
DICTATURE
DICTATURES
DICTED
DICTING
DICTION
DICTIONS
DICTS
DICTUM
DICTY
DICTYOGEN
DICTYOGENS
DICYCLIC
DID
DIDACTIC
DIDACTICS
DIDACTYL
DIDACTYLS
DIDAKAI
DIDAKAIS
DIDAKEI
DIDAKEIS
DIDAPPER
DIDAPPERS
DIDDER
DIDDERED
DIDDERING
DIDDERS
DIDDICOI
DIDDICOIS
DIDDICOY
DIDDICOYS
DIDDLE
DIDDLED
DIDDLER
DIDDLERS
DIDDLES
DIDDLING
DIDDYCOY
DIDDYCOYS
DIDELPHIC
DIDELPHID
DIDELPHIDS
DIDICOI
DIDICOIS
DIDICOY
DIDICOYS
DIDO
DIDOES
DIDOS
DIDRACHM
DIDRACHMA
DIDRACHMAS
DIDRACHMS
DIDST
DIDYMIUM

DIDYMIUMS
DIDYMOUS
DIE
DIEB
DIEBACK
DIEBACKS
DIEBS
DIED
DIEDRAL
DIEDRALS
DIÈDRE
DIÈDRES
DIEGESES
DIEGESIS
DIELDRIN
DIELDRINS
DIELYTRA
DIELYTRAS
DIENE
DIENES
DIERESES
DIERESIS
DIES
DIESEL
DIESELISE
DIESELISED
DIESELISES
DIESELISING
DIESELIZE
DIESELIZED
DIESELIZES
DIESELIZING
DIESELS
DIESES
DIESIS
DIESTRUS
DIESTRUSES
DIET
DIETARIAN
DIETARIANS
DIETARY
DIETED
DIETER
DIETERS
DIETETIC
DIETETICS
DIETHYL
DIETICIAN
DIETICIANS
DIETINE
DIETINES
DIETING
DIETIST
DIETISTS
DIETITIAN
DIETITIANS
DIETS
DIFFER
DIFFERED
DIFFERENT
DIFFERING
DIFFERS
DIFFICILE
DIFFICULT
DIFFIDENT
DIFFLUENT
DIFFORM
DIFFRACT
DIFFRACTED
DIFFRACTING

DIFFRACTS
DIFFUSE
DIFFUSED
DIFFUSELY
DIFFUSER
DIFFUSERS
DIFFUSES
DIFFUSEST
DIFFUSING
DIFFUSION
DIFFUSIONS
DIFFUSIVE
DIG
DIGAMIES
DIGAMIST
DIGAMISTS
DIGAMMA
DIGAMMAS
DIGAMOUS
DIGAMY
DIGASTRIC
DIGEST
DIGESTED
DIGESTER
DIGESTERS
DIGESTING
DIGESTION
DIGESTIONS
DIGESTIVE
DIGESTIVES
DIGESTS
DIGGABLE
DIGGED
DIGGER
DIGGERS
DIGGING
DIGGINGS
DIGHT
DIGHTED
DIGHTING
DIGHTS
DIGIT
DIGITAL
DIGITALIN
DIGITALINS
DIGITALIS
DIGITALISES
DIGITALS
DIGITATE
DIGITATED
DIGITISE
DIGITISED
DIGITISER
DIGITISERS
DIGITISES
DIGITISING
DIGITIZE
DIGITIZED
DIGITIZER
DIGITIZERS
DIGITIZES
DIGITIZING
DIGITS
DIGLOT
DIGLOTS
DIGLYPH
DIGLYPHS
DIGNIFIED
DIGNIFIES
DIGNIFY

DIGNIFYING
DIGNITARIES
DIGNITARY
DIGNITIES
DIGNITY
DIGONAL
DIGRAPH
DIGRAPHS
DIGRESS
DIGRESSED
DIGRESSES
DIGRESSING
DIGS
DIGYNIAN
DIGYNOUS
DIHEDRAL
DIHEDRALS
DIHEDRON
DIHEDRONS
DIHYBRID
DIHYBRIDS
DIHYDRIC
DIKA
DIKAS
DIKAST
DIKASTS
DIKE
DIKED
DIKER
DIKERS
DIKES
DIKEY
DIKIER
DIKIEST
DIKING
DIKTAT
DIKTATS
DILATABLE
DILATANCIES
DILATANCY
DILATANT
DILATATOR
DILATATORS
DILATE
DILATED
DILATER
DILATERS
DILATES
DILATING
DILATION
DILATIONS
DILATIVE
DILATOR
DILATORS
DILATORY
DILDO
DILDOE
DILDOES
DILDOS
DILEMMA
DILEMMAS
DILIGENCE
DILIGENCES
DILIGENT
DILL
DILLI
DILLIES
DILLING
DILLINGS
DILLIS

DILLS
DILLY
DILUENT
DILUENTS
DILUTABLE
DILUTABLES
DILUTE
DILUTED
DILUTEE
DILUTEES
DILUTER
DILUTERS
DILUTES
DILUTING
DILUTION
DILUTIONS
DILUTOR
DILUTORS
DILUVIA
DILUVIAL
DILUVIAN
DILUVION
DILUVIONS
DILUVIUM
DILUVIUMS
DIM
DIMBLE
DIMBLES
DIME
DIMENSION
DIMENSIONED
DIMENSIONING
DIMENSIONS
DIMER
DIMERIC
DIMERISE
DIMERISED
DIMERISES
DIMERISING
DIMERISM
DIMERISMS
DIMERIZE
DIMERIZED
DIMERIZES
DIMERIZING
DIMEROUS
DIMERS
DIMES
DIMETER
DIMETERS
DIMETHYL
DIMETHYLS
DIMETRIC
DIMIDIATE
DIMIDIATED
DIMIDIATES
DIMIDIATING
DIMINISH
DIMINISHED
DIMINISHES
DIMINISHING
DIMINISHINGS
DIMISSORY
DIMITIES
DIMITY
DIMLY
DIMMED
DIMMER
DIMMERS
DIMMEST

DIMMING
DIMMISH
DIMNESS
DIMNESSES
DIMORPH
DIMORPHIC
DIMORPHS
DIMPLE
DIMPLED
DIMPLES
DIMPLIER
DIMPLIEST
DIMPLING
DIMPLY
DIMS
DIMWIT
DIMWITS
DIMYARIAN
DIN
DINAR
DINARCHIES
DINARCHY
DINARS
DINDLE
DINDLED
DINDLES
DINDLING
DINE
DINED
DINER
DINERS
DINES
DINETTE
DINETTES
DINFUL
DING
DINGBAT
DINGBATS
DINGE
DINGED
DINGER
DINGERS
DINGES
DINGESES
DINGEY
DINGEYS
DINGHIES
DINGHY
DINGIER
DINGIES
DINGIEST
DINGINESS
DINGINESSES
DINGING
DINGLE
DINGLES
DINGO
DINGOES
DINGS
DINGUS
DINGUSES
DINGY
DINIC
DINICS
DINING
DINK
DINKED
DINKER
DINKEST
DINKIER

DINKIEST
DINKING
DINKS
DINKUM
DINKY
DINMONT
DINMONTS
DINNED
DINNER
DINNERED
DINNERING
DINNERS
DINNING
DINNLE
DINNLED
DINNLES
DINNLING
DINOSAUR
DINOSAURS
DINS
DINT
DINTED
DINTING
DINTS
DIOCESAN
DIOCESANS
DIOCESE
DIOCESES
DIODE
DIODES
DIOECIOUS
DIOECISM
DIOECISMS
DIOESTRUS
DIOESTRUSES
DIOPSIDE
DIOPSIDES
DIOPTASE
DIOPTASES
DIOPTER
DIOPTERS
DIOPTRATE
DIOPTRE
DIOPTRES
DIOPTRIC
DIOPTRICS
DIORAMA
DIORAMAS
DIORAMIC
DIORISM
DIORISMS
DIORISTIC
DIORITE
DIORITES
DIORITIC
DIOSGENIN
DIOSGENINS
DIOTA
DIOTAS
DIOXAN
DIOXANE
DIOXANES
DIOXANS
DIOXIDE
DIOXIDES
DIOXIN
DIOXINS
DIP
DIPCHICK
DIPCHICKS

DIPEPTIDE
DIPEPTIDES
DIPHENYL
DIPHENYLS
DIPHONE
DIPHONES
DIPHTHONG
DIPHTHONGS
DIPHYSITE
DIPHYSITES
DIPLEX
DIPLOE
DIPLOES
DIPLOGEN
DIPLOGENS
DIPLOID
DIPLOIDIES
DIPLOIDY
DIPLOMA
DIPLOMACIES
DIPLOMACY
DIPLOMAED
DIPLOMAING
DIPLOMAS
DIPLOMAT
DIPLOMATE
DIPLOMATED
DIPLOMATES
DIPLOMATING
DIPLOMATS
DIPLON
DIPLONS
DIPLONT
DIPLONTS
DIPLOPIA
DIPLOPIAS
DIPNOAN
DIPNOANS
DIPNOOUS
DIPODIES
DIPODY
DIPOLAR
DIPOLE
DIPOLES
DIPPED
DIPPER
DIPPERS
DIPPIER
DIPPIEST
DIPPING
DIPPINGS
DIPPY
DIPS
DIPSADES
DIPSAS
DIPSO
DIPSOS
DIPTERAL
DIPTERAN
DIPTERANS
DIPTERIST
DIPTERISTS
DIPTEROI
DIPTEROS
DIPTEROSES
DIPTEROUS
DIPTYCH
DIPTYCHS
DIRDAM
DIRDAMS

DIRDUM
DIRDUMS
DIRE
DIRECT
DIRECTED
DIRECTER
DIRECTEST
DIRECTING
DIRECTION
DIRECTIONS
DIRECTIVE
DIRECTIVES
DIRECTLY
DIRECTOR
DIRECTORIES
DIRECTORS
DIRECTORY
DIRECTRICES
DIRECTRIX
DIRECTRIXES
DIRECTS
DIREFUL
DIREFULLY
DIREMPT
DIREMPTED
DIREMPTING
DIREMPTS
DIRER
DIREST
DIRGE
DIRGES
DIRHAM
DIRHAMS
DIRHEM
DIRHEMS
DIRIGE
DIRIGENT
DIRIGES
DIRIGIBLE
DIRIGIBLES
DIRIGISM
DIRIGISME
DIRIGISMES
DIRIGISMS
DIRIGISTE
DIRIMENT
DIRK
DIRKE
DIRKED
DIRKES
DIRKING
DIRKS
DIRL
DIRLED
DIRLING
DIRLS
DIRNDL
DIRNDLS
DIRT
DIRTED
DIRTIED
DIRTIER
DIRTIES
DIRTIEST
DIRTILY
DIRTINESS
DIRTINESSES
DIRTING
DIRTS
DIRTY

DIRTYING
DISA
DISABLE
DISABLED
DISABLES
DISABLING
DISABUSE
DISABUSED
DISABUSES
DISABUSING
DISACCORD
DISACCORDED
DISACCORDING
DISACCORDS
DISADORN
DISADORNED
DISADORNING
DISADORNS
DISAFFECT
DISAFFECTED
DISAFFECTING
DISAFFECTS
DISAFFIRM
DISAFFIRMED
DISAFFIRMING
DISAFFIRMS
DISAGREE
DISAGREED
DISAGREEING
DISAGREES
DISALLIED
DISALLIES
DISALLOW
DISALLOWED
DISALLOWING
DISALLOWS
DISALLY
DISALLYING
DISANCHOR
DISANCHORED
DISANCHORING
DISANCHORS
DISANNEX
DISANNEXED
DISANNEXES
DISANNEXING
DISANNUL
DISANNULLED
DISANNULLING
DISANNULS
DISANOINT
DISANOINTED
DISANOINTING
DISANOINTS
DISAPPEAR
DISAPPEARED
DISAPPEARING
DISAPPEARS
DISAPPLIED
DISAPPLIES
DISAPPLY
DISAPPLYING
DISARM
DISARMED
DISARMER
DISARMERS
DISARMING
DISARMS
DISARRAY
DISARRAYED

DISARRAYING
DISARRAYS
DISAS
DISASTER
DISASTERS
DISATTIRE
DISATTIRED
DISATTIRES
DISATTIRING
DISATTUNE
DISATTUNED
DISATTUNES
DISATTUNING
DISAVOUCH
DISAVOUCHED
DISAVOUCHES
DISAVOUCHING
DISAVOW
DISAVOWAL
DISAVOWALS
DISAVOWED
DISAVOWING
DISAVOWS
DISBAND
DISBANDED
DISBANDING
DISBANDS
DISBAR
DISBARK
DISBARKED
DISBARKING
DISBARKS
DISBARRED
DISBARRING
DISBARS
DISBELIEF
DISBELIEFS
DISBENCH
DISBENCHED
DISBENCHES
DISBENCHING
DISBODIED
DISBOSOM
DISBOSOMED
DISBOSOMING
DISBOSOMS
DISBOWEL
DISBOWELLED
DISBOWELLING
DISBOWELS
DISBRANCH
DISBRANCHED
DISBRANCHES
DISBRANCHING
DISBUD
DISBUDDED
DISBUDDING
DISBUDS
DISBURDEN
DISBURDENED
DISBURDENING
DISBURDENS
DISBURSAL
DISBURSALS
DISBURSE
DISBURSED
DISBURSES
DISBURSING
DISC
DISCAGE

DISCAGED	DISCOLOURED	DISEASE	DISFLUENT	DISHERITED
DISCAGES	DISCOLOURING	DISEASED	DISFOREST	DISHERITING
DISCAGING	DISCOLOURS	DISEASES	DISFORESTED	DISHERITS
DISCAL	DISCOMFIT	DISEASING	DISFORESTING	DISHES
DISCALCED	DISCOMFITED	DISEDGE	DISFORESTS	DISHEVEL
DISCANDIE	DISCOMFITING	DISEDGED	DISFORM	DISHEVELLED
DISCANDIED	DISCOMFITS	DISEDGES	DISFORMED	DISHEVELLING
DISCANDIES	DISCOMMON	DISEDGING	DISFORMING	DISHEVELS
DISCANDY	DISCOMMONED	DISEMBARK	DISFORMS	DISHFUL
DISCANDYING	DISCOMMONING	DISEMBARKED	DISFROCK	DISHFULS
DISCANT	DISCOMMONS	DISEMBARKING	DISFROCKED	DISHIER
DISCANTED	DISCORD	DISEMBARKS	DISFROCKING	DISHIEST
DISCANTING	DISCORDED	DISEMBODIED	DISFROCKS	DISHING
DISCANTS	DISCORDING	DISEMBODIES	DISGAVEL	DISHINGS
DISCARD	DISCORDS	DISEMBODY	DISGAVELLED	DISHOME
DISCARDED	DISCOS	DISEMBODYING	DISGAVELLING	DISHOMED
DISCARDING	DISCOUNT	DISEMPLOY	DISGAVELS	DISHOMES
DISCARDS	DISCOUNTED	DISEMPLOYED	DISGEST	DISHOMING
DISCASE	DISCOUNTING	DISEMPLOYING	DISGESTED	DISHONEST
DISCASED	DISCOUNTS	DISEMPLOYS	DISGESTING	DISHONOR
DISCASES	DISCOURE	DISENABLE	DISGESTS	DISHONORED
DISCASING	DISCOURED	DISENABLED	DISGODDED	DISHONORING
DISCED	DISCOURES	DISENABLES	DISGORGE	DISHONORS
DISCEPT	DISCOURING	DISENABLING	DISGORGED	DISHONOUR
DISCEPTED	DISCOURSE	DISENDOW	DISGORGES	DISHONOURED
DISCEPTING	DISCOURSED	DISENDOWED	DISGORGING	DISHONOURING
DISCEPTS	DISCOURSES	DISENDOWING	DISGOWN	DISHONOURS
DISCERN	DISCOURSING	DISENDOWS	DISGOWNED	DISHORN
DISCERNED	DISCOVER	DISENGAGE	DISGOWNING	DISHORNED
DISCERNER	DISCOVERED	DISENGAGED	DISGOWNS	DISHORNING
DISCERNERS	DISCOVERIES	DISENGAGES	DISGRACE	DISHORNS
DISCERNING	DISCOVERING	DISENGAGING	DISGRACED	DISHORSE
DISCERNS	DISCOVERS	DISENROL	DISGRACER	DISHORSED
DISCERP	DISCOVERT	DISENROLLED	DISGRACERS	DISHORSES
DISCERPED	DISCOVERY	DISENROLLING	DISGRACES	DISHORSING
DISCERPING	DISCREDIT	DISENROLS	DISGRACING	DISHOUSE
DISCERPS	DISCREDITED	DISENTAIL	DISGRADE	DISHOUSED
DISCHARGE	DISCREDITING	DISENTAILED	DISGRADED	DISHOUSES
DISCHARGED	DISCREDITS	DISENTAILING	DISGRADES	DISHOUSING
DISCHARGES	DISCREET	DISENTAILS	DISGRADING	DISHUMOUR
DISCHARGING	DISCREETER	DISENTOMB	DISGUISE	DISHUMOURED
DISCHURCH	DISCREETEST	DISENTOMBED	DISGUISED	DISHUMOURING
DISCHURCHED	DISCRETE	DISENTOMBING	DISGUISER	DISHUMOURS
DISCHURCHES	DISCRETER	DISENTOMBS	DISGUISERS	DISHY
DISCHURCHING	DISCRETEST	DISESTEEM	DISGUISES	DISILLUDE
DISCIDE	DISCROWN	DISESTEEMED	DISGUISING	DISILLUDED
DISCIDED	DISCROWNED	DISESTEEMING	DISGUISINGS	DISILLUDES
DISCIDES	DISCROWNING	DISESTEEMS	DISGUST	DISILLUDING
DISCIDING	DISCROWNS	DISEUR	DISGUSTED	DISIMMURE
DISCINCT	DISCS	DISEURS	DISGUSTING	DISIMMURED
DISCING	DISCUMBER	DISEUSE	DISGUSTS	DISIMMURES
DISCIPLE	DISCUMBERED	DISEUSES	DISH	DISIMMURING
DISCIPLED	DISCUMBERING	DISFAME	DISHABIT	DISINFECT
DISCIPLES	DISCUMBERS	DISFAMES	DISHABITED	DISINFECTED
DISCIPLING	DISCURE	DISFAVOR	DISHABITING	DISINFECTING
DISCLAIM	DISCURED	DISFAVORED	DISHABITS	DISINFECTS
DISCLAIMED	DISCURES	DISFAVORING	DISHABLE	DISINFEST
DISCLAIMING	DISCURING	DISFAVORS	DISHABLED	DISINFESTED
DISCLAIMS	DISCURSUS	DISFAVOUR	DISHABLES	DISINFESTING
DISCLOSE	DISCURSUSES	DISFAVOURED	DISHABLING	DISINFESTS
DISCLOSED	DISCUS	DISFAVOURING	DISHALLOW	DISINHUME
DISCLOSES	DISCUSES	DISFAVOURS	DISHALLOWED	DISINHUMED
DISCLOSING	DISCUSS	DISFIGURE	DISHALLOWING	DISINHUMES
DISCLOST	DISCUSSED	DISFIGURED	DISHALLOWS	DISINHUMING
DISCO	DISCUSSES	DISFIGURES	DISHED	DISINTER
DISCOER	DISCUSSING	DISFIGURING	DISHELM	DISINTERRED
DISCOERS	DISDAIN	DISFLESH	DISHELMED	DISINTERRING
DISCOID	DISDAINED	DISFLESHED	DISHELMING	DISINTERS
DISCOIDAL	DISDAINING	DISFLESHES	DISHELMS	DISINURE
DISCOLOUR	DISDAINS	DISFLESHING	DISHERIT	DISINURED

DISINURES	DISLOIGN	DISOBLIGED	DISPERSAL	DISPOSTED
DISINURING	DISLOIGNED	DISOBLIGES	DISPERSALS	DISPOSTING
DISINVEST	DISLOIGNING	DISOBLIGING	DISPERSE	DISPOSTS
DISINVESTED	DISLOIGNS	DISORBED	DISPERSED	DISPOSURE
DISINVESTING	DISLOYAL	DISORDER	DISPERSER	DISPOSURES
DISINVESTS	DISLOYALLER	DISORDERED	DISPERSERS	DISPRAD
DISJASKIT	DISLOYALLEST	DISORDERING	DISPERSES	DISPRAISE
DISJECT	DISLUSTRE	DISORDERS	DISPERSING	DISPRAISED
DISJECTED	DISLUSTRED	DISORIENT	DISPIRIT	DISPRAISES
DISJECTING	DISLUSTRES	DISORIENTED	DISPIRITED	DISPRAISING
DISJECTS	DISLUSTRING	DISORIENTING	DISPIRITING	DISPREAD
DISJOIN	DISMAL	DISORIENTS	DISPIRITS	DISPREADING
DISJOINED	DISMALITIES	DISOWN	DISPLACE	DISPREADS
DISJOINING	DISMALITY	DISOWNED	DISPLACED	DISPRED
DISJOINS	DISMALLER	DISOWNING	DISPLACES	DISPREDDEN
DISJOINT	DISMALLEST	DISOWNS	DISPLACING	DISPREDS
DISJOINTED	DISMALLY	DISPACE	DISPLANT	DISPRISON
DISJOINTING	DISMALS	DISPACED	DISPLANTED	DISPRISONED
DISJOINTS	DISMAN	DISPACES	DISPLANTING	DISPRISONING
DISJUNCT	DISMANNED	DISPACING	DISPLANTS	DISPRISONS
DISJUNCTS	DISMANNING	DISPARAGE	DISPLAY	DISPRIZE
DISJUNE	DISMANS	DISPARAGED	DISPLAYED	DISPRIZED
DISJUNES	DISMANTLE	DISPARAGES	DISPLAYER	DISPRIZES
DISK	DISMANTLED	DISPARAGING	DISPLAYERS	DISPRIZING
DISKED	DISMANTLES	DISPARATE	DISPLAYING	DISPROFIT
DISKETTE	DISMANTLING	DISPARATES	DISPLAYS	DISPROFITS
DISKETTES	DISMASK	DISPARITIES	DISPLE	DISPROOF
DISKING	DISMASKED	DISPARITY	DISPLEASE	DISPROOFS
DISKS	DISMASKING	DISPARK	DISPLEASED	DISPROOVE
DISLEAF	DISMASKS	DISPARKED	DISPLEASES	DISPROOVED
DISLEAFED	DISMAST	DISPARKING	DISPLEASING	DISPROOVES
DISLEAFING	DISMASTED	DISPARKS	DISPLED	DISPROOVING
DISLEAFS	DISMASTING	DISPART	DISPLES	DISPROVAL
DISLEAL	DISMASTS	DISPARTED	DISPLING	DISPROVALS
DISLEAVE	DISMAY	DISPARTING	DISPLODE	DISPROVE
DISLEAVED	DISMAYD	DISPARTS	DISPLODED	DISPROVED
DISLEAVES	DISMAYED	DISPATCH	DISPLODES	DISPROVEN
DISLEAVING	DISMAYFUL	DISPATCHED	DISPLODING	DISPROVES
DISLIKE	DISMAYING	DISPATCHES	DISPLUME	DISPROVING
DISLIKED	DISMAYL	DISPATCHING	DISPLUMED	DISPUNGE
DISLIKEN	DISMAYLED	DISPATHIES	DISPLUMES	DISPUNGED
DISLIKENED	DISMAYLING	DISPATHY	DISPLUMING	DISPUNGES
DISLIKENING	DISMAYLS	DISPAUPER	DISPONDEE	DISPUNGING
DISLIKENS	DISMAYS	DISPAUPERED	DISPONDEES	DISPURSE
DISLIKES	DISME	DISPAUPERING	DISPONE	DISPURSED
DISLIKING	DISMEMBER	DISPAUPERS	DISPONED	DISPURSES
DISLIMB	DISMEMBERED	DISPEACE	DISPONEE	DISPURSING
DISLIMBED	DISMEMBERING	DISPEACES	DISPONEES	DISPURVEY
DISLIMBING	DISMEMBERS	DISPEL	DISPONER	DISPURVEYED
DISLIMBS	DISMES	DISPELLED	DISPONERS	DISPURVEYING
DISLIMN	DISMISS	DISPELLING	DISPONES	DISPURVEYS
DISLIMNED	DISMISSAL	DISPELS	DISPONGE	DISPUTANT
DISLIMNING	DISMISSALS	DISPENCE	DISPONGED	DISPUTANTS
DISLIMNS	DISMISSED	DISPENCED	DISPONGES	DISPUTE
DISLINK	DISMISSES	DISPENCES	DISPONGING	DISPUTED
DISLINKED	DISMISSING	DISPENCING	DISPONING	DISPUTER
DISLINKING	DISMODED	DISPEND	DISPORT	DISPUTERS
DISLINKS	DISMOUNT	DISPENDED	DISPORTED	DISPUTES
DISLOAD	DISMOUNTED	DISPENDING	DISPORTING	DISPUTING
DISLOADED	DISMOUNTING	DISPENDS	DISPORTS	DISQUIET
DISLOADING	DISMOUNTS	DISPENSE	DISPOSAL	DISQUIETED
DISLOADS	DISNEST	DISPENSED	DISPOSALS	DISQUIETING
DISLOCATE	DISNESTED	DISPENSER	DISPOSE	DISQUIETS
DISLOCATED	DISNESTING	DISPENSERS	DISPOSED	DISRANK
DISLOCATES	DISNESTS	DISPENSES	DISPOSER	DISRANKED
DISLOCATING	DISOBEY	DISPENSING	DISPOSERS	DISRANKING
DISLODGE	DISOBEYED	DISPEOPLE	DISPOSES	DISRANKS
DISLODGED	DISOBEYING	DISPEOPLED	DISPOSING	DISRATE
DISLODGES	DISOBEYS	DISPEOPLES	DISPOSINGS	DISRATED
DISLODGING	DISOBLIGE	DISPEOPLING	DISPOST	DISRATES

DISRATING
DISREGARD
DISREGARDED
DISREGARDING
DISREGARDS
DISRELISH
DISRELISHED
DISRELISHES
DISRELISHING
DISREPAIR
DISREPAIRS
DISREPUTE
DISREPUTES
DISROBE
DISROBED
DISROBES
DISROBING
DISROOT
DISROOTED
DISROOTING
DISROOTS
DISRUPT
DISRUPTED
DISRUPTER
DISRUPTERS
DISRUPTING
DISRUPTOR
DISRUPTORS
DISRUPTS
DISS
DISSEAT
DISSEATED
DISSEATING
DISSEATS
DISSECT
DISSECTED
DISSECTING
DISSECTINGS
DISSECTOR
DISSECTORS
DISSECTS
DISSEISE
DISSEISED
DISSEISES
DISSEISIN
DISSEISING
DISSEISINS
DISSEISOR
DISSEISORS
DISSEIZE
DISSEIZED
DISSEIZES
DISSEIZIN
DISSEIZING
DISSEIZINS
DISSEIZOR
DISSEIZORS
DISSEMBLE
DISSEMBLED
DISSEMBLES
DISSEMBLIES
DISSEMBLING
DISSEMBLY
DISSENT
DISSENTED
DISSENTER
DISSENTERS
DISSENTING
DISSENTS
DISSERT

DISSERTED
DISSERTING
DISSERTS
DISSERVE
DISSERVED
DISSERVES
DISSERVING
DISSES
DISSEVER
DISSEVERED
DISSEVERING
DISSEVERS
DISSHIVER
DISSHIVERED
DISSHIVERING
DISSHIVERS
DISSIDENT
DISSIDENTS
DISSIGHT
DISSIGHTS
DISSIMILE
DISSIMILES
DISSIPATE
DISSIPATED
DISSIPATES
DISSIPATING
DISSOCIAL
DISSOLUTE
DISSOLUTES
DISSOLVE
DISSOLVED
DISSOLVES
DISSOLVING
DISSONANT
DISSUADE
DISSUADED
DISSUADER
DISSUADERS
DISSUADES
DISSUADING
DISSUNDER
DISSUNDERED
DISSUNDERING
DISSUNDERS
DISTAFF
DISTAFFS
DISTAIN
DISTAINED
DISTAINING
DISTAINS
DISTAL
DISTALLY
DISTANCE
DISTANCED
DISTANCES
DISTANCING
DISTANT
DISTANTLY
DISTASTE
DISTASTED
DISTASTES
DISTASTING
DISTEMPER
DISTEMPERED
DISTEMPERING
DISTEMPERS
DISTEND
DISTENDED
DISTENDING
DISTENDS

DISTENT
DISTHENE
DISTHENES
DISTHRONE
DISTHRONED
DISTHRONES
DISTHRONING
DISTICH
DISTICHAL
DISTICHS
DISTIL
DISTILL
DISTILLED
DISTILLER
DISTILLERS
DISTILLING
DISTILLINGS
DISTILLS
DISTILS
DISTINCT
DISTINCTER
DISTINCTEST
DISTINGUÉ
DISTORT
DISTORTED
DISTORTING
DISTORTS
DISTRACT
DISTRACTED
DISTRACTING
DISTRACTS
DISTRAIN
DISTRAINED
DISTRAINING
DISTRAINS
DISTRAINT
DISTRAINTS
DISTRAIT
DISTRAITE
DISTRESS
DISTRESSED
DISTRESSES
DISTRESSING
DISTRICT
DISTRICTED
DISTRICTING
DISTRICTS
DISTRUST
DISTRUSTED
DISTRUSTING
DISTRUSTS
DISTUNE
DISTUNED
DISTUNES
DISTUNING
DISTURB
DISTURBED
DISTURBER
DISTURBERS
DISTURBING
DISTURBS
DISTYLE
DISTYLES
DISUNION
DISUNIONS
DISUNITE
DISUNITED
DISUNITES
DISUNITIES
DISUNITING

DISUNITY
DISUSAGE
DISUSAGES
DISUSE
DISUSED
DISUSES
DISUSING
DISVALUE
DISVALUED
DISVALUES
DISVALUING
DISVOUCH
DISVOUCHED
DISVOUCHES
DISVOUCHING
DISYOKE
DISYOKED
DISYOKES
DISYOKING
DIT
DITA
DITAL
DITALS
DITAS
DITCH
DITCHED
DITCHER
DITCHERS
DITCHES
DITCHING
DITE
DITED
DITES
DITHECAL
DITHECOUS
DITHEISM
DITHEISMS
DITHEIST
DITHEISTS
DITHELETE
DITHELETES
DITHELISM
DITHELISMS
DITHER
DITHERED
DITHERER
DITHERERS
DITHERING
DITHERS
DITHERY
DITHYRAMB
DITHYRAMBS
DITING
DITOKOUS
DITONE
DITONES
DITROCHEE
DITROCHEES
DITS
DITT
DITTANDER
DITTANDERS
DITTANIES
DITTANY
DITTAY
DITTAYS
DITTED
DITTIED
DITTIES
DITTING

DITTIT
DITTO
DITTOED
DITTOING
DITTOLOGIES
DITTOLOGY
DITTOS
DITTS
DITTY
DITTYING
DIURESES
DIURESIS
DIURETIC
DIURETICS
DIURNAL
DIURNALLY
DIURNALS
DIUTURNAL
DIV
DIVA
DIVAGATE
DIVAGATED
DIVAGATES
DIVAGATING
DIVALENT
DIVALENTS
DIVAN
DIVANS
DIVAS
DIVE
DIVED
DIVELLENT
DIVER
DIVERGE
DIVERGED
DIVERGENT
DIVERGES
DIVERGING
DIVERS
DIVERSE
DIVERSED
DIVERSELY
DIVERSES
DIVERSIFIED
DIVERSIFIES
DIVERSIFY
DIVERSIFYING
DIVERSING
DIVERSION
DIVERSIONS
DIVERSITIES
DIVERSITY
DIVERSLY
DIVERT
DIVERTED
DIVERTING
DIVERTIVE
DIVERTS
DIVES
DIVEST
DIVESTED
DIVESTING
DIVESTS
DIVI
DIVIDABLE
DIVIDANT
DIVIDE
DIVIDED
DIVIDEDLY
DIVIDEND

DIVIDENDS	DIVVY	DOCILER	DODDERERS	DOGES
DIVIDER	DIVVYING	DOCILEST	DODDERIER	DOGESHIP
DIVIDERS	DIWAN	DOCILITIES	DODDERIEST	DOGESHIPS
DIVIDES	DIWANS	DOCILITY	DODDERING	DOGFIGHT
DIVIDING	DIXI	DOCIMASIES	DODDERS	DOGFIGHTS
DIVIDINGS	DIXIE	DOCIMASY	DODDERY	DOGFISH
DIVIDIVI	DIXIES	DOCK	DODDIER	DOGFISHES
DIVIDIVIS	DIXY	DOCKAGE	DODDIES	DOGFOX
DIVIDUAL	DIZAIN	DOCKAGES	DODDIEST	DOGFOXES
DIVIDUOUS	DIZAINS	DOCKED	DODDING	DOGGED
DIVINATOR	DIZEN	DOCKEN	DODDIPOLL	DOGGEDER
DIVINATORS	DIZENED	DOCKENS	DODDIPOLLS	DOGGEDEST
DIVINE	DIZENING	DOCKER	DODDLE	DOGGEDLY
DIVINED	DIZENS	DOCKERS	DODDLES	DOGGER
DIVINELY	DIZYGOTIC	DOCKET	DODDY	DOGGEREL
DIVINER	DIZZARD	DOCKETED	DODDYPOLL	DOGGERELS
DIVINERS	DIZZARDS	DOCKETING	DODDYPOLLS	DOGGERIES
DIVINES	DIZZIED	DOCKETS	DODECAGON	DOGGERMAN
DIVINEST	DIZZIER	DOCKING	DODECAGONS	DOGGERMEN
DIVING	DIZZIES	DOCKINGS	DODGE	DOGGERS
DIVINGS	DIZZIEST	DOCKISE	DODGED	DOGGERY
DIVINIFIED	DIZZILY	DOCKISED	DODGEM	DOGGESS
DIVINIFIES	DIZZINESS	DOCKISES	DODGEMS	DOGGESSES
DIVINIFY	DIZZINESSES	DOCKISING	DODGER	DOGGIE
DIVINIFYING	DIZZY	DOCKIZE	DODGERIES	DOGGIER
DIVINING	DIZZYING	DOCKIZED	DODGERS	DOGGIES
DIVINISE	DJEBEL	DOCKIZES	DODGERY	DOGGIEST
DIVINISED	DJEBELS	DOCKIZING	DODGES	DOGGINESS
DIVINISES	DJELLABA	DOCKLAND	DODGIER	DOGGINESSES
DIVINISING	DJELLABAH	DOCKLANDS	DODGIEST	DOGGING
DIVINITIES	DJELLABAHS	DOCKS	DODGING	DOGGINGS
DIVINITY	DJELLABAS	DOCKYARD	DODGY	DOGGISH
DIVINIZE	DJIBBAH	DOCKYARDS	DODKIN	DOGGISHLY
DIVINIZED	DJIBBAHS	DOCQUET	DODKINS	DOGGO
DIVINIZES	DJINN	DOCQUETED	DODMAN	DOGGONE
DIVINIZING	DJINNI	DOCQUETING	DODMANS	DOGGONED
DIVIS	DO	DOCQUETS	DODO	DOGGREL
DIVISIBLE	DOAB	DOCS	DODOES	DOGGRELS
DIVISIBLY	DOABLE	DOCTOR	DODOS	DOGGY
DIVISIM	DOABS	DOCTORAL	DODS	DOGHOLE
DIVISION	DOAT	DOCTORAND	DOE	DOGHOLES
DIVISIONS	DOATED	DOCTORANDS	DOEN	DOGIE
DIVISIVE	DOATER	DOCTORATE	DOER	DOGIES
DIVISOR	DOATERS	DOCTORATED	DOERS	DOGMA
DIVISORS	DOATING	DOCTORATES	DOES	DOGMAS
DIVORCE	DOATINGS	DOCTORATING	DOEST	DOGMATIC
DIVORCED	DOATS	DOCTORED	DOETH	DOGMATICS
DIVORCEE	DOB	DOCTORESS	DOFF	DOGMATISE
DIVORCEES	DOBBED	DOCTORESSES	DOFFED	DOGMATISED
DIVORCER	DOBBER	DOCTORIAL	DOFFER	DOGMATISES
DIVORCERS	DOBBERS	DOCTORING	DOFFERS	DOGMATISING
DIVORCES	DOBBIE	DOCTORLY	DOFFING	DOGMATISM
DIVORCING	DOBBIES	DOCTORS	DOFFS	DOGMATISMS
DIVORCIVE	DOBBIN	DOCTRESS	DOG	DOGMATIST
DIVOT	DOBBING	DOCTRESSES	DOGARESSA	DOGMATISTS
DIVOTS	DOBBINS	DOCTRINAL	DOGARESSAS	DOGMATIZE
DIVS	DOBBY	DOCTRINE	DOGATE	DOGMATIZED
DIVULGATE	DOBCHICK	DOCTRINES	DOGATES	DOGMATIZES
DIVULGATED	DOBCHICKS	DOCUDRAMA	DOGBANE	DOGMATIZING
DIVULGATES	DOBHASH	DOCUDRAMAS	DOGBANES	DOGMATORY
DIVULGATING	DOBHASHES	DOCUMENT	DOGBERRIES	DOGS
DIVULGE	DOBS	DOCUMENTED	DOGBERRY	DOGSBODIES
DIVULGED	DOC	DOCUMENTING	DOGBOLT	DOGSBODY
DIVULGES	DOCHMIAC	DOCUMENTS	DOGBOLTS	DOGSHIP
DIVULGING	DOCHMII	DOD	DOGCART	DOGSHIPS
DIVULSION	DOCHMIUS	DODDARD	DOGCARTS	DOGSHORES
DIVULSIONS	DOCHMIUSES	DODDED	DOGDAYS	DOGSKIN
DIVULSIVE	DOCHT	DODDER	DOGE	DOGSKINS
DIVVIED	DOCIBLE	DODDERED	DOGEATE	DOGSLEEP
DIVVIES	DOCILE	DODDERER	DOGEATES	DOGSLEEPS

DOGTEETH	DOLLYING	DOMINOES	DONUT	DOORSTEP
DOGTOOTH	DOLMA	DOMINOS	DONUTS	DOORSTEPPED
DOGTOWN	DOLMADES	DOMY	DONZEL	DOORSTEPPING
DOGTOWNS	DOLMAN	DON	DONZELS	DOORSTEPS
DOGTROT	DOLMANS	DONA	DOO	DOORSTONE
DOGTROTS	DOLMAS	DONAH	DOOB	DOORSTONES
DOGVANE	DOLMEN	DONAHS	DOOBS	DOORSTOP
DOGVANES	DOLMENS	DONARIES	DOOCOT	DOORSTOPS
DOGWOOD	DOLOMITE	DONARY	DOOCOTS	DOORWAY
DOGWOODS	DOLOMITES	DONAS	DOODAD	DOORWAYS
DOGY	DOLOMITIC	DONATARIES	DOODADS	DOOS
DOH	DOLORIFIC	DONATARY	DOODAH	DOP
DOHS	DOLOROSO	DONATE	DOODAHS	DOPA
DOILED	DOLOROUS	DONATED	DOODLE	DOPAMINE
DOILEDER	DOLOUR	DONATES	DOODLEBUG	DOPAMINES
DOILEDEST	DOLOURS	DONATING	DOODLEBUGS	DOPANT
DOILIES	DOLPHIN	DONATION	DOODLED	DOPANTS
DOILT	DOLPHINET	DONATIONS	DOODLER	DOPAS
DOILTER	DOLPHINETS	DONATISM	DOODLERS	DOPE
DOILTEST	DOLPHINS	DONATISMS	DOODLES	DOPED
DOILY	DOLT	DONATIVE	DOODLING	DOPER
DOING	DOLTISH	DONATIVES	DOOK	DOPERS
DOINGS	DOLTISHLY	DONATOR	DOOKED	DOPES
DOIT	DOLTS	DONATORIES	DOOKET	DOPEY
DOITED	DOMAIN	DONATORS	DOOKETS	DOPIER
DOITIT	DOMAINAL	DONATORY	DOOKING	DOPIEST
DOITKIN	DOMAINS	DONE	DOOKS	DOPING
DOITKINS	DOMAL	DONEE	DOOL	DOPINGS
DOITS	DOMANIAL	DONEES	DOOLE	DOPPED
DOJO	DOMATIA	DONENESS	DOOLES	DOPPER
DOJOS	DOMATIUM	DONENESSES	DOOLIE	DOPPERS
DOLCE	DOME	DONG	DOOLIES	DOPPIE
DOLCES	DOMED	DONGA	DOOLS	DOPPIES
DOLDRUMS	DOMES	DONGAS	DOOM	DOPPING
DOLE	DOMESTIC	DONGED	DOOMED	DOPPINGS
DOLED	DOMESTICS	DONGING	DOOMFUL	DOPS
DOLEFUL	DOMETT	DONGLE	DOOMIER	DOPY
DOLEFULLY	DOMETTS	DONGLES	DOOMIEST	DOR
DOLENT	DOMICAL	DONGS	DOOMING	DORAD
DOLERITE	DOMICIL	DONING	DOOMS	DORADO
DOLERITES	DOMICILE	DONINGS	DOOMSDAY	DORADOS
DOLERITIC	DOMICILED	DONJON	DOOMSDAYS	DORADS
DOLES	DOMICILES	DONJONS	DOOMSMAN	DOREE
DOLESOME	DOMICILING	DONKEY	DOOMSMEN	DOREES
DOLIA	DOMICILS	DONKEYS	DOOMSTER	DORHAWK
DOLICHOS	DOMIER	DONNARD	DOOMSTERS	DORHAWKS
DOLICHOSES	DOMIEST	DONNART	DOOMWATCH	DORIDOID
DOLING	DOMINANCE	DONNAT	DOOMWATCHED	DORIDOIDS
DOLIUM	DOMINANCES	DONNATS	DOOMWATCHES	DORIES
DOLL	DOMINANCIES	DONNÉ	DOOMWATCHING	DORISE
DOLLAR	DOMINANCY	DONNE	DOOMWATCHINGS	DORISED
DOLLARED	DOMINANT	DONNED	DOOMY	DORISES
DOLLARS	DOMINANTS	DONNÉE	DOOR	DORISING
DOLLDOM	DOMINATE	DONNÉES	DOORBELL	DORIZE
DOLLDOMS	DOMINATED	DONNERD	DOORBELLS	DORIZED
DOLLED	DOMINATES	DONNERED	DOORKNOB	DORIZES
DOLLHOOD	DOMINATING	DONNERT	DOORKNOBS	DORIZING
DOLLHOODS	DOMINATOR	DONNÉS	DOORKNOCK	DORLACH
DOLLIED	DOMINATORS	DONNING	DOORKNOCKED	DORLACHS
DOLLIER	DOMINEER	DONNISH	DOORKNOCKING	DORM
DOLLIERS	DOMINEERED	DONNISM	DOORKNOCKS	DORMANCIES
DOLLIES	DOMINEERING	DONNISMS	DOORMAT	DORMANCY
DOLLINESS	DOMINEERS	DONNOT	DOORMATS	DORMANT
DOLLINESSES	DOMING	DONNOTS	DOORN	DORMANTS
DOLLING	DOMINICAL	DONOR	DOORNAIL	DORMER
DOLLISH	DOMINIE	DONORS	DOORNAILS	DORMERS
DOLLOP	DOMINIES	DONS	DOORNS	DORMICE
DOLLOPS	DOMINION	DONSHIP	DOORPOST	DORMIE
DOLLS	DOMINIONS	DONSHIPS	DOORPOSTS	DORMIENT
DOLLY	DOMINO	DONSIE	DOORS	DORMITION

DORMITIONS
DORMITIVE
DORMITIVES
DORMITORIES
DORMITORY
DORMOUSE
DORMS
DORMY
DORNICK
DORNICKS
DORP
DORPS
DORR
DORRED
DORRING
DORRS
DORS
DORSA
DORSAL
DORSALLY
DORSALS
DORSE
DORSEL
DORSELS
DORSER
DORSERS
DORSES
DORSIFLEX
DORSUM
DORT
DORTED
DORTER
DORTERS
DORTING
DORTOUR
DORTOURS
DORTS
DORTY
DORY
DOS
DOSAGE
DOSAGES
DOSE
DOSED
DOSEH
DOSEHS
DOSES
DOSIMETER
DOSIMETERS
DOSIMETRIES
DOSIMETRY
DOSING
DOSIOLOGIES
DOSIOLOGY
DOSOLOGIES
DOSOLOGY
DOSS
DOSSAL
DOSSALS
DOSSED
DOSSEL
DOSSELS
DOSSER
DOSSERS
DOSSES
DOSSIER
DOSSIERS
DOSSIL
DOSSILS
DOSSING

DOST
DOT
DOTAGE
DOTAGES
DOTAL
DOTANT
DOTANTS
DOTARD
DOTARDS
DOTATION
DOTATIONS
DOTE
DOTED
DOTER
DOTERS
DOTES
DOTH
DOTIER
DOTIEST
DOTING
DOTINGS
DOTISH
DOTS
DOTTED
DOTTEREL
DOTTERELS
DOTTIER
DOTTIEST
DOTTINESS
DOTTINESSES
DOTTING
DOTTIPOLL
DOTTIPOLLS
DOTTLE
DOTTLED
DOTTLER
DOTTLES
DOTTLEST
DOTTREL
DOTTRELS
DOTTY
DOTY
DOUANE
DOUANES
DOUANIER
DOUANIERS
DOUAR
DOUARS
DOUBLE
DOUBLED
DOUBLER
DOUBLERS
DOUBLES
DOUBLET
DOUBLETON
DOUBLETONS
DOUBLETS
DOUBLING
DOUBLINGS
DOUBLOON
DOUBLOONS
DOUBLY
DOUBT
DOUBTABLE
DOUBTED
DOUBTER
DOUBTERS
DOUBTFUL
DOUBTFULS
DOUBTING

DOUBTINGS
DOUBTLESS
DOUBTS
DOUC
DOUCE
DOUCELY
DOUCENESS
DOUCENESSES
DOUCEPERE
DOUCEPERES
DOUCER
DOUCEST
DOUCET
DOUCETS
DOUCEUR
DOUCEURS
DOUCHE
DOUCHED
DOUCHES
DOUCHING
DOUCINE
DOUCINES
DOUCS
DOUGH
DOUGHIER
DOUGHIEST
DOUGHNUT
DOUGHNUTS
DOUGHS
DOUGHT
DOUGHTIER
DOUGHTIEST
DOUGHTILY
DOUGHTY
DOUGHY
DOULEIA
DOULEIAS
DOUMA
DOUMAS
DOUP
DOUPS
DOUR
DOURA
DOURAS
DOURER
DOUREST
DOURINE
DOURINES
DOURNESS
DOURNESSES
DOUSE
DOUSED
DOUSER
DOUSERS
DOUSES
DOUSING
DOUT
DOUTED
DOUTER
DOUTERS
DOUTING
DOUTS
DOUZEPER
DOUZEPERS
DOVE
DOVECOT
DOVECOTE
DOVECOTES
DOVECOTS
DOVED

DOVEISH
DOVEKIE
DOVEKIES
DOVELET
DOVELETS
DOVER
DOVERED
DOVERING
DOVERS
DOVES
DOVETAIL
DOVETAILED
DOVETAILING
DOVETAILINGS
DOVETAILS
DOVIE
DOVIER
DOVIEST
DOVING
DOVISH
DOW
DOWABLE
DOWAGER
DOWAGERS
DOWAR
DOWARS
DOWD
DOWDIER
DOWDIES
DOWDIEST
DOWDILY
DOWDINESS
DOWDINESSES
DOWDS
DOWDY
DOWDYISH
DOWDYISM
DOWDYISMS
DOWED
DOWEL
DOWELLED
DOWELLING
DOWELLINGS
DOWELS
DOWER
DOWERED
DOWERING
DOWERLESS
DOWERS
DOWF
DOWFNESS
DOWFNESSES
DOWIE
DOWIER
DOWIEST
DOWING
DOWL
DOWLAS
DOWLASES
DOWLE
DOWLES
DOWLNE
DOWLNES
DOWLNEY
DOWLNEYS
DOWLS
DOWN
DOWNA
DOWNBEAT
DOWNBEATS

DOWNBOW
DOWNBOWS
DOWNCAST
DOWNCASTS
DOWNED
DOWNER
DOWNERS
DOWNFALL
DOWNFALLS
DOWNFLOW
DOWNFLOWS
DOWNFORCE
DOWNFORCES
DOWNGRADE
DOWNGRADED
DOWNGRADES
DOWNGRADING
DOWNHILL
DOWNHILLS
DOWNIER
DOWNIEST
DOWNINESS
DOWNINESSES
DOWNING
DOWNLAND
DOWNLANDS
DOWNMOST
DOWNPIPE
DOWNPIPES
DOWNPOUR
DOWNPOURS
DOWNRIGHT
DOWNRUSH
DOWNRUSHES
DOWNS
DOWNSTAGE
DOWNSTAIR
DOWNSTAIRS
DOWNSWING
DOWNSWINGS
DOWNTIME
DOWNTIMES
DOWNTREND
DOWNTRENDS
DOWNTURN
DOWNTURNS
DOWNWARD
DOWNWARDS
DOWNWIND
DOWNY
DOWP
DOWPS
DOWRIES
DOWRY
DOWS
DOWSE
DOWSED
DOWSER
DOWSERS
DOWSES
DOWSET
DOWSETS
DOWSING
DOWT
DOWTS
DOXIES
DOXOLOGIES
DOXOLOGY
DOXY
DOYEN

DOYENNE
DOYENNES
DOYENS
DOYLEY
DOYLEYS
DOYLIES
DOYLY
DOZE
DOZED
DOZEN
DOZENED
DOZENING
DOZENS
DOZENTH
DOZENTHS
DOZER
DOZERS
DOZES
DOZIER
DOZIEST
DOZINESS
DOZINESSES
DOZING
DOZINGS
DOZY
DRAB
DRABBED
DRABBER
DRABBERS
DRABBEST
DRABBET
DRABBETS
DRABBIER
DRABBIEST
DRABBING
DRABBISH
DRABBLE
DRABBLED
DRABBLER
DRABBLERS
DRABBLES
DRABBLING
DRABBLINGS
DRABBY
DRABETTE
DRABETTES
DRABLER
DRABLERS
DRABLY
DRABNESS
DRABNESSES
DRABS
DRACHM
DRACHMA
DRACHMAE
DRACHMAI
DRACHMAS
DRACHMS
DRACONE
DRACONES
DRACONIAN
DRACONIC
DRACONISM
DRACONISMS
DRACONTIC
DRAD
DRAFF
DRAFFISH
DRAFFS
DRAFFY

DRAFT
DRAFTED
DRAFTEE
DRAFTEES
DRAFTER
DRAFTERS
DRAFTING
DRAFTS
DRAFTSMAN
DRAFTSMEN
DRAG
DRAGÉE
DRAGÉES
DRAGGED
DRAGGIER
DRAGGIEST
DRAGGING
DRAGGLE
DRAGGLED
DRAGGLES
DRAGGLING
DRAGGY
DRAGHOUND
DRAGHOUNDS
DRAGLINE
DRAGLINES
DRAGOMAN
DRAGOMANS
DRAGON
DRAGONESS
DRAGONESSES
DRAGONET
DRAGONETS
DRAGONFLIES
DRAGONFLY
DRAGONISE
DRAGONISED
DRAGONISES
DRAGONISH
DRAGONISING
DRAGONISM
DRAGONISMS
DRAGONIZE
DRAGONIZED
DRAGONIZES
DRAGONIZING
DRAGONNÉ
DRAGONS
DRAGOON
DRAGOONED
DRAGOONING
DRAGOONS
DRAGS
DRAGSMAN
DRAGSMEN
DRAGSTER
DRAGSTERS
DRAIL
DRAILED
DRAILING
DRAILS
DRAIN
DRAINABLE
DRAINAGE
DRAINAGES
DRAINED
DRAINER
DRAINERS
DRAINING
DRAINS

DRAISENE
DRAISENES
DRAISINE
DRAISINES
DRAKE
DRAKES
DRAM
DRAMA
DRAMAS
DRAMATIC
DRAMATICS
DRAMATISE
DRAMATISED
DRAMATISES
DRAMATISING
DRAMATIST
DRAMATISTS
DRAMATIZE
DRAMATIZED
DRAMATIZES
DRAMATIZING
DRAMATURG
DRAMATURGE
DRAMATURGS
DRAMMACH
DRAMMACHS
DRAMMED
DRAMMING
DRAMMOCK
DRAMMOCKS
DRAMS
DRANK
DRANT
DRANTED
DRANTING
DRANTS
DRAP
DRAPE
DRAPED
DRAPER
DRAPERIED
DRAPERIES
DRAPERS
DRAPERY
DRAPERYING
DRAPES
DRAPET
DRAPETS
DRAPIER
DRAPIERS
DRAPING
DRAPPED
DRAPPIE
DRAPPIES
DRAPPING
DRAPPY
DRAPS
DRASTIC
DRASTICS
DRAT
DRATCHELL
DRATCHELLS
DRATTED
DRAUGHT
DRAUGHTED
DRAUGHTER
DRAUGHTERS
DRAUGHTIER
DRAUGHTIEST
DRAUGHTING

DRAUGHTS
DRAUGHTY
DRAUNT
DRAUNTED
DRAUNTING
DRAUNTS
DRAVE
DRAW
DRAWABLE
DRAWBACK
DRAWBACKS
DRAWEE
DRAWEES
DRAWER
DRAWERS
DRAWING
DRAWINGS
DRAWL
DRAWLED
DRAWLER
DRAWLERS
DRAWLING
DRAWLS
DRAWN
DRAWS
DRAY
DRAYAGE
DRAYAGES
DRAYMAN
DRAYMEN
DRAYS
DRAZEL
DRAZELS
DREAD
DREADED
DREADER
DREADERS
DREADFUL
DREADING
DREADLESS
DREADLY
DREADS
DREAM
DREAMBOAT
DREAMBOATS
DREAMED
DREAMER
DREAMERIES
DREAMERS
DREAMERY
DREAMFUL
DREAMHOLE
DREAMHOLES
DREAMIER
DREAMIEST
DREAMILY
DREAMING
DREAMINGS
DREAMLESS
DREAMS
DREAMT
DREAMY
DREAR
DREARE
DREARER
DREARES
DREAREST
DREARIER
DREARIEST
DREARILY

DREARING
DREARINGS
DREARS
DREARY
DRECK
DRECKS
DREDGE
DREDGED
DREDGER
DREDGERS
DREDGES
DREDGING
DREE
DREED
DREEING
DREES
DREGGIER
DREGGIEST
DREGGY
DREGS
DREICH
DREICHER
DREICHEST
DRENCH
DRENCHED
DRENCHER
DRENCHERS
DRENCHES
DRENCHING
DRENT
DREPANIUM
DREPANIUMS
DRERE
DRERES
DRERYHEAD
DRERYHEADS
DRESS
DRESSAGE
DRESSAGES
DRESSED
DRESSER
DRESSERS
DRESSES
DRESSIER
DRESSIEST
DRESSING
DRESSINGS
DRESSY
DREST
DREVILL
DREVILLS
DREW
DREY
DREYS
DRIB
DRIBBED
DRIBBER
DRIBBERS
DRIBBING
DRIBBLE
DRIBBLED
DRIBBLER
DRIBBLERS
DRIBBLES
DRIBBLET
DRIBBLETS
DRIBBLIER
DRIBBLIEST
DRIBBLING
DRIBBLY

DRIBLET	DRIZZLY	DROOLING	DROWNER	DRUMS
DRIBLETS	DROGER	DROOLS	DROWNERS	DRUMSTICK
DRIBS	DROGERS	DROOME	DROWNING	DRUMSTICKS
DRICKSIE	DROGHER	DROOMES	DROWNINGS	DRUNK
DRIED	DROGHERS	DROOP	DROWNS	DRUNKARD
DRIER	DROGUE	DROOPED	DROWS	DRUNKARDS
DRIERS	DROGUES	DROOPIER	DROWSE	DRUNKEN
DRIES	DROGUET	DROOPIEST	DROWSED	DRUNKENLY
DRIEST	DROGUETS	DROOPILY	DROWSES	DRUNKER
DRIFT	DROICH	DROOPING	DROWSIER	DRUNKEST
DRIFTAGE	DROICHS	DROOPS	DROWSIEST	DRUNKS
DRIFTAGES	DROICHY	DROOPY	DROWSIHED	DRUPE
DRIFTED	DROIL	DROP	DROWSIHEDS	DRUPEL
DRIFTER	DROILED	DROPFLIES	DROWSILY	DRUPELET
DRIFTERS	DROILING	DROPFLY	DROWSING	DRUPELETS
DRIFTIER	DROILS	DROPLET	DROWSY	DRUPELS
DRIFTIEST	DROIT	DROPLETS	DRUB	DRUPES
DRIFTING	DROITS	DROPPED	DRUBBED	DRUSE
DRIFTLESS	DRÔLE	DROPPER	DRUBBING	DRUSES
DRIFTPIN	DRÔLER	DROPPERS	DRUBBINGS	DRUSY
DRIFTPINS	DRÔLES	DROPPING	DRUBS	DRUXY
DRIFTS	DRÔLEST	DROPPINGS	DRUCKEN	DRY
DRIFTY	DROLL	DROPPLE	DRUDGE	DRYAD
DRILL	DROLLED	DROPPLES	DRUDGED	DRYADES
DRILLED	DROLLER	DROPS	DRUDGER	DRYADS
DRILLER	DROLLERIES	DROPSICAL	DRUDGERIES	DRYBEAT
DRILLERS	DROLLERY	DROPSIED	DRUDGERS	DRYBEATEN
DRILLING	DROLLEST	DROPSIES	DRUDGERY	DRYBEATING
DRILLINGS	DROLLING	DROPSTONE	DRUDGES	DRYBEATS
DRILLS	DROLLINGS	DROPSTONES	DRUDGING	DRYER
DRILY	DROLLISH	DROPSY	DRUDGISM	DRYERS
DRINK	DROLLNESS	DROPWISE	DRUDGISMS	DRYING
DRINKABLE	DROLLNESSES	DROSERA	DRUG	DRYINGS
DRINKER	DROLLS	DROSERAS	DRUGGED	DRYISH
DRINKERS	DROLLY	DROSHKIES	DRUGGER	DRYLY
DRINKING	DROME	DROSHKY	DRUGGERS	DRYNESS
DRINKINGS	DROMEDARE	DROSKIES	DRUGGET	DRYNESSES
DRINKS	DROMEDARES	DROSKY	DRUGGETS	DRYSALTER
DRIP	DROMEDARIES	DROSS	DRUGGING	DRYSALTERS
DRIPPED	DROMEDARY	DROSSES	DRUGGIST	DSO
DRIPPIER	DROMES	DROSSIER	DRUGGISTS	DSOBO
DRIPPIEST	DROMIC	DROSSIEST	DRUGS	DSOBOS
DRIPPING	DROMICAL	DROSSY	DRUIDIC	DSOMO
DRIPPINGS	DROMOI	DROSTDIES	DRUIDICAL	DSOMOS
DRIPPY	DROMON	DROSTDY	DRUIDISM	DSOS
DRIPS	DROMOND	DROSTDYS	DRUIDISMS	DUAD
DRISHEEN	DROMONDS	DROUGHT	DRUM	DUADS
DRISHEENS	DROMONS	DROUGHTIER	DRUMBEAT	DUAL
DRIVABLE	DROMOS	DROUGHTIEST	DRUMBEATS	DUALIN
DRIVE	DRONE	DROUGHTS	DRUMBLE	DUALINS
DRIVEABLE	DRONED	DROUGHTY	DRUMBLED	DUALISM
DRIVEL	DRONES	DROUK	DRUMBLES	DUALISMS
DRIVELLED	DRONGO	DROUKED	DRUMBLING	DUALIST
DRIVELLER	DRONGOES	DROUKING	DRUMFIRE	DUALISTIC
DRIVELLERS	DRONGOS	DROUKINGS	DRUMFIRES	DUALISTS
DRIVELLING	DRONIER	DROUKIT	DRUMFISH	DUALITIES
DRIVELS	DRONIEST	DROUKS	DRUMFISHES	DUALITY
DRIVEN	DRONING	DROUTH	DRUMHEAD	DUALLY
DRIVER	DRONINGLY	DROUTHIER	DRUMHEADS	DUALS
DRIVERS	DRONISH	DROUTHIEST	DRUMLIER	DUAN
DRIVES	DRONISHLY	DROUTHS	DRUMLIEST	DUANS
DRIVEWAY	DRONY	DROUTHY	DRUMLIN	DUAR
DRIVEWAYS	DROOK	DROVE	DRUMLINS	DUARCHIES
DRIVING	DROOKED	DROVER	DRUMLY	DUARCHY
DRIZZLE	DROOKING	DROVERS	DRUMMED	DUARS
DRIZZLED	DROOKINGS	DROVES	DRUMMER	DUB
DRIZZLES	DROOKIT	DROW	DRUMMERS	DUBBED
DRIZZLIER	DROOKS	DROWN	DRUMMING	DUBBIN
DRIZZLIEST	DROOL	DROWNDED	DRUMMOCK	DUBBING
DRIZZLING	DROOLED	DROWNED	DRUMMOCKS	DUBBINGS

DUBBINS	DUDE	DUKEDOM	DUMBFOUNDS	DUNGEONING
DUBIETIES	DUDEEN	DUKEDOMS	DUMBING	DUNGEONS
DUBIETY	DUDEENS	DUKELING	DUMBLY	DUNGIER
DUBIOSITIES	DUDES	DUKELINGS	DUMBNESS	DUNGIEST
DUBIOSITY	DUDGEON	DUKERIES	DUMBNESSES	DUNGING
DUBIOUS	DUDGEONS	DUKERY	DUMBS	DUNGMERE
DUBIOUSLY	DUDHEEN	DUKES	DUMDUM	DUNGMERES
DUBITABLE	DUDHEENS	DUKESHIP	DUMDUMS	DUNGS
DUBITABLY	DUDISH	DUKESHIPS	DUMFOUND	DUNGY
DUBITANCIES	DUDISM	DUKING	DUMFOUNDED	DUNITE
DUBITANCY	DUDISMS	DULCAMARA	DUMFOUNDING	DUNITES
DUBITATE	DUDS	DULCAMARAS	DUMFOUNDS	DUNK
DUBITATED	DUE	DULCET	DUMKA	DUNKED
DUBITATES	DUED	DULCIAN	DUMKY	DUNKING
DUBITATING	DUEFUL	DULCIANA	DUMMERER	DUNKS
DUBS	DUEL	DULCIANAS	DUMMERERS	DUNLIN
DUCAL	DUELLED	DULCIANS	DUMMIED	DUNLINS
DUCALLY	DUELLER	DULCIFIED	DUMMIER	DUNNAGE
DUCAT	DUELLERS	DULCIFIES	DUMMIES	DUNNAGES
DUCATOON	DUELLING	DULCIFY	DUMMIEST	DUNNAKIN
DUCATOONS	DUELLINGS	DULCIFYING	DUMMINESS	DUNNAKINS
DUCATS	DUELLIST	DULCIMER	DUMMINESSES	DUNNED
DUCDAME	DUELLISTS	DULCIMERS	DUMMY	DUNNER
DUCE	DUELLO	DULCITE	DUMMYING	DUNNEST
DUCES	DUELLOS	DULCITES	DUMOSE	DUNNIES
DUCHESS	DUELS	DULCITOL	DUMOSITIES	DUNNING
DUCHESSE	DUELSOME	DULCITOLS	DUMOSITY	DUNNINGS
DUCHESSES	DUENNA	DULCITUDE	DUMOUS	DUNNISH
DUCHIES	DUENNAS	DULCITUDES	DUMP	DUNNITE
DUCHY	DUES	DULCOSE	DUMPED	DUNNITES
DUCK	DUET	DULCOSES	DUMPER	DUNNO
DUCKBILL	DUETS	DULE	DUMPERS	DUNNOCK
DUCKBILLS	DUETT	DULES	DUMPIER	DUNNOCKS
DUCKED	DUETTED	DULIA	DUMPIES	DUNNY
DUCKER	DUETTI	DULIAS	DUMPIEST	DUNS
DUCKERS	DUETTING	DULL	DUMPINESS	DUNSH
DUCKIER	DUETTINO	DULLARD	DUMPINESSES	DUNSHED
DUCKIES	DUETTINOS	DULLARDS	DUMPING	DUNSHES
DUCKIEST	DUETTIST	DULLED	DUMPISH	DUNSHING
DUCKING	DUETTISTS	DULLER	DUMPISHLY	DUNT
DUCKINGS	DUETTO	DULLEST	DUMPLE	DUNTED
DUCKLING	DUETTOS	DULLIER	DUMPLED	DUNTING
DUCKLINGS	DUETTS	DULLIEST	DUMPLES	DUNTS
DUCKMOLE	DUFF	DULLING	DUMPLING	DUO
DUCKMOLES	DUFFED	DULLISH	DUMPLINGS	DUODECIMO
DUCKS	DUFFEL	DULLNESS	DUMPS	DUODECIMOS
DUCKSES	DUFFELS	DULLNESSES	DUMPY	DUODENA
DUCKSHOVE	DUFFER	DULLS	DUN	DUODENAL
DUCKSHOVED	DUFFERDOM	DULLY	DUNCE	DUODENARY
DUCKSHOVES	DUFFERDOMS	DULNESS	DUNCEDOM	DUODENUM
DUCKSHOVING	DUFFERISM	DULNESSES	DUNCEDOMS	DUOLOGUE
DUCKWEED	DUFFERISMS	DULOCRACIES	DUNCERIES	DUOLOGUES
DUCKWEEDS	DUFFERS	DULOCRACY	DUNCERY	DUOMI
DUCKY	DUFFEST	DULOSES	DUNCES	DUOMO
DUCT	DUFFING	DULOSIS	DUNCH	DUOMOS
DUCTED	DUFFINGS	DULOTIC	DUNCHED	DUOPOLIES
DUCTILE	DUFFLE	DULSE	DUNCHES	DUOPOLY
DUCTILITIES	DUFFLES	DULSES	DUNCHING	DUOS
DUCTILITY	DUFFS	DULY	DUNDER	DUOTONE
DUCTING	DUG	DUMA	DUNDERS	DUOTONES
DUCTLESS	DUGONG	DUMAIST	DUNE	DUP
DUCTS	DUGONGS	DUMAISTS	DUNES	DUPABLE
DUD	DUGOUT	DUMAS	DUNG	DUPE
DUDDER	DUGOUTS	DUMB	DUNGAREE	DUPED
DUDDERIES	DUGS	DUMBED	DUNGAREES	DUPER
DUDDERS	DUIKER	DUMBER	DUNGED	DUPERIES
DUDDERY	DUIKERS	DUMBEST	DUNGEON	DUPERS
DUDDIE	DUING	DUMBFOUND	DUNGEONED	DUPERY
DUDDIER	DUKE	DUMBFOUNDED	DUNGEONER	DUPES
DUDDIEST	DUKED	DUMBFOUNDING	DUNGEONERS	DUPING

DUPION
DUPIONS
DUPLE
DUPLET
DUPLETS
DUPLEX
DUPLEXES
DUPLICAND
DUPLICANDS
DUPLICATE
DUPLICATED
DUPLICATES
DUPLICATING
DUPLICITIES
DUPLICITY
DUPLIED
DUPLIES
DUPLY
DUPLYING
DUPONDII
DUPONDIUS
DUPPED
DUPPIES
DUPPING
DUPPY
DUPS
DURA
DURABLE
DURABLES
DURABLY
DURAL
DURALS
DURALUMIN
DURALUMINS
DURAMEN
DURAMENS
DURANCE
DURANCES
DURANT
DURANTS
DURAS
DURATION
DURATIONS
DURBAR
DURBARS
DURDUM
DURDUMS
DURE
DURED
DUREFUL
DURES
DURESS
DURESSE
DURESSES
DURGAN
DURGANS
DURGY
DURIAN
DURIANS
DURING
DURION
DURIONS
DURMAST
DURMASTS
DURN
DURNS
DURO
DUROS
DUROY
DUROYS

DURRA
DURRAS
DURRIE
DURRIES
DURST
DURUKULI
DURUKULIS
DURUM
DURUMS
DUSH
DUSHED
DUSHES
DUSHING
DUSK
DUSKED
DUSKEN
DUSKENED
DUSKENING
DUSKENS
DUSKER
DUSKEST
DUSKIER
DUSKIEST
DUSKILY
DUSKINESS
DUSKINESSES
DUSKING
DUSKISH
DUSKISHLY
DUSKLY
DUSKNESS
DUSKNESSES
DUSKS
DUSKY
DUST
DUSTBIN
DUSTBINS
DUSTED
DUSTER
DUSTERS
DUSTIER
DUSTIEST
DUSTILY
DUSTINESS
DUSTINESSES
DUSTING
DUSTLESS
DUSTMAN
DUSTMEN
DUSTPROOF
DUSTS
DUSTY
DUTCH
DUTCHES
DUTEOUS
DUTEOUSLY
DUTIABLE
DUTIED
DUTIES
DUTIFUL
DUTIFULLY
DUTY
DUUMVIR
DUUMVIRAL
DUUMVIRI
DUUMVIRS
DUVET
DUVETINE
DUVETINES
DUVETS

DUVETYN
DUVETYNE
DUVETYNES
DUVETYNS
DUX
DUXELLES
DUXES
DUYKER
DUYKERS
DVANDVA
DVANDVAS
DVORNIK
DVORNIKS
DWALE
DWALES
DWALM
DWALMED
DWALMING
DWALMS
DWAM
DWAMMED
DWAMMMING
DWAMS
DWARF
DWARFED
DWARFING
DWARFISH
DWARFISM
DWARFISMS
DWARFS
DWARVES
DWAUM
DWAUMED
DWAUMING
DWAUMS
DWELL
DWELLED
DWELLER
DWELLERS
DWELLING
DWELLINGS
DWELLS
DWELT
DWINDLE
DWINDLED
DWINDLES
DWINDLING
DWINE
DWINED
DWINES
DWINING
DYABLE
DYAD
DYADIC
DYADS
DYARCHIES
DYARCHY
DYBBUK
DYBBUKS
DYE
DYEABLE
DYED
DYEING
DYEINGS
DYELINE
DYELINES
DYER
DYERS
DYES
DYESTER

DYESTERS
DYESTUFF
DYESTUFFS
DYING
DYINGLY
DYINGNESS
DYINGNESSES
DYINGS
DYKE
DYKED
DYKES
DYKEY
DYKIER
DYKIEST
DYKING
DYNAMIC
DYNAMICAL
DYNAMICS
DYNAMISE
DYNAMISED
DYNAMISES
DYNAMISING
DYNAMISM
DYNAMISMS
DYNAMIST
DYNAMISTS
DYNAMITE
DYNAMITED
DYNAMITER
DYNAMITERS
DYNAMITES
DYNAMITING
DYNAMIZE
DYNAMIZED
DYNAMIZES
DYNAMIZING
DYNAMO
DYNAMOS
DYNAMOTOR
DYNAMOTORS
DYNAST
DYNASTIC
DYNASTIES
DYNASTS
DYNASTY
DYNATRON
DYNATRONS
DYNE
DYNES
DYNODE
DYNODES
DYSCHROA
DYSCHROAS
DYSCHROIA
DYSCHROIAS
DYSCRASIA
DYSCRASIAS
DYSENTERIES
DYSENTERY
DYSGENIC
DYSGENICS
DYSLECTIC
DYSLECTICS
DYSLEXIA
DYSLEXIAS
DYSLEXIC
DYSLEXICS
DYSLOGIES
DYSLOGY
DYSMELIA

DYSMELIAS
DYSMELIC
DYSODIL
DYSODILE
DYSODILES
DYSODILS
DYSODYLE
DYSODYLES
DYSPATHIES
DYSPATHY
DYSPEPSIA
DYSPEPSIAS
DYSPEPSIES
DYSPEPSY
DYSPEPTIC
DYSPEPTICS
DYSPHAGIA
DYSPHAGIAS
DYSPHAGIC
DYSPHAGIES
DYSPHAGY
DYSPHASIA
DYSPHASIAS
DYSPHONIA
DYSPHONIAS
DYSPHONIC
DYSPHORIA
DYSPHORIAS
DYSPHORIC
DYSPLASIA
DYSPLASIAS
DYSPNEA
DYSPNEAL
DYSPNEAS
DYSPNEIC
DYSPNOEA
DYSPNOEAL
DYSPNOEAS
DYSPNOEIC
DYSPRAXIA
DYSPRAXIAS
DYSTECTIC
DYSTHESIA
DYSTHESIAS
DYSTHETIC
DYSTHYMIA
DYSTHYMIAS
DYSTHYMIC
DYSTOPIA
DYSTOPIAN
DYSTOPIAS
DYSTROPHIES
DYSTROPHY
DYSURIA
DYSURIAS
DYSURIC
DYSURIES
DYSURY
DYTISCID
DYTISCIDS
DYVOUR
DYVOURIES
DYVOURS
DYVOURY
DZEREN
DZERENS
DZIGGETAI
DZIGGETAIS
DZO
DZOS

E

EA	EARLS	EARWIGGING	EAVESDRIP	ECBOLES
EACH	EARLY	EARWIGGY	EAVESDRIPS	ECBOLIC
EACHWHERE	EARMARK	EARWIGS	EAVESDROP	ECBOLICS
EADISH	EARMARKED	EAS	EAVESDROPPED	ECCE
EADISHES	EARMARKING	EASE	EAVESDROPPING	ECCENTRIC
EAGER	EARMARKS	EASED	EAVESDROPS	ECCENTRICS
EAGERLY	EARMUFFS	EASEFUL	ÉBAUCHE	ECCLESIA
EAGERNESS	EARN	EASEL	ÉBAUCHES	ECCLESIAL
EAGERNESSES	EARNED	EASELS	EBB	ECCLESIAS
EAGERS	EARNER	EASEMENT	EBBED	ECCO
EAGLE	EARNERS	EASEMENTS	EBBING	ECCRINE
EAGLES	EARNEST	EASES	EBBLESS	ECCRISES
EAGLET	EARNESTLY	EASIER	EBBS	ECCRISIS
EAGLETS	EARNESTS	EASIEST	EBBTIDE	ECCRITIC
EAGLEWOOD	EARNING	EASILY	EBBTIDES	ECCRITICS
EAGLEWOODS	EARNINGS	EASINESS	EBENEZER	ECDYSES
EAGRE	EARNS	EASINESSES	EBENEZERS	ECDYSIAST
EAGRES	EARPHONE	EASING	ÉBÉNISTE	ECDYSIASTS
EALDORMAN	EARPHONES	EASLE	ÉBÉNISTES	ECDYSIS
EALDORMEN	EARPICK	EASLES	EBIONISE	ECH
EALE	EARPICKS	EASSEL	EBIONISED	ÉCHAPPÉ
EALES	EARPIECE	EASSIL	EBIONISES	ÉCHAPPÉS
EAN	EARPIECES	EAST	EBIONISING	ECHE
EANED	EARPLUG	EASTED	EBIONISM	ECHED
EANING	EARPLUGS	EASTER	EBIONISMS	ECHELON
EANLING	EARRING	EASTERLIES	EBIONITIC	ECHELONS
EANLINGS	EARRINGS	EASTERLY	EBIONIZE	ECHES
EANS	EARS	EASTERN	EBIONIZED	ECHIDNA
EAR	EARST	EASTERNER	EBIONIZES	ECHIDNAS
EARACHE	EARTH	EASTERNERS	EBIONIZING	ECHIDNINE
EARACHES	EARTHBORN	EASTING	EBON	ECHIDNINES
EARBASH	EARTHED	EASTINGS	EBONIES	ECHINATE
EARBASHED	EARTHEN	EASTLAND	EBONISE	ECHINATED
EARBASHES	EARTHFALL	EASTLANDS	EBONISED	ECHING
EARBASHING	EARTHFALLS	EASTLIN	EBONISES	ECHINI
EARBOB	EARTHFAST	EASTLING	EBONISING	ECHINOID
EARBOBS	EARTHFLAX	EASTLINGS	EBONIST	ECHINOIDS
EARD	EARTHFLAXES	EASTLINS	EBONISTS	ECHINUS
EARDED	EARTHIER	EASTMOST	EBONITE	ECHINUSES
EARDING	EARTHIEST	EASTS	EBONITES	ECHO
EARDROP	EARTHING	EASTWARD	EBONIZE	ECHOED
EARDROPS	EARTHLIER	EASTWARDS	EBONIZED	ECHOER
EARDRUM	EARTHLIES	EASY	EBONIZES	ECHOERS
EARDRUMS	EARTHLIEST	EAT	EBONIZING	ECHOES
EARDS	EARTHLING	EATABLE	EBONS	ECHOGRAM
EARED	EARTHLINGS	EATABLES	EBONY	ECHOGRAMS
EARFLAP	EARTHLY	EATAGE	EBRIATE	ECHOIC
EARFLAPS	EARTHMAN	EATAGES	EBRIATED	ECHOING
EARFUL	EARTHMEN	EATCHE	EBRIETIES	ECHOISE
EARFULS	EARTHS	EATCHES	EBRIETY	ECHOISED
EARING	EARTHWARD	EATEN	EBRILLADE	ECHOISES
EARINGS	EARTHWAX	EATER	EBRILLADES	ECHOISING
EARL	EARTHWAXES	EATERIES	EBRIOSE	ECHOISM
EARLAP	EARTHWOLF	EATERS	EBRIOSITIES	ECHOISMS
EARLAPS	EARTHWOLVES	EATERY	EBRIOSITY	ECHOIST
EARLDOM	EARTHWORK	EATH	EBULLIENT	ECHOISTS
EARLDOMS	EARTHWORKS	EATHE	EBURNEAN	ECHOIZE
EARLESS	EARTHWORM	EATHLY	EBURNEOUS	ECHOIZED
EARLIER	EARTHWORMS	EATING	ECAD	ECHOIZES
EARLIEST	EARTHY	EATINGS	ECADS	ECHOIZING
EARLINESS	EARWAX	EATS	ÉCARTÉ	ECHOLALIA
EARLINESSES	EARWAXES	EAU	ÉCARTÉS	ECHOLALIAS
EARLOCK	EARWIG	EAUS	ECAUDATE	ECHOLESS
EARLOCKS	EARWIGGED	EAVES	ECBOLE	ECHS

ECHT	ÉCRITOIRE	ECUS	EDITORS	EFFACES
ÉCLAIR	ÉCRITOIRES	ECZEMA	EDITRESS	EFFACING
ÉCLAIRS	ECRU	ECZEMAS	EDITRESSES	EFFECT
ECLAMPSIA	ECRUS	EDACIOUS	EDITS	EFFECTED
ECLAMPSIAS	ECSTASES	EDACITIES	EDUCABLE	EFFECTER
ECLAMPSIES	ECSTASIED	EDACITY	EDUCATE	EFFECTERS
ECLAMPSY	ECSTASIES	EDAPHIC	EDUCATED	EFFECTING
ECLAMPTIC	ECSTASIS	EDDIED	EDUCATES	EFFECTIVE
ÉCLAT	ECSTASISE	EDDIES	EDUCATING	EFFECTIVES
ÉCLATS	ECSTASISED	EDDISH	EDUCATION	EFFECTOR
ECLECTIC	ECSTASISES	EDDISHES	EDUCATIONS	EFFECTORS
ECLECTICS	ECSTASISING	EDDO	EDUCATIVE	EFFECTS
ECLIPSE	ECSTASIZE	EDDOES	EDUCATOR	EFFECTUAL
ECLIPSED	ECSTASIZED	EDDY	EDUCATORS	EFFED
ECLIPSES	ECSTASIZES	EDDYING	EDUCATORY	EFFEIR
ECLIPSING	ECSTASIZING	EDELWEISS	EDUCE	EFFEIRED
ECLIPTIC	ECSTASY	EDELWEISSES	EDUCED	EFFEIRING
ECLIPTICS	ECSTASYING	EDEMA	EDUCEMENT	EFFEIRS
ECLOGITE	ECSTATIC	EDEMAS	EDUCEMENTS	EFFENDI
ECLOGITES	ECSTATICS	EDEMATOSE	EDUCES	EFFENDIS
ECLOGUE	ECTASES	EDEMATOUS	EDUCIBLE	EFFERE
ECLOGUES	ECTASIS	EDENTAL	EDUCING	EFFERED
ECLOSE	ECTHYMA	EDENTATE	EDUCT	EFFERENCE
ECLOSED	ECTHYMAS	EDENTATES	EDUCTION	EFFERENCES
ECLOSES	ECTOBLAST	EDGE	EDUCTIONS	EFFERENT
ECLOSING	ECTOBLASTS	EDGEBONE	EDUCTOR	EFFERES
ECLOSION	ECTOCRINE	EDGEBONES	EDUCTORS	EFFERING
ECLOSIONS	ECTOCRINES	EDGED	EDUCTS	EFFETE
ECOCIDE	ECTODERM	EDGELESS	EDUSKUNTA	EFFETELY
ECOCIDES	ECTODERMS	EDGER	EDUSKUNTAS	EFFETER
ECOFREAK	ECTOGENIC	EDGERS	EE	EFFETEST
ECOFREAKS	ECTOGENIES	EDGES	EECH	EFFICACIES
ECOLOGIC	ECTOGENY	EDGEWAYS	EECHED	EFFICACY
ECOLOGIES	ECTOMORPH	EDGEWISE	EECHES	EFFICIENT
ECOLOGIST	ECTOMORPHS	EDGIER	EECHING	EFFICIENTS
ECOLOGISTS	ECTOPHYTE	EDGIEST	EEK	EFFIERCE
ECOLOGY	ECTOPHYTES	EDGINESS	EEL	EFFIERCED
ECONOMIC	ECTOPIA	EDGINESSES	EELFARE	EFFIERCES
ECONOMICS	ECTOPIAS	EDGING	EELFARES	EFFIERCING
ECONOMIES	ECTOPIC	EDGINGS	EELGRASS	EFFIGIES
ECONOMISE	ECTOPIES	EDGY	EELGRASSES	EFFIGY
ECONOMISED	ECTOPLASM	EDH	EELIER	EFFING
ECONOMISES	ECTOPLASMS	EDHS	EELIEST	EFFLUENCE
ECONOMISING	ECTOPY	EDIBILITIES	EELPOUT	EFFLUENCES
ECONOMISM	ECTOSARC	EDIBILITY	EELPOUTS	EFFLUENT
ECONOMISMS	ECTOSARCS	EDIBLE	EELS	EFFLUENTS
ECONOMIST	ECTOTHERM	EDIBLES	EELWORM	EFFLUVIA
ECONOMISTS	ECTOTHERMS	EDICT	EELWORMS	EFFLUVIAL
ECONOMIZE	ECTOZOA	EDICTAL	EELWRACK	EFFLUVIUM
ECONOMIZED	ECTOZOAN	EDICTALLY	EELWRACKS	EFFLUX
ECONOMIZES	ECTOZOANS	EDICTS	EELY	EFFLUXES
ECONOMIZING	ECTOZOIC	EDIFICE	EEN	EFFLUXION
ECONOMY	ECTOZOON	EDIFICES	EERIE	EFFLUXIONS
ECONUT	ECTROPIC	EDIFICIAL	EERIER	EFFORCE
ECONUTS	ECTROPION	EDIFIED	EERIEST	EFFORCED
ECOPHOBIA	ECTROPIONS	EDIFIER	EERILY	EFFORCES
ECOPHOBIAS	ECTROPIUM	EDIFIERS	EERINESS	EFFORCING
ÉCORCHÉ	ECTROPIUMS	EDIFIES	EERINESSES	EFFORT
ÉCORCHÉS	ECTYPAL	EDIFY	EERY	EFFORTFUL
ECOSPHERE	ECTYPE	EDIFYING	EEVEN	EFFORTS
ECOSPHERES	ECTYPES	EDILE	EEVENS	EFFRAIDE
ÉCOSSAISE	ECU	EDILES	EEVN	EFFRAY
ÉCOSSAISES	ÉCUELLE	EDIT	EEVNING	EFFRAYED
ECOSTATE	ÉCUELLES	EDITED	EEVNINGS	EFFRAYING
ECOSYSTEM	ECUMENIC	EDITING	EEVNS	EFFRAYS
ECOSYSTEMS	ECUMENICS	EDITION	EF	EFFS
ECOTYPE	ECUMENISM	EDITIONS	EFF	EFFULGE
ECOTYPES	ECUMENISMS	EDITOR	EFFABLE	EFFULGED
ÉCRASEUR	ÉCURIE	EDITORIAL	EFFACE	EFFULGENT
ÉCRASEURS	ÉCURIES	EDITORIALS	EFFACED	EFFULGES

EFFULGING	EGOIST	EIGNE	ELAPSED	ELECTRIFY
EFFUSE	EGOISTIC	EIK	ELAPSES	ELECTRIFYING
EFFUSED	EGOISTS	EIKED	ELAPSING	ELECTRISE
EFFUSES	EGOITIES	EIKING	ELASTANCE	ELECTRISED
EFFUSING	EGOITY	EIKON	ELASTANCES	ELECTRISES
EFFUSION	EGOMANIA	EIKONS	ELASTASE	ELECTRISING
EFFUSIONS	EGOMANIAC	EIKS	ELASTASES	ELECTRIZE
EFFUSIVE	EGOMANIACS	EILD	ELASTIC	ELECTRIZED
EFS	EGOMANIAS	EILDING	ELASTICS	ELECTRIZES
EFT	EGOS	EILDINGS	ELASTIN	ELECTRIZING
EFTEST	EGOTHEISM	EILDS	ELASTINS	ELECTRO
EFTS	EGOTHEISMS	EINE	ELASTOMER	ELECTRODE
EFTSOONS	EGOTISE	EIRACK	ELASTOMERS	ELECTRODES
EGAD	EGOTISED	EIRACKS	ELATE	ELECTRON
EGAL	EGOTISES	EIRENIC	ELATED	ELECTRONS
EGALITIES	EGOTISING	EIRENICON	ELATEDLY	ELECTROS
EGALITY	EGOTISM	EIRENICONS	ELATER	ELECTRUM
EGALLY	EGOTISMS	EISEL	ELATERIN	ELECTRUMS
EGAREMENT	EGOTIST	EISELL	ELATERINS	ELECTS
EGAREMENTS	EGOTISTIC	EISELLS	ELATERITE	ELECTUARIES
EGENCE	EGOTISTS	EISELS	ELATERITES	ELECTUARY
EGENCES	EGOTIZE	EITHER	ELATERIUM	ELEGANCE
EGENCIES	EGOTIZED	EJACULATE	ELATERIUMS	ELEGANCES
EGENCY	EGOTIZES	EJACULATED	ELATERS	ELEGANCIES
EGER	EGOTIZING	EJACULATES	ELATES	ELEGANCY
EGERS	EGREGIOUS	EJACULATING	ELATING	ELEGANT
EGEST	EGRESS	EJECT	ELATION	ELEGANTLY
EGESTA	EGRESSES	EJECTA	ELATIONS	ELEGIAC
EGESTED	EGRESSION	EJECTED	ELATIVE	ELEGIACAL
EGESTING	EGRESSIONS	EJECTING	ELATIVES	ELEGIACS
EGESTION	EGRET	EJECTION	ELBOW	ELEGIAST
EGESTIONS	EGRETS	EJECTIONS	ELBOWED	ELEGIASTS
EGESTIVE	EH	EJECTIVE	ELBOWING	ELEGIES
EGESTS	EHED	EJECTMENT	ELBOWS	ELEGISE
EGG	EHING	EJECTMENTS	ELCHEE	ELEGISED
EGGAR	EHS	EJECTOR	ELCHEES	ELEGISES
EGGARS	EIDENT	EJECTORS	ELCHI	ELEGISING
EGGCUP	EIDER	EJECTS	ELCHIS	ELEGIST
EGGCUPS	EIDERDOWN	EKE	ELD	ELEGISTS
EGGED	EIDERDOWNS	EKED	ELDER	ELEGIT
EGGER	EIDERS	EKES	ELDERLY	ELEGITS
EGGERIES	EIDETIC	EKING	ELDERS	ELEGIZE
EGGERS	EIDETICS	EKISTIC	ELDERSHIP	ELEGIZED
EGGERY	EIDOGRAPH	EKISTICS	ELDERSHIPS	ELEGIZES
EGGHEAD	EIDOGRAPHS	EKKA	ELDEST	ELEGIZING
EGGHEADS	EIDOLA	EKKAS	ELDIN	ELEGY
EGGIER	EIDOLON	EKLOGITE	ELDING	ELEMENT
EGGIEST	EIGENTONE	EKLOGITES	ELDINGS	ELEMENTAL
EGGING	EIGENTONES	EKPWELE	ELDINS	ELEMENTALS
EGGLER	EIGHT	EKPWELES	ELDRITCH	ELEMENTS
EGGLERS	EIGHTEEN	EKUELE	ELDS	ELEMI
EGGMASS	EIGHTEENS	EL	ELECT	ELEMIS
EGGMASSES	EIGHTFOIL	ELABORATE	ELECTABLE	ELENCH
EGGNOG	EIGHTFOILS	ELABORATED	ELECTED	ELENCHI
EGGNOGS	EIGHTFOLD	ELABORATES	ELECTING	ELENCHS
EGGS	EIGHTFOOT	ELABORATING	ELECTION	ELENCHUS
EGGSHELL	EIGHTH	ELAEOLITE	ELECTIONS	ELENCTIC
EGGSHELLS	EIGHTHLY	ELAEOLITES	ELECTIVE	ELEPHANT
EGGY	EIGHTHS	ÉLAN	ELECTIVES	ELEPHANTS
EGIS	EIGHTIES	ELANCE	ELECTOR	ELEUTHERI
EGISES	EIGHTIETH	ELANCED	ELECTORAL	ELEVATE
EGLANTINE	EIGHTIETHS	ELANCES	ELECTORS	ELEVATED
EGLANTINES	EIGHTS	ELANCING	ELECTRESS	ELEVATES
EGLATERE	EIGHTSMAN	ELAND	ELECTRESSES	ELEVATING
EGLATERES	EIGHTSMEN	ELANDS	ELECTRET	ELEVATION
EGMA	EIGHTSOME	ELANET	ELECTRETS	ELEVATIONS
EGMAS	EIGHTSOMES	ELANETS	ELECTRIC	ELEVATOR
EGO	EIGHTVO	ÉLANS	ELECTRICS	ELEVATORS
EGOISM	EIGHTVOS	ELAPHINE	ELECTRIFIED	ELEVATORY
EGOISMS	EIGHTY	ELAPSE	ELECTRIFIES	ELEVEN

ELEVENS
ELEVENSES
ELEVENTH
ELEVENTHS
ELEVON
ELEVONS
ELF
ELFED
ELFHOOD
ELFHOODS
ELFIN
ELFING
ELFINS
ELFISH
ELFLAND
ELFLANDS
ELFLOCKS
ELFS
ELIAD
ELIADS
ELICIT
ELICITED
ELICITING
ELICITOR
ELICITORS
ELICITS
ELIDE
ELIDED
ELIDES
ELIDING
ELIGIBLE
ELIGIBLES
ELIGIBLY
ELIMINANT
ELIMINANTS
ELIMINATE
ELIMINATED
ELIMINATES
ELIMINATING
ELISION
ELISIONS
ÉLITE
ÉLITES
ELITISM
ELITISMS
ELITIST
ELITISTS
ELIXIR
ELIXIRS
ELK
ELKHOUND
ELKHOUNDS
ELKS
ELL
ELLAGIC
ELLIPSE
ELLIPSES
ELLIPSIS
ELLIPSOID
ELLIPSOIDS
ELLIPTIC
ELLOPS
ELLOPSES
ELLS
ELLWAND
ELLWANDS
ELM
ELMEN
ELMIER
ELMIEST

ELMS
ELMWOOD
ELMWOODS
ELMY
ELOCUTE
ELOCUTED
ELOCUTES
ELOCUTING
ELOCUTION
ELOCUTIONS
ELOCUTORY
ÉLOGE
ÉLOGES
ELOGIES
ELOGIST
ELOGISTS
ELOGIUM
ELOGIUMS
ELOGY
ELOIGN
ELOIGNED
ELOIGNER
ELOIGNERS
ELOIGNING
ELOIGNS
ELOIN
ELOINED
ELOINER
ELOINERS
ELOINING
ELOINMENT
ELOINMENTS
ELOINS
ELONGATE
ELONGATED
ELONGATES
ELONGATING
ELOPE
ELOPED
ELOPEMENT
ELOPEMENTS
ELOPER
ELOPERS
ELOPES
ELOPING
ELOPS
ELOPSES
ELOQUENCE
ELOQUENCES
ELOQUENT
ELPEE
ELPEES
ELS
ELSE
ELSEWHERE
ELSEWISE
ELSHIN
ELSHINS
ELSIN
ELSINS
ELT
ELTCHI
ELTCHIS
ELTS
ELUANT
ELUANTS
ELUATE
ELUATES
ELUCIDATE
ELUCIDATED

ELUCIDATES
ELUCIDATING
ELUDE
ELUDED
ELUDER
ELUDERS
ELUDES
ELUDIBLE
ELUDING
ELUENT
ELUENTS
ELUSION
ELUSIONS
ELUSIVE
ELUSIVELY
ELUSORY
ELUTE
ELUTED
ELUTES
ELUTING
ELUTION
ELUTIONS
ELUTOR
ELUTORS
ELUTRIATE
ELUTRIATED
ELUTRIATES
ELUTRIATING
ELUVIA
ELUVIAL
ELUVIUM
ELUVIUMS
ELVAN
ELVANITE
ELVANITES
ELVANS
ELVER
ELVERS
ELVES
ELVISH
ELYTRA
ELYTRAL
ELYTRON
ELYTRONS
ELYTRUM
EM
EMACIATE
EMACIATED
EMACIATES
EMACIATING
EMALANGENI
EMANANT
EMANATE
EMANATED
EMANATES
EMANATING
EMANATION
EMANATIONS
EMANATIST
EMANATISTS
EMANATIVE
EMANATORY
EMBACE
EMBACED
EMBACES
EMBACING
EMBAIL
EMBAILED
EMBAILING
EMBAILS

EMBALE
EMBALED
EMBALES
EMBALING
EMBALL
EMBALLED
EMBALLING
EMBALLINGS
EMBALLS
EMBALM
EMBALMED
EMBALMER
EMBALMERS
EMBALMING
EMBALMINGS
EMBALMS
EMBANK
EMBANKED
EMBANKER
EMBANKERS
EMBANKING
EMBANKS
EMBAR
EMBARGO
EMBARGOED
EMBARGOES
EMBARGOING
EMBARGOS
EMBARK
EMBARKED
EMBARKING
EMBARKS
EMBARRASS
EMBARRASSED
EMBARRASSES
EMBARRASSING
EMBARRED
EMBARRING
EMBARRINGS
EMBARS
EMBASE
EMBASED
EMBASES
EMBASING
EMBASSADE
EMBASSADES
EMBASSAGE
EMBASSAGES
EMBASSIES
EMBASSY
EMBASTE
EMBATHE
EMBATHED
EMBATHES
EMBATHING
EMBATTLE
EMBATTLED
EMBATTLES
EMBATTLING
EMBAY
EMBAYED
EMBAYING
EMBAYLD
EMBAYMENT
EMBAYMENTS
EMBAYS
EMBED
EMBEDDED
EMBEDDING
EMBEDMENT

EMBEDMENTS
EMBEDS
EMBELLISH
EMBELLISHED
EMBELLISHES
EMBELLISHING
EMBER
EMBERS
EMBEZZLE
EMBEZZLED
EMBEZZLER
EMBEZZLERS
EMBEZZLES
EMBEZZLING
EMBITTER
EMBITTERED
EMBITTERING
EMBITTERINGS
EMBITTERS
EMBLAZE
EMBLAZED
EMBLAZES
EMBLAZING
EMBLAZON
EMBLAZONED
EMBLAZONING
EMBLAZONS
EMBLEM
EMBLEMA
EMBLEMATA
EMBLEMED
EMBLEMING
EMBLEMISE
EMBLEMISED
EMBLEMISES
EMBLEMISING
EMBLEMIZE
EMBLEMIZED
EMBLEMIZES
EMBLEMIZING
EMBLEMS
EMBLIC
EMBLICS
EMBLOOM
EMBLOOMED
EMBLOOMING
EMBLOOMS
EMBLOSSOM
EMBLOSSOMED
EMBLOSSOMING
EMBLOSSOMS
EMBODIED
EMBODIES
EMBODY
EMBODYING
EMBOG
EMBOGGED
EMBOGGING
EMBOGS
EMBOGUE
EMBOGUED
EMBOGUEING
EMBOGUES
EMBOGUING
EMBOIL
EMBOILED
EMBOILING
EMBOILS
EMBOLDEN
EMBOLDENED

EMBOLDENING
EMBOLDENS
EMBOLI
EMBOLIC
EMBOLIES
EMBOLISM
EMBOLISMS
EMBOLUS
EMBOLUSES
EMBOLY
EMBORDER
EMBORDERED
EMBORDERING
EMBORDERS
EMBOSCATA
EMBOSCATAS
EMBOSOM
EMBOSOMED
EMBOSOMING
EMBOSOMS
EMBOSS
EMBOSSED
EMBOSSER
EMBOSSERS
EMBOSSES
EMBOSSING
EMBOST
EMBOUND
EMBOUNDED
EMBOUNDING
EMBOUNDS
EMBOW
EMBOWED
EMBOWEL
EMBOWELLED
EMBOWELLING
EMBOWELS
EMBOWER
EMBOWERED
EMBOWERING
EMBOWERS
EMBOWING
EMBOWS
EMBOX
EMBOXED
EMBOXES
EMBOXING
EMBRACE
EMBRACED
EMBRACEOR
EMBRACEORS
EMBRACER
EMBRACERIES
EMBRACERS
EMBRACERY
EMBRACES
EMBRACING
EMBRACIVE
EMBRAID
EMBRAIDED
EMBRAIDING
EMBRAIDS
EMBRANGLE
EMBRANGLED
EMBRANGLES
EMBRANGLING
EMBRASOR
EMBRASORS
EMBRASURE
EMBRASURES

EMBRAVE
EMBRAVED
EMBRAVES
EMBRAVING
EMBRAZURE
EMBRAZURES
EMBREAD
EMBREADED
EMBREADING
EMBREADS
EMBREATHE
EMBREATHED
EMBREATHES
EMBREATHING
EMBREWE
EMBREWED
EMBREWES
EMBREWING
EMBRITTLE
EMBRITTLED
EMBRITTLES
EMBRITTLING
EMBROCATE
EMBROCATED
EMBROCATES
EMBROCATING
EMBROGLIO
EMBROGLIOS
EMBROIDER
EMBROIDERED
EMBROIDERING
EMBROIDERS
EMBROIL
EMBROILED
EMBROILING
EMBROILS
EMBROWN
EMBROWNED
EMBROWNING
EMBROWNS
EMBRUE
EMBRUED
EMBRUEING
EMBRUES
EMBRUING
EMBRUTE
EMBRUTED
EMBRUTES
EMBRUTING
EMBRYO
EMBRYON
EMBRYONAL
EMBRYONIC
EMBRYONS
EMBRYOS
EMBRYOTIC
EMBUS
EMBUSIED
EMBUSIES
EMBUSQUÉ
EMBUSQUÉS
EMBUSSED
EMBUSSES
EMBUSSING
EMBUSY
EMBUSYING
EMCEE
EMCEED
EMCEEING
EMCEES

EME
EMEER
EMEERS
EMEND
EMENDABLE
EMENDALS
EMENDATE
EMENDATED
EMENDATES
EMENDATING
EMENDATOR
EMENDATORS
EMENDED
EMENDING
EMENDS
EMERALD
EMERALDS
EMERAUDE
EMERAUDES
EMERGE
EMERGED
EMERGENCE
EMERGENCES
EMERGENCIES
EMERGENCY
EMERGENT
EMERGES
EMERGING
EMERIED
EMERIES
EMERITI
EMERITUS
EMERODS
EMERSED
EMERSION
EMERSIONS
EMERY
EMERYING
EMES
EMESES
EMESIS
EMETIC
EMETICAL
EMETICS
EMETIN
EMETINE
EMETINES
EMETINS
EMEU
EMEUS
ÉMEUTE
ÉMEUTES
EMICANT
EMICATE
EMICATED
EMICATES
EMICATING
EMICATION
EMICATIONS
EMICTION
EMICTIONS
EMICTORY
EMIGRANT
EMIGRANTS
EMIGRATE
EMIGRATED
EMIGRATES
EMIGRATING
ÉMIGRÉ
ÉMIGRÉS

EMINENCE
EMINENCES
EMINENCIES
EMINENCY
EMINENT
EMINENTLY
EMIR
EMIRATE
EMIRATES
EMIRS
EMISSARIES
EMISSARY
EMISSILE
EMISSION
EMISSIONS
EMISSIVE
EMIT
EMITS
EMITTED
EMITTING
EMMA
EMMARBLE
EMMARBLED
EMMARBLES
EMMARBLING
EMMAS
EMMER
EMMERS
EMMESH
EMMESHED
EMMESHES
EMMESHING
EMMET
EMMETROPE
EMMETROPES
EMMETS
EMMEW
EMMEWED
EMMEWING
EMMEWS
EMMOVE
EMMOVED
EMMOVES
EMMOVING
EMOLLIATE
EMOLLIATED
EMOLLIATES
EMOLLIATING
EMOLLIENT
EMOLLIENTS
EMOLUMENT
EMOLUMENTS
EMONG
EMONGES
EMONGEST
EMONGST
EMOTE
EMOTED
EMOTES
EMOTING
EMOTION
EMOTIONAL
EMOTIONS
EMOTIVE
EMOVE
EMOVED
EMOVES
EMOVING
EMPACKET
EMPACKETED

EMPACKETING
EMPACKETS
EMPAESTIC
EMPAIRE
EMPAIRED
EMPAIRES
EMPAIRING
EMPALE
EMPALED
EMPALES
EMPALING
EMPANEL
EMPANELLED
EMPANELLING
EMPANELS
EMPANOPLIED
EMPANOPLIES
EMPANOPLY
EMPANOPLYING
EMPARE
EMPARED
EMPARES
EMPARING
EMPART
EMPARTED
EMPARTING
EMPARTS
EMPATHIC
EMPATHIES
EMPATHISE
EMPATHISED
EMPATHISES
EMPATHISING
EMPATHIZE
EMPATHIZED
EMPATHIZES
EMPATHIZING
EMPATHY
EMPATRON
EMPATRONED
EMPATRONING
EMPATRONS
EMPAYRE
EMPAYRED
EMPAYRES
EMPAYRING
EMPEACH
EMPEACHED
EMPEACHES
EMPEACHING
EMPENNAGE
EMPENNAGES
EMPEOPLE
EMPEOPLED
EMPEOPLES
EMPEOPLING
EMPERCE
EMPERCED
EMPERCES
EMPERCING
EMPERIES
EMPERISE
EMPERISED
EMPERISES
EMPERISH
EMPERISHED
EMPERISHES
EMPERISHING
EMPERISING
EMPERIZE

EMPERIZED	EMPOLDERED	EMULOUS	ENARCHING	ENCHEASONS
EMPERIZES	EMPOLDERING	EMULOUSLY	ENARM	ENCHEER
EMPERIZING	EMPOLDERS	EMULSIFIED	ENARMED	ENCHEERED
EMPEROR	EMPORIA	EMULSIFIES	ENARMING	ENCHEERING
EMPERORS	EMPORIUM	EMULSIFY	ENARMS	ENCHEERS
EMPERY	EMPORIUMS	EMULSIFYING	ENATE	ENCHILADA
EMPHASES	EMPOWER	EMULSIN	ENATION	ENCHILADAS
EMPHASIS	EMPOWERED	EMULSINS	ENATIONS	ENCHORIAL
EMPHASISE	EMPOWERING	EMULSION	ENAUNTER	ENCHORIC
EMPHASISED	EMPOWERS	EMULSIONS	ENCAENIA	ENCIPHER
EMPHASISES	EMPRESS	EMULSIVE	ENCAENIAS	ENCIPHERED
EMPHASISING	EMPRESSE	EMULSOID	ENCAGE	ENCIPHERING
EMPHASIZE	EMPRESSES	EMULSOIDS	ENCAGED	ENCIPHERS
EMPHASIZED	EMPRISE	EMULSOR	ENCAGES	ENCIRCLE
EMPHASIZES	EMPRISES	EMULSORS	ENCAGING	ENCIRCLED
EMPHASIZING	EMPTIED	EMUNCTORIES	ENCALM	ENCIRCLES
EMPHATIC	EMPTIER	EMUNCTORY	ENCALMED	ENCIRCLING
EMPHLYSES	EMPTIERS	EMUNGE	ENCALMING	ENCIRCLINGS
EMPHLYSIS	EMPTIES	EMUNGED	ENCALMS	ENCLASP
EMPHYSEMA	EMPTIEST	EMUNGES	ENCAMP	ENCLASPED
EMPHYSEMAS	EMPTILY	EMUNGING	ENCAMPED	ENCLASPING
EMPIERCE	EMPTINESS	EMURE	ENCAMPING	ENCLASPS
EMPIERCED	EMPTINESSES	EMURED	ENCAMPS	ENCLAVE
EMPIERCES	EMPTION	EMURES	ENCANTHIS	ENCLAVED
EMPIERCING	EMPTIONAL	EMURING	ENCANTHISES	ENCLAVES
EMPIGHT	EMPTIONS	EMUS	ENCARPUS	ENCLAVING
EMPIRE	EMPTY	EMYDES	ENCARPUSES	ENCLISES
EMPIRES	EMPTYING	EMYS	ENCASE	ENCLISIS
EMPIRIC	EMPTYINGS	EN	ENCASED	ENCLITIC
EMPIRICAL	EMPTYSES	ENABLE	ENCASES	ENCLITICS
EMPIRICS	EMPTYSIS	ENABLED	ENCASH	ENCLOSE
EMPLACE	EMPURPLE	ENABLER	ENCASHED	ENCLOSED
EMPLACED	EMPURPLED	ENABLERS	ENCASHES	ENCLOSER
EMPLACES	EMPURPLES	ENABLES	ENCASHING	ENCLOSERS
EMPLACING	EMPURPLING	ENABLING	ENCASING	ENCLOSES
EMPLANE	EMPUSA	ENACT	ENCAUSTIC	ENCLOSING
EMPLANED	EMPUSAS	ENACTED	ENCAUSTICS	ENCLOSURE
EMPLANES	EMPUSE	ENACTING	ENCAVE	ENCLOSURES
EMPLANING	EMPUSES	ENACTION	ENCAVED	ENCLOTHE
EMPLASTER	EMPYEMA	ENACTIONS	ENCAVES	ENCLOTHED
EMPLASTERED	EMPYEMAS	ENACTIVE	ENCAVING	ENCLOTHES
EMPLASTERING	EMPYESES	ENACTMENT	ENCEINTE	ENCLOTHING
EMPLASTERS	EMPYESIS	ENACTMENTS	ENCEINTES	ENCLOUD
EMPLASTIC	EMPYREAL	ENACTOR	ENCHAFE	ENCLOUDED
EMPLASTICS	EMPYREAN	ENACTORS	ENCHAFED	ENCLOUDING
EMPLECTON	EMPYREANS	ENACTS	ENCHAFES	ENCLOUDS
EMPLECTONS	EMPYREUMA	ENACTURE	ENCHAFING	ENCODE
EMPLECTUM	EMPYREUMATA	ENACTURES	ENCHAIN	ENCODED
EMPLECTUMS	EMS	ENALLAGE	ENCHAINED	ENCODES
EMPLONGE	EMU	ENALLAGES	ENCHAINING	ENCODING
EMPLONGED	EMULATE	ENAMEL	ENCHAINS	ENCOLOUR
EMPLONGES	EMULATED	ENAMELLED	ENCHANT	ENCOLOURED
EMPLONGING	EMULATES	ENAMELLER	ENCHANTED	ENCOLOURING
EMPLOY	EMULATING	ENAMELLERS	ENCHANTER	ENCOLOURS
EMPLOYED	EMULATION	ENAMELLING	ENCHANTERS	ENCOLPION
EMPLOYEE	EMULATIONS	ENAMELLINGS	ENCHANTING	ENCOLPIONS
EMPLOYEES	EMULATIVE	ENAMELS	ENCHANTS	ENCOLPIUM
EMPLOYER	EMULATOR	ENAMOR	ENCHARGE	ENCOLPIUMS
EMPLOYERS	EMULATORS	ENAMORADO	ENCHARGED	ENCOLURE
EMPLOYING	EMULE	ENAMORADOS	ENCHARGES	ENCOLURES
EMPLOYS	EMULED	ENAMORED	ENCHARGING	ENCOMIA
EMPLUME	EMULES	ENAMORING	ENCHARM	ENCOMIAST
EMPLUMED	EMULGE	ENAMORS	ENCHARMED	ENCOMIASTS
EMPLUMES	EMULGED	ENAMOUR	ENCHARMING	ENCOMION
EMPLUMING	EMULGENCE	ENAMOURED	ENCHARMS	ENCOMIONS
EMPOISON	EMULGENCES	ENAMOURING	ENCHASE	ENCOMIUM
EMPOISONED	EMULGENT	ENAMOURS	ENCHASED	ENCOMIUMS
EMPOISONING	EMULGES	ENARCH	ENCHASES	ENCOMPASS
EMPOISONS	EMULGING	ENARCHED	ENCHASING	ENCOMPASSED
EMPOLDER	EMULING	ENARCHES	ENCHEASON	ENCOMPASSES

ENCOMPASSING	ENDART	ENDOLYMPH	ENDURED	ENFILADE
ENCORE	ENDARTED	ENDOLYMPHS	ENDURER	ENFILADED
ENCORED	ENDARTING	ENDOMIXES	ENDURERS	ENFILADES
ENCORES	ENDARTS	ENDOMIXIS	ENDURES	ENFILADING
ENCORING	ENDEAR	ENDOMIXISES	ENDURING	ENFILED
ENCOUNTER	ENDEARED	ENDOMORPH	ENDWAYS	ENFIRE
ENCOUNTERED	ENDEARING	ENDOMORPHS	ENDWISE	ENFIRED
ENCOUNTERING	ENDEARS	ENDOPHAGIES	ENE	ENFIRES
ENCOUNTERS	ENDEAVOUR	ENDOPHAGY	ENEMA	ENFIRING
ENCOURAGE	ENDEAVOURED	ENDOPHYTE	ENEMAS	ENFIX
ENCOURAGED	ENDEAVOURING	ENDOPHYTES	ENEMATA	ENFIXED
ENCOURAGES	ENDEAVOURS	ENDOPLASM	ENEMIES	ENFIXES
ENCOURAGING	ENDECAGON	ENDOPLASMS	ENEMY	ENFIXING
ENCOURAGINGS	ENDECAGONS	ENDORPHIN	ENERGETIC	ENFLESH
ENCRADLE	ENDED	ENDORPHINS	ENERGETICS	ENFLESHED
ENCRADLED	ENDEICTIC	ENDORSE	ENERGIC	ENFLESHES
ENCRADLES	ENDEIXES	ENDORSED	ENERGID	ENFLESHING
ENCRADLING	ENDEIXIS	ENDORSEE	ENERGIDS	ENFLOWER
ENCRATIES	ENDEIXISES	ENDORSEES	ENERGIES	ENFLOWERED
ENCRATY	ENDEMIAL	ENDORSER	ENERGISE	ENFLOWERING
ENCREASE	ENDEMIC	ENDORSERS	ENERGISED	ENFLOWERS
ENCREASED	ENDEMICAL	ENDORSES	ENERGISES	ENFOLD
ENCREASES	ENDEMICS	ENDORSING	ENERGISING	ENFOLDED
ENCREASING	ENDEMISM	ENDOSARC	ENERGIZE	ENFOLDING
ENCRIMSON	ENDEMISMS	ENDOSARCS	ENERGIZED	ENFOLDS
ENCRIMSONED	ENDENIZEN	ENDOSCOPE	ENERGIZES	ENFORCE
ENCRIMSONING	ENDENIZENED	ENDOSCOPES	ENERGIZING	ENFORCED
ENCRIMSONS	ENDENIZENING	ENDOSCOPIES	ENERGUMEN	ENFORCES
ENCRINAL	ENDENIZENS	ENDOSCOPY	ENERGUMENS	ENFORCING
ENCRINIC	ENDERMIC	ENDOSMOSE	ENERGY	ENFOREST
ENCRINITE	ENDERON	ENDOSMOSES	ENERVATE	ENFORESTED
ENCRINITES	ENDERONS	ENDOSPERM	ENERVATED	ENFORESTING
ENCROACH	ENDEW	ENDOSPERMS	ENERVATES	ENFORESTS
ENCROACHED	ENDEWED	ENDOSPORE	ENERVATING	ENFORM
ENCROACHES	ENDEWING	ENDOSPORES	ENERVE	ENFORMED
ENCROACHING	ENDEWS	ENDOSS	ENERVED	ENFORMING
ENCRUST	ENDGAME	ENDOSSED	ENERVES	ENFORMS
ENCRUSTED	ENDGAMES	ENDOSSES	ENERVING	ENFRAME
ENCRUSTING	ENDING	ENDOSSING	ENES	ENFRAMED
ENCRUSTS	ENDINGS	ENDOSTEAL	ENEW	ENFRAMES
ENCRYPT	ENDIRON	ENDOSTEUM	ENEWED	ENFRAMING
ENCRYPTED	ENDIRONS	ENDOSTEUMS	ENEWING	ENFREE
ENCRYPTING	ENDITE	ENDOW	ENEWS	ENFREED
ENCRYPTS	ENDITED	ENDOWED	ENFACE	ENFREEDOM
ENCUMBER	ENDITES	ENDOWER	ENFACED	ENFREEDOMED
ENCUMBERED	ENDITING	ENDOWERS	ENFACES	ENFREEDOMING
ENCUMBERING	ENDIVE	ENDOWING	ENFACING	ENFREEDOMS
ENCUMBERS	ENDIVES	ENDOWMENT	ENFANT	ENFREEING
ENCURTAIN	ENDLANG	ENDOWMENTS	ENFANTS	ENFREES
ENCURTAINED	ENDLESS	ENDOWS	ENFEEBLE	ENFREEZE
ENCURTAINING	ENDLESSLY	ENDOZOA	ENFEEBLED	ENFREEZES
ENCURTAINS	ENDLONG	ENDOZOIC	ENFEEBLES	ENFREEZING
ENCYCLIC	ENDMOST	ENDOZOON	ENFEEBLING	ENFROSEN
ENCYCLICS	ENDOBLAST	ENDS	ENFELON	ENFROZE
ENCYST	ENDOBLASTS	ENDSHIP	ENFELONED	ENFROZEN
ENCYSTED	ENDOCARP	ENDSHIPS	ENFELONING	ENG
ENCYSTING	ENDOCARPS	ENDUE	ENFELONS	ENGAGÉ
ENCYSTS	ENDOCRINE	ENDUED	ENFEOFF	ENGAGE
END	ENDOCRINES	ENDUEING	ENFEOFFED	ENGAGED
ENDAMAGE	ENDODERM	ENDUES	ENFEOFFING	ENGAGER
ENDAMAGED	ENDODERMS	ENDUING	ENFEOFFS	ENGAGERS
ENDAMAGES	ENDODYNE	ENDUNGEON	ENFESTED	ENGAGES
ENDAMAGING	ENDOGAMIC	ENDUNGEONED	ENFETTER	ENGAGING
ENDAMOEBA	ENDOGAMIES	ENDUNGEONING	ENFETTERED	ENGAOL
ENDAMOEBAE	ENDOGAMY	ENDUNGEONS	ENFETTERING	ENGAOLED
ENDANGER	ENDOGEN	ENDURABLE	ENFETTERS	ENGAOLING
ENDANGERED	ENDOGENIC	ENDURABLY	ENFIERCE	ENGAOLS
ENDANGERING	ENDOGENIES	ENDURANCE	ENFIERCED	ENGARLAND
ENDANGERS	ENDOGENS	ENDURANCES	ENFIERCES	ENGARLANDED
ENDARCH	ENDOGENY	ENDURE	ENFIERCING	ENGARLANDING

ENGARLANDS	ENGRAFTS	ENHEARSE	ENLARGES	ENOSES
ENGENDER	ENGRAIL	ENHEARSED	ENLARGING	ENOSIS
ENGENDERED	ENGRAILED	ENHEARSES	ENLEVÉ	ENOUGH
ENGENDERING	ENGRAILING	ENHEARSING	ENLIGHT	ENOUGHS
ENGENDERS	ENGRAILS	ENHEARTEN	ENLIGHTED	ENOUNCE
ENGENDURE	ENGRAIN	ENHEARTENED	ENLIGHTEN	ENOUNCED
ENGENDURES	ENGRAINED	ENHEARTENING	ENLIGHTENED	ENOUNCES
ENGILD	ENGRAINER	ENHEARTENS	ENLIGHTENING	ENOUNCING
ENGILDED	ENGRAINERS	ENHUNGER	ENLIGHTENS	ENOW
ENGILDING	ENGRAINING	ENHUNGERED	ENLIGHTING	ENPRINT
ENGILDS	ENGRAINS	ENHUNGERING	ENLIGHTS	ENPRINTS
ENGINE	ENGRAM	ENHUNGERS	ENLINK	ENQUIRE
ENGINED	ENGRAMMA	ENHYDRITE	ENLINKED	ENQUIRED
ENGINEER	ENGRAMMAS	ENHYDRITES	ENLINKING	ENQUIRER
ENGINEERED	ENGRAMS	ENHYDROS	ENLINKS	ENQUIRERS
ENGINEERING	ENGRASP	ENHYDROSES	ENLIST	ENQUIRES
ENGINEERINGS	ENGRASPED	ENHYDROUS	ENLISTED	ENQUIRIES
ENGINEERS	ENGRASPING	ENIAC	ENLISTING	ENQUIRING
ENGINER	ENGRASPS	ENIACS	ENLISTS	ENQUIRY
ENGINERIES	ENGRAVE	ENIGMA	ENLIVEN	ENRACE
ENGINERS	ENGRAVED	ENIGMAS	ENLIVENED	ENRACED
ENGINERY	ENGRAVEN	ENIGMATIC	ENLIVENER	ENRACES
ENGINES	ENGRAVER	ENISLE	ENLIVENERS	ENRACING
ENGINING	ENGRAVERIES	ENISLED	ENLIVENING	ENRAGÉ
ENGIRD	ENGRAVERS	ENISLES	ENLIVENS	ENRAGE
ENGIRDING	ENGRAVERY	ENISLING	ENLOCK	ENRAGED
ENGIRDLE	ENGRAVES	ENJAMB	ENLOCKED	ENRAGES
ENGIRDLED	ENGRAVING	ENJAMBED	ENLOCKING	ENRAGING
ENGIRDLES	ENGRAVINGS	ENJAMBING	ENLOCKS	ENRANCKLE
ENGIRDLING	ENGRENAGE	ENJAMBS	ENLUMINE	ENRANCKLED
ENGIRDS	ENGRENAGES	ENJOIN	ENLUMINED	ENRANCKLES
ENGIRT	ENGRIEVE	ENJOINED	ENLUMINES	ENRANCKLING
ENGISCOPE	ENGRIEVED	ENJOINER	ENLUMINING	ENRANGE
ENGISCOPES	ENGRIEVES	ENJOINERS	ENMESH	ENRANGED
ENGLOBE	ENGRIEVING	ENJOINING	ENMESHED	ENRANGES
ENGLOBED	ENGROOVE	ENJOINS	ENMESHES	ENRANGING
ENGLOBES	ENGROOVED	ENJOY	ENMESHING	ENRANK
ENGLOBING	ENGROOVES	ENJOYABLE	ENMEW	ENRANKED
ENGLOOM	ENGROOVING	ENJOYABLY	ENMEWED	ENRANKING
ENGLOOMED	ENGROSS	ENJOYED	ENMEWING	ENRANKS
ENGLOOMING	ENGROSSED	ENJOYER	ENMEWS	ENRAPT
ENGLOOMS	ENGROSSER	ENJOYERS	ENMITIES	ENRAPTURE
ENGLUT	ENGROSSERS	ENJOYING	ENMITY	ENRAPTURED
ENGLUTS	ENGROSSES	ENJOYMENT	ENMOSSED	ENRAPTURES
ENGLUTTED	ENGROSSING	ENJOYMENTS	ENMOVE	ENRAPTURING
ENGLUTTING	ENGS	ENJOYS	ENMOVED	ENRAUNGE
ENGOBE	ENGUARD	ENKERNEL	ENMOVES	ENRAUNGED
ENGOBES	ENGUARDED	ENKERNELLED	ENMOVING	ENRAUNGES
ENGORE	ENGUARDING	ENKERNELLING	ENNEAD	ENRAUNGING
ENGORED	ENGUARDS	ENKERNELS	ENNEADIC	ENRAVISH
ENGORES	ENGULF	ENKINDLE	ENNEADS	ENRAVISHED
ENGORGE	ENGULFED	ENKINDLED	ENNEAGON	ENRAVISHES
ENGORGED	ENGULFING	ENKINDLES	ENNEAGONS	ENRAVISHING
ENGORGES	ENGULFS	ENKINDLING	ENNOBLE	ENRHEUM
ENGORGING	ENGULPH	ENLACE	ENNOBLED	ENRHEUMED
ENGORING	ENGULPHED	ENLACED	ENNOBLES	ENRHEUMING
ENGOULED	ENGULPHING	ENLACES	ENNOBLING	ENRHEUMS
ENGOÜMENT	ENGULPHS	ENLACING	ENNUI	ENRICH
ENGOÜMENTS	ENGYSCOPE	ENLARD	ENNUIED	ENRICHED
ENGRACE	ENGYSCOPES	ENLARDED	ENNUIS	ENRICHES
ENGRACED	ENHALO	ENLARDING	ENNUYÉ	ENRICHING
ENGRACES	ENHALOED	ENLARDS	ENNUYED	ENRIDGED
ENGRACING	ENHALOES	ENLARGE	ENNUYING	ENRING
ENGRAFF	ENHALOING	ENLARGED	ENODAL	ENRINGED
ENGRAFFED	ENHALOS	ENLARGEN	ENOMOTIES	ENRINGING
ENGRAFFING	ENHANCE	ENLARGENED	ENOMOTY	ENRINGS
ENGRAFFS	ENHANCED	ENLARGENING	ENORM	ENRIVEN
ENGRAFT	ENHANCES	ENLARGENS	ENORMITIES	ENROBE
ENGRAFTED	ENHANCING	ENLARGER	ENORMITY	ENROBED
ENGRAFTING	ENHANCIVE	ENLARGERS	ENORMOUS	ENROBES

ENROBING
ENROL
ENROLL
ENROLLED
ENROLLER
ENROLLERS
ENROLLING
ENROLLS
ENROLMENT
ENROLMENTS
ENROLS
ENROOT
ENROOTED
ENROOTING
ENROOTS
ENROUGH
ENROUGHED
ENROUGHING
ENROUGHS
ENROUND
ENROUNDED
ENROUNDING
ENROUNDS
ENS
ENSAMPLE
ENSAMPLED
ENSAMPLES
ENSAMPLING
ENSATE
ENSCONCE
ENSCONCED
ENSCONCES
ENSCONCING
ENSEAL
ENSEALED
ENSEALING
ENSEALS
ENSEAM
ENSEAMED
ENSEAMING
ENSEAMS
ENSEAR
ENSEARED
ENSEARING
ENSEARS
ENSEMBLE
ENSEMBLES
ENSEW
ENSEWED
ENSEWING
ENSEWS
ENSHEATH
ENSHEATHE
ENSHEATHED
ENSHEATHES
ENSHEATHING
ENSHEATHS
ENSHELL
ENSHELLED
ENSHELLING
ENSHELLS
ENSHELTER
ENSHELTERED
ENSHELTERING
ENSHELTERS
ENSHIELD
ENSHIELDED
ENSHIELDING
ENSHIELDS
ENSHRINE

ENSHRINED
ENSHRINES
ENSHRINING
ENSHROUD
ENSHROUDED
ENSHROUDING
ENSHROUDS
ENSIFORM
ENSIGN
ENSIGNCIES
ENSIGNCY
ENSIGNED
ENSIGNING
ENSIGNS
ENSILAGE
ENSILAGED
ENSILAGES
ENSILAGING
ENSILE
ENSILED
ENSILES
ENSILING
ENSKIED
ENSKIES
ENSKY
ENSKYING
ENSLAVE
ENSLAVED
ENSLAVER
ENSLAVERS
ENSLAVES
ENSLAVING
ENSNARE
ENSNARED
ENSNARES
ENSNARING
ENSNARL
ENSNARLED
ENSNARLING
ENSNARLS
ENSORCELL
ENSORCELLED
ENSORCELLING
ENSORCELLS
ENSOUL
ENSOULED
ENSOULING
ENSOULS
ENSPHERE
ENSPHERED
ENSPHERES
ENSPHERING
ENSTAMP
ENSTAMPED
ENSTAMPING
ENSTAMPS
ENSTATITE
ENSTATITES
ENSTEEP
ENSTEEPED
ENSTEEPING
ENSTEEPS
ENSTYLE
ENSTYLED
ENSTYLES
ENSTYLING
ENSUE
ENSUED
ENSUES
ENSUING

ENSURE
ENSURED
ENSURER
ENSURERS
ENSURES
ENSURING
ENSWATHE
ENSWATHED
ENSWATHES
ENSWATHING
ENSWEEP
ENSWEEPING
ENSWEEPS
ENSWEPT
ENTAIL
ENTAILED
ENTAILER
ENTAILERS
ENTAILING
ENTAILS
ENTAME
ENTAMED
ENTAMES
ENTAMING
ENTAMOEBA
ENTAMOEBAE
ENTANGLE
ENTANGLED
ENTANGLES
ENTANGLING
ENTASES
ENTASIS
ENTAYLE
ENTAYLED
ENTAYLES
ENTAYLING
ENTELECHIES
ENTELECHY
ENTELLUS
ENTELLUSES
ENTENDER
ENTENDERED
ENTENDERING
ENTENDERS
ENTENTE
ENTENTES
ENTER
ENTERA
ENTERABLE
ENTERAL
ENTERATE
ENTERED
ENTERER
ENTERERS
ENTERIC
ENTERICS
ENTERING
ENTERINGS
ENTERITIS
ENTERITISES
ENTERON
ENTERS
ENTERTAIN
ENTERTAINED
ENTERTAINING
ENTERTAININGS
ENTERTAINS
ENTERTAKE
ENTERTAKEN
ENTERTAKES

ENTERTAKING
ENTERTOOK
ENTÊTÉ
ENTÊTÉE
ENTHALPIES
ENTHALPY
ENTHETIC
ENTHRAL
ENTHRALL
ENTHRALLED
ENTHRALLING
ENTHRALLS
ENTHRALS
ENTHRONE
ENTHRONED
ENTHRONES
ENTHRONING
ENTHUSE
ENTHUSED
ENTHUSES
ENTHUSING
ENTHYMEME
ENTHYMEMES
ENTIA
ENTICE
ENTICED
ENTICER
ENTICERS
ENTICES
ENTICING
ENTICINGS
ENTIRE
ENTIRELY
ENTIRES
ENTIRETIES
ENTIRETY
ENTITIES
ENTITLE
ENTITLED
ENTITLES
ENTITLING
ENTITY
ENTOBLAST
ENTOBLASTS
ENTODERM
ENTODERMS
ENTOIL
ENTOILED
ENTOILING
ENTOILS
ENTOMB
ENTOMBED
ENTOMBING
ENTOMBS
ENTOMIC
ENTOPHYTE
ENTOPHYTES
ENTOPIC
ENTOPTIC
ENTOPTICS
ENTOTIC
ENTOURAGE
ENTOURAGES
ENTOZOA
ENTOZOAL
ENTOZOIC
ENTOZOON
ENTRAIL
ENTRAILED
ENTRAILING

ENTRAILS
ENTRAIN
ENTRAINED
ENTRAINING
ENTRAINS
ENTRALL
ENTRALLES
ENTRAMMEL
ENTRAMMELLED
ENTRAMMELLING
ENTRAMMELS
ENTRANCE
ENTRANCED
ENTRANCES
ENTRANCING
ENTRANT
ENTRANTS
ENTRAP
ENTRAPPED
ENTRAPPER
ENTRAPPERS
ENTRAPPING
ENTRAPS
ENTREAT
ENTREATED
ENTREATIES
ENTREATING
ENTREATS
ENTREATY
ENTRECHAT
ENTRECHATS
ENTRECÔTE
ENTRECÔTES
ENTRÉE
ENTRÉES
ENTREMES
ENTREMETS
ENTRENCH
ENTRENCHED
ENTRENCHES
ENTRENCHING
ENTREPOT
ENTREPOTS
ENTRESOL
ENTRESOLS
ENTREZ
ENTRIES
ENTRISM
ENTRISMS
ENTRIST
ENTRISTS
ENTROLD
ENTROPIES
ENTROPION
ENTROPIONS
ENTROPIUM
ENTROPIUMS
ENTROPY
ENTRUST
ENTRUSTED
ENTRUSTING
ENTRUSTS
ENTRY
ENTRYISM
ENTRYISMS
ENTRYIST
ENTRYISTS
ENTWINE
ENTWINED
ENTWINES

ENTWINING
ENTWIST
ENTWISTED
ENTWISTING
ENTWISTS
ENUCLEATE
ENUCLEATED
ENUCLEATES
ENUCLEATING
ENUMERATE
ENUMERATED
ENUMERATES
ENUMERATING
ENUNCIATE
ENUNCIATED
ENUNCIATES
ENUNCIATING
ENURE
ENURED
ENURES
ENURESES
ENURESIS
ENURETIC
ENURETICS
ENURING
ENVASSAL
ENVASSALLED
ENVASSALLING
ENVASSALS
ENVAULT
ENVAULTED
ENVAULTING
ENVAULTS
ENVEIGLE
ENVEIGLED
ENVEIGLES
ENVEIGLING
ENVELOP
ENVELOPE
ENVELOPED
ENVELOPES
ENVELOPING
ENVELOPS
ENVENOM
ENVENOMED
ENVENOMING
ENVENOMS
ENVERMEIL
ENVERMEILED
ENVERMEILING
ENVERMEILS
ENVIABLE
ENVIABLY
ENVIED
ENVIER
ENVIERS
ENVIES
ENVIOUS
ENVIOUSLY
ENVIRON
ENVIRONED
ENVIRONING
ENVIRONS
ENVISAGE
ENVISAGED
ENVISAGES
ENVISAGING
ENVISION
ENVISIONED
ENVISIONING

ENVISIONS
ENVOI
ENVOIS
ENVOY
ENVOYS
ENVOYSHIP
ENVOYSHIPS
ENVY
ENVYING
ENVYINGS
ENWALL
ENWALLED
ENWALLING
ENWALLOW
ENWALLOWED
ENWALLOWING
ENWALLOWS
ENWALLS
ENWHEEL
ENWHEELED
ENWHEELING
ENWHEELS
ENWIND
ENWINDING
ENWINDS
ENWOMB
ENWOMBED
ENWOMBING
ENWOMBS
ENWOUND
ENWRAP
ENWRAPPED
ENWRAPPING
ENWRAPPINGS
ENWRAPS
ENWREATHE
ENWREATHED
ENWREATHES
ENWREATHING
ENZIAN
ENZIANS
ENZONE
ENZONED
ENZONES
ENZONING
ENZOOTIC
ENZOOTICS
ENZYMATIC
ENZYME
ENZYMES
ENZYMIC
EOAN
ÉOLIENNE
ÉOLIENNES
EOLIPILE
EOLIPILES
EOLITH
EOLITHIC
EOLITHS
EON
EONISM
EONISMS
EONS
EORL
EORLS
EOSIN
EOSINS
EOTHEN
EPACRID
EPACRIDS

EPACRIS
EPACRISES
EPACT
EPACTS
EPAENETIC
EPAGOGE
EPAGOGES
EPAGOGIC
EPAINETIC
EPANODOS
EPANODOSES
EPARCH
EPARCHATE
EPARCHATES
EPARCHIES
EPARCHS
EPARCHY
ÉPATANT
EPAULE
EPAULES
EPAULET
EPAULETS
EPAULETTE
EPAULETTES
EPAXIAL
EPEDAPHIC
ÉPÉE
ÉPÉES
EPEIRA
EPEIRAS
EPEIRID
EPEIRIDS
EPEOLATRIES
EPEOLATRY
ÉPERDU
ÉPERDUE
EPERGNE
EPERGNES
EPHA
EPHAH
EPHAHS
EPHAS
EPHEBE
EPHEBI
EPHEBIC
EPHEBOS
EPHEBUS
EPHEDRA
EPHEDRAS
EPHEDRINE
EPHEDRINES
EPHELIDES
EPHELIS
EPHEMERA
EPHEMERAE
EPHEMERAL
EPHEMERALS
EPHEMERAS
EPHEMERID
EPHEMERIDES
EPHEMERIDS
EPHEMERIS
EPHEMERON
EPHIALTES
EPHOD
EPHODS
EPHOR
EPHORALTIES
EPHORALTY
EPHORS

EPIBLAST
EPIBLASTS
EPIC
EPICAL
EPICALLY
EPICALYCES
EPICALYX
EPICALYXES
EPICARP
EPICARPS
EPICEDE
EPICEDES
EPICEDIA
EPICEDIAL
EPICEDIAN
EPICEDIUM
EPICENE
EPICENES
EPICENTRE
EPICENTRES
ÉPICIER
ÉPICIERS
EPICISM
EPICISMS
EPICIST
EPICISTS
EPICLESES
EPICLESIS
EPICOTYL
EPICOTYLS
EPICRITIC
EPICS
EPICURE
EPICUREAN
EPICUREANS
EPICURES
EPICURISE
EPICURISED
EPICURISES
EPICURISING
EPICURISM
EPICURISMS
EPICURIZE
EPICURIZED
EPICURIZES
EPICURIZING
EPICYCLE
EPICYCLES
EPICYCLIC
EPIDEMIC
EPIDEMICS
EPIDERMAL
EPIDERMIC
EPIDERMIS
EPIDERMISES
EPIDOSITE
EPIDOSITES
EPIDOTE
EPIDOTES
EPIDOTIC
EPIDURAL
EPIDURALS
EPIFOCAL
EPIGAEAL
EPIGAEAN
EPIGAEOUS
EPIGAMIC
EPIGEAL
EPIGEAN
EPIGENE

EPIGEOUS
EPIGON
EPIGONE
EPIGONES
EPIGONI
EPIGONS
EPIGRAM
EPIGRAMS
EPIGRAPH
EPIGRAPHED
EPIGRAPHIES
EPIGRAPHING
EPIGRAPHS
EPIGRAPHY
EPIGYNIES
EPIGYNOUS
EPIGYNY
EPILATE
EPILATED
EPILATES
EPILATING
EPILATION
EPILATIONS
EPILATOR
EPILATORS
EPILEPSIES
EPILEPSY
EPILEPTIC
EPILEPTICS
EPILOBIUM
EPILOBIUMS
EPILOGIC
EPILOGISE
EPILOGISED
EPILOGISES
EPILOGISING
EPILOGIZE
EPILOGIZED
EPILOGIZES
EPILOGIZING
EPILOGUE
EPILOGUES
EPIMER
EPIMERIC
EPIMERS
EPINASTIC
EPINASTIES
EPINASTY
EPINICIAN
EPINICION
EPINICIONS
EPINIKIAN
EPINIKION
EPINIKIONS
EPINOSIC
EPIPHANIC
EPIPHRAGM
EPIPHRAGMS
EPIPHYSES
EPIPHYSIS
EPIPHYTAL
EPIPHYTE
EPIPHYTES
EPIPHYTIC
EPIPLOIC
EPIPLOON
EPIPLOONS
EPIPOLIC
EPIPOLISM
EPIPOLISMS

EPIRRHEMA
EPIRRHEMAS
EPISCOPAL
EPISCOPE
EPISCOPES
EPISCOPIES
EPISCOPY
EPISEMON
EPISEMONS
EPISODAL
EPISODE
EPISODES
EPISODIAL
EPISODIC
EPISOME
EPISOMES
EPISPERM
EPISPERMS
EPISPORE
EPISPORES
EPISTASES
EPISTASIS
EPISTATIC
EPISTAXES
EPISTAXIS
EPISTAXISES
EPISTEMIC
EPISTEMICS
EPISTLE
EPISTLED
EPISTLER
EPISTLERS
EPISTLES
EPISTLING
EPISTOLER
EPISTOLERS
EPISTOLET
EPISTOLETS
EPISTOLIC
EPISTYLE
EPISTYLES
EPITAPH
EPITAPHED
EPITAPHER
EPITAPHERS
EPITAPHIC
EPITAPHING
EPITAPHS
EPITASES
EPITASIS
EPITAXIAL
EPITAXIES
EPITAXY
EPITHEM
EPITHEMA
EPITHEMATA
EPITHEMS
EPITHESES
EPITHESIS
EPITHET
EPITHETED
EPITHETIC
EPITHETING
EPITHETON
EPITHETONS
EPITHETS
EPITOME
EPITOMES
EPITOMIC
EPITOMISE

EPITOMISED
EPITOMISES
EPITOMISING
EPITOMIST
EPITOMISTS
EPITOMIZE
EPITOMIZED
EPITOMIZES
EPITOMIZING
EPITONIC
EPITRITE
EPITRITES
EPIZEUXES
EPIZEUXIS
EPIZEUXISES
EPIZOA
EPIZOAN
EPIZOANS
EPIZOIC
EPIZOON
EPIZOOTIC
EPIZOOTICS
EPOCH
EPOCHA
EPOCHAL
EPOCHAS
EPOCHS
EPODE
EPODES
EPODIC
EPONYM
EPONYMOUS
EPONYMS
EPOPEE
EPOPEES
EPOPOEIA
EPOPOEIAS
EPOPT
EPOPTS
EPOS
EPOSES
EPOXIDE
EPOXIDES
EPOXIES
EPOXY
ÉPRIS
ÉPRISE
EPSILON
EPSILONS
EPSOMITE
EPSOMITES
ÉPUISÉ
ÉPUISÉE
EPULARY
EPULATION
EPULATIONS
EPULIDES
EPULIS
EPULISES
EPULOTIC
EPULOTICS
EPURATE
EPURATED
EPURATES
EPURATING
EPURATION
EPURATIONS
EPYLLION
EPYLLIONS
EQUABLE

EQUABLY
EQUAL
EQUALISE
EQUALISED
EQUALISER
EQUALISERS
EQUALISES
EQUALISING
EQUALITIES
EQUALITY
EQUALIZE
EQUALIZED
EQUALIZER
EQUALIZERS
EQUALIZES
EQUALIZING
EQUALLED
EQUALLING
EQUALLY
EQUALNESS
EQUALNESSES
EQUALS
EQUANT
EQUANTS
EQUATE
EQUATED
EQUATES
EQUATING
EQUATION
EQUATIONS
EQUATOR
EQUATORS
EQUERRIES
EQUERRY
EQUINAL
EQUINE
EQUINIA
EQUINIAS
EQUINITIES
EQUINITY
EQUINOX
EQUINOXES
EQUIP
EQUIPAGE
EQUIPAGED
EQUIPAGES
EQUIPAGING
ÉQUIPE
ÉQUIPES
EQUIPMENT
EQUIPMENTS
EQUIPOISE
EQUIPOISED
EQUIPOISES
EQUIPOISING
EQUIPPED
EQUIPPING
EQUIPS
EQUISETA
EQUISETIC
EQUISETUM
EQUISETUMS
EQUITABLE
EQUITABLY
EQUITANT
EQUITIES
EQUITY
EQUIVALVE
EQUIVOCAL
EQUIVOKE

EQUIVOKES
EQUIVOQUE
EQUIVOQUES
ER
ERA
ERADIATE
ERADIATED
ERADIATES
ERADIATING
ERADICATE
ERADICATED
ERADICATES
ERADICATING
ERAS
ERASABLE
ERASE
ERASED
ERASEMENT
ERASEMENTS
ERASER
ERASERS
ERASES
ERASING
ERASION
ERASIONS
ERASURE
ERASURES
ERATHEM
ERATHEMS
ERBIA
ERBIAS
ERBIUM
ERBIUMS
ERE
ERECT
ERECTED
ERECTER
ERECTERS
ERECTILE
ERECTING
ERECTION
ERECTIONS
ERECTIVE
ERECTLY
ERECTNESS
ERECTNESSES
ERECTOR
ERECTORS
ERECTS
ERED
ERELONG
EREMIC
EREMITAL
EREMITE
EREMITES
EREMITIC
EREMITISM
EREMITISMS
ERENOW
EREPSIN
EREPSINS
ERES
ERETHISM
ERETHISMS
ERETHITIC
EREWHILE
ERF
ERG
ERGATANER
ERGATANERS

ERGATE
ERGATES
ERGATOID
ERGO
ERGODIC
ERGOGRAM
ERGOGRAMS
ERGOGRAPH
ERGOGRAPHS
ERGOMETER
ERGOMETERS
ERGON
ERGONOMIC
ERGONOMICS
ERGONS
ERGOT
ERGOTISE
ERGOTISED
ERGOTISES
ERGOTISING
ERGOTISM
ERGOTISMS
ERGOTIZE
ERGOTIZED
ERGOTIZES
ERGOTIZING
ERGOTS
ERGS
ERIACH
ERIACHS
ERIC
ERICA
ERICAS
ERICK
ERICKS
ERICOID
ERICS
ERIGERON
ERIGERONS
ERING
ERINGO
ERINGOES
ERINGOS
ERINITE
ERINITES
ERIOMETER
ERIOMETERS
ERIONITE
ERIONITES
ERISTIC
ERISTICAL
ERK
ERKS
ERMELIN
ERMELINS
ERMINE
ERMINED
ERMINES
ERN
ERNE
ERNED
ERNES
ERNING
ERNS
ERODE
ERODED
ERODENT
ERODENTS
ERODES
ERODING

ERODIUM	ERUDITES	ESCARPED	ESLOYNING	ESSENTIAL
ERODIUMS	ERUDITION	ESCARPING	ESNE	ESSENTIALS
EROGENIC	ERUDITIONS	ESCARPS	ESNECIES	ESSES
EROGENOUS	ERUPT	ESCHALOT	ESNECY	ESSIVE
EROSE	ERUPTED	ESCHALOTS	ESNES	ESSIVES
EROSION	ERUPTING	ESCHAR	ESOPHAGI	ESSOIN
EROSIONS	ERUPTION	ESCHARS	ESOPHAGUS	ESSOINER
EROSIVE	ERUPTIONS	ESCHEAT	ESOTERIC	ESSOINERS
EROSTRATE	ERUPTIVE	ESCHEATED	ESOTERICA	ESSOINS
EROTEMA	ERUPTS	ESCHEATING	ESOTERIES	ESSONITE
EROTEMAS	ERVALENTA	ESCHEATOR	ESOTERISM	ESSONITES
EROTEME	ERVALENTAS	ESCHEATORS	ESOTERISMS	ESSOYNE
EROTEMES	ERVEN	ESCHEATS	ESOTERY	ESSOYNES
EROTESES	ERYNGIUM	ESCHEW	ESPADA	ESTABLISH
EROTESIS	ERYNGIUMS	ESCHEWED	ESPADAS	ESTABLISHED
EROTETIC	ERYNGO	ESCHEWING	ESPAGNOLE	ESTABLISHES
EROTIC	ERYNGOES	ESCHEWS	ESPAGNOLES	ESTABLISHING
EROTICA	ERYNGOS	ESCLANDRE	ESPALIER	ESTACADE
EROTICAL	ERYTHEMA	ESCLANDRES	ESPALIERED	ESTACADES
EROTICALS	ERYTHEMAL	ESCOLAR	ESPALIERING	ESTAFETTE
EROTICISM	ERYTHEMAS	ESCOLARS	ESPALIERS	ESTAFETTES
EROTICISMS	ERYTHRINA	ESCOPETTE	ESPARTO	ESTAMINET
EROTICIST	ERYTHRINAS	ESCOPETTES	ESPARTOS	ESTAMINETS
EROTICISTS	ERYTHRISM	ESCORT	ESPECIAL	ESTANCIA
EROTICS	ERYTHRISMS	ESCORTAGE	ESPERANCE	ESTANCIAS
EROTISM	ERYTHRITE	ESCORTAGES	ESPERANCES	ESTATE
EROTISMS	ERYTHRITES	ESCORTED	ESPIAL	ESTATED
ERR	ES	ESCORTING	ESPIALS	ESTATES
ERRABLE	ESCALADE	ESCORTS	ESPIED	ESTATING
ERRAND	ESCALADED	ESCOT	ESPIÈGLE	ESTEEM
ERRANDS	ESCALADES	ESCOTS	ESPIES	ESTEEMED
ERRANT	ESCALADING	ESCOTTED	ESPIONAGE	ESTEEMING
ERRANTLY	ESCALADO	ESCOTTING	ESPIONAGES	ESTEEMS
ERRANTRIES	ESCALADOES	ESCRIBANO	ESPLANADE	ESTER
ERRANTRY	ESCALATE	ESCRIBANOS	ESPLANADES	ESTERIFIED
ERRANTS	ESCALATED	ESCRIBE	ESPOUSAL	ESTERIFIES
ERRATA	ESCALATES	ESCRIBED	ESPOUSALS	ESTERIFY
ERRATIC	ESCALATING	ESCRIBES	ESPOUSE	ESTERIFYING
ERRATICAL	ESCALATOR	ESCRIBING	ESPOUSED	ESTERS
ERRATICS	ESCALATORS	ESCROC	ESPOUSER	ESTHESES
ERRATUM	ESCALIER	ESCROCS	ESPOUSERS	ESTHESIA
ERRED	ESCALIERS	ESCROL	ESPOUSES	ESTHESIAS
ERRHINE	ESCALLOP	ESCROLL	ESPOUSING	ESTHESIS
ERRHINES	ESCALLOPS	ESCROLLS	ESPRESSO	ESTHETE
ERRING	ESCALOP	ESCROLS	ESPRESSOS	ESTHETES
ERRINGLY	ESCALOPE	ESCROW	ESPRIT	ESTHETIC
ERRINGS	ESCALOPES	ESCROWS	ESPRITS	ESTHETICS
ERRONEOUS	ESCALOPS	ESCUAGE	ESPUMOSO	ESTIMABLE
ERROR	ESCAPABLE	ESCUAGES	ESPUMOSOS	ESTIMABLY
ERRORIST	ESCAPADE	ESCUDO	ESPY	ESTIMATE
ERRORISTS	ESCAPADES	ESCUDOS	ESPYING	ESTIMATED
ERRORS	ESCAPADO	ESCULENT	ESQUIRE	ESTIMATES
ERRS	ESCAPADOES	ESCULENTS	ESQUIRES	ESTIMATING
ERS	ESCAPE	ESEMPLASIES	ESQUISSE	ESTIMATOR
ERSATZ	ESCAPED	ESEMPLASY	ESQUISSES	ESTIMATORS
ERSATZES	ESCAPEE	ESILE	ESS	ESTIVAL
ERSES	ESCAPEES	ESILES	ESSAY	ESTIVATE
ERST	ESCAPER	ESKAR	ESSAYED	ESTIVATED
ERSTWHILE	ESCAPERS	ESKARS	ESSAYER	ESTIVATES
ERUCIFORM	ESCAPES	ESKER	ESSAYERS	ESTIVATING
ERUCT	ESCAPING	ESKERS	ESSAYETTE	ESTOC
ERUCTATE	ESCAPISM	ESKIES	ESSAYETTES	ESTOCS
ERUCTATED	ESCAPISMS	ESKY™	ESSAYING	ESTOILE
ERUCTATES	ESCAPIST	ESLOIN	ESSAYISH	ESTOILES
ERUCTATING	ESCAPISTS	ESLOINED	ESSAYIST	ESTOP
ERUCTED	ESCARGOT	ESLOINING	ESSAYISTS	ESTOPPAGE
ERUCTING	ESCARGOTS	ESLOINS	ESSAYS	ESTOPPAGES
ERUCTS	ESCAROLE	ESLOYNE	ESSE	ESTOPPED
ERUDITE	ESCAROLES	ESLOYNED	ESSENCE	ESTOPPEL
ERUDITELY	ESCARP	ESLOYNES	ESSENCES	ESTOPPELS

ESTOPPING	ÉTATISMES	ETHICISM	ETTIN	EUK
ESTOPS	ÉTATISTE	ETHICISMS	ETTINS	EUKARYON
ESTOVER	ÉTATISTES	ETHICIST	ETTLE	EUKARYONS
ESTOVERS	ÉTATS	ETHICISTS	ETTLED	EUKARYOT
ESTRADE	ETCH	ETHICIZE	ETTLES	EUKARYOTE
ESTRADES	ETCHANT	ETHICIZED	ETTLING	EUKARYOTES
ESTRAL	ETCHANTS	ETHICIZES	ÉTUDE	EUKARYOTS
ESTRANGE	ETCHED	ETHICIZING	ÉTUDES	EUKED
ESTRANGED	ETCHER	ETHICS	ETUI	EUKING
ESTRANGER	ETCHERS	ETHIOPS	ETUIS	EUKS
ESTRANGERS	ETCHES	ETHIOPSES	ETWEE	EULACHON
ESTRANGES	ETCHING	ETHMOID	ETWEES	EULACHONS
ESTRANGING	ETCHINGS	ETHMOIDAL	ETYMA	EULOGIA
ESTRAPADE	ETEN	ETHNARCH	ETYMIC	EULOGIES
ESTRAPADES	ETENS	ETHNARCHIES	ETYMOLOGIES	EULOGISE
ESTRAY	ETERNAL	ETHNARCHS	ETYMOLOGY	EULOGISED
ESTRAYED	ETERNALLY	ETHNARCHY	ETYMON	EULOGISES
ESTRAYING	ETERNE	ETHNIC	ETYMONS	EULOGISING
ESTRAYS	ETERNISE	ETHNICAL	ETYPIC	EULOGIST
ESTREAT	ETERNISED	ETHNICISM	ETYPICAL	EULOGISTS
ESTREATED	ETERNISES	ETHNICISMS	EUCAIN	EULOGIUM
ESTREATING	ETERNISING	ETHNICITIES	EUCAINE	EULOGIUMS
ESTREATS	ETERNITIES	ETHNICITY	EUCAINES	EULOGIZE
ESTREPE	ETERNITY	ETHNICS	EUCAINS	EULOGIZED
ESTREPED	ETERNIZE	ETHNOCIDE	EUCALYPT	EULOGIZES
ESTREPES	ETERNIZED	ETHNOCIDES	EUCALYPTI	EULOGIZING
ESTREPING	ETERNIZES	ETHNOLOGIES	EUCALYPTS	EULOGY
ESTRICH	ETERNIZING	ETHNOLOGY	EUCARYON	EUMELANIN
ESTRICHES	ETESIAN	ETHOLOGIC	EUCARYONS	EUMELANINS
ESTRIDGE	ETH	ETHOLOGIES	EUCARYOT	EUMERISM
ESTRIDGES	ETHAL	ETHOLOGY	EUCARYOTE	EUMERISMS
ESTRILDID	ETHALS	ETHOS	EUCARYOTES	EUNUCH
ESTRILDIDS	ETHANE	ETHOSES	EUCARYOTS	EUNUCHISE
ESTRO	ETHANES	ETHS	EUCHARIS	EUNUCHISED
ESTROGEN	ETHANOL	ETHYL	EUCHARISES	EUNUCHISES
ESTROGENS	ETHANOLS	ETHYLATE	EUCHLORIC	EUNUCHISING
ESTROS	ETHE	ETHYLATED	EUCHOLOGIES	EUNUCHISM
ESTROUS	ETHENE	ETHYLATES	EUCHOLOGY	EUNUCHISMS
ESTRUM	ETHENES	ETHYLATING	EUCHRE	EUNUCHIZE
ESTRUMS	ETHER	ETHYLENE	EUCHRED	EUNUCHIZED
ESTRUS	ETHERCAP	ETHYLENES	EUCHRES	EUNUCHIZES
ESTRUSES	ETHERCAPS	ETHYLS	EUCHRING	EUNUCHIZING
ESTUARIAL	ETHEREAL	ETHYNE	EUCLASE	EUNUCHOID
ESTUARIAN	ETHEREOUS	ETHYNES	EUCLASES	EUNUCHOIDS
ESTUARIES	ETHERIAL	ETIOLATE	EUCRITE	EUNUCHS
ESTUARINE	ETHERIC	ETIOLATED	EUCRITES	EUOI
ESTUARY	ETHERICAL	ETIOLATES	EUCRITIC	EUONYMIN
ESURIENCE	ETHERION	ETIOLATING	EUCYCLIC	EUONYMINS
ESURIENCES	ETHERIONS	ETIOLIN	EUDAEMONIES	EUONYMUS
ESURIENCIES	ETHERISE	ETIOLINS	EUDAEMONY	EUONYMUSES
ESURIENCY	ETHERISED	ETIOLOGIES	EUDEMONIA	EUOUAE
ESURIENT	ETHERISES	ETIOLOGY	EUDEMONIAS	EUOUAES
ETA	ETHERISING	ETIQUETTE	EUDEMONIC	EUPAD
ETACISM	ETHERISM	ETIQUETTES	EUDEMONICS	EUPADS
ETACISMS	ETHERISMS	ETNA	EUDEMONIES	EUPATRID
ETAERIO	ETHERIST	ETNAS	EUDEMONY	EUPATRIDAE
ETAERIOS	ETHERISTS	ÉTOILE	EUDIALYTE	EUPATRIDS
ÉTAGE	ETHERIZE	ÉTOILES	EUDIALYTES	EUPEPSIA
ÉTAGÈRE	ETHERIZED	ÉTOURDI	EUGE	EUPEPSIAS
ÉTAGÈRES	ETHERIZES	ÉTOURDIE	EUGENIC	EUPEPSIES
ÉTAGES	ETHERIZING	ÉTRANGER	EUGENICS	EUPEPSY
ÉTALAGE	ETHERS	ÉTRANGÈRE	EUGENISM	EUPEPTIC
ÉTALAGES	ETHIC	ÉTRANGÈRES	EUGENISMS	EUPHAUSID
ETALON	ETHICAL	ÉTRANGERS	EUGENIST	EUPHAUSIDS
ETALONS	ETHICALLY	ÉTRENNE	EUGENISTS	EUPHEMISE
ÉTAPE	ETHICALS	ÉTRENNES	EUGENOL	EUPHEMISED
ÉTAPES	ETHICISE	ÉTRIER	EUGENOLS	EUPHEMISES
ETAS	ETHICISED	ÉTRIERS	EUGH	EUPHEMISING
ÉTAT	ETHICISES	ETTERCAP	EUGHEN	EUPHEMISM
ÉTATISME	ETHICISING	ETTERCAPS	EUGHS	EUPHEMISMS

EUPHEMIZE
EUPHEMIZED
EUPHEMIZES
EUPHEMIZING
EUPHENICS
EUPHOBIA
EUPHOBIAS
EUPHON
EUPHONIA
EUPHONIAS
EUPHONIC
EUPHONIES
EUPHONISE
EUPHONISED
EUPHONISES
EUPHONISING
EUPHONIUM
EUPHONIUMS
EUPHONIZE
EUPHONIZED
EUPHONIZES
EUPHONIZING
EUPHONS
EUPHONY
EUPHORBIA
EUPHORBIAS
EUPHORIA
EUPHORIAS
EUPHORIC
EUPHORIES
EUPHORY
EUPHRASIES
EUPHRASY
EUPHROE
EUPHROES
EUPHUISE
EUPHUISED
EUPHUISES
EUPHUISING
EUPHUISM
EUPHUISMS
EUPHUIST
EUPHUISTS
EUPHUIZE
EUPHUIZED
EUPHUIZES
EUPHUIZING
EUREKA
EUREKAS
EURHYTHMIES
EURHYTHMY
EURIPI
EURIPUS
EURIPUSES
EURO
EUROPIUM
EUROPIUMS
EUROS
EURYTHERM
EURYTHERMS
EURYTHMIES
EURYTHMY
EUSOL
EUSOLS
EUSTACIES
EUSTACY
EUSTASIES
EUSTASY
EUSTATIC
EUSTYLE

EUSTYLES
EUTAXIES
EUTAXITE
EUTAXITES
EUTAXITIC
EUTAXY
EUTECTIC
EUTECTICS
EUTECTOID
EUTECTOIDS
EUTEXIA
EUTEXIAS
EUTHANASIES
EUTHANASY
EUTHENICS
EUTHENIST
EUTHENISTS
EUTHERIAN
EUTHERIANS
EUTRAPELIES
EUTRAPELY
EUTROPHIC
EUTROPHIES
EUTROPHY
EUTROPIC
EUTROPIES
EUTROPOUS
EUTROPY
EUXENITE
EUXENITES
EVACUANT
EVACUANTS
EVACUATE
EVACUATED
EVACUATES
EVACUATING
EVACUATOR
EVACUATORS
EVACUEE
EVACUEES
EVADABLE
EVADE
EVADED
EVADES
EVADING
EVAGATION
EVAGATIONS
EVAGINATE
EVAGINATED
EVAGINATES
EVAGINATING
EVALUATE
EVALUATED
EVALUATES
EVALUATING
EVANESCE
EVANESCED
EVANESCES
EVANESCING
EVANGEL
EVANGELIC
EVANGELIES
EVANGELS
EVANGELY
EVANISH
EVANISHED
EVANISHES
EVANISHING
EVANITION
EVANITIONS

EVAPORATE
EVAPORATED
EVAPORATES
EVAPORATING
EVAPORITE
EVAPORITES
EVASIBLE
EVASION
EVASIONS
EVASIVE
EVASIVELY
EVE
EVECTION
EVECTIONS
EVEJAR
EVEJARS
EVEN
EVENED
ÉVÉNEMENT
ÉVÉNEMENTS
EVENER
EVENEST
EVENFALL
EVENFALLS
EVENING
EVENINGS
EVENLY
EVENNESS
EVENNESSES
EVENS
EVENSONG
EVENSONGS
EVENT
EVENTER
EVENTERS
EVENTFUL
EVENTIDE
EVENTIDES
EVENTING
EVENTINGS
EVENTS
EVENTUAL
EVENTUATE
EVENTUATED
EVENTUATES
EVENTUATING
EVER
EVERGLADE
EVERGLADES
EVERGREEN
EVERGREENS
EVERMORE
EVERSIBLE
EVERSION
EVERSIONS
EVERT
EVERTED
EVERTING
EVERTS
EVERY
EVERYBODY
EVERYDAY
EVERYDAYS
EVERYONE
EVERYWAY
EVERYWHEN
EVES
EVET
EVETS
EVHOE

EVICT
EVICTED
EVICTING
EVICTION
EVICTIONS
EVICTOR
EVICTORS
EVICTS
EVIDENCE
EVIDENCED
EVIDENCES
EVIDENCING
EVIDENT
EVIDENTLY
EVIDENTS
EVIL
EVILLER
EVILLEST
EVILLY
EVILNESS
EVILNESSES
EVILS
EVINCE
EVINCED
EVINCES
EVINCIBLE
EVINCIBLY
EVINCING
EVINCIVE
EVIRATE
EVIRATED
EVIRATES
EVIRATING
EVITABLE
EVITATE
EVITATED
EVITATES
EVITATING
EVITATION
EVITATIONS
EVITE
EVITED
EVITERNAL
EVITES
EVITING
EVOCATE
EVOCATED
EVOCATES
EVOCATING
EVOCATION
EVOCATIONS
EVOCATIVE
EVOCATORY
EVOE
EVOHE
EVOKE
EVOKED
EVOKES
EVOKING
ÉVOLUÉ
ÉVOLUÉS
EVOLUTE
EVOLUTED
EVOLUTES
EVOLUTING
EVOLUTION
EVOLUTIONS
EVOLUTIVE
EVOLVABLE
EVOLVE

EVOLVED
EVOLVENT
EVOLVES
EVOLVING
EVOVAE
EVOVAES
EVULGATE
EVULGATED
EVULGATES
EVULGATING
EVULSE
EVULSED
EVULSES
EVULSING
EVULSION
EVULSIONS
EVZONE
EVZONES
EWE
EWER
EWERS
EWES
EWEST
EWFTES
EWGHEN
EWHOW
EWK
EWKED
EWKING
EWKS
EWT
EWTS
EX
EXACT
EXACTED
EXACTER
EXACTERS
EXACTEST
EXACTING
EXACTION
EXACTIONS
EXACTLY
EXACTMENT
EXACTMENTS
EXACTNESS
EXACTNESSES
EXACTOR
EXACTORS
EXACTRESS
EXACTRESSES
EXACTS
EXALT
EXALTED
EXALTING
EXALTS
EXAM
EXAMEN
EXAMENS
EXAMINANT
EXAMINANTS
EXAMINATE
EXAMINATES
EXAMINE
EXAMINED
EXAMINEE
EXAMINEES
EXAMINER
EXAMINERS
EXAMINES
EXAMINING

EXAMPLAR	EXCERPTINGS	EXCORIATED	EXECUTRIXES	EXHALING
EXAMPLARS	EXCERPTOR	EXCORIATES	EXECUTRY	EXHAUST
EXAMPLE	EXCERPTORS	EXCORIATING	EXEDRA	EXHAUSTED
EXAMPLED	EXCERPTS	EXCREMENT	EXEDRAE	EXHAUSTER
EXAMPLES	EXCERPTUM	EXCREMENTS	EXEEM	EXHAUSTERS
EXAMPLING	EXCESS	EXCRETA	EXEEMED	EXHAUSTING
EXAMS	EXCESSES	EXCRETE	EXEEMING	EXHAUSTS
EXANIMATE	EXCESSIVE	EXCRETED	EXEEMS	EXHEDRA
EXANTHEM	EXCHANGE	EXCRETES	EXEGESES	EXHEDRAE
EXANTHEMA	EXCHANGED	EXCRETING	EXEGESIS	EXHIBIT
EXANTHEMATA	EXCHANGER	EXCRETION	EXEGETE	EXHIBITED
EXANTHEMS	EXCHANGERS	EXCRETIONS	EXEGETES	EXHIBITER
EXARATE	EXCHANGES	EXCRETIVE	EXEGETIC	EXHIBITERS
EXARATION	EXCHANGING	EXCRETORIES	EXEGETICS	EXHIBITING
EXARATIONS	EXCHEAT	EXCRETORY	EXEGETIST	EXHIBITOR
EXARCH	EXCHEATS	EXCUBANT	EXEGETISTS	EXHIBITORS
EXARCHATE	EXCHEQUER	EXCUDIT	EXEME	EXHIBITS
EXARCHATES	EXCHEQUERED	EXCULPATE	EXEMED	EXHORT
EXARCHIES	EXCHEQUERING	EXCULPATED	EXEMES	EXHORTED
EXARCHIST	EXCHEQUERS	EXCULPATES	EXEMING	EXHORTER
EXARCHISTS	EXCIDE	EXCULPATING	EXEMPLA	EXHORTERS
EXARCHS	EXCIDED	EXCURRENT	EXEMPLAR	EXHORTING
EXARCHY	EXCIDES	EXCURSE	EXEMPLARS	EXHORTS
EXCAMB	EXCIDING	EXCURSED	EXEMPLARY	EXHUMATE
EXCAMBED	EXCIPIENT	EXCURSES	EXEMPLE	EXHUMATED
EXCAMBING	EXCIPIENTS	EXCURSING	EXEMPLES	EXHUMATES
EXCAMBION	EXCISABLE	EXCURSION	EXEMPLIFIED	EXHUMATING
EXCAMBIONS	EXCISE	EXCURSIONED	EXEMPLIFIES	EXHUME
EXCAMBIUM	EXCISED	EXCURSIONING	EXEMPLIFY	EXHUMED
EXCAMBIUMS	EXCISEMAN	EXCURSIONS	EXEMPLIFYING	EXHUMER
EXCAMBS	EXCISEMEN	EXCURSIVE	EXEMPLUM	EXHUMERS
EXCARNATE	EXCISES	EXCURSUS	EXEMPT	EXHUMES
EXCARNATED	EXCISING	EXCURSUSES	EXEMPTED	EXHUMING
EXCARNATES	EXCISION	EXCUSABLE	EXEMPTING	EXIES
EXCARNATING	EXCISIONS	EXCUSABLY	EXEMPTION	EXIGEANT
EXCAUDATE	EXCITABLE	EXCUSAL	EXEMPTIONS	EXIGEANTE
EXCAVATE	EXCITANCIES	EXCUSALS	EXEMPTS	EXIGENCE
EXCAVATED	EXCITANCY	EXCUSE	EXEQUATUR	EXIGENCES
EXCAVATES	EXCITANT	EXCUSED	EXEQUATURS	EXIGENCIES
EXCAVATING	EXCITANTS	EXCUSER	EXEQUIAL	EXIGENCY
EXCAVATOR	EXCITE	EXCUSERS	EXEQUIES	EXIGENT
EXCAVATORS	EXCITED	EXCUSES	EXEQUY	EXIGENTS
EXCEED	EXCITER	EXCUSING	EXERCISE	EXIGIBLE
EXCEEDED	EXCITERS	EXCUSIVE	EXERCISED	EXIGUITIES
EXCEEDING	EXCITES	EXEAT	EXERCISER	EXIGUITY
EXCEEDS	EXCITING	EXEATS	EXERCISERS	EXIGUOUS
EXCEL	EXCITON	EXECRABLE	EXERCISES	EXILE
EXCELLED	EXCITONS	EXECRABLY	EXERCISING	EXILED
EXCELLENT	EXCITOR	EXECRATE	EXERGUAL	EXILEMENT
EXCELLING	EXCITORS	EXECRATED	EXERGUE	EXILEMENTS
EXCELS	EXCLAIM	EXECRATES	EXERGUES	EXILES
EXCELSIOR	EXCLAIMED	EXECRATING	EXERT	EXILIAN
EXCELSIORS	EXCLAIMING	EXECUTANT	EXERTED	EXILIC
EXCENTRIC	EXCLAIMS	EXECUTANTS	EXERTING	EXILING
EXCENTRICS	EXCLAVE	EXECUTE	EXERTION	EXILITIES
EXCEPT	EXCLAVES	EXECUTED	EXERTIONS	EXILITY
EXCEPTANT	EXCLOSURE	EXECUTER	EXERTIVE	EXIMIOUS
EXCEPTANTS	EXCLOSURES	EXECUTERS	EXERTS	EXINE
EXCEPTED	EXCLUDE	EXECUTES	EXES	EXINES
EXCEPTING	EXCLUDED	EXECUTING	EXEUNT	EXIST
EXCEPTION	EXCLUDEE	EXECUTION	EXFOLIATE	EXISTED
EXCEPTIONS	EXCLUDEES	EXECUTIONS	EXFOLIATED	EXISTENCE
EXCEPTIVE	EXCLUDES	EXECUTIVE	EXFOLIATES	EXISTENCES
EXCEPTOR	EXCLUDING	EXECUTIVES	EXFOLIATING	EXISTENT
EXCEPTORS	EXCLUSION	EXECUTOR	EXHALABLE	EXISTING
EXCEPTS	EXCLUSIONS	EXECUTORS	EXHALANT	EXISTS
EXCERPT	EXCLUSIVE	EXECUTORY	EXHALANTS	EXIT
EXCERPTA	EXCLUSIVES	EXECUTRICES	EXHALE	EXITANCE
EXCERPTED	EXCLUSORY	EXECUTRIES	EXHALED	EXITANCES
EXCERPTING	EXCORIATE	EXECUTRIX	EXHALES	EXITED

EXITING
EXITS
EXOCARP
EXOCARPS
EXOCRINE
EXOCRINES
EXODE
EXODERM
EXODERMAL
EXODERMIS
EXODERMISES
EXODERMS
EXODES
EXODIC
EXODIST
EXODISTS
EXODUS
EXODUSES
EXOENZYME
EXOENZYMES
EXOERGIC
EXOGAMIC
EXOGAMIES
EXOGAMOUS
EXOGAMY
EXOGEN
EXOGENOUS
EXOGENS
EXOMION
EXOMIONS
EXOMIS
EXOMISES
EXON
EXONERATE
EXONERATED
EXONERATES
EXONERATING
EXONS
EXONYM
EXONYMS
EXOPHAGIES
EXOPHAGY
EXOPLASM
EXOPLASMS
EXOPOD
EXOPODITE
EXOPODITES
EXOPODS
EXORABLE
EXORATION
EXORATIONS
EXORCISE
EXORCISED
EXORCISER
EXORCISERS
EXORCISES
EXORCISING
EXORCISM
EXORCISMS
EXORCIST
EXORCISTS
EXORCIZE
EXORCIZED
EXORCIZER
EXORCIZERS
EXORCIZES
EXORCIZING
EXORDIA
EXORDIAL
EXORDIUM

EXORDIUMS
EXOSMOSE
EXOSMOSES
EXOSMOSIS
EXOSMOTIC
EXOSPHERE
EXOSPHERES
EXOSPORAL
EXOSPORE
EXOSPORES
EXOSTOSES
EXOSTOSIS
EXOTERIC
EXOTIC
EXOTICA
EXOTICISM
EXOTICISMS
EXOTICS
EXOTOXIC
EXOTOXIN
EXOTOXINS
EXPAND
EXPANDED
EXPANDER
EXPANDERS
EXPANDING
EXPANDOR
EXPANDORS
EXPANDS
EXPANSE
EXPANSES
EXPANSILE
EXPANSION
EXPANSIONS
EXPANSIVE
EXPAT
EXPATIATE
EXPATIATED
EXPATIATES
EXPATIATING
EXPATS
EXPECT
EXPECTANT
EXPECTANTS
EXPECTED
EXPECTER
EXPECTERS
EXPECTING
EXPECTINGS
EXPECTS
EXPEDIENT
EXPEDIENTS
EXPEDITE
EXPEDITED
EXPEDITES
EXPEDITING
EXPEL
EXPELLANT
EXPELLANTS
EXPELLED
EXPELLEE
EXPELLEES
EXPELLENT
EXPELLENTS
EXPELLING
EXPELS
EXPEND
EXPENDED
EXPENDER
EXPENDERS

EXPENDING
EXPENDS
EXPENSE
EXPENSES
EXPENSIVE
EXPERT
EXPERTED
EXPERTING
EXPERTISE
EXPERTISED
EXPERTISES
EXPERTISING
EXPERTIZE
EXPERTIZED
EXPERTIZES
EXPERTIZING
EXPERTLY
EXPERTS
EXPIABLE
EXPIATE
EXPIATED
EXPIATES
EXPIATING
EXPIATION
EXPIATIONS
EXPIATOR
EXPIATORS
EXPIATORY
EXPIRABLE
EXPIRANT
EXPIRANTS
EXPIRE
EXPIRED
EXPIRES
EXPIRIES
EXPIRING
EXPIRY
EXPISCATE
EXPISCATED
EXPISCATES
EXPISCATING
EXPLAIN
EXPLAINED
EXPLAINER
EXPLAINERS
EXPLAINING
EXPLAINS
EXPLANT
EXPLANTED
EXPLANTING
EXPLANTS
EXPLETIVE
EXPLETIVES
EXPLETORY
EXPLICATE
EXPLICATED
EXPLICATES
EXPLICATING
EXPLICIT
EXPLICITS
EXPLODE
EXPLODED
EXPLODER
EXPLODERS
EXPLODES
EXPLODING
EXPLOIT
EXPLOITED
EXPLOITER
EXPLOITERS

EXPLOITING
EXPLOITS
EXPLORE
EXPLORED
EXPLORER
EXPLORERS
EXPLORES
EXPLORING
EXPLOSION
EXPLOSIONS
EXPLOSIVE
EXPLOSIVES
EXPO
EXPONENT
EXPONENTS
EXPONIBLE
EXPORT
EXPORTED
EXPORTER
EXPORTERS
EXPORTING
EXPORTS
EXPOS
EXPOSAL
EXPOSALS
EXPOSE
EXPOSÉ
EXPOSED
EXPOSER
EXPOSERS
EXPOSÉS
EXPOSES
EXPOSING
EXPOSITOR
EXPOSITORS
EXPOSTURE
EXPOSTURES
EXPOSURE
EXPOSURES
EXPOUND
EXPOUNDED
EXPOUNDER
EXPOUNDERS
EXPOUNDING
EXPOUNDS
EXPRESS
EXPRESSED
EXPRESSES
EXPRESSING
EXPRESSLY
EXPRESSO
EXPRESSOS
EXPUGN
EXPUGNED
EXPUGNING
EXPUGNS
EXPULSE
EXPULSED
EXPULSES
EXPULSING
EXPULSION
EXPULSIONS
EXPULSIVE
EXPUNCT
EXPUNCTED
EXPUNCTING
EXPUNCTS
EXPUNGE
EXPUNGED
EXPUNGER

EXPUNGERS
EXPUNGES
EXPUNGING
EXPURGATE
EXPURGATED
EXPURGATES
EXPURGATING
EXPURGE
EXPURGED
EXPURGES
EXPURGING
EXQUISITE
EXQUISITES
EXSCIND
EXSCINDED
EXSCINDING
EXSCINDS
EXSECT
EXSECTED
EXSECTING
EXSECTION
EXSECTIONS
EXSECTS
EXSERT
EXSERTED
EXSERTILE
EXSERTING
EXSERTION
EXSERTIONS
EXSERTS
EXSICCANT
EXSICCATE
EXSICCATED
EXSICCATES
EXSICCATING
EXSUCCOUS
EXTANT
EXTASIES
EXTASY
EXTATIC
EXTATICS
EXTEMPORE
EXTEMPORES
EXTEND
EXTENDANT
EXTENDED
EXTENDER
EXTENDERS
EXTENDING
EXTENDS
EXTENSE
EXTENSILE
EXTENSION
EXTENSIONS
EXTENSITIES
EXTENSITY
EXTENSIVE
EXTENSOR
EXTENSORS
EXTENT
EXTENTS
EXTENUATE
EXTENUATED
EXTENUATES
EXTENUATING
EXTENUATINGS
EXTERIOR
EXTERIORS
EXTERMINE
EXTERMINED

EXTERMINES
EXTERMINING
EXTERN
EXTERNAL
EXTERNALS
EXTERNAT
EXTERNATS
EXTERNE
EXTERNES
EXTERNS
EXTINCT
EXTINCTED
EXTINE
EXTINES
EXTIRP
EXTIRPATE
EXTIRPATED
EXTIRPATES
EXTIRPATING
EXTIRPED
EXTIRPING
EXTIRPS
EXTOL
EXTOLD
EXTOLLED
EXTOLLER
EXTOLLERS
EXTOLLING
EXTOLMENT
EXTOLMENTS
EXTOLS
EXTORSIVE
EXTORT
EXTORTED
EXTORTING
EXTORTION
EXTORTIONS
EXTORTIVE
EXTORTS

EXTRA
EXTRACT
EXTRACTED
EXTRACTING
EXTRACTOR
EXTRACTORS
EXTRACTS
EXTRADITE
EXTRADITED
EXTRADITES
EXTRADITING
EXTRADOS
EXTRADOSES
EXTRAIT
EXTRAITS
EXTRAS
EXTRAUGHT
EXTRAVERT
EXTRAVERTED
EXTRAVERTING
EXTRAVERTS
EXTREAT
EXTREATS
EXTREME
EXTREMELY
EXTREMER
EXTREMES
EXTREMEST
EXTREMISM
EXTREMISMS
EXTREMIST
EXTREMISTS
EXTREMITIES
EXTREMITY
EXTRICATE
EXTRICATED
EXTRICATES
EXTRICATING
EXTRINSIC

EXTRORSE
EXTROVERT
EXTROVERTED
EXTROVERTING
EXTROVERTS
EXTRUDE
EXTRUDED
EXTRUDER
EXTRUDERS
EXTRUDES
EXTRUDING
EXTRUSION
EXTRUSIONS
EXTRUSIVE
EXTRUSORY
EXUBERANT
EXUBERATE
EXUBERATED
EXUBERATES
EXUBERATING
EXUDATE
EXUDATES
EXUDATION
EXUDATIONS
EXUDATIVE
EXUDE
EXUDED
EXUDES
EXUDING
EXUL
EXULS
EXULT
EXULTANCE
EXULTANCES
EXULTANCIES
EXULTANCY
EXULTANT
EXULTED
EXULTING

EXULTS
EXURB
EXURBAN
EXURBIA
EXURBIAS
EXURBS
EXUVIAE
EXUVIAL
EXUVIATE
EXUVIATED
EXUVIATES
EXUVIATING
EYALET
EYALETS
EYAS
EYASES
EYE
EYEBALL
EYEBALLED
EYEBALLING
EYEBALLS
EYEBOLT
EYEBOLTS
EYEBRIGHT
EYEBRIGHTS
EYEBROW
EYEBROWED
EYEBROWING
EYEBROWS
EYED
EYEFUL
EYEFULS
EYEGLASS
EYEGLASSES
EYEHOOK
EYEHOOKS
EYEING
EYELASH
EYELASHES

EYELESS
EYELET
EYELETED
EYELETING
EYELETS
EYELIAD
EYELIADS
EYELID
EYELIDS
EYELINER
EYELINERS
EYES
EYESHADE
EYESHADES
EYESIGHT
EYESIGHTS
EYESORE
EYESORES
EYESTALK
EYESTALKS
EYESTRAIN
EYESTRAINS
EYING
EYLIAD
EYLIADS
EYNE
EYOT
EYOTS
EYRA
EYRAS
EYRE
EYRES
EYRIE
EYRIES
EYRY

F

FA	FACILITIES	FADDIST	FAHLORE	FAIRLY
FAB	FACILITY	FADDISTS	FAHLORES	FAIRNESS
FABACEOUS	FACING	FADDLE	FAHS	FAIRNESSES
FABBER	FACINGS	FADDLED	FAIBLE	FAIRS
FABBEST	FAÇONNÉ	FADDLES	FAIBLES	FAIRWAY
FABLE	FAÇONNÉS	FADDLING	FAÏENCE	FAIRWAYS
FABLED	FACSIMILE	FADDY	FAIENCE	FAIRY
FABLER	FACSIMILED	FADE	FAÏENCES	FAIRYDOM
FABLERS	FACSIMILEING	FADED	FAIENCES	FAIRYDOMS
FABLES	FACSIMILES	FADEDLY	FAIK	FAIRYHOOD
FABLIAU	FACT	FADEDNESS	FAIKED	FAIRYHOODS
FABLIAUX	FACTION	FADEDNESSES	FAIKES	FAIRYISM
FABLING	FACTIONAL	FADELESS	FAIKING	FAIRYISMS
FABLINGS	FACTIONS	FADES	FAIKS	FAIRYLAND
FABRIC	FACTIOUS	FADEUR	FAIL	FAIRYLANDS
FABRICANT	FACTITIVE	FADEURS	FAILED	FAIRYLIKE
FABRICANTS	FACTIVE	FADGE	FAILING	FAITH
FABRICATE	FACTOID	FADGED	FAILINGS	FAITHED
FABRICATED	FACTOIDS	FADGES	FAILLE	FAITHFUL
FABRICATES	FACTOR	FADGING	FAILLES	FAITHING
FABRICATING	FACTORAGE	FADIER	FAILS	FAITHLESS
FABRICKED	FACTORAGES	FADIEST	FAILURE	FAITHS
FABRICKING	FACTORED	FADING	FAILURES	FAITOR
FABRICS	FACTORIAL	FADINGS	FAIN	FAITORS
FABULAR	FACTORIALS	FADO	FAINE	FAITOUR
FABULISE	FACTORIES	FADOS	FAINÉANCE	FAITOURS
FABULISED	FACTORING	FADS	FAINÉANCES	FAIX
FABULISES	FACTORINGS	FADY	FAINÉANCIES	FAKE
FABULISING	FACTORISE	FAECAL	FAINÉANCY	FAKED
FABULIST	FACTORISED	FAECES	FAINÉANT	FAKEMENT
FABULISTS	FACTORISES	FAERIE	FAINÉANTS	FAKEMENTS
FABULIZE	FACTORISING	FAERIES	FAINED	FAKER
FABULIZED	FACTORIZE	FAERY	FAINER	FAKERIES
FABULIZES	FACTORIZED	FAFF	FAINES	FAKERS
FABULIZING	FACTORIZES	FAFFED	FAINEST	FAKERY
FABULOUS	FACTORIZING	FAFFING	FAINING	FAKES
FABURDEN	FACTORS	FAFFS	FAINITES	FAKING
FABURDENS	FACTORY	FAG	FAINLY	FAKIR
FAÇADE	FACTOTUM	FAGACEOUS	FAINNESS	FAKIRISM
FAÇADES	FACTOTUMS	FAGGED	FAINNESSES	FAKIRISMS
FACE	FACTS	FAGGERIES	FAINS	FAKIRS
FACED	FACTUAL	FAGGERY	FAINT	FALAFEL
FACELESS	FACTUM	FAGGING	FAINTED	FALAFELS
FACEMAN	FACTUMS	FAGGINGS	FAINTER	FALAJ
FACEMEN	FACTURE	FAGGOT	FAINTEST	FALANGISM
FACER	FACTURES	FAGGOTED	FAINTIER	FALANGISMS
FACERS	FACULA	FAGGOTING	FAINTIEST	FALANGIST
FACES	FACULAE	FAGGOTINGS	FAINTING	FALANGISTS
FACET	FACULAR	FAGGOTS	FAINTINGS	FALBALA
FACETE	FACULTIES	FAGOT	FAINTISH	FALBALAS
FACETED	FACULTY	FAGOTED	FAINTLY	FALCADE
FACETIAE	FACUNDITIES	FAGOTING	FAINTNESS	FALCADES
FACETING	FACUNDITY	FAGOTINGS	FAINTNESSES	FALCATE
FACETIOUS	FAD	FAGOTS	FAINTS	FALCATED
FACETS	FADABLE	FAGOTTI	FAINTY	FALCATION
FACIA	FADAISE	FAGOTTIST	FAIR	FALCATIONS
FACIAL	FADAISES	FAGOTTISTS	FAIRED	FALCES
FACIALLY	FADDIER	FAGOTTO	FAIRER	FALCHION
FACIALS	FADDIEST	FAGS	FAIREST	FALCHIONS
FACIAS	FADDINESS	FAH	FAIRIES	FALCIFORM
FACIES	FADDINESSES	FAHLBAND	FAIRILY	FALCON
FACIESES	FADDISH	FAHLBANDS	FAIRING	FALCONER
FACILE	FADDISM	FAHLERZ	FAIRINGS	FALCONERS
FACILELY	FADDISMS	FAHLERZES	FAIRISH	FALCONET

FALCONETS
FALCONINE
FALCONRIES
FALCONRY
FALCONS
FALCULA
FALCULAS
FALCULATE
FALDAGE
FALDAGES
FALDERAL
FALDERALS
FALDETTA
FALDETTAS
FALDSTOOL
FALDSTOOLS
FALL
FALLACIES
FALLACY
FALLAL
FALLALERIES
FALLALERY
FALLALS
FALLEN
FALLIBLE
FALLIBLY
FALLING
FALLINGS
FALLOW
FALLOWED
FALLOWER
FALLOWEST
FALLOWING
FALLOWS
FALLS
FALSE
FALSED
FALSEHOOD
FALSEHOODS
FALSELY
FALSENESS
FALSENESSES
FALSER
FALSERS
FALSES
FALSEST
FALSETTO
FALSETTOS
FALSEWORK
FALSEWORKS
FALSIE
FALSIES
FALSIFIED
FALSIFIER
FALSIFIERS
FALSIFIES
FALSIFY
FALSIFYING
FALSING
FALSISH
FALSISM
FALSISMS
FALSITIES
FALSITY
FALTBOAT
FALTBOATS
FALTER
FALTERED
FALTERING
FALTERINGS

FALTERS
FALX
FAME
FAMED
FAMELESS
FAMES
FAMILIAL
FAMILIAR
FAMILIARS
FAMILIES
FAMILISM
FAMILISMS
FAMILY
FAMINE
FAMINES
FAMING
FAMISH
FAMISHED
FAMISHES
FAMISHING
FAMOUS
FAMOUSED
FAMOUSES
FAMOUSING
FAMOUSLY
FAMULUS
FAMULUSES
FAN
FANAL
FANALS
FANATIC
FANATICAL
FANATICS
FANCIED
FANCIER
FANCIERS
FANCIES
FANCIEST
FANCIFUL
FANCILESS
FANCY
FANCYING
FANCYWORK
FANCYWORKS
FAND
FANDANGLE
FANDANGLES
FANDANGO
FANDANGOS
FANDED
FANDING
FANDOM
FANDOMS
FANDS
FANE
FANES
FANFARADE
FANFARADES
FANFARE
FANFARED
FANFARES
FANFARING
FANFARON
FANFARONA
FANFARONAS
FANFARONS
FANFOLD
FANG
FANGED
FANGING

FANGLE
FANGLED
FANGLES
FANGLESS
FANGLING
FANGO
FANGOS
FANGS
FANION
FANIONS
FANK
FANKLE
FANKLED
FANKLES
FANKLING
FANKS
FANLIGHT
FANLIGHTS
FANNED
FANNEL
FANNELL
FANNELLS
FANNELS
FANNER
FANNERS
FANNIES
FANNING
FANNINGS
FANNY
FANON
FANONS
FANS
FANTAD
FANTADS
FANTAIL
FANTAILED
FANTAILS
FANTASIA
FANTASIAS
FANTASIED
FANTASIES
FANTASISE
FANTASISED
FANTASISES
FANTASISING
FANTASIST
FANTASISTS
FANTASIZE
FANTASIZED
FANTASIZES
FANTASIZING
FANTASM
FANTASMS
FANTASQUE
FANTASQUES
FANTAST
FANTASTIC
FANTASTICS
FANTASTRIES
FANTASTRY
FANTASTS
FANTASY
FANTASYING
FANTEEG
FANTEEGS
FANTIGUE
FANTIGUES
FANTOD
FANTODS
FANTOM

FANTOMS
FANTOOSH
FANZINE
FANZINES
FAP
FAQUIR
FAQUIRS
FAR
FARAD
FARADAY
FARADAYS
FARADIC
FARADISE
FARADISED
FARADISES
FARADISING
FARADISM
FARADISMS
FARADIZE
FARADIZED
FARADIZES
FARADIZING
FARADS
FARAND
FARANDINE
FARANDINES
FARANDOLE
FARANDOLES
FARAWAY
FARAWAYS
FARCE
FARCED
FARCES
FARCEUR
FARCEURS
FARCEUSE
FARCEUSES
FARCI
FARCICAL
FARCIED
FARCIES
FARCIFIED
FARCIFIES
FARCIFY
FARCIFYING
FARCIN
FARCING
FARCINGS
FARCINS
FARCY
FARD
FARDAGE
FARDAGES
FARDED
FARDEL
FARDELS
FARDEN
FARDENS
FARDING
FARDINGS
FARDS
FARE
FARED
FARES
FAREWELL
FAREWELLS
FARFET
FARINA
FARINAS
FARING

FARINOSE
FARL
FARLE
FARLES
FARLS
FARM
FARMED
FARMER
FARMERESS
FARMERESSES
FARMERIES
FARMERS
FARMERY
FARMHOUSE
FARMHOUSES
FARMING
FARMINGS
FARMOST
FARMS
FARMSTEAD
FARMSTEADS
FARMYARD
FARMYARDS
FARNESOL
FARNESOLS
FARNESS
FARNESSES
FARO
FAROS
FAROUCHE
FARRAGO
FARRAGOES
FARRAND
FARRANT
FARRED
FARREN
FARRENS
FARRIER
FARRIERIES
FARRIERS
FARRIERY
FARRING
FARROW
FARROWED
FARROWING
FARROWS
FARRUCA
FARRUCAS
FARS
FARSE
FARSED
FARSES
FARSING
FART
FARTED
FARTHEL
FARTHELS
FARTHER
FARTHEST
FARTHING
FARTHINGS
FARTING
FARTS
FAS
FASCES
FASCI
FASCIA
FASCIAL
FASCIAS
FASCIATE

FASCIATED	FATALISTS	FAUCHON	FAWS	FEATURE
FASCICLE	FATALITIES	FAUCHONS	FAX	FEATURED
FASCICLED	FATALITY	FAUCIAL	FAXED	FEATURELY
FASCICLES	FATALLY	FAUGH	FAXES	FEATURES
FASCICULE	FATE	FAULCHIN	FAXING	FEATURING
FASCICULES	FATED	FAULCHINS	FAY	FEBLESSE
FASCICULI	FATEFUL	FAULCHION	FAYALITE	FEBLESSES
FASCINATE	FATEFULLY	FAULCHIONS	FAYALITES	FEBRICITIES
FASCINATED	FATES	FAULT	FAYED	FEBRICITY
FASCINATES	FATHER	FAULTED	FAYENCE	FEBRICULA
FASCINATING	FATHERED	FAULTFUL	FAYENCES	FEBRICULAS
FASCINE	FATHERING	FAULTIER	FAYER	FEBRICULE
FASCINES	FATHERLY	FAULTIEST	FAYEST	FEBRICULES
FASCIO	FATHERS	FAULTILY	FAYING	FEBRIFIC
FASCIOLA	FATHOM	FAULTING	FAYNE	FEBRIFUGE
FASCIOLAS	FATHOMED	FAULTLESS	FAYNED	FEBRIFUGES
FASCIOLE	FATHOMING	FAULTS	FAYNES	FEBRILE
FASCIOLES	FATHOMS	FAULTY	FAYNING	FEBRILITIES
FASCISM	FATIDICAL	FAUN	FAYS	FEBRILITY
FASCiSMI	FATIGABLE	FAUNA	FAZE	FECAL
FASCISMO	FATIGATE	FAUNAE	FAZED	FECES
FASCISMS	FATIGATED	FAUNAL	FAZES	FECHT
FASCIST	FATIGATES	FAUNAS	FAZING	FECHTER
FASCISTA	FATIGATING	FAUNIST	FEAGUE	FECHTERS
FASCISTI	FATIGUE	FAUNISTIC	FEAGUED	FECHTING
FASCISTIC	FATIGUED	FAUNISTS	FEAGUEING	FECHTS
FASCISTS	FATIGUES	FAUNS	FEAGUES	FECIAL
FASH	FATIGUING	FAURD	FEAGUING	FECIT
FASHED	FATISCENT	FAUSTIAN	FEAL	FECK
FASHERIES	FATLING	FAUTEUIL	FEALED	FECKLESS
FASHERY	FATLINGS	FAUTEUILS	FEALING	FECKLY
FASHES	FATLY	FAUTOR	FEALS	FECKS
FASHING	FATNESS	FAUTORS	FEALTIES	FECULA
FASHION	FATNESSES	FAUVETTE	FEALTY	FECULAS
FASHIONED	FATS	FAUVETTES	FEAR	FECULENCE
FASHIONER	FATSO	FAUX	FEARE	FECULENCES
FASHIONERS	FATSOES	FAVEL	FEARED	FECULENCIES
FASHIONING	FATSOS	FAVELA	FEARES	FECULENCY
FASHIONS	FATSTOCK	FAVELAS	FEARFUL	FECULENT
FASHIOUS	FATTED	FAVELL	FEARFULLY	FECUND
FAST	FATTEN	FAVEOLATE	FEARING	FECUNDATE
FASTBACK	FATTENED	FAVISM	FEARLESS	FECUNDATED
FASTBACKS	FATTENER	FAVISMS	FEARS	FECUNDATES
FASTED	FATTENERS	FAVOR	FEARSOME	FECUNDATING
FASTEN	FATTENING	FAVORED	FEARSOMER	FECUNDITIES
FASTENED	FATTENINGS	FAVORING	FEARSOMEST	FECUNDITY
FASTENER	FATTENS	FAVORS	FEASIBLE	FED
FASTENERS	FATTER	FAVOSE	FEASIBLY	FEDARIE
FASTENING	FATTEST	FAVOUR	FEAST	FEDARIES
FASTENINGS	FATTIER	FAVOURED	FEASTED	FEDAYEE
FASTENS	FATTIES	FAVOURER	FEASTER	FEDAYEEN
FASTER	FATTIEST	FAVOURERS	FEASTERS	FEDELINI
FASTERS	FATTINESS	FAVOURING	FEASTFUL	FEDELINIS
FASTEST	FATTINESSES	FAVOURITE	FEASTING	FEDERACIES
FASTI	FATTING	FAVOURITES	FEASTINGS	FEDERACY
FASTIGIUM	FATTISH	FAVOURS	FEASTS	FEDERAL
FASTIGIUMS	FATTRELS	FAVOUS	FEAT	FEDERALS
FASTING	FATTY	FAVRILE	FEATED	FEDERARIE
FASTINGS	FATUITIES	FAVRILES	FEATEOUS	FEDERARIES
FASTISH	FATUITOUS	FAVUS	FEATHER	FEDERARY
FASTLY	FATUITY	FAVUSES	FEATHERED	FEDERATE
FASTNESS	FATUOUS	FAW	FEATHERING	FEDERATED
FASTNESSES	FAUBOURG	FAWN	FEATHERINGS	FEDERATES
FASTS	FAUBOURGS	FAWNED	FEATHERS	FEDERATING
FASTUOUS	FAUCAL	FAWNER	FEATHERY	FEDORA
FAT	FAUCES	FAWNERS	FEATING	FEDORAS
FATAL	FAUCET	FAWNING	FEATLY	FEDS
FATALISM	FAUCETS	FAWNINGLY	FEATOUS	FEE
FATALISMS	FAUCHION	FAWNINGS	FEATS	FÉE
FATALIST	FAUCHIONS	FAWNS	FEATUOUS	FEEBLE

FEEBLED
FEEBLER
FEEBLES
FEEBLEST
FEEBLING
FEEBLISH
FEEBLY
FEED
FEEDBACK
FEEDBACKS
FEEDER
FEEDERS
FEEDING
FEEDINGS
FEEDLOT
FEEDLOTS
FEEDS
FEEDSTOCK
FEEDSTOCKS
FEEDSTUFF
FEEDSTUFFS
FEEING
FEEL
FEELER
FEELERS
FEELING
FEELINGLY
FEELINGS
FEELS
FEER
FEERED
FÉERIE
FÉERIES
FEERIN
FEERING
FEERINGS
FEERINS
FEERS
FEES
FEET
FEETLESS
FEEZE
FEEZED
FEEZES
FEEZING
FEGARIES
FEGARY
FEGS
FEHM
FEHME
FEHMIC
FEIGN
FEIGNED
FEIGNEDLY
FEIGNING
FEIGNINGS
FEIGNS
FEINT
FEINTED
FEINTER
FEINTEST
FEINTING
FEINTS
FEIS
FEISEANNA
FEISTIER
FEISTIEST
FEISTY
FELAFEL
FELAFELS

FELDGRAU
FELDGRAUS
FELDSHER
FELDSHERS
FELDSPAR
FELDSPARS
FELDSPATH
FELDSPATHS
FELICIFIC
FELICITER
FELICITIES
FELICITY
FELINE
FELINES
FELINITIES
FELINITY
FELL
FELLA
FELLABLE
FELLAH
FELLAHÎN
FELLAHS
FELLAS
FELLATE
FELLATED
FELLATES
FELLATING
FELLATIO
FELLATION
FELLATIONS
FELLATIOS
FELLED
FELLER
FELLERS
FELLEST
FELLIER
FELLIES
FELLIEST
FELLING
FELLNESS
FELLNESSES
FELLOE
FELLOES
FELLOW
FELLOWLY
FELLOWS
FELLS
FELLY
FELON
FELONIES
FELONIOUS
FELONOUS
FELONRIES
FELONRY
FELONS
FELONY
FELSITE
FELSITES
FELSITIC
FELSPAR
FELSPARS
FELSTONE
FELSTONES
FELT
FELTED
FELTER
FELTERED
FELTERING
FELTERS
FELTING

FELTINGS
FELTS
FELUCCA
FELUCCAS
FELWORT
FELWORTS
FEMAL
FEMALE
FEMALES
FEMALITIES
FEMALITY
FEMALS
FEME
FEMERALL
FEMERALLS
FEMES
FEMETARIES
FEMETARY
FEMINAL
FEMINEITIES
FEMINEITY
FEMININE
FEMININES
FEMINISE
FEMINISED
FEMINISES
FEMINISING
FEMINISM
FEMINISMS
FEMINIST
FEMINISTS
FEMINITIES
FEMINITY
FEMINIZE
FEMINIZED
FEMINIZES
FEMINIZING
FEMITER
FEMITERS
FEMME
FEMMES
FEMORA
FEMORAL
FEMUR
FEMURS
FEN
FENCE
FENCED
FENCELESS
FENCER
FENCERS
FENCES
FENCIBLE
FENCIBLES
FENCING
FENCINGS
FEND
FENDED
FENDER
FENDERS
FENDIER
FENDIEST
FENDING
FENDS
FENDY
FENESTRA
FENESTRAL
FENESTRALS
FENESTRAS
FENITAR

FENITARS
FENKS
FENLAND
FENLANDS
FENMAN
FENMEN
FENNEC
FENNECS
FENNEL
FENNELS
FENNIER
FENNIEST
FENNISH
FENNY
FENS
FENT
FENTS
FENUGREEK
FENUGREEKS
FEOD
FEODAL
FEODARIES
FEODARY
FEODS
FEOFF
FEOFFED
FEOFFEE
FEOFFEES
FEOFFER
FEOFFERS
FEOFFING
FEOFFMENT
FEOFFMENTS
FEOFFOR
FEOFFORS
FEOFFS
FERACIOUS
FERACITIES
FERACITY
FERAL
FERALISED
FERALIZED
FERE
FERER
FERES
FEREST
FERETORIES
FERETORY
FERIAL
FERINE
FERITIES
FERITY
FERLIED
FERLIES
FERLY
FERLYING
FERM
FERMATA
FERMATAS
FERMENT
FERMENTED
FERMENTING
FERMENTS
FERMI
FERMION
FERMIONS
FERMIS
FERMIUM
FERMIUMS
FERMS

FERN
FERNBIRD
FERNBIRDS
FERNERIES
FERNERY
FERNIER
FERNIEST
FERNING
FERNINGS
FERNS
FERNSHAW
FERNSHAWS
FERNTICLE
FERNTICLES
FERNY
FEROCIOUS
FEROCITIES
FEROCITY
FERRATE
FERRATES
FERREL
FERRELS
FERREOUS
FERRET
FERRETED
FERRETER
FERRETERS
FERRETING
FERRETS
FERRETY
FERRIAGE
FERRIAGES
FERRIC
FERRIED
FERRIES
FERRITE
FERRITES
FERRITIC
FERROGRAM
FERROGRAMS
FERROTYPE
FERROTYPES
FERROUS
FERRUGO
FERRUGOS
FERRULE
FERRULES
FERRY
FERRYING
FERRYMAN
FERRYMEN
FERTILE
FERTILELY
FERTILER
FERTILEST
FERTILISE
FERTILISED
FERTILISES
FERTILISING
FERTILITIES
FERTILITY
FERTILIZE
FERTILIZED
FERTILIZES
FERTILIZING
FERULA
FERULAS
FERULE
FERULES
FERVENCIES

FERVENCY	FETICHIZE	FEUDALISMS	FIAT	FICTIONAL
FERVENT	FETICHIZED	FEUDALIST	FIATED	FICTIONS
FERVENTER	FETICHIZES	FEUDALISTS	FIATING	FICTIVE
FERVENTEST	FETICHIZING	FEUDALITIES	FIATS	FICTOR
FERVENTLY	FETICIDAL	FEUDALITY	FIAUNT	FICTORS
FERVID	FETICIDE	FEUDALIZE	FIAUNTS	FID
FERVIDER	FETICIDES	FEUDALIZED	FIB	FIDDIOUS
FERVIDEST	FETID	FEUDALIZES	FIBBED	FIDDIOUSED
FERVIDITIES	FETIDER	FEUDALIZING	FIBBER	FIDDIOUSES
FERVIDITY	FETIDEST	FEUDALLY	FIBBERIES	FIDDIOUSING
FERVIDLY	FETIDNESS	FEUDARIES	FIBBERS	FIDDLE
FERVOROUS	FETIDNESSES	FEUDARY	FIBBERY	FIDDLED
FERVOUR	FÊTING	FEUDATORIES	FIBBING	FIDDLER
FERVOURS	FETISH	FEUDATORY	FIBER	FIDDLERS
FESCUE	FETISHES	FEUDED	FIBERS	FIDDLES
FESCUES	FETISHISE	FEUDING	FIBRE	FIDDLEY
FESS	FETISHISED	FEUDINGS	FIBRED	FIDDLEYS
FESSE	FETISHISES	FEUDIST	FIBRELESS	FIDDLIER
FESSES	FETISHISING	FEUDISTS	FIBRES	FIDDLIEST
FESTA	FETISHISM	FEUDS	FIBRIFORM	FIDDLING
FESTAL	FETISHISMS	FEUED	FIBRIL	FIDDLY
FESTALLY	FETISHIST	FEUILLETÉ	FIBRILLA	FIDEISM
FESTALS	FETISHISTS	FEUILLETÉS	FIBRILLAE	FIDEISMS
FESTAS	FETISHIZE	FEUING	FIBRILLAR	FIDEISTIC
FESTER	FETISHIZED	FEUS	FIBRILS	FIDELITIES
FESTERED	FETISHIZES	FEUTRE	FIBRIN	FIDELITY
FESTERING	FETISHIZING	FEUTRED	FIBRINOUS	FIDGE
FESTERS	FETLOCK	FEUTRES	FIBRINS	FIDGED
FESTILOGIES	FETLOCKED	FEUTRING	FIBRO	FIDGES
FESTILOGY	FETLOCKS	FEVER	FIBROCYTE	FIDGET
FESTINATE	FETOR	FEVERED	FIBROCYTES	FIDGETED
FESTINATED	FETORS	FEVERFEW	FIBROID	FIDGETING
FESTINATES	FETOSCOPIES	FEVERFEWS	FIBROIDS	FIDGETS
FESTINATING	FETOSCOPY	FEVERING	FIBROIN	FIDGETY
FESTIVAL	FETS	FEVERISH	FIBROINS	FIDGING
FESTIVALS	FETT	FEVEROUS	FIBROLINE	FIDIBUS
FESTIVE	FETTA	FEVERS	FIBROLINES	FIDIBUSES
FESTIVELY	FETTAS	FEW	FIBROLITE	FIDS
FESTIVITIES	FETTED	FEWER	FIBROLITES	FIDUCIAL
FESTIVITY	FETTER	FEWEST	FIBROMA	FIDUCIARIES
FESTIVOUS	FETTERED	FEWMET	FIBROMATA	FIDUCIARY
FESTOLOGIES	FETTERING	FEWMETS	FIBROS	FIE
FESTOLOGY	FETTERS	FEWNESS	FIBROSE	FIEF
FESTOON	FETTING	FEWNESSES	FIBROSED	FIEFS
FESTOONED	FETTLE	FEWTER	FIBROSES	FIELD
FESTOONING	FETTLED	FEWTERED	FIBROSING	FIELDED
FESTOONS	FETTLER	FEWTERING	FIBROSIS	FIELDER
FET	FETTLERS	FEWTERS	FIBROTIC	FIELDERS
FETA	FETTLES	FEWTRILS	FIBROUS	FIELDFARE
FETAL	FETTLING	FEY	FIBS	FIELDFARES
FETAS	FETTLINGS	FEYED	FIBSTER	FIELDING
FETCH	FETTS	FEYER	FIBSTERS	FIELDINGS
FETCHED	FETTUCINE	FEYEST	FIBULA	FIELDMICE
FETCHES	FETTUCINES	FEYING	FIBULAR	FIELDS
FETCHING	FETTUCINI	FEYS	FIBULAS	FIELDSMAN
FÊTE	FETTUCINIS	FEZ	FICHE	FIELDSMEN
FÊTED	FETUS	FEZES	FICHES	FIELDWARD
FÊTES	FETUSES	FEZZED	FICHU	FIELDWORK
FETIAL	FETWA	FEZZES	FICHUS	FIELDWORKS
FETICH	FETWAS	FIACRE	FICKLE	FIEND
FETICHE	FEU	FIACRES	FICKLED	FIENDISH
FETICHES	FEUAR	FIANCÉ	FICKLER	FIENDS
FETICHISE	FEUARS	FIANCÉE	FICKLES	FIENT
FETICHISED	FEUD	FIANCÉES	FICKLEST	FIENTS
FETICHISES	FEUDAL	FIANCÉS	FICKLING	FIERCE
FETICHISING	FEUDALISE	FIAR	FICO	FIERCELY
FETICHISM	FEUDALISED	FIARS	FICOES	FIERCER
FETICHISMS	FEUDALISES	FIASCO	FICOS	FIERCEST
FETICHIST	FEUDALISING	FIASCOES	FICTILE	FIERE
FETICHISTS	FEUDALISM	FIASCOS	FICTION	FIERES

FIERIER
FIERIEST
FIERILY
FIERINESS
FIERINESSES
FIERY
FIESTA
FIESTAS
FIFE
FIFED
FIFER
FIFERS
FIFES
FIFING
FIFTEEN
FIFTEENER
FIFTEENERS
FIFTEENS
FIFTEENTH
FIFTEENTHS
FIFTH
FIFTHLY
FIFTHS
FIFTIES
FIFTIETH
FIFTIETHS
FIFTY
FIFTYISH
FIG
FIGGED
FIGGERIES
FIGGERY
FIGGING
FIGHT
FIGHTABLE
FIGHTBACK
FIGHTBACKS
FIGHTER
FIGHTERS
FIGHTING
FIGHTINGS
FIGHTS
FIGMENT
FIGMENTS
FIGO
FIGOS
FIGS
FIGULINE
FIGULINES
FIGURABLE
FIGURAL
FIGURANT
FIGURANTE
FIGURANTES
FIGURANTS
FIGURATE
FIGURE
FIGURED
FIGURES
FIGURINE
FIGURINES
FIGURING
FIGURIST
FIGURISTS
FIGWORT
FIGWORTS
FIKE
FIKED
FIKERIES
FIKERY

FIKES
FIKIER
FIKIEST
FIKING
FIKISH
FIKY
FIL
FILABEG
FILABEGS
FILACEOUS
FILACER
FILACERS
FILAGREE
FILAGREES
FILAMENT
FILAMENTS
FILANDER
FILANDERS
FILAR
FILARIA
FILARIAL
FILARIAS
FILASSE
FILASSES
FILATORIES
FILATORY
FILATURE
FILATURES
FILAZER
FILAZERS
FILBERD
FILBERDS
FILBERT
FILBERTS
FILCH
FILCHED
FILCHER
FILCHERS
FILCHES
FILCHING
FILCHINGS
FILE
FILED
FILEMOT
FILEMOTS
FILER
FILERS
FILES
FILET
FILETS
FILFOT
FILFOTS
FILIAL
FILIALLY
FILIATE
FILIATED
FILIATES
FILIATING
FILIATION
FILIATIONS
FILIBEG
FILIBEGS
FILICIDE
FILICIDES
FILIFORM
FILIGRAIN
FILIGRAINS
FILIGRANE
FILIGRANES
FILIGREE

FILIGREED
FILIGREES
FILING
FILINGS
FILIOQUE
FILIOQUES
FILL
FILLE
FILLED
FILLER
FILLERS
FILLES
FILLET
FILLETED
FILLETING
FILLETS
FILLIBEG
FILLIBEGS
FILLIES
FILLING
FILLINGS
FILLIP
FILLIPED
FILLIPEEN
FILLIPEENS
FILLIPING
FILLIPS
FILLISTER
FILLISTERS
FILLS
FILLY
FILM
FILMABLE
FILMDOM
FILMDOMS
FILMED
FILMGOER
FILMGOERS
FILMIC
FILMIER
FILMIEST
FILMINESS
FILMINESSES
FILMING
FILMISH
FILMLAND
FILMLANDS
FILMS
FILMSET
FILMSETS
FILMSETTING
FILMSETTINGS
FILMY
FILOPLUME
FILOPLUMES
FILOPODIA
FILOSE
FILOSELLE
FILOSELLES
FILS
FILTER
FILTERED
FILTERING
FILTERS
FILTH
FILTHIER
FILTHIEST
FILTHILY
FILTHS
FILTHY

FILTRABLE
FILTRATE
FILTRATED
FILTRATES
FILTRATING
FIMBLE
FIMBLES
FIMBRIA
FIMBRIAS
FIMBRIATE
FIMBRIATED
FIMBRIATES
FIMBRIATING
FIN
FINABLE
FINAGLE
FINAGLED
FINAGLES
FINAGLING
FINAL
FINALE
FINALES
FINALISE
FINALISED
FINALISES
FINALISING
FINALISM
FINALISMS
FINALIST
FINALISTS
FINALITIES
FINALITY
FINALIZE
FINALIZED
FINALIZES
FINALIZING
FINALLY
FINALS
FINANCE
FINANCED
FINANCES
FINANCIAL
FINANCIER
FINANCIERED
FINANCIERING
FINANCIERS
FINANCING
FINBACK
FINBACKS
FINCH
FINCHED
FINCHES
FIND
FINDER
FINDERS
FINDING
FINDINGS
FINDRAM
FINDRAMS
FINDS
FINE
FINED
FINEER
FINEERED
FINEERING
FINEERS
FINEISH
FINELESS
FINELY
FINENESS

FINENESSES
FINER
FINERIES
FINERS
FINERY
FINES
FINESSE
FINESSED
FINESSER
FINESSERS
FINESSES
FINESSING
FINESSINGS
FINEST
FINGAN
FINGANS
FINGER
FINGERED
FINGERING
FINGERINGS
FINGERS
FINGERTIP
FINGERTIPS
FINIAL
FINIALS
FINICAL
FINICALLY
FINICKING
FINICKINGS
FINICKY
FINIKIN
FINING
FININGS
FINIS
FINISES
FINISH
FINISHED
FINISHER
FINISHERS
FINISHES
FINISHING
FINISHINGS
FINITE
FINITELY
FINITUDE
FINITUDES
FINJAN
FINJANS
FINK
FINKED
FINKING
FINKS
FINLESS
FINNAC
FINNACK
FINNACKS
FINNACS
FINNAN
FINNANS
FINNED
FINNER
FINNERS
FINNESKO
FINNIER
FINNIEST
FINNOCHIO
FINNOCHIOS
FINNOCK
FINNOCKS
FINNSKO

FINNY
FINO
FINOCCHIO
FINOCCHIOS
FINOCHIO
FINOCHIOS
FINOS
FINS
FINSKO
FIORD
FIORDS
FIORIN
FIORINS
FIORITURA
FIORITURE
FIPPENCE
FIPPENCES
FIPPLE
FIPPLES
FIR
FIRE
FIREARM
FIREARMS
FIREBALL
FIREBALLS
FIREBRAND
FIREBRANDS
FIREBRAT
FIREBRATS
FIREBRICK
FIREBRICKS
FIREBUG
FIREBUGS
FIRECREST
FIRECRESTS
FIRED
FIREDAMP
FIREDAMPS
FIREDOG
FIREDOGS
FIREFLIES
FIREFLOAT
FIREFLOATS
FIREFLY
FIREGUARD
FIREGUARDS
FIREHOUSE
FIREHOUSES
FIRELESS
FIRELIGHT
FIRELIGHTS
FIRELOCK
FIRELOCKS
FIREMAN
FIREMARK
FIREMARKS
FIREMEN
FIREPAN
FIREPANS
FIREPLACE
FIREPLACES
FIREPOT
FIREPOTS
FIREPROOF
FIREPROOFED
FIREPROOFING
FIREPROOFINGS
FIREPROOFS
FIRER
FIRERS

FIRES
FIRESHIP
FIRESHIPS
FIRESIDE
FIRESIDES
FIRESTONE
FIRESTONES
FIRETHORN
FIRETHORNS
FIREWEED
FIREWEEDS
FIREWOMAN
FIREWOMEN
FIREWOOD
FIREWOODS
FIREWORK
FIREWORKS
FIREWORM
FIREWORMS
FIRING
FIRINGS
FIRK
FIRKED
FIRKIN
FIRKING
FIRKINS
FIRKS
FIRLOT
FIRLOTS
FIRM
FIRMAMENT
FIRMAMENTS
FIRMAN
FIRMANS
FIRMED
FIRMER
FIRMERS
FIRMEST
FIRMING
FIRMLESS
FIRMLY
FIRMNESS
FIRMNESSES
FIRMS
FIRMWARE
FIRMWARES
FIRN
FIRNS
FIRRIER
FIRRIEST
FIRRING
FIRRINGS
FIRRY
FIRS
FIRST
FIRSTLING
FIRSTLINGS
FIRSTLY
FIRSTS
FIRTH
FIRTHS
FISC
FISCAL
FISCALS
FISCS
FISGIG
FISGIGS
FISH
FISHABLE
FISHBALL

FISHBALLS
FISHCAKE
FISHCAKES
FISHED
FISHER
FISHERIES
FISHERMAN
FISHERMEN
FISHERS
FISHERY
FISHES
FISHEYE
FISHEYES
FISHFUL
FISHGIG
FISHGIGS
FISHIER
FISHIEST
FISHIFIED
FISHIFIES
FISHIFY
FISHIFYING
FISHINESS
FISHINESSES
FISHING
FISHINGS
FISHSKIN
FISHSKINS
FISHWIFE
FISHWIVES
FISHY
FISHYBACK
FISHYBACKS
FISK
FISKED
FISKING
FISKS
FISNOMIE
FISNOMIES
FISSILE
FISSILITIES
FISSILITY
FISSION
FISSIONS
FISSIPED
FISSIPEDE
FISSIPEDES
FISSIPEDS
FISSIVE
FISSLE
FISSLED
FISSLES
FISSLING
FISSURE
FISSURED
FISSURES
FISSURING
FIST
FISTED
FISTFUL
FISTFULS
FISTIANA
FISTIANAS
FISTIC
FISTICAL
FISTICUFF
FISTICUFFS
FISTIER
FISTIEST
FISTING

FISTMELE
FISTMELES
FISTS
FISTULA
FISTULAE
FISTULAR
FISTULAS
FISTULOSE
FISTULOUS
FISTY
FIT
FITCH
FITCHÉ
FITCHÉE
FITCHES
FITCHET
FITCHETS
FITCHEW
FITCHEWS
FITCHY
FITFUL
FITFULLY
FITLIER
FITLIEST
FITLY
FITMENT
FITMENTS
FITNESS
FITNESSES
FITS
FITT
FITTE
FITTED
FITTER
FITTERS
FITTES
FITTEST
FITTING
FITTINGLY
FITTINGS
FITTS
FIVE
FIVEFOLD
FIVEPENCE
FIVEPENCES
FIVEPENNY
FIVEPIN
FIVEPINS
FIVER
FIVERS
FIVES
FIX
FIXABLE
FIXATE
FIXATED
FIXATES
FIXATING
FIXATION
FIXATIONS
FIXATIVE
FIXATIVES
FIXATURE
FIXATURES
FIXED
FIXEDLY
FIXEDNESS
FIXEDNESSES
FIXER
FIXERS
FIXES

FIXING
FIXINGS
FIXITIES
FIXITY
FIXIVE
FIXTURE
FIXTURES
FIXURE
FIXURES
FIZ
FIZGIG
FIZGIGS
FIZZ
FIZZED
FIZZEN
FIZZENS
FIZZER
FIZZERS
FIZZES
FIZZGIG
FIZZGIGS
FIZZIER
FIZZIEST
FIZZING
FIZZINGS
FIZZLE
FIZZLED
FIZZLES
FIZZLING
FIZZY
FJORD
FJORDS
FLAB
FLABBIER
FLABBIEST
FLABBY
FLABELLA
FLABELLUM
FLABELLUMS
FLABS
FLACCID
FLACCIDER
FLACCIDEST
FLACCIDLY
FLACK
FLACKER
FLACKERED
FLACKERING
FLACKERS
FLACKET
FLACKETS
FLACKS
FLACON
FLACONS
FLAFF
FLAFFED
FLAFFER
FLAFFERED
FLAFFERING
FLAFFERS
FLAFFING
FLAFFS
FLAG
FLAGELLA
FLAGELLUM
FLAGEOLET
FLAGEOLETS
FLAGGED
FLAGGIER
FLAGGIEST

FLAGGING	FLAMMED	FLASHING	FLAUNT	FLEDGES
FLAGGINGS	FLAMMING	FLASHINGS	FLAUNTED	FLEDGIER
FLAGGY	FLAMMS	FLASHY	FLAUNTER	FLEDGIEST
FLAGITATE	FLAMMULE	FLASK	FLAUNTERS	FLEDGING
FLAGITATED	FLAMMULES	FLASKET	FLAUNTIER	FLEDGLING
FLAGITATES	FLAMS	FLASKETS	FLAUNTIEST	FLEDGLINGS
FLAGITATING	FLAMY	FLASKS	FLAUNTING	FLEDGY
FLAGON	FLAN	FLAT	FLAUNTS	FLEE
FLAGONS	FLANCH	FLATBACK	FLAUNTY	FLEECE
FLAGPOLE	FLANCHED	FLATBACKS	FLAUTIST	FLEECED
FLAGPOLES	FLANCHES	FLATBOAT	FLAUTISTS	FLEECER
FLAGRANCE	FLANCHING	FLATBOATS	FLAVIN	FLEECERS
FLAGRANCES	FLANCHINGS	FLATFISH	FLAVINE	FLEECES
FLAGRANCIES	FLÂNERIE	FLATFISHES	FLAVINES	FLEECH
FLAGRANCY	FLÂNERIES	FLATHEAD	FLAVINS	FLEECHED
FLAGRANT	FLÂNEUR	FLATHEADS	FLAVONE	FLEECHES
FLAGS	FLÂNEURS	FLATIRON	FLAVONES	FLEECHING
FLAGSHIP	FLANGE	FLATIRONS	FLAVOROUS	FLEECHINGS
FLAGSHIPS	FLANGED	FLATLET	FLAVOUR	FLEECIER
FLAGSTAFF	FLANGES	FLATLETS	FLAVOURED	FLEECIEST
FLAGSTAFFS	FLANGING	FLATLING	FLAVOURING	FLEECING
FLAGSTICK	FLANK	FLATLINGS	FLAVOURINGS	FLEECY
FLAGSTICKS	FLANKED	FLATLONG	FLAVOURS	FLEEING
FLAGSTONE	FLANKER	FLATLY	FLAW	FLEER
FLAGSTONES	FLANKERED	FLATMATE	FLAWED	FLEERED
FLAIL	FLANKERING	FLATMATES	FLAWIER	FLEERER
FLAILED	FLANKERS	FLATNESS	FLAWIEST	FLEERERS
FLAILING	FLANKING	FLATNESSES	FLAWING	FLEERING
FLAILS	FLANKS	FLATS	FLAWLESS	FLEERINGS
FLAIR	FLANNEL	FLATTED	FLAWN	FLEERS
FLAIRS	FLANNELLED	FLATTEN	FLAWNS	FLEES
FLAK	FLANNELLING	FLATTENED	FLAWS	FLEET
FLAKE	FLANNELLY	FLATTENING	FLAWY	FLEETED
FLAKED	FLANNELS	FLATTENS	FLAX	FLEETER
FLAKES	FLANNEN	FLATTER	FLAXEN	FLEETEST
FLAKIER	FLANNENS	FLATTERED	FLAXES	FLEETING
FLAKIEST	FLANS	FLATTERER	FLAXIER	FLEETLIER
FLAKINESS	FLAP	FLATTERERS	FLAXIEST	FLEETLIEST
FLAKINESSES	FLAPJACK	FLATTERIES	FLAXY	FLEETLY
FLAKING	FLAPJACKS	FLATTERING	FLAY	FLEETNESS
FLAKS	FLAPPABLE	FLATTERS	FLAYED	FLEETNESSES
FLAKY	FLAPPED	FLATTERY	FLAYER	FLEETS
FLAM	FLAPPER	FLATTEST	FLAYERS	FLEG
FLAMBÉ	FLAPPERS	FLATTING	FLAYING	FLEGGED
FLAMBEAU	FLAPPING	FLATTINGS	FLAYS	FLEGGING
FLAMBEAUS	FLAPPINGS	FLATTISH	FLEA	FLEGS
FLAMBEAUX	FLAPS	FLATULENT	FLEAM	FLEME
FLAMBÉED	FLAPTRACK	FLATUOUS	FLEAMS	FLEMES
FLAME	FLAPTRACKS	FLATUS	FLEAS	FLEMING
FLAMED	FLARE	FLATUSES	FLEASOME	FLEMISH
FLAMELESS	FLARED	FLATWARE	FLÈCHE	FLEMISHED
FLAMELET	FLARES	FLATWARES	FLÈCHES	FLEMISHES
FLAMELETS	FLARIER	FLATWAYS	FLECHETTE	FLEMISHING
FLAMEN	FLARIEST	FLATWISE	FLÉCHETTE	FLEMIT
FLAMENCO	FLARING	FLATWORM	FLECHETTES	FLENCH
FLAMENCOS	FLARINGLY	FLATWORMS	FLÉCHETTES	FLENCHED
FLAMENS	FLARY	FLAUGHT	FLECK	FLENCHES
FLAMES	FLASER	FLAUGHTED	FLECKED	FLENCHING
FLAMFEW	FLASERS	FLAUGHTER	FLECKER	FLENSE
FLAMFEWS	FLASH	FLAUGHTERED	FLECKERED	FLENSED
FLAMIER	FLASHCUBE	FLAUGHTERING	FLECKERING	FLENSES
FLAMIEST	FLASHCUBES	FLAUGHTERS	FLECKERS	FLENSING
FLAMINES	FLASHED	FLAUGHTING	FLECKING	FLESH
FLAMING	FLASHER	FLAUGHTS	FLECKLESS	FLESHED
FLAMINGLY	FLASHERS	FLAUNCH	FLECKS	FLESHER
FLAMINGO	FLASHES	FLAUNCHED	FLECTION	FLESHERS
FLAMINGOES	FLASHEST	FLAUNCHES	FLECTIONS	FLESHES
FLAMINGOS	FLASHIER	FLAUNCHING	FLED	FLESHIER
FLAMM	FLASHIEST	FLAUNE	FLEDGE	FLESHIEST
FLAMMABLE	FLASHILY	FLAUNES	FLEDGED	FLESHING

FLESHINGS	FLIGHT	FLISKY	FLOODMARK	FLORUITS
FLESHLESS	FLIGHTED	FLIT	FLOODMARKS	FLORY
FLESHLIER	FLIGHTIER	FLITCH	FLOODS	FLOSCULAR
FLESHLIEST	FLIGHTIEST	FLITCHES	FLOODTIDE	FLOSCULE
FLESHLING	FLIGHTILY	FLITE	FLOODTIDES	FLOSCULES
FLESHLINGS	FLIGHTING	FLITED	FLOODWALL	FLOSH
FLESHLY	FLIGHTS	FLITES	FLOODWALLS	FLOSHES
FLESHMENT	FLIGHTY	FLITING	FLOODWAY	FLOSS
FLESHMENTS	FLIMP	FLITS	FLOODWAYS	FLOSSES
FLESHWORM	FLIMPED	FLITT	FLOOR	FLOSSIER
FLESHWORMS	FLIMPING	FLITTED	FLOORED	FLOSSIEST
FLESHY	FLIMPS	FLITTER	FLOORER	FLOSSY
FLETCH	FLIMSIER	FLITTERED	FLOORERS	FLOTA
FLETCHED	FLIMSIES	FLITTERING	FLOORHEAD	FLOTAGE
FLETCHER	FLIMSIEST	FLITTERN	FLOORHEADS	FLOTAGES
FLETCHERS	FLIMSILY	FLITTERNS	FLOORING	FLOTANT
FLETCHES	FLIMSY	FLITTERS	FLOORINGS	FLOTAS
FLETCHING	FLINCH	FLITTING	FLOORS	FLOTATION
FLETTON	FLINCHED	FLITTINGS	FLOOSIE	FLOTATIONS
FLETTONS	FLINCHER	FLIVVER	FLOOSIES	FLOTE
FLEURET	FLINCHERS	FLIVVERS	FLOOSY	FLOTEL
FLEURETS	FLINCHES	FLIX	FLOOZIE	FLOTELS
FLEURETTE	FLINCHING	FLIXED	FLOOZIES	FLOTES
FLEURETTES	FLINCHINGS	FLIXES	FLOOZY	FLOTILLA
FLEURON	FLINDER	FLIXING	FLOP	FLOTILLAS
FLEURONS	FLINDERS	FLOAT	FLOPHOUSE	FLOTSAM
FLEURY	FLING	FLOATABLE	FLOPHOUSES	FLOTSAMS
FLEW	FLINGER	FLOATAGE	FLOPPED	FLOUNCE
FLEWED	FLINGERS	FLOATAGES	FLOPPIER	FLOUNCED
FLEWS	FLINGING	FLOATANT	FLOPPIEST	FLOUNCES
FLEX	FLINGS	FLOATANTS	FLOPPILY	FLOUNCING
FLEXED	FLINT	FLOATED	FLOPPING	FLOUNCINGS
FLEXES	FLINTIER	FLOATEL	FLOPPY	FLOUNDER
FLEXIBLE	FLINTIEST	FLOATELS	FLOPS	FLOUNDERED
FLEXIBLY	FLINTIFIED	FLOATER	FLOR	FLOUNDERING
FLEXILE	FLINTIFIES	FLOATERS	FLORA	FLOUNDERS
FLEXING	FLINTIFY	FLOATIER	FLORAE	FLOUR
FLEXION	FLINTIFYING	FLOATIEST	FLORAL	FLOURED
FLEXIONS	FLINTILY	FLOATING	FLORALLY	FLOURIER
FLEXITIME	FLINTLOCK	FLOATINGS	FLORAS	FLOURIEST
FLEXITIMES	FLINTLOCKS	FLOATS	FLOREAT	FLOURING
FLEXOR	FLINTS	FLOATY	FLOREATED	FLOURISH
FLEXORS	FLINTY	FLOCCI	FLORENCE	FLOURISHED
FLEXUOSE	FLIP	FLOCCOSE	FLORENCES	FLOURISHES
FLEXUOUS	FLIPFLOP	FLOCCULAR	FLORET	FLOURISHING
FLEXURAL	FLIPFLOPS	FLOCCULE	FLORETS	FLOURISHY
FLEXURE	FLIPPANCIES	FLOCCULES	FLORIATED	FLOURS
FLEXURES	FLIPPANCY	FLOCCULI	FLORID	FLOURY
FLEY	FLIPPANT	FLOCCULUS	FLORIDEAN	FLOUSE
FLEYED	FLIPPED	FLOCCUS	FLORIDEANS	FLOUSED
FLEYING	FLIPPER	FLOCK	FLORIDER	FLOUSES
FLEYS	FLIPPERS	FLOCKED	FLORIDEST	FLOUSH
FLIC	FLIPPEST	FLOCKING	FLORIDITIES	FLOUSHED
FLICHTER	FLIPPING	FLOCKS	FLORIDITY	FLOUSHES
FLICHTERED	FLIPS	FLOE	FLORIDLY	FLOUSHING
FLICHTERING	FLIRT	FLOES	FLORIER	FLOUSING
FLICHTERS	FLIRTED	FLOG	FLORIEST	FLOUT
FLICK	FLIRTIER	FLOGGED	FLORIFORM	FLOUTED
FLICKED	FLIRTIEST	FLOGGING	FLORIGEN	FLOUTING
FLICKER	FLIRTING	FLOGGINGS	FLORIGENS	FLOUTS
FLICKERED	FLIRTINGS	FLOGS	FLORIN	FLOW
FLICKERING	FLIRTISH	FLONG	FLORINS	FLOWAGE
FLICKERS	FLIRTS	FLONGS	FLORIST	FLOWAGES
FLICKING	FLIRTY	FLOOD	FLORISTIC	FLOWED
FLICKS	FLISK	FLOODED	FLORISTICS	FLOWER
FLICS	FLISKED	FLOODGATE	FLORISTRIES	FLOWERAGE
FLIER	FLISKIER	FLOODGATES	FLORISTRY	FLOWERAGES
FLIERS	FLISKIEST	FLOODING	FLORISTS	FLOWERED
FLIES	FLISKING	FLOODINGS	FLORS	FLOWERER
FLIEST	FLISKS	FLOODLIT	FLORUIT	FLOWERERS

FLOWERET	FLUIDIZING	FLUSHINGS	FLYPING	FOES
FLOWERETS	FLUIDNESS	FLUSHNESS	FLYTE	FOETAL
FLOWERING	FLUIDNESSES	FLUSHNESSES	FLYTED	FOETICIDE
FLOWERINGS	FLUIDS	FLUSHY	FLYTES	FOETICIDES
FLOWERPOT	FLUIER	FLUSTER	FLYTING	FOETID
FLOWERPOTS	FLUIEST	FLUSTERED	FLYTINGS	FOETIDER
FLOWERS	FLUKE	FLUSTERING	FLYTRAP	FOETIDEST
FLOWERY	FLUKED	FLUSTERS	FLYTRAPS	FOETOR
FLOWING	FLUKES	FLUSTERY	FLYWEIGHT	FOETORS
FLOWINGLY	FLUKEY	FLUSTRATE	FLYWEIGHTS	FOETUS
FLOWMETER	FLUKIER	FLUSTRATED	FLYWHEEL	FOETUSES
FLOWMETERS	FLUKIEST	FLUSTRATES	FLYWHEELS	FOG
FLOWN	FLUKING	FLUSTRATING	FOAL	FOGASH
FLOWS	FLUKY	FLUTE	FOALED	FOGASHES
FLU	FLUME	FLUTED	FOALFOOT	FOGBOUND
FLUATE	FLUMES	FLUTER	FOALFOOTS	FOGEY
FLUATES	FLUMMERIES	FLUTERS	FOALING	FOGEYS
FLUB	FLUMMERY	FLUTES	FOALS	FOGGAGE
FLUBBED	FLUMMOX	FLUTIER	FOAM	FOGGAGED
FLUBBING	FLUMMOXED	FLUTIEST	FOAMED	FOGGAGES
FLUBS	FLUMMOXES	FLUTINA	FOAMIER	FOGGAGING
FLUCTUANT	FLUMMOXING	FLUTINAS	FOAMIEST	FOGGED
FLUCTUATE	FLUMP	FLUTING	FOAMILY	FOGGER
FLUCTUATED	FLUMPED	FLUTINGS	FOAMINESS	FOGGERS
FLUCTUATES	FLUMPING	FLUTIST	FOAMINESSES	FOGGIER
FLUCTUATING	FLUMPS	FLUTISTS	FOAMING	FOGGIEST
FLUE	FLUNG	FLUTTER	FOAMINGLY	FOGGILY
FLUELLIN	FLUNK	FLUTTERED	FOAMINGS	FOGGINESS
FLUELLINS	FLUNKED	FLUTTERING	FOAMLESS	FOGGINESSES
FLUENCE	FLUNKEY	FLUTTERS	FOAMS	FOGGING
FLUENCES	FLUNKEYS	FLUTY	FOAMY	FOGGY
FLUENCIES	FLUNKIES	FLUVIAL	FOB	FOGHORN
FLUENCY	FLUNKING	FLUVIATIC	FOBBED	FOGHORNS
FLUENT	FLUNKS	FLUX	FOBBING	FOGIES
FLUENTLY	FLUNKY	FLUXED	FOBS	FOGLE
FLUENTS	FLUOR	FLUXES	FOCAL	FOGLES
FLUES	FLUORESCE	FLUXING	FOCALISE	FOGLESS
FLUEWORK	FLUORESCED	FLUXION	FOCALISED	FOGMAN
FLUEWORKS	FLUORESCES	FLUXIONAL	FOCALISES	FOGMEN
FLUEY	FLUORESCING	FLUXIONS	FOCALISING	FOGRAM
FLUFF	FLUORIC	FLUXIVE	FOCALIZE	FOGRAMITE
FLUFFED	FLUORIDE	FLY	FOCALIZED	FOGRAMITES
FLUFFIER	FLUORIDES	FLYABLE	FOCALIZES	FOGRAMITIES
FLUFFIEST	FLUORINE	FLYAWAY	FOCALIZING	FOGRAMITY
FLUFFING	FLUORINES	FLYBANE	FOCALLY	FOGRAMS
FLUFFS	FLUORITE	FLYBANES	FOCI	FOGS
FLUFFY	FLUORITES	FLYBELT	FOCIMETER	FOGY
FLUGEL	FLUOROSES	FLYBELTS	FOCIMETERS	FOGYDOM
FLUGELMAN	FLUOROSIS	FLYBLOW	FOCUS	FOGYDOMS
FLUGELMEN	FLUORS	FLYBLOWS	FOCUSED	FOGYISH
FLUGELS	FLUORSPAR	FLYBOAT	FOCUSES	FOGYISM
FLUID	FLUORSPARS	FLYBOATS	FOCUSING	FOGYISMS
FLUIDAL	FLURR	FLYBOOK	FOCUSSED	FOH
FLUIDER	FLURRED	FLYBOOKS	FOCUSSING	FÖHN
FLUIDEST	FLURRIED	FLYER	FODDER	FÖHNS
FLUIDIC	FLURRIES	FLYERS	FODDERED	FOIBLE
FLUIDICS	FLURRING	FLYEST	FODDERER	FOIBLES
FLUIDIFIED	FLURRS	FLYING	FODDERERS	FOIL
FLUIDIFIES	FLURRY	FLYINGS	FODDERING	FOILED
FLUIDIFY	FLURRYING	FLYLEAF	FODDERINGS	FOILING
FLUIDIFYING	FLUS	FLYLEAVES	FODDERS	FOILINGS
FLUIDISE	FLUSH	FLYMAKER	FOE	FOILS
FLUIDISED	FLUSHED	FLYMAKERS	FOEDARIE	FOIN
FLUIDISES	FLUSHER	FLYOVER	FOEDARIES	FOINED
FLUIDISING	FLUSHERS	FLYOVERS	FOEDERATI	FOINING
FLUIDITIES	FLUSHES	FLYPAPER	FOEHN	FOININGLY
FLUIDITY	FLUSHEST	FLYPAPERS	FOEHNS	FOINS
FLUIDIZE	FLUSHIER	FLYPE	FOEMAN	FOISON
FLUIDIZED	FLUSHIEST	FLYPED	FOEMEN	FOISONS
FLUIDIZES	FLUSHING	FLYPES	FOEN	FOIST

FOISTED
FOISTER
FOISTERS
FOISTING
FOISTS
FOLACIN
FOLACINS
FOLD
FOLDABLE
FOLDAWAY
FOLDBOAT
FOLDBOATS
FOLDED
FOLDER
FOLDEROL
FOLDEROLS
FOLDERS
FOLDING
FOLDINGS
FOLDS
FOLIA
FOLIAGE
FOLIAGED
FOLIAGES
FOLIAR
FOLIATE
FOLIATED
FOLIATES
FOLIATING
FOLIATION
FOLIATIONS
FOLIATURE
FOLIATURES
FOLIE
FOLIES
FOLIO
FOLIOED
FOLIOING
FOLIOLATE
FOLIOLE
FOLIOLES
FOLIOLOSE
FOLIOS
FOLIOSE
FOLIUM
FOLK
FOLKLAND
FOLKLANDS
FOLKLORE
FOLKLORES
FOLKLORIC
FOLKMOOT
FOLKMOOTS
FOLKROCK
FOLKROCKS
FOLKS
FOLKSIER
FOLKSIEST
FOLKSY
FOLKWAY
FOLKWAYS
FOLLICLE
FOLLICLES
FOLLIED
FOLLIES
FOLLOW
FOLLOWED
FOLLOWER
FOLLOWERS
FOLLOWING

FOLLOWINGS
FOLLOWS
FOLLY
FOLLYING
FOMENT
FOMENTED
FOMENTER
FOMENTERS
FOMENTING
FOMENTS
FOMES
FOMITES
FON
FOND
FONDA
FONDANT
FONDANTS
FONDAS
FONDED
FONDER
FONDEST
FONDING
FONDLE
FONDLED
FONDLER
FONDLERS
FONDLES
FONDLING
FONDLINGS
FONDLY
FONDNESS
FONDNESSES
FONDS
FONDUE
FONDUES
FONE
FONLY
FONNED
FONNING
FONS
FONT
FONTAL
FONTANEL
FONTANELS
FONTANGE
FONTANGES
FONTLET
FONTLETS
FONTS
FOOD
FOODED
FOODFUL
FOODIE
FOODIES
FOODING
FOODLESS
FOODS
FOODSTUFF
FOODSTUFFS
FOOL
FOOLED
FOOLERIES
FOOLERY
FOOLHARDY
FOOLING
FOOLINGS
FOOLISH
FOOLISHER
FOOLISHEST
FOOLISHLY

FOOLPROOF
FOOLS
FOOLSCAP
FOOLSCAPS
FOOT
FOOTAGE
FOOTAGES
FOOTBALL
FOOTBALLS
FOOTBAR
FOOTBARS
FOOTBOARD
FOOTBOARDS
FOOTBOY
FOOTBOYS
FOOTCLOTH
FOOTCLOTHS
FOOTED
FOOTER
FOOTERS
FOOTFALL
FOOTFALLS
FOOTFAULT
FOOTFAULTED
FOOTFAULTING
FOOTFAULTS
FOOTGEAR
FOOTHILL
FOOTHILLS
FOOTHOLD
FOOTHOLDS
FOOTING
FOOTINGS
FOOTLE
FOOTLED
FOOTLES
FOOTLESS
FOOTLIGHT
FOOTLIGHTS
FOOTLING
FOOTLINGS
FOOTLOOSE
FOOTMAN
FOOTMARK
FOOTMARKS
FOOTMEN
FOOTMUFF
FOOTMUFFS
FOOTNOTE
FOOTNOTES
FOOTPACE
FOOTPACES
FOOTPAD
FOOTPADS
FOOTPAGE
FOOTPAGES
FOOTPATH
FOOTPATHS
FOOTPLATE
FOOTPLATES
FOOTPOST
FOOTPOSTS
FOOTPRINT
FOOTPRINTS
FOOTRA
FOOTRAS
FOOTREST
FOOTRESTS
FOOTROT
FOOTROTS

FOOTRULE
FOOTRULES
FOOTS
FOOTSLOG
FOOTSLOGGED
FOOTSLOGGING
FOOTSLOGGINGS
FOOTSLOGS
FOOTSORE
FOOTSTALK
FOOTSTALKS
FOOTSTEP
FOOTSTEPS
FOOTSTOOL
FOOTSTOOLS
FOOTWAY
FOOTWAYS
FOOTWEAR
FOOTWORK
FOOTWORKS
FOOTWORN
FOOTY
FOOZLE
FOOZLED
FOOZLER
FOOZLERS
FOOZLES
FOOZLING
FOOZLINGS
FOP
FOPLING
FOPLINGS
FOPPERIES
FOPPERY
FOPPISH
FOPPISHLY
FOPS
FOR
FORA
FORAGE
FORAGED
FORAGER
FORAGERS
FORAGES
FORAGING
FORAMEN
FORAMINA
FORAMINAL
FORANE
FORASMUCH
FORAY
FORAYED
FORAYER
FORAYERS
FORAYING
FORAYS
FORBAD
FORBADE
FORBEAR
FORBEARING
FORBEARS
FORBID
FORBIDDAL
FORBIDDALS
FORBIDDEN
FORBIDDER
FORBIDDERS
FORBIDDING
FORBIDDINGS
FORBIDS

FORBODE
FORBODES
FORBORE
FORBORNE
FORBY
FORBYE
FORÇAT
FORÇATS
FORCE
FORCED
FORCEDLY
FORCEFUL
FORCELESS
FORCEMEAT
FORCEMEATS
FORCEPS
FORCEPSES
FORCER
FORCERS
FORCES
FORCIBLE
FORCIBLY
FORCING
FORCIPES
FORD
FORDABLE
FORDED
FORDID
FORDING
FORDO
FORDOES
FORDOING
FORDONE
FORDS
FORE
FOREANENT
FOREARM
FOREARMED
FOREARMING
FOREARMS
FOREBEAR
FOREBEARS
FOREBITT
FOREBITTS
FOREBODE
FOREBODED
FOREBODER
FOREBODERS
FOREBODES
FOREBODING
FOREBODINGS
FOREBY
FORECABIN
FORECABINS
FORECAR
FORECARS
FORECAST
FORECASTED
FORECASTING
FORECASTS
FORECLOSE
FORECLOSED
FORECLOSES
FORECLOSING
FORECLOTH
FORECLOTHS
FORECOURT
FORECOURTS
FOREDATE
FOREDATED

FOREDATES	FORELOCK	FORESHOCK	FORETHINKS	FORGERS
FOREDATING	FORELOCKS	FORESHOCKS	FORETHOUGHT	FORGERY
FOREDECK	FORELS	FORESHORE	FORETIME	FORGES
FOREDECKS	FORELYING	FORESHORES	FORETIMES	FORGET
FOREDOOM	FOREMAN	FORESHOW	FORETOKEN	FORGETFUL
FOREDOOMED	FOREMAST	FORESHOWED	FORETOKENED	FORGETIVE
FOREDOOMING	FOREMASTS	FORESHOWING	FORETOKENING	FORGETS
FOREDOOMS	FOREMEAN	FORESHOWN	FORETOKENINGS	FORGETTER
FOREFEEL	FOREMEANING	FORESHOWS	FORETOKENS	FORGETTERS
FOREFEELING	FOREMEANS	FORESIDE	FORETOLD	FORGETTING
FOREFEELS	FOREMEANT	FORESIDES	FORETOOTH	FORGETTINGS
FOREFEET	FOREMEN	FORESIGHT	FORETOP	FORGING
FOREFELT	FOREMOST	FORESIGHTS	FORETOPS	FORGINGS
FOREFOOT	FORENAME	FORESKIN	FOREVER	FORGIVE
FOREFRONT	FORENAMED	FORESKINS	FOREVERS	FORGIVEN
FOREFRONTS	FORENAMES	FORESKIRT	FOREWARD	FORGIVES
FOREGLEAM	FORENIGHT	FORESKIRTS	FOREWARDS	FORGIVING
FOREGLEAMS	FORENIGHTS	FORESLACK	FOREWARN	FORGO
FOREGO	FORENOON	FORESLACKED	FOREWARNED	FORGOES
FOREGOER	FORENOONS	FORESLACKING	FOREWARNING	FORGOING
FOREGOERS	FORENSIC	FORESLACKS	FOREWARNINGS	FORGONE
FOREGOES	FORENSICS	FORESLOW	FOREWARNS	FORGOT
FOREGOING	FOREPART	FORESLOWED	FOREWEIGH	FORGOTTEN
FOREGOINGS	FOREPARTS	FORESLOWING	FOREWEIGHED	FORHAILE
FOREGONE	FOREPAST	FORESLOWS	FOREWEIGHING	FORHAILED
FOREGUT	FOREPAW	FORESPEAK	FOREWEIGHS	FORHAILES
FOREGUTS	FOREPAWS	FORESPEAKING	FOREWENT	FORHAILING
FOREHAND	FOREPEAK	FORESPEAKS	FOREWIND	FORHENT
FOREHANDS	FOREPEAKS	FORESPEND	FOREWINDS	FORHENTED
FOREHEAD	FOREPLAN	FORESPENDING	FOREWING	FORHENTING
FOREHEADS	FOREPLANNED	FORESPENDS	FOREWINGS	FORHENTS
FOREHENT	FOREPLANNING	FORESPENT	FOREWOMAN	FORHOO
FOREHENTED	FOREPLANS	FORESPOKE	FOREWOMEN	FORHOOED
FOREHENTING	FOREPLAY	FORESPOKEN	FOREWORD	FORHOOIE
FOREHENTS	FOREPLAYS	FOREST	FOREWORDS	FORHOOIED
FOREIGN	FOREPOINT	FORESTAGE	FORFAIR	FORHOOIEING
FOREIGNER	FOREPOINTED	FORESTAGES	FORFAIRED	FORHOOIES
FOREIGNERS	FOREPOINTING	FORESTAIR	FORFAIRING	FORHOOING
FOREJUDGE	FOREPOINTS	FORESTAIRS	FORFAIRN	FORHOOS
FOREJUDGED	FORERAN	FORESTAL	FORFAIRS	FORHOW
FOREJUDGES	FOREREACH	FORESTALL	FORFAULT	FORHOWED
FOREJUDGING	FOREREACHED	FORESTALLED	FORFAULTED	FORHOWING
FOREKING	FOREREACHES	FORESTALLING	FORFAULTING	FORHOWS
FOREKINGS	FOREREACHING	FORESTALLINGS	FORFAULTS	FORINSEC
FOREKNEW	FOREREAD	FORESTALLS	FORFEIT	FORINT
FOREKNOW	FOREREADING	FORESTAY	FORFEITED	FORINTS
FOREKNOWING	FOREREADINGS	FORESTAYS	FORFEITER	FORJASKIT
FOREKNOWN	FOREREADS	FORESTEAL	FORFEITERS	FORJESKIT
FOREKNOWS	FORERUN	FORESTED	FORFEITING	FORJUDGE
FOREL	FORERUNNING	FORESTER	FORFEITS	FORJUDGED
FORELAID	FORERUNS	FORESTERS	FORFEND	FORJUDGES
FORELAND	FORES	FORESTINE	FORFENDED	FORJUDGING
FORELANDS	FORESAID	FORESTING	FORFENDING	FORK
FORELAY	FORESAIL	FORESTRIES	FORFENDS	FORKED
FORELAYING	FORESAILS	FORESTRY	FORFEX	FORKEDLY
FORELAYS	FORESAW	FORESTS	FORFEXES	FORKER
FORELEG	FORESAY	FORETASTE	FORFICATE	FORKERS
FORELEGS	FORESAYING	FORETASTED	FORGAT	FORKHEAD
FORELEND	FORESAYS	FORETASTES	FORGATHER	FORKHEADS
FORELENDING	FORESEE	FORETASTING	FORGATHERED	FORKIER
FORELENDS	FORESEEING	FORETAUGHT	FORGATHERING	FORKIEST
FORELENT	FORESEEN	FORETEACH	FORGATHERS	FORKINESS
FORELIE	FORESEES	FORETEACHES	FORGAVE	FORKINESSES
FORELIES	FORESHEW	FORETEACHING	FORGE	FORKING
FORELIFT	FORESHEWED	FORETEETH	FORGEABLE	FORKS
FORELIFTED	FORESHEWING	FORETELL	FORGED	FORKTAIL
FORELIFTING	FORESHEWN	FORETELLING	FORGEMAN	FORKTAILS
FORELIFTS	FORESHEWS	FORETELLS	FORGEMEN	FORKY
FORELIMB	FORESHIP	FORETHINK	FORGER	FORLANA
FORELIMBS	FORESHIPS	FORETHINKING	FORGERIES	FORLANAS

FORLEND
FORLENDING
FORLENDS
FORLENT
FORLESE
FORLESED
FORLESES
FORLESING
FORLORE
FORLORN
FORLORNER
FORLORNEST
FORLORNLY
FORLORNS
FORM
FORMABLE
FORMAL
FORMALIN
FORMALINS
FORMALISE
FORMALISED
FORMALISES
FORMALISING
FORMALISM
FORMALISMS
FORMALIST
FORMALISTS
FORMALITIES
FORMALITY
FORMALIZE
FORMALIZED
FORMALIZES
FORMALIZING
FORMALLY
FORMANT
FORMANTS
FORMAT
FORMATE
FORMATED
FORMATES
FORMATING
FORMATION
FORMATIONS
FORMATIVE
FORMATIVES
FORMATS
FORMATTED
FORMATTER
FORMATTERS
FORMATTING
FORME
FORMED
FORMER
FORMERLY
FORMERS
FORMES
FORMIATE
FORMIATES
FORMIC
FORMICANT
FORMICARIES
FORMICARY
FORMICATE
FORMING
FORMINGS
FORMLESS
FORMOL
FORMOLS
FORMS
FORMULA

FORMULAE
FORMULAIC
FORMULAR
FORMULARIES
FORMULARY
FORMULAS
FORMULATE
FORMULATED
FORMULATES
FORMULATING
FORMULISE
FORMULISED
FORMULISES
FORMULISING
FORMULISM
FORMULISMS
FORMULIST
FORMULISTS
FORMULIZE
FORMULIZED
FORMULIZES
FORMULIZING
FORMWORK
FORMWORKS
FORNENST
FORNENT
FORNICAL
FORNICATE
FORNICATED
FORNICATES
FORNICATING
FORNIX
FORNIXES
FORPET
FORPETS
FORPINE
FORPINED
FORPINES
FORPINING
FORPIT
FORPITS
FORRAD
FORRADER
FORRAY
FORRAYED
FORRAYING
FORRAYS
FORREN
FORRIT
FORSAID
FORSAKE
FORSAKEN
FORSAKES
FORSAKING
FORSAKINGS
FORSAY
FORSAYING
FORSAYS
FORSLACK
FORSLACKED
FORSLACKING
FORSLACKS
FORSLOE
FORSLOED
FORSLOEING
FORSLOES
FORSLOW
FORSLOWED
FORSLOWING
FORSLOWS

FORSOOK
FORSOOTH
FORSPEAK
FORSPEAKING
FORSPEAKS
FORSPEND
FORSPENDING
FORSPENDS
FORSPENT
FORSPOKE
FORSPOKEN
FORSWATT
FORSWEAR
FORSWEARING
FORSWEARS
FORSWINK
FORSWINKED
FORSWINKING
FORSWINKS
FORSWONCK
FORSWORE
FORSWORN
FORSWUNK
FORSYTHIA
FORSYTHIAS
FORT
FORTALICE
FORTALICES
FORTE
FORTED
FORTES
FORTH
FORTHCAME
FORTHCOME
FORTHCOMES
FORTHCOMING
FORTHINK
FORTHINKING
FORTHINKS
FORTHOUGHT
FORTHWITH
FORTHY
FORTIES
FORTIETH
FORTIETHS
FORTIFIED
FORTIFIER
FORTIFIERS
FORTIFIES
FORTIFY
FORTIFYING
FORTILAGE
FORTILAGES
FORTING
FORTIS
FORTITUDE
FORTITUDES
FORTLET
FORTLETS
FORTNIGHT
FORTNIGHTS
FORTRESS
FORTRESSED
FORTRESSES
FORTRESSING
FORTS
FORTUITIES
FORTUITY
FORTUNATE
FORTUNE

FORTUNED
FORTUNES
FORTUNING
FORTUNIZE
FORTUNIZED
FORTUNIZES
FORTUNIZING
FORTY
FORTYISH
FORUM
FORUMS
FORWANDER
FORWANDERED
FORWANDERING
FORWANDERS
FORWARD
FORWARDED
FORWARDER
FORWARDERS
FORWARDEST
FORWARDING
FORWARDINGS
FORWARDLY
FORWARDS
FORWARN
FORWARNED
FORWARNING
FORWARNS
FORWASTE
FORWASTED
FORWASTES
FORWASTING
FORWEARIED
FORWEARIES
FORWEARY
FORWEARYING
FORWENT
FORWHY
FORWORN
FORZANDI
FORZANDO
FORZANDOS
FORZATI
FORZATO
FORZATOS
FOSS
FOSSA
FOSSAE
FOSSAS
FOSSE
FOSSED
FOSSES
FOSSETTE
FOSSETTES
FOSSICK
FOSSICKED
FOSSICKER
FOSSICKERS
FOSSICKING
FOSSICKINGS
FOSSICKS
FOSSIL
FOSSILISE
FOSSILISED
FOSSILISES
FOSSILISING
FOSSILIZE
FOSSILIZED
FOSSILIZES
FOSSILIZING

FOSSILS
FOSSOR
FOSSORIAL
FOSSORS
FOSSULA
FOSSULAS
FOSSULATE
FOSTER
FOSTERAGE
FOSTERAGES
FOSTERED
FOSTERER
FOSTERERS
FOSTERING
FOSTERINGS
FOSTERS
FOSTRESS
FOSTRESSES
FOTHER
FOTHERED
FOTHERING
FOTHERS
FOU
FOUAT
FOUATS
FOUD
FOUDRIE
FOUDRIES
FOUDS
FOUER
FOUEST
FOUET
FOUETS
FOUETTÉ
FOUETTÉS
FOUGADE
FOUGADES
FOUGASSE
FOUGASSES
FOUGHT
FOUGHTEN
FOUGHTY
FOUL
FOULARD
FOULARDS
FOULDER
FOULDERED
FOULDERING
FOULDERS
FOULÉ
FOULED
FOULER
FOULÉS
FOULEST
FOULING
FOULLY
FOULMART
FOULMARTS
FOULNESS
FOULNESSES
FOULS
FOUMART
FOUMARTS
FOUND
FOUNDED
FOUNDER
FOUNDERED
FOUNDERING
FOUNDERS
FOUNDING

FOUNDINGS	FOXHOUND	FRAGRANCED	FRAPPED	FREE
FOUNDLING	FOXHOUNDS	FRAGRANCES	FRAPPÉE	FREEBEE
FOUNDLINGS	FOXIER	FRAGRANCIES	FRAPPING	FREEBEES
FOUNDRESS	FOXIEST	FRAGRANCING	FRAPS	FREEBIE
FOUNDRESSES	FOXINESS	FRAGRANCY	FRAS	FREEBIES
FOUNDRIES	FOXINESSES	FRAGRANT	FRASS	FREEBOOTIES
FOUNDRY	FOXING	FRAÎCHEUR	FRASSES	FREEBOOTY
FOUNDS	FOXINGS	FRAÎCHEURS	FRATCH	FREEBORN
FOUNT	FOXSHARK	FRAIL	FRATCHES	FREED
FOUNTAIN	FOXSHARKS	FRAILER	FRATCHETY	FREEDMAN
FOUNTAINED	FOXSHIP	FRAILEST	FRATCHING	FREEDMEN
FOUNTAINING	FOXSHIPS	FRAILISH	FRATCHY	FREEDOM
FOUNTAINS	FOXTROT	FRAILLY	FRATE	FREEDOMS
FOUNTFUL	FOXTROTS	FRAILNESS	FRATER	FREEHOLD
FOUNTS	FOXTROTTED	FRAILNESSES	FRATERIES	FREEHOLDS
FOUR	FOXTROTTING	FRAILS	FRATERNAL	FREEING
FOURFOLD	FOXY	FRAILTEE	FRATERS	FREELOAD
FOURGON	FOY	FRAILTEES	FRATERY	FREELOADED
FOURGONS	FOYER	FRAILTIES	FRATI	FREELOADING
FOURPENCE	FOYERS	FRAILTY	FRATRIES	FREELOADINGS
FOURPENCES	FOYLE	FRAIM	FRATRY	FREELOADS
FOURPENNIES	FOYLED	FRAIMS	FRAU	FREELY
FOURPENNY	FOYLES	FRAISE	FRAUD	FREEMAN
FOURS	FOYLING	FRAISED	FRAUDFUL	FREEMASON
FOURSCORE	FOYNE	FRAISES	FRAUDS	FREEMASONS
FOURSES	FOYNED	FRAISING	FRAUDSMAN	FREEMEN
FOURSOME	FOYNES	FRAME	FRAUDSMEN	FREENESS
FOURSOMES	FOYNING	FRAMED	FRAUDSTER	FREENESSES
FOURTEEN	FOYS	FRAMER	FRAUDSTERS	FREER
FOURTEENS	FOZIER	FRAMERS	FRAUGHT	FREERS
FOURTH	FOZIEST	FRAMES	FRAUGHTED	FREES
FOURTHLY	FOZINESS	FRAMEWORK	FRAUGHTER	FREESHEET
FOURTHS	FOZINESSES	FRAMEWORKS	FRAUGHTEST	FREESHEETS
FOUS	FOZY	FRAMING	FRAUGHTING	FREESIA
FOUSSA	FRA	FRAMINGS	FRAUGHTS	FREESIAS
FOUSSAS	FRAB	FRAMPAL	FRÄULEIN	FREEST
FOUTER	FRABBED	FRAMPLER	FRÄULEINS	FREESTONE
FOUTERS	FRABBING	FRAMPLERS	FRAUS	FREESTONES
FOUTH	FRABBIT	FRAMPOLD	FRAUTAGE	FREESTYLE
FOUTHS	FRABJOUS	FRANC	FRAUTAGES	FREESTYLES
FOUTRA	FRABS	FRANCHISE	FRAY	FREET
FOUTRAS	FRACAS	FRANCHISED	FRAYED	FREETIER
FOUTRE	FRACK	FRANCHISES	FRAYING	FREETIEST
FOUTRES	FRACT	FRANCHISING	FRAYINGS	FREETS
FOVEA	FRACTED	FRANCIUM	FRAYS	FREETY
FOVEAE	FRACTING	FRANCIUMS	FRAZIL	FREEWAY
FOVEAL	FRACTION	FRANCO	FRAZILS	FREEWAYS
FOVEATE	FRACTIONS	FRANCOLIN	FRAZZLE	FREEWOMAN
FOVEOLA	FRACTIOUS	FRANCOLINS	FRAZZLED	FREEWOMEN
FOVEOLAS	FRACTS	FRANCS	FRAZZLES	FREEZABLE
FOVEOLE	FRACTURE	FRANGIBLE	FRAZZLING	FREEZE
FOVEOLES	FRACTURED	FRANION	FREAK	FREEZER
FOWL	FRACTURES	FRANIONS	FREAKED	FREEZERS
FOWLED	FRACTURING	FRANK	FREAKFUL	FREEZES
FOWLER	FRAE	FRANKED	FREAKIER	FREEZING
FOWLERS	FRAENA	FRANKER	FREAKIEST	FREEZINGS
FOWLING	FRAENUM	FRANKEST	FREAKING	FREIGHT
FOWLINGS	FRAGILE	FRANKING	FREAKISH	FREIGHTED
FOWLS	FRAGILELY	FRANKLIN	FREAKS	FREIGHTER
FOWTH	FRAGILER	FRANKLINS	FREAKY	FREIGHTERS
FOWTHS	FRAGILEST	FRANKLY	FRECKLE	FREIGHTING
FOX	FRAGILITIES	FRANKNESS	FRECKLED	FREIGHTS
FOXBERRIES	FRAGILITY	FRANKNESSES	FRECKLES	FREIT
FOXBERRY	FRAGMENT	FRANKS	FRECKLIER	FREITIER
FOXED	FRAGMENTED	FRANTIC	FRECKLIEST	FREITIEST
FOXES	FRAGMENTING	FRANTICLY	FRECKLING	FREITS
FOXGLOVE	FRAGMENTS	FRANZY	FRECKLINGS	FREITY
FOXGLOVES	FRAGOR	FRAP	FRECKLY	FREMD
FOXHOLE	FRAGORS	FRAPPANT	FREDAINE	FREMDS
FOXHOLES	FRAGRANCE	FRAPPÉ	FREDAINES	FREMIT

FREMITS	FRETTIEST	FRIGGERS	FRISKS	FROGGIEST
FREMITUS	FRETTING	FRIGGING	FRISKY	FROGGING
FREMITUSES	FRETTINGS	FRIGGINGS	FRISSON	FROGGINGS
FRENA	FRETTY	FRIGHT	FRISSONS	FROGGY
FRENCH	FRETWORK	FRIGHTED	FRIST	FROGLET
FRENETIC	FRETWORKS	FRIGHTEN	FRISTED	FROGLETS
FRENETICS	FRIABLE	FRIGHTENED	FRISTING	FROGLING
FRENNE	FRIAND	FRIGHTENING	FRISTS	FROGLINGS
FRENNES	FRIANDE	FRIGHTENS	FRISURE	FROGMAN
FRENUM	FRIANDES	FRIGHTFUL	FRISURES	FROGMEN
FRENZICAL	FRIANDS	FRIGHTING	FRIT	FROGMOUTH
FRENZIED	FRIAR	FRIGHTS	FRITFLIES	FROGMOUTHS
FRENZIES	FRIARBIRD	FRIGID	FRITFLY	FROGS
FRENZY	FRIARBIRDS	FRIGIDER	FRITH	FROISE
FRENZYING	FRIARIES	FRIGIDEST	FRITHBORH	FROISES
FREON	FRIARLY	FRIGIDITIES	FRITHBORHS	FROLIC
FREONS	FRIARS	FRIGIDITY	FRITHGILD	FROLICKED
FREQUENCE	FRIARY	FRIGIDLY	FRITHGILDS	FROLICKING
FREQUENCES	FRIBBLE	FRIGOT	FRITHS	FROLICS
FREQUENCIES	FRIBBLED	FRIGOTS	FRITS	FROM
FREQUENCY	FRIBBLER	FRIGS	FRITTED	FROMENTIES
FREQUENT	FRIBBLERS	FRIJOL	FRITTER	FROMENTY
FREQUENTED	FRIBBLES	FRIJOLE	FRITTERED	FROND
FREQUENTER	FRIBBLING	FRIJOLES	FRITTERER	FRONDAGE
FREQUENTEST	FRIBBLISH	FRIKKADEL	FRITTERERS	FRONDAGES
FREQUENTING	FRICADEL	FRIKKADELS	FRITTERING	FRONDED
FREQUENTS	FRICADELS	FRILL	FRITTERS	FRONDENT
FRÈRE	FRICASSEE	FRILLED	FRITTING	FRONDEUR
FRÈRES	FRICASSEED	FRILLIER	FRITURE	FRONDEURS
FRESCADE	FRICASSEEING	FRILLIES	FRITURES	FRONDOSE
FRESCADES	FRICASSEES	FRILLIEST	FRIVOL	FRONDS
FRESCO	FRICATIVE	FRILLING	FRIVOLITIES	FRONT
FRESCOED	FRICATIVES	FRILLINGS	FRIVOLITY	FRONTAGE
FRESCOER	FRICHT	FRILLS	FRIVOLLED	FRONTAGER
FRESCOERS	FRICHTED	FRILLY	FRIVOLLING	FRONTAGERS
FRESCOES	FRICHTING	FRINGE	FRIVOLOUS	FRONTAGES
FRESCOING	FRICHTS	FRINGED	FRIVOLS	FRONTAL
FRESCOINGS	FRICTION	FRINGES	FRIZ	FRONTALS
FRESCOIST	FRICTIONS	FRINGIER	FRIZE	FRONTED
FRESCOISTS	FRIDGE	FRINGIEST	FRIZES	FRONTIER
FRESCOS	FRIDGED	FRINGING	FRIZING	FRONTIERED
FRESH	FRIDGES	FRINGY	FRIZZ	FRONTIERING
FRESHED	FRIDGING	FRIPON	FRIZZANTE	FRONTIERS
FRESHEN	FRIED	FRIPONS	FRIZZED	FRONTING
FRESHENED	FRIEDCAKE	FRIPPER	FRIZZES	FRONTLESS
FRESHENER	FRIEDCAKES	FRIPPERER	FRIZZIER	FRONTLET
FRESHENERS	FRIEND	FRIPPERERS	FRIZZIEST	FRONTLETS
FRESHENING	FRIENDED	FRIPPERIES	FRIZZING	FRONTMAN
FRESHENS	FRIENDING	FRIPPERS	FRIZZLE	FRONTMEN
FRESHER	FRIENDINGS	FRIPPERY	FRIZZLED	FRONTON
FRESHERS	FRIENDLIER	FRIS	FRIZZLES	FRONTONS
FRESHES	FRIENDLIES	FRISES	FRIZZLIER	FRONTOON
FRESHEST	FRIENDLIEST	FRISETTE	FRIZZLIEST	FRONTOONS
FRESHET	FRIENDLY	FRISETTES	FRIZZLING	FRONTS
FRESHETS	FRIENDS	FRISEUR	FRIZZLY	FRONTWARD
FRESHING	FRIER	FRISEURS	FRIZZY	FRONTWAYS
FRESHISH	FRIERS	FRISK	FRO	FRONTWISE
FRESHLY	FRIES	FRISKA	FROCK	FRORE
FRESHMAN	FRIEZE	FRISKAS	FROCKED	FROREN
FRESHMEN	FRIEZED	FRISKED	FROCKING	FRORN
FRESHNESS	FRIEZES	FRISKER	FROCKINGS	FRORNE
FRESHNESSES	FRIEZING	FRISKERS	FROCKLESS	FRORY
FRET	FRIG	FRISKET	FROCKS	FROST
FRETFUL	FRIGATE	FRISKETS	FROG	FROSTBIT
FRETFULLY	FRIGATES	FRISKFUL	FROGBIT	FROSTBITE
FRETS	FRIGATOON	FRISKIER	FROGBITS	FROSTBITES
FRETSAW	FRIGATOONS	FRISKIEST	FROGGED	FROSTBITING
FRETSAWS	FRIGES	FRISKILY	FROGGERIES	FROSTBITTEN
FRETTED	FRIGGED	FRISKING	FROGGERY	FROSTED
FRETTIER	FRIGGER	FRISKINGS	FROGGIER	FROSTIER

FROSTIEST	FRUGALITIES	FRYERS	FUGGING	FULMAR
FROSTILY	FRUGALITY	FRYING	FUGGY	FULMARS
FROSTING	FRUGALLY	FRYINGS	FUGHETTA	FULMINANT
FROSTINGS	FRUICT	FUB	FUGHETTAS	FULMINANTS
FROSTLESS	FRUICTED	FUBBED	FUGIE	FULMINATE
FROSTS	FRUICTING	FUBBERIES	FUGIES	FULMINATED
FROSTWORK	FRUICTS	FUBBERY	FUGITIVE	FULMINATES
FROSTWORKS	FRUIT	FUBBING	FUGITIVES	FULMINATING
FROSTY	FRUITAGE	FUBBY	FUGLE	FULMINE
FROTH	FRUITAGES	FUBS	FUGLED	FULMINED
FROTHED	FRUITED	FUBSY	FUGLEMAN	FULMINES
FROTHERIES	FRUITER	FUCHSIA	FUGLEMEN	FULMINING
FROTHERY	FRUITERER	FUCHSIAS	FUGLES	FULMINOUS
FROTHIER	FRUITERERS	FUCHSINE	FUGLING	FULNESS
FROTHIEST	FRUITERIES	FUCHSINES	FUGS	FULNESSES
FROTHILY	FRUITERS	FUCHSITE	FUGUE	FULSOME
FROTHING	FRUITERY	FUCHSITES	FUGUES	FULSOMELY
FROTHLESS	FRUITFUL	FUCI	FUGUIST	FULSOMER
FROTHS	FRUITIER	FUCK	FUGUISTS	FULSOMEST
FROTHY	FRUITIEST	FUCKED	FULCRA	FULVID
FROTTAGE	FRUITING	FUCKER	FULCRATE	FULVIDER
FROTTAGES	FRUITINGS	FUCKERS	FULCRUM	FULVIDEST
FROTTEUR	FRUITION	FUCKING	FULCRUMS	FULVOUS
FROTTEURS	FRUITIONS	FUCKINGS	FULFIL	FUM
FROUGHY	FRUITIVE	FUCKS	FULFILLED	FUMADO
FROUNCE	FRUITLESS	FUCOID	FULFILLER	FUMADOES
FROUNCED	FRUITLET	FUCOIDAL	FULFILLERS	FUMADOS
FROUNCES	FRUITLETS	FUCOIDS	FULFILLING	FUMAGE
FROUNCING	FRUITS	FUCUS	FULFILLINGS	FUMAGES
FROW	FRUITWOOD	FUCUSED	FULFILS	FUMAROLE
FROWARD	FRUITWOODS	FUCUSES	FULGENCIES	FUMAROLES
FROWARDLY	FRUITY	FUD	FULGENCY	FUMATORIA
FROWARDS	FRUMENTIES	FUDDLE	FULGENT	FUMATORIES
FROWIE	FRUMENTY	FUDDLED	FULGENTLY	FUMATORY
FROWN	FRUMP	FUDDLER	FULGID	FUMBLE
FROWNED	FRUMPED	FUDDLERS	FULGIDER	FUMBLED
FROWNING	FRUMPIER	FUDDLES	FULGIDEST	FUMBLER
FROWNS	FRUMPIEST	FUDDLING	FULGOR	FUMBLERS
FROWS	FRUMPING	FUDDLINGS	FULGOROUS	FUMBLES
FROWST	FRUMPISH	FUDGE	FULGORS	FUMBLING
FROWSTED	FRUMPLE	FUDGED	FULGOUR	FUME
FROWSTER	FRUMPLED	FUDGES	FULGOURS	FUMED
FROWSTERS	FRUMPLES	FUDGING	FULGURAL	FUMEROLE
FROWSTIER	FRUMPLING	FUDS	FULGURANT	FUMEROLES
FROWSTIEST	FRUMPS	FUEL	FULGURATE	FUMES
FROWSTING	FRUMPY	FUELLED	FULGURATED	FUMET
FROWSTS	FRUSH	FUELLER	FULGURATES	FUMETS
FROWSTY	FRUSHED	FUELLERS	FULGURATING	FUMETTE
FROWSY	FRUSHES	FUELLING	FULGURITE	FUMETTES
FROWY	FRUSHING	FUELS	FULGURITES	FUMETTI
FROWZY	FRUST	FUERO	FULGUROUS	FUMETTO
FROZE	FRUSTA	FUEROS	FULHAM	FUMIER
FROZEN	FRUSTRATE	FUFF	FULHAMS	FUMIEST
FRUCTED	FRUSTRATED	FUFFED	FULL	FUMIGANT
FRUCTIFIED	FRUSTRATES	FUFFIER	FULLAGE	FUMIGANTS
FRUCTIFIES	FRUSTRATING	FUFFIEST	FULLAGES	FUMIGATE
FRUCTIFY	FRUSTS	FUFFING	FULLAM	FUMIGATED
FRUCTIFYING	FRUSTULE	FUFFS	FULLAMS	FUMIGATES
FRUCTOSE	FRUSTULES	FUFFY	FULLAN	FUMIGATING
FRUCTOSES	FRUSTUM	FUG	FULLANS	FUMIGATOR
FRUCTUARIES	FRUSTUMS	FUGACIOUS	FULLED	FUMIGATORS
FRUCTUARY	FRUTEX	FUGACITIES	FULLER	FUMING
FRUCTUATE	FRUTICES	FUGACITY	FULLERS	FUMITORIES
FRUCTUATED	FRUTICOSE	FUGAL	FULLEST	FUMITORY
FRUCTUATES	FRUTIFIED	FUGALLY	FULLING	FUMOSITIES
FRUCTUATING	FRUTIFIES	FUGATO	FULLISH	FUMOSITY
FRUCTUOUS	FRUTIFY	FUGATOS	FULLNESS	FUMOUS
FRUGAL	FRUTIFYING	FUGGED	FULLNESSES	FUMS
FRUGALIST	FRY	FUGGIER	FULLS	FUMY
FRUGALISTS	FRYER	FUGGIEST	FULLY	FUN

FUNCTION	FUNNIEST	FURLOUGHING	FURZIER	FUSTING
FUNCTIONED	FUNNILY	FURLOUGHS	FURZIEST	FUSTOC
FUNCTIONING	FUNNINESS	FURLS	FURZY	FUSTOCS
FUNCTIONS	FUNNINESSES	FURMENTIES	FUSAIN	FUSTS
FUND	FUNNING	FURMENTY	FUSAINS	FUSTY
FUNDABLE	FUNNY	FURMETIES	FUSAROL	FUTCHEL
FUNDAMENT	FUNS	FURMETY	FUSAROLE	FUTCHELS
FUNDAMENTS	FUR	FURMITIES	FUSAROLES	FUTHARK
FUNDED	FURACIOUS	FURMITY	FUSAROLS	FUTHARKS
FUNDER	FURACITIES	FURNACE	FUSC	FUTHORC
FUNDERS	FURACITY	FURNACED	FUSCOUS	FUTHORCS
FUNDI	FURAL	FURNACES	FUSE	FUTHORK
FUNDING	FURALS	FURNACING	FUSED	FUTHORKS
FUNDINGS	FURAN	FURNIMENT	FUSEE	FUTILE
FUNDIS	FURANE	FURNIMENTS	FUSEES	FUTILELY
FUNDLESS	FURANES	FURNISH	FUSELAGE	FUTILER
FUNDS	FURANS	FURNISHED	FUSELAGES	FUTILEST
FUNDUS	FURBELOW	FURNISHER	FUSES	FUTILITIES
FUNEBRAL	FURBELOWED	FURNISHERS	FUSHION	FUTILITY
FUNÈBRE	FURBELOWING	FURNISHES	FUSHIONS	FUTON
FUNEBRIAL	FURBELOWS	FURNISHING	FUSIBLE	FUTONS
FUNERAL	FURBISH	FURNISHINGS	FUSIFORM	FUTTOCK
FUNERALS	FURBISHED	FURNITURE	FUSIL	FUTTOCKS
FUNERARY	FURBISHER	FURNITURES	FUSILE	FUTURE
FUNEREAL	FURBISHERS	FUROL	FUSILEER	FUTURES
FUNEST	FURBISHES	FUROLE	FUSILEERS	FUTURISM
FUNFAIR	FURBISHING	FUROLES	FUSILIER	FUTURISMS
FUNFAIRS	FURCAL	FUROLS	FUSILIERS	FUTURIST
FUNG	FURCATE	FUROR	FUSILLADE	FUTURISTS
FUNGAL	FURCATED	FURORE	FUSILLADES	FUTURITIES
FUNGI	FURCATION	FURORES	FUSILS	FUTURITY
FUNGIBLES	FURCATIONS	FURORS	FUSING	FUZE
FUNGICIDE	FURCULA	FURPHIES	FUSION	FUZEE
FUNGICIDES	FURCULAR	FURPHY	FUSIONISM	FUZEES
FUNGIFORM	FURCULAS	FURR	FUSIONISMS	FUZES
FUNGOID	FURDER	FURRED	FUSIONIST	FUZZ
FUNGOIDAL	FUREUR	FURRIER	FUSIONISTS	FUZZED
FUNGOSITIES	FUREURS	FURRIERIES	FUSIONS	FUZZES
FUNGOSITY	FURFAIR	FURRIERS	FUSS	FUZZIER
FUNGOUS	FURFAIRS	FURRIERY	FUSSED	FUZZIEST
FUNGS	FURFUR	FURRIEST	FUSSER	FUZZILY
FUNGUS	FURFURAL	FURRING	FUSSERS	FUZZINESS
FUNGUSES	FURFURALS	FURRINGS	FUSSES	FUZZINESSES
FUNICLE	FURFURAN	FURROW	FUSSIER	FUZZING
FUNICLES	FURFURANS	FURROWED	FUSSIEST	FUZZLE
FUNICULAR	FURFUROL	FURROWING	FUSSILY	FUZZLED
FUNICULI	FURFUROLE	FURROWS	FUSSINESS	FUZZLES
FUNICULUS	FURFUROLES	FURROWY	FUSSINESSES	FUZZLING
FUNK	FURFUROLS	FURRS	FUSSING	FUZZY
FUNKED	FURFUROUS	FURRY	FUSSY	FY
FUNKHOLE	FURFURS	FURS	FUST	FYKE
FUNKHOLES	FURIBUND	FURTH	FUSTED	FYKED
FUNKIA	FURIES	FURTHER	FUSTET	FYKES
FUNKIAS	FURIOSITIES	FURTHERED	FUSTETS	FYKING
FUNKIER	FURIOSITY	FURTHERER	FUSTIAN	FYLE
FUNKIEST	FURIOSO	FURTHERERS	FUSTIANS	FYLES
FUNKINESS	FURIOSOS	FURTHERING	FUSTIC	FYLFOT
FUNKINESSES	FURIOUS	FURTHERS	FUSTICS	FYLFOTS
FUNKING	FURIOUSLY	FURTHEST	FUSTIER	FYNBOS
FUNKS	FURL	FURTIVE	FUSTIEST	FYNBOSES
FUNKY	FURLANA	FURTIVELY	FUSTIGATE	FYRD
FUNNED	FURLANAS	FURTIVER	FUSTIGATED	FYRDS
FUNNEL	FURLED	FURTIVEST	FUSTIGATES	FYTTE
FUNNELLED	FURLING	FURUNCLE	FUSTIGATING	FYTTES
FUNNELLING	FURLONG	FURUNCLES	FUSTILUGS	
FUNNELS	FURLONGS	FURY	FUSTILY	
FUNNIER	FURLOUGH	FURZE	FUSTINESS	
FUNNIES	FURLOUGHED	FURZES	FUSTINESSES	

G

GAB
GABARDINE
GABARDINES
GABBARD
GABBARDS
GABBART
GABBARTS
GABBED
GABBER
GABBERS
GABBIER
GABBIEST
GABBING
GABBLE
GABBLED
GABBLER
GABBLERS
GABBLES
GABBLING
GABBLINGS
GABBRO
GABBROIC
GABBROID
GABBROS
GABBY
GABELLE
GABELLER
GABELLERS
GABELLES
GABERDINE
GABERDINES
GABFEST
GABFESTS
GABIES
GABION
GABIONADE
GABIONADES
GABIONAGE
GABIONED
GABIONS
GABLE
GABLED
GABLES
GABLET
GABLETS
GABNASH
GABNASHES
GABS
GABY
GAD
GADABOUT
GADABOUTS
GADDED
GADDER
GADDERS
GADDING
GADE
GADES
GADFLIES
GADFLY
GADGE
GADGES
GADGET
GADGETEER

GADGETEERS
GADGETRIES
GADGETRY
GADGETS
GADGIE
GADGIES
GADI
GADIS
GADJE
GADJES
GADLING
GADLINGS
GADOID
GADOIDS
GADROON
GADROONED
GADROONS
GADS
GADSMAN
GADSMEN
GADSO
GADSOS
GADWALL
GADWALLS
GADZOOKS
GAE
GAED
GAEING
GAELICISE
GAELICISED
GAELICISES
GAELICISING
GAELICISM
GAELICISMS
GAELICIZE
GAELICIZED
GAELICIZES
GAELICIZING
GAES
GAFF
GAFFE
GAFFED
GAFFER
GAFFERS
GAFFES
GAFFING
GAFFINGS
GAFFS
GAG
GAGA
GAGAKU
GAGAKUS
GAGE
GAGED
GAGES
GAGGED
GAGGER
GAGGERS
GAGGING
GAGGLE
GAGGLED
GAGGLES
GAGGLING
GAGGLINGS

GAGING
GAGMAN
GAGMEN
GAGS
GAGSTER
GAGSTERS
GAHNITE
GAHNITES
GAID
GAIDS
GAIETIES
GAIETY
GAILLARD
GAILLARDS
GAILY
GAIN
GAINABLE
GAINED
GAINER
GAINERS
GAINEST
GAINFUL
GAINFULLY
GAINING
GAININGS
GAINLESS
GAINLY
GAINS
GAINSAID
GAINSAY
GAINSAYER
GAINSAYERS
GAINSAYING
GAINSAYINGS
GAINSAYS
GAINST
GAIR
GAIRFOWL
GAIRFOWLS
GAIRS
GAIT
GAITED
GAITER
GAITERS
GAITS
GAITT
GAITTS
GAJO
GAJOS
GAL
GALA
GALABEA
GALABEAH
GALABEAHS
GALABEAS
GALABIA
GALABIAH
GALABIAHS
GALABIAS
GALABIEH
GALABIEHS
GALABIYA
GALABIYAH
GALABIYAHS

GALABIYAS
GALABIYEH
GALABIYEHS
GALACTIC
GALACTOSE
GALACTOSES
GALAGE
GALAGES
GALAH
GALAHS
GALANGA
GALANGAL
GALANGALS
GALANGAS
GALANT
GALANTINE
GALANTINES
GALAPAGO
GALAPAGOS
GALAS
GALATEA
GALATEAS
GALAXIES
GALAXY
GALBANUM
GALBANUMS
GALDRAGON
GALDRAGONS
GALE
GALEA
GALEAS
GALEATE
GALEATED
GALENA
GALENAS
GALENGALE
GALENGALES
GALENITE
GALENITES
GALENOID
GALÈRE
GALÈRES
GALES
GALILEE
GALILEES
GALINGALE
GALINGALES
GALIONGEE
GALIONGEES
GALIOT
GALIOTS
GALIPOT
GALIPOTS
GALL
GALLABEA
GALLABEAH
GALLABEAHS
GALLABEAS
GALLABIA
GALLABIAH
GALLABIAHS
GALLABIAS
GALLABIEH
GALLABIEHS

GALLABIYA
GALLABIYAS
GALLANT
GALLANTER
GALLANTEST
GALLANTLY
GALLANTRIES
GALLANTRY
GALLANTS
GALLATE
GALLATES
GALLEASS
GALLEASSES
GALLED
GALLEON
GALLEONS
GALLERIED
GALLERIES
GALLERY
GALLERYING
GALLET
GALLETED
GALLETING
GALLETS
GALLEY
GALLEYS
GALLIARD
GALLIARDS
GALLIASS
GALLIASSES
GALLICISE
GALLICISED
GALLICISES
GALLICISING
GALLICISM
GALLICISMS
GALLICIZE
GALLICIZED
GALLICIZES
GALLICIZING
GALLIED
GALLIES
GALLINAZO
GALLINAZOS
GALLING
GALLINGLY
GALLINULE
GALLINULES
GALLIOT
GALLIOTS
GALLIPOT
GALLIPOTS
GALLISE
GALLISED
GALLISES
GALLISING
GALLISISE
GALLISISED
GALLISISES
GALLISISING
GALLISIZE
GALLISIZED
GALLISIZES
GALLISIZING

GALLIUM
GALLIUMS
GALLIVANT
GALLIVANTED
GALLIVANTING
GALLIVANTS
GALLIVAT
GALLIVATS
GALLIWASP
GALLIWASPS
GALLIZE
GALLIZED
GALLIZES
GALLIZING
GALLON
GALLONAGE
GALLONAGES
GALLONS
GALLOON
GALLOONED
GALLOONS
GALLOP
GALLOPADE
GALLOPADED
GALLOPADES
GALLOPADING
GALLOPED
GALLOPER
GALLOPERS
GALLOPHIL
GALLOPHILS
GALLOPING
GALLOPS
GALLOW
GALLOWED
GALLOWING
GALLOWS
GALLOWSES
GALLS
GALLUMPH
GALLUMPHED
GALLUMPHING
GALLUMPHS
GALLUS
GALLUSES
GALLY
GALLYING
GALOCHE
GALOCHED
GALOCHES
GALOCHING
GALOOT
GALOOTS
GALOP
GALOPED
GALOPIN
GALOPING
GALOPINS
GALOPPED
GALOPPING
GALOPS
GALORE
GALOSH
GALOSHED
GALOSHES
GALOSHING
GALOWSES
GALRAVAGE
GALRAVAGED
GALRAVAGES

GALRAVAGING
GALS
GALTONIA
GALTONIAS
GALUMPH
GALUMPHED
GALUMPHER
GALUMPHERS
GALUMPHING
GALUMPHS
GALUT
GALUTH
GALUTHS
GALUTS
GALVANIC
GALVANISE
GALVANISED
GALVANISES
GALVANISING
GALVANISM
GALVANISMS
GALVANIST
GALVANISTS
GALVANIZE
GALVANIZED
GALVANIZES
GALVANIZING
GAM
GAMASH
GAMASHES
GAMB
GAMBA
GAMBADO
GAMBADOES
GAMBADOS
GAMBAS
GAMBESON
GAMBESONS
GAMBET
GAMBETS
GAMBIER
GAMBIERS
GAMBIR
GAMBIRS
GAMBIST
GAMBISTS
GAMBIT
GAMBITED
GAMBITING
GAMBITS
GAMBLE
GAMBLED
GAMBLER
GAMBLERS
GAMBLES
GAMBLING
GAMBLINGS
GAMBOGE
GAMBOGES
GAMBOGIAN
GAMBOGIC
GAMBOL
GAMBOLLED
GAMBOLLING
GAMBOLS
GAMBREL
GAMBRELS
GAMBROON
GAMBROONS
GAMBS

GAME
GAMED
GAMELAN
GAMELANS
GAMELY
GAMENESS
GAMENESSES
GAMER
GAMES
GAMESIER
GAMESIEST
GAMESOME
GAMEST
GAMESTER
GAMESTERS
GAMESY
GAMETAL
GAMETE
GAMETES
GAMETIC
GAMIC
GAMIER
GAMIEST
GAMIN
GAMINE
GAMINERIE
GAMINERIES
GAMINES
GAMING
GAMINGS
GAMINS
GAMMA
GAMMADION
GAMMADIONS
GAMMAS
GAMMATION
GAMMATIONS
GAMME
GAMMED
GAMMER
GAMMERS
GAMMES
GAMMIER
GAMMIEST
GAMMING
GAMMOCK
GAMMOCKED
GAMMOCKING
GAMMOCKS
GAMMON
GAMMONED
GAMMONER
GAMMONERS
GAMMONING
GAMMONINGS
GAMMONS
GAMMY
GAMP
GAMPISH
GAMPS
GAMS
GAMUT
GAMUTS
GAMY
GAN
GANCH
GANCHED
GANCHES
GANCHING
GANDER

GANDERISM
GANDERISMS
GANDERS
GANE
GANG
GANGBOARD
GANGBOARDS
GANGED
GANGER
GANGERS
GANGING
GANGINGS
GANGLAND
GANGLANDS
GANGLIA
GANGLIAR
GANGLIATE
GANGLIER
GANGLIEST
GANGLING
GANGLION
GANGLIONS
GANGLY
GANGPLANK
GANGPLANKS
GANGREL
GANGRELS
GANGRENE
GANGRENED
GANGRENES
GANGRENING
GANGS
GANGSMAN
GANGSMEN
GANGSTER
GANGSTERS
GANGUE
GANGUES
GANGWAY
GANGWAYS
GANISTER
GANISTERS
GANJA
GANJAS
GANNET
GANNETRIES
GANNETRY
GANNETS
GANNISTER
GANNISTERS
GANOID
GANOIDS
GANOIN
GANOINS
GANT
GANTED
GANTING
GANTLET
GANTLETS
GANTLINE
GANTLINES
GANTLOPE
GANTLOPES
GANTRIES
GANTRY
GANTS
GAOL
GAOLED
GAOLER
GAOLERESS

GAOLERESSES
GAOLERS
GAOLING
GAOLS
GAP
GAPE
GAPED
GAPER
GAPERS
GAPES
GAPESEED
GAPESEEDS
GAPEWORM
GAPEWORMS
GAPING
GAPINGLY
GAPINGS
GAPO
GAPOS
GAPPED
GAPPIER
GAPPIEST
GAPPING
GAPPY
GAPS
GAR
GARAGE
GARAGED
GARAGES
GARAGING
GARAGINGS
GARB
GARBAGE
GARBAGES
GARBANZO
GARBANZOS
GARBE
GARBED
GARBES
GARBING
GARBLE
GARBLED
GARBLER
GARBLERS
GARBLES
GARBLING
GARBLINGS
GARBO
GARBOARD
GARBOARDS
GARBOIL
GARBOILS
GARBOS
GARBS
GARÇON
GARÇONS
GARDA
GARDAI
GARDANT
GARDANTS
GARDEN
GARDENED
GARDENER
GARDENERS
GARDENIA
GARDENIAS
GARDENING
GARDENINGS
GARDENS
GARDEROBE

GARDEROBES
GARDYLOO
GARDYLOOS
GARE
GAREFOWL
GAREFOWLS
GARFISH
GARFISHES
GARGANEY
GARGANEYS
GARGARISE
GARGARISED
GARGARISES
GARGARISING
GARGARISM
GARGARISMS
GARGARIZE
GARGARIZED
GARGARIZES
GARGARIZING
GARGET
GARGETS
GARGLE
GARGLED
GARGLES
GARGLING
GARGOYLE
GARGOYLES
GARIAL
GARIALS
GARIBALDI
GARIBALDIS
GARIGUE
GARIGUES
GARISH
GARISHED
GARISHES
GARISHING
GARISHLY
GARJAN
GARJANS
GARLAND
GARLANDED
GARLANDING
GARLANDRY
GARLANDS
GARLIC
GARLICKY
GARLICS
GARMENT
GARMENTED
GARMENTING
GARMENTS
GARNER
GARNERED
GARNERING
GARNERS
GARNET
GARNETS
GARNI
GARNISH
GARNISHED
GARNISHEE
GARNISHEED
GARNISHEEING
GARNISHEES
GARNISHER
GARNISHERS
GARNISHES
GARNISHING

GARNISHINGS
GARNISHRIES
GARNISHRY
GARNITURE
GARNITURES
GAROTTE
GAROTTED
GAROTTER
GAROTTERS
GAROTTES
GAROTTING
GAROTTINGS
GARPIKE
GARPIKES
GARRAN
GARRANS
GARRE
GARRED
GARRES
GARRET
GARRETED
GARRETEER
GARRETEERS
GARRETS
GARRIGUE
GARRIGUES
GARRING
GARRISON
GARRISONED
GARRISONING
GARRISONS
GARRON
GARRONS
GARROT
GARROTE
GARROTED
GARROTES
GARROTING
GARROTS
GARROTTE
GARROTTED
GARROTTER
GARROTTERS
GARROTTES
GARROTTING
GARROTTINGS
GARRULITIES
GARRULITY
GARRULOUS
GARRYA
GARRYAS
GARRYOWEN
GARRYOWENS
GARS
GART
GARTER
GARTERED
GARTERING
GARTERS
GARTH
GARTHS
GARUDA
GARUDAS
GARUM
GARUMS
GARVIE
GARVIES
GARVOCK
GARVOCKS
GAS

GASAHOL
GASAHOLS
GASALIER
GASALIERS
GASCON
GASCONADE
GASCONADED
GASCONADES
GASCONADING
GASCONISM
GASCONISMS
GASCONS
GASEITIES
GASEITY
GASELIER
GASELIERS
GASEOUS
GASES
GASFIELD
GASFIELDS
GASH
GASHED
GASHES
GASHFUL
GASHING
GASHLY
GASIFIED
GASIFIER
GASIFIERS
GASIFIES
GASIFORM
GASIFY
GASIFYING
GASKET
GASKETS
GASKIN
GASKINS
GASLIGHT
GASLIGHTS
GASLIT
GASMAN
GASMEN
GASOGENE
GASOGENES
GASOHOL
GASOHOLS
GASOLENE
GASOLENES
GASOLIER
GASOLIERS
GASOLINE
GASOLINES
GASOMETER
GASOMETERS
GASOMETRIES
GASOMETRY
GASP
GASPED
GASPER
GASPEREAU
GASPEREAUS
GASPERS
GASPIER
GASPIEST
GASPINESS
GASPINESSES
GASPING
GASPINGLY
GASPINGS
GASPS

GASPY
GASSED
GASSES
GASSIER
GASSIEST
GASSINESS
GASSINESSES
GASSING
GASSINGS
GASSY
GAST
GASTED
GASTFULL
GASTING
GASTNESS
GASTNESSE
GASTNESSES
GASTRAEA
GASTRAEAS
GASTRAEUM
GASTRAEUMS
GASTRIC
GASTRIN
GASTRINS
GASTRITIS
GASTRITISES
GASTROPOD
GASTROPODS
GASTRULA
GASTRULAE
GASTRULAS
GASTS
GAT
GATE
GÂTEAU
GÂTEAUS
GÂTEAUX
GATECRASH
GATECRASHED
GATECRASHES
GATECRASHING
GATED
GATEFOLD
GATEFOLDS
GATELEG
GATELESS
GATES
GATEWAY
GATEWAYS
GATH
GATHER
GATHERED
GATHERER
GATHERERS
GATHERING
GATHERINGS
GATHERS
GATHS
GATING
GATINGS
GATS
GAU
GAUCHE
GAUCHER
GAUCHERIE
GAUCHERIES
GAUCHESCO
GAUCHEST
GAUCHO
GAUCHOS

GAUCIE
GAUCIER
GAUCIEST
GAUCY
GAUD
GAUDEAMUS
GAUDEAMUSES
GAUDED
GAUDERIES
GAUDERY
GAUDGIE
GAUDGIES
GAUDIER
GAUDIES
GAUDIEST
GAUDILY
GAUDINESS
GAUDINESSES
GAUDING
GAUDS
GAUDY
GAUFER
GAUFERS
GAUFRE
GAUFRES
GAUGE
GAUGEABLE
GAUGED
GAUGER
GAUGERS
GAUGES
GAUGING
GAUGINGS
GAUJE
GAUJES
GAULEITER
GAULEITERS
GAULT
GAULTER
GAULTERS
GAULTS
GAUM
GAUMED
GAUMIER
GAUMIEST
GAUMING
GAUMLESS
GAUMS
GAUMY
GAUN
GAUNCH
GAUNCHED
GAUNCHES
GAUNCHING
GAUNT
GAUNTED
GAUNTER
GAUNTEST
GAUNTING
GAUNTLET
GAUNTLETS
GAUNTLY
GAUNTNESS
GAUNTNESSES
GAUNTREE
GAUNTREES
GAUNTRIES
GAUNTRY
GAUNTS
GAUP

GAUPED	GAYNESS	GEATS	GELT	GENERALE
GAUPER	GAYNESSES	GEBUR	GELTED	GENERALIA
GAUPERS	GAYS	GEBURS	GELTING	GENERALLED
GAUPING	GAYSOME	GECK	GELTS	GENERALLING
GAUPS	GAZAL	GECKED	GEM	GENERALLY
GAUPUS	GAZALS	GECKING	GEMATRIA	GENERALS
GAUPUSES	GAZE	GECKO	GEMATRIAS	GENERANT
GAUR	GAZEBO	GECKOES	GEMEL	GENERANTS
GAURS	GAZEBOES	GECKOS	GEMELS	GENERATE
GAUS	GAZEBOS	GECKS	GEMINATE	GENERATED
GAUSS	GAZED	GED	GEMINATED	GENERATES
GAUSSES	GAZEFUL	GEDS	GEMINATES	GENERATING
GAUSSIAN	GAZEL	GEE	GEMINATING	GENERATOR
GAUZE	GAZELLE	GEEBUNG	GEMINI	GENERATORS
GAUZES	GAZELLES	GEEBUNGS	GEMINIES	GENERIC
GAUZIER	GAZELS	GEED	GEMINIS	GENERICAL
GAUZIEST	GAZEMENT	GEEING	GEMINOUS	GENERICS
GAUZINESS	GAZEMENTS	GEES	GEMINY	GENEROUS
GAUZINESSES	GAZER	GEESE	GEMMA	GENES
GAUZY	GAZERS	GEEZER	GEMMAE	GENESES
GAVAGE	GAZES	GEEZERS	GEMMAN	GENESIS
GAVAGES	GAZETTE	GEFUFFLE	GEMMATE	GENET
GAVE	GAZETTED	GEFUFFLED	GEMMATED	GENETIC
GAVEL	GAZETTEER	GEFUFFLES	GEMMATES	GENETICAL
GAVELKIND	GAZETTEERED	GEFUFFLING	GEMMATING	GENETICS
GAVELKINDS	GAZETTEERING	GEISHA	GEMMATION	GENETRICES
GAVELMAN	GAZETTEERS	GEISHAS	GEMMATIONS	GENETRIX
GAVELMEN	GAZETTES	GEIST	GEMMATIVE	GENETRIXES
GAVELOCK	GAZETTING	GEISTS	GEMMED	GENETS
GAVELOCKS	GAZIER	GEIT	GEMMEN	GENETTE
GAVELS	GAZIEST	GEITS	GEMMEOUS	GENETTES
GAVIAL	GAZING	GEL	GEMMERY	GENEVA
GAVIALS	GAZOGENE	GELADA	GEMMIER	GENEVAS
GAVOTTE	GAZOGENES	GELADAS	GEMMIEST	GENIAL
GAVOTTES	GAZON	GELASTIC	GEMMING	GENIALISE
GAWCIER	GAZONS	GELATI	GEMMOLOGIES	GENIALISED
GAWCIEST	GAZOO	GELATIN	GEMMOLOGY	GENIALISES
GAWCY	GAZOOKA	GELATINE	GEMMULE	GENIALISING
GAWD	GAZOOKAS	GELATINES	GEMMULES	GENIALITIES
GAWDS	GAZOON	GELATINS	GEMMY	GENIALITY
GAWK	GAZOONS	GELATION	GEMOLOGIES	GENIALIZE
GAWKED	GAZOOS	GELATIONS	GEMOLOGY	GENIALIZED
GAWKER	GAZPACHO	GELATO	GEMONIES	GENIALIZES
GAWKERS	GAZPACHOS	GELD	GEMONY	GENIALIZING
GAWKIER	GAZUMP	GELDED	GEMOT	GENIALLY
GAWKIES	GAZUMPED	GELDER	GEMOTS	GENIC
GAWKIEST	GAZUMPING	GELDERS	GEMS	GENIE
GAWKIHOOD	GAZUMPS	GELDING	GEMSBOK	GENIES
GAWKIHOODS	GAZY	GELDINGS	GEMSBOKS	GENII
GAWKINESS	GEAL	GELDS	GEMSTONE	GENIP
GAWKINESSES	GEALED	GELID	GEMSTONES	GENIPAP
GAWKING	GEALING	GELIDER	GEMÜTLICH	GENIPAPS
GAWKS	GEALOUS	GELIDEST	GEN	GENIPS
GAWKY	GEALOUSIES	GELIDITIES	GENA	GENISTA
GAWP	GEALOUSY	GELIDITY	GENAL	GENISTAS
GAWPED	GEALS	GELIDLY	GENAPPE	GENITAL
GAWPER	GEAN	GELIDNESS	GENAPPES	GENITALIA
GAWPERS	GEANS	GELIDNESSES	GENAS	GENITALS
GAWPING	GEAR	GELIGNITE	GENDARME	GENITIVAL
GAWPS	GEARBOX	GELIGNITES	GENDARMES	GENITIVE
GAWPUS	GEARBOXES	GELLED	GENDER	GENITIVES
GAWPUSES	GEARE	GELLING	GENDERED	GENITOR
GAWSIER	GEARED	GELLY	GENDERING	GENITORS
GAWSIEST	GEARES	GELOSIES	GENDERS	GENITRICES
GAWSY	GEARING	GELOSY	GENE	GENITRIX
GAY	GEARINGS	GELS	GENEALOGIES	GENITRIXES
GAYAL	GEARLESS	GELSEMINE	GENEALOGY	GENITURE
GAYALS	GEARS	GELSEMINES	GENERA	GENITURES
GAYER	GEASON	GELSEMIUM	GENERABLE	GENIUS
GAYEST	GEAT	GELSEMIUMS	GENERAL	GENIUSES

GENIZAH	GENUFLECTING	GEOPHILIC	GERMICIDES	GEWGAW
GENIZAHS	GENUFLECTS	GEOPHONE	GERMIN	GEWGAWS
GENNET	GENUINE	GEOPHONES	GERMINAL	GEY
GENNETS	GENUINELY	GEOPHYTE	GERMINANT	GEYAN
GENOA	GENUS	GEOPHYTES	GERMINATE	GEYER
GENOAS	GENUSES	GEOPHYTIC	GERMINATED	GEYEST
GENOCIDAL	GEO	GEOPONIC	GERMINATES	GEYSER
GENOCIDE	GEOCARPIC	GEOPONICS	GERMINATING	GEYSERITE
GENOCIDES	GEOCARPIES	GEORDIE	GERMING	GEYSERITES
GENOM	GEOCARPY	GEORDIES	GERMINS	GEYSERS
GENOME	GEODE	GEORGETTE	GERMS	GHARIAL
GENOMES	GEODES	GEORGETTES	GERNE	GHARIALS
GENOMS	GEODESIC	GEORGIC	GERNED	GHARRI
GENOTYPE	GEODESIES	GEORGICS	GERNES	GHARRIES
GENOTYPES	GEODESIST	GEOS	GERNING	GHARRIS
GENOTYPIC	GEODESISTS	GEOSPHERE	GERONTIC	GHARRY
GENRE	GEODESY	GEOSPHERES	GEROPIGA	GHAST
GENRES	GEODETIC	GEOSTATIC	GEROPIGAS	GHASTED
GENS	GEODETICS	GEOSTATICS	GERUND	GHASTFUL
GENSDARMES	GEODIC	GEOTACTIC	GERUNDIAL	GHASTFULL
GENT	GEOGENIES	GEOTAXES	GERUNDIVE	GHASTING
GENTEEL	GEOGENY	GEOTAXIS	GERUNDIVES	GHASTLIER
GENTEELER	GEOGNOSES	GEOTROPIC	GERUNDS	GHASTLIEST
GENTEELEST	GEOGNOSIES	GERAH	GESNERIA	GHASTLY
GENTEELLY	GEOGNOSIS	GERAHS	GESNERIAS	GHASTNESS
GENTES	GEOGNOST	GERANIOL	GESSAMINE	GHASTNESSES
GENTIAN	GEOGNOSTS	GERANIOLS	GESSAMINES	GHASTS
GENTIANS	GEOGNOSY	GERANIUM	GESSE	GHAT
GENTIER	GEOGONIC	GERANIUMS	GESSED	GHATS
GENTIEST	GEOGONIES	GERBE	GESSES	GHAUT
GENTILE	GEOGONY	GERBERA	GESSING	GHAUTS
GENTILES	GEOGRAPHIES	GERBERAS	GESSO	GHAZAL
GENTILIC	GEOGRAPHY	GERBES	GESSOES	GHAZALS
GENTILISE	GEOID	GERBIL	GEST	GHAZEL
GENTILISED	GEOIDAL	GERBILLE	GESTALT	GHAZELS
GENTILISES	GEOIDS	GERBILLES	GESTALTS	GHAZI
GENTILISH	GEOLATRIES	GERBILS	GESTANT	GHAZIS
GENTILISING	GEOLATRY	GERE	GESTATE	GHEE
GENTILISM	GEOLOGER	GERENT	GESTATED	GHEES
GENTILISMS	GEOLOGERS	GERENTS	GESTATES	GHERAO
GENTILITIES	GEOLOGIAN	GERENUK	GESTATING	GHERAOED
GENTILITY	GEOLOGIANS	GERENUKS	GESTATION	GHERAOING
GENTILIZE	GEOLOGIC	GERES	GESTATIONS	GHERAOS
GENTILIZED	GEOLOGIES	GERFALCON	GESTATIVE	GHERKIN
GENTILIZES	GEOLOGISE	GERFALCONS	GESTATORY	GHERKINS
GENTILIZING	GEOLOGISED	GERIATRIC	GESTE	GHESSE
GENTLE	GEOLOGISES	GERIATRICS	GESTES	GHESSED
GENTLED	GEOLOGISING	GERIATRIES	GESTIC	GHESSES
GENTLEMAN	GEOLOGIST	GERIATRY	GESTS	GHESSING
GENTLEMEN	GEOLOGISTS	GERLE	GESTURAL	GHEST
GENTLER	GEOLOGIZE	GERLES	GESTURE	GHETTO
GENTLES	GEOLOGIZED	GERM	GESTURED	GHETTOES
GENTLEST	GEOLOGIZES	GERMAIN	GESTURES	GHETTOISE
GENTLING	GEOLOGIZING	GERMAINE	GESTURING	GHETTOISED
GENTLY	GEOLOGY	GERMAINES	GET	GHETTOISES
GENTOO	GEOMANCER	GERMAINS	GETA	GHETTOISING
GENTOOS	GEOMANCERS	GERMAN	GETAS	GHETTOIZE
GENTRICE	GEOMANCIES	GERMANDER	GETAWAY	GHETTOIZED
GENTRICES	GEOMANCY	GERMANDERS	GETAWAYS	GHETTOIZES
GENTRIES	GEOMANTIC	GERMANE	GETS	GHETTOIZING
GENTRIFIED	GEOMETER	GERMANELY	GETTABLE	GHETTOS
GENTRIFIES	GEOMETERS	GERMANER	GETTER	GHI
GENTRIFY	GEOMETRIC	GERMANEST	GETTERED	GHILGAI
GENTRIFYING	GEOMETRID	GERMANIUM	GETTERING	GHILGAIS
GENTRY	GEOMETRIDS	GERMANIUMS	GETTERINGS	GHILLIE
GENTS	GEOMETRIES	GERMANS	GETTERS	GHILLIED
GENTY	GEOMETRY	GERMED	GETTING	GHILLIES
GENU	GEOMYOID	GERMEN	GETTINGS	GHILLYING
GENUFLECT	GEOPHAGIES	GERMENS	GEUM	GHIS
GENUFLECTED	GEOPHAGY	GERMICIDE	GEUMS	GHOST

GHOSTED	GIDDIED	GILCUP	GIMP	GIRAFFE
GHOSTIER	GIDDIER	GILCUPS	GIMPED	GIRAFFES
GHOSTIEST	GIDDIES	GILD	GIMPING	GIRAFFID
GHOSTING	GIDDIEST	GILDED	GIMPS	GIRAFFINE
GHOSTLIER	GIDDILY	GILDEN	GIN	GIRAFFOID
GHOSTLIEST	GIDDINESS	GILDER	GING	GIRANDOLA
GHOSTLY	GIDDINESSES	GILDERS	GINGAL	GIRANDOLAS
GHOSTS	GIDDY	GILDING	GINGALL	GIRANDOLE
GHOSTY	GIDDYING	GILDINGS	GINGALLS	GIRANDOLES
GHOUL	GIDGEE	GILDS	GINGALS	GIRASOL
GHOULISH	GIDGEES	GILET	GINGELLIES	GIRASOLE
GHOULS	GIDJEE	GILETS	GINGELLY	GIRASOLES
GHYLL	GIDJEES	GILGAI	GINGER	GIRASOLS
GHYLLS	GIDS	GILGAIS	GINGERADE	GIRD
GI	GIE	GILGIE	GINGERADES	GIRDED
GIAMBEUX	GIED	GILGIES	GINGERED	GIRDER
GIANT	GIEN	GILL	GINGERING	GIRDERS
GIANTESS	GIES	GILLAROO	GINGERLY	GIRDING
GIANTESSES	GIF	GILLAROOS	GINGEROUS	GIRDINGS
GIANTHOOD	GIFT	GILLED	GINGERS	GIRDLE
GIANTHOODS	GIFTED	GILLET	GINGERY	GIRDLED
GIANTISM	GIFTEDLY	GILLETS	GINGHAM	GIRDLER
GIANTISMS	GIFTING	GILLFLIRT	GINGHAMS	GIRDLERS
GIANTLIER	GIFTS	GILLFLIRTS	GINGILI	GIRDLES
GIANTLIEST	GIG	GILLIE	GINGILIS	GIRDLING
GIANTLY	GIGA	GILLIED	GINGIVAL	GIRDS
GIANTRIES	GIGAHERTZ	GILLIES	GINGKO	GIRKIN
GIANTRY	GIGAHERTZES	GILLING	GINGKOES	GIRKINS
GIANTS	GIGANTEAN	GILLION	GINGLE	GIRL
GIANTSHIP	GIGANTIC	GILLIONS	GINGLED	GIRLHOOD
GIANTSHIPS	GIGANTISM	GILLS	GINGLES	GIRLHOODS
GIAOUR	GIGANTISMS	GILLY	GINGLING	GIRLIE
GIAOURS	GIGAS	GILLYING	GINGLYMI	GIRLIES
GIB	GIGAWATT	GILLYVOR	GINGLYMUS	GIRLISH
GIBBED	GIGAWATTS	GILLYVORS	GINGS	GIRLISHLY
GIBBER	GIGGED	GILPEY	GINHOUSE	GIRLOND
GIBBERED	GIGGING	GILPEYS	GINHOUSES	GIRLONDS
GIBBERING	GIGGIT	GILPIES	GINK	GIRLS
GIBBERISH	GIGGITED	GILPY	GINKGO	GIRLY
GIBBERISHES	GIGGITING	GILRAVAGE	GINKGOES	GIRN
GIBBERS	GIGGITS	GILRAVAGED	GINKS	GIRNED
GIBBET	GIGGLE	GILRAVAGES	GINN	GIRNEL
GIBBETED	GIGGLED	GILRAVAGING	GINNED	GIRNELS
GIBBETING	GIGGLER	GILT	GINNEL	GIRNIE
GIBBETS	GIGGLERS	GILTCUP	GINNELS	GIRNIER
GIBBING	GIGGLES	GILTCUPS	GINNER	GIRNIEST
GIBBON	GIGGLIER	GILTS	GINNERIES	GIRNING
GIBBONS	GIGGLIEST	GILTWOOD	GINNERS	GIRNS
GIBBOSE	GIGGLING	GIMBAL	GINNERY	GIRO
GIBBOSITIES	GIGGLINGS	GIMBALS	GINNING	GIRON
GIBBOSITY	GIGGLY	GIMCRACK	GINS	GIRONS
GIBBOUS	GIGLET	GIMCRACKS	GINSENG	GIROS
GIBBOUSLY	GIGLETS	GIMLET	GINSENGS	GIROSOL
GIBBSITE	GIGLOT	GIMLETED	GINSHOP	GIROSOLS
GIBBSITES	GIGLOTS	GIMLETING	GINSHOPS	GIRR
GIBE	GIGMAN	GIMLETS	GIO	GIRRS
GIBED	GIGMANITIES	GIMMAL	GIOCOSO	GIRT
GIBEL	GIGMANITY	GIMMALLED	GIOS	GIRTED
GIBELS	GIGMEN	GIMMALS	GIP	GIRTH
GIBER	GIGOLO	GIMME	GIPPIES	GIRTHED
GIBERS	GIGOLOS	GIMMER	GIPPO	GIRTHING
GIBES	GIGOT	GIMMERS	GIPPOS	GIRTHLINE
GIBING	GIGOTS	GIMMES	GIPPY	GIRTHLINES
GIBINGLY	GIGS	GIMMICK	GIPS	GIRTHS
GIBLET	GIGUE	GIMMICKRIES	GIPSEN	GIRTING
GIBLETS	GIGUES	GIMMICKRY	GIPSENS	GIRTLINE
GIBS	GILA	GIMMICKS	GIPSIED	GIRTLINES
GIBUS	GILAS	GIMMICKY	GIPSIES	GIRTS
GIBUSES	GILBERT	GIMMOR	GIPSY	GIS
GID	GILBERTS	GIMMORS	GIPSYING	GISARME

GISARMES	GLADDENED	GLANCES	GLAZIEST	GLENTS
GISM	GLADDENING	GLANCING	GLAZING	GLEY
GISMO	GLADDENS	GLANCINGS	GLAZINGS	GLEYED
GISMOS	GLADDER	GLAND	GLAZY	GLEYING
GISMS	GLADDEST	GLANDERED	GLEAM	GLEYS
GIST	GLADDIE	GLANDERS	GLEAMED	GLIA
GISTS	GLADDIES	GLANDES	GLEAMIER	GLIADIN
GIT	GLADDING	GLANDS	GLEAMIEST	GLIADINE
GITANA	GLADDON	GLANDULAR	GLEAMING	GLIADINES
GITANAS	GLADDONS	GLANDULE	GLEAMINGS	GLIADINS
GITANO	GLADE	GLANDULES	GLEAMS	GLIAL
GITANOS	GLADES	GLANS	GLEAMY	GLIAS
GITE	GLADFUL	GLARE	GLEAN	GLIB
GITES	GLADIATE	GLAREAL	GLEANED	GLIBBED
GITS	GLADIATOR	GLARED	GLEANER	GLIBBER
GITTERN	GLADIATORS	GLAREOUS	GLEANERS	GLIBBERY
GITTERNED	GLADIER	GLARES	GLEANING	GLIBBEST
GITTERNING	GLADIEST	GLARIER	GLEANINGS	GLIBBING
GITTERNS	GLADIOLE	GLARIEST	GLEANS	GLIBLY
GIUST	GLADIOLES	GLARING	GLEAVE	GLIBNESS
GIUSTED	GLADIOLI	GLARINGLY	GLEAVES	GLIBNESSES
GIUSTING	GLADIOLUS	GLARY	GLEBE	GLIBS
GIUSTO	GLADIOLUSES	GLASNOST	GLEBES	GLID
GIUSTS	GLADIUSES	GLASNOSTS	GLEBOUS	GLIDDER
GIVE	GLADIUS	GLASS	GLEBY	GLIDDERY
GIVEAWAY	GLADLY	GLASSED	GLED	GLIDDEST
GIVEAWAYS	GLADNESS	GLASSEN	GLEDE	GLIDE
GIVED	GLADNESSES	GLASSES	GLEDES	GLIDED
GIVEN	GLADS	GLASSFUL	GLEDGE	GLIDER
GIVENNESS	GLADSOME	GLASSFULS	GLEDGED	GLIDERS
GIVENNESSES	GLADSOMER	GLASSIER	GLEDGES	GLIDES
GIVER	GLADSOMEST	GLASSIEST	GLEDGING	GLIDING
GIVERS	GLADY	GLASSIFIED	GLEDS	GLIDINGLY
GIVES	GLAIK	GLASSIFIES	GLEE	GLIDINGS
GIVING	GLAIKET	GLASSIFY	GLEED	GLIFF
GIVINGS	GLAIKIT	GLASSIFYING	GLEEDED	GLIFFING
GIZMO	GLAIKS	GLASSILY	GLEEDING	GLIFFINGS
GIZMOS	GLAIR	GLASSINE	GLEEDS	GLIFFS
GIZZ	GLAIRED	GLASSINES	GLEEFUL	GLIFT
GIZZARD	GLAIREOUS	GLASSING	GLEEING	GLIFTS
GIZZARDS	GLAIRIER	GLASSLIKE	GLEEK	GLIKE
GIZZEN	GLAIRIEST	GLASSMAN	GLEEKED	GLIKES
GIZZENED	GLAIRIN	GLASSMEN	GLEEKING	GLIM
GIZZENING	GLAIRING	GLASSWARE	GLEEKS	GLIMMER
GIZZENS	GLAIRINS	GLASSWARES	GLEEMAN	GLIMMERED
GIZZES	GLAIRS	GLASSWORK	GLEEMEN	GLIMMERING
GJU	GLAIRY	GLASSWORKS	GLEES	GLIMMERINGS
GJUS	GLAIVE	GLASSWORT	GLEESOME	GLIMMERS
GLABELLA	GLAIVED	GLASSWORTS	GLEET	GLIMMERY
GLABELLAE	GLAIVES	GLASSY	GLEETED	GLIMPSE
GLABELLAR	GLAM	GLAUCOMA	GLEETIER	GLIMPSED
GLABRATE	GLAMOR	GLAUCOMAS	GLEETIEST	GLIMPSES
GLABROUS	GLAMORED	GLAUCOUS	GLEETING	GLIMPSING
GLACÉ	GLAMORING	GLAUM	GLEETS	GLIMS
GLACÉED	GLAMORISE	GLAUMED	GLEETY	GLINT
GLACÉING	GLAMORISED	GLAUMING	GLEG	GLINTED
GLACÉS	GLAMORISES	GLAUMS	GLEGGER	GLINTING
GLACIAL	GLAMORISING	GLAUR	GLEGGEST	GLINTS
GLACIALS	GLAMORIZE	GLAURIER	GLEI	GLIOMA
GLACIATE	GLAMORIZED	GLAURIEST	GLEIS	GLIOMAS
GLACIATED	GLAMORIZES	GLAURS	GLEN	GLIOMATA
GLACIATES	GLAMORIZING	GLAURY	GLENGARRIES	GLIOSES
GLACIATING	GLAMOROUS	GLAZE	GLENGARRY	GLIOSIS
GLACIER	GLAMORS	GLAZED	GLENOID	GLISK
GLACIERS	GLAMOUR	GLAZEN	GLENOIDAL	GLISKS
GLACIS	GLAMOURED	GLAZER	GLENOIDS	GLISSADE
GLACISES	GLAMOURING	GLAZERS	GLENS	GLISSADED
GLAD	GLAMOURS	GLAZES	GLENT	GLISSADES
GLADDED	GLANCE	GLAZIER	GLENTED	GLISSADING
GLADDEN	GLANCED	GLAZIERS	GLENTING	GLISSANDO

GLISSANDOS
GLISTEN
GLISTENED
GLISTENING
GLISTENS
GLISTER
GLISTERED
GLISTERING
GLISTERS
GLIT
GLITCH
GLITCHES
GLITS
GLITTER
GLITTERED
GLITTERING
GLITTERINGS
GLITTERS
GLITTERY
GLITZ
GLITZES
GLITZIER
GLITZIEST
GLITZY
GLOAMING
GLOAMINGS
GLOAT
GLOATED
GLOATING
GLOATS
GLOB
GLOBAL
GLOBALISE
GLOBALISED
GLOBALISES
GLOBALISING
GLOBALIZE
GLOBALIZED
GLOBALIZES
GLOBALIZING
GLOBALLY
GLOBATE
GLOBATED
GLOBE
GLOBED
GLOBES
GLOBIN
GLOBING
GLOBINS
GLOBOID
GLOBOIDS
GLOBOSE
GLOBOSES
GLOBOSITIES
GLOBOSITY
GLOBOUS
GLOBS
GLOBULAR
GLOBULE
GLOBULES
GLOBULET
GLOBULETS
GLOBULIN
GLOBULINS
GLOBULITE
GLOBULITES
GLOBULOUS
GLOBY
GLODE
GLOGG

GLOGGS
GLOIRE
GLOIRES
GLOM
GLOMERATE
GLOMERATED
GLOMERATES
GLOMERATING
GLOMERULE
GLOMERULES
GLOMERULI
GLOMMED
GLOMMING
GLOMS
GLONOIN
GLONOINS
GLOOM
GLOOMED
GLOOMFUL
GLOOMIER
GLOOMIEST
GLOOMILY
GLOOMING
GLOOMINGS
GLOOMS
GLOOMY
GLORIA
GLORIAS
GLORIED
GLORIES
GLORIFIED
GLORIFIES
GLORIFY
GLORIFYING
GLORIOLE
GLORIOLES
GLORIOSA
GLORIOSAS
GLORIOUS
GLORY
GLORYBOX
GLORYBOXES
GLORYING
GLOSS
GLOSSA
GLOSSAE
GLOSSAL
GLOSSARIES
GLOSSARY
GLOSSAS
GLOSSATOR
GLOSSATORS
GLOSSED
GLOSSEME
GLOSSEMES
GLOSSER
GLOSSERS
GLOSSES
GLOSSIER
GLOSSIES
GLOSSIEST
GLOSSILY
GLOSSINA
GLOSSINAS
GLOSSING
GLOSSITIS
GLOSSITISES
GLOSSY
GLOTTAL
GLOTTIC

GLOTTIDES
GLOTTIS
GLOTTISES
GLOUT
GLOUTED
GLOUTING
GLOUTS
GLOVE
GLOVED
GLOVER
GLOVERS
GLOVES
GLOVING
GLOW
GLOWED
GLOWER
GLOWERED
GLOWERING
GLOWERS
GLOWING
GLOWINGLY
GLOWLAMP
GLOWLAMPS
GLOWS
GLOXINIA
GLOXINIAS
GLOZE
GLOZED
GLOZES
GLOZING
GLOZINGS
GLUCAGON
GLUCAGONS
GLUCINA
GLUCINAS
GLUCINIUM
GLUCINIUMS
GLUCINUM
GLUCINUMS
GLUCOSE
GLUCOSES
GLUCOSIDE
GLUCOSIDES
GLUE
GLUED
GLUER
GLUERS
GLUES
GLUEY
GLUEYNESS
GLUEYNESSES
GLUG
GLUGGED
GLUGGING
GLUGS
GLÜHWEIN
GLÜHWEINS
GLUIER
GLUIEST
GLUING
GLUISH
GLUM
GLUME
GLUMELLA
GLUMELLAS
GLUMES
GLUMLY
GLUMMER
GLUMMEST
GLUMNESS

GLUMNESSES
GLUMPISH
GLUMPS
GLUMPY
GLUON
GLUONS
GLUT
GLUTAEAL
GLUTAEI
GLUTAEUS
GLUTAMATE
GLUTAMATES
GLUTAMINE
GLUTAMINES
GLUTEAL
GLUTEI
GLUTELIN
GLUTELINS
GLUTEN
GLUTENOUS
GLUTENS
GLUTEUS
GLUTINOUS
GLUTS
GLUTTED
GLUTTING
GLUTTON
GLUTTONIES
GLUTTONS
GLUTTONY
GLYCERIC
GLYCERIDE
GLYCERIDES
GLYCERIN
GLYCERINE
GLYCERINES
GLYCERINS
GLYCEROL
GLYCEROLS
GLYCERYL
GLYCERYLS
GLYCIN
GLYCINE
GLYCINES
GLYCINS
GLYCOCOLL
GLYCOCOLLS
GLYCOGEN
GLYCOGENS
GLYCOL
GLYCOLIC
GLYCOLLIC
GLYCOLS
GLYCONIC
GLYCONICS
GLYCOSE
GLYCOSES
GLYCOSIDE
GLYCOSIDES
GLYCOSYL
GLYCOSYLS
GLYPH
GLYPHIC
GLYPHS
GLYPTIC
GLYPTICS
GMELINITE
GMELINITES
GNAR
GNARL

GNARLED
GNARLIER
GNARLIEST
GNARLING
GNARLS
GNARLY
GNARR
GNARRED
GNARRING
GNARRS
GNARS
GNASH
GNASHED
GNASHER
GNASHERS
GNASHES
GNASHING
GNAT
GNATHAL
GNATHIC
GNATHITE
GNATHITES
GNATHONIC
GNATLING
GNATLINGS
GNATS
GNAW
GNAWED
GNAWER
GNAWERS
GNAWING
GNAWN
GNAWS
GNEISS
GNEISSES
GNEISSIC
GNEISSOID
GNEISSOSE
GNOCCHI
GNOCCHIS
GNOMAE
GNOME
GNOMES
GNOMIC
GNOMISH
GNOMIST
GNOMISTS
GNOMON
GNOMONIC
GNOMONICS
GNOMONS
GNOSES
GNOSIS
GNOSTIC
GNOSTICAL
GNU
GNUS
GO
GOA
GOAD
GOADED
GOADING
GOADS
GOADSMAN
GOADSMEN
GOADSTER
GOADSTERS
GOAF
GOAFS
GOAL

GOALED	GODDESSES	GOFFS	GOLES	GONADIC
GOALIE	GODDING	GOG	GOLF	GONADS
GOALIES	GODET	GOGGLE	GOLFED	GONDELAY
GOALING	GODETIA	GOGGLED	GOLFER	GONDELAYS
GOALLESS	GODETIAS	GOGGLER	GOLFERS	GONDOLA
GOALMOUTH	GODETS	GOGGLERS	GOLFIANA	GONDOLAS
GOALMOUTHS	GODFATHER	GOGGLES	GOLFIANAS	GONDOLIER
GOALPOST	GODFATHERS	GOGGLIER	GOLFING	GONDOLIERS
GOALPOSTS	GODHEAD	GOGGLIEST	GOLFINGS	GONE
GOALS	GODHEADS	GOGGLING	GOLFS	GONENESS
GOANNA	GODHOOD	GOGGLINGS	GOLIARD	GONENESSES
GOANNAS	GODHOODS	GOGGLY	GOLIARDIC	GONER
GOARY	GODLESS	GOGLET	GOLIARDIES	GONERS
GOAS	GODLESSLY	GOGLETS	GOLIARDS	GONFALON
GOAT	GODLIER	GOGO	GOLIARDY	GONFALONS
GOATEE	GODLIEST	GOGS	GOLIAS	GONFANON
GOATEED	GODLIKE	GOING	GOLIASED	GONFANONS
GOATEES	GODLILY	GOINGS	GOLIASES	GONG
GOATFISH	GODLINESS	GOITER	GOLIASING	GONGED
GOATFISHES	GODLINESSES	GOITERS	GOLLAN	GONGING
GOATHERD	GODLING	GOITRE	GOLLAND	GONGS
GOATHERDS	GODLINGS	GOITRED	GOLLANDS	GONGSTER
GOATIER	GODLY	GOITRES	GOLLANS	GONGSTERS
GOATIEST	GODMOTHER	GOITROUS	GOLLAR	GONIA
GOATISH	GODMOTHERS	GOLD	GOLLARED	GONIATITE
GOATLING	GODOWN	GOLDARN	GOLLARING	GONIATITES
GOATLINGS	GODOWNS	GOLDCREST	GOLLARS	GONIDIA
GOATS	GODPARENT	GOLDCRESTS	GOLLIES	GONIDIAL
GOATSKIN	GODPARENTS	GOLDEN	GOLLIWOG	GONIDIC
GOATSKINS	GODROON	GOLDENED	GOLLIWOGS	GONIDIUM
GOATWEED	GODROONS	GOLDENER	GOLLOP	GONION
GOATWEEDS	GODS	GOLDENEST	GOLLOPED	GONK
GOATY	GODSEND	GOLDENING	GOLLOPING	GONKS
GOB	GODSENDS	GOLDENLY	GOLLOPS	GONNA
GOBANG	GODSHIP	GOLDENROD	GOLLY	GONOCOCCI
GOBANGS	GODSHIPS	GOLDENRODS	GOLLYWOG	GONOCYTE
GOBBELINE	GODSO	GOLDENS	GOLLYWOGS	GONOCYTES
GOBBELINES	GODSON	GOLDER	GOLOMYNKA	GONOPHORE
GOBBET	GODSONS	GOLDEST	GOLOMYNKAS	GONOPHORES
GOBBETS	GODSOS	GOLDEYE	GOLOSH	GONORRHEA
GOBBI	GODSPEED	GOLDEYES	GOLOSHED	GONORRHEAS
GOBBLE	GODSPEEDS	GOLDFIELD	GOLOSHES	GONS
GOBBLED	GODWARD	GOLDFIELDS	GOLOSHING	GOO
GOBBLER	GODWARDS	GOLDFINCH	GOLP	GOOBER
GOBBLERS	GODWIT	GOLDFINCHES	GOLPE	GOOBERS
GOBBLES	GODWITS	GOLDFINNIES	GOLPES	GOOD
GOBBLING	GOE	GOLDFINNY	GOLPS	GOODFACED
GOBBO	GOEIER	GOLDFISH	GOMBEEN	GOODIER
GOBIES	GOEIEST	GOLDFISHES	GOMBEENS	GOODIES
GOBIOID	GOEL	GOLDIER	GOMBO	GOODIEST
GOBLET	GOELS	GOLDIEST	GOMBOS	GOODINESS
GOBLETS	GOER	GOLDISH	GOMBRO	GOODINESSES
GOBLIN	GOERS	GOLDLESS	GOMBROS	GOODISH
GOBLINS	GOES	GOLDS	GOMERAL	GOODLIER
GOBO	GOETHITE	GOLDSINNIES	GOMERALS	GOODLIEST
GOBOES	GOETHITES	GOLDSINNY	GOMERIL	GOODLY
GOBONY	GOETIC	GOLDSIZE	GOMERILS	GOODMAN
GOBOS	GOETIES	GOLDSIZES	GOMOKU	GOODMEN
GOBS	GOETY	GOLDSMITH	GOMOKUS	GOODNESS
GOBURRA	GOEY	GOLDSMITHS	GOMPA	GOODNESSES
GOBURRAS	GOFER	GOLDSPINK	GOMPAS	GOODNIGHT
GOBY	GOFERS	GOLDSPINKS	GOMPHOSES	GOODNIGHTS
GQD	GOFF	GOLDSTICK	GOMPHOSIS	GOODS
GODCHILD	GOFFED	GOLDSTICKS	GOMUTI	GOODSIRE
GODCHILDREN	GOFFER	GOLDSTONE	GOMUTIS	GOODSIRES
GODDAM	GOFFERED	GOLDSTONES	GOMUTO	GOODTIME
GODDAMN	GOFFERING	GOLDY	GOMUTOS	GOODWIFE
GODDAMNED	GOFFERINGS	GOLE	GON	GOODWILL
GODDED	GOFFERS	GOLEM	GONAD	GOODWILLS
GODDESS	GOFFING	GOLEMS	GONADIAL	GOODWIVES

GOODY	GOOSY	GORSEDD	GOUACHE	GOWF
GOODYEAR	GOPAK	GORSEDDS	GOUACHES	GOWFED
GOODYEARS	GOPAKS	GORSES	GOUGE	GOWFER
GOOEY	GOPHER	GORSIER	GOUGED	GOWFERS
GOOF	GOPHERED	GORSIEST	GOUGÈRE	GOWFING
GOOFBALL	GOPHERING	GORSOON	GOUGÈRES	GOWFS
GOOFBALLS	GOPHERS	GORSOONS	GOUGES	GOWK
GOOFED	GOPURA	GORSY	GOUGING	GOWKS
GOOFIER	GOPURAM	GORY	GOUJEERS	GOWL
GOOFIEST	GOPURAMS	GOS	GOUJONS	GOWLAND
GOOFILY	GOPURAS	GOSH	GOUK	GOWLANDS
GOOFINESS	GORAL	GOSHAWK	GOUKS	GOWLED
GOOFINESSES	GORALS	GOSHAWKS	GOULASH	GOWLING
GOOFING	GORAMIES	GOSLARITE	GOULASHES	GOWLS
GOOFS	GORAMY	GOSLARITES	GOURAMI	GOWN
GOOFY	GORBLIMEY	GOSLET	GOURAMIS	GOWNBOY
GOOGLE	GORBLIMY	GOSLETS	GOURD	GOWNBOYS
GOOGLED	GORCOCK	GOSLING	GOURDE	GOWNED
GOOGLES	GORCOCKS	GOSLINGS	GOURDES	GOWNING
GOOGLIES	GORCROW	GOSPEL	GOURDS	GOWNMAN
GOOGLING	GORCROWS	GOSPELISE	GOURDY	GOWNMEN
GOOGLY	GORE	GOSPELISED	GOURMAND	GOWNS
GOOGOL	GORED	GOSPELISES	GOURMANDS	GOWNSMAN
GOOGOLS	GORES	GOSPELISING	GOURMET	GOWNSMEN
GOOIER	GORGE	GOSPELIZE	GOURMETS	GOWPEN
GOOIEST	GORGED	GOSPELIZED	GOUSTIER	GOWPENFUL
GOOK	GORGEOUS	GOSPELIZES	GOUSTIEST	GOWPENFULS
GOOKS	GORGERIN	GOSPELIZING	GOUSTROUS	GOWPENS
GOOL	GORGERINS	GOSPELLED	GOUSTY	GOY
GOOLD	GORGES	GOSPELLER	GOUT	GOYIM
GOOLDS	GORGET	GOSPELLERS	GOUTFLIES	GOYISCH
GOOLEY	GORGETS	GOSPELLING	GOUTFLY	GOYISH
GOOLEYS	GORGIA	GOSPELS	GOUTIER	GOZZAN
GOOLIE	GORGIAS	GOSPODAR	GOUTIEST	GOZZANS
GOOLIES	GORGING	GOSPODARS	GOUTINESS	GRAAL
GOOLS	GORGIO	GOSSAMER	GOUTINESSES	GRAALS
GOOLY	GORGIOS	GOSSAMERS	GOUTS	GRAB
GOON	GORGON	GOSSAMERY	GOUTTE	GRABBED
GOONEY	GORGONEIA	GOSSAN	GOUTTES	GRABBER
GOONEYS	GORGONIAN	GOSSANS	GOUTWEED	GRABBERS
GOONS	GORGONIANS	GOSSE	GOUTWEEDS	GRABBING
GOOP	GORGONISE	GOSSES	GOUTWORT	GRABBLE
GOOPS	GORGONISED	GOSSIB	GOUTWORTS	GRABBLED
GOOPY	GORGONISES	GOSSIBS	GOUTY	GRABBLER
GOOR	GORGONISING	GOSSIP	GOV	GRABBLERS
GOOROO	GORGONIZE	GOSSIPED	GOVERN	GRABBLES
GOOROOS	GORGONIZED	GOSSIPING	GOVERNALL	GRABBLING
GOORS	GORGONIZES	GOSSIPINGS	GOVERNALLS	GRABEN
GOOS	GORGONIZING	GOSSIPRIES	GOVERNED	GRABENS
GOOSANDER	GORGONS	GOSSIPRY	GOVERNESS	GRABS
GOOSANDERS	GORIER	GOSSIPS	GOVERNESSED	GRACE
GOOSE	GORIEST	GOSSIPY	GOVERNESSES	GRACED
GOOSED	GORILLA	GOSSOON	GOVERNESSING	GRACEFUL
GOOSEFOOT	GORILLAS	GOSSOONS	GOVERNING	GRACELESS
GOOSEFOOTS	GORILLIAN	GOSSYPINE	GOVERNOR	GRACES
GOOSEGOB	GORILLINE	GOSSYPOL	GOVERNORS	GRACILE
GOOSEGOBS	GORILY	GOSSYPOLS	GOVERNS	GRACILITIES
GOOSEGOG	GORING	GOT	GOVS	GRACILITY
GOOSEGOGS	GORINGS	GOTHICISE	GOWAN	GRACING
GOOSEHERD	GORM	GOTHICISED	GOWANED	GRACIOSO
GOOSEHERDS	GORMAND	GOTHICISES	GOWANS	GRACIOSOS
GOOSERIES	GORMANDS	GOTHICISING	GOWANY	GRACIOUS
GOOSERY	GORMED	GOTHICIZE	GOWD	GRACKLE
GOOSES	GORMIER	GOTHICIZED	GOWDED	GRACKLES
GOOSEY	GORMIEST	GOTHICIZES	GOWDER	GRADABLE
GOOSEYS	GORMING	GOTHICIZING	GOWDEST	GRADABLES
GOOSIER	GORMLESS	GÖTHITE	GOWDING	GRADATE
GOOSIES	GORMS	GÖTHITES	GOWDS	GRADATED
GOOSIEST	GORMY	GOTTA	GOWDSPINK	GRADATES
GOOSING	GORSE	GOTTEN	GOWDSPINKS	GRADATIM

GRADATING
GRADATION
GRADATIONS
GRADATORY
GRADDAN
GRADDANED
GRADDANING
GRADDANS
GRADE
GRADED
GRADELY
GRADER
GRADERS
GRADES
GRADIENT
GRADIENTS
GRADIN
GRADINE
GRADINES
GRADING
GRADINI
GRADINO
GRADINOS
GRADINS
GRADUAL
GRADUALLY
GRADUALS
GRADUAND
GRADUANDS
GRADUATE
GRADUATED
GRADUATES
GRADUATING
GRADUATOR
GRADUATORS
GRADUS
GRADUSES
GRAFF
GRAFFED
GRAFFING
GRAFFITI
GRAFFITIS
GRAFFITO
GRAFFS
GRAFT
GRAFTED
GRAFTER
GRAFTERS
GRAFTING
GRAFTINGS
GRAFTS
GRAIL
GRAILE
GRAILES
GRAILS
GRAIN
GRAINAGE
GRAINAGES
GRAINE
GRAINED
GRAINER
GRAINERS
GRAINES
GRAINIER
GRAINIEST
GRAINING
GRAININGS
GRAINS
GRAINY
GRAIP

GRAIPS
GRAITH
GRAITHED
GRAITHING
GRAITHLY
GRAITHS
GRAKLE
GRAKLES
GRALLOCH
GRALLOCHED
GRALLOCHING
GRALLOCHS
GRAM
GRAMA
GRAMARIES
GRAMARY
GRAMARYE
GRAMARYES
GRAMAS
GRAMASH
GRAMASHES
GRAME
GRAMERCIES
GRAMERCY
GRAMES
GRAMMAR
GRAMMARS
GRAMMATIC
GRAMME
GRAMMES
GRAMOCHE
GRAMOCHES
GRAMPUS
GRAMPUSES
GRAMS
GRAN
GRANARIES
GRANARY
GRAND
GRANDAD
GRANDADDIES
GRANDADDY
GRANDADS
GRANDAM
GRANDAMS
GRANDDAD
GRANDDADS
GRANDE
GRANDEE
GRANDEES
GRANDER
GRANDEST
GRANDEUR
GRANDEURS
GRANDIOSE
GRANDLY
GRANDMA
GRANDMAMA
GRANDMAMAS
GRANDMAS
GRANDNESS
GRANDNESSES
GRANDPA
GRANDPAPA
GRANDPAPAS
GRANDPAS
GRANDS
GRANDSIRE
GRANDSIRES
GRANDSON

GRANDSONS
GRANFER
GRANFERS
GRANGE
GRANGER
GRANGERS
GRANGES
GRANITE
GRANITES
GRANITIC
GRANITISE
GRANITISED
GRANITISES
GRANITISING
GRANITITE
GRANITITES
GRANITIZE
GRANITIZED
GRANITIZES
GRANITIZING
GRANITOID
GRANIVORE
GRANIVORES
GRANNAM
GRANNAMS
GRANNIE
GRANNIES
GRANNY
GRANS
GRANT
GRANTABLE
GRANTED
GRANTEE
GRANTEES
GRANTER
GRANTERS
GRANTING
GRANTOR
GRANTORS
GRANTS
GRANULAR
GRANULARY
GRANULATE
GRANULATED
GRANULATES
GRANULATING
GRANULE
GRANULES
GRANULITE
GRANULITES
GRANULOMA
GRANULOMAS
GRANULOMATA
GRANULOSE
GRANULOUS
GRAPE
GRAPED
GRAPELESS
GRAPERIES
GRAPERY
GRAPES
GRAPESEED
GRAPESEEDS
GRAPESHOT
GRAPESHOTS
GRAPETREE
GRAPETREES
GRAPEVINE
GRAPEVINES
GRAPEY

GRAPH
GRAPHED
GRAPHEME
GRAPHEMES
GRAPHEMIC
GRAPHEMICS
GRAPHIC
GRAPHICAL
GRAPHICLY
GRAPHICS
GRAPHING
GRAPHITE
GRAPHITES
GRAPHITIC
GRAPHIUM
GRAPHIUMS
GRAPHS
GRAPIER
GRAPIEST
GRAPING
GRAPLE
GRAPLED
GRAPLES
GRAPLING
GRAPNEL
GRAPNELS
GRAPPA
GRAPPAS
GRAPPLE
GRAPPLED
GRAPPLES
GRAPPLING
GRAPY
GRASP
GRASPABLE
GRASPED
GRASPER
GRASPERS
GRASPING
GRASPLESS
GRASPS
GRASS
GRASSED
GRASSER
GRASSERS
GRASSES
GRASSHOOK
GRASSHOOKS
GRASSIER
GRASSIEST
GRASSING
GRASSINGS
GRASSLAND
GRASSLANDS
GRASSUM
GRASSUMS
GRASSY
GRASTE
GRAT
GRATE
GRATED
GRATEFUL
GRATER
GRATERS
GRATES
GRATICULE
GRATICULES
GRATIFIED
GRATIFIER
GRATIFIERS

GRATIFIES
GRATIFY
GRATIFYING
GRATING
GRATINGLY
GRATINGS
GRATIS
GRATITUDE
GRATITUDES
GRATTOIR
GRATTOIRS
GRATUITIES
GRATUITY
GRATULANT
GRATULATE
GRATULATED
GRATULATES
GRATULATING
GRAUPEL
GRAUPELS
GRAVAMEN
GRAVAMINA
GRAVE
GRAVED
GRAVEL
GRAVELESS
GRAVELLED
GRAVELLING
GRAVELLY
GRAVELS
GRAVELY
GRAVEN
GRAVENESS
GRAVENESSES
GRAVER
GRAVERS
GRAVES
GRAVEST
GRAVEYARD
GRAVEYARDS
GRAVID
GRAVIDITIES
GRAVIDITY
GRAVIES
GRAVING
GRAVINGS
GRAVITAS
GRAVITASES
GRAVITATE
GRAVITATED
GRAVITATES
GRAVITATING
GRAVITIES
GRAVITON
GRAVITONS
GRAVITY
GRAVURE
GRAVURES
GRAVY
GRAY
GRAYED
GRAYER
GRAYEST
GRAYFLIES
GRAYFLY
GRAYING
GRAYLE
GRAYLES
GRAYLING
GRAYLINGS

GRAYS
GRAYWACKE
GRAYWACKES
GRAZE
GRAZED
GRAZER
GRAZERS
GRAZES
GRAZIER
GRAZIERS
GRAZING
GRAZINGS
GRAZIOSO
GREASE
GREASED
GREASER
GREASERS
GREASES
GREASIER
GREASIEST
GREASILY
GREASING
GREASY
GREAT
GREATCOAT
GREATCOATS
GREATEN
GREATENED
GREATENING
GREATENS
GREATER
GREATEST
GREATLY
GREATNESS
GREATNESSES
GREATS
GREAVE
GREAVED
GREAVES
GREAVING
GREBE
GREBES
GRECE
GRECES
GRECIAN
GRECIANS
GRECQUE
GRECQUES
GREE
GREECE
GREECES
GREED
GREEDIER
GREEDIEST
GREEDILY
GREEDS
GREEDY
GREEGREE
GREEGREES
GREEING
GREEN
GREENBACK
GREENBACKS
GREENED
GREENER
GREENERIES
GREENERY
GREENEST
GREENFLIES
GREENFLY

GREENGAGE
GREENGAGES
GREENHAND
GREENHANDS
GREENHORN
GREENHORNS
GREENIER
GREENIEST
GREENING
GREENINGS
GREENISH
GREENLET
GREENLETS
GREENLY
GREENMAIL
GREENMAILS
GREENNESS
GREENNESSES
GREENROOM
GREENROOMS
GREENS
GREENSAND
GREENSANDS
GREENTH
GREENTHS
GREENWEED
GREENWEEDS
GREENWOOD
GREENWOODS
GREENY
GREES
GREESE
GREESES
GREESING
GREESINGS
GREET
GREETE
GREETED
GREETES
GREETING
GREETINGS
GREETS
GREFFIER
GREFFIERS
GREGALE
GREGALES
GREGARIAN
GREGARINE
GREGARINES
GREGATIM
GRÈGE
GREGO
GREGORIES
GREGORY
GREGOS
GREIGE
GREIN
GREINED
GREINING
GREINS
GREISEN
GREISENS
GREISLY
GREMIAL
GREMIALS
GREMLIN
GREMLINS
GREN
GRENADE
GRENADES

GRENADIER
GRENADIERS
GRENADINE
GRENADINES
GRENNED
GRENNING
GRENS
GRESE
GRESES
GRESSING
GRESSINGS
GREVE
GREVES
GREW
GREWED
GREWHOUND
GREWHOUNDS
GREWING
GREWS
GREY
GREYBEARD
GREYBEARDS
GREYED
GREYER
GREYEST
GREYHEN
GREYHENS
GREYHOUND
GREYHOUNDS
GREYING
GREYISH
GREYLY
GREYNESS
GREYNESSES
GREYS
GREYWACKE
GREYWACKES
GRIBBLE
GRIBBLES
GRICE
GRICER
GRICERS
GRICES
GRICING
GRICINGS
GRID
GRIDDLE
GRIDDLES
GRIDE
GRIDED
GRIDELIN
GRIDELINS
GRIDES
GRIDING
GRIDIRON
GRIDIRONED
GRIDIRONING
GRIDIRONS
GRIDLOCK
GRIDLOCKS
GRIDS
GRIECE
GRIECED
GRIECES
GRIEF
GRIEFFUL
GRIEFLESS
GRIEFS
GRIESIE
GRIESLY

GRIESY
GRIEVANCE
GRIEVANCES
GRIEVE
GRIEVED
GRIEVER
GRIEVERS
GRIEVES
GRIEVING
GRIEVOUS
GRIFF
GRIFFE
GRIFFES
GRIFFIN
GRIFFINS
GRIFFON
GRIFFONS
GRIFFS
GRIFT
GRIFTED
GRIFTER
GRIFTERS
GRIFTING
GRIFTS
GRIG
GRIGGED
GRIGGING
GRIGRI
GRIGRIS
GRIGS
GRIKE
GRIKES
GRILL
GRILLADE
GRILLADES
GRILLAGE
GRILLAGES
GRILLE
GRILLED
GRILLES
GRILLING
GRILLINGS
GRILLS
GRILSE
GRILSES
GRIM
GRIMACE
GRIMACED
GRIMACES
GRIMACING
GRIMALKIN
GRIMALKINS
GRIME
GRIMED
GRIMES
GRIMIER
GRIMIEST
GRIMILY
GRIMINESS
GRIMINESSES
GRIMING
GRIMLY
GRIMMER
GRIMMEST
GRIMNESS
GRIMNESSES
GRIMOIRE
GRIMOIRES
GRIMY
GRIN

GRIND
GRINDED
GRINDER
GRINDERIES
GRINDERS
GRINDERY
GRINDING
GRINDINGS
GRINDS
GRINGO
GRINGOS
GRINNED
GRINNER
GRINNERS
GRINNING
GRINS
GRIOT
GRIOTS
GRIP
GRIPE
GRIPED
GRIPER
GRIPERS
GRIPES
GRIPING
GRIPINGLY
GRIPLE
GRIPLES
GRIPPE
GRIPPED
GRIPPER
GRIPPERS
GRIPPES
GRIPPIER
GRIPPIEST
GRIPPING
GRIPPLE
GRIPPLES
GRIPPY
GRIPS
GRIPSACK
GRIPSACKS
GRIS
GRISAILLE
GRISAILLES
GRISE
GRISED
GRISELY
GRISEOUS
GRISES
GRISETTE
GRISETTES
GRISGRIS
GRISING
GRISKIN
GRISKINS
GRISLED
GRISLIER
GRISLIEST
GRISLY
GRISON
GRISONS
GRIST
GRISTLE
GRISTLES
GRISTLIER
GRISTLIEST
GRISTLY
GRISTS
GRISY

GRIT	GRONEFULL	GROUCHY	GROWLS	GRUMOSE
GRITH	GRONES	GROUF	GROWLY	GRUMOUS
GRITHS	GRONING	GROUFS	GROWN	GRUMPH
GRITS	GROOF	GROUND	GROWS	GRUMPHED
GRITSTONE	GROOFS	GROUNDAGE	GROWTH	GRUMPHIE
GRITSTONES	GROOLY	GROUNDAGES	GROWTHIST	GRUMPHIES
GRITTED	GROOM	GROUNDED	GROWTHISTS	GRUMPHING
GRITTER	GROOMED	GROUNDEN	GROWTHS	GRUMPHS
GRITTERS	GROOMING	GROUNDER	GROYNE	GRUMPIER
GRITTEST	GROOMS	GROUNDERS	GROYNES	GRUMPIEST
GRITTIER	GROOMSMAN	GROUNDING	GRUB	GRUMPILY
GRITTIEST	GROOMSMEN	GROUNDINGS	GRUBBED	GRUMPY
GRITTING	GROOVE	GROUNDMAN	GRUBBER	GRUNGIER
GRITTY	GROOVED	GROUNDMEN	GRUBBERS	GRUNGIEST
GRIVET	GROOVES	GROUNDS	GRUBBIER	GRUNGY
GRIVETS	GROOVIER	GROUNDSEL	GRUBBIEST	GRUNION
GRIZE	GROOVIEST	GROUNDSELS	GRUBBING	GRUNIONS
GRIZES	GROOVING	GROUP	GRUBBLE	GRUNT
GRIZZLE	GROOVY	GROUPAGE	GRUBBLED	GRUNTED
GRIZZLED	GROPE	GROUPAGES	GRUBBLES	GRUNTER
GRIZZLER	GROPED	GROUPED	GRUBBLING	GRUNTERS
GRIZZLERS	GROPER	GROUPER	GRUBBY	GRUNTING
GRIZZLES	GROPERS	GROUPERS	GRUBS	GRUNTINGS
GRIZZLIER	GROPES	GROUPIE	GRUDGE	GRUNTLE
GRIZZLIES	GROPING	GROUPIES	GRUDGED	GRUNTLED
GRIZZLIEST	GROPINGLY	GROUPING	GRUDGEFUL	GRUNTLES
GRIZZLING	GROSBEAK	GROUPINGS	GRUDGES	GRUNTLING
GRIZZLY	GROSBEAKS	GROUPIST	GRUDGING	GRUNTS
GROAN	GROSCHEN	GROUPISTS	GRUDGINGS	GRUPPETTI
GROANED	GROSCHENS	GROUPLET	GRUE	GRUPPETTO
GROANER	GROSER	GROUPLETS	GRUED	GRUTCH
GROANERS	GROSERS	GROUPS	GRUEING	GRUTCHED
GROANFUL	GROSERT	GROUPY	GRUEL	GRUTCHES
GROANING	GROSERTS	GROUSE	GRUELLED	GRUTCHING
GROANINGS	GROSET	GROUSED	GRUELLING	GRUTTEN
GROANS	GROSETS	GROUSER	GRUELLINGS	GRYCE
GROAT	GROSGRAIN	GROUSERS	GRUELS	GRYCES
GROATS	GROSGRAINS	GROUSES	GRUES	GRYDE
GROCER	GROSS	GROUSING	GRUESOME	GRYDED
GROCERIES	GROSSART	GROUT	GRUESOMER	GRYDES
GROCERS	GROSSARTS	GROUTED	GRUESOMEST	GRYDING
GROCERY	GROSSED	GROUTIER	GRUFF	GRYESLY
GROCKLE	GROSSER	GROUTIEST	GRUFFER	GRYESY
GROCKLES	GROSSES	GROUTING	GRUFFEST	GRYFON
GROG	GROSSEST	GROUTINGS	GRUFFISH	GRYFONS
GROGGED	GROSSING	GROUTS	GRUFFLY	GRYKE
GROGGERIES	GROSSLY	GROUTY	GRUFFNESS	GRYKES
GROGGERY	GROSSNESS	GROVE	GRUFFNESSES	GRYPE
GROGGIER	GROSSNESSES	GROVEL	GRUFTED	GRYPES
GROGGIEST	GROSSULAR	GROVELLED	GRUING	GRYPHON
GROGGING	GROSSULARS	GROVELLER	GRUM	GRYPHONS
GROGGY	GROT	GROVELLERS	GRUMBLE	GRYPT
GROGRAM	GROTESQUE	GROVELLING	GRUMBLED	GRYSBOK
GROGRAMS	GROTESQUER	GROVELS	GRUMBLER	GRYSBOKS
GROGS	GROTESQUES	GROVES	GRUMBLERS	GRYSELY
GROIN	GROTESQUEST	GROW	GRUMBLES	GRYSIE
GROINED	GROTS	GROWER	GRUMBLIER	GU
GROINING	GROTTIER	GROWERS	GRUMBLIEST	GUACAMOLE
GROININGS	GROTTIEST	GROWING	GRUMBLING	GUACAMOLES
GROINS	GROTTO	GROWINGS	GRUMBLINGS	GUACHARO
GROMA	GROTTOES	GROWL	GRUMBLY	GUACHAROS
GROMAS	GROTTOS	GROWLED	GRUME	GUACO
GROMET	GROTTY	GROWLER	GRUMES	GUACOS
GROMETS	GROUCH	GROWLERIES	GRUMLY	GUAIACUM
GROMMET	GROUCHED	GROWLERS	GRUMMER	GUAIACUMS
GROMMETS	GROUCHES	GROWLERY	GRUMMEST	GUAN
GROMWELL	GROUCHIER	GROWLIER	GRUMMET	GUANA
GROMWELLS	GROUCHIEST	GROWLIEST	GRUMMETS	GUANACO
GRONE	GROUCHILY	GROWLING	GRUMNESS	GUANACOS
GRONED	GROUCHING	GROWLINGS	GRUMNESSES	GUANAS

GUANAZOLO
GUANAZOLOS
GUANIN
GUANINE
GUANINES
GUANINS
GUANO
GUANOS
GUANS
GUAR
GUARANÁ
GUARANÁS
GUARANI
GUARANIES
GUARANTEE
GUARANTEED
GUARANTEEING
GUARANTEES
GUARANTIED
GUARANTIES
GUARANTOR
GUARANTORS
GUARANTY
GUARANTYING
GUARD
GUARDABLE
GUARDAGE
GUARDAGES
GUARDANT
GUARDANTS
GUARDED
GUARDEDLY
GUARDEE
GUARDEES
GUARDIAN
GUARDIANS
GUARDING
GUARDLESS
GUARDS
GUARDSMAN
GUARDSMEN
GUARISH
GUARISHED
GUARISHES
GUARISHING
GUARS
GUAVA
GUAVAS
GUAYULE
GUAYULES
GUB
GUBBAH
GUBBAHS
GUBBINS
GUBS
GUCK
GUCKIER
GUCKIEST
GUCKS
GUCKY
GUDDLE
GUDDLED
GUDDLES
GUDDLING
GUDE
GUDEMAN
GUDEMEN
GUDESIRE
GUDESIRES
GUDEWIFE

GUDEWIVES
GUDGEON
GUDGEONED
GUDGEONING
GUDGEONS
GUE
GUENON
GUENONS
GUERDON
GUERDONED
GUERDONING
GUERDONS
GUEREZA
GUEREZAS
GUÉRIDON
GUÉRIDONS
GUERILLA
GUERILLAS
GUERNSEY
GUERNSEYS
GUERRILLA
GUERRILLAS
GUES
GUESS
GUESSABLE
GUESSED
GUESSER
GUESSERS
GUESSES
GUESSING
GUESSINGS
GUEST
GUESTED
GUESTEN
GUESTENED
GUESTENING
GUESTENS
GUESTING
GUESTS
GUESTWISE
GUFF
GUFFAW
GUFFAWED
GUFFAWING
GUFFAWS
GUFFS
GUGGLE
GUGGLED
GUGGLES
GUGGLING
GUICHET
GUICHETS
GUID
GUIDABLE
GUIDAGE
GUIDAGES
GUIDANCE
GUIDANCES
GUIDE
GUIDED
GUIDELESS
GUIDELINE
GUIDELINES
GUIDER
GUIDERS
GUIDES
GUIDESHIP
GUIDESHIPS
GUIDING
GUIDINGS

GUIDON
GUIDONS
GUILD
GUILDER
GUILDERS
GUILDHALL
GUILDHALLS
GUILDRIES
GUILDRY
GUILDS
GUILE
GUILED
GUILEFUL
GUILELESS
GUILER
GUILERS
GUILES
GUILING
GUILLEMOT
GUILLEMOTS
GUILLOCHE
GUILLOCHED
GUILLOCHES
GUILLOCHING
GUILT
GUILTIER
GUILTIEST
GUILTILY
GUILTLESS
GUILTS
GUILTY
GUIMBARD
GUIMBARDS
GUIMP
GUIMPE
GUIMPED
GUIMPES
GUIMPING
GUIMPS
GUINEA
GUINEAS
GUIPURE
GUIPURES
GUIRO
GUIROS
GUISARD
GUISARDS
GUISE
GUISED
GUISER
GUISERS
GUISES
GUISING
GUITAR
GUITARIST
GUITARISTS
GUITARS
GUIZER
GUIZERS
GULA
GULAG
GULAGS
GULAR
GULAS
GULCH
GULCHED
GULCHES
GULCHING
GULDEN
GULDENS

GULE
GULES
GULF
GULFED
GULFIER
GULFIEST
GULFING
GULFS
GULFWEED
GULFWEEDS
GULFY
GULL
GULLABLE
GULLED
GULLER
GULLERIES
GULLERS
GULLERY
GULLET
GULLETS
GULLEY
GULLEYED
GULLEYING
GULLEYS
GULLIBLE
GULLIED
GULLIES
GULLING
GULLISH
GULLS
GULLY
GULLYING
GULOSITIES
GULOSITY
GULP
GULPED
GULPER
GULPERS
GULPH
GULPHED
GULPHING
GULPHS
GULPING
GULPS
GULY
GUM
GUMBO
GUMBOIL
GUMBOILS
GUMBOOT
GUMBOOTS
GUMBOS
GUMDROP
GUMDROPS
GUMMA
GUMMATA
GUMMATOUS
GUMMED
GUMMIER
GUMMIEST
GUMMINESS
GUMMINESSES
GUMMING
GUMMINGS
GUMMITE
GUMMITES
GUMMOSES
GUMMOSIS
GUMMOSITIES
GUMMOSITY

GUMMOUS
GUMMY
GUMP
GUMPED
GUMPHION
GUMPHIONS
GUMPING
GUMPS
GUMPTION
GUMPTIONS
GUMPTIOUS
GUMS
GUMSHIELD
GUMSHIELDS
GUMSHOE
GUMSHOED
GUMSHOEING
GUMSHOES
GUN
GUNBOAT
GUNBOATS
GUNCOTTON
GUNCOTTONS
GUNDIES
GUNDY
GUNFIGHT
GUNFIGHTING
GUNFIGHTS
GUNFIRE
GUNFIRES
GUNFLINT
GUNFLINTS
GUNFOUGHT
GUNGE
GUNGES
GUNGIER
GUNGIEST
GUNGY
GUNITE
GUNITES
GUNK
GUNKS
GUNLAYER
GUNLAYERS
GUNMAKER
GUNMAKERS
GUNMAN
GUNMEN
GUNMETAL
GUNMETALS
GUNNAGE
GUNNAGES
GUNNED
GUNNEL
GUNNELS
GUNNER
GUNNERA
GUNNERAS
GUNNERIES
GUNNERS
GUNNERY
GUNNIES
GUNNING
GUNNINGS
GUNNY
GUNPLAY
GUNPLAYS
GUNPORT
GUNPORTS
GUNPOWDER

GUNPOWDERS	GURNEYS	GUTCHERS	GYELDS	GYPSYDOM
GUNROOM	GURNING	GUTLESS	GYLDEN	GYPSYDOMS
GUNROOMS	GURNS	GUTS	GYM	GYPSYING
GUNRUNNER	GURRAH	GUTSIER	GYMBAL	GYPSYISM
GUNRUNNERS	GURRAHS	GUTSIEST	GYMBALS	GYPSYISMS
GUNS	GURRIES	GUTSINESS	GYMKHANA	GYPSYWORT
GUNSEL	GURRY	GUTSINESSES	GYMKHANAS	GYPSYWORTS
GUNSELS	GURS	GUTSY	GYMMAL	GYRAL
GUNSHIP	GURU	GUTTA	GYMMALS	GYRALLY
GUNSHIPS	GURUDOM	GUTTAE	GYMNASIA	GYRANT
GUNSHOT	GURUDOMS	GUTTAS	GYMNASIAL	GYRATE
GUNSHOTS	GURUISM	GUTTATE	GYMNASIC	GYRATED
GUNSMITH	GURUISMS	GUTTATED	GYMNASIEN	GYRATES
GUNSMITHS	GURUS	GUTTATES	GYMNASIUM	GYRATING
GUNSTICK	GURUSHIP	GUTTATING	GYMNASIUMS	GYRATION
GUNSTICKS	GURUSHIPS	GUTTATION	GYMNAST	GYRATIONS
GUNSTOCK	GUS	GUTTATIONS	GYMNASTIC	GYRATORY
GUNSTOCKS	GUSH	GUTTED	GYMNASTICS	GYRE
GUNSTONE	GUSHED	GUTTER	GYMNASTS	GYRED
GUNSTONES	GUSHER	GUTTERED	GYMNIC	GYRES
GUNTER	GUSHERS	GUTTERING	GYMNOSOPH	GYRFALCON
GUNTERS	GUSHES	GUTTERINGS	GYMNOSOPHS	GYRFALCONS
GUNWALE	GUSHIER	GUTTERS	GYMP	GYRI
GUNWALES	GUSHIEST	GUTTIES	GYMPED	GYRING
GUNYAH	GUSHING	GUTTING	GYMPING	GYRO
GUNYAHS	GUSHINGLY	GUTTLE	GYMPS	GYROCAR
GUP	GUSHY	GUTTLED	GYMS	GYROCARS
GUPPIES	GUSLA	GUTTLES	GYNAE	GYRODYNE
GUPPY	GUSLAR	GUTTLING	GYNAECEUM	GYRODYNES
GUPS	GUSLARS	GUTTURAL	GYNAECEUMS	GYROIDAL
GUR	GUSLAS	GUTTURALS	GYNAECOID	GYROMANCIES
GURAMI	GUSLE	GUTTY	GYNAES	GYROMANCY
GURAMIS	GUSLES	GUY	GYNANDRIES	GYRON
GURDWARA	GUSLI	GUYED	GYNANDRY	GYRONNY
GURDWARAS	GUSLIS	GUYING	GYNECIUM	GYRONS
GURGE	GUSSET	GUYLE	GYNECIUMS	GYROPLANE
GURGES	GUSSETED	GUYLER	GYNIES	GYROPLANES
GURGLE	GUSSETING	GUYLERS	GYNNEY	GYROS
GURGLED	GUSSETS	GUYLES	GYNNY	GYROSCOPE
GURGLES	GUST	GUYOT	GYNOCRACIES	GYROSCOPES
GURGLING	GUSTABLE	GUYOTS	GYNOCRACY	GYROSE
GURGOYLE	GUSTABLES	GUYS	GYNOECIUM	GYROSTAT
GURGOYLES	GUSTATION	GUYSE	GYNOECIUMS	GYROSTATS
GURJUN	GUSTATIONS	GUYSES	GYNOPHORE	GYROUS
GURJUNS	GUSTATIVE	GUZZLE	GYNOPHORES	GYROVAGUE
GURL	GUSTATORY	GUZZLED	GYNY	GYROVAGUES
GURLED	GUSTED	GUZZLER	GYP	GYRUS
GURLET	GUSTFUL	GUZZLERS	GYPPED	GYRUSES
GURLETS	GUSTIER	GUZZLES	GYPPIE	GYTE
GURLIER	GUSTIEST	GUZZLING	GYPPIES	GYTER
GURLIEST	GUSTINESS	GWINIAD	GYPPING	GYTES
GURLING	GUSTINESSES	GWINIADS	GYPPO	GYTEST
GURLS	GUSTING	GWYNIAD	GYPPOS	GYTRASH
GURLY	GUSTO	GWYNIADS	GYPPY	GYTRASHES
GURN	GUSTOS	GYAL	GYPS	GYVE
GURNARD	GUSTS	GYALS	GYPSEOUS	GYVED
GURNARDS	GUSTY	GYBE	GYPSIED	GYVES
GURNED	GUT	GYBED	GYPSIES	GYVING
GURNET	GUTBUCKET	GYBES	GYPSUM	
GURNETS	GUTBUCKETS	GYBING	GYPSUMS	
GURNEY	GUTCHER	GYELD	GYPSY	

H

HA	HACKERS	HAEMIC	HAGS	HAJ
HAAF	HACKERY	HAEMIN	HAH	HAJES
HAAFS	HACKETTE	HAEMINS	HAHNIUM	HAJI
HAANEPOOT	HACKETTES	HAEMOCYTE	HAHNIUMS	HAJIS
HAANEPOOTS	HACKING	HAEMOCYTES	HAICK	HAJJ
HAAR	HACKINGS	HAEMONIES	HAICKS	HAJJES
HAARS	HACKLE	HAEMONY	HAIDUK	HAJJI
HABANERA	HACKLED	HAEMOSTAT	HAIDUKS	HAJJIS
HABANERAS	HACKLER	HAEMOSTATS	HAIK	HAKA
HABDABS	HACKLERS	HAEMS	HAIKAI	HAKAM
HABERDINE	HACKLES	HAET	HAIKS	HAKAMS
HABERDINES	HACKLET	HAETS	HAIKU	HAKAS
HABERGEON	HACKLETS	HAFF	HAIL	HAKE
HABERGEONS	HACKLIER	HAFFET	HAILED	HAKES
HABILABLE	HACKLIEST	HAFFETS	HAILER	HAKIM
HABILE	HACKLING	HAFFIT	HAILERS	HAKIMS
HABIT	HACKLY	HAFFITS	HAILIER	HALAL
HABITABLE	HACKNEY	HAFFLIN	HAILIEST	HALALLED
HABITABLY	HACKNEYED	HAFFLINS	HAILING	HALALLING
HABITANS	HACKNEYING	HAFFS	HAILS	HALALS
HABITANT	HACKNEYS	HAFNIUM	HAILSHOT	HALATION
HABITANTS	HACKS	HAFNIUMS	HAILSHOTS	HALATIONS
HABITAT	HACQUETON	HAFT	HAILSTONE	HALAVAH
HABITATS	HACQUETONS	HAFTED	HAILSTONES	HALAVAHS
HABITED	HAD	HAFTING	HAILY	HALBERD
HABITING	HADAL	HAFTS	HAIN	HALBERDS
HABITS	HADDEN	HAG	HAINCH	HALBERT
HABITUAL	HADDIE	HAGBERRIES	HAINCHED	HALBERTS
HABITUALS	HADDIES	HAGBERRY	HAINCHES	HALCYON
HABITUATE	HADDING	HAGBOLT	HAINCHING	HALCYONS
HABITUATED	HADDOCK	HAGBOLTS	HAINED	HALE
HABITUATES	HADDOCKS	HAGBUT	HAINING	HALED
HABITUATING	HADE	HAGBUTS	HAININGS	HALENESS
HABITUDE	HADED	HAGDEN	HAINS	HALENESSES
HABITUDES	HADES	HAGDENS	HAIQUE	HALER
HABITUÉ	HADING	HAGDON	HAIQUES	HALERS
HABITUÉS	HADITH	HAGDONS	HAIR	HALES
HABITUS	HADITHS	HAGDOWN	HAIRBELL	HALEST
HABLE	HADJ	HAGDOWNS	HAIRBELLS	HALF
HABOOB	HADJES	HAGFISH	HAIRCLOTH	HALFA
HABOOBS	HADJI	HAGFISHES	HAIRCLOTHS	HALFAS
HACEK	HADJIS	HAGG	HAIRCUT	HALFEN
HACEKS	HADROME	HAGGARD	HAIRCUTS	HALFLIN
HACHIS	HADROMES	HAGGARDLY	HAIRED	HALFLING
HACHURE	HADRON	HAGGARDS	HAIRIER	HALFLINGS
HACHURED	HADRONIC	HAGGED	HAIRIEST	HALFLINS
HACHURES	HADRONS	HAGGING	HAIRINESS	HALFPACE
HACHURING	HADROSAUR	HAGGIS	HAIRINESSES	HALFPACES
HACIENDA	HADROSAURS	HAGGISES	HAIRING	HALFPENCE
HACIENDAS	HADS	HAGGISH	HAIRLESS	HALFPENNIES
HACK	HADST	HAGGISHLY	HAIRLIKE	HALFPENNY
HACKAMORE	HAE	HAGGLE	HAIRLINE	HALFWAY
HACKAMORES	HAECCEITIES	HAGGLED	HAIRLINES	HALIBUT
HACKBERRIES	HAECCEITY	HAGGLER	HAIRPIN	HALIBUTS
HACKBERRY	HAEM	HAGGLERS	HAIRPINS	HALICORE
HACKBOLT	HAEMAL	HAGGLES	HAIRS	HALICORES
HACKBOLTS	HAEMATIC	HAGGLING	HAIRST	HALIDE
HACKBUT	HAEMATIN	HAGGS	HAIRSTED	HALIDES
HACKBUTS	HAEMATINS	HAGIARCHIES	HAIRSTING	HALIDOM
HACKED	HAEMATITE	HAGIARCHY	HAIRSTS	HALIDOMS
HACKEE	HAEMATITES	HAGIOLOGIES	HAIRSTYLE	HALIEUTIC
HACKEES	HAEMATOID	HAGIOLOGY	HAIRSTYLES	HALIEUTICS
HACKER	HAEMATOMA	HAGLET	HAIRY	HALIMOT
HACKERIES	HAEMATOMAS	HAGLETS	HAITH	HALIMOTE

HALIMOTES	HALOGENS	HAMMALS	HANDCLAP	HANDSHAKE
HALIMOTS	HALOID	HAMMAM	HANDCLAPS	HANDSHAKES
HALING	HALOIDS	HAMMAMS	HANDCLASP	HANDSOME
HALIOTIS	HALOING	HAMMED	HANDCLASPS	HANDSOMER
HALITE	HALOPHILE	HAMMER	HANDCRAFT	HANDSOMEST
HALITES	HALOPHILIES	HAMMERED	HANDCRAFTS	HANDSPIKE
HALITOSES	HALOPHILY	HAMMERER	HANDCUFF	HANDSPIKES
HALITOSIS	HALOPHOBE	HAMMERERS	HANDCUFFED	HANDSTAFF
HALITOUS	HALOPHOBES	HAMMERING	HANDCUFFING	HANDSTAFFS
HALITUS	HALOPHYTE	HAMMERINGS	HANDCUFFS	HANDSTAND
HALITUSES	HALOPHYTES	HAMMERKOP	HANDED	HANDSTANDS
HALL	HALOS	HAMMERKOPS	HANDER	HANDSTAVES
HALLAL	HALOTHANE	HAMMERMAN	HANDERS	HANDSTURN
HALLALI	HALOTHANES	HAMMERMEN	HANDFAST	HANDSTURNS
HALLALIS	HALSE	HAMMERS	HANDFASTED	HANDTOWEL
HALLALLED	HALSED	HAMMIER	HANDFASTING	HANDTOWELS
HALLALLING	HALSER	HAMMIEST	HANDFASTINGS	HANDWORK
HALLALOO	HALSERS	HAMMILY	HANDFASTS	HANDWORKS
HALLALOOS	HALSES	HAMMING	HANDFUL	HANDY
HALLALS	HALSING	HAMMOCK	HANDFULS	HANDYMAN
HALLAN	HALT	HAMMOCKS	HANDGRIP	HANDYMEN
HALLANS	HALTED	HAMMY	HANDGRIPS	HANDYWORK
HALLIAN	HALTER	HAMOSE	HANDHOLD	HANDYWORKS
HALLIANS	HALTERED	HAMOUS	HANDHOLDS	HANEPOOT
HALLIARD	HALTERES	HAMPER	HANDICAP	HANEPOOTS
HALLIARDS	HALTERING	HAMPERED	HANDICAPPED	HANG
HALLING	HALTERS	HAMPERING	HANDICAPPING	HANGABLE
HALLINGS	HALTING	HAMPERS	HANDICAPS	HANGAR
HALLION	HALTINGLY	HAMPSTER	HANDIER	HANGARS
HALLIONS	HALTINGS	HAMPSTERS	HANDIEST	HANGBIRD
HALLMARK	HALTS	HAMS	HANDILY	HANGBIRDS
HALLMARKED	HALVA	HAMSTER	HANDINESS	HANGDOG
HALLMARKING	HALVAH	HAMSTERS	HANDINESSES	HANGDOGS
HALLMARKS	HALVAHS	HAMSTRING	HANDING	HANGED
HALLO	HALVAS	HAMSTRINGED	HANDIWORK	HANGER
HALLOA	HALVE	HAMSTRINGING	HANDIWORKS	HANGERS
HALLOAED	HALVED	HAMSTRINGS	HANDJAR	HANGFIRE
HALLOAING	HALVER	HAMSTRUNG	HANDJARS	HANGFIRES
HALLOAS	HALVERS	HAMULAR	HANDLE	HANGING
HALLOED	HALVES	HAMULATE	HANDLEBAR	HANGINGS
HALLOES	HALVING	HAMULI	HANDLEBARS	HANGMAN
HALLOING	HALYARD	HAMULUS	HANDLED	HANGMEN
HALLOO	HALYARDS	HAMZA	HANDLER	HANGNAIL
HALLOOED	HAM	HAMZAH	HANDLERS	HANGNAILS
HALLOOING	HAMADRYAD	HAMZAHS	HANDLES	HANGNEST
HALLOOS	HAMADRYADES	HAMZAS	HANDLESS	HANGNESTS
HALLOS	HAMADRYADS	HAN	HANDLING	HANGOUT
HALLOW	HAMAL	HANAP	HANDLINGS	HANGOUTS
HALLOWED	HAMALS	HANAPER	HANDLIST	HANGOVER
HALLOWING	HAMARTIA	HANAPERS	HANDLISTS	HANGOVERS
HALLOWS	HAMARTIAS	HANAPS	HANDMADE	HANGS
HALLS	HAMATE	HANCE	HANDMAID	HANJAR
HALLSTAND	HAMBLE	HANCES	HANDMAIDS	HANJARS
HALLSTANDS	HAMBLED	HANCH	HANDOUT	HANK
HALLUCES	HAMBLES	HANCHED	HANDOUTS	HANKED
HALLUX	HAMBLING	HANCHES	HANDOVER	HANKER
HALLWAY	HAMBURGER	HANCHING	HANDOVERS	HANKERED
HALLWAYS	HAMBURGERS	HAND	HANDPLAY	HANKERING
HALLYON	HAME	HANDBAG	HANDPLAYS	HANKERINGS
HALLYONS	HAMED	HANDBAGS	HANDRAIL	HANKERS
HALM	HAMES	HANDBALL	HANDRAILS	HANKIE
HALMA	HAMEWITH	HANDBALLS	HANDS	HANKIES
HALMAS	HAMFATTER	HANDBELL	HANDSAW	HANKING
HALMS	HAMFATTERED	HANDBELLS	HANDSAWS	HANKS
HALO	HAMFATTERING	HANDBILL	HANDSEL	HANKY
HALOBIONT	HAMFATTERS	HANDBILLS	HANDSELLED	HANSEL
HALOBIONTS	HAMING	HANDBOOK	HANDSELLING	HANSELLED
HALOED	HAMLET	HANDBOOKS	HANDSELS	HANSELLING
HALOES	HAMLETS	HANDCAR	HANDSET	HANSELS
HALOGEN	HAMMAL	HANDCARS	HANDSETS	HANSOM

HANSOMS	HARD	HAREMS	HARMONIUM	HARSHNESSES
HANTLE	HARDBACK	HARES	HARMONIUMS	HARSLET
HANTLES	HARDBACKS	HAREWOOD	HARMONIZE	HARSLETS
HANUMAN	HARDBAKE	HAREWOODS	HARMONIZED	HART
HANUMANS	HARDBAKES	HARICOT	HARMONIZES	HARTAL
HAOMA	HARDBEAM	HARICOTS	HARMONIZING	HARTALS
HAOMAS	HARDBEAMS	HARIGALDS	HARMONY	HARTBEES
HAP	HARDBOARD	HARIGALS	HARMOST	HARTBEESES
HAPHAZARD	HARDBOARDS	HARIM	HARMOSTIES	HARTELY
HAPHAZARDS	HARDCORE	HARIMS	HARMOSTS	HARTEN
HAPLESS	HARDCORES	HARING	HARMOSTY	HARTENED
HAPLESSLY	HARDEN	HARIOLATE	HARMOTOME	HARTENING
HAPLOID	HARDENED	HARIOLATED	HARMOTOMES	HARTENS
HAPLOIDIES	HARDENER	HARIOLATES	HARMS	HARTLESSE
HAPLOIDY	HARDENERS	HARIOLATING	HARN	HARTS
HAPLOLOGIES	HARDENING	HARISH	HARNESS	HARTSHORN
HAPLOLOGY	HARDENINGS	HARK	HARNESSED	HARTSHORNS
HAPLY	HARDENS	HARKED	HARNESSES	HARUSPEX
HAPPED	HARDER	HARKEN	HARNESSING	HARUSPICES
HAPPEN	HARDEST	HARKENED	HARNS	HARUSPICIES
HAPPENED	HARDFACE	HARKENING	HARO	HARUSPICY
HAPPENING	HARDFACES	HARKENS	HAROS	HARVEST
HAPPENINGS	HARDGRASS	HARKING	HAROSET	HARVESTED
HAPPENS	HARDGRASSES	HARKS	HAROSETH	HARVESTER
HAPPIED	HARDHACK	HARL	HAROSETHS	HARVESTERS
HAPPIER	HARDHACKS	HARLED	HAROSETS	HARVESTING
HAPPIES	HARDHEAD	HARLEQUIN	HARP	HARVESTS
HAPPIEST	HARDHEADS	HARLEQUINED	HARPED	HAS
HAPPILY	HARDIER	HARLEQUINING	HARPER	HASH
HAPPINESS	HARDIEST	HARLEQUINS	HARPERS	HASHED
HAPPINESSES	HARDIHEAD	HARLING	HARPIES	HASHEESH
HAPPING	HARDIHEADS	HARLINGS	HARPING	HASHEESHES
HAPPY	HARDIHOOD	HARLOT	HARPINGS	HASHES
HAPPYING	HARDIHOODS	HARLOTRIES	HARPIST	HASHIER
HAPS	HARDILY	HARLOTRY	HARPISTS	HASHIEST
HAPTERON	HARDIMENT	HARLOTS	HARPOON	HASHING
HAPTERONS	HARDIMENTS	HARLS	HARPOONED	HASHISH
HAPTIC	HARDINESS	HARM	HARPOONER	HASHISHES
HAPTICS	HARDINESSES	HARMALA	HARPOONERS	HASHY
HAQUETON	HARDISH	HARMALAS	HARPOONING	HASK
HAQUETONS	HARDLINE	HARMALIN	HARPOONS	HASKS
HARAM	HARDLINER	HARMALINE	HARPS	HASLET
HARAMS	HARDLINERS	HARMALINES	HARPY	HASLETS
HARANGUE	HARDLY	HARMALINS	HARQUEBUS	HASP
HARANGUED	HARDNESS	HARMAN	HARQUEBUSES	HASPED
HARANGUER	HARDNESSES	HARMANS	HARRIDAN	HASPING
HARANGUERS	HARDNOSED	HARMATTAN	HARRIDANS	HASPS
HARANGUES	HARDOKE	HARMATTANS	HARRIED	HASSAR
HARANGUING	HARDOKES	HARMED	HARRIER	HASSARS
HARASS	HARDPARTS	HARMEL	HARRIERS	HASSLE
HARASSED	HARDS	HARMELS	HARRIES	HASSLED
HARASSER	HARDSHELL	HARMFUL	HARROW	HASSLES
HARASSERS	HARDSHIP	HARMFULLY	HARROWED	HASSLING
HARASSES	HARDSHIPS	HARMIN	HARROWING	HASSOCK
HARASSING	HARDTACK	HARMINE	HARROWS	HASSOCKS
HARASSINGS	HARDTACKS	HARMINES	HARRUMPH	HASSOCKY
HARBINGER	HARDWARE	HARMING	HARRUMPHED	HAST
HARBINGERED	HARDWARES	HARMINS	HARRUMPHING	HASTA
HARBINGERING	HARDWOOD	HARMLESS	HARRUMPHS	HASTATE
HARBINGERS	HARDWOODS	HARMONIC	HARRY	HASTATED
HARBOR	HARDY	HARMONICA	HARRYING	HASTE
HARBORED	HARE	HARMONICAS	HARSH	HASTED
HARBORING	HAREBELL	HARMONICS	HARSHEN	HASTEN
HARBORS	HAREBELLS	HARMONIES	HARSHENED	HASTENED
HARBOUR	HARED	HARMONISE	HARSHENING	HASTENER
HARBOURED	HAREEM	HARMONISED	HARSHENS	HASTENERS
HARBOURER	HAREEMS	HARMONISES	HARSHER	HASTENING
HARBOURERS	HARELD	HARMONISING	HARSHEST	HASTENS
HARBOURING	HARELDS	HARMONIST	HARSHLY	HASTES
HARBOURS	HAREM	HARMONISTS	HARSHNESS	HASTIER

HASTIEST	HATTERED	HAVENING	HAWTHORN	HEADACHY
HASTILY	HATTERING	HAVENS	HAWTHORNS	HEADBAND
HASTINESS	HATTERS	HAVEOUR	HAY	HEADBANDS
HASTINESSES	HATTING	HAVEOURS	HAYBAND	HEADBOARD
HASTING	HATTINGS	HAVER	HAYBANDS	HEADBOARDS
HASTINGS	HATTOCK	HAVERED	HAYBOX	HEADCHAIR
HASTY	HATTOCKS	HAVEREL	HAYBOXES	HEADCHAIRS
HAT	HAUBERK	HAVERELS	HAYCOCK	HEADCLOTH
HATABLE	HAUBERKS	HAVERING	HAYCOCKS	HEADCLOTHS
HATBAND	HAUD	HAVERINGS	HAYED	HEADED
HATBANDS	HAUDING	HAVERS	HAYFIELD	HEADER
HATBOX	HAUDS	HAVERSACK	HAYFIELDS	HEADERS
HATBOXES	HAUGH	HAVERSACKS	HAYFORK	HEADFAST
HATBRUSH	HAUGHS	HAVERSINE	HAYFORKS	HEADFASTS
HATBRUSHES	HAUGHT	HAVERSINES	HAYING	HEADFRAME
HATCH	HAUGHTIER	HAVES	HAYINGS	HEADFRAMES
HATCHBACK	HAUGHTIEST	HAVILDAR	HAYLE	HEADGEAR
HATCHBACKS	HAUGHTILY	HAVILDARS	HAYLES	HEADGEARS
HATCHED	HAUGHTY	HAVING	HAYLOFT	HEADHUNT
HATCHEL	HAUL	HAVINGS	HAYLOFTS	HEADHUNTED
HATCHELLED	HAULAGE	HAVIOUR	HAYMAKER	HEADHUNTING
HATCHELLING	HAULAGES	HAVIOURS	HAYMAKERS	HEADHUNTINGS
HATCHELS	HAULD	HAVOC	HAYMAKING	HEADHUNTS
HATCHER	HAULDS	HAVOCKED	HAYMAKINGS	HEADIER
HATCHERIES	HAULED	HAVOCKING	HAYMOW	HEADIEST
HATCHERS	HAULER	HAVOCS	HAYMOWS	HEADILY
HATCHERY	HAULERS	HAW	HAYRICK	HEADINESS
HATCHES	HAULIER	HAWBUCK	HAYRICKS	HEADINESSES
HATCHET	HAULIERS	HAWBUCKS	HAYS	HEADING
HATCHETS	HAULING	HAWED	HAYSEED	HEADINGS
HATCHETY	HAULM	HAWFINCH	HAYSEEDS	HEADLAMP
HATCHING	HAULMS	HAWFINCHES	HAYSEL	HEADLAMPS
HATCHINGS	HAULS	HAWING	HAYSELS	HEADLAND
HATCHLING	HAULST	HAWK	HAYSTACK	HEADLANDS
HATCHLINGS	HAULT	HAWKBELL	HAYSTACKS	HEADLESS
HATCHMENT	HAUNCH	HAWKBELLS	HAYWARD	HEADLIGHT
HATCHMENTS	HAUNCHED	HAWKBIT	HAYWARDS	HEADLIGHTS
HATCHWAY	HAUNCHES	HAWKBITS	HAYWIRE	HEADLINE
HATCHWAYS	HAUNCHING	HAWKED	HAYWIRES	HEADLINED
HATE	HAUNT	HAWKER	HAZARD	HEADLINER
HATEABLE	HAUNTED	HAWKERS	HAZARDED	HEADLINERS
HATED	HAUNTER	HAWKEY	HAZARDING	HEADLINES
HATEFUL	HAUNTERS	HAWKEYS	HAZARDIZE	HEADLINING
HATEFULLY	HAUNTING	HAWKIE	HAZARDIZES	HEADLOCK
HATELESS	HAUNTINGS	HAWKIES	HAZARDOUS	HEADLOCKS
HATER	HAUNTS	HAWKING	HAZARDRIES	HEADLONG
HATERENT	HAURIANT	HAWKINGS	HAZARDRY	HEADMAN
HATERENTS	HAURIENT	HAWKISH	HAZARDS	HEADMARK
HATERS	HAUSE	HAWKISHLY	HAZE	HEADMARKS
HATES	HAUSED	HAWKIT	HAZED	HEADMEN
HATFUL	HAUSES	HAWKS	HAZEL	HEADMOST
HATFULS	HAUSFRAU	HAWKSBILL	HAZELLY	HEADNOTE
HATGUARD	HAUSFRAUS	HAWKSBILLS	HAZELNUT	HEADNOTES
HATGUARDS	HAUSING	HAWKWEED	HAZELNUTS	HEADPEACE
HATH	HAUSTELLA	HAWKWEEDS	HAZELS	HEADPEACES
HATING	HAUSTORIA	HAWM	HAZER	HEADPHONE
HATLESS	HAUT	HAWMED	HAZERS	HEADPHONES
HATPEG	HAUTBOIS	HAWMING	HAZES	HEADPIECE
HATPEGS	HAUTBOY	HAWMS	HAZIER	HEADPIECES
HATPIN	HAUTBOYS	HAWS	HAZIEST	HEADRACE
HATPINS	HAUTE	HAWSE	HAZILY	HEADRACES
HATRACK	HAUTEUR	HAWSED	HAZINESS	HEADRAIL
HATRACKS	HAUTEURS	HAWSEHOLE	HAZINESSES	HEADRAILS
HATRED	HAÜYNE	HAWSEHOLES	HAZING	HEADREACH
HATREDS	HAÜYNES	HAWSEPIPE	HAZINGS	HEADREACHED
HATS	HAVE	HAWSEPIPES	HAZY	HEADREACHES
HATSTAND	HAVELOCK	HAWSER	HE	HEADREACHING
HATSTANDS	HAVELOCKS	HAWSERS	HEAD	HEADREST
HATTED	HAVEN	HAWSES	HEADACHE	HEADRESTS
HATTER	HAVENED	HAWSING	HEADACHES	HEADRIG

HEADRIGS	HEARES	HEATHEN	HECOGENINS	HEELS
HEADRING	HEARIE	HEATHENRIES	HECTARE	HEEZE
HEADRINGS	HEARING	HEATHENRY	HECTARES	HEEZED
HEADROOM	HEARINGS	HEATHENS	HECTIC	HEEZES
HEADROOMS	HEARKEN	HEATHER	HECTICAL	HEEZIE
HEADROPE	HEARKENED	HEATHERS	HECTICS	HEEZIES
HEADROPES	HEARKENER	HEATHERY	HECTOGRAM	HEEZING
HEADS	HEARKENERS	HEATHIER	HECTOGRAMS	HEFT
HEADSCARF	HEARKENING	HEATHIEST	HECTOR	HEFTE
HEADSCARVES	HEARKENS	HEATHS	HECTORED	HEFTED
HEADSET	HEARS	HEATHY	HECTORER	HEFTIER
HEADSETS	HEARSAY	HEATING	HECTORERS	HEFTIEST
HEADSHAKE	HEARSAYS	HEATINGS	HECTORING	HEFTING
HEADSHAKES	HEARSE	HEATS	HECTORINGS	HEFTS
HEADSHIP	HEARSED	HEATSPOT	HECTORISM	HEFTY
HEADSHIPS	HEARSES	HEATSPOTS	HECTORISMS	HEGEMONIC
HEADSMAN	HEARSIER	HEAUME	HECTORLY	HEGEMONIES
HEADSMEN	HEARSIEST	HEAUMES	HECTORS	HEGEMONY
HEADSTALL	HEARSING	HEAVE	HEDDLE	HEGIRA
HEADSTALLS	HEARSY	HEAVED	HEDDLED	HEGIRAS
HEADSTICK	HEART	HEAVEN	HEDDLES	HEID
HEADSTICKS	HEARTACHE	HEAVENLIER	HEDDLING	HEIDS
HEADSTOCK	HEARTACHES	HEAVENLIEST	HEDERAL	HEIFER
HEADSTOCKS	HEARTBURN	HEAVENLY	HEDERATED	HEIFERS
HEADSTONE	HEARTBURNS	HEAVENS	HEDGE	HEIGH
HEADSTONES	HEARTED	HEAVER	HEDGEBILL	HEIGHT
HEADWAY	HEARTEN	HEAVERS	HEDGEBILLS	HEIGHTEN
HEADWAYS	HEARTENED	HEAVES	HEDGED	HEIGHTENED
HEADWORD	HEARTENING	HEAVIER	HEDGEHOG	HEIGHTENING
HEADWORDS	HEARTENS	HEAVIES	HEDGEHOGS	HEIGHTENS
HEADWORK	HEARTFELT	HEAVIEST	HEDGEPIG	HEIGHTS
HEADWORKS	HEARTH	HEAVILY	HEDGEPIGS	HEIL
HEADY	HEARTHS	HEAVINESS	HEDGER	HEINOUS
HEAL	HEARTIER	HEAVINESSES	HEDGEROW	HEINOUSLY
HEALABLE	HEARTIES	HEAVING	HEDGEROWS	HEIR
HEALD	HEARTIEST	HEAVINGS	HEDGERS	HEIRDOM
HEALDED	HEARTIKIN	HEAVY	HEDGES	HEIRDOMS
HEALDING	HEARTIKINS	HEBDOMAD	HEDGIER	HEIRED
HEALDS	HEARTILY	HEBDOMADS	HEDGIEST	HEIRESS
HEALED	HEARTING	HEBE	HEDGING	HEIRESSES
HEALER	HEARTLAND	HEBEN	HEDGINGS	HEIRING
HEALERS	HEARTLANDS	HEBENON	HEDGY	HEIRLESS
HEALING	HEARTLESS	HEBENONS	HEDONIC	HEIRLOOM
HEALINGLY	HEARTLET	HEBENS	HEDONICS	HEIRLOOMS
HEALINGS	HEARTLETS	HEBES	HEDONISM	HEIRS
HEALS	HEARTLING	HEBETANT	HEDONISMS	HEIRSHIP
HEALSOME	HEARTLINGS	HEBETATE	HEDONIST	HEIRSHIPS
HEALTH	HEARTLY	HEBETATED	HEDONISTS	HEIST
HEALTHFUL	HEARTPEA	HEBETATES	HEDYPHANE	HEISTED
HEALTHIER	HEARTPEAS	HEBETATING	HEDYPHANES	HEISTER
HEALTHIEST	HEARTS	HEBETUDE	HEED	HEISTERS
HEALTHILY	HEARTSEED	HEBETUDES	HEEDED	HEISTING
HEALTHS	HEARTSEEDS	HEBONA	HEEDFUL	HEISTS
HEALTHY	HEARTSOME	HEBONAS	HEEDFULLY	HEJAB
HEAME	HEARTWOOD	HECATOMB	HEEDINESS	HEJABS
HEAP	HEARTWOODS	HECATOMBS	HEEDINESSES	HEJIRA
HEAPED	HEARTY	HECH	HEEDING	HEJIRAS
HEAPIER	HEAST	HECHT	HEEDLESS	HEJRA
HEAPIEST	HEASTE	HECHTING	HEEDS	HEJRAS
HEAPING	HEASTES	HECHTS	HEEDY	HELCOID
HEAPS	HEASTS	HECK	HEEHAW	HELD
HEAPSTEAD	HEAT	HECKLE	HEEHAWED	HELE
HEAPSTEADS	HEATED	HECKLED	HEEHAWING	HELED
HEAPY	HEATER	HECKLER	HEEHAWS	HELES
HEAR	HEATERS	HECKLERS	HEEL	HELIAC
HEARD	HEATH	HECKLES	HEELED	HELIACAL
HEARDS	HEATHBIRD	HECKLING	HEELER	HELIBUS
HEARE	HEATHBIRDS	HECKLINGS	HEELERS	HELIBUSES
HEARER	HEATHCOCK	HECKS	HEELING	HELICAL
HEARERS	HEATHCOCKS	HECOGENIN	HEELINGS	HELICALLY

HELICES
HELICOID
HELICTITE
HELICTITES
HELIDROME
HELIDROMES
HELIMAN
HELIMEN
HELING
HELIODOR
HELIODORS
HELIOLOGIES
HELIOLOGY
HELIOSES
HELIOSIS
HELIOSTAT
HELIOSTATS
HELIOTYPE
HELIOTYPES
HELIOTYPIES
HELIOTYPY
HELIOZOAN
HELIOZOANS
HELIOZOIC
HELIPAD
HELIPADS
HELIPILOT
HELIPILOTS
HELIPORT
HELIPORTS
HELISCOOP
HELISCOOPS
HELISTOP
HELISTOPS
HELIUM
HELIUMS
HELIX
HELIXES
HELL
HELLEBORE
HELLEBORES
HELLED
HELLENISE
HELLENISED
HELLENISES
HELLENISING
HELLENIZE
HELLENIZED
HELLENIZES
HELLENIZING
HELLER
HELLERS
HELLHOUND
HELLHOUNDS
HELLICAT
HELLICATS
HELLIER
HELLIERS
HELLING
HELLION
HELLIONS
HELLISH
HELLISHLY
HELLO
HELLOED
HELLOES
HELLOING
HELLOS
HELLOVA
HELLS

HELLUVA
HELLWARD
HELLWARDS
HELM
HELMED
HELMET
HELMETED
HELMETS
HELMING
HELMINTH
HELMINTHS
HELMLESS
HELMS
HELMSMAN
HELMSMEN
HELOT
HELOTAGE
HELOTAGES
HELOTISM
HELOTISMS
HELOTRIES
HELOTRY
HELOTS
HELP
HELPABLE
HELPED
HELPER
HELPERS
HELPFUL
HELPING
HELPINGS
HELPLESS
HELPLINE
HELPLINES
HELPMATE
HELPMATES
HELPMEET
HELPMEETS
HELPS
HELVE
HELVED
HELVES
HELVETIUM
HELVETIUMS
HELVING
HEM
HEMAL
HEMATITE
HEMATITES
HEME
HEMES
HEMIALGIA
HEMIALGIAS
HEMICYCLE
HEMICYCLES
HEMIHEDRIES
HEMIHEDRY
HEMINA
HEMINAS
HEMIOLA
HEMIOLAS
HEMIOLIA
HEMIOLIAS
HEMIOLIC
HEMIONE
HEMIONES
HEMIONUS
HEMIONUSES
HEMIOPIA
HEMIOPIAS

HEMIOPIC
HEMIOPSIA
HEMIOPSIAS
HEMISPACE
HEMISPACES
HEMISTICH
HEMISTICHS
HEMITROPE
HEMITROPES
HEMLOCK
HEMLOCKS
HEMMED
HEMMING
HEMP
HEMPBUSH
HEMPBUSHES
HEMPEN
HEMPIER
HEMPIES
HEMPIEST
HEMPS
HEMPY
HEMS
HEN
HENBANE
HENBANES
HENCE
HENCHMAN
HENCHMEN
HEND
HENDED
HENDIADYS
HENDIADYSES
HENDING
HENDS
HENEQUEN
HENEQUENS
HENEQUIN
HENEQUINS
HENGE
HENGES
HENIQUIN
HENIQUINS
HENNA
HENNAED
HENNAS
HENNED
HENNER
HENNERIES
HENNERS
HENNERY
HENNIER
HENNIES
HENNIEST
HENNIN
HENNING
HENNINS
HENNY
HENOTIC
HENPECK
HENPECKED
HENPECKING
HENPECKS
HENRIES
HENRY
HENRYS
HENS
HENT
HENTING
HENTS

HEP
HEPAR
HEPARIN
HEPARINS
HEPARS
HEPATIC
HEPATICAL
HEPATICS
HEPATISE
HEPATISED
HEPATISES
HEPATISING
HEPATITE
HEPATITES
HEPATITIS
HEPATITISES
HEPATIZE
HEPATIZED
HEPATIZES
HEPATIZING
HEPPER
HEPPEST
HEPS
HEPSTER
HEPSTERS
HEPT
HEPTAD
HEPTADS
HEPTAGLOT
HEPTAGLOTS
HEPTAGON
HEPTAGONS
HEPTANE
HEPTANES
HEPTAPODIES
HEPTAPODY
HEPTARCH
HEPTARCHIES
HEPTARCHS
HEPTARCHY
HER
HERALD
HERALDED
HERALDIC
HERALDING
HERALDRIES
HERALDRY
HERALDS
HERB
HERBAGE
HERBAGED
HERBAGES
HERBAL
HERBALIST
HERBALISTS
HERBALS
HERBAR
HERBARIA
HERBARIAN
HERBARIANS
HERBARIES
HERBARIUM
HERBARIUMS
HERBARS
HERBARY
HERBELET
HERBELETS
HERBICIDE
HERBICIDES
HERBIER

HERBIEST
HERBIST
HERBISTS
HERBIVORA
HERBIVORE
HERBIVORES
HERBIVORIES
HERBIVORY
HERBLESS
HERBLET
HERBLETS
HERBORISE
HERBORISED
HERBORISES
HERBORISING
HERBORIST
HERBORISTS
HERBORIZE
HERBORIZED
HERBORIZES
HERBORIZING
HERBOSE
HERBOUS
HERBS
HERBY
HERCOGAMIES
HERCOGAMY
HERCULEAN
HERCYNITE
HERCYNITES
HERD
HERDBOY
HERDBOYS
HERDED
HERDEN
HERDENS
HERDESS
HERDESSES
HERDIC
HERDICS
HERDING
HERDMAN
HERDMEN
HERDS
HERDSMAN
HERDSMEN
HERDWICK
HERDWICKS
HERE
HEREABOUT
HEREAFTER
HEREAFTERS
HEREAT
HEREAWAY
HEREBY
HEREDITIES
HEREDITY
HEREFROM
HEREIN
HERENESS
HERENESSES
HEREOF
HEREON
HERESIES
HERESY
HERETIC
HERETICAL
HERETICS
HERETO
HEREUNDER

HEREUNTO	HERON	HETAERAE	HEXAGON	HICCOUGH
HEREUPON	HERONRIES	HETAERAS	HEXAGONAL	HICCOUGHED
HEREWITH	HERONRY	HETAERIA	HEXAGONS	HICCOUGHING
HERIED	HERONS	HETAERIAS	HEXAGRAM	HICCOUGHS
HERIES	HERONSEW	HETAERISM	HEXAGRAMS	HICCUP
HERIOT	HERONSEWS	HETAERISMS	HEXAHEDRA	HICCUPED
HERIOTS	HERONSHAW	HETAERIST	HEXAMETER	HICCUPING
HÉRISSÉ	HERONSHAWS	HETAERISTS	HEXAMETERS	HICCUPS
HERISSON	HEROON	HETAIRA	HEXANE	HICCUPY
HERISSONS	HEROONS	HETAIRAI	HEXANES	HICK
HERITABLE	HEROSHIP	HETAIRIA	HEXAPLA	HICKEY
HERITABLY	HEROSHIPS	HETAIRIAS	HEXAPLAR	HICKEYS
HERITAGE	HERPES	HETAIRISM	HEXAPLAS	HICKORIES
HERITAGES	HERPETIC	HETAIRISMS	HEXAPLOID	HICKORY
HERITOR	HERPETOID	HETAIRIST	HEXAPLOIDS	HICKS
HERITORS	HERRIED	HETAIRISTS	HEXAPOD	HICKWALL
HERITRESS	HERRIES	HETE	HEXAPODIES	HICKWALLS
HERITRESSES	HERRIMENT	HETERODOX	HEXAPODS	HID
HERITRICES	HERRIMENTS	HETERONYM	HEXAPODY	HIDAGE
HERITRIX	HERRING	HETERONYMS	HEXARCH	HIDAGES
HERITRIXES	HERRINGER	HETEROPOD	HEXASTICH	HIDALGA
HERKOGAMIES	HERRINGERS	HETEROPODS	HEXASTICHS	HIDALGAS
HERKOGAMY	HERRINGS	HETEROSES	HEXASTYLE	HIDALGO
HERL	HERRY	HETEROSIS	HEXASTYLES	HIDALGOS
HERLING	HERRYING	HETEROTIC	HEXED	HIDDEN
HERLINGS	HERRYMENT	HETES	HEXENE	HIDDENITE
HERLS	HERRYMENTS	HETHER	HEXENES	HIDDENITES
HERM	HERS	HETING	HEXES	HIDDENLY
HERMA	HERSALL	HETMAN	HEXING	HIDDER
HERMAE	HERSALLS	HETMANATE	HEXINGS	HIDDERS
HERMANDAD	HERSE	HETMANATES	HEXOSE	HIDE
HERMANDADS	HERSED	HETMANS	HEXOSES	HIDED
HERMETIC	HERSELF	HETS	HEXPLARIC	HIDEOSITIES
HERMETICS	HERSES	HETTED	HEXYLENE	HIDEOSITY
HERMIT	HERSHIP	HETTING	HEXYLENES	HIDEOUS
HERMITAGE	HERSHIPS	HEUCH	HEY	HIDEOUSLY
HERMITAGES	HERTZ	HEUCHS	HEYDAY	HIDEOUT
HERMITESS	HERTZES	HEUGH	HEYDAYS	HIDEOUTS
HERMITESSES	HERY	HEUGHS	HEYDUCK	HIDES
HERMITS	HERYE	HEUREKA	HEYDUCKS	HIDING
HERMS	HERYED	HEUREKAS	HEYED	HIDINGS
HERN	HERYES	HEURETIC	HEYING	HIDLING
HERNIA	HERYING	HEURETICS	HEYS	HIDLINGS
HERNIAL	HES	HEURISM	HI	HIDLINS
HERNIAS	HESITANCE	HEURISMS	HIANT	HIDROSES
HERNIATED	HESITANCES	HEURISTIC	HIATUS	HIDROSIS
HERNS	HESITANCIES	HEURISTICS	HIATUSES	HIDROTIC
HERNSHAW	HESITANCY	HEVEA	HIBACHI	HIDROTICS
HERNSHAWS	HESITANT	HEVEAS	HIBACHIS	HIE
HERO	HESITATE	HEW	HIBAKUSHA	HIED
HEROE	HESITATED	HEWED	HIBERNAL	HIEING
HEROES	HESITATES	HEWEDS	HIBERNATE	HIELAMAN
HEROIC	HESITATING	HEWER	HIBERNATED	HIELAMANS
HEROICAL	HESITATOR	HEWERS	HIBERNATES	HIEMAL
HEROICLY	HESITATORS	HEWGH	HIBERNATING	HIEMS
HEROICS	HESP	HEWING	HIBERNISE	HIERACIUM
HEROIN	HESPED	HEWINGS	HIBERNISED	HIERACIUMS
HEROINE	HESPERID	HEWN	HIBERNISES	HIERARCH
HEROINES	HESPERIDS	HEWS	HIBERNISING	HIERARCHIES
HEROINS	HESPING	HEX	HIBERNIZE	HIERARCHS
HEROISE	HESPS	HEXACHORD	HIBERNIZED	HIERARCHY
HEROISED	HESSIAN	HEXACHORDS	HIBERNIZES	HIERATIC
HEROISES	HESSIANS	HEXACT	HIBERNIZING	HIERATICA
HEROISING	HESSONITE	HEXACTS	HIBISCUS	HIERATICAS
HEROISM	HESSONITES	HEXAD	HIBISCUSES	HIEROCRAT
HEROISMS	HEST	HEXADIC	HIC	HIEROCRATS
HEROIZE	HESTERNAL	HEXADS	HICATEE	HIERODULE
HEROIZED	HESTS	HEXAFOIL	HICATEES	HIERODULES
HEROIZES	HET	HEXAFOILS	HICCATEE	HIEROGRAM
HEROIZING	HETAERA	HEXAGLOT	HICCATEES	HIEROGRAMS

HIEROLOGIES
HIEROLOGY
HIERURGIES
HIERURGY
HIES
HIGGLE
HIGGLED
HIGGLER
HIGGLERS
HIGGLES
HIGGLING
HIGGLINGS
HIGH
HIGHBALL
HIGHBALLED
HIGHBALLING
HIGHBALLS
HIGHBOY
HIGHBOYS
HIGHBROW
HIGHBROWS
HIGHED
HIGHER
HIGHERED
HIGHERING
HIGHERS
HIGHEST
HIGHING
HIGHISH
HIGHJACK
HIGHJACKED
HIGHJACKING
HIGHJACKS
HIGHLAND
HIGHLANDS
HIGHLIGHT
HIGHLIGHTED
HIGHLIGHTING
HIGHLIGHTS
HIGHLY
HIGHMAN
HIGHMEN
HIGHMOST
HIGHNESS
HIGHNESSES
HIGHROAD
HIGHROADS
HIGHS
HIGHT
HIGHTAIL
HIGHTAILED
HIGHTAILING
HIGHTAILS
HIGHTH
HIGHTHS
HIGHTING
HIGHTS
HIGHWAY
HIGHWAYS
HIJACK
HIJACKED
HIJACKER
HIJACKERS
HIJACKING
HIJACKS
HIJINKS
HIJRA
HIJRAH
HIJRAHS
HIJRAS

HIKE
HIKED
HIKER
HIKERS
HIKES
HIKING
HILA
HILAR
HILARIOUS
HILARITIES
HILARITY
HILCH
HILCHED
HILCHES
HILCHING
HILD
HILDING
HILDINGS
HILI
HILL
HILLED
HILLFOLK
HILLFOLKS
HILLIER
HILLIEST
HILLINESS
HILLINESSES
HILLING
HILLMEN
HILLO
HILLOCK
HILLOCKS
HILLOCKY
HILLOED
HILLOING
HILLOS
HILLS
HILLSIDE
HILLSIDES
HILLTOP
HILLTOPS
HILLY
HILT
HILTED
HILTING
HILTS
HILUM
HILUS
HIM
HIMATIA
HIMATION
HIMATIONS
HIMSEEMED
HIMSEEMS
HIMSELF
HIN
HIND
HINDBERRIES
HINDBERRY
HINDER
HINDERED
HINDERER
HINDERERS
HINDERING
HINDERS
HINDFEET
HINDFOOT
HINDHEAD
HINDHEADS
HINDLEG

HINDLEGS
HINDMOST
HINDRANCE
HINDRANCES
HINDS
HINDSIGHT
HINDSIGHTS
HINDWARD
HING
HINGE
HINGED
HINGES
HINGING
HINGS
HINNIED
HINNIES
HINNY
HINNYING
HINS
HINT
HINTED
HINTING
HINTINGLY
HINTS
HIP
HIPPARCH
HIPPARCHS
HIPPED
HIPPER
HIPPEST
HIPPIATRIES
HIPPIATRY
HIPPIC
HIPPIE
HIPPIEDOM
HIPPIEDOMS
HIPPIER
HIPPIES
HIPPIEST
HIPPING
HIPPINGS
HIPPISH
HIPPO
HIPPOCRAS
HIPPOCRASES
HIPPODAME
HIPPODAMES
HIPPOLOGIES
HIPPOLOGY
HIPPOS
HIPPURIC
HIPPURITE
HIPPURITES
HIPPUS
HIPPUSES
HIPPY
HIPPYDOM
HIPPYDOMS
HIPS
HIPSTER
HIPSTERS
HIPT
HIRABLE
HIRCINE
HIRCOSITIES
HIRCOSITY
HIRE
HIREABLE
HIRED
HIRELING

HIRELINGS
HIRER
HIRERS
HIRES
HIRING
HIRINGS
HIRLING
HIRLINGS
HIRPLE
HIRPLED
HIRPLES
HIRPLING
HIRRIENT
HIRRIENTS
HIRSEL
HIRSELLED
HIRSELLING
HIRSELS
HIRSLE
HIRSLED
HIRSLES
HIRSLING
HIRSTIE
HIRSUTE
HIRSUTER
HIRSUTEST
HIRUDIN
HIRUDINS
HIRUNDINE
HIS
HISH
HISHED
HISHES
HISHING
HISN
HISPID
HISPIDITIES
HISPIDITY
HISS
HISSED
HISSES
HISSING
HISSINGLY
HISSINGS
HIST
HISTAMINE
HISTAMINES
HISTED
HISTIDINE
HISTIDINES
HISTIE
HISTING
HISTIOID
HISTOGEN
HISTOGENIES
HISTOGENS
HISTOGENY
HISTOGRAM
HISTOGRAMS
HISTOID
HISTOLOGIES
HISTOLOGY
HISTONE
HISTONES
HISTORIAN
HISTORIANS
HISTORIC
HISTORIED
HISTORIES
HISTORIFIED

HISTORIFIES
HISTORIFY
HISTORIFYING
HISTORISM
HISTORISMS
HISTORY
HISTORYING
HISTRIO
HISTRION
HISTRIONS
HISTRIOS
HISTS
HIT
HITCH
HITCHED
HITCHER
HITCHERS
HITCHES
HITCHIER
HITCHIEST
HITCHILY
HITCHING
HITCHY
HITHE
HITHER
HITHERED
HITHERING
HITHERS
HITHERTO
HITHES
HITS
HITTER
HITTERS
HITTING
HIVE
HIVED
HIVELESS
HIVELIKE
HIVER
HIVERS
HIVES
HIVEWARD
HIVEWARDS
HIVING
HIYA
HIZEN
HIZENS
HIZZ
HIZZED
HIZZES
HIZZING
HO
HOA
HOACTZIN
HOACTZINS
HOAED
HOAING
HOAR
HOARD
HOARDED
HOARDER
HOARDERS
HOARDING
HOARDINGS
HOARDS
HOARED
HOARHEAD
HOARHEADS
HOARHOUND
HOARHOUNDS

HOARIER	HOBNOBBING	HOGGED	HOKIER	HOLLOWER
HOARIEST	HOBNOBBINGS	HOGGER	HOKIEST	HOLLOWEST
HOARILY	HOBNOBBY	HOGGEREL	HOKING	HOLLOWING
HOARINESS	HOBNOBS	HOGGERELS	HOKKU	HOLLOWLY
HOARINESSES	HOBO	HOGGERIES	HOKUM	HOLLOWS
HOARING	HOBODOM	HOGGERS	HOKUMS	HOLLY
HOARS	HOBODOMS	HOGGERY	HOLD	HOLLYHOCK
HOARSE	HOBOED	HOGGET	HOLDBACK	HOLLYHOCKS
HOARSELY	HOBOES	HOGGETS	HOLDBACKS	HOLM
HOARSEN	HOBOING	HOGGIN	HOLDEN	HOLMIA
HOARSENED	HOBOISM	HOGGING	HOLDER	HOLMIAS
HOARSENING	HOBOISMS	HOGGINGS	HOLDERBAT	HOLMIC
HOARSENS	HOBS	HOGGINS	HOLDERBATS	HOLMIUM
HOARSER	HOC	HOGGISH	HOLDERS	HOLMIUMS
HOARSEST	HOCK	HOGGISHLY	HOLDFAST	HOLMS
HOARY	HOCKED	HOGGS	HOLDFASTS	HOLOCAUST
HOAS	HOCKER	HOGH	HOLDING	HOLOCAUSTS
HOAST	HOCKERS	HOGHOOD	HOLDINGS	HOLOCRINE
HOASTED	HOCKEY	HOGHOODS	HOLDOVER	HOLOGRAM
HOASTING	HOCKEYS	HOGHS	HOLDOVERS	HOLOGRAMS
HOASTMAN	HOCKING	HOGS	HOLDS	HOLOGRAPH
HOASTMEN	HOCKS	HOGSHEAD	HOLE	HOLOGRAPHED
HOASTS	HOCUS	HOGSHEADS	HOLED	HOLOGRAPHING
HOATZIN	HOCUSED	HOGTIE	HOLES	HOLOGRAPHS
HOATZINS	HOCUSES	HOGTIED	HOLESOM	HOLOPHOTE
HOAX	HOCUSING	HOGTIES	HOLESOME	HOLOPHOTES
HOAXED	HOCUSSED	HOGTYING	HOLEY	HOLOPHYTE
HOAXER	HOCUSSES	HOGWARD	HOLIBUT	HOLOPHYTES
HOAXERS	HOCUSSING	HOGWARDS	HOLIBUTS	HOLOPTIC
HOAXES	HOD	HOGWASH	HOLIDAY	HOLOTYPE
HOAXING	HODDED	HOGWASHES	HOLIDAYED	HOLOTYPES
HOB	HODDEN	HOGWEED	HOLIDAYING	HOLOTYPIC
HOBBIES	HODDENS	HOGWEEDS	HOLIDAYS	HOLOZOIC
HOBBISH	HODDING	HOH	HOLIER	HOLP
HOBBIT	HODDLE	HOHED	HOLIES	HOLPEN
HOBBITRIES	HODDLED	HOHING	HOLIEST	HOLS
HOBBITRY	HODDLES	HOHS	HOLILY	HOLSTER
HOBBITS	HODDLING	HOI	HOLINESS	HOLSTERED
HOBBLE	HODIERNAL	HOICK	HOLINESSES	HOLSTERS
HOBBLED	HODJA	HOICKED	HOLING	HOLT
HOBBLER	HODJAS	HOICKING	HOLINGS	HOLTS
HOBBLERS	HODMAN	HOICKS	HOLISM	HOLY
HOBBLES	HODMANDOD	HOICKSED	HOLISMS	HOLYDAM
HOBBLING	HODMANDODS	HOICKSES	HOLIST	HOLYDAME
HOBBLINGS	HODMEN	HOICKSING	HOLISTIC	HOLYDAMES
HOBBY	HODOGRAPH	HOIDEN	HOLISTS	HOLYDAMS
HOBBYISM	HODOGRAPHS	HOIDENS	HOLLA	HOLYSTONE
HOBBYISMS	HODOMETER	HOIK	HOLLAND	HOLYSTONED
HOBBYIST	HODOMETERS	HOIKED	HOLLANDS	HOLYSTONES
HOBBYISTS	HODOMETRIES	HOIKING	HOLLAS	HOLYSTONING
HOBBYLESS	HODOMETRY	HOIKS	HOLLER	HOMAGE
HOBDAY	HODOSCOPE	HOING	HOLLERED	HOMAGED
HOBDAYED	HODOSCOPES	HOISE	HOLLERING	HOMAGER
HOBDAYING	HODS	HOISED	HOLLERS	HOMAGERS
HOBDAYS	HOE	HOISES	HOLLIDAM	HOMAGES
HOBGOBLIN	HOED	HOISING	HOLLIDAMS	HOMAGING
HOBGOBLINS	HOEDOWN	HOIST	HOLLIES	HOMALOID
HOBJOB	HOEDOWNS	HOISTED	HOLLO	HOMALOIDS
HOBJOBBED	HOEING	HOISTER	HOLLOA	HOMBRE
HOBJOBBER	HOER	HOISTERS	HOLLOAED	HOMBRES
HOBJOBBERS	HOERS	HOISTING	HOLLOAING	HOME
HOBJOBBING	HOES	HOISTMAN	HOLLOAS	HOMEBOUND
HOBJOBBINGS	HOG	HOISTMEN	HOLLOED	HOMECRAFT
HOBJOBS	HOGAN	HOISTS	HOLLOES	HOMECRAFTS
HOBNAIL	HOGANS	HOISTWAY	HOLLOING	HOMED
HOBNAILED	HOGBACK	HOISTWAYS	HOLLOS	HOMEFELT
HOBNAILING	HOGBACKS	HOKE	HOLLOW	HOMELAND
HOBNAILS	HOGEN	HOKED	HOLLOWARE	HOMELANDS
HOBNOB	HOGENS	HOKES	HOLLOWARES	HOMELESS
HOBNOBBED	HOGG	HOKEY	HOLLOWED	HOMELIER

HOMELIEST	HOMOLOGUES	HONEYPOTS	HOOFROT	HOOVED
HOMELIKE	HOMOLOGY	HONEYS	HOOFROTS	HOOVEN
HOMELILY	HOMOMORPH	HONEYSEED	HOOFS	HOOVER
HOMELY	HOMOMORPHS	HONEYSEEDS	HOOK	HOOVERED
HOMELYN	HOMONYM	HONG	HOOKA	HOOVERING
HOMELYNS	HOMONYMIC	HONGING	HOOKAH	HOOVERS
HOMEMAKER	HOMONYMIES	HONGS	HOOKAHS	HOOVES
HOMEMAKERS	HOMONYMS	HONIED	HOOKAS	HOOVING
HOMEOMERIES	HOMONYMY	HONING	HOOKED	HOP
HOMEOMERY	HOMOPHILE	HONK	HOOKER	HOPBIND
HOMEOPATH	HOMOPHILES	HONKED	HOOKERS	HOPBINDS
HOMEOPATHS	HOMOPHOBE	HONKER	HOOKEY	HOPBINE
HOMEOSES	HOMOPHOBES	HONKERS	HOOKEYS	HOPBINES
HOMEOSIS	HOMOPHONE	HONKIE	HOOKIER	HOPDOG
HOMER	HOMOPHONES	HONKIES	HOOKIES	HOPDOGS
HOMERS	HOMOPHONIES	HONKING	HOOKIEST	HOPE
HOMES	HOMOPHONY	HONKS	HOOKING	HOPED
HOMESICK	HOMOPHYLIES	HONKY	HOOKS	HOPEFUL
HOMESPUN	HOMOPHYLY	HONOR	HOOKY	HOPEFULLY
HOMESPUNS	HOMOPLASIES	HONORAND	HOOLACHAN	HOPEFULS
HOMESTALL	HOMOPLASY	HONORANDS	HOOLACHANS	HOPELESS
HOMESTALLS	HOMOPOLAR	HONORARIA	HOOLEY	HOPER
HOMESTEAD	HOMOS	HONORARIES	HOOLEYS	HOPERS
HOMESTEADS	HOMOTAXES	HONORARY	HOOLICAN	HOPES
HOMEWARD	HOMOTAXIC	HONORED	HOOLICANS	HOPING
HOMEWARDS	HOMOTAXIS	HONORIFIC	HOOLIER	HOPINGLY
HOMEWORK	HOMOTONIC	HONORIFICS	HOOLIEST	HOPLITE
HOMEWORKS	HOMOTONIES	HONORING	HOOLIGAN	HOPLITES
HOMEY	HOMOTONY	HONORS	HOOLIGANS	HOPLOLOGIES
HOMICIDAL	HOMOTYPAL	HONOUR	HOOLOCK	HOPLOLOGY
HOMICIDE	HOMOTYPE	HONOURED	HOOLOCKS	HOPPED
HOMICIDES	HOMOTYPES	HONOURER	HOOLY	HOPPER
HOMIER	HOMOTYPIC	HONOURERS	HOOP	HOPPERS
HOMIEST	HOMOTYPIES	HONOURING	HOOPED	HOPPIER
HOMILETIC	HOMOTYPY	HONOURS	HOOPER	HOPPIEST
HOMILETICS	HOMOUSIAN	HONS	HOOPERS	HOPPING
HOMILIES	HOMOUSIANS	HONYSEED	HOOPING	HOPPINGS
HOMILIST	HOMUNCLE	HONYSEEDS	HOOPOE	HOPPLE
HOMILISTS	HOMUNCLES	HOO	HOOPOES	HOPPLED
HOMILY	HOMUNCULE	HOOCH	HOOPS	HOPPLES
HOMING	HOMUNCULES	HOOCHES	HOORAH	HOPPLING
HOMINGS	HOMUNCULI	HOOD	HOORAHED	HOPPY
HOMINID	HOMY	HOODED	HOORAHING	HOPS
HOMINIDS	HON	HOODING	HOORAHS	HOPSACK
HOMINIES	HOND	HOODLESS	HOORAY	HOPSACKS
HOMINOID	HONDS	HOODLUM	HOORAYED	HORAL
HOMINOIDS	HONE	HOODLUMS	HOORAYING	HORARY
HOMINY	HONED	HOODMAN	HOORAYS	HORDE
HOMME	HONES	HOODMEN	HOORD	HORDED
HOMMES	HONEST	HOODOO	HOORDS	HORDEIN
HOMMOCK	HONESTER	HOODOOED	HOOROO	HORDEINS
HOMMOCKS	HONESTEST	HOODOOING	HOOSEGOW	HORDEOLUM
HOMO	HONESTIES	HOODOOS	HOOSEGOWS	HORDEOLUMS
HOMODONT	HONESTLY	HOODS	HOOSGOW	HORDES
HOMODYNE	HONESTY	HOODWINK	HOOSGOWS	HORDING
HOMOEOSES	HONEY	HOODWINKED	HOOSH	HORDOCK
HOMOEOSIS	HONEYBUN	HOODWINKING	HOOSHED	HORDOCKS
HOMOGAMIC	HONEYBUNS	HOODWINKS	HOOSHES	HORE
HOMOGAMIES	HONEYCOMB	HOOEY	HOOSHING	HOREHOUND
HOMOGAMY	HONEYCOMBED	HOOEYS	HOOT	HOREHOUNDS
HOMOGENIES	HONEYCOMBING	HOOF	HOOTCH	HORIZON
HOMOGENY	HONEYCOMBS	HOOFBEAT	HOOTCHES	HORIZONS
HOMOGRAFT	HONEYED	HOOFBEATS	HOOTED	HORKEY
HOMOGRAFTS	HONEYING	HOOFED	HOOTER	HORKEYS
HOMOGRAPH	HONEYLESS	HOOFER	HOOTERS	HORME
HOMOGRAPHS	HONEYMOON	HOOFERS	HOOTING	HORMES
HOMOLOG	HONEYMOONED	HOOFING	HOOTNANNIES	HORMONAL
HOMOLOGIES	HONEYMOONING	HOOFLESS	HOOTNANNY	HORMONE
HOMOLOGS	HONEYMOONS	HOOFPRINT	HOOTS	HORMONES
HOMOLOGUE	HONEYPOT	HOOFPRINTS	HOOVE	HORMONIC

HORN	HORRID	HOSEPIPES	HOTHOUSE	HOUSETOPS
HORNBEAK	HORRIDER	HOSES	HOTHOUSES	HOUSEWIFE
HORNBEAKS	HORRIDEST	HOSIER	HOTLY	HOUSEWIVES
HORNBEAM	HORRIDLY	HOSIERIES	HOTNESS	HOUSEWORK
HORNBEAMS	HORRIFIC	HOSIERS	HOTNESSES	HOUSEWORKS
HORNBILL	HORRIFIED	HOSIERY	HOTPOT	HOUSING
HORNBILLS	HORRIFIES	HOSING	HOTPOTS	HOUSINGS
HORNBOOK	HORRIFY	HOSPICE	HOTS	HOUSLING
HORNBOOKS	HORRIFYING	HOSPICES	HOTSHOT	HOUT
HORNBUG	HORROR	HOSPITAGE	HOTSHOTS	HOUTS
HORNBUGS	HORRORS	HOSPITAGES	HOTTED	HOVE
HORNED	HORS	HOSPITAL	HOTTENTOT	HOVED
HORNER	HORSE	HOSPITALE	HOTTENTOTS	HOVEL
HORNERS	HORSEBACK	HOSPITALES	HOTTER	HOVELED
HORNET	HORSEBACKS	HOSPITALS	HOTTERED	HOVELLED
HORNETS	HORSECAR	HOSPITIA	HOTTERING	HOVELLER
HORNFELS	HORSECARS	HOSPITIUM	HOTTERS	HOVELLERS
HORNFELSES	HORSED	HOSPODAR	HOTTEST	HOVELLING
HORNFUL	HORSEFLIES	HOSPODARS	HOTTIE	HOVELS
HORNFULS	HORSEFLY	HOSS	HOTTIES	HOVEN
HORNGELD	HORSEHAIR	HOSSES	HOTTING	HOVER
HORNGELDS	HORSEHAIRS	HOST	HOTTISH	HOVERED
HORNIER	HORSEHIDE	HOSTA	HOUDAH	HOVERING
HORNIEST	HORSEHIDES	HOSTAGE	HOUDAHS	HOVERPORT
HORNINESS	HORSELESS	HOSTAGES	HOUDAN	HOVERPORTS
HORNINESSES	HORSEMAN	HOSTAS	HOUDANS	HOVERS
HORNING	HORSEMEAT	HOSTED	HOUF	HOVES
HORNINGS	HORSEMEATS	HOSTEL	HOUFED	HOVING
HORNISH	HORSEMEN	HOSTELER	HOUFF	HOW
HORNIST	HORSEMINT	HOSTELERS	HOUFFED	HOWBE
HORNISTS	HORSEMINTS	HOSTELLER	HOUFFING	HOWBEIT
HORNITO	HORSEPLAY	HOSTELLERS	HOUFFS	HOWDAH
HORNITOS	HORSEPLAYS	HOSTELRIES	HOUFING	HOWDAHS
HORNLESS	HORSEPOND	HOSTELRY	HOUFS	HOWDIE
HORNLET	HORSEPONDS	HOSTELS	HOUGH	HOWDIES
HORNLETS	HORSES	HOSTESS	HOUGHED	HOWDY
HORNPIPE	HORSESHOE	HOSTESSED	HOUGHING	HOWE
HORNPIPES	HORSESHOES	HOSTESSES	HOUGHS	HOWES
HORNS	HORSETAIL	HOSTESSING	HOUND	HOWEVER
HORNSTONE	HORSETAILS	HOSTILE	HOUNDED	HOWF
HORNSTONES	HORSEWAY	HOSTILELY	HOUNDING	HOWFED
HORNTAIL	HORSEWAYS	HOSTILITIES	HOUNDS	HOWFF
HORNTAILS	HORSEWHIP	HOSTILITY	HOUR	HOWFFED
HORNWORK	HORSEWHIPPED	HOSTING	HOURI	HOWFFING
HORNWORKS	HORSEWHIPPING	HOSTINGS	HOURIS	HOWFFS
HORNWORM	HORSEWHIPS	HOSTLER	HOURLONG	HOWFING
HORNWORMS	HORSIER	HOSTLERS	HOURLY	HOWFS
HORNWORT	HORSIEST	HOSTLESSE	HOURPLATE	HOWITZER
HORNWORTS	HORSINESS	HOSTRIES	HOURPLATES	HOWITZERS
HORNWRACK	HORSINESSES	HOSTRY	HOURS	HOWK
HORNWRACKS	HORSING	HOSTS	HOUSE	HOWKED
HORNY	HORSINGS	HOT	HOUSEBOY	HOWKER
HORNYHEAD	HORSON	HOTBED	HOUSEBOYS	HOWKERS
HORNYHEADS	HORSONS	HOTBEDS	HOUSED	HOWKING
HOROLOGE	HORST	HOTCH	HOUSEFUL	HOWKS
HOROLOGER	HORSTS	HOTCHED	HOUSEFULS	HOWL
HOROLOGERS	HORSY	HOTCHES	HOUSEHOLD	HOWLED
HOROLOGES	HORTATION	HOTCHING	HOUSEHOLDS	HOWLER
HOROLOGIC	HORTATIONS	HOTCHPOT	HOUSEL	HOWLERS
HOROLOGIES	HORTATIVE	HOTCHPOTS	HOUSELESS	HOWLET
HOROLOGY	HORTATORY	HOTE	HOUSELLED	HOWLETS
HOROMETRIES	HOS	HOTEL	HOUSELLING	HOWLING
HOROMETRY	HOSANNA	HOTELIER	HOUSELLINGS	HOWLINGS
HOROSCOPE	HOSANNAS	HOTELIERS	HOUSELS	HOWLS
HOROSCOPES	HOSE	HOTELS	HOUSEMAID	HOWRE
HOROSCOPIES	HOSED	HOTEN	HOUSEMAIDS	HOWRES
HOROSCOPY	HOSEMAN	HOTFOOT	HOUSEMAN	HOWS
HORRENT	HOSEMEN	HOTHEAD	HOUSEMEN	HOWSO
HORRIBLE	HOSEN	HOTHEADED	HOUSES	HOWSOEVER
HORRIBLY	HOSEPIPE	HOTHEADS	HOUSETOP	HOWTOWDIE

HOWTOWDIES	HUGELY	HUMAS	HUMILIATED	HUMUS
HOWZAT	HUGENESS	HUMBLE	HUMILIATES	HUMUSES
HOX	HUGENESSES	HUMBLED	HUMILIATING	HUMUSY
HOXED	HUGEOUS	HUMBLER	HUMILITIES	HUNCH
HOXES	HUGEOUSLY	HUMBLES	HUMILITY	HUNCHBACK
HOXING	HUGER	HUMBLESSE	HUMITE	HUNCHBACKS
HOY	HUGEST	HUMBLESSES	HUMITES	HUNCHED
HOYA	HUGGABLE	HUMBLEST	HUMLIE	HUNCHES
HOYAS	HUGGED	HUMBLING	HUMLIES	HUNCHING
HOYDEN	HUGGING	HUMBLINGS	HUMMABLE	HUNDRED
HOYDENISH	HUGS	HUMBLY	HUMMAUM	HUNDREDER
HOYDENISM	HUGY	HUMBUG	HUMMAUMS	HUNDREDERS
HOYDENISMS	HUH	HUMBUGGED	HUMMED	HUNDREDOR
HOYDENS	HUIA	HUMBUGGER	HUMMEL	HUNDREDORS
HOYED	HUIAS	HUMBUGGERS	HUMMELLED	HUNDREDS
HOYING	HUISSIER	HUMBUGGING	HUMMELLER	HUNDREDTH
HOYS	HUISSIERS	HUMBUGS	HUMMELLERS	HUNDREDTHS
HUANACO	HUITAIN	HUMBUZZ	HUMMELLING	HUNG
HUANACOS	HUITAINS	HUMBUZZES	HUMMELS	HUNGER
HUB	HULA	HUMDINGER	HUMMER	HUNGERED
HUBBIES	HULAS	HUMDINGERS	HUMMERS	HUNGERFUL
HUBBUB	HULE	HUMDRUM	HUMMING	HUNGERING
HUBBUBOO	HULES	HUMDRUMS	HUMMINGS	HUNGERLY
HUBBUBOOS	HULK	HUMECT	HUMMOCK	HUNGERS
HUBBUBS	HULKIER	HUMECTANT	HUMMOCKED	HUNGRIER
HUBBY	HULKIEST	HUMECTANTS	HUMMOCKS	HUNGRIEST
HUBRIS	HULKING	HUMECTATE	HUMMOCKY	HUNGRILY
HUBRISES	HULKS	HUMECTATED	HUMMUM	HUNGRY
HUBRISTIC	HULKY	HUMECTATES	HUMMUMS	HUNK
HUBS	HULL	HUMECTATING	HUMMUS	HUNKER
HUCK	HULLED	HUMECTED	HUMMUSES	HUNKERED
HUCKABACK	HULLIER	HUMECTING	HUMOGEN	HUNKERING
HUCKABACKS	HULLIEST	HUMECTIVE	HUMOGENS	HUNKERS
HUCKLE	HULLING	HUMECTIVES	HUMOR	HUNKIER
HUCKLES	HULLO	HUMECTS	HUMORAL	HUNKIES
HUCKS	HULLOED	HUMEFIED	HUMORALLY	HUNKIEST
HUCKSTER	HULLOES	HUMEFIES	HUMORED	HUNKS
HUCKSTERED	HULLOING	HUMEFY	HUMORESK	HUNKSES
HUCKSTERIES	HULLOS	HUMEFYING	HUMORESKS	HUNKY
HUCKSTERING	HULLS	HUMERAL	HUMORING	HUNT
HUCKSTERS	HULLY	HUMERALS	HUMORIST	HUNTED
HUCKSTERY	HUM	HUMERI	HUMORISTS	HUNTER
HUDDEN	HUMA	HUMERUS	HUMOROUS	HUNTERS
HUDDLE	HUMAN	HUMF	HUMORS	HUNTING
HUDDLED	HUMANE	HUMFED	HUMOUR	HUNTINGS
HUDDLES	HUMANELY	HUMFING	HUMOURED	HUNTRESS
HUDDLING	HUMANER	HUMFS	HUMOURING	HUNTRESSES
HUDDUP	HUMANEST	HUMHUM	HUMOURS	HUNTS
HUE	HUMANISE	HUMHUMS	HUMOUS	HUNTSMAN
HUED	HUMANISED	HUMIC	HUMP	HUNTSMEN
HUELESS	HUMANISES	HUMID	HUMPBACK	HUP
HUER	HUMANISING	HUMIDER	HUMPBACKS	HUPPED
HUERS	HUMANISM	HUMIDEST	HUMPED	HUPPING
HUES	HUMANISMS	HUMIDIFIED	HUMPEN	HUPS
HUFF	HUMANIST	HUMIDIFIES	HUMPENS	HURCHEON
HUFFED	HUMANISTS	HUMIDIFY	HUMPH	HURCHEONS
HUFFIER	HUMANITIES	HUMIDIFYING	HUMPHED	HURDEN
HUFFIEST	HUMANITY	HUMIDITIES	HUMPHING	HURDENS
HUFFILY	HUMANIZE	HUMIDITY	HUMPHS	HURDIES
HUFFINESS	HUMANIZED	HUMIDLY	HUMPIER	HURDLE
HUFFINESSES	HUMANIZES	HUMIDNESS	HUMPIES	HURDLED
HUFFING	HUMANIZING	HUMIDNESSES	HUMPIEST	HURDLER
HUFFISH	HUMANKIND	HUMIDOR	HUMPING	HURDLERS
HUFFISHLY	HUMANLIKE	HUMIDORS	HUMPS	HURDLES
HUFFKIN	HUMANLY	HUMIFIED	HUMPTIES	HURDLING
HUFFKINS	HUMANNESS	HUMIFIES	HUMPTY	HURDLINGS
HUFFS	HUMANNESSES	HUMIFY	HUMPY	HURDS
HUFFY	HUMANOID	HUMIFYING	HUMS	HURL
HUG	HUMANOIDS	HUMILIANT	HUMSTRUM	HURLED
HUGE	HUMANS	HUMILIATE	HUMSTRUMS	HURLER

HURLERS	HUSKIER	HYALITES	HYDROLYSE	HYKE
HURLEY	HUSKIES	HYALOID	HYDROLYSED	HYKES
HURLEYS	HUSKIEST	HYALONEMA	HYDROLYSES	HYLDING
HURLIES	HUSKILY	HYALONEMAS	HYDROLYSING	HYLDINGS
HURLING	HUSKINESS	HYBRID	HYDROLYTE	HYLE
HURLINGS	HUSKINESSES	HYBRIDISE	HYDROLYTES	HYLEG
HURLS	HUSKING	HYBRIDISED	HYDROLYZE	HYLEGS
HURLY	HUSKINGS	HYBRIDISES	HYDROLYZED	HYLES
HURRA	HUSKS	HYBRIDISING	HYDROLYZES	HYLIC
HURRAED	HUSKY	HYBRIDISM	HYDROLYZING	HYLICISM
HURRAH	HUSO	HYBRIDISMS	HYDROMEL	HYLICISMS
HURRAHED	HUSOS	HYBRIDITIES	HYDROMELS	HYLICIST
HURRAHING	HUSS	HYBRIDITY	HYDRONAUT	HYLICISTS
HURRAHS	HUSSAR	HYBRIDIZE	HYDRONAUTS	HYLISM
HURRAING	HUSSARS	HYBRIDIZED	HYDROPIC	HYLISMS
HURRAS	HUSSES	HYBRIDIZES	HYDROPSIES	HYLIST
HURRAY	HUSSIES	HYBRIDIZING	HYDROPSY	HYLISTS
HURRAYED	HUSSIF	HYBRIDOMA	HYDROPTIC	HYLOBATE
HURRAYING	HUSSIFS	HYBRIDOMAS	HYDROPULT	HYLOBATES
HURRAYS	HUSSY	HYBRIDOUS	HYDROPULTS	HYLOIST
HURRICANE	HUSTINGS	HYBRIDS	HYDROS	HYLOISTS
HURRICANES	HUSTLE	HYBRIS	HYDROSKI	HYLOPHYTE
HURRICANO	HUSTLED	HYBRISES	HYDROSKIS	HYLOPHYTES
HURRICANOES	HUSTLER	HYDATHODE	HYDROSOMA	HYLOZOISM
HURRIED	HUSTLERS	HYDATHODES	HYDROSOMATA	HYLOZOISMS
HURRIEDLY	HUSTLES	HYDATID	HYDROSOME	HYLOZOIST
HURRIES	HUSTLING	HYDATIDS	HYDROSOMES	HYLOZOISTS
HURRY	HUSTLINGS	HYDATOID	HYDROSTAT	HYMEN
HURRYING	HUSWIFE	HYDRA	HYDROSTATS	HYMENAEAL
HURRYINGS	HUSWIVES	HYDRAEMIA	HYDROUS	HYMENAEAN
HURST	HUT	HYDRAEMIAS	HYDROVANE	HYMENAL
HURSTS	HUTCH	HYDRANGEA	HYDROVANES	HYMENEAL
HURT	HUTCHED	HYDRANGEAS	HYDROXIDE	HYMENEALS
HURTER	HUTCHES	HYDRANT	HYDROXIDES	HYMENEAN
HURTERS	HUTCHING	HYDRANTH	HYDROXY	HYMENIA
HURTFUL	HUTIA	HYDRANTHS	HYDROXYL	HYMENIAL
HURTFULLY	HUTIAS	HYDRANTS	HYDROXYLS	HYMENIUM
HURTING	HUTMENT	HYDRAS	HYDROZOA	HYMENIUMS
HURTLE	HUTMENTS	HYDRATE	HYDROZOAN	HYMENS
HURTLED	HUTS	HYDRATED	HYDROZOANS	HYMN
HURTLES	HUTTED	HYDRATES	HYDROZOON	HYMNAL
HURTLESS	HUTTING	HYDRATING	HYDYNE	HYMNALS
HURTLING	HUTTINGS	HYDRATION	HYDYNES	HYMNARIES
HURTS	HUZOOR	HYDRATIONS	HYE	HYMNARY
HUSBAND	HUZOORS	HYDRAULIC	HYED	HYMNED
HUSBANDED	HUZZA	HYDRAULICKED	HYEING	HYMNIC
HUSBANDING	HUZZAED	HYDRAULICKING	HYEN	HYMNING
HUSBANDLY	HUZZAING	HYDRAULICS	HYENA	HYMNIST
HUSBANDRIES	HUZZAS	HYDRAZINE	HYENAS	HYMNISTS
HUSBANDRY	HUZZIES	HYDRAZINES	HYENS	HYMNODIES
HUSBANDS	HUZZY	HYDREMIA	HYES	HYMNODIST
HUSH	HWYL	HYDREMIAS	HYETAL	HYMNODISTS
HUSHABIED	HWYLS	HYDRIA	HYETOLOGIES	HYMNODY
HUSHABIES	HYACINE	HYDRIAE	HYETOLOGY	HYMNOLOGIES
HUSHABY	HYACINES	HYDRIAS	HYGIENE	HYMNOLOGY
HUSHABYING	HYACINTH	HYDRIC	HYGIENES	HYMNS
HUSHED	HYACINTHS	HYDRIDE	HYGIENIC	HYNDE
HUSHER	HYAENA	HYDRIDES	HYGIENICS	HYNDES
HUSHERED	HYAENAS	HYDRIODIC	HYGIENIST	HYOID
HUSHERING	HYALINE	HYDRO	HYGIENISTS	HYOSCINE
HUSHERS	HYALINES	HYDROCELE	HYGRISTOR	HYOSCINES
HUSHES	HYALINISE	HYDROCELES	HYGRISTORS	HYP
HUSHIER	HYALINISED	HYDROFOIL	HYGRODEIK	HYPALGIA
HUSHIEST	HYALINISES	HYDROFOILS	HYGRODEIKS	HYPALGIAS
HUSHING	HYALINISING	HYDROGEN	HYGROLOGIES	HYPALLAGE
HUSHY	HYALINIZE	HYDROGENS	HYGROLOGY	HYPALLAGES
HUSK	HYALINIZED	HYDROID	HYGROPHIL	HYPATE
HUSKED	HYALINIZES	HYDROIDS	HYGROSTAT	HYPATES
HUSKER	HYALINIZING	HYDROLOGIES	HYGROSTATS	HYPE
HUSKERS	HYALITE	HYDROLOGY	HYING	HYPED

HYPER
HYPERBOLA
HYPERBOLAS
HYPERBOLE
HYPERBOLES
HYPERCUBE
HYPERCUBES
HYPEREMIA
HYPEREMIAS
HYPERGAMIES
HYPERGAMY
HYPERMART
HYPERMARTS
HYPERON
HYPERONS
HYPEROPIA
HYPEROPIAS
HYPERS
HYPES
HYPHA
HYPHAE
HYPHAL
HYPHEN
HYPHENATE
HYPHENATED
HYPHENATEDS
HYPHENATES
HYPHENATING
HYPHENED
HYPHENIC
HYPHENING

HYPHENISE
HYPHENISED
HYPHENISES
HYPHENISING
HYPHENISM
HYPHENISMS
HYPHENIZE
HYPHENIZED
HYPHENIZES
HYPHENIZING
HYPHENS
HYPING
HYPINOSES
HYPINOSIS
HYPNA
HYPNIC
HYPNICS
HYPNOGENIES
HYPNOGENY
HYPNOID
HYPNOIDAL
HYPNOLOGIES
HYPNOLOGY
HYPNONE
HYPNONES
HYPNOSES
HYPNOSIS
HYPNOTEE
HYPNOTEES
HYPNOTIC
HYPNOTICS

HYPNOTISE
HYPNOTISED
HYPNOTISES
HYPNOTISING
HYPNOTISM
HYPNOTISMS
HYPNOTIST
HYPNOTISTS
HYPNOTIZE
HYPNOTIZED
HYPNOTIZES
HYPNOTIZING
HYPNOTOID
HYPNUM
HYPNUMS
HYPO
HYPOBLAST
HYPOBLASTS
HYPOBOLE
HYPOBOLES
HYPOCAUST
HYPOCAUSTS
HYPOCIST
HYPOCISTS
HYPOCOTYL
HYPOCOTYLS
HYPOCRISIES
HYPOCRISY
HYPOCRITE
HYPOCRITES
HYPODERM

HYPODERMA
HYPODERMAS
HYPODERMS
HYPOGAEA
HYPOGAEAL
HYPOGAEAN
HYPOGAEUM
HYPOGEA
HYPOGEAL
HYPOGEAN
HYPOGENE
HYPOGEOUS
HYPOGEUM
HYPOGYNIES
HYPOGYNY
HYPOID
HYPOMANIA
HYPOMANIAS
HYPOMANIC
HYPONASTIES
HYPONASTY
HYPONYM
HYPONYMS
HYPOS
HYPOSTYLE
HYPOSTYLES
HYPOTAXES
HYPOTAXIS
HYPOTHEC
HYPOTHECS
HYPOTONIA

HYPOTONIAS
HYPOTONIC
HYPOXEMIA
HYPOXEMIAS
HYPOXEMIC
HYPOXIA
HYPOXIAS
HYPOXIC
HYPPED
HYPPING
HYPS
HYPURAL
HYRACES
HYRACOID
HYRAX
HYRAXES
HYSON
HYSONS
HYSSOP
HYSSOPS
HYSTERIA
HYSTERIAS
HYSTERIC
HYSTERICS
HYSTEROID
HYTHE
HYTHES

I

IAIDO	ICIEST	IDEALLESS	IDIOTISMS	IGNAROS
IAIDOS	ICILY	IDEALLY	IDIOTS	IGNEOUS
IAMB	ICINESS	IDEALOGUE	IDLE	IGNESCENT
IAMBI	ICINESSES	IDEALOGUES	IDLED	IGNESCENTS
IAMBIC	ICING	IDEALS	IDLEHOOD	IGNITABLE
IAMBICS	ICINGS	IDEAS	IDLEHOODS	IGNITE
IAMBIST	ICKER	IDEATE	IDLENESS	IGNITED
IAMBISTS	ICKERS	IDEATED	IDLENESSES	IGNITER
IAMBS	ICKIER	IDEATES	IDLER	IGNITERS
IAMBUS	ICKIEST	IDEATING	IDLERS	IGNITES
IAMBUSES	ICKY	IDEATION	IDLES	IGNITIBLE
IANTHINE	ICON	IDEATIONS	IDLESSE	IGNITING
IATRIC	ICONIC	IDEATIVE	IDLESSES	IGNITION
IATRICAL	ICONISE	IDÉE	IDLEST	IGNITIONS
IATROGENIES	ICONISED	IDÉES	IDLING	IGNITRON
IATROGENY	ICONISES	IDEM	IDLY	IGNITRONS
IBEX	ICONISING	IDENTIC	IDOCRASE	IGNOBLE
IBEXES	ICONIZE	IDENTICAL	IDOCRASES	IGNOBLED
IBICES	ICONIZED	IDENTIFIED	IDOL	IGNOBLER
IBIDEM	ICONIZES	IDENTIFIES	IDOLATER	IGNOBLES
IBIS	ICONIZING	IDENTIFY	IDOLATERS	IGNOBLEST
IBISES	ICONOLOGIES	IDENTIFYING	IDOLATRIES	IGNOBLING
IBUPROFEN	ICONOLOGY	IDENTIKIT	IDOLATRY	IGNOBLY
IBUPROFENS	ICONOSTAS	IDENTIKITS	IDOLISE	IGNOMIES
ICE	ICONOSTASES	IDENTITIES	IDOLISED	IGNOMINIES
ICEBERG	ICONS	IDENTITY	IDOLISER	IGNOMINY
ICEBERGS	ICTAL	IDEOGRAM	IDOLISERS	IGNOMY
ICEBLINK	ICTERIC	IDEOGRAMS	IDOLISES	IGNORABLE
ICEBLINKS	ICTERICAL	IDEOGRAPH	IDOLISING	IGNORAMUS
ICEBOX	ICTERICALS	IDEOGRAPHS	IDOLISM	IGNORAMUSES
ICEBOXES	ICTERICS	IDEOLOGIC	IDOLISMS	IGNORANCE
ICED	ICTERINE	IDEOLOGIES	IDOLIST	IGNORANCES
ICEMAN	ICTERUS	IDEOLOGUE	IDOLISTS	IGNORANT
ICEMEN	ICTERUSES	IDEOLOGUES	IDOLIZE	IGNORANTS
ICEPACK	ICTIC	IDEOLOGY	IDOLIZED	IGNORE
ICEPACKS	ICTUS	IDEOPHONE	IDOLIZER	IGNORED
ICEPLANT	ICTUSES	IDEOPHONES	IDOLIZERS	IGNORER
ICEPLANTS	ICY	IDES	IDOLIZES	IGNORERS
ICER	ID	IDIOBLAST	IDOLIZING	IGNORES
ICERS	IDANT	IDIOBLASTS	IDOLS	IGNORING
ICES	IDANTS	IDIOCIES	IDS	IGUANA
ICH	IDE	IDIOCY	IDYL	IGUANAS
ICHABOD	IDEA	IDIOGRAPH	IDYLL	IGUANID
ICHED	IDEAED	IDIOGRAPHS	IDYLLIAN	IGUANIDS
ICHING	IDEAL	IDIOLECT	IDYLLIC	IHRAM
ICHNEUMON	IDEALESS	IDIOLECTS	IDYLLIST	IHRAMS
ICHNEUMONS	IDEALISE	IDIOM	IDYLLISTS	IKAT
ICHNITE	IDEALISED	IDIOMATIC	IDYLLS	IKATS
ICHNITES	IDEALISER	IDIOMS	IDYLS	IKEBANA
ICHNOLITE	IDEALISERS	IDIOPATHIES	IF	IKEBANAS
ICHNOLITES	IDEALISES	IDIOPATHY	IFF	IKON
ICHNOLOGIES	IDEALISING	IDIOPHONE	IFFIER	IKONS
ICHNOLOGY	IDEALISM	IDIOPHONES	IFFIEST	ILEA
ICHOR	IDEALISMS	IDIOPLASM	IFFY	ILEAC
ICHOROUS	IDEALIST	IDIOPLASMS	IFS	ILEITIS
ICHORS	IDEALISTS	IDIOT	IGAD	ILEITISES
ICHTHIC	IDEALITIES	IDIOTCIES	IGAPO	ILEUM
ICHTHYOID	IDEALITY	IDIOTCY	IGAPOS	ILEUS
ICHTHYOIDS	IDEALIZE	IDIOTIC	IGARAPÉ	ILEUSES
ICHTHYS	IDEALIZED	IDIOTICAL	IGARAPÉS	ILEX
ICHTHYSES	IDEALIZER	IDIOTICON	IGLOO	ILEXES
ICICLE	IDEALIZERS	IDIOTICONS	IGLOOS	ILIA
ICICLES	IDEALIZES	IDIOTISH	IGNARO	ILIAC
ICIER	IDEALIZING	IDIOTISM	IGNAROES	ILICES

ILIUM	IMAGELESS	IMBODY	IMITATION	IMMISSION
ILK	IMAGERIES	IMBODYING	IMITATIONS	IMMISSIONS
ILKA	IMAGERY	IMBORDER	IMITATIVE	IMMIT
ILKADAY	IMAGES	IMBORDERED	IMITATOR	IMMITS
ILKADAYS	IMAGINAL	IMBORDERING	IMITATORS	IMMITTED
ILKS	IMAGINARY	IMBORDERS	IMMANACLE	IMMITTING
ILL	IMAGINE	IMBOSK	IMMANACLED	IMMIX
ILLAPSE	IMAGINED	IMBOSKED	IMMANACLES	IMMIXED
ILLAPSED	IMAGINER	IMBOSKING	IMMANACLING	IMMIXES
ILLAPSES	IMAGINERS	IMBOSKS	IMMANE	IMMIXING
ILLAPSING	IMAGINES	IMBOSOM	IMMANELY	IMMOBILE
ILLATION	IMAGING	IMBOSOMED	IMMANENCE	IMMODEST
ILLATIONS	IMAGINGS	IMBOSOMING	IMMANENCES	IMMODESTIES
ILLATIVE	IMAGINING	IMBOSOMS	IMMANENCIES	IMMODESTY
ILLATIVES	IMAGININGS	IMBOSS	IMMANENCY	IMMOLATE
ILLEGAL	IMAGINIST	IMBOSSED	IMMANENT	IMMOLATED
ILLEGALLY	IMAGINISTS	IMBOSSES	IMMANITIES	IMMOLATES
ILLEGIBLE	IMAGISM	IMBOSSING	IMMANITY	IMMOLATING
ILLEGIBLY	IMAGISMS	IMBOWER	IMMANTLE	IMMOLATOR
ILLER	IMAGIST	IMBOWERED	IMMANTLED	IMMOLATORS
ILLEST	IMAGISTIC	IMBOWERING	IMMANTLES	IMMOMENT
ILLIAD	IMAGISTS	IMBOWERS	IMMANTLING	IMMORAL
ILLIADS	IMAGO	IMBRANGLE	IMMASK	IMMORALLY
ILLIBERAL	IMAGOES	IMBRANGLED	IMMASKED	IMMORTAL
ILLICIT	IMAGOS	IMBRANGLES	IMMASKING	IMMORTALS
ILLICITLY	IMAM	IMBRANGLING	IMMASKS	IMMOVABLE
ILLIMITED	IMAMATE	IMBRAST	IMMATURE	IMMOVABLY
ILLINIUM	IMAMATES	IMBREX	IMMATURED	IMMUNE
ILLINIUMS	IMAMS	IMBRICATE	IMMEDIACIES	IMMUNES
ILLIPE	IMARI	IMBRICATED	IMMEDIACY	IMMUNISE
ILLIPES	IMARIS	IMBRICATES	IMMEDIATE	IMMUNISED
ILLIQUID	IMAUM	IMBRICATING	IMMENSE	IMMUNISES
ILLISION	IMAUMS	IMBRICES	IMMENSELY	IMMUNISING
ILLISIONS	IMBALANCE	IMBROGLIO	IMMENSER	IMMUNITIES
ILLITE	IMBALANCES	IMBROGLIOS	IMMENSEST	IMMUNITY
ILLITES	IMBAR	IMBROWN	IMMENSITIES	IMMUNIZE
ILLNESS	IMBARK	IMBROWNED	IMMENSITY	IMMUNIZED
ILLNESSES	IMBARKED	IMBROWNING	IMMERGE	IMMUNIZES
ILLOGIC	IMBARKING	IMBROWNS	IMMERGED	IMMUNIZING
ILLOGICAL	IMBARKS	IMBRUE	IMMERGES	IMMUNOGEN
ILLOGICS	IMBARRED	IMBRUED	IMMERGING	IMMUNOGENS
ILLS	IMBARRING	IMBRUEING	IMMERSE	IMMURE
ILLTH	IMBARS	IMBRUES	IMMERSED	IMMURED
ILLTHS	IMBASE	IMBRUING	IMMERSES	IMMURES
ILLUDE	IMBASED	IMBRUTE	IMMERSING	IMMURING
ILLUDED	IMBASES	IMBRUTED	IMMERSION	IMMUTABLE
ILLUDES	IMBASING	IMBRUTES	IMMERSIONS	IMMUTABLY
ILLUDING	IMBATHE	IMBRUTING	IMMESH	IMP
ILLUME	IMBATHED	IMBUE	IMMESHED	IMPACABLE
ILLUMED	IMBATHES	IMBUED	IMMESHES	IMPACT
ILLUMES	IMBATHING	IMBUEING	IMMESHING	IMPACTED
ILLUMINE	IMBECILE	IMBUES	IMMEW	IMPACTING
ILLUMINED	IMBECILES	IMBUING	IMMEWED	IMPACTION
ILLUMINER	IMBECILIC	IMBURSE	IMMEWING	IMPACTIONS
ILLUMINERS	IMBED	IMBURSED	IMMEWS	IMPACTITE
ILLUMINES	IMBEDDED	IMBURSES	IMMIGRANT	IMPACTITES
ILLUMING	IMBEDDING	IMBURSING	IMMIGRANTS	IMPACTS
ILLUMINING	IMBEDS	IMIDE	IMMIGRATE	IMPAINT
ILLUPI	IMBIBE	IMIDES	IMMIGRATED	IMPAINTED
ILLUPIS	IMBIBED	IMINE	IMMIGRATES	IMPAINTING
ILLUSION	IMBIBER	IMINES	IMMIGRATING	IMPAINTS
ILLUSIONS	IMBIBERS	IMITABLE	IMMINENCE	IMPAIR
ILLUSIVE	IMBIBES	IMITANCIES	IMMINENCES	IMPAIRED
ILLUSORY	IMBIBING	IMITANCY	IMMINENCIES	IMPAIRING
ILLY	IMBITTER	IMITANT	IMMINENCY	IMPAIRS
ILMENITE	IMBITTERED	IMITANTS	IMMINENT	IMPALA
ILMENITES	IMBITTERING	IMITATE	IMMINGLE	IMPALAS
IMAGE	IMBITTERS	IMITATED	IMMINGLED	IMPALE
IMAGEABLE	IMBODIED	IMITATES	IMMINGLES	IMPALED
IMAGED	IMBODIES	IMITATING	IMMINGLING	IMPALES

IMPALING
IMPANATE
IMPANEL
IMPANELLED
IMPANELLING
IMPANELS
IMPANNEL
IMPANNELLED
IMPANNELLING
IMPANNELS
IMPARITIES
IMPARITY
IMPARK
IMPARKED
IMPARKING
IMPARKS
IMPARL
IMPARLED
IMPARLING
IMPARLS
IMPART
IMPARTED
IMPARTER
IMPARTERS
IMPARTIAL
IMPARTING
IMPARTS
IMPASSE
IMPASSES
IMPASSION
IMPASSIONED
IMPASSIONING
IMPASSIONS
IMPASSIVE
IMPASTE
IMPASTED
IMPASTES
IMPASTING
IMPASTO
IMPASTOED
IMPASTOS
IMPATIENS
IMPATIENT
IMPAVE
IMPAVED
IMPAVES
IMPAVID
IMPAVIDLY
IMPAVING
IMPAWN
IMPAWNED
IMPAWNING
IMPAWNS
IMPEACH
IMPEACHED
IMPEACHER
IMPEACHERS
IMPEACHES
IMPEACHING
IMPEARL
IMPEARLED
IMPEARLING
IMPEARLS
IMPECCANT
IMPED
IMPEDANCE
IMPEDANCES
IMPEDE
IMPEDED
IMPEDES

IMPEDING
IMPEL
IMPELLED
IMPELLENT
IMPELLENTS
IMPELLER
IMPELLERS
IMPELLING
IMPELS
IMPEND
IMPENDED
IMPENDENT
IMPENDING
IMPENDS
IMPERATOR
IMPERATORS
IMPERFECT
IMPERFECTS
IMPERIAL
IMPERIALS
IMPERIL
IMPERILLED
IMPERILLING
IMPERILS
IMPERIOUS
IMPERIUM
IMPERIUMS
IMPETICOS
IMPETICOSED
IMPETICOSES
IMPETICOSING
IMPETIGINES
IMPETIGO
IMPETIGOS
IMPETRATE
IMPETRATED
IMPETRATES
IMPETRATING
IMPETUOUS
IMPETUS
IMPETUSES
IMPI
IMPIETIES
IMPIETY
IMPING
IMPINGE
IMPINGED
IMPINGENT
IMPINGES
IMPINGING
IMPIOUS
IMPIOUSLY
IMPIS
IMPISH
IMPISHLY
IMPLANT
IMPLANTED
IMPLANTING
IMPLANTS
IMPLATE
IMPLATED
IMPLATES
IMPLATING
IMPLEACH
IMPLEACHED
IMPLEACHES
IMPLEACHING
IMPLEAD
IMPLEADED
IMPLEADER

IMPLEADERS
IMPLEADING
IMPLEADS
IMPLEDGE
IMPLEDGED
IMPLEDGES
IMPLEDGING
IMPLEMENT
IMPLEMENTED
IMPLEMENTING
IMPLEMENTS
IMPLETE
IMPLETED
IMPLETES
IMPLETING
IMPLETION
IMPLETIONS
IMPLEX
IMPLEXES
IMPLEXION
IMPLEXIONS
IMPLICATE
IMPLICATED
IMPLICATES
IMPLICATING
IMPLICIT
IMPLIED
IMPLIEDLY
IMPLIES
IMPLODE
IMPLODED
IMPLODENT
IMPLODENTS
IMPLODES
IMPLODING
IMPLORE
IMPLORED
IMPLORER
IMPLORERS
IMPLORES
IMPLORING
IMPLOSION
IMPLOSIONS
IMPLOSIVE
IMPLOSIVES
IMPLUNGE
IMPLUNGED
IMPLUNGES
IMPLUNGING
IMPLUVIA
IMPLUVIUM
IMPLY
IMPLYING
IMPOCKET
IMPOCKETED
IMPOCKETING
IMPOCKETS
IMPOLDER
IMPOLDERED
IMPOLDERING
IMPOLDERS
IMPOLICIES
IMPOLICY
IMPOLITE
IMPOLITER
IMPOLITEST
IMPOLITIC
IMPONE
IMPONED
IMPONENT

IMPONENTS
IMPONES
IMPONING
IMPORT
IMPORTANT
IMPORTED
IMPORTER
IMPORTERS
IMPORTING
IMPORTS
IMPORTUNE
IMPORTUNED
IMPORTUNES
IMPORTUNING
IMPORTUNINGS
IMPOSABLE
IMPOSE
IMPOSED
IMPOSER
IMPOSERS
IMPOSES
IMPOSING
IMPOST
IMPOSTER
IMPOSTERS
IMPOSTOR
IMPOSTORS
IMPOSTS
IMPOSTUME
IMPOSTUMES
IMPOSTURE
IMPOSTURES
IMPOT
IMPOTENCE
IMPOTENCES
IMPOTENCIES
IMPOTENCY
IMPOTENT
IMPOTS
IMPOUND
IMPOUNDED
IMPOUNDER
IMPOUNDERS
IMPOUNDING
IMPOUNDS
IMPRECATE
IMPRECATED
IMPRECATES
IMPRECATING
IMPRECISE
IMPREGN
IMPREGNED
IMPREGNING
IMPREGNS
IMPRESA
IMPRESARI
IMPRESAS
IMPRESE
IMPRESES
IMPRESS
IMPRESSE
IMPRESSED
IMPRESSES
IMPRESSING
IMPREST
IMPRESTED
IMPRESTING
IMPRESTS
IMPRIMIS
IMPRINT

IMPRINTED
IMPRINTING
IMPRINTINGS
IMPRINTS
IMPRISON
IMPRISONED
IMPRISONING
IMPRISONS
IMPROBITIES
IMPROBITY
IMPROMPTU
IMPROMPTUS
IMPROPER
IMPROVE
IMPROVED
IMPROVER
IMPROVERS
IMPROVES
IMPROVING
IMPROVISE
IMPROVISED
IMPROVISES
IMPROVISING
IMPRUDENT
IMPS
IMPUDENCE
IMPUDENCES
IMPUDENT
IMPUGN
IMPUGNED
IMPUGNER
IMPUGNERS
IMPUGNING
IMPUGNS
IMPULSE
IMPULSES
IMPULSION
IMPULSIONS
IMPULSIVE
IMPULSORY
IMPUNITIES
IMPUNITY
IMPURE
IMPURELY
IMPURER
IMPUREST
IMPURITIES
IMPURITY
IMPURPLE
IMPURPLED
IMPURPLES
IMPURPLING
IMPUTABLE
IMPUTABLY
IMPUTE
IMPUTED
IMPUTER
IMPUTERS
IMPUTES
IMPUTING
IMSHI
IMSHY
IN
INABILITIES
INABILITY
INACTION
INACTIONS
INACTIVE
INAIDABLE
INAMORATA

INAMORATAS	INCASE	INCISION	INCONY	INCURVED
INAMORATO	INCASED	INCISIONS	INCORPSE	INCURVES
INAMORATOS	INCASES	INCISIVE	INCORPSED	INCURVING
INANE	INCASING	INCISOR	INCORPSES	INCURVITIES
INANELY	INCAUTION	INCISORS	INCORPSING	INCURVITY
INANENESS	INCAUTIONS	INCISORY	INCORRECT	INCUS
INANENESSES	INCAVE	INCISURE	INCORRUPT	INCUSE
INANER	INCAVED	INCISURES	INCREASE	INCUSED
INANES	INCAVES	INCITANT	INCREASED	INCUSES
INANEST	INCAVI	INCITANTS	INCREASER	INCUSING
INANIMATE	INCAVING	INCITE	INCREASERS	INCUT
INANITIES	INCAVO	INCITED	INCREASES	INDABA
INANITION	INCAVOS	INCITER	INCREASING	INDABAS
INANITIONS	INCEDE	INCITERS	INCREASINGS	INDAGATE
INANITY	INCEDED	INCITES	INCREATE	INDAGATED
INAPT	INCEDES	INCITING	INCREMATE	INDAGATES
INAPTLY	INCEDING	INCIVIL	INCREMATED	INDAGATING
INAPTNESS	INCENSE	INCIVISM	INCREMATES	INDAGATOR
INAPTNESSES	INCENSED	INCIVISMS	INCREMATING	INDAGATORS
INARABLE	INCENSER	INCLASP	INCREMENT	INDART
INARCH	INCENSERS	INCLASPED	INCREMENTS	INDARTED
INARCHED	INCENSES	INCLASPING	INCROSS	INDARTING
INARCHES	INCENSING	INCLASPS	INCROSSED	INDARTS
INARCHING	INCENSOR	INCLE	INCROSSES	INDEBTED
INARM	INCENSORIES	INCLEMENT	INCROSSING	INDECENCIES
INARMED	INCENSORS	INCLES	INCRUST	INDECENCY
INARMING	INCENSORY	INCLINE	INCRUSTED	INDECENT
INARMS	INCENTIVE	INCLINED	INCRUSTING	INDECENTER
INAUDIBLE	INCENTIVES	INCLINES	INCRUSTS	INDECENTEST
INAUDIBLY	INCENTRE	INCLINING	INCUBATE	INDECORUM
INAUGURAL	INCENTRES	INCLININGS	INCUBATED	INDECORUMS
INAUGURALS	INCEPT	INCLIP	INCUBATES	INDEED
INAURATE	INCEPTED	INCLIPPED	INCUBATING	INDELIBLE
INBEING	INCEPTING	INCLIPPING	INCUBATOR	INDELIBLY
INBEINGS	INCEPTION	INCLIPS	INCUBATORS	INDEMNIFIED
INBENT	INCEPTIONS	INCLOSE	INCUBI	INDEMNIFIES
INBOARD	INCEPTIVE	INCLOSED	INCUBOUS	INDEMNIFY
INBORN	INCEPTIVES	INCLOSER	INCUBUS	INDEMNIFYING
INBREAK	INCEPTOR	INCLOSERS	INCUBUSES	INDEMNITIES
INBREAKS	INCEPTORS	INCLOSES	INCUDES	INDEMNITY
INBREATHE	INCEPTS	INCLOSING	INCULCATE	INDENE
INBREATHED	INCERTAIN	INCLOSURE	INCULCATED	INDENES
INBREATHES	INCESSANT	INCLOSURES	INCULCATES	INDENT
INBREATHING	INCEST	INCLUDE	INCULCATING	INDENTED
INBRED	INCESTS	INCLUDED	INCULPATE	INDENTER
INBREED	INCH	INCLUDES	INCULPATED	INDENTERS
INBREEDING	INCHASE	INCLUDING	INCULPATES	INDENTING
INBREEDINGS	INCHASED	INCLUSION	INCULPATING	INDENTION
INBREEDS	INCHASES	INCLUSIONS	INCULT	INDENTIONS
INBRING	INCHASING	INCLUSIVE	INCUMBENT	INDENTS
INBRINGING	INCHED	INCOGNITA	INCUMBENTS	INDENTURE
INBRINGINGS	INCHES	INCOGNITAS	INCUNABLE	INDENTURED
INBRINGS	INCHING	INCOGNITO	INCUNABLES	INDENTURES
INBROUGHT	INCHMEAL	INCOGNITOS	INCUR	INDENTURING
INBURNING	INCHOATE	INCOME	INCURABLE	INDEW
INBURST	INCHOATED	INCOMER	INCURABLES	INDEWED
INBURSTS	INCHOATES	INCOMERS	INCURABLY	INDEWING
INBY	INCHOATING	INCOMES	INCURIOUS	INDEWS
INBYE	INCHPIN	INCOMING	INCURRED	INDEX
INCAGE	INCHPINS	INCOMINGS	INCURRENT	INDEXED
INCAGED	INCIDENCE	INCOMMODE	INCURRING	INDEXER
INCAGES	INCIDENCES	INCOMMODED	INCURS	INDEXERS
INCAGING	INCIDENT	INCOMMODES	INCURSION	INDEXES
INCAPABLE	INCIDENTS	INCOMMODING	INCURSIONS	INDEXICAL
INCAPABLES	INCIPIENT	INCONDITE	INCURSIVE	INDEXING
INCAPABLY	INCIPIT	INCONIE	INCURVATE	INDEXINGS
INCARNATE	INCISE	INCONNU	INCURVATED	INDEXLESS
INCARNATED	INCISED	INCONNUE	INCURVATES	INDICAN
INCARNATES	INCISES	INCONNUES	INCURVATING	INDICANS
INCARNATING	INCISING	INCONNUS	INCURVE	INDICANT

INDICANTS	INDORSE	INDWELLINGS	INFANCY	INFILTERING
INDICATE	INDORSED	INDWELLS	INFANT	INFILTERS
INDICATED	INDORSES	INDWELT	INFANTA	INFINITE
INDICATES	INDORSING	INEARTH	INFANTAS	INFINITES
INDICATING	INDRAFT	INEARTHED	INFANTE	INFINITIES
INDICATOR	INDRAFTS	INEARTHING	INFANTED	INFINITY
INDICATORS	INDRAUGHT	INEARTHS	INFANTES	INFIRM
INDICES	INDRAUGHTS	INEBRIANT	INFANTILE	INFIRMARIES
INDICIA	INDRAWN	INEBRIANTS	INFANTINE	INFIRMARY
INDICIUM	INDRENCH	INEBRIATE	INFANTING	INFIRMER
INDICT	INDRENCHED	INEBRIATED	INFANTRIES	INFIRMEST
INDICTED	INDRENCHES	INEBRIATES	INFANTRY	INFIRMITIES
INDICTEE	INDRENCHING	INEBRIATING	INFANTS	INFIRMITY
INDICTEES	INDRI	INEBRIETIES	INFARCT	INFIRMLY
INDICTING	INDRIS	INEBRIETY	INFARCTS	INFIX
INDICTION	INDRISES	INEBRIOUS	INFARE	INFIXED
INDICTIONS	INDUBIOUS	INEDIBLE	INFARES	INFIXES
INDICTS	INDUCE	INEDITED	INFATUATE	INFIXING
INDIGENCE	INDUCED	INEFFABLE	INFATUATED	INFLAME
INDIGENCES	INDUCER	INEFFABLY	INFATUATES	INFLAMED
INDIGENCIES	INDUCERS	INELASTIC	INFATUATING	INFLAMER
INDIGENCY	INDUCES	INELEGANT	INFAUST	INFLAMERS
INDIGENE	INDUCIAE	INEPT	INFECT	INFLAMES
INDIGENES	INDUCIBLE	INEPTER	INFECTED	INFLAMING
INDIGENT	INDUCING	INEPTEST	INFECTING	INFLATE
INDIGEST	INDUCT	INEPTLY	INFECTION	INFLATED
INDIGESTS	INDUCTED	INEPTNESS	INFECTIONS	INFLATES
INDIGN	INDUCTILE	INEPTNESSES	INFECTIVE	INFLATING
INDIGNANT	INDUCTING	INEQUABLE	INFECTOR	INFLATION
INDIGNIFIED	INDUCTION	INEQUITIES	INFECTORS	INFLATIONS
INDIGNIFIES	INDUCTIONS	INEQUITY	INFECTS	INFLATIVE
INDIGNIFY	INDUCTIVE	INERM	INFECUND	INFLATOR
INDIGNIFYING	INDUCTOR	INERRABLE	INFEFT	INFLATORS
INDIGNITIES	INDUCTORS	INERRABLY	INFEFTED	INFLATUS
INDIGNITY	INDUCTS	INERRANCIES	INFEFTING	INFLATUSES
INDIGO	INDUE	INERRANCY	INFEFTS	INFLECT
INDIGOES	INDUED	INERRANT	INFELT	INFLECTED
INDIGOS	INDUEING	INERT	INFER	INFLECTING
INDIGOTIN	INDUES	INERTER	INFERABLE	INFLECTS
INDIGOTINS	INDUING	INERTEST	INFERE	INFLEXED
INDIRECT	INDULGE	INERTIA	INFERENCE	INFLEXION
INDIRECTER	INDULGED	INERTIAL	INFERENCES	INFLEXIONS
INDIRECTEST	INDULGENT	INERTIAS	INFERIAE	INFLEXURE
INDIRUBIN	INDULGER	INERTLY	INFERIOR	INFLEXURES
INDIRUBINS	INDULGERS	INERTNESS	INFERIORS	INFLICT
INDISPOSE	INDULGES	INERTNESSES	INFERNAL	INFLICTED
INDISPOSED	INDULGING	INERUDITE	INFERNO	INFLICTING
INDISPOSES	INDULINE	INESSIVE	INFERNOS	INFLICTS
INDISPOSING	INDULINES	INESSIVES	INFERRED	INFLOW
INDITE	INDULT	INEXACT	INFERRING	INFLOWING
INDITED	INDULTS	INEXACTLY	INFERS	INFLOWS
INDITER	INDUNA	INEXPERT	INFERTILE	INFLUENCE
INDITERS	INDUNAS	INFALL	INFEST	INFLUENCED
INDITES	INDURATE	INFALLS	INFESTED	INFLUENCES
INDITING	INDURATED	INFAME	INFESTING	INFLUENCING
INDIUM	INDURATES	INFAMED	INFESTS	INFLUENT
INDIUMS	INDURATING	INFAMES	INFICETE	INFLUENTS
INDOCIBLE	INDUSIA	INFAMIES	INFIDEL	INFLUENZA
INDOCILE	INDUSIAL	INFAMING	INFIDELS	INFLUENZAS
INDOL	INDUSIATE	INFAMISE	INFIELD	INFLUX
INDOLE	INDUSIUM	INFAMISED	INFIELDER	INFLUXES
INDOLENCE	INDUSTRIES	INFAMISES	INFIELDERS	INFLUXION
INDOLENCES	INDUSTRY	INFAMISING	INFIELDS	INFLUXIONS
INDOLENCIES	INDUVIAE	INFAMIZE	INFILL	INFO
INDOLENCY	INDUVIAL	INFAMIZED	INFILLED	INFOLD
INDOLENT	INDUVIATE	INFAMIZES	INFILLING	INFOLDED
INDOLES	INDWELL	INFAMIZING	INFILLINGS	INFOLDING
INDOLS	INDWELLER	INFAMOUS	INFILLS	INFOLDS
INDOOR	INDWELLERS	INFAMY	INFILTER	INFORCE
INDOORS	INDWELLING	INFANCIES	INFILTERED	INFORCED

INFORCES	INGLE	INHARMONY	INITIATED	INLACE
INFORCING	INGLES	INHAUST	INITIATES	INLACED
INFORM	INGLOBE	INHAUSTED	INITIATING	INLACES
INFORMAL	INGLOBED	INHAUSTING	INITIATOR	INLACING
INFORMANT	INGLOBES	INHAUSTS	INITIATORS	INLAID
INFORMANTS	INGLOBING	INHEARSE	INJECT	INLAND
INFORMED	INGLUVIAL	INHEARSED	INJECTED	INLANDER
INFORMER	INGLUVIES	INHEARSES	INJECTING	INLANDERS
INFORMERS	INGLUVIESES	INHEARSING	INJECTION	INLANDS
INFORMING	INGO	INHERCE	INJECTIONS	INLAY
INFORMS	INGOES	INHERCED	INJECTOR	INLAYER
INFORTUNE	INGOING	INHERCES	INJECTORS	INLAYERS
INFORTUNES	INGOINGS	INHERCING	INJECTS	INLAYING
INFOS	INGOT	INHERE	INJELLIED	INLAYINGS
INFRA	INGOTS	INHERED	INJELLIES	INLAYS
INFRACT	INGOWES	INHERENCE	INJELLY	INLET
INFRACTED	INGRAFT	INHERENCES	INJELLYING	INLETS
INFRACTING	INGRAFTED	INHERENCIES	INJOINT	INLIER
INFRACTOR	INGRAFTING	INHERENCY	INJOINTED	INLIERS
INFRACTORS	INGRAFTS	INHERENT	INJOINTING	INLIEST
INFRACTS	INGRAIN	INHERES	INJOINTS	INLOCK
INFRINGE	INGRAINED	INHERING	INJUNCT	INLOCKED
INFRINGED	INGRAINING	INHERIT	INJUNCTED	INLOCKING
INFRINGES	INGRAINS	INHERITED	INJUNCTING	INLOCKS
INFRINGING	INGRAM	INHERITING	INJUNCTS	INLY
INFULA	INGRATE	INHERITOR	INJURANT	INLYING
INFULAE	INGRATES	INHERITORS	INJURANTS	INMATE
INFURIATE	INGRESS	INHERITS	INJURE	INMATES
INFURIATED	INGRESSES	INHESION	INJURED	INMESH
INFURIATES	INGROOVE	INHESIONS	INJURER	INMESHED
INFURIATING	INGROOVED	INHIBIT	INJURERS	INMESHES
INFUSCATE	INGROOVES	INHIBITED	INJURES	INMESHING
INFUSE	INGROOVING	INHIBITING	INJURIES	INMOST
INFUSED	INGROSS	INHIBITOR	INJURING	INN
INFUSER	INGROSSED	INHIBITORS	INJURIOUS	INNARDS
INFUSERS	INGROSSES	INHIBITS	INJURY	INNATE
INFUSES	INGROSSING	INHOLDER	INJUSTICE	INNATELY
INFUSIBLE	INGROUP	INHOLDERS	INJUSTICES	INNATIVE
INFUSING	INGROUPS	INHOOP	INK	INNED
INFUSION	INGROWING	INHOOPED	INKBERRIES	INNER
INFUSIONS	INGROWN	INHOOPING	INKBERRY	INNERMOST
INFUSIVE	INGROWTH	INHOOPS	INKED	INNERS
INFUSORIA	INGROWTHS	INHUMAN	INKER	INNERVATE
INFUSORY	INGRUM	INHUMANE	INKERS	INNERVATED
INGAN	INGUINAL	INHUMANER	INKHOLDER	INNERVATES
INGANS	INGULF	INHUMANEST	INKHOLDERS	INNERVATING
INGATE	INGULFED	INHUMANLY	INKHORN	INNERVE
INGATES	INGULFING	INHUMATE	INKHORNS	INNERVED
INGENER	INGULFS	INHUMATED	INKIER	INNERVES
INGENERS	INGULPH	INHUMATES	INKIEST	INNERVING
INGENIOUS	INGULPHED	INHUMATING	INKINESS	INNHOLDER
INGENIUM	INGULPHING	INHUME	INKINESSES	INNHOLDERS
INGENIUMS	INGULPHS	INHUMED	INKING	INNING
INGÉNU	INHABIT	INHUMES	INKLE	INNINGS
INGÉNUE	INHABITED	INHUMING	INKLED	INNKEEPER
INGÉNUES	INHABITING	INIA	INKLES	INNKEEPERS
INGENUITIES	INHABITOR	INIMICAL	INKLING	INNOCENCE
INGENUITY	INHABITORS	INION	INKLINGS	INNOCENCES
INGENUOUS	INHABITS	INIQUITIES	INKPOT	INNOCENCIES
INGÉNUS	INHALANT	INIQUITY	INKPOTS	INNOCENCY
INGEST	INHALANTS	INISLE	INKS	INNOCENT
INGESTA	INHALATOR	INISLED	INKSPOT	INNOCENTS
INGESTED	INHALATORS	INISLES	INKSPOTS	INNOCUITIES
INGESTING	INHALE	INISLING	INKSTAND	INNOCUITY
INGESTION	INHALED	INITIAL	INKSTANDS	INNOCUOUS
INGESTIONS	INHALER	INITIALLED	INKSTONE	INNOVATE
INGESTIVE	INHALERS	INITIALLING	INKSTONES	INNOVATED
INGESTS	INHALES	INITIALLY	INKWELL	INNOVATES
INGINE	INHALING	INITIALS	INKWELLS	INNOVATING
INGINES	INHARMONIES	INITIATE	INKY	INNOVATOR

INNOVATORS	INRUSHING	INSETTING	INSOLVENT	INSTIGATED
INNOXIOUS	INRUSHINGS	INSHALLAH	INSOLVENTS	INSTIGATES
INNS	INS	INSHEATHE	INSOMNIA	INSTIGATING
INNUENDO	INSANE	INSHEATHED	INSOMNIAC	INSTIL
INNUENDOED	INSANELY	INSHEATHES	INSOMNIACS	INSTILL
INNUENDOES	INSANER	INSHEATHING	INSOMNIAS	INSTILLED
INNUENDOING	INSANEST	INSHELL	INSOMUCH	INSTILLING
INNUENDOS	INSANIE	INSHELLED	INSOOTH	INSTILLS
INNYARD	INSANIES	INSHELLING	INSOUL	INSTILS
INNYARDS	INSANITIES	INSHELLS	INSOULED	INSTINCT
INOCULATE	INSANITY	INSHELTER	INSOULING	INSTINCTS
INOCULATED	INSATIATE	INSHELTERED	INSOULS	INSTITUTE
INOCULATES	INSATIETIES	INSHELTERING	INSPAN	INSTITUTED
INOCULATING	INSATIETY	INSHELTERS	INSPANNED	INSTITUTES
INOCULUM	INSCAPE	INSHIP	INSPANNING	INSTITUTING
INOCULUMS	INSCAPES	INSHIPPED	INSPANS	INSTRESS
INODOROUS	INSCIENCE	INSHIPPING	INSPECT	INSTRESSED
INOPINATE	INSCIENCES	INSHIPS	INSPECTED	INSTRESSES
INORB	INSCIENT	INSHORE	INSPECTING	INSTRESSING
INORBED	INSCONCE	INSHRINE	INSPECTOR	INSTRUCT
INORBING	INSCONCED	INSHRINED	INSPECTORS	INSTRUCTED
INORBS	INSCONCES	INSHRINES	INSPECTS	INSTRUCTING
INORGANIC	INSCONCING	INSHRINING	INSPHEARE	INSTRUCTS
INORNATE	INSCRIBE	INSIDE	INSPHERE	INSUCKEN
INOSITOL	INSCRIBED	INSIDER	INSPHERED	INSULA
INOSITOLS	INSCRIBER	INSIDERS	INSPHERES	INSULAE
INOTROPIC	INSCRIBERS	INSIDES	INSPHERING	INSULANCE
INPAYMENT	INSCRIBES	INSIDIOUS	INSPIRE	INSULANCES
INPAYMENTS	INSCRIBING	INSIGHT	INSPIRED	INSULANT
INPHASE	INSCROLL	INSIGHTS	INSPIRER	INSULANTS
INPOURING	INSCROLLED	INSIGNE	INSPIRERS	INSULAR
INPOURINGS	INSCROLLING	INSIGNES	INSPIRES	INSULARLY
INPUT	INSCROLLS	INSIGNIA	INSPIRING	INSULAS
INPUTS	INSCULP	INSIGNIAS	INSPIRIT	INSULATE
INPUTTER	INSCULPED	INSINCERE	INSPIRITED	INSULATED
INPUTTERS	INSCULPING	INSINEW	INSPIRITING	INSULATES
INPUTTING	INSCULPS	INSINEWED	INSPIRITS	INSULATING
INQILAB	INSCULPT	INSINEWING	INSPYRE	INSULATOR
INQILABS	INSEAM	INSINEWS	INSPYRED	INSULATORS
INQUERE	INSEAMED	INSINUATE	INSPYRES	INSULIN
INQUERED	INSEAMING	INSINUATED	INSPYRING	INSULINS
INQUERES	INSEAMS	INSINUATES	INSTABLE	INSULSE
INQUERING	INSECT	INSINUATING	INSTAL	INSULSITIES
INQUEST	INSECTARIES	INSIPID	INSTALL	INSULSITY
INQUESTS	INSECTARY	INSIPIDER	INSTALLED	INSULT
INQUIET	INSECTILE	INSIPIDEST	INSTALLING	INSULTANT
INQUIETED	INSECTION	INSIPIDLY	INSTALLS	INSULTED
INQUIETING	INSECTIONS	INSIPIENT	INSTALS	INSULTER
INQUIETLY	INSECTS	INSIST	INSTANCE	INSULTERS
INQUIETS	INSECTY	INSISTED	INSTANCED	INSULTING
INQUILINE	INSECURE	INSISTENT	INSTANCES	INSULTS
INQUILINES	INSECURER	INSISTING	INSTANCIES	INSURABLE
INQUINATE	INSECUREST	INSISTS	INSTANCING	INSURANCE
INQUINATED	INSEEM	INSISTURE	INSTANCY	INSURANCES
INQUINATES	INSEEMED	INSISTURES	INSTANT	INSURANT
INQUINATING	INSEEMING	INSNARE	INSTANTER	INSURANTS
INQUIRE	INSEEMS	INSNARED	INSTANTLY	INSURE
INQUIRED	INSELBERG	INSNARES	INSTANTS	INSURED
INQUIRER	INSELBERGE	INSNARING	INSTAR	INSURER
INQUIRERS	INSENSATE	INSOLATE	INSTARRED	INSURERS
INQUIRES	INSERT	INSOLATED	INSTARRING	INSURES
INQUIRIES	INSERTED	INSOLATES	INSTARS	INSURGENT
INQUIRING	INSERTER	INSOLATING	INSTATE	INSURGENTS
INQUIRY	INSERTERS	INSOLE	INSTATED	INSURING
INQUORATE	INSERTING	INSOLENCE	INSTATES	INSWATHE
INRO	INSERTION	INSOLENCES	INSTATING	INSWATHED
INROAD	INSERTIONS	INSOLENT	INSTEAD	INSWATHES
INROADS	INSERTS	INSOLES	INSTEP	INSWATHING
INRUSH	INSET	INSOLUBLE	INSTEPS	INSWING
INRUSHES	INSETS	INSOLUBLY	INSTIGATE	INSWINGER

INSWINGERS
INSWINGS
INTACT
INTAGLIO
INTAGLIOED
INTAGLIOING
INTAGLIOS
INTAKE
INTAKES
INTARSI
INTARSIA
INTARSIAS
INTARSIO
INTARSIOS
INTEGER
INTEGERS
INTEGRAL
INTEGRALS
INTEGRAND
INTEGRANDS
INTEGRANT
INTEGRATE
INTEGRATED
INTEGRATES
INTEGRATING
INTEGRITIES
INTEGRITY
INTELLECT
INTELLECTS
INTENABLE
INTEND
INTENDANT
INTENDANTS
INTENDED
INTENDEDS
INTENDER
INTENDERED
INTENDERING
INTENDERS
INTENDING
INTENDS
INTENIBLE
INTENSATE
INTENSATED
INTENSATES
INTENSATING
INTENSE
INTENSELY
INTENSER
INTENSEST
INTENSIFIED
INTENSIFIES
INTENSIFY
INTENSIFYING
INTENSION
INTENSIONS
INTENSITIES
INTENSITY
INTENSIVE
INTENSIVES
INTENT
INTENTER
INTENTEST
INTENTION
INTENTIONS
INTENTIVE
INTENTLY
INTENTS
INTER
INTERACT

INTERACTED
INTERACTING
INTERACTS
INTERBANK
INTERBRED
INTERCEDE
INTERCEDED
INTERCEDES
INTERCEDING
INTERCEPT
INTERCEPTED
INTERCEPTING
INTERCEPTS
INTERCITY
INTERCOM
INTERCOMS
INTERCROP
INTERCROPPED
INTERCROPPING
INTERCROPS
INTERCUT
INTERCUTS
INTERCUTTING
INTERDASH
INTERDASHED
INTERDASHES
INTERDASHING
INTERDEAL
INTERDEALING
INTERDEALS
INTERDEALT
INTERDICT
INTERDICTED
INTERDICTING
INTERDICTS
INTERDINE
INTERDINED
INTERDINES
INTERDINING
INTERESS
INTERESSE
INTERESSED
INTERESSES
INTERESSING
INTEREST
INTERESTED
INTERESTING
INTERESTS
INTERFACE
INTERFACED
INTERFACES
INTERFACING
INTERFACINGS
INTERFERE
INTERFERED
INTERFERES
INTERFERING
INTERFLOW
INTERFLOWED
INTERFLOWING
INTERFLOWS
INTERFOLD
INTERFOLDED
INTERFOLDING
INTERFOLDS
INTERFUSE
INTERFUSED
INTERFUSES
INTERFUSING
INTERGREW

INTERGROW
INTERGROWING
INTERGROWN
INTERGROWS
INTERIM
INTERIMS
INTERIOR
INTERIORS
INTERJECT
INTERJECTED
INTERJECTING
INTERJECTS
INTERJOIN
INTERJOINED
INTERJOINING
INTERJOINS
INTERKNIT
INTERKNITS
INTERKNITTED
INTERKNITTING
INTERLACE
INTERLACED
INTERLACES
INTERLACING
INTERLAID
INTERLARD
INTERLARDED
INTERLARDING
INTERLARDS
INTERLAY
INTERLAYING
INTERLAYS
INTERLEAF
INTERLEAVES
INTERLINE
INTERLINED
INTERLINES
INTERLINING
INTERLININGS
INTERLINK
INTERLINKED
INTERLINKING
INTERLINKS
INTERLOCK
INTERLOCKED
INTERLOCKING
INTERLOCKS
INTERLOPE
INTERLOPED
INTERLOPES
INTERLOPING
INTERLUDE
INTERLUDED
INTERLUDES
INTERLUDING
INTERMENT
INTERMENTS
INTERMIT
INTERMITS
INTERMITTED
INTERMITTING
INTERMIX
INTERMIXED
INTERMIXES
INTERMIXING
INTERMURE
INTERMURED
INTERMURES
INTERMURING
INTERN

INTERNAL
INTERNALS
INTERNE
INTERNED
INTERNEE
INTERNEES
INTERNES
INTERNING
INTERNIST
INTERNISTS
INTERNODE
INTERNODES
INTERNS
INTERPAGE
INTERPAGED
INTERPAGES
INTERPAGING
INTERPLAY
INTERPLAYS
INTERPONE
INTERPONED
INTERPONES
INTERPONING
INTERPOSE
INTERPOSED
INTERPOSES
INTERPOSING
INTERPRET
INTERPRETED
INTERPRETING
INTERPRETS
INTERRED
INTERREGES
INTERREX
INTERRING
INTERRUPT
INTERRUPTED
INTERRUPTING
INTERRUPTS
INTERS
INTERSECT
INTERSECTED
INTERSECTING
INTERSECTS
INTERSERT
INTERSERTED
INTERSERTING
INTERSERTS
INTERSEX
INTERSEXES
INTERTIE
INTERTIES
INTERVAL
INTERVALE
INTERVALES
INTERVALS
INTERVEIN
INTERVEINED
INTERVEINING
INTERVEINS
INTERVENE
INTERVENED
INTERVENES
INTERVENING
INTERVIEW
INTERVIEWED
INTERVIEWING
INTERVIEWS
INTERWAR
INTERWIND

INTERWINDING
INTERWINDS
INTERWORK
INTERWORKED
INTERWORKING
INTERWORKS
INTERWOUND
INTERZONE
INTERZONES
INTESTACIES
INTESTACY
INTESTATE
INTESTATES
INTESTINE
INTESTINES
INTHRAL
INTHRALL
INTHRALLED
INTHRALLING
INTHRALLS
INTHRALS
INTIL
INTIMA
INTIMACIES
INTIMACY
INTIMAE
INTIMATE
INTIMATED
INTIMATES
INTIMATING
INTIME
INTIMISM
INTIMISMS
INTIMIST
INTIMISTE
INTIMISTES
INTIMISTS
INTIMITIES
INTIMITY
INTINE
INTINES
INTIRE
INTITULE
INTITULED
INTITULES
INTITULING
INTO
INTOED
INTOMB
INTOMBED
INTOMBING
INTOMBS
INTONATE
INTONATED
INTONATES
INTONATING
INTONATOR
INTONATORS
INTONE
INTONED
INTONER
INTONERS
INTONES
INTONING
INTONINGS
INTORSION
INTORSIONS
INTORTED
INTORTION
INTORTIONS

INTOWN	INTUBATE	INVALIDS	INVISIBLES	INWREATHES
INTRA	INTUBATED	INVARIANT	INVISIBLY	INWREATHING
INTRADOS	INTUBATES	INVARIANTS	INVITE	INWROUGHT
INTRADOSES	INTUBATING	INVASION	INVITED	INYALA
INTRANT	INTUIT	INVASIONS	INVITEE	INYALAS
INTRANTS	INTUITED	INVASIVE	INVITEES	IO
INTREAT	INTUITING	INVEAGLE	INVITER	IODATE
INTREATED	INTUITION	INVEAGLED	INVITERS	IODATES
INTREATING	INTUITIONS	INVEAGLES	INVITES	IODIC
INTREATS	INTUITIVE	INVEAGLING	INVITING	IODIDE
INTRENCH	INTUITS	INVECKED	INVITINGS	IODIDES
INTRENCHED	INTUMESCE	INVECTED	INVOCATE	IODINE
INTRENCHES	INTUMESCED	INVECTIVE	INVOCATED	IODINES
INTRENCHING	INTUMESCES	INVECTIVES	INVOCATES	IODISE
INTREPID	INTUMESCING	INVEIGH	INVOCATING	IODISED
INTREPIDER	INTUSE	INVEIGHED	INVOICE	IODISES
INTREPIDEST	INTUSES	INVEIGHING	INVOICED	IODISING
INTRICACIES	INTWINE	INVEIGHS	INVOICES	IODISM
INTRICACY	INTWINED	INVEIGLE	INVOICING	IODISMS
INTRICATE	INTWINES	INVEIGLED	INVOKE	IODIZE
INTRIGANT	INTWINING	INVEIGLER	INVOKED	IODIZED
INTRIGANTS	INTWIST	INVEIGLERS	INVOKES	IODIZES
INTRIGUE	INTWISTED	INVEIGLES	INVOKING	IODIZING
INTRIGUED	INTWISTING	INVEIGLING	INVOLUCEL	IODOFORM
INTRIGUER	INTWISTS	INVENIT	INVOLUCELS	IODOFORMS
INTRIGUERS	INULA	INVENT	INVOLUCRE	IODOPHILE
INTRIGUES	INULAS	INVENTED	INVOLUCRES	IODOUS
INTRIGUING	INULASE	INVENTING	INVOLUTE	IODURET
INTRINCE	INULASES	INVENTION	INVOLUTED	IODURETS
INTRINSIC	INULIN	INVENTIONS	INVOLUTES	IODYRITE
INTRO	INULINS	INVENTIVE	INVOLUTING	IODYRITES
INTRODUCE	INUMBRATE	INVENTOR	INVOLVE	IOLITE
INTRODUCED	INUMBRATED	INVENTORIED	INVOLVED	IOLITES
INTRODUCES	INUMBRATES	INVENTORIES	INVOLVES	ION
INTRODUCING	INUMBRATING	INVENTORS	INVOLVING	IONIC
INTROIT	INUNCTION	INVENTORY	INWALL	IONISE
INTROITS	INUNCTIONS	INVENTORYING	INWALLED	IONISED
INTROITUS	INUNDANT	INVENTS	INWALLING	IONISER
INTROITUSES	INUNDATE	INVERSE	INWALLS	IONISERS
INTROJECT	INUNDATED	INVERSED	INWARD	IONISES
INTROJECTED	INUNDATES	INVERSELY	INWARDLY	IONISING
INTROJECTING	INUNDATING	INVERSES	INWARDS	IONIUM
INTROJECTS	INURBANE	INVERSING	INWEAVE	IONIUMS
INTROLD	INURE	INVERSION	INWEAVES	IONIZE
INTROMIT	INURED	INVERSIONS	INWEAVING	IONIZED
INTROMITS	INUREMENT	INVERSIVE	INWICK	IONIZER
INTROMITTED	INUREMENTS	INVERT	INWICKED	IONIZERS
INTROMITTING	INURES	INVERTASE	INWICKING	IONIZES
INTRON	INURING	INVERTASES	INWICKS	IONIZING
INTRONS	INURN	INVERTED	INWIND	IONOMER
INTRORSE	INURNED	INVERTER	INWINDING	IONOMERS
INTROS	INURNING	INVERTERS	INWINDS	IONONE
INTROVERT	INURNS	INVERTIN	INWIT	IONONES
INTROVERTED	INUSITATE	INVERTING	INWITH	IONOPAUSE
INTROVERTING	INUST	INVERTINS	INWITS	IONOPAUSES
INTROVERTS	INUSTION	INVERTOR	INWORK	IONS
INTRUDE	INUSTIONS	INVERTORS	INWORKED	IOS
INTRUDED	INUTILITIES	INVERTS	INWORKING	IOTA
INTRUDER	INUTILITY	INVEST	INWORKINGS	IOTACISM
INTRUDERS	INVADE	INVESTED	INWORKS	IOTACISMS
INTRUDES	INVADED	INVESTING	INWORN	IOTAS
INTRUDING	INVADER	INVESTOR	INWOUND	IPECAC
INTRUSION	INVADERS	INVESTORS	INWOVE	IPECACS
INTRUSIONS	INVADES	INVESTS	INWOVEN	IPOMOEA
INTRUSIVE	INVADING	INVEXED	INWRAP	IPOMOEAS
INTRUSIVES	INVALID	INVIABLE	INWRAPPED	IRACUND
INTRUST	INVALIDED	INVIDIOUS	INWRAPPING	IRADE
INTRUSTED	INVALIDING	INVIOLATE	INWRAPS	IRADES
INTRUSTING	INVALIDINGS	INVIOUS	INWREATHE	IRASCIBLE
INTRUSTS	INVALIDLY	INVISIBLE	INWREATHED	IRASCIBLY

IRATE
IRATELY
IRATER
IRATEST
IRE
IREFUL
IREFULLY
IRENIC
IRENICAL
IRENICISM
IRENICISMS
IRENICON
IRENICONS
IRENICS
IRENOLOGIES
IRENOLOGY
IRES
IRID
IRIDAL
IRIDEAL
IRIDES
IRIDIAL
IRIDIAN
IRIDIC
IRIDISE
IRIDISED
IRIDISES
IRIDISING
IRIDIUM
IRIDIUMS
IRIDIZE
IRIDIZED
IRIDIZES
IRIDIZING
IRIDOLOGIES
IRIDOLOGY
IRIDOTOMIES
IRIDOTOMY
IRIDS
IRIS
IRISATE
IRISATED
IRISATES
IRISATING
IRISATION
IRISATIONS
IRISCOPE
IRISCOPES
IRISED
IRISES
IRISING
IRITIC
IRITIS
IRITISES
IRK
IRKED
IRKING
IRKS
IRKSOME
IRKSOMELY
IROKO
IROKOS
IRON
IRONBARK
IRONBARKS
IRONED
IRONER
IRONERS
IRONIC
IRONICAL

IRONIES
IRONING
IRONINGS
IRONISE
IRONISED
IRONISES
IRONISING
IRONIST
IRONISTS
IRONIZE
IRONIZED
IRONIZES
IRONIZING
IRONS
IRONSMITH
IRONSMITHS
IRONSTONE
IRONSTONES
IRONWARE
IRONWARES
IRONWOOD
IRONWOODS
IRONWORK
IRONWORKS
IRONY
IRRADIANT
IRRADIATE
IRRADIATED
IRRADIATES
IRRADIATING
IRREALITIES
IRREALITY
IRREGULAR
IRREGULARS
IRRELATED
IRRIGABLE
IRRIGATE
IRRIGATED
IRRIGATES
IRRIGATING
IRRIGATOR
IRRIGATORS
IRRIGUOUS
IRRISION
IRRISIONS
IRRISORY
IRRITABLE
IRRITABLY
IRRITANCIES
IRRITANCY
IRRITANT
IRRITANTS
IRRITATE
IRRITATED
IRRITATES
IRRITATING
IRRITATOR
IRRITATORS
IRRUPT
IRRUPTED
IRRUPTING
IRRUPTION
IRRUPTIONS
IRRUPTIVE
IRRUPTS
IS
ISABEL
ISABELLA
ISABELLAS
ISABELS

ISAGOGE
ISAGOGES
ISAGOGIC
ISAGOGICS
ISALLOBAR
ISALLOBARS
ISATIN
ISATINE
ISATINES
ISATINS
ISCHAEMIA
ISCHAEMIAS
ISCHAEMIC
ISCHEMIA
ISCHEMIAS
ISCHEMIC
ISCHIA
ISCHIADIC
ISCHIAL
ISCHIATIC
ISCHIUM
ISCHURIA
ISCHURIAS
ISENERGIC
ISH
ISHES
ISINGLASS
ISINGLASSES
ISLAND
ISLANDED
ISLANDER
ISLANDERS
ISLANDING
ISLANDS
ISLE
ISLED
ISLEMAN
ISLEMEN
ISLES
ISLESMAN
ISLESMEN
ISLET
ISLETS
ISLING
ISM
ISMATIC
ISMATICAL
ISMS
ISMY
ISOBAR
ISOBARE
ISOBARES
ISOBARIC
ISOBARS
ISOBASE
ISOBASES
ISOBATH
ISOBATHIC
ISOBATHS
ISOBRONT
ISOBRONTS
ISOCHASM
ISOCHASMS
ISOCHEIM
ISOCHEIMS
ISOCHIMAL
ISOCHIMALS
ISOCHIME
ISOCHIMES
ISOCHOR

ISOCHORE
ISOCHORES
ISOCHORIC
ISOCHORS
ISOCHRONE
ISOCHRONES
ISOCLINAL
ISOCLINALS
ISOCLINE
ISOCLINES
ISOCLINIC
ISOCLINICS
ISOCRACIES
ISOCRACY
ISOCRATIC
ISOCRYMAL
ISOCRYMALS
ISOCRYME
ISOCRYMES
ISOCYCLIC
ISODICON
ISODICONS
ISODOMA
ISODOMON
ISODOMONS
ISODOMOUS
ISODOMUM
ISODONT
ISODONTAL
ISODONTS
ISOETES
ISOGAMETE
ISOGAMETES
ISOGAMIC
ISOGAMIES
ISOGAMOUS
ISOGAMY
ISOGENIES
ISOGENOUS
ISOGENY
ISOGLOSS
ISOGLOSSES
ISOGON
ISOGONAL
ISOGONALS
ISOGONIC
ISOGONICS
ISOGONS
ISOGRAM
ISOGRAMS
ISOHEL
ISOHELS
ISOHYET
ISOHYETAL
ISOHYETALS
ISOHYETS
ISOKONT
ISOKONTAN
ISOKONTANS
ISOKONTS
ISOLABLE
ISOLATE
ISOLATED
ISOLATES
ISOLATING
ISOLATION
ISOLATIONS
ISOLATIVE
ISOLATOR
ISOLATORS

ISOLINE
ISOLINES
ISOLOGOUS
ISOLOGUE
ISOLOGUES
ISOMER
ISOMERE
ISOMERES
ISOMERIC
ISOMERISE
ISOMERISED
ISOMERISES
ISOMERISING
ISOMERISM
ISOMERISMS
ISOMERIZE
ISOMERIZED
ISOMERIZES
ISOMERIZING
ISOMEROUS
ISOMERS
ISOMETRIC
ISOMETRICS
ISOMETRIES
ISOMETRY
ISOMORPH
ISOMORPHS
ISONIAZID
ISONIAZIDS
ISONOMIC
ISONOMIES
ISONOMOUS
ISONOMY
ISOPLETH
ISOPLETHS
ISOPOD
ISOPODAN
ISOPODOUS
ISOPODS
ISOPOLITIES
ISOPOLITY
ISOPRENE
ISOPRENES
ISOPROPYL
ISOPROPYLS
ISOSCELES
ISOSPIN
ISOSPINS
ISOSPORIES
ISOSPORY
ISOSTASIES
ISOSTASY
ISOSTATIC
ISOSTERIC
ISOTACTIC
ISOTHERAL
ISOTHERALS
ISOTHERE
ISOTHERES
ISOTHERM
ISOTHERMS
ISOTONE
ISOTONES
ISOTONIC
ISOTOPE
ISOTOPES
ISOTOPIC
ISOTOPIES
ISOTOPY
ISOTRON

ISOTRONS   ISTHMUSES   ITCHIEST   ITERATE   IVORIED
ISOTROPIC   ISTLE   ITCHINESS   ITERATED   IVORIES
ISOTROPIES   ISTLES   ITCHINESSES   ITERATES   IVORIST
ISOTROPY   IT   ITCHING   ITERATING   IVORISTS
ISOTYPE   ITA   ITCHWEED   ITERATION   IVORY
ISOTYPES   ITACISM   ITCHWEEDS   ITERATIONS   IVRESSE
ISSEI   ITACISMS   ITCHY   ITERATIVE   IVRESSES
ISSEIS   ITALIC   ITEM   ITERUM   IVY
ISSUABLE   ITALICISE   ITEMED   ITINERACIES   IWIS
ISSUABLY   ITALICISED   ITEMING   ITINERACY   IXIA
ISSUANCE   ITALICISES   ITEMISE   ITINERANT   IXIAS
ISSUANCES   ITALICISING   ITEMISED   ITINERANTS   IXTLE
ISSUANT   ITALICIZE   ITEMISES   ITINERARIES   IXTLES
ISSUE   ITALICIZED   ITEMISING   ITINERARY   IYNX
ISSUED   ITALICIZES   ITEMIZE   ITINERATE   IYNXES
ISSUELESS   ITALICIZING   ITEMIZED   ITINERATED   IZARD
ISSUER   ITALICS   ITEMIZES   ITINERATES   IZARDS
ISSUERS   ITAS   ITEMIZING   ITINERATING   IZZARD
ISSUES   ITCH   ITEMS   ITS   IZZARDS
ISSUING   ITCHED   ITERANCE   ITSELF   IZZET
ISTHMIAN   ITCHES   ITERANCES   IVIED   IZZETS
ISTHMUS   ITCHIER   ITERANT   IVIES

J

JAB	JACKPOT	JAILER	JAMBOOLS	JANTIER
JABBED	JACKPOTS	JAILERESS	JAMBOREE	JANTIES
JABBER	JACKS	JAILERESSES	JAMBOREES	JANTIEST
JABBERED	JACKSIE	JAILERS	JAMBOS	JANTY
JABBERER	JACKSIES	JAILHOUSE	JAMBS	JAP
JABBERERS	JACKSMITH	JAILHOUSES	JAMBU	JAPAN
JABBERING	JACKSMITHS	JAILING	JAMBUL	JAPANNED
JABBERINGS	JACKSY	JAILOR	JAMBULS	JAPANNER
JABBERS	JACOBUS	JAILORESS	JAMBUS	JAPANNERS
JABBING	JACOBUSES	JAILORESSES	JAMDANI	JAPANNING
JABBLE	JACONET	JAILORS	JAMDANIS	JAPANS
JABBLED	JACONETS	JAILS	JAMES	JAPE
JABBLES	JACQUARD	JAK	JAMESES	JAPED
JABBLING	JACQUARDS	JAKE	JAMJAR	JAPES
JABERS	JACTATION	JAKES	JAMJARS	JAPING
JABIRU	JACTATIONS	JAKESES	JAMMED	JAPONICA
JABIRUS	JACULATE	JAKS	JAMMER	JAPONICAS
JABORANDI	JACULATED	JALAP	JAMMERS	JAPPED
JABORANDIS	JACULATES	JALAPIC	JAMMIER	JAPPING
JABOT	JACULATING	JALAPIN	JAMMIEST	JAPS
JABOTS	JACULATOR	JALAPINS	JAMMING	JAR
JABS	JACULATORS	JALAPS	JAMMY	JARARACA
JACAMAR	JACUZZI	JALOPIES	JAMPAN	JARARACAS
JACAMARS	JACUZZIS	JALOPPIES	JAMPANEE	JARARAKA
JACANA	JADE	JALOPPY	JAMPANEES	JARARAKAS
JAÇANA	JADED	JALOPY	JAMPANI	JARFUL
JACANAS	JADEDLY	JALOUSE	JAMPANIS	JARFULS
JAÇANAS	JADEITE	JALOUSED	JAMPANS	JARGON
JACARANDA	JADEITES	JALOUSES	JAMPOT	JARGONED
JACARANDAS	JADERIES	JALOUSIE	JAMPOTS	JARGONEER
JACCHUS	JADERY	JALOUSIED	JAMS	JARGONEERS
JACCHUSES	JADES	JALOUSIES	JANE	JARGONING
JACENT	JADING	JALOUSING	JANES	JARGONISE
JACINTH	JADISH	JAM	JANGLE	JARGONISED
JACINTHS	JAEGER	JAMADAR	JANGLED	JARGONISES
JACK	JAEGERS	JAMADARS	JANGLER	JARGONISING
JACKAL	JAG	JAMB	JANGLERS	JARGONIST
JACKALLED	JAGANNATH	JAMBE	JANGLES	JARGONISTS
JACKALLING	JAGANNATHS	JAMBEAU	JANGLIER	JARGONIZE
JACKALS	JÄGER	JAMBEAUX	JANGLIEST	JARGONIZED
JACKAROO	JÄGERS	JAMBEE	JANGLING	JARGONIZES
JACKAROOED	JAGGED	JAMBEES	JANGLINGS	JARGONIZING
JACKAROOING	JAGGEDLY	JAMBER	JANGLY	JARGONS
JACKAROOS	JAGGER	JAMBERS	JANISSARIES	JARGOON
JACKASS	JAGGERIES	JAMBES	JANISSARY	JARGOONS
JACKASSES	JAGGERS	JAMBEUX	JANITOR	JARK
JACKBOOT	JAGGERY	JAMBIER	JANITORS	JARKMAN
JACKBOOTED	JAGGIER	JAMBIERS	JANITRESS	JARKMEN
JACKBOOTING	JAGGIEST	JAMBIYA	JANITRESSES	JARKS
JACKBOOTS	JAGGING	JAMBIYAH	JANITRIX	JARL
JACKDAW	JAGGY	JAMBIYAHS	JANITRIXES	JARLS
JACKDAWS	JAGHIR	JAMBIYAS	JANIZAR	JAROOL
JACKED	JAGHIRDAR	JAMBO	JANIZARIES	JAROOLS
JACKEROO	JAGHIRDARS	JAMBOK	JANIZARS	JAROSITE
JACKEROOED	JAGHIRE	JAMBOKKED	JANIZARY	JAROSITES
JACKEROOING	JAGHIRES	JAMBOKKING	JANKER	JARRAH
JACKEROOS	JAGHIRS	JAMBOKS	JANKERS	JARRAHS
JACKET	JAGIR	JAMBOLAN	JANN	JARRED
JACKETED	JAGIRS	JAMBOLANA	JANNOCK	JARRING
JACKETING	JAGS	JAMBOLANAS	JANNOCKS	JARRINGLY
JACKETS	JAGUAR	JAMBOLANS	JANNS	JARRINGS
JACKING	JAGUARS	JAMBONE	JANSKIES	JARS
JACKMAN	JAIL	JAMBONES	JANSKY	JARTA
JACKMEN	JAILED	JAMBOOL	JANTEE	JARTAS

JARUL	JAWARIS	JEELY	JEOFAILS	JESTBOOK
JARULS	JAWBATION	JEELYING	JEOPARD	JESTBOOKS
JARVEY	JAWBATIONS	JEEP	JEOPARDED	JESTED
JARVEYS	JAWBONE	JEEPERS	JEOPARDER	JESTEE
JARVIE	JAWBONED	JEEPNEY	JEOPARDERS	JESTEES
JARVIES	JAWBONES	JEEPNEYS	JEOPARDIED	JESTER
JASEY	JAWBONING	JEEPS	JEOPARDIES	JESTERS
JASEYS	JAWBONINGS	JEER	JEOPARDING	JESTFUL
JASIES	JAWBOX	JEERED	JEOPARDS	JESTING
JASMINE	JAWBOXES	JEERER	JEOPARDY	JESTINGLY
JASMINES	JAWED	JEERERS	JEOPARDYING	JESTINGS
JASP	JAWFALL	JEERING	JEQUIRITIES	JESTS
JASPÉ	JAWFALLS	JEERINGLY	JEQUIRITY	JÉSUS
JASPER	JAWHOLE	JEERINGS	JERBIL	JET
JASPERISE	JAWHOLES	JEERS	JERBILS	JETÉ
JASPERISED	JAWING	JEES	JERBOA	JETÉS
JASPERISES	JAWINGS	JEFF	JERBOAS	JETFOIL
JASPERISING	JAWS	JEFFED	JEREED	JETFOILS
JASPERIZE	JAY	JEFFING	JEREEDS	JETLINER
JASPERIZED	JAYS	JEFFS	JEREMIAD	JETLINERS
JASPERIZES	JAYWALK	JEHAD	JEREMIADS	JETON
JASPERIZING	JAYWALKED	JEHADS	JERFALCON	JETONS
JASPEROUS	JAYWALKER	JEJUNA	JERFALCONS	JETPLANE
JASPERS	JAYWALKERS	JEJUNE	JERID	JETPLANES
JASPERY	JAYWALKING	JEJUNELY	JERIDS	JETS
JASPES	JAYWALKINGS	JEJUNITIES	JFRK	JETSAM
JASPIDEAN	JAYWALKS	JEJUNITY	JERKED	JETSAMS
JASPIS	JAZERANT	JEJUNUM	JERKER	JETSOM
JASPISES	JAZERANTS	JELAB	JERKERS	JETSOMS
JASPS	JAZIES	JELABS	JERKIER	JETSON
JASY	JAZY	JELL	JERKIES	JETSONS
JATAKA	JAZZ	JELLABA	JERKIEST	JETSTREAM
JATAKAS	JAZZED	JELLABAS	JERKIN	JETSTREAMS
JATO	JAZZES	JELLED	JERKINESS	JETTATURA
JATOS	JAZZIER	JELLIED	JERKINESSES	JETTATURAS
JAUNCE	JAZZIEST	JELLIES	JERKING	JETTED
JAUNCED	JAZZILY	JELLIFIED	JERKINGS	JETTIES
JAUNCES	JAZZINESS	JELLIFIES	JERKINS	JETTINESS
JAUNCING	JAZZINESSES	JELLIFORM	JERKS	JETTINESSES
JAUNDICE	JAZZING	JELLIFY	JERKY	JETTING
JAUNDICED	JAZZMAN	JELLIFYING	JEROBOAM	JETTISON
JAUNDICES	JAZZMEN	JELLING	JEROBOAMS	JETTISONED
JAUNDICING	JAZZY	JELLO	JERQUE	JETTISONING
JAUNSE	JEALOUS	JELLOS	JERQUED	JETTISONS
JAUNSED	JEALOUSE	JELLS	JERQUER	JETTON
JAUNSES	JEALOUSED	JELLY	JERQUERS	JETTONS
JAUNSING	JEALOUSES	JELLYBEAN	JERQUES	JETTY
JAUNT	JEALOUSIES	JELLYBEANS	JERQUING	JEU
JAUNTED	JEALOUSING	JELLYFISH	JERQUINGS	JEUNE
JAUNTEE	JEALOUSLY	JELLYFISHES	JERRICAN	JEUX
JAUNTIE	JEALOUSY	JELLYING	JERRICANS	JEWEL
JAUNTIER	JEAN	JELUTONG	JERRIES	JEWELFISH
JAUNTIES	JEANETTE	JELUTONGS	JERRY	JEWELFISHES
JAUNTIEST	JEANETTES	JEMADAR	JERRYCAN	JEWELLED
JAUNTILY	JEANS	JEMADARS	JERRYCANS	JEWELLER
JAUNTING	JEAT	JEMIDAR	JERSEY	JEWELLERIES
JAUNTS	JEATS	JEMIDARS	JERSEYS	JEWELLERS
JAUNTY	JEBEL	JEMIMA	JESS	JEWELLERY
JAUP	JEBELS	JEMIMAS	JESSAMIES	JEWELLING
JAUPED	JEE	JEMMIES	JESSAMINE	JEWELRIES
JAUPING	JEED	JEMMINESS	JESSAMINES	JEWELRY
JAUPS	JEEING	JEMMINESSES	JESSAMY	JEWELS
JAVEL	JEEL	JEMMY	JESSANT	JEWFISH
JAVELIN	JEELED	JENNET	JESSED	JEWFISHES
JAVELINS	JEELIE	JENNETING	JESSERANT	JEZAIL
JAVELS	JEELIED	JENNETINGS	JESSERANTS	JEZAILS
JAW	JEELIEING	JENNETS	JESSES	JHALA
JAWAN	JEELIES	JENNIES	JESSIE	JHALAS
JAWANS	JEELING	JENNY	JESSIES	JIAO
JAWARI	JEELS	JEOFAIL	JEST	JIAOS

JIB	JIMCRACK	JITNEYS	JOCULATOR	JOKER
JIBBAH	JIMCRACKS	JITTER	JOCULATORS	JOKERS
JIBBAHS	JIMINIES	JITTERBUG	JOCUND	JOKES
JIBBED	JIMINY	JITTERBUGGED	JOCUNDITIES	JOKESMITH
JIBBER	JIMJAM	JITTERBUGGING	JOCUNDITY	JOKESMITHS
JIBBERED	JIMJAMS	JITTERBUGS	JOCUNDLY	JOKESOME
JIBBERING	JIMMIES	JITTERED	JODEL	JOKEY
JIBBERS	JIMMY	JITTERING	JODELLED	JOKIER
JIBBING	JIMP	JITTERS	JODELLING	JOKIEST
JIBBINGS	JIMPER	JITTERY	JODELS	JOKING
JIBE	JIMPEST	JIVE	JODHPURS	JOKINGLY
JIBED	JIMPIER	JIVED	JOE	JOKOL
JIBER	JIMPIEST	JIVER	JOES	JOKY
JIBERS	JIMPLY	JIVERS	JOEY	JOLE
JIBES	JIMPNESS	JIVES	JOEYS	JOLED
JIBING	JIMPNESSES	JIVING	JOG	JOLES
JIBS	JIMPY	JIZ	JOGGED	JOLING
JICKAJOG	JINGAL	JIZZ	JOGGER	JOLL
JICKAJOGS	JINGALS	JIZZES	JOGGERS	JOLLED
JIFF	JINGBANG	JO	JOGGING	JOLLIED
JIFFIES	JINGBANGS	JOANNA	JOGGINGS	JOLLIER
JIFFS	JINGLE	JOANNAS	JOGGLE	JOLLIES
JIFFY	JINGLED	JOANNES	JOGGLED	JOLLIEST
JIG	JINGLER	JOANNESES	JOGGLES	JOLLIFIED
JIGAJIG	JINGLERS	JOB	JOGGLING	JOLLIFIES
JIGAJIGS	JINGLES	JOBATION	JOGS	JOLLIFY
JIGAJOG	JINGLET	JOBATIONS	JOGTROT	JOLLIFYING
JIGAJOGS	JINGLETS	JOBBED	JOGTROTS	JOLLILY
JIGAMAREE	JINGLIER	JOBBER	JOHANNES	JOLLIMENT
JIGAMAREES	JINGLIEST	JOBBERIES	JOHANNESES	JOLLIMENTS
JIGGED	JINGLING	JOBBERS	JOHN	JOLLINESS
JIGGER	JINGLINGS	JOBBERY	JOHNNIE	JOLLINESSES
JIGGERED	JINGLY	JOBBING	JOHNNIES	JOLLING
JIGGERING	JINGO	JOBBINGS	JOHNNY	JOLLITIES
JIGGERS	JINGOES	JOBCENTRE	JOHNS	JOLLITY
JIGGING	JINGOISH	JOBCENTRES	JOIN	JOLLS
JIGGINGS	JINGOISM	JOBE	JOINDER	JOLLY
JIGGISH	JINGOISMS	JOBED	JOINDERS	JOLLYBOAT
JIGGLE	JINGOIST	JOBERNOWL	JOINED	JOLLYBOATS
JIGGLED	JINGOISTS	JOBERNOWLS	JOINER	JOLLYHEAD
JIGGLES	JINJILI	JOBES	JOINERIES	JOLLYHEADS
JIGGLING	JINJILIS	JOBING	JOINERS	JOLLYING
JIGGUMBOB	JINK	JOBLESS	JOINERY	JOLT
JIGGUMBOBS	JINKED	JOBS	JOINING	JOLTED
JIGJIG	JINKER	JOBSWORTH	JOININGS	JOLTER
JIGJIGS	JINKERS	JOBSWORTHS	JOINS	JOLTERS
JIGOT	JINKING	JOCK	JOINT	JOLTHEAD
JIGOTS	JINKS	JOCKETTE	JOINTED	JOLTHEADS
JIGS	JINN	JOCKETTES	JOINTER	JOLTIER
JIGSAW	JINNEE	JOCKEY	JOINTERS	JOLTIEST
JIGSAWED	JINNI	JOCKEYED	JOINTING	JOLTING
JIGSAWING	JINNS	JOCKEYING	JOINTLESS	JOLTINGLY
JIGSAWN	JINX	JOCKEYISM	JOINTLY	JOLTS
JIGSAWS	JINXED	JOCKEYISMS	JOINTNESS	JOLTY
JIHAD	JINXES	JOCKEYS	JOINTNESSES	JOMO
JIHADS	JIRBLE	JOCKO	JOINTRESS	JOMOS
JILGIE	JIRBLED	JOCKOS	JOINTRESSES	JONCANOE
JILGIES	JIRBLES	JOCKS	JOINTS	JONCANOES
JILL	JIRBLING	JOCKSTRAP	JOINTURE	JONGLEUR
JILLAROO	JIRD	JOCKSTRAPS	JOINTURED	JONGLEURS
JILLAROOS	JIRDS	JOCKTELEG	JOINTURES	JONQUIL
JILLET	JIRGA	JOCKTELEGS	JOINTURING	JONQUILS
JILLETS	JIRGAS	JOCO	JOIST	JONTIES
JILLFLIRT	JIRKINET	JOCOROUS	JOISTED	JONTY
JILLFLIRTS	JIRKINETS	JOCOSE	JOISTING	JOOK
JILLS	JISM	JOCOSELY	JOISTS	JOOKED
JILT	JISMS	JOCOSITIES	JOJOBA	JOOKERIES
JILTED	JISSOM	JOCOSITY	JOJOBAS	JOOKERY
JILTING	JISSOMS	JOCULAR	JOKE	JOOKING
JILTS	JITNEY	JOCULARLY	JOKED	JOOKS

JOR	JOURNO	JUDGEMENT	JUKE	JUNGLIER
JORAM	JOURNOS	JUDGEMENTS	JUKED	JUNGLIEST
JORAMS	JOURS	JUDGES	JUKES	JUNGLIS
JORDAN	JOUST	JUDGESHIP	JUKING	JUNGLY
JORDANS	JOUSTED	JUDGESHIPS	JULEP	JUNIOR
JORDELOO	JOUSTER	JUDGING	JULEPS	JUNIORITIES
JORDELOOS	JOUSTERS	JUDGMENT	JULIENNE	JUNIORITY
JORS	JOUSTING	JUDGMENTS	JULIENNES	JUNIORS
JORUM	JOUSTS	JUDICABLE	JUMAR	JUNIPER
JORUMS	JOUYSANCE	JUDICATOR	JUMARED	JUNIPERS
JOSEPH	JOUYSANCES	JUDICATORS	JUMARING	JUNK
JOSEPHS	JOVIAL	JUDICIAL	JUMARS	JUNKANOO
JOSH	JOVIALITIES	JUDICIARIES	JUMART	JUNKANOOS
JOSHED	JOVIALITY	JUDICIARY	JUMARTS	JUNKED
JOSHER	JOVIALLY	JUDICIOUS	JUMBAL	JUNKER
JOSHERS	JOW	JUDIES	JUMBALS	JUNKERDOM
JOSHES	JOWAR	JUDO	JUMBIE	JUNKERDOMS
JOSHING	JOWARI	JUDOGI	JUMBIES	JUNKERISM
JOSKIN	JOWARIS	JUDOGIS	JUMBLE	JUNKERISMS
JOSKINS	JOWARS	JUDOIST	JUMBLED	JUNKERS
JOSS	JOWED	JUDOISTS	JUMBLER	JUNKET
JOSSER	JOWING	JUDOKA	JUMBLERS	JUNKETED
JOSSERS	JOWL	JUDOKAS	JUMBLES	JUNKETING
JOSSES	JOWLED	JUDOS	JUMBLIER	JUNKETINGS
JOSTLE	JOWLER	JUDS	JUMBLIEST	JUNKETS
JOSTLED	JOWLERS	JUDY	JUMBLING	JUNKIE
JOSTLES	JOWLING	JUG	JUMBLY	JUNKIER
JOSTLING	JOWLS	JUGA	JUMBO	JUNKIES
JOSTLINGS	JOWS	JUGAL	JUMBOISE	JUNKIEST
JOT	JOY	JUGALS	JUMBOISED	JUNKING
JOTA	JOYANCE	JUGATE	JUMBOISES	JUNKMAN
JOTAS	JOYANCES	JUGFUL	JUMBOISING	JUNKMEN
JOTS	JOYED	JUGFULS	JUMBOIZE	JUNKS
JOTTED	JOYFUL	JUGGED	JUMBOIZED	JUNKY
JOTTER	JOYFULLER	JUGGING	JUMBOIZES	JUNTA
JOTTERS	JOYFULLEST	JUGGINS	JUMBOIZING	JUNTAS
JOTTING	JOYFULLY	JUGGINSES	JUMBOS	JUNTO
JOTTINGS	JOYING	JUGGLE	JUMBUCK	JUNTOS
JOTUN	JOYLESS	JUGGLED	JUMBUCKS	JUPATI
JÖTUNN	JOYLESSLY	JUGGLER	JUMBY	JUPATIS
JÖTUNNS	JOYOUS	JUGGLERIES	JUMELLE	JUPON
JOTUNS	JOYOUSLY	JUGGLERS	JUMELLES	JUPONS
JOUGS	JOYS	JUGGLERY	JUMP	JURA
JOUISANCE	JUBA	JUGGLES	JUMPED	JURAL
JOUISANCES	JUBAS	JUGGLING	JUMPER	JURALLY
JOUK	JUBATE	JUGGLINGS	JUMPERS	JURANT
JOUKED	JUBBAH	JUGS	JUMPIER	JURANTS
JOUKERIES	JUBBAHS	JUGULAR	JUMPIEST	JURAT
JOUKERY	JUBE	JUGULARS	JUMPILY	JURATORY
JOUKING	JUBES	JUGULATE	JUMPINESS	JURATS
JOUKS	JUBILANCE	JUGULATED	JUMPINESSES	JURE
JOULE	JUBILANCES	JUGULATES	JUMPING	JURIDIC
JOULED	JUBILANCIES	JUGULATING	JUMPS	JURIDICAL
JOULES	JUBILANCY	JUGUM	JUMPY	JURIES
JOULING	JUBILANT	JUICE	JUNCATE	JURIST
JOUNCE	JUBILATE	JUICED	JUNCATES	JURISTIC
JOUNCED	JUBILATED	JUICELESS	JUNCO	JURISTS
JOUNCES	JUBILATES	JUICER	JUNCOES	JUROR
JOUNCING	JUBILATING	JUICERS	JUNCOS	JURORS
JOUR	JUBILEE	JUICES	JUNCTION	JURY
JOURNAL	JUBILEES	JUICIER	JUNCTIONS	JURYMAN
JOURNALLED	JUD	JUICIEST	JUNCTURE	JURYMAST
JOURNALLING	JUDAS	JUICINESS	JUNCTURES	JURYMASTS
JOURNALS	JUDASES	JUICINESSES	JUNCUS	JURYMEN
JOURNEY	JUDDER	JUICING	JUNCUSES	JURYWOMAN
JOURNEYED	JUDDERED	JUICY	JUNEATING	JURYWOMEN
JOURNEYER	JUDDERING	JUJU	JUNEATINGS	JUS
JOURNEYERS	JUDDERS	JUJUBE	JUNGLE	JUSSIVE
JOURNEYING	JUDGE	JUJUBES	JUNGLES	JUSSIVES
JOURNEYS	JUDGED	JUJUS	JUNGLI	JUST

JUSTED	JUSTIFIER	JUSTLY	JUTTIES	JUXTAPOSE
JUSTER	JUSTIFIERS	JUSTNESS	JUTTING	JUXTAPOSED
JUSTEST	JUSTIFIES	JUSTNESSES	JUTTINGLY	JUXTAPOSES
JUSTICE	JUSTIFY	JUSTS	JUTTY	JUXTAPOSING
JUSTICER	JUSTIFYING	JUT	JUTTYING	JYMOLD
JUSTICERS	JUSTING	JUTE	JUVENAL	JYNX
JUSTICES	JUSTLE	JUTES	JUVENALS	JYNXES
JUSTICIAR	JUSTLED	JUTS	JUVENILE	
JUSTICIARS	JUSTLES	JUTTED	JUVENILES	
JUSTIFIED	JUSTLING	JUTTIED	JUVENILIA	

K

KA
KAAMA
KAAMAS
KABAB
KABABS
KABALA
KABALAS
KABAYA
KABAYAS
KABBALA
KABBALAH
KABBALAHS
KABBALAS
KABELE
KABELES
KABELJOU
KABELJOUS
KABELJOUW
KABELJOUWS
KABOB
KABOBS
KABUKI
KABUKIS
KACCHA
KACCHAS
KACHA
KACHAHRI
KACHAHRIS
KACHCHA
KACHERI
KACHERIS
KACHINA
KACHINAS
KADE
KADES
KADI
KADIS
KAE
KAED
KAEING
KAES
KAFFIYEH
KAFFIYEHS
KAFILA
KAFILAS
KAFTAN
KAFTANS
KAGO
KAGOOL
KAGOOLS
KAGOS
KAGOUL
KAGOULE
KAGOULES
KAGOULS
KAHAL
KAHALS
KAI
KAIAK
KAIAKS
KAID
KAIDS
KAIE
KAIES

KAIF
KAIFS
KAIKAI
KAIKAIED
KAIKAIING
KAIKAIS
KAIL
KAILS
KAILYAIRD
KAILYAIRDS
KAILYARD
KAILYARDS
KAIM
KAIMAKAM
KAIMAKAMS
KAIMS
KAIN
KAING
KAINITE
KAINITES
KAINS
KAIS
KAISER
KAISERDOM
KAISERDOMS
KAISERIN
KAISERINS
KAISERISM
KAISERISMS
KAISERS
KAJAWAH
KAJAWAHS
KAKA
KAKAPO
KAKAPOS
KAKAS
KAKEMONO
KAKEMONOS
KAKI
KAKIS
KAKODYL
KAKODYLS
KALAMDAN
KALAMDANS
KALAMKARI
KALAMKARIS
KALE
KALENDAR
KALENDARED
KALENDARING
KALENDARS
KALENDS
KALES
KALI
KALIAN
KALIANS
KALIF
KALIFS
KALINITE
KALINITES
KALIS
KALIUM
KALIUMS
KALLITYPE

KALLITYPES
KALMIA
KALMIAS
KALONG
KALONGS
KALOTYPE
KALOTYPES
KALPA
KALPAK
KALPAKS
KALPAS
KALPIS
KALPISES
KALUMPIT
KALUMPITS
KALYPTRA
KALYPTRAS
KAM
KAMACITE
KAMACITES
KAMALA
KAMALAS
KAME
KAMEES
KAMEESES
KAMELA
KAMELAS
KAMERAD
KAMERADED
KAMERADING
KAMERADS
KAMES
KAMI
KAMICHI
KAMICHIS
KAMIK
KAMIKAZE
KAMIKAZES
KAMIKS
KAMILA
KAMILAS
KAMIS
KAMISES
KAMME
KAMPONG
KAMPONGS
KAMSEEN
KAMSEENS
KAMSIN
KAMSINS
KANA
KANAKA
KANAKAS
KANAS
KANDIES
KANDY
KANEH
KANEHS
KANG
KANGA
KANGAROO
KANGAROOS
KANGAS
KANGHA

KANGHAS
KANGS
KANS
KANSES
KANT
KANTAR
KANTARS
KANTED
KANTELA
KANTELAS
KANTELE
KANTELES
KANTEN
KANTENS
KANTHA
KANTHAS
KANTICOY
KANTICOYED
KANTICOYING
KANTICOYS
KANTIKOY
KANTIKOYED
KANTIKOYING
KANTIKOYS
KANTING
KANTS
KANZU
KANZUS
KAOLIANG
KAOLIANGS
KAOLIN
KAOLINE
KAOLINES
KAOLINISE
KAOLINISED
KAOLINISES
KAOLINISING
KAOLINITE
KAOLINITES
KAOLINIZE
KAOLINIZED
KAOLINIZES
KAOLINIZING
KAOLINS
KAON
KAONS
KAPOK
KAPOKS
KAPPA
KAPPAS
KAPUT
KAPUTT
KARA
KARABINER
KARABINERS
KARAIT
KARAITS
KARAKA
KARAKAS
KARAKUL
KARAKULS
KARAS
KARAT
KARATE

KARATEIST
KARATEISTS
KARATEKA
KARATEKAS
KARATES
KARATS
KARITE
KARITES
KARMA
KARMAS
KARMIC
KAROSS
KAROSSES
KARRI
KARRIS
KARSEY
KARSEYS
KARSIES
KARST
KARSTS
KARSY
KART
KARTING
KARTINGS
KARTS
KARYOLOGIES
KARYOLOGY
KARYOSOME
KARYOSOMES
KARZIES
KARZY
KAS
KASBA
KASBAH
KASBAHS
KASBAS
KAT
KATABASES
KATABASIS
KATABATIC
KATABOLIC
KATAKANA
KATAKANAS
KATHAK
KATHAKALI
KATHAKALIS
KATHAKS
KATHARSES
KATHARSIS
KATHODE
KATHODES
KATI
KATION
KATIONS
KATIS
KATORGA
KATORGAS
KATS
KATTI
KATTIS
KATYDID
KATYDIDS
KAUGH
KAUGHS

KAURI
KAURIS
KAVA
KAVAS
KAVASS
KAVASSES
KAW
KAWED
KAWING
KAWS
KAY
KAYAK
KAYAKS
KAYLE
KAYLES
KAYO
KAYOE
KAYOED
KAYOEING
KAYOES
KAYOING
KAYOS
KAYS
KAZATZKA
KAZATZKAS
KAZI
KAZIS
KAZOO
KAZOOS
KEA
KEAS
KEASAR
KEASARS
KEB
KEBAB
KEBABS
KEBBED
KEBBIE
KEBBIES
KEBBING
KEBBOCK
KEBBOCKS
KEBBUCK
KEBBUCKS
KEBELE
KEBELES
KEBLAH
KEBLAHS
KEBOB
KEBOBS
KEBS
KECK
KECKED
KECKING
KECKLE
KECKLED
KECKLES
KECKLING
KECKLINGS
KECKS
KECKSES
KECKSIES
KECKSY
KED
KEDDAH
KEDDAHS
KEDGE
KEDGED
KEDGER
KEDGEREE

KEDGEREES
KEDGERS
KEDGES
KEDGING
KEDGY
KEDS
KEECH
KEECHES
KEEK
KEEKED
KEEKER
KEEKERS
KEEKING
KEEKS
KEEL
KEELAGE
KEELAGES
KEELBOAT
KEELBOATS
KEELED
KEELER
KEELERS
KEELHAUL
KEELHAULED
KEELHAULING
KEELHAULINGS
KEELHAULS
KEELIE
KEELIES
KEELING
KEELINGS
KEELIVINE
KEELIVINES
KEELMAN
KEELMEN
KEELS
KEELSON
KEELSONS
KEELYVINE
KEELYVINES
KEEN
KEENED
KEENER
KEENERS
KEENEST
KEENING
KEENINGS
KEENLY
KEENNESS
KEENNESSES
KEENS
KEEP
KEEPER
KEEPERS
KEEPING
KEEPINGS
KEEPNET
KEEPNETS
KEEPS
KEEPSAKE
KEEPSAKES
KEEPSAKY
KEESHOND
KEESHONDS
KEEVE
KEEVES
KEF
KEFFEL
KEFFELS
KEFFIYEH

KEFFIYEHS
KEFIR
KEFIRS
KEFS
KEFUFFLE
KEFUFFLED
KEFUFFLES
KEFUFFLING
KEG
KEGS
KEIGHT
KEIR
KEIRS
KEITLOA
KEITLOAS
KEKSYE
KEKSYES
KELIM
KELIMS
KELL
KELLAUT
KELLAUTS
KELLIES
KELLS
KELLY
KELOID
KELOIDAL
KELOIDS
KELP
KELPER
KELPERS
KELPIE
KELPIES
KELPS
KELPY
KELSON
KELSONS
KELT
KELTER
KELTERS
KELTIE
KELTIES
KELTS
KELTY
KELVIN
KELVINS
KEMB
KEMBED
KEMBING
KEMBO
KEMBOED
KEMBOING
KEMBOS
KEMBS
KEMP
KEMPED
KEMPER
KEMPERS
KEMPING
KEMPINGS
KEMPLE
KEMPLES
KEMPS
KEMPT
KEN
KENAF
KENAFS
KENDO
KENDOS
KENNED

KENNEL
KENNELLED
KENNELLING
KENNELS
KENNER
KENNERS
KENNET
KENNETS
KENNING
KENNINGS
KENOSES
KENOSIS
KENOTIC
KENS
KENSPECK
KENT
KENTED
KENTING
KENTLEDGE
KENTLEDGES
KENTS
KEP
KEPHALIC
KEPHALICS
KEPHIR
KEPHIRS
KEPI
KEPIS
KEPPING
KEPPIT
KEPS
KEPT
KERAMIC
KERATIN
KERATINS
KERATITIS
KERATITISES
KERATOID
KERATOSE
KERATOSES
KERATOSIS
KERB
KERBS
KERBSIDE
KERBSIDES
KERBSTONE
KERBSTONES
KERCHIEF
KERCHIEFED
KERCHIEFING
KERCHIEFS
KERF
KERFS
KERFUFFLE
KERFUFFLED
KERFUFFLES
KERFUFFLING
KERMES
KERMESES
KERMESITE
KERMESITES
KERMESS
KERMESSE
KERMESSES
KERMIS
KERMISES
KERN
KERNE
KERNED
KERNEL

KERNELLED
KERNELLING
KERNELLY
KERNELS
KERNES
KERNING
KERNISH
KERNITE
KERNITES
KERNS
KEROGEN
KEROGENS
KEROSENE
KEROSENES
KEROSINE
KEROSINES
KERRIA
KERRIAS
KERSEY
KERSEYS
KERVE
KERVED
KERVES
KERVING
KERYGMA
KERYGMAS
KESAR
KESARS
KESH
KESHES
KEST
KESTING
KESTREL
KESTRELS
KESTS
KET
KETA
KETAS
KETCH
KETCHES
KETCHING
KETCHUP
KETCHUPS
KETONE
KETONES
KETOSE
KETOSES
KETOSIS
KETS
KETTLE
KETTLEFUL
KETTLEFULS
KETTLES
KEVEL
KEVELS
KEX
KEXES
KEY
KEYBOARD
KEYBOARDED
KEYBOARDING
KEYBOARDS
KEYBUGLE
KEYBUGLES
KEYED
KEYHOLE
KEYHOLES
KEYING
KEYLESS
KEYNOTE

KEYNOTED	KHOJA	KIDDYWINK	KILLOGIE	KINDLED
KEYNOTES	KHOJAS	KIDDYWINKS	KILLOGIES	KINDLER
KEYNOTING	KHOR	KIDEL	KILLS	KINDLERS
KEYS	KHORS	KIDELS	KILLUT	KINDLES
KEYSTONE	KHOTBAH	KIDGE	KILLUTS	KINDLESS
KEYSTONED	KHOTBAHS	KIDLING	KILN	KINDLIER
KEYSTONES	KHOTBEH	KIDLINGS	KILNED	KINDLIEST
KEYSTONING	KHOTBEHS	KIDNAP	KILNING	KINDLILY
KEYSTROKE	KHUD	KIDNAPPED	KILNS	KINDLING
KEYSTROKES	KHUDS	KIDNAPPER	KILO	KINDLINGS
KGOTLA	KHURTA	KIDNAPPERS	KILOBAR	KINDLY
KGOTLAS	KHURTAS	KIDNAPPING	KILOBARS	KINDNESS
KHADDAR	KHUSKHUS	KIDNAPPINGS	KILOBIT	KINDNESSES
KHADDARS	KHUSKHUSES	KIDNAPS	KILOBITS	KINDRED
KHADI	KHUTBAH	KIDNEY	KILOBYTE	KINDREDS
KHADIS	KHUTBAHS	KIDNEYS	KILOBYTES	KINDS
KHAKI	KIANG	KIDOLOGIES	KILOGRAM	KINE
KHAKIS	KIANGS	KIDOLOGY	KILOGRAMS	KINEMA
KHALAT	KIAUGH	KIDS	KILOHERTZ	KINEMAS
KHALATS	KIAUGHS	KIER	KILOHERTZES	KINEMATIC
KHALIF	KIBBLE	KIERIE	KILOJOULE	KINEMATICS
KHALIFA	KIBBLED	KIERIES	KILOJOULES	KINESES
KHALIFAH	KIBBLES	KIERS	KILOMETRE	KINESICS
KHALIFAHS	KIBBLING	KIESERITE	KILOMETRES	KINESIS
KHALIFAS	KIBBUTZ	KIESERITES	KILOS	KINETIC
KHALIFAT	KIBBUTZIM	KIEVE	KILOTON	KINETICAL
KHALIFATE	KIBE	KIEVES	KILOTONNE	KINETICS
KHALIFATES	KIBES	KIF	KILOTONNES	KINFOLK
KHALIFATS	KIBITKA	KIFS	KILOTONS	KINFOLKS
KHALIFS	KIBITKAS	KIGHT	KILOVOLT	KING
KHAMSIN	KIBITZ	KIGHTS	KILOVOLTS	KINGCRAFT
KHAMSINS	KIBITZED	KIKE	KILOWATT	KINGCRAFTS
KHAN	KIBITZER	KIKES	KILOWATTS	KINGCUP
KHANATE	KIBITZERS	KIKUMON	KILP	KINGCUPS
KHANATES	KIBITZES	KIKUMONS	KILPS	KINGDOM
KHANGA	KIBITZING	KIKUYU	KILT	KINGDOMED
KHANGAS	KIBLAH	KIKUYUS	KILTED	KINGDOMS
KHANJAR	KIBLAHS	KILD	KILTER	KINGED
KHANJARS	KIBOSH	KILDERKIN	KILTERS	KINGFISH
KHANS	KIBOSHED	KILDERKINS	KILTIE	KINGFISHES
KHANSAMA	KIBOSHES	KILERG	KILTIES	KINGHOOD
KHANSAMAH	KIBOSHING	KILERGS	KILTING	KINGHOODS
KHANSAMAHS	KICK	KILEY	KILTS	KINGING
KHANSAMAS	KICKABLE	KILEYS	KILTY	KINGLE
KHANUM	KICKBACK	KILIM	KIMBO	KINGLES
KHANUMS	KICKBACKS	KILIMS	KIMBOED	KINGLESS
KHARIF	KICKDOWN	KILL	KIMBOING	KINGLET
KHARIFS	KICKDOWNS	KILLADAR	KIMBOS	KINGLETS
KHAT	KICKED	KILLADARS	KIMMER	KINGLIER
KHATS	KICKER	KILLAS	KIMMERS	KINGLIEST
KHAYA	KICKERS	KILLASES	KIMONO	KINGLING
KHAYAS	KICKING	KILLCOW	KIMONOS	KINGLINGS
KHEDA	KICKS	KILLCOWS	KIN	KINGLY
KHEDAS	KICKSHAW	KILLCROP	KINA	KINGMAKER
KHEDIVA	KICKSHAWS	KILLCROPS	KINAKINA	KINGMAKERS
KHEDIVAL	KID	KILLDEE	KINAKINAS	KINGPOST
KHEDIVAS	KIDDED	KILLDEER	KINAS	KINGPOSTS
KHEDIVATE	KIDDER	KILLDEERS	KINASE	KINGS
KHEDIVATES	KIDDERS	KILLDEES	KINASES	KINGSHIP
KHEDIVE	KIDDIED	KILLED	KINCHIN	KINGSHIPS
KHEDIVES	KIDDIER	KILLER	KINCHINS	KINGWOOD
KHEDIVIAL	KIDDIERS	KILLERS	KINCOB	KINGWOODS
KHILAFAT	KIDDIES	KILLICK	KINCOBS	KININ
KHILAFATS	KIDDING	KILLICKS	KIND	KININS
KHILAT	KIDDLE	KILLING	KINDA	KINK
KHILATS	KIDDLES	KILLINGS	KINDED	KINKAJOU
KHILIM	KIDDUSH	KILLJOY	KINDER	KINKAJOUS
KHILIMS	KIDDUSHES	KILLJOYS	KINDEST	KINKED
KHODJA	KIDDY	KILLOCK	KINDING	KINKIER
KHODJAS	KIDDYING	KILLOCKS	KINDLE	KINKIEST

KINKING
KINKLE
KINKLES
KINKS
KINKY
KINLESS
KINO
KINONE
KINONES
KINOS
KINRED
KINREDS
KINS
KINSFOLK
KINSFOLKS
KINSHIP
KINSHIPS
KINSMAN
KINSMEN
KINSWOMAN
KINSWOMEN
KINTLEDGE
KINTLEDGES
KIOSK
KIOSKS
KIP
KIPE
KIPES
KIPP
KIPPAGE
KIPPAGES
KIPPED
KIPPER
KIPPERED
KIPPERER
KIPPERERS
KIPPERING
KIPPERS
KIPPING
KIPPS
KIPS
KIR
KIRBEH
KIRBEHS
KIRBIGRIP
KIRBIGRIPS
KIRI
KIRIMON
KIRIMONS
KIRIS
KIRK
KIRKED
KIRKING
KIRKINGS
KIRKS
KIRKTON
KIRKTONS
KIRKTOWN
KIRKTOWNS
KIRKWARD
KIRKYAIRD
KIRKYAIRDS
KIRKYARD
KIRKYARDS
KIRMESS
KIRMESSES
KIRN
KIRNS
KIRPAN
KIRPANS

KIRS
KIRSCH
KIRSCHES
KIRTLE
KIRTLED
KIRTLES
KISAN
KISANS
KISH
KISHES
KISMET
KISMETS
KISS
KISSABLE
KISSED
KISSER
KISSERS
KISSES
KISSING
KIST
KISTED
KISTING
KISTS
KISTVAEN
KISTVAENS
KIT
KITCHEN
KITCHENED
KITCHENER
KITCHENERS
KITCHENING
KITCHENS
KITE
KITED
KITES
KITH
KITHARA
KITHARAS
KITHE
KITHED
KITHES
KITHING
KITHS
KITING
KITLING
KITLINGS
KITS
KITSCH
KITSCHES
KITSCHIER
KITSCHIEST
KITSCHLY
KITSCHY
KITTED
KITTEN
KITTENED
KITTENING
KITTENISH
KITTENS
KITTENY
KITTIES
KITTING
KITTIWAKE
KITTIWAKES
KITTLE
KITTLED
KITTLER
KITTLES
KITTLEST
KITTLIER

KITTLIEST
KITTLING
KITTLY
KITTUL
KITTULS
KITTY
KIWI
KIWIS
KLANG
KLANGS
KLAVIER
KLAVIERS
KLAXON
KLAXONS
KLENDUSIC
KLEPHT
KLEPHTIC
KLEPHTISM
KLEPHTISMS
KLEPHTS
KLINKER
KLINKERS
KLINOSTAT
KLINOSTATS
KLIPDAS
KLIPDASES
KLONDIKE
KLONDIKED
KLONDIKES
KLONDIKING
KLONDYKE
KLONDYKED
KLONDYKER
KLONDYKERS
KLONDYKES
KLONDYKING
KLOOF
KLOOFS
KLUDGE
KLUDGES
KLUTZ
KLUTZES
KLYSTRON
KLYSTRONS
KNACK
KNACKER
KNACKERED
KNACKERIES
KNACKERING
KNACKERS
KNACKERY
KNACKIER
KNACKIEST
KNACKISH
KNACKS
KNACKY
KNAG
KNAGGIER
KNAGGIEST
KNAGGY
KNAGS
KNAP
KNAPPED
KNAPPER
KNAPPERS
KNAPPING
KNAPPLE
KNAPPLED
KNAPPLES
KNAPPLING

KNAPS
KNAPSACK
KNAPSACKS
KNAPSCAL
KNAPSCALS
KNAPSCULL
KNAPSCULLS
KNAPSKULL
KNAPSKULLS
KNAPWEED
KNAPWEEDS
KNAR
KNARL
KNARLS
KNARRED
KNARRING
KNARS
KNAVE
KNAVERIES
KNAVERY
KNAVES
KNAVESHIP
KNAVESHIPS
KNAVISH
KNAVISHLY
KNAWEL
KNAWELS
KNEAD
KNEADED
KNEADER
KNEADERS
KNEADING
KNEADS
KNEE
KNEED
KNEEHOLE
KNEEHOLES
KNEEING
KNEEL
KNEELED
KNEELER
KNEELERS
KNEELING
KNEELS
KNEES
KNELL
KNELLED
KNELLING
KNELLS
KNELT
KNEVELL
KNEVELLED
KNEVELLING
KNEVELLS
KNEW
KNICKER
KNICKERED
KNICKERS
KNICKS
KNIFE
KNIFED
KNIFELESS
KNIFES
KNIFING
KNIFINGS
KNIGHT
KNIGHTAGE
KNIGHTAGES
KNIGHTED
KNIGHTING

KNIGHTLIER
KNIGHTLIEST
KNIGHTLY
KNIGHTS
KNISH
KNISHES
KNIT
KNITCH
KNITCHES
KNITS
KNITTED
KNITTER
KNITTERS
KNITTING
KNITTINGS
KNITTLE
KNITTLES
KNITWEAR
KNITWEARS
KNIVE
KNIVED
KNIVES
KNIVING
KNOB
KNOBBED
KNOBBER
KNOBBERS
KNOBBIER
KNOBBIEST
KNOBBLE
KNOBBLED
KNOBBLES
KNOBBLIER
KNOBBLIEST
KNOBBLING
KNOBBLY
KNOBBY
KNOBS
KNOCK
KNOCKED
KNOCKER
KNOCKERS
KNOCKING
KNOCKINGS
KNOCKOUT
KNOCKOUTS
KNOCKS
KNOLL
KNOLLED
KNOLLING
KNOLLS
KNOP
KNOPS
KNOSP
KNOSPS
KNOT
KNOTGRASS
KNOTGRASSES
KNOTLESS
KNOTS
KNOTTED
KNOTTER
KNOTTERS
KNOTTIER
KNOTTIEST
KNOTTING
KNOTTINGS
KNOTTY
KNOTWEED
KNOTWEEDS

KNOTWORK
KNOTWORKS
KNOUT
KNOUTED
KNOUTING
KNOUTS
KNOW
KNOWABLE
KNOWE
KNOWER
KNOWERS
KNOWES
KNOWING
KNOWINGLY
KNOWLEDGE
KNOWLEDGED
KNOWLEDGES
KNOWLEDGING
KNOWN
KNOWS
KNUB
KNUBBIER
KNUBBIEST
KNUBBLE
KNUBBLED
KNUBBLES
KNUBBLIER
KNUBBLIEST
KNUBBLING
KNUBBLY
KNUBBY
KNUBS
KNUCKLE
KNUCKLED
KNUCKLES
KNUCKLING
KNUR
KNURL
KNURLED
KNURLIER
KNURLIEST
KNURLING
KNURLINGS
KNURLS
KNURLY
KNURR
KNURRS
KNURS
KNUT
KNUTS
KO
KOA
KOALA
KOALAS
KOAN
KOANS
KOAS
KOB
KOBAN
KOBANG
KOBANGS
KOBANS
KOBOLD
KOBOLDS
KOBS
KOFF
KOFFS
KOFTA
KOFTAS
KOFTGAR
KOFTGARI

KOFTGARIS
KOFTGARS
KOFTWORK
KOFTWORKS
KOHL
KOHLRABI
KOHLRABIS
KOHLS
KOINE
KOINES
KOKRA
KOKRAS
KOKUM
KOKUMS
KOLA
KOLAS
KOLINSKIES
KOLINSKY
KOLKHOZ
KOLKHOZES
KOLO
KOLOS
KOMISSAR
KOMISSARS
KOMITAJI
KOMITAJIS
KON
KOND
KONFYT
KONFYTS
KONIMETER
KONIMETERS
KONIOLOGIES
KONIOLOGY
KONISCOPE
KONISCOPES
KONK
KONKED
KONKING
KONKS
KONNING
KONS
KOODOO
KOODOOS
KOOK
KOOKED
KOOKIE
KOOKIER
KOOKIEST
KOOKING
KOOKS
KOOKY
KOOLAH
KOOLAHS
KOP
KOPECK
KOPECKS
KOPJE
KOPJES
KOPPA
KOPPAS
KOPPIE
KOPPIES
KOPS
KORA
KORAS
KORFBALL
KORFBALLS
KORKIR
KORKIRS

KORMA
KORMAS
KORORA
KORORAS
KORUNA
KORUNAS
KOS
KOSES
KOSHER
KOSHERS
KOSMOS
KOSMOSES
KOSS
KOSSES
KOTO
KOTOS
KOTOW
KOTOWED
KOTOWING
KOTOWS
KOTTABOS
KOTTABOSES
KOTWAL
KOTWALS
KOULAN
KOULANS
KOUMISS
KOUMISSES
KOURBASH
KOURBASHED
KOURBASHES
KOURBASHING
KOUSKOUS
KOUSKOUSES
KOW
KOWHAI
KOWHAIS
KOWS
KOWTOW
KOWTOWED
KOWTOWING
KOWTOWS
KRAAL
KRAALED
KRAALING
KRAALS
KRAFT
KRAFTS
KRAIT
KRAITS
KRAKEN
KRAKENS
KRAKOWIAK
KRAKOWIAKS
KRAMERIA
KRAMERIAS
KRANG
KRANGS
KRANS
KRANSES
KRANTZ
KRANTZES
KRANZ
KRANZES
KRAUT
KRAUTS
KREASOTE
KREASOTED
KREASOTES
KREASOTING

KREATINE
KREATINES
KREESE
KREESED
KREESES
KREESING
KREMLIN
KREMLINS
KRENG
KRENGS
KREOSOTE
KREOSOTED
KREOSOTES
KREOSOTING
KREPLACH
KREUTZER
KREUTZERS
KRILL
KRILLS
KRIMMER
KRIMMERS
KRIS
KRISED
KRISES
KRISING
KROMESKIES
KROMESKY
KRONA
KRONE
KRONEN
KRONER
KRONOR
KRONUR
KRUMHORN
KRUMHORNS
KRUMMHORN
KRUMMHORNS
KRYOMETER
KRYOMETERS
KRYPSES
KRYPSIS
KRYPTON
KRYPTONS
KSAR
KSARS
KUCHCHA
KUDOS
KUDOSES
KUDU
KUDUS
KUDZU
KUDZUS
KUFFIAH
KUFFIAHS
KUFFIEH
KUFFIEHS
KUFFIYEH
KUFFIYEHS
KUFIAH
KUFIAHS
KUFIYA
KUFIYAH
KUFIYAHS
KUFIYAS
KUKRI
KUKRIS
KUKU
KUKUS
KULAK
KULAKS

KULAN
KULANS
KUMARA
KUMARAS
KUMARI
KUMARIS
KUMISS
KUMISSES
KÜMMEL
KÜMMELS
KUMQUAT
KUMQUATS
KUNKAR
KUNKARS
KUNKUR
KUNKURS
KURBASH
KURBASHED
KURBASHES
KURBASHING
KURGAN
KURGANS
KURRAJONG
KURRAJONGS
KURRE
KURRES
KURSAAL
KURSAALS
KURTA
KURTAS
KURTOSES
KURTOSIS
KURVEY
KURVEYED
KURVEYING
KURVEYOR
KURVEYORS
KURVEYS
KUTCH
KUTCHA
KUTCHES
KVASS
KVASSES
KVETCH
KVETCHED
KVETCHER
KVETCHERS
KVETCHES
KVETCHING
KWACHA
KWACHAS
KWELA
KWELAS
KY
KYANG
KYANGS
KYANISE
KYANISED
KYANISES
KYANISING
KYANITE
KYANITES
KYANIZE
KYANIZED
KYANIZES
KYANIZING
KYAT
KYATS
KYBOSH
KYBOSHED

KYBOSHES	KYLICES	KYLOE	KYNDED	KYRIELLE
KYBOSHING	KYLIE	KYLOES	KYNDES	KYRIELLES
KYDST	KYLIES	KYMOGRAM	KYNDING	KYTE
KYE	KYLIN	KYMOGRAMS	KYNDS	KYTES
KYLE	KYLINS	KYMOGRAPH	KYNE	KYTHE
KYLES	KYLIX	KYMOGRAPHS	KYPHOSES	KYTHED
KYLEY	KYLLOSES	KYND	KYPHOSIS	KYTHES
KYLEYS	KYLLOSIS	KYNDE	KYPHOTIC	KYTHING

L

LA	LABRID	LACONICAL	LADIFYING	LAGNIAPPE
LAAGER	LABRIDS	LACONISM	LADING	LAGNIAPPES
LAAGERED	LABROID	LACONISMS	LADINGS	LAGOMORPH
LAAGERING	LABROIDS	LACQUER	LADLE	LAGOMORPHS
LAAGERS	LABROSE	LACQUERED	LADLED	LAGOON
LAB	LABRUM	LACQUERER	LADLEFUL	LAGOONAL
LABARA	LABRYS	LACQUERERS	LADLEFULS	LAGOONS
LABARUM	LABRYSES	LACQUERING	LADLES	LAGRIMOSO
LABARUMS	LABS	LACQUERS	LADLING	LAGS
LABDA	LABURNUM	LACQUEY	LADRONE	LAGUNE
LABDACISM	LABURNUMS	LACQUEYED	LADRONES	LAGUNES
LABDACISMS	LABYRINTH	LACQUEYING	LADS	LAH
LABDANUM	LABYRINTHS	LACQUEYS	LADY	LAHAR
LABDANUMS	LAC	LACRIMAL	LADYBIRD	LAHARS
LABDAS	LACCOLITE	LACRIMALS	LADYBIRDS	LAHS
LABEL	LACCOLITES	LACROSSE	LADYBUG	LAIC
LABELLA	LACCOLITH	LACROSSES	LADYBUGS	LAICAL
LABELLED	LACCOLITHS	LACRYMAL	LADYCOW	LAICISE
LABELLING	LACE	LACRYMALS	LADYCOWS	LAICISED
LABELLOID	LACEBARK	LACS	LADYFIED	LAICISES
LABELLUM	LACEBARKS	LACTASE	LADYFIES	LAICISING
LABELS	LACED	LACTASES	LADYFLIES	LAICITIES
LABIA	LACERABLE	LACTASESD	LADYFLY	LAICITY
LABIAL	LACERANT	LACTATE	LADYFY	LAICIZE
LABIALISE	LACERATE	LACTATED	LADYFYING	LAICIZED
LABIALISED	LACERATED	LACTATES	LADYHOOD	LAICIZES
LABIALISES	LACERATES	LACTATING	LADYHOODS	LAICIZING
LABIALISING	LACERATING	LACTATION	LADYISH	LAICS
LABIALISM	LACERTIAN	LACTATIONS	LADYISM	LAID
LABIALISMS	LACERTINE	LACTEAL	LADYISMS	LAIDED
LABIALIZE	LACES	LACTEALS	LADYKIN	LAIDEN
LABIALIZED	LACET	LACTEOUS	LADYKINS	LAIDING
LABIALIZES	LACETS	LACTIC	LADYLIKE	LAIDLY
LABIALIZING	LACEY	LACTIFIC	LADYSHIP	LAIDS
LABIALLY	LACHES	LACTOSE	LADYSHIPS	LAIGH
LABIALS	LACHESES	LACTOSES	LAER	LAIGHER
LABIATE	LACHRYMAL	LACUNA	LAESIE	LAIGHEST
LABIATES	LACHRYMALS	LACUNAE	LAETARE	LAIGHS
LABILE	LACIER	LACUNAL	LAETARES	LAIK
LABILITIES	LACIEST	LACUNAR	LAEVIGATE	LAIKA
LABILITY	LACING	LACUNARIA	LAEVIGATED	LAIKAS
LABIS	LACINGS	LACUNARS	LAEVIGATES	LAIKED
LABISES	LACINIA	LACUNARY	LAEVIGATING	LAIKING
LABIUM	LACINIAE	LACUNATE	LAEVULOSE	LAIKS
LABLAB	LACINIATE	LACUNOSE	LAEVULOSES	LAIN
LABLABS	LACINIATED	LACY	LAG	LAIR
LABOR	LACK	LAD	LAGAN	LAIRAGE
LABORED	LACKADAY	LADANUM	LAGANS	LAIRAGES
LABORING	LACKED	LADANUMS	LAGENA	LAIRD
LABORIOUS	LACKER	LADDER	LAGENAS	LAIRDS
LABORS	LACKERED	LADDERED	LAGER	LAIRDSHIP
LABOUR	LACKERING	LADDERING	LAGERS	LAIRDSHIPS
LABOURED	LACKERS	LADDERS	LAGGARD	LAIRED
LABOURER	LACKEY	LADDERY	LAGGARDS	LAIRIER
LABOURERS	LACKEYED	LADDIE	LAGGED	LAIRIEST
LABOURING	LACKEYING	LADDIES	LAGGEN	LAIRING
LABOURISM	LACKEYS	LADE	LAGGENS	LAIRISE
LABOURISMS	LACKING	LADED	LAGGER	LAIRISED
LABOURIST	LACKLAND	LADEN	LAGGERS	LAIRISES
LABOURISTS	LACKLANDS	LADES	LAGGIN	LAIRISING
LABOURS	LACKS	LADIES	LAGGING	LAIRIZE
LABRA	LACMUS	LADIFIED	LAGGINGLY	LAIRIZED
LABRET	LACMUSES	LADIFIES	LAGGINGS	LAIRIZES
LABRETS	LACONIC	LADIFY	LAGGINS	LAIRIZING

LAIRS
LAIRY
LAISSE
LAISSES
LAITANCE
LAITANCES
LAITH
LAITIES
LAITY
LAKE
LAKED
LAKELET
LAKELETS
LAKER
LAKERS
LAKES
LAKH
LAKHS
LAKIER
LAKIEST
LAKIN
LAKING
LAKINS
LAKISH
LAKY
LALANG
LALANGS
LALDIE
LALDIES
LALDY
LALLAN
LALLANS
LALLATION
LALLATIONS
LALLING
LALLINGS
LALLYGAG
LALLYGAGGED
LALLYGAGGING
LALLYGAGS
LAM
LAMA
LAMAISTIC
LAMANTIN
LAMANTINS
LAMAS
LAMASERAI
LAMASERAIS
LAMASERIES
LAMASERY
LAMB
LAMBAST
LAMBASTE
LAMBASTED
LAMBASTES
LAMBASTING
LAMBASTS
LAMBDA
LAMBDAS
LAMBDOID
LAMBED
LAMBENCIES
LAMBENCY
LAMBENT
LAMBENTLY
LAMBER
LAMBERS
LAMBERT
LAMBERTS
LAMBIE

LAMBIES
LAMBING
LAMBITIVE
LAMBITIVES
LAMBKIN
LAMBKINS
LAMBLING
LAMBLINGS
LAMBOYS
LAMBS
LAMBSKIN
LAMBSKINS
LAME
LAMED
LAMELLA
LAMELLAE
LAMELLAR
LAMELLATE
LAMELLATED
LAMELLOID
LAMELLOSE
LAMELY
LAMENESS
LAMENESSES
LAMENT
LAMENTED
LAMENTING
LAMENTINGS
LAMENTS
LAMER
LAMES
LAMEST
LAMETER
LAMETERS
LAMIA
LAMIAE
LAMIAS
LAMIGER
LAMIGERS
LAMINA
LAMINABLE
LAMINAE
LAMINAR
LAMINARY
LAMINATE
LAMINATED
LAMINATES
LAMINATING
LAMINATOR
LAMINATORS
LAMING
LAMINGTON
LAMINGTONS
LAMINITIS
LAMINITISES
LAMISH
LAMITER
LAMITERS
LAMMED
LAMMER
LAMMERS
LAMMIE
LAMMIES
LAMMIGER
LAMMIGERS
LAMMING
LAMMINGS
LAMMY
LAMP
LAMPAD

LAMPADARIES
LAMPADARY
LAMPADIST
LAMPADISTS
LAMPADS
LAMPAS
LAMPASES
LAMPASSE
LAMPASSES
LAMPED
LAMPERN
LAMPERNS
LAMPHOLE
LAMPHOLES
LAMPING
LAMPION
LAMPIONS
LAMPLIGHT
LAMPLIGHTS
LAMPOON
LAMPOONED
LAMPOONER
LAMPOONERS
LAMPOONING
LAMPOONS
LAMPPOST
LAMPPOSTS
LAMPREY
LAMPREYS
LAMPS
LAMPSHADE
LAMPSHADES
LAMPUKA
LAMPUKAS
LAMPUKI
LAMPUKIS
LAMS
LANA
LANAS
LANATE
LANCE
LANCED
LANCEGAY
LANCEGAYS
LANCELET
LANCELETS
LANCEOLAR
LANCER
LANCERS
LANCES
LANCET
LANCETED
LANCETS
LANCH
LANCHED
LANCHES
LANCHING
LANCIFORM
LANCINATE
LANCINATED
LANCINATES
LANCINATING
LANCING
LAND
LANDAMMAN
LANDAMMANS
LANDAU
LANDAULET
LANDAULETS
LANDAULETTE

LANDAULETTES
LANDAUS
LANDDAMNE
LANDDAMNED
LANDDAMNES
LANDDAMNING
LANDDROS
LANDDROSES
LANDDROST
LANDDROSTS
LANDE
LANDED
LANDER
LANDERS
LANDES
LANDFALL
LANDFALLS
LANDFILL
LANDFILLS
LANDFORCE
LANDFORCES
LANDFORM
LANDFORMS
LANDGRAVE
LANDGRAVES
LANDING
LANDINGS
LANDLADIES
LANDLADY
LÄNDLER
LÄNDLERS
LANDLESS
LANDLOPER
LANDLOPERS
LANDLORD
LANDLORDS
LANDMAN
LANDMARK
LANDMARKS
LANDMASS
LANDMASSES
LANDMEN
LANDOWNER
LANDOWNERS
LANDRACE
LANDRACES
LANDRAIL
LANDRAILS
LANDS
LANDSCAPE
LANDSCAPED
LANDSCAPES
LANDSCAPING
LANDSKIP
LANDSKIPS
LANDSLIDE
LANDSLIDES
LANDSLIP
LANDSLIPS
LANDSMAN
LANDSMEN
LANDWARD
LANDWARDS
LANDWIND
LANDWINDS
LANE
LANES
LANEWAY
LANEWAYS
LANG

LANGAHA
LANGAHAS
LANGER
LANGEST
LANGLAUF
LANGLAUFS
LANGOUSTE
LANGOUSTES
LANGRAGE
LANGRAGES
LANGREL
LANGRELS
LANGRIDGE
LANGRIDGES
LANGSPEL
LANGSPELS
LANGSPIEL
LANGSPIELS
LANGUAGE
LANGUAGED
LANGUAGES
LANGUAGING
LANGUE
LANGUED
LANGUES
LANGUET
LANGUETS
LANGUETTE
LANGUETTES
LANGUID
LANGUIDER
LANGUIDEST
LANGUIDLY
LANGUISH
LANGUISHED
LANGUISHES
LANGUISHING
LANGUOR
LANGUORS
LANGUR
LANGURS
LANIARD
LANIARDS
LANIARY
LANK
LANKED
LANKER
LANKEST
LANKIER
LANKIEST
LANKINESS
LANKINESSES
LANKING
LANKLY
LANKNESS
LANKNESSES
LANKS
LANKY
LANNER
LANNERET
LANNERETS
LANNERS
LANOLIN
LANOLINE
LANOLINES
LANOLINS
LANOSE
LANT
LANTANA
LANTANAS

LANTERLOO
LANTERLOOS
LANTERN
LANTERNED
LANTERNING
LANTERNS
LANTHANUM
LANTHANUMS
LANTHORN
LANTHORNS
LANTS
LANTSKIP
LANTSKIPS
LANUGO
LANUGOS
LANX
LANYARD
LANYARDS
LAP
LAPDOG
LAPDOGS
LAPEL
LAPELLED
LAPELS
LAPFUL
LAPFULS
LAPIDARIES
LAPIDARY
LAPIDATE
LAPIDATED
LAPIDATES
LAPIDATING
LAPIDEOUS
LAPIDIFIC
LAPIDIFIED
LAPIDIFIES
LAPIDIFY
LAPIDIFYING
LAPILLI
LAPIS
LAPISES
LAPJE
LAPJES
LAPPED
LAPPEL
LAPPELS
LAPPER
LAPPERS
LAPPET
LAPPETED
LAPPETS
LAPPIE
LAPPIES
LAPPING
LAPPINGS
LAPS
LAPSABLE
LAPSANG
LAPSANGS
LAPSE
LAPSED
LAPSES
LAPSING
LAPSTONE
LAPSTONES
LAPSTREAK
LAPSTREAKS
LAPSUS
LAPSUSES
LAPTOP

LAPTOPS
LAPWING
LAPWINGS
LAPWORK
LAPWORKS
LAQUEARIA
LAR
LARBOARD
LARBOARDS
LARCENER
LARCENERS
LARCENIES
LARCENIST
LARCENISTS
LARCENOUS
LARCENY
LARCH
LARCHEN
LARCHES
LARD
LARDALITE
LARDALITES
LARDED
LARDER
LARDERER
LARDERERS
LARDERS
LARDIER
LARDIEST
LARDING
LARDON
LARDONS
LARDOON
LARDOONS
LARDS
LARDY
LARE
LARES
LARGE
LARGELY
LARGEN
LARGENED
LARGENESS
LARGENESSES
LARGENING
LARGENS
LARGER
LARGES
LARGESS
LARGESSE
LARGESSES
LARGEST
LARGHETTO
LARGHETTOS
LARGISH
LARGITION
LARGITIONS
LARGO
LARGOS
LARIAT
LARIATS
LARINE
LARK
LARKED
LARKER
LARKERS
LARKIER
LARKIEST
LARKINESS
LARKINESSES

LARKING
LARKISH
LARKS
LARKSPUR
LARKSPURS
LARKY
LARMIER
LARMIERS
LARN
LARNAKES
LARNAX
LARNED
LARNING
LARNS
LAROID
LARRIGAN
LARRIGANS
LARRIKIN
LARRIKINS
LARRUP
LARRUPED
LARRUPING
LARRUPS
LARUM
LARUMS
LARVA
LARVAE
LARVAL
LARVATE
LARVATED
LARVICIDE
LARVICIDES
LARVIFORM
LARVIKITE
LARVIKITES
LARYNGAL
LARYNGEAL
LARYNGES
LARYNX
LARYNXES
LAS
LASAGNA
LASAGNAS
LASAGNE
LASAGNES
LASCAR
LASCARS
LASE
LASED
LASER
LASERS
LASERWORT
LASERWORTS
LASES
LASH
LASHED
LASHER
LASHERS
LASHES
LASHING
LASHINGS
LASHKAR
LASHKARS
LASING
LASINGS
LASKET
LASKETS
LASQUE
LASQUES
LASS

LASSES
LASSIE
LASSIES
LASSITUDE
LASSITUDES
LASSLORN
LASSO
LASSOCK
LASSOCKS
LASSOED
LASSOES
LASSOING
LASSOS
LASSU
LASSUS
LAST
LASTAGE
LASTAGES
LASTED
LASTER
LASTERS
LASTING
LASTINGLY
LASTINGS
LASTLY
LASTS
LAT
LATCH
LATCHED
LATCHES
LATCHET
LATCHETS
LATCHING
LATCHKEY
LATCHKEYS
LATE
LATED
LATEEN
LATELY
LATEN
LATENCE
LATENCES
LATENCIES
LATENCY
LATENED
LATENESS
LATENESSES
LATENING
LATENS
LATENT
LATENTLY
LATER
LATERAL
LATERALLY
LATERALS
LATERITE
LATERITES
LATESCENT
LATEST
LATESTS
LATEWAKE
LATEWAKES
LATEX
LATEXES
LATH
LATHE
LATHED
LATHEE
LATHEES
LATHEN

LATHER
LATHERED
LATHERING
LATHERS
LATHERY
LATHES
LATHI
LATHIER
LATHIEST
LATHING
LATHINGS
LATHIS
LATHS
LATHY
LATHYRISM
LATHYRISMS
LATHYRUS
LATHYRUSES
LATICES
LATICLAVE
LATICLAVES
LATIFONDI
LATISH
LATITANCIES
LATITANCY
LATITANT
LATITAT
LATITATS
LATITUDE
LATITUDES
LATKE
LATKES
LATRANT
LATRATION
LATRATIONS
LATRIA
LATRIAS
LATRINE
LATRINES
LATROCINIES
LATROCINY
LATRON
LATRONS
LATS
LATTEN
LATTENS
LATTER
LATTERLY
LATTICE
LATTICED
LATTICES
LATTICING
LATTICINI
LATTICINO
LAUCH
LAUCHING
LAUCHS
LAUD
LAUDABLE
LAUDABLY
LAUDANUM
LAUDANUMS
LAUDATION
LAUDATIONS
LAUDATIVE
LAUDATIVES
LAUDATORIES
LAUDATORY
LAUDED
LAUDER

LAUDERS
LAUDING
LAUDS
LAUF
LAUFS
LAUGH
LAUGHABLE
LAUGHABLY
LAUGHED
LAUGHER
LAUGHERS
LAUGHFUL
LAUGHING
LAUGHINGS
LAUGHS
LAUGHSOME
LAUGHTER
LAUGHTERS
LAUGHY
LAUNCE
LAUNCED
LAUNCES
LAUNCH
LAUNCHED
LAUNCHER
LAUNCHERS
LAUNCHES
LAUNCHING
LAUNCING
LAUND
LAUNDER
LAUNDERED
LAUNDERER
LAUNDERERS
LAUNDERING
LAUNDERS
LAUNDRESS
LAUNDRESSES
LAUNDRIES
LAUNDRY
LAUNDS
LAURA
LAURAS
LAUREATE
LAUREATED
LAUREATES
LAUREATING
LAUREL
LAURELLED
LAURELS
LAUWINE
LAUWINES
LAV
LAVA
LAVABO
LAVABOES
LAVABOS
LAVAFORM
LAVAGE
LAVAGES
LAVALIERE
LAVALIERES
LAVAS
LAVATERA
LAVATERAS
LAVATION
LAVATIONS
LAVATORIES
LAVATORY
LAVE

LAVED
LAVEER
LAVEERED
LAVEERING
LAVEERS
LAVEMENT
LAVEMENTS
LAVENDER
LAVENDERED
LAVENDERING
LAVENDERS
LAVER
LAVEROCK
LAVEROCKED
LAVEROCKING
LAVEROCKS
LAVERS
LAVES
LAVING
LAVISH
LAVISHED
LAVISHER
LAVISHES
LAVISHEST
LAVISHING
LAVISHLY
LAVOLT
LAVOLTA
LAVOLTAS
LAVOLTED
LAVOLTING
LAVOLTS
LAVRA
LAVRAS
LAVS
LAW
LAWED
LAWER
LAWEST
LAWFUL
LAWFULLY
LAWING
LAWINGS
LAWK
LAWKS
LAWLAND
LAWLANDS
LAWLESS
LAWLESSLY
LAWMAN
LAWMEN
LAWMONGER
LAWMONGERS
LAWN
LAWNS
LAWNY
LAWS
LAWSUIT
LAWSUITS
LAWYER
LAWYERLY
LAWYERS
LAX
LAXATIVE
LAXATIVES
LAXATOR
LAXATORS
LAXER
LAXES
LAXEST

LAXISM
LAXISMS
LAXIST
LAXISTS
LAXITIES
LAXITY
LAXLY
LAXNESS
LAXNESSES
LAY
LAYABOUT
LAYABOUTS
LAYAWAY
LAYAWAYS
LAYBACK
LAYBACKED
LAYBACKING
LAYBACKS
LAYER
LAYERED
LAYERING
LAYERINGS
LAYERS
LAYETTE
LAYETTES
LAYING
LAYINGS
LAYLOCK
LAYLOCKS
LAYMAN
LAYMEN
LAYPERSON
LAYPERSONS
LAYS
LAYSTALL
LAYSTALLS
LAYTIME
LAYTIMES
LAZAR
LAZARET
LAZARETS
LAZARETTO
LAZARETTOS
LAZARS
LAZE
LAZED
LAZES
LAZIER
LAZIEST
LAZILY
LAZINESS
LAZINESSES
LAZING
LAZULITE
LAZULITES
LAZURITE
LAZURITES
LAZY
LAZZARONE
LAZZARONI
LAZZI
LAZZO
LEA
LEACH
LEACHATE
LEACHATES
LEACHED
LEACHES
LEACHIER
LEACHIEST

LEACHING
LEACHINGS
LEACHOUR
LEACHOURS
LEACHY
LEAD
LEADED
LEADEN
LEADENED
LEADENING
LEADENLY
LEADENS
LEADER
LEADERS
LEADIER
LEADIEST
LEADING
LEADINGS
LEADLESS
LEADS
LEADSMAN
LEADSMEN
LEADY
LEAF
LEAFAGE
LEAFAGES
LEAFBUD
LEAFBUDS
LEAFED
LEAFERIES
LEAFERY
LEAFIER
LEAFIEST
LEAFINESS
LEAFINESSES
LEAFING
LEAFLESS
LEAFLET
LEAFLETED
LEAFLETING
LEAFLETS
LEAFLETTED
LEAFLETTING
LEAFS
LEAFY
LEAGUE
LEAGUED
LEAGUER
LEAGUERED
LEAGUERING
LEAGUERS
LEAGUES
LEAGUING
LEAK
LEAKAGE
LEAKAGES
LEAKED
LEAKER
LEAKERS
LEAKIER
LEAKIEST
LEAKINESS
LEAKINESSES
LEAKING
LEAKS
LEAKY
LEAL
LEALTIES
LEALTY
LEAM

LEAMED
LEAMING
LEAMS
LEAN
LEANED
LEANER
LEANEST
LEANING
LEANINGS
LEANLY
LEANNESS
LEANNESSES
LEANS
LEANT
LEANY
LEAP
LEAPED
LEAPER
LEAPEROUS
LEAPERS
LEAPING
LEAPOROUS
LEAPROUS
LEAPS
LEAPT
LEAR
LEARE
LEARED
LEARES
LEARIER
LEARIEST
LEARING
LEARN
LEARNABLE
LEARNED
LEARNEDLY
LEARNER
LEARNERS
LEARNING
LEARNINGS
LEARNS
LEARNT
LEARS
LEARY
LEAS
LEASABLE
LEASE
LEASEBACK
LEASEBACKS
LEASED
LEASEHOLD
LEASEHOLDS
LEASER
LEASERS
LEASES
LEASH
LEASHED
LEASHES
LEASHING
LEASING
LEASINGS
LEASOW
LEASOWE
LEASOWED
LEASOWES
LEASOWING
LEASOWS
LEAST
LEASTS
LEASTWAYS

LEASTWISE	LEDDEN	LEGALESES	LEGIST	LEMELS
LEASURE	LEDDENS	LEGALISE	LEGISTS	LEMES
LEASURES	LEDGE	LEGALISED	LEGIT	LEMING
LEAT	LEDGER	LEGALISES	LEGITIM	LEMMA
LEATHER	LEDGERED	LEGALISING	LEGITIMS	LEMMAS
LEATHERED	LEDGERING	LEGALISM	LEGLAN	LEMMATA
LEATHERING	LEDGERS	LEGALISMS	LEGLANS	LEMMING
LEATHERINGS	LEDGES	LEGALIST	LEGLEN	LEMMINGS
LEATHERN	LEDGIER	LEGALISTS	LEGLENS	LEMON
LEATHERS	LEDGIEST	LEGALITIES	LEGLESS	LEMONADE
LEATHERY	LEDGY	LEGALITY	LEGLET	LEMONADES
LEATS	LEDUM	LEGALIZE	LEGLETS	LEMONED
LEAVE	LEDUMS	LEGALIZED	LEGLIN	LEMONING
LEAVED	LEE	LEGALIZES	LEGLINS	LEMONS
LEAVEN	LEEAR	LEGALIZING	LEGROOM	LEMONY
LEAVENED	LEEARS	LEGALLY	LEGROOMS	LEMPIRA
LEAVENING	LEECH	LEGATARIES	LEGS	LEMPIRAS
LEAVENINGS	LEECHDOM	LEGATARY	LEGUME	LEMUR
LEAVENOUS	LEECHDOMS	LEGATE	LEGUMES	LEMURES
LEAVENS	LEECHED	LEGATEE	LEGUMIN	LEMURIAN
LEAVES	LEECHEE	LEGATEES	LEGUMINS	LEMURIANS
LEAVIER	LEECHEES	LEGATES	LEGWORK	LEMURINE
LEAVIEST	LEECHES	LEGATINE	LEGWORKS	LEMURINES
LEAVING	LEECHING	LEGATION	LEHR	LEMUROID
LEAVINGS	LEED	LEGATIONS	LEHREJAHRE	LEMUROIDS
LEAVY	LEEING	LEGATO	LEHRS	LEMURS
LEAZE	LEEK	LEGATOR	LEI	LEND
LEAZES	LEEKS	LEGATORS	LEIDGER	LENDER
LEBBEK	LEEP	LEGATOS	LEIDGERS	LENDERS
LEBBEKS	LEEPED	LEGEND	LEIGER	LENDING
LECANORA	LEEPING	LEGENDARIES	LEIGERS	LENDINGS
LECANORAS	LEEPS	LEGENDARY	LEIPOA	LENDS
LECH	LEER	LEGENDIST	LEIPOAS	LENES
LECHED	LEERED	LEGENDISTS	LEIR	LENG
LECHER	LEERIER	LEGENDRIES	LEIRED	LENGED
LECHERED	LEERIEST	LEGENDRY	LEIRING	LENGER
LECHERIES	LEERING	LEGENDS	LEIRS	LENGEST
LECHERING	LEERINGLY	LEGER	LEIS	LENGING
LECHEROUS	LEERINGS	LEGERING	LEISH	LENGS
LECHERS	LEERS	LEGERINGS	LEISHER	LENGTH
LECHERY	LEERY	LEGERITIES	LEISHEST	LENGTHEN
LECHES	LEES	LEGERITY	LEISLER	LENGTHENED
LECHING	LEESE	LEGERS	LEISLERS	LENGTHENING
LECHWE	LEESES	LEGGE	LEISTER	LENGTHENS
LECHWES	LEESING	LEGGED	LEISTERED	LENGTHFUL
LECITHIN	LEET	LEGGER	LEISTERING	LENGTHIER
LECITHINS	LEETLE	LEGGERS	LEISTERS	LENGTHIEST
LECTERN	LEETS	LEGGES	LEISURE	LENGTHILY
LECTERNS	LEEWARD	LEGGIER	LEISURED	LENGTHS
LECTIN	LEEWARDS	LEGGIEST	LEISURELY	LENGTHY
LECTINS	LEEWAY	LEGGINESS	LEISURES	LENIENCE
LECTION	LEEWAYS	LEGGINESSES	LEISURING	LENIENCES
LECTIONS	LEEZE	LEGGING	LEITMOTIF	LENIENCIES
LECTOR	LEFT	LEGGINGS	LEITMOTIFS	LENIENCY
LECTORATE	LEFTE	LEGGISM	LEITMOTIV	LENIENT
LECTORATES	LEFTIE	LEGGISMS	LEITMOTIVS	LENIENTLY
LECTORS	LEFTIES	LEGGY	LEK	LENIENTS
LECTRESS	LEFTISM	LEGHORN	LEKE	LENIFIED
LECTRESSES	LEFTISMS	LEGHORNS	LEKKED	LENIFIES
LECTURE	LEFTIST	LEGIBLE	LEKKING	LENIFY
LECTURED	LEFTISTS	LEGIBLY	LEKKINGS	LENIFYING
LECTURER	LEFTS	LEGION	LEKS	LENIS
LECTURERS	LEFTWARD	LEGIONARIES	LEKYTHOI	LENITIES
LECTURES	LEFTWARDS	LEGIONARY	LEKYTHOS	LENITION
LECTURING	LEFTY	LEGIONED	LEMAN	LENITIONS
LECTURN	LEG	LEGIONS	LEMANS	LENITIVE
LECTURNS	LEGACIES	LEGISLATE	LEME	LENITIVES
LECYTHI	LEGACY	LEGISLATED	LEMED	LENITY
LECYTHUS	LEGAL	LEGISLATES	LEMEL	LENO
LED	LEGALESE	LEGISLATING		

LENOS	LESBIAN	LEUCOCYTE	LEVULOSES	LIBATORY
LENS	LESBIANS	LEUCOCYTES	LEVY	LIBBARD
LENSES	LESBIC	LEUCOMA	LEVYING	LIBBARDS
LENT	LESES	LEUCOMAS	LEW	LIBBED
LENTANDO	LESION	LEUCOTOME	LEWD	LIBBER
LENTEN	LESIONS	LEUCOTOMES	LEWDER	LIBBERS
LENTI	LESS	LEUCOTOMIES	LEWDEST	LIBBING
LENTIC	LESSEE	LEUCOTOMY	LEWDLY	LIBECCHIO
LENTICEL	LESSEES	LEUGH	LEWDNESS	LIBECCHIOS
LENTICELS	LESSEN	LEUGHEN	LEWDNESSES	LIBECCIO
LENTICLE	LESSENED	LEUKAEMIA	LEWDSBIES	LIBECCIOS
LENTICLES	LESSENING	LEUKAEMIAS	LEWDSBY	LIBEL
LENTIFORM	LESSENS	LEV	LEWDSTER	LIBELLANT
LENTIGINES	LESSER	LEVA	LEWDSTERS	LIBELLANTS
LENTIGO	LESSES	LEVANT	LEWIS	LIBELLED
LENTIL	LESSON	LEVANTED	LEWISES	LIBELLEE
LENTILS	LESSONED	LEVANTER	LEWISITE	LIBELLEES
LENTISK	LESSONING	LEVANTERS	LEWISITES	LIBELLER
LENTISKS	LESSONINGS	LEVANTINE	LEWISSON	LIBELLERS
LENTO	LESSONS	LEVANTINES	LEWISSONS	LIBELLING
LENTOID	LESSOR	LEVANTING	LEX	LIBELLINGS
LENTOR	LESSORS	LEVANTS	LEXEME	LIBELLOUS
LENTORS	LEST	LEVATOR	LEXEMES	LIBELS
LENTOS	LET	LEVATORS	LEXES	LIBER
LENTOUS	LETCH	LEVE	LEXICAL	LIBERAL
LENVOY	LETCHED	LEVEE	LEXICALLY	LIBERALLY
LENVOYS	LETCHES	LEVEED	LEXICON	LIBERALS
LEONE	LETCHING	LEVEEING	LEXICONS	LIBERATE
LEONES	LETHAL	LEVEES	LEXIGRAM	LIBERATED
LEONINE	LETHALITIES	LEVEL	LEXIGRAMS	LIBERATES
LEOPARD	LETHALITY	LEVELLED	LEXIS	LIBERATING
LEOPARDS	LETHALLY	LEVELLER	LEXISES	LIBERATOR
LEOTARD	LETHARGIC	LEVELLERS	LEY	LIBERATORS
LEOTARDS	LETHARGIES	LEVELLEST	LEYS	LIBERS
LEP	LETHARGY	LEVELLING	LEZ	LIBERTIES
LEPER	LETHEAN	LEVELS	LEZES	LIBERTINE
LEPERS	LETHEE	LEVER	LEZZ	LIBERTINES
LEPID	LETHEES	LEVERAGE	LEZZES	LIBERTY
LEPIDOTE	LETHIED	LEVERAGES	LEZZIES	LIBIDINAL
LEPORINE	LETS	LEVERED	LEZZY	LIBIDO
LEPPED	LETTABLE	LEVERET	LI	LIBIDOS
LEPPING	LETTED	LEVERETS	LIABILITIES	LIBKEN
LEPRA	LETTER	LEVERING	LIABILITY	LIBKENS
LEPRAS	LETTERED	LEVERS	LIABLE	LIBRA
LEPROSE	LETTERER	LEVIABLE	LIAISE	LIBRAIRE
LEPROSERIES	LETTERERS	LEVIATHAN	LIAISED	LIBRAIRES
LEPROSERY	LETTERING	LEVIATHANS	LIAISES	LIBRAIRIE
LEPROSIES	LETTERINGS	LEVIED	LIAISING	LIBRARIAN
LEPROSITIES	LETTERN	LEVIES	LIAISON	LIBRARIANS
LEPROSITY	LETTERNS	LEVIGABLE	LIAISONS	LIBRARIES
LEPROSY	LETTERS	LEVIGATE	LIANA	LIBRARY
LEPROUS	LETTING	LEVIGATED	LIANAS	LIBRAS
LEPS	LETTINGS	LEVIGATES	LIANE	LIBRATE
LEPTA	LETTRE	LEVIGATING	LIANES	LIBRATED
LEPTOME	LETTRES	LEVIN	LIANG	LIBRATES
LEPTOMES	LETTUCE	LEVINS	LIANGS	LIBRATING
LEPTON	LETTUCES	LEVIRATE	LIANOID	LIBRATION
LEPTONIC	LEU	LEVIRATES	LIAR	LIBRATIONS
LEPTONS	LEUCAEMIA	LEVIS	LIARD	LIBRATORY
LEPTOSOME	LEUCAEMIAS	LEVITATE	LIARDS	LIBRETTI
LEPTOSOMES	LEUCAEMIC	LEVITATED	LIARS	LIBRETTO
LEPTOTENE	LEUCH	LEVITATES	LIART	LIBRETTOS
LEPTOTENES	LEUCHEN	LEVITATING	LIB	LIBS
LERE	LEUCIN	LEVITE	LIBANT	LICE
LERED	LEUCINE	LEVITES	LIBATE	LICENCE
LERES	LEUCINES	LEVITIC	LIBATED	LICENCED
LERING	LEUCINS	LEVITICAL	LIBATES	LICENCES
LERNAEAN	LEUCITE	LEVITIES	LIBATING	LICENCING
LERNEAN	LEUCITES	LEVITY	LIBATION	LICENSE
LES	LEUCITIC	LEVULOSE	LIBATIONS	LICENSED

LICENSEE
LICENSEES
LICENSER
LICENSERS
LICENSES
LICENSING
LICENSOR
LICENSORS
LICENSURE
LICENSURES
LICH
LICHANOS
LICHANOSES
LICHED
LICHEE
LICHEES
LICHEN
LICHENED
LICHENIN
LICHENINS
LICHENISM
LICHENISMS
LICHENIST
LICHENISTS
LICHENOID
LICHENOSE
LICHENOUS
LICHENS
LICHES
LICHGATE
LICHGATES
LICHI
LICHING
LICHIS
LICHT
LICHTED
LICHTER
LICHTEST
LICHTING
LICHTLIED
LICHTLIES
LICHTLY
LICHTLYING
LICHTS
LICHWAKE
LICHWAKES
LICHWAY
LICHWAYS
LICIT
LICITLY
LICK
LICKED
LICKER
LICKERISH
LICKERS
LICKING
LICKINGS
LICKPENNIES
LICKPENNY
LICKS
LICORICE
LICORICES
LICTOR
LICTORS
LID
LIDDED
LIDGER
LIDGERS
LIDLESS
LIDO

LIDOCAINE
LIDOCAINES
LIDOS
LIDS
LIE
LIED
LIEDER
LIEF
LIEFER
LIEFEST
LIEFS
LIEGE
LIEGEDOM
LIEGEDOMS
LIEGELESS
LIEGEMAN
LIEGEMEN
LIEGER
LIEGERS
LIEGES
LIEN
LIENAL
LIENS
LIENTERIC
LIENTERIES
LIENTERY
LIER
LIERNE
LIERNES
LIERS
LIES
LIEU
LIEUS
LIEVE
LIEVER
LIEVEST
LIFE
LIFEBELT
LIFEBELTS
LIFEBOAT
LIFEBOATS
LIFEFUL
LIFEGUARD
LIFEGUARDS
LIFEHOLD
LIFELESS
LIFELIKE
LIFELONG
LIFER
LIFERS
LIFESOME
LIFESPAN
LIFESPANS
LIFETIME
LIFETIMES
LIFT
LIFTABLE
LIFTED
LIFTER
LIFTERS
LIFTING
LIFTS
LIFULL
LIG
LIGAMENT
LIGAMENTS
LIGAN
LIGAND
LIGANDS
LIGANS

LIGATE
LIGATED
LIGATES
LIGATING
LIGATION
LIGATIONS
LIGATURE
LIGATURES
LIGER
LIGERS
LIGGE
LIGGED
LIGGEING
LIGGEN
LIGGER
LIGGERS
LIGGES
LIGGING
LIGGINGS
LIGHT
LIGHTED
LIGHTEN
LIGHTENED
LIGHTENING
LIGHTENS
LIGHTER
LIGHTERS
LIGHTEST
LIGHTFAST
LIGHTFUL
LIGHTING
LIGHTINGS
LIGHTISH
LIGHTLESS
LIGHTLIED
LIGHTLIES
LIGHTLY
LIGHTLYING
LIGHTNESS
LIGHTNESSES
LIGHTNING
LIGHTNINGS
LIGHTS
LIGHTSHIP
LIGHTSHIPS
LIGHTSOME
LIGNAGE
LIGNAGES
LIGNALOES
LIGNE
LIGNEOUS
LIGNES
LIGNIFIED
LIGNIFIES
LIGNIFORM
LIGNIFY
LIGNIFYING
LIGNIN
LIGNINS
LIGNITE
LIGNITES
LIGNITIC
LIGNUM
LIGNUMS
LIGROIN
LIGROINS
LIGS
LIGULA
LIGULAE
LIGULAR

LIGULAS
LIGULATE
LIGULE
LIGULES
LIGULOID
LIGURE
LIGURES
LIKABLE
LIKE
LIKEABLE
LIKED
LIKELIER
LIKELIEST
LIKELY
LIKEN
LIKENED
LIKENESS
LIKENESSES
LIKENING
LIKENS
LIKER
LIKERS
LIKES
LIKEWAKE
LIKEWAKES
LIKEWALK
LIKEWALKS
LIKEWISE
LIKIN
LIKING
LIKINGS
LIKINS
LILAC
LILACS
LILANGENI
LILIED
LILIES
LILL
LILLED
LILLING
LILLS
LILO
LILOS
LILT
LILTED
LILTING
LILTS
LILY
LIMA
LIMACEL
LIMACELS
LIMACEOUS
LIMACES
LIMACINE
LIMAÇON
LIMAÇONS
LIMAIL
LIMAILS
LIMAS
LIMATION
LIMATIONS
LIMAX
LIMB
LIMBATE
LIMBEC
LIMBECK
LIMBECKS
LIMBECS
LIMBED
LIMBER

LIMBERED
LIMBERING
LIMBERS
LIMBIC
LIMBING
LIMBLESS
LIMBMEAL
LIMBO
LIMBOS
LIMBOUS
LIMBS
LIME
LIMED
LIMEKILN
LIMEKILNS
LIMELIGHT
LIMELIGHTED
LIMELIGHTING
LIMELIGHTS
LIMELIT
LIMEN
LIMENS
LIMEPIT
LIMEPITS
LIMERICK
LIMERICKS
LIMES
LIMESTONE
LIMESTONES
LIMEWASH
LIMEWASHES
LIMEWATER
LIMEWATERS
LIMEY
LIMEYS
LIMIER
LIMIEST
LIMINAL
LIMINESS
LIMINESSES
LIMING
LIMINGS
LIMIT
LIMITABLE
LIMITARY
LIMITED
LIMITEDLY
LIMITEDS
LIMITER
LIMITERS
LIMITES
LIMITING
LIMITINGS
LIMITLESS
LIMITS
LIMMA
LIMMAS
LIMMER
LIMMERS
LIMN
LIMNAEID
LIMNAEIDS
LIMNED
LIMNER
LIMNERS
LIMNETIC
LIMNING
LIMNOLOGIES
LIMNOLOGY
LIMNS

LIMONITE	LINEATION	LINKED	LIONIZES	LIQUIDATED
LIMONITES	LINEATIONS	LINKING	LIONIZING	LIQUIDATES
LIMONITIC	LINED	LINKMAN	LIONLY	LIQUIDATING
LIMOSES	LINEMAN	LINKMEN	LIONS	LIQUIDER
LIMOSIS	LINEMEN	LINKS	LIP	LIQUIDEST
LIMOSISES	LINEN	LINKSTER	LIPARITE	LIQUIDISE
LIMOUS	LINENS	LINKSTERS	LIPARITES	LIQUIDISED
LIMOUSINE	LINEOLATE	LINKWORK	LIPASE	LIQUIDISES
LIMOUSINES	LINER	LINKWORKS	LIPASES	LIQUIDISING
LIMP	LINERS	LINN	LIPECTOMIES	LIQUIDITIES
LIMPED	LINES	LINNED	LIPECTOMY	LIQUIDITY
LIMPER	LINESMAN	LINNET	LIPGLOSS	LIQUIDIZE
LIMPEST	LINESMEN	LINNETS	LIPGLOSSES	LIQUIDIZED
LIMPET	LINEY	LINNIES	LIPID	LIQUIDIZES
LIMPETS	LING	LINNING	LIPIDE	LIQUIDIZING
LIMPID	LINGA	LINNS	LIPIDES	LIQUIDLY
LIMPIDITIES	LINGAM	LINNY	LIPIDS	LIQUIDS
LIMPIDITY	LINGAMS	LINO	LIPLESS	LIQUIDUS
LIMPIDLY	LINGAS	LINOCUT	LIPOGRAM	LIQUIDUSES
LIMPING	LINGEL	LINOCUTS	LIPOGRAMS	LIQUIFIED
LIMPINGLY	LINGELS	LINOLEUM	LIPOID	LIQUOR
LIMPINGS	LINGER	LINOLEUMS	LIPOIDS	LIQUORED
LIMPKIN	LINGERED	LINOS	LIPOMA	LIQUORICE
LIMPKINS	LINGERER	LINS	LIPOMATA	LIQUORICES
LIMPS	LINGERERS	LINSANG	LIPOSOMAL	LIQUORING
LIMULI	LINGERIE	LINSANGS	LIPOSOME	LIQUORISH
LIMULUS	LINGERIES	LINSEED	LIPOSOMES	LIQUORS
LIMULUSES	LINGERING	LINSEEDS	LIPPED	LIRA
LIMY	LINGERINGS	LINSEY	LIPPEN	LIRAS
LIN	LINGERS	LINSEYS	LIPPENED	LIRE
LINAC	LINGIER	LINSTOCK	LIPPENING	LIRIPIPE
LINAGE	LINGIEST	LINSTOCKS	LIPPENS	LIRIPIPES
LINAGES	LINGLE	LINT	LIPPIE	LIRIPOOP
LINALOOL	LINGLES	LINTEL	LIPPIER	LIRIPOOPS
LINALOOLS	LINGO	LINTELLED	LIPPIES	LIRK
LINCH	LINGOES	LINTELS	LIPPIEST	LIRKED
LINCHES	LINGOT	LINTER	LIPPING	LIRKING
LINCHET	LINGOTS	LINTERS	LIPPITUDE	LIRKS
LINCHETS	LINGS	LINTIE	LIPPITUDES	LIS
LINCHPIN	LINGSTER	LINTIER	LIPPY	LISK
LINCHPINS	LINGSTERS	LINTIES	LIPS	LISKS
LINCRUSTA	LINGUA	LINTIEST	LIPSALVE	LISLE
LINCRUSTAS	LINGUAE	LINTS	LIPSALVES	LISLES
LINCTURE	LINGUAL	LINTSEED	LIPSTICK	LISP
LINCTURES	LINGUALLY	LINTSEEDS	LIPSTICKED	LISPED
LINCTUS	LINGUAS	LINTSTOCK	LIPSTICKING	LISPER
LINCTUSES	LINGUINI	LINTSTOCKS	LIPSTICKS	LISPERS
LIND	LINGUIST	LINTWHITE	LIQUABLE	LISPING
LINDANE	LINGUISTS	LINTWHITES	LIQUATE	LISPINGLY
LINDANES	LINGULA	LINTY	LIQUATED	LISPINGS
LINDEN	LINGULAE	LINY	LIQUATES	LISPOUND
LINDENS	LINGULAR	LION	LIQUATING	LISPOUNDS
LINDS	LINGULAS	LIONCEL	LIQUATION	LISPS
LINDWORM	LINGULATE	LIONCELLE	LIQUATIONS	LISPUND
LINDWORMS	LINGY	LIONCELLES	LIQUEFIED	LISPUNDS
LINE	LINHAY	LIONCELS	LIQUEFIER	LISSES
LINEAGE	LINHAYS	LIONEL	LIQUEFIERS	LISSOM
LINEAGES	LINIER	LIONELS	LIQUEFIES	LISSOME
LINEAL	LINIEST	LIONESS	LIQUEFY	LISSOMER
LINEALITIES	LINIMENT	LIONESSES	LIQUEFYING	LISSOMEST
LINEALITY	LINIMENTS	LIONET	LIQUESCE	LIST
LINEALLY	LININ	LIONETS	LIQUESCED	LISTED
LINEAMENT	LINING	LIONISE	LIQUESCES	LISTEL
LINEAMENTS	LININGS	LIONISED	LIQUESCING	LISTELS
LINEAR	LININS	LIONISES	LIQUEUR	LISTEN
LINEARITIES	LINK	LIONISING	LIQUEURED	LISTENED
LINEARITY	LINKAGE	LIONISM	LIQUEURING	LISTENER
LINEARLY	LINKAGES	LIONISMS	LIQUEURS	LISTENERS
LINEATE	LINKBOY	LIONIZE	LIQUID	LISTENING
LINEATED	LINKBOYS	LIONIZED	LIQUIDATE	LISTENS

LISTER	LITHOTOMES	LIVERYMAN	LOAMING	LOBSCOUSES
LISTERS	LITHOTOMIES	LIVERYMEN	LOAMS	LOBSTER
LISTETH	LITHOTOMY	LIVES	LOAMY	LOBSTERS
LISTFUL	LITHS	LIVESTOCK	LOAN	LOBULAR
LISTING	LITIGABLE	LIVESTOCKS	LOANABLE	LOBULATE
LISTINGS	LITIGANT	LIVEWARE	LOANED	LOBULATED
LISTLESS	LITIGANTS	LIVEWARES	LOANING	LOBULE
LISTS	LITIGATE	LIVID	LOANINGS	LOBULES
LIT	LITIGATED	LIVIDER	LOANS	LOBULI
LITANIES	LITIGATES	LIVIDEST	LOAST	LOBULUS
LITANY	LITIGATING	LIVIDITIES	LOATH	LOBUS
LITCHI	LITIGIOUS	LIVIDITY	LOATHE	LOBWORM
LITCHIS	LITMUS	LIVIDNESS	LOATHED	LOBWORMS
LITE	LITMUSES	LIVIDNESSES	LOATHEING	LOCAL
LITER	LITOTES	LIVING	LOATHER	LOCALE
LITERACIES	LITRE	LIVINGS	LOATHERS	LOCALES
LITERACY	LITRES	LIVOR	LOATHES	LOCALISE
LITERAL	LITTEN	LIVORS	LOATHEST	LOCALISED
LITERALLY	LITTER	LIVRAISON	LOATHFUL	LOCALISER
LITERALS	LITTERED	LIVRAISONS	LOATHING	LOCALISERS
LITERARY	LITTERING	LIVRE	LOATHINGS	LOCALISES
LITERATE	LITTERS	LIVRES	LOATHLY	LOCALISING
LITERATES	LITTERY	LIXIVIAL	LOATHSOME	LOCALISM
LITERATI	LITTLE	LIXIVIATE	LOATHSOMER	LOCALISMS
LITERATIM	LITTLEANE	LIXIVIATED	LOATHSOMEST	LOCALIST
LITERATO	LITTLEANES	LIXIVIATES	LOATHY	LOCALISTS
LITERATOR	LITTLER	LIXIVIATING	LOAVE	LOCALITIES
LITERATORS	LITTLES	LIXIVIOUS	LOAVED	LOCALITY
LITERATUS	LITTLEST	LIXIVIUM	LOAVES	LOCALIZE
LITEROSE	LITTLIN	LIXIVIUMS	LOAVING	LOCALIZED
LITERS	LITTLING	LIZARD	LOB	LOCALIZER
LITES	LITTLINGS	LIZARDS	LOBAR	LOCALIZERS
LITH	LITTLINS	LLAMA	LOBATE	LOCALIZES
LITHARGE	LITTORAL	LLAMAS	LOBATION	LOCALIZING
LITHARGES	LITTORALS	LLANERO	LOBATIONS	LOCALLY
LITHATE	LITURGIC	LLANEROS	LOBBED	LOCALS
LITHATES	LITURGICS	LLANO	LOBBIED	LOCATE
LITHE	LITURGIES	LLANOS	LOBBIES	LOCATED
LITHED	LITURGIST	LO	LOBBING	LOCATES
LITHELY	LITURGISTS	LOACH	LOBBY	LOCATING
LITHENESS	LITURGY	LOACHES	LOBBYER	LOCATION
LITHENESSES	LITUUS	LOAD	LOBBYERS	LOCATIONS
LITHER	LITUUSES	LOADED	LOBBYING	LOCATIVE
LITHERLY	LIVABLE	LOADEN	LOBBYINGS	LOCATIVES
LITHES	LIVE	LOADENED	LOBBYIST	LOCELLATE
LITHESOME	LIVEABLE	LOADENING	LOBBYISTS	LOCH
LITHEST	LIVED	LOADENS	LOBE	LOCHAN
LITHIA	LIVELIER	LOADER	LOBECTOMIES	LOCHANS
LITHIAS	LIVELIEST	LOADERS	LOBECTOMY	LOCHIA
LITHIASES	LIVELILY	LOADING	LOBED	LOCHIAL
LITHIASIS	LIVELOD	LOADINGS	LOBELET	LOCHS
LITHIC	LIVELODS	LOADS	LOBELETS	LOCI
LITHING	LIVELONG	LOADSTAR	LOBELIA	LOCK
LITHISTID	LIVELONGS	LOADSTARS	LOBELIAS	LOCKAGE
LITHISTIDS	LIVELOOD	LOADSTONE	LOBELINE	LOCKAGES
LITHITE	LIVELOODS	LOADSTONES	LOBELINES	LOCKAWAY
LITHITES	LIVELY	LOAF	LOBES	LOCKAWAYS
LITHIUM	LIVEN	LOAFED	LOBI	LOCKED
LITHIUMS	LIVENED	LOAFER	LOBING	LOCKER
LITHO	LIVENING	LOAFERISH	LOBINGS	LOCKERS
LITHOCYST	LIVENS	LOAFERS	LOBIPED	LOCKET
LITHOCYSTS	LIVER	LOAFING	LOBLOLLIES	LOCKETS
LITHOID	LIVERED	LOAFINGS	LOBLOLLY	LOCKFAST
LITHOIDAL	LIVERIED	LOAFS	LOBO	LOCKFUL
LITHOLOGIES	LIVERIES	LOAM	LOBOS	LOCKFULS
LITHOLOGY	LIVERISH	LOAMED	LOBOSE	LOCKHOUSE
LITHOPONE	LIVERS	LOAMIER	LOBOTOMIES	LOCKHOUSES
LITHOPONES	LIVERWORT	LOAMIEST	LOBOTOMY	LOCKING
LITHOS	LIVERWORTS	LOAMINESS	LOBS	LOCKMAN
LITHOTOME	LIVERY	LOAMINESSES	LOBSCOUSE	LOCKMEN

LOCKOUT	LODICULA	LOGOGRIPHS	LONENESSES	LOOFAS
LOCKOUTS	LODICULAE	LOGOMACHIES	LONER	LOOFED
LOCKPICK	LODICULE	LOGOMACHY	LONERS	LOOFFUL
LOCKPICKS	LODICULES	LOGORRHEA	LONESOME	LOOFFULS
LOCKRAM	LOESS	LOGORRHEAS	LONESOMER	LOOFING
LOCKRAMS	LOESSES	LOGOS	LONESOMEST	LOOFS
LOCKS	LOFT	LOGOTHETE	LONG	LOOING
LOCKSMAN	LOFTED	LOGOTHETES	LONGA	LOOK
LOCKSMEN	LOFTER	LOGOTYPE	LONGAEVAL	LOOKED
LOCKSMITH	LOFTERS	LOGOTYPES	LONGAN	LOOKER
LOCKSMITHS	LOFTIER	LOGS	LONGANS	LOOKERS
LOCKSTEP	LOFTIEST	LOGWOOD	LONGAS	LOOKING
LOCKSTEPS	LOFTILY	LOGWOODS	LONGBOAT	LOOKINGS
LOCO	LOFTINESS	LOID	LONGBOATS	LOOKOUT
LOCOED	LOFTINESSES	LOIDED	LONGBOW	LOOKOUTS
LOCOES	LOFTING	LOIDING	LONGBOWS	LOOKS
LOCOFOCO	LOFTS	LOIDS	LONGCLOTH	LOOM
LOCOFOCOS	LOFTY	LOIN	LONGCLOTHES	LOOMED
LOCOMAN	LOG	LOINS	LONGCOATS	LOOMING
LOCOMEN	LOGAN	LOIPE	LONGE	LOOMS
LOCOMOTE	LOGANS	LOIPES	LONGED	LOON
LOCOMOTED	LOGAOEDIC	LOIR	LONGEING	LOONIE
LOCOMOTES	LOGARITHM	LOIRS	LONGER	LOONIER
LOCOMOTING	LOGARITHMS	LOITER	LONGERON	LOONIES
LOCOMOTOR	LOGBOARD	LOITERED	LONGERONS	LOONIEST
LOCOMOTORS	LOGBOARDS	LOITERER	LONGES	LOONING
LOCOS	LOGE	LOITERERS	LONGEST	LOONINGS
LOCULAR	LOGES	LOITERING	LONGEVAL	LOONS
LOCULATE	LOGGAT	LOITERINGS	LONGEVITIES	LOONY
LOCULE	LOGGATS	LOITERS	LONGEVITY	LOOP
LOCULES	LOGGED	LOKE	LONGEVOUS	LOOPED
LOCULI	LOGGER	LOKES	LONGHAND	LOOPER
LOCULUS	LOGGERS	LOKSHEN	LONGHANDS	LOOPERS
LOCUM	LOGGIA	LOLL	LONGHORN	LOOPHOLE
LOCUMS	LOGGIAS	LOLLED	LONGHORNS	LOOPHOLED
LOCUPLETE	LOGGIE	LOLLER	LONGICORN	LOOPHOLES
LOCUS	LOGGING	LOLLERS	LONGICORNS	LOOPHOLING
LOCUST	LOGGINGS	LOLLIES	LONGING	LOOPIER
LOCUSTA	LOGIA	LOLLING	LONGINGLY	LOOPIEST
LOCUSTAE	LOGIC	LOLLINGLY	LONGINGS	LOOPING
LOCUSTED	LOGICAL	LOLLIPOP	LONGISH	LOOPINGS
LOCUSTING	LOGICALLY	LOLLIPOPS	LONGITUDE	LOOPS
LOCUSTS	LOGICIAN	LOLLOP	LONGITUDES	LOOPY
LOCUTION	LOGICIANS	LOLLOPED	LONGLY	LOOR
LOCUTIONS	LOGICISE	LOLLOPING	LONGNESS	LOORD
LOCUTORIES	LOGICISED	LOLLOPS	LONGNESSES	LOORDS
LOCUTORY	LOGICISES	LOLLS	LONGS	LOOS
LODE	LOGICISING	LOLLY	LONGSHIP	LOOSE
LODEN	LOGICIZE	LOLLYGAG	LONGSHIPS	LOOSED
LODENS	LOGICIZED	LOLLYGAGGED	LONGSHORE	LOOSELY
LODES	LOGICIZES	LOLLYGAGGING	LONGSOME	LOOSEN
LODESMAN	LOGICIZING	LOLLYGAGS	LONGTAIL	LOOSENED
LODESMEN	LOGICS	LOLOG	LONGTAILS	LOOSENER
LODESTAR	LOGIE	LOLOGS	LONGUEUR	LOOSENERS
LODESTARS	LOGIES	LOMA	LONGUEURS	LOOSENESS
LODESTONE	LOGION	LOMAS	LONGWALL	LOOSENESSES
LODESTONES	LOGISTIC	LOME	LONGWALLS	LOOSENING
LODGE	LOGISTICS	LOMED	LONGWAYS	LOOSENS
LODGED	LOGJUICE	LOMENT	LONGWISE	LOOSER
LODGEMENT	LOGJUICES	LOMENTA	LONICERA	LOOSES
LODGEMENTS	LOGLINE	LOMENTS	LONICERAS	LOOSEST
LODGEPOLE	LOGLINES	LOMENTUM	LOO	LOOSING
LODGEPOLES	LOGLOG	LOMES	LOOBIES	LOOT
LODGER	LOGLOGS	LOMING	LOOBILY	LOOTED
LODGERS	LOGO	LOMPISH	LOOBY	LOOTEN
LODGES	LOGOGRAM	LONE	LOOED	LOOTER
LODGING	LOGOGRAMS	LONELIER	LOOF	LOOTERS
LODGINGS	LOGOGRAPH	LONELIEST	LOOFA	LOOTING
LODGMENT	LOGOGRAPHS	LONELY	LOOFAH	LOOTS
LODGMENTS	LOGOGRIPH	LONENESS	LOOFAHS	LOOVES

LOP	LORINER	LOUDLY	LOVE	LOWNESSES
LOPE	LORINERS	LOUDMOUTH	LOVEABLE	LOWNING
LOPED	LORING	LOUDMOUTHS	LOVEBIRD	LOWNS
LOPER	LORINGS	LOUDNESS	LOVEBIRDS	LOWS
LOPERS	LORIOT	LOUDNESSES	LOVEBITE	LOWSE
LOPES	LORIOTS	LOUGH	LOVEBITES	LOWSER
LOPGRASS	LORIS	LOUGHS	LOVED	LOWSES
LOPGRASSES	LORISES	LOUIS	LOVELESS	LOWSEST
LOPHODONT	LORN	LOUN	LOVELIER	LOWSING
LOPING	LORRELL	LOUND	LOVELIES	LOWSIT
LOPPED	LORRELLS	LOUNDED	LOVELIEST	LOWT
LOPPER	LORRIES	LOUNDERED	LOVELIGHT	LOWTED
LOPPERS	LORRY	LOUNDERING	LOVELIGHTS	LOWTING
LOPPING	LORY	LOUNDERS	LOVELILY	LOWTS
LOPPINGS	LOS	LOUNDING	LOVELOCK	LOWVELD
LOPS	LOSABLE	LOUNDS	LOVELOCKS	LOWVELDS
LOQUACITIES	LOSE	LOUNED	LOVELORN	LOX
LOQUACITY	LOSEL	LOUNGE	LOVELY	LOXES
LOQUAT	LOSELS	LOUNGED	LOVER	LOXODROME
LOQUATS	LOSEN	LOUNGER	LOVERED	LOXODROMES
LOQUITUR	LOSER	LOUNGERS	LOVERLESS	LOXODROMIES
LOR	LOSERS	LOUNGES	LOVERLY	LOXODROMY
LORAL	LOSES	LOUNGING	LOVERS	LOXYGEN
LORAN	LOSH	LOUNGINGS	LOVES	LOXYGENS
LORANS	LOSING	LOUNING	LOVESICK	LOY
LORATE	LOSINGLY	LOUNS	LOVESOME	LOYAL
LORCHA	LOSINGS	LOUP	LOVEY	LOYALIST
LORCHAS	LOSS	LOUPE	LOVEYS	LOYALISTS
LORD	LOSSES	LOUPED	LOVING	LOYALLER
LORDED	LOSSIER	LOUPEN	LOVINGLY	LOYALLEST
LORDING	LOSSIEST	LOUPES	LOVINGS	LOYALLY
LORDINGS	LOSSY	LOUPING	LOW	LOYALTIES
LORDKIN	LOST	LOUPIT	LOWAN	LOYALTY
LORDKINS	LOT	LOUPS	LOWANS	LOYS
LORDLESS	LOTA	LOUR	LOWBOY	LOZELL
LORDLIER	LOTAH	LOURE	LOWBOYS	LOZELLS
LORDLIEST	LOTAHS	LOURED	LOWE	LOZEN
LORDLING	LOTAS	LOURES	LOWED	LOZENGE
LORDLINGS	LOTE	LOURING	LOWER	LOZENGED
LORDLY	LOTES	LOURINGLY	LOWERED	LOZENGES
LORDOSES	LOTH	LOURINGS	LOWERING	LOZENGY
LORDOSIS	LOTHEFULL	LOURS	LOWERINGS	LOZENS
LORDOTIC	LOTHER	LOURY	LOWERMOST	LUAU
LORDS	LOTHEST	LOUSE	LOWERS	LUAUS
LORDSHIP	LOTHFULL	LOUSED	LOWERY	LUBBARD
LORDSHIPS	LOTIC	LOUSES	LOWES	LUBBARDS
LORDY	LOTION	LOUSIER	LOWEST	LUBBER
LORE	LOTIONS	LOUSIEST	LOWING	LUBBERLY
LOREL	LOTO	LOUSILY	LOWINGS	LUBBERS
LORELS	LOTOS	LOUSINESS	LOWLAND	LUBFISH
LORES	LOTOSES	LOUSINESSES	LOWLANDER	LUBFISHES
LORETTE	LOTS	LOUSING	LOWLANDERS	LUBRA
LORETTES	LOTTED	LOUSY	LOWLANDS	LUBRAS
LORGNETTE	LOTTERIES	LOUT	LOWLIER	LUBRIC
LORGNETTES	LOTTERY	LOUTED	LOWLIEST	LUBRICAL
LORGNON	LOTTING	LOUTING	LOWLIHEAD	LUBRICANT
LORGNONS	LOTTO	LOUTISH	LOWLIHEADS	LUBRICANTS
LORIC	LOTTOS	LOUTISHLY	LOWLILY	LUBRICATE
LORICA	LOTUS	LOUTS	LOWLINESS	LUBRICATED
LORICAE	LOTUSES	LOUVER	LOWLINESSES	LUBRICATES
LORICATE	LOUCHE	LOUVERED	LOWLY	LUBRICATING
LORICATED	LOUCHELY	LOUVERS	LOWN	LUBRICITIES
LORICATES	LOUD	LOUVRE	LOWND	LUBRICITY
LORICATING	LOUDEN	LOUVRED	LOWNDED	LUBRICOUS
LORICS	LOUDENED	LOUVRES	LOWNDING	LUCARNE
LORIES	LOUDENING	LOVABLE	LOWNDS	LUCARNES
LORIKEET	LOUDENS	LOVAGE	LOWNE	LUCE
LORIKEETS	LOUDER	LOVAGES	LOWNED	LUCENCIES
LORIMER	LOUDEST	LOVAT	LOWNES	LUCENCY
LORIMERS	LOUDISH	LOVATS	LOWNESS	LUCENT

LUCERN	LUGGAGES	LUMINIST	LUNGIE	LURRY
LUCERNE	LUGGED	LUMINISTS	LUNGIES	LURS
LUCERNES	LUGGER	LUMINOUS	LUNGING	LUSCIOUS
LUCERNS	LUGGERS	LUMME	LUNGIS	LUSH
LUCES	LUGGIE	LUMMOX	LUNGS	LUSHED
LUCID	LUGGIES	LUMMOXES	LUNGWORT	LUSHER
LUCIDER	LUGGING	LUMMY	LUNGWORTS	LUSHERS
LUCIDEST	LUGING	LUMP	LUNISOLAR	LUSHES
LUCIDITY	LUGINGS	LUMPED	LUNITIDAL	LUSHEST
LUCIDLY	LUGS	LUMPEN	LUNKER	LUSHING
LUCIDNESS	LUGSAIL	LUMPENLY	LUNKERS	LUSHLY
LUCIFER	LUGSAILS	LUMPER	LUNKHEAD	LUSHNESS
LUCIFERIN	LUGWORM	LUMPERS	LUNKHEADS	LUSHNESSES
LUCIFERINS	LUGWORMS	LUMPFISH	LUNT	LUSHY
LUCIFERS	LUIT	LUMPFISHES	LUNTED	LUSK
LUCIGEN	LUITEN	LUMPIER	LUNTING	LUSKED
LUCIGENS	LUKE	LUMPIEST	LUNTS	LUSKING
LUCK	LUKEWARM	LUMPILY	LUNULA	LUSKISH
LUCKEN	LULL	LUMPINESS	LUNULAR	LUSKS
LUCKIE	LULLABIED	LUMPINESSES	LUNULAS	LUST
LUCKIER	LULLABIES	LUMPING	LUNULATE	LUSTED
LUCKIES	LULLABY	LUMPISH	LUNULATED	LUSTER
LUCKIEST	LULLABYING	LUMPISHLY	LUNULE	LUSTERED
LUCKILY	LULLED	LUMPKIN	LUNULES	LUSTERING
LUCKINESS	LULLING	LUMPKINS	LUNYIE	LUSTERS
LUCKINESSES	LULLS	LUMPS	LUNYIES	LUSTFUL
LUCKLESS	LULU	LUMPY	LUPIN	LUSTFULLY
LUCKS	LULUS	LUMS	LUPINE	LUSTICK
LUCKY	LUM	LUNACIES	LUPINES	LUSTIER
LUCRATIVE	LUMBAGO	LUNACY	LUPINS	LUSTIEST
LUCRE	LUMBAGOS	LUNANAUT	LUPPEN	LUSTIHEAD
LUCRES	LUMBANG	LUNANAUTS	LUPULIN	LUSTIHEADS
LUCTATION	LUMBANGS	LUNAR	LUPULINE	LUSTIHOOD
LUCTATIONS	LUMBAR	LUNARIAN	LUPULINIC	LUSTIHOODS
LUCUBRATE	LUMBER	LUNARIANS	LUPULINS	LUSTILY
LUCUBRATED	LUMBERED	LUNARIES	LUPUS	LUSTINESS
LUCUBRATES	LUMBERER	LUNARIST	LUPUSES	LUSTINESSES
LUCUBRATING	LUMBERERS	LUNARISTS	LUR	LUSTING
LUCULENT	LUMBERING	LUNARNAUT	LURCH	LUSTIQUE
LUCUMA	LUMBERINGS	LUNARNAUTS	LURCHED	LUSTLESS
LUCUMAS	LUMBERLY	LUNARS	LURCHER	LUSTRA
LUCUMO	LUMBERMAN	LUNARY	LURCHERS	LUSTRAL
LUCUMONES	LUMBERMEN	LUNATE	LURCHES	LUSTRATE
LUCUMOS	LUMBERS	LUNATED	LURCHING	LUSTRATED
LUD	LUMBRICAL	LUNATIC	LURDAN	LUSTRATES
LUDIC	LUMBRICALS	LUNATICS	LURDANE	LUSTRATING
LUDICROUS	LUMBRICI	LUNATION	LURDANES	LUSTRE
LUDO	LUMBRICUS	LUNATIONS	LURDANS	LUSTRED
LUDOS	LUMBRICUSES	LUNCH	LURDEN	LUSTRES
LUDS	LUMEN	LUNCHED	LURDENS	LUSTRINE
LUDSHIP	LUMENAL	LUNCHEON	LURE	LUSTRINES
LUDSHIPS	LUMENS	LUNCHEONED	LURED	LUSTRING
LUES	LUMINA	LUNCHEONING	LURES	LUSTRINGS
LUESES	LUMINAIRE	LUNCHEONS	LURGIES	LUSTROUS
LUETIC	LUMINAIRES	LUNCHER	LURGY	LUSTRUM
LUFF	LUMINAL	LUNCHERS	LURID	LUSTRUMS
LUFFA	LUMINANCE	LUNCHES	LURIDER	LUSTS
LUFFAS	LUMINANCES	LUNCHING	LURIDEST	LUSTY
LUFFED	LUMINANT	LUNE	LURIDLY	LUTANIST
LUFFING	LUMINANTS	LUNES	LURIDNESS	LUTANISTS
LUFFS	LUMINARIES	LUNETTE	LURIDNESSES	LUTE
LUFTWAFFE	LUMINARY	LUNETTES	LURING	LUTEAL
LUFTWAFFES	LUMINE	LUNG	LURK	LUTECIUM
LUG	LUMINED	LUNGE	LURKED	LUTECIUMS
LUGE	LUMINES	LUNGED	LURKER	LUTED
LUGED	LUMINESCE	LUNGEING	LURKERS	LUTEIN
LUGEING	LUMINESCED	LUNGES	LURKING	LUTEINISE
LUGEINGS	LUMINESCES	LUNGFUL	LURKINGS	LUTEINISED
LUGES	LUMINESCING	LUNGFULS	LURKS	LUTEINISES
LUGGAGE	LUMINING	LUNGI	LURRIES	LUTEINISING

LUTEINIZE	LUXATION	LYCOPODS	LYNCHES	LYSE
LUTEINIZED	LUXATIONS	LYDDITE	LYNCHET	LYSED
LUTEINIZES	LUXES	LYDDITES	LYNCHETS	LYSERGIDE
LUTEINIZING	LUXMETER	LYE	LYNCHING	LYSERGIDES
LUTEINS	LUXMETERS	LYES	LYNCHPIN	LYSES
LUTENIST	LUXURIANT	LYFULL	LYNCHPINS	LYSIGENIC
LUTENISTS	LUXURIATE	LYING	LYNE	LYSIMETER
LUTEOLIN	LUXURIATED	LYINGLY	LYNES	LYSIMETERS
LUTEOLINS	LUXURIATES	LYINGS	LYNX	LYSIN
LUTEOLOUS	LUXURIATING	LYKEWAKE	LYNXES	LYSINE
LUTEOUS	LUXURIES	LYKEWAKES	LYOMEROUS	LYSINES
LUTER	LUXURIOUS	LYKEWALK	LYOPHIL	LYSING
LUTERS	LUXURIST	LYKEWALKS	LYOPHILE	LYSINS
LUTES	LUXURISTS	LYM	LYOPHILIC	LYSIS
LUTESCENT	LUXURY	LYME	LYOPHOBE	LYSOL
LUTETIUM	LUZ	LYMES	LYOPHOBIC	LYSOLS
LUTETIUMS	LUZERN	LYMITER	LYRATE	LYSOSOME
LUTHERN	LUZERNS	LYMITERS	LYRATED	LYSOSOMES
LUTHERNS	LUZZES	LYMPH	LYRE	LYSOZYME
LUTHIER	LYAM	LYMPHAD	LYRES	LYSOZYMES
LUTHIERS	LYAMS	LYMPHADS	LYRIC	LYSSA
LUTING	LYART	LYMPHATIC	LYRICAL	LYSSAS
LUTINGS	LYCÉE	LYMPHATICS	LYRICALLY	LYTE
LUTIST	LYCÉES	LYMPHOID	LYRICISM	LYTED
LUTISTS	LYCEUM	LYMPHOMA	LYRICISMS	LYTES
LUTTEN	LYCEUMS	LYMPHOMAS	LYRICIST	LYTHE
LUTZ	LYCHEE	LYMPHS	LYRICISTS	LYTHES
LUTZES	LYCHEES	LYMS	LYRICS	LYTING
LUX	LYCHGATE	LYNAGE	LYRIFORM	LYTTA
LUXATE	LYCHGATES	LYNAGES	LYRISM	LYTTAS
LUXATED	LYCHNIS	LYNCEAN	LYRISMS	
LUXATES	LYCHNISES	LYNCH	LYRIST	
LUXATING	LYCOPOD	LYNCHED	LYRISTS	

M

MA	MACHINISTS	MACULE	MADREPORE	MAGIC
MAAR	MACHISMO	MACULES	MADREPORES	MAGICAL
MAARS	MACHISMOES	MACULOSE	MADRIGAL	MAGICALLY
MAC	MACHISMOS	MAD	MADRIGALS	MAGICIAN
MACABRE	MACHMETER	MADAM	MADROÑA	MAGICIANS
MACACO	MACHMETERS	MADAME	MADROÑAS	MAGICKED
MACACOS	MACHO	MADAMED	MADROÑO	MAGICKING
MACADAM	MACHOS	MADAMING	MADROÑOS	MAGICS
MACADAMIA	MACHREE	MADAMS	MADS	MAGILP
MACADAMIAS	MACHREES	MADAROSES	MADWOMAN	MAGILPS
MACADAMS	MACHZOR	MADAROSIS	MADWOMEN	MAGISTER
MACAHUBA	MACHZORIM	MADBRAIN	MADWORT	MAGISTERIES
MACAHUBAS	MACINTOSH	MADBRAINED	MADWORTS	MAGISTERS
MACAQUE	MACINTOSHES	MADCAP	MADZOON	MAGISTERY
MACAQUES	MACK	MADCAPS	MADZOONS	MAGISTRAL
MACARISE	MACKEREL	MADDED	MAE	MAGISTRALS
MACARISED	MACKERELS	MADDEN	MAELSTROM	MAGLEV
MACARISES	MACKINAW	MADDENED	MAELSTROMS	MAGMA
MACARISING	MACKINAWS	MADDENING	MAENAD	MAGMAS
MACARISM	MACKLE	MADDENS	MAENADIC	MAGMATA
MACARISMS	MACKLED	MADDER	MAENADS	MAGMATIC
MACARIZE	MACKLES	MADDERS	MAESTOSO	MAGNALIUM
MACARIZED	MACKLING	MADDEST	MAESTRI	MAGNALIUMS
MACARIZES	MACKS	MADDING	MAESTRO	MAGNATE
MACARIZING	MACLE	MADDINGLY	MAESTROS	MAGNATES
MACARONI	MACLED	MADE	MAFFIA	MAGNES
MACARONIC	MACLES	MADEFIED	MAFFIAS	MAGNESES
MACARONICS	MACOYA	MADEFIES	MAFFICK	MAGNESIA
MACARONIES	MACOYAS	MADEFY	MAFFICKED	MAGNESIAN
MACARONIS	MACRAMÉ	MADEFYING	MAFFICKER	MAGNESIAS
MACAROON	MACRAMÉS	MADELEINE	MAFFICKERS	MAGNESITE
MACAROONS	MACRAMI	MADELEINES	MAFFICKING	MAGNESITES
MACAW	MACRAMIS	MADERISE	MAFFICKINGS	MAGNESIUM
MACAWS	MACRO	MADERISED	MAFFICKS	MAGNESIUMS
MACCHIE	MACROBIAN	MADERISES	MAFFLED	MAGNET
MACE	MACROCODE	MADERISING	MAFFLIN	MAGNETIC
MACÉDOINE	MACROCODES	MADERIZE	MAFFLING	MAGNETICS
MACÉDOINES	MACROCOPIES	MADERIZED	MAFFLINGS	MAGNETISE
MACER	MACROCOPY	MADERIZES	MAFFLINS	MAGNETISED
MACERATE	MACROCOSM	MADERIZING	MAFIA	MAGNETISES
MACERATED	MACROCOSMS	MADGE	MAFIAS	MAGNETISING
MACERATES	MACROCYTE	MADGES	MAFIOSI	MAGNETISM
MACERATING	MACROCYTES	MADHOUSE	MAFIOSO	MAGNETISMS
MACERATOR	MACRODOME	MADHOUSES	MAG	MAGNETIST
MACERATORS	MACRODOMES	MADID	MAGAZINE	MAGNETISTS
MACERS	MACROLOGIES	MADLING	MAGAZINES	MAGNETITE
MACES	MACROLOGY	MADLINGS	MAGDALEN	MAGNETITES
MACHAIR	MACRON	MADLY	MAGDALENE	MAGNETIZE
MACHAIRS	MACRONS	MADMAN	MAGDALENES	MAGNETIZED
MACHAN	MACROPOD	MADMEN	MAGDALENS	MAGNETIZES
MACHANS	MACROPODS	MADNESS	MAGE	MAGNETIZING
MACHETE	MACROS	MADNESSES	MAGENTA	MAGNETO
MACHETES	MACRURAL	MADOQUA	MAGENTAS	MAGNETON
MACHINATE	MACRUROUS	MADOQUAS	MAGES	MAGNETONS
MACHINATED	MACS	MADRAS	MAGESHIP	MAGNETOS
MACHINATES	MACTATION	MADRASA	MAGESHIPS	MAGNETRON
MACHINATING	MACTATIONS	MADRASAH	MAGG	MAGNETRONS
MACHINE	MACULA	MADRASAHS	MAGGED	MAGNETS
MACHINED	MACULAE	MADRASAS	MAGGING	MAGNIFIC
MACHINERIES	MACULAR	MADRASES	MAGGOT	MAGNIFICO
MACHINERY	MACULATE	MADRASSA	MAGGOTS	MAGNIFICOES
MACHINES	MACULATED	MADRASSAH	MAGGOTY	MAGNIFIED
MACHINING	MACULATES	MADRASSAHS	MAGGS	MAGNIFIER
MACHINIST	MACULATING	MADRASSAS	MAGI	MAGNIFIERS

MAGNIFIES	MAIDLESS	MAINSTAYS	MALACHITES	MALIGN
MAGNIFY	MAIDS	MAINTAIN	MALACIA	MALIGNANT
MAGNIFYING	MAIEUTIC	MAINTAINED	MALACIAS	MALIGNANTS
MAGNITUDE	MAIEUTICS	MAINTAINING	MALADIES	MALIGNED
MAGNITUDES	MAIGRE	MAINTAINS	MALADROIT	MALIGNER
MAGNOLIA	MAIGRES	MAINTOP	MALADY	MALIGNERS
MAGNOLIAS	MAIK	MAINTOPS	MALAGUEÑA	MALIGNING
MAGNOX	MAIKO	MAINYARD	MALAGUEÑAS	MALIGNITIES
MAGNOXES	MAIKOS	MAINYARDS	MALAISE	MALIGNITY
MAGNUM	MAIKS	MAIOLICA	MALAISES	MALIGNLY
MAGNUMS	MAIL	MAIOLICAS	MALAMUTE	MALIGNS
MAGOT	MAILABLE	MAIRE	MALAMUTES	MALINGER
MAGOTS	MAILE	MAIRES	MALANDER	MALINGERED
MAGPIE	MAILED	MAISE	MALANDERS	MALINGERIES
MAGPIES	MAILER	MAISES	MALAPERT	MALINGERING
MAGS	MAILERS	MAIST	MALAR	MALINGERS
MAGSMAN	MAILES	MAISTER	MALARIA	MALINGERY
MAGSMEN	MAILING	MAISTERED	MALARIAL	MALIS
MAGUEY	MAILINGS	MAISTERING	MALARIAN	MALISON
MAGUEYS	MAILLOT	MAISTERS	MALARIAS	MALISONS
MAGUS	MAILLOTS	MAISTRIES	MALARIOUS	MALIST
MAGYAR	MAILMAN	MAISTRING	MALARKEY	MALKIN
MAHARAJA	MAILMEN	MAISTRINGS	MALARKEYS	MALKINS
MAHARAJAH	MAILMERGE	MAISTRY	MALARKIES	MALL
MAHARAJAHS	MAILMERGED	MAIZE	MALARKY	MALLAM
MAHARAJAS	MAILMERGES	MAIZES	MALARS	MALLAMS
MAHARANEE	MAILMERGING	MAJESTIC	MALATE	MALLANDER
MAHARANEES	MAILS	MAJESTIES	MALATES	MALLANDERS
MAHARANI	MAIM	MAJESTY	MALAX	MALLARD
MAHARANIS	MAIMED	MAJOLICA	MALAXAGE	MALLARDS
MAHARISHI	MAIMING	MAJOLICAS	MALAXAGES	MALLEABLE
MAHARISHIS	MAIMINGS	MAJOR	MALAXATE	MALLEATE
MAHATMA	MAIMS	MAJORAT	MALAXATED	MALLEATED
MAHATMAS	MAIN	MAJORATS	MALAXATES	MALLEATES
MAHLSTICK	MAINBOOM	MAJORED	MALAXATING	MALLEATING
MAHLSTICKS	MAINBOOMS	MAJORETTE	MALAXATOR	MALLECHO
MAHMAL	MAINBRACE	MAJORETTES	MALAXATORS	MALLECHOES
MAHMALS	MAINBRACES	MAJORING	MALAXED	MALLECHOS
MAHOE	MAINDOOR	MAJORITIES	MALAXES	MALLED
MAHOES	MAINDOORS	MAJORITY	MALAXING	MALLEE
MAHOGANIES	MAINED	MAJORS	MALE	MALLEES
MAHOGANY	MAINER	MAJORSHIP	MALEATE	MALLEI
MAHONIA	MAINEST	MAJORSHIPS	MALEATES	MALLEMUCK
MAHONIAS	MAINFRAME	MAJUSCULE	MALEDICT	MALLEMUCKS
MAHOUT	MAINFRAMES	MAJUSCULES	MALEDICTED	MALLENDER
MAHOUTS	MAINING	MAK	MALEDICTING	MALLENDERS
MAHSEER	MAINLAND	MAKABLE	MALEDICTS	MALLEOLAR
MAHSEERS	MAINLANDS	MAKAR	MALEFIC	MALLEOLI
MAHSIR	MAINLINE	MAKARS	MALEFICE	MALLEOLUS
MAHSIRS	MAINLINED	MAKE	MALEFICES	MALLEOLUSES
MAHUA	MAINLINER	MAKEABLE	MALEIC	MALLET
MAHUAS	MAINLINERS	MAKEBATE	MALEMUTE	MALLETS
MAHWA	MAINLINES	MAKEBATES	MALEMUTES	MALLEUS
MAHWAS	MAINLINING	MAKELESS	MALENGINE	MALLEUSES
MAHZOR	MAINLININGS	MAKER	MALENGINES	MALLING
MAHZORIM	MAINLY	MAKERS	MALES	MALLOW
MAID	MAINMAST	MAKES	MALFORMED	MALLOWS
MAIDAN	MAINMASTS	MAKESHIFT	MALGRADO	MALLS
MAIDANS	MAINOR	MAKESHIFTS	MALGRE	MALM
MAIDED	MAINORS	MAKIMONO	MALGRES	MALMAG
MAIDEN	MAINOUR	MAKIMONOS	MALI	MALMAGS
MAIDENISH	MAINOURS	MAKING	MALIC	MALMS
MAIDENLY	MAINPRISE	MAKINGS	MALICE	MALMSEY
MAIDENS	MAINPRISES	MAKO	MALICED	MALMSEYS
MAIDHOOD	MAINS	MAKOMAKO	MALICES	MALODOUR
MAIDHOODS	MAINSAIL	MAKOMAKOS	MALICHO	MALODOURS
MAIDING	MAINSAILS	MAKOS	MALICHOES	MALONATE
MAIDISH	MAINSHEET	MAKS	MALICHOS	MALONATES
MAIDISM	MAINSHEETS	MAL	MALICING	MALS
MAIDISMS	MAINSTAY	MALACHITE	MALICIOUS	MALSTICK

MALSTICKS
MALT
MALTALENT
MALTALENTS
MALTASE
MALTASES
MALTED
MALTHA
MALTHAS
MALTIER
MALTIEST
MALTING
MALTINGS
MALTMAN
MALTMEN
MALTOSE
MALTOSES
MALTREAT
MALTREATED
MALTREATING
MALTREATS
MALTS
MALTSTER
MALTSTERS
MALTWORM
MALTWORMS
MALTY
MALVA
MALVAS
MALVASIA
MALVASIAS
MALVESIE
MALVESIES
MALVOISIE
MALVOISIES
MAM
MAMA
MAMAS
MAMBA
MAMBAS
MAMBO
MAMBOED
MAMBOING
MAMBOS
MAMELON
MAMELONS
MAMELUCO
MAMELUCOS
MAMILLA
MAMILLAE
MAMILLAR
MAMILLARY
MAMILLATE
MAMMA
MAMMAE
MAMMAL
MAMMALIAN
MAMMALOGIES
MAMMALOGY
MAMMALS
MAMMARY
MAMMAS
MAMMATE
MAMMEE
MAMMEES
MAMMER
MAMMERED
MAMMERING
MAMMERS
MAMMET

MAMMETRIES
MAMMETRY
MAMMETS
MAMMIES
MAMMIFER
MAMMIFERS
MAMMIFORM
MAMMILLA
MAMMILLAE
MAMMOCK
MAMMOCKED
MAMMOCKING
MAMMOCKS
MAMMOGRAM
MAMMOGRAMS
MAMMON
MAMMONISH
MAMMONISM
MAMMONISMS
MAMMONIST
MAMMONISTS
MAMMONITE
MAMMONITES
MAMMONS
MAMMOTH
MAMMOTHS
MAMMY
MAMS
MAMSELLE
MAMSELLES
MAN
MANA
MANACLE
MANACLED
MANACLES
MANACLING
MANAGE
MANAGED
MANAGER
MANAGERS
MANAGES
MANAGING
MANAKIN
MANAKINS
MAÑANA
MAÑANAS
MANAS
MANATEE
MANATEES
MANATI
MANATIS
MANCANDO
MANCHE
MANCHES
MANCHET
MANCHETS
MANCIPATE
MANCIPATED
MANCIPATES
MANCIPATING
MANCIPLE
MANCIPLES
MANCUS
MANCUSES
MAND
MANDALA
MANDALAS
MANDAMUS
MANDAMUSES
MANDARIN

MANDARINE
MANDARINES
MANDARINS
MANDATARIES
MANDATARY
MANDATE
MANDATED
MANDATES
MANDATING
MANDATOR
MANDATORIES
MANDATORS
MANDATORY
MANDIBLE
MANDIBLES
MANDILION
MANDILIONS
MANDIOC
MANDIOCA
MANDIOCAS
MANDIOCCA
MANDIOCCAS
MANDIOCS
MANDIR
MANDIRA
MANDIRAS
MANDIRS
MANDOLA
MANDOLAS
MANDOLIN
MANDOLINE
MANDOLINES
MANDOLINS
MANDOM
MANDOMS
MANDORA
MANDORAS
MANDORLA
MANDORLAS
MANDRAKE
MANDRAKES
MANDREL
MANDRELS
MANDRIL
MANDRILL
MANDRILLS
MANDRILS
MANDUCATE
MANDUCATED
MANDUCATES
MANDUCATING
MANDYLION
MANDYLIONS
MANE
MANED
MANÈGE
MANÈGED
MANÈGES
MANÈGING
MANEH
MANEHS
MANELESS
MANENT
MANES
MANET
MANEUVER
MANEUVERED
MANEUVERING
MANEUVERS
MANFUL

MANFULLY
MANGABEY
MANGABEYS
MANGAL
MANGALS
MANGANATE
MANGANATES
MANGANESE
MANGANESES
MANGANIC
MANGANIN
MANGANITE
MANGANITES
MANGANOUS
MANGE
MANGEL
MANGELS
MANGER
MANGERS
MANGES
MANGETOUT
MANGETOUTS
MANGEY
MANGIER
MANGIEST
MANGINESS
MANGINESSES
MANGLE
MANGLED
MANGLER
MANGLERS
MANGLES
MANGLING
MANGO
MANGOES
MANGOLD
MANGOLDS
MANGONEL
MANGONELS
MANGOSTAN
MANGOSTANS
MANGOUSTE
MANGOUSTES
MANGROVE
MANGROVES
MANGY
MANHANDLE
MANHANDLED
MANHANDLES
MANHANDLING
MANHOLE
MANHOLES
MANHOOD
MANHOODS
MANHUNT
MANHUNTS
MANIA
MANIAC
MANIACAL
MANIACS
MANIAS
MANIC
MANICALLY
MANICURE
MANICURED
MANICURES
MANICURING
MANIES
MANIFEST
MANIFESTED

MANIFESTING
MANIFESTO
MANIFESTOED
MANIFESTOES
MANIFESTOING
MANIFESTOS
MANIFESTS
MANIFOLD
MANIFOLDED
MANIFOLDING
MANIFOLDS
MANIFORM
MANIHOC
MANIHOCS
MANIKIN
MANIKINS
MANILA
MANILAS
MANILLA
MANILLAS
MANILLE
MANILLES
MANIOC
MANIOCS
MANIPLE
MANIPLES
MANIPLIES
MANIPULAR
MANIPULARS
MANITO
MANITOS
MANITOU
MANITOUS
MANJACK
MANJACKS
MANKIER
MANKIEST
MANKIND
MANKY
MANLIER
MANLIEST
MANLINESS
MANLINESSES
MANLY
MANNA
MANNAS
MANNED
MANNEQUIN
MANNEQUINS
MANNER
MANNERED
MANNERISM
MANNERISMS
MANNERIST
MANNERISTS
MANNERLY
MANNERS
MANNIKIN
MANNIKINS
MANNING
MANNISH
MANNITE
MANNITES
MANNITOL
MANNITOLS
MANNOSE
MANNOSES
MANOAO
MANOAOS
MANOEUVRE

MANOEUVRED
MANOEUVRES
MANOEUVRING
MANOMETER
MANOMETERS
MANOMETRIES
MANOMETRY
MANOR
MANORIAL
MANORS
MANPACK
MANPACKS
MANPOWER
MANPOWERS
MANQUÉ
MANRED
MANREDS
MANRENT
MANRENTS
MANRIDER
MANRIDERS
MANS
MANSARD
MANSARDS
MANSE
MANSES
MANSHIFT
MANSHIFTS
MANSION
MANSIONS
MANSONRIES
MANSONRY
MANSUETE
MANSWORN
MANTA
MANTAS
MANTEAU
MANTEAUS
MANTEAUX
MANTEEL
MANTEELS
MANTEL
MANTELET
MANTELETS
MANTELS
MANTIC
MANTICORA
MANTICORAS
MANTICORE
MANTICORES
MANTID
MANTIDS
MANTIES
MANTILLA
MANTILLAS
MANTIS
MANTISES
MANTISSA
MANTISSAS
MANTLE
MANTLED
MANTLES
MANTLET
MANTLETS
MANTLING
MANTLINGS
MANTO
MANTOES
MANTOS
MANTRA

MANTRAM
MANTRAMS
MANTRAP
MANTRAPS
MANTRAS
MANTUA
MANTUAS
MANTY
MANUAL
MANUALLY
MANUALS
MANUBRIA
MANUBRIAL
MANUBRIUM
MANUKA
MANUKAS
MANUL
MANULS
MANUMIT
MANUMITS
MANUMITTED
MANUMITTING
MANURANCE
MANURANCES
MANURE
MANURED
MANURER
MANURERS
MANURES
MANURIAL
MANURING
MANURINGS
MANUS
MANY
MANYFOLD
MANYPLIES
MANZANITA
MANZANITAS
MANZELLO
MANZELLOS
MAORMOR
MAORMORS
MAP
MAPLE
MAPLES
MAPPED
MAPPEMOND
MAPPEMONDS
MAPPER
MAPPERIES
MAPPERS
MAPPERY
MAPPING
MAPPIST
MAPPISTS
MAPS
MAPSTICK
MAPSTICKS
MAPWISE
MAQUETTE
MAQUETTES
MAQUI
MAQUIS
MAQUISARD
MAQUISARDS
MAR
MARA
MARABOU
MARABOUS
MARABOUT

MARABOUTS
MARACA
MARACAS
MARAGING
MARAGINGS
MARAH
MARAHS
MARAS
MARASMIC
MARASMUS
MARASMUSES
MARATHON
MARATHONS
MARAUD
MARAUDED
MARAUDER
MARAUDERS
MARAUDING
MARAUDS
MARAVEDI
MARAVEDIS
MARBLE
MARBLED
MARBLER
MARBLERS
MARBLES
MARBLIER
MARBLIEST
MARBLING
MARBLINGS
MARBLY
MARC
MARCASITE
MARCASITES
MARCATO
MARCEL
MARCELLA
MARCELLAS
MARCELLED
MARCELLING
MARCELS
MARCH
MARCHED
MARCHER
MARCHERS
MARCHES
MARCHESA
MARCHESAS
MARCHESE
MARCHESES
MARCHESI
MARCHING
MARCHMAN
MARCHMEN
MARCHPANE
MARCHPANES
MARCONI
MARCONIED
MARCONIES
MARCONIING
MARCS
MARD
MARDIED
MARDIES
MARDY
MARDYING
MARE
MAREMMA
MAREMMAS
MARES

MARESCHAL
MARESCHALLED
MARESCHALLING
MARESCHALS
MARG
MARGARIC
MARGARIN
MARGARINE
MARGARINES
MARGARINS
MARGARITA
MARGARITAS
MARGARITE
MARGARITES
MARGAY
MARGAYS
MARGE
MARGENT
MARGENTED
MARGENTING
MARGENTS
MARGES
MARGIN
MARGINAL
MARGINALS
MARGINATE
MARGINATED
MARGINED
MARGINING
MARGINS
MARGOSA
MARGOSAS
MARGRAVE
MARGRAVES
MARGS
MARIA
MARIACHI
MARIACHIS
MARIALITE
MARIALITES
MARID
MARIDS
MARIGOLD
MARIGOLDS
MARIGRAM
MARIGRAMS
MARIGRAPH
MARIGRAPHS
MARIHUANA
MARIHUANAS
MARIJUANA
MARIJUANAS
MARIMBA
MARIMBAS
MARINA
MARINADE
MARINADED
MARINADES
MARINADING
MARINAS
MARINATE
MARINATED
MARINATES
MARINATING
MARINE
MARINER
MARINERS
MARINES
MARINIÈRE
MARIPOSA

MARIPOSAS
MARISCHAL
MARISCHALLED
MARISCHALLING
MARISCHALS
MARISH
MARISHES
MARITAGE
MARITAGES
MARITAL
MARITALLY
MARITIME
MARJORAM
MARJORAMS
MARK
MARKED
MARKEDLY
MARKER
MARKERS
MARKET
MARKETED
MARKETEER
MARKETEERS
MARKETER
MARKETERS
MARKETING
MARKETINGS
MARKETS
MARKHOR
MARKHORS
MARKING
MARKINGS
MARKKA
MARKKAA
MARKKAS
MARKMAN
MARKMEN
MARKS
MARKSMAN
MARKSMEN
MARL
MARLE
MARLED
MARLES
MARLIER
MARLIEST
MARLIN
MARLINE
MARLINES
MARLING
MARLINGS
MARLINS
MARLS
MARLSTONE
MARLSTONES
MARLY
MARM
MARMALADE
MARMALADES
MARMARISE
MARMARISED
MARMARISES
MARMARISING
MARMARIZE
MARMARIZED
MARMARIZES
MARMARIZING
MARMITE
MARMITES
MARMOREAL

MARMOSE	MARSHIER	MASCON	MASSACRES	MASTIFFS
MARMOSES	MARSHIEST	MASCONS	MASSACRING	MASTING
MARMOSET	MARSHLAND	MASCOT	MASSAGE	MASTITIS
MARMOSETS	MARSHLANDS	MASCOTS	MASSAGED	MASTITISES
MARMOT	MARSHWORT	MASCULINE	MASSAGES	MASTLESS
MARMOTS	MARSHWORTS	MASCULINES	MASSAGING	MASTODON
MARMS	MARSHY	MASCULY	MASSAGIST	MASTODONS
MAROCAIN	MARSUPIA	MASE	MASSAGISTS	MASTOID
MAROCAINS	MARSUPIAL	MASED	MASSAS	MASTOIDAL
MAROON	MARSUPIALS	MASER	MASSÉ	MASTOIDS
MAROONED	MARSUPIUM	MASERS	MASSED	MASTS
MAROONER	MARSUPIUMS	MASES	MASSES	MASTY
MAROONERS	MART	MASH	MASSÉS	MASU
MAROONING	MARTAGON	MASHALLAH	MASSETER	MASULA
MAROONINGS	MARTAGONS	MASHED	MASSETERS	MASULAS
MAROONS	MARTED	MASHER	MASSEUR	MASURIUM
MAROQUIN	MARTEL	MASHERS	MASSEURS	MASURIUMS
MAROQUINS	MARTELLED	MASHES	MASSEUSE	MASUS
MAROR	MARTELLING	MASHIE	MASSEUSES	MAT
MARORS	MARTELLO	MASHIER	MASSICOT	MATACHIN
MARPLOT	MARTELLOS	MASHIES	MASSICOTS	MATACHINS
MARPLOTS	MARTELS	MASHIEST	MASSIER	MATADOR
MARQUE	MARTEN	MASHING	MASSIEST	MATADORE
MARQUEE	MARTENOT	MASHINGS	MASSIF	MATADORES
MARQUEES	MARTENOTS	MASHLAM	MASSIFS	MATADORS
MARQUES	MARTENS	MASHLAMS	MASSINESS	MATAMATA
MARQUESS	MARTIAL	MASHLIM	MASSINESSES	MATAMATAS
MARQUESSES	MARTIALLY	MASHLIMS	MASSING	MATCH
MARQUETRIES	MARTIN	MASHLIN	MASSIVE	MATCHABLE
MARQUETRY	MARTINET	MASHLINS	MASSIVELY	MATCHBOX
MARQUIS	MARTINETS	MASHLOCH	MASSOOLA	MATCHBOXES
MARQUISE	MARTING	MASHLOCHS	MASSOOLAS	MATCHED
MARQUISES	MARTINI	MASHLUM	MASSY	MATCHER
MARRAM	MARTINIS	MASHLUMS	MASSYMORE	MATCHERS
MARRAMS	MARTINS	MASHMAN	MASSYMORES	MATCHES
MARRED	MARTLET	MASHMEN	MAST	MATCHING
MARRELS	MARTLETS	MASHY	MASTABA	MATCHLESS
MARRIAGE	MARTS	MASING	MASTABAS	MATCHLOCK
MARRIAGES	MARTYR	MASJID	MASTED	MATCHLOCKS
MARRIED	MARTYRDOM	MASJIDS	MASTER	MATCHWOOD
MARRIER	MARTYRDOMS	MASK	MASTERATE	MATCHWOODS
MARRIERS	MARTYRED	MASKED	MASTERATES	MATE
MARRIES	MARTYRIES	MASKER	MASTERDOM	MATÉ
MARRING	MARTYRING	MASKERS	MASTERDOMS	MATED
MARROW	MARTYRISE	MASKING	MASTERED	MATELASSÉ
MARROWED	MARTYRISED	MASKS	MASTERFUL	MATELASSÉS
MARROWFAT	MARTYRISES	MASLIN	MASTERIES	MATELESS
MARROWFATS	MARTYRISING	MASLINS	MASTERING	MATELOT
MARROWING	MARTYRIZE	MASOCHISM	MASTERINGS	MATELOTE
MARROWISH	MARTYRIZED	MASOCHISMS	MASTERLY	MATELOTES
MARROWS	MARTYRIZES	MASOCHIST	MASTERS	MATELOTS
MARROWSKIED	MARTYRIZING	MASOCHISTS	MASTERY	MATER
MARROWSKIES	MARTYRS	MASON	MASTFUL	MATERIAL
MARROWSKY	MARTYRY	MASONED	MASTHEAD	MATERIALS
MARROWSKYING	MARVEL	MASONIC	MASTHEADED	MATÉRIEL
MARROWY	MARVELLED	MASONING	MASTHEADING	MATÉRIELS
MARRUM	MARVELLING	MASONRIED	MASTHEADS	MATERNAL
MARRUMS	MARVELS	MASONRIES	MASTHOUSE	MATERNITIES
MARRY	MARYBUD	MASONRY	MASTHOUSES	MATERNITY
MARRYING	MARYBUDS	MASONS	MASTIC	MATERS
MARRYINGS	MARZIPAN	MASOOLAH	MASTICATE	MATES
MARS	MARZIPANS	MASOOLAHS	MASTICATED	MATÉS
MARSH	MAS	MASQUE	MASTICATES	MATEY
MARSHAL	MASCARA	MASQUER	MASTICATING	MATFELON
MARSHALCIES	MASCARAS	MASQUERS	MASTICH	MATFELONS
MARSHALCY	MASCARON	MASQUES	MASTICHS	MATGRASS
MARSHALLED	MASCARONS	MASS	MASTICOT	MATGRASSES
MARSHALLING	MASCLE	MASSA	MASTICOTS	MATH
MARSHALS	MASCLED	MASSACRE	MASTICS	MATHESES
MARSHES	MASCLES	MASSACRED	MASTIFF	MATHESIS

MATHESISES	MATTOCK	MAUNNA	MAXIMISTS	MAZUMAS
MATHS	MATTOCKS	MAUSOLEAN	MAXIMIZE	MAZURKA
MATICO	MATTOID	MAUSOLEUM	MAXIMIZED	MAZURKAS
MATICOS	MATTOIDS	MAUSOLEUMS	MAXIMIZES	MAZUT
MATIER	MATTRESS	MAUTHER	MAXIMIZING	MAZUTS
MATIEST	MATTRESSES	MAUTHERS	MAXIMS	MAZY
MATIN	MATURABLE	MAUVAIS	MAXIMUM	MAZZARD
MATINAL	MATURATE	MAUVAISE	MAXIS	MAZZARDS
MATINEE	MATURATED	MAUVE	MAXIXE	ME
MATINÉE	MATURATES	MAUVEIN	MAXIXES	MEACOCK
MATINEES	MATURATING	MAUVEINE	MAXWELL	MEACOCKS
MATINÉES	MATURE	MAUVEINES	MAXWELLS	MEAD
MATING	MATURED	MAUVEINS	MAY	MEADOW
MATINS	MATURELY	MAUVER	MAYA	MEADOWS
MATLO	MATURER	MAUVES	MAYAS	MEADOWY
MATLOS	MATURES	MAUVEST	MAYBE	MEADS
MATLOW	MATUREST	MAUVIN	MAYBES	MEAGRE
MATLOWS	MATURING	MAUVINE	MAYDAY	MEAGRELY
MATRASS	MATURITIES	MAUVINES	MAYDAYS	MEAGRER
MATRASSES	MATURITY	MAUVINS	MAYED	MEAGRES
MATRIARCH	MATUTINAL	MAVERICK	MAYEST	MEAGREST
MATRIARCHS	MATUTINE	MAVERICKED	MAYFLIES	MEAL
MATRIC	MATWEED	MAVERICKING	MAYFLOWER	MEALED
MATRICE	MATWEEDS	MAVERICKS	MAYFLOWERS	MEALER
MATRICES	MATY	MAVIN	MAYFLY	MEALERS
MATRICIDE	MATZA	MAVINS	MAYHAP	MEALIE
MATRICIDES	MATZAH	MAVIS	MAYHEM	MEALIER
MATRICS	MATZAHS	MAVISES	MAYHEMS	MEALIES
MATRICULA	MATZAS	MAW	MAYING	MEALIEST
MATRICULAS	MATZO	MAWBOUND	MAYINGS	MEALINESS
MATRILINIES	MATZOH	MAWK	MAYOR	MEALINESSES
MATRILINY	MATZOON	MAWKIN	MAYORAL	MEALING
MATRIMONIES	MATZOONS	MAWKINS	MAYORALTIES	MEALS
MATRIMONY	MATZOS	MAWKISH	MAYORALTY	MEALY
MATRIX	MATZOT	MAWKISHLY	MAYORESS	MEAN
MATRIXES	MATZOTH	MAWKS	MAYORESSES	MEANDER
MATRON	MAUD	MAWKY	MAYORS	MEANDERED
MATRONAGE	MAUDLIN	MAWMET	MAYORSHIP	MEANDERING
MATRONAGES	MAUDS	MAWMETRIES	MAYORSHIPS	MEANDERS
MATRONAL	MAUGRE	MAWMETRY	MAYPOLE	MEANDRIAN
MATRONISE	MAUGRES	MAWMETS	MAYPOLES	MEANDROUS
MATRONISED	MAUL	MAWPUS	MAYS	MEANE
MATRONISES	MAULED	MAWPUSES	MAYST	MEANED
MATRONISING	MAULERS	MAWR	MAYSTER	MEANER
MATRONIZE	MAULGRE	MAWRS	MAYSTERS	MEANES
MATRONIZED	MAULGRES	MAWS	MAYWEED	MEANEST
MATRONIZES	MAULING	MAWSEED	MAYWEEDS	MEANIE
MATRONIZING	MAULS	MAWSEEDS	MAZARD	MEANIES
MATRONLY	MAULSTICK	MAWTHER	MAZARDS	MEANING
MATRONS	MAULSTICKS	MAWTHERS	MAZARINE	MEANINGLY
MATROSS	MAULVI	MAX	MAZARINES	MEANINGS
MATROSSES	MAULVIS	MAXES	MAZE	MEANLY
MATS	MAUMET	MAXI	MAZED	MEANNESS
MATT	MAUMETRIES	MAXILLA	MAZEFUL	MEANNESSES
MATTAMORE	MAUMETRY	MAXILLAE	MAZEMENT	MEANS
MATTAMORES	MAUMETS	MAXILLARY	MAZEMENTS	MEANT
MATTE	MAUN	MAXILLULA	MAZER	MEANTIME
MATTED	MAUND	MAXILLULAE	MAZERS	MEANTIMES
MATTER	MAUNDED	MAXILLULAS	MAZES	MEANWHILE
MATTERED	MAUNDER	MAXIM	MAZHBI	MEANWHILES
MATTERFUL	MAUNDERED	MAXIMA	MAZHBIS	MEANY
MATTERING	MAUNDERER	MAXIMAL	MAZIER	MEARE
MATTERS	MAUNDERERS	MAXIMALLY	MAZIEST	MEARES
MATTERY	MAUNDERING	MAXIMIN	MAZILY	MEASE
MATTES	MAUNDERINGS	MAXIMINS	MAZINESS	MEASED
MATTIE	MAUNDERS	MAXIMISE	MAZINESSES	MEASES
MATTIES	MAUNDIES	MAXIMISED	MAZING	MEASING
MATTING	MAUNDING	MAXIMISES	MAZOUT	MEASLE
MATTINGS	MAUNDS	MAXIMISING	MAZOUTS	MEASLED
MATTINS	MAUNDY	MAXIMIST	MAZUMA	MEASLES

MEASLIER
MEASLIEST
MEASLING
MEASLY
MEASURE
MEASURED
MEASURER
MEASURERS
MEASURES
MEASURING
MEASURINGS
MEAT
MEATAL
MEATH
MEATHE
MEATHEAD
MEATHEADS
MEATHES
MEATHS
MEATIER
MEATIEST
MEATINESS
MEATINESSES
MEATLESS
MEATS
MEATUS
MEATUSES
MEATY
MEAWES
MEAWESS
MEAZEL
MEAZELS
MEBOS
MEBOSES
MECHANIC
MECHANICS
MECHANISE
MECHANISED
MECHANISES
MECHANISING
MECHANISM
MECHANISMS
MECHANIST
MECHANISTS
MECHANIZE
MECHANIZED
MECHANIZES
MECHANIZING
MECONATE
MECONATES
MECONIC
MECONIN
MECONINS
MECONIUM
MECONIUMS
MEDAEWART
MEDAEWARTS
MEDAL
MEDALET
MEDALETS
MEDALLED
MEDALLIC
MEDALLING
MEDALLION
MEDALLIONED
MEDALLIONING
MEDALLIONS
MEDALLIST
MEDALLISTS
MEDALS

MEDDLE
MEDDLED
MEDDLER
MEDDLERS
MEDDLES
MEDDLING
MEDDLINGS
MEDIA
MEDIACIES
MEDIACY
MEDIAE
MEDIAEVAL
MEDIAL
MEDIALLY
MEDIALS
MEDIAN
MEDIANS
MEDIANT
MEDIANTS
MEDIATE
MEDIATED
MEDIATELY
MEDIATES
MEDIATING
MEDIATION
MEDIATIONS
MEDIATISE
MEDIATISED
MEDIATISES
MEDIATISING
MEDIATIVE
MEDIATIZE
MEDIATIZED
MEDIATIZES
MEDIATIZING
MEDIATOR
MEDIATORS
MEDIATORY
MEDIATRICES
MEDIATRIX
MEDIC
MEDICABLE
MEDICAID
MEDICAIDS
MEDICAL
MEDICALLY
MEDICALS
MEDICARE
MEDICARES
MEDICATE
MEDICATED
MEDICATES
MEDICATING
MEDICINAL
MEDICINE
MEDICINED
MEDICINER
MEDICINERS
MEDICINES
MEDICINING
MEDICK
MEDICKS
MEDICO
MEDICOS
MEDICS
MEDIEVAL
MEDII
MEDINA
MEDINAS
MEDIOCRE

MEDITATE
MEDITATED
MEDITATES
MEDITATING
MEDIUM
MEDIUMS
MEDIUS
MEDIUSES
MEDLAR
MEDLARS
MEDLE
MEDLED
MEDLES
MEDLEY
MEDLEYS
MEDLING
MEDRESSEH
MEDRESSEHS
MEDULLA
MEDULLAE
MEDULLAR
MEDULLARY
MEDULLAS
MEDULLATE
MEDUSA
MEDUSAE
MEDUSAN
MEDUSANS
MEDUSAS
MEDUSOID
MEDUSOIDS
MEED
MEEDS
MEEK
MEEKEN
MEEKENED
MEEKENING
MEEKENS
MEEKER
MEEKEST
MEEKLY
MEEKNESS
MEEKNESSES
MEER
MEERCAT
MEERCATS
MEERKAT
MEERKATS
MEERS
MEET
MEETER
MEETEST
MEETING
MEETINGS
MEETLY
MEETNESS
MEETNESSES
MEETS
MEGABAR
MEGABARS
MEGABIT
MEGABITS
MEGABYTE
MEGABYTES
MEGACURIE
MEGACURIES
MEGACYCLE
MEGACYCLES
MEGADEATH
MEGADEATHS

MEGADYNE
MEGADYNES
MEGAFARAD
MEGAFARADS
MEGAFAUNA
MEGAFLORA
MEGAFOG
MEGAFOGS
MEGAGAUSS
MEGAGAUSSES
MEGAHERTZ
MEGAHERTZES
MEGAJOULE
MEGAJOULES
MEGALITH
MEGALITHS
MEGAPHONE
MEGAPHONED
MEGAPHONES
MEGAPHONING
MEGAPODE
MEGAPODES
MEGARA
MEGARAD
MEGARADS
MEGARON
MEGARONS
MEGASCOPE
MEGASCOPES
MEGASPORE
MEGASPORES
MEGASS
MEGASSE
MEGASSES
MEGASTORE
MEGASTORES
MEGATON
MEGATONNE
MEGATONNES
MEGATONS
MEGAVOLT
MEGAVOLTS
MEGAWATT
MEGAWATTS
MEGILP
MEGILPS
MEGOHM
MEGOHMS
MEGRIM
MEGRIMS
MEIN
MEINED
MEINEY
MEINEYS
MEINIE
MEINIES
MEINING
MEINS
MEINT
MEINY
MEIOFAUNA
MEIONITE
MEIONITES
MEIOSES
MEIOSIS
MEIOTIC
MEITH
MEITHS
MEKOMETER
MEKOMETERS

MEL
MELAMINE
MELAMINES
MELAMPODE
MELAMPODES
MÉLANGE
MÉLANGES
MELANIC
MELANIN
MELANINS
MELANISM
MELANISMS
MELANITE
MELANITES
MELANO
MELANOMA
MELANOMAS
MELANOMATA
MELANOS
MELANOSIS
MELANOSISES
MELANOTIC
MELANOUS
MELANURIA
MELANURIAS
MELANURIC
MELAPHYRE
MELAPHYRES
MELATONIN
MELATONINS
MELD
MELDED
MELDER
MELDERS
MELDING
MELDS
MÊLÉE
MÊLÉES
MELIC
MELICS
MELILITE
MELILITES
MELILOT
MELILOTS
MELINITE
MELINITES
MELIORATE
MELIORATED
MELIORATES
MELIORATING
MELIORISM
MELIORISMS
MELIORIST
MELIORISTS
MELIORITIES
MELIORITY
MELISMA
MELISMAS
MELISMATA
MELL
MELLAY
MELLAYS
MELLED
MELLING
MELLITE
MELLITES
MELLITIC
MELLOW
MELLOWED
MELLOWER

MELLOWEST
MELLOWING
MELLOWLY
MELLOWS
MELLOWY
MELLS
MELOCOTON
MELOCOTONS
MELODEON
MELODEONS
MELODIC
MELODICS
MELODIES
MELODION
MELODIONS
MELODIOUS
MELODISE
MELODISED
MELODISES
MELODISING
MELODIST
MELODISTS
MELODIZE
MELODIZED
MELODIZES
MELODIZING
MELODRAMA
MELODRAMAS
MELODRAME
MELODRAMES
MELODY
MELOMANIA
MELOMANIAS
MELOMANIC
MELON
MELONS
MELS
MELT
MELTDOWN
MELTDOWNS
MELTED
MELTING
MELTINGLY
MELTINGS
MELTITH
MELTITHS
MELTON
MELTONS
MELTS
MEMBER
MEMBERED
MEMBERS
MEMBRAL
MEMBRANE
MEMBRANES
MEMENTO
MEMENTOES
MEMENTOS
MEMO
MEMOIR
MEMOIRISM
MEMOIRISMS
MEMOIRIST
MEMOIRISTS
MEMOIRS
MEMORABLE
MEMORABLY
MEMORANDA
MEMORIAL
MEMORIALS

MEMORIES
MEMORISE
MEMORISED
MEMORISES
MEMORISING
MEMORITER
MEMORIZE
MEMORIZED
MEMORIZES
MEMORIZING
MEMORY
MEMOS
MEN
MENACE
MENACED
MENACER
MENACERS
MENACES
MENACING
MENADIONE
MENADIONES
MÉNAGE
MENAGERIE
MENAGERIES
MÉNAGES
MENARCHE
MENARCHES
MEND
MENDACITIES
MENDACITY
MENDED
MENDER
MENDERS
MENDICANT
MENDICANTS
MENDICITIES
MENDICITY
MENDING
MENDINGS
MENDS
MENE
MENED
MENEER
MENEERS
MENES
MENFOLK
MENFOLKS
MENG
MENGE
MENGED
MENGES
MENGING
MENGS
MENHADEN
MENHADENS
MENHIR
MENHIRS
MENIAL
MENIALS
MENING
MENINGEAL
MENINGES
MENINX
MENISCI
MENISCOID
MENISCUS
MENISCUSES
MENOLOGIES
MENOLOGY
MENOMINEE

MENOMINEES
MENOPAUSE
MENOPAUSES
MENOPOME
MENOPOMES
MENORAH
MENORAHS
MENORRHEA
MENORRHEAS
MENSAL
MENSCH
MENSCHES
MENSE
MENSED
MENSEFUL
MENSELESS
MENSES
MENSH
MENSHED
MENSHES
MENSHING
MENSING
MENSTRUA
MENSTRUAL
MENSTRUUM
MENSTRUUMS
MENSUAL
MENSURAL
MENSWEAR
MENSWEARS
MENT
MENTAL
MENTALISM
MENTALISMS
MENTALIST
MENTALISTS
MENTALITIES
MENTALITY
MENTALLY
MENTATION
MENTATIONS
MENTHOL
MENTHOLS
MENTICIDE
MENTICIDES
MENTION
MENTIONED
MENTIONING
MENTIONS
MENTOR
MENTORIAL
MENTORING
MENTORINGS
MENTORS
MENTUM
MENTUMS
MENU
MENUS
MEOW
MEOWED
MEOWING
MEOWS
MEPACRINE
MEPACRINES
MEPHITIC
MEPHITIS
MEPHITISES
MEPHITISM
MEPHITISMS
MERC

MERCAPTAN
MERCAPTANS
MERCAT
MERCATS
MERCENARIES
MERCENARY
MERCER
MERCERIES
MERCERISE
MERCERISED
MERCERISES
MERCERISING
MERCERIZE
MERCERIZED
MERCERIZES
MERCERIZING
MERCERS
MERCERY
MERCHANT
MERCHANTED
MERCHANTING
MERCHANTS
MERCHET
MERCHETS
MERCHILD
MERCHILDREN
MERCIABLE
MERCIES
MERCIFIDE
MERCIFIED
MERCIFIES
MERCIFUL
MERCIFY
MERCIFYING
MERCILESS
MERCS
MERCURATE
MERCURATED
MERCURATES
MERCURATING
MERCURIAL
MERCURIC
MERCURIES
MERCUROUS
MERCURY
MERCY
MERE
MERED
MEREL
MERELL
MERELLS
MERELS
MERELY
MERER
MERES
MERESMAN
MERESMEN
MEREST
MERESTONE
MERESTONES
MERFOLK
MERFOLKS
MERGANSER
MERGANSERS
MERGE
MERGED
MERGENCE
MERGENCES
MERGER
MERGERS

MERGES
MERGING
MERI
MERICARP
MERICARPS
MERIDIAN
MERIDIANS
MERIL
MERILS
MERIMAKE
MERIMAKES
MERING
MERINGUE
MERINGUES
MERINO
MERINOS
MERIS
MERISM
MERISMS
MERISTEM
MERISTEMS
MERISTIC
MERIT
MERITED
MERITING
MERITS
MERK
MERKIN
MERKINS
MERKS
MERL
MERLE
MERLES
MERLIN
MERLING
MERLINGS
MERLINS
MERLON
MERLONS
MERLS
MERMAID
MERMAIDEN
MERMAIDENS
MERMAIDS
MERMAN
MERMEN
MEROGONIES
MEROGONY
MEROISTIC
MEROME
MEROMES
MEROPIDAN
MEROPIDANS
MEROSOME
MEROSOMES
MEROZOITE
MEROZOITES
MERPEOPLE
MERRIER
MERRIES
MERRIEST
MERRILY
MERRIMENT
MERRIMENTS
MERRINESS
MERRINESSES
MERRY
MERRYMADE
MERRYMAKER
MERRYMAKERS

MERRYMAKING	MESODERM	METALLING	METHANES	METRICATING
MERRYMAKINGS	MESODERMS	METALLINGS	METHANOL	METRICIAN
MERRYMAN	MESOGLOEA	METALLISE	METHANOLS	METRICIANS
MERRYMEN	MESOGLOEAS	METALLISED	METHEGLIN	METRICISE
MERSALYL	MESOLITE	METALLISES	METHEGLINS	METRICISED
MERSALYLS	MESOLITES	METALLISING	METHINK	METRICISES
MERSE	MESOMORPH	METALLIST	METHINKS	METRICISING
MERSES	MESOMORPHS	METALLISTS	METHOD	METRICIST
MERSION	MESON	METALLIZE	METHODIC	METRICISTS
MERSIONS	MESONIC	METALLIZED	METHODISE	METRICIZE
MERYCISM	MESONS	METALLIZES	METHODISED	METRICIZED
MERYCISMS	MESOPHYLL	METALLIZING	METHODISES	METRICIZES
MES	MESOPHYLLS	METALLOID	METHODISING	METRICIZING
MESA	MESOPHYTE	METALLOIDS	METHODIST	METRICS
MESAIL	MESOPHYTES	METALLY	METHODISTS	METRIFIER
MESAILS	MESOTRON	METALS	METHODIZE	METRIFIERS
MESAL	MESOTRONS	METAMER	METHODIZED	METRING
MESALLY	MESPRISE	METAMERE	METHODIZES	METRIST
MESARAIC	MESPRISES	METAMERES	METHODIZING	METRISTS
MESARCH	MESPRIZE	METAMERIC	METHODS	METRITIS
MESAS	MESPRIZES	METAMERS	METHOUGHT	METRITISES
MESCAL	MESQUIN	METANOIA	METHS	METRO
MESCALIN	MESQUINE	METANOIAS	METHYL	MÉTRO
MESCALINS	MESQUIT	METAPHASE	METHYLATE	METROLOGIES
MESCALISM	MESQUITE	METAPHASES	METHYLATED	METROLOGY
MESCALISMS	MESQUITES	METAPHOR	METHYLATES	METRONOME
MESCALS	MESQUITS	METAPHORS	METHYLATING	METRONOMES
MESDAMES	MESS	METAPLASM	METHYLENE	METROS
MESE	MESSAGE	METAPLASMS	METHYLENES	MÉTROS
MESEEMED	MESSAGED	MÉTAYAGE	METHYLIC	METTLE
MESEEMS	MESSAGES	MÉTAYAGES	METHYLS	METTLED
MESEL	MESSAGING	MÉTAYER	METHYSES	METTLES
MESELED	MESSAN	MÉTAYERS	METHYSIS	MEU
MESELS	MESSANS	METAZOA	METHYSTIC	MEUNIÈRE
MESENTERIES	MESSED	METAZOAN	METIC	MEUS
MESENTERY	MESSENGER	METAZOANS	METICAL	MEUSE
MESES	MESSENGERS	METAZOIC	METICALS	MEUSED
MESH	MESSES	METAZOON	METICS	MEUSES
MESHED	MESSIER	METCAST	MÉTIER	MEUSING
MESHES	MESSIEST	METCASTS	MÉTIERS	MEVE
MESHIER	MESSIEURS	METE	METIF	MEVED
MESHIEST	MESSILY	METED	METIFS	MEVES
MESHING	MESSINESS	METEOR	METING	MEVING
MESHINGS	MESSINESSES	METEORIC	MÉTIS	MEW
MESHUGA	MESSING	METEORISM	MÉTISSE	MEWED
MESHUGGA	MESSMATE	METEORISMS	MÉTISSES	MEWING
MESHUGGE	MESSMATES	METEORIST	METOL	MEWL
MESHY	MESSUAGE	METEORISTS	METOLS	MEWLED
MESIAL	MESSUAGES	METEORITE	METONYM	MEWLING
MESIALLY	MESSY	METEORITES	METONYMIC	MEWLS
MESIAN	MESTEE	METEOROID	METONYMIES	MEWS
MESIC	MESTEES	METEOROIDS	METONYMS	MEWSED
MESMERIC	MESTIZA	METEOROUS	METONYMY	MEWSES
MESMERISE	MESTIZAS	METEORS	METOPE	MEWSING
MESMERISED	MESTIZO	METER	METOPES	MEYNT
MESMERISES	MESTIZOS	METERED	METOPIC	MEZAIL
MESMERISING	MESTO	METERING	METOPISM	MEZAILS
MESMERISM	MET	METERS	METOPISMS	MÉZÉ
MESMERISMS	METABASES	METES	METOPON	MEZE
MESMERIST	METABASIS	METESTICK	METOPONS	MEZEREON
MESMERISTS	METABATIC	METESTICKS	METOPRYL	MEZEREONS
MESMERIZE	METABOLIC	METEWAND	METOPRYLS	MEZEREUM
MESMERIZED	METAGE	METEWANDS	METRE	MEZEREUMS
MESMERIZES	METAGES	METEYARD	METRED	MÉZÉS
MESMERIZING	MÉTAIRIE	METEYARDS	METRES	MEZES
MESNE	MÉTAIRIES	METHADON	METRIC	MEZUZA
MESOBLAST	METAL	METHADONE	METRICAL	MEZUZAH
MESOBLASTS	METALLED	METHADONES	METRICATE	MEZUZAHS
MESOCARP	METALLIC	METHADONS	METRICATED	MEZUZOTH
MESOCARPS	METALLINE	METHANE	METRICATES	MEZZANINE

MEZZANINES	MICROCHIPS	MIDFIELDS	MIGNONNE	MILITATE
MEZZO	MICROCODE	MIDGE	MIGRAINE	MILITATED
MEZZOS	MICROCODES	MIDGES	MIGRAINES	MILITATES
MEZZOTINT	MICROCOPIES	MIDGET	MIGRANT	MILITATING
MEZZOTINTS	MICROCOPY	MIDGETS	MIGRANTS	MILITIA
MGANGA	MICROCOSM	MIDI	MIGRATE	MILITIAS
MGANGAS	MICROCOSMS	MIDINETTE	MIGRATED	MILK
MHO	MICROCYTE	MIDINETTES	MIGRATES	MILKED
MHORR	MICROCYTES	MIDIRON	MIGRATING	MILKEN
MHORRS	MICRODOT	MIDIRONS	MIGRATION	MILKER
MHOS	MICRODOTS	MIDIS	MIGRATIONS	MILKERS
MI	MICROFILM	MIDLAND	MIGRATOR	MILKFISH
MIAOW	MICROFILMED	MIDLANDS	MIGRATORS	MILKFISHES
MIAOWED	MICROFILMING	MIDMOST	MIGRATORY	MILKIER
MIAOWING	MICROFILMS	MIDMOSTS	MIHRAB	MILKIEST
MIAOWS	MICROFORM	MIDNIGHT	MIHRABS	MILKILY
MIASM	MICROFORMS	MIDNIGHTS	MIKADO	MILKINESS
MIASMA	MICROGRAM	MIDNOON	MIKADOS	MILKINESSES
MIASMAL	MICROGRAMS	MIDNOONS	MIKE	MILKING
MIASMAS	MICROLITE	MIDRIB	MIKES	MILKINGS
MIASMATA	MICROLITES	MIDRIBS	MIKRON	MILKLESS
MIASMATIC	MICROLITH	MIDRIFF	MIKRONS	MILKLIKE
MIASMIC	MICROLITHS	MIDRIFFS	MIL	MILKMAID
MIASMOUS	MICROLOGIES	MIDS	MILADI	MILKMAIDS
MIASMS	MICROLOGY	MIDSHIP	MILADIES	MILKMAN
MIAUL	MICRON	MIDSHIPS	MILADIS	MILKMEN
MIAULED	MICRONS	MIDST	MILADY	MILKS
MIAULING	MICROPSIA	MIDSTREAM	MILAGE	MILKWOOD
MIAULS	MICROPSIAS	MIDSTREAMS	MILAGES	MILKWOODS
MICA	MICROPYLE	MIDSTS	MILCH	MILKWORT
MICACEOUS	MICROPYLES	MIDSUMMER	MILD	MILKWORTS
MICAS	MICROS	MIDSUMMERS	MILDEN	MILKY
MICATE	MICROSOME	MIDWAY	MILDENED	MILL
MICATED	MICROSOMES	MIDWAYS	MILDENING	MILLDAM
MICATES	MICROTOME	MIDWIFE	MILDENS	MILLDAMS
MICATING	MICROTOMES	MIDWIFED	MILDER	MILLE
MICE	MICROTOMIES	MIDWIFERIES	MILDEST	MILLED
MICELLA	MICROTOMY	MIDWIFERY	MILDEW	MILLENARIES
MICELLAR	MICROTONE	MIDWIFES	MILDEWED	MILLENARY
MICELLAS	MICROTONES	MIDWIFING	MILDEWING	MILLENNIA
MICELLE	MICROWAVE	MIDWIVE	MILDEWS	MILLEPED
MICELLES	MICROWAVES	MIDWIVED	MILDEWY	MILLEPEDE
MICHE	MICROWIRE	MIDWIVES	MILDLY	MILLEPEDES
MICHED	MICROWIRES	MIDWIVING	MILDNESS	MILLEPEDS
MICHER	MICRURGIES	MIEN	MILDNESSES	MILLEPORE
MICHERS	MICRURGY	MIENS	MILDS	MILLEPORES
MICHES	MICTION	MIEVE	MILE	MILLER
MICHING	MICTIONS	MIEVED	MILEAGE	MILLERITE
MICHINGS	MICTURATE	MIEVES	MILEAGES	MILLERITES
MICK	MICTURATED	MIEVING	MILER	MILLERS
MICKEY	MICTURATES	MIFF	MILERS	MILLES
MICKEYS	MICTURATING	MIFFED	MILES	MILLET
MICKIES	MID	MIFFIER	MILESTONE	MILLETS
MICKLE	MIDBRAIN	MIFFIEST	MILESTONES	MILLIARD
MICKLES	MIDBRAINS	MIFFINESS	MILFOIL	MILLIARDS
MICKS	MIDDAY	MIFFINESSES	MILFOILS	MILLIARE
MICKY	MIDDAYS	MIFFING	MILIARIA	MILLIARES
MICO	MIDDEN	MIFFS	MILIARIAS	MILLIARIES
MICOS	MIDDENS	MIFFY	MILIARY	MILLIARY
MICRO	MIDDEST	MIFTY	MILIEU	MILLIBAR
MICROBAR	MIDDIES	MIGHT	MILIEUS	MILLIBARS
MICROBARS	MIDDLE	MIGHTEST	MILIEUX	MILLIÈME
MICROBE	MIDDLED	MIGHTFUL	MILITANCIES	MILLIÈMES
MICROBES	MIDDLEMAN	MIGHTIER	MILITANCY	MILLIME
MICROBIAL	MIDDLEMEN	MIGHTIEST	MILITANT	MILLIMES
MICROBIAN	MIDDLES	MIGHTILY	MILITANTS	MILLINER
MICROBIC	MIDDLING	MIGHTS	MILITAR	MILLINERIES
MICROCARD	MIDDLINGS	MIGHTST	MILITARIA	MILLINERS
MICROCARDS	MIDDY	MIGHTY	MILITARIES	MILLINERY
MICROCHIP	MIDFIELD	MIGNON	MILITARY	MILLING

MILLINGS	MIMING	MINGLES	MINK	MINYANS
MILLION	MIMMER	MINGLING	MINKE	MIOSES
MILLIONS	MIMMEST	MINGLINGS	MINKES	MIOSIS
MILLIONTH	MIMMICK	MINGS	MINKS	MIR
MILLIONTHS	MIMMICKED	MINGY	MINNEOLA	MIRABELLE
MILLIPED	MIMMICKING	MINI	MINNEOLAS	MIRABELLES
MILLIPEDE	MIMMICKS	MINIATE	MINNICK	MIRABILIA
MILLIPEDES	MIMOSA	MINIATED	MINNICKED	MIRABILIS
MILLIPEDS	MIMOSAS	MINIATES	MINNICKING	MIRABILISES
MILLOCRAT	MIMULUS	MINIATING	MINNICKS	MIRABLE
MILLOCRATS	MIMULUSES	MINIATION	MINNIE	MIRACLE
MILLPOND	MINA	MINIATIONS	MINNIES	MIRACLES
MILLPONDS	MINACIOUS	MINIATURE	MINNOCK	MIRADOR
MILLRACE	MINACITIES	MINIATURED	MINNOCKED	MIRADORS
MILLRACES	MINACITY	MINIATURES	MINNOCKING	MIRAGE
MILLRIND	MINAE	MINIATURING	MINNOCKS	MIRAGES
MILLRINDS	MINAR	MINIBUS	MINNOW	MIRBANE
MILLS	MINARET	MINIBUSES	MINNOWS	MIRE
MILLSTONE	MINARETS	MINIFIED	MINO	MIRED
MILLSTONES	MINARS	MINIFIES	MINOR	MIREPOIX
MILLTAIL	MINAS	MINIFY	MINORESS	MIRES
MILLTAILS	MINATORY	MINIFYING	MINORESSES	MIRIER
MILO	MINBAR	MINIKIN	MINORITE	MIRIEST
MILOMETER	MINBARS	MINIKINS	MINORITES	MIRIFIC
MILOMETERS	MINCE	MINIM	MINORITIES	MIRIFICAL
MILOR	MINCED	MINIMA	MINORITY	MIRINESS
MILORD	MINCEMEAT	MINIMAL	MINORS	MIRINESSES
MILORDS	MINCEMEATS	MINIMENT	MINORSHIP	MIRING
MILORS	MINCER	MINIMENTS	MINORSHIPS	MIRITI
MILOS	MINCERS	MINIMISE	MINOS	MIRITIS
MILREIS	MINCES	MINIMISED	MINSTER	MIRK
MILS	MINCING	MINIMISES	MINSTERS	MIRKER
MILSEY	MINCINGLY	MINIMISING	MINSTREL	MIRKEST
MILSEYS	MINCINGS	MINIMISM	MINSTRELS	MIRKIER
MILT	MIND	MINIMISMS	MINT	MIRKIEST
MILTED	MINDED	MINIMIST	MINTAGE	MIRKS
MILTER	MINDER	MINIMISTS	MINTAGES	MIRKSOME
MILTERS	MINDERS	MINIMIZE	MINTED	MIRKY
MILTING	MINDFUL	MINIMIZED	MINTER	MIRLIGOES
MILTONIA	MINDFULLY	MINIMIZES	MINTERS	MIRLITON
MILTONIAS	MINDING	MINIMIZING	MINTIER	MIRLITONS
MILTS	MINDINGS	MINIMS	MINTIEST	MIRLY
MILTZ	MINDLESS	MINIMUM	MINTING	MIRROR
MILTZES	MINDS	MINIMUS	MINTS	MIRRORED
MILVINE	MINDSET	MINIMUSES	MINTY	MIRRORING
MIM	MINDSETS	MINING	MINUEND	MIRRORS
MIMBAR	MINE	MININGS	MINUENDS	MIRS
MIMBARS	MINED	MINION	MINUET	MIRTH
MIME	MINEOLA	MINIONS	MINUETS	MIRTHFUL
MIMED	MINEOLAS	MINIPILL	MINUS	MIRTHLESS
MIMER	MINER	MINIPILLS	MINUSCULE	MIRTHS
MIMERS	MINERAL	MINIS	MINUSCULES	MIRY
MIMES	MINERALS	MINISCULE	MINUSES	MIS
MIMESES	MINERS	MINISCULES	MINUTE	MISADVISE
MIMESIS	MINES	MINISH	MINUTED	MISADVISED
MIMESTER	MINETTE	MINISHED	MINUTELY	MISADVISES
MIMESTERS	MINETTES	MINISHES	MINUTEMAN	MISADVISING
MIMETIC	MINEVER	MINISHING	MINUTEMEN	MISAIM
MIMETICAL	MINEVERS	MINISTER	MINUTER	MISAIMED
MIMETITE	MING	MINISTERED	MINUTES	MISAIMING
MIMETITES	MINGED	MINISTERING	MINUTEST	MISAIMS
MIMIC	MINGIER	MINISTERS	MINUTIA	MISALLEGE
MIMICAL	MINGIEST	MINISTRIES	MINUTIAE	MISALLEGED
MIMICKED	MINGINESS	MINISTRY	MINUTING	MISALLEGES
MIMICKER	MINGINESSES	MINIUM	MINUTIOSE	MISALLEGING
MIMICKERS	MINGING	MINIUMS	MINX	MISALLIED
MIMICKING	MINGLE	MINIVER	MINXES	MISALLOT
MIMICRIES	MINGLED	MINIVERS	MINY	MISALLOTS
MIMICRY	MINGLER	MINIVET	MINYAN	MISALLOTTED
MIMICS	MINGLERS	MINIVETS	MINYANIM	MISALLOTTING

MISANDRIES	MISCOLOURED	MISDRAWN	MISGIVEN	MISJOINS
MISANDRY	MISCOLOURING	MISDRAWS	MISGIVES	MISJUDGE
MISAPPLIED	MISCOLOURS	MISDREAD	MISGIVING	MISJUDGED
MISAPPLIES	MISCOPIED	MISDREADS	MISGIVINGS	MISJUDGES
MISAPPLY	MISCOPIES	MISDREW	MISGO	MISJUDGING
MISAPPLYING	MISCOPY	MISE	MISGOES	MISKEN
MISARRAY	MISCOPYING	MISEASE	MISGOING	MISKENNED
MISARRAYS	MISCOUNT	MISEASES	MISGONE	MISKENNING
MISASSIGN	MISCOUNTED	MISED	MISGOTTEN	MISKENS
MISASSIGNED	MISCOUNTING	MISEMPLOY	MISGOVERN	MISKENT
MISASSIGNING	MISCOUNTS	MISEMPLOYED	MISGOVERNED	MISKNEW
MISASSIGNS	MISCREANT	MISEMPLOYING	MISGOVERNING	MISKNOW
MISAUNTER	MISCREANTS	MISEMPLOYS	MISGOVERNS	MISKNOWING
MISAUNTERS	MISCREATE	MISENTRIES	MISGRAFF	MISKNOWN
MISAVISED	MISCREDIT	MISENTRY	MISGRAFFED	MISKNOWS
MISBECAME	MISCREDITED	MISER	MISGRAFFING	MISLAID
MISBECOME	MISCREDITING	MISERABLE	MISGRAFFS	MISLAY
MISBECOMES	MISCREDITS	MISERABLES	MISGRAFT	MISLAYING
MISBECOMING	MISCREED	MISERABLY	MISGROWTH	MISLAYS
MISBEGOT	MISCREEDS	MISERE	MISGROWTHS	MISLEAD
MISBEHAVE	MISCUE	MISÈRE	MISGUGGLE	MISLEADER
MISBEHAVED	MISCUED	MISERERE	MISGUGGLED	MISLEADERS
MISBEHAVES	MISCUEING	MISERERES	MISGUGGLES	MISLEADING
MISBEHAVING	MISCUES	MISÈRES	MISGUGGLING	MISLEADS
MISBELIEF	MISCUING	MISERIES	MISGUIDE	MISLEARED
MISBELIEFS	MISDATE	MISERLY	MISGUIDED	MISLED
MISBESEEM	MISDATED	MISERS	MISGUIDER	MISLEEKE
MISBESEEMED	MISDATES	MISERY	MISGUIDERS	MISLEEKED
MISBESEEMING	MISDATING	MISES	MISGUIDES	MISLEEKES
MISBESEEMS	MISDEAL	MISESTEEM	MISGUIDING	MISLEEKING
MISBESTOW	MISDEALING	MISESTEEMED	MISHANDLE	MISLETOE
MISBESTOWED	MISDEALS	MISESTEEMING	MISHANDLED	MISLETOES
MISBESTOWING	MISDEALT	MISESTEEMS	MISHANDLES	MISLIGHT
MISBESTOWS	MISDEED	MISFAITH	MISHANDLING	MISLIGHTING
MISBIRTH	MISDEEDS	MISFAITHS	MISHANTER	MISLIGHTS
MISBIRTHS	MISDEEM	MISFALL	MISHANTERS	MISLIKE
MISBORN	MISDEEMED	MISFALLEN	MISHAP	MISLIKED
MISCALL	MISDEEMING	MISFALLING	MISHAPPED	MISLIKER
MISCALLED	MISDEEMINGS	MISFALLS	MISHAPPEN	MISLIKERS
MISCALLING	MISDEEMS	MISFALNE	MISHAPPENED	MISLIKES
MISCALLS	MISDEMEAN	MISFARE	MISHAPPENING	MISLIKING
MISCARRIED	MISDEMEANED	MISFARED	MISHAPPENS	MISLIKINGS
MISCARRIES	MISDEMEANING	MISFARES	MISHAPPING	MISLIPPEN
MISCARRY	MISDEMEANS	MISFARING	MISHAPS	MISLIPPENED
MISCARRYING	MISDEMPT	MISFARINGS	MISHAPT	MISLIPPENING
MISCAST	MISDESERT	MISFEASOR	MISHEAR	MISLIPPENS
MISCASTED	MISDESERTS	MISFEASORS	MISHEARD	MISLIT
MISCASTING	MISDID	MISFEIGN	MISHEARING	MISLIVE
MISCASTS	MISDIET	MISFEIGNED	MISHEARS	MISLIVED
MISCEGEN	MISDIETS	MISFEIGNING	MISHIT	MISLIVES
MISCEGENE	MISDIGHT	MISFEIGNS	MISHITS	MISLIVING
MISCEGENES	MISDIRECT	MISFELL	MISHITTING	MISLUCK
MISCEGENS	MISDIRECTED	MISFILE	MISHMASH	MISLUCKED
MISCEGINE	MISDIRECTING	MISFILED	MISHMASHES	MISLUCKING
MISCEGINES	MISDIRECTS	MISFILES	MISHMEE	MISLUCKS
MISCHANCE	MISDO	MISFILING	MISHMEES	MISMADE
MISCHANCED	MISDOER	MISFIRE	MISHMI	MISMAKE
MISCHANCES	MISDOERS	MISFIRED	MISHMIS	MISMAKES
MISCHANCING	MISDOES	MISFIRES	MISINFORM	MISMAKING
MISCHANCY	MISDOING	MISFIRING	MISINFORMED	MISMANAGE
MISCHARGE	MISDOINGS	MISFIT	MISINFORMING	MISMANAGED
MISCHARGED	MISDONE	MISFITS	MISINFORMS	MISMANAGES
MISCHARGES	MISDONNE	MISFITTED	MISING	MISMANAGING
MISCHARGING	MISDOUBT	MISFITTING	MISINTEND	MISMARRIED
MISCHIEF	MISDOUBTED	MISFORM	MISINTENDED	MISMARRIES
MISCHIEFED	MISDOUBTING	MISFORMED	MISINTENDING	MISMARRY
MISCHIEFING	MISDOUBTS	MISFORMING	MISINTENDS	MISMARRYING
MISCHIEFS	MISDRAW	MISFORMS	MISJOIN	MISMATCH
MISCIBLE	MISDRAWING	MISGAVE	MISJOINED	MISMATCHED
MISCOLOUR	MISDRAWINGS	MISGIVE	MISJOINING	MISMATCHES

MISMATCHING	MISPRIZE	MISSHAPEN	MISTEMPERED	MISTUNING
MISMATE	MISPRIZED	MISSHAPES	MISTEMPERING	MISTY
MISMATED	MISPRIZES	MISSHAPING	MISTEMPERS	MISUSAGE
MISMATES	MISPRIZING	MISSHOOD	MISTER	MISUSAGES
MISMATING	MISPROUD	MISSHOODS	MISTERED	MISUSE
MISMETRE	MISQUOTE	MISSIES	MISTERIES	MISUSED
MISMETRED	MISQUOTED	MISSILE	MISTERING	MISUSER
MISMETRES	MISQUOTES	MISSILERIES	MISTERM	MISUSERS
MISMETRING	MISQUOTING	MISSILERY	MISTERMED	MISUSES
MISNAME	MISRATE	MISSILES	MISTERMING	MISUSING
MISNAMED	MISRATED	MISSILRIES	MISTERMS	MISUST
MISNAMES	MISRATES	MISSILRY	MISTERS	MISWEEN
MISNAMING	MISRATING	MISSING	MISTERY	MISWEENED
MISNOMER	MISREAD	MISSINGLY	MISTFUL	MISWEENING
MISNOMERED	MISREADING	MISSION	MISTHINK	MISWEENS
MISNOMERING	MISREADINGS	MISSIONED	MISTHINKING	MISWEND
MISNOMERS	MISREADS	MISSIONER	MISTHINKS	MISWENDING
MISO	MISRECKON	MISSIONERS	MISTHOUGHT	MISWENDS
MISOCLERE	MISRECKONED	MISSIONING	MISTHOUGHTS	MISWENT
MISOGAMIES	MISRECKONING	MISSIONS	MISTICO	MISWORD
MISOGAMY	MISRECKONINGS	MISSIS	MISTICOS	MISWORDED
MISOGYNIES	MISRECKONS	MISSISES	MISTIER	MISWORDING
MISOGYNY	MISREGARD	MISSISH	MISTIEST	MISWORDINGS
MISOLOGIES	MISREGARDS	MISSIVE	MISTIGRIS	MISWORDS
MISOLOGY	MISRELATE	MISSIVES	MISTIGRISES	MISWRITE
MISONEISM	MISRELATED	MISSPEAK	MISTILY	MISWRITES
MISONEISMS	MISRELATES	MISSPEAKING	MISTIME	MISWRITING
MISONEIST	MISRELATING	MISSPEAKS	MISTIMED	MISWRITTEN
MISONEISTS	MISREPORT	MISSPELL	MISTIMES	MISWROTE
MISORDER	MISREPORTED	MISSPELLED	MISTIMING	MISYOKE
MISORDERED	MISREPORTING	MISSPELLING	MISTINESS	MISYOKED
MISORDERING	MISREPORTS	MISSPELLINGS	MISTINESSES	MISYOKES
MISORDERS	MISRULE	MISSPELLS	MISTING	MISYOKING
MISOS	MISRULED	MISSPELT	MISTINGS	MITCH
MISPICKEL	MISRULES	MISSPEND	MISTITLE	MITCHED
MISPICKELS	MISRULING	MISSPENDING	MISTITLED	MITCHES
MISPLACE	MISS	MISSPENDS	MISTITLES	MITCHING
MISPLACED	MISSA	MISSPENT	MISTITLING	MITE
MISPLACES	MISSABLE	MISSPOKE	MISTLE	MITER
MISPLACING	MISSAID	MISSPOKEN	MISTLED	MITERED
MISPLAY	MISSAL	MISSTATE	MISTLES	MITERING
MISPLAYED	MISSALS	MISSTATED	MISTLETOE	MITERS
MISPLAYING	MISSAS	MISSTATES	MISTLETOES	MITES
MISPLAYS	MISSAW	MISSTATING	MISTLING	MITHER
MISPLEAD	MISSAY	MISSTEP	MISTOLD	MITHERED
MISPLEADED	MISSAYING	MISSTEPPED	MISTOOK	MITHERING
MISPLEADING	MISSAYINGS	MISSTEPPING	MISTRAL	MITHERS
MISPLEADINGS	MISSAYS	MISSTEPS	MISTRALS	MITICIDAL
MISPLEADS	MISSED	MISSUIT	MISTREAT	MITICIDE
MISPLEASE	MISSEE	MISSUITED	MISTREATED	MITICIDES
MISPLEASED	MISSEEING	MISSUITING	MISTREATING	MITIER
MISPLEASES	MISSEEM	MISSUITS	MISTREATS	MITIEST
MISPLEASING	MISSEEMED	MISSUS	MISTRESS	MITIGABLE
MISPLED	MISSEEMING	MISSUSES	MISTRESSED	MITIGANT
MISPOINT	MISSEEMINGS	MISSY	MISTRESSES	MITIGATE
MISPOINTED	MISSEEMS	MIST	MISTRESSING	MITIGATED
MISPOINTING	MISSEEN	MISTAKE	MISTRIAL	MITIGATES
MISPOINTS	MISSEES	MISTAKEN	MISTRIALS	MITIGATING
MISPRAISE	MISSEL	MISTAKES	MISTRUST	MITIGATOR
MISPRAISED	MISSELS	MISTAKING	MISTRUSTED	MITIGATORS
MISPRAISES	MISSEND	MISTAKINGS	MISTRUSTING	MITOGEN
MISPRAISING	MISSENDING	MISTAUGHT	MISTRUSTS	MITOGENIC
MISPRINT	MISSENDS	MISTEACH	MISTRYST	MITOGENS
MISPRINTED	MISSENT	MISTEACHES	MISTRYSTED	MITOSES
MISPRINTING	MISSES	MISTEACHING	MISTRYSTING	MITOSIS
MISPRINTS	MISSET	MISTED	MISTRYSTS	MITOTIC
MISPRISE	MISSETS	MISTELL	MISTS	MITRAILLE
MISPRISED	MISSETTING	MISTELLING	MISTUNE	MITRAILLES
MISPRISES	MISSHAPE	MISTELLS	MISTUNED	MITRAL
MISPRISING	MISSHAPED	MISTEMPER	MISTUNES	MITRE

MITRED	MOAN	MOCKINGS	MODIFYING	MOILER
MITRES	MOANED	MOCKS	MODII	MOILERS
MITRIFORM	MOANER	MOCOCK	MODILLION	MOILING
MITRING	MOANERS	MOCOCKS	MODILLIONS	MOILS
MITT	MOANFUL	MOCUCK	MODIOLAR	MOINEAU
MITTEN	MOANFULLY	MOCUCKS	MODIOLI	MOINEAUS
MITTENED	MOANING	MOCUDDUM	MODIOLUS	MOIRE
MITTENS	MOANS	MOCUDDUMS	MODIOLUSES	MOIRÉ
MITTIMUS	MOAS	MOD	MODISH	MOIRES
MITTIMUSES	MOAT	MODAL	MODISHLY	MOIRÉS
MITTS	MOATED	MODALISM	MODIST	MOIST
MITY	MOATING	MODALISMS	MODISTE	MOISTED
MITZVAH	MOATS	MODALIST	MODISTES	MOISTEN
MITZVAHS	MOB	MODALISTS	MODISTS	MOISTENED
MITZVOTH	MOBBED	MODALITIES	MODIUS	MOISTENING
MIURUS	MOBBIE	MODALITY	MODIWORT	MOISTENS
MIURUSES	MOBBIES	MODALLY	MODIWORTS	MOISTER
MIX	MOBBING	MODE	MODS	MOISTEST
MIXABLE	MOBBISH	MODEL	MODULAR	MOISTIFIED
MIXED	MOBBLE	MODELLED	MODULATE	MOISTIFIES
MIXEDLY	MOBBLED	MODELLER	MODULATED	MOISTIFY
MIXEDNESS	MOBBLES	MODELLERS	MODULATES	MOISTIFYING
MIXEDNESSES	MOBBLING	MODELLING	MODULATING	MOISTING
MIXEN	MOBBY	MODELLINGS	MODULATOR	MOISTLY
MIXENS	MOBILE	MODELS	MODULATORS	MOISTNESS
MIXER	MOBILES	MODEM	MODULE	MOISTNESSES
MIXERS	MOBILISE	MODEMS	MODULES	MOISTS
MIXES	MOBILISED	MODENA	MODULI	MOISTURE
MIXIER	MOBILISES	MODENAS	MODULO	MOISTURES
MIXIEST	MOBILISING	MODERATE	MODULUS	MOIT
MIXING	MOBILITIES	MODERATED	MODUS	MOITHER
MIXT	MOBILITY	MODERATES	MOE	MOITHERED
MIXTION	MOBILIZE	MODERATING	MOED	MOITHERING
MIXTIONS	MOBILIZED	MODERATO	MOEING	MOITHERS
MIXTURE	MOBILIZES	MODERATOR	MOELLON	MOITS
MIXTURES	MOBILIZING	MODERATORS	MOELLONS	MOKADDAM
MIXY	MOBLE	MODERN	MOES	MOKADDAMS
MIZ	MOBLED	MODERNER	MOFETTE	MOKE
MIZEN	MOBLES	MODERNEST	MOFETTES	MOKES
MIZENS	MOBLING	MODERNISE	MOFUSSIL	MOKO
MIZES	MOBOCRACIES	MODERNISED	MOFUSSILS	MOKOS
MIZMAZE	MOBOCRACY	MODERNISES	MOG	MOLAL
MIZMAZES	MOBOCRAT	MODERNISING	MOGGAN	MOLALITIES
MIZZ	MOBOCRATS	MODERNISM	MOGGANS	MOLALITY
MIZZEN	MOBS	MODERNISMS	MOGGIE	MOLAR
MIZZENS	MOBSMAN	MODERNIST	MOGGIES	MOLARITIES
MIZZES	MOBSMEN	MODERNISTS	MOGGY	MOLARITY
MIZZLE	MOBSTER	MODERNITIES	MOGS	MOLARS
MIZZLED	MOBSTERS	MODERNITY	MOGUL	MOLASSES
MIZZLES	MOCASSIN	MODERNIZE	MOGULS	MOLD
MIZZLIER	MOCASSINS	MODERNIZED	MOHAIR	MOLDED
MIZZLIEST	MOCCASIN	MODERNIZES	MOHAIRS	MOLDING
MIZZLING	MOCCASINS	MODERNIZING	MOHAWK	MOLDS
MIZZLINGS	MOCHA	MODERNLY	MOHAWKS	MOLDWARP
MIZZLY	MOCHAS	MODERNS	MOHEL	MOLDWARPS
MIZZONITE	MOCHELL	MODES	MOHELS	MOLE
MIZZONITES	MOCHELLS	MODEST	MOHR	MOLECAST
MNA	MOCK	MODESTER	MOHRS	MOLECASTS
MNAS	MOCKABLE	MODESTEST	MOHUR	MOLECULAR
MNEME	MOCKADO	MODESTIES	MOHURS	MOLECULE
MNEMES	MOCKADOES	MODESTLY	MOIDER	MOLECULES
MNEMIC	MOCKAGE	MODESTY	MOIDERED	MOLEHILL
MNEMON	MOCKAGES	MODI	MOIDERING	MOLEHILLS
MNEMONIC	MOCKED	MODICUM	MOIDERS	MOLERAT
MNEMONICS	MOCKER	MODICUMS	MOIDORE	MOLERATS
MNEMONIST	MOCKERIES	MODIFIED	MOIDORES	MOLES
MNEMONISTS	MOCKERS	MODIFIER	MOIETIES	MOLESKIN
MNEMONS	MOCKERY	MODIFIERS	MOIETY	MOLESKINS
MO	MOCKING	MODIFIES	MOIL	MOLEST
MOA	MOCKINGLY	MODIFY	MOILED	MOLESTED

MOLESTER	MOMMAS	MONETIZES	MONKFISHES	MONOLOGIC
MOLESTERS	MOMMET	MONETIZING	MONKHOOD	MONOLOGIES
MOLESTFUL	MOMMETS	MONEY	MONKHOODS	MONOLOGUE
MOLESTING	MOMMIES	MONEYED	MONKISH	MONOLOGUES
MOLESTS	MOMMY	MONEYER	MONKS	MONOLOGY
MOLIES	MOMS	MONEYERS	MONKSHOOD	MONOMACHIES
MOLIMEN	MONA	MONEYLESS	MONKSHOODS	MONOMACHY
MOLIMENS	MONACHAL	MONEYS	MONO	MONOMANIA
MOLINE	MONACHISM	MONEYWORT	MONOACID	MONOMANIAS
MOLINES	MONACHISMS	MONEYWORTS	MONOAMINE	MONOMARK
MOLL	MONACHIST	MONG	MONOAMINES	MONOMARKS
MOLLA	MONACID	MONGCORN	MONOBASIC	MONOMER
MOLLAH	MONACT	MONGCORNS	MONOCARP	MONOMERIC
MOLLAHS	MONACTINE	MONGER	MONOCARPS	MONOMERS
MOLLAS	MONAD	MONGERIES	MONOCEROS	MONOMETER
MOLLIE	MONADES	MONGERING	MONOCEROSES	MONOMETERS
MOLLIES	MONADIC	MONGERINGS	MONOCHORD	MONOMIAL
MOLLIFIED	MONADICAL	MONGERS	MONOCHORDS	MONOMIALS
MOLLIFIER	MONADISM	MONGERY	MONOCLE	MONOMODE
MOLLIFIERS	MONADISMS	MONGOL	MONOCLED	MONOPHAGIES
MOLLIFIES	MONADS	MONGOLISM	MONOCLES	MONOPHAGY
MOLLIFY	MONAL	MONGOLISMS	MONOCLINE	MONOPHASE
MOLLIFYING	MONALS	MONGOLOID	MONOCLINES	MONOPHONIES
MOLLITIES	MONANDRIES	MONGOLOIDS	MONOCOQUE	MONOPHONY
MOLLS	MONANDRY	MONGOLS	MONOCOQUES	MONOPITCH
MOLLUSC	MONARCH	MONGOOSE	MONOCOT	MONOPLANE
MOLLUSCAN	MONARCHAL	MONGOOSES	MONOCOTS	MONOPLANES
MOLLUSCS	MONARCHIC	MONGREL	MONOCRACIES	MONOPODE
MOLLUSK	MONARCHIES	MONGRELLY	MONOCRACY	MONOPODES
MOLLUSKS	MONARCHS	MONGRELS	MONOCRAT	MONOPOLE
MOLLY	MONARCHY	MONGS	MONOCRATS	MONOPOLES
MOLLYMAWK	MONARDA	MONIAL	MONOCULAR	MONOPOLIES
MOLLYMAWKS	MONARDAS	MONIALS	MONOCYTE	MONOPOLY
MOLOCH	MONAS	MONICKER	MONOCYTES	MONOPSONIES
MOLOCHISE	MONASES	MONICKERS	MONODIC	MONOPSONY
MOLOCHISED	MONASTERIES	MONIED	MONODICAL	MONOPTOTE
MOLOCHISES	MONASTERY	MONIES	MONODIES	MONOPTOTES
MOLOCHISING	MONASTIC	MONIKER	MONODIST	MONORAIL
MOLOCHIZE	MONASTICS	MONIKERS	MONODISTS	MONORAILS
MOLOCHIZED	MONATOMIC	MONILIA	MONODONT	MONORCHID
MOLOCHIZES	MONAUL	MONILIAS	MONODRAMA	MONORHINE
MOLOCHIZING	MONAULS	MONIMENT	MONODRAMAS	MONORHYME
MOLOCHS	MONAURAL	MONIMENTS	MONODY	MONORHYMES
MOLOSSI	MONAXIAL	MONIPLIES	MONOECISM	MONOS
MOLOSSUS	MONAXON	MONISM	MONOECISMS	MONOSES
MOLT	MONAXONIC	MONISMS	MONOFIL	MONOSIES
MOLTED	MONAXONS	MONIST	MONOFILS	MONOSIS
MOLTEN	MONAZITE	MONISTIC	MONOGAMIC	MONOSTICH
MOLTENLY	MONAZITES	MONISTS	MONOGAMIES	MONOSTICHES
MOLTING	MONDAIN	MONITION	MONOGAMY	MONOSTICHS
MOLTO	MONDAINE	MONITIONS	MONOGENIES	MONOSTYLE
MOLTS	MONDAINES	MONITIVE	MONOGENY	MONOSY
MOLY	MONDAINS	MONITOR	MONOGLOT	MONOTINT
MOLYBDATE	MONDIAL	MONITORED	MONOGLOTS	MONOTINTS
MOLYBDATES	MONECIOUS	MONITORING	MONOGONIES	MONOTONE
MOLYBDIC	MONER	MONITORS	MONOGONY	MONOTONED
MOLYBDOUS	MONERA	MONITORY	MONOGRAM	MONOTONES
MOM	MONERGISM	MONITRESS	MONOGRAMS	MONOTONIC
MOME	MONERGISMS	MONITRESSES	MONOGRAPH	MONOTONIES
MOMENT	MONERON	MONK	MONOGRAPHS	MONOTONING
MOMENTA	MONERONS	MONKERIES	MONOGYNIES	MONOTONY
MOMENTANIES	MONETARY	MONKERY	MONOGYNY	MONOTREME
MOMENTANY	MONETH	MONKEY	MONOHULL	MONOTREMES
MOMENTARY	MONETHS	MONKEYED	MONOHULLS	MONOTROCH
MOMENTLY	MONETISE	MONKEYING	MONOLATER	MONOTROCHS
MOMENTOUS	MONETISED	MONKEYISH	MONOLATERS	MONOTYPE
MOMENTS	MONETISES	MONKEYISM	MONOLATRIES	MONOTYPES
MOMENTUM	MONETISING	MONKEYISMS	MONOLATRY	MONOTYPIC
MOMES	MONETIZE	MONKEYS	MONOLITH	MONOXIDE
MOMMA	MONETIZED	MONKFISH	MONOLITHS	MONOXIDES

MONOXYLON	MOOI	MOOPED	MOPPED	MORBUSES
MONOXYLONS	MOOING	MOOPING	MOPPER	MORCEAU
MONSIEUR	MOOKTAR	MOOPS	MOPPERS	MORCEAUX
MONSOON	MOOKTARS	MOOR	MOPPET	MORDACITIES
MONSOONAL	MOOL	MOORAGE	MOPPETS	MORDACITY
MONSOONS	MOOLA	MOORAGES	MOPPIER	MORDANCIES
MONSTER	MOOLAH	MOORCOCK	MOPPIEST	MORDANCY
MONSTERA	MOOLAHS	MOORCOCKS	MOPPING	MORDANT
MONSTERAS	MOOLAS	MOORED	MOPPY	MORDANTED
MONSTERS	MOOLED	MOORFOWL	MOPS	MORDANTING
MONSTROUS	MOOLEY	MOORFOWLS	MOPSIES	MORDANTLY
MONTAGE	MOOLEYS	MOORHEN	MOPSTICK	MORDANTS
MONTAGES	MOOLI	MOORHENS	MOPSTICKS	MORDENT
MONTANE	MOOLIES	MOORIER	MOPSY	MORDENTS
MONTANT	MOOLING	MOORIEST	MOPUS	MORE
MONTANTO	MOOLIS	MOORILL	MOPUSES	MOREEN
MONTANTOES	MOOLS	MOORILLS	MOPY	MOREENS
MONTANTOS	MOOLY	MOORING	MOQUETTE	MOREISH
MONTANTS	MOON	MOORINGS	MOQUETTES	MOREL
MONTARIA	MOONBEAM	MOORISH	MOR	MORELLO
MONTARIAS	MOONBEAMS	MOORLAND	MORA	MORELLOS
MONTE	MOONBLIND	MOORLANDS	MORACEOUS	MORELS
MONTEITH	MOONCALF	MOORLOG	MORAINAL	MORENDO
MONTEITHS	MOONCALVES	MOORLOGS	MORAINE	MOREOVER
MONTEM	MOONED	MOORMAN	MORAINES	MOREPORK
MONTEMS	MOONER	MOORMEN	MORAINIC	MOREPORKS
MONTERO	MOONERS	MOORS	MORAL	MORES
MONTEROS	MOONEYE	MOORVA	MORALE	MORGANITE
MONTES	MOONEYES	MOORVAS	MORALES	MORGANITES
MONTH	MOONFACE	MOORY	MORALISE	MORGAY
MONTHLIES	MOONFACES	MOOS	MORALISED	MORGAYS
MONTHLING	MOONIER	MOOSE	MORALISER	MORGEN
MONTHLINGS	MOONIES	MOOSEYARD	MORALISERS	MORGENS
MONTHLY	MOONIEST	MOOSEYARDS	MORALISES	MORGUE
MONTHS	MOONING	MOOT	MORALISING	MORGUES
MONTICLE	MOONISH	MOOTABLE	MORALISM	MORIA
MONTICLES	MOONLESS	MOOTED	MORALISMS	MORIAS
MONTICULE	MOONLET	MOOTER	MORALIST	MORIBUND
MONTICULES	MOONLETS	MOOTERS	MORALISTS	MORICHE
MONTRE	MOONLIGHT	MOOTEST	MORALITIES	MORICHES
MONTRES	MOONLIGHTS	MOOTING	MORALITY	MORION
MONTURE	MOONLIT	MOOTINGS	MORALIZE	MORIONS
MONTURES	MOONQUAKE	MOOTMAN	MORALIZED	MORISCO
MONUMENT	MOONQUAKES	MOOTMEN	MORALIZES	MORISCOES
MONUMENTED	MOONRAKER	MOOTS	MORALIZING	MORISCOS
MONUMENTING	MOONRAKERS	MOOVE	MORALL	MORISH
MONUMENTS	MOONRISE	MOOVED	MORALLED	MORKIN
MONY	MOONRISES	MOOVES	MORALLER	MORKINS
MONYPLIES	MOONS	MOOVING	MORALLERS	MORLING
MONZONITE	MOONSAIL	MOP	MORALLING	MORLINGS
MONZONITES	MOONSAILS	MOPANE	MORALLS	MORMAOR
MOO	MOONSCAPE	MOPANES	MORALLY	MORMAORS
MOOCH	MOONSCAPES	MOPBOARD	MORALS	MORN
MOOCHED	MOONSEED	MOPBOARDS	MORAS	MORNAY
MOOCHER	MOONSEEDS	MOPE	MORASS	MORNAYS
MOOCHERS	MOONSET	MOPED	MORASSES	MORNE
MOOCHES	MOONSETS	MOPEDS	MORASSY	MORNÉ
MOOCHING	MOONSHEE	MOPEHAWK	MORAT	MORNED
MOOD	MOONSHEES	MOPEHAWKS	MORATORIA	MORNES
MOODIED	MOONSHINE	MOPER	MORATORY	MORNING
MOODIER	MOONSHINES	MOPERS	MORATS	MORNINGS
MOODIES	MOONSHINY	MOPES	MORAY	MORNS
MOODIEST	MOONSHOT	MOPIER	MORAYS	MOROCCO
MOODILY	MOONSHOTS	MOPIEST	MORBID	MOROCCOS
MOODINESS	MOONSTONE	MOPING	MORBIDITIES	MORON
MOODINESSES	MOONSTONES	MOPINGLY	MORBIDITY	MORONIC
MOODS	MOONWORT	MOPISH	MORBIDLY	MORONS
MOODY	MOONWORTS	MOPISHLY	MORBIFIC	MOROSE
MOODYING	MOONY	MOPOKE	MORBILLI	MOROSELY
MOOED	MOOP	MOPOKES	MORBUS	MOROSER

MOROSEST	MORTGAGE	MOSS	MOTIVED	MOUCHER
MOROSITIES	MORTGAGED	MOSSED	MOTIVES	MOUCHERS
MOROSITY	MORTGAGEE	MOSSES	MOTIVIC	MOUCHES
MORPH	MORTGAGEES	MOSSIE	MOTIVING	MOUCHING
MORPHEAN	MORTGAGER	MOSSIER	MOTIVITIES	MOUCHOIR
MORPHEME	MORTGAGERS	MOSSIES	MOTIVITY	MOUCHOIRS
MORPHEMES	MORTGAGES	MOSSIEST	MOTLEY	MOUDIWART
MORPHEMIC	MORTGAGING	MOSSINESS	MOTLEYER	MOUDIWARTS
MORPHETIC	MORTGAGOR	MOSSINESSES	MOTLEYEST	MOUDIWORT
MORPHEW	MORTGAGORS	MOSSING	MOTLEYS	MOUDIWORTS
MORPHEWS	MORTICE	MOSSLAND	MOTLIER	MOUE
MORPHIA	MORTICED	MOSSLANDS	MOTLIEST	MOUES
MORPHIAS	MORTICER	MOSSPLANT	MOTMOT	MOUFFLON
MORPHIC	MORTICERS	MOSSPLANTS	MOTMOTS	MOUFFLONS
MORPHINE	MORTICES	MOSSY	MOTOCROSS	MOUFLON
MORPHINES	MORTICIAN	MOST	MOTOCROSSES	MOUFLONS
MORPHO	MORTICIANS	MOSTLY	MOTOR	MOUGHT
MORPHOS	MORTICING	MOSTS	MOTORABLE	MOUILLÉ
MORPHOSES	MORTIFIC	MOSTWHAT	MOTORAIL	MOUJIK
MORPHOSIS	MORTIFIED	MOT	MOTORAILS	MOUJIKS
MORPHOTIC	MORTIFIER	MOTE	MOTORCADE	MOULAGE
MORPHS	MORTIFIERS	MOTED	MOTORCADES	MOULAGES
MORRA	MORTIFIES	MOTEL	MOTORED	MOULD
MORRAS	MORTIFY	MOTELIER	MOTORIAL	MOULDABLE
MORRHUA	MORTIFYING	MOTELIERS	MOTORING	MOULDED
MORRHUAS	MORTIFYINGS	MOTELS	MOTORISE	MOULDER
MORRICE	MORTISE	MOTEN	MOTORISED	MOULDERED
MORRICES	MORTISED	MOTES	MOTORISES	MOULDERING
MORRION	MORTISER	MOTET	MOTORISING	MOULDERS
MORRIONS	MORTISERS	MOTETS	MOTORIST	MOULDIER
MORRIS	MORTISES	MOTETT	MOTORISTS	MOULDIEST
MORRISED	MORTISING	MOTETTIST	MOTORIUM	MOULDING
MORRISES	MORTLING	MOTETTISTS	MOTORIUMS	MOULDINGS
MORRISING	MORTLINGS	MOTETTS	MOTORIZE	MOULDS
MORRO	MORTMAIN	MOTEY	MOTORIZED	MOULDWARP
MORROS	MORTMAINS	MOTH	MOTORIZES	MOULDWARPS
MORROW	MORTS	MOTHBALL	MOTORIZING	MOULDY
MORROWS	MORTUARIES	MOTHBALLED	MOTORMAN	MOULIN
MORS	MORTUARY	MOTHBALLING	MOTORMEN	MOULINET
MORSAL	MORULA	MOTHBALLS	MOTORS	MOULINETS
MORSE	MORULAR	MOTHED	MOTORWAY	MOULINS
MORSEL	MORULAS	MOTHER	MOTORWAYS	MOULS
MORSELLED	MORWONG	MOTHERED	MOTORY	MOULT
MORSELLING	MORWONGS	MOTHERING	MOTOSCAFI	MOULTED
MORSELS	MOSAIC	MOTHERINGS	MOTOSCAFO	MOULTEN
MORSES	MOSAICISM	MOTHERLY	MOTS	MOULTING
MORSURE	MOSAICISMS	MOTHERS	MOTSER	MOULTINGS
MORSURES	MOSAICIST	MOTHERY	MOTSERS	MOULTS
MORT	MOSAICISTS	MOTHIER	MOTT	MOUND
MORTAL	MOSAICS	MOTHIEST	MOTTE	MOUNDED
MORTALISE	MOSCHATEL	MOTHS	MOTTES	MOUNDING
MORTALISED	MOSCHATELS	MOTHY	MOTTLE	MOUNDS
MORTALISES	MOSE	MOTIF	MOTTLED	MOUNSEER
MORTALISING	MOSED	MOTIFS	MOTTLES	MOUNSEERS
MORTALITIES	MOSES	MOTILE	MOTTLING	MOUNT
MORTALITY	MOSEY	MOTILES	MOTTLINGS	MOUNTAIN
MORTALIZE	MOSEYED	MOTILITIES	MOTTO	MOUNTAINS
MORTALIZED	MOSEYING	MOTILITY	MOTTOED	MOUNTANT
MORTALIZES	MOSEYS	MOTION	MOTTOES	MOUNTANTS
MORTALIZING	MOSHAV	MOTIONAL	MOTTS	MOUNTED
MORTALLY	MOSHAVIM	MOTIONED	MOTTY	MOUNTER
MORTALS	MOSING	MOTIONING	MOTUCA	MOUNTERS
MORTAR	MOSKONFYT	MOTIONIST	MOTUCAS	MOUNTIE
MORTARED	MOSKONFYTS	MOTIONISTS	MOTZA	MOUNTIES
MORTARING	MOSLINGS	MOTIONS	MOTZAS	MOUNTING
MORTARS	MOSQUE	MOTIVATE	MOU	MOUNTINGS
MORTBELL	MOSQUES	MOTIVATED	MOUCH	MOUNTS
MORTBELLS	MOSQUITO	MOTIVATES	MOUCHARD	MOUNTY
MORTCLOTH	MOSQUITOES	MOTIVATING	MOUCHARDS	MOUP
MORTCLOTHS	MOSQUITOS	MOTIVE	MOUCHED	MOUPED

MOUPING
MOUPS
MOURN
MOURNED
MOURNER
MOURNERS
MOURNFUL
MOURNING
MOURNINGS
MOURNIVAL
MOURNIVALS
MOURNS
MOUS
MOUSAKA
MOUSAKAS
MOUSE
MOUSED
MOUSEKIN
MOUSEKINS
MOUSER
MOUSERIES
MOUSERS
MOUSERY
MOUSES
MOUSEY
MOUSIE
MOUSIER
MOUSIES
MOUSIEST
MOUSING
MOUSINGS
MOUSLE
MOUSLED
MOUSLES
MOUSLING
MOUSMÉ
MOUSMEE
MOUSMEES
MOUSMÉS
MOUSSAKA
MOUSSAKAS
MOUSSE
MOUSSES
MOUST
MOUSTACHE
MOUSTACHES
MOUSTED
MOUSTING
MOUSTS
MOUSY
MOUTAN
MOUTANS
MOUTER
MOUTERED
MOUTERER
MOUTERERS
MOUTERING
MOUTERS
MOUTH
MOUTHABLE
MOUTHED
MOUTHER
MOUTHERS
MOUTHFUL
MOUTHFULS
MOUTHIER
MOUTHIEST
MOUTHING
MOUTHLESS
MOUTHS

MOUTHWASH
MOUTHWASHES
MOUTHY
MOUTON
MOUTONS
MOVABLE
MOVABLES
MOVABLY
MOVE
MOVEABLE
MOVEABLES
MOVEABLY
MOVED
MOVELESS
MOVEMENT
MOVEMENTS
MOVER
MOVERS
MOVES
MOVIE
MOVIES
MOVING
MOVINGLY
MOVY
MOW
MOWA
MOWAS
MOWBURN
MOWBURNED
MOWBURNING
MOWBURNS
MOWBURNT
MOWDIWART
MOWDIWARTS
MOWDIWORT
MOWDIWORTS
MOWED
MOWER
MOWERS
MOWING
MOWINGS
MOWN
MOWRA
MOWRAS
MOWS
MOXA
MOXAS
MOXIE
MOXIES
MOY
MOYA
MOYAS
MOYGASHEL
MOYGASHELS
MOYITIES
MOYITY
MOYL
MOYLE
MOYLES
MOYLS
MOYS
MOZ
MOZE
MOZED
MOZES
MOZETTA
MOZETTAS
MOZING
MOZZ
MOZZES

MOZZETTA
MOZZETTAS
MOZZIE
MOZZIES
MOZZLE
MOZZLES
MPRET
MPRETS
MRIDAMGAM
MRIDAMGAMS
MRIDANGAM
MRIDANGAMS
MU
MUCATE
MUCATES
MUCH
MUCHEL
MUCHELL
MUCHELLS
MUCHELS
MUCHES
MUCHLY
MUCHNESS
MUCHNESSES
MUCIC
MUCID
MUCIGEN
MUCIGENS
MUCILAGE
MUCILAGES
MUCIN
MUCINS
MUCK
MUCKED
MUCKENDER
MUCKENDERS
MUCKER
MUCKERED
MUCKERING
MUCKERS
MUCKIER
MUCKIEST
MUCKINESS
MUCKINESSES
MUCKING
MUCKLE
MUCKLES
MUCKLUCK
MUCKLUCKS
MUCKS
MUCKY
MUCLUC
MUCLUCS
MUCOID
MUCOR
MUCORS
MUCOSA
MUCOSAE
MUCOSITIES
MUCOSITY
MUCOUS
MUCRO
MUCRONATE
MUCRONES
MUCROS
MUCULENT
MUCUS
MUCUSES
MUD
MUDDED

MUDDIED
MUDDIER
MUDDIES
MUDDIEST
MUDDILY
MUDDINESS
MUDDINESSES
MUDDING
MUDDLE
MUDDLED
MUDDLER
MUDDLERS
MUDDLES
MUDDLING
MUDDY
MUDDYING
MUDÉJAR
MUDÉJARES
MUDIR
MUDIRIA
MUDIRIAS
MUDIRIEH
MUDIRIEHS
MUDIRS
MUDLARK
MUDLARKED
MUDLARKING
MUDLARKS
MUDPACK
MUDPACKS
MUDRA
MUDRAS
MUDS
MUDSCOW
MUDSCOWS
MUDSTONE
MUDSTONES
MUDWORT
MUDWORTS
MUEDDIN
MUEDDINS
MUESLI
MUESLIS
MUEZZIN
MUEZZINS
MUFF
MUFFED
MUFFETTEE
MUFFETTEES
MUFFIN
MUFFINEER
MUFFINEERS
MUFFING
MUFFINS
MUFFLE
MUFFLED
MUFFLER
MUFFLERS
MUFFLES
MUFFLING
MUFFS
MUFLON
MUFLONS
MUFTI
MUFTIS
MUG
MUGEARITE
MUGEARITES
MUGFUL
MUGFULS

MUGGED
MUGGER
MUGGERS
MUGGIER
MUGGIEST
MUGGINESS
MUGGINESSES
MUGGING
MUGGINGS
MUGGINS
MUGGINSES
MUGGISH
MUGGY
MUGS
MUGSHOT
MUGSHOTS
MUGWORT
MUGWORTS
MUGWUMP
MUGWUMPS
MUID
MUIDS
MUIL
MUILS
MUIR
MUIRS
MUIST
MUISTED
MUISTING
MUISTS
MUJAHEDIN
MUJAHIDIN
MUJIK
MUJIKS
MUKHTAR
MUKHTARS
MUKLUK
MUKLUKS
MULATTA
MULATTAS
MULATTO
MULATTOS
MULBERRIES
MULBERRY
MULCH
MULCHED
MULCHES
MULCHING
MULCT
MULCTED
MULCTING
MULCTS
MULE
MULES
MULETEER
MULETEERS
MULEY
MULEYS
MULGA
MULGAS
MULISH
MULISHLY
MULL
MULLAH
MULLAHS
MULLED
MULLEIN
MULLEINS
MULLER
MULLERS

MULLET
MULLETS
MULLEY
MULLEYS
MULLIGAN
MULLIGANS
MULLING
MULLION
MULLIONED
MULLIONS
MULLOCK
MULLOCKS
MULLOWAY
MULLOWAYS
MULLS
MULMUL
MULMULL
MULMULLS
MULMULS
MULSE
MULSES
MULSH
MULSHED
MULSHES
MULSHING
MULTEITIES
MULTEITY
MULTIFID
MULTIFIL
MULTIFILS
MULTIFOIL
MULTIFOILS
MULTIFORM
MULTIFORMS
MULTIHULL
MULTIHULLS
MULTIPARA
MULTIPARAE
MULTIPARAS
MULTIPED
MULTIPEDE
MULTIPEDES
MULTIPEDS
MULTIPLE
MULTIPLES
MULTIPLET
MULTIPLETS
MULTIPLEX
MULTIPLEXED
MULTIPLEXES
MULTIPLEXING
MULTIPLIED
MULTIPLIES
MULTIPLY
MULTIPLYING
MULTITUDE
MULTITUDES
MULTUM
MULTUMS
MULTURE
MULTURED
MULTURER
MULTURERS
MULTURES
MULTURING
MUM
MUMBLE
MUMBLED
MUMBLER
MUMBLERS

MUMBLES
MUMBLING
MUMBLINGS
MUMCHANCE
MUMCHANCES
MUMM
MUMMED
MUMMER
MUMMERIES
MUMMERS
MUMMERY
MUMMIA
MUMMIAS
MUMMIED
MUMMIES
MUMMIFIED
MUMMIFIES
MUMMIFORM
MUMMIFY
MUMMIFYING
MUMMING
MUMMINGS
MUMMOCK
MUMMOCKS
MUMMS
MUMMY
MUMMYING
MUMP
MUMPED
MUMPER
MUMPERS
MUMPING
MUMPISH
MUMPISHLY
MUMPS
MUMPSIMUS
MUMPSIMUSES
MUMS
MUN
MUNCH
MUNCHED
MUNCHER
MUNCHERS
MUNCHES
MUNCHING
MUNDANE
MUNDANELY
MUNDANER
MUNDANEST
MUNDANITIES
MUNDANITY
MUNDIC
MUNDICS
MUNDIFIED
MUNDIFIES
MUNDIFY
MUNDIFYING
MUNDUNGUS
MUNDUNGUSES
MUNGCORN
MUNGCORNS
MUNGO
MUNGOOSE
MUNGOOSES
MUNGOS
MUNICIPAL
MUNIFIED
MUNIFIES
MUNIFY
MUNIFYING

MUNIMENT
MUNIMENTS
MUNITE
MUNITED
MUNITES
MUNITING
MUNITION
MUNITIONED
MUNITIONING
MUNITIONS
MUNNION
MUNNIONS
MUNSHI
MUNSHIS
MUNSTER
MUNSTERS
MUNTIN
MUNTING
MUNTINGS
MUNTINS
MUNTJAC
MUNTJACS
MUNTJAK
MUNTJAKS
MUON
MUONIC
MUONIUM
MUONIUMS
MUONS
MUQADDAM
MUQADDAMS
MURAENA
MURAENAS
MURAGE
MURAGES
MURAL
MURALIST
MURALISTS
MURALS
MURDER
MURDERED
MURDERER
MURDERERS
MURDERESS
MURDERESSES
MURDERING
MURDEROUS
MURDERS
MURE
MURED
MURENA
MURENAS
MURES
MUREX
MUREXES
MUREXS
MURGEON
MURGEONED
MURGEONING
MURGEONS
MURIATE
MURIATED
MURIATES
MURIATIC
MURICATE
MURICATED
MURICES
MURIFORM
MURINE
MURINES

MURING
MURK
MURKER
MURKEST
MURKIER
MURKIEST
MURKILY
MURKINESS
MURKINESSES
MURKISH
MURKS
MURKSOME
MURKY
MURL
MURLAIN
MURLAINS
MURLAN
MURLANS
MURLED
MURLIER
MURLIEST
MURLIN
MURLING
MURLINS
MURLS
MURLY
MURMUR
MURMURED
MURMURER
MURMURERS
MURMURING
MURMURINGS
MURMUROUS
MURMURS
MURPHIES
MURPHY
MURRA
MURRAIN
MURRAINED
MURRAINS
MURRAM
MURRAMS
MURRAS
MURRAY
MURRAYS
MURRE
MURRELET
MURRELETS
MURREN
MURRENS
MURRES
MURREY
MURREYS
MURRHA
MURRHAS
MURRHINE
MURRIES
MURRIN
MURRINE
MURRINS
MURRION
MURRIONS
MURRY
MURTHER
MURTHERED
MURTHERER
MURTHERERS
MURTHERING
MURTHERS
MURVA

MURVAS
MUS
MUSACEOUS
MUSANG
MUSANGS
MUSCADEL
MUSCADELS
MUSCADIN
MUSCADINE
MUSCADINES
MUSCADINS
MUSCARINE
MUSCARINES
MUSCAT
MUSCATEL
MUSCATELS
MUSCATS
MUSCID
MUSCIDS
MUSCLE
MUSCLED
MUSCLES
MUSCLING
MUSCLINGS
MUSCOID
MUSCOLOGIES
MUSCOLOGY
MUSCOSE
MUSCOVADO
MUSCOVADOS
MUSCOVITE
MUSCOVITES
MUSCULAR
MUSCULOUS
MUSE
MUSED
MUSEFUL
MUSEFULLY
MUSEOLOGIES
MUSEOLOGY
MUSER
MUSERS
MUSES
MUSET
MUSETS
MUSETTE
MUSETTES
MUSEUM
MUSEUMS
MUSH
MUSHA
MUSHED
MUSHER
MUSHERS
MUSHES
MUSHIER
MUSHIEST
MUSHILY
MUSHINESS
MUSHINESSES
MUSHING
MUSHROOM
MUSHROOMED
MUSHROOMING
MUSHROOMS
MUSHY
MUSIC
MUSICAL
MUSICALE
MUSICALES

MUSICALLY	MUSTACHE	MUTINING	MYALLS	MYOLOGY
MUSICALS	MUSTACHES	MUTINOUS	MYCELIA	MYOMA
MUSICIAN	MUSTACHIO	MUTINY	MYCELIAL	MYOMANCIES
MUSICIANS	MUSTACHIOS	MUTINYING	MYCELIUM	MYOMANCY
MUSICKED	MUSTANG	MUTISM	MYCETES	MYOMANTIC
MUSICKER	MUSTANGS	MUTISMS	MYCETOMA	MYOMAS
MUSICKERS	MUSTARD	MUTON	MYCETOMAS	MYOPE
MUSICKING	MUSTARDS	MUTONS	MYCOLOGIC	MYOPES
MUSICS	MUSTED	MUTOSCOPE	MYCOLOGIES	MYOPIA
MUSIMON	MUSTEE	MUTOSCOPES	MYCOLOGY	MYOPIAS
MUSIMONS	MUSTEES	MUTT	MYCOPHAGIES	MYOPIC
MUSING	MUSTELINE	MUTTER	MYCOPHAGY	MYOPICS
MUSINGLY	MUSTELINES	MUTTERED	MYCORHIZA	MYOPS
MUSINGS	MUSTER	MUTTERER	MYCORHIZAS	MYOPSES
MUSIT	MUSTERED	MUTTERERS	MYCOSES	MYOSES
MUSITS	MUSTERING	MUTTERING	MYCOSIS	MYOSIN
MUSIVE	MUSTERS	MUTTERINGS	MYCOTIC	MYOSINS
MUSK	MUSTH	MUTTERS	MYCOTOXIN	MYOSIS
MUSKED	MUSTHS	MUTTON	MYCOTOXINS	MYOSITES
MUSKEG	MUSTIER	MUTTONS	MYDRIASES	MYOSITIC
MUSKEGS	MUSTIEST	MUTTONY	MYDRIASIS	MYOSITICS
MUSKET	MUSTING	MUTTS	MYDRIATIC	MYOSITIS
MUSKETEER	MUSTS	MUTUAL	MYDRIATICS	MYOSOTE
MUSKETEERS	MUSTY	MUTUALISE	MYELIN	MYOSOTES
MUSKETOON	MUTABLE	MUTUALISED	MYELINS	MYOSOTIS
MUSKETOONS	MUTABLY	MUTUALISES	MYELITES	MYOSOTISES
MUSKETRIES	MUTAGEN	MUTUALISING	MYELITIS	MYOTIC
MUSKETRY	MUTAGENIC	MUTUALISM	MYELOID	MYOTICS
MUSKETS	MUTAGENS	MUTUALISMS	MYELOMA	MYOTUBE
MUSKIER	MUTANDA	MUTUALITIES	MYELOMAS	MYOTUBES
MUSKIEST	MUTANDUM	MUTUALITY	MYELON	MYRBANE
MUSKILY	MUTANT	MUTUALIZE	MYELONS	MYRIAD
MUSKINESS	MUTANTS	MUTUALIZED	MYGALE	MYRIADS
MUSKINESSES	MUTATE	MUTUALIZES	MYGALES	MYRIADTH
MUSKING	MUTATED	MUTUALIZING	MYIASES	MYRIADTHS
MUSKLE	MUTATES	MUTUALLY	MYIASIS	MYRIAPOD
MUSKLES	MUTATING	MUTUCA	MYLODON	MYRIAPODS
MUSKONE	MUTATION	MUTUCAS	MYLODONS	MYRINGA
MUSKONES	MUTATIONS	MUTULE	MYLODONT	MYRINGAS
MUSKS	MUTATIVE	MUTULES	MYLODONTS	MYRIOPOD
MUSKY	MUTATORY	MUTUUM	MYLOHYOID	MYRIOPODS
MUSLIN	MUTCH	MUTUUMS	MYLOHYOIDS	MYRIORAMA
MUSLINED	MUTCHES	MUX	MYLONITE	MYRIORAMAS
MUSLINET	MUTCHKIN	MUXED	MYLONITES	MYRISTIC
MUSLINETS	MUTCHKINS	MUXES	MYLONITIC	MYRMECOID
MUSLINS	MUTE	MUXING	MYNA	MYRMIDON
MUSMON	MUTED	MUZHIK	MYNAH	MYRMIDONS
MUSMONS	MUTELY	MUZHIKS	MYNAHS	MYROBALAN
MUSQUASH	MUTENESS	MUZZIER	MYNAS	MYROBALANS
MUSQUASHES	MUTENESSES	MUZZIEST	MYNHEER	MYRRH
MUSROL	MUTER	MUZZILY	MYNHEERS	MYRRHIC
MUSROLS	MUTES	MUZZINESS	MYOBLAST	MYRRHINE
MUSS	MUTEST	MUZZINESSES	MYOBLASTS	MYRRHOL
MUSSE	MUTICOUS	MUZZLE	MYOFIBRIL	MYRRHOLS
MUSSED	MUTILATE	MUZZLED	MYOFIBRILS	MYRRHS
MUSSEL	MUTILATED	MUZZLER	MYOGEN	MYRTLE
MUSSELLED	MUTILATES	MUZZLERS	MYOGENIC	MYRTLES
MUSSELS	MUTILATING	MUZZLES	MYOGENS	MYSELF
MUSSES	MUTILATOR	MUZZLING	MYOGLOBIN	MYSTAGOGIES
MUSSIER	MUTILATORS	MUZZY	MYOGLOBINS	MYSTAGOGY
MUSSIEST	MUTINE	MVULE	MYOGRAM	MYSTERIES
MUSSINESS	MUTINED	MVULES	MYOGRAMS	MYSTERY
MUSSINESSES	MUTINEER	MY	MYOGRAPH	MYSTIC
MUSSING	MUTINEERED	MYAL	MYOGRAPHIES	MYSTICAL
MUSSITATE	MUTINEERING	MYALGIA	MYOGRAPHS	MYSTICISM
MUSSITATED	MUTINEERS	MYALGIAS	MYOGRAPHY	MYSTICISMS
MUSSITATES	MUTINES	MYALGIC	MYOID	MYSTICS
MUSSITATING	MUTING	MYALISM	MYOLOGIES	MYSTIFIED
MUSSY	MUTINIED	MYALISMS	MYOLOGIST	MYSTIFIER
MUST	MUTINIES	MYALL	MYOLOGISTS	MYSTIFIERS

MYSTIFIES	MYTHICISING	MYTHISES	MYTHOLOGY	MYXEDEMA
MYSTIFY	MYTHICISM	MYTHISING	MYTHOMANE	MYXEDEMAS
MYSTIFYING	MYTHICISMS	MYTHISM	MYTHOMANES	MYXOEDEMA
MYSTIQUE	MYTHICIST	MYTHISMS	MYTHOPOET	MYXOEDEMAS
MYSTIQUES	MYTHICISTS	MYTHIST	MYTHOPOETS	MYXOMA
MYTH	MYTHICIZE	MYTHISTS	MYTHOS	MYXOMATA
MYTHIC	MYTHICIZED	MYTHIZE	MYTHOSES	MYXOVIRUS
MYTHICAL	MYTHICIZES	MYTHIZED	MYTHS	MYXOVIRUSES
MYTHICISE	MYTHICIZING	MYTHIZES	MYTHUS	MZUNGU
MYTHICISED	MYTHISE	MYTHIZING	MYTHUSES	MZUNGUS
MYTHICISES	MYTHISED	MYTHOLOGIES	MYTILOID	

N

NA
NAAM
NAAMS
NAAN
NAANS
NAARTJE
NAARTJES
NAB
NABBED
NABBER
NABBERS
NABBING
NABK
NABKS
NABLA
NABLAS
NABOB
NABOBS
NABS
NABSES
NACARAT
NACARATS
NACELLE
NACELLES
NACH
NACHE
NACHES
NACHTMAAL
NACHTMAALS
NACKET
NACKETS
NACRE
NACREOUS
NACRES
NACRITE
NACRITES
NACROUS
NADA
NADAS
NADIR
NADIRS
NAE
NAEBODIES
NAEBODY
NAETHING
NAETHINGS
NAEVE
NAEVES
NAEVI
NAEVOID
NAEVUS
NAFF
NAFFING
NAFFS
NAG
NAGA
NAGANA
NAGANAS
NAGAPIE
NAGAPIES
NAGARI
NAGARIS
NAGAS
NAGGED

NAGGER
NAGGERS
NAGGIER
NAGGIEST
NAGGING
NAGGY
NAGMAAL
NAGMAALS
NAGOR
NAGORS
NAGS
NAHAL
NAHALS
NAIAD
NAIADES
NAIADS
NAIANT
NAÏF
NAÏFER
NAÏFEST
NAIK
NAIKS
NAIL
NAILED
NAILER
NAILERIES
NAILERS
NAILERY
NAILING
NAILINGS
NAILS
NAIN
NAINSELL
NAINSELLS
NAINSOOK
NAINSOOKS
NAIRA
NAIRAS
NAISSANT
NAÏVE
NAÏVELY
NAÏVER
NAÏVEST
NAÏVETÉ
NAÏVETÉS
NAÏVETIES
NAÏVETY
NAKED
NAKEDER
NAKEDEST
NAKEDLY
NAKEDNESS
NAKEDNESSES
NAKER
NAKERS
NALA
NALAS
NALLA
NALLAH
NALLAHS
NALLAS
NALOXONE
NALOXONES
NAM

NAMABLE
NAMASKAR
NAMASKARS
NAMASTE
NAMASTES
NAME
NAMEABLE
NAMED
NAMELESS
NAMELY
NAMER
NAMERS
NAMES
NAMESAKE
NAMESAKES
NAMING
NAMINGS
NAMS
NAN
NANA
NANAS
NANCE
NANCES
NANCIES
NANCY
NANDINE
NANDINES
NANDOO
NANDOOS
NANDU
NANDUS
NANISM
NANISMS
NANKEEN
NANKEENS
NANKIN
NANKINS
NANNA
NANNAS
NANNIED
NANNIES
NANNY
NANNYING
NANNYISH
NANOGRAM
NANOGRAMS
NANOMETRE
NANOMETRES
NANS
NAOS
NAOSES
NAP
NAPA
NAPALM
NAPALMS
NAPAS
NAPE
NAPERIES
NAPERY
NAPES
NAPHTHA
NAPHTHAS
NAPHTHOL
NAPHTHOLS

NAPIFORM
NAPKIN
NAPKINS
NAPLESS
NAPOLEON
NAPOLEONS
NAPOO
NAPOOED
NAPOOING
NAPOOS
NAPPA
NAPPAS
NAPPE
NAPPED
NAPPER
NAPPERS
NAPPES
NAPPIER
NAPPIES
NAPPIEST
NAPPINESS
NAPPINESSES
NAPPING
NAPPY
NAPRON
NAPRONS
NAPS
NARAS
NARASES
NARCISSI
NARCISSUS
NARCISSUSES
NARCOSES
NARCOSIS
NARCOTIC
NARCOTICS
NARCOTINE
NARCOTINES
NARCOTISE
NARCOTISED
NARCOTISES
NARCOTISING
NARCOTISM
NARCOTISMS
NARCOTIST
NARCOTISTS
NARD
NARDED
NARDING
NARDOO
NARDOOS
NARDS
NARE
NARES
NARGHILE
NARGHILES
NARGHILIES
NARGHILLIES
NARGHILLY
NARGHILY
NARGILE
NARGILEH
NARGILEHS
NARGILES

NARGILIES
NARGILLIES
NARGILLY
NARGILY
NARIAL
NARICORN
NARICORNS
NARINE
NARK
NARKED
NARKIER
NARKIEST
NARKING
NARKS
NARKY
NARQUOIS
NARRAS
NARRASES
NARRATE
NARRATED
NARRATES
NARRATING
NARRATION
NARRATIONS
NARRATIVE
NARRATIVES
NARRATOR
NARRATORS
NARRATORY
NARRE
NARROW
NARROWED
NARROWER
NARROWEST
NARROWING
NARROWINGS
NARROWLY
NARROWS
NARTHEX
NARTHEXES
NARTJIE
NARTJIES
NARWHAL
NARWHALS
NARY
NAS
NASAL
NASALISE
NASALISED
NASALISES
NASALISING
NASALITIES
NASALITY
NASALIZE
NASALIZED
NASALIZES
NASALIZING
NASALLY
NASALS
NASARD
NASARDS
NASCENCE
NASCENCES
NASCENCIES

NASCENCY	NATURALLY	NAVICULARS	NEBBICHES	NECKWEEDS
NASCENT	NATURALS	NAVICULAS	NEBBING	NECROLOGIES
NASEBERRIES	NATURE	NAVIES	NEBBISH	NECROLOGY
NASEBERRY	NATURED	NAVIGABLE	NEBBISHE	NECROPSIES
NASHGAB	NATURES	NAVIGATE	NEBBISHER	NECROPSY
NASHGABS	NATURING	NAVIGATED	NEBBISHERS	NECROSE
NASION	NATURISM	NAVIGATES	NEBBISHES	NECROSED
NASIONS	NATURISMS	NAVIGATING	NEBBUK	NECROSES
NASTALIK	NATURIST	NAVIGATOR	NEBBUKS	NECROSING
NASTALIKS	NATURISTS	NAVIGATORS	NEBECK	NECROSIS
NASTIC	NAUGHT	NAVVIED	NEBECKS	NECROTIC
NASTIER	NAUGHTIER	NAVVIES	NEBEK	NECROTISE
NASTIES	NAUGHTIEST	NAVVY	NEBEKS	NECROTISED
NASTIEST	NAUGHTILY	NAVVYING	NEBEL	NECROTISES
NASTILY	NAUGHTS	NAVY	NEBELS	NECROTISING
NASTINESS	NAUGHTY	NAWAB	NEBISH	NECROTIZE
NASTINESSES	NAUMACHIA	NAWABS	NEBISHES	NECROTIZED
NASTY	NAUMACHIAE	NAY	NEBRIS	NECROTIZES
NASUTE	NAUMACHIAS	NAYS	NEBRISES	NECROTIZING
NASUTES	NAUMACHIES	NAYTHLES	NEBS	NECROTOMIES
NAT	NAUMACHY	NAYWARD	NEBULA	NECROTOMY
NATAL	NAUNT	NAYWARDS	NEBULAE	NECTAR
NATALITIES	NAUNTS	NAYWORD	NEBULAR	NECTAREAL
NATALITY	NAUPLII	NAYWORDS	NEBULE	NECTAREAN
NATANT	NAUPLIOID	NAZE	NEBULÉ	NECTARED
NATATION	NAUPLIUS	NAZES	NEBULES	NECTARIAL
NATATIONS	NAUSEA	NAZIR	NEBULISE	NECTARIES
NATATORY	NAUSEANT	NAZIRS	NEBULISED	NECTARINE
NATCH	NAUSEANTS	NE	NEBULISER	NECTARINES
NATCHES	NAUSEAS	NEAFE	NEBULISERS	NECTAROUS
NATES	NAUSEATE	NEAFES	NEBULISES	NECTARS
NATHELESS	NAUSEATED	NEAFFE	NEBULISING	NECTARY
NATHEMO	NAUSEATES	NEAFFES	NEBULIUM	NED
NATHEMORE	NAUSEATING	NEAL	NEBULIUMS	NEDDIES
NATHLESS	NAUSEOUS	NEALED	NEBULIZE	NEDDY
NATIFORM	NAUTCH	NEALING	NEBULIZED	NEDS
NATION	NAUTCHES	NEALS	NEBULIZER	NÉE
NATIONAL	NAUTIC	NEANIC	NEBULIZERS	NEED
NATIONALS	NAUTICAL	NEAP	NEBULIZES	NEEDED
NATIONS	NAUTICS	NEAPED	NEBULIZING	NEEDER
NATIVE	NAUTILI	NEAPING	NEBULOUS	NEEDERS
NATIVELY	NAUTILUS	NEAPS	NEBULY	NEEDFUL
NATIVES	NAUTILUSES	NEAPTIDE	NECESSARIES	NEEDFULLY
NATIVISM	NAVAID	NEAPTIDES	NECESSARY	NEEDIER
NATIVISMS	NAVAIDS	NEAR	NECESSITIES	NEEDIEST
NATIVIST	NAVAL	NEARED	NECESSITY	NEEDILY
NATIVISTS	NAVALISM	NEARER	NECK	NEEDINESS
NATIVITIES	NAVALISMS	NEAREST	NECKATEE	NEEDINESSES
NATIVITY	NAVARCH	NEARING	NECKATEES	NEEDING
NATRIUM	NAVARCHIES	NEARLY	NECKBEEF	NEEDLE
NATRIUMS	NAVARCHS	NEARNESS	NECKBEEFS	NEEDLED
NATROLITE	NAVARCHY	NEARNESSES	NECKED	NEEDLEFUL
NATROLITES	NAVARHO	NEARS	NECKGEAR	NEEDLEFULS
NATRON	NAVARHOS	NEARSIDE	NECKGEARS	NEEDLER
NATRONS	NAVARIN	NEARSIDES	NECKING	NEEDLERS
NATS	NAVARINS	NEAT	NECKINGS	NEEDLES
NATTER	NAVE	NEATEN	NECKLACE	NEEDLESS
NATTERED	NAVEL	NEATENED	NECKLACES	NEEDLIER
NATTERING	NAVELS	NEATENING	NECKLET	NEEDLIEST
NATTERS	NAVELWORT	NEATENS	NECKLETS	NEEDLING
NATTERY	NAVELWORTS	NEATER	NECKLINE	NEEDLY
NATTIER	NAVES	NEATEST	NECKLINES	NEEDMENT
NATTIEST	NAVETTE	NEATH	NECKS	NEEDMENTS
NATTILY	NAVETTES	NEATLY	NECKTIE	NEEDS
NATTINESS	NAVEW	NEATNESS	NECKTIES	NEEDY
NATTINESSES	NAVEWS	NEATNESSES	NECKVERSE	NEELD
NATTY	NAVICERT	NEATS	NECKVERSES	NEELDS
NATURA	NAVICERTS	NEB	NECKWEAR	NEELE
NATURAE	NAVICULA	NEBBED	NECKWEARS	NEELES
NATURAL	NAVICULAR	NEBBICH	NECKWEED	NEEM

NEEMS	NEIGHBOURING	NEOLOGIZED	NEPHRITE	NESSES
NEEP	NEIGHBOURS	NEOLOGIZES	NEPHRITES	NEST
NEEPS	NEIGHED	NEOLOGIZING	NEPHRITIC	NESTED
NEESBERRIES	NEIGHING	NEOLOGY	NEPHRITIS	NESTER
NEESBERRY	NEIGHS	NEOMYCIN	NEPHROID	NESTERS
NEESE	NEIST	NEOMYCINS	NEPHRON	NESTING
NEESED	NEITHER	NEON	NEPHRONS	NESTLE
NEESES	NEIVE	NEONATAL	NEPHROSES	NESTLED
NEESING	NEIVES	NEONATE	NEPHROSIS	NESTLES
NEEZE	NEK	NEONATES	NEPHROTIC	NESTLING
NEEZED	NEKS	NEONOMIAN	NEPIONIC	NESTLINGS
NEEZES	NEKTON	NEONOMIANS	NEPIT	NESTS
NEEZING	NEKTONS	NEONS	NEPITS	NET
NEF	NELIES	NEOPAGAN	NEPOTIC	NETBALL
NEFANDOUS	NELIS	NEOPAGANS	NEPOTISM	NETBALLS
NEFARIOUS	NELLIE	NEOPHILE	NEPOTISMS	NETE
NEFAST	NELLIES	NEOPHILES	NEPOTIST	NETES
NEFS	NELLY	NEOPHILIA	NEPOTISTS	NETFUL
NEGATE	NELSON	NEOPHILIAS	NEPS	NETFULS
NEGATED	NELSONS	NEOPHOBIA	NEPTUNIUM	NETHELESS
NEGATES	NELUMBIUM	NEOPHOBIAS	NEPTUNIUMS	NETHER
NEGATING	NELUMBIUMS	NEOPHYTE	NERD	NETS
NEGATION	NELUMBO	NEOPHYTES	NERDS	NETSUKE
NEGATIONS	NELUMBOS	NEOPHYTIC	NEREID	NETSUKES
NEGATIVE	NEMATIC	NEOPLASM	NEREIDS	NETT
NEGATIVED	NEMATODE	NEOPLASMS	NERINE	NETTED
NEGATIVES	NEMATODES	NEOPRENE	NERINES	NETTIER
NEGATIVING	NEMATOID	NEOPRENES	NERITE	NETTIEST
NEGATORY	NEMERTEAN	NEOTEINIA	NERITES	NETTING
NEGATRON	NEMERTEANS	NEOTEINIAS	NERITIC	NETTINGS
NEGATRONS	NEMERTIAN	NEOTEINIC	NERKA	NETTLE
NEGLECT	NEMERTIANS	NEOTENIC	NERKAS	NETTLED
NEGLECTED	NEMERTINE	NEOTENIES	NEROLI	NETTLES
NEGLECTER	NEMERTINES	NEOTENOUS	NEROLIS	NETTLING
NEGLECTERS	NEMESES	NEOTENY	NERVAL	NETTS
NEGLECTING	NEMESIA	NEOTERIC	NERVATE	NETTY
NEGLECTS	NEMESIAS	NEOTERISE	NERVATION	NETWORK
NÉGLIGÉ	NEMESIS	NEOTERISED	NERVATIONS	NETWORKED
NEGLIGEE	NEMN	NEOTERISES	NERVATURE	NETWORKING
NEGLIGEES	NEMNED	NEOTERISING	NERVATURES	NETWORKS
NEGLIGENT	NEMNING	NEOTERISM	NERVE	NEUK
NÉGLIGÉS	NEMNS	NEOTERISMS	NERVED	NEUKS
NÉGOCIANT	NEMOPHILA	NEOTERIST	NERVELESS	NEUM
NÉGOCIANTS	NEMOPHILAS	NEOTERISTS	NERVELET	NEUME
NEGOTIATE	NEMORAL	NEOTORIZE	NERVELETS	NEUMES
NEGOTIATED	NEMOROUS	NEOTORIZED	NERVER	NEUMS
NEGOTIATES	NEMPT	NEOTORIZES	NERVERS	NEURAL
NEGOTIATING	NENE	NEOTORIZING	NERVES	NEURALGIA
NEGRESS	NENES	NEP	NERVIER	NEURALGIAS
NEGRESSES	NENUPHAR	NEPENTHE	NERVIEST	NEURALGIC
NEGRITUDE	NENUPHARS	NEPENTHES	NERVINE	NEURATION
NEGRITUDES	NEOBLAST	NEPER	NERVINES	NEURATIONS
NEGRO	NEOBLASTS	NEPERS	NERVINESS	NEURILITIES
NEGROES	NEODYMIUM	NEPHALISM	NERVINESSES	NEURILITY
NEGROHEAD	NEODYMIUMS	NEPHALISMS	NERVING	NEURINE
NEGROHEADS	NEOLITH	NEPHALIST	NERVOUS	NEURINES
NEGROID	NEOLITHS	NEPHALISTS	NERVOUSLY	NEURISM
NEGROIDAL	NEOLOGIAN	NEPHELINE	NERVULAR	NEURISMS
NEGROIDS	NEOLOGIANS	NEPHELINES	NERVULE	NEURITE
NEGROISM	NEOLOGIC	NEPHELITE	NERVULES	NEURITES
NEGROISMS	NEOLOGIES	NEPHELITES	NERVURE	NEURITIC
NEGROPHIL	NEOLOGISE	NEPHEW	NERVURES	NEURITICS
NEGROPHILS	NEOLOGISED	NEPHEWS	NERVY	NEURITIS
NEGUS	NEOLOGISES	NEPHOGRAM	NESCIENCE	NEUROGLIA
NEGUSES	NEOLOGISING	NEPHOGRAMS	NESCIENCES	NEUROGLIAS
NEIF	NEOLOGISM	NEPHOLOGIES	NESCIENT	NEUROGRAM
NEIFS	NEOLOGISMS	NEPHOLOGY	NESH	NEUROGRAMS
NEIGH	NEOLOGIST	NEPHRALGIES	NESHNESS	NEUROLOGIES
NEIGHBOUR	NEOLOGISTS	NEPHRALGY	NESHNESSES	NEUROLOGY
NEIGHBOURED	NEOLOGIZE	NEPHRIC	NESS	NEUROMA

NEUROMAS	NEWSGIRL	NICHER	NIDGET	NIGGLED
NEURON	NEWSGIRLS	NICHERED	NIDGETS	NIGGLER
NEURONAL	NEWSHAWK	NICHERING	NIDI	NIGGLERS
NEURONE	NEWSHAWKS	NICHERS	NIDIFIED	NIGGLES
NEURONES	NEWSHOUND	NICHES	NIDIFIES	NIGGLIER
NEURONS	NEWSHOUNDS	NICHING	NIDIFY	NIGGLIEST
NEUROPATH	NEWSIER	NICK	NIDIFYING	NIGGLING
NEUROPATHS	NEWSIES	NICKAR	NIDING	NIGGLINGS
NEUROSES	NEWSIEST	NICKARS	NIDOR	NIGGLY
NEUROSIS	NEWSINESS	NICKED	NIDOROUS	NIGH
NEUROTIC	NEWSINESSES	NICKEL	NIDORS	NIGHED
NEUROTICS	NEWSING	NICKELIC	NIDS	NIGHING
NEUROTOMIES	NEWSMAN	NICKELINE	NIDUS	NIGHLY
NEUROTOMY	NEWSMEN	NICKELINES	NIE	NIGHNESS
NEUSTON	NEWSPAPER	NICKELISE	NIECE	NIGHNESSES
NEUSTONS	NEWSPAPERS	NICKELISED	NIECES	NIGHS
NEUTER	NEWSPEAK	NICKELISES	NIEF	NIGHT
NEUTERED	NEWSPEAKS	NICKELISING	NIEFS	NIGHTCAP
NEUTERING	NEWSPRINT	NICKELIZE	NIELLATED	NIGHTCAPS
NEUTERS	NEWSPRINTS	NICKELIZED	NIELLI	NIGHTED
NEUTRAL	NEWSREEL	NICKELIZES	NIELLIST	NIGHTFALL
NEUTRALLY	NEWSREELS	NICKELIZING	NIELLISTS	NIGHTFALLS
NEUTRALS	NEWSROOM	NICKELLED	NIELLO	NIGHTFIRE
NEUTRETTO	NEWSROOMS	NICKELLING	NIELLOED	NIGHTFIRES
NEUTRETTOS	NEWSTRADE	NICKELOUS	NIELLOING	NIGHTGEAR
NEUTRINO	NEWSTRADES	NICKELS	NIELLOS	NIGHTGEARS
NEUTRINOS	NEWSWOMAN	NICKER	NIEVE	NIGHTGOWN
NEUTRON	NEWSWOMEN	NICKERED	NIEVEFUL	NIGHTGOWNS
NEUTRONS	NEWSY	NICKERING	NIEVEFULS	NIGHTHAWK
NÉVÉ	NEWT	NICKERS	NIEVES	NIGHTHAWKS
NEVEL	NEWTON	NICKING	NIFE	NIGHTIE
NEVELLED	NEWTONS	NICKNAME	NIFES	NIGHTIES
NEVELLING	NEWTS	NICKNAMED	NIFF	NIGHTJAR
NEVELS	NEXT	NICKNAMES	NIFFER	NIGHTJARS
NEVER	NEXTLY	NICKNAMING	NIFFERED	NIGHTLESS
NEVERMORE	NEXTNESS	NICKS	NIFFERING	NIGHTLONG
NÉVÉS	NEXTNESSES	NICKSTICK	NIFFERS	NIGHTLY
NEW	NEXUS	NICKSTICKS	NIFFIER	NIGHTMARE
NEWBORN	NEXUSES	NICKUM	NIFFIEST	NIGHTMARES
NEWCOME	NGAIO	NICKUMS	NIFFNAFF	NIGHTMARY
NEWCOMER	NGAIOS	NICOL	NIFFNAFFED	NIGHTS
NEWCOMERS	NGWEE	NICOLS	NIFFNAFFING	NIGHTSPOT
NEWED	NIACIN	NICOMPOOP	NIFFNAFFS	NIGHTSPOTS
NEWEL	NIACINS	NICOMPOOPS	NIFFS	NIGHTWARD
NEWELL	NIB	NICOTIAN	NIFFY	NIGHTWEAR
NEWELLED	NIBBED	NICOTIANA	NIFTIER	NIGHTWEARS
NEWELLS	NIBBING	NICOTIANAS	NIFTIEST	NIGHTY
NEWELS	NIBBLE	NICOTIANS	NIFTINESS	NIGRICANT
NEWER	NIBBLED	NICOTINE	NIFTINESSES	NIGRIFIED
NEWEST	NIBBLER	NICOTINES	NIFTY	NIGRIFIES
NEWFANGLE	NIBBLERS	NICOTINIC	NIGELLA	NIGRIFY
NEWFANGLED	NIBBLES	NICTATE	NIGELLAS	NIGRIFYING
NEWING	NIBBLING	NICTATED	NIGER	NIGRITUDE
NEWISH	NIBBLINGS	NICTATES	NIGERS	NIGRITUDES
NEWLY	NIBLICK	NICTATING	NIGGARD	NIGROSINE
NEWMARKET	NIBLICKS	NICTATION	NIGGARDED	NIGROSINES
NEWMARKETS	NIBS	NICTATIONS	NIGGARDING	NIHIL
NEWNESS	NICCOLITE	NICTITATE	NIGGARDLY	NIHILISM
NEWNESSES	NICCOLITES	NICTITATED	NIGGARDS	NIHILISMS
NEWS	NICE	NICTITATES	NIGGER	NIHILIST
NEWSAGENT	NICEISH	NICTITATING	NIGGERDOM	NIHILISTS
NEWSAGENTS	NICELY	NID	NIGGERDOMS	NIHILITIES
NEWSBOY	NICENESS	NIDAL	NIGGERED	NIHILITY
NEWSBOYS	NICENESSES	NIDATION	NIGGERING	NIHILS
NEWSCAST	NICER	NIDATIONS	NIGGERISH	NIL
NEWSCASTS	NICEST	NIDDERING	NIGGERISM	NILGAI
NEWSED	NICETIES	NIDE	NIGGERISMS	NILGAIS
NEWSES	NICETY	NIDERING	NIGGERS	NILGAU
NEWSFLASH	NICHE	NIDERLING	NIGGERY	NILGAUS
NEWSFLASHES	NICHED	NIDES	NIGGLE	NILL

NILLED
NILLING
NILLS
NILS
NIM
NIMBED
NIMBI
NIMBLE
NIMBLER
NIMBLESSE
NIMBLESSES
NIMBLEST
NIMBLY
NIMBUS
NIMBUSED
NIMBUSES
NIMIETIES
NIMIETY
NIMIOUS
NIMMED
NIMMER
NIMMERS
NIMMING
NIMONIC
NIMS
NINCOM
NINCOMS
NINCUM
NINCUMS
NINE
NINEFOLD
NINEHOLES
NINEPENCE
NINEPENCES
NINEPENNIES
NINEPENNY
NINEPINS
NINES
NINESCORE
NINESCORES
NINETEEN
NINETEENS
NINETIES
NINETIETH
NINETIETHS
NINETY
NINJA
NINJAS
NINNIES
NINNY
NINON
NINONS
NINTH
NINTHLY
NINTHS
NIOBATE
NIOBATES
NIOBIC
NIOBITE
NIOBITES
NIOBIUM
NIOBIUMS
NIOBOUS
NIP
NIPPED
NIPPER
NIPPERED
NIPPERING
NIPPERKIN
NIPPERKINS

NIPPERS
NIPPIER
NIPPIEST
NIPPING
NIPPINGLY
NIPPLE
NIPPLED
NIPPLES
NIPPLING
NIPPY
NIPS
NIPTER
NIPTERS
NIRL
NIRLED
NIRLIE
NIRLIER
NIRLIEST
NIRLING
NIRLIT
NIRLS
NIRLY
NIRVANA
NIRVANAS
NIS
NISBERRIES
NISBERRY
NISEI
NISEIS
NISES
NISI
NISSE
NISSES
NISUS
NIT
NITERIE
NITERIES
NITERY
NITHING
NITHINGS
NITID
NITON
NITONS
NITRATE
NITRATED
NITRATES
NITRATINE
NITRATINES
NITRATING
NITRATION
NITRATIONS
NITRE
NITRES
NITRIC
NITRIDE
NITRIDED
NITRIDES
NITRIDING
NITRIDINGS
NITRIFIED
NITRIFIES
NITRIFY
NITRIFYING
NITRILE
NITRILES
NITRITE
NITRITES
NITROGEN
NITROGENS
NITROUS

NITROXYL
NITROXYLS
NITRY
NITRYL
NITRYLS
NITS
NITTIER
NITTIEST
NITTY
NITWIT
NITWITS
NITWITTED
NIVAL
NIVEOUS
NIX
NIXES
NIXIE
NIXIES
NIXY
NIZAM
NIZAMS
NO
NOB
NOBBIER
NOBBIEST
NOBBILY
NOBBINESS
NOBBINESSES
NOBBLE
NOBBLED
NOBBLER
NOBBLERS
NOBBLES
NOBBLING
NOBBUT
NOBBY
NOBELIUM
NOBELIUMS
NOBILESSE
NOBILESSES
NOBILIARY
NOBILITIES
NOBILITY
NOBLE
NOBLEMAN
NOBLEMEN
NOBLENESS
NOBLENESSES
NOBLER
NOBLES
NOBLESSE
NOBLESSES
NOBLEST
NOBLY
NOBODIES
NOBODY
NOBS
NOCAKE
NOCAKES
NOCENT
NOCENTLY
NOCENTS
NOCHEL
NOCHELLED
NOCHELLING
NOCHELS
NOCK
NOCKED
NOCKET
NOCKETS

NOCKING
NOCKS
NOCTILUCA
NOCTILUCAS
NOCTUA
NOCTUARIES
NOCTUARY
NOCTUAS
NOCTUID
NOCTUIDS
NOCTULE
NOCTULES
NOCTURN
NOCTURNAL
NOCTURNALS
NOCTURNE
NOCTURNES
NOCTURNS
NOCUOUS
NOCUOUSLY
NOD
NODAL
NODALISE
NODALISED
NODALISES
NODALISING
NODALITIES
NODALITY
NODALIZE
NODALIZED
NODALIZES
NODALIZING
NODATED
NODATION
NODATIONS
NODDED
NODDER
NODDERS
NODDIES
NODDING
NODDINGS
NODDLE
NODDLED
NODDLES
NODDLING
NODDY
NODE
NODES
NODI
NODICAL
NODOSE
NODOSITIES
NODOSITY
NODOUS
NODS
NODULAR
NODULATED
NODULE
NODULED
NODULES
NODULOSE
NODULOUS
NODUS
NOËL
NOËLS
NOES
NOESES
NOESIS
NOETIC
NOG

NOGAKU
NOGGIN
NOGGING
NOGGINGS
NOGGINS
NOGS
NOH
NOHOW
NOHOWISH
NOIL
NOILS
NOINT
NOINTED
NOINTING
NOINTS
NOISE
NOISED
NOISEFUL
NOISELESS
NOISES
NOISETTE
NOISETTES
NOISIER
NOISIEST
NOISILY
NOISINESS
NOISINESSES
NOISING
NOISOME
NOISOMELY
NOISY
NOLE
NOLES
NOLITION
NOLITIONS
NOLL
NOLLS
NOM
NOMA
NOMAD
NOMADE
NOMADES
NOMADIC
NOMADIES
NOMADISE
NOMADISED
NOMADISES
NOMADISING
NOMADISM
NOMADISMS
NOMADIZE
NOMADIZED
NOMADIZES
NOMADIZING
NOMADS
NOMADY
NOMARCH
NOMARCHIES
NOMARCHS
NOMARCHY
NOMAS
NOMBRIL
NOMBRILS
NOME
NOMEN
NOMES
NOMIC
NOMINA
NOMINABLE
NOMINAL

NOMINALLY	NONSENSES	NORMALITIES	NOSTOC	NOTICED
NOMINALS	NONSUCH	NORMALITY	NOSTOCS	NOTICES
NOMINATE	NONSUCHES	NORMALIZE	NOSTOI	NOTICING
NOMINATED	NONSUIT	NORMALIZED	NOSTOLOGIES	NOTIFIED
NOMINATES	NONSUITED	NORMALIZES	NOSTOLOGY	NOTIFIER
NOMINATING	NONSUITING	NORMALIZING	NOSTOS	NOTIFIERS
NOMINATOR	NONSUITS	NORMALLY	NOSTRIL	NOTIFIES
NOMINATORS	NONUPLE	NORMALS	NOSTRILS	NOTIFY
NOMINEE	NONUPLET	NORMAN	NOSTRUM	NOTIFYING
NOMINEES	NONUPLETS	NORMANS	NOSTRUMS	NOTING
NOMISM	NOODLE	NORMAS	NOSY	NOTION
NOMISMS	NOODLED	NORMATIVE	NOT	NOTIONAL
NOMISTIC	NOODLEDOM	NORMS	NOTABILIA	NOTIONIST
NOMOCRACIES	NOODLEDOMS	NORSEL	NOTABLE	NOTIONISTS
NOMOCRACY	NOODLES	NORSELLED	NOTABLES	NOTIONS
NOMOGENIES	NOODLING	NORSELLER	NOTABLY	NOTITIA
NOMOGENY	NOOK	NORSELLERS	NOTAEUM	NOTITIAS
NOMOGRAM	NOOKIE	NORSELLING	NOTAEUMS	NOTOCHORD
NOMOGRAMS	NOOKIER	NORSELS	NOTAL	NOTOCHORDS
NOMOGRAPH	NOOKIES	NORTH	NOTANDA	NOTORIETIES
NOMOGRAPHS	NOOKIEST	NORTHED	NOTANDUM	NOTORIETY
NOMOI	NOOKS	NORTHER	NOTAPHILIES	NOTORIOUS
NOMOLOGIES	NOOKY	NORTHERED	NOTAPHILY	NOTORNIS
NOMOLOGY	NOOLOGIES	NORTHERING	NOTARIAL	NOTORNISES
NOMOS	NOOLOGY	NORTHERLY	NOTARIES	NOTOUR
NOMOTHETE	NOOMETRIES	NORTHERN	NOTARISE	NOTT
NOMOTHETES	NOOMETRY	NORTHERNS	NOTARISED	NOTUM
NOMS	NOON	NORTHERS	NOTARISES	NOTUMS
NON	NOONDAY	NORTHING	NOTARISING	NOUGAT
NONAGE	NOONDAYS	NORTHINGS	NOTARIZE	NOUGATS
NONAGED	NOONED	NORTHLAND	NOTARIZED	NOUGHT
NONAGES	NOONING	NORTHLANDS	NOTARIZES	NOUGHTS
NONAGON	NOONINGS	NORTHMOST	NOTARIZING	NOUL
NONAGONS	NOONS	NORTHS	NOTARY	NOULD
NONANE	NOONTIDE	NORTHWARD	NOTATE	NOULDE
NONANES	NOONTIDES	NORWARD	NOTATED	NOULE
NONARY	NOOP	NORWARDS	NOTATES	NOULES
NONCE	NOOPS	NOSE	NOTATING	NOULS
NONCES	NOOSE	NOSEAN	NOTATION	NOUMENA
NONE	NOOSED	NOSEANS	NOTATIONS	NOUMENAL
NONENTITIES	NOOSES	NOSEBAG	NOTCH	NOUMENON
NONENTITY	NOOSING	NOSEBAGS	NOTCHBACK	NOUN
NONES	NOOSPHERE	NOSED	NOTCHBACKS	NOUNAL
NONESUCH	NOOSPHERES	NOSEGAY	NOTCHED	NOUNS
NONESUCHES	NOPAL	NOSEGAYS	NOTCHEL	NOUNY
NONET	NOPALS	NOSELESS	NOTCHELLED	NOUP
NONETS	NOPE	NOSELITE	NOTCHELLING	NOUPS
NONETTE	NOPES	NOSELITES	NOTCHELS	NOURICE
NONETTES	NOR	NOSER	NOTCHES	NOURICES
NONETTI	NORI	NOSERS	NOTCHING	NOURISH
NONETTO	NORIA	NOSES	NOTCHINGS	NOURISHED
NONETTOS	NORIAS	NOSEY	NOTCHY	NOURISHER
NONG	NORIMON	NOSEYS	NOTE	NOURISHERS
NONGS	NORIMONS	NOSH	NOTEBOOK	NOURISHES
NONILLION	NORIS	NOSHED	NOTEBOOKS	NOURISHING
NONILLIONS	NORITE	NOSHES	NOTED	NOURITURE
NONJURING	NORITES	NOSHING	NOTEDLY	NOURITURES
NONJUROR	NORK	NOSIER	NOTEDNESS	NOURSLE
NONJURORS	NORKS	NOSIES	NOTEDNESSES	NOURSLED
NONNIES	NORLAND	NOSIEST	NOTELESS	NOURSLES
NONNY	NORLANDS	NOSILY	NOTELET	NOURSLING
NONPAREIL	NORM	NOSINESS	NOTELETS	NOUS
NONPAREILS	NORMA	NOSINESSES	NOTEPAPER	NOUSELL
NONPAROUS	NORMAL	NOSING	NOTEPAPERS	NOUSES
NONPLUS	NORMALCIES	NOSINGS	NOTER	NOUSLE
NONPLUSSED	NORMALCY	NOSOLOGIES	NOTERS	NOUSLED
NONPLUSSES	NORMALISE	NOSOLOGY	NOTES	NOUSLES
NONPLUSSING	NORMALISED	NOSTALGIA	NOTHING	NOUSLING
NONPOLAR	NORMALISES	NOSTALGIAS	NOTHINGS	NOUT
NONSENSE	NORMALISING	NOSTALGIC	NOTICE	NOUVEAU

NOUVELLE	NOWLS	NUCLEATE	NULLING	NUNCLE
NOUVELLES	NOWN	NUCLEATED	NULLINGS	NUNCLES
NOVA	NOWNESS	NUCLEATES	NULLIPARA	NUNCUPATE
NOVAE	NOWNESSES	NUCLEATING	NULLIPARAE	NUNCUPATED
NOVALIA	NOWS	NUCLEI	NULLIPARAS	NUNCUPATES
NOVAS	NOWT	NUCLEIDE	NULLIPORE	NUNCUPATING
NOVATION	NOWTS	NUCLEIDES	NULLIPORES	NUNDINAL
NOVATIONS	NOWY	NUCLEIN	NULLITIES	NUNDINE
NOVEL	NOXAL	NUCLEINS	NULLITY	NUNDINES
NOVELDOM	NOXIOUS	NUCLEOLAR	NULLNESS	NUNHOOD
NOVELDOMS	NOXIOUSLY	NUCLEOLE	NULLNESSES	NUNHOODS
NOVELESE	NOY	NUCLEOLES	NULLS	NUNNATION
NOVELESES	NOYADE	NUCLEOLI	NUMB	NUNNATIONS
NOVELETTE	NOYADES	NUCLEOLUS	NUMBAT	NUNNERIES
NOVELETTES	NOYANCE	NUCLEON	NUMBATS	NUNNERY
NOVELISE	NOYANCES	NUCLEONS	NUMBED	NUNNISH
NOVELISED	NOYAU	NUCLEUS	NUMBER	NUNS
NOVELISER	NOYAUS	NUCLIDE	NUMBERED	NUNSHIP
NOVELISERS	NOYED	NUCLIDES	NUMBERER	NUNSHIPS
NOVELISES	NOYES	NUCULE	NUMBERERS	NUPTIAL
NOVELISH	NOYESES	NUCULES	NUMBERING	NUPTIALS
NOVELISING	NOYING	NUDATION	NUMBERS	NUR
NOVELISM	NOYOUS	NUDATIONS	NUMBEST	NURAGHE
NOVELISMS	NOYS	NUDE	NUMBING	NURAGHI
NOVELIST	NOYSOME	NUDELY	NUMBLES	NURAGHIC
NOVELISTS	NOZZLE	NUDENESS	NUMBS	NURHAG
NOVELIZE	NOZZLES	NUDENESSES	NUMBSKULL	NURHAGS
NOVELIZED	NTH	NUDER	NUMBSKULLS	NURL
NOVELIZER	NU	NUDES	NUMDAH	NURLED
NOVELIZERS	NUANCE	NUDEST	NUMDAHS	NURLING
NOVELIZES	NUANCED	NUDGE	NUMEN	NURLS
NOVELIZING	NUANCES	NUDGED	NUMERABLE	NURR
NOVELLA	NUANCING	NUDGES	NUMERABLY	NURRS
NOVELLAE	NUB	NUDGING	NUMERACIES	NURS
NOVELLAS	NUBBED	NUDICAUL	NUMERACY	NURSE
NOVELLE	NUBBIER	NUDIE	NUMERAIRE	NURSED
NOVELS	NUBBIEST	NUDIES	NUMERAIRES	NURSELIKE
NOVELTIES	NUBBIN	NUDISM	NUMERAL	NURSELING
NOVELTY	NUBBING	NUDISMS	NUMERALLY	NURSELINGS
NOVENA	NUBBINS	NUDIST	NUMERALS	NURSEMAID
NOVENARIES	NUBBLE	NUDISTS	NUMERARY	NURSEMAIDS
NOVENARY	NUBBLED	NUDITIES	NUMERATE	NURSER
NOVENAS	NUBBLES	NUDITY	NUMERATED	NURSERIES
NOVENNIAL	NUBBLIER	NUGAE	NUMERATES	NURSERS
NOVERCAL	NUBBLIEST	NUGATORY	NUMERATING	NURSERY
NOVERINT	NUBBLING	NUGGAR	NUMERATOR	NURSES
NOVERINTS	NUBBLY	NUGGARS	NUMERATORS	NURSING
NOVICE	NUBBY	NUGGET	NUMERIC	NURSLE
NOVICES	NUBECULA	NUGGETS	NUMERICAL	NURSLING
NOVICIATE	NUBECULAE	NUGGETY	NUMEROUS	NURSLINGS
NOVICIATES	NUBIA	NUISANCE	NUMINA	NURTURAL
NOVITIATE	NUBIAS	NUISANCER	NUMINOUS	NURTURANT
NOVITIATES	NUBIFORM	NUISANCERS	NUMMARY	NURTURE
NOVITIES	NUBILE	NUISANCES	NUMMULAR	NURTURED
NOVITY	NUBILITIES	NUKE	NUMMULARY	NURTURER
NOVODAMUS	NUBILITY	NUKED	NUMMULINE	NURTURERS
NOVODAMUSES	NUBILOUS	NUKES	NUMMULITE	NURTURES
NOVUM	NUBS	NUKING	NUMMULITES	NURTURING
NOVUMS	NUCELLAR	NULL	NUMNAH	NUS
NOW	NUCELLI	NULLA	NUMNAHS	NUT
NOWADAYS	NUCELLUS	NULLAH	NUMSKULL	NUTANT
NOWAY	NUCELLUSES	NULLAHS	NUMSKULLS	NUTARIAN
NOWAYS	NUCHA	NULLAS	NUN	NUTARIANS
NOWED	NUCHAL	NULLED	NUNATAK	NUTATE
NOWHENCE	NUCHAS	NULLIFIED	NUNATAKER	NUTATED
NOWHERE	NUCLEAL	NULLIFIER	NUNATAKS	NUTATES
NOWHERES	NUCLEAR	NULLIFIERS	NUNCHEON	NUTATING
NOWHITHER	NUCLEARY	NULLIFIES	NUNCHEONS	NUTATION
NOWISE	NUCLEASE	NULLIFY	NUNCIO	NUTATIONS
NOWL	NUCLEASES	NULLIFYING	NUNCIOS	NUTCASE

NUTCASES
NUTHATCH
NUTHATCHES
NUTJOBBER
NUTJOBBERS
NUTLET
NUTLETS
NUTMEAL
NUTMEALS
NUTMEG
NUTMEGGED
NUTMEGGY
NUTMEGS
NUTPECKER
NUTPECKERS
NUTRIA
NUTRIAS
NUTRIENT

NUTRIENTS
NUTRIMENT
NUTRIMENTS
NUTRITION
NUTRITIONS
NUTRITIVE
NUTS
NUTSHELL
NUTSHELLS
NUTTED
NUTTER
NUTTERIES
NUTTERS
NUTTERY
NUTTIER
NUTTIEST
NUTTINESS
NUTTINESSES

NUTTING
NUTTINGS
NUTTY
NUZZER
NUZZERS
NUZZLE
NUZZLED
NUZZLES
NUZZLING
NY
NYAFF
NYAFFED
NYAFFING
NYAFFS
NYALA
NYALAS
NYANZA
NYANZAS

NYAS
NYASES
NYCTALOPES
NYCTALOPS
NYE
NYES
NYING
NYLGHAU
NYLGHAUS
NYLON
NYLONS
NYMPH
NYMPHAE
NYMPHAEA
NYMPHAEUM
NYMPHAEUMS
NYMPHAL
NYMPHALID

NYMPHALIDS
NYMPHEAN
NYMPHET
NYMPHETS
NYMPHIC
NYMPHICAL
NYMPHISH
NYMPHLY
NYMPHO
NYMPHOS
NYMPHS
NYS
NYSTAGMIC
NYSTAGMUS
NYSTAGMUSES

O

OAF	OBDURING	OBITUARY	OBOE	OBSIGNED
OAFISH	OBEAH	OBJECT	OBOES	OBSIGNING
OAFS	OBEAHED	OBJECTED	OBOIST	OBSIGNS
OAK	OBEAHING	OBJECTIFIED	OBOISTS	OBSOLESCE
OAKEN	OBEAHISM	OBJECTIFIES	OBOL	OBSOLESCED
OAKENSHAW	OBEAHISMS	OBJECTIFY	OBOLARY	OBSOLESCES
OAKENSHAWS	OBEAHS	OBJECTIFYING	OBOLI	OBSOLESCING
OAKER	OBECHE	OBJECTING	OBOLS	OBSOLETE
OAKERS	OBECHES	OBJECTION	OBOLUS	OBSTACLE
OAKIER	OBEDIENCE	OBJECTIONS	OBOVATE	OBSTACLES
OAKIEST	OBEDIENCES	OBJECTIVE	OBOVATELY	OBSTETRIC
OAKLING	OBEDIENT	OBJECTIVES	OBOVOID	OBSTETRICS
OAKLINGS	OBEISANCE	OBJECTOR	OBREPTION	OBSTINACIES
OAKS	OBEISANCES	OBJECTORS	OBREPTIONS	OBSTINACY
OAKUM	OBEISANT	OBJECTS	OBS	OBSTINATE
OAKUMS	OBEISM	OBJET	OBSCENE	OBSTRUCT
OAKY	OBEISMS	OBJETS	OBSCENELY	OBSTRUCTED
OAR	OBELI	OBJURE	OBSCENER	OBSTRUCTING
OARAGE	OBELION	OBJURED	OBSCENEST	OBSTRUCTS
OARAGES	OBELIONS	OBJURES	OBSCENITIES	OBSTRUENT
OARED	OBELISCAL	OBJURGATE	OBSCENITY	OBSTRUENTS
OARING	OBELISE	OBJURGATED	OBSCURANT	OBTAIN
OARLESS	OBELISED	OBJURGATES	OBSCURANTS	OBTAINED
OARS	OBELISES	OBJURGATING	OBSCURE	OBTAINER
OARSMAN	OBELISING	OBJURING	OBSCURED	OBTAINERS
OARSMEN	OBELISK	OBLAST	OBSCURELY	OBTAINING
OARSWOMAN	OBELISKS	OBLASTS	OBSCURER	OBTAINS
OARSWOMEN	OBELIZE	OBLATE	OBSCURERS	OBTECT
OARWEED	OBELIZED	OBLATES	OBSCURES	OBTECTED
OARWEEDS	OBELIZES	OBLATION	OBSCUREST	OBTEMPER
OARY	OBELIZING	OBLATIONS	OBSCURING	OBTEMPERED
OASES	OBELUS	OBLATORY	OBSCURITIES	OBTEMPERING
OASIS	OBESE	OBLIGANT	OBSCURITY	OBTEMPERS
OAST	OBESENESS	OBLIGANTS	OBSECRATE	OBTEND
OASTS	OBESENESSES	OBLIGATE	OBSECRATED	OBTENDED
OAT	OBESER	OBLIGATED	OBSECRATES	OBTENDING
OATCAKE	OBESEST	OBLIGATES	OBSECRATING	OBTENDS
OATCAKES	OBESITIES	OBLIGATING	OBSEQUENT	OBTENTION
OATEN	OBESITY	OBLIGE	OBSEQUIAL	OBTENTIONS
OATH	OBEY	OBLIGED	OBSEQUIE	OBTEST
OATHABLE	OBEYED	OBLIGEE	OBSEQUIES	OBTESTED
OATHS	OBEYER	OBLIGEES	OBSEQUY	OBTESTING
OATMEAL	OBEYERS	OBLIGES	OBSERVANT	OBTESTS
OATMEALS	OBEYING	OBLIGING	OBSERVANTS	OBTRUDE
OATS	OBEYS	OBLIGOR	OBSERVE	OBTRUDED
OAVES	OBFUSCATE	OBLIGORS	OBSERVED	OBTRUDER
OB	OBFUSCATED	OBLIQUE	OBSERVER	OBTRUDERS
OBANG	OBFUSCATES	OBLIQUED	OBSERVERS	OBTRUDES
OBANGS	OBFUSCATING	OBLIQUELY	OBSERVES	OBTRUDING
OBBLIGATI	OBI	OBLIQUER	OBSERVING	OBTRUDINGS
OBBLIGATO	OBIA	OBLIQUES	OBSESS	OBTRUSION
OBBLIGATOS	OBIAS	OBLIQUEST	OBSESSED	OBTRUSIONS
OBCONIC	OBIED	OBLIQUID	OBSESSES	OBTRUSIVE
OBCONICAL	OBIING	OBLIQUING	OBSESSING	OBTUND
OBCORDATE	OBIISM	OBLIQUITIES	OBSESSION	OBTUNDED
OBDURACIES	OBIISMS	OBLIQUITY	OBSESSIONS	OBTUNDENT
OBDURACY	OBIIT	OBLIVION	OBSESSIVE	OBTUNDENTS
OBDURATE	OBIS	OBLIVIONS	OBSIDIAN	OBTUNDING
OBDURATED	OBIT	OBLIVIOUS	OBSIDIANS	OBTUNDS
OBDURATES	OBITAL	OBLONG	OBSIGN	OBTURATE
OBDURATING	OBITER	OBLONGS	OBSIGNATE	OBTURATED
OBDURE	OBITS	OBLOQUIES	OBSIGNATED	OBTURATES
OBDURED	OBITUAL	OBLOQUY	OBSIGNATES	OBTURATING
OBDURES	OBITUARIES	OBNOXIOUS	OBSIGNATING	OBTURATOR

OBTURATORS	OCCULTS	OCOTILLOS	OCTUPLET	ODONTIST
OBTUSE	OCCUPANCE	OCREA	OCTUPLETS	ODONTISTS
OBTUSELY	OCCUPANCES	OCREAE	OCTUPLING	ODONTOID
OBTUSER	OCCUPANCIES	OCREATE	OCULAR	ODONTOMA
OBTUSEST	OCCUPANCY	OCTACHORD	OCULARIST	ODONTOMAS
OBTUSITIES	OCCUPANT	OCTACHORDS	OCULARISTS	ODONTOMATA
OBTUSITY	OCCUPANTS	OCTAD	OCULARLY	ODOR
OBUMBRATE	OCCUPATE	OCTADIC	OCULARS	ODORANT
OBUMBRATED	OCCUPATED	OCTADS	OCULATE	ODORATE
OBUMBRATES	OCCUPATES	OCTAGON	OCULATED	ODOROUS
OBUMBRATING	OCCUPATING	OCTAGONAL	OCULI	ODOROUSLY
OBVENTION	OCCUPIED	OCTAGONS	OCULIST	ODORS
OBVENTIONS	OCCUPIER	OCTAHEDRA	OCULISTS	ODOUR
OBVERSE	OCCUPIERS	OCTAL	OCULUS	ODOURED
OBVERSELY	OCCUPIES	OCTAMETER	OD	ODOURLESS
OBVERSES	OCCUPY	OCTAMETERS	ODA	ODOURS
OBVERSION	OCCUPYING	OCTANE	ODAL	ODS
OBVERSIONS	OCCUR	OCTANES	ODALIQUE	ODSO
OBVERT	OCCURRED	OCTANT	ODALIQUES	ODSOS
OBVERTED	OCCURRENT	OCTANTAL	ODALISK	ODYL
OBVERTING	OCCURRENTS	OCTANTS	ODALISKS	ODYLE
OBVERTS	OCCURRING	OCTAPLA	ODALISQUE	ODYLES
OBVIATE	OCCURS	OCTAPLOID	ODALISQUES	ODYLISM
OBVIATED	OCEAN	OCTAPLOIDS	ODALLER	ODYLISMS
OBVIATES	OCEANAUT	OCTAPODIC	ODALLERS	ODYLS
OBVIATING	OCEANAUTS	OCTAPODIES	ODALS	ODYSSEY
OBVIATION	OCEANIC	OCTAPODY	ODAS	ODYSSEYS
OBVIATIONS	OCEANID	OCTAROON	ODD	ODZOOKS
OBVIOUS	OCEANIDES	OCTAROONS	ODDBALL	OE
OBVIOUSLY	OCEANIDS	OCTASTICH	ODDBALLS	OECIST
OBVOLUTE	OCEANS	OCTASTICHS	ODDER	OECISTS
OBVOLUTED	OCELLAR	OCTASTYLE	ODDEST	OECOLOGIES
OBVOLVENT	OCELLATE	OCTASTYLES	ODDISH	OECOLOGY
OCA	OCELLATED	OCTAVAL	ODDITIES	OECUMENIC
OCARINA	OCELLI	OCTAVE	ODDITY	OEDEMA
OCARINAS	OCELLUS	OCTAVES	ODDLY	OEDEMAS
OCAS	OCELOID	OCTAVO	ODDMENT	OEILLADE
OCCAMIES	OCELOT	OCTAVOS	ODDMENTS	OEILLADES
OCCAMY	OCELOTS	OCTENNIAL	ODDNESS	OENANTHIC
OCCASION	OCH	OCTET	ODDNESSES	OENOLOGIES
OCCASIONED	OCHE	OCTETS	ODDS	OENOLOGY
OCCASIONING	OCHER	OCTETT	ODDSMAN	OENOMANCIES
OCCASIONS	OCHERED	OCTETTE	ODDSMEN	OENOMANCY
OCCIDENT	OCHERING	OCTETTES	ODE	OENOMANIA
OCCIDENTS	OCHEROUS	OCTETTS	ODEA	OENOMANIAS
OCCIPITAL	OCHERS	OCTILLION	ODEON	OENOMEL
OCCIPITALS	OCHERY	OCTILLIONS	ODEONS	OENOMELS
OCCIPUT	OCHES	OCTOFID	ODES	OENOMETER
OCCIPUTS	OCHIDORE	OCTONARIES	ODEUM	OENOMETERS
OCCLUDE	OCHIDORES	OCTONARII	ODEUMS	OENOPHIL
OCCLUDED	OCHLOCRAT	OCTONARY	ODIC	OENOPHILE
OCCLUDENT	OCHLOCRATS	OCTOPI	ODIOUS	OENOPHILES
OCCLUDENTS	OCHONE	OCTOPLOID	ODIOUSLY	OENOPHILIES
OCCLUDES	OCHRE	OCTOPLOIDS	ODISM	OENOPHILS
OCCLUDING	OCHREA	OCTOPOD	ODISMS	OENOPHILY
OCCLUSAL	OCHREAE	OCTOPODES	ODIST	OERLIKON
OCCLUSION	OCHREATE	OCTOPODS	ODISTS	OERLIKONS
OCCLUSIONS	OCHRED	OCTOPUS	ODIUM	OERSTED
OCCLUSIVE	OCHREOUS	OCTOPUSES	ODIUMS	OERSTEDS
OCCLUSIVES	OCHRES	OCTOROON	ODOGRAPH	OES
OCCLUSOR	OCHREY	OCTOROONS	ODOGRAPHS	OESOPHAGI
OCCLUSORS	OCHRING	OCTOSTYLE	ODOMETER	OESTRAL
OCCULT	OCHROID	OCTOSTYLES	ODOMETERS	OESTROGEN
OCCULTED	OCHROUS	OCTROI	ODOMETRIES	OESTROGENS
OCCULTING	OCHRY	OCTROIS	ODOMETRY	OESTROUS
OCCULTISM	OCKER	OCTUOR	ODONATIST	OESTRUM
OCCULTISMS	OCKERISM	OCTUORS	ODONATISTS	OESTRUMS
OCCULTIST	OCKERISMS	OCTUPLE	ODONTALGIES	OESTRUS
OCCULTISTS	OCKERS	OCTUPLED	ODONTALGY	OESTRUSES
OCCULTLY	OCOTILLO	OCTUPLES	ODONTIC	OEUVRE

OEUVRES	OFFPUTS	OHOS	OLDSQUAWS	OLIVINES
OF	OFFS	OI	OLDSTER	OLLA
OFAY	OFFSADDLE	OIDIA	OLDSTERS	OLLAMH
OFAYS	OFFSADDLED	OIDIUM	OLDY	OLLAMHS
OFF	OFFSADDLES	OIK	OLÉ	OLLAS
OFFAL	OFFSADDLING	OIKIST	OLEACEOUS	OLLAV
OFFALS	OFFSCUM	OIKISTS	OLEANDER	OLLAVS
OFFBEAT	OFFSCUMS	OIKS	OLEANDERS	OLM
OFFCUT	OFFSEASON	OIL	OLEARIA	OLMS
OFFCUTS	OFFSEASONS	OILCAN	OLEARIAS	OLOGIES
OFFED	OFFSET	OILCANS	OLEASTER	OLOGY
OFFENCE	OFFSETS	OILCLOTH	OLEASTERS	OLOROSO
OFFENCES	OFFSETTING	OILCLOTHS	OLEATE	OLOROSOS
OFFEND	OFFSHOOT	OILED	OLEATES	OLPAE
OFFENDED	OFFSHOOTS	OILER	OLECRANAL	OLPE
OFFENDER	OFFSHORE	OILERIES	OLECRANON	OLPES
OFFENDERS	OFFSIDE	OILERS	OLECRANONS	OLYCOOK
OFFENDING	OFFSIDER	OILERY	OLEFIANT	OLYCOOKS
OFFENDRESS	OFFSIDERS	OILIER	OLEFIN	OLYKOEK
OFFENDRESSES	OFFSIDES	OILIEST	OLEFINE	OLYKOEKS
OFFENDS	OFFSPRING	OILILY	OLEFINES	OLYMPIAD
OFFENSE	OFFSPRINGS	OILINESS	OLEFINS	OLYMPIADS
OFFENSED	OFFTAKE	OILINESSES	OLEIC	OLYMPICS
OFFENSES	OFFTAKES	OILING	OLEIN	OM
OFFENSING	OFLAG	OILLET	OLEINS	OMADHAUN
OFFENSIVE	OFLAGS	OILLETS	OLENT	OMADHAUNS
OFFENSIVES	OFT	OILNUT	OLEO	OMASA
OFFER	OFTEN	OILNUTS	OLEOGRAPH	OMASAL
OFFERABLE	OFTENER	OILS	OLEOGRAPHS	OMASUM
OFFERED	OFTENEST	OILSKIN	OLEOS	OMBRE
OFFEREE	OFTENNESS	OILSKINS	OLEPHILIC	OMBRÉ
OFFEREES	OFTENNESSES	OILSTONE	OLEUM	OMBRELLA
OFFERER	OFTTIMES	OILSTONES	OLEUMS	OMBRELLAS
OFFERERS	OGAM	OILY	OLFACT	OMBRES
OFFERING	OGAMIC	OINT	OLFACTED	OMBROPHIL
OFFERINGS	OGAMS	OINTED	OLFACTING	OMBROPHILS
OFFEROR	OGDOAD	OINTING	OLFACTION	OMBU
OFFERORS	OGDOADS	OINTMENT	OLFACTIONS	OMBÚ
OFFERS	OGEE	OINTMENTS	OLFACTIVE	OMBUDSMAN
OFFERTORIES	OGEES	OINTS	OLFACTORY	OMBUDSMEN
OFFERTORY	OGGIN	OITICICA	OLFACTS	OMBÚS
OFFHAND	OGGINS	OITICICAS	OLIBANUM	OMBUS
OFFHANDED	OGHAM	OJIME	OLIBANUMS	OMEGA
OFFICE	OGHAMIC	OJIMES	OLID	OMEGAS
OFFICER	OGHAMS	OKAPI	OLIGAEMIA	OMELET
OFFICERED	OGIVAL	OKAPIS	OLIGAEMIAS	OMELETS
OFFICERING	OGIVE	OKAY	OLIGARCH	OMELETTE
OFFICERS	OGIVES	OKAYED	OLIGARCHIES	OMELETTES
OFFICES	OGLE	OKAYING	OLIGARCHS	OMEN
OFFICIAL	OGLED	OKAYS	OLIGARCHY	OMENED
OFFICIALS	OGLER	OKE	OLIGIST	OMENING
OFFICIANT	OGLERS	OKES	OLIGISTS	OMENS
OFFICIANTS	OGLES	OKIMONO	OLIGOPOLIES	OMENTA
OFFICIATE	OGLING	OKIMONOS	OLIGOPOLY	OMENTAL
OFFICIATED	OGLINGS	OKRA	OLIO	OMENTUM
OFFICIATES	OGMIC	OKRAS	OLIOS	OMER
OFFICIATING	OGRE	OLD	OLIPHANT	OMERS
OFFICINAL	OGREISH	OLDEN	OLIPHANTS	OMERTÀ
OFFICIOUS	OGRES	OLDENED	OLITORIES	OMERTÀS
OFFING	OGRESS	OLDENING	OLITORY	OMICRON
OFFINGS	OGRESSES	OLDENS	OLIVARY	OMICRONS
OFFISH	OGRISH	OLDER	OLIVE	OMINOUS
OFFLOAD	OH	OLDEST	OLIVENITE	OMINOUSLY
OFFLOADED	OHM	OLDIE	OLIVENITES	OMISSIBLE
OFFLOADING	OHMIC	OLDIES	OLIVER	OMISSION
OFFLOADS	OHMMETER	OLDISH	OLIVERS	OMISSIONS
OFFPEAK	OHMMETERS	OLDNESS	OLIVES	OMISSIVE
OFFPRINT	OHMS	OLDNESSES	OLIVET	OMIT
OFFPRINTS	OHO	OLDS	OLIVETS	OMITS
OFFPUT	OHONE	OLDSQUAW	OLIVINE	OMITTANCE

OMITTANCES
OMITTED
OMITTER
OMITTERS
OMITTING
OMLAH
OMLAHS
OMMATEA
OMMATEUM
OMMATIDIA
OMNEITIES
OMNEITY
OMNIANA
OMNIBUS
OMNIBUSES
OMNIETIES
OMNIETY
OMNIFIC
OMNIFIED
OMNIFIES
OMNIFORM
OMNIFY
OMNIFYING
OMNIUM
OMNIUMS
OMNIVORE
OMNIVORES
OMOHYOID
OMOHYOIDS
OMOPHAGIA
OMOPHAGIAS
OMOPHAGIC
OMOPHAGIES
OMOPHAGY
OMOPLATE
OMOPLATES
OMPHACITE
OMPHACITES
OMPHALIC
OMPHALOID
OMPHALOS
OMPHALOSES
OMRAH
OMRAHS
OMS
ON
ONAGER
ONAGERS
ONANISM
ONANISMS
ONANIST
ONANISTIC
ONANISTS
ONBOARD
ONCE
ONCER
ONCERS
ONCES
ONCIDIUM
ONCIDIUMS
ONCOGEN
ONCOGENE
ONCOGENES
ONCOGENIC
ONCOGENS
ONCOLOGIES
ONCOLOGY
ONCOME
ONCOMES
ONCOMETER

ONCOMETERS
ONCOMING
ONCOMINGS
ONCOST
ONCOSTMAN
ONCOSTMEN
ONCOSTS
ONCOTOMIES
ONCOTOMY
ONCUS
ONDATRA
ONDATRAS
ONDINE
ONDINES
ONDING
ONDINGS
ONE
ONEFOLD
ONEIRIC
ONELY
ONENESS
ONENESSES
ONER
ONEROUS
ONEROUSLY
ONERS
ONES
ONESELF
ONESTEP
ONESTEPPED
ONESTEPPING
ONESTEPS
ONEYER
ONEYERS
ONEYRE
ONEYRES
ONFALL
ONFALLS
ONFLOW
ONFLOWS
ONGOING
ONGOINGS
ONION
ONIONED
ONIONING
ONIONS
ONIONY
ONIRIC
ONISCOID
ONKUS
ONLOOKER
ONLOOKERS
ONLOOKING
ONLY
ONNED
ONNING
ONOMASTIC
ONOMASTICS
ONRUSH
ONRUSHES
ONS
ONSET
ONSETS
ONSETTER
ONSETTERS
ONSETTING
ONSETTINGS
ONSHORE
ONSIDE
ONSIDES

ONSLAUGHT
ONSLAUGHTS
ONST
ONSTEAD
ONSTEADS
ONTO
ONTOGENIC
ONTOGENIES
ONTOGENY
ONTOLOGIC
ONTOLOGIES
ONTOLOGY
ONUS
ONUSES
ONWARD
ONWARDLY
ONWARDS
ONYCHA
ONYCHAS
ONYCHIA
ONYCHIAS
ONYCHITE
ONYCHITES
ONYCHITIS
ONYCHIUM
ONYCHIUMS
ONYMOUS
ONYX
ONYXES
OO
OOBIT
OOBITS
OOCYTE
OOCYTES
OODLES
OODLINS
OOF
OOFS
OOFTISH
OOFTISHES
OOGAMIES
OOGAMOUS
OOGAMY
OOGENESES
OOGENESIS
OOGENETIC
OOGENIES
OOGENY
OOGONIA
OOGONIAL
OOGONIUM
OOH
OOHED
OOHING
OOHS
OOIDAL
OOLAKAN
OOLAKANS
OOLITE
OOLITES
OOLITIC
OOLOGIES
OOLOGIST
OOLOGISTS
OOLOGY
OOLONG
OOLONGS
OOM
OOMIAC
OOMIACK

OOMIACKS
OOMIACS
OOMIAK
OOMIAKS
OOMPAH
OOMPAHED
OOMPAHING
OOMPAHS
OOMPH
OOMPHS
OOMS
OON
OONS
OONT
OONTS
OOP
OOPED
OOPHORON
OOPHORONS
OOPHYTE
OOPHYTES
OOPING
OOPS
OOR
OORIAL
OORIALS
OORIE
OOS
OOSE
OOSES
OOSIER
OOSIEST
OOSPHERE
OOSPHERES
OOSPORE
OOSPORES
OOSY
OOZE
OOZED
OOZES
OOZIER
OOZIEST
OOZILY
OOZINESS
OOZINESSES
OOZING
OOZY
OP
OPACITIES
OPACITY
OPACOUS
OPAH
OPAHS
OPAL
OPALED
OPALINE
OPALINES
OPALISED
OPALIZED
OPALS
OPAQUE
OPAQUED
OPAQUELY
OPAQUER
OPAQUES
OPAQUEST
OPAQUING
OPE
OPED
OPEN

OPENABLE
OPENED
OPENER
OPENERS
OPENEST
OPENING
OPENINGS
OPENLY
OPENNESS
OPENNESSES
OPENS
OPERA
OPERABLE
OPERAND
OPERANDS
OPERANT
OPERANTS
OPERAS
OPERATE
OPERATED
OPERATES
OPERATIC
OPERATING
OPERATION
OPERATIONS
OPERATIVE
OPERATIVES
OPERATOR
OPERATORS
OPERCULA
OPERCULAR
OPERCULUM
OPERETTA
OPERETTAS
OPEROSE
OPEROSELY
OPEROSITIES
OPEROSITY
OPES
OPHIDIAN
OPHIDIANS
OPHIOLITE
OPHIOLITES
OPHIOLOGIES
OPHIOLOGY
OPHITE
OPHITES
OPHITIC
OPHIURAN
OPHIURANS
OPHIURID
OPHIURIDS
OPHIUROID
OPHIUROIDS
OPIATE
OPIATED
OPIATES
OPIATING
OPIFICER
OPIFICERS
OPINABLE
OPINE
OPINED
OPINES
OPING
OPINICUS
OPINICUSES
OPINING
OPINION
OPINIONED

OPINIONS	OPTICALLY	ORANGE	ORCHESTIC	ORDUROUS
OPIOID	OPTICIAN	ORANGEADE	ORCHESTRA	ORE
OPIUM	OPTICIANS	ORANGEADES	ORCHESTRAS	OREAD
OPIUMS	OPTICS	ORANGER	ORCHID	OREADES
OPOBALSAM	OPTIMA	ORANGERIES	ORCHIDIST	OREADS
OPOBALSAMS	OPTIMAL	ORANGERY	ORCHIDISTS	ORECROWE
OPODELDOC	OPTIMATE	ORANGES	ORCHIDS	ORECTIC
OPODELDOCS	OPTIMATES	ORANGEST	ORCHIL	OREGANO
OPOPANAX	OPTIME	ORANGS	ORCHILLA	OREGANOS
OPOPANAXES	OPTIMES	ORANT	ORCHILLAS	OREIDE
OPORICE	OPTIMISE	ORANTS	ORCHILS	OREIDES
OPORICES	OPTIMISED	ORARIA	ORCHIS	OREOLOGIES
OPOSSUM	OPTIMISES	ORARIAN	ORCHISES	OREOLOGY
OPOSSUMS	OPTIMISING	ORARIANS	ORCHITIC	OREPEARCH
OPPIDAN	OPTIMISM	ORARION	ORCHITIS	ORES
OPPIDANS	OPTIMISMS	ORARIONS	ORCHITISES	ORESTUNCK
OPPILATE	OPTIMIST	ORARIUM	ORCIN	OREWEED
OPPILATED	OPTIMISTS	ORARIUMS	ORCINE	OREWEEDS
OPPILATES	OPTIMIZE	ORATE	ORCINES	OREXIS
OPPILATING	OPTIMIZED	ORATED	ORCINOL	OREXISES
OPPO	OPTIMIZES	ORATES	ORCINOLS	ORF
OPPONENCIES	OPTIMIZING	ORATING	ORCINS	ORFE
OPPONENCY	OPTIMUM	ORATION	ORCS	ORFES
OPPONENT	OPTING	ORATIONS	ORD	ORFS
OPPONENTS	OPTION	ORATOR	ORDAIN	ORGAN
OPPORTUNE	OPTIONAL	ORATORIAL	ORDAINED	ORGANA
OPPOS	OPTIONS	ORATORIAN	ORDAINER	ORGANDIE
OPPOSABLE	OPTOLOGIES	ORATORIANS	ORDAINERS	ORGANDIES
OPPOSE	OPTOLOGY	ORATORIES	ORDAINING	ORGANELLE
OPPOSED	OPTOMETER	ORATORIO	ORDAINS	ORGANELLES
OPPOSER	OPTOMETERS	ORATORIOS	ORDALIAN	ORGANIC
OPPOSERS	OPTOMETRIES	ORATORS	ORDALIUM	ORGANICAL
OPPOSES	OPTOMETRY	ORATORY	ORDALIUMS	ORGANISE
OPPOSING	OPTOPHONE	ORATRESS	ORDEAL	ORGANISED
OPPOSITE	OPTOPHONES	ORATRESSES	ORDEALS	ORGANISER
OPPOSITES	OPTS	ORATRIX	ORDER	ORGANISERS
OPPRESS	OPULENCE	ORATRIXES	ORDERED	ORGANISES
OPPRESSED	OPULENCES	ORB	ORDERER	ORGANISING
OPPRESSES	OPULENT	ORBED	ORDERERS	ORGANISM
OPPRESSING	OPULENTLY	ORBICULAR	ORDERING	ORGANISMS
OPPRESSOR	OPULUS	ORBIER	ORDERINGS	ORGANIST
OPPRESSORS	OPULUSES	ORBIEST	ORDERLESS	ORGANISTS
OPPUGN	OPUNTIA	ORBING	ORDERLIES	ORGANITIES
OPPUGNANT	OPUNTIAS	ORBIT	ORDERLY	ORGANITY
OPPUGNANTS	OPUS	ORBITA	ORDERS	ORGANIZE
OPPUGNED	OPUSCLE	ORBITAL	ORDINAIRE	ORGANIZED
OPPUGNER	OPUSCLES	ORBITALS	ORDINAIRES	ORGANIZER
OPPUGNERS	OPUSCULA	ORBITAS	ORDINAL	ORGANIZERS
OPPUGNING	OPUSCULE	ORBITED	ORDINALS	ORGANIZES
OPPUGNS	OPUSCULES	ORBITER	ORDINANCE	ORGANIZING
OPS	OPUSCULUM	ORBITERS	ORDINANCES	ORGANON
OPSIMATH	OPUSES	ORBITIES	ORDINAND	ORGANS
OPSIMATHIES	OR	ORBITING	ORDINANDS	ORGANUM
OPSIMATHS	ORACH	ORBITS	ORDINANT	ORGANZA
OPSIMATHY	ORACHE	ORBITY	ORDINANTS	ORGANZAS
OPSOMANIA	ORACHES	ORBS	ORDINAR	ORGANZINE
OPSOMANIAS	ORACHS	ORBY	ORDINARIES	ORGANZINES
OPSONIC	ORACIES	ORC	ORDINARS	ORGASM
OPSONIN	ORACLE	ORCEIN	ORDINARY	ORGASMED
OPSONINS	ORACLED	ORCEINS	ORDINATE	ORGASMIC
OPSONIUM	ORACLES	ORCHARD	ORDINATED	ORGASMING
OPSONIUMS	ORACLING	ORCHARDS	ORDINATES	ORGASMS
OPT	ORACULAR	ORCHAT	ORDINATING	ORGASTIC
OPTANT	ORACULOUS	ORCHATS	ORDINEE	ORGEAT
OPTANTS	ORACY	ORCHEL	ORDINEES	ORGEATS
OPTATIVE	ORAGIOUS	ORCHELLA	ORDNANCE	ORGIA
OPTATIVES	ORAL	ORCHELLAS	ORDNANCES	ORGIAS
OPTED	ORALLY	ORCHELS	ORDS	ORGIAST
OPTIC	ORALS	ORCHESES	ORDURE	ORGIASTIC
OPTICAL	ORANG	ORCHESIS	ORDURES	ORGIASTS

ORGIC	ORMER	ORTHODOXY	OSMOMETRIES	OSTINATO
ORGIES	ORMERS	ORTHOEPIC	OSMOMETRY	OSTINATOS
ORGILLOUS	ORMOLU	ORTHOEPIES	OSMOSE	OSTIOLATE
ORGONE	ORMOLUS	ORTHOEPY	OSMOSED	OSTIOLE
ORGONES	ORNAMENT	ORTHOPEDIES	OSMOSES	OSTIOLES
ORGUE	ORNAMENTED	ORTHOPEDY	OSMOSING	OSTIUM
ORGUES	ORNAMENTING	ORTHOPOD	OSMOSIS	OSTLER
ORGULOUS	ORNAMENTS	ORTHOPODS	OSMOTIC	OSTLERESS
ORGY	ORNATE	ORTHOPTIC	OSMOUS	OSTLERESSES
ORIBI	ORNATELY	ORTHOS	OSMUND	OSTLERS
ORIBIS	ORNATER	ORTHOSES	OSMUNDA	OSTRACA
ORICALCHE	ORNATEST	ORTHOSIS	OSMUNDAS	OSTRACEAN
ORICALCHES	ORNERY	ORTHOTIC	OSMUNDS	OSTRACISE
ORICHALC	ORNIS	ORTHOTICS	OSNABURG	OSTRACISED
ORICHALCS	ORNISES	ORTHOTIST	OSNABURGS	OSTRACISES
ORIEL	ORNITHIC	ORTHOTISTS	OSPREY	OSTRACISING
ORIELLED	ORNITHOID	ORTHOTONE	OSPREYS	OSTRACISM
ORIELS	OROGENIC	ORTHROS	OSSA	OSTRACISMS
ORIENCIES	OROGENIES	ORTHROSES	OSSARIUM	OSTRACIZE
ORIENCY	OROGENY	ORTOLAN	OSSARIUMS	OSTRACIZED
ORIENT	OROGRAPHIES	ORTOLANS	OSSEIN	OSTRACIZES
ORIENTAL	OROGRAPHY	ORTS	OSSEINS	OSTRACIZING
ORIENTALS	OROIDE	ORVAL	OSSELET	OSTRACOD
ORIENTATE	OROIDES	ORVALS	OSSELETS	OSTRACODS
ORIENTATED	OROLOGIES	ORYX	OSSEOUS	OSTRACON
ORIENTATES	OROLOGIST	ORYXES	OSSETER	OSTRAKA
ORIENTATING	OROLOGISTS	OS	OSSETERS	OSTRAKON
ORIENTED	OROLOGY	OSCHEAL	OSSIA	OSTREGER
ORIENTEER	OROPESA	OSCILLATE	OSSICLE	OSTREGERS
ORIENTEERED	OROPESAS	OSCILLATED	OSSICLES	OSTRICH
ORIENTEERING	OROROTUND	OSCILLATES	OSSICULAR	OSTRICHES
ORIENTEERINGS	OROTUND	OSCILLATING	OSSIFIC	OTALGIA
ORIENTEERS	ORPHAN	OSCINE	OSSIFIED	OTALGIAS
ORIENTING	ORPHANAGE	OSCININE	OSSIFIES	OTALGIES
ORIENTS	ORPHANAGES	OSCITANCIES	OSSIFRAGA	OTALGY
ORIFEX	ORPHANED	OSCITANCY	OSSIFRAGAS	OTARIES
ORIFEXES	ORPHANING	OSCITANT	OSSIFRAGE	OTARINE
ORIFICE	ORPHANISM	OSCITATE	OSSIFRAGES	OTARY
ORIFICES	ORPHANISMS	OSCITATED	OSSIFY	OTHER
ORIFICIAL	ORPHANS	OSCITATES	OSSIFYING	OTHERNESS
ORIFLAMME	ORPHARION	OSCITATING	OSSUARIES	OTHERNESSES
ORIFLAMMES	ORPHARIONS	OSCULA	OSSUARY	OTHERS
ORIGAMI	ORPHREY	OSCULANT	OSTEAL	OTHERWISE
ORIGAMIS	ORPHREYS	OSCULAR	OSTEITIS	OTIC
ORIGAN	ORPIMENT	OSCULATE	OSTEITISES	OTIOSE
ORIGANE	ORPIMENTS	OSCULATED	OSTENSIVE	OTIOSITIES
ORIGANES	ORPIN	OSCULATES	OSTENSORIES	OTIOSITY
ORIGANS	ORPINE	OSCULATING	OSTENSORY	OTITIS
ORIGANUM	ORPINES	OSCULE	OSTENT	OTITISES
ORIGANUMS	ORPINS	OSCULES	OSTENTS	OTOCYST
ORIGIN	ORRA	OSCULUM	OSTEODERM	OTOCYSTS
ORIGINAL	ORRERIES	OSCULUMS	OSTEODERMS	OTOLITH
ORIGINALS	ORRERY	OSHAC	OSTEOGENIES	OTOLITHS
ORIGINATE	ORRIS	OSHACS	OSTEOGENY	OTOLOGIES
ORIGINATED	ORRISES	OSIER	OSTEOID	OTOLOGIST
ORIGINATES	ORS	OSIERED	OSTEOLOGIES	OTOLOGISTS
ORIGINATING	ORSEILLE	OSIERIES	OSTEOLOGY	OTOLOGY
ORIGINS	ORSEILLES	OSIERS	OSTEOMA	OTORRHOEA
ORILLION	ORSELLIC	OSIERY	OSTEOMAS	OTORRHOEAS
ORILLIONS	ORT	OSMATE	OSTEOPATH	OTOSCOPE
ORIOLE	ORTANIQUE	OSMATES	OSTEOPATHS	OTOSCOPES
ORIOLES	ORTANIQUES	OSMETERIA	OSTEOTOME	OTTAR
ORISON	ORTHIAN	OSMIATE	OSTEOTOMES	OTTARS
ORISONS	ORTHICON	OSMIATES	OSTEOTOMIES	OTTAVA
ORLE	ORTHICONS	OSMIC	OSTEOTOMY	OTTAVAS
ORLEANS	ORTHO	OSMIOUS	OSTIA	OTTAVINO
ORLEANSES	ORTHOAXES	OSMIUM	OSTIAL	OTTAVINOS
ORLES	ORTHOAXIS	OSMIUMS	OSTIARIES	OTTER
ORLOP	ORTHODOX	OSMOMETER	OSTIARY	OTTERED
ORLOPS	ORTHODOXIES	OSMOMETERS	OSTIATE	OTTERING

OTTERS	OURS	OUTCASTING	OUTERMOST	OUTGLARED
OTTO	OURSELF	OUTCASTS	OUTERS	OUTGLARES
OTTOMAN	OURSELVES	OUTCLASS	OUTERWEAR	OUTGLARING
OTTOMANS	OUSEL	OUTCLASSED	OUTERWEARS	OUTGO
OTTOS	OUSELS	OUTCLASSES	OUTFACE	OUTGOER
OTTRELITE	OUST	OUTCLASSING	OUTFACED	OUTGOERS
OTTRELITES	OUSTED	OUTCOME	OUTFACES	OUTGOES
OU	OUSTER	OUTCOMES	OUTFACING	OUTGOING
OUABAIN	OUSTERS	OUTCRAFTIED	OUTFALL	OUTGOINGS
OUABAINS	OUSTING	OUTCRAFTIES	OUTFALLS	OUTGONE
OUBIT	OUSTITI	OUTCRAFTY	OUTFIELD	OUTGREW
OUBITS	OUSTITIS	OUTCRAFTYING	OUTFIELDS	OUTGROW
OUBLIETTE	OUSTS	OUTCRIED	OUTFIGHT	OUTGROWING
OUBLIETTES	OUT	OUTCRIES	OUTFIGHTING	OUTGROWN
OUCH	OUTACT	OUTCROP	OUTFIGHTS	OUTGROWS
OUCHES	OUTACTED	OUTCROPPED	OUTFIT	OUTGROWTH
OUCHT	OUTACTING	OUTCROPPING	OUTFITS	OUTGROWTHS
OUCHTS	OUTACTS	OUTCROPS	OUTFITTED	OUTGUARD
OUGHLIED	OUTAGE	OUTCROSS	OUTFITTER	OUTGUARDS
OUGHLIES	OUTAGES	OUTCROSSED	OUTFITTERS	OUTGUN
OUGHLY	OUTATE	OUTCROSSES	OUTFITTING	OUTGUNNED
OUGHLYING	OUTBACK	OUTCROSSING	OUTFLANK	OUTGUNNING
OUGHT	OUTBACKER	OUTCRY	OUTFLANKED	OUTGUNS
OUGHTNESS	OUTBACKERS	OUTCRYING	OUTFLANKING	OUTGUSH
OUGHTNESSES	OUTBACKS	OUTDANCE	OUTFLANKS	OUTGUSHED
OUGHTS	OUTBAR	OUTDANCED	OUTFLASH	OUTGUSHES
OUGLIE	OUTBARRED	OUTDANCES	OUTFLASHED	OUTGUSHING
OUGLIED	OUTBARRING	OUTDANCING	OUTFLASHES	OUTHAUL
OUGLIEING	OUTBARS	OUTDARE	OUTFLASHING	OUTHAULER
OUGLIES	OUTBID	OUTDARED	OUTFLEW	OUTHAULERS
OUIJA	OUTBIDDING	OUTDARES	OUTFLIES	OUTHAULS
OUIJAS	OUTBIDS	OUTDARING	OUTFLING	OUTHER
OUISTITI	OUTBOARD	OUTDATE	OUTFLINGS	OUTHIRE
OUISTITIS	OUTBOUND	OUTDATED	OUTFLOW	OUTHIRED
OUK	OUTBOUNDS	OUTDATES	OUTFLOWED	OUTHIRES
OUKS	OUTBOX	OUTDATING	OUTFLOWING	OUTHIRING
OULACHON	OUTBOXED	OUTDID	OUTFLOWN	OUTHIT
OULACHONS	OUTBOXES	OUTDO	OUTFLOWS	OUTHITS
OULAKAN	OUTBOXING	OUTDOES	OUTFLUSH	OUTHITTING
OULAKANS	OUTBRAG	OUTDOING	OUTFLUSHED	OUTHOUSE
OULK	OUTBRAGGED	OUTDONE	OUTFLUSHES	OUTHOUSES
OULKS	OUTBRAGGING	OUTDOOR	OUTFLUSHING	OUTHYRE
OULONG	OUTBRAGS	OUTDOORS	OUTFLY	OUTING
OULONGS	OUTBRAVE	OUTDOORSY	OUTFLYING	OUTINGS
OUNCE	OUTBRAVED	OUTDRANK	OUTFOOT	OUTJEST
OUNCES	OUTBRAVES	OUTDRINK	OUTFOOTED	OUTJESTED
OUNDY	OUTBRAVING	OUTDRINKING	OUTFOOTING	OUTJESTING
OUP	OUTBREAK	OUTDRINKS	OUTFOOTS	OUTJESTS
OUPED	OUTBREAKING	OUTDRIVE	OUTFOUGHT	OUTJET
OUPH	OUTBREAKS	OUTDRIVEN	OUTFOX	OUTJETS
OUPHE	OUTBRED	OUTDRIVES	OUTFOXED	OUTJUMP
OUPHES	OUTBREED	OUTDRIVING	OUTFOXES	OUTJUMPED
OUPHS	OUTBREEDING	OUTDROVE	OUTFOXING	OUTJUMPING
OUPING	OUTBREEDS	OUTDRUNK	OUTFROWN	OUTJUMPS
OUPS	OUTBROKE	OUTDURE	OUTFROWNED	OUTJUT
OUR	OUTBROKEN	OUTDURED	OUTFROWNING	OUTJUTS
OURALI	OUTBURN	OUTDURES	OUTFROWNS	OUTLAID
OURALIS	OUTBURNED	OUTDURING	OUTGAS	OUTLAND
OURARI	OUTBURNING	OUTDWELL	OUTGASES	OUTLANDER
OURARIS	OUTBURNS	OUTDWELLED	OUTGASSED	OUTLANDERS
OUREBI	OUTBURNT	OUTDWELLING	OUTGASSING	OUTLANDS
OUREBIS	OUTBURST	OUTDWELLS	OUTGATE	OUTLASH
OURIE	OUTBURSTING	OUTEAT	OUTGATES	OUTLASHES
OURN	OUTBURSTS	OUTEATEN	OUTGAVE	OUTLAST
OUROBOROS	OUTBY	OUTEATING	OUTGIVE	OUTLASTED
OUROBOROSES	OUTBYE	OUTEATS	OUTGIVEN	OUTLASTING
OUROLOGIES	OUTCAST	OUTED	OUTGIVES	OUTLASTS
OUROLOGY	OUTCASTE	OUTEDGE	OUTGIVING	OUTLAUNCE
OUROSCOPIES	OUTCASTED	OUTEDGES	OUTGIVINGS	OUTLAUNCH
OUROSCOPY	OUTCASTES	OUTER	OUTGLARE	OUTLAUNCHED

OUTLAUNCHES
OUTLAUNCHING
OUTLAW
OUTLAWED
OUTLAWING
OUTLAWRIES
OUTLAWRY
OUTLAWS
OUTLAY
OUTLAYING
OUTLAYS
OUTLEAP
OUTLEAPED
OUTLEAPING
OUTLEAPS
OUTLEAPT
OUTLEARN
OUTLEARNED
OUTLEARNING
OUTLEARNS
OUTLEARNT
OUTLER
OUTLERS
OUTLET
OUTLETS
OUTLIE
OUTLIED
OUTLIER
OUTLIERS
OUTLIES
OUTLINE
OUTLINEAR
OUTLINED
OUTLINES
OUTLINING
OUTLIVE
OUTLIVED
OUTLIVES
OUTLIVING
OUTLOOK
OUTLOOKED
OUTLOOKING
OUTLOOKS
OUTLUSTRE
OUTLUSTRED
OUTLUSTRES
OUTLUSTRING
OUTLYING
OUTMAN
OUTMANNED
OUTMANNING
OUTMANS
OUTMANTLE
OUTMANTLED
OUTMANTLES
OUTMANTLING
OUTMARCH
OUTMARCHED
OUTMARCHES
OUTMARCHING
OUTMATCH
OUTMATCHED
OUTMATCHES
OUTMATCHING
OUTMODE
OUTMODED
OUTMODES
OUTMODING
OUTMOST
OUTMOVE

OUTMOVED
OUTMOVES
OUTMOVING
OUTNAME
OUTNAMED
OUTNAMES
OUTNAMING
OUTNESS
OUTNESSES
OUTNIGHT
OUTNIGHTED
OUTNIGHTING
OUTNIGHTS
OUTNUMBER
OUTNUMBERED
OUTNUMBERING
OUTNUMBERS
OUTPACE
OUTPACED
OUTPACES
OUTPACING
OUTPART
OUTPARTS
OUTPEEP
OUTPEEPED
OUTPEEPING
OUTPEEPS
OUTPEER
OUTPEERED
OUTPEERING
OUTPEERS
OUTPLAY
OUTPLAYED
OUTPLAYING
OUTPLAYS
OUTPOINT
OUTPOINTED
OUTPOINTING
OUTPOINTS
OUTPORT
OUTPORTS
OUTPOST
OUTPOSTS
OUTPOUR
OUTPOURED
OUTPOURER
OUTPOURERS
OUTPOURING
OUTPOURS
OUTPOWER
OUTPOWERED
OUTPOWERING
OUTPOWERS
OUTPRAY
OUTPRAYED
OUTPRAYING
OUTPRAYS
OUTPRICE
OUTPRICED
OUTPRICES
OUTPRICING
OUTPRIZE
OUTPRIZED
OUTPRIZES
OUTPRIZING
OUTPUT
OUTPUTS
OUTPUTTED
OUTPUTTING
OUTRACE

OUTRACED
OUTRACES
OUTRACING
OUTRAGE
OUTRAGED
OUTRAGES
OUTRAGING
OUTRAIGNE
OUTRAN
OUTRANCE
OUTRANCES
OUTRANK
OUTRANKED
OUTRANKING
OUTRANKS
OUTRATE
OUTRATED
OUTRATES
OUTRATING
OUTRÉ
OUTREACH
OUTREACHED
OUTREACHES
OUTREACHING
OUTRED
OUTREDDED
OUTREDDEN
OUTREDDENED
OUTREDDENING
OUTREDDENS
OUTREDDING
OUTREDS
OUTREIGN
OUTREIGNED
OUTREIGNING
OUTREIGNS
OUTRELIEF
OUTRELIEFS
OUTREMER
OUTREMERS
OUTRIDDEN
OUTRIDE
OUTRIDER
OUTRIDERS
OUTRIDES
OUTRIDING
OUTRIGGER
OUTRIGGERS
OUTRIGHT
OUTRIVAL
OUTRIVALLED
OUTRIVALLING
OUTRIVALS
OUTROAR
OUTROARED
OUTROARING
OUTROARS
OUTRODE
OUTROOP
OUTROOPER
OUTROOPERS
OUTROOPS
OUTROOT
OUTROOTED
OUTROOTING
OUTROOTS
OUTROPE
OUTROPER
OUTROPERS
OUTROPES

OUTRUN
OUTRUNNER
OUTRUNNERS
OUTRUNNING
OUTRUNS
OUTRUSH
OUTRUSHED
OUTRUSHES
OUTRUSHING
OUTS
OUTSAIL
OUTSAILED
OUTSAILING
OUTSAILS
OUTSAT
OUTSCOLD
OUTSCOLDED
OUTSCOLDING
OUTSCOLDS
OUTSCORN
OUTSCORNED
OUTSCORNING
OUTSCORNS
OUTSELL
OUTSELLING
OUTSELLS
OUTSET
OUTSETS
OUTSHINE
OUTSHINES
OUTSHINING
OUTSHONE
OUTSHOOT
OUTSHOOTING
OUTSHOOTS
OUTSHOT
OUTSHOTS
OUTSIDE
OUTSIDER
OUTSIDERS
OUTSIDES
OUTSIGHT
OUTSIGHTS
OUTSIT
OUTSITS
OUTSITTING
OUTSIZE
OUTSIZED
OUTSIZES
OUTSKIRT
OUTSKIRTS
OUTSLEEP
OUTSLEEPING
OUTSLEEPS
OUTSLEPT
OUTSMART
OUTSMARTED
OUTSMARTING
OUTSMARTS
OUTSOAR
OUTSOARED
OUTSOARING
OUTSOARS
OUTSOLD
OUTSOLE
OUTSOLES
OUTSPAN
OUTSPANNED
OUTSPANNING
OUTSPANS

OUTSPEAK
OUTSPEAKING
OUTSPEAKS
OUTSPEND
OUTSPENDING
OUTSPENDS
OUTSPENT
OUTSPOKE
OUTSPOKEN
OUTSPORT
OUTSPORTED
OUTSPORTING
OUTSPORTS
OUTSPREAD
OUTSPREADING
OUTSPREADS
OUTSPRING
OUTSPRINGING
OUTSPRINGS
OUTSPRUNG
OUTSTAND
OUTSTANDING
OUTSTANDS
OUTSTARE
OUTSTARED
OUTSTARES
OUTSTARING
OUTSTAY
OUTSTAYED
OUTSTAYING
OUTSTAYS
OUTSTEP
OUTSTEPPED
OUTSTEPPING
OUTSTEPS
OUTSTOOD
OUTSTRAIN
OUTSTRAINED
OUTSTRAINING
OUTSTRAINS
OUTSTRIKE
OUTSTRIKES
OUTSTRIKING
OUTSTRIP
OUTSTRIPPED
OUTSTRIPPING
OUTSTRIPS
OUTSTRUCK
OUTSUM
OUTSUMMED
OUTSUMMING
OUTSUMS
OUTSWEAR
OUTSWEARING
OUTSWEARS
OUTSWELL
OUTSWELLED
OUTSWELLING
OUTSWELLS
OUTSWING
OUTSWINGS
OUTSWOLLEN
OUTSWORE
OUTSWORN
OUTTAKE
OUTTAKEN
OUTTAKES
OUTTAKING
OUTTALK
OUTTALKED

OUTTALKING	OUTWEEPING	OVARIOLE	OVERBOUNDING	OVERCROPS
OUTTALKS	OUTWEEPS	OVARIOLES	OVERBOUNDS	OVERCROW
OUTTELL	OUTWEIGH	OVARIOUS	OVERBROW	OVERCROWD
OUTTELLING	OUTWEIGHED	OVARITIS	OVERBROWED	OVERCROWDED
OUTTELLS	OUTWEIGHING	OVARITISES	OVERBROWING	OVERCROWDING
OUTTHINK	OUTWEIGHS	OVARY	OVERBROWS	OVERCROWDS
OUTTHINKING	OUTWELL	OVATE	OVERBUILD	OVERCROWED
OUTTHINKS	OUTWELLED	OVATED	OVERBUILDING	OVERCROWING
OUTTHOUGHT	OUTWELLING	OVATES	OVERBUILDS	OVERCROWS
OUTTOLD	OUTWELLS	OVATING	OVERBUILT	OVERDATED
OUTTONGUE	OUTWENT	OVATION	OVERBULK	OVERDID
OUTTONGUED	OUTWEPT	OVATIONS	OVERBULKED	OVERDIGHT
OUTTONGUES	OUTWICK	OVATOR	OVERBULKING	OVERDO
OUTTONGUING	OUTWICKED	OVATORS	OVERBULKS	OVERDOER
OUTTOOK	OUTWICKING	OVEN	OVERBURN	OVERDOERS
OUTTOP	OUTWICKS	OVENS	OVERBURNED	OVERDOES
OUTTOPPED	OUTWIN	OVENWARE	OVERBURNING	OVERDOING
OUTTOPPING	OUTWIND	OVENWARES	OVERBURNS	OVERDONE
OUTTOPS	OUTWINDING	OVENWOOD	OVERBURNT	OVERDOSE
OUTTRAVEL	OUTWINDS	OVENWOODS	OVERBUSIED	OVERDOSED
OUTTRAVELLED	OUTWING	OVER	OVERBUSIES	OVERDOSES
OUTTRAVELLING	OUTWINGED	OVERACT	OVERBUSY	OVERDOSING
OUTTRAVELS	OUTWINGING	OVERACTED	OVERBUSYING	OVERDRAFT
OUTTURN	OUTWINGS	OVERACTING	OVERBUY	OVERDRAFTS
OUTTURNS	OUTWINNING	OVERACTS	OVERBUYING	OVERDRAW
OUTVALUE	OUTWINS	OVERALL	OVERBUYS	OVERDRAWING
OUTVALUED	OUTWIT	OVERALLED	OVERBY	OVERDRAWN
OUTVALUES	OUTWITH	OVERALLS	OVERCALL	OVERDRAWS
OUTVALUING	OUTWITS	OVERARCH	OVERCALLED	OVERDRESS
OUTVENOM	OUTWITTED	OVERARCHED	OVERCALLING	OVERDRESSED
OUTVENOMED	OUTWITTING	OVERARCHES	OVERCALLS	OVERDRESSES
OUTVENOMING	OUTWON	OVERARCHING	OVERCAME	OVERDRESSING
OUTVENOMS	OUTWORE	OVERARM	OVERCARRIED	OVERDREW
OUTVIE	OUTWORK	OVERATE	OVERCARRIES	OVERDRIVE
OUTVIED	OUTWORKED	OVERAWE	OVERCARRY	OVERDRIVEN
OUTVIES	OUTWORKER	OVERAWED	OVERCARRYING	OVERDRIVES
OUTVOICE	OUTWORKERS	OVERAWES	OVERCAST	OVERDRIVING
OUTVOICED	OUTWORKING	OVERAWING	OVERCASTING	OVERDROVE
OUTVOICES	OUTWORKS	OVERBEAR	OVERCASTS	OVERDUE
OUTVOICING	OUTWORN	OVERBEARING	OVERCATCH	OVERDUST
OUTVOTE	OUTWORTH	OVERBEARS	OVERCATCHES	OVERDUSTED
OUTVOTED	OUTWORTHED	OVERBEAT	OVERCATCHING	OVERDUSTING
OUTVOTER	OUTWORTHING	OVERBEATEN	OVERCAUGHT	OVERDUSTS
OUTVOTERS	OUTWORTHS	OVERBEATING	OVERCHECK	OVERDYE
OUTVOTES	OUTWOUND	OVERBEATS	OVERCHECKS	OVERDYED
OUTVOTING	OUTWREST	OVERBID	OVERCLAD	OVERDYEING
OUTVYING	OUTWRESTED	OVERBIDDING	OVERCLOUD	OVERDYES
OUTWALK	OUTWRESTING	OVERBIDS	OVERCLOUDED	OVEREAT
OUTWALKED	OUTWRESTS	OVERBITE	OVERCLOUDING	OVEREATEN
OUTWALKING	OUTWROUGHT	OVERBITES	OVERCLOUDS	OVEREATING
OUTWALKS	OUVERT	OVERBLEW	OVERCLOY	OVEREATS
OUTWARD	OUVERTE	OVERBLOW	OVERCLOYED	OVERED
OUTWARDLY	OUVRAGE	OVERBLOWING	OVERCLOYING	OVEREXERT
OUTWARDS	OUVRAGES	OVERBLOWN	OVERCLOYS	OVEREXERTED
OUTWATCH	OUVRIER	OVERBLOWS	OVERCOAT	OVEREXERTING
OUTWATCHED	OUVRIÈRE	OVERBOARD	OVERCOATS	OVEREXERTS
OUTWATCHES	OUVRIÈRES	OVERBOIL	OVERCOME	OVEREYE
OUTWATCHING	OUVRIERS	OVERBOILED	OVERCOMES	OVEREYED
OUTWEAR	OUZEL	OVERBOILING	OVERCOMING	OVEREYEING
OUTWEARIED	OUZELS	OVERBOILS	OVERCOUNT	OVEREYES
OUTWEARIES	OUZO	OVERBOLD	OVERCOUNTED	OVEREYING
OUTWEARING	OUZOS	OVERBOOK	OVERCOUNTING	OVERFALL
OUTWEARS	OVA	OVERBOOKED	OVERCOUNTS	OVERFALLEN
OUTWEARY	OVAL	OVERBOOKING	OVERCOVER	OVERFALLING
OUTWEARYING	OVALBUMIN	OVERBOOKS	OVERCOVERED	OVERFALLS
OUTWEED	OVALBUMINS	OVERBORE	OVERCOVERING	OVERFAR
OUTWEEDED	OVALLY	OVERBORNE	OVERCOVERS	OVERFED
OUTWEEDING	OVALS	OVERBOUGHT	OVERCROP	OVERFEED
OUTWEEDS	OVARIAN	OVERBOUND	OVERCROPPED	OVERFEEDING
OUTWEEP	OVARIES	OVERBOUNDED	OVERCROPPING	OVERFEEDS

OVERFELL
OVERFILL
OVERFILLED
OVERFILLING
OVERFILLS
OVERFINE
OVERFIRE
OVERFIRED
OVERFIRES
OVERFIRING
OVERFISH
OVERFISHED
OVERFISHES
OVERFISHING
OVERFLEW
OVERFLIES
OVERFLOW
OVERFLOWED
OVERFLOWING
OVERFLOWN
OVERFLOWS
OVERFLUSH
OVERFLUSHED
OVERFLUSHES
OVERFLUSHING
OVERFLY
OVERFLYING
OVERFOLD
OVERFOLDED
OVERFOLDING
OVERFOLDS
OVERFOND
OVERFREE
OVERFULL
OVERGALL
OVERGALLED
OVERGALLING
OVERGALLS
OVERGANG
OVERGANGED
OVERGANGING
OVERGANGS
OVERGAVE
OVERGET
OVERGETS
OVERGETTING
OVERGIVE
OVERGIVES
OVERGIVING
OVERGLAZE
OVERGLAZED
OVERGLAZES
OVERGLAZING
OVERGLOOM
OVERGLOOMED
OVERGLOOMING
OVERGLOOMS
OVERGO
OVERGOES
OVERGOING
OVERGOINGS
OVERGONE
OVERGORGE
OVERGORGED
OVERGORGES
OVERGORGING
OVERGOT
OVERGOTTEN
OVERGRAIN
OVERGRAINED

OVERGRAINING
OVERGRAINS
OVERGRASS
OVERGRASSED
OVERGRASSES
OVERGRASSING
OVERGRAZE
OVERGRAZED
OVERGRAZES
OVERGRAZING
OVERGREAT
OVERGREEN
OVERGREENED
OVERGREENING
OVERGREENS
OVERGREW
OVERGROW
OVERGROWING
OVERGROWN
OVERGROWS
OVERHAILE
OVERHAILED
OVERHAILES
OVERHAILING
OVERHAIR
OVERHAIRS
OVERHALE
OVERHALED
OVERHALES
OVERHALING
OVERHAND
OVERHANDED
OVERHANDING
OVERHANDS
OVERHANG
OVERHANGING
OVERHANGS
OVERHAPPY
OVERHASTE
OVERHASTES
OVERHASTY
OVERHAUL
OVERHAULED
OVERHAULING
OVERHAULS
OVERHEAD
OVERHEADS
OVERHEAR
OVERHEARD
OVERHEARING
OVERHEARS
OVERHEAT
OVERHEATED
OVERHEATING
OVERHEATS
OVERHELD
OVERHENT
OVERHENTED
OVERHENTING
OVERHENTS
OVERHIT
OVERHITS
OVERHITTING
OVERHOLD
OVERHOLDING
OVERHOLDS
OVERHUNG
OVERING
OVERINKED
OVERISSUE

OVERISSUED
OVERISSUES
OVERISSUING
OVERJOY
OVERJOYED
OVERJOYING
OVERJOYS
OVERJUMP
OVERJUMPED
OVERJUMPING
OVERJUMPS
OVERKEEP
OVERKEEPING
OVERKEEPS
OVERKEPT
OVERKEST
OVERKILL
OVERKILLS
OVERKIND
OVERKING
OVERKINGS
OVERKNEE
OVERLADE
OVERLADED
OVERLADEN
OVERLADES
OVERLADING
OVERLAID
OVERLAIN
OVERLAND
OVERLANDED
OVERLANDING
OVERLANDS
OVERLAP
OVERLAPPED
OVERLAPPING
OVERLAPS
OVERLARD
OVERLARDED
OVERLARDING
OVERLARDS
OVERLAY
OVERLAYING
OVERLAYS
OVERLEAF
OVERLEAP
OVERLEAPED
OVERLEAPING
OVERLEAPS
OVERLEAPT
OVERLEND
OVERLENDING
OVERLENDS
OVERLENT
OVERLIE
OVERLIER
OVERLIERS
OVERLIES
OVERLIVE
OVERLIVED
OVERLIVES
OVERLIVING
OVERLOAD
OVERLOADED
OVERLOADING
OVERLOADS
OVERLONG
OVERLOOK
OVERLOOKED
OVERLOOKING

OVERLOOKS
OVERLORD
OVERLORDED
OVERLORDING
OVERLORDS
OVERLUSTY
OVERLY
OVERLYING
OVERMAN
OVERMANNED
OVERMANNING
OVERMANS
OVERMAST
OVERMASTED
OVERMASTING
OVERMASTS
OVERMATCH
OVERMATCHED
OVERMATCHES
OVERMATCHING
OVERMEN
OVERMERRY
OVERMOUNT
OVERMOUNTED
OVERMOUNTING
OVERMOUNTS
OVERMUCH
OVERNAME
OVERNAMED
OVERNAMES
OVERNAMING
OVERNEAT
OVERNET
OVERNETS
OVERNETTED
OVERNETTING
OVERNICE
OVERNIGHT
OVERNIGHTS
OVERPAGE
OVERPAID
OVERPAINT
OVERPAINTED
OVERPAINTING
OVERPAINTS
OVERPART
OVERPARTED
OVERPARTING
OVERPARTS
OVERPASS
OVERPASSED
OVERPASSES
OVERPASSING
OVERPAST
OVERPAY
OVERPAYING
OVERPAYS
OVERPEDAL
OVERPEDALLED
OVERPEDALLING
OVERPEDALS
OVERPEER
OVERPEERED
OVERPEERING
OVERPEERS
OVERPERCH
OVERPERCHED
OVERPERCHES
OVERPERCHING
OVERPITCH

OVERPITCHED
OVERPITCHES
OVERPITCHING
OVERPLAST
OVERPLAY
OVERPLAYED
OVERPLAYING
OVERPLAYS
OVERPLIED
OVERPLIES
OVERPLUS
OVERPLUSES
OVERPLY
OVERPLYING
OVERPOISE
OVERPOISED
OVERPOISES
OVERPOISING
OVERPOST
OVERPOSTED
OVERPOSTING
OVERPOSTS
OVERPOWER
OVERPOWERED
OVERPOWERING
OVERPOWERS
OVERPRESS
OVERPRESSED
OVERPRESSES
OVERPRESSING
OVERPRINT
OVERPRINTED
OVERPRINTING
OVERPRINTS
OVERPRIZE
OVERPRIZED
OVERPRIZES
OVERPRIZING
OVERPROOF
OVERPROUD
OVERRACK
OVERRACKED
OVERRACKING
OVERRACKS
OVERRAKE
OVERRAKED
OVERRAKES
OVERRAKING
OVERRAN
OVERRANK
OVERRASH
OVERRATE
OVERRATED
OVERRATES
OVERRATING
OVERREACH
OVERREACHED
OVERREACHES
OVERREACHING
OVERREACT
OVERREACTED
OVERREACTING
OVERREACTS
OVERREAD
OVERREADING
OVERREADS
OVERRED
OVERREDDED
OVERREDDING
OVERREDS

OVERREN OVERSHIRTS OVERSTAYS OVERTHROWING OVERWASHES
OVERRENNED OVERSHOE OVERSTEER OVERTHROWN OVERWATCH
OVERRENNING OVERSHOES OVERSTEERED OVERTHROWS OVERWATCHED
OVERRENS OVERSHONE OVERSTEERING OVERTIME OVERWATCHES
OVERRIDDEN OVERSHOOT OVERSTEERS OVERTIMED OVERWATCHING
OVERRIDE OVERSHOOTING OVERSTEP OVERTIMER OVERWEAR
OVERRIDER OVERSHOOTS OVERSTEPPED OVERTIMERS OVERWEARIED
OVERRIDERS OVERSHOT OVERSTEPPING OVERTIMES OVERWEARIES
OVERRIDES OVERSIDE OVERSTEPS OVERTIMING OVERWEARING
OVERRIDING OVERSIGHT OVERSTINK OVERTIRE OVERWEARS
OVERRIPE OVERSIGHTS OVERSTINKING OVERTIRED OVERWEARY
OVERRIPEN OVERSIZE OVERSTINKS OVERTIRES OVERWEARYING
OVERRIPENED OVERSIZED OVERSTOCK OVERTIRING OVERWEEN
OVERRIPENING OVERSIZES OVERSTOCKED OVERTLY OVERWEENED
OVERRIPENS OVERSIZING OVERSTOCKING OVERTOIL OVERWEENING
OVERROAST OVERSKIP OVERSTOCKS OVERTOILED OVERWEENS
OVERROASTED OVERSKIPPED OVERSTOOD OVERTOILING OVERWEIGH
OVERROASTING OVERSKIPPING OVERSTREW OVERTOILS OVERWEIGHED
OVERROASTS OVERSKIPS OVERSTREWING OVERTONE OVERWEIGHING
OVERRODE OVERSKIRT OVERSTREWN OVERTONES OVERWEIGHS
OVERRUFF OVERSKIRTS OVERSTREWS OVERTOOK OVERWENT
OVERRUFFED OVERSLEEP OVERSTUDIED OVERTOP OVERWHELM
OVERRUFFING OVERSLEEPING OVERSTUDIES OVERTOPPED OVERWHELMED
OVERRUFFS OVERSLEEPS OVERSTUDY OVERTOPPING OVERWHELMING
OVERRULE OVERSLEPT OVERSTUDYING OVERTOPS OVERWHELMS
OVERRULED OVERSLIP OVERSTUFF OVERTOWER OVERWIND
OVERRULER OVERSLIPPED OVERSTUFFED OVERTOWERED OVERWINDING
OVERRULERS OVERSLIPPING OVERSTUFFING OVERTOWERING OVERWINDS
OVERRULES OVERSLIPS OVERSTUFFS OVERTOWERS OVERWING
OVERRULING OVERSMAN OVERSTUNK OVERTRAIN OVERWINGED
OVERRUN OVERSMEN OVERSWAM OVERTRAINED OVERWINGING
OVERRUNNING OVERSOLD OVERSWAY OVERTRAINING OVERWINGS
OVERRUNS OVERSOUL OVERSWAYED OVERTRAINS OVERWISE
OVERS OVERSOULS OVERSWAYING OVERTRICK OVERWORD
OVERSAIL OVERSOW OVERSWAYS OVERTRICKS OVERWORDS
OVERSAILED OVERSOWED OVERSWEAR OVERTRIP OVERWORE
OVERSAILING OVERSOWING OVERSWEARING OVERTRIPPED OVERWORK
OVERSAILS OVERSOWN OVERSWEARS OVERTRIPPING OVERWORKED
OVERSAW OVERSOWS OVERSWELL OVERTRIPS OVERWORKING
OVERSCORE OVERSPEND OVERSWELLED OVERTRUMP OVERWORKS
OVERSCORED OVERSPENDING OVERSWELLING OVERTRUMPED OVERWORN
OVERSCORES OVERSPENDS OVERSWELLS OVERTRUMPING OVERWOUND
OVERSCORING OVERSPENT OVERSWIM OVERTRUMPS OVERWREST
OVERSEA OVERSPILL OVERSWIMMING OVERTRUST OVERWRESTED
OVERSEAS OVERSPILLS OVERSWIMS OVERTRUSTED OVERWRESTING
OVERSEE OVERSPIN OVERSWORE OVERTRUSTING OVERWRESTS
OVERSEEING OVERSPINS OVERSWORN OVERTRUSTS OVERWRITE
OVERSEEN OVERSTAFF OVERSWUM OVERTURE OVERWRITES
OVERSEER OVERSTAFFED OVERT OVERTURED OVERWRITING
OVERSEERS OVERSTAFFING OVERTAKE OVERTURES OVERWRITTEN
OVERSEES OVERSTAFFS OVERTAKEN OVERTURING OVERWROUGHT
OVERSELL OVERSTAIN OVERTAKES OVERTURN OVERYEAR
OVERSELLING OVERSTAINED OVERTAKING OVERTURNED OVERYEARED
OVERSELLS OVERSTAINING OVERTALK OVERTURNING OVERYEARING
OVERSET OVERSTAINS OVERTALKED OVERTURNS OVERYEARS
OVERSETS OVERSTAND OVERTALKING OVERUSE OVIBOS
OVERSETTING OVERSTANDING OVERTALKS OVERUSED OVIBOSES
OVERSEW OVERSTANDS OVERTASK OVERUSES OVIBOVINE
OVERSEWING OVERSTANK OVERTASKED OVERUSING OVICIDE
OVERSEWN OVERSTARE OVERTASKING OVERVALUE OVICIDES
OVERSEWS OVERSTARED OVERTASKS OVERVALUED OVIDUCAL
OVERSEXED OVERSTARES OVERTAX OVERVALUES OVIDUCT
OVERSHADE OVERSTARING OVERTAXED OVERVALUING OVIDUCTAL
OVERSHADED OVERSTATE OVERTAXES OVERVEIL OVIDUCTS
OVERSHADES OVERSTATED OVERTAXING OVERVEILED OVIFEROUS
OVERSHADING OVERSTATES OVERTEEM OVERVEILING OVIFORM
OVERSHINE OVERSTATING OVERTEEMED OVERVEILS OVIGEROUS
OVERSHINES OVERSTAY OVERTEEMING OVERVIEW OVINE
OVERSHINING OVERSTAYED OVERTEEMS OVERVIEWS OVIPARITIES
OVERSHIRT OVERSTAYING OVERTHROW OVERWASH OVIPARITY

OVIPAROUS
OVIPOSIT
OVIPOSITED
OVIPOSITING
OVIPOSITS
OVISAC
OVISACS
OVIST
OVISTS
OVOID
OVOIDAL
OVOIDS
OVOLI
OVOLO
OVOTESTES
OVOTESTIS
OVULAR
OVULATE
OVULATED
OVULATES
OVULATING
OVULATION
OVULATIONS
OVULE
OVULES
OVUM
OW
OWCHE
OWCHES
OWE
OWED
OWELTIES
OWELTY
OWER
OWERBY
OWERING
OWERLOUP
OWERLOUPED
OWERLOUPING
OWERLOUPS

OWERS
OWES
OWING
OWL
OWLED
OWLER
OWLERIES
OWLERS
OWLERY
OWLET
OWLETS
OWLING
OWLISH
OWLS
OWLY
OWN
OWNED
OWNER
OWNERLESS
OWNERS
OWNERSHIP
OWNERSHIPS
OWNING
OWNS
OWRE
OWRECOME
OWRECOMES
OWRED
OWRES
OWREWORD
OWREWORDS
OWRIE
OWRING
OWSEN
OWT
OWTS
OX
OXALATE
OXALATES
OXALIC

OXALIS
OXALISES
OXAZINE
OXAZINES
OXBLOOD
OXBLOODS
OXEN
OXER
OXERS
OXGANG
OXGANGS
OXGATE
OXGATES
OXHEAD
OXHEADS
OXIDANT
OXIDANTS
OXIDASE
OXIDASES
OXIDATE
OXIDATED
OXIDATES
OXIDATING
OXIDATION
OXIDATIONS
OXIDE
OXIDES
OXIDISE
OXIDISED
OXIDISER
OXIDISERS
OXIDISES
OXIDISING
OXIDIZE
OXIDIZED
OXIDIZER
OXIDIZERS
OXIDIZES
OXIDIZING
OXIME

OXIMES
OXIMETER
OXIMETERS
OXLAND
OXLANDS
OXLIP
OXLIPS
OXONIUM
OXONIUMS
OXSLIP
OXSLIPS
OXTAIL
OXTAILS
OXTER
OXTERED
OXTERING
OXTERS
OXYGEN
OXYGENATE
OXYGENATED
OXYGENATES
OXYGENATING
OXYGENISE
OXYGENISED
OXYGENISES
OXYGENISING
OXYGENIZE
OXYGENIZED
OXYGENIZES
OXYGENIZING
OXYGENOUS
OXYGENS
OXYMEL
OXYMELS
OXYMORON
OXYMORONS
OXYTOCIC
OXYTOCICS
OXYTOCIN
OXYTOCINS

OXYTONE
OXYTONES
OY
OYE
OYER
OYERS
OYES
OYESES
OYEZ
OYEZES
OYS
OYSTER
OYSTERS
OYSTRIGE
OYSTRIGES
OZAENA
OZAENAS
OZEKI
OZEKIS
OZOCERITE
OZOCERITES
OZOKERITE
OZOKERITES
OZONATION
OZONATIONS
OZONE
OZONES
OZONISE
OZONISED
OZONISER
OZONISERS
OZONISES
OZONISING
OZONIZE
OZONIZED
OZONIZER
OZONIZERS
OZONIZES
OZONIZING

P

PA
PABOUCHE
PABOUCHES
PABULAR
PABULOUS
PABULUM
PABULUMS
PACA
PACABLE
PACAS
PACATION
PACATIONS
PACE
PACED
PACEMAKER
PACEMAKERS
PACER
PACERS
PACES
PACEY
PACHA
PACHAK
PACHAKS
PACHALIC
PACHALICS
PACHAS
PACHINKO
PACHINKOS
PACHISI
PACHISIS
PACHYDERM
PACHYDERMS
PACIER
PACIEST
PACIFIC
PACIFICAL
PACIFIED
PACIFIER
PACIFIERS
PACIFIES
PACIFISM
PACIFISMS
PACIFIST
PACIFISTS
PACIFY
PACIFYING
PACING
PACK
PACKAGE
PACKAGED
PACKAGER
PACKAGERS
PACKAGES
PACKAGING
PACKAGINGS
PACKED
PACKER
PACKERS
PACKET
PACKETED
PACKETING
PACKETS
PACKFONG
PACKFONGS

PACKING
PACKINGS
PACKMAN
PACKMEN
PACKS
PACKSHEET
PACKSHEETS
PACKSTAFF
PACKSTAFFS
PACKWAY
PACKWAYS
PACO
PACOS
PACT
PACTA
PACTION
PACTIONAL
PACTIONED
PACTIONING
PACTIONS
PACTS
PACTUM
PACY
PAD
PADANG
PADANGS
PADAUK
PADAUKS
PADDED
PADDER
PADDERS
PADDIES
PADDING
PADDINGS
PADDLE
PADDLED
PADDLER
PADDLERS
PADDLES
PADDLING
PADDLINGS
PADDOCK
PADDOCKS
PADDY
PADELLA
PADELLAS
PADEMELON
PADEMELONS
PADERERO
PADEREROES
PADEREROS
PADISHAH
PADISHAHS
PADLE
PADLES
PADLOCK
PADLOCKED
PADLOCKING
PADLOCKS
PADMA
PADMAS
PADOUK
PADOUKS
PADRE

PADRES
PADRONE
PADRONI
PADS
PADUASOY
PADUASOYS
PADYMELON
PADYMELONS
PAEAN
PAEANS
PAEDERAST
PAEDERASTS
PAEDEUTIC
PAEDEUTICS
PAEDIATRIES
PAEDIATRY
PAEDOLOGIES
PAEDOLOGY
PAELLA
PAELLAS
PAENULA
PAENULAE
PAENULAS
PAEON
PAEONIC
PAEONICS
PAEONIES
PAEONS
PAEONY
PAGAN
PAGANISE
PAGANISED
PAGANISES
PAGANISH
PAGANISING
PAGANISM
PAGANISMS
PAGANIZE
PAGANIZED
PAGANIZES
PAGANIZING
PAGANS
PAGE
PAGEANT
PAGEANTRIES
PAGEANTRY
PAGEANTS
PAGED
PAGEHOOD
PAGEHOODS
PAGER
PAGERS
PAGES
PAGINAL
PAGINATE
PAGINATED
PAGINATES
PAGINATING
PAGING
PAGINGS
PAGLE
PAGLES
PAGOD
PAGODA

PAGODAS
PAGODS
PAGRI
PAGRIS
PAGURIAN
PAGURIANS
PAGURID
PAGURIDS
PAH
PAHOEHOE
PAHOEHOES
PAHS
PAID
PAIDEUTIC
PAIDEUTICS
PAIDLE
PAIDLES
PAIGLE
PAIGLES
PAIK
PAIKED
PAIKING
PAIKS
PAIL
PAILFUL
PAILFULS
PAILLASSE
PAILLASSES
PAILLETTE
PAILLETTES
PAILLON
PAILLONS
PAILS
PAIN
PAINED
PAINFUL
PAINFULLER
PAINFULLEST
PAINFULLY
PAINIM
PAINIMS
PAINING
PAINLESS
PAINS
PAINT
PAINTABLE
PAINTED
PAINTER
PAINTERLY
PAINTERS
PAINTIER
PAINTIEST
PAINTING
PAINTINGS
PAINTRESS
PAINTRESSES
PAINTS
PAINTURE
PAINTURES
PAINTY
PAIOCK
PAIOCKE
PAIOCKES
PAIOCKS

PAIR
PAIRE
PAIRED
PAIRIAL
PAIRIALS
PAIRING
PAIRINGS
PAIRS
PAIRWISE
PAIS
PAISA
PAISANO
PAISANOS
PAISAS
PAISE
PAISES
PAISLEY
PAISLEYS
PAITRICK
PAITRICKS
PAJAMAS
PAJOCK
PAJOCKE
PAJOCKES
PAJOCKS
PAKAPOO
PAKAPOOS
PAKEHA
PAKEHAS
PAKFONG
PAKFONGS
PAKKA
PAKORA
PAKORAS
PAKTONG
PAKTONGS
PAL
PALABRA
PALABRAS
PALACE
PALACES
PALADIN
PALADINS
PALAESTRA
PALAESTRAE
PALAESTRAS
PALAFITTE
PALAFITTES
PALAMA
PALAMAE
PALAMATE
PALAMINO
PALAMINOS
PALAMPORE
PALAMPORES
PALANKEEN
PALANKEENS
PALANQUIN
PALANQUINS
PALAS
PALASES
PALATABLE
PALATABLY
PALATAL

PALATALS
PALATE
PALATED
PALATES
PALATIAL
PALATINE
PALATINES
PALATING
PALAVER
PALAVERED
PALAVERER
PALAVERERS
PALAVERING
PALAVERS
PALAY
PALAYS
PALAZZI
PALAZZO
PALE
PALEA
PALEAE
PALEBUCK
PALEBUCKS
PALED
PALEFACE
PALEFACES
PALELY
PALEMPORE
PALEMPORES
PALENESS
PALENESSES
PALER
PALES
PALEST
PALESTRA
PALESTRAE
PALESTRAS
PALET
PALETOT
PALETOTS
PALETS
PALETTE
PALETTES
PALEWISE
PALFREY
PALFREYED
PALFREYS
PALIER
PALIEST
PALIFORM
PALILALIA
PALILALIAS
PALILLOGIES
PALILLOGY
PALIMONIES
PALIMONY
PALING
PALINGS
PALINODE
PALINODES
PALINODIES
PALINODY
PALISADE
PALISADED
PALISADES
PALISADING
PALISADO
PALISADOES
PALISH
PALKEE

PALKEES
PALKI
PALKIS
PALL
PALLA
PALLADIC
PALLADIUM
PALLADIUMS
PALLADOUS
PALLAE
PALLAH
PALLAHS
PALLED
PALLET
PALLETED
PALLETISE
PALLETISED
PALLETISES
PALLETISING
PALLETIZE
PALLETIZED
PALLETIZES
PALLETIZING
PALLETS
PALLIA
PALLIAL
PALLIARD
PALLIARDS
PALLIASSE
PALLIASSES
PALLIATE
PALLIATED
PALLIATES
PALLIATING
PALLID
PALLIDER
PALLIDEST
PALLIDITIES
PALLIDITY
PALLIDLY
PALLIER
PALLIEST
PALLING
PALLIUM
PALLONE
PALLONES
PALLOR
PALLORS
PALLS
PALLY
PALM
PALMAR
PALMARIAN
PALMARY
PALMATE
PALMATED
PALMATELY
PALMATION
PALMATIONS
PALMED
PALMER
PALMERS
PALMETTE
PALMETTES
PALMETTO
PALMETTOES
PALMETTOS
PALMFUL
PALMFULS
PALMHOUSE

PALMHOUSES
PALMIER
PALMIES
PALMIEST
PALMIET
PALMIETS
PALMING
PALMIPED
PALMIPEDE
PALMIPEDES
PALMIPEDS
PALMIST
PALMISTRIES
PALMISTRY
PALMISTS
PALMITATE
PALMITATES
PALMITIN
PALMITINS
PALMS
PALMY
PALMYRA
PALMYRAS
PALOLO
PALOLOS
PALOMINO
PALOMINOS
PALOOKA
PALOOKAS
PALP
PALPABLE
PALPABLY
PALPAL
PALPATE
PALPATED
PALPATES
PALPATING
PALPATION
PALPATIONS
PALPEBRAL
PALPED
PALPI
PALPING
PALPITANT
PALPITATE
PALPITATED
PALPITATES
PALPITATING
PALPS
PALPUS
PALS
PALSGRAVE
PALSGRAVES
PALSIED
PALSIER
PALSIES
PALSIEST
PALSTAFF
PALSTAFFS
PALSTAVE
PALSTAVES
PALSY
PALSYING
PALTER
PALTERED
PALTERER
PALTERERS
PALTERING
PALTERS
PALTRIER

PALTRIEST
PALTRILY
PALTRY
PALUDAL
PALUDIC
PALUDINAL
PALUDINE
PALUDISM
PALUDISMS
PALUDOSE
PALUDOUS
PALUSTRAL
PALY
PAM
PAMPA
PAMPAS
PAMPEAN
PAMPER
PAMPERED
PAMPERER
PAMPERERS
PAMPERING
PAMPERO
PAMPEROS
PAMPERS
PAMPHLET
PAMPHLETS
PAMS
PAN
PANACEA
PANACEAN
PANACEAS
PANACHAEA
PANACHAEAS
PANACHE
PANACHES
PANADA
PANADAS
PANAMA
PANAMAS
PANARIES
PANARY
PANATELLA
PANATELLAS
PANAX
PANAXES
PANCAKE
PANCAKED
PANCAKES
PANCAKING
PANCE
PANCES
PANCHAX
PANCHAXES
PANCHAYAT
PANCHAYATS
PANCHEON
PANCHEONS
PANCHION
PANCHIONS
PANCOSMIC
PANCRATIC
PANCREAS
PANCREASES
PAND
PANDA
PANDAR
PANDARS
PANDAS
PANDATION

PANDATIONS
PANDECT
PANDECTS
PANDEMIA
PANDEMIAN
PANDEMIAS
PANDEMIC
PANDEMICS
PANDER
PANDERED
PANDERESS
PANDERESSES
PANDERING
PANDERISM
PANDERISMS
PANDERLY
PANDEROUS
PANDERS
PANDIED
PANDIES
PANDIT
PANDITS
PANDOOR
PANDOORS
PANDORA
PANDORAS
PANDORE
PANDORES
PANDOUR
PANDOURS
PANDOWDIES
PANDOWDY
PANDS
PANDURA
PANDURAS
PANDURATE
PANDY
PANDYING
PANE
PANED
PANEGOISM
PANEGOISMS
PANEGYRIC
PANEGYRICS
PANEGYRIES
PANEGYRY
PANEITIES
PANEITY
PANEL
PANELLED
PANELLING
PANELLINGS
PANELLIST
PANELLISTS
PANELS
PANES
PANETTONE
PANETTONI
PANFUL
PANFULS
PANG
PANGA
PANGAMIC
PANGAMIES
PANGAMY
PANGAS
PANGED
PANGEN
PANGENE
PANGENES

PANGENS	PANORAMAS	PANZER	PAPISHERS	PARADISAL
PANGING	PANORAMIC	PANZERS	PAPISHES	PARADISE
PANGLESS	PANS	PAOLI	PAPISM	PARADISES
PANGOLIN	PANSEXUAL	PAOLO	PAPISMS	PARADISIC
PANGOLINS	PANSIED	PAP	PAPIST	PARADOS
PANGRAM	PANSIES	PAPA	PAPISTIC	PARADOSES
PANGRAMS	PANSOPHIC	PAPABLE	PAPISTRIES	PARADOX
PANGS	PANSOPHIES	PAPACIES	PAPISTRY	PARADOXAL
PANHANDLE	PANSOPHY	PAPACY	PAPISTS	PARADOXER
PANHANDLED	PANSPERMIES	PAPAIN	PAPOOSE	PARADOXERS
PANHANDLES	PANSPERMY	PAPAINS	PAPOOSES	PARADOXES
PANHANDLING	PANSY	PAPAL	PAPPADOM	PARADOXIES
PANIC	PANT	PAPALISE	PAPPADOMS	PARADOXY
PANICK	PANTABLE	PAPALISED	PAPPED	PARADROP
PANICKED	PANTABLES	PAPALISES	PAPPIER	PARADROPS
PANICKING	PANTAGAMIES	PAPALISING	PAPPIES	PARAFFIN
PANICKS	PANTAGAMY	PAPALISM	PAPPIEST	PARAFFINE
PANICKY	PANTALEON	PAPALISMS	PAPPING	PARAFFINED
PANICLE	PANTALEONS	PAPALIST	PAPPOOSE	PARAFFINES
PANICLED	PANTALETS	PAPALISTS	PAPPOOSES	PARAFFINING
PANICLES	PANTALON	PAPALIZE	PAPPOSE	PARAFFINS
PANICS	PANTALONS	PAPALIZED	PAPPOUS	PARAFFINY
PANIM	PANTALOON	PAPALIZES	PAPPUS	PARAFFLE
PANIMS	PANTALOONS	PAPALIZING	PAPPUSES	PARAFFLES
PANING	PANTED	PAPALLY	PAPPY	PARAFLE
PANISC	PANTER	PAPARAZZI	PAPRIKA	PARAFLES
PANISCS	PANTERS	PAPARAZZO	PAPRIKAS	PARAFOIL
PANISK	PANTHEISM	PAPAS	PAPS	PARAFOILS
PANISKS	PANTHEISMS	PAPAW	PAPULA	PARAGE
PANISLAM	PANTHEIST	PAPAWS	PAPULAE	PARAGES
PANISLAMS	PANTHEISTS	PAPAYA	PAPULAR	PARAGOGE
PANLOGISM	PANTHENOL	PAPAYAS	PAPULE	PARAGOGES
PANLOGISMS	PANTHENOLS	PAPE	PAPULES	PARAGOGIC
PANMICTIC	PANTHER	PAPER	PAPULOSE	PARAGOGUE
PANMIXIA	PANTHERS	PAPERBACK	PAPULOUS	PARAGOGUES
PANMIXIAS	PANTIES	PAPERBACKED	PAPYRI	PARAGON
PANMIXIS	PANTIHOSE	PAPERBACKING	PAPYRUS	PARAGONED
PANMIXISES	PANTILE	PAPERBACKS	PAR	PARAGONING
PANNAGE	PANTILED	PAPERED	PARA	PARAGONS
PANNAGES	PANTILES	PAPERER	PARABASES	PARAGRAM
PANNE	PANTILING	PAPERERS	PARABASIS	PARAGRAMS
PANNED	PANTILINGS	PAPERING	PARABEMA	PARAGRAPH
PANNELLED	PANTINE	PAPERINGS	PARABEMATA	PARAGRAPHED
PANNES	PANTINES	PAPERLESS	PARABLE	PARAGRAPHING
PANNICK	PANTING	PAPERS	PARABLED	PARAGRAPHS
PANNICKS	PANTINGLY	PAPERWARE	PARABLES	PARAKEET
PANNICLE	PANTINGS	PAPERWARES	PARABLING	PARAKEETS
PANNICLES	PANTLER	PAPERY	PARABOLA	PARALALIA
PANNIER	PANTLERS	PAPES	PARABOLAS	PARALALIAS
PANNIERED	PANTO	PAPETERIE	PARABOLE	PARALEGAL
PANNIERS	PANTOFFLE	PAPETERIES	PARABOLES	PARALEGALS
PANNIKEL	PANTOFFLES	PAPILIO	PARABOLIC	PARALEXIA
PANNIKELL	PANTOFLE	PAPILIOS	PARABRAKE	PARALEXIAS
PANNIKELLS	PANTOFLES	PAPILLA	PARABRAKES	PARALLAX
PANNIKELS	PANTOMIME	PAPILLAE	PARACHUTE	PARALLAXES
PANNIKIN	PANTOMIMES	PAPILLAR	PARACHUTED	PARALLEL
PANNIKINS	PANTON	PAPILLARY	PARACHUTES	PARALLELED
PANNING	PANTONS	PAPILLATE	PARACHUTING	PARALLELING
PANNINGS	PANTOS	PAPILLOMA	PARACLETE	PARALLELS
PANNOSE	PANTOUFLE	PAPILLOMAS	PARACLETES	PARALOGIA
PANNUS	PANTOUFLES	PAPILLON	PARACME	PARALOGIAS
PANNUSES	PANTOUM	PAPILLONS	PARACMES	PARALOGIES
PANOCHA	PANTOUMS	PAPILLOSE	PARACUSES	PARALOGY
PANOCHAS	PANTRIES	PAPILLOTE	PARACUSIS	PARALYSE
PANOISTIC	PANTRY	PAPILLOTES	PARADE	PARALYSED
PANOPLIED	PANTRYMAN	PAPILLOUS	PARADED	PARALYSER
PANOPLIES	PANTRYMEN	PAPILLULE	PARADES	PARALYSERS
PANOPLY	PANTS	PAPILLULES	PARADIGM	PARALYSES
PANOPTIC	PANTUN	PAPISH	PARADIGMS	PARALYSING
PANORAMA	PANTUNS	PAPISHER	PARADING	PARALYSIS

PARALYTIC
PARALYTICS
PARALYZE
PARALYZED
PARALYZER
PARALYZERS
PARALYZES
PARALYZING
PARAMATTA
PARAMATTAS
PARAMECIA
PARAMEDIC
PARAMEDICS
PARAMENT
PARAMENTS
PARAMESE
PARAMESES
PARAMETER
PARAMETERS
PARAMO
PARAMORPH
PARAMORPHS
PARAMOS
PARAMOUNT
PARAMOUNTS
PARAMOUR
PARAMOURS
PARANETE
PARANETES
PARANG
PARANGS
PARANOEA
PARANOEAS
PARANOEIC
PARANOEICS
PARANOIA
PARANOIAC
PARANOIACS
PARANOIAS
PARANOIC
PARANOICS
PARANOID
PARANYM
PARANYMPH
PARANYMPHS
PARANYMS
PARAPET
PARAPETED
PARAPETS
PARAPH
PARAPHED
PARAPHING
PARAPHS
PARAPODIA
PARAQUAT
PARAQUATS
PARAQUITO
PARAQUITOS
PARARHYME
PARARHYMES
PARAS
PARASANG
PARASANGS
PARASCEVE
PARASCEVES
PARASITE
PARASITES
PARASITIC
PARASOL
PARASOLS

PARATAXES
PARATAXIS
PARATHA
PARATHAS
PARATONIC
PARAVAIL
PARAVANE
PARAVANES
PARAVANT
PARAVAUNT
PARAZOA
PARAZOAN
PARAZOANS
PARAZOON
PARBOIL
PARBOILED
PARBOILING
PARBOILS
PARBREAK
PARBREAKED
PARBREAKING
PARBREAKS
PARBUCKLE
PARBUCKLED
PARBUCKLES
PARBUCKLING
PARCEL
PARCELLED
PARCELLING
PARCELS
PARCENARIES
PARCENARY
PARCENER
PARCENERS
PARCH
PARCHED
PARCHEDLY
PARCHES
PARCHESI
PARCHESIS
PARCHING
PARCHMENT
PARCHMENTS
PARCIMONIES
PARCIMONY
PARCLOSE
PARCLOSES
PARD
PARDAL
PARDALE
PARDALES
PARDALIS
PARDALISES
PARDALS
PARDED
PARDI
PARDIE
PARDINE
PARDNER
PARDNERS
PARDON
PARDONED
PARDONER
PARDONERS
PARDONING
PARDONINGS
PARDONS
PARDS
PARDY
PARE

PARECIOUS
PARED
PAREGORIC
PAREGORICS
PAREIRA
PAREIRAS
PARELLA
PARELLAS
PARELLE
PARELLES
PARENESES
PARENESIS
PARENT
PARENTAGE
PARENTAGES
PARENTAL
PARENTED
PARENTING
PARENTS
PARER
PARERGA
PARERGON
PARERS
PARES
PARESES
PARESIS
PARETIC
PAREU
PAREUS
PARFAIT
PARFAITS
PARFLECHE
PARFLECHES
PARGANA
PARGANAS
PARGASITE
PARGASITES
PARGE
PARGED
PARGES
PARGET
PARGETED
PARGETER
PARGETERS
PARGETING
PARGETINGS
PARGETS
PARGING
PARHELIA
PARHELIC
PARHELION
PARHYPATE
PARHYPATES
PARIAH
PARIAHS
PARIAL
PARIALS
PARIETAL
PARIETALS
PARING
PARINGS
PARISCHAN
PARISCHANS
PARISH
PARISHEN
PARISHENS
PARISHES
PARISON
PARISONS
PARITIES

PARITOR
PARITORS
PARITY
PARK
PARKA
PARKAS
PARKED
PARKEE
PARKEES
PARKER
PARKERS
PARK!
PARKIER
PARKIEST
PARKIN
PARKING
PARKINGS
PARKINS
PARKIS
PARKISH
PARKLAND
PARKLANDS
PARKLIKE
PARKLY
PARKS
PARKWARD
PARKWARDS
PARKWAY
PARKWAYS
PARKY
PARLAID
PARLANCE
PARLANCES
PARLANDO
PARLAY
PARLAYING
PARLAYS
PARLE
PARLED
PARLES
PARLEY
PARLEYED
PARLEYING
PARLEYS
PARLEYVOO
PARLEYVOOED
PARLEYVOOING
PARLEYVOOS
PARLIES
PARLING
PARLOUR
PARLOURS
PARLOUS
PARLY
PAROCHIAL
PAROCHIN
PAROCHINE
PAROCHINES
PAROCHINS
PARODIC
PARODICAL
PAROD!ED
PARODIES
PARODIST
PARODISTS
PARODY
PARODYING
PAROEMIA
PAROEMIAC
PAROEMIACS

PAROEMIAL
PAROEMIAS
PAROICOUS
PAROL
PAROLE
PAROLED
PAROLEE
PAROLEES
PAROLES
PAROLING
PARONYM
PARONYMIES
PARONYMS
PARONYMY
PAROQUET
PAROQUETS
PAROTIC
PAROTID
PAROTIDS
PAROTIS
PAROTISES
PAROTITIS
PAROTITISES
PAROUSIA
PAROUSIAS
PAROXYSM
PAROXYSMS
PARPANE
PARPANES
PARPEN
PARPEND
PARPENDS
PARPENS
PARPENT
PARPENTS
PARPOINT
PARPOINTS
PARQUET
PARQUETED
PARQUETING
PARQUETRIES
PARQUETRY
PARQUETS
PARQUETTED
PARR
PARRAKEET
PARRAKEETS
PARRAL
PARRALS
PARREL
PARRELS
PARRHESIA
PARRHESIAS
PARRICIDE
PARRICIDES
PARRIED
PARRIES
PARRITCH
PARRITCHES
PARROCK
PARROCKED
PARROCKING
PARROCKS
PARROQUET
PARROQUETS
PARROT
PARROTED
PARROTER
PARROTERS
PARROTING

PATIENCES

PARROTRIES
PARROTRY
PARROTS
PARROTY
PARRS
PARRY
PARRYING
PARS
PARSE
PARSEC
PARSECS
PARSED
PARSER
PARSERS
PARSES
PARSIMONIES
PARSIMONY
PARSING
PARSINGS
PARSLEY
PARSLEYS
PARSNEP
PARSNEPS
PARSNIP
PARSNIPS
PARSON
PARSONAGE
PARSONAGES
PARSONIC
PARSONISH
PARSONS
PART
PARTAKE
PARTAKEN
PARTAKER
PARTAKERS
PARTAKES
PARTAKING
PARTAKINGS
PARTAN
PARTANS
PARTED
PARTER
PARTERRE
PARTERRES
PARTERS
PARTI
PARTIAL
PARTIALLY
PARTIALS
PARTIBLE
PARTICLE
PARTICLES
PARTIED
PARTIES
PARTIM
PARTING
PARTINGS
PARTIS
PARTISAN
PARTISANS
PARTITA
PARTITAS
PARTITE
PARTITION
PARTITIONED
PARTITIONING
PARTITIONS
PARTITIVE
PARTITIVES

PARTITUR
PARTITURA
PARTITURAS
PARTITURS
PARTIZAN
PARTIZANS
PARTLET
PARTLETS
PARTLY
PARTNER
PARTNERED
PARTNERING
PARTNERS
PARTON
PARTONS
PARTOOK
PARTRIDGE
PARTRIDGES
PARTS
PARTURE
PARTURES
PARTWORK
PARTWORKS
PARTY
PARTYING
PARTYISM
PARTYISMS
PARULIS
PARULISES
PARURE
PARURES
PARVENU
PARVENUS
PARVIS
PARVISE
PARVISES
PAS
PASCAL
PASCALS
PASCHAL
PASCUAL
PASEAR
PASEARED
PASEARING
PASEARS
PASEO
PASEOS
PASH
PASHA
PASHALIK
PASHALIKS
PASHAS
PASHED
PASHES
PASHIM
PASHIMS
PASHING
PASHM
PASHMINA
PASHMINAS
PASHMS
PASPALUM
PASPALUMS
PASPIES
PASPY
PASQUILER
PASQUILERS
PASS
PASSABLE
PASSABLY

PASSADE
PASSADES
PASSADO
PASSADOES
PASSADOS
PASSAGE
PASSAGED
PASSAGES
PASSAGING
PASSAMENT
PASSAMENTED
PASSAMENTING
PASSAMENTS
PASSANT
PASSÉ
PASSED
PASSÉE
PASSEMENT
PASSEMENTED
PASSEMENTING
PASSEMENTS
PASSENGER
PASSENGERS
PASSEPIED
PASSEPIEDS
PASSER
PASSERINE
PASSERINES
PASSERS
PASSES
PASSIBLE
PASSIBLY
PASSIM
PASSING
PASSINGS
PASSION
PASSIONAL
PASSIONALS
PASSIONED
PASSIONING
PASSIONS
PASSIVE
PASSIVELY
PASSIVES
PASSIVISM
PASSIVISMS
PASSIVIST
PASSIVISTS
PASSIVITIES
PASSIVITY
PASSKEY
PASSKEYS
PASSLESS
PASSMAN
PASSMEN
PASSMENT
PASSMENTED
PASSMENTING
PASSMENTS
PASSOUT
PASSPORT
PASSPORTS
PASSUS
PASSUSES
PASSWORD
PASSWORDS
PAST
PASTA
PASTANCE
PASTANCES

PASTAS
PASTE
PASTED
PASTEL
PASTELS
PASTER
PASTERN
PASTERNS
PASTERS
PASTES
PASTICCI
PASTICCIO
PASTICHE
PASTICHES
PASTIER
PASTIES
PASTIEST
PASTIL
PASTILLE
PASTILLES
PASTILS
PASTIME
PASTIMES
PASTINESS
PASTINESSES
PASTING
PASTINGS
PASTIS
PASTISES
PASTOR
PASTORAL
PASTORALE
PASTORALES
PASTORALS
PASTORATE
PASTORATES
PASTORLY
PASTORS
PASTRAMI
PASTRAMIS
PASTRIES
PASTRY
PASTS
PASTURAGE
PASTURAGES
PASTURAL
PASTURE
PASTURED
PASTURES
PASTURING
PASTY
PAT
PATACA
PATACAS
PATAGIA
PATAGIAL
PATAGIUM
PATAMAR
PATAMARS
PATBALL
PATBALLS
PATCH
PATCHABLE
PATCHED
PATCHER
PATCHERIES
PATCHERS
PATCHERY
PATCHES
PATCHIER

PATCHIEST
PATCHILY
PATCHING
PATCHINGS
PATCHOCKE
PATCHOCKES
PATCHOULI
PATCHOULIES
PATCHOULIS
PATCHOULY
PATCHWORK
PATCHWORKS
PATCHY
PÂTÉ
PATE
PATED
PATELLA
PATELLAE
PATELLAR
PATELLAS
PATELLATE
PATEN
PATENCIES
PATENCY
PATENS
PATENT
PATENTED
PATENTEE
PATENTEES
PATENTING
PATENTLY
PATENTOR
PATENTORS
PATENTS
PATER
PATERA
PATERAE
PATERCOVE
PATERCOVES
PATERERO
PATEREROES
PATEREROS
PATERNAL
PATERNITIES
PATERNITY
PATERS
PATES
PÂTÉS
PATH
PATHED
PATHETIC
PATHETICS
PATHIC
PATHICS
PATHING
PATHLESS
PATHOGEN
PATHOGENIES
PATHOGENS
PATHOGENY
PATHOLOGIES
PATHOLOGY
PATHOS
PATHOSES
PATHS
PATHWAY
PATHWAYS
PATIBLE
PATIENCE
PATIENCES

PATIENT

PATIENT	PATRONIZED	PAUPERIZED	PAWKY	PEACHIER
PATIENTED	PATRONIZES	PAUPERIZES	PAWL	PEACHIEST
PATIENTING	PATRONIZING	PAUPERIZING	PAWLS	PEACHING
PATIENTLY	PATRONNE	PAUPERS	PAWN	PEACHY
PATIENTS	PATRONNES	PAUSAL	PAWNCE	PEACING
PATIN	PATRONS	PAUSE	PAWNCES	PEACOCK
PATINA	PATROON	PAUSED	PAWNED	PEACOCKED
PATINAS	PATROONS	PAUSEFUL	PAWNEE	PEACOCKING
PATINATED	PATS	PAUSELESS	PAWNEES	PEACOCKS
PATINE	PATSIES	PAUSER	PAWNER	PEACOCKY
PATINED	PATSY	PAUSERS	PAWNERS	PEACOD
PATINES	PATTE	PAUSES	PAWNING	PEACODS
PATINS	PATTÉ	PAUSING	PAWNS	PEAG
PATIO	PATTED	PAUSINGLY	PAWNSHOP	PEAGS
PATIOS	PATTÉE	PAUSINGS	PAWNSHOPS	PEAK
PATLY	PATTEN	PAVAGE	PAWPAW	PEAKED
PATNESS	PATTENED	PAVAGES	PAWPAWS	PEAKIER
PATNESSES	PATTENING	PAVAN	PAWS	PEAKIEST
PATOIS	PATTENS	PAVANE	PAX	PEAKING
PATONCE	PATTER	PAVANES	PAXES	PEAKS
PATRERO	PATTERED	PAVANS	PAXIUBA	PEAKY
PATREROES	PATTERER	PAVE	PAXIUBAS	PEAL
PATREROS	PATTERERS	PAVED	PAXWAX	PEALED
PATRIAL	PATTERING	PAVEMENT	PAXWAXES	PEALING
PATRIALS	PATTERN	PAVEMENTED	PAY	PEALS
PATRIARCH	PATTERNED	PAVEMENTING	PAYABLE	PEAN
PATRIARCHS	PATTERNING	PAVEMENTS	PAYED	PEANED
PATRIATE	PATTERNS	PAVEN	PAYEE	PEANING
PATRIATED	PATTERS	PAVENS	PAYEES	PEANS
PATRIATES	PATTES	PAVER	PAYER	PEANUT
PATRIATING	PATTIES	PAVERS	PAYERS	PEANUTS
PATRICIAN	PATTING	PAVES	PAYING	PEAR
PATRICIANS	PATTLE	PAVID	PAYINGS	PEARCE
PATRICIDE	PATTLES	PAVILION	PAYMASTER	PEARCED
PATRICIDES	PATTY	PAVILIONED	PAYMASTERS	PEARCES
PATRICK	PATULIN	PAVILIONING	PAYMENT	PEARCING
PATRICKS	PATULINS	PAVILIONS	PAYMENTS	PEARE
PATRICO	PATULOUS	PAVIN	PAYNIM	PEARES
PATRICOES	PATZER	PAVING	PAYNIMRIES	PEARL
PATRILINIES	PATZERS	PAVINGS	PAYNIMRY	PEARLED
PATRILINY	PAUA	PAVINS	PAYNIMS	PEARLER
PATRIMONIES	PAUAS	PAVIOR	PAYOLA	PEARLERS
PATRIMONY	PAUCITIES	PAVIORS	PAYOLAS	PEARLIER
PATRIOT	PAUCITY	PAVIOUR	PAYS	PEARLIES
PATRIOTIC	PAUGHTY	PAVIOURS	PAYSAGE	PEARLIEST
PATRIOTS	PAUL	PAVIS	PAYSAGES	PEARLIN
PATRISTIC	PAULDRON	PAVISE	PAYSAGIST	PEARLING
PATROL	PAULDRONS	PAVISES	PAYSAGISTS	PEARLINGS
PATROLLED	PAULOWNIA	PAVLOVA	PAYSD	PEARLINS
PATROLLER	PAULOWNIAS	PAVLOVAS	PAZAZZ	PEARLISED
PATROLLERS	PAULS	PAVONAZZO	PAZAZZES	PEARLITE
PATROLLING	PAUNCE	PAVONAZZOS	PEA	PEARLITES
PATROLMAN	PAUNCES	PAVONE	PEABERRIES	PEARLITIC
PATROLMEN	PAUNCH	PAVONES	PEABERRY	PEARLIZED
PATROLOGIES	PAUNCHED	PAVONIAN	PEACE	PEARLS
PATROLOGY	PAUNCHES	PAVONINE	PEACEABLE	PEARLY
PATROLS	PAUNCHIER	PAW	PEACEABLY	PEARMAIN
PATRON	PAUNCHIEST	PAWA	PEACED	PEARMAINS
PATRONAGE	PAUNCHING	PAWAS	PEACEFUL	PEARS
PATRONAGED	PAUNCHY	PAWAW	PEACELESS	PEARST
PATRONAGES	PAUPER	PAWAWS	PEACENIK	PEART
PATRONAGING	PAUPERESS	PAWED	PEACENIKS	PEARTLY
PATRONAL	PAUPERESSES	PAWING	PEACES	PEAS
PATRONESS	PAUPERISE	PAWK	PEACETIME	PEASANT
PATRONESSES	PAUPERISED	PAWKIER	PEACETIMES	PEASANTRIES
PATRONISE	PAUPERISES	PAWKIEST	PEACH	PEASANTRY
PATRONISED	PAUPERISING	PAWKILY	PEACHED	PEASANTS
PATRONISES	PAUPERISM	PAWKINESS	PEACHER	PEASANTY
PATRONISING	PAUPERISMS	PAWKINESSES	PEACHERS	PEASCOD
PATRONIZE	PAUPERIZE	PAWKS	PEACHES	PEASCODS

PEASE
PEASECOD
PEASECODS
PEASED
PEASES
PEASEWEEP
PEASEWEEPS
PEASING
PEASON
PEAT
PEATARIES
PEATARY
PEATERIES
PEATERY
PEATIER
PEATIEST
PEATMAN
PEATMEN
PEATS
PEATSHIP
PEATSHIPS
PEATY
PEAVEY
PEAVEYS
PEAVIES
PEAVY
PEAZE
PEAZED
PEAZES
PEAZING
PEBA
PEBAS
PEBBLE
PEBBLED
PEBBLES
PEBBLIER
PEBBLIEST
PEBBLING
PEBBLINGS
PEBBLY
PÉBRINE
PÉBRINES
PEC
PECAN
PECANS
PECCABLE
PECCANCIES
PECCANCY
PECCANT
PECCANTLY
PECCARIES
PECCARY
PECCAVI
PECCAVIS
PECH
PECHED
PECHING
PECHS
PECK
PECKE
PECKED
PECKER
PECKERS
PECKES
PECKING
PECKINGS
PECKISH
PECKS
PECS
PECTEN

PECTIC
PECTIN
PECTINAL
PECTINATE
PECTINATED
PECTINEAL
PECTINES
PECTINS
PECTISE
PECTISED
PECTISES
PECTISING
PECTIZE
PECTIZED
PECTIZES
PECTIZING
PECTOLITE
PECTOLITES
PECTORAL
PECTORALS
PECTOSE
PECTOSES
PECULATE
PECULATED
PECULATES
PECULATING
PECULATOR
PECULATORS
PECULIAR
PECULIARS
PECULIUM
PECULIUMS
PECUNIARY
PECUNIOUS
PED
PEDAGOGIC
PEDAGOGIES
PEDAGOGUE
PEDAGOGUED
PEDAGOGUES
PEDAGOGUING
PEDAGOGY
PEDAL
PEDALIER
PEDALIERS
PEDALLED
PEDALLER
PEDALLERS
PEDALLING
PEDALLINGS
PEDALO
PEDALOES
PEDALOS
PEDALS
PEDANT
PEDANTIC
PEDANTISE
PEDANTISED
PEDANTISES
PEDANTISING
PEDANTISM
PEDANTISMS
PEDANTIZE
PEDANTIZED
PEDANTIZES
PEDANTIZING
PEDANTRIES
PEDANTRY
PEDANTS
PEDATE

PEDATELY
PEDATIFID
PEDDER
PEDDERS
PEDDLE
PEDDLED
PEDDLER
PEDDLERS
PEDDLES
PEDDLING
PEDDLINGS
PEDERERO
PEDEREROES
PEDEREROS
PEDESES
PEDESIS
PEDESTAL
PEDESTALLED
PEDESTALLING
PEDESTALS
PEDETIC
PEDICAB
PEDICABS
PEDICEL
PEDICELS
PEDICLE
PEDICLED
PEDICLES
PEDICULAR
PEDICULUS
PEDICULUSES
PEDICURE
PEDICURED
PEDICURES
PEDICURING
PEDIGREE
PEDIGREED
PEDIGREES
PEDIMENT
PEDIMENTS
PEDIPALP
PEDIPALPS
PEDLAR
PEDLARIES
PEDLARS
PEDLARY
PEDOLOGIES
PEDOLOGY
PEDOMETER
PEDOMETERS
PEDRAIL
PEDRAILS
PEDRERO
PEDREROES
PEDREROS
PEDRO
PEDROS
PEDS
PEDUNCLE
PEDUNCLES
PEE
PEECE
PEECES
PEED
PEEING
PEEK
PEEKABO
PEEKABOO
PEEKABOOS
PEEKABOS

PEEKED
PEEKING
PEEKS
PEEL
PEELED
PEELER
PEELERS
PEELING
PEELINGS
PEELS
PEEN
PEENED
PEENGE
PEENGED
PEENGEING
PEENGES
PEENING
PEENS
PEEOY
PEEOYS
PEEP
PEEPE
PEEPED
PEEPER
PEEPERS
PEEPES
PEEPING
PEEPS
PEEPUL
PEEPULS
PEER
PEERAGE
PEERAGES
PEERED
PEERESS
PEERESSES
PEERIE
PEERIER
PEERIES
PEERIEST
PEERING
PEERLESS
PEERS
PEERY
PEES
PEESWEEP
PEESWEEPS
PEETWEET
PEETWEETS
PEEVE
PEEVED
PEEVER
PEEVERS
PEEVES
PEEVING
PEEVISH
PEEVISHLY
PEEWEE
PEEWEES
PEEWIT
PEEWITS
PEG
PEGASUS
PEGASUSES
PEGBOARD
PEGBOARDS
PEGGED
PEGGIES
PEGGING
PEGGINGS

PEGGY
PEGH
PEGHED
PEGHING
PEGHS
PEGMATITE
PEGMATITES
PEGS
PEIGNOIR
PEIGNOIRS
PEIN
PEINCT
PEINCTS
PEINED
PEINING
PEINS
PEIRASTIC
PEISE
PEISED
PEISES
PEISHWA
PEISHWAH
PEISHWAHS
PEISHWAS
PEISING
PEIZE
PEIZED
PEIZES
PEIZING
PEJORATE
PEJORATED
PEJORATES
PEJORATING
PEKAN
PEKANS
PEKE
PEKES
PEKOE
PEKOES
PELA
PELAGE
PELAGES
PELAGIAN
PELAGIC
PELAS
PELE
PELERINE
PELERINES
PELES
PELF
PELFS
PELHAM
PELHAMS
PELICAN
PELICANS
PELISSE
PELISSES
PELITE
PELITES
PELITIC
PELL
PELLACH
PELLACHS
PELLACK
PELLACKS
PELLAGRA
PELLAGRAS
PELLAGRIN
PELLAGRINS
PELLET

PELLETED
PELLETIFIED
PELLETIFIES
PELLETIFY
PELLETIFYING
PELLETING
PELLETISE
PELLETISED
PELLETISES
PELLETISING
PELLETIZE
PELLETIZED
PELLETIZES
PELLETIZING
PELLETS
PELLICLE
PELLICLES
PELLITORIES
PELLITORY
PELLOCK
PELLOCKS
PELLS
PELLUCID
PELMA
PELMANISM
PELMANISMS
PELMAS
PELMATIC
PELMET
PELMETS
PELOID
PELOIDS
PELOLOGIES
PELOLOGY
PELORIA
PELORIAS
PELORIC
PELORIES
PELORISED
PELORISM
PELORISMS
PELORIZED
PELORUS
PELORUSES
PELORY
PELOTA
PELOTAS
PELT
PELTA
PELTAE
PELTAS
PELTAST
PELTASTS
PELTATE
PELTED
PELTER
PELTERED
PELTERING
PELTERS
PELTING
PELTINGLY
PELTINGS
PELTRIES
PELTRY
PELTS
PELVES
PELVIC
PELVIFORM
PELVIS
PELVISES

PEMBROKE
PEMBROKES
PEMICAN
PEMICANS
PEMMICAN
PEMMICANS
PEMOLINE
PEMOLINES
PEMPHIGUS
PEMPHIGUSES
PEN
PENAL
PENALISE
PENALISED
PENALISES
PENALISING
PENALIZE
PENALIZED
PENALIZES
PENALIZING
PENALLY
PENALTIES
PENALTY
PENANCE
PENANCED
PENANCES
PENANCING
PENATES
PENCE
PENCEL
PENCELS
PENCES
PENCHANT
PENCHANTS
PENCIL
PENCILLED
PENCILLER
PENCILLERS
PENCILLING
PENCILS
PENCRAFT
PENCRAFTS
PEND
PENDANT
PENDANTS
PENDED
PENDENCIES
PENDENCY
PENDENT
PENDENTLY
PENDENTS
PENDICLE
PENDICLER
PENDICLERS
PENDICLES
PENDING
PENDRAGON
PENDRAGONS
PENDS
PENDULAR
PENDULATE
PENDULATED
PENDULATES
PENDULATING
PENDULINE
PENDULOUS
PENDULUM
PENDULUMS
PENE
PENED

PENEPLAIN
PENEPLAINS
PENEPLANE
PENEPLANES
PENES
PENETRANT
PENETRANTS
PENETRATE
PENETRATED
PENETRATES
PENETRATING
PENFOLD
PENFOLDS
PENFUL
PENFULS
PENGUIN
PENGUINRIES
PENGUINRY
PENGUINS
PENHOLDER
PENHOLDERS
PENI
PENIAL
PENIE
PENIES
PENILE
PENILLION
PENING
PENINSULA
PENINSULAS
PENIS
PENISES
PENISTONE
PENISTONES
PENITENCE
PENITENCES
PENITENCIES
PENITENCY
PENITENT
PENITENTS
PENK
PENKNIFE
PENKNIVES
PENKS
PENLIGHT
PENLIGHTS
PENMAN
PENMEN
PENNA
PENNAE
PENNAL
PENNALISM
PENNALISMS
PENNALS
PENNANT
PENNANTS
PENNATE
PENNATULA
PENNATULAE
PENNATULAS
PENNE
PENNED
PENNEECH
PENNEECHES
PENNEECK
PENNEECKS
PENNER
PENNERS
PENNES
PENNIED

PENNIES
PENNIFORM
PENNILESS
PENNILL
PENNILLION
PENNINE
PENNINES
PENNING
PENNINITE
PENNINITES
PENNON
PENNONCEL
PENNONCELS
PENNONED
PENNONS
PENNY
PENNYLAND
PENNYLANDS
PENOLOGIES
PENOLOGY
PENONCEL
PENONCELS
PENS
PENSÉE
PENSÉES
PENSEL
PENSELS
PENSIL
PENSILE
PENSILITIES
PENSILITY
PENSILS
PENSION
PENSIONED
PENSIONER
PENSIONERS
PENSIONING
PENSIONS
PENSIVE
PENSIVELY
PENSTEMON
PENSTEMONS
PENSTOCK
PENSTOCKS
PENSUM
PENSUMS
PENT
PENTACLE
PENTACLES
PENTACT
PENTACTS
PENTAD
PENTADIC
PENTADS
PENTAGON
PENTAGONS
PENTAGRAM
PENTAGRAMS
PENTALOGIES
PENTALOGY
PENTALPHA
PENTALPHAS
PENTAMERIES
PENTAMERY
PENTANE
PENTANES
PENTANGLE
PENTANGLES
PENTAPODIES
PENTAPODY

PENTARCH
PENTARCHIES
PENTARCHS
PENTARCHY
PENTEL™
PENTELS™
PENTENE
PENTENES
PENTHIA
PENTHIAS
PENTHOUSE
PENTHOUSED
PENTHOUSES
PENTHOUSING
PENTICE
PENTICED
PENTICES
PENTICING
PENTISE
PENTISED
PENTISES
PENTISING
PENTODE
PENTODES
PENTOMIC
PENTOSAN
PENTOSANE
PENTOSANES
PENTOSANS
PENTOSE
PENTOSES
PENTOXIDE
PENTOXIDES
PENTROOF
PENTROOFS
PENTS
PENTYLENE
PENTYLENES
PENUCHE
PENUCHES
PENUCHI
PENUCHIS
PENUCHLE
PENUCHLES
PENULT
PENULTIMA
PENULTIMAS
PENULTS
PENUMBRA
PENUMBRAL
PENUMBRAS
PENURIES
PENURIOUS
PENURY
PENWOMAN
PENWOMEN
PEON
PEONAGE
PEONAGES
PEONIES
PEONISM
PEONISMS
PEONS
PEONY
PEOPLE
PEOPLED
PEOPLES
PEOPLING
PEP
PEPERINO

PEPERINOS	PERAIS	PERENNATE	PERIAKTOI	PERINAEUMS
PEPEROMIA	PERCALE	PERENNATED	PERIAKTOS	PERINATAL
PEPEROMIAS	PERCALES	PERENNATES	PERIANTH	PERINEAL
PEPERONI	PERCALINE	PERENNATING	PERIANTHS	PERINEUM
PEPERONIS	PERCALINES	PERENNIAL	PERIAPT	PERINEUMS
PEPFUL	PERCASE	PERENNIALS	PERIAPTS	PERIOD
PEPLOS	PERCE	PERENNITIES	PERIBLAST	PERIODATE
PEPLOSES	PERCEABLE	PERENNITY	PERIBLASTS	PERIODATES
PEPLUM	PERCEANT	PÈRES	PERIBLEM	PERIODED
PEPLUMS	PERCEIVE	PERFAY	PERIBLEMS	PERIODIC
PEPLUS	PERCEIVED	PERFECT	PERIBOLI	PERIODING
PEPLUSES	PERCEIVER	PERFECTED	PERIBOLOI	PERIODS
PEPO	PERCEIVERS	PERFECTER	PERIBOLOS	PERIOST
PEPOS	PERCEIVES	PERFECTERS	PERIBOLUS	PERIOSTS
PEPPED	PERCEIVING	PERFECTEST	PERICARP	PERIOTIC
PEPPER	PERCEIVINGS	PERFECTI	PERICARPS	PERIOTICS
PEPPERED	PERCEN	PERFECTING	PERICLASE	PERIPATUS
PEPPERER	PERCENTAL	PERFECTLY	PERICLASES	PERIPATUSES
PEPPERERS	PERCEPT	PERFECTO	PERICLINE	PERIPETIA
PEPPERING	PERCEPTS	PERFECTOR	PERICLINES	PERIPETIAS
PEPPERINGS	PERCH	PERFECTORS	PERICON	PERIPETIES
PEPPERONI	PERCHANCE	PERFECTOS	PERICONES	PERIPETY
PEPPERONIS	PERCHED	PERFECTS	PERICOPE	PERIPHERIES
PEPPERS	PERCHER	PERFERVID	PERICOPES	PERIPHERY
PEPPERY	PERCHERON	PERFERVOR	PERICRANIES	PERIPLAST
PEPPIER	PERCHERONS	PERFERVORS	PERICRANY	PERIPLASTS
PEPPIEST	PERCHERS	PERFET	PERICYCLE	PERIPLUS
PEPPING	PERCHES	PERFIDIES	PERICYCLES	PERIPLUSES
PEPPY	PERCHING	PERFIDY	PERIDERM	PERIPROCT
PEPS	PERCHINGS	PERFORANS	PERIDERMS	PERIPROCTS
PEPSIN	PERCIFORM	PERFORANSES	PERIDIA	PERIPTERIES
PEPSINATE	PERCINE	PERFORANT	PERIDIAL	PERIPTERY
PEPSINATED	PERCOCT	PERFORATE	PERIDINIA	PERIQUE
PEPSINATES	PERCOID	PERFORATED	PERIDIUM	PERIQUES
PEPSINATING	PERCOLATE	PERFORATES	PERIDIUMS	PERIS
PEPSINE	PERCOLATED	PERFORATING	PERIDOT	PERISARC
PEPSINES	PERCOLATES	PERFORCE	PERIDOTE	PERISARCS
PEPSINS	PERCOLATING	PERFORM	PERIDOTES	PERISCIAN
PEPTIC	PERCOLIN	PERFORMED	PERIDOTIC	PERISCIANS
PEPTICITIES	PERCOLINS	PERFORMER	PERIDOTS	PERISCOPE
PEPTICITY	PERCUSS	PERFORMERS	PERIDROME	PERISCOPES
PEPTICS	PERCUSSED	PERFORMING	PERIDROMES	PERISH
PEPTIDE	PERCUSSES	PERFORMINGS	PERIGEAL	PERISHED
PEPTIDES	PERCUSSING	PERFORMS	PERIGEAN	PERISHER
PEPTISE	PERCUSSOR	PERFUME	PERIGEE	PERISHERS
PEPTISED	PERCUSSORS	PERFUMED	PERIGEES	PERISHES
PEPTISES	PERDENDO	PERFUMER	PERIGON	PERISHING
PEPTISING	PERDIE	PERFUMERIES	PERIGONE	PERISPERM
PEPTIZE	PERDITION	PERFUMERS	PERIGONES	PERISPERMS
PEPTIZED	PERDITIONS	PERFUMERY	PERIGONS	PERISTOME
PEPTIZES	PERDU	PERFUMES	PERIGYNIES	PERISTOMES
PEPTIZING	PERDUE	PERFUMING	PERIGYNY	PERISTYLE
PEPTONE	PERDUES	PERFUMY	PERIKARYA	PERISTYLES
PEPTONES	PERDURE	PERFUSATE	PERIL	PERITI
PEPTONISE	PERDURED	PERFUSATES	PERILLED	PERITRICH
PEPTONISED	PERDURES	PERFUSE	PERILLING	PERITRICHA
PEPTONISES	PERDURING	PERFUSED	PERILOUS	PERITUS
PEPTONISING	PERDUS	PERFUSES	PERILS	PERIWIG
PEPTONIZE	PERDY	PERFUSING	PERILUNE	PERIWIGGED
PEPTONIZED	PÈRE	PERFUSION	PERILUNES	PERIWIGGING
PEPTONIZES	PEREGAL	PERFUSIONS	PERILYMPH	PERIWIGS
PEPTONIZING	PEREGALS	PERFUSIVE	PERILYMPHS	PERJINK
PER	PEREGRINE	PERGOLA	PERIMETER	PERJINKER
PERACUTE	PEREGRINES	PERGOLAS	PERIMETERS	PERJINKEST
PERAEA	PEREIA	PERGUNNAH	PERIMETRIES	PERJURE
PERAEON	PEREION	PERGUNNAHS	PERIMETRY	PERJURED
PERAEONS	PEREIOPOD	PERHAPS	PERIMORPH	PERJURER
PERAEOPOD	PEREIOPODS	PERI	PERIMORPHS	PERJURERS
PERAEOPODS	PEREIRA	PERIAGUA	PERINAEAL	PERJURES
PERAI	PEREIRAS	PERIAGUAS	PERINAEUM	PERJURIES

PERJURING	PERPENDS	PERSONIZE	PERVASIVE	PETALISM
PERJUROUS	PERPENT	PERSONIZED	PERVERSE	PETALISMS
PERJURY	PERPENTS	PERSONIZES	PERVERSER	PETALLED
PERK	PERPETUAL	PERSONIZING	PERVERSEST	PETALODIES
PERKED	PERPETUALS	PERSONNEL	PERVERT	PETALODY
PERKIER	PERPLEX	PERSONNELS	PERVERTED	PETALOID
PERKIEST	PERPLEXED	PERSONS	PERVERTER	PETALOUS
PERKILY	PERPLEXES	PERSPIRE	PERVERTERS	PETALS
PERKIN	PERPLEXING	PERSPIRED	PERVERTING	PÉTANQUE
PERKINESS	PERRADIAL	PERSPIRES	PERVERTS	PÉTANQUES
PERKINESSES	PERRADII	PERSPIRING	PERVES	PETAR
PERKING	PERRADIUS	PERST	PERVIATE	PETARA
PERKINS	PERRIER	PERSUADE	PERVIATED	PETARAS
PERKS	PERRIERS	PERSUADED	PERVIATES	PETARD
PERKY	PERRIES	PERSUADER	PERVIATING	PETARDS
PERLITE	PERRON	PERSUADERS	PERVICACIES	PETARIES
PERLITES	PERRONS	PERSUADES	PERVICACY	PETARS
PERLITIC	PERRUQUE	PERSUADING	PERVIOUS	PETARY
PERLOUS	PERRUQUES	PERSUE	PERVS	PETASUS
PERM	PERRY	PERSUES	PESADE	PETASUSES
PERMALLOY	PERSANT	PERSWADE	PESADES	PETAURINE
PERMALLOYS	PERSAUNT	PERT	PESANT	PETAURIST
PERMANENT	PERSE	PERTAIN	PESANTE	PETAURISTS
PERMEABLE	PERSECUTE	PERTAINED	PESANTS	PETCHARIES
PERMEABLY	PERSECUTED	PERTAINING	PESAUNT	PETCHARY
PERMEANCE	PERSECUTES	PERTAINS	PESAUNTS	PETCOCK
PERMEANCES	PERSECUTING	PERTAKE	PESETA	PETCOCKS
PERMEASE	PERSED	PERTER	PESETAS	PETECHIA
PERMEASES	PERSEITIES	PERTEST	PESEWA	PETECHIAE
PERMEATE	PERSEITY	PERTHITE	PESEWAS	PETECHIAL
PERMEATED	PERSELINE	PERTHITES	PESHWA	PETER
PERMEATES	PERSELINES	PERTHITIC	PESHWAS	PETERED
PERMEATING	PERSES	PERTINENT	PESKIER	PETERING
PERMED	PERSEVERE	PERTINENTS	PESKIEST	PETERMAN
PERMING	PERSEVERED	PERTLY	PESKILY	PETERMEN
PERMIT	PERSEVERES	PERTNESS	PESKY	PETERS
PERMITS	PERSEVERING	PERTNESSES	PESO	PETERSHAM
PERMITTED	PERSICO	PERTS	PESOS	PETERSHAMS
PERMITTER	PERSICOS	PERTURB	PESSARIES	PETHER
PERMITTERS	PERSICOT	PERTURBED	PESSARY	PETHERS
PERMITTING	PERSICOTS	PERTURBER	PESSIMISM	PETHIDINE
PERMS	PERSIENNE	PERTURBERS	PESSIMISMS	PETHIDINES
PERMUTATE	PERSIENNES	PERTURBING	PESSIMIST	PÉTILLANT
PERMUTATED	PERSIMMON	PERTURBS	PESSIMISTS	PETIOLAR
PERMUTATES	PERSIMMONS	PERTUSATE	PEST	PETIOLATE
PERMUTATING	PERSING	PERTUSE	PESTER	PETIOLATED
PERMUTE	PERSIST	PERTUSED	PESTERED	PETIOLE
PERMUTED	PERSISTED	PERTUSION	PESTERER	PETIOLED
PERMUTES	PERSISTING	PERTUSIONS	PESTERERS	PETIOLES
PERMUTING	PERSISTS	PERTUSSAL	PESTERING	PETIOLULE
PERN	PERSON	PERTUSSIS	PESTEROUS	PETIOLULES
PERNANCIES	PERSONA	PERTUSSISES	PESTERS	PETIT
PERNANCY	PERSONAE	PERUKE	PESTFUL	PETITE
PERNS	PERSONAGE	PERUKED	PESTHOUSE	PETITION
PERONE	PERSONAGES	PERUKES	PESTHOUSES	PETITIONED
PERONEAL	PERSONAL	PERUSAL	PESTICIDE	PETITIONING
PERONES	PERSONAS	PERUSALS	PESTICIDES	PETITIONS
PERONEUS	PERSONATE	PERUSE	PESTILENT	PETITORY
PERONEUSES	PERSONATED	PERUSED	PESTLE	PETRARIES
PERORATE	PERSONATES	PERUSER	PESTLED	PETRARY
PERORATED	PERSONATING	PERUSERS	PESTLES	PETRE
PERORATES	PERSONATINGS	PERUSES	PESTLING	PETREL
PERORATING	PERSONIFIED	PERUSING	PESTO	PETRELS
PEROXIDE	PERSONIFIES	PERV	PESTOLOGIES	PETRES
PEROXIDED	PERSONIFY	PERVADE	PESTOLOGY	PETRIFIC
PEROXIDES	PERSONIFYING	PERVADED	PESTOS	PETRIFIED
PEROXIDING	PERSONISE	PERVADES	PESTS	PETRIFIES
PERPEND	PERSONISED	PERVADING	PET	PETRIFY
PERPENDED	PERSONISES	PERVASION	PETAL	PETRIFYING
PERPENDING	PERSONISING	PERVASIONS	PETALINE	PETROGRAM

PETROGRAMS	PEYOTISTS	PHARISAIC	PHENOTYPING	PHLEGMON
PETROL	PEYSE	PHARMACIES	PHENYL	PHLEGMONS
PETROLAGE	PEYSED	PHARMACY	PHENYLIC	PHLEGMS
PETROLAGES	PEYSES	PHAROS	PHENYLS	PHLEGMY
PETROLEUM	PEYSING	PHAROSES	PHEON	PHLOEM
PETROLEUMS	PEZANT	PHARYNGAL	PHEONS	PHLOEMS
PETROLEUR	PEZANTS	PHARYNGES	PHEROMONE	PHLOX
PETROLEURS	PEZIZOID	PHARYNX	PHEROMONES	PHLOXES
PETROLIC	PFENNIG	PHARYNXES	PHESE	PHLYCTENA
PETROLLED	PFENNIGE	PHASE	PHESED	PHLYCTENAE
PETROLLING	PFENNIGS	PHASED	PHESES	PHO
PETROLOGIES	PFENNING	PHASELESS	PHESING	PHOBIA
PETROLOGY	PFENNINGS	PHASES	PHEW	PHOBIAS
PETROLS	PHACOID	PHASIC	PHI	PHOBIC
PETRONEL	PHACOIDAL	PHASING	PHIAL	PHOBISM
PETRONELS	PHACOLITE	PHASIS	PHIALLED	PHOBISMS
PETROSAL	PHACOLITES	PHASMID	PHIALLING	PHOBIST
PETROSALS	PHACOLITH	PHASMIDS	PHIALS	PHOBISTS
PETROUS	PHACOLITHS	PHATIC	PHILABEG	PHOCA
PETS	PHAEIC	PHEASANT	PHILABEGS	PHOCAE
PETTED	PHAEISM	PHEASANTS	PHILAMOT	PHOCAS
PETTEDLY	PHAEISMS	PHEAZAR	PHILAMOTS	PHOCINE
PETTER	PHAENOGAM	PHEAZARS	PHILANDER	PHOEBE
PETTERS	PHAENOGAMS	PHEER	PHILANDERED	PHOEBES
PETTICOAT	PHAETON	PHEERE	PHILANDERING	PHOENIX
PETTICOATS	PHAETONS	PHEERES	PHILANDERS	PHOENIXES
PETTIER	PHAGE	PHEERS	PHILATELIES	PHOH
PETTIES	PHAGEDENA	PHEESE	PHILATELY	PHOLADES
PETTIEST	PHAGEDENAS	PHEESED	PHILHORSE	PHOLAS
PETTIFOG	PHAGES	PHEESES	PHILHORSES	PHON
PETTIFOGGED	PHAGOCYTE	PHEESING	PHILIBEG	PHONAL
PETTIFOGGING	PHAGOCYTES	PHEEZE	PHILIBEGS	PHONATE
PETTIFOGS	PHALANGAL	PHEEZED	PHILIPPIC	PHONATED
PETTILY	PHALANGE	PHEEZES	PHILIPPICS	PHONATES
PETTINESS	PHALANGER	PHEEZING	PHILISTER	PHONATING
PETTINESSES	PHALANGERS	PHELLEM	PHILISTERS	PHONATION
PETTING	PHALANGES	PHELLEMS	PHILLABEG	PHONATIONS
PETTINGS	PHALANGID	PHELLOGEN	PHILLABEGS	PHONATORY
PETTISH	PHALANGIDS	PHELLOGENS	PHILLIBEG	PHONE
PETTISHLY	PHALANX	PHELLOID	PHILLIBEGS	PHONECARD
PETTITOES	PHALANXES	PHELONION	PHILOGYNIES	PHONECARDS
PETTLE	PHALAROPE	PHELONIONS	PHILOGYNY	PHONED
PETTLED	PHALAROPES	PHENACITE	PHILOLOGIES	PHONEME
PETTLES	PHALLI	PHENACITES	PHILOLOGY	PHONEMES
PETTLING	PHALLIC	PHENAKISM	PHILOMATH	PHONEMIC
PETTY	PHALLIN	PHENAKISMS	PHILOMATHS	PHONEMICS
PETULANCE	PHALLINS	PHENAKITE	PHILOMOT	PHONES
PETULANCES	PHALLISM	PHENAKITES	PHILOMOTS	PHONETIC
PETULANCIES	PHALLISMS	PHENATE	PHILOPENA	PHONETICS
PETULANCY	PHALLOID	PHENATES	PHILOPENAS	PHONETISM
PETULANT	PHALLUS	PHENE	PHILTER	PHONETISMS
PETUNIA	PHALLUSES	PHENES	PHILTERS	PHONETIST
PETUNIAS	PHANG	PHENETIC	PHILTRE	PHONETISTS
PETUNTSE	PHANGS	PHENETICS	PHILTRES	PHONEY
PETUNTSES	PHANTASIES	PHENGITE	PHIMOSES	PHONEYED
PETUNTZE	PHANTASIM	PHENGITES	PHIMOSIS	PHONEYING
PETUNTZES	PHANTASIMS	PHENIC	PHINNOCK	PHONEYS
PEW	PHANTASM	PHENOGAM	PHINNOCKS	PHONIC
PEWIT	PHANTASMA	PHENOGAMS	PHIS	PHONICS
PEWITS	PHANTASMATA	PHENOL	PHISNOMIES	PHONIED
PEWS	PHANTASMS	PHENOLATE	PHISNOMY	PHONIER
PEWTER	PHANTASY	PHENOLATES	PHIZ	PHONIES
PEWTERER	PHANTOM	PHENOLIC	PHIZOG	PHONIEST
PEWTERERS	PHANTOMS	PHENOLOGIES	PHIZOGS	PHONINESS
PEWTERS	PHANTOMY	PHENOLOGY	PHIZZES	PHONINESSES
PEYOTE	PHANTOSME	PHENOLS	PHLEBITIS	PHONING
PEYOTES	PHANTOSMES	PHENOMENA	PHLEBITISES	PHONMETER
PEYOTISM	PHARAONIC	PHENOTYPE	PHLEGM	PHONMETERS
PEYOTISMS	PHARE	PHENOTYPED	PHLEGMIER	PHONOGRAM
PEYOTIST	PHARES	PHENOTYPES	PHLEGMIEST	PHONOGRAMS

PHONOLITE	PHOTOPHIL	PHYLLARIES	PIANISTIC	PICKETING
PHONOLITES	PHOTOPHILS	PHYLLARY	PIANISTS	PICKETS
PHONOLOGIES	PHOTOPIA	PHYLLITE	PIANO	PICKIER
PHONOLOGY	PHOTOPIAS	PHYLLITES	PIANOS	PICKIEST
PHONON	PHOTOPIC	PHYLLO	PIARIST	PICKING
PHONONS	PHOTOPSIA	PHYLLODE	PIARISTS	PICKINGS
PHONOPORE	PHOTOPSIAS	PHYLLODES	PIAS	PICKLE
PHONOPORES	PHOTOPSIES	PHYLLODIES	PIASSABA	PICKLED
PHONOTYPE	PHOTOPSY	PHYLLODY	PIASSABAS	PICKLER
PHONOTYPED	PHOTOS	PHYLLOID	PIASSAVA	PICKLERS
PHONOTYPES	PHOTOTYPE	PHYLLOME	PIASSAVAS	PICKLES
PHONOTYPIES	PHOTOTYPED	PHYLLOMES	PIASTRE	PICKLING
PHONOTYPING	PHOTOTYPES	PHYLLOPOD	PIASTRES	PICKLOCK
PHONOTYPY	PHOTOTYPIES	PHYLLOPODS	PIAZZA	PICKLOCKS
PHONS	PHOTOTYPING	PHYLLOS	PIAZZAS	PICKMAW
PHONY	PHOTOTYPY	PHYLOGENIES	PIAZZIAN	PICKMAWS
PHONYING	PHOTS	PHYLOGENY	PIBROCH	PICKS
PHOOEY	PHRASAL	PHYLUM	PIBROCHS	PICKY
PHORMINGES	PHRASE	PHYSALIA	PIC	PICNIC
PHORMINX	PHRASED	PHYSALIAS	PICA	PICNICKED
PHORMIUM	PHRASEMAN	PHYSALIS	PICADOR	PICNICKER
PHORMIUMS	PHRASEMEN	PHYSALISES	PICADORS	PICNICKERS
PHOS	PHRASER	PHYSIC	PICAMAR	PICNICKING
PHOSGENE	PHRASERS	PHYSICAL	PICAMARS	PICNICKY
PHOSGENES	PHRASES	PHYSICALS	PICARIAN	PICNICS
PHOSPHATE	PHRASING	PHYSICIAN	PICARIANS	PICOT
PHOSPHATED	PHRASINGS	PHYSICIANS	PICAROON	PICOTÉ
PHOSPHATES	PHRASY	PHYSICISM	PICAROONS	PICOTED
PHOSPHATING	PHRATRIES	PHYSICISMS	PICAS	PICOTEE
PHOSPHENE	PHRATRY	PHYSICIST	PICAYUNE	PICOTEES
PHOSPHENES	PHREATIC	PHYSICISTS	PICAYUNES	PICOTING
PHOSPHIDE	PHRENESES	PHYSICKED	PICCADILL	PICOTITE
PHOSPHIDES	PHRENESIS	PHYSICKING	PICCADILLS	PICOTITES
PHOSPHINE	PHRENETIC	PHYSICKY	PICCANIN	PICOTS
PHOSPHINES	PHRENETICS	PHYSICS	PICCANINS	PICQUET
PHOSPHITE	PHRENIC	PHYSIO	PICCOLO	PICQUETED
PHOSPHITES	PHRENISM	PHYSIOS	PICCOLOS	PICQUETING
PHOSPHOR	PHRENISMS	PHYSIQUE	PICE	PICQUETS
PHOSPHORS	PHRENITIC	PHYSIQUES	PICENE	PICRA
PHOT	PHRENITIS	PHYTOGENIES	PICENES	PICRAS
PHOTIC	PHRENITISES	PHYTOGENY	PICEOUS	PICRATE
PHOTICS	PHRENSIES	PHYTOLOGIES	PICHURIM	PICRATES
PHOTISM	PHRENSY	PHYTOLOGY	PICHURIMS	PICRIC
PHOTISMS	PHRENTICK	PHYTON	PICINE	PICRITE
PHOTO	PHTHALATE	PHYTONS	PICK	PICRITES
PHOTOCALL	PHTHALATES	PHYTOSES	PICKABACK	PICS
PHOTOCALLS	PHTHALEIN	PHYTOSIS	PICKABACKS	PICTARNIE
PHOTOCELL	PHTHALEINS	PHYTOTOMIES	PICKAPACK	PICTARNIES
PHOTOCELLS	PHTHALIC	PHYTOTOMY	PICKAPACKS	PICTOGRAM
PHOTOCOPIED	PHTHALIN	PHYTOTRON	PICKAXE	PICTOGRAMS
PHOTOCOPIES	PHTHALINS	PHYTOTRONS	PICKAXES	PICTORIAL
PHOTOCOPY	PHTHISES	PI	PICKBACK	PICTORIALS
PHOTOCOPYING	PHTHISIC	PIA	PICKBACKS	PICTURAL
PHOTOED	PHTHISICS	PIACEVOLE	PICKED	PICTURALS
PHOTOGEN	PHTHISIS	PIACULAR	PICKEER	PICTURE
PHOTOGENE	PHUT	PIAFFE	PICKEERED	PICTURED
PHOTOGENES	PHUTS	PIAFFED	PICKEERER	PICTURES
PHOTOGENIES	PHYCOCYAN	PIAFFER	PICKEERERS	PICTURING
PHOTOGENS	PHYCOCYANS	PIAFFERS	PICKEERING	PICUL
PHOTOGENY	PHYCOLOGIES	PIAFFES	PICKEERS	PICULS
PHOTOGRAM	PHYCOLOGY	PIAFFING	PICKER	PIDDLE
PHOTOGRAMS	PHYLA	PIANETTE	PICKEREL	PIDDLED
PHOTOING	PHYLAE	PIANETTES	PICKERELS	PIDDLER
PHOTOLYSE	PHYLARCH	PIANINO	PICKERIES	PIDDLERS
PHOTOLYSED	PHYLARCHIES	PIANINOS	PICKERS	PIDDLES
PHOTOLYSES	PHYLARCHS	PIANISM	PICKERY	PIDDLING
PHOTOLYSING	PHYLARCHY	PIANISMS	PICKET	PIDDOCK
PHOTON	PHYLE	PIANIST	PICKETED	PIDDOCKS
PHOTONICS	PHYLES	PIANISTE	PICKETER	PIDGEON
PHOTONS	PHYLETIC	PIANISTES	PICKETERS	PIDGEONS

PIDGIN
PIDGINS
PIE
PIEBALD
PIEBALDS
PIECE
PIECED
PIECELESS
PIECEMEAL
PIECEMEALED
PIECEMEALING
PIECEMEALS
PIECEN
PIECENED
PIECENER
PIECENERS
PIECENING
PIECENS
PIECER
PIECERS
PIECES
PIECING
PIECRUST
PIECRUSTS
PIED
PIEDISH
PIEDISHES
PIEDMONT
PIEDMONTS
PIEDNESS
PIEDNESSES
PIEING
PIEMAN
PIEMEN
PIEND
PIENDS
PIEPOWDER
PIEPOWDERS
PIER
PIERAGE
PIERAGES
PIERCE
PIERCED
PIERCER
PIERCERS
PIERCES
PIERCING
PIERID
PIERIDINE
PIERIDS
PIERROT
PIERROTS
PIERS
PIERST
PIERT
PIES
PIET
PIETÀ
PIETÀS
PIETIES
PIETISM
PIETISMS
PIETIST
PIETISTIC
PIETISTS
PIETS
PIETY
PIEZO
PIFFERARI
PIFFERARO

PIFFERO
PIFFEROS
PIFFLE
PIFFLED
PIFFLER
PIFFLERS
PIFFLES
PIFFLING
PIG
PIGBOAT
PIGBOATS
PIGEON
PIGEONED
PIGEONING
PIGEONRIES
PIGEONRY
PIGEONS
PIGFEED
PIGFEEDS
PIGGED
PIGGERIES
PIGGERY
PIGGIE
PIGGIER
PIGGIES
PIGGIEST
PIGGIN
PIGGING
PIGGINGS
PIGGINS
PIGGISH
PIGGISHLY
PIGGY
PIGGYBACK
PIGGYBACKS
PIGHEADED
PIGHT
PIGHTLE
PIGHTLES
PIGLET
PIGLETS
PIGLING
PIGLINGS
PIGMEAN
PIGMEAT
PIGMEATS
PIGMENT
PIGMENTAL
PIGMENTED
PIGMENTS
PIGMIES
PIGMY
PIGNERATE
PIGNERATED
PIGNERATES
PIGNERATING
PIGNORATE
PIGNORATED
PIGNORATES
PIGNORATING
PIGPEN
PIGPENS
PIGS
PIGSCONCE
PIGSCONCES
PIGSKIN
PIGSKINS
PIGSNEY
PIGSNEYS
PIGSNIE

PIGSNIES
PIGSNY
PIGSTIES
PIGSTY
PIGSWILL
PIGSWILLS
PIGTAIL
PIGTAILS
PIGWASH
PIGWASHES
PIGWEED
PIGWEEDS
PIKA
PIKADELL
PIKADELLS
PIKAS
PIKE
PIKED
PIKELET
PIKELETS
PIKEMAN
PIKEMEN
PIKER
PIKERS
PIKES
PIKESTAFF
PIKESTAFFS
PIKING
PIKUL
PIKULS
PILA
PILAFF
PILAFFS
PILASTER
PILASTERS
PILAU
PILAUS
PILAW
PILAWS
PILCH
PILCHARD
PILCHARDS
PILCHER
PILCHERS
PILCHES
PILCORN
PILCORNS
PILCROW
PILCROWS
PILE
PILEA
PILEATE
PILEATED
PILED
PILEI
PILEOUS
PILER
PILERS
PILES
PILEUM
PILEUS
PILEWORK
PILEWORKS
PILEWORT
PILEWORTS
PILFER
PILFERAGE
PILFERAGES
PILFERED
PILFERER

PILFERERS
PILFERIES
PILFERING
PILFERINGS
PILFERS
PILFERY
PILGRIM
PILGRIMER
PILGRIMERS
PILGRIMS
PILHORSE
PILHORSES
PILI
PILIFORM
PILING
PILIS
PILL
PILLAGE
PILLAGED
PILLAGER
PILLAGERS
PILLAGES
PILLAGING
PILLAR
PILLARIST
PILLARISTS
PILLARS
PILLAU
PILLAUS
PILLED
PILLHEAD
PILLHEADS
PILLICOCK
PILLICOCKS
PILLING
PILLION
PILLIONED
PILLIONING
PILLIONS
PILLOCK
PILLOCKS
PILLORIED
PILLORIES
PILLORISE
PILLORISED
PILLORISES
PILLORISING
PILLORIZE
PILLORIZED
PILLORIZES
PILLORIZING
PILLORY
PILLORYING
PILLOW
PILLOWED
PILLOWING
PILLOWS
PILLOWY
PILLS
PILLWORM
PILLWORMS
PILLWORT
PILLWORTS
PILOSE
PILOSITIES
PILOSITY
PILOT
PILOTAGE
PILOTAGES
PILOTED

PILOTING
PILOTLESS
PILOTS
PILOUS
PILOW
PILOWS
PILSENER
PILSENERS
PILSNER
PILSNERS
PILULA
PILULAR
PILULAS
PILULE
PILULES
PILUM
PILUS
PIMENT
PIMENTO
PIMENTOS
PIMENTS
PIMIENTO
PIMIENTOS
PIMP
PIMPED
PIMPERNEL
PIMPERNELS
PIMPING
PIMPLE
PIMPLED
PIMPLES
PIMPLIER
PIMPLIEST
PIMPLY
PIMPS
PIN
PIÑA
PINACOID
PINACOIDS
PINAFORE
PINAFORED
PINAFORES
PINAKOID
PINAKOIDS
PIÑAS
PINASTER
PINASTERS
PINBALL
PINBALLS
PINCASE
PINCASES
PINCER
PINCERED
PINCERING
PINCERS
PINCH
PINCHBECK
PINCHBECKS
PINCHCOCK
PINCHCOCKS
PINCHED
PINCHER
PINCHERS
PINCHES
PINCHFIST
PINCHFISTS
PINCHGUT
PINCHGUTS
PINCHING
PINCHINGS

PINDAREE
PINDAREES
PINDARI
PINDARIS
PINDER
PINDERS
PINE
PINEAL
PINEAPPLE
PINEAPPLES
PINED
PINERIES
PINERY
PINES
PINETA
PINETUM
PINEY
PINFISH
PINFISHES
PINFOLD
PINFOLDED
PINFOLDING
PINFOLDS
PING
PINGED
PINGER
PINGERS
PINGING
PINGLE
PINGLED
PINGLER
PINGLERS
PINGLES
PINGLING
PINGO
PINGOES
PINGOS
PINGS
PINGUEFIED
PINGUEFIES
PINGUEFY
PINGUEFYING
PINGUID
PINGUIN
PINGUINS
PINHEAD
PINHEADS
PINHOLE
PINHOLES
PINIER
PINIES
PINIEST
PINING
PINION
PINIONED
PINIONING
PINIONS
PINITE
PINITES
PINK
PINKED
PINKER
PINKERTON
PINKERTONS
PINKEST
PINKIE
PINKIER
PINKIES
PINKIEST
PINKINESS

PINKINESSES
PINKING
PINKINGS
PINKISH
PINKNESS
PINKNESSES
PINKO
PINKOES
PINKOS
PINKROOT
PINKROOTS
PINKS
PINKY
PINNA
PINNACE
PINNACES
PINNACLE
PINNACLED
PINNACLES
PINNACLING
PINNAE
PINNATE
PINNATED
PINNATELY
PINNED
PINNER
PINNERS
PINNET
PINNETS
PINNIE
PINNIES
PINNING
PINNINGS
PINNIPED
PINNIPEDE
PINNIPEDES
PINNIPEDS
PINNOCK
PINNOCKS
PINNOED
PINNULA
PINNULAS
PINNULATE
PINNULE
PINNULES
PINNY
PINOCHLE
PINOCHLES
PINOCLE
PINOCLES
PINOLE
PINOLES
PIÑON
PIÑONS
PINOT
PINOTS
PINS
PINT
PINTA
PINTABLE
PINTABLES
PINTADO
PINTADOS
PINTAIL
PINTAILED
PINTAILS
PINTAS
PINTLE
PINTLES
PINTO

PINTOS
PINTS
PINXIT
PINY
PIOLET
PIOLETS
PION
PIONED
PIONEER
PIONEERED
PIONEERING
PIONEERS
PIONER
PIONERS
PIONEY
PIONEYS
PIONIES
PIONING
PIONINGS
PIONS
PIONY
PIOTED
PIOUS
PIOUSLY
PIOY
PIOYE
PIOYES
PIOYS
PIP
PIPA
PIPAGE
PIPAGES
PIPAL
PIPALS
PIPAS
PIPE
PIPECLAY
PIPECLAYED
PIPECLAYING
PIPECLAYS
PIPED
PIPEFISH
PIPEFISHES
PIPEFUL
PIPEFULS
PIPELESS
PIPELIKE
PIPELINE
PIPELINES
PIPER
PIPERIC
PIPERINE
PIPERINES
PIPERONAL
PIPERONALS
PIPERS
PIPES
PIPESTONE
PIPESTONES
PIPETTE
PIPETTED
PIPETTES
PIPETTING
PIPEWORK
PIPEWORKS
PIPEWORT
PIPEWORTS
PIPI
PIPIER
PIPIEST

PIPING
PIPINGS
PIPIS
PIPIT
PIPITS
PIPKIN
PIPKINS
PIPLESS
PIPPED
PIPPIER
PIPPIEST
PIPPIN
PIPPING
PIPPINS
PIPPY
PIPS
PIPSQUEAK
PIPSQUEAKS
PIPUL
PIPULS
PIPY
PIQUANCIES
PIQUANCY
PIQUANT
PIQUANTLY
PIQUE
PIQUED
PIQUES
PIQUET
PIQUETED
PIQUETING
PIQUETS
PIQUING
PIR
PIRACIES
PIRACY
PIRAGUA
PIRAGUAS
PIRAI
PIRAIS
PIRANA
PIRAÑAS
PIRAÑHA
PIRANHAS
PIRARUCU
PIRARUCUS
PIRATE
PIRATED
PIRATES
PIRATIC
PIRATICAL
PIRATING
PIRAYA
PIRAYAS
PIRL
PIRLICUE
PIRLICUED
PIRLICUES
PIRLICUING
PIRLS
PIRN
PIRNIE
PIRNIES
PIRNIT
PIRNS
PIROGUE
PIROGUES
PIROSHKI
PIROUETTE
PIROUETTED

PIROUETTES
PIROUETTING
PIROZHKI
PIRS
PIS
PISCARIES
PISCARY
PISCATOR
PISCATORS
PISCATORY
PISCATRIX
PISCATRIXES
PISCIFORM
PISCINA
PISCINAE
PISCINAS
PISCINE
PISCINES
PISÉ
PISÉS
PISH
PISHED
PISHES
PISHING
PISHOGUE
PISHOGUES
PISIFORM
PISIFORMS
PISKIES
PISKY
PISMIRE
PISMIRES
PISOLITE
PISOLITES
PISOLITIC
PISS
PISSED
PISSES
PISSING
PISSOIR
PISSOIRS
PISTACHIO
PISTACHIOS
PISTAREEN
PISTAREENS
PISTE
PISTES
PISTIL
PISTILS
PISTOL
PISTOLE
PISTOLEER
PISTOLEERS
PISTOLES
PISTOLET
PISTOLETS
PISTOLLED
PISTOLLING
PISTOLS
PISTON
PISTONS
PIT
PITA
PITAPAT
PITAPATS
PITAPATTED
PITAPATTING
PITARA
PITARAH
PITARAHS

PITARAS	PITTING	PLACCATS	PLAINER	PLANKTONS
PITAS	PITTINGS	PLACE	PLAINEST	PLANLESS
PITCH	PITTITE	PLACEBO	PLAINFUL	PLANNED
PITCHED	PITTITES	PLACEBOS	PLAINING	PLANNER
PITCHER	PITUITA	PLACED	PLAININGS	PLANNERS
PITCHERS	PITUITARY	PLACELESS	PLAINISH	PLANNING
PITCHES	PITUITAS	PLACEMAN	PLAINLY	PLANS
PITCHFORK	PITUITE	PLACEMEN	PLAINNESS	PLANT
PITCHFORKED	PITUITES	PLACEMENT	PLAINNESSES	PLANTA
PITCHFORKING	PITUITRIN	PLACEMENTS	PLAINS	PLANTABLE
PITCHFORKS	PITUITRINS	PLACENTA	PLAINSMAN	PLANTAGE
PITCHIER	PITURI	PLACENTAE	PLAINSMEN	PLANTAGES
PITCHIEST	PITURIS	PLACENTAL	PLAINSONG	PLANTAIN
PITCHING	PITY	PLACENTALS	PLAINSONGS	PLANTAINS
PITCHINGS	PITYING	PLACENTAS	PLAINT	PLANTAR
PITCHMAN	PITYINGLY	PLACER	PLAINTFUL	PLANTAS
PITCHMEN	PITYROID	PLACERS	PLAINTIFF	PLANTED
PITCHPINE	PIÙ	PLACES	PLAINTIFFS	PLANTER
PITCHPINES	PIUM	PLACET	PLAINTIVE	PLANTERS
PITCHPIPE	PIUMS	PLACETS	PLAINTS	PLANTING
PITCHPIPES	PIUPIU	PLACID	PLAINWORK	PLANTINGS
PITCHY	PIUPIUS	PLACIDER	PLAINWORKS	PLANTLESS
PITEOUS	PIVOT	PLACIDEST	PLAISTER	PLANTLET
PITEOUSLY	PIVOTAL	PLACIDITIES	PLAISTERS	PLANTLETS
PITFALL	PIVOTALLY	PLACIDITY	PLAIT	PLANTLING
PITFALLS	PIVOTED	PLACIDLY	PLAITED	PLANTLINGS
PITH	PIVOTER	PLACING	PLAITER	PLANTS
PITHBALL	PIVOTERS	PLACINGS	PLAITERS	PLANTSMAN
PITHBALLS	PIVOTING	PLACIT	PLAITING	PLANTSMEN
PITHEAD	PIVOTINGS	PLACITA	PLAITINGS	PLANTULE
PITHEADS	PIVOTS	PLACITORY	PLAITS	PLANTULES
PITHECOID	PIX	PLACITS	PLAN	PLANULA
PITHED	PIXED	PLACITUM	PLANAR	PLANULAE
PITHFUL	PIXEL	PLACK	PLANARIAN	PLANULAR
PITHIER	PIXELS	PLACKET	PLANARIANS	PLANULOID
PITHIEST	PIXES	PLACKETS	PLANATION	PLANURIA
PITHILY	PIXIE	PLACKLESS	PLANATIONS	PLANURIAS
PITHINESS	PIXIES	PLACKS	PLANCH	PLANURIES
PITHINESSES	PIXILATED	PLACODERM	PLANCHED	PLANURY
PITHING	PIXING	PLACODERMS	PLANCHES	PLANXTIES
PITHLESS	PIXY	PLACOID	PLANCHET	PLANXTY
PITHLIKE	PIZAZZ	PLAFOND	PLANCHETS	PLAP
PITHOI	PIZAZZES	PLAFONDS	PLANCHING	PLAPPED
PITHOS	PIZE	PLAGAL	PLANE	PLAPPING
PITHS	PIZES	PLAGE	PLANED	PLAPS
PITHY	PIZZA	PLAGES	PLANER	PLAQUE
PITIABLE	PIZZAIOLA	PLAGIARIES	PLANERS	PLAQUES
PITIABLY	PIZZAS	PLAGIARY	PLANES	PLAQUETTE
PITIED	PIZZERIA	PLAGIUM	PLANET	PLAQUETTES
PITIER	PIZZERIAS	PLAGIUMS	PLANETARY	PLASH
PITIERS	PIZZICATO	PLAGUE	PLANETIC	PLASHED
PITIES	PIZZICATOS	PLAGUED	PLANETOID	PLASHES
PITIFUL	PIZZLE	PLAGUES	PLANETOIDS	PLASHET
PITIFULLY	PIZZLES	PLAGUEY	PLANETS	PLASHETS
PITILESS	PLACABLE	PLAGUILY	PLANGENCIES	PLASHIER
PITMAN	PLACABLY	PLAGUING	PLANGENCY	PLASHIEST
PITMEN	PLACARD	PLAGUY	PLANGENT	PLASHING
PITON	PLACARDED	PLAICE	PLANING	PLASHINGS
PITONS	PLACARDING	PLAICES	PLANISH	PLASHY
PITS	PLACARDS	PLAID	PLANISHED	PLASM
PITTA	PLACATE	PLAIDED	PLANISHER	PLASMA
PITTANCE	PLACATED	PLAIDING	PLANISHERS	PLASMAS
PITTANCES	PLACATES	PLAIDINGS	PLANISHES	PLASMATIC
PITTAS	PLACATING	PLAIDMAN	PLANISHING	PLASMIC
PITTED	PLACATION	PLAIDMEN	PLANK	PLASMID
PITTEN	PLACATIONS	PLAIDS	PLANKED	PLASMIDS
PITTER	PLACATORY	PLAIN	PLANKING	PLASMIN
PITTERED	PLACCAT	PLAINANT	PLANKINGS	PLASMINS
PITTERING	PLACCATE	PLAINANTS	PLANKS	PLASMODIA
PITTERS	PLACCATES	PLAINED	PLANKTON	PLASMS

PLAST
PLASTE
PLASTER
PLASTERED
PLASTERER
PLASTERERS
PLASTERING
PLASTERINGS
PLASTERS
PLASTERY
PLASTIC
PLASTICS
PLASTID
PLASTIDS
PLASTIQUE
PLASTIQUES
PLASTISOL
PLASTISOLS
PLASTRAL
PLASTRON
PLASTRONS
PLAT
PLATAN
PLATANE
PLATANES
PLATANNA
PLATANNAS
PLATANS
PLATBAND
PLATBANDS
PLATE
PLATEASM
PLATEASMS
PLATEAU
PLATEAUED
PLATEAUING
PLATEAUS
PLATEAUX
PLATED
PLATEFUL
PLATEFULS
PLATELET
PLATELETS
PLATEMAN
PLATEMARK
PLATEMARKS
PLATEMEN
PLATEN
PLATENS
PLATER
PLATERS
PLATES
PLATFORM
PLATFORMED
PLATFORMING
PLATFORMINGS
PLATFORMS
PLATIER
PLATIEST
PLATINA
PLATINAS
PLATING
PLATINGS
PLATINIC
PLATINISE
PLATINISED
PLATINISES
PLATINISING
PLATINIZE
PLATINIZED

PLATINIZES
PLATINIZING
PLATINOID
PLATINOIDS
PLATINOUS
PLATINUM
PLATINUMS
PLATITUDE
PLATITUDES
PLATONIC
PLATONICS
PLATOON
PLATOONS
PLATS
PLATTED
PLATTER
PLATTERS
PLATTING
PLATTINGS
PLATY
PLATYPUS
PLATYPUSES
PLATYSMA
PLATYSMAS
PLAUDIT
PLAUDITE
PLAUDITS
PLAUSIBLE
PLAUSIBLY
PLAUSIVE
PLAUSTRAL
PLAY
PLAYA
PLAYABLE
PLAYAS
PLAYBACK
PLAYBACKS
PLAYBILL
PLAYBILLS
PLAYBOOK
PLAYBOOKS
PLAYBOY
PLAYBOYS
PLAYBUS
PLAYBUSES
PLAYED
PLAYER
PLAYERS
PLAYFUL
PLAYFULLER
PLAYFULLEST
PLAYFULLY
PLAYGIRL
PLAYGIRLS
PLAYGROUP
PLAYGROUPS
PLAYHOUSE
PLAYHOUSES
PLAYING
PLAYLET
PLAYLETS
PLAYMATE
PLAYMATES
PLAYROOM
PLAYROOMS
PLAYS
PLAYSOME
PLAYSUIT
PLAYSUITS
PLAYTHING

PLAYTHINGS
PLAYTIME
PLAYTIMES
PLAZA
PLAZAS
PLEA
PLEACH
PLEACHED
PLEACHES
PLEACHING
PLEAD
PLEADABLE
PLEADED
PLEADER
PLEADERS
PLEADING
PLEADINGS
PLEADS
PLEAED
PLEAING
PLEAS
PLEASANCE
PLEASANCES
PLEASANT
PLEASANTER
PLEASANTEST
PLEASE
PLEASED
PLEASEMAN
PLEASEMEN
PLEASER
PLEASERS
PLEASES
PLEASETH
PLEASING
PLEASINGS
PLEASURE
PLEASURED
PLEASURER
PLEASURERS
PLEASURES
PLEASURING
PLEAT
PLEATED
PLEATING
PLEATS
PLEB
PLEBBIER
PLEBBIEST
PLEBBY
PLEBEAN
PLEBEIAN
PLEBEIANS
PLEBIFIED
PLEBIFIES
PLEBIFY
PLEBIFYING
PLEBS
PLECTRA
PLECTRE
PLECTRES
PLECTRON
PLECTRONS
PLECTRUM
PLECTRUMS
PLED
PLEDGE
PLEDGED
PLEDGEE
PLEDGEES

PLEDGEOR
PLEDGEORS
PLEDGER
PLEDGERS
PLEDGES
PLEDGET
PLEDGETS
PLEDGING
PLEDGOR
PLEDGORS
PLEIOMERIES
PLEIOMERY
PLENARILY
PLENARTIES
PLENARTY
PLENARY
PLENILUNE
PLENILUNES
PLENIPO
PLENIPOES
PLENIPOS
PLENISH
PLENISHED
PLENISHES
PLENISHING
PLENISHINGS
PLENIST
PLENISTS
PLENITUDE
PLENITUDES
PLENTEOUS
PLENTIES
PLENTIFUL
PLENTY
PLENUM
PLENUMS
PLEON
PLEONASM
PLEONASMS
PLEONAST
PLEONASTE
PLEONASTES
PLEONASTS
PLEONEXIA
PLEONEXIAS
PLEONS
PLEOPOD
PLEOPODS
PLEROMA
PLEROMAS
PLEROME
PLEROMES
PLESH
PLESHES
PLESSOR
PLESSORS
PLETHORA
PLETHORAS
PLETHORIC
PLEUCH
PLEUCHS
PLEUGH
PLEUGHS
PLEURA
PLEURAE
PLEURAL
PLEURISIES
PLEURISY
PLEURITIC
PLEURITIS

PLEURITISES
PLEURON
PLEXIFORM
PLEXOR
PLEXORS
PLEXURE
PLEXURES
PLEXUS
PLEXUSES
PLIABLE
PLIABLY
PLIANCIES
PLIANCY
PLIANT
PLIANTLY
PLICA
PLICAE
PLICAL
PLICATE
PLICATED
PLICATELY
PLICATES
PLICATING
PLICATION
PLICATIONS
PLICATURE
PLICATURES
PLIÉ
PLIED
PLIER
PLIERS
PLIÉS
PLIES
PLIGHT
PLIGHTED
PLIGHTER
PLIGHTERS
PLIGHTFUL
PLIGHTING
PLIGHTS
PLIM
PLIMMED
PLIMMING
PLIMS
PLIMSOLE
PLIMSOLES
PLIMSOLL
PLIMSOLLS
PLINK
PLINKED
PLINKING
PLINKS
PLINTH
PLINTHS
PLISKIE
PLISKIES
PLISSÉ
PLOAT
PLOATED
PLOATING
PLOATS
PLOD
PLODDED
PLODDER
PLODDERS
PLODDING
PLODDINGS
PLODS
PLONG
PLONGD

PLONGE	PLUCKING	PLUMP	PLUSES	POCHOIRS
PLONK	PLUCKS	PLUMPED	PLUSH	POCK
PLONKED	PLUCKY	PLUMPEN	PLUSHER	POCKARD
PLONKER	PLUFF	PLUMPENED	PLUSHES	POCKARDS
PLONKERS	PLUFFED	PLUMPENING	PLUSHEST	POCKED
PLONKING	PLUFFING	PLUMPENS	PLUSHIER	POCKET
PLONKS	PLUFFS	PLUMPER	PLUSHIEST	POCKETED
PLOOK	PLUFFY	PLUMPERS	PLUSHY	POCKETFUL
PLOOKIE	PLUG	PLUMPEST	PLUSSAGE	POCKETFULS
PLOOKS	PLUGGED	PLUMPIE	PLUSSAGES	POCKETING
PLOP	PLUGGER	PLUMPING	PLUSSED	POCKETS
PLOPPED	PLUGGERS	PLUMPISH	PLUSSES	POCKIER
PLOPPING	PLUGGING	PLUMPLY	PLUSSING	POCKIEST
PLOPS	PLUGGINGS	PLUMPNESS	PLUTEAL	POCKMANKIES
PLOSION	PLUGS	PLUMPNESSES	PLUTEUS	POCKMANKY
PLOSIONS	PLUM	PLUMPS	PLUTEUSES	POCKMARK
PLOSIVE	PLUMAGE	PLUMPY	PLUTOCRAT	POCKMARKS
PLOSIVES	PLUMAGED	PLUMS	PLUTOCRATS	POCKPIT
PLOT	PLUMAGES	PLUMULA	PLUTOLOGIES	POCKPITS
PLOTFUL	PLUMATE	PLUMULAE	PLUTOLOGY	POCKS
PLOTLESS	PLUMB	PLUMULAR	PLUTON	POCKY
PLOTS	PLUMBAGO	PLUMULATE	PLUTONIUM	POCO
PLOTTED	PLUMBAGOS	PLUMULE	PLUTONIUMS	POD
PLOTTER	PLUMBATE	PLUMULES	PLUTONOMIES	PODAGRA
PLOTTERED	PLUMBATES	PLUMULOSE	PLUTONOMY	PODAGRAL
PLOTTERING	PLUMBED	PLUMY	PLUTONS	PODAGRAS
PLOTTERS	PLUMBEOUS	PLUNDER	PLUVIAL	PODAGRIC
PLOTTIE	PLUMBER	PLUNDERED	PLUVIALS	PODAGROUS
PLOTTIES	PLUMBERIES	PLUNDERER	PLUVIOSE	PODAL
PLOTTING	PLUMBERS	PLUNDERERS	PLUVIOUS	PODALIC
PLOTTINGS	PLUMBERY	PLUNDERING	PLY	PODDED
PLOTTY	PLUMBIC	PLUNDERS	PLYING	PODDIER
PLOUGH	PLUMBING	PLUNGE	PLYWOOD	PODDIEST
PLOUGHBOY	PLUMBINGS	PLUNGED	PLYWOODS	PODDING
PLOUGHBOYS	PLUMBISM	PLUNGER	PNEUMA	PODDY
PLOUGHED	PLUMBISMS	PLUNGERS	PNEUMAS	PODESTA
PLOUGHER	PLUMBITE	PLUNGES	PNEUMATIC	PODESTAS
PLOUGHERS	PLUMBITES	PLUNGING	PNEUMATICS	PODEX
PLOUGHING	PLUMBLESS	PLUNGINGS	PNEUMONIA	PODEXES
PLOUGHINGS	PLUMBOUS	PLUNK	PNEUMONIAS	PODGE
PLOUGHMAN	PLUMBS	PLUNKED	PNEUMONIC	PODGES
PLOUGHMEN	PLUMBUM	PLUNKER	PNEUMONICS	PODGIER
PLOUGHS	PLUMBUMS	PLUNKERS	PO	PODGIEST
PLOUK	PLUMCOT	PLUNKING	POA	PODGINESS
PLOUKIE	PLUMCOTS	PLUNKS	POACEOUS	PODGINESSES
PLOUKS	PLUMDAMAS	PLURAL	POACH	PODGY
PLOUTER	PLUMDAMASES	PLURALISE	POACHED	PODIA
PLOUTERED	PLUME	PLURALISED	POACHER	PODIAL
PLOUTERING	PLUMED	PLURALISES	POACHERS	PODIATRIES
PLOUTERS	PLUMELESS	PLURALISING	POACHES	PODIATRY
PLOVER	PLUMELET	PLURALISM	POACHIER	PODITE
PLOVERS	PLUMELETS	PLURALISMS	POACHIEST	PODITES
PLOVERY	PLUMERIES	PLURALIST	POACHING	PODIUM
PLOW	PLUMERY	PLURALISTS	POACHINGS	PODLEY
PLOWED	PLUMES	PLURALITIES	POACHY	PODLEYS
PLOWING	PLUMIER	PLURALITY	POAKA	PODOLOGIES
PLOWS	PLUMIEST	PLURALIZE	POAKAS	PODOLOGY
PLOWTER	PLUMING	PLURALIZED	POAKE	PODS
PLOWTERED	PLUMIPED	PLURALIZES	POAKES	PODSOL
PLOWTERING	PLUMIST	PLURALIZING	POAS	PODSOLIC
PLOWTERS	PLUMISTS	PLURALLY	POCAS	PODSOLS
PLOY	PLUMMET	PLURALS	POCHARD	PODZOL
PLOYS	PLUMMETED	PLURIPARA	POCHARDS	PODZOLS
PLUCK	PLUMMETING	PLURIPARAE	POCHAY	POEM
PLUCKED	PLUMMETS	PLURIPARAS	POCHAYED	POEMATIC
PLUCKER	PLUMMIER	PLURISIE	POCHAYING	POEMS
PLUCKERS	PLUMMIEST	PLURISIES	POCHAYS	POENOLOGIES
PLUCKIER	PLUMMY	PLUS	POCHETTE	POENOLOGY
PLUCKIEST	PLUMOSE	PLUSAGE	POCHETTES	POESIED
PLUCKILY	PLUMOUS	PLUSAGES	POCHOIR	POESIES

POESY	POINTELS	POLARONS	POLITIES	POLLYWIG
POESYING	POINTER	POLARS	POLITIQUE	POLLYWIGS
POET	POINTERS	POLDER	POLITIQUES	POLLYWOG
POETASTER	POINTES	POLDERED	POLITY	POLLYWOGS
POETASTERS	POINTIER	POLDERING	POLK	POLO
POETASTRIES	POINTIEST	POLDERS	POLKA	POLOIST
POETASTRY	POINTILLÉ	POLE	POLKAS	POLOISTS
POETESS	POINTING	POLECAT	POLKED	POLONAISE
POETESSES	POINTINGS	POLECATS	POLKING	POLONAISES
POETIC	POINTLESS	POLED	POLKS	POLONIE
POETICAL	POINTS	POLEMARCH	POLL	POLONIES
POETICISE	POINTSMAN	POLEMARCHS	POLLACK	POLONISE
POETICISED	POINTSMEN	POLEMIC	POLLACKS	POLONISED
POETICISES	POINTY	POLEMICAL	POLLAN	POLONISES
POETICISING	POIS	POLEMICS	POLLANS	POLONISING
POETICISM	POISE	POLEMISE	POLLARD	POLONISM
POETICISMS	POISED	POLEMISED	POLLARDED	POLONISMS
POETICIZE	POISER	POLEMISES	POLLARDING	POLONIUM
POETICIZED	POISERS	POLEMISING	POLLARDS	POLONIUMS
POETICIZES	POISES	POLEMIST	POLLED	POLONIZE
POETICIZING	POISING	POLEMISTS	POLLEN	POLONIZED
POETICS	POISON	POLEMIZE	POLLENED	POLONIZES
POETICULE	POISONED	POLEMIZED	POLLENING	POLONIZING
POETICULES	POISONER	POLEMIZES	POLLENS	POLONY
POETISE	POISONERS	POLEMIZING	POLLENT	POLOS
POETISED	POISONING	POLENTA	POLLER	POLT
POETISES	POISONOUS	POLENTAS	POLLERS	POLTED
POETISING	POISONS	POLES	POLLEX	POLTFEET
POETIZE	POISSON	POLEY	POLLICAL	POLTFOOT
POETIZED	POISSONS	POLEYN	POLLICES	POLTING
POETIZES	POITREL	POLEYNS	POLLICIE	POLTROON
POETIZING	POITRELS	POLIANITE	POLLICIES	POLTROONS
POETRESSE	POKAL	POLIANITES	POLLICY	POLTS
POETRESSES	POKALS	POLICE	POLLIES	POLVERINE
POETRIES	POKE	POLICED	POLLINATE	POLVERINES
POETRY	POKEBERRIES	POLICEMAN	POLLINATED	POLY
POETS	POKEBERRY	POLICEMEN	POLLINATES	POLYACID
POETSHIP	POKED	POLICES	POLLINATING	POLYACT
POETSHIPS	POKEFUL	POLICIES	POLLING	POLYAMIDE
POFFLE	POKEFULS	POLICING	POLLINGS	POLYAMIDES
POFFLES	POKER	POLICY	POLLINIA	POLYANDRIES
POGGE	POKERISH	POLING	POLLINIC	POLYANDRY
POGGES	POKERS	POLINGS	POLLINIUM	POLYARCH
POGROM	POKES	POLIO	POLLIWIG	POLYARCHIES
POGROMS	POKEWEED	POLIOS	POLLIWIGS	POLYARCHY
POH	POKEWEEDS	POLISH	POLLIWOG	POLYAXIAL
POI	POKIER	POLISHED	POLLIWOGS	POLYAXON
POIGNADO	POKIEST	POLISHER	POLLMAN	POLYAXONS
POIGNADOS	POKING	POLISHERS	POLLMEN	POLYBASIC
POIGNANCIES	POKY	POLISHES	POLLOCK	POLYCONIC
POIGNANCY	POLACCA	POLISHING	POLLOCKS	POLYESTER
POIGNANT	POLACCAS	POLISHINGS	POLLS	POLYESTERS
POILU	POLACRE	POLITE	POLLSTER	POLYGALA
POILUS	POLACRES	POLITELY	POLLSTERS	POLYGALAS
POINADO	POLAR	POLITER	POLLUSION	POLYGAM
POINADOS	POLARISE	POLITESSE	POLLUSIONS	POLYGAMIC
POINCIANA	POLARISED	POLITESSES	POLLUTANT	POLYGAMIES
POINCIANAS	POLARISER	POLITEST	POLLUTANTS	POLYGAMS
POIND	POLARISERS	POLITIC	POLLUTE	POLYGAMY
POINDED	POLARISES	POLITICAL	POLLUTED	POLYGENE
POINDER	POLARISING	POLITICK	POLLUTER	POLYGENES
POINDERS	POLARITIES	POLITICKED	POLLUTERS	POLYGENIC
POINDING	POLARITY	POLITICKING	POLLUTES	POLYGENIES
POINDINGS	POLARIZE	POLITICKINGS	POLLUTING	POLYGENY
POINDS	POLARIZED	POLITICKS	POLLUTION	POLYGLOT
POINT	POLARIZER	POLITICLY	POLLUTIONS	POLYGLOTS
POINTE	POLARIZERS	POLITICO	POLLUTIVE	POLYGLOTT
POINTED	POLARIZES	POLITICOES	POLLY	POLYGLOTTS
POINTEDLY	POLARIZING	POLITICOS	POLLYANNA	POLYGON
POINTEL	POLARON	POLITICS	POLLYANNAS	POLYGONAL

POLYGONIES
POLYGONS
POLYGONUM
POLYGONUMS
POLYGONY
POLYGRAPH
POLYGRAPHS
POLYGYNIES
POLYGYNY
POLYHEDRA
POLYLEMMA
POLYLEMMAS
POLYMASTIES
POLYMASTY
POLYMATH
POLYMATHIES
POLYMATHS
POLYMATHY
POLYMER
POLYMERIC
POLYMERIES
POLYMERS
POLYMERY
POLYMORPH
POLYMORPHS
POLYNIA
POLYNIAS
POLYNYA
POLYNYAS
POLYOMINO
POLYOMINOS
POLYONYM
POLYONYMIES
POLYONYMS
POLYONYMY
POLYP
POLYPARIES
POLYPARY
POLYPE
POLYPES
POLYPHAGIES
POLYPHAGY
POLYPHASE
POLYPHON
POLYPHONE
POLYPHONES
POLYPHONIES
POLYPHONS
POLYPHONY
POLYPI
POLYPIDE
POLYPIDES
POLYPIDOM
POLYPIDOMS
POLYPINE
POLYPITE
POLYPITES
POLYPLOID
POLYPOD
POLYPODIES
POLYPODS
POLYPODY
POLYPOID
POLYPOSES
POLYPOSIS
POLYPOUS
POLYPS
POLYPTYCH
POLYPTYCHS
POLYPUS

POLYS
POLYSEME
POLYSEMES
POLYSEMIES
POLYSEMY
POLYSOME
POLYSOMES
POLYSOMIES
POLYSOMY
POLYSTYLE
POLYTENE
POLYTHENE
POLYTHENES
POLYTONAL
POLYTYPIC
POLYURIA
POLYURIAS
POLYVINYL
POLYVINYLS
POLYWATER
POLYWATERS
POLYZOA
POLYZOAN
POLYZOANS
POLYZOARIES
POLYZOARY
POLYZOIC
POLYZONAL
POLYZOOID
POLYZOON
POLYZOONS
POM
POMACE
POMACEOUS
POMACES
POMADE
POMADED
POMADES
POMADING
POMANDER
POMANDERS
POMATO
POMATOES
POMATUM
POMATUMS
POMBE
POMBES
POME
POMELO
POMELOS
POMEROY
POMEROYS
POMES
POMFRET
POMFRETS
POMMEL
POMMELE
POMMELLED
POMMELLING
POMMELS
POMMETTY
POMMIES
POMMY
POMOERIUM
POMOERIUMS
POMOLOGIES
POMOLOGY
POMP
POMPADOUR
POMPADOURS

POMPANO
POMPANOS
POMPELO
POMPELOS
POMPEY
POMPEYED
POMPEYING
POMPEYS
POMPHOLYX
POMPHOLYXES
POMPIER
POMPION
POMPIONS
POMPOM
POMPOMS
POMPON
POMPONS
POMPOON
POMPOONS
POMPOSITIES
POMPOSITY
POMPOUS
POMPOUSLY
POMPS
POMROY
POMROYS
POMS
POMWATER
POMWATERS
PONCE
PONCEAU
PONCEAUS
PONCEAUX
PONCED
PONCES
PONCHO
PONCHOS
PONCING
POND
PONDAGE
PONDAGES
PONDED
PONDER
PONDERAL
PONDERATE
PONDERATED
PONDERATES
PONDERATING
PONDERED
PONDERER
PONDERERS
PONDERING
PONDEROUS
PONDERS
PONDING
PONDOK
PONDOKKIE
PONDOKKIES
PONDOKS
PONDS
PONDWEED
PONDWEEDS
PONE
PONENT
PONES
PONEY
PONEYED
PONEYING
PONEYS
PONG

PONGED
PONGEE
PONGEES
PONGID
PONGIDS
PONGIER
PONGIEST
PONGING
PONGO
PONGOES
PONGOS
PONGS
PONGY
PONIARD
PONIARDED
PONIARDING
PONIARDS
PONIED
PONIES
PONK
PONKED
PONKING
PONKS
PONS
PONTAGE
PONTAGES
PONTAL
PONTES
PONTIANAC
PONTIANACS
PONTIANAK
PONTIANAKS
PONTIC
PONTIE
PONTIES
PONTIFEX
PONTIFF
PONTIFFS
PONTIFIC
PONTIFICE
PONTIFICES
PONTIFIED
PONTIFIES
PONTIFY
PONTIFYING
PONTIL
PONTILE
PONTILS
PONTLEVIS
PONTLEVISES
PONTON
PONTONED
PONTONEER
PONTONEERS
PONTONIER
PONTONIERS
PONTONING
PONTONS
PONTOON
PONTOONED
PONTOONER
PONTOONERS
PONTOONING
PONTOONS
PONTY
PONY
PONYING
POO
POOCH
POOCHES

POOD
POODLE
POODLES
POODS
POOED
POOF
POOFS
POOFTAH
POOFTAHS
POOFTER
POOFTERS
POOGYE
POOGYEE
POOGYEES
POOGYES
POOH
POOING
POOJA
POOJAH
POOJAHS
POOJAS
POOK
POOKA
POOKAS
POOKED
POOKING
POOKIT
POOKS
POOL
POOLED
POOLING
POOLS
POOLSIDE
POOLSIDES
POON
POONAC
POONACS
POONS
POONTANG
POONTANGS
POOP
POOPED
POOPING
POOPS
POOR
POORER
POOREST
POORHOUSE
POORHOUSES
POORISH
POORLIER
POORLIEST
POORLY
POORNESS
POORNESSES
POORT
POORTITH
POORTITHS
POORTS
POORWILL
POORWILLS
POOS
POOT
POOTED
POOTER
POOTERS
POOTING
POOTS
POOVE
POOVERIES

POOVERY	POPSY	POROSCOPIES	PORTESSES	POSADA
POOVES	POPULACE	POROSCOPY	PORTFOLIO	POSADAS
POOVIER	POPULACES	POROSE	PORTFOLIOS	POSAUNE
POOVIEST	POPULAR	POROSES	PORTHOLE	POSAUNES
POOVY	POPULARLY	POROSIS	PORTHOLES	POSE
POP	POPULARS	POROSITIES	PORTHORS	POSÉ
POPADUM	POPULATE	POROSITY	PORTHORSES	POSEABLE
POPADUMS	POPULATED	POROUS	PORTHOS	POSED
POPCORN	POPULATES	PORPESS	PORTHOSES	POSER
POPCORNS	POPULATING	PORPESSE	PORTHOUSE	POSERS
POPE	POPULISM	PORPESSES	PORTHOUSES	POSES
POPEDOM	POPULISMS	PORPHYRIA	PORTICO	POSEUR
POPEDOMS	POPULIST	PORPHYRIAS	PORTICOED	POSEURS
POPEHOOD	POPULISTS	PORPHYRIES	PORTICOES	POSEUSE
POPEHOODS	POPULOUS	PORPHYRIO	PORTICOS	POSEUSES
POPELING	PORAL	PORPHYRIOS	PORTIÈRE	POSH
POPELINGS	PORBEAGLE	PORPHYRY	PORTIÈRES	POSHED
POPERIES	PORBEAGLES	PORPOISE	PORTIGUE	POSHER
POPERIN	PORCELAIN	PORPOISED	PORTIGUES	POSHES
POPERINS	PORCELAINS	PORPOISES	PORTING	POSHEST
POPERY	PORCH	PORPOISING	PORTION	POSHING
POPES	PORCHES	PORPORATE	PORTIONED	POSHLY
POPESHIP	PORCINE	PORRECT	PORTIONER	POSHNESS
POPESHIPS	PORCPISCE	PORRECTED	PORTIONERS	POSHNESSES
POPINJAY	PORCPISCES	PORRECTING	PORTIONING	POSHTEEN
POPINJAYS	PORCUPINE	PORRECTS	PORTIONS	POSHTEENS
POPISH	PORCUPINES	PORRENGER	PORTLAND	POSIES
POPISHLY	PORE	PORRENGERS	PORTLANDS	POSIGRADE
POPJOY	PORED	PORRIDGE	PORTLAST	POSING
POPJOYED	PORER	PORRIDGES	PORTLASTS	POSINGLY
POPJOYING	PORERS	PORRIGO	PORTLIER	POSINGS
POPJOYS	PORES	PORRIGOS	PORTLIEST	POSIT
POPLAR	PORGE	PORRINGER	PORTLY	POSITED
POPLARS	PORGED	PORRINGERS	PORTMAN	POSITING
POPLIN	PORGES	PORT	PORTMEN	POSITION
POPLINS	PORGIE	PORTA	PORTOISE	POSITIONED
POPLITEAL	PORGIES	PORTABLE	PORTOISES	POSITIONING
POPLITIC	PORGING	PORTABLES	PORTOLAN	POSITIONS
POPOVER	PORGY	PORTAGE	PORTOLANI	POSITIVE
POPOVERS	PORIFER	PORTAGES	PORTOLANO	POSITIVES
POPPA	PORIFERAL	PORTAGUE	PORTOLANOS	POSITON
POPPADUM	PORIFERAN	PORTAGUES	PORTOLANS	POSITONS
POPPADUMS	PORIFERS	PORTAL	PORTOUS	POSITRON
POPPAS	PORINESS	PORTALS	PORTOUSES	POSITRONS
POPPED	PORINESSES	PORTANCE	PORTRAIT	POSITS
POPPER	PORING	PORTANCES	PORTRAITED	POSNET
POPPERING	PORISM	PORTAS	PORTRAITING	POSNETS
POPPERINGS	PORISMS	PORTASES	PORTRAITS	POSOLOGIES
POPPERS	PORISTIC	PORTATE	PORTRAY	POSOLOGY
POPPET	PORK	PORTATILE	PORTRAYAL	POSS
POPPETS	PORKER	PORTATIVE	PORTRAYALS	POSSE
POPPIED	PORKERS	PORTATIVES	PORTRAYED	POSSED
POPPIES	PORKIER	PORTED	PORTRAYER	POSSER
POPPING	PORKIEST	PORTEND	PORTRAYERS	POSSERS
POPPIT	PORKLING	PORTENDED	PORTRAYING	POSSES
POPPITS	PORKLINGS	PORTENDING	PORTRAYS	POSSESS
POPPLE	PORKS	PORTENDS	PORTREEVE	POSSESSED
POPPLED	PORKY	PORTENT	PORTREEVES	POSSESSES
POPPLES	PORN	PORTENTS	PORTRESS	POSSESSING
POPPLIER	PORNO	PORTEOUS	PORTRESSES	POSSESSOR
POPPLIEST	PORNOMAG	PORTEOUSES	PORTS	POSSESSORS
POPPLING	PORNOMAGS	PORTER	PORTULACA	POSSET
POPPLY	PORNOS	PORTERAGE	PORTULACAS	POSSETED
POPPY	PORNS	PORTERAGES	PORTULAN	POSSETING
POPPYCOCK	POROGAMIC	PORTERESS	PORTULANS	POSSETS
POPPYCOCKS	POROGAMIES	PORTERESSES	PORTY	POSSIBLE
POPRIN	POROGAMY	PORTERLY	PORWIGGLE	POSSIBLES
POPRINS	POROMERIC	PORTERS	PORWIGGLES	POSSIBLY
POPS	POROSCOPE	PORTESS	PORY	POSSIE
POPSIES	POROSCOPES	PORTESSE	POS	POSSIES

POSSING
POSSUM
POSSUMED
POSSUMING
POSSUMS
POST
POSTAGE
POSTAGES
POSTAL
POSTALS
POSTCARD
POSTCARDED
POSTCARDING
POSTCARDS
POSTCODE
POSTCODED
POSTCODES
POSTCODING
POSTDATE
POSTDATED
POSTDATES
POSTDATING
POSTED
POSTEEN
POSTEENS
POSTER
POSTERED
POSTERING
POSTERIOR
POSTERIORS
POSTERITIES
POSTERITY
POSTERN
POSTERNS
POSTERS
POSTFACE
POSTFACES
POSTFIX
POSTFIXED
POSTFIXES
POSTFIXING
POSTHASTE
POSTHORSE
POSTHORSES
POSTHOUSE
POSTHOUSES
POSTICHE
POSTICHES
POSTICOUS
POSTIE
POSTIES
POSTIL
POSTILION
POSTILIONS
POSTILLED
POSTILLER
POSTILLERS
POSTILLING
POSTILS
POSTING
POSTINGS
POSTLUDE
POSTLUDES
POSTMAN
POSTMARK
POSTMARKS
POSTMEN
POSTPONE
POSTPONED
POSTPONER

POSTPONERS
POSTPONES
POSTPONING
POSTS
POSTULANT
POSTULANTS
POSTULATE
POSTULATED
POSTULATES
POSTULATING
POSTURAL
POSTURE
POSTURED
POSTURER
POSTURERS
POSTURES
POSTURING
POSTURIST
POSTURISTS
POSTWOMAN
POSTWOMEN
POSY
POT
POTABLE
POTABLES
POTAGE
POTAGES
POTAMIC
POTASH
POTASHED
POTASHES
POTASHING
POTASS
POTASSA
POTASSAS
POTASSES
POTASSIC
POTASSIUM
POTASSIUMS
POTATION
POTATIONS
POTATO
POTATOES
POTATORY
POTCH
POTCHE
POTCHED
POTCHER
POTCHERS
POTCHES
POTCHING
POTCHY
POTE
POTED
POTEEN
POTEENS
POTENCE
POTENCÉ
POTENCES
POTENCÉS
POTENCIES
POTENCY
POTENT
POTENTATE
POTENTATES
POTENTIAL
POTENTIALS
POTENTISE
POTENTISED
POTENTISES

POTENTISING
POTENTIZE
POTENTIZED
POTENTIZES
POTENTIZING
POTENTLY
POTENTS
POTES
POTFUL
POTFULS
POTGUN
POTGUNS
POTHECARIES
POTHECARY
POTHEEN
POTHEENS
POTHER
POTHERED
POTHERING
POTHERS
POTHERY
POTHOLE
POTHOLER
POTHOLERS
POTHOLES
POTHOLING
POTHOLINGS
POTHOOK
POTHOOKS
POTHOUSE
POTHOUSES
POTICARIES
POTICARY
POTICHE
POTICHES
POTIN
POTING
POTINS
POTION
POTIONS
POTLACH
POTLACHES
POTOMETER
POTOMETERS
POTOROO
POTOROOS
POTS
POTSHERD
POTSHERDS
POTSTONE
POTSTONES
POTT
POTTAGE
POTTAGES
POTTED
POTTER
POTTERED
POTTERER
POTTERERS
POTTERIES
POTTERING
POTTERINGS
POTTERS
POTTERY
POTTIER
POTTIES
POTTIEST
POTTINESS
POTTINESSES
POTTING

POTTINGAR
POTTINGARS
POTTINGER
POTTINGERS
POTTLE
POTTLES
POTTO
POTTOS
POTTS
POTTY
POUCH
POUCHED
POUCHES
POUCHFUL
POUCHFULS
POUCHIER
POUCHIEST
POUCHING
POUCHY
POUDER
POUDERS
POUDRE
POUDRES
POUF
POUFED
POUFFE
POUFFES
POUFS
POUFTAH
POUFTAHS
POUFTER
POUFTERS
POUK
POUKE
POUKED
POUKES
POUKING
POUKIT
POUKS
POULAINE
POULAINES
POULARD
POULARDS
POULDER
POULDERS
POULDRE
POULDRES
POULDRON
POULDRONS
POULE
POULES
POULP
POULPE
POULPES
POULPS
POULT
POULTER
POULTERER
POULTERERS
POULTERS
POULTICE
POULTICED
POULTICES
POULTICING
POULTRIES
POULTRY
POULTS
POUNCE
POUNCED
POUNCES

POUNCET
POUNCETS
POUNCING
POUND
POUNDAGE
POUNDAGES
POUNDAL
POUNDALS
POUNDED
POUNDER
POUNDERS
POUNDING
POUNDS
POUPE
POUPED
POUPES
POUPING
POUPT
POUR
POURABLE
POURBOIRE
POURBOIRES
POURED
POURER
POURERS
POURIE
POURIES
POURING
POURINGS
POURPOINT
POURPOINTS
POURS
POURSEW
POURSUE
POURSUIT
POURSUITS
POURSUITT
POURSUITTS
POURTRAY
POURTRAYD
POURTRAYED
POURTRAYING
POURTRAYS
POUSOWDIE
POUSOWDIES
POUSSE
POUSSES
POUSSETTE
POUSSETTED
POUSSETTES
POUSSETTING
POUSSIN
POUSSINS
POUT
POUTED
POUTER
POUTERS
POUTHER
POUTHERED
POUTHERING
POUTHERS
POUTIER
POUTIEST
POUTING
POUTINGLY
POUTINGS
POUTS
POUTY
POVERTIES
POVERTY

POW	POYSED	PRAISES	PRATTLED	PRECEPITS
POWAN	POYSES	PRAISING	PRATTLER	PRECEPT
POWANS	POYSING	PRAISINGS	PRATTLERS	PRECEPTOR
POWDER	POYSON	PRALINE	PRATTLES	PRECEPTORS
POWDERED	POYSONED	PRALINES	PRATTLING	PRECEPTS
POWDERING	POYSONING	PRAM	PRATY	PRECESS
POWDERS	POYSONS	PRAMS	PRAU	PRECESSED
POWDERY	POZ	PRANA	PRAUNCE	PRECESSES
POWELLISE	POZZ	PRANAS	PRAUS	PRECESSING
POWELLISED	POZZIES	PRANAYAMA	PRAVITIES	PRÉCIEUSE
POWELLISES	POZZOLANA	PRANAYAMAS	PRAVITY	PRÉCIEUSES
POWELLISING	POZZOLANAS	PRANCE	PRAWLE	PRECINCT
POWELLITE	POZZY	PRANCED	PRAWLES	PRECINCTS
POWELLITES	PRAAM	PRANCER	PRAWLIN	PRECIOUS
POWELLIZE	PRAAMS	PRANCERS	PRAWLINS	PRECIOUSES
POWELLIZED	PRABBLE	PRANCES	PRAWN	PRECIPICE
POWELLIZES	PRABBLES	PRANCING	PRAWNED	PRECIPICES
POWELLIZING	PRACTIC	PRANCINGS	PRAWNING	PRÉCIS
POWER	PRACTICAL	PRANCK	PRAWNS	PRECISE
POWERBOAT	PRACTICALS	PRANCKE	PRAXES	PRÉCISED
POWERBOATS	PRACTICE	PRANCKED	PRAXIS	PRECISELY
POWERED	PRACTICED	PRANCKES	PRAY	PRECISER
POWERFUL	PRACTICES	PRANCKING	PRAYED	PRÉCISES
POWERING	PRACTICING	PRANCKS	PRAYER	PRECISEST
POWERLESS	PRACTICK	PRANDIAL	PRAYERFUL	PRECISIAN
POWERPLAY	PRACTICKS	PRANG	PRAYERS	PRECISIANS
POWERPLAYS	PRACTICS	PRANGED	PRAYING	PRÉCISING
POWERS	PRACTICUM	PRANGING	PRAYINGLY	PRECISION
POWIN	PRACTICUMS	PRANGS	PRAYINGS	PRECISIONS
POWINS	PRACTIQUE	PRANK	PRAYS	PRECISIVE
POWN	PRACTIQUES	PRANKED	PRE	PRECLUDE
POWND	PRACTISE	PRANKFUL	PREACE	PRECLUDED
POWNEY	PRACTISED	PRANKIER	PREACH	PRECLUDES
POWNEYED	PRACTISER	PRANKIEST	PREACHED	PRECLUDING
POWNEYING	PRACTISERS	PRANKING	PREACHER	PRECOCIAL
POWNEYS	PRACTISES	PRANKINGS	PREACHERS	PRECOCITIES
POWNIE	PRACTISING	PRANKISH	PREACHES	PRECOCITY
POWNIED	PRACTIVE	PRANKLE	PREACHIER	PRECONISE
POWNIES	PRACTOLOL	PRANKLED	PREACHIEST	PRECONISED
POWNS	PRACTOLOLS	PRANKLES	PREACHIFIED	PRECONISES
POWNY	PRAD	PRANKLING	PREACHIFIES	PRECONISING
POWNYING	PRADS	PRANKS	PREACHIFY	PRECONIZE
POWRE	PRAEAMBLE	PRANKSOME	PREACHIFYING	PRECONIZED
POWS	PRAEAMBLES	PRANKSTER	PREACHILY	PRECONIZES
POWSOWDIES	PRAECOCES	PRANKSTERS	PREACHING	PRECONIZING
POWSOWDY	PRAEDIAL	PRANKY	PREACHINGS	PRECOOK
POWTER	PRAEDIALS	PRASE	PREACHY	PRECOOKED
POWTERED	PRAEFECT	PRASES	PREAMBLE	PRECOOKING
POWTERING	PRAEFECTS	PRAT	PREAMBLED	PRECOOKS
POWTERS	PRAENOMEN	PRATE	PREAMBLES	PRECURRER
POWWAW	PRAENOMENS	PRATED	PREAMBLING	PRECURRERS
POWWOW	PRAENOMINA	PRATER	PREASE	PRECURSE
POWWOWED	PRAESES	PRATERS	PREASSE	PRECURSES
POWWOWING	PRAESIDIA	PRATES	PREBEND	PRECURSOR
POWWOWS	PRAETOR	PRATFALL	PREBENDAL	PRECURSORS
POX	PRAETORS	PRATFALLEN	PREBENDS	PREDACITIES
POXED	PRAGMATIC	PRATFALLING	PREBIOTIC	PREDACITY
POXES	PRAGMATICS	PRATFALLS	PRECAST	PREDATE
POXIER	PRAHU	PRATFELL	PRECATIVE	PREDATED
POXIEST	PRAHUS	PRATIE	PRECATORY	PREDATES
POXING	PRAIRIE	PRATIES	PRECEDE	PREDATING
POXVIRUS	PRAIRIED	PRATING	PRECEDED	PREDATION
POXVIRUSES	PRAIRIES	PRATINGLY	PRECEDENT	PREDATIONS
POXY	PRAISE	PRATINGS	PRECEDENTS	PREDATIVE
POYNANT	PRAISEACH	PRATIQUE	PRECEDES	PREDATOR
POYNT	PRAISEACHS	PRATIQUES	PRECEDING	PREDATORS
POYNTED	PRAISED	PRATS	PRECEESE	PREDATORY
POYNTING	PRAISEFUL	PRATTED	PRECENTOR	PREDEFINE
POYNTS	PRAISER	PRATTING	PRECENTORS	PREDEFINED
POYSE	PRAISERS	PRATTLE	PRECEPIT	PREDEFINES

PREDEFINING	PREFERRING	PRELATISM	PREMY	PRESAGE
PREDELLA	PREFERS	PRELATISMS	PRENASAL	PRESAGED
PREDELLAS	PREFIGURE	PRELATIST	PRENASALS	PRESAGER
PREDESIGN	PREFIGURED	PRELATISTS	PRENATAL	PRESAGERS
PREDESIGNED	PREFIGURES	PRELATIZE	PRENOTION	PRESAGES
PREDESIGNING	PREFIGURING	PRELATIZED	PRENOTIONS	PRESAGING
PREDESIGNS	PREFIX	PRELATIZES	PRENT	PRESBYOPE
PREDEVOTE	PREFIXED	PRELATIZING	PRENTICE	PRESBYOPES
PREDIAL	PREFIXES	PRELATURE	PRENTICES	PRESBYOPIES
PREDIALS	PREFIXING	PRELATURES	PRENTS	PRESBYOPY
PREDICANT	PREFIXION	PRELATY	PRENUBILE	PRESBYTE
PREDICANTS	PREFIXIONS	PRELECT	PRENZIE	PRESBYTER
PREDICATE	PREFLIGHT	PRELECTED	PREOCCUPIED	PRESBYTERS
PREDICATED	PREFORM	PRELECTING	PREOCCUPIES	PRESBYTES
PREDICATES	PREFORMED	PRELECTOR	PREOCCUPY	PRESCHOOL
PREDICATING	PREFORMING	PRELECTORS	PREOCCUPYING	PRESCIENT
PREDICT	PREFORMS	PRELECTS	PREOPTION	PRESCIND
PREDICTED	PREGGERS	PRELIM	PREOPTIONS	PRESCINDED
PREDICTING	PREGNABLE	PRELIMS	PREORAL	PRESCINDING
PREDICTOR	PREGNANCE	PRELUDE	PREORALLY	PRESCINDS
PREDICTORS	PREGNANCES	PRELUDED	PREORDAIN	PRESCIOUS
PREDICTS	PREGNANCIES	PRELUDES	PREORDAINED	PRESCRIBE
PREDIED	PREGNANCY	PRELUDI	PREORDAINING	PRESCRIBED
PREDIES	PREGNANT	PRELUDIAL	PREORDAINS	PRESCRIBES
PREDIGEST	PREHALLUX	PRELUDING	PREORDER	PRESCRIBING
PREDIGESTED	PREHALLUXES	PRELUDIO	PREORDERED	PRESCRIPT
PREDIGESTING	PREHEAT	PRELUSION	PREORDERING	PRESCRIPTS
PREDIGESTS	PREHEATED	PRELUSIONS	PREORDERS	PRESCUTA
PREDIKANT	PREHEATING	PRELUSIVE	PREP	PRESCUTUM
PREDIKANTS	PREHEATS	PRELUSORY	PREPACK	PRESE
PREDILECT	PREHEND	PREMATURE	PREPACKED	PRESELECT
PREDOOM	PREHENDED	PREMED	PREPACKING	PRESELECTED
PREDOOMED	PREHENDING	PREMEDIC	PREPACKS	PRESELECTING
PREDOOMING	PREHENDS	PREMEDICS	PREPAID	PRESELECTS
PREDOOMS	PREHENSOR	PREMEDS	PREPARE	PRESENCE
PREDY	PREHENSORS	PREMIA	PREPARED	PRESENCES
PREDYING	PREHNITE	PREMIER	PREPARER	PRESENT
PREE	PREHNITES	PREMIÈRE	PREPARERS	PRESENTED
PREED	PREHUMAN	PREMIÈRED	PREPARES	PRESENTEE
PREEING	PREIF	PREMIÈRES	PREPARING	PRESENTEES
PREEMIE	PREIFE	PREMIÈRING	PREPAY	PRESENTER
PREEMIES	PREIFES	PREMIERS	PREPAYING	PRESENTERS
PREEN	PREIFS	PREMIES	PREPAYS	PRESENTING
PREENED	PREJINK	PREMISE	PREPENSE	PRESENTLY
PREENING	PREJUDGE	PREMISED	PREPENSED	PRESENTS
PREENS	PREJUDGED	PREMISES	PREPENSES	PRESERVE
PREES	PREJUDGES	PREMISING	PREPENSING	PRESERVED
PREEVE	PREJUDGING	PREMISS	PREPOLLEX	PRESERVER
PREEVED	PREJUDICE	PREMISSED	PREPOLLEXES	PRESERVERS
PREEVES	PREJUDICED	PREMISSES	PREPOTENT	PRESERVES
PREEVING	PREJUDICES	PREMIUM	PREPPED	PRESERVING
PREFAB	PREJUDICING	PREMIUMS	PREPPIER	PRESES
PREFABS	PREJUDIZE	PREMIX	PREPPIES	PRESET
PREFACE	PREJUDIZES	PREMIXED	PREPPIEST	PRESETS
PREFACED	PRELACIES	PREMIXES	PREPPING	PRESETTING
PREFACES	PRELACY	PREMIXING	PREPPY	PRESIDE
PREFACIAL	PRELATE	PREMOLAR	PREPS	PRESIDED
PREFACING	PRELATES	PREMOLARS	PREPUCE	PRESIDENT
PREFADE	PRELATESS	PREMONISH	PREPUCES	PRESIDENTS
PREFADED	PRELATESSES	PREMONISHED	PREPUTIAL	PRESIDES
PREFADES	PRELATIAL	PREMONISHES	PREQUEL	PRESIDIA
PREFADING	PRELATIC	PREMONISHING	PREQUELS	PRESIDIAL
PREFARD	PRELATIES	PREMORSE	PRERECORD	PRESIDING
PREFATORY	PRELATION	PREMOSAIC	PRERECORDED	PRESIDIO
PREFECT	PRELATIONS	PREMOTION	PRERECORDING	PRESIDIOS
PREFECTS	PRELATISE	PREMOTIONS	PRERECORDS	PRESIDIUM
PREFER	PRELATISED	PREMOVE	PREROSION	PRESIDIUMS
PREFERRED	PRELATISES	PREMOVED	PREROSIONS	PRESS
PREFERRER	PRELATISH	PREMOVES	PRERUPT	PRESSED
PREFERRERS	PRELATISING	PREMOVING	PRESA	PRESSER

PRESSERS	PREVAILING	PRICKLIEST	PRIMED	PRINCIPLE
PRESSES	PREVAILS	PRICKLING	PRIMELY	PRINCIPLED
PRESSFAT	PREVALENT	PRICKLINGS	PRIMENESS	PRINCIPLES
PRESSFATS	PREVE	PRICKLY	PRIMENESSES	PRINCIPLING
PRESSFUL	PREVENE	PRICKS	PRIMER	PRINCOCK
PRESSFULS	PREVENED	PRICKWOOD	PRIMERO	PRINCOCKS
PRESSING	PREVENES	PRICKWOODS	PRIMEROS	PRINCOX
PRESSINGS	PREVENING	PRICY	PRIMERS	PRINCOXES
PRESSION	PREVENT	PRIDE	PRIMES	PRINK
PRESSIONS	PREVENTED	PRIDED	PRIMEUR	PRINKED
PRESSMAN	PREVENTER	PRIDEFUL	PRIMEURS	PRINKING
PRESSMEN	PREVENTERS	PRIDELESS	PRIMEVAL	PRINKS
PRESSOR	PREVENTING	PRIDES	PRIMINE	PRINT
PRESSURE	PREVENTS	PRIDIAN	PRIMINES	PRINTABLE
PRESSURED	PREVERBAL	PRIDING	PRIMING	PRINTED
PRESSURES	PREVIEW	PRIED	PRIMINGS	PRINTER
PRESSURING	PREVIEWED	PRIEF	PRIMIPARA	PRINTERS
PREST	PREVIEWING	PRIEFE	PRIMIPARAE	PRINTING
PRESTED	PREVIEWS	PRIEFES	PRIMIPARAS	PRINTINGS
PRESTIGE	PREVIOUS	PRIEFS	PRIMITIAE	PRINTLESS
PRESTIGES	PREVISE	PRIER	PRIMITIAL	PRINTS
PRESTING	PREVISED	PRIERS	PRIMITIAS	PRION
PRESTO	PREVISES	PRIES	PRIMITIVE	PRIONS
PRESTOS	PREVISING	PRIEST	PRIMITIVES	PRIOR
PRESTS	PREVISION	PRIESTED	PRIMLY	PRIORATE
PRESUME	PREVISIONS	PRIESTESS	PRIMMED	PRIORATES
PRESUMED	PREWYN	PRIESTESSES	PRIMMER	PRIORESS
PRESUMER	PREWYNS	PRIESTING	PRIMMEST	PRIORESSES
PRESUMERS	PREX	PRIESTLY	PRIMMING	PRIORIES
PRESUMES	PREXES	PRIESTS	PRIMNESS	PRIORITIES
PRESUMING	PREXIES	PRIEVE	PRIMNESSES	PRIORITY
PRETENCE	PREXY	PRIEVED	PRIMO	PRIORS
PRETENCES	PREY	PRIEVES	PRIMOS	PRIORSHIP
PRETEND	PREYED	PRIEVING	PRIMP	PRIORSHIPS
PRETENDED	PREYFUL	PRIG	PRIMPED	PRIORY
PRETENDER	PREYING	PRIGGED	PRIMPING	PRISAGE
PRETENDERS	PREYS	PRIGGER	PRIMPS	PRISAGES
PRETENDING	PREZZIE	PRIGGERIES	PRIMROSE	PRISE
PRETENDS	PREZZIES	PRIGGERS	PRIMROSED	PRISED
PRETENSE	PRIAL	PRIGGERY	PRIMROSES	PRISER
PRETENSES	PRIALS	PRIGGING	PRIMROSING	PRISERS
PRETERIST	PRIAPIC	PRIGGINGS	PRIMROSY	PRISES
PRETERISTS	PRIAPISM	PRIGGISH	PRIMS	PRISING
PRETERIT	PRIAPISMS	PRIGGISM	PRIMSIE	PRISM
PRETERITE	PRIBBLE	PRIGGISMS	PRIMULA	PRISMATIC
PRETERITES	PRIBBLES	PRIGS	PRIMULAS	PRISMOID
PRETERITS	PRICE	PRILL	PRIMULINE	PRISMOIDS
PRETERM	PRICED	PRILLED	PRIMULINES	PRISMS
PRETERMIT	PRICELESS	PRILLING	PRIMUS	PRISMY
PRETERMITS	PRICER	PRILLS	PRIMUSES	PRISON
PRETERMITTED	PRICERS	PRIM	PRIMY	PRISONED
PRETERMITTING	PRICES	PRIMA	PRINCE	PRISONER
PRETEXT	PRICEY	PRIMACIES	PRINCED	PRISONERS
PRETEXTS	PRICIER	PRIMACY	PRINCEDOM	PRISONING
PRETTIER	PRICIEST	PRIMAEVAL	PRINCEDOMS	PRISONOUS
PRETTIES	PRICINESS	PRIMAGE	PRINCEKIN	PRISONS
PRETTIEST	PRICINESSES	PRIMAGES	PRINCEKINS	PRISSIER
PRETTIFIED	PRICING	PRIMAL	PRINCELET	PRISSIEST
PRETTIFIES	PRICK	PRIMALITIES	PRINCELETS	PRISSY
PRETTIFY	PRICKED	PRIMALITY	PRINCELIER	PRISTINE
PRETTIFYING	PRICKER	PRIMALLY	PRINCELIEST	PRITHEE
PRETTILY	PRICKERS	PRIMARIES	PRINCELY	PRIVACIES
PRETTY	PRICKET	PRIMARILY	PRINCES	PRIVACY
PRETTYISH	PRICKETS	PRIMARY	PRINCESS	PRIVADO
PRETTYISM	PRICKING	PRIMATAL	PRINCESSE	PRIVADOES
PRETTYISMS	PRICKINGS	PRIMATE	PRINCESSES	PRIVADOS
PRETZEL	PRICKLE	PRIMATES	PRINCING	PRIVATE
PRETZELS	PRICKLED	PRIMATIAL	PRINCIPAL	PRIVATEER
PREVAIL	PRICKLES	PRIMATIC	PRINCIPALS	PRIVATEERED
PREVAILED	PRICKLIER	PRIME	PRINCIPIA	PRIVATEERING

PRIVATEERS
PRIVATELY
PRIVATES
PRIVATION
PRIVATIONS
PRIVATISE
PRIVATISED
PRIVATISES
PRIVATISING
PRIVATIVE
PRIVATIVES
PRIVATIZE
PRIVATIZED
PRIVATIZES
PRIVATIZING
PRIVET
PRIVETS
PRIVIES
PRIVILEGE
PRIVILEGED
PRIVILEGES
PRIVILEGING
PRIVILY
PRIVITIES
PRIVITY
PRIVY
PRIZABLE
PRIZE
PRIZED
PRIZER
PRIZERS
PRIZES
PRIZING
PRO
PROA
PROAS
PROBABLE
PROBABLES
PROBABLY
PROBALL
PROBAND
PROBANDS
PROBANG
PROBANGS
PROBATE
PROBATED
PROBATES
PROBATING
PROBATION
PROBATIONS
PROBATIVE
PROBATORY
PROBE
PROBED
PROBES
PROBING
PROBIT
PROBITIES
PROBITS
PROBITY
PROBLEM
PROBLEMS
PROBOSCIDES
PROBOSCIS
PROBOSCISES
PROCACITIES
PROCACITY
PROCAINE
PROCAINES
PROCARYON

PROCARYONS
PROCEDURE
PROCEDURES
PROCEED
PROCEEDED
PROCEEDER
PROCEEDERS
PROCEEDING
PROCEEDINGS
PROCEEDS
PROCERITIES
PROCERITY
PROCESS
PROCESSED
PROCESSES
PROCESSING
PROCESSOR
PROCESSORS
PROCIDENT
PROCINCT
PROCINCTS
PROCLAIM
PROCLAIMED
PROCLAIMING
PROCLAIMS
PROCLISES
PROCLISIS
PROCLITIC
PROCLITICS
PROCLIVE
PROCONSUL
PROCONSULS
PROCREANT
PROCREANTS
PROCREATE
PROCREATED
PROCREATES
PROCREATING
PROCTAL
PROCTITIS
PROCTITISES
PROCTOR
PROCTORS
PROCURACIES
PROCURACY
PROCURE
PROCURED
PROCURER
PROCURERS
PROCURES
PROCURESS
PROCURESSES
PROCUREUR
PROCUREURS
PROCURING
PROD
PRODDED
PRODDING
PRODIGAL
PRODIGALS
PRODIGIES
PRODIGY
PRODITOR
PRODITORS
PRODITORY
PRODNOSE
PRODNOSED
PRODNOSES
PRODNOSING
PRODROMAL

PRODROME
PRODROMES
PRODROMI
PRODROMIC
PRODROMUS
PRODS
PRODUCE
PRODUCED
PRODUCER
PRODUCERS
PRODUCES
PRODUCING
PRODUCT
PRODUCTS
PROEM
PROEMBRYO
PROEMBRYOS
PROEMIAL
PROEMS
PROENZYME
PROENZYMES
PROF
PROFACE
PROFANE
PROFANED
PROFANELY
PROFANER
PROFANERS
PROFANES
PROFANEST
PROFANING
PROFANITIES
PROFANITY
PROFESS
PROFESSED
PROFESSES
PROFESSING
PROFESSOR
PROFESSORS
PROFFER
PROFFERED
PROFFERER
PROFFERERS
PROFFERING
PROFFERS
PROFILE
PROFILED
PROFILER
PROFILERS
PROFILES
PROFILING
PROFILIST
PROFILISTS
PROFIT
PROFITED
PROFITEER
PROFITEERED
PROFITEERING
PROFITEERINGS
PROFITEERS
PROFITER
PROFITERS
PROFITING
PROFITINGS
PROFITS
PROFLUENT
PROFORMA
PROFORMAS
PROFOUND
PROFOUNDER

PROFOUNDEST
PROFOUNDS
PROFS
PROFUSE
PROFUSELY
PROFUSERS
PROFUSION
PROFUSIONS
PROG
PROGENIES
PROGENY
PROGERIA
PROGERIAS
PROGESTIN
PROGESTINS
PROGGED
PROGGING
PROGGINS
PROGGINSES
PROGNOSES
PROGNOSIS
PROGRADE
PROGRADED
PROGRADES
PROGRADING
PROGRAM
PROGRAMME
PROGRAMMED
PROGRAMMES
PROGRAMMING
PROGRAMS
PROGRESS
PROGRESSED
PROGRESSES
PROGRESSING
PROGS
PROHIBIT
PROHIBITED
PROHIBITING
PROHIBITS
PROIGN
PROIGNS
PROIN
PROINE
PROINES
PROINS
PROJECT
PROJECTED
PROJECTING
PROJECTINGS
PROJECTOR
PROJECTORS
PROJECTS
PROKARYON
PROKARYONS
PROKARYOT
PROKARYOTS
PROKE
PROKED
PROKER
PROKERS
PROKES
PROKING
PROLACTIN
PROLACTINS
PROLAMIN
PROLAMINE
PROLAMINES
PROLAMINS
PROLAPSE

PROLAPSED
PROLAPSES
PROLAPSING
PROLAPSUS
PROLAPSUSES
PROLATE
PROLATED
PROLATELY
PROLATES
PROLATING
PROLATION
PROLATIONS
PROLATIVE
PROLE
PROLEG
PROLEGS
PROLEPSES
PROLEPSIS
PROLEPTIC
PROLER
PROLERS
PROLES
PROLETARIES
PROLETARY
PROLICIDE
PROLICIDES
PROLIFIC
PROLINE
PROLINES
PROLIX
PROLIXITIES
PROLIXITY
PROLIXLY
PROLL
PROLLER
PROLLERS
PROLOGISE
PROLOGISED
PROLOGISES
PROLOGISING
PROLOGIZE
PROLOGIZED
PROLOGIZES
PROLOGIZING
PROLOGUE
PROLOGUED
PROLOGUES
PROLOGUING
PROLONG
PROLONGE
PROLONGED
PROLONGER
PROLONGERS
PROLONGES
PROLONGING
PROLONGS
PROLUSION
PROLUSIONS
PROLUSORY
PROM
PROMACHOS
PROMACHOSES
PROMENADE
PROMENADED
PROMENADES
PROMENADING
PROMETAL
PROMETALS
PROMINENT
PROMISE

PROMISED	PRONGS	PROPHESIES	PROROGUED	PROSTRATE
PROMISEE	PRONOTA	PROPHESY	PROROGUES	PROSTRATED
PROMISEES	PRONOTAL	PROPHESYING	PROROGUING	PROSTRATES
PROMISER	PRONOTUM	PROPHET	PROS	PROSTRATING
PROMISERS	PRONOUN	PROPHETIC	PROSAIC	PROSTYLE
PROMISES	PRONOUNCE	PROPHETS	PROSAICAL	PROSTYLES
PROMISING	PRONOUNCED	PROPHYLL	PROSAISM	PROSY
PROMISOR	PRONOUNCES	PROPHYLLS	PROSAISMS	PROTAMINE
PROMISORS	PRONOUNCING	PROPINE	PROSAIST	PROTAMINES
PROMISSOR	PRONOUNCINGS	PROPINED	PROSAISTS	PROTANDRIES
PROMISSORS	PRONOUNS	PROPINES	PROSATEUR	PROTANDRY
PROMMER	PRONTO	PROPINING	PROSATEURS	PROTANOPE
PROMMERS	PRONUCLEI	PROPODEON	PROSCRIBE	PROTANOPES
PROMO	PROO	PROPODEONS	PROSCRIBED	PROTASES
PROMOS	PROOEMION	PROPODEUM	PROSCRIBES	PROTASIS
PROMOTE	PROOEMIONS	PROPODEUMS	PROSCRIBING	PROTATIC
PROMOTED	PROOEMIUM	PROPOLIS	PROSCRIPT	PROTEA
PROMOTER	PROOEMIUMS	PROPOLISES	PROSCRIPTS	PROTEAN
PROMOTERS	PROOF	PROPONE	PROSE	PROTEAS
PROMOTES	PROOFED	PROPONED	PROSECTOR	PROTEASE
PROMOTING	PROOFING	PROPONENT	PROSECTORS	PROTEASES
PROMOTION	PROOFINGS	PROPONENTS	PROSECUTE	PROTECT
PROMOTIONS	PROOFLESS	PROPONES	PROSECUTED	PROTECTED
PROMOTIVE	PROOFS	PROPONING	PROSECUTES	PROTECTING
PROMOTOR	PROOTIC	PROPOSAL	PROSECUTING	PROTECTOR
PROMOTORS	PROOTICS	PROPOSALS	PROSED	PROTECTORS
PROMPT	PROP	PROPOSE	PROSELYTE	PROTECTS
PROMPTED	PROPAGATE	PROPOSED	PROSELYTED	PROTÉGÉ
PROMPTER	PROPAGATED	PROPOSER	PROSELYTES	PROTÉGÉE
PROMPTERS	PROPAGATES	PROPOSERS	PROSELYTING	PROTÉGÉES
PROMPTEST	PROPAGATING	PROPOSES	PROSEMAN	PROTÉGÉS
PROMPTING	PROPAGE	PROPOSING	PROSEMEN	PROTEID
PROMPTINGS	PROPAGED	PROPOUND	PROSER	PROTEIDS
PROMPTLY	PROPAGES	PROPOUNDED	PROSERS	PROTEIN
PROMPTS	PROPAGING	PROPOUNDING	PROSES	PROTEINIC
PROMPTURE	PROPAGULE	PROPOUNDS	PROSEUCHA	PROTEINS
PROMPTURES	PROPAGULES	PROPPED	PROSEUCHAE	PROTEND
PROMS	PROPALE	PROPPING	PROSEUCHE	PROTENDED
PROMULGE	PROPALED	PROPRIETIES	PROSIER	PROTENDING
PROMULGED	PROPALES	PROPRIETY	PROSIEST	PROTENDS
PROMULGES	PROPALING	PROPS	PROSILY	PROTENSE
PROMULGING	PROPANE	PROPSES	PROSIMIAN	PROTENSES
PROMUSCIS	PROPANES	PROPTOSES	PROSIMIANS	PROTEST
PROMUSCISES	PROPEL	PROPTOSIS	PROSINESS	PROTESTED
PRONAOI	PROPELLED	PROPYL	PROSINESSES	PROTESTER
PRONAOS	PROPELLER	PROPYLA	PROSING	PROTESTERS
PRONATE	PROPELLERS	PROPYLAEA	PROSINGS	PROTESTING
PRONATED	PROPELLING	PROPYLENE	PROSIT	PROTESTOR
PRONATES	PROPELS	PROPYLENES	PROSODIAL	PROTESTORS
PRONATING	PROPEND	PROPYLIC	PROSODIAN	PROTESTS
PRONATION	PROPENDED	PROPYLITE	PROSODIANS	PROTEUS
PRONATIONS	PROPENDING	PROPYLITES	PROSODIC	PROTEUSES
PRONATOR	PROPENDS	PROPYLON	PROSODIES	PROTHALLI
PRONATORS	PROPENE	PROPYLONS	PROSODIST	PROTHESES
PRONE	PROPENES	PROPYLS	PROSODISTS	PROTHESIS
PRONELY	PROPENSE	PRORATE	PROSODY	PROTHETIC
PRONENESS	PROPER	PRORATED	PROSOPON	PROTHORACES
PRONENESSES	PROPERDIN	PRORATES	PROSOPONS	PROTHORAX
PRONER	PROPERDINS	PRORATING	PROSPECT	PROTHORAXES
PRONES	PROPERLY	PRORATION	PROSPECTED	PROTHYL
PRONEST	PROPERS	PRORATIONS	PROSPECTING	PROTHYLE
PRONEUR	PROPERTIED	PRORE	PROSPECTINGS	PROTHYLES
PRONEURS	PROPERTIES	PRORECTOR	PROSPECTS	PROTHYLS
PRONG	PROPERTY	PRORECTORS	PROSPER	PROTIST
PRONGBUCK	PROPERTYING	PRORES	PROSPERED	PROTISTIC
PRONGBUCKS	PROPHASE	PROROGATE	PROSPERING	PROTISTS
PRONGED	PROPHASES	PROROGATED	PROSPERS	PROTIUM
PRONGHORN	PROPHECIES	PROROGATES	PROSTATE	PROTIUMS
PRONGHORNS	PROPHECY	PROROGATING	PROSTATES	PROTOCOL
PRONGING	PROPHESIED	PROROGUE	PROSTATIC	PROTOCOLLED

PROTOCOLLING
PROTOCOLS
PROTOGINE
PROTOGINES
PROTOGYNIES
PROTOGYNY
PROTON
PROTONEMA
PROTONEMATA
PROTONIC
PROTONS
PROTOSTAR
PROTOSTARS
PROTOTYPE
PROTOTYPED
PROTOTYPES
PROTOTYPING
PROTOXIDE
PROTOXIDES
PROTOZOA
PROTOZOAN
PROTOZOANS
PROTOZOIC
PROTOZOON
PROTRACT
PROTRACTED
PROTRACTING
PROTRACTS
PROTRUDE
PROTRUDED
PROTRUDES
PROTRUDING
PROTYL
PROTYLE
PROTYLES
PROTYLS
PROUD
PROUDER
PROUDEST
PROUDISH
PROUDLY
PROUDNESS
PROUDNESSES
PROUL
PROULED
PROULER
PROULERS
PROULING
PROULS
PROUSTITE
PROUSTITES
PROVABLE
PROVABLY
PROVAND
PROVANDS
PROVANT
PROVE
PROVEABLE
PROVEABLY
PROVED
PROVEDOR
PROVEDORE
PROVEDORES
PROVEDORS
PROVEN
PROVEND
PROVENDER
PROVENDERED
PROVENDERING
PROVENDERS

PROVENDS
PROVER
PROVERB
PROVERBED
PROVERBING
PROVERBS
PROVERS
PROVES
PROVIANT
PROVIANTS
PROVIDE
PROVIDED
PROVIDENT
PROVIDER
PROVIDERS
PROVIDES
PROVIDING
PROVIDOR
PROVIDORS
PROVINCE
PROVINCES
PROVINE
PROVINED
PROVINES
PROVING
PROVINING
PROVIRAL
PROVIRUS
PROVIRUSES
PROVISION
PROVISIONED
PROVISIONING
PROVISIONS
PROVISO
PROVISOES
PROVISOR
PROVISORS
PROVISORY
PROVISOS
PROVOCANT
PROVOCANTS
PROVOKE
PROVOKED
PROVOKER
PROVOKERS
PROVOKES
PROVOKING
PROVOST
PROVOSTRIES
PROVOSTRY
PROVOSTS
PROW
PROWESS
PROWESSED
PROWESSES
PROWEST
PROWL
PROWLED
PROWLER
PROWLERS
PROWLING
PROWLINGS
PROWLS
PROWS
PROXIES
PROXIMAL
PROXIMATE
PROXIMITIES
PROXIMITY
PROXIMO

PROXY
PROYN
PROYNE
PROYNES
PROYNS
PROZYMITE
PROZYMITES
PRUDE
PRUDENCE
PRUDENCES
PRUDENT
PRUDENTLY
PRUDERIES
PRUDERY
PRUDES
PRUDISH
PRUDISHLY
PRUH
PRUINA
PRUINAS
PRUINE
PRUINES
PRUINOSE
PRUNE
PRUNED
PRUNELLA
PRUNELLAS
PRUNELLE
PRUNELLES
PRUNELLO
PRUNELLOS
PRUNER
PRUNERS
PRUNES
PRUNING
PRUNINGS
PRUNT
PRUNTED
PRUNTS
PRURIENCE
PRURIENCES
PRURIENCIES
PRURIENCY
PRURIENT
PRURIGO
PRURIGOS
PRURITIC
PRURITUS
PRURITUSES
PRUSSIAN
PRUSSIANS
PRUSSIATE
PRUSSIATES
PRUSSIC
PRY
PRYER
PRYERS
PRYING
PRYINGLY
PRYINGS
PRYS
PRYSE
PRYSES
PRYTANEA
PRYTANEUM
PRYTHEE
PSALM
PSALMIST
PSALMISTS
PSALMODIC

PSALMODIES
PSALMODY
PSALMS
PSALTER
PSALTERIA
PSALTERIES
PSALTERS
PSALTERY
PSALTRESS
PSALTRESSES
PSAMMITE
PSAMMITES
PSAMMITIC
PSELLISM
PSELLISMS
PSEPHISM
PSEPHISMS
PSEPHITE
PSEPHITES
PSEPHITIC
PSEUD
PSEUDAXES
PSEUDAXIS
PSEUDERIES
PSEUDERY
PSEUDISH
PSEUDO
PSEUDONYM
PSEUDONYMS
PSEUDOPOD
PSEUDOPODS
PSEUDOS
PSEUDS
PSHAW
PSHAWED
PSHAWING
PSHAWS
PSI
PSILOSES
PSILOSIS
PSILOTIC
PSIONIC
PSIS
PSOAS
PSOASES
PSORA
PSORAS
PSORIASES
PSORIASIS
PSORIATIC
PSORIC
PSST
PST
PSYCH
PSYCHE
PSYCHED
PSYCHES
PSYCHIC
PSYCHICAL
PSYCHICS
PSYCHING
PSYCHISM
PSYCHISMS
PSYCHIST
PSYCHISTS
PSYCHO
PSYCHOGAS
PSYCHOGASES
PSYCHOID
PSYCHOIDS

PSYCHOS
PSYCHOSES
PSYCHOSIS
PSYCHOTIC
PSYCHOTICS
PSYCHS
PSYOP
PSYOPS
PSYWAR
PSYWARS
PTARMIC
PTARMICS
PTARMIGAN
PTARMIGANS
PTERIA
PTERIN
PTERINS
PTERION
PTEROPOD
PTEROPODS
PTEROSAUR
PTEROSAURS
PTERYGIA
PTERYGIAL
PTERYGIUM
PTERYGOID
PTERYGOIDS
PTERYLA
PTERYLAE
PTILOSES
PTILOSIS
PTISAN
PTISANS
PTOMAINE
PTOMAINES
PTOSES
PTOSIS
PTYALIN
PTYALINS
PTYALISE
PTYALISED
PTYALISES
PTYALISING
PTYALISM
PTYALISMS
PTYALIZE
PTYALIZED
PTYALIZES
PTYALIZING
PTYXES
PTYXIS
PTYXISES
PUB
PUBBED
PUBBING
PUBERAL
PUBERTAL
PUBERTIES
PUBERTY
PUBES
PUBESCENT
PUBIC
PUBIS
PUBISES
PUBLIC
PUBLICAN
PUBLICANS
PUBLICISE
PUBLICISED
PUBLICISES

PUBLICISING
PUBLICIST
PUBLICISTS
PUBLICITIES
PUBLICITY
PUBLICIZE
PUBLICIZED
PUBLICIZES
PUBLICIZING
PUBLICLY
PUBLICS
PUBLISH
PUBLISHED
PUBLISHER
PUBLISHERS
PUBLISHES
PUBLISHING
PUBS
PUCCOON
PUCCOONS
PUCE
PUCELAGE
PUCELAGES
PUCELLE
PUCELLES
PUCES
PUCK
PUCKA
PUCKER
PUCKERED
PUCKERING
PUCKERS
PUCKERY
PUCKFIST
PUCKFISTS
PUCKISH
PUCKS
PUD
PUDDED
PUDDEN
PUDDENING
PUDDENINGS
PUDDENS
PUDDER
PUDDERED
PUDDERING
PUDDERS
PUDDIES
PUDDING
PUDDINGS
PUDDINGY
PUDDLE
PUDDLED
PUDDLER
PUDDLERS
PUDDLES
PUDDLIER
PUDDLIEST
PUDDLING
PUDDLINGS
PUDDLY
PUDDOCK
PUDDOCKS
PUDDY
PUDENCIES
PUDENCY
PUDENDA
PUDENDAL
PUDENDOUS
PUDENDUM

PUDENT
PUDGE
PUDGES
PUDGIER
PUDGIEST
PUDGINESS
PUDGINESSES
PUDGY
PUDIBUND
PUDIC
PUDICITIES
PUDICITY
PUDOR
PUDORS
PUDS
PUDSEY
PUDSY
PUEBLO
PUEBLOS
PUER
PUERED
PUERILE
PUERILISM
PUERILISMS
PUERILITIES
PUERILITY
PUERING
PUERPERAL
PUERS
PUFF
PUFFBALL
PUFFBALLS
PUFFED
PUFFER
PUFFERIES
PUFFERS
PUFFERY
PUFFIER
PUFFIEST
PUFFILY
PUFFIN
PUFFINESS
PUFFINESSES
PUFFING
PUFFINGLY
PUFFINGS
PUFFINS
PUFFS
PUFFY
PUG
PUGGAREE
PUGGAREES
PUGGED
PUGGERIES
PUGGERY
PUGGIER
PUGGIES
PUGGIEST
PUGGING
PUGGINGS
PUGGISH
PUGGREE
PUGGREES
PUGGY
PUGH
PUGIL
PUGILISM
PUGILISMS
PUGILIST
PUGILISTS

PUGILS
PUGNACITIES
PUGNACITY
PUGS
PUH
PUIR
PUIRER
PUIREST
PUISNE
PUISNES
PUISNIES
PUISNY
PUISSANCE
PUISSANCES
PUISSANT
PUISSAUNT
PUJA
PUJAS
PUKE
PUKED
PUKER
PUKERS
PUKES
PUKING
PUKKA
PULDRON
PULDRONS
PULE
PULED
PULER
PULERS
PULES
PULICIDE
PULICIDES
PULING
PULINGLY
PULINGS
PULK
PULKA
PULKAS
PULKHA
PULKHAS
PULKS
PULL
PULLED
PULLER
PULLERS
PULLET
PULLETS
PULLEY
PULLEYS
PULLING
PULLOVER
PULLOVERS
PULLS
PULLULATE
PULLULATED
PULLULATES
PULLULATING
PULMO
PULMONARY
PULMONATE
PULMONATES
PULMONES
PULMONIC
PULMONICS
PULP
PULPBOARD
PULPBOARDS
PULPED

PULPER
PULPERS
PULPIER
PULPIEST
PULPIFIED
PULPIFIES
PULPIFY
PULPIFYING
PULPILY
PULPINESS
PULPINESSES
PULPING
PULPIT
PULPITED
PULPITEER
PULPITEERS
PULPITER
PULPITERS
PULPITRIES
PULPITRY
PULPITS
PULPITUM
PULPITUMS
PULPMILL
PULPMILLS
PULPOUS
PULPS
PULPSTONE
PULPSTONES
PULPWOOD
PULPWOODS
PULPY
PULQUE
PULQUES
PULSAR
PULSARS
PULSATE
PULSATED
PULSATES
PULSATILE
PULSATING
PULSATION
PULSATIONS
PULSATIVE
PULSATOR
PULSATORS
PULSATORY
PULSE
PULSED
PULSEJET
PULSEJETS
PULSELESS
PULSES
PULSIDGE
PULSIDGES
PULSIFIC
PULSING
PULSOJET
PULSOJETS
PULTAN
PULTANS
PULTON
PULTONS
PULTOON
PULTOONS
PULTUN
PULTUNS
PULTURE
PULTURES
PULU

PULUS
PULVER
PULVERED
PULVERINE
PULVERINES
PULVERING
PULVERISE
PULVERISED
PULVERISES
PULVERISING
PULVERIZE
PULVERIZED
PULVERIZES
PULVERIZING
PULVEROUS
PULVERS
PULVIL
PULVILIO
PULVILIOS
PULVILLAR
PULVILLE
PULVILLED
PULVILLES
PULVILLI
PULVILLING
PULVILLIO
PULVILLIOS
PULVILLUS
PULVILS
PULVINAR
PULVINATE
PULVINI
PULVINULE
PULVINULES
PULVINUS
PULWAR
PULWARS
PULY
PUMA
PUMAS
PUMELO
PUMELOS
PUMICATE
PUMICATED
PUMICATES
PUMICATING
PUMICE
PUMICED
PUMICEOUS
PUMICES
PUMICING
PUMIE
PUMIES
PUMMEL
PUMMELLED
PUMMELLING
PUMMELS
PUMP
PUMPED
PUMPER
PUMPERS
PUMPING
PUMPION
PUMPIONS
PUMPKIN
PUMPKINS
PUMPS
PUMY
PUN
PUNA

PUNALUA	PUNKINESS	PUPPYISMS	PURITIES	PURSINESSES
PUNALUAN	PUNKINESSES	PUPS	PURITY	PURSING
PUNALUAS	PUNKS	PUPUNHA	PURL	PURSLAIN
PUNAS	PUNNED	PUPUNHAS	PURLED	PURSLAINS
PUNCE	PUNNER	PUR	PURLER	PURSLANE
PUNCES	PUNNERS	PURBLIND	PURLERS	PURSLANES
PUNCH	PUNNET	PURCHASE	PURLICUE	PURSUABLE
PUNCHED	PUNNETS	PURCHASED	PURLICUED	PURSUAL
PUNCHEON	PUNNING	PURCHASER	PURLICUES	PURSUALS
PUNCHEONS	PUNNINGS	PURCHASERS	PURLICUING	PURSUANCE
PUNCHER	PUNS	PURCHASES	PURLIEU	PURSUANCES
PUNCHERS	PUNSTER	PURCHASING	PURLIEUS	PURSUANT
PUNCHES	PUNSTERS	PURDAH	PURLIN	PURSUE
PUNCHIER	PUNT	PURDAHS	PURLINE	PURSUED
PUNCHIEST	PUNTED	PURDONIUM	PURLINES	PURSUER
PUNCHING	PUNTEE	PURDONIUMS	PURLING	PURSUERS
PUNCHY	PUNTEES	PURE	PURLINGS	PURSUES
PUNCTA	PUNTER	PURED	PURLINS	PURSUING
PUNCTATE	PUNTERS	PURÉE	PURLOIN	PURSUINGS
PUNCTATED	PUNTIES	PURÉED	PURLOINED	PURSUIT
PUNCTATOR	PUNTING	PURÉEING	PURLOINER	PURSUITS
PUNCTATORS	PUNTO	PURÉES	PURLOINERS	PURSY
PUNCTILIO	PUNTOS	PURELY	PURLOINING	PURTRAID
PUNCTILIOS	PUNTS	PURENESS	PURLOINS	PURTRAYD
PUNCTO	PUNTSMAN	PURENESSES	PURLS	PURTY
PUNCTOS	PUNTSMEN	PURER	PURPIE	PURULENCE
PUNCTUAL	PUNTY	PURES	PURPIES	PURULENCES
PUNCTUATE	PUNY	PUREST	PURPLE	PURULENCIES
PUNCTUATED	PUP	PURFLE	PURPLED	PURULENCY
PUNCTUATES	PUPA	PURFLED	PURPLES	PURULENT
PUNCTUATING	PUPAE	PURFLES	PURPLING	PURVEY
PUNCTULE	PUPAL	PURFLING	PURPLISH	PURVEYED
PUNCTULES	PUPARIA	PURFLINGS	PURPLY	PURVEYING
PUNCTUM	PUPARIAL	PURFLY	PURPORT	PURVEYOR
PUNCTURE	PUPARIUM	PURGATION	PURPORTED	PURVEYORS
PUNCTURED	PUPAS	PURGATIONS	PURPORTING	PURVEYS
PUNCTURES	PUPATE	PURGATIVE	PURPORTS	PURVIEW
PUNCTURING	PUPATED	PURGATIVES	PURPOSE	PURVIEWS
PUNDIT	PUPATES	PURGATORIES	PURPOSED	PUS
PUNDITRIES	PUPATING	PURGATORY	PURPOSELY	PUSES
PUNDITRY	PUPATION	PURGE	PURPOSES	PUSH
PUNDITS	PUPATIONS	PURGED	PURPOSING	PUSHED
PUNDONOR	PUPFISH	PURGER	PURPOSIVE	PUSHER
PUNDONORES	PUPFISHES	PURGERS	PURPURA	PUSHERS
PUNGENCE	PUPIL	PURGES	PURPURAS	PUSHES
PUNGENCES	PUPILLAGE	PURGING	PURPURE	PUSHFUL
PUNGENCIES	PUPILLAGES	PURGINGS	PURPUREAL	PUSHFULLY
PUNGENCY	PUPILLARY	PURI	PURPURES	PUSHIER
PUNGENT	PUPILLATE	PURIFIED	PURPURIC	PUSHIEST
PUNGENTLY	PUPILS	PURIFIER	PURPURIN	PUSHINESS
PUNIER	PUPPED	PURIFIERS	PURPURINS	PUSHINESSES
PUNIEST	PUPPET	PURIFIES	PURPY	PUSHING
PUNILY	PUPPETEER	PURIFY	PURR	PUSHINGLY
PUNINESS	PUPPETEERS	PURIFYING	PURRED	PUSHROD
PUNINESSES	PUPPETRIES	PURIM	PURRING	PUSHRODS
PUNISH	PUPPETRY	PURIMS	PURRINGLY	PUSHY
PUNISHED	PUPPETS	PURIN	PURRINGS	PUSLE
PUNISHER	PUPPIED	PURINE	PURRS	PUSLED
PUNISHERS	PUPPIES	PURINES	PURS	PUSLES
PUNISHES	PUPPING	PURING	PURSE	PUSLING
PUNISHING	PUPPODUM	PURINS	PURSED	PUSS
PUNITION	PUPPODUMS	PURIS	PURSEFUL	PUSSEL
PUNITIONS	PUPPY	PURISM	PURSEFULS	PUSSELS
PUNITIVE	PUPPYDOM	PURISMS	PURSER	PUSSES
PUNITORY	PUPPYDOMS	PURIST	PURSERS	PUSSIES
PUNK	PUPPYHOOD	PURISTIC	PURSES	PUSSY
PUNKA	PUPPYHOODS	PURISTS	PURSEW	PUSSYFOOT
PUNKAH	PUPPYING	PURITAN	PURSIER	PUSSYFOOTED
PUNKAHS	PUPPYISH	PURITANIC	PURSIEST	PUSSYFOOTING
PUNKAS	PUPPYISM	PURITANS	PURSINESS	PUSSYFOOTS

PUSTULANT	PUTTIERS	PYET	PYRAMISES	PYROMANCIES
PUSTULANTS	PUTTIES	PYETS	PYRE	PYROMANCY
PUSTULAR	PUTTING	PYGAL	PYRENE	PYROMANIA
PUSTULATE	PUTTINGS	PYGALS	PYRENEITE	PYROMANIAS
PUSTULATED	PUTTO	PYGARG	PYRENEITES	PYROMETER
PUSTULATES	PUTTOCK	PYGARGS	PYRENES	PYROMETERS
PUSTULATING	PUTTOCKS	PYGIDIA	PYRENOID	PYROMETRIES
PUSTULE	PUTTS	PYGIDIAL	PYRENOIDS	PYROMETRY
PUSTULES	PUTTY	PYGIDIUM	PYRES	PYROPE
PUSTULOUS	PUTTYING	PYGIDIUMS	PYRETHRIN	PYROPES
PUT	PUTURE	PYGMAEAN	PYRETHRINS	PYROPHONE
PUTAMEN	PUTURES	PYGMEAN	PYRETHRUM	PYROPHONES
PUTAMINA	PUTZ	PYGMIES	PYRETHRUMS	PYROPUS
PUTATIVE	PUTZES	PYGMOID	PYRETIC	PYROPUSES
PUTCHER	PUY	PYGMY	PYREXIA	PYROS
PUTCHERS	PUYS	PYGOSTYLE	PYREXIAL	PYROSCOPE
PUTCHOCK	PUZEL	PYGOSTYLES	PYREXIAS	PYROSCOPES
PUTCHOCKS	PUZELS	PYJAMAED	PYREXIC	PYROSES
PUTCHUK	PUZZEL	PYJAMAS	PYRIDINE	PYROSIS
PUTCHUKS	PUZZELS	PYKNIC	PYRIDINES	PYROSOME
PUTEAL	PUZZLE	PYKNOSOME	PYRIDOXIN	PYROSOMES
PUTEALS	PUZZLED	PYKNOSOMES	PYRIDOXINS	PYROSTAT
PUTELI	PUZZLEDOM	PYLON	PYRIFORM	PYROSTATS
PUTELIS	PUZZLEDOMS	PYLONS	PYRITE	PYROXENE
PUTID	PUZZLER	PYLORIC	PYRITES	PYROXENES
PUTLOCK	PUZZLERS	PYLORUS	PYRITESES	PYROXENIC
PUTLOCKS	PUZZLES	PYLORUSES	PYRITIC	PYROXYLE
PUTLOG	PUZZLING	PYNE	PYRITICAL	PYROXYLES
PUTLOGS	PUZZOLANA	PYNED	PYRITISE	PYROXYLIC
PUTOIS	PUZZOLANAS	PYNES	PYRITISED	PYROXYLIN
PUTOISES	PYAEMIA	PYNING	PYRITISES	PYROXYLINS
PUTREFIED	PYAEMIAS	PYOGENIC	PYRITISING	PYRRHIC
PUTREFIES	PYAEMIC	PYOID	PYRITIZE	PYRRHICS
PUTREFY	PYAT	PYONER	PYRITIZED	PYRRHOUS
PUTREFYING	PYATS	PYONERS	PYRITIZES	PYRROLE
PUTRID	PYCNIC	PYONINGS	PYRITIZING	PYRROLES
PUTRIDER	PYCNIDIA	PYORRHOEA	PYRITOUS	PYRUVATE
PUTRIDEST	PYCNIDIUM	PYORRHOEAS	PYRO	PYRUVATES
PUTRIDITIES	PYCNIDIUMS	PYOT	PYROCLAST	PYTHIUM
PUTRIDITY	PYCNITE	PYOTS	PYROCLASTS	PYTHIUMS
PUTRIDLY	PYCNITES	PYRACANTH	PYROGEN	PYTHON
PUTS	PYCNON	PYRACANTHS	PYROGENIC	PYTHONESS
PUTSCH	PYCNONS	PYRAL	PYROGENS	PYTHONESSES
PUTSCHES	PYE	PYRALID	PYROLATER	PYTHONIC
PUTT	PYEBALD	PYRALIDS	PYROLATERS	PYTHONS
PUTTED	PYEBALDS	PYRALIS	PYROLATRIES	PYURIA
PUTTEE	PYEING	PYRALISES	PYROLATRY	PYURIAS
PUTTEES	PYELITIC	PYRAMID	PYROLYSE	PYX
PUTTEN	PYELITIS	PYRAMIDAL	PYROLYSED	PYXED
PUTTER	PYELITISES	PYRAMIDED	PYROLYSES	PYXES
PUTTERED	PYELOGRAM	PYRAMIDES	PYROLYSING	PYXIDES
PUTTERING	PYELOGRAMS	PYRAMIDIC	PYROLYSIS	PYXIDIA
PUTTERS	PYEMIA	PYRAMIDING	PYROLYTIC	PYXIDIUM
PUTTI	PYEMIAS	PYRAMIDON	PYROLYZE	PYXING
PUTTIE	PYENGADU	PYRAMIDONS	PYROLYZED	PYXIS
PUTTIED	PYENGADUS	PYRAMIDS	PYROLYZES	PZAZZ
PUTTIER	PYES	PYRAMIS	PYROLYZING	PZAZZES

Q

QADI
QADIS
QALAMDAN
QALAMDANS
QANAT
QANATS
QAT
QATS
QIBLA
QIBLAS
QIGONG
QIGONGS
QINTAR
QINTARS
QUA
QUACK
QUACKED
QUACKERIES
QUACKERY
QUACKING
QUACKLE
QUACKLED
QUACKLES
QUACKLING
QUACKS
QUAD
QUADDED
QUADDING
QUADRANS
QUADRANT
QUADRANTES
QUADRANTS
QUADRAT
QUADRATE
QUADRATED
QUADRATES
QUADRATIC
QUADRATICS
QUADRATING
QUADRATS
QUADRATUS
QUADRATUSES
QUADRELLA
QUADRELLAS
QUADRIC
QUADRIFID
QUADRIGA
QUADRIGAE
QUADRILLE
QUADRILLED
QUADRILLES
QUADRILLING
QUADROON
QUADROONS
QUADRUMAN
QUADRUMANS
QUADRUPED
QUADRUPEDS
QUADRUPLE
QUADRUPLED
QUADRUPLES
QUADRUPLIES
QUADRUPLING
QUADRUPLY
QUADS
QUAERE

QUAERED
QUAERES
QUAERING
QUAERITUR
QUAESITUM
QUAESITUMS
QUAESTOR
QUAESTORS
QUAFF
QUAFFED
QUAFFER
QUAFFERS
QUAFFING
QUAFFS
QUAG
QUAGGA
QUAGGAS
QUAGGIER
QUAGGIEST
QUAGGY
QUAGMIRE
QUAGMIRED
QUAGMIRES
QUAGMIRIER
QUAGMIRIEST
QUAGMIRING
QUAGMIRY
QUAGS
QUAHAUG
QUAHAUGS
QUAHOG
QUAHOGS
QUAICH
QUAICHS
QUAIGH
QUAIGHS
QUAIL
QUAILED
QUAILING
QUAILINGS
QUAILS
QUAINT
QUAINTER
QUAINTEST
QUAINTLY
QUAIR
QUAIRS
QUAKE
QUAKED
QUAKES
QUAKIER
QUAKIEST
QUAKINESS
QUAKINESSES
QUAKING
QUAKINGLY
QUAKINGS
QUAKY
QUALAMDAN
QUALAMDANS
QUALE
QUALIA
QUALIFIED
QUALIFIER

QUALIFIERS
QUALIFIES
QUALIFY
QUALIFYING
QUALIFYINGS
QUALITIED
QUALITIES
QUALITY
QUALM
QUALMIER
QUALMIEST
QUALMING
QUALMISH
QUALMLESS
QUALMS
QUALMY
QUAMASH
QUAMASHES
QUANDANG
QUANDANGS
QUANDARIES
QUANDARY
QUANDONG
QUANDONGS
QUANGO
QUANGOS
QUANNET
QUANNETS
QUANT
QUANTA
QUANTAL
QUANTED
QUANTIC
QUANTICAL
QUANTICS
QUANTIFIED
QUANTIFIES
QUANTIFY
QUANTIFYING
QUANTING
QUANTISE
QUANTISED
QUANTISES
QUANTISING
QUANTITIES
QUANTITY
QUANTIZE
QUANTIZED
QUANTIZES
QUANTIZING
QUANTONG
QUANTONGS
QUANTS
QUANTUM
QUARENDEN
QUARENDENS
QUARENDER
QUARENDERS
QUARK
QUARKS
QUARLE
QUARLES
QUARREL
QUARRELLED

QUARRELLING
QUARRELLINGS
QUARRELS
QUARRIED
QUARRIER
QUARRIERS
QUARRIES
QUARRY
QUARRYING
QUARRYMAN
QUARRYMEN
QUART
QUARTAN
QUARTANS
QUARTE
QUARTER
QUARTERED
QUARTERING
QUARTERINGS
QUARTERLIES
QUARTERLY
QUARTERN
QUARTERNS
QUARTERS
QUARTES
QUARTET
QUARTETS
QUARTETT
QUARTETTE
QUARTETTES
QUARTETTI
QUARTETTO
QUARTETTS
QUARTIC
QUARTICS
QUARTIER
QUARTIERS
QUARTILE
QUARTILES
QUARTO
QUARTOS
QUARTS
QUARTZ
QUARTZES
QUARTZITE
QUARTZITES
QUARTZOSE
QUARTZY
QUASAR
QUASARS
QUASH
QUASHED
QUASHEE
QUASHEES
QUASHES
QUASHIE
QUASHIES
QUASHING
QUASI
QUASSIA
QUASSIAS
QUAT
QUATCH
QUATCHED

QUATCHES
QUATCHING
QUATORZE
QUATORZES
QUATRAIN
QUATRAINS
QUATS
QUAVER
QUAVERED
QUAVERER
QUAVERERS
QUAVERING
QUAVERINGS
QUAVERS
QUAVERY
QUAY
QUAYAGE
QUAYAGES
QUAYD
QUAYS
QUAYSIDE
QUAYSIDES
QUEACH
QUEACHES
QUEACHY
QUEAN
QUEANS
QUEASIER
QUEASIEST
QUEASILY
QUEASY
QUEAZIER
QUEAZIEST
QUEAZY
QUEBRACHO
QUEBRACHOS
QUEECHY
QUEEN
QUEENDOM
QUEENDOMS
QUEENED
QUEENHOOD
QUEENHOODS
QUEENING
QUEENINGS
QUEENITE
QUEENITES
QUEENLESS
QUEENLET
QUEENLETS
QUEENLIER
QUEENLIEST
QUEENLY
QUEENS
QUEENSHIP
QUEENSHIPS
QUEER
QUEERDOM
QUEERDOMS
QUEERED
QUEERER
QUEEREST
QUEERING
QUEERISH

QUEERITIES
QUEERITY
QUEERLY
QUEERNESS
QUEERNESSES
QUEERS
QUEEST
QUEESTS
QUEINT
QUELCH
QUELCHED
QUELCHES
QUELCHING
QUELEA
QUELEAS
QUELL
QUELLED
QUELLER
QUELLERS
QUELLING
QUELLS
QUEME
QUEMED
QUEMES
QUEMING
QUENA
QUENAS
QUENCH
QUENCHED
QUENCHER
QUENCHERS
QUENCHES
QUENCHING
QUENCHINGS
QUENELLE
QUENELLES
QUEP
QUERCETUM
QUERCETUMS
QUERIED
QUERIES
QUERIMONIES
QUERIMONY
QUERIST
QUERISTS
QUERN
QUERNS
QUERULOUS
QUERY
QUERYING
QUERYINGS
QUEST
QUESTANT
QUESTANTS
QUESTED
QUESTER
QUESTERS
QUESTING
QUESTINGS
QUESTION
QUESTIONED
QUESTIONING
QUESTIONS
QUESTOR
QUESTORS
QUESTRIST
QUESTRISTS
QUESTS
QUETCH
QUETCHED

QUETCHES
QUETCHING
QUETHE
QUETHES
QUETHING
QUETSCH
QUETSCHES
QUETZAL
QUETZALS
QUEUE
QUEUED
QUEUEING
QUEUEINGS
QUEUES
QUEUING
QUEUINGS
QUEY
QUEYN
QUEYNIE
QUEYNIES
QUEYNS
QUEYS
QUIBBLE
QUIBBLED
QUIBBLER
QUIBBLERS
QUIBBLES
QUIBBLING
QUIBBLINGS
QUIBLIN
QUIBLINS
QUICH
QUICHE
QUICHED
QUICHES
QUICHING
QUICK
QUICKBEAM
QUICKBEAMS
QUICKEN
QUICKENED
QUICKENER
QUICKENERS
QUICKENING
QUICKENINGS
QUICKENS
QUICKER
QUICKEST
QUICKIE
QUICKIES
QUICKLIME
QUICKLIMES
QUICKLY
QUICKNESS
QUICKNESSES
QUICKS
QUICKSAND
QUICKSANDS
QUICKSET
QUICKSETS
QUICKSTEP
QUICKSTEPPED
QUICKSTEPPING
QUICKSTEPS
QUID
QUIDAM
QUIDAMS
QUIDDANIES
QUIDDANY
QUIDDIT

QUIDDITIES
QUIDDITS
QUIDDITY
QUIDDLE
QUIDDLED
QUIDDLER
QUIDDLERS
QUIDDLES
QUIDDLING
QUIDNUNC
QUIDNUNCS
QUIDS
QUIESCE
QUIESCED
QUIESCENT
QUIESCES
QUIESCING
QUIET
QUIETED
QUIETEN
QUIETENED
QUIETENING
QUIETENINGS
QUIETENS
QUIETER
QUIETERS
QUIETEST
QUIETING
QUIETINGS
QUIETISM
QUIETISMS
QUIETIST
QUIETISTS
QUIETIVE
QUIETIVES
QUIETLY
QUIETNESS
QUIETNESSES
QUIETS
QUIETSOME
QUIETUDE
QUIETUDES
QUIETUS
QUIETUSES
QUIFF
QUIFFS
QUIGHT
QUILL
QUILLAI
QUILLAIA
QUILLAIAS
QUILLAIS
QUILLAJA
QUILLAJAS
QUILLED
QUILLET
QUILLETS
QUILLING
QUILLINGS
QUILLMAN
QUILLMEN
QUILLON
QUILLONS
QUILLS
QUILLWORT
QUILLWORTS
QUILT
QUILTED
QUILTER
QUILTERS

QUILTING
QUILTINGS
QUILTS
QUIM
QUIMS
QUIN
QUINA
QUINARY
QUINAS
QUINATE
QUINCE
QUINCES
QUINCHE
QUINCHED
QUINCHES
QUINCHING
QUINCUNX
QUINCUNXES
QUINE
QUINELLA
QUINELLAS
QUINES
QUINIC
QUINIDINE
QUINIDINES
QUINIE
QUINIES
QUININE
QUININES
QUINNAT
QUINNATS
QUINOA
QUINOAS
QUINOL
QUINOLINE
QUINOLINES
QUINOLS
QUINONE
QUINONES
QUINQUINA
QUINQUINAS
QUINS
QUINSIED
QUINSIES
QUINSY
QUINT
QUINTA
QUINTAIN
QUINTAINS
QUINTAL
QUINTALS
QUINTAN
QUINTAS
QUINTE
QUINTES
QUINTET
QUINTETS
QUINTETT
QUINTETTE
QUINTETTES
QUINTETTI
QUINTETTO
QUINTETTS
QUINTIC
QUINTILE
QUINTILES
QUINTROON
QUINTROONS
QUINTS
QUINTUPLE

QUINTUPLED
QUINTUPLES
QUINTUPLING
QUINZE
QUINZES
QUIP
QUIPO
QUIPOS
QUIPPED
QUIPPING
QUIPPISH
QUIPS
QUIPSTER
QUIPSTERS
QUIPU
QUIPUS
QUIRE
QUIRED
QUIRES
QUIRING
QUIRISTER
QUIRISTERS
QUIRK
QUIRKED
QUIRKIER
QUIRKIEST
QUIRKING
QUIRKISH
QUIRKS
QUIRKY
QUIRT
QUIRTED
QUIRTING
QUIRTS
QUISLING
QUISLINGS
QUIST
QUISTS
QUIT
QUITCH
QUITCHED
QUITCHES
QUITCHING
QUITE
QUITED
QUITES
QUITING
QUITS
QUITTAL
QUITTALS
QUITTANCE
QUITTANCED
QUITTANCES
QUITTANCING
QUITTED
QUITTER
QUITTERS
QUITTING
QUITTOR
QUITTORS
QUIVER
QUIVERED
QUIVERFUL
QUIVERFULS
QUIVERING
QUIVERINGS
QUIVERISH
QUIVERS
QUIVERY
QUIXOTIC

QUIXOTISM	QUOAD	QUOISTS	QUOPPED	QUOTES
QUIXOTISMS	QUOD	QUOIT	QUOPPING	QUOTH
QUIXOTRIES	QUODDED	QUOITED	QUOPS	QUOTHA
QUIXOTRY	QUODDING	QUOITER	QUORATE	QUOTIDIAN
QUIZ	QUODLIBET	QUOITERS	QUORUM	QUOTIDIANS
QUIZZED	QUODLIBETS	QUOITING	QUORUMS	QUOTIENT
QUIZZER	QUODLIN	QUOITS	QUOTA	QUOTIENTS
QUIZZERIES	QUODLINS	QUOKKA	QUOTABLE	QUOTING
QUIZZERS	QUODS	QUOKKAS	QUOTABLY	QUOTITION
QUIZZERY	QUOIF	QUOLL	QUOTAS	QUOTITIONS
QUIZZES	QUOIFED	QUOLLS	QUOTATION	QUOTUM
QUIZZICAL	QUOIFING	QUONDAM	QUOTATIONS	QUOTUMS
QUIZZIFIED	QUOIFS	QUONK	QUOTATIVE	QUYTE
QUIZZIFIES	QUOIN	QUONKED	QUOTATIVES	QWERTIES
QUIZZIFY	QUOINED	QUONKING	QUOTE	QWERTY
QUIZZIFYING	QUOINING	QUONKS	QUOTED	QWERTYS
QUIZZING	QUOINS	QUOOKE	QUOTER	
QUIZZINGS	QUOIST	QUOP	QUOTERS	

R

RABANNA
RABANNAS
RABAT
RABATINE
RABATINES
RABATMENT
RABATMENTS
RABATO
RABATOES
RABATS
RABATTE
RABATTED
RABATTES
RABATTING
RABATTINGS
RABBET
RABBETED
RABBETING
RABBETS
RABBI
RABBIN
RABBINATE
RABBINATES
RABBINIC
RABBINISM
RABBINISMS
RABBINIST
RABBINISTS
RABBINITE
RABBINITES
RABBINS
RABBIS
RABBIT
RABBITED
RABBITER
RABBITERS
RABBITING
RABBITRIES
RABBITRY
RABBITS
RABBITY
RABBLE
RABBLED
RABBLER
RABBLERS
RABBLES
RABBLING
RABBLINGS
RABBONI
RABBONIS
RABI
RABIC
RABID
RABIDER
RABIDEST
RABIDITIES
RABIDITY
RABIDLY
RABIDNESS
RABIDNESSES
RABIES
RABIS
RACA
RACAHOUT

RACAHOUTS
RACCAHOUT
RACCAHOUTS
RACCOON
RACCOONS
RACE
RACED
RACEGOER
RACEGOERS
RACEGOING
RACEGOINGS
RACEHORSE
RACEHORSES
RACEMATE
RACEMATES
RACEME
RACEMED
RACEMES
RACEMIC
RACEMISE
RACEMISED
RACEMISES
RACEMISING
RACEMISM
RACEMISMS
RACEMIZE
RACEMIZED
RACEMIZES
RACEMIZING
RACEMOSE
RACER
RACERS
RACES
RACEWAY
RACEWAYS
RACH
RACHE
RACHES
RACHIAL
RACHIDES
RACHIDIAL
RACHIDIAN
RACHILLA
RACHILLAS
RACHIS
RACHISES
RACHITIC
RACHITIS
RACHITISES
RACIAL
RACIALISM
RACIALISMS
RACIALIST
RACIALISTS
RACIALLY
RACIATION
RACIATIONS
RACIER
RACIEST
RACILY
RACINESS
RACINESSES
RACING
RACINGS

RACISM
RACISMS
RACIST
RACISTS
RACK
RACKED
RACKER
RACKERS
RACKET
RACKETED
RACKETEER
RACKETEERED
RACKETEERING
RACKETEERS
RACKETER
RACKETERS
RACKETING
RACKETRIES
RACKETRY
RACKETS
RACKETT
RACKETTS
RACKETY
RACKING
RACKINGS
RACKS
RACKWORK
RACKWORKS
RACLETTE
RACLETTES
RACLOIR
RACLOIRS
RACON
RACONS
RACONTEUR
RACONTEURS
RACOON
RACOONS
RACQUET
RACQUETED
RACQUETING
RACQUETS
RACY
RAD
RADAR
RADARS
RADDLE
RADDLED
RADDLEMAN
RADDLEMEN
RADDLES
RADDLING
RADDOCKE
RADDOCKES
RADE
RADIAL
RADIALE
RADIALIA
RADIALISE
RADIALISED
RADIALISES
RADIALISING
RADIALITIES
RADIALITY

RADIALIZE
RADIALIZED
RADIALIZES
RADIALIZING
RADIALLY
RADIALS
RADIAN
RADIANCE
RADIANCES
RADIANCIES
RADIANCY
RADIANS
RADIANT
RADIANTLY
RADIANTS
RADIATE
RADIATED
RADIATELY
RADIATES
RADIATING
RADIATION
RADIATIONS
RADIATIVE
RADIATOR
RADIATORS
RADIATORY
RADICAL
RADICALLY
RADICALS
RADICANT
RADICATE
RADICATED
RADICATES
RADICATING
RADICEL
RADICELS
RADICES
RADICLE
RADICLES
RADICULAR
RADICULE
RADICULES
RADII
RADIO
RADIOED
RADIOGRAM
RADIOGRAMS
RADIOING
RADIOLOGIES
RADIOLOGY
RADIONICS
RADIOS
RADISH
RADISHES
RADIUM
RADIUMS
RADIUS
RADIUSES
RADIX
RADOME
RADOMES
RADON
RADONS
RADS

RADULA
RADULAE
RADULAR
RADULATE
RAFALE
RAFALES
RAFF
RAFFIA
RAFFIAS
RAFFINATE
RAFFINATES
RAFFINOSE
RAFFINOSES
RAFFISH
RAFFISHLY
RAFFLE
RAFFLED
RAFFLER
RAFFLERS
RAFFLES
RAFFLING
RAFFS
RAFT
RAFTED
RAFTER
RAFTERED
RAFTERING
RAFTERINGS
RAFTERS
RAFTING
RAFTMAN
RAFTMEN
RAFTS
RAFTSMAN
RAFTSMEN
RAG
RAGA
RAGAS
RAGBOLT
RAGBOLTS
RAGDE
RAGE
RAGED
RAGEFUL
RAGER
RAGERS
RAGES
RAGG
RAGGED
RAGGEDER
RAGGEDEST
RAGGEDLY
RAGGEDY
RAGGEE
RAGGEES
RAGGERIES
RAGGERY
RAGGIER
RAGGIES
RAGGIEST
RAGGING
RAGGINGS
RAGGLE
RAGGLED

RAGGLES	RAILLY	RAJAHSHIPS	RAMEQUINS	RANA
RAGGLING	RAILMAN	RAJAS	RAMFEEZLE	RANARIAN
RAGGS	RAILMEN	RAJASHIP	RAMFEEZLED	RANARIUM
RAGGY	RAILROAD	RAJASHIPS	RAMFEEZLES	RANARIUMS
RAGI	RAILROADED	RAJES	RAMFEEZLING	RANAS
RAGING	RAILROADING	RAKE	RAMI	RANCE
RAGINGLY	RAILROADS	RAKED	RAMIE	RANCED
RAGINI	RAILS	RAKEE	RAMIES	RANCEL
RAGINIS	RAILWAY	RAKEES	RAMIFIED	RANCELS
RAGIS	RAILWAYS	RAKEHELL	RAMIFIES	RANCES
RAGLAN	RAIMENT	RAKEHELLS	RAMIFORM	RANCH
RAGLANS	RAIMENTS	RAKEHELLY	RAMIFY	RANCHED
RAGMAN	RAIN	RAKER	RAMIFYING	RANCHER
RAGMEN	RAINBAND	RAKERIES	RAMIS	RANCHERIA
RAGMENT	RAINBANDS	RAKERS	RAMMED	RANCHERIAS
RAGMENTS	RAINBOW	RAKERY	RAMMER	RANCHERO
RAGOUT	RAINBOWED	RAKES	RAMMERS	RANCHEROS
RAGOUTED	RAINBOWS	RAKESHAME	RAMMIES	RANCHERS
RAGOUTING	RAINBOWY	RAKESHAMES	RAMMING	RANCHES
RAGOUTS	RAINCHECK	RAKI	RAMMISH	RANCHING
RAGS	RAINCHECKS	RAKING	RAMMY	RANCHINGS
RAGSTONE	RAINCOAT	RAKINGS	RAMOSE	RANCHMAN
RAGSTONES	RAINCOATS	RAKIS	RAMOUS	RANCHMEN
RAGTIME	RAINDROP	RAKISH	RAMP	RANCHO
RAGTIMER	RAINDROPS	RAKISHLY	RAMPAGE	RANCHOS
RAGTIMERS	RAINE	RAKSHAS	RAMPAGED	RANCID
RAGTIMES	RAINED	RAKSHASA	RAMPAGES	RANCIDER
RAGULED	RAINES	RAKSHASAS	RAMPAGING	RANCIDEST
RAGULY	RAINFALL	RAKSHASES	RAMPANCIES	RANCIDITIES
RAGWEED	RAINFALLS	RALE	RAMPANCY	RANCIDITY
RAGWEEDS	RAINIER	RÂLE	RAMPANT	RANCING
RAGWHEEL	RAINIEST	RALES	RAMPANTLY	RANCOR
RAGWHEELS	RAININESS	RÂLES	RAMPART	RANCOROUS
RAGWORK	RAININESSES	RALLIED	RAMPARTED	RANCORS
RAGWORKS	RAINING	RALLIER	RAMPARTING	RANCOUR
RAGWORM	RAINLESS	RALLIERS	RAMPARTS	RANCOURS
RAGWORMS	RAINPROOF	RALLIES	RAMPAUGE	RAND
RAGWORT	RAINPROOFED	RALLINE	RAMPAUGED	RANDAN
RAGWORTS	RAINPROOFING	RALLY	RAMPAUGES	RANDANS
RAH	RAINPROOFS	RALLYE	RAMPAUGING	RANDED
RAHED	RAINS	RALLYES	RAMPED	RANDEM
RAHING	RAINSTORM	RALLYING	RAMPER	RANDEMS
RAHS	RAINSTORMS	RALLYINGS	RAMPERS	RANDIE
RAID	RAINTIGHT	RALLYIST	RAMPICK	RANDIER
RAIDED	RAINY	RALLYISTS	RAMPICKED	RANDIES
RAIDER	RAIRD	RAM	RAMPICKS	RANDIEST
RAIDERS	RAIRDS	RAMAKIN	RAMPIKE	RANDING
RAIDING	RAISABLE	RAMAKINS	RAMPIKES	RANDOM
RAIDS	RAISE	RAMAL	RAMPING	RANDOMISE
RAIK	RAISEABLE	RAMATE	RAMPION	RANDOMISED
RAIKED	RAISED	RAMBLE	RAMPIONS	RANDOMISES
RAIKING	RAISER	RAMBLED	RAMPIRE	RANDOMISING
RAIKS	RAISERS	RAMBLER	RAMPIRED	RANDOMIZE
RAIL	RAISES	RAMBLERS	RAMPIRES	RANDOMIZED
RAILBUS	RAISIN	RAMBLES	RAMPS	RANDOMIZES
RAILBUSES	RAISING	RAMBLING	RAMPSMAN	RANDOMIZING
RAILBUSSES	RAISINGS	RAMBLINGS	RAMPSMEN	RANDOMLY
RAILCARD	RAISINS	RAMBUTAN	RAMROD	RANDOMS
RAILCARDS	RAISONNÉ	RAMBUTANS	RAMRODS	RANDON
RAILE	RAIT	RAMCAT	RAMS	RANDONS
RAILED	RAITED	RAMCATS	RAMSON	RANDS
RAILER	RAITING	RAMEAL	RAMSONS	RANDY
RAILERS	RAITS	RAMEE	RAMSTAM	RANEE
RAILING	RAIYAT	RAMEES	RAMULAR	RANEES
RAILINGLY	RAIYATS	RAMEKIN	RAMULI	RANG
RAILINGS	RAJ	RAMEKINS	RAMULOSE	RANGE
RAILLERIES	RAJA	RAMENTA	RAMULOUS	RANGED
RAILLERY	RAJAH	RAMENTUM	RAMULUS	RANGELAND
RAILLESS	RAJAHS	RAMEOUS	RAMUS	RANGELANDS
RAILLIES	RAJAHSHIP	RAMEQUIN	RAN	RANGER

RANGERS
RANGES
RANGIER
RANGIEST
RANGINESS
RANGINESSES
RANGING
RANGY
RANI
RANIFORM
RANINE
RANIS
RANK
RANKE
RANKED
RANKER
RANKERS
RANKES
RANKEST
RANKING
RANKINGS
RANKLE
RANKLED
RANKLES
RANKLING
RANKLY
RANKNESS
RANKNESSES
RANKS
RANSACK
RANSACKED
RANSACKER
RANSACKERS
RANSACKING
RANSACKS
RANSEL
RANSELS
RANSHAKLE
RANSHAKLED
RANSHAKLES
RANSHAKLING
RANSOM
RANSOMED
RANSOMER
RANSOMERS
RANSOMING
RANSOMS
RANT
RANTED
RANTER
RANTERISM
RANTERISMS
RANTERS
RANTING
RANTINGLY
RANTIPOLE
RANTIPOLED
RANTIPOLES
RANTIPOLING
RANTS
RANULA
RANULAS
RANUNCULI
RANZEL
RANZELMAN
RANZELMEN
RANZELS
RAP
RAPACIOUS
RAPACITIES

RAPACITY
RAPE
RAPED
RAPER
RAPERS
RAPES
RAPHANIA
RAPHANIAS
RAPHE
RAPHES
RAPHIA
RAPHIAS
RAPHIDE
RAPHIDES
RAPHIS
RAPID
RAPIDER
RAPIDEST
RAPIDITIES
RAPIDITY
RAPIDLY
RAPIDNESS
RAPIDNESSES
RAPIDS
RAPIER
RAPIERS
RAPINE
RAPINES
RAPING
RAPIST
RAPISTS
RAPLOCH
RAPLOCHS
RAPPAREE
RAPPAREES
RAPPED
RAPPEE
RAPPEES
RAPPEL
RAPPELLED
RAPPELLING
RAPPELS
RAPPER
RAPPERS
RAPPING
RAPPINGS
RAPPORT
RAPPORTS
RAPS
RAPT
RAPTOR
RAPTORIAL
RAPTORS
RAPTURE
RAPTURED
RAPTURES
RAPTURING
RAPTURISE
RAPTURISED
RAPTURISES
RAPTURISING
RAPTURIST
RAPTURISTS
RAPTURIZE
RAPTURIZED
RAPTURIZES
RAPTURIZING
RAPTUROUS
RARE
RAREBIT

RAREBITS
RAREFIED
RAREFIES
RAREFY
RAREFYING
RARELY
RARENESS
RARENESSES
RARER
RAREST
RARING
RARITIES
RARITY
RAS
RASCAILLE
RASCAILLES
RASCAL
RASCALDOM
RASCALDOMS
RASCALISM
RASCALISMS
RASCALITIES
RASCALITY
RASCALLY
RASCALS
RASCHEL
RASCHELS
RASE
RASED
RASES
RASH
RASHED
RASHER
RASHERS
RASHES
RASHEST
RASHING
RASHLY
RASHNESS
RASHNESSES
RASING
RASORIAL
RASP
RASPATORIES
RASPATORY
RASPBERRIES
RASPBERRY
RASPED
RASPER
RASPERS
RASPIER
RASPIEST
RASPING
RASPINGLY
RASPINGS
RASPS
RASPY
RASSE
RASSES
RAST
RASTA
RASTAFARI
RASTER
RASTERS
RASTRUM
RASTRUMS
RASURE
RASURES
RAT
RATA

RATABLE
RATABLY
RATAFIA
RATAFIAS
RATAN
RATANS
RATAPLAN
RATAPLANS
RATAS
RATBAG
RATBAGS
RATCH
RATCHES
RATCHET
RATCHETS
RATE
RATEABLE
RATEABLY
RATED
RATEL
RATELS
RATEPAYER
RATEPAYERS
RATER
RATERS
RATES
RATFINK
RATFINKS
RATH
RATHE
RATHER
RATHEREST
RATHERIPE
RATHERIPES
RATHERISH
RATHEST
RATHRIPE
RATHRIPES
RATHS
RATIFIED
RATIFIER
RATIFIERS
RATIFIES
RATIFY
RATIFYING
RATINE
RATINES
RATING
RATINGS
RATIO
RATION
RATIONAL
RATIONALE
RATIONALES
RATIONALS
RATIONED
RATIONING
RATIONS
RATIOS
RATITE
RATLIN
RATLINE
RATLINES
RATLING
RATLINGS
RATLINS
RATOON
RATOONED
RATOONER
RATOONERS

RATOONING
RATOONS
RATPACK
RATPACKS
RATPROOF
RATS
RATSBANE
RATSBANES
RATTAN
RATTANS
RATTED
RATTEEN
RATTEENS
RATTEN
RATTENED
RATTENING
RATTENINGS
RATTENS
RATTER
RATTERIES
RATTERS
RATTERY
RATTIER
RATTIEST
RATTING
RATTINGS
RATTISH
RATTLE
RATTLEBAG
RATTLEBAGS
RATTLED
RATTLER
RATTLERS
RATTLES
RATTLIN
RATTLINE
RATTLINES
RATTLING
RATTLINGS
RATTLINS
RATTLY
RATTON
RATTONS
RATTY
RAUCID
RAUCLE
RAUCLER
RAUCLEST
RAUCOUS
RAUCOUSLY
RAUGHT
RAUN
RAUNCH
RAUNCHES
RAUNCHIER
RAUNCHIEST
RAUNCHY
RAUNGE
RAUNS
RAVAGE
RAVAGED
RAVAGER
RAVAGERS
RAVAGES
RAVAGING
RAVE
RAVED
RAVEL
RAVELIN
RAVELINS

RAVELLED	RAZE	READDRESSES	REALISTIC	REAPPEARED
RAVELLING	RAZED	READDRESSING	REALISTS	REAPPEARING
RAVELLINGS	RAZEE	READER	REALITIES	REAPPEARS
RAVELMENT	RAZEED	READERS	REALITY	REAPPLIED
RAVELMENTS	RAZEEING	READIED	REALIZE	REAPPLIES
RAVELS	RAZEES	READIER	REALIZED	REAPPLY
RAVEN	RAZES	READIES	REALIZER	REAPPLYING
RAVENED	RAZING	READIEST	REALIZERS	REAPPOINT
RAVENER	RAZMATAZ	READILY	REALIZES	REAPPOINTED
RAVENERS	RAZMATAZES	READINESS	REALIZING	REAPPOINTING
RAVENING	RAZMATAZZ	READINESSES	REALLIE	REAPPOINTS
RAVENOUS	RAZMATAZZES	READING	REALLIED	REAPS
RAVENS	RAZOR	READINGS	REALLIES	REAR
RAVER	RAZORABLE	READJUST	REALLOT	REARED
RAVERS	RAZORS	READJUSTED	REALLOTS	REARER
RAVES	RAZURE	READJUSTING	REALLOTTED	REARERS
RAVIN	RAZURES	READJUSTS	REALLOTTING	REARHORSE
RAVINE	RAZZ	READMIT	REALLY	REARHORSES
RAVINED	RAZZED	READMITS	REALLYING	REARING
RAVINES	RAZZES	READMITTED	REALM	REARISE
RAVING	RAZZIA	READMITTING	REALMLESS	REARISEN
RAVINGLY	RAZZIAS	READOPT	REALMS	REARISES
RAVINGS	RAZZING	READOPTED	REALNESS	REARISING
RAVINING	RAZZLE	READOPTING	REALNESSES	REARLY
RAVINS	RAZZLES	READOPTS	REALS	REARM
RAVIOLI	RAZZMATAZ	READS	REALTIE	REARMED
RAVIOLIS	RAZZMATAZES	READVANCE	REALTIES	REARMICE
RAVISH	RE	READVANCED	REALTIME	REARMING
RAVISHED	REABSORB	READVANCES	REALTOR	REARMOST
RAVISHER	REABSORBED	READVANCING	REALTORS	REARMOUSE
RAVISHERS	REABSORBING	READVISE	REALTY	REARMS
RAVISHES	REABSORBS	READVISED	REAM	REAROSE
RAVISHING	REACH	READVISES	REAME	REAROUSAL
RAW	REACHABLE	READVISING	REAMED	REAROUSALS
RAWBONE	REACHED	READY	REAMEND	REAROUSE
RAWBONED	REACHER	READYING	REAMENDED	REAROUSED
RAWER	REACHERS	REAEDIFIED	REAMENDING	REAROUSES
RAWEST	REACHES	REAEDIFIES	REAMENDS	REAROUSING
RAWHEAD	REACHING	REAEDIFY	REAMER	REARRANGE
RAWHEADS	REACHLESS	REAEDIFYE	REAMERS	REARRANGED
RAWHIDE	REACQUIRE	REAEDIFYING	REAMES	REARRANGES
RAWHIDES	REACQUIRED	REAFFIRM	REAMIER	REARRANGING
RAWING	REACQUIRES	REAFFIRMED	REAMIEST	REARREST
RAWINGS	REACQUIRING	REAFFIRMING	REAMING	REARRESTED
RAWISH	REACT	REAFFIRMS	REAMS	REARRESTING
RAWLY	REACTANCE	REAGENCIES	REAMY	REARRESTS
RAWN	REACTANCES	REAGENCY	REAN	REARS
RAWNESS	REACTANT	REAGENT	REANIMATE	REARWARD
RAWNESSES	REACTANTS	REAGENTS	REANIMATED	REARWARDS
RAWNS	REACTED	REAK	REANIMATES	REASCEND
RAWS	REACTING	REAKS	REANIMATING	REASCENDED
RAX	REACTION	REAL	REANNEX	REASCENDING
RAXED	REACTIONS	REALER	REANNEXED	REASCENDS
RAXES	REACTIVE	REALEST	REANNEXES	REASCENT
RAXING	REACTOR	REALGAR	REANNEXING	REASCENTS
RAY	REACTORS	REALGARS	REANS	REASON
RAYAH	REACTS	REALIA	REANSWER	REASONED
RAYAHS	REACTUATE	REALIGN	REANSWERED	REASONER
RAYED	REACTUATED	REALIGNED	REANSWERING	REASONERS
RAYING	REACTUATES	REALIGNING	REANSWERS	REASONING
RAYLE	REACTUATING	REALIGNS	REAP	REASONINGS
RAYLES	READ	REALISE	REAPED	REASONS
RAYLESS	READABLE	REALISED	REAPER	REASSERT
RAYLET	READABLY	REALISER	REAPERS	REASSERTED
RAYLETS	READAPT	REALISERS	REAPING	REASSERTING
RAYNE	READAPTED	REALISES	REAPPAREL	REASSERTS
RAYNES	READAPTING	REALISING	REAPPARELLED	REASSESS
RAYON	READAPTS	REALISM	REAPPARELLING	REASSESSED
RAYONS	READDRESS	REALISMS	REAPPARELS	REASSESSES
RAYS	READDRESSED	REALIST	REAPPEAR	REASSESSING

REASSIGN
REASSIGNED
REASSIGNING
REASSIGNS
REASSUME
REASSUMED
REASSUMES
REASSUMING
REASSURE
REASSURED
REASSURER
REASSURERS
REASSURES
REASSURING
REAST
REASTED
REASTIER
REASTIEST
REASTING
REASTS
REASTY
REATA
REATAS
REATE
REATES
REATTACH
REATTACHED
REATTACHES
REATTACHING
REATTAIN
REATTAINED
REATTAINING
REATTAINS
REATTEMPT
REATTEMPTED
REATTEMPTING
REATTEMPTS
REAVE
REAVER
REAVERS
REAVES
REAVING
REAWAKE
REAWAKED
REAWAKEN
REAWAKENED
REAWAKENING
REAWAKENINGS
REAWAKENS
REAWAKES
REAWAKING
REAWOKE
REAWOKEN
REBACK
REBACKED
REBACKING
REBACKS
REBAPTISE
REBAPTISED
REBAPTISES
REBAPTISING
REBAPTISM
REBAPTISMS
REBAPTIZE
REBAPTIZED
REBAPTIZES
REBAPTIZING
REBATE
REBATED
REBATER

REBATERS
REBATES
REBATING
REBATO
REBATOES
REBEC
REBECK
REBECKS
REBECS
REBEL
REBELDOM
REBELDOMS
REBELLED
REBELLER
REBELLERS
REBELLING
REBELLION
REBELLIONS
REBELLOW
REBELLOWED
REBELLOWING
REBELLOWS
REBELS
REBID
REBIDDING
REBIDS
REBIND
REBINDING
REBINDS
REBIRTH
REBIRTHS
REBIT
REBITE
REBITES
REBITING
REBITTEN
REBLOOM
REBLOOMED
REBLOOMING
REBLOOMS
REBLOSSOM
REBLOSSOMED
REBLOSSOMING
REBLOSSOMS
REBOANT
REBOATION
REBOATIONS
REBOIL
REBOILED
REBOILING
REBOILS
REBORE
REBORED
REBORES
REBORING
REBORN
REBOUND
REBOUNDED
REBOUNDING
REBOUNDS
REBRACE
REBRACED
REBRACES
REBRACING
REBUFF
REBUFFED
REBUFFING
REBUFFS
REBUILD
REBUILDING

REBUILDS
REBUILT
REBUKABLE
REBUKE
REBUKED
REBUKEFUL
REBUKER
REBUKERS
REBUKES
REBUKING
REBURIAL
REBURIALS
REBURIED
REBURIES
REBURY
REBURYING
REBUS
REBUSES
REBUT
REBUTMENT
REBUTMENTS
REBUTS
REBUTTAL
REBUTTALS
REBUTTED
REBUTTER
REBUTTERS
REBUTTING
REBUTTON
REBUTTONED
REBUTTONING
REBUTTONS
RECAL
RECALESCE
RECALESCED
RECALESCES
RECALESCING
RECALL
RECALLED
RECALLING
RECALLS
RECALMENT
RECALMENTS
RECALS
RECANT
RECANTED
RECANTER
RECANTERS
RECANTING
RECANTS
RECAP
RECAPPED
RECAPPING
RECAPS
RECAPTION
RECAPTIONS
RECAPTOR
RECAPTORS
RECAPTURE
RECAPTURED
RECAPTURES
RECAPTURING
RECAST
RECASTING
RECASTS
RECATCH
RECATCHES
RECATCHING
RECAUGHT
RECCE

RECCED
RECCEED
RECCEING
RECCES
RECCIED
RECCIES
RECCO
RECCOS
RECCY
RECCYING
RECEDE
RECEDED
RECEDES
RECEDING
RECEIPT
RECEIPTED
RECEIPTING
RECEIPTS
RECEIVAL
RECEIVALS
RECEIVE
RECEIVED
RECEIVER
RECEIVERS
RECEIVES
RECEIVING
RECEIVINGS
RECENCIES
RECENCY
RECENSE
RECENSED
RECENSES
RECENSING
RECENSION
RECENSIONS
RECENT
RECENTER
RECENTEST
RECENTLY
RECENTRE
RECENTRED
RECENTRES
RECENTRING
RECEPT
RECEPTION
RECEPTIONS
RECEPTIVE
RECEPTOR
RECEPTORS
RECEPTS
RECESS
RECESSED
RECESSES
RECESSING
RECESSION
RECESSIONS
RECESSIVE
RECHARGE
RECHARGED
RECHARGES
RECHARGING
RECHART
RECHARTED
RECHARTER
RECHARTERED
RECHARTERING
RECHARTERS
RECHARTING
RECHARTS
RECHATE

RECHATES
RÉCHAUFFÉ
RÉCHAUFFÉS
RECHEAT
RECHEATS
RECHECK
RECHECKED
RECHECKING
RECHECKS
RECHERCHÉ
RECHIE
RECHLESSE
RECIPE
RECIPES
RECIPIENT
RECIPIENTS
RECISION
RECISIONS
RÉCIT
RECITAL
RECITALS
RECITE
RECITED
RECITER
RECITERS
RECITES
RECITING
RÉCITS
RECK
RECKAN
RECKED
RECKING
RECKLESS
RECKLING
RECKLINGS
RECKON
RECKONED
RECKONER
RECKONERS
RECKONING
RECKONINGS
RECKONS
RECKS
RECLAIM
RECLAIMED
RECLAIMER
RECLAIMERS
RECLAIMING
RECLAIMS
RÉCLAME
RÉCLAMES
RECLIMB
RECLIMBED
RECLIMBING
RECLIMBS
RECLINATE
RECLINE
RECLINED
RECLINER
RECLINERS
RECLINES
RECLINING
RECLOSE
RECLOSED
RECLOSES
RECLOSING
RECLOTHE
RECLOTHED
RECLOTHES
RECLOTHING

RECLUSE	RECONQUERS	RECRUITED	RECUSED	REDEFINED
RECLUSELY	RECONVENE	RECRUITER	RECUSES	REDEFINES
RECLUSES	RECONVENED	RECRUITERS	RECUSING	REDEFINING
RECLUSION	RECONVENES	RECRUITING	RECYCLE	REDELESS
RECLUSIONS	RECONVENING	RECRUITS	RECYCLED	REDELIVER
RECLUSIVE	RECONVERT	RECTA	RECYCLES	REDELIVERED
RECLUSORIES	RECONVERTED	RECTAL	RECYCLING	REDELIVERING
RECLUSORY	RECONVERTING	RECTALLY	RED	REDELIVERS
RECOGNISE	RECONVERTS	RECTANGLE	REDACT	REDEPLOY
RECOGNISED	RECONVEY	RECTANGLES	REDACTED	REDEPLOYED
RECOGNISES	RECONVEYED	RECTI	REDACTING	REDEPLOYING
RECOGNISING	RECONVEYING	RECTIFIED	REDACTION	REDEPLOYS
RECOGNIZE	RECONVEYS	RECTIFIER	REDACTIONS	REDES
RECOGNIZED	RECORD	RECTIFIERS	REDACTOR	REDESCEND
RECOGNIZES	RECORDED	RECTIFIES	REDACTORS	REDESCENDED
RECOGNIZING	RECORDER	RECTIFY	REDACTS	REDESCENDING
RECOIL	RECORDERS	RECTIFYING	REDAN	REDESCENDS
RECOILED	RECORDING	RECTION	REDANS	REDESIGN
RECOILER	RECORDINGS	RECTIONS	REDARGUE	REDESIGNED
RECOILERS	RECORDIST	RECTITIC	REDARGUED	REDESIGNING
RECOILING	RECORDISTS	RECTITIS	REDARGUES	REDESIGNS
RECOILS	RECORDS	RECTITISES	REDARGUING	REDEVELOP
RECOINAGE	RECOUNT	RECTITUDE	REDBACK	REDEVELOPED
RECOINAGES	RECOUNTAL	RECTITUDES	REDBACKS	REDEVELOPING
RECOLLECT	RECOUNTALS	RECTO	REDBREAST	REDEVELOPS
RECOLLECTED	RECOUNTED	RECTOR	REDBREASTS	REDEYE
RECOLLECTING	RECOUNTING	RECTORAL	REDBRICK	REDEYES
RECOLLECTS	RECOUNTS	RECTORATE	REDCOAT	REDFISH
RÉCOLLET	RECOUP	RECTORATES	REDCOATS	REDFISHES
RÉCOLLETS	RECOUPED	RECTORESS	REDD	REDHANDED
RECOMBINE	RECOUPING	RECTORESSES	REDDED	REDIA
RECOMBINED	RECOUPS	RECTORIAL	REDDEN	REDIAE
RECOMBINES	RECOURE	RECTORIALS	REDDENDA	REDID
RECOMBINING	RECOURSE	RECTORIES	REDDENDO	REDING
RECOMFORT	RECOURSED	RECTORS	REDDENDOS	REDINGOTE
RECOMFORTED	RECOURSES	RECTORY	REDDENDUM	REDINGOTES
RECOMFORTING	RECOURSING	RECTOS	REDDENED	REDIP
RECOMFORTS	RECOVER	RECTRESS	REDDENING	REDIPPED
RECOMMEND	RECOVERED	RECTRESSES	REDDENS	REDIPPING
RECOMMENDED	RECOVEREE	RECTRICES	REDDER	REDIPS
RECOMMENDING	RECOVEREES	RECTRIX	REDDERS	REDIRECT
RECOMMENDS	RECOVERER	RECTUM	REDDEST	REDIRECTED
RECOMMIT	RECOVERERS	RECTUMS	REDDIER	REDIRECTING
RECOMMITS	RECOVERIES	RECTUS	REDDIEST	REDIRECTS
RECOMMITTED	RECOVERING	RECUILE	REDDING	REDISTIL
RECOMMITTING	RECOVEROR	RECULE	REDDINGS	REDISTILLED
RECOMPACT	RECOVERORS	RECUMBENT	REDDISH	REDISTILLING
RECOMPACTED	RECOVERS	RECUR	REDDLE	REDISTILS
RECOMPACTING	RECOVERY	RECURE	REDDLED	REDIVIDE
RECOMPACTS	RECOWER	RECURED	REDDLEMAN	REDIVIDED
RECOMPOSE	RECOYLE	RECURES	REDDLEMEN	REDIVIDES
RECOMPOSED	RECREANCE	RECURING	REDDLES	REDIVIDING
RECOMPOSES	RECREANCES	RECURRED	REDDLING	REDIVIVUS
RECOMPOSING	RECREANCIES	RECURRENT	REDDS	REDLEG
RECONCILE	RECREANCY	RECURRING	REDDY	REDLEGS
RECONCILED	RECREANT	RECURS	REDE	REDLY
RECONCILES	RECREANTS	RECURSION	REDEAL	REDNECK
RECONCILING	RECREATE	RECURSIONS	REDEALING	REDNECKS
RECONDITE	RECREATED	RECURSIVE	REDEALS	REDNESS
RECONFIRM	RECREATES	RECURVE	REDEALT	REDNESSES
RECONFIRMED	RECREATING	RECURVED	REDECRAFT	REDO
RECONFIRMING	RECREMENT	RECURVES	REDECRAFTS	REDOES
RECONFIRMS	RECREMENTS	RECURVING	REDED	REDOING
RECONNECT	RECROSS	RECUSANCE	REDEEM	REDOLENCE
RECONNECTED	RECROSSED	RECUSANCES	REDEEMED	REDOLENCES
RECONNECTING	RECROSSES	RECUSANCIES	REDEEMER	REDOLENCIES
RECONNECTS	RECROSSING	RECUSANCY	REDEEMERS	REDOLENCY
RECONQUER	RECRUIT	RECUSANT	REDEEMING	REDOLENT
RECONQUERED	RECRUITAL	RECUSANTS	REDEEMS	REDONE
RECONQUERING	RECRUITALS	RECUSE	REDEFINE	REDOUBLE

REDOUBLED	REDWINGS	REEVES	REFLATE	REFOUNDERS
REDOUBLES	REDWOOD	REEVING	REFLATED	REFOUNDING
REDOUBLING	REDWOODS	REF	REFLATES	REFOUNDS
REDOUBT	REE	REFACE	REFLATING	REFRACT
REDOUBTED	REEBOK	REFACED	REFLATION	REFRACTED
REDOUBTING	REEBOKS	REFACES	REFLATIONS	REFRACTING
REDOUBTS	REECH	REFACING	REFLECT	REFRACTOR
REDOUND	REECHED	REFASHION	REFLECTED	REFRACTORS
REDOUNDED	REECHES	REFASHIONED	REFLECTER	REFRACTS
REDOUNDING	REECHIE	REFASHIONING	REFLECTERS	REFRAIN
REDOUNDINGS	REECHIER	REFASHIONS	REFLECTING	REFRAINED
REDOUNDS	REECHIEST	REFECT	REFLECTOR	REFRAINING
REDOWA	REECHING	REFECTED	REFLECTORS	REFRAINS
REDOWAS	REECHY	REFECTING	REFLECTS	REFRAME
REDOX	REED	REFECTION	REFLET	REFRAMED
REDPOLL	REEDE	REFECTIONS	REFLETS	REFRAMES
REDPOLLS	REEDED	REFECTORIES	REFLEX	REFRAMING
REDRAFT	REEDEN	REFECTORY	REFLEXED	REFREEZE
REDRAFTED	REEDER	REFECTS	REFLEXES	REFREEZES
REDRAFTING	REEDERS	REFEL	REFLEXING	REFREEZING
REDRAFTS	REEDES	REFELLED	REFLEXION	REFRESH
REDRAW	REEDIER	REFELLING	REFLEXIONS	REFRESHED
REDRAWING	REEDIEST	REFELS	REFLEXIVE	REFRESHEN
REDRAWN	REEDINESS	REFER	REFLEXLY	REFRESHENED
REDRAWS	REEDINESSES	REFERABLE	REFLOAT	REFRESHENING
REDRESS	REEDING	REFEREE	REFLOATED	REFRESHENS
REDRESSED	REEDINGS	REFEREED	REFLOATING	REFRESHER
REDRESSER	REEDLING	REFEREEING	REFLOATS	REFRESHERS
REDRESSERS	REEDLINGS	REFEREES	REFLOW	REFRESHES
REDRESSES	REEDS	REFERENCE	REFLOWED	REFRESHING
REDRESSING	REEDSTOP	REFERENCED	REFLOWER	REFRINGE
REDREW	REEDSTOPS	REFERENCES	REFLOWERED	REFRINGED
REDRIVE	REEDY	REFERENCING	REFLOWERING	REFRINGES
REDRIVEN	REEF	REFERENDA	REFLOWERS	REFRINGING
REDRIVES	REEFED	REFERENT	REFLOWING	REFROZE
REDRIVING	REEFER	REFERENTS	REFLOWINGS	REFROZEN
REDROVE	REEFERS	REFERRAL	REFLOWS	REFS
REDS	REEFING	REFERRALS	REFLUENCE	REFT
REDSEAR	REEFINGS	REFERRED	REFLUENCES	REFUEL
REDSHANK	REEFS	REFERRING	REFLUENT	REFUELLED
REDSHANKS	REEK	REFERS	REFLUX	REFUELLING
REDSHARE	REEKED	REFFED	REFLUXED	REFUELS
REDSHIRE	REEKIE	REFFING	REFLUXES	REFUGE
REDSHORT	REEKIER	REFFO	REFLUXING	REFUGED
REDSKIN	REEKIEST	REFFOS	REFOOT	REFUGEE
REDSKINS	REEKING	REFIGURE	REFOOTED	REFUGEES
REDSTART	REEKS	REFIGURED	REFOOTING	REFUGES
REDSTARTS	REEKY	REFIGURES	REFOOTS	REFUGIA
REDSTREAK	REEL	REFIGURING	REFORM	REFUGING
REDSTREAKS	REELED	REFILL	REFORMADE	REFUGIUM
REDTOP	REELER	REFILLED	REFORMADES	REFULGENT
REDTOPS	REELERS	REFILLING	REFORMADO	REFUND
REDUCE	REELING	REFILLS	REFORMADOES	REFUNDED
REDUCED	REELINGLY	REFINE	REFORMADOS	REFUNDER
REDUCER	REELINGS	REFINED	REFORMED	REFUNDERS
REDUCERS	REELMAN	REFINEDLY	REFORMER	REFUNDING
REDUCES	REELMEN	REFINER	REFORMERS	REFUNDS
REDUCIBLE	REELS	REFINERIES	REFORMING	REFURBISH
REDUCING	REEN	REFINERS	REFORMISM	REFURBISHED
REDUCTANT	REENS	REFINERY	REFORMISMS	REFURBISHES
REDUCTANTS	REES	REFINES	REFORMIST	REFURBISHING
REDUCTASE	REEST	REFINING	REFORMISTS	REFURNISH
REDUCTASES	REESTED	REFININGS	REFORMS	REFURNISHED
REDUCTION	REESTIER	REFIT	REFORTIFIED	REFURNISHES
REDUCTIONS	REESTIEST	REFITMENT	REFORTIFIES	REFURNISHING
REDUCTIVE	REESTING	REFITMENTS	REFORTIFY	REFUSABLE
REDUIT	REESTS	REFITS	REFORTIFYING	REFUSAL
REDUITS	REESTY	REFITTED	REFOUND	REFUSALS
REDUNDANT	REEVE	REFITTING	REFOUNDED	REFUSE
REDWING	REEVED	REFITTINGS	REFOUNDER	REFUSED

REFUSENIK
REFUSENIKS
REFUSER
REFUSERS
REFUSES
REFUSING
REFUSION
REFUSIONS
REFUSNIK
REFUSNIKS
REFUTABLE
REFUTABLY
REFUTAL
REFUTALS
REFUTE
REFUTED
REFUTER
REFUTERS
REFUTES
REFUTING
REGAIN
REGAINED
REGAINER
REGAINERS
REGAINING
REGAINS
REGAL
REGALE
REGALED
REGALES
REGALIA
REGALIAN
REGALIAS
REGALING
REGALISM
REGALISMS
REGALIST
REGALISTS
REGALITIES
REGALITY
REGALLY
REGALS
REGAR
REGARD
REGARDANT
REGARDED
REGARDER
REGARDERS
REGARDFUL
REGARDING
REGARDS
REGARS
REGATHER
REGATHERED
REGATHERING
REGATHERS
REGATTA
REGATTAS
REGAVE
REGELATE
REGELATED
REGELATES
REGELATING
REGENCE
REGENCES
REGENCIES
REGENCY
REGENT
REGENTS
REGEST

REGESTS
REGGAE
REGGAES
REGICIDAL
REGICIDE
REGICIDES
RÉGIE
RÉGIES
RÉGIME
REGIMEN
REGIMENS
REGIMENT
REGIMENTED
REGIMENTING
REGIMENTS
RÉGIMES
REGIMINAL
REGINA
REGINAE
REGINAL
REGINAS
REGION
REGIONAL
REGIONARY
REGIONS
REGISSEUR
REGISSEURS
REGISTER
REGISTERED
REGISTERING
REGISTERS
REGISTRAR
REGISTRARS
REGISTRIES
REGISTRY
REGIUS
REGIVE
REGIVEN
REGIVES
REGIVING
REGLET
REGLETS
REGMA
REGMATA
REGNAL
REGNANT
REGOLITH
REGOLITHS
REGORGE
REGORGED
REGORGES
REGORGING
REGRADE
REGRADED
REGRADES
REGRADING
REGRANT
REGRANTED
REGRANTING
REGRANTS
REGRATE
REGRATED
REGRATER
REGRATERS
REGRATES
REGRATING
REGRATINGS
REGRATOR
REGRATORS
REGREDE

REGREDED
REGREDES
REGREDING
REGREET
REGREETED
REGREETING
REGREETS
REGRESS
REGRESSED
REGRESSES
REGRESSING
REGRET
REGRETFUL
REGRETS
REGRETTED
REGRETTING
REGRIND
REGRINDING
REGRINDS
REGROUND
REGROUP
REGROUPED
REGROUPING
REGROUPS
REGROWTH
REGROWTHS
REGUERDON
REGUERDONED
REGUERDONING
REGUERDONS
REGULA
REGULAE
REGULAR
REGULARLY
REGULARS
REGULATE
REGULATED
REGULATES
REGULATING
REGULATOR
REGULATORS
REGULINE
REGULISE
REGULISED
REGULISES
REGULISING
REGULIZE
REGULIZED
REGULIZES
REGULIZING
REGULO®
REGULOS®
REGULUS
REGULUSES
REGUR
REGURS
REH
REHANDLE
REHANDLED
REHANDLES
REHANDLING
REHANDLINGS
REHASH
REHASHED
REHASHES
REHASHING
REHEAR
REHEARD
REHEARING
REHEARINGS

REHEARS
REHEARSAL
REHEARSALS
REHEARSE
REHEARSED
REHEARSER
REHEARSERS
REHEARSES
REHEARSING
REHEARSINGS
REHEAT
REHEATED
REHEATER
REHEATERS
REHEATING
REHEATS
REHEEL
REHEELED
REHEELING
REHEELS
REHOBOAM
REHOBOAMS
REHOUSE
REHOUSED
REHOUSES
REHOUSING
REHOUSINGS
REHS
REIF
REIFIED
REIFIES
REIFS
REIFY
REIFYING
REIGN
REIGNED
REIGNING
REIGNS
REIK
REIKS
REILLUME
REILLUMED
REILLUMES
REILLUMING
REIMBURSE
REIMBURSED
REIMBURSES
REIMBURSING
REIMPLANT
REIMPLANTED
REIMPLANTING
REIMPLANTS
REIMPORT
REIMPORTED
REIMPORTING
REIMPORTS
REIMPOSE
REIMPOSED
REIMPOSES
REIMPOSING
REIN
REINDEER
REINDEERS
REINED
REINETTE
REINETTES
REINFORCE
REINFORCED
REINFORCES
REINFORCING

REINFORM
REINFORMED
REINFORMING
REINFORMS
REINFUND
REINFUNDED
REINFUNDING
REINFUNDS
REINFUSE
REINFUSED
REINFUSES
REINFUSING
REINHABIT
REINHABITED
REINHABITING
REINHABITS
REINING
REINLESS
REINS
REINSERT
REINSERTED
REINSERTING
REINSERTS
REINSMAN
REINSMEN
REINSPECT
REINSPECTED
REINSPECTING
REINSPECTS
REINSPIRE
REINSPIRED
REINSPIRES
REINSPIRING
REINSTALL
REINSTALLED
REINSTALLING
REINSTALLS
REINSTATE
REINSTATED
REINSTATES
REINSTATING
REINSURE
REINSURED
REINSURER
REINSURERS
REINSURES
REINSURING
REINTER
REINTERRED
REINTERRING
REINTERS
REINVEST
REINVESTED
REINVESTING
REINVESTS
REINVOLVE
REINVOLVED
REINVOLVES
REINVOLVING
REIRD
REIRDS
REIS
REISES
REISSUE
REISSUED
REISSUES
REISSUING
REIST
REISTAFEL
REISTAFELS

REISTED	RELÂCHE	RELICTS	RELUME	REMEASURED
REISTIER	RELÂCHES	RELIDE	RELUMED	REMEASURES
REISTIEST	RELAID	RELIE	RELUMES	REMEASURING
REISTING	RELAPSE	RELIED	RELUMINE	REMEDE
REISTS	RELAPSED	RELIEF	RELUMINED	REMEDED
REISTY	RELAPSER	RELIEFS	RELUMINES	REMEDES
REITER	RELAPSERS	RELIER	RELUMING	REMEDIAL
REITERANT	RELAPSES	RELIERS	RELUMINING	REMEDIAT
REITERATE	RELAPSING	RELIES	RELY	REMEDIATE
REITERATED	RELATE	RELIEVE	RELYING	REMEDIED
REITERATES	RELATED	RELIEVED	REM	REMEDIES
REITERATING	RELATER	RELIEVER	REMADE	REMEDING
REITERS	RELATERS	RELIEVERS	REMADES	REMEDY
REIVE	RELATES	RELIEVES	REMAIN	REMEDYING
REIVER	RELATING	RELIEVING	REMAINDER	REMEID
REIVERS	RELATION	RELIEVO	REMAINDERED	REMEIDED
REIVES	RELATIONS	RELIEVOS	REMAINDERING	REMEIDING
REIVING	RELATIVAL	RELIGHT	REMAINDERS	REMEIDS
REJECT	RELATIVE	RELIGHTING	REMAINED	REMEMBER
REJECTED	RELATIVES	RELIGHTS	REMAINING	REMEMBERED
REJECTER	RELATOR	RELIGION	REMAINS	REMEMBERING
REJECTERS	RELATORS	RELIGIONS	REMAKE	REMEMBERS
REJECTING	RELAX	RELIGIOSE	REMAKES	REMEN
REJECTION	RELAXANT	RELIGIOSO	REMAKING	REMENS
REJECTIONS	RELAXANTS	RELIGIOUS	REMAN	REMERCIED
REJECTIVE	RELAXED	RELIGIOUSES	REMAND	REMERCIES
REJECTOR	RELAXES	RELINE	REMANDED	REMERCY
REJECTORS	RELAXIN	RELINED	REMANDING	REMERCYING
REJECTS	RELAXING	RELINES	REMANDS	REMERGE
REJIG	RELAXINS	RELINING	REMANENCE	REMERGED
REJIGGED	RELAY	RELIQUARIES	REMANENCES	REMERGES
REJIGGER	RELAYED	RELIQUARY	REMANENCIES	REMERGING
REJIGGERED	RELAYING	RELIQUE	REMANENCY	REMEX
REJIGGERING	RELAYS	RELIQUES	REMANENT	REMIGATE
REJIGGERS	RELEASE	RELIQUIAE	REMANENTS	REMIGATED
REJIGGING	RELEASED	RELISH	REMANET	REMIGATES
REJIGS	RELEASEE	RELISHED	REMANETS	REMIGATING
REJOICE	RELEASEES	RELISHES	REMANIÉ	REMIGES
REJOICED	RELEASER	RELISHING	REMANIÉS	REMIGIAL
REJOICER	RELEASERS	RELIT	REMANNED	REMIGRATE
REJOICERS	RELEASES	RELIVE	REMANNING	REMIGRATED
REJOICES	RELEASING	RELIVED	REMANS	REMIGRATES
REJOICING	RELEASOR	RELIVER	REMARK	REMIGRATING
REJOICINGS	RELEASORS	RELIVERED	REMARKED	REMIND
REJOIN	RELEGABLE	RELIVERING	REMARKER	REMINDED
REJOINDER	RELEGATE	RELIVERS	REMARKERS	REMINDER
REJOINDERS	RELEGATED	RELIVES	REMARKING	REMINDERS
REJOINED	RELEGATES	RELIVING	REMARKS	REMINDFUL
REJOINING	RELEGATING	RELLISH	REMARQUÉ	REMINDING
REJOINS	RELENT	RELLISHED	REMARQUED	REMINDS
REJÓN	RELENTED	RELLISHES	REMARQUÉS	REMINISCE
REJONEO	RELENTING	RELLISHING	REMARRIED	REMINISCED
REJONEOS	RELENTINGS	RELOAD	REMARRIES	REMINISCES
REJONES	RELENTS	RELOADED	REMARRY	REMINISCING
REJOURN	RELET	RELOADING	REMARRYING	REMISE
REJOURNED	RELETS	RELOADS	REMATCH	REMISED
REJOURNING	RELETTING	RELOCATE	REMATCHED	REMISES
REJOURNS	RELEVANCE	RELOCATED	REMATCHES	REMISING
REJUDGE	RELEVANCES	RELOCATES	REMATCHING	REMISS
REJUDGED	RELEVANCIES	RELOCATING	REMBLAI	REMISSION
REJUDGES	RELEVANCY	RELUCENT	REMBLAIS	REMISSIONS
REJUDGING	RELEVANT	RELUCT	REMBLE	REMISSIVE
REKE	RELIABLE	RELUCTANT	REMBLED	REMISSLY
REKED	RELIABLY	RELUCTATE	REMBLES	REMISSORY
REKES	RELIANCE	RELUCTATED	REMBLING	REMIT
REKINDLE	RELIANCES	RELUCTATES	REMEAD	REMITMENT
REKINDLED	RELIANT	RELUCTATING	REMEADED	REMITMENTS
REKINDLES	RELIC	RELUCTED	REMEADING	REMITS
REKINDLING	RELICS	RELUCTING	REMEADS	REMITTAL
REKING	RELICT	RELUCTS	REMEASURE	REMITTALS

REMITTED	RENAGUING	RENGAS	RENVOYS	REPASTURES
REMITTEE	RENAL	RENIED	RENY	REPAY
REMITTEES	RENAME	RENIES	RENYING	REPAYABLE
REMITTENT	RENAMED	RENIFORM	REOCCUPIED	REPAYING
REMITTER	RENAMES	RENIG	REOCCUPIES	REPAYMENT
REMITTERS	RENAMING	RENIGGED	REOCCUPY	REPAYMENTS
REMITTING	RENASCENT	RENIGGING	REOCCUPYING	REPAYS
REMITTOR	RENAY	RENIGS	REOFFEND	REPEAL
REMITTORS	RENAYED	RENIN	REOFFENDED	REPEALED
REMNANT	RENAYING	RENINS	REOFFENDING	REPEALER
REMNANTS	RENAYS	RENITENCIES	REOFFENDS	REPEALERS
REMODEL	RENCONTRE	RENITENCY	REOPEN	REPEALING
REMODELLED	RENCONTRED	RENITENT	REOPENED	REPEALS
REMODELLING	RENCONTRES	RENMINBI	REOPENER	REPEAT
REMODELS	RENCONTRING	RENMINBIS	REOPENERS	REPEATED
REMODIFIED	REND	RENNE	REOPENING	REPEATER
REMODIFIES	RENDER	RENNED	REOPENS	REPEATERS
REMODIFY	RENDERED	RENNES	REORDAIN	REPEATING
REMODIFYING	RENDERER	RENNET	REORDAINED	REPEATINGS
REMONTANT	RENDERERS	RENNETS	REORDAINING	REPEATS
REMONTANTS	RENDERING	RENNIN	REORDAINS	REPECHAGE
REMORA	RENDERINGS	RENNING	REORDER	REPEL
REMORAS	RENDERS	RENNINGS	REORDERED	REPELLANT
REMORSE	RENDING	RENNINS	REORDERING	REPELLANTS
REMORSES	RENDITION	RENOUNCE	REORDERS	REPELLED
REMOTE	RENDITIONS	RENOUNCED	REORIENT	REPELLENT
REMOTELY	RENDS	RENOUNCER	REORIENTED	REPELLENTS
REMOTER	RENDZINA	RENOUNCERS	REORIENTING	REPELLER
REMOTES	RENDZINAS	RENOUNCES	REORIENTS	REPELLERS
REMOTEST	RENEGADE	RENOUNCING	REP	REPELLING
REMOTION	RENEGADED	RENOVATE	REPACK	REPELS
REMOTIONS	RENEGADES	RENOVATED	REPACKED	REPENT
REMOUD	RENEGADING	RENOVATES	REPACKING	REPENTANT
REMOULADE	RENEGADO	RENOVATING	REPACKS	REPENTANTS
RÉMOULADE	RENEGADOS	RENOVATOR	REPAID	REPENTED
REMOULADES	RENEGATE	RENOVATORS	REPAINT	REPENTER
RÉMOULADES	RENEGATES	RENOWN	REPAINTED	REPENTERS
REMOULD	RENEGE	RENOWNED	REPAINTING	REPENTING
REMOULDED	RENEGED	RENOWNER	REPAINTINGS	REPENTS
REMOULDING	RENEGER	RENOWNERS	REPAINTS	REPEOPLE
REMOULDS	RENEGERS	RENOWNING	REPAIR	REPEOPLED
REMOUNT	RENEGES	RENOWNS	REPAIRED	REPEOPLES
REMOUNTED	RENEGING	RENS	REPAIRER	REPEOPLING
REMOUNTING	RENEGUE	RENT	REPAIRERS	REPERCUSS
REMOUNTS	RENEGUED	RENTABLE	REPAIRING	REPERCUSSED
REMOVABLE	RENEGUER	RENTAL	REPAIRMAN	REPERCUSSES
REMOVABLY	RENEGUERS	RENTALLER	REPAIRMEN	REPERCUSSING
REMOVAL	RENEGUES	RENTALLERS	REPAIRS	REPERTORIES
REMOVALS	RENEGUING	RENTALS	REPAND	REPERTORY
REMOVE	RENEW	RENTE	REPAPER	REPERUSAL
REMOVED	RENEWABLE	RENTED	REPAPERED	REPERUSALS
REMOVER	RENEWAL	RENTER	REPAPERING	REPERUSE
REMOVERS	RENEWALS	RENTERS	REPAPERS	REPERUSED
REMOVES	RENEWED	RENTES	REPARABLE	REPERUSES
REMOVING	RENEWER	RENTIER	REPARABLY	REPERUSING
REMS	RENEWERS	RENTIERS	REPARTEE	REPETEND
REMUAGE	RENEWING	RENTING	REPARTEED	REPETENDS
REMUAGES	RENEWINGS	RENTS	REPARTEEING	REPHRASE
REMUDA	RENEWS	RENUMBER	REPARTEES	REPHRASED
REMUDAS	RENEY	RENUMBERED	REPARTEEING	REPHRASES
REMUEUR	RENEYED	RENUMBERING	REPASS	REPHRASING
REMUEURS	RENEYING	RENUMBERS	REPASSAGE	REPINE
REMURMUR	RENEYS	RENVERSE	REPASSAGES	REPINED
REMURMURED	RENFIERST	RENVERSED	REPASSED	REPINER
REMURMURING	RENFORCE	RENVERSES	REPASSES	REPINERS
REMURMURS	RENFORCED	RENVERSING	REPASSING	REPINES
REN	RENFORCES	RENVERST	REPAST	REPINING
RENAGUE	RENFORCING	RENVOI	REPASTED	REPININGS
RENAGUED	RENFORST	RENVOIS	REPASTING	REPIQUE
RENAGUES	RENGA	RENVOY	REPASTS	REPIQUED

REPIQUES	REPOS	REPRINTED	REPUGNS	REQUOYLE
REPIQUING	REPOSAL	REPRINTING	REPULP	RERADIATE
REPLA	REPOSALL	REPRINTS	REPULPED	RERADIATED
REPLACE	REPOSALLS	REPRISAL	REPULPING	RERADIATES
REPLACED	REPOSALS	REPRISALS	REPULPS	RERADIATING
REPLACER	REPOSE	REPRISE	REPULSE	RERAIL
REPLACERS	REPOSED	REPRISED	REPULSED	RERAILED
REPLACES	REPOSEDLY	REPRISES	REPULSES	RERAILING
REPLACING	REPOSEFUL	REPRISING	REPULSING	RERAILS
REPLAN	REPOSES	REPRIVE	REPULSION	RERAN
REPLANNED	REPOSING	REPRIZE	REPULSIONS	REREAD
REPLANNING	REPOSIT	REPRIZED	REPULSIVE	REREADING
REPLANS	REPOSITED	REPRIZES	REPURE	REREADS
REPLANT	REPOSITING	REPRIZING	REPURED	REREBRACE
REPLANTED	REPOSITOR	REPRO	REPURES	REREBRACES
REPLANTING	REPOSITORS	REPROACH	REPURIFIED	REREDORSE
REPLANTS	REPOSITS	REPROACHED	REPURIFIES	REREDORSES
REPLAY	REPOSSESS	REPROACHES	REPURIFY	REREDOS
REPLAYED	REPOSSESSED	REPROACHING	REPURIFYING	REREDOSES
REPLAYING	REPOSSESSES	REPROBACIES	REPURING	REREDOSSE
REPLAYS	REPOSSESSING	REPROBACY	REPUTABLE	REREDOSSES
REPLENISH	REPOST	REPROBATE	REPUTABLY	REREMICE
REPLENISHED	REPOSTED	REPROBATED	REPUTE	REREMOUSE
REPLENISHES	REPOSTING	REPROBATES	REPUTED	REREVISE
REPLENISHING	REPOSTS	REPROBATING	REPUTEDLY	REREVISED
REPLETE	REPOSURE	REPROCESS	REPUTES	REREVISES
REPLETED	REPOSURES	REPROCESSED	REPUTING	REREVISING
REPLETES	REPOT	REPROCESSES	REPUTINGS	REREWARD
REPLETING	REPOTS	REPROCESSING	REQUERE	REREWARDS
REPLETION	REPOTTED	REPRODUCE	REQUERED	REROUTE
REPLETIONS	REPOTTING	REPRODUCED	REQUERES	REROUTED
REPLEVIED	REPOTTINGS	REPRODUCES	REQUERING	REROUTES
REPLEVIES	REPOUSSÉ	REPRODUCING	REQUEST	REROUTING
REPLEVIN	REPOUSSÉS	REPROOF	REQUESTED	RERUN
REPLEVINED	REPP	REPROOFED	REQUESTER	RERUNNING
REPLEVINING	REPPED	REPROOFING	REQUESTERS	RERUNS
REPLEVINS	REPPING	REPROOFS	REQUESTING	RES
REPLEVY	REPPS	REPROS	REQUESTS	RESAID
REPLEVYING	REPREEVE	REPROVAL	REQUICKEN	RESALE
REPLICA	REPREHEND	REPROVALS	REQUICKENED	RESALES
REPLICAS	REPREHENDED	REPROVE	REQUICKENING	RESALGAR
REPLICATE	REPREHENDING	REPROVED	REQUICKENS	RESALGARS
REPLICATED	REPREHENDS	REPROVER	REQUIEM	RESALUTE
REPLICATES	REPRESENT	REPROVERS	REQUIEMS	RESALUTED
REPLICATING	REPRESENTED	REPROVES	REQUIGHT	RESALUTES
REPLIED	REPRESENTING	REPROVING	REQUIRE	RESALUTING
REPLIER	REPRESENTS	REPROVINGS	REQUIRED	RESAT
REPLIERS	REPRESS	REPRYVE	REQUIRER	RESAY
REPLIES	REPRESSED	REPS	REQUIRERS	RESAYING
REPLUM	REPRESSES	REPTANT	REQUIRES	RESAYS
REPLY	REPRESSING	REPTATION	REQUIRING	RESCALE
REPLYING	REPRESSOR	REPTATIONS	REQUIRINGS	RESCALED
REPO	REPRESSORS	REPTILE	REQUISITE	RESCALES
REPOINT	REPRIEFE	REPTILES	REQUISITES	RESCALING
REPOINTED	REPRIEFES	REPTILIAN	REQUIT	RESCIND
REPOINTING	REPRIEVAL	REPTILOID	REQUITAL	RESCINDED
REPOINTS	REPRIEVALS	REPUBLIC	REQUITALS	RESCINDING
REPONE	REPRIEVE	REPUBLICS	REQUITE	RESCINDS
REPONED	REPRIEVED	REPUBLISH	REQUITED	RESCORE
REPONES	REPRIEVES	REPUBLISHED	REQUITER	RESCORED
REPONING	REPRIEVING	REPUBLISHES	REQUITERS	RESCORES
REPORT	REPRIMAND	REPUBLISHING	REQUITES	RESCORING
REPORTAGE	REPRIMANDED	REPUDIATE	REQUITING	RESCRIPT
REPORTAGES	REPRIMANDING	REPUDIATED	REQUITS	RESCRIPTED
REPORTED	REPRIMANDS	REPUDIATES	REQUITTED	RESCRIPTING
REPORTER	REPRIME	REPUDIATING	REQUITTING	RESCRIPTS
REPORTERS	REPRIMED	REPUGN	REQUOTE	RESCUABLE
REPORTING	REPRIMES	REPUGNANT	REQUOTED	RESCUE
REPORTINGS	REPRIMING	REPUGNED	REQUOTES	RESCUED
REPORTS	REPRINT	REPUGNING	REQUOTING	RESCUER

RESCUERS
RESCUES
RESCUING
RESEAL
RESEALED
RESEALING
RESEALS
RESEARCH
RESEARCHED
RESEARCHES
RESEARCHING
RESEAT
RESEATED
RESEATING
RESEATS
RÉSEAU
RÉSEAUS
RÉSEAUX
RESECT
RESECTED
RESECTING
RESECTION
RESECTIONS
RESECTS
RESEDA
RESEDAS
RESEIZE
RESEIZED
RESEIZES
RESEIZING
RESELECT
RESELECTED
RESELECTING
RESELECTS
RESELL
RESELLING
RESELLS
RESEMBLE
RESEMBLED
RESEMBLER
RESEMBLERS
RESEMBLES
RESEMBLING
RESENT
RESENTED
RESENTER
RESENTERS
RESENTFUL
RESENTING
RESENTIVE
RESENTS
RESERPINE
RESERPINES
RESERVE
RESERVED
RESERVES
RESERVING
RESERVIST
RESERVISTS
RESERVOIR
RESERVOIRED
RESERVOIRING
RESERVOIRS
RESET
RESETS
RESETTER
RESETTERS
RESETTING
RESETTLE
RESETTLED

RESETTLES
RESETTLING
RESHAPE
RESHAPED
RESHAPES
RESHAPING
RESHIP
RESHIPPED
RESHIPPING
RESHIPS
RESHUFFLE
RESHUFFLED
RESHUFFLES
RESHUFFLING
RESIANCE
RESIANCES
RESIANT
RESIANTS
RESIDE
RESIDED
RESIDENCE
RESIDENCES
RESIDENCIES
RESIDENCY
RESIDENT
RESIDENTS
RESIDER
RESIDERS
RESIDES
RESIDING
RESIDUA
RESIDUAL
RESIDUALS
RESIDUARY
RESIDUE
RESIDUES
RESIDUOUS
RESIDUUM
RESIGN
RESIGNED
RESIGNER
RESIGNERS
RESIGNING
RESIGNS
RESILE
RESILED
RESILES
RESILIENT
RESILING
RESIN
RESINATA
RESINATAS
RESINATE
RESINATES
RESINED
RESINER
RESINERS
RESINIFIED
RESINIFIES
RESINIFY
RESINIFYING
RESINING
RESINISE
RESINISED
RESINISES
RESINISING
RESINIZE
RESINIZED
RESINIZES
RESINIZING

RESINOID
RESINOIDS
RESINOSES
RESINOSIS
RESINOUS
RESINS
RESIST
RESISTANT
RESISTANTS
RESISTED
RESISTENT
RESISTENTS
RESISTING
RESISTIVE
RESISTOR
RESISTORS
RESISTS
RESIT
RESITS
RESITTING
RESKEW
RESKUE
RESNATRON
RESNATRONS
RESOLD
RESOLE
RESOLED
RESOLES
RESOLING
RESOLUBLE
RESOLUTE
RESOLUTES
RESOLVE
RESOLVED
RESOLVENT
RESOLVENTS
RESOLVER
RESOLVERS
RESOLVES
RESOLVING
RESONANCE
RESONANCES
RESONANT
RESONATE
RESONATED
RESONATES
RESONATING
RESONATOR
RESONATORS
RESORB
RESORBED
RESORBENT
RESORBING
RESORBS
RESORCIN
RESORCINS
RESORT
RESORTED
RESORTER
RESORTERS
RESORTING
RESORTS
RESOUND
RESOUNDED
RESOUNDING
RESOUNDS
RESOURCE
RESOURCED
RESOURCES
RESOURCING

RESPEAK
RESPEAKING
RESPEAKS
RESPECT
RESPECTED
RESPECTER
RESPECTERS
RESPECTING
RESPECTS
RESPELL
RESPELLED
RESPELLING
RESPELLS
RESPELT
RESPIRE
RESPIRED
RESPIRES
RESPIRING
RESPITE
RESPITED
RESPITES
RESPITING
RESPLEND
RESPLENDED
RESPLENDING
RESPLENDS
RESPOKE
RESPOKEN
RESPOND
RESPONDED
RESPONDER
RESPONDERS
RESPONDING
RESPONDS
RESPONSA
RESPONSE
RESPONSER
RESPONSERS
RESPONSES
RESPONSOR
RESPONSORS
RESPONSUM
RESPONSUMS
RESPRAY
RESPRAYED
RESPRAYING
RESPRAYS
RESSALDAR
RESSALDARS
REST
RESTAFF
RESTAFFED
RESTAFFING
RESTAFFS
RESTAGE
RESTAGED
RESTAGES
RESTAGING
RESTART
RESTARTED
RESTARTER
RESTARTERS
RESTARTING
RESTARTS
RESTATE
RESTATED
RESTATES
RESTATING
RESTED
RESTEM

RESTEMMED
RESTEMMING
RESTEMS
RESTER
RESTERS
RESTFUL
RESTFULLER
RESTFULLEST
RESTFULLY
RESTIER
RESTIEST
RESTIFF
RESTIFORM
RESTING
RESTINGS
RESTITUTE
RESTITUTED
RESTITUTES
RESTITUTING
RESTIVE
RESTIVELY
RESTLESS
RESTOCK
RESTOCKED
RESTOCKING
RESTOCKS
RESTORE
RESTORED
RESTORER
RESTORERS
RESTORES
RESTORING
RESTRAIN
RESTRAINED
RESTRAINING
RESTRAININGS
RESTRAINS
RESTRAINT
RESTRAINTS
RESTRICT
RESTRICTED
RESTRICTING
RESTRICTS
RESTRING
RESTRINGE
RESTRINGED
RESTRINGEING
RESTRINGES
RESTRINGING
RESTRINGS
RESTRUNG
RESTS
RESTY
RESTYLE
RESTYLED
RESTYLES
RESTYLING
RESUBMIT
RESUBMITS
RESUBMITTED
RESUBMITTING
RESULT
RESULTANT
RESULTANTS
RESULTED
RESULTFUL
RESULTING
RESULTS
RESUMABLE
RESUME

RÉSUMÉ
RESUMED
RESUMES
RÉSUMÉS
RESUMING
RESUPINE
RESURGE
RESURGED
RESURGENT
RESURGES
RESURGING
RESURRECT
RESURRECTED
RESURRECTING
RESURRECTS
RESURVEY
RESURVEYED
RESURVEYING
RESURVEYS
RET
RETABLE
RETABLES
RETAIL
RETAILED
RETAILER
RETAILERS
RETAILING
RETAILS
RETAIN
RETAINED
RETAINER
RETAINERS
RETAINING
RETAINS
RETAKE
RETAKEN
RETAKER
RETAKERS
RETAKES
RETAKING
RETAKINGS
RETALIATE
RETALIATED
RETALIATES
RETALIATING
RETAMA
RETAMAS
RETARD
RETARDANT
RETARDANTS
RETARDATE
RETARDATES
RETARDED
RETARDER
RETARDERS
RETARDING
RETARDS
RETCH
RETCHED
RETCHES
RETCHING
RETCHLESS
RETE
RETELL
RETELLER
RETELLERS
RETELLING
RETELLS
RETENE
RETENES

RETENTION
RETENTIONS
RETENTIVE
RETES
RETEXTURE
RETEXTURED
RETEXTURES
RETEXTURING
RETHINK
RETHINKING
RETHINKS
RETHOUGHT
RETIAL
RETIARII
RETIARIUS
RETIARIUSES
RETIARY
RETICENCE
RETICENCES
RETICENCIES
RETICENCY
RETICENT
RETICLE
RETICLES
RETICULAR
RETICULE
RETICULES
RETICULUM
RETICULUMS
RETIE
RETIED
RETIES
RETIFORM
RETILE
RETILED
RETILES
RETILING
RETINA
RETINAE
RETINAL
RETINAS
RETINITE
RETINITES
RETINITIS
RETINITISES
RETINOL
RETINOLS
RETINUE
RETINUES
RETINULA
RETINULAE
RETINULAR
RETIRACIES
RETIRACY
RETIRAL
RETIRALS
RETIRE
RETIRED
RETIREDLY
RETIREE
RETIREES
RETIRER
RETIRERS
RETIRES
RETIRING
RETITLE
RETITLED
RETITLES
RETITLING
RETOLD

RETOOK
RETOOL
RETOOLED
RETOOLING
RETOOLS
RETORSION
RETORSIONS
RETORT
RETORTED
RETORTER
RETORTERS
RETORTING
RETORTION
RETORTIONS
RETORTIVE
RETORTS
RETOUCH
RETOUCHED
RETOUCHER
RETOUCHERS
RETOUCHES
RETOUCHING
RETOUR
RETOURED
RETOURING
RETOURS
RETRACE
RETRACED
RETRACES
RETRACING
RETRACT
RETRACTED
RETRACTING
RETRACTOR
RETRACTORS
RETRACTS
RETRAICT
RETRAIN
RETRAINED
RETRAINING
RETRAINS
RETRAIT
RETRAITE
RETRAITES
RETRAITS
RETRAITT
RETRAITTS
RETRAL
RETRALLY
RETRATE
RETRATES
RETREAD
RETREADED
RETREADING
RETREADS
RETREAT
RETREATED
RETREATING
RETREATS
RETREE
RETREES
RETRENCH
RETRENCHED
RETRENCHES
RETRENCHING
RETRIAL
RETRIALS
RETRIBUTE
RETRIBUTED
RETRIBUTES

RETRIBUTING
RETRIED
RETRIES
RETRIEVAL
RETRIEVALS
RETRIEVE
RETRIEVED
RETRIEVER
RETRIEVERS
RETRIEVES
RETRIEVING
RETRIEVINGS
RETRIM
RETRIMMED
RETRIMMING
RETRIMS
RETRO
RETROACT
RETROACTED
RETROACTING
RETROACTS
RETROCEDE
RETROCEDED
RETROCEDES
RETROCEDING
RETROD
RETRODDEN
RETROFIT
RETROFITS
RETROFITTED
RETROFITTING
RETROFLEX
RETROJECT
RETROJECTED
RETROJECTING
RETROJECTS
RETRORSE
RETROS
RETROUSSÉ
RETROVERT
RETROVERTED
RETROVERTING
RETROVERTS
RETRY
RETRYING
RETS
RETSINA
RETSINAS
RETTED
RETTERIES
RETTERY
RETTING
RETUND
RETUNDED
RETUNDING
RETUNDS
RETUNE
RETUNED
RETUNES
RETUNING
RETURF
RETURFED
RETURFING
RETURFS
RETURN
RETURNED
RETURNEE
RETURNEES
RETURNING
RETURNS

RETUSE
RETYING
REUNIFIED
REUNIFIES
REUNIFY
REUNIFYING
REUNION
REUNIONS
REUNITE
REUNITED
REUNITES
REUNITING
REURGE
REURGED
REURGES
REURGING
REUSABLE
REUSE
REUSED
REUSES
REUSING
REUTTER
REUTTERED
REUTTERING
REUTTERS
REV
REVALENTA
REVALENTAS
REVALUE
REVALUED
REVALUES
REVALUING
REVAMP
REVAMPED
REVAMPING
REVAMPS
REVANCHE
REVANCHES
REVEAL
REVEALED
REVEALER
REVEALERS
REVEALING
REVEALINGS
REVEALS
REVEILLE
REVEILLES
REVEL
REVELATOR
REVELATORS
REVELLED
REVELLER
REVELLERS
REVELLING
REVELLINGS
REVELRIES
REVELRY
REVELS
REVENANT
REVENANTS
REVENGE
REVENGED
REVENGER
REVENGERS
REVENGES
REVENGING
REVENGINGS
REVENGIVE
REVENUE
REVENUED

REVENUES	REVIEWED	REVULSION	RHAPSODE	RHIPIDIUM
REVERABLE	REVIEWER	REVULSIONS	RHAPSODES	RHIPIDIUMS
REVERB	REVIEWERS	REVULSIVE	RHAPSODIC	RHIZIC
REVERBED	REVIEWING	REVVED	RHAPSODIES	RHIZINE
REVERBING	REVIEWS	REVVING	RHAPSODY	RHIZINES
REVERBS	REVILE	REVYING	RHATANIES	RHIZOBIA
REVERE	REVILED	REW	RHATANY	RHIZOBIUM
REVERED	REVILER	REWARD	RHEA	RHIZOCARP
REVERENCE	REVILERS	REWARDED	RHEAS	RHIZOCARPS
REVERENCES	REVILES	REWARDER	RHEMATIC	RHIZOCAUL
REVEREND	REVILING	REWARDERS	RHENIUM	RHIZOCAULS
REVERENDS	REVILINGS	REWARDFUL	RHENIUMS	RHIZOID
REVERENT	REVISABLE	REWARDING	RHEOCHORD	RHIZOIDAL
REVERER	REVISAL	REWARDS	RHEOCHORDS	RHIZOIDS
REVERERS	REVISALS	REWAREWA	RHEOCORD	RHIZOME
REVERES	REVISE	REWAREWAS	RHEOCORDS	RHIZOMES
REVERIE	REVISED	REWEIGH	RHEOLOGIC	RHIZOPI
REVERIES	REVISER	REWEIGHED	RHEOLOGIES	RHIZOPOD
REVERING	REVISERS	REWEIGHING	RHEOLOGY	RHIZOPODS
REVERIST	REVISES	REWEIGHS	RHEOMETER	RHIZOPUS
REVERISTS	REVISING	REWIND	RHEOMETERS	RHIZOPUSES
REVERS	REVISION	REWINDING	RHEOSTAT	RHO
REVERSAL	REVISIONS	REWINDS	RHEOSTATS	RHODAMINE
REVERSALS	REVISIT	REWIRE	RHEOTAXIS	RHODAMINES
REVERSE	REVISITED	REWIRED	RHEOTAXISES	RHODANATE
REVERSED	REVISITING	REWIRES	RHEOTOME	RHODANATES
REVERSELY	REVISITS	REWIRING	RHEOTOMES	RHODANIC
REVERSER	REVISOR	REWORD	RHEOTROPE	RHODANISE
REVERSERS	REVISORS	REWORDED	RHEOTROPES	RHODANISED
REVERSES	REVISORY	REWORDING	RHESUS	RHODANISES
REVERSI	REVIVABLE	REWORDS	RHESUSES	RHODANISING
REVERSING	REVIVABLY	REWORK	RHETOR	RHODANIZE
REVERSINGS	REVIVAL	REWORKED	RHETORIC	RHODANIZED
REVERSION	REVIVALS	REWORKING	RHETORICS	RHODANIZES
REVERSIONS	REVIVE	REWORKS	RHETORISE	RHODANIZING
REVERSIS	REVIVED	REWOUND	RHETORISED	RHODIC
REVERSO	REVIVER	REWRAP	RHETORISES	RHODIUM
REVERSOS	REVIVERS	REWRAPPED	RHETORISING	RHODIUMS
REVERT	REVIVES	REWRAPPING	RHETORIZE	RHODOLITE
REVERTED	REVIVIFIED	REWRAPS	RHETORIZED	RHODOLITES
REVERTING	REVIVIFIES	REWRITE	RHETORIZES	RHODONITE
REVERTIVE	REVIVIFY	REWRITES	RHETORIZING	RHODONITES
REVERTS	REVIVIFYING	REWRITING	RHETORS	RHODOPSIN
REVERY	REVIVING	REWRITTEN	RHEUM	RHODOPSINS
REVEST	REVIVINGS	REWROTE	RHEUMATIC	RHODORA
REVESTED	REVIVOR	REWS	RHEUMATICS	RHODORAS
REVESTING	REVIVORS	REWTH	RHEUMATIZ	RHODOUS
REVESTRIES	REVOCABLE	REWTHS	RHEUMATIZES	RHOEADINE
REVESTRY	REVOCABLY	REX	RHEUMED	RHOEADINES
REVESTS	REVOKE	REYNARD	RHEUMS	RHOMB
REVET	REVOKED	REYNARDS	RHEUMY	RHOMBI
REVETMENT	REVOKES	RHABDOID	RHEXES	RHOMBIC
REVETMENTS	REVOKING	RHABDOIDS	RHEXIS	RHOMBOI
REVETS	REVOLT	RHABDOM	RHEXISES	RHOMBOID
REVETTED	REVOLTED	RHABDOMS	RHIME	RHOMBOIDS
REVETTING	REVOLTER	RHABDUS	RHIMES	RHOMBOS
RÊVEUR	REVOLTERS	RHABDUSES	RHINAL	RHOMBS
RÊVEURS	REVOLTING	RHACHIDES	RHINE	RHOMBUS
RÊVEUSE	REVOLTS	RHACHIS	RHINES	RHOMBUSES
RÊVEUSES	REVOLUTE	RHACHISES	RHINITIS	RHONCHAL
REVICTUAL	REVOLVE	RHACHITIS	RHINITISES	RHONCHI
REVICTUALLED	REVOLVED	RHACHITISES	RHINO	RHONCHIAL
REVICTUALLING	REVOLVER	RHAMPHOID	RHINOLITH	RHONCHUS
REVICTUALS	REVOLVERS	RHAPHE	RHINOLITHS	RHONE
REVIE	REVOLVES	RHAPHES	RHINOLOGIES	RHONES
REVIED	REVOLVING	RHAPHIDE	RHINOLOGY	RHOPALIC
REVIES	REVOLVINGS	RHAPHIDES	RHINOS	RHOPALISM
REVIEW	REVS	RHAPHIS	RHIPIDATE	RHOPALISMS
REVIEWAL	REVUE	RHAPONTIC	RHIPIDION	RHOS
REVIEWALS	REVUES	RHAPONTICS	RHIPIDIONS	RHOTACISE

RHOTACISED
RHOTACISES
RHOTACISING
RHOTACISM
RHOTACISMS
RHOTACIZE
RHOTACIZED
RHOTACIZES
RHOTACIZING
RHOTIC
RHUBARB
RHUBARBS
RHUBARBY
RHUMB
RHUMBA
RHUMBAS
RHUMBS
RHUS
RHUSES
RHY
RHYME
RHYMED
RHYMELESS
RHYMER
RHYMERS
RHYMES
RHYMESTER
RHYMESTERS
RHYMING
RHYMIST
RHYMISTS
RHYOLITE
RHYOLITES
RHYOLITIC
RHYS
RHYTA
RHYTHM
RHYTHMAL
RHYTHMED
RHYTHMI
RHYTHMIC
RHYTHMICS
RHYTHMING
RHYTHMISE
RHYTHMISED
RHYTHMISES
RHYTHMISING
RHYTHMIST
RHYTHMISTS
RHYTHMIZE
RHYTHMIZED
RHYTHMIZES
RHYTHMIZING
RHYTHMS
RHYTHMUS
RHYTHMUSES
RHYTINA
RHYTINAS
RHYTON
RIA
RIAL
RIALS
RIANCIES
RIANCY
RIANT
RIAS
RIATA
RIATAS
RIB
RIBALD

RIBALDRIES
RIBALDRY
RIBALDS
RIBAND
RIBANDED
RIBANDING
RIBANDS
RIBATTUTA
RIBATTUTAS
RIBAUD
RIBAUDRED
RIBAUDRIES
RIBAUDRY
RIBAUDS
RIBBAND
RIBBANDED
RIBBANDING
RIBBANDS
RIBBED
RIBBIER
RIBBIEST
RIBBING
RIBBINGS
RIBBON
RIBBONED
RIBBONING
RIBBONRIES
RIBBONRY
RIBBONS
RIBBONY
RIBBY
RIBCAGE
RIBCAGES
RIBIBE
RIBIBES
RIBIBLE
RIBIBLES
RIBLESS
RIBLIKE
RIBOSE
RIBOSES
RIBOSOME
RIBOSOMES
RIBS
RIBSTON
RIBSTONE
RIBSTONES
RIBSTONS
RIBWORK
RIBWORKS
RIBWORT
RIBWORTS
RICE
RICED
RICER
RICERCAR
RICERCARE
RICERCARES
RICERCARS
RICERCATA
RICERCATAS
RICERS
RICES
RICEY
RICH
RICHED
RICHEN
RICHENED
RICHENING
RICHENS

RICHER
RICHES
RICHESSE
RICHESSES
RICHEST
RICHING
RICHLY
RICHNESS
RICHNESSES
RICHT
RICHTED
RICHTER
RICHTEST
RICHTING
RICHTS
RICIER
RICIEST
RICIN
RICING
RICINS
RICK
RICKED
RICKER
RICKERS
RICKETILY
RICKETS
RICKETTY
RICKETY
RICKING
RICKLE
RICKLES
RICKLY
RICKS
RICKSHA
RICKSHAS
RICKSHAW
RICKSHAWS
RICKSTAND
RICKSTANDS
RICKSTICK
RICKSTICKS
RICKYARD
RICKYARDS
RICOCHET
RICOCHETED
RICOCHETING
RICOCHETS
RICOCHETTED
RICOCHETTING
RICOTTA
RICOTTAS
RICTAL
RICTUS
RICTUSES
RICY
RID
RIDABLE
RIDDANCE
RIDDANCES
RIDDED
RIDDEN
RIDDER
RIDDERS
RIDDING
RIDDLE
RIDDLED
RIDDLER
RIDDLERS
RIDDLES
RIDDLING

RIDDLINGS
RIDE
RIDEABLE
RIDENT
RIDER
RIDERED
RIDERLESS
RIDERS
RIDES
RIDGE
RIDGEBACK
RIDGEBACKS
RIDGED
RIDGEL
RIDGELS
RIDGES
RIDGEWAY
RIDGEWAYS
RIDGIER
RIDGIEST
RIDGIL
RIDGILS
RIDGING
RIDGINGS
RIDGLING
RIDGLINGS
RIDGY
RIDICULE
RIDICULED
RIDICULER
RIDICULERS
RIDICULES
RIDICULING
RIDING
RIDINGS
RIDOTTO
RIDOTTOS
RIDS
RIEL
RIELS
RIEM
RIEMPIE
RIEMPIES
RIEMS
RIEVE
RIEVER
RIEVERS
RIEVES
RIEVING
RIFE
RIFELY
RIFENESS
RIFENESSES
RIFER
RIFEST
RIFF
RIFFLE
RIFFLED
RIFFLER
RIFFLERS
RIFFLES
RIFFLING
RIFFS
RIFLE
RIFLED
RIFLEMAN
RIFLEMEN
RIFLER
RIFLERS
RIFLES

RIFLING
RIFLINGS
RIFT
RIFTE
RIFTED
RIFTING
RIFTLESS
RIFTS
RIFTY
RIG
RIGADOON
RIGADOONS
RIGG
RIGGALD
RIGGALDS
RIGGED
RIGGER
RIGGERS
RIGGING
RIGGINGS
RIGGISH
RIGGS
RIGHT
RIGHTABLE
RIGHTED
RIGHTEN
RIGHTENED
RIGHTENING
RIGHTENS
RIGHTEOUS
RIGHTER
RIGHTERS
RIGHTEST
RIGHTFUL
RIGHTING
RIGHTINGS
RIGHTIST
RIGHTISTS
RIGHTLESS
RIGHTLY
RIGHTNESS
RIGHTNESSES
RIGHTO
RIGHTOS
RIGHTS
RIGHTWARD
RIGHTWARDS
RIGID
RIGIDER
RIGIDEST
RIGIDIFIED
RIGIDIFIES
RIGIDIFY
RIGIDIFYING
RIGIDISE
RIGIDISED
RIGIDISES
RIGIDISING
RIGIDITIES
RIGIDITY
RIGIDIZE
RIGIDIZED
RIGIDIZES
RIGIDIZING
RIGIDLY
RIGIDNESS
RIGIDNESSES
RIGIDS
RIGLIN
RIGLING

RIGLINGS
RIGLINS
RIGMAROLE
RIGMAROLES
RIGOL
RIGOLL
RIGOLLS
RIGOLS
RIGOR
RIGORISM
RIGORISMS
RIGORIST
RIGORISTS
RIGOROUS
RIGORS
RIGOUR
RIGOURS
RIGS
RIGWIDDIE
RIGWIDDIES
RIGWOODIE
RIGWOODIES
RIJSTAFEL
RIJSTAFELS
RILE
RILED
RILES
RILEY
RILIEVI
RILIEVO
RILING
RILL
RILLE
RILLED
RILLES
RILLET
RILLETS
RILLETTES
RILLING
RILLMARK
RILLMARKS
RILLS
RIM
RIMA
RIMAE
RIME
RIMED
RIMER
RIMERS
RIMES
RIMIER
RIMIEST
RIMING
RIMLESS
RIMMED
RIMMING
RIMOSE
RIMOUS
RIMS
RIMU
RIMUS
RIMY
RIN
RIND
RINDED
RINDIER
RINDIEST
RINDING
RINDLESS
RINDS

RINDY
RINE
RINES
RING
RINGBIT
RINGBITS
RINGBONE
RINGBONES
RINGED
RINGENT
RINGER
RINGERS
RINGGIT
RINGGITS
RINGHALS
RINGHALSES
RINGING
RINGINGLY
RINGINGS
RINGLESS
RINGLET
RINGLETED
RINGLETS
RINGMAN
RINGMEN
RINGS
RINGSIDE
RINGSIDER
RINGSIDERS
RINGSIDES
RINGSTAND
RINGSTANDS
RINGSTER
RINGSTERS
RINGTAIL
RINGTAILS
RINGWAY
RINGWAYS
RINGWISE
RINGWORK
RINGWORKS
RINGWORM
RINGWORMS
RINK
RINKED
RINKHALS
RINKHALSES
RINKING
RINKS
RINNING
RINS
RINSABLE
RINSE
RINSED
RINSER
RINSERS
RINSES
RINSIBLE
RINSING
RINSINGS
RIOT
RIOTED
RIOTER
RIOTERS
RIOTING
RIOTINGS
RIOTISE
RIOTISES
RIOTIZE
RIOTIZES

RIOTOUS
RIOTOUSLY
RIOTRIES
RIOTRY
RIOTS
RIP
RIPARIAL
RIPARIAN
RIPARIANS
RIPE
RIPECK
RIPECKS
RIPED
RIPELY
RIPEN
RIPENED
RIPENESS
RIPENESSES
RIPENING
RIPENS
RIPER
RIPERS
RIPES
RIPEST
RIPIENI
RIPIENIST
RIPIENISTS
RIPIENO
RIPIENOS
RIPING
RIPOSTE
RIPOSTED
RIPOSTES
RIPOSTING
RIPP
RIPPED
RIPPER
RIPPERS
RIPPIER
RIPPIERS
RIPPING
RIPPINGLY
RIPPLE
RIPPLED
RIPPLER
RIPPLERS
RIPPLES
RIPPLET
RIPPLETS
RIPPLIER
RIPPLIEST
RIPPLING
RIPPLINGS
RIPPLY
RIPPS
RIPRAP
RIPRAPS
RIPS
RIPT
RIPTIDE
RIPTIDES
RISALDAR
RISALDARS
RISE
RISEN
RISER
RISERS
RISES
RISHI
RISHIS

RISIBLE
RISING
RISINGS
RISK
RISKED
RISKER
RISKERS
RISKFUL
RISKIER
RISKIEST
RISKILY
RISKINESS
RISKINESSES
RISKING
RISKS
RISKY
RISOLUTO
RISOTTO
RISOTTOS
RISP
RISPED
RISPETTI
RISPETTO
RISPING
RISPINGS
RISPS
RISQUE
RISQUÉ
RISQUES
RISSOLE
RISSOLES
RISUS
RISUSES
RIT
RITE
RITELESS
RITENUTO
RITENUTOS
RITES
RITORNEL
RITORNELL
RITORNELLS
RITORNELS
RITS
RITT
RITTED
RITTER
RITTERS
RITTING
RITTS
RITUAL
RITUALISE
RITUALISED
RITUALISES
RITUALISING
RITUALISM
RITUALISMS
RITUALIST
RITUALISTS
RITUALIZE
RITUALIZED
RITUALIZES
RITUALIZING
RITUALLY
RITUALS
RITZIER
RITZIEST
RITZY
RIVA
RIVAGE

RIVAGES
RIVAL
RIVALESS
RIVALESSES
RIVALISE
RIVALISED
RIVALISES
RIVALISING
RIVALITIES
RIVALITY
RIVALIZE
RIVALIZED
RIVALIZES
RIVALIZING
RIVALLED
RIVALLESS
RIVALLING
RIVALRIES
RIVALRY
RIVALS
RIVALSHIP
RIVALSHIPS
RIVAS
RIVE
RIVED
RIVEL
RIVELLED
RIVELLING
RIVELS
RIVEN
RIVER
RIVERAIN
RIVERAINS
RIVERED
RIVERET
RIVERETS
RIVERINE
RIVERLESS
RIVERLIKE
RIVERMAN
RIVERMEN
RIVERS
RIVERSIDE
RIVERSIDES
RIVERWAY
RIVERWAYS
RIVERWEED
RIVERWEEDS
RIVERY
RIVES
RIVET
RIVETED
RIVETER
RIVETERS
RIVETING
RIVETINGS
RIVETS
RIVETTED
RIVETTING
RIVIERA
RIVIERAS
RIVIÈRE
RIVIÈRES
RIVING
RIVLIN
RIVLINS
RIVO
RIVOS
RIVULET
RIVULETS

RIYAL	ROASTER	ROCKERY	ROESTONE	ROLLMOP
RIYALS	ROASTERS	ROCKET	ROESTONES	ROLLMOPS
RIZ	ROASTING	ROCKETED	ROGATION	ROLLOCK
RIZARD	ROASTINGS	ROCKETEER	ROGATIONS	ROLLOCKS
RIZARDS	ROASTS	ROCKETEERS	ROGATORY	ROLLS
RIZZAR	ROATE	ROCKETER	ROGER	ROM
RIZZARED	ROATED	ROCKETERS	ROGERED	ROMA
RIZZARING	ROATES	ROCKETING	ROGERING	ROMAGE
RIZZARS	ROATING	ROCKETRIES	ROGERS	ROMAGES
RIZZART	ROB	ROCKETRY	ROGUE	ROMAIKA
RIZZARTS	ROBALO	ROCKETS	ROGUED	ROMAIKAS
RIZZER	ROBALOS	ROCKIER	ROGUERIES	ROMAL
RIZZERED	ROBBED	ROCKIERS	ROGUERY	ROMALS
RIZZERING	ROBBER	ROCKIEST	ROGUES	ROMAN
RIZZERS	ROBBERIES	ROCKILY	ROGUESHIP	ROMANCE
RIZZOR	ROBBERS	ROCKINESS	ROGUESHIPS	ROMANCED
RIZZORED	ROBBERY	ROCKINESSES	ROGUING	ROMANCER
RIZZORING	ROBBING	ROCKING	ROGUISH	ROMANCERS
RIZZORS	ROBE	ROCKINGS	ROGUISHLY	ROMANCES
ROACH	ROBED	ROCKLAY	ROGUY	ROMANCING
ROACHED	ROBES	ROCKLAYS	ROIL	ROMANCINGS
ROACHES	ROBIN	ROCKLING	ROILED	ROMANS
ROACHING	ROBING	ROCKLINGS	ROILIER	ROMANTIC
ROAD	ROBINGS	ROCKS	ROILIEST	ROMANTICS
ROADBLOCK	ROBINIA	ROCKWATER	ROILING	ROMAS
ROADBLOCKS	ROBINIAS	ROCKWATERS	ROILS	ROMAUNT
ROADHOUSE	ROBINS	ROCKWEED	ROILY	ROMAUNTS
ROADHOUSES	ROBLE	ROCKWEEDS	ROIN	ROMNEYA
ROADIE	ROBLES	ROCKWORK	ROINISH	ROMNEYAS
ROADIES	ROBORANT	ROCKWORKS	ROINS	ROMP
ROADING	ROBORANTS	ROCKY	ROIST	ROMPED
ROADINGS	ROBOT	ROCOCO	ROISTED	ROMPER
ROADLESS	ROBOTIC	ROCOCOS	ROISTER	ROMPERS
ROADMAN	ROBOTICS	ROCQUET	ROISTERED	ROMPING
ROADMEN	ROBOTISE	ROCQUETS	ROISTERER	ROMPINGLY
ROADS	ROBOTISED	ROCS	ROISTERERS	ROMPISH
ROADSHOW	ROBOTISES	ROD	ROISTERING	ROMPISHLY
ROADSHOWS	ROBOTISING	RODDED	ROISTERS	ROMPS
ROADSIDE	ROBOTIZE	RODDING	ROISTING	RONCADOR
ROADSIDES	ROBOTIZED	RODE	ROISTS	RONCADORS
ROADSMAN	ROBOTIZES	RODED	ROK	RONDACHE
ROADSMEN	ROBOTIZING	RODENT	ROKE	RONDACHES
ROADSTEAD	ROBOTS	RODENTS	ROKED	RONDAVEL
ROADSTEADS	ROBS	RODEO	ROKELAY	RONDAVELS
ROADSTER	ROBURITE	RODEOS	ROKELAYS	RONDE
ROADSTERS	ROBURITES	RODES	ROKER	RONDEAU
ROADWAY	ROBUST	RODEWAY	ROKERS	RONDEAUX
ROADWAYS	ROBUSTA	RODEWAYS	ROKES	RONDEL
ROAM	ROBUSTAS	RODFISHER	ROKIER	RONDELS
ROAMED	ROBUSTER	RODFISHERS	ROKIEST	RONDES
ROAMER	ROBUSTEST	RODING	ROKING	RONDINO
ROAMERS	ROBUSTLY	RODINGS	ROKS	RONDINOS
ROAMING	ROC	RODLESS	ROKY	RONDO
ROAMS	ROCAILLE	RODLIKE	ROLAG	RONDOS
ROAN	ROCAILLES	RODMAN	ROLAGS	RONDURE
ROANS	ROCAMBOLE	RODMEN	RÔLE	RONDURES
ROAR	ROCAMBOLES	RODS	ROLE	RONE
ROARED	ROCH	RODSMAN	RÔLES	RONEO
ROARER	ROCHES	RODSMEN	ROLES	RONEOED
ROARERS	ROCHET	RODSTER	ROLL	RONEOING
ROARIE	ROCHETS	RODSTERS	ROLLABLE	RONEOS
ROARIER	ROCK	ROE	ROLLED	RONES
ROARIEST	ROCKAWAY	ROEBUCK	ROLLER	RONG
ROARING	ROCKAWAYS	ROEBUCKS	ROLLERS	RONGGENG
ROARINGLY	ROCKCRESS	ROED	ROLLICK	RONGGENGS
ROARINGS	ROCKCRESSES	ROEMER	ROLLICKED	RONNE
ROARS	ROCKED	ROEMERS	ROLLICKING	RONNING
ROARY	ROCKER	ROENTGEN	ROLLICKS	RONT
ROAST	ROCKERIES	ROENTGENS	ROLLING	RONTE
ROASTED	ROCKERS	ROES	ROLLINGS	RONTES

RÖNTGEN	ROOSTERS	RORTER	ROSINING	ROTCHIES
RÖNTGENS	ROOSTING	RORTERS	ROSINS	ROTE
RONTS	ROOSTS	RORTIER	ROSINY	ROTED
RONYON	ROOT	RORTIEST	ROSIT	ROTENONE
RONYONS	ROOTAGE	RORTS	ROSITED	ROTENONES
ROO	ROOTAGES	RORTY	ROSITING	ROTES
ROOD	ROOTED	RORY	ROSITS	ROTGRASS
ROODS	ROOTEDLY	ROSACE	ROSITTY	ROTGRASSES
ROOF	ROOTER	ROSACEA	ROSITY	ROTGUT
ROOFED	ROOTERS	ROSACEAS	ROSMARINE	ROTGUTS
ROOFER	ROOTHOLD	ROSACEOUS	ROSMARINES	ROTHER
ROOFERS	ROOTHOLDS	ROSACES	ROSOGLIO	ROTHERS
ROOFIER	ROOTIER	ROSAKER	ROSOGLIOS	ROTI
ROOFIEST	ROOTIES	ROSAKERS	ROSOLIO	ROTIFER
ROOFING	ROOTIEST	ROSALIA	ROSOLIOS	ROTIFERAL
ROOFINGS	ROOTING	ROSALIAS	ROSSER	ROTIFERS
ROOFLESS	ROOTINGS	ROSARIAN	ROSSERS	ROTING
ROOFS	ROOTLE	ROSARIANS	ROST	ROTIS
ROOFY	ROOTLED	ROSARIES	ROSTED	ROTL
ROOINEK	ROOTLES	ROSARIUM	ROSTELLAR	ROTLS
ROOINEKS	ROOTLESS	ROSARIUMS	ROSTELLUM	ROTOGRAPH
ROOK	ROOTLET	ROSARY	ROSTELLUMS	ROTOGRAPHED
ROOKED	ROOTLETS	ROSCID	ROSTER	ROTOGRAPHING
ROOKERIES	ROOTLIKE	ROSE	ROSTERED	ROTOGRAPHS
ROOKERY	ROOTLING	ROSÉ	ROSTERING	ROTOLO
ROOKIE	ROOTS	ROSEAL	ROSTERINGS	ROTOLOS
ROOKIER	ROOTSTOCK	ROSEATE	ROSTERS	ROTOR
ROOKIES	ROOTSTOCKS	ROSED	ROSTING	ROTORS
ROOKIEST	ROOTY	ROSEFISH	ROSTRA	ROTOVATE
ROOKING	ROPABLE	ROSEFISHES	ROSTRAL	ROTOVATED
ROOKISH	ROPE	ROSELESS	ROSTRATE	ROTOVATES
ROOKS	ROPEABLE	ROSELIKE	ROSTRATED	ROTOVATING
ROOKY	ROPED	ROSELLA	ROSTRUM	ROTOVATOR
ROOM	ROPER	ROSELLAS	ROSTS	ROTOVATORS
ROOMED	ROPERIES	ROSELLE	ROSULA	ROTS
ROOMER	ROPERS	ROSELLES	ROSULAS	ROTTAN
ROOMERS	ROPERY	ROSEMARIES	ROSULATE	ROTTANS
ROOMETTE	ROPES	ROSEMARY	ROSY	ROTTED
ROOMETTES	ROPEWAY	ROSEOLA	ROSYING	ROTTEN
ROOMFUL	ROPEWAYS	ROSEOLAS	ROT	ROTTENER
ROOMFULS	ROPEWORK	ROSERIES	ROTA	ROTTENEST
ROOMIER	ROPEWORKS	ROSERY	ROTAL	ROTTENLY
ROOMIEST	ROPEY	ROSES	ROTAPLANE	ROTTENS
ROOMILY	ROPIER	ROSÉS	ROTAPLANES	ROTTER
ROOMINESS	ROPIEST	ROSET	ROTARIES	ROTTERS
ROOMINESSES	ROPILY	ROSETED	ROTARY	ROTTING
ROOMING	ROPINESS	ROSETING	ROTAS	ROTULA
ROOMS	ROPINESSES	ROSETS	ROTATABLE	ROTULAS
ROOMSOME	ROPING	ROSETTE	ROTATE	ROTUND
ROOMY	ROPINGS	ROSETTED	ROTATED	ROTUNDA
ROON	ROPY	ROSETTES	ROTATES	ROTUNDAS
ROONS	ROQUE	ROSETTY	ROTATING	ROTUNDATE
ROOP	ROQUES	ROSETY	ROTATION	ROTUNDED
ROOPED	ROQUET	ROSEWOOD	ROTATIONS	ROTUNDER
ROOPIER	ROQUETED	ROSEWOODS	ROTATIVE	ROTUNDEST
ROOPIEST	ROQUETING	ROSIED	ROTATOR	ROTUNDING
ROOPING	ROQUETS	ROSIER	ROTATORS	ROTUNDITIES
ROOPIT	ROQUETTE	ROSIERE	ROTATORY	ROTUNDITY
ROOPS	ROQUETTES	ROSIERES	ROTAVATE	ROTUNDLY
ROOPY	RORAL	ROSIERS	ROTAVATED	ROTUNDS
ROOS	RORE	ROSIES	ROTAVATES	ROTURIER
ROOSA	RORES	ROSIEST	ROTAVATING	ROTURIERS
ROOSAS	RORIC	ROSILY	ROTAVATOR	ROUBLE
ROOSE	RORID	ROSIN	ROTAVATORS	ROUBLES
ROOSED	RORIE	ROSINATE	ROTAVIRUS	ROUCOU
ROOSES	RORIER	ROSINATES	ROTAVIRUSES	ROUCOUS
ROOSING	RORIEST	ROSINED	ROTCH	ROUÉ
ROOST	RORQUAL	ROSINESS	ROTCHE	ROUÉS
ROOSTED	RORQUALS	ROSINESSES	ROTCHES	ROUGE
ROOSTER	RORT	ROSING	ROTCHIE	ROUGED

ROUGES	ROUNDNESSES	ROVED	ROYALLER	RUBEFIES
ROUGH	ROUNDS	ROVER	ROYALLEST	RUBEFY
ROUGHAGE	ROUNDSMAN	ROVERS	ROYALLY	RUBEFYING
ROUGHAGES	ROUNDSMEN	ROVES	ROYALS	RUBELLA
ROUGHCAST	ROUNDURE	ROVING	ROYALTIES	RUBELLAN
ROUGHCASTING	ROUNDURES	ROVINGLY	ROYALTY	RUBELLANS
ROUGHCASTS	ROUP	ROVINGS	ROYNE	RUBELLAS
ROUGHED	ROUPED	ROW	ROYNED	RUBELLITE
ROUGHEN	ROUPIER	ROWABLE	ROYNES	RUBELLITES
ROUGHENED	ROUPIEST	ROWAN	ROYNING	RUBEOLA
ROUGHENING	ROUPING	ROWANS	ROYNISH	RUBEOLAS
ROUGHENS	ROUPIT	ROWBOAT	ROYST	RUBES
ROUGHER	ROUPS	ROWBOATS	ROYSTED	RUBESCENT
ROUGHERS	ROUPY	ROWDEDOW	ROYSTER	RUBICELLE
ROUGHEST	ROUSANT	ROWDEDOWS	ROYSTERED	RUBICELLES
ROUGHIE	ROUSE	ROWDIER	ROYSTERER	RUBICON
ROUGHIES	ROUSED	ROWDIES	ROYSTERERS	RUBICONNED
ROUGHING	ROUSEMENT	ROWDIEST	ROYSTERING	RUBICONNING
ROUGHISH	ROUSEMENTS	ROWDILY	ROYSTERS	RUBICONS
ROUGHLY	ROUSER	ROWDINESS	ROYSTING	RUBICUND
ROUGHNECK	ROUSERS	ROWDINESSES	ROYSTS	RUBIDIUM
ROUGHNECKS	ROUSES	ROWDY	ROZELLE	RUBIDIUMS
ROUGHNESS	ROUSING	ROWDYDOW	ROZELLES	RUBIED
ROUGHNESSES	ROUSINGLY	ROWDYDOWS	ROZET	RUBIER
ROUGHS	ROUSSETTE	ROWDYISH	ROZETED	RUBIES
ROUGHT	ROUSSETTES	ROWDYISM	ROZETING	RUBIEST
ROUGHY	ROUST	ROWDYISMS	ROZETS	RUBIFIED
ROUGING	ROUSTED	ROWED	ROZIT	RUBIFIES
ROUL	ROUSTER	ROWEL	ROZITED	RUBIFY
ROULADE	ROUSTERS	ROWELLED	ROZITING	RUBIFYING
ROULADES	ROUSTING	ROWELLING	ROZITS	RUBIN
ROULE	ROUSTS	ROWELS	ROZZER	RUBINE
ROULEAU	ROUT	ROWEN	ROZZERS	RUBINEOUS
ROULEAUS	ROUTE	ROWENS	RUB	RUBINES
ROULEAUX	ROUTED	ROWER	RUBAIYAT	RUBINS
ROULES	ROUTEING	ROWERS	RUBAIYATS	RUBIOUS
ROULETTE	ROUTEMAN	ROWING	RUBATI	RUBLE
ROULETTES	ROUTEMEN	ROWINGS	RUBATO	RUBLES
ROULS	ROUTER	ROWLOCK	RUBATOS	RUBRIC
ROUM	ROUTERS	ROWLOCKS	RUBBED	RUBRICAL
ROUMING	ROUTES	ROWME	RUBBER	RUBRICATE
ROUMINGS	ROUTH	ROWMES	RUBBERED	RUBRICATED
ROUMS	ROUTHIE	ROWND	RUBBERING	RUBRICATES
ROUNCE	ROUTHIER	ROWNDED	RUBBERISE	RUBRICATING
ROUNCES	ROUTHIEST	ROWNDELL	RUBBERISED	RUBRICIAN
ROUNCEVAL	ROUTHS	ROWNDELLS	RUBBERISES	RUBRICIANS
ROUNCEVALS	ROUTINE	ROWNDING	RUBBERISING	RUBRICS
ROUNCIES	ROUTINEER	ROWNDS	RUBBERIZE	RUBS
ROUNCY	ROUTINEERS	ROWS	RUBBERIZED	RUBSTONE
ROUND	ROUTINELY	ROWT	RUBBERIZES	RUBSTONES
ROUNDARCH	ROUTINES	ROWTED	RUBBERIZING	RUBY
ROUNDED	ROUTING	ROWTH	RUBBERS	RUBYING
ROUNDEL	ROUTINGS	ROWTHS	RUBBERY	RUC
ROUNDELAY	ROUTINISE	ROWTING	RUBBET	RUCHE
ROUNDELAYS	ROUTINISED	ROWTS	RUBBING	RUCHED
ROUNDELS	ROUTINISES	ROYAL	RUBBINGS	RUCHES
ROUNDER	ROUTINISING	ROYALET	RUBBISH	RUCHING
ROUNDERS	ROUTINISM	ROYALETS	RUBBISHED	RUCHINGS
ROUNDEST	ROUTINISMS	ROYALISE	RUBBISHES	RUCK
ROUNDHAND	ROUTINIST	ROYALISED	RUBBISHING	RUCKED
ROUNDHANDS	ROUTINISTS	ROYALISES	RUBBISHLY	RUCKING
ROUNDING	ROUTINIZE	ROYALISING	RUBBISHY	RUCKLE
ROUNDINGS	ROUTINIZED	ROYALISM	RUBBIT	RUCKLED
ROUNDISH	ROUTINIZES	ROYALISMS	RUBBLE	RUCKLES
ROUNDLE	ROUTINIZING	ROYALIST	RUBBLES	RUCKLING
ROUNDLES	ROUTOUS	ROYALISTS	RUBBLY	RUCKS
ROUNDLET	ROUTOUSLY	ROYALIZE	RUBDOWN	RUCKSACK
ROUNDLETS	ROUTS	ROYALIZED	RUBDOWNS	RUCKSACKS
ROUNDLY	ROUX	ROYALIZES	RUBE	RUCKUS
ROUNDNESS	ROVE	ROYALIZING	RUBEFIED	RUCKUSES

RUCS
RUCTATION
RUCTATIONS
RUCTION
RUCTIONS
RUD
RUDAS
RUDASES
RUDBECKIA
RUDBECKIAS
RUDD
RUDDED
RUDDER
RUDDERS
RUDDIED
RUDDIER
RUDDIES
RUDDIEST
RUDDILY
RUDDINESS
RUDDINESSES
RUDDING
RUDDLE
RUDDLED
RUDDLEMAN
RUDDLEMEN
RUDDLES
RUDDLING
RUDDOCK
RUDDOCKS
RUDDS
RUDDY
RUDDYING
RUDE
RUDELY
RUDENESS
RUDENESSES
RUDER
RUDERAL
RUDERALS
RUDERIES
RUDERY
RUDESBIES
RUDESBY
RUDEST
RUDIMENT
RUDIMENTS
RUDISH
RUDS
RUE
RUED
RUEFUL
RUEFULLY
RUEING
RUEINGS
RUELLE
RUELLES
RUELLIA
RUELLIAS
RUES
RUFESCENT
RUFF
RUFFE
RUFFED
RUFFES
RUFFIAN
RUFFIANED
RUFFIANING
RUFFIANLY
RUFFIANS

RUFFIN
RUFFING
RUFFINS
RUFFLE
RUFFLED
RUFFLER
RUFFLERS
RUFFLES
RUFFLING
RUFFLINGS
RUFFS
RUFOUS
RUG
RUGATE
RUGBIES
RUGBY
RUGGED
RUGGEDER
RUGGEDEST
RUGGEDISE
RUGGEDISED
RUGGEDISES
RUGGEDISING
RUGGEDIZE
RUGGEDIZED
RUGGEDIZES
RUGGEDIZING
RUGGEDLY
RUGGER
RUGGERS
RUGGIER
RUGGIEST
RUGGING
RUGGINGS
RUGGY
RUGOSE
RUGOSELY
RUGOSITIES
RUGOSITY
RUGOUS
RUGS
RUGULOSE
RUIN
RUINABLE
RUINATE
RUINATED
RUINATES
RUINATING
RUINATION
RUINATIONS
RUINED
RUINER
RUINERS
RUING
RUINGS
RUINING
RUININGS
RUINOUS
RUINOUSLY
RUINS
RUKH
RUKHS
RULABLE
RULE
RULED
RULELESS
RULER
RULERED
RULERING
RULERS

RULERSHIP
RULERSHIPS
RULES
RULESSE
RULIER
RULIEST
RULING
RULINGS
RULLION
RULLIONS
RULLOCK
RULLOCKS
RULY
RUM
RUMAL
RUMALS
RUMBA
RUMBAS
RUMBELOW
RUMBELOWS
RUMBLE
RUMBLED
RUMBLER
RUMBLERS
RUMBLES
RUMBLING
RUMBLINGS
RUMBLY
RUMBO
RUMBOS
RUME
RUMEN
RUMES
RUMINA
RUMINANT
RUMINANTS
RUMINATE
RUMINATED
RUMINATES
RUMINATING
RUMINATOR
RUMINATORS
RUMKIN
RUMKINS
RUMLY
RUMMAGE
RUMMAGED
RUMMAGER
RUMMAGERS
RUMMAGES
RUMMAGING
RUMMER
RUMMERS
RUMMEST
RUMMIER
RUMMIES
RUMMIEST
RUMMILY
RUMMINESS
RUMMINESSES
RUMMISH
RUMMY
RUMOR
RUMORED
RUMORING
RUMOROUS
RUMORS
RUMOUR
RUMOURED
RUMOURER

RUMOURERS
RUMOURING
RUMOURS
RUMP
RUMPED
RUMPING
RUMPLE
RUMPLED
RUMPLES
RUMPLESS
RUMPLING
RUMPS
RUMPUS
RUMPUSES
RUMS
RUN
RUNABOUT
RUNABOUTS
RUNAGATE
RUNAGATES
RUNAROUND
RUNAROUNDS
RUNAWAY
RUNAWAYS
RUNCH
RUNCHES
RUNCIBLE
RUNCINATE
RUND
RUNDALE
RUNDALES
RUNDLE
RUNDLED
RUNDLES
RUNDLET
RUNDLETS
RUNDOWN
RUNDOWNS
RUNDS
RUNE
RUNED
RUNES
RUNFLAT
RUNG
RUNGS
RUNIC
RUNKLE
RUNKLED
RUNKLES
RUNKLING
RUNLET
RUNLETS
RUNNABLE
RUNNEL
RUNNELS
RUNNER
RUNNERS
RUNNET
RUNNETS
RUNNIER
RUNNIEST
RUNNING
RUNNINGLY
RUNNINGS
RUNNION
RUNNIONS
RUNNY
RUNRIG
RUNRIGS
RUNS

RUNT
RUNTED
RUNTIER
RUNTIEST
RUNTISH
RUNTS
RUNTY
RUNWAY
RUNWAYS
RUPEE
RUPEES
RUPIA
RUPIAH
RUPIAHS
RUPIAS
RUPTURE
RUPTURED
RUPTURES
RUPTURING
RURAL
RURALISE
RURALISED
RURALISES
RURALISING
RURALISM
RURALISMS
RURALIST
RURALISTS
RURALITIES
RURALITY
RURALIZE
RURALIZED
RURALIZES
RURALIZING
RURALLY
RURALNESS
RURALNESSES
RURALS
RURP
RURPS
RUSA
RUSALKA
RUSALKAS
RUSAS
RUSCUS
RUSCUSES
RUSE
RUSÉ
RUSES
RUSH
RUSHED
RUSHEN
RUSHER
RUSHERS
RUSHES
RUSHIER
RUSHIEST
RUSHINESS
RUSHINESSES
RUSHING
RUSHLIGHT
RUSHLIGHTS
RUSHY
RUSINE
RUSK
RUSKS
RUSMA
RUSMAS
RUSSEL
RUSSELS

RUSSET
RUSSETED
RUSSETING
RUSSETINGS
RUSSETS
RUSSETY
RUSSIA
RUSSIAS
RUST
RUSTED
RUSTIC
RUSTICAL
RUSTICALS
RUSTICATE
RUSTICATED
RUSTICATES
RUSTICATING
RUSTICIAL
RUSTICISE
RUSTICISED
RUSTICISES
RUSTICISING
RUSTICISM
RUSTICISMS
RUSTICITIES

RUSTICITY
RUSTICIZE
RUSTICIZED
RUSTICIZES
RUSTICIZING
RUSTICS
RUSTIER
RUSTIEST
RUSTILY
RUSTINESS
RUSTINESSES
RUSTING
RUSTINGS
RUSTLE
RUSTLED
RUSTLER
RUSTLERS
RUSTLES
RUSTLESS
RUSTLING
RUSTLINGS
RUSTRE
RUSTRED
RUSTRES
RUSTS

RUSTY
RUT
RUTABAGA
RUTABAGAS
RUTACEOUS
RUTH
RUTHENIC
RUTHENIUM
RUTHENIUMS
RUTHFUL
RUTHFULLY
RUTHLESS
RUTHS
RUTILANT
RUTILATED
RUTILE
RUTILES
RUTIN
RUTINS
RUTS
RUTTED
RUTTER
RUTTERS
RUTTIER
RUTTIEST

RUTTING
RUTTINGS
RUTTISH
RUTTY
RYA
RYAL
RYALS
RYAS
RYBAT
RYBATS
RYBAUDRYE
RYBAUDRYES
RYBAULD
RYBAULDS
RYE
RYEPECK
RYEPECKS
RYES
RYFE
RYKE
RYKED
RYKES
RYKING
RYMME
RYMMED

RYMMES
RYMMING
RYND
RYNDS
RYOKAN
RYOKANS
RYOT
RYOTS
RYOTWARI
RYOTWARIS
RYPE
RYPECK
RYPECKS
RYPER
RYTHME
RYTHMED
RYTHMES
RYTHMING
RYVE
RYVED
RYVES
RYVING

S

SAB
SABADILLA
SABADILLAS
SABATON
SABATONS
SABBAT
SABBATIC
SABBATINE
SABBATISE
SABBATISED
SABBATISES
SABBATISING
SABBATISM
SABBATISMS
SABBATIZE
SABBATIZED
SABBATIZES
SABBATIZING
SABBATS
SABELLA
SABELLAS
SABER
SABERED
SABERING
SABERS
SABIN
SABINS
SABLE
SABLED
SABLES
SABLING
SABOT
SABOTAGE
SABOTAGED
SABOTAGES
SABOTAGING
SABOTEUR
SABOTEURS
SABOTIER
SABOTIERS
SABOTS
SABRA
SABRAS
SABRE
SABRED
SABRES
SABRING
SABS
SABULOSE
SABULOUS
SABURRA
SABURRAL
SABURRAS
SAC
SACCADE
SACCADES
SACCADIC
SACCATE
SACCHARIC
SACCHARIN
SACCHARINS
SACCIFORM
SACCOI
SACCOS

SACCOSES
SACCULAR
SACCULE
SACCULES
SACCULI
SACCULUS
SACELLA
SACELLUM
SACHEM
SACHEMDOM
SACHEMDOMS
SACHEMS
SACHET
SACHETS
SACK
SACKAGE
SACKAGES
SACKBUT
SACKBUTS
SACKCLOTH
SACKCLOTHS
SACKED
SACKFUL
SACKFULS
SACKING
SACKINGS
SACKLESS
SACKS
SACLESS
SACQUE
SACQUES
SACRA
SACRAL
SACRALISE
SACRALISED
SACRALISES
SACRALISING
SACRALIZE
SACRALIZED
SACRALIZES
SACRALIZING
SACRAMENT
SACRAMENTED
SACRAMENTING
SACRAMENTS
SACRARIA
SACRARIUM
SACRED
SACREDLY
SACRIFICE
SACRIFICED
SACRIFICES
SACRIFICING
SACRIFIDE
SACRIFIED
SACRIFIES
SACRIFY
SACRIFYING
SACRILEGE
SACRILEGES
SACRING
SACRINGS
SACRIST
SACRISTAN

SACRISTANS
SACRISTIES
SACRISTS
SACRISTY
SACRUM
SACS
SAD
SADDEN
SADDENED
SADDENING
SADDENS
SADDER
SADDEST
SADDHU
SADDHUS
SADDISH
SADDLE
SADDLED
SADDLER
SADDLERIES
SADDLERS
SADDLERY
SADDLES
SADDLING
SADHU
SADHUS
SADISM
SADISMS
SADIST
SADISTIC
SADISTS
SADLY
SADNESS
SADNESSES
SAE
SAECULUM
SAECULUMS
SAETER
SAETERS
SAFARI
SAFARIED
SAFARIING
SAFARIS
SAFE
SAFED
SAFEGUARD
SAFEGUARDED
SAFEGUARDING
SAFEGUARDINGS
SAFEGUARDS
SAFELY
SAFENESS
SAFENESSES
SAFER
SAFES
SAFEST
SAFETIES
SAFETY
SAFFIAN
SAFFIANS
SAFFLOWER
SAFFLOWERS
SAFFRON
SAFFRONED

SAFFRONS
SAFFRONY
SAFING
SAFRANIN
SAFRANINE
SAFRANINES
SAFRANINS
SAFROLE
SAFROLES
SAG
SAGA
SAGACIOUS
SAGACITIES
SAGACITY
SAGAMAN
SAGAMEN
SAGAMORE
SAGAMORES
SAGAPENUM
SAGAPENUMS
SAGAS
SAGATHIES
SAGATHY
SAGE
SAGEBRUSH
SAGEBRUSHES
SAGELY
SAGENE
SAGENES
SAGENESS
SAGENESSES
SAGENITE
SAGENITES
SAGENITIC
SAGER
SAGES
SAGEST
SAGGAR
SAGGARD
SAGGARDS
SAGGARS
SAGGED
SAGGER
SAGGERS
SAGGIER
SAGGIEST
SAGGING
SAGGINGS
SAGGY
SAGIER
SAGIEST
SAGINATE
SAGINATED
SAGINATES
SAGINATING
SAGITTA
SAGITTAL
SAGITTARIES
SAGITTARY
SAGITTAS
SAGITTATE
SAGO
SAGOIN
SAGOINS

SAGOS
SAGOUIN
SAGOUINS
SAGS
SAGUARO
SAGUAROS
SAGUIN
SAGUINS
SAGUM
SAGY
SAHIB
SAHIBA
SAHIBAH
SAHIBAHS
SAHIBAS
SAHIBS
SAI
SAIBLING
SAIBLINGS
SAIC
SAICE
SAICES
SAICK
SAICKS
SAICS
SAID
SAIDEST
SAIDS
SAIDST
SAIGA
SAIGAS
SAIKEI
SAIKEIS
SAIKLESS
SAIL
SAILABLE
SAILBOARD
SAILBOARDS
SAILED
SAILER
SAILERS
SAILIER
SAILIEST
SAILING
SAILINGS
SAILLESS
SAILOR
SAILORING
SAILORINGS
SAILORLY
SAILORS
SAILPLANE
SAILPLANES
SAILS
SAILY
SAIM
SAIMIRI
SAIMIRIS
SAIMS
SAIN
SAINE
SAINED
SAINFOIN
SAINFOINS

SAINING	SALAD	SALIFYING	SALPICON	SALUKI
SAINS	SALADE	SALIGOT	SALPICONS	SALUKIS
SAINT	SALADES	SALIGOTS	SALPIFORM	SALUTARY
SAINTDOM	SALADING	SALIMETER	SALPINGES	SALUTE
SAINTDOMS	SALADINGS	SALIMETERS	SALPINX	SALUTED
SAINTED	SALADS	SALINA	SALPINXES	SALUTER
SAINTESS	SALAL	SALINAS	SALPS	SALUTERS
SAINTESSES	SALALS	SALINE	SALS	SALUTES
SAINTFOIN	SALAME	SALINES	SALSA	SALUTING
SAINTFOINS	SALAMI	SALINITIES	SALSAED	SALVABLE
SAINTHOOD	SALAMIS	SALINITY	SALSAFIES	SALVAGE
SAINTHOODS	SALAMON	SALIVA	SALSAFY	SALVAGED
SAINTING	SALAMONS	SALIVAL	SALSAING	SALVAGES
SAINTISH	SALANGANE	SALIVARY	SALSAS	SALVAGING
SAINTISM	SALANGANES	SALIVAS	SALSE	SALVARSAN
SAINTISMS	SALARIAT	SALIVATE	SALSES	SALVARSANS
SAINTLIER	SALARIATS	SALIVATED	SALSIFIES	SALVATION
SAINTLIEST	SALARIED	SALIVATES	SALSIFY	SALVATIONS
SAINTLIKE	SALARIES	SALIVATING	SALT	SALVATORIES
SAINTLING	SALARY	SALIX	SALTANDO	SALVATORY
SAINTLINGS	SALARYING	SALLAD	SALTANT	SALVE
SAINTLY	SALBAND	SALLADS	SALTANTS	SALVED
SAINTS	SALBANDS	SALLAL	SALTATE	SALVER
SAINTSHIP	SALCHOW	SALLALS	SALTATED	SALVERS
SAINTSHIPS	SALCHOWS	SALLE	SALTATES	SALVES
SAIQUE	SALE	SALLEE	SALTATING	SALVETE
SAIQUES	SALEABLE	SALLEES	SALTATION	SALVETES
SAIR	SALEABLY	SALLES	SALTATIONS	SALVIA
SAIRED	SALEP	SALLET	SALTATO	SALVIAS
SAIRER	SALEPS	SALLETS	SALTATORY	SALVIFIC
SAIREST	SALERATUS	SALLIED	SALTED	SALVING
SAIRING	SALERATUSES	SALLIES	SALTER	SALVINGS
SAIRS	SALES	SALLOW	SALTERN	SALVO
SAIS	SALESGIRL	SALLOWED	SALTERNS	SALVOES
SAIST	SALESGIRLS	SALLOWER	SALTERS	SALVOR
SAITH	SALESLADIES	SALLOWEST	SALTEST	SALVORS
SAITHE	SALESLADY	SALLOWING	SALTIER	SALVOS
SAITHES	SALESMAN	SALLOWISH	SALTIERS	SAM
SAITHS	SALESMEN	SALLOWS	SALTIEST	SAMAAN
SAJOU	SALET	SALLOWY	SALTILY	SAMAANS
SAJOUS	SALETS	SALLY	SALTINESS	SAMAN
SAKE	SALEWD	SALLYING	SALTINESSES	SAMANS
SAKER	SALEWORK	SALLYPORT	SALTING	SAMARA
SAKERET	SALEWORKS	SALLYPORTS	SALTINGS	SAMARAS
SAKERETS	SALFERN	SALMI	SALTIRE	SAMARIUM
SAKERS	SALFERNS	SALMIS	SALTIRES	SAMARIUMS
SAKES	SALIAUNCE	SALMON	SALTISH	SAMBA
SAKI	SALIAUNCES	SALMONET	SALTISHLY	SAMBAL
SAKIA	SALIC	SALMONETS	SALTLESS	SAMBALS
SAKIAS	SALICES	SALMONID	SALTLY	SAMBAR
SAKIEH	SALICET	SALMONIDS	SALTNESS	SAMBARS
SAKIEHS	SALICETA	SALMONOID	SALTNESSES	SAMBAS
SAKIS	SALICETS	SALMONOIDS	SALTO	SAMBO
SAKIYEH	SALICETUM	SALMONS	SALTOED	SAMBOS
SAKIYEHS	SALICETUMS	SALON	SALTOING	SAMBUCA
SAKKOI	SALICIN	SALONS	SALTOS	SAMBUCAS
SAKKOS	SALICINE	SALOON	SALTPETER	SAMBUR
SAKKOSES	SALICINES	SALOONIST	SALTPETERS	SAMBURS
SAKSAUL	SALICINS	SALOONISTS	SALTPETRE	SAME
SAKSAULS	SALICYLIC	SALOONS	SALTPETRES	SAMEL
SAL	SALIENCE	SALOOP	SALTS	SAMELY
SALAAM	SALIENCES	SALOOPS	SALTUS	SAMEN
SALAAMED	SALIENCIES	SALOP	SALTUSES	SAMENESS
SALAAMING	SALIENCY	SALOPETTE	SALTY	SAMENESSES
SALAAMS	SALIENT	SALOPETTES	SALUBRITIES	SAMES
SALABLE	SALIENTLY	SALOPIAN	SALUBRITY	SAMEY
SALABLY	SALIENTS	SALOPS	SALUE	SAMFOO
SALACIOUS	SALIFIED	SALP	SALUED	SAMFOOS
SALACITIES	SALIFIES	SALPIAN	SALUES	SAMFU
SALACITY	SALIFY	SALPIANS	SALUING	SAMFUS

SAMIEL	SANDALS	SANGUINER	SAPAJOUS	SAPS
SAMIELS	SANDARAC	SANGUINES	SAPAN	SAPSAGO
SAMIER	SANDARACH	SANGUINEST	SAPANS	SAPSAGOS
SAMIEST	SANDARACHS	SANGUINING	SAPEGO	SAPSUCKER
SAMISEN	SANDARACS	SANICLE	SAPEGOES	SAPSUCKERS
SAMISENS	SANDBAG	SANICLES	SAPELE	SAPUCAIA
SAMITE	SANDBAGGED	SANIDINE	SAPELES	SAPUCAIAS
SAMITES	SANDBAGGING	SANIDINES	SAPFUL	SAPWOOD
SAMIZDAT	SANDBAGS	SANIES	SAPHEAD	SAPWOODS
SAMIZDATS	SANDED	SANIFIED	SAPHEADED	SAR
SAMLET	SANDER	SANIFIES	SAPHEADS	SARABAND
SAMLETS	SANDERS	SANIFY	SAPID	SARABANDS
SAMLOR	SANDERSES	SANIFYING	SAPIDITIES	SARAFAN
SAMLORS	SANDHI	SANIOUS	SAPIDITY	SARAFANS
SAMNITIS	SANDHIS	SANITARIA	SAPIDLESS	SARANGI
SAMNITISES	SANDIER	SANITARY	SAPIENCE	SARANGIS
SAMOSA	SANDIEST	SANITATE	SAPIENCES	SARBACANE
SAMOSAS	SANDINESS	SANITATED	SAPIENT	SARBACANES
SAMOVAR	SANDINESSES	SANITATES	SAPIENTLY	SARCASM
SAMOVARS	SANDING	SANITATING	SAPLESS	SARCASMS
SAMP	SANDINGS	SANITIES	SAPLING	SARCASTIC
SAMPAN	SANDIVER	SANITISE	SAPLINGS	SARCENET
SAMPANS	SANDIVERS	SANITISED	SAPODILLA	SARCENETS
SAMPHIRE	SANDLING	SANITISES	SAPODILLAS	SARCOCARP
SAMPHIRES	SANDLINGS	SANITISING	SAPOGENIN	SARCOCARPS
SAMPI	SANDMAN	SANITIZE	SAPOGENINS	SARCODE
SAMPIRE	SANDMEN	SANITIZED	SAPONIFIED	SARCODES
SAMPIRES	SANDPAPER	SANITIZES	SAPONIFIES	SARCODIC
SAMPIS	SANDPAPERED	SANITIZING	SAPONIFY	SARCOID
SAMPLE	SANDPAPERING	SANITY	SAPONIFYING	SARCOIDS
SAMPLED	SANDPAPERS	SANJAK	SAPONIN	SARCOLOGIES
SAMPLER	SANDPIPER	SANJAKS	SAPONINS	SARCOLOGY
SAMPLERIES	SANDPIPERS	SANK	SAPONITE	SARCOMA
SAMPLERS	SANDS	SANKO	SAPONITES	SARCOMAS
SAMPLERY	SANDSTONE	SANKOS	SAPOR	SARCOMATA
SAMPLES	SANDSTONES	SANNUP	SAPOROUS	SARCOMERE
SAMPLING	SANDWICH	SANNUPS	SAPORS	SARCOMERES
SAMPLINGS	SANDWICHED	SANNYASI	SAPOTA	SARCOPTIC
SAMPS	SANDWICHES	SANNYASIN	SAPOTAS	SARCOUS
SAMSHOO	SANDWICHING	SANNYASINS	SAPPAN	SARD
SAMSHOOS	SANDWORT	SANNYASIS	SAPPANS	SARDANA
SAMSHU	SANDWORTS	SANPAN	SAPPED	SARDANAS
SAMSHUS	SANDY	SANPANS	SAPPER	SARDEL
SAMURAI	SANDYISH	SANS	SAPPERS	SARDELLE
SAN	SANE	SANSA	SAPPHIC	SARDELLES
SANATIVE	SANEI	SANSAS	SAPPHICS	SARDELS
SANATORIA	SANEIS	SANSERIF	SAPPHIRE	SARDINE
SANATORY	SANELY	SANSERIFS	SAPPHIRED	SARDINES
SANBENITO	SANENESS	SANTAL	SAPPHIRES	SARDIUS
SANBENITOS	SANENESSES	SANTALIN	SAPPHISM	SARDIUSES
SANCHO	SANER	SANTALINS	SAPPHISMS	SARDONIAN
SANCHOS	SANEST	SANTALS	SAPPHIST	SARDONIC
SANCTIFIED	SANG	SANTIR	SAPPHISTS	SARDONYX
SANCTIFIES	SANGAR	SANTIRS	SAPPIER	SARDONYXES
SANCTIFY	SANGAREE	SANTOLINA	SAPPIEST	SARDS
SANCTIFYING	SANGAREES	SANTOLINAS	SAPPINESS	SARED
SANCTIFYINGS	SANGARS	SANTON	SAPPINESSES	SAREE
SANCTION	SANGFROID	SANTONICA	SAPPING	SAREES
SANCTIONED	SANGFROIDS	SANTONICAS	SAPPLES	SARGASSO
SANCTIONING	SANGLIER	SANTONIN	SAPPY	SARGASSOS
SANCTIONS	SANGLIERS	SANTONINS	SAPRAEMIA	SARGE
SANCTITIES	SANGRIA	SANTONS	SAPRAEMIAS	SARGES
SANCTITY	SANGRIAS	SANTOUR	SAPRAEMIC	SARGO
SANCTUARIES	SANGS	SANTOURS	SAPROBE	SARGOS
SANCTUARY	SANGUIFIED	SANTUR	SAPROBES	SARGUS
SANCTUM	SANGUIFIES	SANTURS	SAPROLITE	SARGUSES
SANCTUMS	SANGUIFY	SAOUARI	SAPROLITES	SARI
SAND	SANGUIFYING	SAOUARIS	SAPROPEL	SARIN
SANDAL	SANGUINE	SAP	SAPROPELS	SARING
SANDALLED	SANGUINED	SAPAJOU	SAPROZOIC	SARINS

SARIS	SASKATOONS	SATINY	SAUCER	SAVAGEDOM
SARK	SASQUATCH	SATIRE	SAUCERFUL	SAVAGEDOMS
SARKFUL	SASQUATCHES	SATIRES	SAUCERFULS	SAVAGELY
SARKFULS	SASS	SATIRIC	SAUCERS	SAVAGER
SARKIER	SASSABIES	SATIRICAL	SAUCES	SAVAGERIES
SARKIEST	SASSABY	SATIRISE	SAUCH	SAVAGERY
SARKING	SASSAFRAS	SATIRISED	SAUCHS	SAVAGES
SARKINGS	SASSAFRASES	SATIRISES	SAUCIER	SAVAGEST
SARKS	SASSARARA	SATIRISING	SAUCIEST	SAVAGING
SARKY	SASSARARAS	SATIRIST	SAUCILY	SAVAGISM
SARMENT	SASSE	SATIRISTS	SAUCINESS	SAVAGISMS
SARMENTA	SASSED	SATIRIZE	SAUCINESSES	SAVANNA
SARMENTS	SASSES	SATIRIZED	SAUCING	SAVANNAH
SARMENTUM	SASSIER	SATIRIZES	SAUCISSE	SAVANNAHS
SARNEY	SASSIEST	SATIRIZING	SAUCISSES	SAVANNAS
SARNEYS	SASSING	SATIS	SAUCISSON	SAVANT
SARNIE	SASSOLIN	SATISFIED	SAUCISSONS	SAVANTS
SARNIES	SASSOLINS	SATISFIER	SAUCY	SAVARIN
SAROD	SASSOLITE	SATISFIERS	SAUFGARD	SAVARINS
SARODS	SASSOLITES	SATISFIES	SAUFGARDS	SAVATE
SARONG	SASSY	SATISFY	SAUGER	SAVATES
SARONGS	SASTRUGA	SATISFYING	SAUGERS	SAVE
SARONIC	SASTRUGI	SATIVE	SAUGH	SAVED
SAROS	SAT	SATORI	SAUGHS	SAVEGARD
SAROSES	SATANIC	SATORIS	SAUL	SAVEGARDED
SARPANCH	SATANICAL	SATRAP	SAULGE	SAVEGARDING
SARPANCHES	SATANISM	SATRAPAL	SAULGES	SAVEGARDS
SARRASIN	SATANISMS	SATRAPIC	SAULIE	SAVELOY
SARRASINS	SATANITIES	SATRAPIES	SAULIES	SAVELOYS
SARRAZIN	SATANITY	SATRAPS	SAULS	SAVER
SARRAZINS	SATARA	SATRAPY	SAULT	SAVERS
SARS	SATARAS	SATSUMA	SAULTS	SAVES
SARSA	SATCHEL	SATSUMAS	SAUNA	SAVEY
SARSAS	SATCHELS	SATURABLE	SAUNAS	SAVEYED
SARSDEN	SATE	SATURANT	SAUNT	SAVEYING
SARSDENS	SATED	SATURANTS	SAUNTED	SAVEYS
SARSEN	SATEDNESS	SATURATE	SAUNTER	SAVIN
SARSENET	SATEDNESSES	SATURATED	SAUNTERED	SAVINE
SARSENETS	SATEEN	SATURATES	SAUNTERER	SAVINES
SARSENS	SATEENS	SATURATING	SAUNTERERS	SAVING
SARSNET	SATELESS	SATURATOR	SAUNTERING	SAVINGLY
SARSNETS	SATELLES	SATURATORS	SAUNTERINGS	SAVINGS
SARTOR	SATELLITE	SATURNIC	SAUNTERS	SAVINS
SARTORIAL	SATELLITED	SATURNINE	SAUNTING	SAVIOUR
SARTORIAN	SATELLITES	SATURNISM	SAUNTS	SAVIOURS
SARTORII	SATELLITING	SATURNISMS	SAUREL	SAVOR
SARTORIUS	SATES	SATURNIST	SAURELS	SAVORED
SARTORIUSES	SATI	SATURNISTS	SAURIAN	SAVORIES
SARTORS	SATIABLE	SATYR	SAURIANS	SAVORING
SARUS	SATIATE	SATYRA	SAURIES	SAVOROUS
SARUSES	SATIATED	SATYRAL	SAUROID	SAVORS
SARZA	SATIATES	SATYRALS	SAUROPOD	SAVORY
SARZAS	SATIATING	SATYRAS	SAUROPODS	SAVOUR
SASARARA	SATIATION	SATYRESS	SAURY	SAVOURED
SASARARAS	SATIATIONS	SATYRESSES	SAUSAGE	SAVOURIES
SASH	SATIETIES	SATYRIC	SAUSAGES	SAVOURILY
SASHAY	SATIETY	SATYRICAL	SAUT	SAVOURING
SASHAYED	SATIN	SATYRID	SAUTÉ	SAVOURLY
SASHAYING	SATINED	SATYRIDS	SAUTÉD	SAVOURS
SASHAYS	SATINET	SATYRISK	SAUTED	SAVOURY
SASHED	SATINETS	SATYRISKS	SAUTÉED	SAVOY
SASHES	SATINETTA	SATYRS	SAUTÉING	SAVOYS
SASHIMI	SATINETTAS	SAUBA	SAUTÉS	SAVVEY
SASHIMIS	SATINETTE	SAUBAS	SAUTING	SAVVEYED
SASHING	SATINETTES	SAUCE	SAUTOIR	SAVVEYING
SASIN	SATING	SAUCED	SAUTOIRS	SAVVEYS
SASINE	SATINING	SAUCEMAN	SAUTS	SAVVIED
SASINES	SATINS	SAUCEMEN	SAVABLE	SAVVIES
SASINS	SATINWOOD	SAUCEPAN	SAVAGE	SAVVY
SASKATOON	SATINWOODS	SAUCEPANS	SAVAGED	SAVVYING

SAW	SCAB	SCALELESS	SCANDIUMS	SCARCELY
SAWAH	SCABBARD	SCALELIKE	SCANNED	SCARCER
SAWAHS	SCABBARDED	SCALENE	SCANNER	SCARCEST
SAWDER	SCABBARDING	SCALER	SCANNERS	SCARCITIES
SAWDERED	SCABBARDS	SCALERS	SCANNING	SCARCITY
SAWDERING	SCABBED	SCALES	SCANNINGS	SCARE
SAWDERS	SCABBIER	SCALIER	SCANS	SCARECROW
SAWDUST	SCABBIEST	SCALIEST	SCANSION	SCARECROWS
SAWDUSTED	SCABBING	SCALINESS	SCANSIONS	SCARED
SAWDUSTING	SCABBLE	SCALINESSES	SCANT	SCAREDER
SAWDUSTS	SCABBLED	SCALING	SCANTED	SCAREDEST
SAWDUSTY	SCABBLES	SCALINGS	SCANTER	SCARER
SAWED	SCABBLING	SCALL	SCANTEST	SCARERS
SAWER	SCABBY	SCALLAWAG	SCANTIER	SCARES
SAWERS	SCABIES	SCALLAWAGS	SCANTIES	SCAREY
SAWING	SCABIOUS	SCALLED	SCANTIEST	SCARF
SAWINGS	SCABIOUSES	SCALLION	SCANTILY	SCARFED
SAWN	SCABRID	SCALLIONS	SCANTING	SCARFING
SAWNEY	SCABROUS	SCALLOP	SCANTITIES	SCARFINGS
SAWNEYS	SCABS	SCALLOPED	SCANTITY	SCARFISH
SAWPIT	SCAD	SCALLOPING	SCANTLE	SCARFISHES
SAWPITS	SCADS	SCALLOPS	SCANTLED	SCARFS
SAWS	SCAFF	SCALLS	SCANTLES	SCARFSKIN
SAWYER	SCAFFIE	SCALLYWAG	SCANTLING	SCARFSKINS
SAWYERS	SCAFFIES	SCALLYWAGS	SCANTLINGS	SCARIER
SAX	SCAFFOLD	SCALP	SCANTLY	SCARIEST
SAXATILE	SCAFFOLDED	SCALPED	SCANTNESS	SCARIFIED
SAXAUL	SCAFFOLDING	SCALPEL	SCANTNESSES	SCARIFIER
SAXAULS	SCAFFOLDINGS	SCALPELS	SCANTS	SCARIFIERS
SAXES	SCAFFOLDS	SCALPER	SCANTY	SCARIFIES
SAXHORN	SCAFFS	SCALPERS	SCAPA	SCARIFY
SAXHORNS	SCAG	SCALPING	SCAPAED	SCARIFYING
SAXIFRAGE	SCAGLIA	SCALPLESS	SCAPAING	SCARING
SAXIFRAGES	SCAGLIAS	SCALPRUM	SCAPAS	SCARIOUS
SAXITOXIN	SCAGLIOLA	SCALPRUMS	SCAPE	SCARLESS
SAXITOXINS	SCAGLIOLAS	SCALPS	SCAPED	SCARLET
SAXONIES	SCAGS	SCALY	SCAPEGOAT	SCARLETED
SAXONITE	SCAIL	SCAM	SCAPEGOATS	SCARLETING
SAXONITES	SCAILED	SCAMBLE	SCAPELESS	SCARLETS
SAXONY	SCAILING	SCAMBLED	SCAPEMENT	SCARMOGE
SAXOPHONE	SCAILS	SCAMBLER	SCAPEMENTS	SCARMOGES
SAXOPHONES	SCAITH	SCAMBLERS	SCAPES	SCARP
SAY	SCAITHED	SCAMBLES	SCAPHOID	SCARPED
SAYABLE	SCAITHING	SCAMBLING	SCAPHOIDS	SCARPER
SAYED	SCAITHS	SCAMBLINGS	SCAPHOPOD	SCARPERED
SAYEDS	SCALA	SCAMEL	SCAPHOPODS	SCARPERING
SAYER	SCALABLE	SCAMELS	SCAPI	SCARPERS
SAYERS	SCALADE	SCAMMONIES	SCAPING	SCARPETTI
SAYEST	SCALADES	SCAMMONY	SCAPOLITE	SCARPETTO
SAYID	SCALADO	SCAMP	SCAPOLITES	SCARPINES
SAYIDS	SCALADOS	SCAMPED	SCAPPLE	SCARPING
SAYING	SCALAE	SCAMPER	SCAPPLED	SCARPINGS
SAYINGS	SCALAR	SCAMPERED	SCAPPLES	SCARPS
SAYNE	SCALARS	SCAMPERING	SCAPPLING	SCARRE
SAYON	SCALAWAG	SCAMPERS	SCAPULA	SCARRED
SAYONARA	SCALAWAGS	SCAMPI	SCAPULAE	SCARRES
SAYONARAS	SCALD	SCAMPING	SCAPULAR	SCARRIER
SAYONS	SCALDED	SCAMPINGS	SCAPULARIES	SCARRIEST
SAYS	SCALDER	SCAMPIS	SCAPULARS	SCARRING
SAYST	SCALDERS	SCAMPISH	SCAPULARY	SCARRINGS
SAYYID	SCALDFISH	SCAMPS	SCAPULAS	SCARRY
SAYYIDS	SCALDFISHES	SCAMS	SCAPUS	SCARS
SAZ	SCALDIC	SCAN	SCAR	SCART
SAZERAC®	SCALDING	SCAND	SCARAB	SCARTED
SAZERACS®	SCALDINGS	SCANDAL	SCARABEE	SCARTH
SAZES	SCALDINI	SCANDALLED	SCARABEES	SCARTHS
SAZHEN	SCALDINO	SCANDALLING	SCARABOID	SCARTING
SAZHENS	SCALDS	SCANDALS	SCARABOIDS	SCARTS
SBIRRI	SCALE	SCANDENT	SCARABS	SCARVES
SBIRRO	SCALED	SCANDIUM	SCARCE	SCARY

SCAT
SCATCH
SCATCHES
SCATH
SCATHE
SCATHED
SCATHEFUL
SCATHES
SCATHING
SCATHS
SCATOLE
SCATOLES
SCATOLOGIES
SCATOLOGY
SCATS
SCATT
SCATTED
SCATTER
SCATTERED
SCATTERER
SCATTERERS
SCATTERING
SCATTERINGS
SCATTERS
SCATTERY
SCATTIER
SCATTIEST
SCATTING
SCATTS
SCATTY
SCAUD
SCAUDED
SCAUDING
SCAUDS
SCAUP
SCAUPER
SCAUPERS
SCAUPS
SCAUR
SCAURED
SCAURIES
SCAURING
SCAURS
SCAURY
SCAVAGE
SCAVAGER
SCAVAGERS
SCAVAGES
SCAVENGE
SCAVENGED
SCAVENGER
SCAVENGERED
SCAVENGERING
SCAVENGERINGS
SCAVENGERS
SCAVENGES
SCAVENGING
SCAVENGINGS
SCAW
SCAWS
SCAZON
SCAZONS
SCAZONTIC
SCAZONTICS
SCEAT
SCEATT
SCEATTAS
SCEDULE
SCEDULES
SCELERAT

SCELERATE
SCELERATES
SCELERATS
SCENA
SCENARIES
SCENARIO
SCENARIOS
SCENARISE
SCENARISED
SCENARISES
SCENARISING
SCENARIST
SCENARISTS
SCENARIZE
SCENARIZED
SCENARIZES
SCENARIZING
SCENARY
SCEND
SCENDED
SCENDING
SCENDS
SCENE
SCENED
SCENERIES
SCENERY
SCENES
SCENIC
SCENICAL
SCENING
SCENT
SCENTED
SCENTFUL
SCENTING
SCENTINGS
SCENTLESS
SCENTS
SCEPSES
SCEPSIS
SCEPSISES
SCEPTIC
SCEPTICAL
SCEPTICS
SCEPTRAL
SCEPTRE
SCEPTRED
SCEPTRES
SCEPTRY
SCERNE
SCERNED
SCERNES
SCERNING
SCHAPPE
SCHAPPED
SCHAPPES
SCHAPPING
SCHAPSKA
SCHAPSKAS
SCHECHITA
SCHECHITAS
SCHEDULE
SCHEDULED
SCHEDULES
SCHEDULING
SCHEELITE
SCHEELITES
SCHELLUM
SCHELLUMS
SCHELM
SCHELMS

SCHEMA
SCHEMATA
SCHEMATIC
SCHEME
SCHEMED
SCHEMER
SCHEMERS
SCHEMES
SCHEMING
SCHEMINGS
SCHERZI
SCHERZO
SCHERZOS
SCHIAVONE
SCHIAVONES
SCHIEDAM
SCHIEDAMS
SCHILLER
SCHILLERS
SCHILLING
SCHILLINGS
SCHIMMEL
SCHIMMELS
SCHISM
SCHISMA
SCHISMAS
SCHISMS
SCHIST
SCHISTOSE
SCHISTOUS
SCHISTS
SCHIZO
SCHIZOID
SCHIZOIDS
SCHIZONT
SCHIZONTS
SCHIZOPOD
SCHIZOPODS
SCHIZOS
SCHLÄGER
SCHLÄGERS
SCHLEMIEL
SCHLEMIELS
SCHLEMIHL
SCHLEMIHLS
SCHLEP
SCHLEPP
SCHLEPPED
SCHLEPPIER
SCHLEPPIEST
SCHLEPPING
SCHLEPPS
SCHLEPPY
SCHLEPS
SCHLICH
SCHLICHS
SCHLIEREN
SCHLOCK
SCHLOCKS
SCHLOSS
SCHLOSSES
SCHMALTZ
SCHMALTZES
SCHMALTZIER
SCHMALTZIEST
SCHMALTZY
SCHMELZ
SCHMELZES
SCHMO
SCHMOCK

SCHMOCKS
SCHMOE
SCHMOES
SCHMOOZE
SCHMOOZED
SCHMOOZES
SCHMOOZING
SCHMUCK
SCHMUCKS
SCHMUTTER
SCHMUTTERS
SCHNAPPER
SCHNAPPERS
SCHNAPPS
SCHNAPPSES
SCHNAPS
SCHNAPSES
SCHNAUZER
SCHNAUZERS
SCHNELL
SCHNITZEL
SCHNITZELS
SCHNOOK
SCHNOOKS
SCHNORKEL
SCHNORKELS
SCHNORR
SCHNORRED
SCHNORRER
SCHNORRERS
SCHNORRING
SCHNORRS
SCHNOZZLE
SCHNOZZLES
SCHOLAR
SCHOLARCH
SCHOLARCHS
SCHOLARLY
SCHOLARS
SCHOLIA
SCHOLIAST
SCHOLIASTS
SCHOLION
SCHOLIUM
SCHOOL
SCHOOLBAG
SCHOOLBAGS
SCHOOLBOY
SCHOOLBOYS
SCHOOLE
SCHOOLED
SCHOOLERIES
SCHOOLERY
SCHOOLES
SCHOOLING
SCHOOLINGS
SCHOOLMAN
SCHOOLMEN
SCHOOLS
SCHOONER
SCHOONERS
SCHORL
SCHORLS
SCHOUT
SCHOUTS
SCHTICK
SCHTICKS
SCHTIK
SCHTIKS
SCHTOOK

SCHTOOKS
SCHTOOM
SCHTUCK
SCHTUCKS
SCHUIT
SCHUITS
SCHUL
SCHULS
SCHUSS
SCHUSSED
SCHUSSES
SCHUSSING
SCHUYT
SCHUYTS
SCHWA
SCHWAS
SCIAENID
SCIAENOID
SCIAMACHIES
SCIAMACHY
SCIARID
SCIARIDS
SCIATIC
SCIATICA
SCIATICAL
SCIATICAS
SCIENCE
SCIENCED
SCIENCES
SCIENT
SCIENTER
SCIENTIAL
SCIENTISE
SCIENTISED
SCIENTISES
SCIENTISING
SCIENTISM
SCIENTISMS
SCIENTIST
SCIENTISTS
SCIENTIZE
SCIENTIZED
SCIENTIZES
SCIENTIZING
SCILICET
SCILLA
SCILLAS
SCIMITAR
SCIMITARS
SCINCOID
SCINTILLA
SCINTILLAS
SCIOLISM
SCIOLISMS
SCIOLIST
SCIOLISTS
SCIOLOUS
SCIOLTO
SCION
SCIONS
SCIOSOPHIES
SCIOSOPHY
SCIROC
SCIROCCO
SCIROCCOS
SCIROCS
SCIRRHOID
SCIRRHOUS
SCIRRHUS
SCIRRHUSES

SCISSEL
SCISSELS
SCISSIL
SCISSILE
SCISSILS
SCISSION
SCISSIONS
SCISSOR
SCISSORED
SCISSORER
SCISSORERS
SCISSORING
SCISSORS
SCISSURE
SCISSURES
SCIURINE
SCIUROID
SCLAFF
SCLAFFED
SCLAFFING
SCLAFFS
SCLATE
SCLATED
SCLATES
SCLATING
SCLAUNDER
SCLAUNDERS
SCLAVE
SCLAVES
SCLERA
SCLERAL
SCLERAS
SCLERE
SCLEREID
SCLEREIDE
SCLEREIDES
SCLEREIDS
SCLEREMA
SCLEREMAS
SCLERES
SCLERITE
SCLERITES
SCLERITIS
SCLERITISES
SCLEROID
SCLEROMA
SCLEROMAS
SCLEROSE
SCLEROSED
SCLEROSES
SCLEROSING
SCLEROSIS
SCLEROTAL
SCLEROTALS
SCLEROTIA
SCLEROTIC
SCLEROTICS
SCLEROUS
SCLIFF
SCLIFFS
SCLIM
SCLIMMED
SCLIMMING
SCLIMS
SCOFF
SCOFFED
SCOFFER
SCOFFERS
SCOFFING
SCOFFINGS

SCOFFLAW
SCOFFLAWS
SCOFFS
SCOG
SCOGGED
SCOGGING
SCOGS
SCOINSON
SCOINSONS
SCOLD
SCOLDED
SCOLDER
SCOLDERS
SCOLDING
SCOLDINGS
SCOLDS
SCOLECES
SCOLECID
SCOLECITE
SCOLECITES
SCOLECOID
SCOLEX
SCOLICES
SCOLIOMA
SCOLIOMAS
SCOLIOSES
SCOLIOSIS
SCOLIOTIC
SCOLLOP
SCOLLOPED
SCOLLOPING
SCOLLOPS
SCOLYTOID
SCOMBROID
SCOMFISH
SCOMFISHED
SCOMFISHES
SCOMFISHING
SCONCE
SCONCED
SCONCES
SCONCHEON
SCONCHEONS
SCONCING
SCONE
SCONES
SCONTION
SCONTIONS
SCOOG
SCOOGED
SCOOGING
SCOOGS
SCOOP
SCOOPED
SCOOPER
SCOOPERS
SCOOPFUL
SCOOPFULS
SCOOPING
SCOOPINGS
SCOOPS
SCOOT
SCOOTED
SCOOTER
SCOOTERS
SCOOTING
SCOOTS
SCOPA
SCOPAE
SCOPATE

SCOPE
SCOPES
SCOPULA
SCOPULAS
SCOPULATE
SCORBUTIC
SCORCH
SCORCHED
SCORCHER
SCORCHERS
SCORCHES
SCORCHING
SCORCHINGS
SCORDATO
SCORE
SCORED
SCORELINE
SCORELINES
SCORER
SCORERS
SCORES
SCORIA
SCORIAC
SCORIAE
SCORIFIED
SCORIFIER
SCORIFIERS
SCORIFIES
SCORIFY
SCORIFYING
SCORING
SCORINGS
SCORIOUS
SCORN
SCORNED
SCORNER
SCORNERS
SCORNFUL
SCORNING
SCORNINGS
SCORNS
SCORODITE
SCORODITES
SCORPER
SCORPERS
SCORPIO
SCORPIOID
SCORPION
SCORPIONS
SCORPIOS
SCORSE
SCORSED
SCORSER
SCORSERS
SCORSES
SCORSING
SCOT
SCOTCH
SCOTCHED
SCOTCHES
SCOTCHING
SCOTER
SCOTERS
SCOTIA
SCOTIAS
SCOTOMA
SCOTOMAS
SCOTOMATA
SCOTOMIES
SCOTOMY

SCOTOPIA
SCOTOPIAS
SCOTOPIC
SCOTS
SCOUG
SCOUGED
SCOUGING
SCOUGS
SCOUNDREL
SCOUNDRELS
SCOUP
SCOUPED
SCOUPING
SCOUPS
SCOUR
SCOURED
SCOURER
SCOURERS
SCOURGE
SCOURGED
SCOURGER
SCOURGERS
SCOURGES
SCOURGING
SCOURIE
SCOURIES
SCOURING
SCOURINGS
SCOURS
SCOURSE
SCOURSED
SCOURSES
SCOURSING
SCOUSE
SCOUSES
SCOUT
SCOUTED
SCOUTER
SCOUTERS
SCOUTH
SCOUTHER
SCOUTHERED
SCOUTHERING
SCOUTHERINGS
SCOUTHERS
SCOUTHERY
SCOUTHS
SCOUTING
SCOUTINGS
SCOUTS
SCOW
SCOWDER
SCOWDERED
SCOWDERING
SCOWDERINGS
SCOWDERS
SCOWL
SCOWLED
SCOWLING
SCOWLS
SCOWP
SCOWPED
SCOWPING
SCOWPS
SCOWRER
SCOWRERS
SCOWRIE
SCOWRIES
SCOWS
SCOWTH

SCOWTHER
SCOWTHERED
SCOWTHERING
SCOWTHERS
SCOWTHS
SCRAB
SCRABBED
SCRABBING
SCRABBLE
SCRABBLED
SCRABBLER
SCRABBLERS
SCRABBLES
SCRABBLING
SCRABS
SCRAE
SCRAES
SCRAG
SCRAGGED
SCRAGGIER
SCRAGGIEST
SCRAGGILY
SCRAGGING
SCRAGGLY
SCRAGGY
SCRAGS
SCRAICH
SCRAICHED
SCRAICHING
SCRAICHS
SCRAIGH
SCRAIGHED
SCRAIGHING
SCRAIGHS
SCRAM
SCRAMBLE
SCRAMBLED
SCRAMBLER
SCRAMBLERS
SCRAMBLES
SCRAMBLING
SCRAMBLINGS
SCRAMJET
SCRAMJETS
SCRAMMED
SCRAMMING
SCRAMS
SCRAN
SCRANCH
SCRANCHED
SCRANCHES
SCRANCHING
SCRANNEL
SCRANNY
SCRANS
SCRAP
SCRAPE
SCRAPED
SCRAPER
SCRAPERS
SCRAPES
SCRAPIE
SCRAPIES
SCRAPING
SCRAPINGS
SCRAPPED
SCRAPPIER
SCRAPPIEST
SCRAPPILY
SCRAPPING

SCRAPPY	SCREECHING	SCRIENE	SCROGS	SCRUMMING
SCRAPS	SCREECHY	SCRIENES	SCROLL	SCRUMMY
SCRAT	SCREED	SCRIES	SCROLLED	SCRUMP
SCRATCH	SCREEDED	SCRIEVE	SCROLLERIES	SCRUMPED
SCRATCHED	SCREEDER	SCRIEVED	SCROLLERY	SCRUMPIES
SCRATCHER	SCREEDERS	SCRIEVES	SCROLLING	SCRUMPING
SCRATCHERS	SCREEDING	SCRIEVING	SCROLLS	SCRUMPS
SCRATCHES	SCREEDINGS	SCRIGGLE	SCROOGE	SCRUMPY
SCRATCHIER	SCREEDS	SCRIGGLED	SCROOGED	SCRUMS
SCRATCHIEST	SCREEN	SCRIGGLES	SCROOGES	SCRUNCH
SCRATCHING	SCREENED	SCRIGGLING	SCROOGING	SCRUNCHED
SCRATCHINGS	SCREENER	SCRIGGLY	SCROOP	SCRUNCHES
SCRATCHY	SCREENERS	SCRIKE	SCROOPED	SCRUNCHIER
SCRATS	SCREENING	SCRIKED	SCROOPING	SCRUNCHIEST
SCRATTED	SCREENINGS	SCRIKES	SCROOPS	SCRUNCHING
SCRATTING	SCREENS	SCRIKING	SCROTAL	SCRUNCHY
SCRATTLE	SCREES	SCRIM	SCROTUM	SCRUNT
SCRATTLED	SCREEVE	SCRIMMAGE	SCROTUMS	SCRUNTS
SCRATTLES	SCREEVED	SCRIMMAGED	SCROUGE	SCRUNTY
SCRATTLING	SCREEVER	SCRIMMAGES	SCROUGED	SCRUPLE
SCRAUCH	SCREEVERS	SCRIMMAGING	SCROUGER	SCRUPLED
SCRAUCHED	SCREEVES	SCRIMP	SCROUGERS	SCRUPLER
SCRAUCHING	SCREEVING	SCRIMPED	SCROUGES	SCRUPLERS
SCRAUCHS	SCREEVINGS	SCRIMPIER	SCROUGING	SCRUPLES
SCRAUGH	SCREICH	SCRIMPIEST	SCROUNGE	SCRUPLING
SCRAUGHED	SCREICHED	SCRIMPILY	SCROUNGED	SCRUTABLE
SCRAUGHING	SCREICHING	SCRIMPING	SCROUNGER	SCRUTATOR
SCRAUGHS	SCREICHS	SCRIMPLY	SCROUNGERS	SCRUTATORS
SCRAW	SCREIGH	SCRIMPS	SCROUNGES	SCRUTINIES
SCRAWL	SCREIGHED	SCRIMPY	SCROUNGING	SCRUTINY
SCRAWLED	SCREIGHING	SCRIMS	SCROUNGINGS	SCRUTO
SCRAWLER	SCREIGHS	SCRIMSHAW	SCROW	SCRUTOIRE
SCRAWLERS	SCREW	SCRIMSHAWED	SCROWDGE	SCRUTOIRES
SCRAWLIER	SCREWBALL	SCRIMSHAWING	SCROWDGED	SCRUTOS
SCRAWLIEST	SCREWBALLS	SCRIMSHAWS	SCROWDGES	SCRUZE
SCRAWLING	SCREWED	SCRIMURE	SCROWDGING	SCRUZED
SCRAWLINGS	SCREWER	SCRIMURES	SCROWL	SCRUZES
SCRAWLS	SCREWERS	SCRINE	SCROWLE	SCRUZING
SCRAWLY	SCREWIER	SCRINES	SCROWLED	SCRY
SCRAWM	SCREWIEST	SCRIP	SCROWLES	SCRYDE
SCRAWMED	SCREWING	SCRIPPAGE	SCROWLING	SCRYER
SCRAWMING	SCREWINGS	SCRIPPAGES	SCROWLS	SCRYERS
SCRAWMS	SCREWS	SCRIPS	SCROWS	SCRYING
SCRAWNIER	SCREWTOP	SCRIPT	SCROYLE	SCRYINGS
SCRAWNIEST	SCREWTOPS	SCRIPTED	SCROYLES	SCRYNE
SCRAWNY	SCREWY	SCRIPTING	SCRUB	SCRYNES
SCRAWS	SCRIBABLE	SCRIPTORY	SCRUBBED	SCUBA
SCRAY	SCRIBAL	SCRIPTS	SCRUBBER	SCUBAS
SCRAYE	SCRIBBLE	SCRIPTURE	SCRUBBERS	SCUCHIN
SCRAYES	SCRIBBLED	SCRIPTURES	SCRUBBIER	SCUCHINS
SCRAYS	SCRIBBLER	SCRITCH	SCRUBBIEST	SCUCHION
SCREAK	SCRIBBLERS	SCRITCHED	SCRUBBING	SCUCHIONS
SCREAKED	SCRIBBLES	SCRITCHES	SCRUBBINGS	SCUD
SCREAKING	SCRIBBLING	SCRITCHING	SCRUBBY	SCUDDALER
SCREAKS	SCRIBBLINGS	SCRIVE	SCRUBLAND	SCUDDALERS
SCREAKY	SCRIBBLY	SCRIVED	SCRUBLANDS	SCUDDED
SCREAM	SCRIBE	SCRIVENER	SCRUBS	SCUDDER
SCREAMED	SCRIBED	SCRIVENERS	SCRUFF	SCUDDERS
SCREAMER	SCRIBER	SCRIVES	SCRUFFIER	SCUDDING
SCREAMERS	SCRIBERS	SCRIVING	SCRUFFIEST	SCUDDLE
SCREAMING	SCRIBES	SCROBE	SCRUFFS	SCUDDLED
SCREAMS	SCRIBING	SCROBES	SCRUFFY	SCUDDLES
SCREE	SCRIBINGS	SCRODDLED	SCRUM	SCUDDLING
SCREECH	SCRIBISM	SCROFULA	SCRUMMAGE	SCUDI
SCREECHED	SCRIBISMS	SCROFULAS	SCRUMMAGED	SCUDLER
SCREECHER	SCRIECH	SCROG	SCRUMMAGES	SCUDLERS
SCREECHERS	SCRIECHED	SCROGGIE	SCRUMMAGING	SCUDO
SCREECHES	SCRIECHING	SCROGGIER	SCRUMMED	SCUDS
SCREECHIER	SCRIECHS	SCROGGIEST	SCRUMMIER	SCUFF
SCREECHIEST	SCRIED	SCROGGY	SCRUMMIEST	SCUFFED

SCUFFIER	SCUMMED	SCUTCHES	SEADROME	SEARATS
SCUFFIEST	SCUMMER	SCUTCHING	SEADROMES	SEARCE
SCUFFING	SCUMMERS	SCUTCHINGS	SEAFARER	SEARCED
SCUFFLE	SCUMMIER	SCUTE	SEAFARERS	SEARCES
SCUFFLED	SCUMMIEST	SCUTELLA	SEAFARING	SEARCH
SCUFFLER	SCUMMING	SCUTELLAR	SEAFARINGS	SEARCHED
SCUFFLERS	SCUMMINGS	SCUTELLUM	SEAFOOD	SEARCHER
SCUFFLES	SCUMMY	SCUTES	SEAFOODS	SEARCHERS
SCUFFLING	SCUMS	SCUTIFORM	SEAGULL	SEARCHES
SCUFFS	SCUNCHEON	SCUTIGER	SEAGULLS	SEARCHING
SCUFFY	SCUNCHEONS	SCUTIGERS	SEAHORSE	SEARCING
SCUFT	SCUNGE	SCUTS	SEAHORSES	SEARE
SCUFTS	SCUNGED	SCUTTER	SEAL	SEARED
SCUG	SCUNGES	SCUTTERED	SEALANT	SEARER
SCUGGED	SCUNGIER	SCUTTERING	SEALANTS	SEARES
SCUGGING	SCUNGIEST	SCUTTERS	SEALCH	SEAREST
SCUGS	SCUNGING	SCUTTLE	SEALCHS	SEARING
SCUL	SCUNGY	SCUTTLED	SEALED	SEARINGS
SCULK	SCUNNER	SCUTTLER	SEALER	SEARNESS
SCULKED	SCUNNERED	SCUTTLERS	SEALERIES	SEARNESSES
SCULKING	SCUNNERING	SCUTTLES	SEALERS	SEARS
SCULKS	SCUNNERS	SCUTTLING	SEALERY	SEAS
SCULL	SCUP	SCUTUM	SEALGH	SEASATYR
SCULLE	SCUPPAUG	SCYBALA	SEALGHS	SEASATYRS
SCULLED	SCUPPAUGS	SCYBALOUS	SEALING	SEASCAPE
SCULLER	SCUPPER	SCYBALUM	SEALINGS	SEASCAPES
SCULLERIES	SCUPPERED	SCYE	SEALS	SEASD
SCULLERS	SCUPPERING	SCYES	SEALSKIN	SEASE
SCULLERY	SCUPPERS	SCYPHI	SEALSKINS	SEASED
SCULLES	SCUPS	SCYPHUS	SEALYHAM	SEASES
SCULLING	SCUR	SCYTALE	SEALYHAMS	SEASHELL
SCULLINGS	SCURF	SCYTALES	SEAM	SEASHELLS
SCULLION	SCURFIER	SCYTHE	SEAMAN	SEASHORE
SCULLIONS	SCURFIEST	SCYTHED	SEAMANLY	SEASHORES
SCULLS	SCURFS	SCYTHEMAN	SEAMARK	SEASICK
SCULP	SCURFY	SCYTHEMEN	SEAMARKS	SEASICKER
SCULPED	SCURRED	SCYTHER	SEAME	SEASICKEST
SCULPIN	SCURRIED	SCYTHERS	SEAMED	SEASIDE
SCULPING	SCURRIER	SCYTHES	SEAMEN	SEASIDES
SCULPINS	SCURRIERS	SCYTHING	SEAMER	SEASING
SCULPS	SCURRIES	SDAINE	SEAMERS	SEASON
SCULPSIT	SCURRIL	SDAINED	SEAMES	SEASONAL
SCULPT	SCURRILE	SDAINES	SEAMIER	SEASONED
SCULPTED	SCURRING	SDAINING	SEAMIEST	SEASONER
SCULPTING	SCURRIOUR	SDAYN	SEAMINESS	SEASONERS
SCULPTOR	SCURRIOURS	SDAYNED	SEAMINESSES	SEASONING
SCULPTORS	SCURRY	SDAYNING	SEAMING	SEASONINGS
SCULPTS	SCURRYING	SDAYNS	SEAMLESS	SEASONS
SCULPTURE	SCURS	SDEIGNE	SEAMOUNT	SEASURE
SCULPTURED	SCURVIER	SDEIGNED	SEAMOUNTS	SEASURES
SCULPTURES	SCURVIES	SDEIGNES	SEAMS	SEAT
SCULPTURING	SCURVIEST	SDEIGNING	SEAMSTER	SEATED
SCULPTURINGS	SCURVILY	SDEIN	SEAMSTERS	SEATER
SCULS	SCURVY	SDEINED	SEAMY	SEATERS
SCUM	SCUSE	SDEINING	SEAN	SEATING
SCUMBAG	SCUSED	SDEINS	SÉANCE	SEATINGS
SCUMBAGS	SCUSES	SEA	SÉANCES	SEATLESS
SCUMBER	SCUSING	SEABED	SEANED	SEATS
SCUMBERED	SCUT	SEABEDS	SEANING	SEAWARD
SCUMBERING	SCUTA	SEABERRIES	SEANNACHIES	SEAWARDLY
SCUMBERS	SCUTAGE	SEABERRY	SEANNACHY	SEAWARDS
SCUMBLE	SCUTAGES	SEABOARD	SEANS	SEAWAY
SCUMBLED	SCUTAL	SEABOARDS	SEAPLANE	SEAWAYS
SCUMBLES	SCUTATE	SEABORNE	SEAPLANES	SEAWEED
SCUMBLING	SCUTCH	SEACOAST	SEAPORT	SEAWEEDS
SCUMBLINGS	SCUTCHED	SEACOASTS	SEAPORTS	SEAWORTHY
SCUMFISH	SCUTCHEON	SEACRAFT	SEAQUAKE	SEAZE
SCUMFISHED	SCUTCHEONS	SEACRAFTS	SEAQUAKES	SEAZED
SCUMFISHES	SCUTCHER	SEACUNNIES	SEAR	SEAZES
SCUMFISHING	SCUTCHERS	SEACUNNY	SEARAT	SEAZING

SEBACEOUS	SECRETE	SEDATING	SEEDNESS	SEGHOL
SEBACIC	SECRETED	SEDATION	SEEDNESSES	SEGHOLATE
SEBATE	SECRETES	SEDATIONS	SEEDS	SEGHOLATES
SEBATES	SECRETIN	SEDATIVE	SEEDSMAN	SEGHOLS
SEBESTEN	SECRETING	SEDATIVES	SEEDSMEN	SEGMENT
SEBESTENS	SECRETINS	SEDENT	SEEDY	SEGMENTAL
SEBIFIC	SECRETION	SEDENTARY	SEEING	SEGMENTED
SEBUM	SECRETIONS	SEDERUNT	SEEINGS	SEGMENTING
SEBUMS	SECRETIVE	SEDERUNTS	SEEK	SEGMENTS
SEBUNDIES	SECRETLY	SEDES	SEEKER	SEGNO
SEBUNDY	SECRETORY	SEDGE	SEEKERS	SEGNOS
SEC	SECRETS	SEDGED	SEEKING	SEGO
SECANT	SECS	SEDGELAND	SEEKS	SEGOL
SECANTS	SECT	SEDGELANDS	SEEL	SEGOLATE
SECATEUR	SECTARIAL	SEDGES	SEELD	SEGOLATES
SECATEURS	SECTARIAN	SEDGIER	SEELED	SEGOLS
SECCO	SECTARIANS	SEDGIEST	SEELING	SEGOS
SECCOS	SECTARIES	SEDGY	SEELINGS	SEGREANT
SECEDE	SECTARY	SEDILE	SEELS	SEGREGATE
SECEDED	SECTATOR	SEDILIA	SEELY	SEGREGATED
SECEDER	SECTATORS	SEDIMENT	SEEM	SEGREGATES
SECEDERS	SECTILE	SEDIMENTED	SEEMED	SEGREGATING
SECEDES	SECTILITIES	SEDIMENTING	SEEMELESS	SEGS
SECEDING	SECTILITY	SEDIMENTS	SEEMER	SEGUE
SECERN	SECTION	SEDITION	SEEMERS	SEGUED
SECERNED	SECTIONAL	SEDITIONS	SEEMING	SEGUEING
SECERNENT	SECTIONED	SEDITIOUS	SEEMINGLY	SEGUES
SECERNENTS	SECTIONING	SEDUCE	SEEMINGS	SEI
SECERNING	SECTIONS	SEDUCED	SEEMLESS	SEICENTO
SECERNS	SECTOR	SEDUCER	SEEMLESSE	SEICENTOS
SECESH	SECTORAL	SEDUCERS	SEEMLIER	SEICHE
SECESHER	SECTORED	SEDUCES	SEEMLIEST	SEICHES
SECESHERS	SECTORIAL	SEDUCING	SEEMLIHED	SEIF
SECESHES	SECTORIALS	SEDUCINGS	SEEMLIHEDS	SEIFS
SECESSION	SECTORING	SEDUCTION	SEEMLY	SEIGNEUR
SECESSIONS	SECTORS	SEDUCTIONS	SEEMLYHED	SEIGNEURS
SECKEL	SECTS	SEDUCTIVE	SEEMLYHEDS	SEIGNIOR
SECKELS	SECULAR	SEDUCTOR	SEEMS	SEIGNIORIES
SECLUDE	SECULARLY	SEDUCTORS	SEEN	SEIGNIORS
SECLUDED	SECULARS	SEDULITIES	SEEP	SEIGNIORY
SECLUDES	SECULUM	SEDULITY	SEEPAGE	SEIGNORAL
SECLUDING	SECULUMS	SEDULOUS	SEEPAGES	SEIGNORIES
SECLUSION	SECUND	SEDUM	SEEPED	SEIGNORY
SECLUSIONS	SECUNDINE	SEDUMS	SEEPIER	SEIL
SECLUSIVE	SECUNDINES	SEE	SEEPIEST	SEILED
SECODONT	SECUNDUM	SEEABLE	SEEPING	SEILING
SECODONTS	SECURABLE	SEECATCH	SEEPS	SEILS
SECOND	SECURANCE	SEECATCHIE	SEEPY	SEINE
SECONDARIES	SECURANCES	SEED	SEER	SEINED
SECONDARY	SECURE	SEEDBED	SEERESS	SEINER
SECONDE	SECURED	SEEDBEDS	SEERESSES	SEINERS
SECONDED	SECURELY	SEEDBOX	SEERS	SEINES
SECONDEE	SECURER	SEEDBOXES	SEES	SEINING
SECONDEES	SECURERS	SEEDCAKE	SEESAW	SEININGS
SECONDER	SECURES	SEEDCAKES	SEESAWED	SEIS
SECONDERS	SECUREST	SEEDED	SEESAWING	SEISE
SECONDES	SECURING	SEEDER	SEESAWS	SEISED
SECONDI	SECURITAN	SEEDERS	SEETHE	SEISES
SECONDING	SECURITANS	SEEDIER	SEETHED	SEISIN
SECONDLY	SECURITIES	SEEDIEST	SEETHER	SEISING
SECONDO	SECURITY	SEEDILY	SEETHERS	SEISINS
SECONDS	SED	SEEDINESS	SEETHES	SEISM
SECRECIES	SEDAN	SEEDINESSES	SEETHING	SEISMAL
SECRECY	SEDANS	SEEDING	SEETHINGS	SEISMIC
SECRET	SEDATE	SEEDINGS	SEEWING	SEISMICAL
SECRETA	SEDATED	SEEDLESS	SEG	SEISMISM
SECRETAGE	SEDATELY	SEEDLING	SEGAR	SEISMISMS
SECRETAGES	SEDATER	SEEDLINGS	SEGARS	SEISMS
SECRETARIES	SEDATES	SEEDLIP	SEGGAR	SEITIES
SECRETARY	SEDATEST	SEEDLIPS	SEGGARS	SEITY

SEIZABLE	SELKIE	SEMIBULL	SENATES	SENSOR
SEIZE	SELKIES	SEMIBULLS	SENATOR	SENSORIAL
SEIZED	SELL	SEMICOLON	SENATORS	SENSORIES
SEIZER	SELLABLE	SEMICOLONS	SEND	SENSORIUM
SEIZERS	SELLE	SEMICOMA	SENDAL	SENSORIUMS
SEIZES	SELLER	SEMICOMAS	SENDALS	SENSORS
SEIZIN	SELLERS	SEMIE	SENDED	SENSORY
SEIZING	SELLES	SEMIES	SENDER	SENSUAL
SEIZINGS	SELLING	SEMIFINAL	SENDERS	SENSUALLY
SEIZINS	SELLOTAPE	SEMIFINALS	SENDING	SENSUALTIES
SEIZURE	SELLOTAPED	SEMIFLUID	SENDINGS	SENSUALTY
SEIZURES	SELLOTAPES	SEMIFLUIDS	SENDS	SENSUISM
SEJANT	SELLOTAPING	SEMILOG	SENECIO	SENSUISMS
SEJEANT	SELLS	SEMILOGS	SENECIOS	SENSUIST
SEKOS	SELS	SEMILUNE	SENEGA	SENSUISTS
SEKOSES	SELTZER	SEMILUNES	SENEGAS	SENSUM
SEKT	SELTZERS	SEMINAL	SENESCENT	SENSUOUS
SEKTS	SELVA	SEMINALLY	SENESCHAL	SENT
SEL	SELVAGE	SEMINAR	SENESCHALS	SENTED
SELACHIAN	SELVAGED	SEMINARIES	SENGREEN	SENTENCE
SELACHIANS	SELVAGEE	SEMINARS	SENGREENS	SENTENCED
SELADANG	SELVAGEES	SEMINARY	SENILE	SENTENCER
SELADANGS	SELVAGES	SEMINATE	SENILITIES	SENTENCERS
SELAH	SELVAGING	SEMINATED	SENILITY	SENTENCES
SELAHS	SELVAS	SEMINATES	SENIOR	SENTENCING
SELCOUTH	SELVEDGE	SEMINATING	SENIORITIES	SENTIENCE
SELD	SELVEDGED	SEMIOLOGIES	SENIORITY	SENTIENCES
SELDOM	SELVEDGES	SEMIOLOGY	SENIORS	SENTIENCIES
SELDSEEN	SELVEDGING	SEMIOTIC	SENNA	SENTIENCY
SELDSHOWN	SELVES	SEMIOTICS	SENNACHIE	SENTIENT
SELE	SEMANTEME	SEMIPED	SENNACHIES	SENTIENTS
SELECT	SEMANTEMES	SEMIPEDS	SENNAS	SENTIMENT
SELECTED	SEMANTIC	SEMIPLUME	SENNET	SENTIMENTS
SELECTING	SEMANTICS	SEMIPLUMES	SENNETS	SENTINEL
SELECTION	SEMANTRA	SEMIS	SENNIGHT	SENTINELLED
SELECTIONS	SEMANTRON	SEMISES	SENNIGHTS	SENTINELLING
SELECTIVE	SEMAPHORE	SEMITAR	SENNIT	SENTINELS
SELECTOR	SEMAPHORED	SEMITARS	SENNITS	SENTING
SELECTORS	SEMAPHORES	SEMITAUR	SENS	SENTRIES
SELECTS	SEMAPHORING	SEMITAURS	SENSA	SENTRY
SELENATE	SEMATIC	SEMITONE	SENSATION	SENTS
SELENATES	SEMBLABLE	SEMITONES	SENSATIONS	SENVIES
SELENIC	SEMBLABLES	SEMITONIC	SENSE	SENVY
SELENIDE	SEMBLABLY	SEMIVOWEL	SENSED	SENZA
SELENIDES	SEMBLANCE	SEMIVOWELS	SENSEFUL	SEPAD
SELENIOUS	SEMBLANCES	SEMMIT	SENSELESS	SEPADDED
SELENITE	SEMBLANT	SEMMITS	SENSES	SEPADDING
SELENITES	SEMBLANTS	SEMOLINA	SENSIBLE	SEPADS
SELENITIC	SEMBLE	SEMOLINAS	SENSIBLER	SEPAL
SELENIUM	SEMBLED	SEMPER	SENSIBLEST	SEPALINE
SELENIUMS	SEMBLES	SEMPITERN	SENSIBLY	SEPALODIES
SELENOUS	SEMBLING	SEMPLE	SENSILE	SEPALODY
SELES	SEMÉ	SEMPLER	SENSILLA	SEPALOID
SELF	SEMÉE	SEMPLEST	SENSILLUM	SEPALOUS
SELFED	SEMEIA	SEMPLICE	SENSING	SEPALS
SELFHOOD	SEMEION	SEMPRE	SENSINGS	SEPARABLE
SELFHOODS	SEMEIOTIC	SEMPSTER	SENSISM	SEPARABLY
SELFING	SEMEIOTICS	SEMPSTERS	SENSISMS	SEPARATE
SELFISH	SEMEME	SEMSEM	SENSIST	SEPARATED
SELFISHLY	SEMEMES	SEMSEMS	SENSISTS	SEPARATES
SELFISM	SEMEN	SEMUNCIA	SENSITISE	SEPARATING
SELFISMS	SEMENS	SEMUNCIAE	SENSITISED	SEPARATOR
SELFIST	SEMESTER	SEMUNCIAL	SENSITISES	SEPARATORS
SELFISTS	SEMESTERS	SEMUNCIAS	SENSITISING	SEPARATUM
SELFLESS	SEMESTRAL	SEN	SENSITIVE	SEPARATUMS
SELFNESS	SEMI	SENARIES	SENSITIVES	SEPHEN
SELFNESSES	SEMIANGLE	SENARII	SENSITIZE	SEPHENS
SELFS	SEMIANGLES	SENARIUS	SENSITIZED	SEPIA
SELICTAR	SEMIBREVE	SENARY	SENSITIZES	SEPIAS
SELICTARS	SEMIBREVES	SENATE	SENSITIZING	SEPIMENT

SEPIMENTS
SEPIOLITE
SEPIOLITES
SEPIOST
SEPIOSTS
SEPIUM
SEPIUMS
SEPOY
SEPOYS
SEPPUKU
SEPPUKUS
SEPS
SEPSES
SEPSIS
SEPT
SEPTA
SEPTAL
SEPTARIA
SEPTARIAN
SEPTARIUM
SEPTATE
SEPTATION
SEPTATIONS
SEPTEMFID
SEPTEMVIR
SEPTEMVIRI
SEPTEMVIRS
SEPTENARIES
SEPTENARY
SEPTENNIA
SEPTET
SEPTETS
SEPTETT
SEPTETTE
SEPTETTES
SEPTETTS
SEPTIC
SEPTICITIES
SEPTICITY
SEPTIFORM
SEPTIMAL
SEPTIME
SEPTIMES
SEPTIMOLE
SEPTIMOLES
SEPTLEVA
SEPTLEVAS
SEPTS
SEPTUM
SEPTUOR
SEPTUORS
SEPTUPLE
SEPTUPLED
SEPTUPLES
SEPTUPLET
SEPTUPLETS
SEPTUPLING
SEPULCHRE
SEPULCHRED
SEPULCHRES
SEPULCHRING
SEPULTURE
SEPULTURED
SEPULTURES
SEPULTURING
SEQUACITIES
SEQUACITY
SEQUEL
SEQUELA
SEQUELAE

SEQUELS
SEQUENCE
SEQUENCED
SEQUENCES
SEQUENCING
SEQUENT
SEQUENTS
SEQUESTER
SEQUESTERED
SEQUESTERING
SEQUESTERS
SEQUIN
SEQUINS
SEQUOIA
SEQUOIAS
SERA
SÉRAC
SÉRACS
SERAFILE
SERAFILES
SERAGLIO
SERAGLIOS
SERAI
SERAIL
SERAILS
SERAIS
SERAL
SERANG
SERANGS
SERAPE
SERAPES
SERAPH
SERAPHIC
SERAPHIM
SERAPHIMS
SERAPHIN
SERAPHINE
SERAPHINES
SERAPHINS
SERAPHS
SERASKIER
SERASKIERS
SERDAB
SERDABS
SERE
SERED
SEREIN
SEREINS
SERENADE
SERENADED
SERENADER
SERENADERS
SERENADES
SERENADING
SERENATA
SERENATAS
SERENATE
SERENATES
SERENE
SERENED
SERENELY
SERENER
SERENES
SERENESS
SERENESSES
SERENEST
SERENING
SERENITIES
SERENITY
SERER

SERES
SEREST
SERF
SERFAGE
SERFAGES
SERFDOM
SERFDOMS
SERFHOOD
SERFHOODS
SERFISH
SERFS
SERFSHIP
SERFSHIPS
SERGE
SERGEANCIES
SERGEANCY
SERGEANT
SERGEANTS
SERGES
SERIAL
SERIALISE
SERIALISED
SERIALISES
SERIALISING
SERIALISM
SERIALISMS
SERIALIST
SERIALISTS
SERIALITIES
SERIALITY
SERIALIZE
SERIALIZED
SERIALIZES
SERIALIZING
SERIALLY
SERIALS
SERIATE
SERIATED
SERIATELY
SERIATES
SERIATIM
SERIATING
SERIATION
SERIATIONS
SERIC
SERICEOUS
SERICIN
SERICINS
SERICITE
SERICITES
SERICITIC
SERICON
SERICONS
SERIEMA
SERIEMAS
SERIES
SERIF
SERIFS
SERIGRAPH
SERIGRAPHS
SERIN
SERINETTE
SERINETTES
SERING
SERINGA
SERINGAS
SERINS
SERIOUS
SERIOUSLY
SERIPH

SERIPHS
SERJEANCIES
SERJEANCY
SERJEANT
SERJEANTIES
SERJEANTS
SERJEANTY
SERK
SERKALI
SERKALIS
SERKS
SERMON
SERMONED
SERMONEER
SERMONEERS
SERMONER
SERMONERS
SERMONET
SERMONETS
SERMONIC
SERMONING
SERMONINGS
SERMONISE
SERMONISED
SERMONISES
SERMONISH
SERMONISING
SERMONIZE
SERMONIZED
SERMONIZES
SERMONIZING
SERMONS
SEROLOGIES
SEROLOGY
SERON
SERONS
SEROON
SEROONS
SEROSA
SEROSAE
SEROSAS
SEROSITIES
SEROSITY
SEROTINE
SEROTINES
SEROTONIN
SEROTONINS
SEROTYPE
SEROTYPED
SEROTYPES
SEROTYPING
SEROUS
SEROW
SEROWS
SERPENT
SERPENTED
SERPENTING
SERPENTRIES
SERPENTRY
SERPENTS
SERPIGINES
SERPIGO
SERPIGOES
SERPULA
SERPULAE
SERPULITE
SERPULITES
SERR
SERRA
SERRAE

SERRAN
SERRANID
SERRANIDS
SERRANOID
SERRANOIDS
SERRANS
SERRAS
SERRATE
SERRATED
SERRATES
SERRATING
SERRATION
SERRATIONS
SERRATURE
SERRATURES
SERRATUS
SERRATUSES
SERRE
SERRED
SERREFILE
SERREFILES
SERRES
SERRICORN
SERRIED
SERRIES
SERRING
SERRS
SERRULATE
SERRY
SERRYING
SERUEWE
SERUEWED
SERUEWES
SERUEWING
SERUM
SERUMS
SERVAL
SERVALS
SERVANT
SERVANTED
SERVANTING
SERVANTRIES
SERVANTRY
SERVANTS
SERVE
SERVED
SERVER
SERVERIES
SERVERS
SERVERY
SERVES
SERVEWE
SERVEWED
SERVEWES
SERVEWING
SERVICE
SERVICED
SERVICES
SERVICING
SERVIENT
SERVIETTE
SERVIETTES
SERVILE
SERVILELY
SERVILES
SERVILISM
SERVILISMS
SERVILITIES
SERVILITY
SERVING

SERVINGS	SETUALE	SEXING	SFORZATO	SHAGGY
SERVITOR	SETUALES	SEXISM	SFORZATOS	SHAGREEN
SERVITORS	SETWALL	SEXISMS	SFUMATO	SHAGREENS
SERVITUDE	SETWALLS	SEXIST	SFUMATOS	SHAGROON
SERVITUDES	SEVEN	SEXISTS	SGRAFFITI	SHAGROONS
SERVO	SEVENFOLD	SEXLESS	SGRAFFITO	SHAGS
SESAME	SEVENS	SEXOLOGIES	SH	SHAH
SESAMES	SEVENTEEN	SEXOLOGY	SHABBIER	SHAHS
SESAMOID	SEVENTEENS	SEXPOT	SHABBIEST	SHAIKH
SESAMOIDS	SEVENTH	SEXPOTS	SHABBILY	SHAIKHS
SESE	SEVENTHLY	SEXT	SHABBLE	SHAIRN
SESELI	SEVENTHS	SEXTAN	SHABBLES	SHAIRNS
SESELIS	SEVENTIES	SEXTANS	SHABBY	SHAITAN
SESEY	SEVENTY	SEXTANSES	SHABRACK	SHAITANS
SESS	SEVER	SEXTANT	SHABRACKS	SHAKABLE
SESSA	SEVERABLE	SEXTANTAL	SHACK	SHAKE
SESSILE	SEVERAL	SEXTANTS	SHACKLE	SHAKEABLE
SESSION	SEVERALLY	SEXTET	SHACKLED	SHAKED
SESSIONAL	SEVERALS	SEXTETS	SHACKLES	SHAKEN
SESSIONS	SEVERALTIES	SEXTETT	SHACKLING	SHAKER
SESSPOOL	SEVERALTY	SEXTETTE	SHACKS	SHAKERISM
SESSPOOLS	SEVERANCE	SEXTETTES	SHAD	SHAKERISMS
SESTERCE	SEVERANCES	SEXTETTS	SHADBERRIES	SHAKERS
SESTERCES	SEVERE	SEXTILE	SHADBERRY	SHAKES
SESTERTIA	SEVERED	SEXTILES	SHADBUSH	SHAKIER
SESTET	SEVERELY	SEXTOLET	SHADBUSHES	SHAKIEST
SESTETS	SEVERER	SEXTOLETS	SHADDOCK	SHAKILY
SESTETT	SEVEREST	SEXTON	SHADDOCKS	SHAKINESS
SESTETTE	SEVERIES	SEXTONESS	SHADE	SHAKINESSES
SESTETTES	SEVERING	SEXTONESSES	SHADED	SHAKING
SESTETTO	SEVERITIES	SEXTONS	SHADELESS	SHAKINGS
SESTETTOS	SEVERITY	SEXTS	SHADES	SHAKO
SESTETTS	SEVERS	SEXTUOR	SHADIER	SHAKOES
SESTINA	SEVERY	SEXTUORS	SHADIEST	SHAKOS
SESTINAS	SEW	SEXTUPLE	SHADILY	SHAKT
SESTINE	SEWAGE	SEXTUPLED	SHADINESS	SHAKUDO
SESTINES	SEWAGES	SEXTUPLES	SHADINESSES	SHAKUDOS
SESTON	SEWED	SEXTUPLET	SHADING	SHAKY
SESTONS	SEWEL	SEXTUPLETS	SHADINGS	SHALE
SET	SEWELLEL	SEXTUPLING	SHADOOF	SHALED
SETA	SEWELLELS	SEXUAL	SHADOOFS	SHALES
SETACEOUS	SEWELS	SEXUALISE	SHADOW	SHALIER
SETAE	SEWEN	SEXUALISED	SHADOWED	SHALIEST
SETBACK	SEWENS	SEXUALISES	SHADOWER	SHALING
SETBACKS	SEWER	SEXUALISING	SHADOWERS	SHALL
SETNESS	SEWERAGE	SEXUALISM	SHADOWIER	SHALLI
SETNESSES	SEWERAGES	SEXUALISMS	SHADOWIEST	SHALLIS
SETON	SEWERED	SEXUALIST	SHADOWING	SHALLON
SETONS	SEWERING	SEXUALISTS	SHADOWINGS	SHALLONS
SETOSE	SEWERINGS	SEXUALITIES	SHADOWS	SHALLOON
SETS	SEWERS	SEXUALITY	SHADOWY	SHALLOONS
SETT	SEWIN	SEXUALIZE	SHADS	SHALLOP
SETTEE	SEWING	SEXUALIZED	SHADUF	SHALLOPS
SETTEES	SEWINGS	SEXUALIZES	SHADUFS	SHALLOT
SETTER	SEWINS	SEXUALIZING	SHADY	SHALLOTS
SETTERED	SEWN	SEXUALLY	SHAFT	SHALLOW
SETTERING	SEWS	SEXVALENT	SHAFTED	SHALLOWED
SETTERS	SEX	SEXY	SHAFTER	SHALLOWER
SETTING	SEXED	SEY	SHAFTERS	SHALLOWEST
SETTINGS	SEXENNIAL	SEYEN	SHAFTING	SHALLOWING
SETTLE	SEXER	SEYENS	SHAFTINGS	SHALLOWINGS
SETTLED	SEXERS	SEYS	SHAFTLESS	SHALLOWLY
SETTLER	SEXES	SEYSURE	SHAFTS	SHALLOWS
SETTLERS	SEXFID	SEYSURES	SHAG	SHALM
SETTLES	SEXFOIL	SEZ	SHAGEARED	SHALMS
SETTLING	SEXFOILS	SFERICS	SHAGGED	SHALOM
SETTLINGS	SEXIER	SFORZANDI	SHAGGIER	SHALOT
SETTLOR	SEXIEST	SFORZANDO	SHAGGIEST	SHALOTS
SETTLORS	SEXINESS	SFORZANDOS	SHAGGILY	SHALT
SETTS	SEXINESSES	SFORZATI	SHAGGING	SHALWAR

SHALWARS
SHALY
SHAM
SHAMA
SHAMAN
SHAMANIC
SHAMANISM
SHAMANISMS
SHAMANIST
SHAMANISTS
SHAMANS
SHAMAS
SHAMATEUR
SHAMATEURS
SHAMBLE
SHAMBLED
SHAMBLES
SHAMBLING
SHAMBLINGS
SHAMBOLIC
SHAME
SHAMED
SHAMEFAST
SHAMEFUL
SHAMELESS
SHAMER
SHAMERS
SHAMES
SHAMIANA
SHAMIANAH
SHAMIANAHS
SHAMIANAS
SHAMING
SHAMISEN
SHAMISENS
SHAMMED
SHAMMER
SHAMMERS
SHAMMIES
SHAMMING
SHAMMY
SHAMOY
SHAMOYED
SHAMOYING
SHAMOYS
SHAMPOO
SHAMPOOED
SHAMPOOER
SHAMPOOERS
SHAMPOOING
SHAMPOOS
SHAMROCK
SHAMROCKS
SHAMS
SHAMUS
SHAMUSES
SHAN
SHANACHIE
SHANACHIES
SHAND
SHANDIES
SHANDRIES
SHANDRY
SHANDS
SHANDY
SHANGHAI
SHANGHAIED
SHANGHAIING
SHANGHAIS
SHANK

SHANKED
SHANKING
SHANKS
SHANNIES
SHANNY
SHANS
SHANTIES
SHANTUNG
SHANTUNGS
SHANTY
SHANTYMAN
SHANTYMEN
SHAPABLE
SHAPE
SHAPEABLE
SHAPED
SHAPELESS
SHAPELIER
SHAPELIEST
SHAPELY
SHAPEN
SHAPER
SHAPERS
SHAPES
SHAPING
SHAPINGS
SHAPS
SHARD
SHARDED
SHARDS
SHARE
SHARECROP
SHARECROPPED
SHARECROPPING
SHARECROPS
SHARED
SHAREMAN
SHAREMEN
SHARER
SHARERS
SHARES
SHARESMAN
SHARESMEN
SHARIA
SHARIAS
SHARIAT
SHARIATS
SHARING
SHARINGS
SHARK
SHARKED
SHARKER
SHARKERS
SHARKING
SHARKINGS
SHARKS
SHARKSKIN
SHARKSKINS
SHARN
SHARNS
SHARNY
SHARP
SHARPED
SHARPEN
SHARPENED
SHARPENER
SHARPENERS
SHARPENING
SHARPENS
SHARPER

SHARPERS
SHARPEST
SHARPIE
SHARPIES
SHARPING
SHARPINGS
SHARPISH
SHARPLY
SHARPNESS
SHARPNESSES
SHARPS
SHASH
SHASHES
SHASHLIK
SHASHLIKS
SHASTER
SHASTERS
SHASTRA
SHASTRAS
SHAT
SHATTER
SHATTERED
SHATTERING
SHATTERS
SHATTERY
SHAUCHLE
SHAUCHLED
SHAUCHLES
SHAUCHLIER
SHAUCHLIEST
SHAUCHLING
SHAUCHLY
SHAVE
SHAVED
SHAVELING
SHAVELINGS
SHAVEN
SHAVER
SHAVERS
SHAVES
SHAVIE
SHAVIES
SHAVING
SHAVINGS
SHAW
SHAWED
SHAWING
SHAWL
SHAWLED
SHAWLING
SHAWLINGS
SHAWLLESS
SHAWLS
SHAWM
SHAWMS
SHAWS
SHAY
SHAYA
SHAYAS
SHAYS
SHCHI
SHCHIS
SHE
SHEA
SHEADING
SHEADINGS
SHEAF
SHEAFED
SHEAFIER
SHEAFIEST

SHEAFING
SHEAFS
SHEAFY
SHEAL
SHEALED
SHEALING
SHEALINGS
SHEALS
SHEAR
SHEARED
SHEARER
SHEARERS
SHEARING
SHEARINGS
SHEARLING
SHEARLINGS
SHEARMAN
SHEARMEN
SHEARS
SHEAS
SHEATH
SHEATHE
SHEATHED
SHEATHES
SHEATHIER
SHEATHIEST
SHEATHING
SHEATHINGS
SHEATHS
SHEATHY
SHEAVE
SHEAVED
SHEAVES
SHEAVING
SHEBANG
SHEBANGS
SHEBEEN
SHEBEENED
SHEBEENER
SHEBEENERS
SHEBEENING
SHEBEENINGS
SHEBEENS
SHECHITA
SHECHITAH
SHECHITAHS
SHECHITAS
SHED
SHEDDER
SHEDDERS
SHEDDING
SHEDDINGS
SHEDS
SHEEL
SHEELED
SHEELING
SHEELINGS
SHEELS
SHEEN
SHEENED
SHEENIER
SHEENIES
SHEENIEST
SHEENING
SHEENS
SHEENY
SHEEP
SHEEPDOG
SHEEPDOGS
SHEEPFOLD

SHEEPFOLDS
SHEEPIER
SHEEPIEST
SHEEPISH
SHEEPMEAT
SHEEPMEATS
SHEEPSKIN
SHEEPSKINS
SHEEPWALK
SHEEPWALKS
SHEEPY
SHEER
SHEERED
SHEERER
SHEEREST
SHEERING
SHEERLY
SHEERS
SHEET
SHEETED
SHEETIER
SHEETIEST
SHEETING
SHEETINGS
SHEETS
SHEETY
SHEHITA
SHEHITAH
SHEHITAHS
SHEHITAS
SHEIK
SHEIKDOM
SHEIKDOMS
SHEIKH
SHEIKHDOM
SHEIKHDOMS
SHEIKHS
SHEIKS
SHEILA
SHEILAS
SHEILING
SHEILINGS
SHEKEL
SHEKELS
SHELDDUCK
SHELDDUCKS
SHELDRAKE
SHELDRAKES
SHELDUCK
SHELDUCKS
SHELF
SHELFED
SHELFIER
SHELFIEST
SHELFING
SHELFROOM
SHELFROOMS
SHELFS
SHELFY
SHELL
SHELLAC
SHELLACKED
SHELLACKING
SHELLACKINGS
SHELLACS
SHELLBACK
SHELLBACKS
SHELLBARK
SHELLBARKS
SHELLDUCK

SHELLDUCKS	SHET	SHIKARI	SHINTIES	SHIT
SHELLED	SHETLAND	SHIKARIS	SHINTY	SHITE
SHELLER	SHETS	SHIKARS	SHINY	SHITES
SHELLERS	SHETTING	SHIKSA	SHIP	SHITING
SHELLFIRE	SHEUCH	SHIKSAS	SHIPBOARD	SHITS
SHELLFIRES	SHEUCHED	SHIKSE	SHIPBOARDS	SHITTAH
SHELLFISH	SHEUCHING	SHIKSES	SHIPFUL	SHITTAHS
SHELLFISHES	SHEUCHS	SHILL	SHIPFULS	SHITTIER
SHELLFUL	SHEUGH	SHILLABER	SHIPLAP	SHITTIEST
SHELLFULS	SHEUGHED	SHILLABERS	SHIPLAPPED	SHITTIM
SHELLIER	SHEUGHING	SHILLED	SHIPLAPPING	SHITTIMS
SHELLIEST	SHEUGHS	SHILLELAH	SHIPLAPS	SHITTING
SHELLING	SHEVA	SHILLELAHS	SHIPLESS	SHITTY
SHELLINGS	SHEVAS	SHILLING	SHIPMAN	SHIV
SHELLS	SHEW	SHILLINGS	SHIPMATE	SHIVAREE
SHELLWORK	SHEWBREAD	SHILLS	SHIPMATES	SHIVAREED
SHELLWORKS	SHEWBREADS	SHILPIT	SHIPMEN	SHIVAREEING
SHELLY	SHEWED	SHILY	SHIPMENT	SHIVAREES
SHELTER	SHEWEL	SHIM	SHIPMENTS	SHIVE
SHELTERED	SHEWELS	SHIMMER	SHIPPED	SHIVER
SHELTERER	SHEWING	SHIMMERED	SHIPPEN	SHIVERED
SHELTERERS	SHEWN	SHIMMERING	SHIPPENS	SHIVERING
SHELTERING	SHEWS	SHIMMERINGS	SHIPPER	SHIVERINGS
SHELTERINGS	SHIATSU	SHIMMERS	SHIPPERS	SHIVERS
SHELTERS	SHIATSUS	SHIMMERY	SHIPPING	SHIVERY
SHELTERY	SHIBUICHI	SHIMMIED	SHIPPINGS	SHIVES
SHELTIE	SHIBUICHIS	SHIMMIES	SHIPPO	SHIVOO
SHELTIES	SHICKER	SHIMMY	SHIPPON	SHIVOOS
SHELTY	SHICKERED	SHIMMYING	SHIPPONS	SHIVS
SHELVE	SHICKERS	SHIMOZZLE	SHIPPOS	SHIVVED
SHELVED	SHICKSA	SHIMOZZLED	SHIPPOUND	SHIVVING
SHELVES	SHICKSAS	SHIMOZZLES	SHIPPOUNDS	SHLEMIEL
SHELVIER	SHIDDER	SHIMOZZLING	SHIPS	SHLEMIELS
SHELVIEST	SHIDDERS	SHIMS	SHIPSHAPE	SHLEP
SHELVING	SHIED	SHIN	SHIPWRECK	SHLEPPED
SHELVINGS	SHIEL	SHINDIES	SHIPWRECKED	SHLEPPING
SHELVY	SHIELD	SHINDIG	SHIPWRECKING	SHLEPS
SHEMOZZLE	SHIELDED	SHINDIGS	SHIPWRECKS	SHLIMAZEL
SHEMOZZLED	SHIELDER	SHINDY	SHIPYARD	SHLIMAZELS
SHEMOZZLES	SHIELDERS	SHINE	SHIPYARDS	SHLOK
SHEMOZZLING	SHIELDING	SHINED	SHIR	SHLOKS
SHEND	SHIELDS	SHINELESS	SHIRALEE	SHMOOSE
SHENDING	SHIELDUCK	SHINER	SHIRALEES	SHMOOSED
SHENDS	SHIELDUCKS	SHINERS	SHIRE	SHMOOSES
SHENT	SHIELED	SHINES	SHIREMAN	SHMOOSING
SHEPHERD	SHIELING	SHINESS	SHIREMEN	SHMOOZE
SHEPHERDED	SHIELINGS	SHINESSES	SHIRES	SHMOOZED
SHEPHERDING	SHIELS	SHINGLE	SHIRK	SHMOOZES
SHEPHERDS	SHIER	SHINGLED	SHIRKED	SHMOOZING
SHERBET	SHIERS	SHINGLER	SHIRKER	SHOAL
SHERBETS	SHIES	SHINGLERS	SHIRKERS	SHOALED
SHERD	SHIEST	SHINGLES	SHIRKING	SHOALER
SHERDS	SHIFT	SHINGLIER	SHIRKS	SHOALEST
SHERE	SHIFTED	SHINGLIEST	SHIRR	SHOALIER
SHEREEF	SHIFTER	SHINGLING	SHIRRA	SHOALIEST
SHEREEFS	SHIFTERS	SHINGLINGS	SHIRRAS	SHOALING
SHERIA	SHIFTIER	SHINGLY	SHIRRED	SHOALINGS
SHERIAS	SHIFTIEST	SHINIER	SHIRRING	SHOALNESS
SHERIAT	SHIFTILY	SHINIEST	SHIRRINGS	SHOALNESSES
SHERIATS	SHIFTING	SHINING	SHIRRS	SHOALS
SHERIF	SHIFTINGS	SHININGLY	SHIRS	SHOALWISE
SHERIFF	SHIFTLESS	SHINNE	SHIRT	SHOALY
SHERIFFS	SHIFTS	SHINNED	SHIRTED	SHOAT
SHERIFIAN	SHIFTY	SHINNES	SHIRTIER	SHOATS
SHERIFS	SHIGELLA	SHINNIED	SHIRTIEST	SHOCHET
SHERRIES	SHIGELLAS	SHINNIES	SHIRTING	SHOCHETIM
SHERRIS	SHIITAKE	SHINNING	SHIRTINGS	SHOCK
SHERRISES	SHIKAR	SHINNY	SHIRTLESS	SHOCKED
SHERRY	SHIKAREE	SHINNYING	SHIRTS	SHOCKER
SHES	SHIKAREES	SHINS	SHIRTY	SHOCKERS

SHOCKING	SHOOTABLE	SHORTHANDS	SHOWCARD	SHREWS
SHOCKS	SHOOTER	SHORTIE	SHOWCARDS	SHRIECH
SHOD	SHOOTERS	SHORTIES	SHOWCASE	SHRIECHED
SHODDIER	SHOOTING	SHORTING	SHOWCASED	SHRIECHES
SHODDIES	SHOOTINGS	SHORTISH	SHOWCASES	SHRIECHING
SHODDIEST	SHOOTIST	SHORTLY	SHOWCASING	SHRIEK
SHODDILY	SHOOTISTS	SHORTNESS	SHOWED	SHRIEKED
SHODDY	SHOOTS	SHORTNESSES	SHOWER	SHRIEKER
SHODER	SHOP	SHORTS	SHOWERED	SHRIEKERS
SHODERS	SHOPBOARD	SHORTY	SHOWERFUL	SHRIEKING
SHOE	SHOPBOARDS	SHOT	SHOWERING	SHRIEKINGS
SHOEBLACK	SHOPE	SHOTE	SHOWERINGS	SHRIEKS
SHOEBLACKS	SHOPFUL	SHOTES	SHOWERS	SHRIEVAL
SHOED	SHOPFULS	SHOTFIRER	SHOWERY	SHRIEVE
SHOEHORN	SHOPHAR	SHOTFIRERS	SHOWGHE	SHRIEVED
SHOEHORNED	SHOPHARS	SHOTGUN	SHOWGHES	SHRIEVES
SHOEHORNING	SHOPHROTH	SHOTGUNS	SHOWGIRL	SHRIEVING
SHOEHORNS	SHOPMAN	SHOTMAKER	SHOWGIRLS	SHRIFT
SHOEING	SHOPMEN	SHOTMAKERS	SHOWIER	SHRIFTS
SHOEINGS	SHOPPED	SHOTPROOF	SHOWIEST	SHRIGHT
SHOELESS	SHOPPER	SHOTS	SHOWILY	SHRIGHTS
SHOEMAKER	SHOPPERS	SHOTT	SHOWINESS	SHRIKE
SHOEMAKERS	SHOPPIER	SHOTTED	SHOWINESSES	SHRIKED
SHOER	SHOPPIEST	SHOTTEN	SHOWING	SHRIKES
SHOERS	SHOPPING	SHOTTING	SHOWINGS	SHRIKING
SHOES	SHOPPINGS	SHOTTLE	SHOWMAN	SHRILL
SHOESHINE	SHOPPY	SHOTTLES	SHOWMANLY	SHRILLED
SHOESHINES	SHOPS	SHOTTS	SHOWMEN	SHRILLER
SHOFAR	SHOPWORN	SHOUGH	SHOWN	SHRILLEST
SHOFARS	SHORAN	SHOUGHS	SHOWPIECE	SHRILLING
SHOFROTH	SHORANS	SHOULD	SHOWPIECES	SHRILLINGS
SHOG	SHORE	SHOULDER	SHOWPLACE	SHRILLS
SHOGGED	SHORED	SHOULDERED	SHOWPLACES	SHRILLY
SHOGGING	SHORELESS	SHOULDERING	SHOWROOM	SHRIMP
SHOGGLE	SHORELINE	SHOULDERINGS	SHOWROOMS	SHRIMPED
SHOGGLY	SHORELINES	SHOULDERS	SHOWS	SHRIMPER
SHOGS	SHOREMAN	SHOULDEST	SHOWY	SHRIMPERS
SHOGUN	SHOREMEN	SHOULDST	SHRADDHA	SHRIMPING
SHOGUNAL	SHORER	SHOUT	SHRADDHAS	SHRIMPINGS
SHOGUNATE	SHORERS	SHOUTED	SHRANK	SHRIMPS
SHOGUNATES	SHORES	SHOUTER	SHRAPNEL	SHRINAL
SHOGUNS	SHORESMAN	SHOUTERS	SHRAPNELS	SHRINE
SHOJI	SHORESMEN	SHOUTHER	SHRED	SHRINED
SHOJIS	SHOREWARD	SHOUTHERED	SHREDDED	SHRINES
SHOLA	SHOREWARDS	SHOUTHERING	SHREDDER	SHRINING
SHOLAS	SHORING	SHOUTHERS	SHREDDERS	SHRINK
SHONE	SHORINGS	SHOUTING	SHREDDIER	SHRINKAGE
SHOO	SHORN	SHOUTINGS	SHREDDIEST	SHRINKAGES
SHOOED	SHORT	SHOUTS	SHREDDING	SHRINKER
SHOOGIE	SHORTAGE	SHOVE	SHREDDINGS	SHRINKERS
SHOOGIED	SHORTAGES	SHOVED	SHREDDY	SHRINKING
SHOOGIEING	SHORTCAKE	SHOVEL	SHREDLESS	SHRINKS
SHOOGIES	SHORTCAKES	SHOVELER	SHREDS	SHRITCH
SHOOGLE	SHORTCUT	SHOVELERS	SHREEK	SHRITCHED
SHOOGLED	SHORTCUTS	SHOVELFUL	SHREEKED	SHRITCHES
SHOOGLES	SHORTED	SHOVELFULS	SHREEKING	SHRITCHING
SHOOGLIER	SHORTEN	SHOVELLED	SHREEKS	SHRIVE
SHOOGLIEST	SHORTENED	SHOVELLER	SHREIK	SHRIVED
SHOOGLING	SHORTENER	SHOVELLERS	SHREIKED	SHRIVEL
SHOOGLY	SHORTENERS	SHOVELLING	SHREIKING	SHRIVELLED
SHOOING	SHORTENING	SHOVELS	SHREIKS	SHRIVELLING
SHOOK	SHORTENINGS	SHOVER	SHREW	SHRIVELS
SHOOKS	SHORTENS	SHOVERS	SHREWD	SHRIVEN
SHOOL	SHORTER	SHOVES	SHREWDER	SHRIVER
SHOOLED	SHORTEST	SHOVING	SHREWDEST	SHRIVERS
SHOOLING	SHORTFALL	SHOW	SHREWDLY	SHRIVES
SHOOLS	SHORTFALLS	SHOWBIZ	SHREWED	SHRIVING
SHOON	SHORTGOWN	SHOWBIZZY	SHREWING	SHRIVINGS
SHOOS	SHORTGOWNS	SHOWBREAD	SHREWISH	SHROFF
SHOOT	SHORTHAND	SHOWBREADS	SHREWMICE	SHROFFAGE

SHROFFAGES	SHUFFLING	SIB	SICKNESSES	SIEMENS
SHROFFED	SHUFFLINGS	SIBB	SICKNURSE	SIEN
SHROFFING	SHUFTI	SIBBS	SICKNURSES	SIENNA
SHROFFS	SHUFTIES	SIBILANCE	SICKROOM	SIENNAS
SHROUD	SHUFTIS	SIBILANCES	SICKROOMS	SIENS
SHROUDED	SHUFTY	SIBILANCIES	SICKS	SIENT
SHROUDIER	SHUL	SIBILANCY	SICLIKE	SIENTS
SHROUDIEST	SHULS	SIBILANT	SICS	SIERRA
SHROUDING	SHUN	SIBILANTS	SIDA	SIERRAN
SHROUDINGS	SHUNLESS	SIBILATE	SIDALCEA	SIERRAS
SHROUDS	SHUNNED	SIBILATED	SIDALCEAS	SIESTA
SHROUDY	SHUNNING	SIBILATES	SIDAS	SIESTAS
SHROVE	SHUNS	SIBILATING	SIDDHA	SIETH
SHROVED	SHUNT	SIBILOUS	SIDDHAS	SIETHS
SHROVES	SHUNTED	SIBLING	SIDDHI	SIEVE
SHROVING	SHUNTER	SIBLINGS	SIDDHIS	SIEVED
SHROW	SHUNTERS	SIBS	SIDDUR	SIEVERT
SHROWD	SHUNTING	SIBSHIP	SIDDURIM	SIEVERTS
SHROWED	SHUNTINGS	SIBSHIPS	SIDE	SIEVES
SHROWING	SHUNTS	SIBYL	SIDEARM	SIEVING
SHROWS	SHUSH	SIBYLS	SIDEARMS	SIFAKA
SHRUB	SHUSHED	SIC	SIDEBOARD	SIFAKAS
SHRUBBED	SHUSHES	SICCAN	SIDEBOARDS	SIFFLE
SHRUBBERIES	SHUSHING	SICCAR	SIDEBURNS	SIFFLED
SHRUBBERY	SHUT	SICCATIVE	SIDECAR	SIFFLES
SHRUBBIER	SHUTS	SICCATIVES	SIDECARS	SIFFLING
SHRUBBIEST	SHUTTER	SICCED	SIDED	SIFT
SHRUBBING	SHUTTERED	SICCING	SIDELIGHT	SIFTED
SHRUBBY	SHUTTERING	SICCITIES	SIDELIGHTS	SIFTER
SHRUBLESS	SHUTTERINGS	SICCITY	SIDELING	SIFTERS
SHRUBS	SHUTTERS	SICE	SIDELOCK	SIFTING
SHRUG	SHUTTING	SICES	SIDELOCKS	SIFTINGLY
SHRUGGED	SHUTTLE	SICH	SIDELONG	SIFTINGS
SHRUGGING	SHUTTLED	SICILIANA	SIDER	SIFTS
SHRUGS	SHUTTLES	SICILIANAS	SIDERAL	SIGH
SHRUNK	SHUTTLING	SICILIANE	SIDEREAL	SIGHED
SHRUNKEN	SHWA	SICILIANO	SIDERITE	SIGHER
SHTCHI	SHWAS	SICILIANOS	SIDERITES	SIGHERS
SHTCHIS	SHY	SICK	SIDERITIC	SIGHFUL
SHTETL	SHYER	SICKED	SIDEROSES	SIGHING
SHTETLS	SHYERS	SICKEN	SIDEROSIS	SIGHINGLY
SHTICK	SHYEST	SICKENED	SIDEROSISES	SIGHS
SHTICKS	SHYING	SICKENER	SIDERS	SIGHT
SHTOOK	SHYISH	SICKENERS	SIDES	SIGHTED
SHTOOKS	SHYLY	SICKENING	SIDESMAN	SIGHTER
SHTOOM	SHYNESS	SICKENINGS	SIDESMEN	SIGHTERS
SHTUCK	SHYNESSES	SICKENS	SIDESWIPE	SIGHTING
SHTUCKS	SHYSTER	SICKER	SIDESWIPES	SIGHTLESS
SHTUM	SHYSTERS	SICKERLY	SIDEWALK	SIGHTLIER
SHTUMM	SI	SICKEST	SIDEWALKS	SIGHTLIEST
SHUBUNKIN	SIAL	SICKIE	SIDEWARD	SIGHTLY
SHUBUNKINS	SIALIC	SICKIES	SIDEWARDS	SIGHTS
SHUCK	SIALOGRAM	SICKING	SIDEWAY	SIGHTSAW
SHUCKED	SIALOGRAMS	SICKISH	SIDEWAYS	SIGHTSEE
SHUCKER	SIALOID	SICKISHLY	SIDEWISE	SIGHTSEEING
SHUCKERS	SIALOLITH	SICKLE	SIDHA	SIGHTSEEINGS
SHUCKING	SIALOLITHS	SICKLED	SIDHAS	SIGHTSEEN
SHUCKINGS	SIALON	SICKLEMAN	SIDING	SIGHTSEER
SHUCKS	SIALONS	SICKLEMEN	SIDINGS	SIGHTSEERS
SHUDDER	SIALS	SICKLES	SIDLE	SIGHTSEES
SHUDDERED	SIAMANG	SICKLIED	SIDLED	SIGIL
SHUDDERING	SIAMANGS	SICKLIER	SIDLES	SIGILLARY
SHUDDERINGS	SIAMESE	SICKLIES	SIDLING	SIGILLATE
SHUDDERS	SIAMESED	SICKLIEST	SIEGE	SIGILS
SHUDDERY	SIAMESES	SICKLILY	SIEGED	SIGISBEI
SHUFFLE	SIAMESING	SICKLY	SIEGER	SIGISBEO
SHUFFLED	SIAMEZE	SICKLYING	SIEGERS	SIGLA
SHUFFLER	SIAMEZED	SICKMAN	SIEGES	SIGMA
SHUFFLERS	SIAMEZES	SICKMEN	SIEGING	SIGMAS
SHUFFLES	SIAMEZING	SICKNESS	SIELD	SIGMATE

SIGMATED	SIGNORIES	SILICLES	SILTIEST	SIMNELS
SIGMATES	SIGNORINA	SILICON	SILTING	SIMONIAC
SIGMATIC	SIGNORINAS	SILICONE	SILTS	SIMONIACS
SIGMATING	SIGNORS	SILICONES	SILTSTONE	SIMONIES
SIGMATION	SIGNORY	SILICONS	SILTSTONES	SIMONIOUS
SIGMATIONS	SIGNPOST	SILICOSES	SILTY	SIMONIST
SIGMATISM	SIGNPOSTED	SILICOSIS	SILURID	SIMONISTS
SIGMATISMS	SIGNPOSTING	SILICOTIC	SILURIDS	SIMONY
SIGMATRON	SIGNPOSTS	SILICOTICS	SILURIST	SIMOOM
SIGMATRONS	SIGNS	SILICULA	SILURISTS	SIMOOMS
SIGMOID	SIKA	SILICULAS	SILUROID	SIMOON
SIGMOIDAL	SIKAS	SILICULE	SILUROIDS	SIMOONS
SIGN	SIKE	SILICULES	SILVA	SIMORG
SIGNAL	SIKES	SILING	SILVAE	SIMORGS
SIGNALISE	SILAGE	SILIQUA	SILVAN	SIMP
SIGNALISED	SILAGED	SILIQUAS	SILVANS	SIMPAI
SIGNALISES	SILAGES	SILIQUE	SILVAS	SIMPAIS
SIGNALISING	SILAGING	SILIQUES	SILVATIC	SIMPATICO
SIGNALIZE	SILANE	SILIQUOSE	SILVER	SIMPER
SIGNALIZED	SILANES	SILK	SILVERED	SIMPERED
SIGNALIZES	SILASTIC	SILKED	SILVERING	SIMPERER
SIGNALIZING	SILASTICS	SILKEN	SILVERINGS	SIMPERERS
SIGNALLED	SILD	SILKENED	SILVERISE	SIMPERING
SIGNALLER	SILDS	SILKENING	SILVERISED	SIMPERINGS
SIGNALLERS	SILE	SILKENS	SILVERISES	SIMPERS
SIGNALLING	SILED	SILKIE	SILVERISING	SIMPKIN
SIGNALLINGS	SILEN	SILKIER	SILVERIZE	SIMPKINS
SIGNALLY	SILENCE	SILKIES	SILVERIZED	SIMPLE
SIGNALMAN	SILENCED	SILKIEST	SILVERIZES	SIMPLED
SIGNALMEN	SILENCER	SILKILY	SILVERIZING	SIMPLER
SIGNALS	SILENCERS	SILKINESS	SILVERLY	SIMPLERS
SIGNARIES	SILENCES	SILKINESSES	SILVERN	SIMPLES
SIGNARY	SILENCING	SILKING	SILVERS	SIMPLESSE
SIGNATORIES	SILENE	SILKS	SILVERY	SIMPLESSES
SIGNATORY	SILENES	SILKTAIL	SIM	SIMPLEST
SIGNATURE	SILENS	SILKTAILS	SIMA	SIMPLETON
SIGNATURES	SILENT	SILKWEED	SIMAR	SIMPLETONS
SIGNBOARD	SILENTER	SILKWEEDS	SIMARRE	SIMPLEX
SIGNBOARDS	SILENTEST	SILKWORM	SIMARRES	SIMPLICES
SIGNED	SILENTLY	SILKWORMS	SIMARS	SIMPLIFIED
SIGNER	SILENTS	SILKY	SIMAS	SIMPLIFIES
SIGNERS	SILENUS	SILL	SIMI	SIMPLIFY
SIGNET	SILENUSES	SILLABUB	SIMIAL	SIMPLIFYING
SIGNETED	SILER	SILLABUBS	SIMIAN	SIMPLING
SIGNETS	SILERS	SILLADAR	SIMICUS	SIMPLINGS
SIGNEUR	SILES	SILLADARS	SIMILAR	SIMPLISM
SIGNEURIE	SILESIA	SILLER	SIMILARLY	SIMPLISMS
SIGNEURIES	SILESIAS	SILLERS	SIMILE	SIMPLIST
SIGNIEUR	SILEX	SILLIER	SIMILES	SIMPLISTE
SIGNIEURS	SILEXES	SILLIES	SIMILISE	SIMPLISTS
SIGNIFICS	SILICA	SILLIEST	SIMILISED	SIMPLY
SIGNIFIED	SILICANE	SILLILY	SIMILISES	SIMPS
SIGNIFIER	SILICANES	SILLINESS	SIMILISING	SIMS
SIGNIFIERS	SILICAS	SILLINESSES	SIMILIZE	SIMULACRA
SIGNIFIES	SILICATE	SILLOCK	SIMILIZED	SIMULACRE
SIGNIFY	SILICATED	SILLOCKS	SIMILIZES	SIMULACRES
SIGNIFYING	SILICATES	SILLS	SIMILIZING	SIMULANT
SIGNING	SILICATING	SILLY	SIMILOR	SIMULANTS
SIGNIOR	SILICEOUS	SILO	SIMILORS	SIMULAR
SIGNIORS	SILICIC	SILOED	SIMIOUS	SIMULARS
SIGNLESS	SILICIDE	SILOING	SIMIS	SIMULATE
SIGNOR	SILICIDES	SILOS	SIMITAR	SIMULATED
SIGNORA	SILICIFIED	SILPHIA	SIMITARS	SIMULATES
SIGNORAS	SILICIFIES	SILPHIUM	SIMKIN	SIMULATING
SIGNORE	SILICIFY	SILPHIUMS	SIMKINS	SIMULATOR
SIGNORES	SILICIFYING	SILT	SIMMER	SIMULATORS
SIGNORI	SILICIOUS	SILTATION	SIMMERED	SIMULCAST
SIGNORIA	SILICIUM	SILTATIONS	SIMMERING	SIMULCASTED
SIGNORIAL	SILICIUMS	SILTED	SIMMERS	SIMULCASTING
SIGNORIAS	SILICLE	SILTIER	SIMNEL	SIMULCASTS

SIMULIUM	SINGULTUS	SIPED	SIRUP	SITTING
SIMULIUMS	SINGULTUSES	SIPES	SIRUPED	SITTINGS
SIMURG	SINICAL	SIPHON	SIRUPING	SITUATE
SIMURGH	SINICISE	SIPHONAGE	SIRUPS	SITUATED
SIMURGHS	SINICISED	SIPHONAGES	SIRVENTE	SITUATES
SIMURGS	SINICISES	SIPHONAL	SIRVENTES	SITUATING
SIN	SINICISING	SIPHONATE	SIS	SITUATION
SINAPISM	SINICIZE	SIPHONED	SISAL	SITUATIONS
SINAPISMS	SINICIZED	SIPHONET	SISALS	SITULA
SINCE	SINICIZES	SIPHONETS	SISERARIES	SITULAE
SINCERE	SINICIZING	SIPHONIC	SISERARY	SITUS
SINCERELY	SINISTER	SIPHONING	SISES	SITUTUNGA
SINCERER	SINISTRAL	SIPHONS	SISKIN	SITUTUNGAS
SINCEREST	SINISTRALS	SIPHUNCLE	SISKINS	SITZKRIEG
SINCERITIES	SINK	SIPHUNCLES	SISS	SITZKRIEGS
SINCERITY	SINKAGE	SIPING	SISSERARIES	SIVER
SINCIPUT	SINKAGES	SIPPED	SISSERARY	SIVERS
SINCIPUTS	SINKER	SIPPER	SISSES	SIWASH
SIND	SINKERS	SIPPERS	SISSIER	SIWASHES
SINDED	SINKIER	SIPPET	SISSIES	SIX
SINDING	SINKIEST	SIPPETS	SISSIEST	SIXAINE
SINDINGS	SINKING	SIPPING	SISSOO	SIXAINES
SINDON	SINKINGS	SIPPLE	SISSOOS	SIXER
SINDONS	SINKS	SIPPLED	SISSY	SIXERS
SINDS	SINKY	SIPPLES	SIST	SIXES
SINE	SINLESS	SIPPLING	SISTED	SIXFOLD
SINECURE	SINLESSLY	SIPS	SISTER	SIXPENCE
SINECURES	SINNED	SIR	SISTERED	SIXPENCES
SINES	SINNER	SIRCAR	SISTERING	SIXPENNIES
SINEW	SINNERED	SIRCARS	SISTERLY	SIXPENNY
SINEWED	SINNERING	SIRDAR	SISTERS	SIXSCORE
SINEWING	SINNERS	SIRDARS	SISTING	SIXSCORES
SINEWLESS	SINNET	SIRE	SISTRA	SIXTE
SINEWS	SINNETS	SIRED	SISTRUM	SIXTEEN
SINEWY	SINNING	SIREN	SISTS	SIXTEENER
SINFONIA	SINOEKETE	SIRENE	SIT	SIXTEENERS
SINFONIAS	SINOEKETES	SIRENES	SITAR	SIXTEENMO
SINFUL	SINOPIA	SIRENIAN	SITARS	SIXTEENMOS
SING	SINOPIAS	SIRENIANS	SITATUNGA	SIXTEENS
SINGABLE	SINOPIS	SIRENIC	SITATUNGAS	SIXTEENTH
SINGE	SINOPISES	SIRENS	SITCOM	SIXTEENTHS
SINGED	SINOPITE	SIRES	SITCOMS	SIXTES
SINGEING	SINOPITES	SIRGANG	SITDOWN	SIXTH
SINGER	SINS	SIRGANGS	SITDOWNS	SIXTHLY
SINGERS	SINSYNE	SIRI	SITE	SIXTHS
SINGES	SINTER	SIRIASES	SITED	SIXTIES
SINGING	SINTERED	SIRIASIS	SITES	SIXTIETH
SINGINGLY	SINTERING	SIRIH	SITFAST	SIXTIETHS
SINGINGS	SINTERS	SIRIHS	SITFASTS	SIXTY
SINGLE	SINTERY	SIRING	SITH	SIZABLE
SINGLED	SINUATE	SIRIS	SITHE	SIZAR
SINGLES	SINUATED	SIRKAR	SITHED	SIZARS
SINGLET	SINUATELY	SIRKARS	SITHEN	SIZARSHIP
SINGLETON	SINUATION	SIRLOIN	SITHENCE	SIZARSHIPS
SINGLETONS	SINUATIONS	SIRLOINS	SITHENS	SIZE
SINGLETS	SINUITIS	SIRNAME	SITHES	SIZEABLE
SINGLING	SINUITISES	SIRNAMED	SITHING	SIZED
SINGLINGS	SINUOSE	SIRNAMES	SITING	SIZEL
SINGLY	SINUOSITIES	SIRNAMING	SITIOLOGIES	SIZELS
SINGS	SINUOSITY	SIROC	SITIOLOGY	SIZER
SINGSONG	SINUOUS	SIROCCO	SITOLOGIES	SIZERS
SINGSONGED	SINUOUSLY	SIROCCOS	SITOLOGY	SIZES
SINGSONGING	SINUS	SIROCS	SITREP	SIZIER
SINGSONGS	SINUSES	SIRRAH	SITREPS	SIZIEST
SINGSPIEL	SINUSITIS	SIRRAHS	SITS	SIZINESS
SINGSPIELS	SINUSITISES	SIRRED	SITTAR	SIZINESSES
SINGULAR	SINUSOID	SIRREE	SITTARS	SIZING
SINGULARS	SINUSOIDS	SIRREES	SITTER	SIZINGS
SINGULT	SIP	SIRRING	SITTERS	SIZY
SINGULTS	SIPE	SIRS	SITTINE	SIZZLE

SIZZLED
SIZZLER
SIZZLERS
SIZZLES
SIZZLING
SIZZLINGS
SJAMBOK
SJAMBOKKED
SJAMBOKKING
SJAMBOKS
SKA
SKAIL
SKAILED
SKAILING
SKAILS
SKAITH
SKAITHED
SKAITHING
SKAITHS
SKALD
SKALDIC
SKALDS
SKART
SKARTH
SKARTHS
SKARTS
SKAS
SKAT
SKATE
SKATED
SKATER
SKATERS
SKATES
SKATING
SKATINGS
SKATOLE
SKATOLES
SKATOLOGIES
SKATOLOGY
SKATS
SKATT
SKATTS
SKAW
SKAWS
SKEAN
SKEANS
SKEAR
SKEARED
SKEARING
SKEARS
SKEARY
SKEDADDLE
SKEDADDLED
SKEDADDLES
SKEDADDLING
SKEELIER
SKEELIEST
SKEELY
SKEER
SKEERED
SKEERING
SKEERS
SKEERY
SKEESICKS
SKEET
SKEETER
SKEETERS
SKEETS
SKEG
SKEGGER

SKEGGERS
SKEGS
SKEIGH
SKEIGHER
SKEIGHEST
SKEIN
SKEINS
SKELDER
SKELDERED
SKELDERING
SKELDERS
SKELETAL
SKELETON
SKELETONS
SKELF
SKELFS
SKELLIE
SKELLIED
SKELLIER
SKELLIES
SKELLIEST
SKELLOCH
SKELLOCHED
SKELLOCHING
SKELLOCHS
SKELLUM
SKELLUMS
SKELLY
SKELLYING
SKELM
SKELMS
SKELP
SKELPED
SKELPING
SKELPINGS
SKELPS
SKELTER
SKELTERED
SKELTERING
SKELTERS
SKENE
SKENES
SKEO
SKEOS
SKEP
SKEPFUL
SKEPFULS
SKEPPED
SKEPPING
SKEPS
SKEPSES
SKEPSIS
SKEPTIC
SKEPTICS
SKER
SKERRED
SKERRICK
SKERRICKS
SKERRIES
SKERRING
SKERRY
SKERS
SKETCH
SKETCHED
SKETCHER
SKETCHERS
SKETCHES
SKETCHIER
SKETCHIEST
SKETCHILY

SKETCHING
SKETCHY
SKEW
SKEWBALD
SKEWBALDS
SKEWED
SKEWER
SKEWERED
SKEWERING
SKEWERS
SKEWEST
SKEWING
SKEWS
SKI
SKIABLE
SKIAGRAM
SKIAGRAMS
SKIAGRAPH
SKIAGRAPHS
SKIAMACHIES
SKIAMACHY
SKIASCOPIES
SKIASCOPY
SKIATRON
SKIATRONS
SKID
SKIDDED
SKIDDING
SKIDOO
SKIDOOS
SKIDPAN
SKIDPANS
SKIDS
SKIED
SKIER
SKIERS
SKIES
SKIEY
SKIEYER
SKIEYEST
SKIFF
SKIFFED
SKIFFING
SKIFFLE
SKIFFLES
SKIFFS
SKIING
SKIINGS
SKIJORING
SKIJORINGS
SKILFUL
SKILFULLY
SKILL
SKILLED
SKILLESS
SKILLET
SKILLETS
SKILLIER
SKILLIES
SKILLIEST
SKILLING
SKILLINGS
SKILLION
SKILLIONS
SKILLS
SKILLY
SKIM
SKIMMED
SKIMMER
SKIMMERS

SKIMMIA
SKIMMIAS
SKIMMING
SKIMMINGS
SKIMP
SKIMPED
SKIMPIER
SKIMPIEST
SKIMPILY
SKIMPING
SKIMPS
SKIMPY
SKIMS
SKIN
SKINFLICK
SKINFLICKS
SKINFLINT
SKINFLINTS
SKINFOOD
SKINFOODS
SKINFUL
SKINFULS
SKINHEAD
SKINHEADS
SKINK
SKINKED
SKINKER
SKINKERS
SKINKING
SKINKS
SKINLESS
SKINNED
SKINNER
SKINNERS
SKINNIER
SKINNIEST
SKINNING
SKINNY
SKINS
SKINT
SKINTER
SKINTEST
SKIO
SKIOS
SKIP
SKIPJACK
SKIPJACKS
SKIPPED
SKIPPER
SKIPPERED
SKIPPERING
SKIPPERS
SKIPPET
SKIPPETS
SKIPPING
SKIPPINGS
SKIPS
SKIRL
SKIRLED
SKIRLING
SKIRLINGS
SKIRLS
SKIRMISH
SKIRMISHED
SKIRMISHES
SKIRMISHING
SKIRMISHINGS
SKIRR
SKIRRED
SKIRRET

SKIRRETS
SKIRRING
SKIRRS
SKIRT
SKIRTED
SKIRTER
SKIRTERS
SKIRTING
SKIRTINGS
SKIRTLESS
SKIRTS
SKIS
SKIT
SKITE
SKITED
SKITES
SKITING
SKITS
SKITTER
SKITTERED
SKITTERING
SKITTERS
SKITTISH
SKITTLE
SKITTLED
SKITTLES
SKITTLING
SKIVE
SKIVED
SKIVER
SKIVERED
SKIVERING
SKIVERS
SKIVES
SKIVIE
SKIVIER
SKIVIEST
SKIVING
SKIVINGS
SKIVVIES
SKIVVY
SKIVY
SKLATE
SKLATED
SKLATES
SKLATING
SKLENT
SKLENTED
SKLENTING
SKLENTS
SKLIFF
SKLIFFS
SKLIM
SKLIMMED
SKLIMMING
SKLIMS
SKOAL
SKOFF
SKOFFED
SKOFFING
SKOFFS
SKOKIAAN
SKOKIAANS
SKOL
SKOLIA
SKOLION
SKOLLIE
SKOLLIES
SKOLLY
SKRAN

SKRANS	SKURRYING	SLABSTONES	SLANGIEST	SLAVERING
SKREAKY	SKUTTLE	SLACK	SLANGILY	SLAVERS
SKREEN	SKUTTLED	SLACKED	SLANGING	SLAVERY
SKREENE	SKUTTLES	SLACKEN	SLANGINGS	SLAVES
SKREENES	SKUTTLING	SLACKENED	SLANGISH	SLAVEY
SKREENS	SKY	SLACKENING	SLANGS	SLAVEYS
SKREIGH	SKYBORN	SLACKENINGS	SLANGULAR	SLAVING
SKREIGHED	SKYCLAD	SLACKENS	SLANGY	SLAVISH
SKREIGHING	SKYER	SLACKER	SLANT	SLAVISHLY
SKREIGHS	SKYERS	SLACKERS	SLANTED	SLAVOCRAT
SKRIECH	SKYEY	SLACKEST	SLANTING	SLAVOCRATS
SKRIECHED	SKYIER	SLACKING	SLANTLY	SLAW
SKRIECHING	SKYIEST	SLACKLY	SLANTS	SLAWS
SKRIECHS	SKYING	SLACKNESS	SLANTWAYS	SLAY
SKRIED	SKYISH	SLACKNESSES	SLANTWISE	SLAYED
SKRIEGH	SKYJACK	SLACKS	SLAP	SLAYER
SKRIEGHED	SKYJACKED	SLADANG	SLAPJACK	SLAYERS
SKRIEGHING	SKYJACKER	SLADANGS	SLAPJACKS	SLAYING
SKRIEGHS	SKYJACKERS	SLADE	SLAPPED	SLAYS
SKRIES	SKYJACKING	SLADES	SLAPPER	SLEAVE
SKRIK	SKYJACKINGS	SLAE	SLAPPERS	SLEAVED
SKRIKS	SKYJACKS	SLAES	SLAPPING	SLEAVES
SKRIMMAGE	SKYLARK	SLAG	SLAPS	SLEAVING
SKRIMMAGED	SKYLARKED	SLAGGED	SLAPSTICK	SLEAZE
SKRIMMAGES	SKYLARKING	SLAGGIER	SLAPSTICKS	SLEAZES
SKRIMMAGING	SKYLARKINGS	SLAGGIEST	SLASH	SLEAZIER
SKRIMP	SKYLARKS	SLAGGING	SLASHED	SLEAZIEST
SKRIMPED	SKYLIGHT	SLAGGY	SLASHER	SLEAZILY
SKRIMPING	SKYLIGHTS	SLAGS	SLASHERS	SLEAZY
SKRIMPS	SKYLINE	SLAID	SLASHES	SLED
SKRUMP	SKYLINES	SLAIN	SLASHING	SLEDDED
SKRUMPED	SKYMAN	SLÀINTE	SLASHINGS	SLEDDING
SKRUMPING	SKYMEN	SLAIRG	SLAT	SLEDDINGS
SKRUMPS	SKYR	SLAIRGED	SLATE	SLEDED
SKRY	SKYRE	SLAIRGING	SLATED	SLEDGE
SKRYER	SKYRED	SLAIRGS	SLATER	SLEDGED
SKRYERS	SKYRES	SLAISTER	SLATERS	SLEDGER
SKRYING	SKYRING	SLAISTERED	SLATES	SLEDGERS
SKUA	SKYROCKET	SLAISTERIES	SLATHER	SLEDGES
SKUAS	SKYROCKETED	SLAISTERING	SLATHERED	SLEDGING
SKUDLER	SKYROCKETING	SLAISTERS	SLATHERING	SLEDGINGS
SKUDLERS	SKYROCKETS	SLAISTERY	SLATHERS	SLEDS
SKUG	SKYRS	SLAKE	SLATIER	SLEE
SKUGGED	SKYSAIL	SLAKED	SLATIEST	SLEECH
SKUGGING	SKYSAILS	SLAKELESS	SLATINESS	SLEECHES
SKUGS	SKYSCAPE	SLAKES	SLATINESSES	SLEECHY
SKULK	SKYSCAPES	SLAKING	SLATING	SLEEK
SKULKED	SKYTE	SLALOM	SLATINGS	SLEEKED
SKULKER	SKYTED	SLALOMED	SLATS	SLEEKEN
SKULKERS	SKYTES	SLALOMING	SLATTED	SLEEKENED
SKULKING	SKYTING	SLALOMS	SLATTER	SLEEKENING
SKULKINGS	SKYWARD	SLAM	SLATTERED	SLEEKENS
SKULKS	SKYWARDS	SLAMMAKIN	SLATTERING	SLEEKER
SKULL	SKYWAY	SLAMMAKINS	SLATTERN	SLEEKERS
SKULLCAP	SKYWAYS	SLAMMED	SLATTERNS	SLEEKEST
SKULLCAPS	SLAB	SLAMMER	SLATTERS	SLEEKIER
SKULLS	SLABBED	SLAMMERS	SLATTERY	SLEEKIEST
SKULPIN	SLABBER	SLAMMING	SLATTING	SLEEKING
SKULPINS	SLABBERED	SLAMS	SLATY	SLEEKINGS
SKUMMER	SLABBERER	SLANDER	SLAUGHTER	SLEEKIT
SKUMMERED	SLABBERERS	SLANDERED	SLAUGHTERED	SLEEKLY
SKUMMERING	SLABBERING	SLANDERER	SLAUGHTERING	SLEEKNESS
SKUMMERS	SLABBERS	SLANDERERS	SLAUGHTERS	SLEEKNESSES
SKUNK	SLABBERY	SLANDERING	SLAVE	SLEEKS
SKUNKED	SLABBIER	SLANDERS	SLAVED	SLEEKY
SKUNKING	SLABBIEST	SLANE	SLAVER	SLEEP
SKUNKS	SLABBING	SLANES	SLAVERED	SLEEPER
SKURRIED	SLABBY	SLANG	SLAVERER	SLEEPERS
SKURRIES	SLABS	SLANGED	SLAVERERS	SLEEPERY
SKURRY	SLABSTONE	SLANGIER	SLAVERIES	SLEEPIER

SLEEPIEST
SLEEPILY
SLEEPING
SLEEPINGS
SLEEPLESS
SLEEPRY
SLEEPS
SLEEPY
SLEER
SLEEST
SLEET
SLEETED
SLEETIER
SLEETIEST
SLEETING
SLEETS
SLEETY
SLEEVE
SLEEVED
SLEEVER
SLEEVERS
SLEEVES
SLEEVING
SLEEVINGS
SLEEZIER
SLEEZIEST
SLEEZY
SLEIDED
SLEIGH
SLEIGHED
SLEIGHING
SLEIGHINGS
SLEIGHS
SLEIGHT
SLEIGHTS
SLENDER
SLENDERER
SLENDEREST
SLENDERLY
SLEPT
SLEUTH
SLEUTHED
SLEUTHING
SLEUTHS
SLEW
SLEWED
SLEWING
SLEWS
SLEY
SLEYS
SLICE
SLICED
SLICER
SLICERS
SLICES
SLICING
SLICINGS
SLICK
SLICKED
SLICKEN
SLICKENED
SLICKENING
SLICKENS
SLICKER
SLICKERS
SLICKEST
SLICKING
SLICKINGS
SLICKLY
SLICKNESS

SLICKNESSES
SLICKS
SLID
SLIDDEN
SLIDDER
SLIDDERED
SLIDDERING
SLIDDERS
SLIDDERY
SLIDE
SLIDED
SLIDER
SLIDERS
SLIDES
SLIDING
SLIDINGLY
SLIDINGS
SLIER
SLIEST
SLIGHT
SLIGHTED
SLIGHTER
SLIGHTEST
SLIGHTING
SLIGHTISH
SLIGHTLY
SLIGHTS
SLILY
SLIM
SLIME
SLIMED
SLIMES
SLIMIER
SLIMIEST
SLIMILY
SLIMINESS
SLIMINESSES
SLIMING
SLIMLINE
SLIMLY
SLIMMED
SLIMMER
SLIMMERS
SLIMMEST
SLIMMING
SLIMMINGS
SLIMMISH
SLIMNESS
SLIMNESSES
SLIMS
SLIMSY
SLIMY
SLING
SLINGER
SLINGERS
SLINGING
SLINGS
SLINGSHOT
SLINGSHOTS
SLINK
SLINKER
SLINKERS
SLINKIER
SLINKIEST
SLINKING
SLINKS
SLINKSKIN
SLINKSKINS
SLINKWEED
SLINKWEEDS

SLINKY
SLIP
SLIPE
SLIPES
SLIPFORM
SLIPPAGE
SLIPPAGES
SLIPPED
SLIPPER
SLIPPERED
SLIPPERIER
SLIPPERIEST
SLIPPERING
SLIPPERS
SLIPPERY
SLIPPIER
SLIPPIEST
SLIPPING
SLIPPY
SLIPRAIL
SLIPRAILS
SLIPS
SLIPSHOD
SLIPSLOP
SLIPSLOPS
SLIPT
SLIPWARE
SLIPWARES
SLIPWAY
SLIPWAYS
SLISH
SLISHES
SLIT
SLITHER
SLITHERED
SLITHERIER
SLITHERIEST
SLITHERING
SLITHERS
SLITHERY
SLITS
SLITTER
SLITTERS
SLITTING
SLIVE
SLIVED
SLIVEN
SLIVER
SLIVERED
SLIVERING
SLIVERS
SLIVES
SLIVING
SLIVOVIC
SLIVOVICA
SLIVOVICAS
SLIVOVICS
SLIVOVITZ
SLIVOVITZES
SLIVOWITZ
SLIVOWITZES
SLOAN
SLOANS
SLOB
SLOBBER
SLOBBERED
SLOBBERING
SLOBBERS
SLOBBERY
SLOBBIER

SLOBBIEST
SLOBBY
SLOBLAND
SLOBLANDS
SLOBS
SLOCKEN
SLOCKENED
SLOCKENING
SLOCKENS
SLOE
SLOEBUSH
SLOEBUSHES
SLOES
SLOETHORN
SLOETHORNS
SLOETREE
SLOETREES
SLOG
SLOGAN
SLOGANEER
SLOGANEERED
SLOGANEERING
SLOGANEERINGS
SLOGANEERS
SLOGANISE
SLOGANISED
SLOGANISES
SLOGANISING
SLOGANISINGS
SLOGANIZE
SLOGANIZED
SLOGANIZES
SLOGANIZING
SLOGANIZINGS
SLOGANS
SLOGGED
SLOGGER
SLOGGERS
SLOGGING
SLOGGORNE
SLOGGORNES
SLOGHORNE
SLOGHORNES
SLOGORNE
SLOGORNES
SLOGS
SLOID
SLOIDS
SLOKEN
SLOKENED
SLOKENING
SLOKENS
SLOOM
SLOOMED
SLOOMING
SLOOMS
SLOOMY
SLOOP
SLOOPS
SLOOT
SLOOTS
SLOP
SLOPE
SLOPED
SLOPES
SLOPEWISE
SLOPIER
SLOPIEST
SLOPING
SLOPINGLY

SLOPPED
SLOPPIER
SLOPPIEST
SLOPPILY
SLOPPING
SLOPPY
SLOPS
SLOPWORK
SLOPWORKS
SLOPY
SLOSH
SLOSHED
SLOSHES
SLOSHIER
SLOSHIEST
SLOSHING
SLOSHY
SLOT
SLOTH
SLOTHED
SLOTHFUL
SLOTHING
SLOTHS
SLOTS
SLOTTED
SLOTTER
SLOTTERS
SLOTTING
SLOUCH
SLOUCHED
SLOUCHER
SLOUCHERS
SLOUCHES
SLOUCHIER
SLOUCHIEST
SLOUCHING
SLOUCHY
SLOUGH
SLOUGHED
SLOUGHIER
SLOUGHIEST
SLOUGHING
SLOUGHS
SLOUGHY
SLOVE
SLOVEN
SLOVENLY
SLOVENRIES
SLOVENRY
SLOVENS
SLOW
SLOWBACK
SLOWBACKS
SLOWCOACH
SLOWCOACHES
SLOWED
SLOWER
SLOWEST
SLOWING
SLOWINGS
SLOWISH
SLOWLY
SLOWNESS
SLOWNESSES
SLOWPOKE
SLOWPOKES
SLOWS
SLOYD
SLOYDS
SLUB

SLUBB	SLUMMOCKS	SMALLS	SMEARILY	SMILEFUL
SLUBBED	SLUMMY	SMALM	SMEARING	SMILELESS
SLUBBER	SLUMP	SMALMED	SMEARS	SMILER
SLUBBERED	SLUMPED	SMALMIER	SMEARY	SMILERS
SLUBBERING	SLUMPIER	SMALMIEST	SMEATH	SMILES
SLUBBERINGS	SLUMPIEST	SMALMILY	SMEATHS	SMILET
SLUBBERS	SLUMPING	SMALMING	SMECTIC	SMILETS
SLUBBIER	SLUMPS	SMALMS	SMEDDUM	SMILING
SLUBBIEST	SLUMPY	SMALMY	SMEDDUMS	SMILINGLY
SLUBBING	SLUMS	SMALT	SMEE	SMILINGS
SLUBBINGS	SLUNG	SMALTI	SMEECH	SMILODON
SLUBBS	SLUNK	SMALTITE	SMEECHED	SMILODONS
SLUBBY	SLUR	SMALTITES	SMEECHES	SMIR
SLUBS	SLURB	SMALTO	SMEECHING	SMIRCH
SLUDGE	SLURBS	SMALTOS	SMEEK	SMIRCHED
SLUDGES	SLURP	SMALTS	SMEEKED	SMIRCHES
SLUDGIER	SLURPED	SMARAGD	SMEEKING	SMIRCHING
SLUDGIEST	SLURPING	SMARAGDS	SMEEKS	SMIRK
SLUDGY	SLURPS	SMARM	SMEES	SMIRKED
SLUE	SLURRED	SMARMED	SMEETH	SMIRKIER
SLUED	SLURRIES	SMARMIER	SMEETHS	SMIRKIEST
SLUEING	SLURRING	SMARMIEST	SMEGMA	SMIRKING
SLUES	SLURRY	SMARMILY	SMEGMAS	SMIRKS
SLUG	SLURS	SMARMING	SMELL	SMIRKY
SLUGFEST	SLUSE	SMARMS	SMELLED	SMIRR
SLUGFESTS	SLUSES	SMARMY	SMELLER	SMIRRED
SLUGGABED	SLUSH	SMART	SMELLERS	SMIRRIER
SLUGGABEDS	SLUSHED	SMARTARSE	SMELLIER	SMIRRIEST
SLUGGARD	SLUSHES	SMARTARSES	SMELLIEST	SMIRRING
SLUGGARDS	SLUSHIER	SMARTASS	SMELLING	SMIRRS
SLUGGED	SLUSHIEST	SMARTASSES	SMELLINGS	SMIRRY
SLUGGER	SLUSHING	SMARTED	SMELLS	SMIRS
SLUGGERS	SLUSHY	SMARTEN	SMELLY	SMIT
SLUGGING	SLUT	SMARTENED	SMELT	SMITE
SLUGGISH	SLUTS	SMARTENING	SMELTED	SMITER
SLUGHORN	SLUTTERIES	SMARTENS	SMELTER	SMITERS
SLUGHORNE	SLUTTERY	SMARTER	SMELTERIES	SMITES
SLUGHORNES	SLUTTISH	SMARTEST	SMELTERS	SMITH
SLUGHORNS	SLY	SMARTIE	SMELTERY	SMITHED
SLUGS	SLYBOOTS	SMARTIES	SMELTING	SMITHERIES
SLUICE	SLYER	SMARTING	SMELTINGS	SMITHERS
SLUICED	SLYEST	SMARTLY	SMELTS	SMITHERY
SLUICES	SLYISH	SMARTNESS	SMEUSE	SMITHIED
SLUICIER	SLYLY	SMARTNESSES	SMEUSES	SMITHIES
SLUICIEST	SLYNESS	SMARTS	SMEW	SMITHING
SLUICING	SLYNESSES	SMARTY	SMEWS	SMITHS
SLUICY	SLYPE	SMASH	SMICKER	SMITHY
SLUIT	SLYPES	SMASHED	SMICKERED	SMITHYING
SLUITS	SMA	SMASHER	SMICKERING	SMITING
SLUM	SMACK	SMASHEROO	SMICKERINGS	SMITS
SLUMBER	SMACKED	SMASHEROOS	SMICKERS	SMITTED
SLUMBERED	SMACKER	SMASHERS	SMICKET	SMITTEN
SLUMBERER	SMACKERS	SMASHES	SMICKETS	SMITTING
SLUMBERERS	SMACKING	SMASHING	SMICKLY	SMITTLE
SLUMBERING	SMACKINGS	SMASHINGS	SMIDDIES	SMOCK
SLUMBERINGS	SMACKS	SMATCH	SMIDDY	SMOCKED
SLUMBERS	SMAIK	SMATCHED	SMIDGEN	SMOCKING
SLUMBERY	SMAIKS	SMATCHES	SMIDGENS	SMOCKINGS
SLUMBROUS	SMALL	SMATCHING	SMIDGEON	SMOCKS
SLUMBRY	SMALLAGE	SMATTER	SMIDGEONS	SMOG
SLUMMED	SMALLAGES	SMATTERED	SMIDGIN	SMOGGIER
SLUMMER	SMALLED	SMATTERER	SMIDGINS	SMOGGIEST
SLUMMERS	SMALLER	SMATTERERS	SMIGHT	SMOGGY
SLUMMIER	SMALLEST	SMATTERING	SMIGHTED	SMOGS
SLUMMIEST	SMALLING	SMATTERINGS	SMIGHTING	SMOILE
SLUMMING	SMALLISH	SMATTERS	SMIGHTS	SMOILED
SLUMMINGS	SMALLNESS	SMEAR	SMILAX	SMOILES
SLUMMOCK	SMALLNESSES	SMEARED	SMILAXES	SMOILING
SLUMMOCKED	SMALLPOX	SMEARIER	SMILE	SMOKABLE
SLUMMOCKING	SMALLPOXES	SMEARIEST	SMILED	SMOKE

SMOKED	SMOUCHED	SMYTRIE	SNAPPING	SNEAKSBIES
SMOKELESS	SMOUCHES	SMYTRIES	SNAPPINGS	SNEAKSBY
SMOKER	SMOUCHING	SNAB	SNAPPISH	SNEAKY
SMOKERS	SMOULDER	SNABBLE	SNAPPY	SNEAP
SMOKES	SMOULDERED	SNABBLED	SNAPS	SNEAPED
SMOKIER	SMOULDERING	SNABBLES	SNAPSHOT	SNEAPING
SMOKIES	SMOULDERS	SNABBLING	SNAPSHOTS	SNEAPS
SMOKIEST	SMOULDRY	SNABS	SNAR	SNEATH
SMOKILY	SMOUS	SNACK	SNARE	SNEATHS
SMOKINESS	SMOUSE	SNACKED	SNARED	SNEB
SMOKINESSES	SMOUSED	SNACKING	SNARER	SNEBBE
SMOKING	SMOUSER	SNACKS	SNARERS	SNEBBED
SMOKINGS	SMOUSERS	SNAFFLE	SNARES	SNEBBES
SMOKO	SMOUSES	SNAFFLED	SNARIER	SNEBBING
SMOKOS	SMOUSING	SNAFFLES	SNARIEST	SNEBS
SMOKY	SMOUT	SNAFFLING	SNARING	SNECK
SMOLDER	SMOUTED	SNAFU	SNARINGS	SNECKED
SMOLDERED	SMOUTING	SNAFUS	SNARK	SNECKING
SMOLDERING	SMOUTS	SNAG	SNARKS	SNECKS
SMOLDERS	SMOWT	SNAGGED	SNARL	SNED
SMOLT	SMOWTS	SNAGGIER	SNARLED	SNEDDED
SMOLTS	SMOYLE	SNAGGIEST	SNARLER	SNEDDING
SMOOCH	SMOYLED	SNAGGING	SNARLERS	SNEDS
SMOOCHED	SMOYLES	SNAGGY	SNARLIER	SNEE
SMOOCHES	SMOYLING	SNAGS	SNARLIEST	SNEED
SMOOCHING	SMUDGE	SNAIL	SNARLING	SNEEING
SMOOR	SMUDGED	SNAILED	SNARLINGS	SNEER
SMOORED	SMUDGER	SNAILERIES	SNARLS	SNEERED
SMOORING	SMUDGERS	SNAILERY	SNARLY	SNEERER
SMOORS	SMUDGES	SNAILIER	SNARRED	SNEERERS
SMOOT	SMUDGIER	SNAILIEST	SNARRING	SNEERIER
SMOOTED	SMUDGIEST	SNAILING	SNARS	SNEERIEST
SMOOTH	SMUDGILY	SNAILS	SNARY	SNEERING
SMOOTHE	SMUDGING	SNAILY	SNASH	SNEERINGS
SMOOTHED	SMUDGY	SNAKE	SNASHED	SNEERS
SMOOTHEN	SMUG	SNAKEBIRD	SNASHES	SNEERY
SMOOTHENED	SMUGGED	SNAKEBIRDS	SNASHING	SNEES
SMOOTHENING	SMUGGER	SNAKEBITE	SNASTE	SNEESH
SMOOTHENS	SMUGGEST	SNAKEBITES	SNASTES	SNEESHAN
SMOOTHER	SMUGGING	SNAKED	SNATCH	SNEESHANS
SMOOTHERS	SMUGGLE	SNAKELIKE	SNATCHED	SNEESHES
SMOOTHES	SMUGGLED	SNAKEROOT	SNATCHER	SNEESHIN
SMOOTHEST	SMUGGLER	SNAKEROOTS	SNATCHERS	SNEESHING
SMOOTHIE	SMUGGLERS	SNAKES	SNATCHES	SNEESHINGS
SMOOTHIES	SMUGGLES	SNAKESKIN	SNATCHIER	SNEESHINS
SMOOTHING	SMUGGLING	SNAKESKINS	SNATCHIEST	SNEEZE
SMOOTHINGS	SMUGGLINGS	SNAKEWEED	SNATCHILY	SNEEZED
SMOOTHISH	SMUGLY	SNAKEWEEDS	SNATCHING	SNEEZER
SMOOTHLY	SMUGNESS	SNAKEWISE	SNATCHY	SNEEZERS
SMOOTHS	SMUGNESSES	SNAKEWOOD	SNATH	SNEEZES
SMOOTING	SMUGS	SNAKEWOODS	SNATHE	SNEEZIER
SMOOTS	SMUR	SNAKIER	SNATHES	SNEEZIEST
SM0RBR0D	SMURRED	SNAKIEST	SNATHS	SNEEZING
SM0RBR0DS	SMURRIER	SNAKILY	SNAZZIER	SNEEZINGS
SMORE	SMURRIEST	SNAKINESS	SNAZZIEST	SNEEZY
SMORED	SMURRING	SNAKINESSES	SNAZZY	SNELL
SMORES	SMURRY	SNAKING	SNEAD	SNELLED
SMORING	SMURS	SNAKISH	SNEADS	SNELLER
SMORZANDO	SMUT	SNAKY	SNEAK	SNELLEST
SMORZATO	SMUTCH	SNAP	SNEAKED	SNELLING
SMOTE	SMUTCHED	SNAPHANCE	SNEAKER	SNELLS
SMOTHER	SMUTCHES	SNAPHANCES	SNEAKERS	SNELLY
SMOTHERED	SMUTCHING	SNAPPED	SNEAKEUP	SNIB
SMOTHERER	SMUTS	SNAPPER	SNEAKEUPS	SNIBBED
SMOTHERERS	SMUTTED	SNAPPERED	SNEAKIER	SNIBBING
SMOTHERING	SMUTTIER	SNAPPERING	SNEAKIEST	SNIBS
SMOTHERINGS	SMUTTIEST	SNAPPERS	SNEAKILY	SNICK
SMOTHERS	SMUTTILY	SNAPPIER	SNEAKING	SNICKED
SMOTHERY	SMUTTING	SNAPPIEST	SNEAKISH	SNICKER
SMOUCH	SMUTTY	SNAPPILY	SNEAKS	SNICKERED

SOAR

317

SNICKERING
SNICKERS
SNICKET
SNICKETS
SNICKING
SNICKS
SNIDE
SNIDELY
SNIDENESS
SNIDENESSES
SNIDER
SNIDES
SNIDEST
SNIFF
SNIFFED
SNIFFER
SNIFFERS
SNIFFIER
SNIFFIEST
SNIFFILY
SNIFFING
SNIFFINGS
SNIFFLE
SNIFFLED
SNIFFLER
SNIFFLERS
SNIFFLES
SNIFFLING
SNIFFS
SNIFFY
SNIFT
SNIFTED
SNIFTER
SNIFTERED
SNIFTERING
SNIFTERS
SNIFTIER
SNIFTIEST
SNIFTING
SNIFTS
SNIFTY
SNIG
SNIGGED
SNIGGER
SNIGGERED
SNIGGERER
SNIGGERERS
SNIGGERING
SNIGGERINGS
SNIGGERS
SNIGGING
SNIGGLE
SNIGGLED
SNIGGLER
SNIGGLERS
SNIGGLES
SNIGGLING
SNIGGLINGS
SNIGS
SNIP
SNIPE
SNIPED
SNIPER
SNIPERS
SNIPES
SNIPIER
SNIPIEST
SNIPING
SNIPINGS
SNIPPED

SNIPPER
SNIPPERS
SNIPPET
SNIPPETS
SNIPPETY
SNIPPIER
SNIPPIEST
SNIPPING
SNIPPINGS
SNIPPY
SNIPS
SNIPY
SNIRT
SNIRTLE
SNIRTLED
SNIRTLES
SNIRTLING
SNIRTS
SNITCH
SNITCHED
SNITCHER
SNITCHERS
SNITCHES
SNITCHING
SNIVEL
SNIVELLED
SNIVELLER
SNIVELLERS
SNIVELLING
SNIVELLY
SNIVELS
SNOB
SNOBBERIES
SNOBBERY
SNOBBIER
SNOBBIEST
SNOBBISH
SNOBBISM
SNOBBISMS
SNOBBY
SNOBLING
SNOBLINGS
SNOBS
SNOD
SNODDED
SNODDING
SNODDIT
SNODS
SNOEK
SNOEKS
SNOG
SNOGGED
SNOGGING
SNOGS
SNOKE
SNOKED
SNOKES
SNOKING
SNOOD
SNOODED
SNOODING
SNOODS
SNOOK
SNOOKED
SNOOKER
SNOOKERED
SNOOKERING
SNOOKERS
SNOOKING
SNOOKS

SNOOKSES
SNOOL
SNOOLED
SNOOLING
SNOOLS
SNOOP
SNOOPED
SNOOPER
SNOOPERS
SNOOPING
SNOOPS
SNOOT
SNOOTED
SNOOTFUL
SNOOTFULS
SNOOTIER
SNOOTIEST
SNOOTING
SNOOTS
SNOOTY
SNOOZE
SNOOZED
SNOOZER
SNOOZERS
SNOOZES
SNOOZING
SNOOZLE
SNOOZLED
SNOOZLES
SNOOZLING
SNORE
SNORED
SNORER
SNORERS
SNORES
SNORING
SNORINGS
SNORKEL
SNORKELS
SNORT
SNORTED
SNORTER
SNORTERS
SNORTIER
SNORTIEST
SNORTING
SNORTINGS
SNORTS
SNORTY
SNOT
SNOTS
SNOTTED
SNOTTER
SNOTTERED
SNOTTERIES
SNOTTERING
SNOTTERS
SNOTTERY
SNOTTIER
SNOTTIES
SNOTTIEST
SNOTTILY
SNOTTING
SNOTTY
SNOUT
SNOUTED
SNOUTIER
SNOUTIEST
SNOUTING
SNOUTS

SNOUTY
SNOW
SNOWBALL
SNOWBALLED
SNOWBALLING
SNOWBALLS
SNOWCAP
SNOWCAPS
SNOWDRIFT
SNOWDRIFTS
SNOWDROP
SNOWDROPS
SNOWED
SNOWFALL
SNOWFALLS
SNOWFLAKE
SNOWFLAKES
SNOWFLECK
SNOWFLECKS
SNOWFLICK
SNOWFLICKS
SNOWIER
SNOWIEST
SNOWILY
SNOWINESS
SNOWINESSES
SNOWING
SNOWISH
SNOWK
SNOWKED
SNOWKING
SNOWKS
SNOWLESS
SNOWLIKE
SNOWLINE
SNOWLINES
SNOWMAN
SNOWMEN
SNOWS
SNOWSCAPE
SNOWSCAPES
SNOWSLIP
SNOWSLIPS
SNOWSTORM
SNOWSTORMS
SNOWY
SNUB
SNUBBE
SNUBBED
SNUBBER
SNUBBERS
SNUBBES
SNUBBIER
SNUBBIEST
SNUBBING
SNUBBINGS
SNUBBISH
SNUBBY
SNUBS
SNUCK
SNUDGE
SNUDGED
SNUDGES
SNUDGING
SNUFF
SNUFFBOX
SNUFFBOXES
SNUFFED
SNUFFER
SNUFFERS

SNUFFIER
SNUFFIEST
SNUFFING
SNUFFINGS
SNUFFLE
SNUFFLED
SNUFFLER
SNUFFLERS
SNUFFLES
SNUFFLING
SNUFFLINGS
SNUFFS
SNUFFY
SNUG
SNUGGED
SNUGGER
SNUGGERIES
SNUGGERY
SNUGGEST
SNUGGING
SNUGGLE
SNUGGLED
SNUGGLES
SNUGGLING
SNUGLY
SNUGNESS
SNUGNESSES
SNUGS
SNUSH
SNUSHED
SNUSHES
SNUSHING
SNUZZLE
SNUZZLED
SNUZZLES
SNUZZLING
SO
SOAK
SOAKAGE
SOAKAGES
SOAKAWAY
SOAKAWAYS
SOAKED
SOAKEN
SOAKER
SOAKERS
SOAKING
SOAKINGLY
SOAKINGS
SOAKS
SOAP
SOAPBERRIES
SOAPBERRY
SOAPBOX
SOAPBOXES
SOAPED
SOAPIER
SOAPIEST
SOAPILY
SOAPINESS
SOAPINESSES
SOAPING
SOAPLESS
SOAPS
SOAPSTONE
SOAPSTONES
SOAPWORT
SOAPWORTS
SOAPY
SOAR

SOARAWAY	SOCIATIVE	SODOMIZING	SOILING	SOLDAN
SOARE	SOCIETAL	SODOMY	SOILINGS	SOLDANS
SOARED	SOCIETARY	SODS	SOILLESS	SOLDE
SOARES	SOCIETIES	SOEVER	SOILS	SOLDER
SOARING	SOCIETY	SOFA	SOILURE	SOLDERED
SOARINGLY	SOCIOGRAM	SOFAR	SOILURES	SOLDERER
SOARINGS	SOCIOGRAMS	SOFARS	SOILY	SOLDERERS
SOARS	SOCIOLOGIES	SOFAS	SOIRÉE	SOLDERING
SOB	SOCIOLOGY	SOFFIONI	SOIRÉES	SOLDERINGS
SOBBED	SOCIOPATH	SOFFIT	SOJA	SOLDERS
SOBBING	SOCIOPATHS	SOFFITS	SOJAS	SOLDES
SOBBINGLY	SOCK	SOFT	SOJOURN	SOLDI
SOBBINGS	SOCKED	SOFTA	SOJOURNED	SOLDIER
SOBEIT	SOCKER	SOFTAS	SOJOURNER	SOLDIERED
SOBER	SOCKERS	SOFTBACK	SOJOURNERS	SOLDIERIES
SOBERED	SOCKET	SOFTBACKS	SOJOURNING	SOLDIERING
SOBERER	SOCKETED	SOFTBALL	SOJOURNINGS	SOLDIERINGS
SOBEREST	SOCKETING	SOFTBALLS	SOJOURNS	SOLDIERLY
SOBERING	SOCKETS	SOFTED	SOKE	SOLDIERS
SOBERISE	SOCKEYE	SOFTEN	SOKEMAN	SOLDIERY
SOBERISED	SOCKEYES	SOFTENED	SOKEMANRIES	SOLDO
SOBERISES	SOCKING	SOFTENER	SOKEMANRY	SOLDS
SOBERISING	SOCKO	SOFTENERS	SOKEMEN	SOLE
SOBERIZE	SOCKS	SOFTENING	SOKEN	SOLECISE
SOBERIZED	SOCLE	SOFTENINGS	SOKENS	SOLECISED
SOBERIZES	SOCLES	SOFTENS	SOKES	SOLECISES
SOBERIZING	SOCMAN	SOFTER	SOL	SOLECISING
SOBERLY	SOCMEN	SOFTEST	SOLA	SOLECISM
SOBERNESS	SOCS	SOFTHEAD	SOLACE	SOLECISMS
SOBERNESSES	SOD	SOFTHEADS	SOLACED	SOLECIST
SOBERS	SODA	SOFTIE	SOLACES	SOLECISTS
SOBOLE	SODAIC	SOFTIES	SOLACING	SOLECIZE
SOBOLES	SODAIN	SOFTING	SOLACIOUS	SOLECIZED
SOBRIETIES	SODAINE	SOFTISH	SOLAH	SOLECIZES
SOBRIETY	SODALITE	SOFTLING	SOLAHS	SOLECIZING
SOBRIQUET	SODALITES	SOFTLINGS	SOLAN	SOLED
SOBRIQUETS	SODALITIES	SOFTLY	SOLAND	SOLEIN
SOBS	SODALITY	SOFTNESS	SOLANDER	SOLELY
SOC	SODAMIDE	SOFTNESSES	SOLANDERS	SOLEMN
SOCAGE	SODAMIDES	SOFTS	SOLANDS	SOLEMNER
SOCAGER	SODAS	SOFTWARE	SOLANINE	SOLEMNESS
SOCAGERS	SODDED	SOFTWARES	SOLANINES	SOLEMNESSES
SOCAGES	SODDEN	SOFTWOOD	SOLANO	SOLEMNEST
SOCCAGE	SODDENED	SOFTWOODS	SOLANOS	SOLEMNIFIED
SOCCAGES	SODDENER	SOFTY	SOLANS	SOLEMNIFIES
SOCCER	SODDENEST	SOG	SOLANUM	SOLEMNIFY
SOCCERS	SODDENING	SOGER	SOLANUMS	SOLEMNIFYING
SOCIABLE	SODDENS	SOGERED	SOLAR	SOLEMNISE
SOCIABLY	SODDIER	SOGERING	SOLARISE	SOLEMNISED
SOCIAL	SODDIEST	SOGERS	SOLARISED	SOLEMNISES
SOCIALISE	SODDING	SOGGED	SOLARISES	SOLEMNISING
SOCIALISED	SODDY	SOGGIER	SOLARISING	SOLEMNITIES
SOCIALISES	SODGER	SOGGIEST	SOLARISM	SOLEMNITY
SOCIALISING	SODGERED	SOGGILY	SOLARIST	SOLEMNIZE
SOCIALISM	SODGERING	SOGGINESS	SOLARISTS	SOLEMNIZED
SOCIALISMS	SODGERS	SOGGINESSES	SOLARIUM	SOLEMNIZES
SOCIALIST	SODIC	SOGGING	SOLARIUMS	SOLEMNIZING
SOCIALISTS	SODIUM	SOGGINGS	SOLARIZE	SOLEMNLY
SOCIALITE	SODIUMS	SOGGY	SOLARIZED	SOLEN
SOCIALITES	SODOMIES	SOGS	SOLARIZES	SOLENESS
SOCIALITIES	SODOMISE	SOH	SOLARIZING	SOLENESSES
SOCIALITY	SODOMISED	SOHS	SOLARS	SOLENETTE
SOCIALIZE	SODOMISES	SOIGNÉ	SOLAS	SOLENETTES
SOCIALIZED	SODOMISING	SOIGNÉE	SOLATION	SOLENODON
SOCIALIZES	SODOMITE	SOIL	SOLATIONS	SOLENODONS
SOCIALIZING	SODOMITES	SOILED	SOLATIUM	SOLENOID
SOCIALLY	SODOMITIC	SOILIER	SOLATIUMS	SOLENOIDS
SOCIALS	SODOMIZE	SOILIEST	SOLD	SOLENS
SOCIATE	SODOMIZED	SOILINESS	SOLDADO	SOLER
SOCIATES	SODOMIZES	SOILINESSES	SOLDADOS	SOLERA

SOLERAS	SOLLAR	SOMEBODY	SONGMAN	SOOJEYING
SOLERS	SOLLARS	SOMEDAY	SONGMEN	SOOJEYS
SOLES	SOLLER	SOMEDEAL	SONGS	SOOK
SOLEUS	SOLLERET	SOMEDELE	SONGSMITH	SOOKS
SOLEUSES	SOLLERETS	SOMEGATE	SONGSMITHS	SOOLE
SOLFATARA	SOLLERS	SOMEHOW	SONGSTER	SOOLED
SOLFATARAS	SOLO	SOMEONE	SONGSTERS	SOOLES
SOLFEGGI	SOLOED	SOMEONES	SONIC	SOOLING
SOLFEGGIO	SOLOING	SOMEPLACE	SONICS	SOOM
SOLFERINO	SOLOIST	SOMERSET	SONLESS	SOOMED
SOLFERINOS	SOLOISTS	SOMERSETS	SONNE	SOOMING
SOLI	SOLONCHAK	SOMERSETTED	SONNES	SOOMS
SOLICIT	SOLONCHAKS	SOMERSETTING	SONNET	SOON
SOLICITED	SOLONETS	SOMETHING	SONNETARY	SOONER
SOLICITIES	SOLONETSES	SOMETHINGS	SONNETED	SOONEST
SOLICITING	SOLONETZ	SOMETIME	SONNETEER	SOOP
SOLICITINGS	SOLONETZES	SOMETIMES	SONNETEERED	SOOPED
SOLICITOR	SOLOS	SOMEWAY	SONNETEERING	SOOPING
SOLICITORS	SOLS	SOMEWAYS	SONNETEERINGS	SOOPINGS
SOLICITS	SOLSTICE	SOMEWHAT	SONNETEERS	SOOPS
SOLICITY	SOLSTICES	SOMEWHATS	SONNETING	SOOPSTAKE
SOLID	SOLUBLE	SOMEWHEN	SONNETINGS	SOOT
SOLIDARE	SOLUM	SOMEWHERE	SONNETISE	SOOTE
SOLIDARES	SOLUMS	SOMEWHILE	SONNETISED	SOOTED
SOLIDARY	SOLUS	SOMEWHY	SONNETISES	SOOTERKIN
SOLIDATE	SOLUTE	SOMEWISE	SONNETISING	SOOTERKINS
SOLIDATED	SOLUTES	SOMITAL	SONNETIST	SOOTES
SOLIDATES	SOLUTION	SOMITE	SONNETISTS	SOOTFLAKE
SOLIDATING	SOLUTIONED	SOMITES	SONNETIZE	SOOTFLAKES
SOLIDER	SOLUTIONING	SOMITIC	SONNETIZED	SOOTH
SOLIDEST	SOLUTIONS	SOMMELIER	SONNETIZES	SOOTHE
SOLIDI	SOLUTIVE	SOMMELIERS	SONNETIZING	SOOTHED
SOLIDIFIED	SOLVABLE	SOMNIAL	SONNETRIES	SOOTHER
SOLIDIFIES	SOLVATE	SOMNIFIC	SONNETRY	SOOTHERS
SOLIDIFY	SOLVATED	SOMNOLENT	SONNETS	SOOTHES
SOLIDIFYING	SOLVATES	SON	SONNIES	SOOTHEST
SOLIDISH	SOLVATING	SONANCE	SONNY	SOOTHFAST
SOLIDISM	SOLVATION	SONANCES	SONOBUOY	SOOTHFUL
SOLIDISMS	SOLVATIONS	SONANCIES	SONOBUOYS	SOOTHING
SOLIDIST	SOLVE	SONANCY	SONOGRAPH	SOOTHINGS
SOLIDISTS	SOLVED	SONANT	SONOGRAPHS	SOOTHLICH
SOLIDITIES	SOLVENCIES	SONANTS	SONORANT	SOOTHLY
SOLIDITY	SOLVENCY	SONAR	SONORANTS	SOOTHS
SOLIDLY	SOLVENT	SONARS	SONORITIES	SOOTHSAID
SOLIDNESS	SOLVENTS	SONATA	SONORITY	SOOTHSAY
SOLIDNESSES	SOLVER	SONATAS	SONOROUS	SOOTHSAYING
SOLIDS	SOLVERS	SONATINA	SONS	SOOTHSAYINGS
SOLIDUM	SOLVES	SONATINAS	SONSE	SOOTHSAYS
SOLIDUMS	SOLVING	SONCE	SONSES	SOOTIER
SOLIDUS	SOMA	SONCES	SONSHIP	SOOTIEST
SOLILOQUIES	SOMAS	SONDAGE	SONSHIPS	SOOTILY
SOLILOQUY	SOMASCOPE	SONDAGES	SONSIE	SOOTINESS
SOLING	SOMASCOPES	SONDE	SONSIER	SOOTINESSES
SOLIPED	SOMATIC	SONDELI	SONSIEST	SOOTING
SOLIPEDS	SOMATISM	SONDELIS	SONSY	SOOTLESS
SOLIPSISM	SOMATISMS	SONDES	SONTAG	SOOTS
SOLIPSISMS	SOMATIST	SONE	SONTAGS	SOOTY
SOLIPSIST	SOMATISTS	SONERI	SONTIES	SOP
SOLIPSISTS	SOMBRE	SONERIS	SONUANCE	SOPH
SOLITAIRE	SOMBRED	SONES	SONUANCES	SOPHA
SOLITAIRES	SOMBRELY	SONG	SOOGEE	SOPHAS
SOLITARIES	SOMBRER	SONGBIRD	SOOGEED	SOPHERIC
SOLITARY	SOMBRERO	SONGBIRDS	SOOGEEING	SOPHERIM
SOLITO	SOMBREROS	SONGBOOK	SOOGEES	SOPHIA
SOLITON	SOMBRES	SONGBOOKS	SOOGIE	SOPHIAS
SOLITONS	SOMBREST	SONGCRAFT	SOOGIED	SOPHIC
SOLITUDE	SOMBRING	SONGCRAFTS	SOOGIEING	SOPHICAL
SOLITUDES	SOMBROUS	SONGFUL	SOOGIES	SOPHISM
SOLIVE	SOME	SONGFULLY	SOOJEY	SOPHISMS
SOLIVES	SOMEBODIES	SONGLESS	SOOJEYED	SOPHIST

SOPHISTER	SORDA	SORORITIES	SOTTISHLY	SOUPSPOONS
SOPHISTERS	SORDES	SORORITY	SOTTISIER	SOUPY
SOPHISTIC	SORDID	SORORIZE	SOTTISIERS	SOUR
SOPHISTICS	SORDIDER	SORORIZED	SOU	SOURCE
SOPHISTRIES	SORDIDEST	SORORIZES	SOUARI	SOURCED
SOPHISTRY	SORDIDLY	SORORIZING	SOUARIS	SOURCES
SOPHISTS	SORDINE	SOROSES	SOUBISE	SOURCING
SOPHOMORE	SORDINES	SOROSIS	SOUBISES	SOURCINGS
SOPHOMORES	SORDINI	SOROSISES	SOUBRETTE	SOURDINE
SOPHS	SORDINO	SORPTION	SOUBRETTES	SOURDINES
SOPITE	SORDO	SORPTIONS	SOUCE	SOURDOUGH
SOPITED	SORDOR	SORRA	SOUCED	SOURDOUGHS
SOPITES	SORDORS	SORRAS	SOUCES	SOURED
SOPITING	SORDS	SORREL	SOUCHONG	SOURER
SOPOR	SORE	SORRELS	SOUCHONGS	SOUREST
SOPORIFIC	SORED	SORRIER	SOUCING	SOURING
SOPORIFICS	SOREDIA	SORRIEST	SOUCT	SOURINGS
SOPOROSE	SOREDIAL	SORRILY	SOUFFLE	SOURISH
SOPOROUS	SOREDIATE	SORRINESS	SOUFFLÉ	SOURISHLY
SOPORS	SOREDIUM	SORRINESSES	SOUFFLES	SOURLY
SOPPED	SOREE	SORROW	SOUFFLÉS	SOURNESS
SOPPIER	SOREES	SORROWED	SOUGH	SOURNESSES
SOPPIEST	SOREHEAD	SORROWER	SOUGHED	SOUROCK
SOPPILY	SOREHEADS	SORROWERS	SOUGHING	SOUROCKS
SOPPINESS	SOREHON	SORROWFUL	SOUGHS	SOURPUSS
SOPPINESSES	SOREHONS	SORROWING	SOUGHT	SOURPUSSES
SOPPING	SOREL	SORROWINGS	SOUK	SOURS
SOPPINGS	SORELL	SORROWS	SOUKS	SOURSE
SOPPY	SORELLS	SORRY	SOUL	SOURSES
SOPRA	SORELS	SORRYISH	SOULDAN	SOUS
SOPRANI	SORELY	SORT	SOULDANS	SOUSE
SOPRANINI	SORENESS	SORTABLE	SOULDIER	SOUSED
SOPRANINO	SORENESSES	SORTANCE	SOULDIERED	SOUSES
SOPRANINOS	SORER	SORTANCES	SOULDIERING	SOUSEWIFE
SOPRANIST	SORES	SORTATION	SOULDIERS	SOUSEWIVES
SOPRANISTS	SOREST	SORTATIONS	SOULED	SOUSING
SOPRANO	SOREX	SORTED	SOULFUL	SOUSINGS
SOPRANOS	SOREXES	SORTER	SOULFULLY	SOUSLIK
SOPS	SORGHO	SORTERS	SOULLESS	SOUSLIKS
SORA	SORGHOS	SORTES	SOULS	SOUT
SORAGE	SORGHUM	SORTIE	SOUM	SOUTACHE
SORAGES	SORGHUMS	SORTIED	SOUMED	SOUTACHES
SORAL	SORGO	SORTIEING	SOUMING	SOUTANE
SORAS	SORGOS	SORTIES	SOUMINGS	SOUTANES
SORB	SORI	SORTILEGE	SOUMS	SOUTAR
SORBARIA	SORICINE	SORTILEGES	SOUND	SOUTARS
SORBARIAS	SORICOID	SORTILEGIES	SOUNDED	SOUTENEUR
SORBATE	SORING	SORTILEGY	SOUNDER	SOUTENEURS
SORBATES	SORITES	SORTING	SOUNDERS	SOUTER
SORBED	SORITIC	SORTINGS	SOUNDEST	SOUTERLY
SORBENT	SORITICAL	SORTITION	SOUNDING	SOUTERS
SORBENTS	SORN	SORTITIONS	SOUNDINGS	SOUTH
SORBET	SORNED	SORTMENT	SOUNDLESS	SOUTHED
SORBETS	SORNER	SORTMENTS	SOUNDLY	SOUTHER
SORBING	SORNERS	SORTS	SOUNDNESS	SOUTHERED
SORBITOL	SORNING	SORUS	SOUNDNESSES	SOUTHERING
SORBITOLS	SORNINGS	SOS	SOUNDS	SOUTHERLY
SORBO	SORNS	SOSS	SOUP	SOUTHERN
SORBOS	SOROBAN	SOSSED	SOUPÇON	SOUTHERNS
SORBS	SOROBANS	SOSSES	SOUPÇONS	SOUTHERS
SORBUS	SOROCHE	SOSSING	SOUPER	SOUTHING
SORBUSES	SOROCHES	SOSSINGS	SOUPERS	SOUTHINGS
SORCERER	SORORAL	SOSTENUTO	SOUPIER	SOUTHLAND
SORCERERS	SORORATE	SOT	SOUPIEST	SOUTHLANDS
SORCERESS	SORORATES	SOTERIAL	SOUPLE	SOUTHMOST
SORCERESSES	SORORIAL	SOTS	SOUPLED	SOUTHPAW
SORCERIES	SORORISE	SOTTED	SOUPLES	SOUTHPAWS
SORCEROUS	SORORISED	SOTTING	SOUPLING	SOUTHRON
SORCERY	SORORISES	SOTTINGS	SOUPS	SOUTHRONS
SORD	SORORISING	SOTTISH	SOUPSPOON	SOUTHS

SOUTHSAID	SOWN	SPADEWORKS	SPALTED	SPARENESSES
SOUTHSAY	SOWND	SPADGER	SPALTING	SPARER
SOUTHSAYING	SOWNDED	SPADGERS	SPALTS	SPARERS
SOUTHSAYS	SOWNDING	SPADICES	SPAMMY	SPARES
SOUTHWARD	SOWNDS	SPADILLE	SPAN	SPAREST
SOUTHWARDS	SOWNE	SPADILLES	SPANAEMIA	SPARGE
SOUTS	SOWNES	SPADILLIO	SPANAEMIAS	SPARGED
SOUVENIR	SOWP	SPADILLIOS	SPANAEMIC	SPARGER
SOUVENIRED	SOWPS	SPADILLO	SPANCEL	SPARGERS
SOUVENIRING	SOWS	SPADILLOS	SPANCELLED	SPARGES
SOUVENIRS	SOWSE	SPADING	SPANCELLING	SPARGING
SOV	SOWSED	SPADIX	SPANCELS	SPARID
SOVENANCE	SOWSES	SPADO	SPANDREL	SPARIDS
SOVENANCES	SOWSING	SPADOES	SPANDRELS	SPARING
SOVEREIGN	SOWSSE	SPADONES	SPANDRIL	SPARINGLY
SOVEREIGNS	SOWSSED	SPADOS	SPANDRILS	SPARK
SOVIET	SOWSSES	SPADROON	SPANE	SPARKE
SOVIETIC	SOWSSING	SPADROONS	SPANED	SPARKED
SOVIETISE	SOWTER	SPAE	SPANES	SPARKES
SOVIETISED	SOWTERS	SPAED	SPANG	SPARKING
SOVIETISES	SOWTH	SPAEING	SPANGED	SPARKISH
SOVIETISING	SOWTHED	SPAEMAN	SPANGHEW	SPARKLE
SOVIETISM	SOWTHING	SPAEMEN	SPANGHEWED	SPARKLED
SOVIETISMS	SOWTHS	SPAER	SPANGHEWING	SPARKLER
SOVIETIZE	SOX	SPAERS	SPANGHEWS	SPARKLERS
SOVIETIZED	SOY	SPAES	SPANGING	SPARKLES
SOVIETIZES	SOYA	SPAEWIFE	SPANGLE	SPARKLESS
SOVIETIZING	SOYAS	SPAEWIVES	SPANGLED	SPARKLET
SOVIETS	SOYLE	SPAGERIC	SPANGLER	SPARKLETS
SOVRAN	SOYLED	SPAGERICS	SPANGLERS	SPARKLIES
SOVRANS	SOYLES	SPAGERIST	SPANGLES	SPARKLING
SOVRANTIES	SOYS	SPAGERISTS	SPANGLET	SPARKLINGS
SOVRANTY	SOZZLE	SPAGHETTI	SPANGLETS	SPARKLY
SOVS	SOZZLED	SPAGHETTIS	SPANGLIER	SPARKS
SOW	SOZZLES	SPAGIRIC	SPANGLIEST	SPARLING
SOWANS	SOZZLING	SPAGIRICS	SPANGLING	SPARLINGS
SOWAR	SOZZLY	SPAGIRIST	SPANGLINGS	SPAROID
SOWARREE	SPA	SPAGIRISTS	SPANGLY	SPAROIDS
SOWARREES	SPACE	SPAGYRIC	SPANGS	SPARRE
SOWARRIES	SPACED	SPAGYRICS	SPANIEL	SPARRED
SOWARRY	SPACELESS	SPAGYRIST	SPANIELLED	SPARRER
SOWARS	SPACEMAN	SPAGYRISTS	SPANIELLING	SPARRERS
SOWCE	SPACEMEN	SPAHEE	SPANIELS	SPARRES
SOWCED	SPACER	SPAHEES	SPANING	SPARRING
SOWCES	SPACERS	SPAHI	SPANK	SPARRINGS
SOWCING	SPACES	SPAHIS	SPANKED	SPARROW
SOWED	SPACESHIP	SPAIN	SPANKER	SPARROWS
SOWENS	SPACESHIPS	SPAINED	SPANKERS	SPARRY
SOWER	SPACEY	SPAING	SPANKING	SPARS
SOWERS	SPACIAL	SPAINGS	SPANKINGS	SPARSE
SOWF	SPACIER	SPAINING	SPANKS	SPARSEDLY
SOWFED	SPACIEST	SPAINS	SPANLESS	SPARSELY
SOWFF	SPACING	SPAIRGE	SPANNED	SPARSER
SOWFFED	SPACINGS	SPAIRGED	SPANNER	SPARSEST
SOWFFING	SPACIOUS	SPAIRGES	SPANNERS	SPARSITIES
SOWFFS	SPACY	SPAIRGING	SPANNING	SPARSITY
SOWFING	SPADASSIN	SPAKE	SPANS	SPART
SOWFS	SPADASSINS	SPALD	SPANSULE	SPARTAN
SOWING	SPADE	SPALDS	SPANSULES	SPARTEINE
SOWINGS	SPADED	SPALE	SPAR	SPARTEINES
SOWL	SPADEFUL	SPALES	SPARABLE	SPARTERIE
SOWLE	SPADEFULS	SPALL	SPARABLES	SPARTERIES
SOWLED	SPADEMAN	SPALLE	SPARAXIS	SPARTH
SOWLES	SPADEMEN	SPALLED	SPARAXISES	SPARTHE
SOWLING	SPADER	SPALLES	SPARD	SPARTHES
SOWLS	SPADERS	SPALLING	SPARE	SPARTHS
SOWM	SPADES	SPALLS	SPARED	SPARTS
SOWMED	SPADESMAN	SPALPEEN	SPARELESS	SPAS
SOWMING	SPADESMEN	SPALPEENS	SPARELY	SPASM
SOWMS	SPADEWORK	SPALT	SPARENESS	SPASMATIC

SPASMED	SPEAKERS	SPECTATED	SPEKBOOM	SPERMATICS
SPASMIC	SPEAKING	SPECTATES	SPEKBOOMS	SPERMATID
SPASMING	SPEAKINGS	SPECTATING	SPELAEAN	SPERMATIDS
SPASMODIC	SPEAKS	SPECTATOR	SPELD	SPERMIC
SPASMS	SPEAL	SPECTATORS	SPELDED	SPERMOUS
SPASTIC	SPEALS	SPECTER	SPELDER	SPERMS
SPASTICS	SPEAN	SPECTERS	SPELDERED	SPERRE
SPAT	SPEANED	SPECTRA	SPELDERING	SPERRED
SPATE	SPEANING	SPECTRAL	SPELDERS	SPERRES
SPATES	SPEANS	SPECTRE	SPELDIN	SPERRING
SPATFALL	SPEAR	SPECTRES	SPELDING	SPERSE
SPATFALLS	SPEARED	SPECTRUM	SPELDINGS	SPERSED
SPATHE	SPEARFISH	SPECULA	SPELDINS	SPERSES
SPATHED	SPEARFISHES	SPECULAR	SPELDRIN	SPERSING
SPATHES	SPEARHEAD	SPECULATE	SPELDRING	SPERST
SPATHIC	SPEARHEADED	SPECULATED	SPELDRINGS	SPERTHE
SPATHOSE	SPEARHEADING	SPECULATES	SPELDRINS	SPERTHES
SPATIAL	SPEARHEADS	SPECULATING	SPELDS	SPET
SPATIALLY	SPEARIER	SPECULUM	SPELEAN	SPETCH
SPÄTLESE	SPEARIEST	SPED	SPELIKIN	SPETCHES
SPÄTLESEN	SPEARING	SPEECH	SPELIKINS	SPETS
SPÄTLESES	SPEARMAN	SPEECHED	SPELK	SPETSNAZ
SPATS	SPEARMEN	SPEECHES	SPELKS	SPETSNAZES
SPATTED	SPEARMINT	SPEECHFUL	SPELL	SPETTING
SPATTEE	SPEARMINTS	SPEECHIFIED	SPELLABLE	SPETZNAZ
SPATTEES	SPEARS	SPEECHIFIES	SPELLBIND	SPETZNAZES
SPATTER	SPEARWORT	SPEECHIFY	SPELLBINDING	SPEW
SPATTERED	SPEARWORTS	SPEECHIFYING	SPELLBINDS	SPEWED
SPATTERING	SPEARY	SPEECHING	SPELLBOUND	SPEWER
SPATTERS	SPEAT	SPEED	SPELLDOWN	SPEWERS
SPATTING	SPEATS	SPEEDBALL	SPELLDOWNS	SPEWIER
SPATULA	SPEC	SPEEDBALLS	SPELLED	SPEWIEST
SPATULAR	SPECCIES	SPEEDED	SPELLER	SPEWINESS
SPATULAS	SPECCY	SPEEDER	SPELLERS	SPEWINESSES
SPATULATE	SPECIAL	SPEEDERS	SPELLFUL	SPEWING
SPATULE	SPECIALLY	SPEEDFUL	SPELLICAN	SPEWS
SPATULES	SPECIALS	SPEEDIER	SPELLICANS	SPEWY
SPAUL	SPECIALTIES	SPEEDIEST	SPELLIKIN	SPHACELUS
SPAULD	SPECIALTY	SPEEDILY	SPELLIKINS	SPHACELUSES
SPAULDS	SPECIATE	SPEEDING	SPELLING	SPHAER
SPAULS	SPECIATED	SPEEDINGS	SPELLINGS	SPHAERE
SPAVIE	SPECIATES	SPEEDLESS	SPELLS	SPHAERES
SPAVIES	SPECIATING	SPEEDO	SPELT	SPHAERITE
SPAVIN	SPECIE	SPEEDOS	SPELTER	SPHAERITES
SPAVINED	SPECIES	SPEEDS	SPELTERS	SPHAERS
SPAVINS	SPECIFIC	SPEEDSTER	SPELTS	SPHAGNOUS
SPAW	SPECIFICS	SPEEDSTERS	SPENCE	SPHEAR
SPAWL	SPECIFIED	SPEEDWAY	SPENCER	SPHEARE
SPAWLED	SPECIFIES	SPEEDWAYS	SPENCERS	SPHEARES
SPAWLING	SPECIFY	SPEEDWELL	SPENCES	SPHEARS
SPAWLS	SPECIFYING	SPEEDWELLS	SPEND	SPHENDONE
SPAWN	SPECIMEN	SPEEDY	SPENDABLE	SPHENDONES
SPAWNED	SPECIMENS	SPEEL	SPENDALL	SPHENE
SPAWNER	SPECIOUS	SPEELED	SPENDALLS	SPHENES
SPAWNERS	SPECK	SPEELER	SPENDER	SPHENIC
SPAWNING	SPECKED	SPEELERS	SPENDERS	SPHENODON
SPAWNINGS	SPECKIER	SPEELING	SPENDING	SPHENODONS
SPAWNS	SPECKIEST	SPEELS	SPENDINGS	SPHENOID
SPAWS	SPECKING	SPEER	SPENDS	SPHENOIDS
SPAY	SPECKLE	SPEERED	SPENT	SPHERAL
SPAYAD	SPECKLED	SPEERING	SPEOS	SPHERE
SPAYADS	SPECKLES	SPEERINGS	SPEOSES	SPHERED
SPAYD	SPECKLESS	SPEERS	SPERLING	SPHERES
SPAYDS	SPECKLING	SPEIR	SPERLINGS	SPHERIC
SPAYED	SPECKS	SPEIRED	SPERM	SPHERICAL
SPAYING	SPECKY	SPEIRING	SPERMARIA	SPHERICS
SPAYS	SPECS	SPEIRINGS	SPERMARIES	SPHERIER
SPEAK	SPECTACLE	SPEIRS	SPERMARY	SPHERIEST
SPEAKABLE	SPECTACLES	SPEISS	SPERMATIA	SPHERING
SPEAKER	SPECTATE	SPEISSES	SPERMATIC	SPHEROID

SPHEROIDS
SPHERULAR
SPHERULE
SPHERULES
SPHERY
SPHINCTER
SPHINCTERS
SPHINGES
SPHINGID
SPHINGIDS
SPHINX
SPHINXES
SPHYGMIC
SPHYGMOID
SPHYGMUS
SPHYGMUSES
SPIAL
SPIALS
SPIC
SPICA
SPICAS
SPICATE
SPICATED
SPICCATO
SPICCATOS
SPICE
SPICED
SPICER
SPICERIES
SPICERS
SPICERY
SPICES
SPICIER
SPICIEST
SPICILEGE
SPICILEGES
SPICILY
SPICINESS
SPICINESSES
SPICING
SPICK
SPICKER
SPICKEST
SPICKNEL
SPICKNELS
SPICKS
SPICS
SPICULA
SPICULAR
SPICULAS
SPICULATE
SPICULE
SPICULES
SPICULUM
SPICY
SPIDE
SPIDER
SPIDERIER
SPIDERIEST
SPIDERS
SPIDERY
SPIE
SPIED
SPIEL
SPIELED
SPIELER
SPIELERS
SPIELING
SPIELS
SPIES

SPIFF
SPIFFIER
SPIFFIEST
SPIFFING
SPIFFY
SPIGHT
SPIGHTED
SPIGHTING
SPIGHTS
SPIGNEL
SPIGNELS
SPIGOT
SPIGOTS
SPIK
SPIKE
SPIKED
SPIKELET
SPIKELETS
SPIKENARD
SPIKENARDS
SPIKES
SPIKIER
SPIKIEST
SPIKILY
SPIKINESS
SPIKINESSES
SPIKING
SPIKS
SPIKY
SPILE
SPILED
SPILES
SPILIKIN
SPILIKINS
SPILING
SPILINGS
SPILITE
SPILITES
SPILITIC
SPILL
SPILLAGE
SPILLAGES
SPILLED
SPILLER
SPILLERS
SPILLIKIN
SPILLIKINS
SPILLING
SPILLINGS
SPILLOVER
SPILLOVERS
SPILLS
SPILLWAY
SPILLWAYS
SPILOSITE
SPILOSITES
SPILT
SPILTH
SPILTHS
SPIN
SPINA
SPINACH
SPINACHES
SPINAE
SPINAGE
SPINAGES
SPINAL
SPINAR
SPINARS
SPINAS

SPINATE
SPINDLE
SPINDLED
SPINDLES
SPINDLIER
SPINDLIEST
SPINDLING
SPINDLINGS
SPINDLY
SPINDRIFT
SPINDRIFTS
SPINE
SPINED
SPINEL
SPINELESS
SPINELS
SPINES
SPINET
SPINETS
SPINETTE
SPINETTES
SPINIER
SPINIEST
SPINIFEX
SPINIFEXES
SPINIFORM
SPININESS
SPININESSES
SPINK
SPINKS
SPINNAKER
SPINNAKERS
SPINNER
SPINNERET
SPINNERETS
SPINNERIES
SPINNERS
SPINNERY
SPINNET
SPINNETS
SPINNEY
SPINNEYS
SPINNIES
SPINNING
SPINNINGS
SPINNY
SPINODE
SPINODES
SPINOSE
SPINOSITIES
SPINOSITY
SPINOUS
SPINOUT
SPINOUTS
SPINS
SPINSTER
SPINSTERS
SPINTEXT
SPINTEXTS
SPINULATE
SPINULE
SPINULES
SPINULOSE
SPINULOUS
SPINY
SPIRACLE
SPIRACLES
SPIRACULA
SPIRAEA
SPIRAEAS

SPIRAL
SPIRALISM
SPIRALISMS
SPIRALIST
SPIRALISTS
SPIRALITIES
SPIRALITY
SPIRALLED
SPIRALLING
SPIRALLY
SPIRALS
SPIRANT
SPIRANTS
SPIRASTER
SPIRASTERS
SPIRATED
SPIRATION
SPIRATIONS
SPIRE
SPIREA
SPIREAS
SPIRED
SPIRELESS
SPIREME
SPIREMES
SPIRES
SPIREWISE
SPIRIC
SPIRICS
SPIRIER
SPIRIEST
SPIRILLA
SPIRILLAR
SPIRILLUM
SPIRING
SPIRIT
SPIRITED
SPIRITFUL
SPIRITING
SPIRITINGS
SPIRITISM
SPIRITISMS
SPIRITIST
SPIRITISTS
SPIRITOSO
SPIRITOUS
SPIRITS
SPIRITUAL
SPIRITUALS
SPIRITUEL
SPIRITUS
SPIRITUSES
SPIRITY
SPIRLING
SPIRLINGS
SPIROID
SPIRT
SPIRTED
SPIRTING
SPIRTLE
SPIRTLES
SPIRTS
SPIRY
SPIT
SPITAL
SPITALS
SPITCHER
SPITE
SPITED
SPITEFUL

SPITEFULLER
SPITEFULLEST
SPITES
SPITFIRE
SPITFIRES
SPITING
SPITS
SPITTED
SPITTEN
SPITTER
SPITTERS
SPITTING
SPITTINGS
SPITTLE
SPITTLES
SPITTOON
SPITTOONS
SPITZ
SPITZES
SPIV
SPIVS
SPIVVERIES
SPIVVERY
SPIVVIER
SPIVVIEST
SPIVVY
SPLASH
SPLASHED
SPLASHER
SPLASHERS
SPLASHES
SPLASHIER
SPLASHIEST
SPLASHILY
SPLASHING
SPLASHINGS
SPLASHY
SPLAT
SPLATCH
SPLATCHED
SPLATCHES
SPLATCHING
SPLATS
SPLATTED
SPLATTER
SPLATTERED
SPLATTERING
SPLATTERS
SPLATTING
SPLATTINGS
SPLAY
SPLAYED
SPLAYING
SPLAYS
SPLEEN
SPLEENFUL
SPLEENIER
SPLEENIEST
SPLEENISH
SPLEENS
SPLEENY
SPLENDENT
SPLENDID
SPLENDOR
SPLENDORS
SPLENDOUR
SPLENDOURS
SPLENETIC
SPLENETICS
SPLENIA

SPLENIAL	SPLUTTERING	SPONTOON	SPOROGENY	SPRACK
SPLENIC	SPLUTTERINGS	SPONTOONS	SPOROPHYL	SPRACKLE
SPLENII	SPLUTTERS	SPOOF	SPOROPHYLS	SPRACKLED
SPLENITIS	SPLUTTERY	SPOOFED	SPORRAN	SPRACKLES
SPLENITISES	SPODE	SPOOFER	SPORRANS	SPRACKLING
SPLENIUM	SPODES	SPOOFERIES	SPORT	SPRAD
SPLENIUMS	SPODIUM	SPOOFERS	SPORTABLE	SPRAG
SPLENIUS	SPODIUMS	SPOOFERY	SPORTANCE	SPRAGGED
SPLENIUSES	SPODUMENE	SPOOFING	SPORTANCES	SPRAGGING
SPLENT	SPODUMENES	SPOOFS	SPORTED	SPRAGS
SPLENTED	SPOFFISH	SPOOK	SPORTER	SPRAICKLE
SPLENTING	SPOFFY	SPOOKED	SPORTERS	SPRAICKLED
SPLENTS	SPOIL	SPOOKERIES	SPORTFUL	SPRAICKLES
SPLEUCHAN	SPOILAGE	SPOOKERY	SPORTIER	SPRAICKLING
SPLEUCHANS	SPOILED	SPOOKIER	SPORTIEST	SPRAID
SPLICE	SPOILER	SPOOKIEST	SPORTILY	SPRAIN
SPLICED	SPOILERS	SPOOKILY	SPORTING	SPRAINED
SPLICES	SPOILFUL	SPOOKING	SPORTIVE	SPRAINING
SPLICING	SPOILING	SPOOKISH	SPORTLESS	SPRAINS
SPLIFF	SPOILS	SPOOKS	SPORTS	SPRAINT
SPLIFFS	SPOILSMAN	SPOOKY	SPORTSMAN	SPRAINTS
SPLINE	SPOILSMEN	SPOOL	SPORTSMEN	SPRANG
SPLINED	SPOILT	SPOOLED	SPORTY	SPRANGLE
SPLINES	SPOKE	SPOOLER	SPORULAR	SPRANGLED
SPLINING	SPOKEN	SPOOLERS	SPORULATE	SPRANGLES
SPLINT	SPOKES	SPOOLING	SPORULATED	SPRANGLING
SPLINTED	SPOKESMAN	SPOOLS	SPORULATES	SPRAT
SPLINTER	SPOKESMEN	SPOOM	SPORULATING	SPRATS
SPLINTERED	SPOKEWISE	SPOOMED	SPORULE	SPRATTLE
SPLINTERING	SPOLIATE	SPOOMING	SPORULES	SPRATTLED
SPLINTERS	SPOLIATED	SPOOMS	SPOSH	SPRATTLES
SPLINTERY	SPOLIATES	SPOON	SPOSHES	SPRATTLING
SPLINTING	SPOLIATING	SPOONBILL	SPOSHY	SPRAUCHLE
SPLINTS	SPOLIATOR	SPOONBILLS	SPOT	SPRAUCHLED
SPLIT	SPOLIATORS	SPOONED	SPOTLESS	SPRAUCHLES
SPLITS	SPONDAIC	SPOONEY	SPOTLIGHT	SPRAUCHLING
SPLITTED	SPONDEE	SPOONEYS	SPOTLIGHTED	SPRAUNCIER
SPLITTER	SPONDEES	SPOONFUL	SPOTLIGHTING	SPRAUNCIEST
SPLITTERS	SPONDULIX	SPOONFULS	SPOTLIGHTS	SPRAUNCY
SPLITTING	SPONDYL	SPOONIER	SPOTLIT	SPRAWL
SPLODGE	SPONDYLS	SPOONIES	SPOTS	SPRAWLED
SPLODGED	SPONGE	SPOONIEST	SPOTTE	SPRAWLER
SPLODGES	SPONGED	SPOONILY	SPOTTED	SPRAWLERS
SPLODGIER	SPONGEOUS	SPOONING	SPOTTER	SPRAWLIER
SPLODGIEST	SPONGER	SPOONMEAT	SPOTTERS	SPRAWLIEST
SPLODGILY	SPONGERS	SPOONMEATS	SPOTTES	SPRAWLING
SPLODGING	SPONGES	SPOONS	SPOTTIER	SPRAWLS
SPLODGY	SPONGIER	SPOONWAYS	SPOTTIEST	SPRAWLY
SPLORE	SPONGIEST	SPOONWISE	SPOTTILY	SPRAY
SPLORES	SPONGILY	SPOONY	SPOTTING	SPRAYED
SPLOSH	SPONGIN	SPOOR	SPOTTINGS	SPRAYER
SPLOSHED	SPONGING	SPOORED	SPOTTY	SPRAYERS
SPLOSHES	SPONGINS	SPOORER	SPOUSAGE	SPRAYEY
SPLOSHING	SPONGIOSE	SPOORERS	SPOUSAGES	SPRAYIER
SPLOTCH	SPONGIOUS	SPOORING	SPOUSAL	SPRAYIEST
SPLOTCHED	SPONGOID	SPOORS	SPOUSALS	SPRAYING
SPLOTCHES	SPONGY	SPORADIC	SPOUSE	SPRAYS
SPLOTCHIER	SPONSAL	SPORANGIA	SPOUSED	SPREAD
SPLOTCHIEST	SPONSALIA	SPORE	SPOUSES	SPREADER
SPLOTCHING	SPONSIBLE	SPORES	SPOUSING	SPREADERS
SPLOTCHY	SPONSING	SPORIDESM	SPOUT	SPREADING
SPLURGE	SPONSINGS	SPORIDESMS	SPOUTED	SPREADINGS
SPLURGED	SPONSION	SPORIDIA	SPOUTER	SPREADS
SPLURGES	SPONSIONS	SPORIDIAL	SPOUTERS	SPREAGH
SPLURGIER	SPONSON	SPORIDIUM	SPOUTIER	SPREAGHS
SPLURGIEST	SPONSONS	SPOROCARP	SPOUTIEST	SPREATHE
SPLURGING	SPONSOR	SPOROCARPS	SPOUTING	SPREATHED
SPLURGY	SPONSORED	SPOROCYST	SPOUTLESS	SPREATHES
SPLUTTER	SPONSORING	SPOROCYSTS	SPOUTS	SPREATHING
SPLUTTERED	SPONSORS	SPOROGENIES	SPOUTY	SPREAZE

SPREAZED
SPREAZES
SPREAZING
SPRECHERIES
SPRECHERY
SPRECKLED
SPRED
SPREDD
SPREDDE
SPREDDEN
SPREDDES
SPREDDING
SPREDDS
SPREDS
SPREE
SPREED
SPREEING
SPREES
SPREETHE
SPREETHED
SPREETHES
SPREETHING
SPREEZE
SPREEZED
SPREEZES
SPREEZING
SPRENT
SPRIG
SPRIGGED
SPRIGGIER
SPRIGGIEST
SPRIGGING
SPRIGGY
SPRIGHT
SPRIGHTED
SPRIGHTING
SPRIGHTLIER
SPRIGHTLIEST
SPRIGHTLY
SPRIGHTS
SPRIGS
SPRING
SPRINGAL
SPRINGALD
SPRINGALDS
SPRINGALS
SPRINGBOK
SPRINGBOKS
SPRINGE
SPRINGED
SPRINGER
SPRINGERS
SPRINGES
SPRINGIER
SPRINGIEST
SPRINGILY
SPRINGING
SPRINGINGS
SPRINGLE
SPRINGLES
SPRINGLET
SPRINGLETS
SPRINGS
SPRINGY
SPRINKLE
SPRINKLED
SPRINKLER
SPRINKLERS
SPRINKLES
SPRINKLING

SPRINKLINGS
SPRINT
SPRINTED
SPRINTER
SPRINTERS
SPRINTING
SPRINTINGS
SPRINTS
SPRIT
SPRITE
SPRITEFUL
SPRITELY
SPRITES
SPRITS
SPRITSAIL
SPRITSAILS
SPRITZER
SPRITZERS
SPRITZIG
SPRITZIGS
SPROCKET
SPROCKETS
SPROD
SPRODS
SPROG
SPROGS
SPRONG
SPROUT
SPROUTED
SPROUTING
SPROUTINGS
SPROUTS
SPRUCE
SPRUCED
SPRUCELY
SPRUCER
SPRUCES
SPRUCEST
SPRUCING
SPRUE
SPRUES
SPRUG
SPRUGS
SPRUIK
SPRUIKED
SPRUIKER
SPRUIKERS
SPRUIKING
SPRUIKS
SPRUIT
SPRUITS
SPRUNG
SPRUSH
SPRUSHED
SPRUSHES
SPRUSHING
SPRY
SPRYER
SPRYEST
SPRYLY
SPRYNESS
SPRYNESSES
SPUD
SPUDDED
SPUDDIER
SPUDDIEST
SPUDDING
SPUDDINGS
SPUDDY
SPUDS

SPUE
SPUED
SPUEING
SPUES
SPUILZIE
SPUILZIED
SPUILZIEING
SPUILZIES
SPULE
SPULEBANE
SPULEBANES
SPULEBONE
SPULEBONES
SPULES
SPULYE
SPULYED
SPULYEING
SPULYES
SPULYIE
SPULYIED
SPULYIEING
SPULYIES
SPULZIE
SPULZIED
SPULZIEING
SPULZIES
SPUME
SPUMED
SPUMES
SPUMIER
SPUMIEST
SPUMING
SPUMOUS
SPUMY
SPUN
SPUNGE
SPUNGES
SPUNK
SPUNKED
SPUNKIE
SPUNKIER
SPUNKIES
SPUNKIEST
SPUNKING
SPUNKS
SPUNKY
SPUR
SPURGE
SPURGES
SPURIAE
SPURIOUS
SPURLESS
SPURLING
SPURLINGS
SPURN
SPURNE
SPURNED
SPURNER
SPURNERS
SPURNES
SPURNING
SPURNINGS
SPURNS
SPURRED
SPURRER
SPURRERS
SPURREY
SPURREYS
SPURRIER
SPURRIERS

SPURRIES
SPURRING
SPURRINGS
SPURRY
SPURS
SPURT
SPURTED
SPURTING
SPURTLE
SPURTLES
SPURTS
SPUTA
SPUTNIK
SPUTNIKS
SPUTTER
SPUTTERED
SPUTTERER
SPUTTERERS
SPUTTERING
SPUTTERINGS
SPUTTERS
SPUTTERY
SPUTUM
SPY
SPYAL
SPYALS
SPYGLASS
SPYGLASSES
SPYING
SPYINGS
SPYMASTER
SPYMASTERS
SPYRE
SPYRES
SQUAB
SQUABASH
SQUABASHED
SQUABASHES
SQUABASHING
SQUABBED
SQUABBER
SQUABBEST
SQUABBIER
SQUABBIEST
SQUABBING
SQUABBISH
SQUABBLE
SQUABBLED
SQUABBLER
SQUABBLERS
SQUABBLES
SQUABBLING
SQUABBY
SQUABS
SQUACCO
SQUACCOS
SQUAD
SQUADDIES
SQUADDY
SQUADRON
SQUADRONE
SQUADRONED
SQUADRONES
SQUADRONING
SQUADRONS
SQUADS
SQUAIL
SQUAILED
SQUAILER
SQUAILERS

SQUAILING
SQUAILINGS
SQUAILS
SQUALID
SQUALIDER
SQUALIDEST
SQUALIDLY
SQUALL
SQUALLED
SQUALLER
SQUALLERS
SQUALLIER
SQUALLIEST
SQUALLING
SQUALLINGS
SQUALLS
SQUALLY
SQUALOID
SQUALOR
SQUALORS
SQUAMA
SQUAMAE
SQUAMATE
SQUAME
SQUAMELLA
SQUAMELLAS
SQUAMES
SQUAMOSAL
SQUAMOSALS
SQUAMOSE
SQUAMOUS
SQUAMULA
SQUAMULAS
SQUAMULE
SQUAMULES
SQUANDER
SQUANDERED
SQUANDERING
SQUANDERINGS
SQUANDERS
SQUARE
SQUARED
SQUARELY
SQUARER
SQUARERS
SQUARES
SQUAREST
SQUARING
SQUARINGS
SQUARISH
SQUARROSE
SQUARSON
SQUARSONS
SQUASH
SQUASHED
SQUASHER
SQUASHERS
SQUASHES
SQUASHIER
SQUASHIEST
SQUASHILY
SQUASHING
SQUASHY
SQUAT
SQUATNESS
SQUATNESSES
SQUATS
SQUATTED
SQUATTER
SQUATTERED

SQUATTERING
SQUATTERS
SQUATTEST
SQUATTIER
SQUATTIEST
SQUATTING
SQUATTLE
SQUATTLED
SQUATTLES
SQUATTLING
SQUATTY
SQUAW
SQUAWK
SQUAWKED
SQUAWKER
SQUAWKERS
SQUAWKIER
SQUAWKIEST
SQUAWKING
SQUAWKINGS
SQUAWKS
SQUAWKY
SQUAWMAN
SQUAWMEN
SQUAWS
SQUEAK
SQUEAKED
SQUEAKER
SQUEAKERIES
SQUEAKERS
SQUEAKERY
SQUEAKIER
SQUEAKIEST
SQUEAKILY
SQUEAKING
SQUEAKINGS
SQUEAKS
SQUEAKY
SQUEAL
SQUEALED
SQUEALER
SQUEALERS
SQUEALING
SQUEALINGS
SQUEALS
SQUEAMISH
SQUEEDGE
SQUEEDGED
SQUEEDGES
SQUEEDGING
SQUEEGEE
SQUEEGEED
SQUEEGEEING
SQUEEGEES
SQUEEZE
SQUEEZED
SQUEEZER
SQUEEZERS
SQUEEZES
SQUEEZIER
SQUEEZIEST
SQUEEZING
SQUEEZINGS
SQUEEZY
SQUEG
SQUEGGED
SQUEGGER
SQUEGGERS
SQUEGGING
SQUEGGINGS

SQUEGS
SQUELCH
SQUELCHED
SQUELCHER
SQUELCHERS
SQUELCHES
SQUELCHIER
SQUELCHIEST
SQUELCHING
SQUELCHINGS
SQUELCHY
SQUIB
SQUIBBED
SQUIBBING
SQUIBBINGS
SQUIBS
SQUID
SQUIDDED
SQUIDDING
SQUIDGE
SQUIDGED
SQUIDGES
SQUIDGIER
SQUIDGIEST
SQUIDGING
SQUIDGY
SQUIDS
SQUIER
SQUIERS
SQUIFF
SQUIFFER
SQUIFFERS
SQUIFFIER
SQUIFFIEST
SQUIFFY
SQUIGGLE
SQUIGGLED
SQUIGGLES
SQUIGGLIER
SQUIGGLIEST
SQUIGGLING
SQUIGGLY
SQUILGEE
SQUILGEED
SQUILGEEING
SQUILGEES
SQUILL
SQUILLS
SQUINANCIES
SQUINANCY
SQUINCH
SQUINCHES
SQUINIED
SQUINIES
SQUINNIED
SQUINNIES
SQUINNY
SQUINNYING
SQUINT
SQUINTED
SQUINTER
SQUINTERS
SQUINTEST
SQUINTING
SQUINTINGS
SQUINTS
SQUINY
SQUINYING
SQUIRAGE
SQUIRAGES

SQUIRALTIES
SQUIRALTY
SQUIRARCH
SQUIRARCHS
SQUIRE
SQUIREAGE
SQUIREAGES
SQUIRED
SQUIREDOM
SQUIREDOMS
SQUIREEN
SQUIREENS
SQUIRELY
SQUIRES
SQUIRESS
SQUIRESSES
SQUIRING
SQUIRM
SQUIRMED
SQUIRMIER
SQUIRMIEST
SQUIRMING
SQUIRMS
SQUIRMY
SQUIRR
SQUIRRED
SQUIRREL
SQUIRRELLED
SQUIRRELLING
SQUIRRELS
SQUIRRELY
SQUIRRING
SQUIRRS
SQUIRT
SQUIRTED
SQUIRTER
SQUIRTERS
SQUIRTING
SQUIRTINGS
SQUIRTS
SQUISH
SQUISHED
SQUISHES
SQUISHIER
SQUISHIEST
SQUISHING
SQUISHY
SQUIT
SQUITCH
SQUITCHES
SQUITS
SRADDHA
SRADDHAS
ST
STAB
STABBED
STABBER
STABBERS
STABBING
STABBINGS
STABILE
STABILES
STABILISE
STABILISED
STABILISES
STABILISING
STABILITIES
STABILITY
STABILIZE
STABILIZED

STABILIZES
STABILIZING
STABLE
STABLED
STABLER
STABLERS
STABLES
STABLEST
STABLING
STABLINGS
STABLISH
STABLISHED
STABLISHES
STABLISHING
STABLY
STABS
STACCATO
STACCATOS
STACK
STACKED
STACKER
STACKERS
STACKET
STACKETS
STACKING
STACKINGS
STACKS
STACKYARD
STACKYARDS
STACTE
STACTES
STADDA
STADDAS
STADDLE
STADDLES
STADE
STADES
STADIA
STADIAL
STADIALS
STADIAS
STADIUM
STADIUMS
STAFF
STAFFAGE
STAFFAGES
STAFFED
STAFFER
STAFFERS
STAFFING
STAFFROOM
STAFFROOMS
STAFFS
STAG
STAGE
STAGED
STAGER
STAGERIES
STAGERS
STAGERY
STAGES
STAGEY
STAGGARD
STAGGARDS
STAGGED
STAGGER
STAGGERED
STAGGERER
STAGGERERS
STAGGERING

STAGGERINGS
STAGGERS
STAGGING
STAGHORN
STAGHORNS
STAGHOUND
STAGHOUNDS
STAGIER
STAGIEST
STAGILY
STAGINESS
STAGINESSES
STAGING
STAGINGS
STAGNANCIES
STAGNANCY
STAGNANT
STAGNATE
STAGNATED
STAGNATES
STAGNATING
STAGS
STAGY
STAID
STAIDER
STAIDEST
STAIDLY
STAIDNESS
STAIDNESSES
STAIG
STAIGS
STAIN
STAINED
STAINER
STAINERS
STAINING
STAININGS
STAINLESS
STAINS
STAIR
STAIRCASE
STAIRCASES
STAIRED
STAIRFOOT
STAIRFOOTS
STAIRHEAD
STAIRHEADS
STAIRS
STAIRWAY
STAIRWAYS
STAIRWISE
STAITH
STAITHE
STAITHES
STAITHS
STAKE
STAKED
STAKES
STAKING
STALACTIC
STALAG
STALAGMA
STALAGMAS
STALAGS
STALE
STALED
STALELY
STALEMATE
STALEMATED
STALEMATES

STALEMATING
STALENESS
STALENESSES
STALER
STALES
STALEST
STALING
STALK
STALKED
STALKER
STALKERS
STALKIER
STALKIEST
STALKING
STALKINGS
STALKLESS
STALKO
STALKOES
STALKS
STALKY
STALL
STALLAGE
STALLAGES
STALLED
STALLING
STALLINGS
STALLION
STALLIONS
STALLMAN
STALLMEN
STALLS
STALWART
STALWARTS
STALWORTH
STALWORTHS
STAMEN
STAMENED
STAMENS
STAMINA
STAMINAL
STAMINAS
STAMINATE
STAMINEAL
STAMINODE
STAMINODES
STAMINODIES
STAMINODY
STAMINOID
STAMMEL
STAMMELS
STAMMER
STAMMERED
STAMMERER
STAMMERERS
STAMMERING
STAMMERINGS
STAMMERS
STAMNOI
STAMNOS
STAMP
STAMPED
STAMPEDE
STAMPEDED
STAMPEDES
STAMPEDING
STAMPEDO
STAMPEDOED
STAMPEDOES
STAMPEDOING
STAMPER

STAMPERS
STAMPING
STAMPINGS
STAMPS
STANCE
STANCES
STANCH
STANCHED
STANCHEL
STANCHELLED
STANCHELLING
STANCHELS
STANCHER
STANCHERED
STANCHERING
STANCHERS
STANCHES
STANCHEST
STANCHING
STANCHINGS
STANCHION
STANCHIONED
STANCHIONING
STANCHIONS
STANCHLY
STANCK
STAND
STANDARD
STANDARDS
STANDEN
STANDER
STANDERS
STANDGALE
STANDGALES
STANDING
STANDINGS
STANDISH
STANDISHES
STANDS
STANE
STANED
STANES
STANG
STANGED
STANGING
STANGS
STANHOPE
STANHOPES
STANIEL
STANIELS
STANING
STANK
STANKS
STANNARIES
STANNARY
STANNATE
STANNATES
STANNATOR
STANNATORS
STANNEL
STANNELS
STANNIC
STANNITE
STANNITES
STANNOUS
STANYEL
STANYELS
STANZA
STANZAIC
STANZAS

STANZE
STANZES
STANZO
STANZOES
STANZOS
STAP
STAPEDES
STAPEDIAL
STAPEDII
STAPEDIUS
STAPEDIUSES
STAPELIA
STAPELIAS
STAPES
STAPH
STAPHS
STAPHYLE
STAPHYLES
STAPLE
STAPLED
STAPLER
STAPLERS
STAPLES
STAPLING
STAPPED
STAPPING
STAPPLE
STAPPLES
STAPS
STAR
STARAGEN
STARAGENS
STARBOARD
STARBOARDED
STARBOARDING
STARBOARDS
STARCH
STARCHED
STARCHER
STARCHERS
STARCHES
STARCHIER
STARCHIEST
STARCHILY
STARCHING
STARCHY
STARDOM
STARDOMS
STARE
STARED
STARER
STARERS
STARES
STARETS
STARETSES
STARETZ
STARETZES
STARFISH
STARFISHES
STARING
STARINGLY
STARINGS
STARK
STARKED
STARKEN
STARKENED
STARKENING
STARKENS
STARKER
STARKERS

STARKEST
STARKING
STARKLY
STARKNESS
STARKNESSES
STARKS
STARLESS
STARLET
STARLETS
STARLIGHT
STARLIGHTS
STARLIKE
STARLING
STARLINGS
STARLIT
STARN
STARNED
STARNIE
STARNIES
STARNING
STARNS
STAROSTA
STAROSTAS
STAROSTIES
STAROSTY
STARR
STARRED
STARRIER
STARRIEST
STARRILY
STARRING
STARRINGS
STARRS
STARRY
STARS
STARSHINE
STARSHINES
STARSPOT
STARSPOTS
START
STARTED
STARTER
STARTERS
STARTFUL
STARTING
STARTINGS
STARTISH
STARTLE
STARTLED
STARTLER
STARTLERS
STARTLES
STARTLING
STARTLINGS
STARTLISH
STARTLY
STARTS
STARVE
STARVED
STARVES
STARVING
STARVINGS
STARWORT
STARWORTS
STASES
STASH
STASHED
STASHES
STASHIE
STASHIES

STASHING
STASIDION
STASIDIONS
STASIMA
STASIMON
STASIS
STATABLE
STATAL
STATANT
STATE
STATED
STATEDLY
STATEHOOD
STATEHOODS
STATELESS
STATELIER
STATELIEST
STATELILY
STATELY
STATEMENT
STATEMENTS
STATER
STATEROOM
STATEROOMS
STATERS
STATES
STATESIDE
STATESMAN
STATESMEN
STATEWIDE
STATIC
STATICAL
STATICS
STATING
STATION
STATIONAL
STATIONED
STATIONER
STATIONERS
STATIONING
STATIONS
STATISM
STATISMS
STATIST
STATISTIC
STATISTICS
STATISTS
STATIVE
STATOCYST
STATOCYSTS
STATOLITH
STATOLITHS
STATOR
STATORS
STATUA
STATUARIES
STATUARY
STATUAS
STATUE
STATUED
STATUES
STATUETTE
STATUETTES
STATURE
STATURED
STATURES
STATUS
STATUTE
STATUTES
STATUTORY

STAUNCH	STEAMIEST	STEELBOW	STEEVING	STENCHES
STAUNCHED	STEAMILY	STEELBOWS	STEEVINGS	STENCHIER
STAUNCHER	STEAMING	STEELD	STEGNOSES	STENCHIEST
STAUNCHES	STEAMINGS	STEELED	STEGNOSIS	STENCHING
STAUNCHEST	STEAMS	STEELIER	STEGNOTIC	STENCHY
STAUNCHING	STEAMSHIP	STEELIEST	STEGODON	STENCIL
STAUNCHLY	STEAMSHIPS	STEELING	STEGODONS	STENCILLED
STAVE	STEAMY	STEELINGS	STEGODONT	STENCILLING
STAVED	STEAN	STEELS	STEGODONTS	STENCILLINGS
STAVES	STEANE	STEELWORK	STEGOMYIA	STENCILS
STAVING	STEANED	STEELWORKS	STEGOMYIAS	STEND
STAW	STEANES	STEELY	STEGOSAUR	STENDED
STAWED	STEANING	STEELYARD	STEGOSAURS	STENDING
STAWING	STEANINGS	STEELYARDS	STEIL	STENDS
STAWS	STEANS	STEEM	STEILS	STENGAH
STAY	STEAR	STEEMED	STEIN	STENGAHS
STAYED	STEARAGE	STEEMING	STEINBOCK	STENLOCK
STAYER	STEARAGES	STEEMS	STEINBOCKS	STENLOCKS
STAYERS	STEARATE	STEEN	STEINED	STENNED
STAYING	STEARATES	STEENBOK	STEINING	STENNING
STAYINGS	STEARD	STEENBOKS	STEININGS	STENOPAIC
STAYLESS	STEARE	STEENBRAS	STEINS	STENOSED
STAYNE	STEARED	STEENBRASES	STELA	STENOSES
STAYNED	STEARES	STEENED	STELAE	STENOSIS
STAYNES	STEARIC	STEENING	STELAR	STENOTIC
STAYNING	STEARIN	STEENINGS	STELE	STENOTYPE
STAYRE	STEARINE	STEENKIRK	STELENE	STENOTYPES
STAYRES	STEARINES	STEENKIRKS	STELL	STENOTYPIES
STAYS	STEARING	STEENS	STELLAR	STENOTYPY
STAYSAIL	STEARINS	STEEP	STELLATE	STENS
STAYSAILS	STEARS	STEEPED	STELLATED	STENT
STEAD	STEARSMAN	STEEPEN	STELLED	STENTED
STEADED	STEARSMEN	STEEPENED	STELLIFIED	STENTING
STEADFAST	STEATITE	STEEPENING	STELLIFIES	STENTOR
STEADIED	STEATITES	STEEPENS	STELLIFY	STENTORS
STEADIER	STEATITIC	STEEPER	STELLIFYING	STENTOUR
STEADIES	STEATOMA	STEEPERS	STELLIFYINGS	STENTOURS
STEADIEST	STEATOMAS	STEEPEST	STELLING	STENTS
STEADILY	STEATOSES	STEEPING	STELLION	STEP
STEADING	STEATOSIS	STEEPISH	STELLIONS	STEPBAIRN
STEADINGS	STED	STEEPLE	STELLS	STEPBAIRNS
STEADS	STEDD	STEEPLED	STELLULAR	STEPCHILD
STEADY	STEDDE	STEEPLES	STEM	STEPCHILDREN
STEADYING	STEDDED	STEEPLY	STEMBOK	STEPDAME
STEAK	STEDDES	STEEPNESS	STEMBOKS	STEPDAMES
STEAKS	STEDDIED	STEEPNESSES	STEMBUCK	STEPHANE
STEAL	STEDDIES	STEEPS	STEMBUCKS	STEPHANES
STEALE	STEDDING	STEEPY	STEME	STEPNEY
STEALED	STEDDS	STEER	STEMED	STEPNEYS
STEALER	STEDDY	STEERABLE	STEMES	STEPPE
STEALERS	STEDDYING	STEERAGE	STEMING	STEPPED
STEALES	STEDE	STEERAGES	STEMLESS	STEPPER
STEALING	STEDED	STEERED	STEMLET	STEPPERS
STEALINGS	STEDES	STEERER	STEMLETS	STEPPES
STEALS	STEDFAST	STEERERS	STEMMA	STEPPING
STEALT	STEDING	STEERIES	STEMMATA	STEPS
STEALTH	STEDS	STEERING	STEMME	STEPSON
STEALTHIER	STEED	STEERINGS	STEMMED	STEPSONS
STEALTHIEST	STEEDED	STEERLING	STEMMES	STEPT
STEALTHS	STEEDIED	STEERLINGS	STEMMING	STEPWISE
STEALTHY	STEEDIES	STEERS	STEMPEL	STERADIAN
STEAM	STEEDING	STEERSMAN	STEMPELS	STERADIANS
STEAMBOAT	STEEDS	STEERSMEN	STEMPLE	STERCORAL
STEAMBOATS	STEEDY	STEERY	STEMPLES	STERCULIA
STEAMED	STEEDYING	STEEVE	STEMS	STERCULIAS
STEAMER	STEEK	STEEVED	STEMSON	STERE
STEAMERS	STEEKING	STEEVELY	STEMSONS	STEREO
STEAMIE	STEEKIT	STEEVER	STEN	STEREOED
STEAMIER	STEEKS	STEEVES	STENCH	STEREOING
STEAMIES	STEEL	STEEVEST	STENCHED	STEREOME

STITCHERS

STEREOMES	STEWARDRY	STICKS	STILLER	STINTEDLY
STEREOS	STEWARDS	STICKUP	STILLERS	STINTER
STERES	STEWARTRIES	STICKUPS	STILLEST	STINTERS
STERIC	STEWARTRY	STICKWORK	STILLIER	STINTIER
STERIGMA	STEWED	STICKWORKS	STILLIEST	STINTIEST
STERIGMATA	STEWER	STICKY	STILLING	STINTING
STERILE	STEWERS	STICKYING	STILLINGS	STINTINGS
STERILISE	STEWIER	STIDDIE	STILLION	STINTLESS
STERILISED	STEWIEST	STIDDIED	STILLIONS	STINTS
STERILISES	STEWING	STIDDIES	STILLNESS	STINTY
STERILISING	STEWINGS	STIDDYING	STILLNESSES	STIPA
STERILITIES	STEWPAN	STIE	STILLS	STIPAS
STERILITY	STEWPANS	STIED	STILLY	STIPE
STERILIZE	STEWPOND	STIEING	STILT	STIPEL
STERILIZED	STEWPONDS	STIES	STILTED	STIPELS
STERILIZES	STEWPOT	STIEVE	STILTEDLY	STIPEND
STERILIZING	STEWPOTS	STIEVELY	STILTER	STIPENDS
STERLET	STEWS	STIEVER	STILTERS	STIPES
STERLETS	STEWY	STIEVEST	STILTIER	STIPITATE
STERLING	STEY	STIFF	STILTIEST	STIPITES
STERLINGS	STEYER	STIFFED	STILTING	STIPPLE
STERN	STEYEST	STIFFEN	STILTINGS	STIPPLED
STERNAGE	STHENIC	STIFFENED	STILTISH	STIPPLER
STERNAGES	STIBBLE	STIFFENER	STILTS	STIPPLERS
STERNAL	STIBBLER	STIFFENERS	STILTY	STIPPLES
STERNEBRA	STIBBLERS	STIFFENING	STIME	STIPPLING
STERNEBRAE	STIBBLES	STIFFENINGS	STIMED	STIPPLINGS
STERNED	STIBIAL	STIFFENS	STIMES	STIPULAR
STERNER	STIBINE	STIFFER	STIMIE	STIPULARY
STERNEST	STIBINES	STIFFEST	STIMIED	STIPULATE
STERNING	STIBIUM	STIFFING	STIMIES	STIPULATED
STERNITE	STIBIUMS	STIFFISH	STIMING	STIPULATES
STERNITES	STIBNITE	STIFFLY	STIMULANT	STIPULATING
STERNITIC	STIBNITES	STIFFNESS	STIMULANTS	STIPULE
STERNLY	STICCADO	STIFFNESSES	STIMULATE	STIPULED
STERNMOST	STICCADOES	STIFFS	STIMULATED	STIPULES
STERNNESS	STICCADOS	STIFLE	STIMULATES	STIR
STERNNESSES	STICCATO	STIFLED	STIMULATING	STIRABOUT
STERNPORT	STICCATOES	STIFLER	STIMULI	STIRABOUTS
STERNPORTS	STICCATOS	STIFLERS	STIMULUS	STIRE
STERNS	STICH	STIFLES	STIMY	STIRED
STERNSON	STICHERON	STIFLING	STIMYING	STIRES
STERNSONS	STICHERONS	STIFLINGS	STING	STIRING
STERNUM	STICHIC	STIGMA	STINGAREE	STIRK
STERNUMS	STICHIDIA	STIGMAS	STINGAREES	STIRKS
STERNWARD	STICHOI	STIGMATA	STINGED	STIRLESS
STERNWARDS	STICHOS	STIGMATIC	STINGER	STIRP
STERNWAY	STICHS	STIGMATICS	STINGERS	STIRPES
STERNWAYS	STICK	STIGME	STINGIER	STIRPS
STEROID	STICKED	STIGMES	STINGIEST	STIRRA
STEROIDS	STICKER	STILB	STINGILY	STIRRAH
STEROL	STICKERS	STILBENE	STINGING	STIRRAHS
STEROLS	STICKFUL	STILBENES	STINGINGS	STIRRAS
STERVE	STICKFULS	STILBITE	STINGLESS	STIRRE
STERVED	STICKIED	STILBITES	STINGO	STIRRED
STERVES	STICKIER	STILBS	STINGOS	STIRRER
STERVING	STICKIES	STILE	STINGS	STIRRERS
STET	STICKIEST	STILED	STINGY	STIRRES
STETS	STICKILY	STILES	STINK	STIRRING
STETTED	STICKING	STILET	STINKARD	STIRRINGS
STETTING	STICKINGS	STILETS	STINKARDS	STIRRUP
STEVEDORE	STICKIT	STILETTO	STINKER	STIRRUPS
STEVEDORED	STICKJAW	STILETTOED	STINKERS	STIRS
STEVEDORES	STICKJAWS	STILETTOING	STINKHORN	STISHIE
STEVEDORING	STICKLE	STILETTOS	STINKHORNS	STISHIES
STEVEN	STICKLED	STILING	STINKING	STITCH
STEVENS	STICKLER	STILL	STINKINGS	STITCHED
STEW	STICKLERS	STILLAGE	STINKS	STITCHER
STEWARD	STICKLES	STILLAGES	STINT	STITCHERIES
STEWARDRIES	STICKLING	STILLED	STINTED	STITCHERS

STITCHERY	STODGY	STONECROP	STOOP	STORMY
STITCHES	STOEP	STONECROPS	STOOPE	STORNELLI
STITCHING	STOEPS	STONED	STOOPED	STORNELLO
STITCHINGS	STOGEY	STONEFISH	STOOPER	STORY
STITHIED	STOGEYS	STONEFISHES	STOOPERS	STORYETTE
STITHIES	STOGIE	STONEHAND	STOOPES	STORYETTES
STITHY	STOGIES	STONEHANDS	STOOPING	STORYING
STITHYING	STOGY	STONELESS	STOOPS	STORYINGS
STIVE	STOIC	STONEN	STOOR.	STOT
STIVED	STOICAL	STONER	STOORS	STOTINKA
STIVER	STOICALLY	STONERN	STOOSHIE	STOTINKI
STIVERS	STOICISM	STONERS	STOOSHIES	STOTIOUS
STIVES	STOICISMS	STONES	STOP	STOTS
STIVING	STOIT	STONESHOT	STOPE	STOTTED
STIVY	STOITED	STONESHOTS	STOPED	STOTTER
STOA	STOITER	STONEWALL	STOPES	STOTTERED
STOAE	STOITERED	STONEWALLED	STOPING	STOTTERING
STOAI	STOITERING	STONEWALLING	STOPINGS	STOTTERS
STOAS	STOITERS	STONEWALLINGS	STOPLESS	STOTTING
STOAT	STOITING	STONEWALLS	STOPPAGE	STOUN
STOATS	STOITS	STONEWARE	STOPPAGES	STOUND
STOB	STOKE	STONEWARES	STOPPED	STOUNDED
STOBS	STOKED	STONEWORK	STOPPER	STOUNDING
STOCCADO	STOKEHOLD	STONEWORKS	STOPPERED	STOUNDS
STOCCADOS	STOKEHOLDS	STONEWORT	STOPPERING	STOUNING
STOCCATA	STOKER	STONEWORTS	STOPPERS	STOUNS
STOCCATAS	STOKERS	STONG	STOPPING	STOUP
STOCK	STOKES	STONIED	STOPPINGS	STOUPS
STOCKADE	STOKING	STONIER	STOPPLE	STOUR
STOCKADED	STOLA	STONIES	STOPPLED	STOURIER
STOCKADES	STOLAS	STONIEST	STOPPLES	STOURIEST
STOCKADING	STOLE	STONILY	STOPPLING	STOURS
STOCKED	STOLED	STONINESS	STOPS	STOURY
STOCKFISH	STOLEN	STONINESSES	STORABLE	STOUSH
STOCKFISHES	STOLES	STONING	STORAGE	STOUSHED
STOCKIER	STOLID	STONINGS	STORAGES	STOUSHES
STOCKIEST	STOLIDER	STONK	STORAX	STOUSHING
STOCKILY	STOLIDEST	STONKER	STORAXES	STOUT
STOCKINET	STOLIDITIES	STONKERED	STORE	STOUTEN
STOCKINETS	STOLIDITY	STONKERING	STORED	STOUTENED
STOCKING	STOLIDLY	STONKERS	STOREMAN	STOUTENING
STOCKINGS	STOLN	STONKS	STOREMEN	STOUTENS
STOCKISH	STOLON	STONN	STORER	STOUTER
STOCKIST	STOLONS	STONNE	STOREROOM	STOUTEST
STOCKISTS	STOMA	STONNED	STOREROOMS	STOUTH
STOCKLESS	STOMACH	STONNES	STORERS	STOUTHRIE
STOCKMAN	STOMACHAL	STONNING	STORES	STOUTHRIES
STOCKMEN	STOMACHED	STONNS	STOREY	STOUTHS
STOCKPILE	STOMACHER	STONY	STOREYED	STOUTISH
STOCKPILED	STOMACHERS	STONYING	STOREYS	STOUTLY
STOCKPILES	STOMACHIC	STOOD	STORGE	STOUTNESS
STOCKPILING	STOMACHICS	STOODEN	STORGES	STOUTNESSES
STOCKPILINGS	STOMACHING	STOOGE	STORIATED	STOUTS
STOCKS	STOMACHS	STOOGED	STORIED	STOVAINE
STOCKTAKE	STOMACHY	STOOGES	STORIES	STOVAINES
STOCKTAKES	STOMATA	STOOGING	STORIETTE	STOVE
STOCKWORK	STOMATAL	STOOK	STORIETTES	STOVED
STOCKWORKS	STOMATIC	STOOKED	STORING	STOVEPIPE
STOCKY	STOMODEA	STOOKER	STORK	STOVEPIPES
STOCKYARD	STOMODEUM	STOOKERS	STORKS	STOVER
STOCKYARDS	STOMODEUMS	STOOKING	STORM	STOVERS
STODGE	STOMP	STOOKS	STORMED	STOVES
STODGED	STOMPED	STOOL	STORMFUL	STOVIES
STODGER	STOMPING	STOOLBALL	STORMIER	STOVING
STODGERS	STOMPS	STOOLBALLS	STORMIEST	STOVINGS
STODGES	STOND	STOOLED	STORMILY	STOW
STODGIER	STONDS	STOOLIE	STORMING	STOWAGE
STODGIEST	STONE	STOOLIES	STORMINGS	STOWAGES
STODGILY	STONECHAT	STOOLING	STORMLESS	STOWAWAY
STODGING	STONECHATS	STOOLS	STORMS	STOWAWAYS

STOWDOWN	STRAINT	STRATEGICS	STREAMLET	STREWING
STOWDOWNS	STRAINTS	STRATEGIES	STREAMLETS	STREWINGS
STOWED	STRAIT	STRATEGY	STREAMS	STREWMENT
STOWER	STRAITED	STRATH	STREAMY	STREWMENTS
STOWERS	STRAITEN	STRATHS	STREEK	STREWN
STOWING	STRAITENED	STRATIFIED	STREEKED	STREWS
STOWINGS	STRAITENING	STRATIFIES	STREEKING	STREWTH
STOWLINS	STRAITENS	STRATIFY	STREEKS	STRIA
STOWN	STRAITER	STRATIFYING	STREEL	STRIAE
STOWND	STRAITEST	STRATONIC	STREELED	STRIATA
STOWNDED	STRAITING	STRATOSE	STREELING	STRIATE
STOWNDING	STRAITLY	STRATOUS	STREELS	STRIATED
STOWNDS	STRAITS	STRATUM	STREET	STRIATES
STOWNLINS	STRAK	STRATUS	STREETAGE	STRIATING
STOWRE	STRAKE	STRATUSES	STREETAGES	STRIATION
STOWRES	STRAKES	STRAUCHT	STREETED	STRIATIONS
STOWS	STRAMAÇON	STRAUCHTED	STREETFUL	STRIATUM
STRABISM	STRAMAÇONS	STRAUCHTER	STREETFULS	STRIATUMS
STRABISMS	STRAMASH	STRAUCHTEST	STREETIER	STRIATURE
STRACK	STRAMASHED	STRAUCHTING	STREETIEST	STRIATURES
STRAD	STRAMASHES	STRAUCHTS	STREETS	STRICH
STRADDLE	STRAMASHING	STRAUGHT	STREETWAY	STRICHES
STRADDLED	STRAMAZON	STRAUGHTED	STREETWAYS	STRICKEN
STRADDLES	STRAMAZONS	STRAUGHTER	STREETY	STRICKLE
STRADDLING	STRAMMEL	STRAUGHTEST	STREIGHT	STRICKLED
STRADIOT	STRAMMELS	STRAUGHTING	STREIGNE	STRICKLES
STRADIOTS	STRAMP	STRAUGHTS	STREIGNED	STRICKLING
STRADS	STRAMPED	STRAUNGE	STREIGNES	STRICT
STRAE	STRAMPING	STRAVAIG	STREIGNING	STRICTER
STRAES	STRAMPS	STRAVAIGED	STRELITZ	STRICTEST
STRAFE	STRAND	STRAVAIGING	STRELITZES	STRICTISH
STRAFED	STRANDED	STRAVAIGS	STRELITZI	STRICTLY
STRAFES	STRANDING	STRAW	STRENE	STRICTURE
STRAFF	STRANDS	STRAWED	STRENES	STRICTURES
STRAFFED	STRANGE	STRAWEN	STRENGTH	STRID
STRAFFING	STRANGELY	STRAWIER	STRENGTHS	STRIDDEN
STRAFFS	STRANGER	STRAWIEST	STRENUITIES	STRIDDLE
STRAFING	STRANGERED	STRAWING	STRENUITY	STRIDDLED
STRAG	STRANGERING	STRAWLESS	STRENUOUS	STRIDDLES
STRAGGLE	STRANGERS	STRAWN	STREP	STRIDDLING
STRAGGLED	STRANGEST	STRAWS	STREPENT	STRIDE
STRAGGLER	STRANGLE	STRAWY	STREPS	STRIDENCE
STRAGGLERS	STRANGLED	STRAY	STRESS	STRIDENCES
STRAGGLES	STRANGLER	STRAYED	STRESSED	STRIDENCIES
STRAGGLIER	STRANGLERS	STRAYER	STRESSES	STRIDENCY
STRAGGLIEST	STRANGLES	STRAYERS	STRESSFUL	STRIDENT
STRAGGLING	STRANGLING	STRAYING	STRESSING	STRIDES
STRAGGLINGS	STRANGURIES	STRAYINGS	STRESSOR	STRIDING
STRAGGLY	STRANGURY	STRAYLING	STRESSORS	STRIDLING
STRAGS	STRAP	STRAYLINGS	STRETCH	STRIDOR
STRAICHT	STRAPLESS	STRAYS	STRETCHED	STRIDORS
STRAICHTER	STRAPPADO	STREAK	STRETCHER	STRIDS
STRAICHTEST	STRAPPADOED	STREAKED	STRETCHERED	STRIFE
STRAIGHT	STRAPPADOING	STREAKER	STRETCHERING	STRIFEFUL
STRAIGHTED	STRAPPADOS	STREAKERS	STRETCHERS	STRIFES
STRAIGHTER	STRAPPED	STREAKIER	STRETCHES	STRIFT
STRAIGHTEST	STRAPPER	STREAKIEST	STRETCHIER	STRIFTS
STRAIGHTING	STRAPPERS	STREAKILY	STRETCHIEST	STRIG
STRAIGHTS	STRAPPING	STREAKING	STRETCHING	STRIGA
STRAIK	STRAPPINGS	STREAKINGS	STRETCHY	STRIGAE
STRAIKED	STRAPPY	STREAKS	STRETTA	STRIGATE
STRAIKING	STRAPS	STREAKY	STRETTE	STRIGGED
STRAIKS	STRAPWORT	STREAM	STRETTI	STRIGGING
STRAIN	STRAPWORTS	STREAMED	STRETTO	STRIGIL
STRAINED	STRASS	STREAMER	STREW	STRIGILS
STRAINER	STRASSES	STREAMERS	STREWAGE	STRIGINE
STRAINERS	STRATA	STREAMIER	STREWAGES	STRIGOSE
STRAINING	STRATAGEM	STREAMIEST	STREWED	STRIGS
STRAININGS	STRATAGEMS	STREAMING	STREWER	STRIKE
STRAINS	STRATEGIC	STREAMINGS	STREWERS	STRIKEOUT

STRIKEOUTS
STRIKER
STRIKERS
STRIKES
STRIKING
STRIKINGS
STRING
STRINGED
STRINGENT
STRINGER
STRINGERS
STRINGIER
STRINGIEST
STRINGILY
STRINGING
STRINGINGS
STRINGS
STRINGY
STRINKLE
STRINKLED
STRINKLES
STRINKLING
STRINKLINGS
STRIP
STRIPE
STRIPED
STRIPES
STRIPEY
STRIPIER
STRIPIEST
STRIPING
STRIPINGS
STRIPLING
STRIPLINGS
STRIPPED
STRIPPER
STRIPPERS
STRIPPING
STRIPPINGS
STRIPS
STRIPY
STRIVE
STRIVED
STRIVEN
STRIVER
STRIVERS
STRIVES
STRIVING
STRIVINGS
STROAM
STROAMED
STROAMING
STROAMS
STROBE
STROBES
STROBIC
STROBILA
STROBILAE
STROBILE
STROBILES
STROBILI
STROBILUS
STRODDLE
STRODDLED
STRODDLES
STRODDLING
STRODE
STRODLE
STRODLED
STRODLES

STRODLING
STROKE
STROKED
STROKEN
STROKER
STROKERS
STROKES
STROKING
STROKINGS
STROLL
STROLLED
STROLLER
STROLLERS
STROLLING
STROLLINGS
STROLLS
STROMA
STROMATA
STROMATIC
STROMB
STROMBS
STROMBUS
STROMBUSES
STROND
STRONDS
STRONG
STRONGARM
STRONGARMED
STRONGARMING
STRONGARMS
STRONGER
STRONGEST
STRONGISH
STRONGLY
STRONGMAN
STRONGMEN
STRONGYLE
STRONGYLES
STRONTIA
STRONTIAN
STRONTIANS
STRONTIAS
STRONTIUM
STRONTIUMS
STROOK
STROOKE
STROOKEN
STROOKES
STROP
STROPHE
STROPHES
STROPHIC
STROPPED
STROPPIER
STROPPIEST
STROPPING
STROPPY
STROPS
STROSSERS
STROUD
STROUDING
STROUDINGS
STROUDS
STROUP
STROUPS
STROUT
STROUTED
STROUTING
STROUTS
STROVE

STROW
STROWED
STROWER
STROWERS
STROWING
STROWINGS
STROWN
STROWS
STROY
STROYED
STROYING
STROYS
STRUCK
STRUCKEN
STRUCTURE
STRUCTURED
STRUCTURES
STRUCTURING
STRUDEL
STRUDELS
STRUGGLE
STRUGGLED
STRUGGLER
STRUGGLERS
STRUGGLES
STRUGGLING
STRUGGLINGS
STRUM
STRUMA
STRUMAE
STRUMATIC
STRUMITIS
STRUMITISES
STRUMMED
STRUMMEL
STRUMMELS
STRUMMING
STRUMOSE
STRUMOUS
STRUMPET
STRUMPETED
STRUMPETING
STRUMPETS
STRUMS
STRUNG
STRUNT
STRUNTED
STRUNTING
STRUNTS
STRUT
STRUTS
STRUTTED
STRUTTER
STRUTTERS
STRUTTING
STRUTTINGS
STRYCHNIA
STRYCHNIAS
STRYCHNIC
STRYFULL
STUB
STUBBED
STUBBIER
STUBBIES
STUBBIEST
STUBBING
STUBBLE
STUBBLED
STUBBLES
STUBBLIER

STUBBLIEST
STUBBLY
STUBBORN
STUBBORNED
STUBBORNING
STUBBORNS
STUBBY
STUBS
STUCCO
STUCCOED
STUCCOER
STUCCOERS
STUCCOING
STUCCOS
STUCK
STUCKS
STUD
STUDDED
STUDDEN
STUDDING
STUDDINGS
STUDDLE
STUDDLES
STUDENT
STUDENTRIES
STUDENTRY
STUDENTS
STUDIED
STUDIEDLY
STUDIER
STUDIERS
STUDIES
STUDIO
STUDIOS
STUDIOUS
STUDS
STUDWORK
STUDWORKS
STUDY
STUDYING
STUFF
STUFFED
STUFFER
STUFFERS
STUFFIER
STUFFIEST
STUFFILY
STUFFING
STUFFINGS
STUFFS
STUFFY
STUGGY
STULL
STULLS
STULM
STULMS
STULTIFIED
STULTIFIES
STULTIFY
STULTIFYING
STUM
STUMBLE
STUMBLED
STUMBLER
STUMBLERS
STUMBLES
STUMBLIER
STUMBLIEST
STUMBLING
STUMBLY

STUMER
STUMERS
STUMM
STUMMED
STUMMEL
STUMMELS
STUMMING
STUMMS
STUMP
STUMPAGE
STUMPAGES
STUMPED
STUMPER
STUMPERS
STUMPIER
STUMPIES
STUMPIEST
STUMPILY
STUMPING
STUMPS
STUMPY
STUMS
STUN
STUNG
STUNK
STUNKARD
STUNNED
STUNNER
STUNNERS
STUNNING
STUNNINGS
STUNS
STUNSAIL
STUNSAILS
STUNT
STUNTED
STUNTING
STUNTMAN
STUNTMEN
STUNTS
STUPA
STUPAS
STUPE
STUPED
STUPEFIED
STUPEFIER
STUPEFIERS
STUPEFIES
STUPEFY
STUPEFYING
STUPENT
STUPES
STUPID
STUPIDER
STUPIDEST
STUPIDITIES
STUPIDITY
STUPIDLY
STUPIDS
STUPING
STUPOR
STUPOROUS
STUPORS
STUPRATE
STUPRATED
STUPRATES
STUPRATING
STURDIED
STURDIER
STURDIES

STURDIEST	STYMYING	SUBBING	SUBERISING	SUBLIMATE
STURDILY	STYPSIS	SUBBINGS	SUBERIZE	SUBLIMATED
STURDY	STYPSISES	SUBBRANCH	SUBERIZED	SUBLIMATES
STURE	STYPTIC	SUBBRANCHES	SUBERIZES	SUBLIMATING
STURGEON	STYPTICAL	SUBBREED	SUBERIZING	SUBLIME
STURGEONS	STYPTICS	SUBBREEDS	SUBEROSE	SUBLIMED
STURMER	STYRAX	SUBCANTOR	SUBEROUS	SUBLIMELY
STURMERS	STYRAXES	SUBCANTORS	SUBERS	SUBLIMER
STURNINE	STYRE	SUBCAUDAL	SUBFAMILIES	SUBLIMES
STURNOID	STYRED	SUBCLASS	SUBFAMILY	SUBLIMEST
STURT	STYRENE	SUBCLASSES	SUBFEU	SUBLIMING
STURTED	STYRENES	SUBCLAUSE	SUBFEUED	SUBLIMINGS
STURTING	STYRES	SUBCLAUSES	SUBFEUING	SUBLIMISE
STURTS	STYRING	SUBCOSTA	SUBFEUS	SUBLIMISED
STUSHIE	SUABILITIES	SUBCOSTAL	SUBFLOOR	SUBLIMISES
STUSHIES	SUABILITY	SUBCOSTALS	SUBFLOORS	SUBLIMISING
STUTTER	SUABLE	SUBCOSTAS	SUBFUSC	SUBLIMITIES
STUTTERED	SUASIBLE	SUBDEACON	SUBFUSCS	SUBLIMITY
STUTTERER	SUASION	SUBDEACONS	SUBFUSK	SUBLIMIZE
STUTTERERS	SUASIONS	SUBDEAN	SUBFUSKS	SUBLIMIZED
STUTTERING	SUASIVE	SUBDEANS	SUBGENERA	SUBLIMIZES
STUTTERINGS	SUASIVELY	SUBDEW	SUBGENUS	SUBLIMIZING
STUTTERS	SUASORY	SUBDEWED	SUBGENUSES	SUBLINEAR
STY	SUAVE	SUBDEWING	SUBGRADE	SUBLUNAR
STYE	SUAVELY	SUBDEWS	SUBGRADES	SUBLUNARIES
STYED	SUAVER	SUBDIVIDE	SUBGROUP	SUBLUNARS
STYES	SUAVEST	SUBDIVIDED	SUBGROUPS	SUBLUNARY
STYING	SUAVITIES	SUBDIVIDES	SUBHUMAN	SUBLUNATE
STYLAR	SUAVITY	SUBDIVIDING	SUBIMAGINES	SUBMAN
STYLATE	SUB	SUBDOLOUS	SUBIMAGO	SUBMARINE
STYLE	SUBACID	SUBDUABLE	SUBIMAGOS	SUBMARINED
STYLED	SUBACRID	SUBDUAL	SUBINCISE	SUBMARINES
STYLELESS	SUBACT	SUBDUALS	SUBINCISED	SUBMARINING
STYLES	SUBACTED	SUBDUCE	SUBINCISES	SUBMEN
STYLET	SUBACTING	SUBDUCED	SUBINCISING	SUBMENTAL
STYLETS	SUBACTION	SUBDUCES	SUBITO	SUBMENTUM
STYLI	SUBACTIONS	SUBDUCING	SUBJACENT	SUBMENTUMS
STYLIFORM	SUBACTS	SUBDUCT	SUBJECT	SUBMERGE
STYLING	SUBACUTE	SUBDUCTED	SUBJECTED	SUBMERGED
STYLISE	SUBADAR	SUBDUCTING	SUBJECTING	SUBMERGES
STYLISED	SUBADARS	SUBDUCTS	SUBJECTS	SUBMERGING
STYLISES	SUBADULT	SUBDUE	SUBJOIN	SUBMERSE
STYLISH	SUBADULTS	SUBDUED	SUBJOINED	SUBMERSED
STYLISHLY	SUBAERIAL	SUBDUEDLY	SUBJOINING	SUBMERSES
STYLISING	SUBAGENCIES	SUBDUER	SUBJOINS	SUBMERSING
STYLIST	SUBAGENCY	SUBDUERS	SUBJUGATE	SUBMICRON
STYLISTIC	SUBAGENT	SUBDUES	SUBJUGATED	SUBMICRONS
STYLISTICS	SUBAGENTS	SUBDUING	SUBJUGATES	SUBMISS
STYLISTS	SUBAH	SUBDUPLE	SUBJUGATING	SUBMISSLY
STYLITE	SUBAHDAR	SUBEDAR	SUBLATE	SUBMIT
STYLITES	SUBAHDARIES	SUBEDARS	SUBLATED	SUBMITS
STYLIZE	SUBAHDARS	SUBEDIT	SUBLATES	SUBMITTED
STYLIZED	SUBAHDARY	SUBEDITED	SUBLATING	SUBMITTER
STYLIZES	SUBAHS	SUBEDITING	SUBLATION	SUBMITTERS
STYLIZING	SUBAHSHIP	SUBEDITOR	SUBLATIONS	SUBMITTING
STYLO	SUBAHSHIPS	SUBEDITORS	SUBLEASE	SUBMITTINGS
STYLOBATE	SUBALPINE	SUBEDITS	SUBLEASED	SUBMUCOSA
STYLOBATES	SUBALTERN	SUBENTIRE	SUBLEASES	SUBMUCOSAE
STYLOID	SUBALTERNS	SUBEQUAL	SUBLEASING	SUBMUCOUS
STYLOIDS	SUBAQUA	SUBER	SUBLESSEE	SUBNEURAL
STYLOS	SUBARCTIC	SUBERATE	SUBLESSEES	SUBNIVEAL
STYLUS	SUBARID	SUBERATES	SUBLESSOR	SUBNIVEAN
STYLUSES	SUBASTRAL	SUBERECT	SUBLESSORS	SUBNORMAL
STYME	SUBATOM	SUBEREOUS	SUBLET	SUBNORMALS
STYMED	SUBATOMIC	SUBERIC	SUBLETHAL	SUBOCTAVE
STYMES	SUBATOMICS	SUBERIN	SUBLETS	SUBOCTAVES
STYMIE	SUBATOMS	SUBERINS	SUBLETTER	SUBOCULAR
STYMIED	SUBBASAL	SUBERISE	SUBLETTERS	SUBOFFICE
STYMIES	SUBBASALS	SUBERISED	SUBLETTING	SUBOFFICES
STYMING	SUBBED	SUBERISES	SUBLETTINGS	SUBORDER

SUBORDERS	SUBSOILER	SUBTITLED	SUBZONE	SUCK
SUBORN	SUBSOILERS	SUBTITLES	SUBZONES	SUCKED
SUBORNED	SUBSOILING	SUBTITLING	SUCCADE	SUCKEN
SUBORNER	SUBSOILINGS	SUBTLE	SUCCADES	SUCKENER
SUBORNERS	SUBSOILS	SUBTLER	SUCCEED	SUCKENERS
SUBORNING	SUBSOLAR	SUBTLEST	SUCCEEDED	SUCKENS
SUBORNS	SUBSONIC	SUBTLETIES	SUCCEEDER	SUCKER
SUBOVATE	SUBSTAGE	SUBTLETY	SUCCEEDERS	SUCKERED
SUBOXIDE	SUBSTAGES	SUBTLIST	SUCCEEDING	SUCKERING
SUBOXIDES	SUBSTANCE	SUBTLISTS	SUCCEEDS	SUCKERS
SUBPHYLA	SUBSTANCES	SUBTLY	SUCCENTOR	SUCKET
SUBPHYLUM	SUBSTRACT	SUBTONIC	SUCCENTORS	SUCKETS
SUBPLOT	SUBSTRACTED	SUBTONICS	SUCCÈS	SUCKING
SUBPLOTS	SUBSTRACTING	SUBTOPIA	SUCCESS	SUCKINGS
SUBPOENA	SUBSTRACTS	SUBTOPIAN	SUCCESSES	SUCKLE
SUBPOENAED	SUBSTRATA	SUBTOPIAS	SUCCESSOR	SUCKLED
SUBPOENAING	SUBSTRATE	SUBTOTAL	SUCCESSORS	SUCKLER
SUBPOENAS	SUBSTRATES	SUBTOTALLED	SUCCI	SUCKLERS
SUBPRIOR	SUBSTRUCT	SUBTOTALLING	SUCCINATE	SUCKLES
SUBPRIORS	SUBSTRUCTED	SUBTOTALS	SUCCINATES	SUCKLING
SUBREGION	SUBSTRUCTING	SUBTRACT	SUCCINCT	SUCKLINGS
SUBREGIONS	SUBSTRUCTS	SUBTRACTED	SUCCINCTER	SUCKS
SUBROGATE	SUBSTYLAR	SUBTRACTING	SUCCINCTEST	SUCRASE
SUBROGATED	SUBSTYLE	SUBTRACTS	SUCCINIC	SUCRASES
SUBROGATES	SUBSTYLES	SUBTRIBE	SUCCINITE	SUCRE
SUBROGATING	SUBSULTUS	SUBTRIBES	SUCCINITES	SUCRES
SUBS	SUBSULTUSES	SUBTRIST	SUCCINUM	SUCRIER
SUBSACRAL	SUBSUME	SUBTROPIC	SUCCINUMS	SUCRIERS
SUBSCRIBE	SUBSUMED	SUBTROPICS	SUCCOR	SUCROSE
SUBSCRIBED	SUBSUMES	SUBTRUDE	SUCCORED	SUCROSES
SUBSCRIBES	SUBSUMING	SUBTRUDED	SUCCORIES	SUCTION
SUBSCRIBING	SUBSYSTEM	SUBTRUDES	SUCCORING	SUCTIONS
SUBSCRIBINGS	SUBSYSTEMS	SUBTRUDING	SUCCORS	SUCTORIAL
SUBSCRIPT	SUBTACK	SUBTYPE	SUCCORY	SUCTORIAN
SUBSCRIPTS	SUBTACKS	SUBTYPES	SUCCOSE	SUCTORIANS
SUBSEA	SUBTEEN	SUBUCULA	SUCCOTASH	SUCURUJÚ
SUBSECIVE	SUBTEENS	SUBUCULAS	SUCCOTASHES	SUCURUJÚS
SUBSELLIA	SUBTENANT	SUBULATE	SUCCOUR	SUD
SUBSERE	SUBTENANTS	SUBUNGUAL	SUCCOURED	SUDAMEN
SUBSERIES	SUBTEND	SUBUNIT	SUCCOURER	SUDAMINA
SUBSERVE	SUBTENDED	SUBUNITS	SUCCOURERS	SUDAMINAL
SUBSERVED	SUBTENDING	SUBURB	SUCCOURING	SUDANIC
SUBSERVES	SUBTENDS	SUBURBAN	SUCCOURS	SUDARIES
SUBSERVING	SUBTENSE	SUBURBANS	SUCCOUS	SUDARIUM
SUBSET	SUBTENSES	SUBURBIA	SUCCUBA	SUDARIUMS
SUBSETS	SUBTEXT	SUBURBIAS	SUCCUBAE	SUDARY
SUBSHRUB	SUBTEXTS	SUBURBS	SUCCUBAS	SUDATE
SUBSHRUBS	SUBTIL	SUBURSINE	SUCCUBI	SUDATED
SUBSIDE	SUBTILE	SUBVASSAL	SUCCUBINE	SUDATES
SUBSIDED	SUBTILELY	SUBVASSALS	SUCCUBOUS	SUDATING
SUBSIDES	SUBTILER	SUBVERSAL	SUCCUBUS	SUDATION
SUBSIDIES	SUBTILEST	SUBVERSALS	SUCCUBUSES	SUDATIONS
SUBSIDING	SUBTILETIES	SUBVERSE	SUCCULENT	SUDATORIES
SUBSIDISE	SUBTILETY	SUBVERSED	SUCCULENTS	SUDATORY
SUBSIDISED	SUBTILISE	SUBVERSES	SUCCUMB	SUDD
SUBSIDISES	SUBTILISED	SUBVERSING	SUCCUMBED	SUDDEN
SUBSIDISING	SUBTILISES	SUBVERST	SUCCUMBING	SUDDENLY
SUBSIDIZE	SUBTILISING	SUBVERT	SUCCUMBS	SUDDENTIES
SUBSIDIZED	SUBTILIST	SUBVERTED	SUCCURSAL	SUDDENTY
SUBSIDIZES	SUBTILISTS	SUBVERTER	SUCCURSALS	SUDDER
SUBSIDIZING	SUBTILITIES	SUBVERTERS	SUCCUS	SUDDERS
SUBSIDY	SUBTILITY	SUBVERTING	SUCCUSS	SUDDS
SUBSIST	SUBTILIZE	SUBVERTS	SUCCUSSED	SUDOR
SUBSISTED	SUBTILIZED	SUBVIRAL	SUCCUSSES	SUDORAL
SUBSISTING	SUBTILIZES	SUBWARDEN	SUCCUSSING	SUDORIFIC
SUBSISTS	SUBTILIZING	SUBWARDENS	SUCH	SUDORIFICS
SUBSIZAR	SUBTILLY	SUBWAY	SUCHLIKE	SUDOROUS
SUBSIZARS	SUBTILTIES	SUBWAYS	SUCHNESS	SUDORS
SUBSOIL	SUBTILTY	SUBZERO	SUCHNESSES	SUDS
SUBSOILED	SUBTITLE	SUBZONAL	SUCHWISE	SUDSER

SUDSERS
SUDSIER
SUDSIEST
SUDSY
SUE
SUEABLE
SUED
SUEDE
SUÈDE
SUEDED
SUÈDED
SUEDES
SUÈDES
SUEDETTE
SUEDETTES
SUEDING
SUÈDING
SUER
SUERS
SUES
SUET
SUETS
SUETTY
SUETY
SUFFER
SUFFERED
SUFFERER
SUFFERERS
SUFFERING
SUFFERINGS
SUFFERS
SUFFETE
SUFFETES
SUFFICE
SUFFICED
SUFFICER
SUFFICERS
SUFFICES
SUFFICING
SUFFIX
SUFFIXAL
SUFFIXED
SUFFIXES
SUFFIXING
SUFFLATE
SUFFLATED
SUFFLATES
SUFFLATING
SUFFOCATE
SUFFOCATED
SUFFOCATES
SUFFOCATING
SUFFOCATINGS
SUFFRAGAN
SUFFRAGANS
SUFFRAGE
SUFFRAGES
SUFFUSE
SUFFUSED
SUFFUSES
SUFFUSING
SUFFUSION
SUFFUSIONS
SUGAR
SUGARED
SUGARIER
SUGARIEST
SUGARING
SUGARINGS
SUGARLESS

SUGARS
SUGARY
SUGGEST
SUGGESTED
SUGGESTER
SUGGESTERS
SUGGESTING
SUGGESTS
SUI
SUICIDAL
SUICIDE
SUICIDES
SUIDIAN
SUILLINE
SUING
SUINGS
SUINT
SUINTS
SUIT
SUITABLE
SUITABLY
SUITE
SUITED
SUITES
SUITING
SUITINGS
SUITOR
SUITORED
SUITORING
SUITORS
SUITRESS
SUITRESSES
SUITS
SUIVEZ
SUJEE
SUJEED
SUJEEING
SUJEES
SUK
SUKH
SUKHS
SUKIYAKI
SUKIYAKIS
SUKS
SULCAL
SULCALISE
SULCALISED
SULCALISES
SULCALISING
SULCALIZE
SULCALIZED
SULCALIZES
SULCALIZING
SULCATE
SULCATED
SULCATION
SULCATIONS
SULCI
SULCUS
SULFA
SULFATE
SULFATED
SULFATES
SULFATING
SULFUR
SULFURED
SULFURING
SULFURS
SULK
SULKED

SULKIER
SULKIES
SULKIEST
SULKILY
SULKINESS
SULKINESSES
SULKING
SULKS
SULKY
SULLAGE
SULLAGES
SULLEN
SULLENER
SULLENEST
SULLENLY
SULLENS
SULLIED
SULLIES
SULLY
SULLYING
SULPHA
SULPHATE
SULPHATED
SULPHATES
SULPHATIC
SULPHATING
SULPHIDE
SULPHIDES
SULPHITE
SULPHITES
SULPHONE
SULPHONES
SULPHONIC
SULPHUR
SULPHURED
SULPHURET
SULPHURETS
SULPHURIC
SULPHURING
SULPHURS
SULPHURY
SULTAN
SULTANA
SULTANAS
SULTANATE
SULTANATES
SULTANESS
SULTANESSES
SULTANIC
SULTANS
SULTRIER
SULTRIEST
SULTRILY
SULTRY
SUM
SUMAC
SUMACH
SUMACHS
SUMACS
SUMATRA
SUMATRAS
SUMLESS
SUMMA
SUMMAE
SUMMAND
SUMMANDS
SUMMAR
SUMMARIES
SUMMARILY
SUMMARISE

SUMMARISED
SUMMARISES
SUMMARISING
SUMMARIST
SUMMARISTS
SUMMARIZE
SUMMARIZED
SUMMARIZES
SUMMARIZING
SUMMARY
SUMMAS
SUMMAT
SUMMATE
SUMMATED
SUMMATES
SUMMATING
SUMMATION
SUMMATIONS
SUMMATIVE
SUMMATS
SUMMED
SUMMER
SUMMERED
SUMMERIER
SUMMERIEST
SUMMERING
SUMMERINGS
SUMMERLY
SUMMERS
SUMMERSET
SUMMERSETS
SUMMERSETTED
SUMMERSETTING
SUMMERY
SUMMING
SUMMINGS
SUMMIST
SUMMISTS
SUMMIT
SUMMITRIES
SUMMITRY
SUMMITS
SUMMON
SUMMONED
SUMMONER
SUMMONERS
SUMMONING
SUMMONS
SUMMONSED
SUMMONSES
SUMMONSING
SUMO
SUMOS
SUMP
SUMPH
SUMPHISH
SUMPHS
SUMPIT
SUMPITAN
SUMPITANS
SUMPITS
SUMPS
SUMPSIMUS
SUMPSIMUSES
SUMPTER
SUMPTERS
SUMPTUARY
SUMPTUOUS
SUMS
SUN

SUNBATH
SUNBATHE
SUNBATHED
SUNBATHER
SUNBATHERS
SUNBATHES
SUNBATHING
SUNBATHINGS
SUNBATHS
SUNBEAM
SUNBEAMED
SUNBEAMS
SUNBEAMY
SUNBED
SUNBEDS
SUNBELT
SUNBELTS
SUNBLOCK
SUNBLOCKS
SUNBOW
SUNBOWS
SUNBRIGHT
SUNBURN
SUNBURNED
SUNBURNING
SUNBURNS
SUNBURNT
SUNBURST
SUNBURSTS
SUNDAE
SUNDAES
SUNDARI
SUNDARIS
SUNDER
SUNDERED
SUNDERER
SUNDERERS
SUNDERING
SUNDERINGS
SUNDERS
SUNDIAL
SUNDIALS
SUNDOWN
SUNDOWNS
SUNDRA
SUNDRAS
SUNDRI
SUNDRIES
SUNDRIS
SUNDRY
SUNFAST
SUNFLOWER
SUNFLOWERS
SUNG
SUNGAR
SUNGARS
SUNGLASS
SUNGLASSES
SUNGLOW
SUNGLOWS
SUNHAT
SUNHATS
SUNK
SUNKEN
SUNKET
SUNKETS
SUNKIE
SUNKIES
SUNKS
SUNLESS

SUNLIGHT
SUNLIGHTS
SUNLIKE
SUNLIT
SUNN
SUNNED
SUNNIER
SUNNIEST
SUNNILY
SUNNINESS
SUNNINESSES
SUNNING
SUNNS
SUNNY
SUNPROOF
SUNRAY
SUNRAYS
SUNRISE
SUNRISES
SUNRISING
SUNRISINGS
SUNS
SUNSET
SUNSETS
SUNSHINE
SUNSHINES
SUNSHINY
SUNSPOT
SUNSPOTS
SUNSTONE
SUNSTONES
SUNSTROKE
SUNSTROKES
SUNSTRUCK
SUNSUIT
SUNSUITS
SUNTAN
SUNTANNED
SUNTANS
SUNTRAP
SUNTRAPS
SUNWARD
SUNWARDS
SUNWISE
SUP
SUPAWN
SUPAWNS
SUPER
SUPERABLE
SUPERABLY
SUPERADD
SUPERADDED
SUPERADDING
SUPERADDS
SUPERATE
SUPERATED
SUPERATES
SUPERATING
SUPERB
SUPERBER
SUPERBEST
SUPERBITIES
SUPERBITY
SUPERBLY
SUPERCOLD
SUPERCOOL
SUPERCOOLED
SUPERCOOLING
SUPERCOOLS
SUPERED

SUPERETTE
SUPERETTES
SUPERFINE
SUPERFLUX
SUPERFLUXES
SUPERFUSE
SUPERFUSED
SUPERFUSES
SUPERFUSING
SUPERGLUE
SUPERGLUES
SUPERHEAT
SUPERHEATED
SUPERHEATING
SUPERHEATS
SUPERHET
SUPERHETS
SUPERHIVE
SUPERHIVES
SUPERING
SUPERIOR
SUPERIORS
SUPERMAN
SUPERMART
SUPERMARTS
SUPERMEN
SUPERNAL
SUPERNOVA
SUPERNOVAE
SUPERNOVAS
SUPERPLUS
SUPERPLUSES
SUPERPOSE
SUPERPOSED
SUPERPOSES
SUPERPOSING
SUPERS
SUPERSALT
SUPERSALTS
SUPERSEDE
SUPERSEDED
SUPERSEDES
SUPERSEDING
SUPERSTAR
SUPERSTARS
SUPERTAX
SUPERTAXES
SUPERVENE
SUPERVENED
SUPERVENES
SUPERVENING
SUPERVISE
SUPERVISED
SUPERVISES
SUPERVISING
SUPINATE
SUPINATED
SUPINATES
SUPINATING
SUPINATOR
SUPINATORS
SUPINE
SUPINELY
SUPINES
SUPPAWN
SUPPAWNS
SUPPEAGO
SUPPEAGOES
SUPPED
SUPPER

SUPPERED
SUPPERING
SUPPERS
SUPPING
SUPPLANT
SUPPLANTED
SUPPLANTING
SUPPLANTS
SUPPLE
SUPPLED
SUPPLER
SUPPLES
SUPPLEST
SUPPLIAL
SUPPLIALS
SUPPLIANT
SUPPLIANTS
SUPPLICAT
SUPPLICATS
SUPPLIED
SUPPLIER
SUPPLIERS
SUPPLIES
SUPPLING
SUPPLY
SUPPLYING
SUPPORT
SUPPORTED
SUPPORTER
SUPPORTERS
SUPPORTING
SUPPORTINGS
SUPPORTS
SUPPOSAL
SUPPOSALS
SUPPOSE
SUPPOSED
SUPPOSER
SUPPOSERS
SUPPOSES
SUPPOSING
SUPPOSINGS
SUPPRESS
SUPPRESSED
SUPPRESSES
SUPPRESSING
SUPPURATE
SUPPURATED
SUPPURATES
SUPPURATING
SUPREMACIES
SUPREMACY
SUPRÊME
SUPREME
SUPREMELY
SUPREMER
SUPREMES
SUPRÊMES
SUPREMEST
SUPREMITIES
SUPREMITY
SUPREMO
SUPREMOS
SUPS
SUQ
SUQS
SUR
SURA
SURAH
SURAHS

SURAL
SURANCE
SURANCES
SURAS
SURAT
SURATS
SURBASE
SURBASED
SURBASES
SURBATE
SURBATED
SURBATES
SURBATING
SURBED
SURBEDDED
SURBEDDING
SURBEDS
SURBET
SURCEASE
SURCEASED
SURCEASES
SURCEASING
SURCHARGE
SURCHARGED
SURCHARGES
SURCHARGING
SURCINGLE
SURCINGLED
SURCINGLES
SURCINGLING
SURCOAT
SURCOATS
SURCULI
SURCULOSE
SURCULUS
SURCULUSES
SURD
SURDITIES
SURDITY
SURDS
SURE
SURED
SURELY
SURENESS
SURENESSES
SURER
SURES
SUREST
SURETIED
SURETIES
SURETY
SURETYING
SURF
SURFACE
SURFACED
SURFACER
SURFACERS
SURFACES
SURFACING
SURFACINGS
SURFBOARD
SURFBOARDS
SURFED
SURFEIT
SURFEITED
SURFEITER
SURFEITERS
SURFEITING
SURFEITINGS
SURFEITS

SURFER
SURFERS
SURFICIAL
SURFIER
SURFIEST
SURFING
SURFINGS
SURFMAN
SURFMEN
SURFS
SURFY
SURGE
SURGED
SURGEFUL
SURGELESS
SURGENT
SURGEON
SURGEONCIES
SURGEONCY
SURGEONS
SURGERIES
SURGERY
SURGES
SURGICAL
SURGING
SURGINGS
SURGY
SURICATE
SURICATES
SURING
SURLIER
SURLIEST
SURLILY
SURLINESS
SURLINESSES
SURLOIN
SURLOINS
SURLY
SURMASTER
SURMASTERS
SURMISAL
SURMISALS
SURMISE
SURMISED
SURMISER
SURMISERS
SURMISES
SURMISING
SURMISINGS
SURMOUNT
SURMOUNTED
SURMOUNTING
SURMOUNTINGS
SURMOUNTS
SURMULLET
SURMULLETS
SURNAME
SURNAMED
SURNAMES
SURNAMING
SURPASS
SURPASSED
SURPASSES
SURPASSING
SURPLICE
SURPLICED
SURPLICES
SURPLUS
SURPLUSES
SURPRISAL

SURPRISALS	SURVIEWING	SUTORS	SWAINISH	SWARAJIST
SURPRISE	SURVIEWS	SUTRA	SWAINS	SWARAJISTS
SURPRISED	SURVIVAL	SUTRAS	SWALE	SWARD
SURPRISER	SURVIVALS	SUTTEE	SWALED	SWARDED
SURPRISERS	SURVIVE	SUTTEEISM	SWALES	SWARDING
SURPRISES	SURVIVED	SUTTEEISMS	SWALIER	SWARDS
SURPRISING	SURVIVES	SUTTEES	SWALIEST	SWARDY
SURPRISINGS	SURVIVING	SUTTLE	SWALING	SWARE
SURQUEDIES	SURVIVOR	SUTTLED	SWALINGS	SWARF
SURQUEDRIES	SURVIVORS	SUTTLES	SWALLET	SWARFED
SURQUEDRY	SUS	SUTTLETIE	SWALLETS	SWARFING
SURQUEDY	SUSCEPTOR	SUTTLETIES	SWALLOW	SWARFS
SURRA	SUSCEPTORS	SUTTLING	SWALLOWED	SWARM
SURRAS	SUSCITATE	SUTURAL	SWALLOWER	SWARMED
SURREAL	SUSCITATED	SUTURALLY	SWALLOWERS	SWARMER
SURREBUT	SUSCITATES	SUTURE	SWALLOWING	SWARMERS
SURREBUTS	SUSCITATING	SUTURED	SWALLOWS	SWARMING
SURREBUTTED	SUSHI	SUTURES	SWALY	SWARMINGS
SURREBUTTING	SUSHIS	SUTURING	SWAM	SWARMS
SURREINED	SUSLIK	SUVERSED	SWAMI	SWART
SURREJOIN	SUSLIKS	SUZERAIN	SWAMIS	SWARTH
SURREJOINED	SUSPECT	SUZERAINS	SWAMP	SWARTHIER
SURREJOINING	SUSPECTED	SVASTIKA	SWAMPED	SWARTHIEST
SURREJOINS	SUSPECTING	SVASTIKAS	SWAMPER	SWARTHS
SURRENDER	SUSPECTS	SVELTE	SWAMPERS	SWARTHY
SURRENDERED	SUSPENCE	SVELTER	SWAMPIER	SWARTNESS
SURRENDERING	SUSPEND	SVELTEST	SWAMPIEST	SWARTNESSES
SURRENDERS	SUSPENDED	SWAB	SWAMPING	SWARTY
SURRENDRIES	SUSPENDER	SWABBED	SWAMPLAND	SWARVE
SURRENDRY	SUSPENDERS	SWABBER	SWAMPLANDS	SWARVED
SURREY	SUSPENDING	SWABBERS	SWAMPS	SWARVES
SURREYS	SUSPENDS	SWABBING	SWAMPY	SWARVING
SURROGATE	SUSPENS	SWABS	SWAN	SWASH
SURROGATES	SUSPENSE	SWACK	SWANG	SWASHED
SURROUND	SUSPENSES	SWAD	SWANHERD	SWASHER
SURROUNDED	SUSPENSOR	SWADDIES	SWANHERDS	SWASHERS
SURROUNDING	SUSPENSORS	SWADDLE	SWANK	SWASHES
SURROUNDINGS	SUSPICION	SWADDLED	SWANKED	SWASHIER
SURROUNDS	SUSPICIONED	SWADDLER	SWANKER	SWASHIEST
SURROYAL	SUSPICIONING	SWADDLERS	SWANKERS	SWASHING
SURROYALS	SUSPICIONS	SWADDLES	SWANKEST	SWASHINGS
SURTAX	SUSPIRE	SWADDLING	SWANKEY	SWASHWORK
SURTAXED	SUSPIRED	SWADDY	SWANKEYS	SWASHWORKS
SURTAXES	SUSPIRES	SWADS	SWANKIER	SWASHY
SURTAXING	SUSPIRING	SWAG	SWANKIES	SWASTIKA
SURTOUT	SUSS	SWAGE	SWANKIEST	SWASTIKAS
SURTOUTS	SUSSARARA	SWAGED	SWANKING	SWAT
SURUCUCU	SUSSARARAS	SWAGES	SWANKS	SWATCH
SURUCUCUS	SUSSED	SWAGGED	SWANKY	SWATCHES
SURVEILLE	SUSSES	SWAGGER	SWANLIKE	SWATH
SURVEILLED	SUSSING	SWAGGERED	SWANNERIES	SWATHE
SURVEILLES	SUSTAIN	SWAGGERER	SWANNERY	SWATHED
SURVEILLING	SUSTAINED	SWAGGERERS	SWANNIER	SWATHES
SURVEW	SUSTAINER	SWAGGERING	SWANNIEST	SWATHIER
SURVEWE	SUSTAINERS	SWAGGERINGS	SWANNY	SWATHIEST
SURVEWED	SUSTAINING	SWAGGERS	SWANS	SWATHING
SURVEWES	SUSTAININGS	SWAGGIE	SWANSDOWN	SWATHS
SURVEWING	SUSTAINS	SWAGGIES	SWANSDOWNS	SWATHY
SURVEWS	SUSTINENT	SWAGGING	SWAP	SWATS
SURVEY	SUSURRANT	SWAGING	SWAPPED	SWATTED
SURVEYAL	SUSURRUS	SWAGMAN	SWAPPER	SWATTER
SURVEYALS	SUSURRUSES	SWAGMEN	SWAPPERS	SWATTERED
SURVEYED	SUTILE	SWAGS	SWAPPING	SWATTERING
SURVEYING	SUTLER	SWAGSHOP	SWAPPINGS	SWATTERS
SURVEYINGS	SUTLERIES	SWAGSHOPS	SWAPS	SWATTING
SURVEYOR	SUTLERS	SWAGSMAN	SWAPT	SWAY
SURVEYORS	SUTLERY	SWAGSMEN	SWARAJ	SWAYBACK
SURVEYS	SUTOR	SWAIN	SWARAJES	SWAYBACKS
SURVIEW	SUTORIAL	SWAINING	SWARAJISM	SWAYED
SURVIEWED	SUTORIAN	SWAININGS	SWARAJISMS	SWAYER

SWAYERS
SWAYING
SWAYINGS
SWAYL
SWAYLED
SWAYLING
SWAYLINGS
SWAYLS
SWAYS
SWEAL
SWEALED
SWEALING
SWEALINGS
SWEALS
SWEAR
SWEARD
SWEARDS
SWEARER
SWEARERS
SWEARING
SWEARINGS
SWEARS
SWEAT
SWEATED
SWEATER
SWEATERS
SWEATIER
SWEATIEST
SWEATING
SWEATINGS
SWEATS
SWEATY
SWEDE
SWEDES
SWEE
SWEED
SWEEING
SWEEL
SWEELED
SWEELING
SWEELS
SWEENEY
SWEENEYS
SWEENIES
SWEENY
SWEEP
SWEEPBACK
SWEEPBACKS
SWEEPER
SWEEPERS
SWEEPIER
SWEEPIEST
SWEEPING
SWEEPINGS
SWEEPS
SWEEPY
SWEER
SWEERED
SWEERT
SWEES
SWEET
SWEETED
SWEETEN
SWEETENED
SWEETENER
SWEETENERS
SWEETENING
SWEETENINGS
SWEETENS
SWEETER

SWEETEST
SWEETFISH
SWEETFISHES
SWEETIE
SWEETIES
SWEETING
SWEETINGS
SWEETISH
SWEETLY
SWEETMEAL
SWEETMEAT
SWEETMEATS
SWEETNESS
SWEETNESSES
SWEETPEA
SWEETPEAS
SWEETS
SWEETWOOD
SWEETWOODS
SWEETY
SWEIR
SWEIRNESS
SWEIRNESSES
SWEIRT
SWELCHIE
SWELCHIES
SWELL
SWELLDOM
SWELLDOMS
SWELLED
SWELLER
SWELLERS
SWELLEST
SWELLING
SWELLINGS
SWELLISH
SWELLS
SWELT
SWELTED
SWELTER
SWELTERED
SWELTERING
SWELTERINGS
SWELTERS
SWELTING
SWELTRIER
SWELTRIEST
SWELTRY
SWELTS
SWEPT
SWERF
SWERFED
SWERFING
SWERFS
SWERVE
SWERVED
SWERVER
SWERVERS
SWERVES
SWERVING
SWERVINGS
SWEVEN
SWEVENS
SWIES
SWIFT
SWIFTED
SWIFTER
SWIFTERS
SWIFTEST
SWIFTING

SWIFTLET
SWIFTLETS
SWIFTLY
SWIFTNESS
SWIFTNESSES
SWIFTS
SWIG
SWIGGED
SWIGGER
SWIGGERS
SWIGGING
SWIGS
SWILL
SWILLED
SWILLER
SWILLERS
SWILLING
SWILLINGS
SWILLS
SWIM
SWIMMABLE
SWIMMER
SWIMMERET
SWIMMERETS
SWIMMERS
SWIMMIER
SWIMMIEST
SWIMMING
SWIMMINGS
SWIMMY
SWIMS
SWIMSUIT
SWIMSUITS
SWIMWEAR
SWINDGE
SWINDGED
SWINDGES
SWINDGING
SWINDLE
SWINDLED
SWINDLER
SWINDLERS
SWINDLES
SWINDLING
SWINDLINGS
SWINE
SWINEHERD
SWINEHERDS
SWINEHOOD
SWINEHOODS
SWINERIES
SWINERY
SWING
SWINGBOAT
SWINGBOATS
SWINGE
SWINGED
SWINGEING
SWINGER
SWINGERS
SWINGES
SWINGING
SWINGINGS
SWINGISM
SWINGISMS
SWINGLE
SWINGLED
SWINGLES
SWINGLING
SWINGLINGS

SWINGS
SWINGTREE
SWINGTREES
SWINISH
SWINISHLY
SWINK
SWINKED
SWINKING
SWINKS
SWIPE
SWIPED
SWIPER
SWIPERS
SWIPES
SWIPEY
SWIPING
SWIPPLE
SWIPPLES
SWIRE
SWIRES
SWIRL
SWIRLED
SWIRLIER
SWIRLIEST
SWIRLING
SWIRLS
SWIRLY
SWISH
SWISHED
SWISHER
SWISHERS
SWISHES
SWISHEST
SWISHIER
SWISHIEST
SWISHING
SWISHINGS
SWISHY
SWISSING
SWISSINGS
SWITCH
SWITCHED
SWITCHEL
SWITCHELS
SWITCHES
SWITCHING
SWITCHINGS
SWITCHMAN
SWITCHMEN
SWITCHY
SWITH
SWITHER
SWITHERED
SWITHERING
SWITHERS
SWITS
SWITSES
SWIVEL
SWIVELLED
SWIVELLING
SWIVELS
SWIZ
SWIZZES
SWIZZLE
SWIZZLED
SWIZZLES
SWIZZLING
SWOB
SWOBBED
SWOBBER

SWOBBERS
SWOBBING
SWOBS
SWOLLEN
SWOLN
SWONE
SWONES
SWOON
SWOONED
SWOONING
SWOONINGS
SWOONS
SWOOP
SWOOPED
SWOOPING
SWOOPS
SWOOSH
SWOOSHED
SWOOSHES
SWOOSHING
SWOP
SWOPPED
SWOPPER
SWOPPERS
SWOPPING
SWOPPINGS
SWOPS
SWOPT
SWORD
SWORDED
SWORDER
SWORDERS
SWORDFISH
SWORDFISHES
SWORDING
SWORDLESS
SWORDMAN
SWORDMEN
SWORDPLAY
SWORDPLAYS
SWORDS
SWORDSMAN
SWORDSMEN
SWORE
SWORN
SWOT
SWOTS
SWOTTED
SWOTTER
SWOTTERS
SWOTTING
SWOTTINGS
SWOUN
SWOUND
SWOUNDED
SWOUNDING
SWOUNDS
SWOUNE
SWOUNED
SWOUNES
SWOUNING
SWOUNS
SWOWND
SWOWNDS
SWOWNE
SWOWNES
SWUM
SWUNG
SWY
SYBARITE

SYBARITES	SYLLEPSIS	SYMITARES	SYNCHS	SYNGAMOUS
SYBARITIC	SYLLEPTIC	SYMITARS	SYNCHYSES	SYNGAMY
SYBBE	SYLLOGISE	SYMMETRAL	SYNCHYSIS	SYNGRAPH
SYBBES	SYLLOGISED	SYMMETRIC	SYNCING	SYNGRAPHS
SYBIL	SYLLOGISES	SYMMETRIES	SYNCLINAL	SYNING
SYBILS	SYLLOGISING	SYMMETRY	SYNCLINALS	SYNIZESES
SYBO	SYLLOGISM	SYMPATHIES	SYNCLINE	SYNIZESIS
SYBOE	SYLLOGISMS	SYMPATHY	SYNCLINES	SYNOD
SYBOES	SYLLOGIZE	SYMPHILE	SYNCOPAL	SYNODAL
SYBOTIC	SYLLOGIZED	SYMPHILES	SYNCOPATE	SYNODALS
SYBOTISM	SYLLOGIZES	SYMPHILIES	SYNCOPATED	SYNODIC
SYBOTISMS	SYLLOGIZING	SYMPHILY	SYNCOPATES	SYNODICAL
SYBOW	SYLPH	SYMPHONIC	SYNCOPATING	SYNODS
SYBOWS	SYLPHID	SYMPHONIES	SYNCOPE	SYNODSMAN
SYCAMINE	SYLPHIDE	SYMPHONY	SYNCOPES	SYNODSMEN
SYCAMINES	SYLPHIDES	SYMPHYSES	SYNCOPIC	SYNOECETE
SYCAMORE	SYLPHIDS	SYMPHYSIS	SYNCOPTIC	SYNOECETES
SYCAMORES	SYLPHINE	SYMPHYTIC	SYNCRETIC	SYNOECISE
SYCE	SYLPHISH	SYMPLOCE	SYNCS	SYNOECISED
SYCEE	SYLPHS	SYMPLOCES	SYNCYTIA	SYNOECISES
SYCEES	SYLVA	SYMPODIA	SYNCYTIAL	SYNOECISING
SYCES	SYLVAE	SYMPODIAL	SYNCYTIUM	SYNOECISM
SYCOMORE	SYLVAN	SYMPODIUM	SYNCYTIUMS	SYNOECISMS
SYCOMORES	SYLVANITE	SYMPOSIA	SYND	SYNOECIZE
SYCONIUM	SYLVANITES	SYMPOSIAC	SYNDACTYL	SYNOECIZED
SYCONIUMS	SYLVANS	SYMPOSIAL	SYNDED	SYNOECIZES
SYCOPHANT	SYLVAS	SYMPOSIUM	SYNDESES	SYNOECIZING
SYCOPHANTS	SYLVATIC	SYMPTOM	SYNDESIS	SYNOICOUS
SYCOSES	SYLVIA	SYMPTOMS	SYNDET	SYNONYM
SYCOSIS	SYLVIAS	SYMPTOSES	SYNDETIC	SYNONYMIC
SYE	SYLVIINE	SYMPTOSIS	SYNDETS	SYNONYMIES
SYED	SYLVINE	SYMPTOTIC	SYNDIC	SYNONYMS
SYEING	SYLVINES	SYNAGOGAL	SYNDICAL	SYNONYMY
SYEN	SYLVINITE	SYNAGOGUE	SYNDICATE	SYNOPSES
SYENITE	SYLVINITES	SYNAGOGUES	SYNDICATED	SYNOPSIS
SYENITES	SYLVITE	SYNANGIA	SYNDICATES	SYNOPTIC
SYENITIC	SYLVITES	SYNANGIUM	SYNDICATING	SYNOPTIST
SYENS	SYMAR	SYNANGIUMS	SYNDICS	SYNOPTISTS
SYES	SYMARS	SYNANTHIC	SYNDING	SYNOVIA
SYKE	SYMBION	SYNANTHIES	SYNDINGS	SYNOVIAL
SYKER	SYMBIONS	SYNANTHY	SYNDROME	SYNOVIAS
SYKES	SYMBIONT	SYNAPHEA	SYNDROMES	SYNOVITIS
SYLLABARIES	SYMBIONTS	SYNAPHEAS	SYNDROMIC	SYNOVITISES
SYLLABARY	SYMBIOSES	SYNAPHEIA	SYNDS	SYNTACTIC
SYLLABI	SYMBIOSIS	SYNAPHEIAS	SYNE	SYNTAGMA
SYLLABIC	SYMBIOTIC	SYNAPSE	SYNECHIA	SYNTAGMATA
SYLLABICS	SYMBOL	SYNAPSES	SYNECHIAS	SYNTAN
SYLLABIFIED	SYMBOLE	SYNAPSIS	SYNECTIC	SYNTANS
SYLLABIFIES	SYMBOLES	SYNAPTASE	SYNECTICS	SYNTAX
SYLLABIFY	SYMBOLIC	SYNAPTASES	SYNED	SYNTAXES
SYLLABIFYING	SYMBOLICS	SYNAPTE	SYNEDRIA	SYNTECTIC
SYLLABISE	SYMBOLISE	SYNAPTES	SYNEDRIAL	SYNTEXIS
SYLLABISED	SYMBOLISED	SYNAPTIC	SYNEDRION	SYNTEXISES
SYLLABISES	SYMBOLISES	SYNARCHIES	SYNEDRIUM	SYNTHESES
SYLLABISING	SYMBOLISING	SYNARCHY	SYNERESES	SYNTHESIS
SYLLABISM	SYMBOLISM	SYNASTRIES	SYNERESIS	SYNTHETIC
SYLLABISMS	SYMBOLISMS	SYNASTRY	SYNERGIC	SYNTHETICS
SYLLABIZE	SYMBOLIST	SYNAXES	SYNERGID	SYNTONIC
SYLLABIZED	SYMBOLISTS	SYNAXIS	SYNERGIDS	SYNTONIES
SYLLABIZES	SYMBOLIZE	SYNC	SYNERGIES	SYNTONIN
SYLLABIZING	SYMBOLIZED	SYNCARP	SYNERGISM	SYNTONINS
SYLLABLE	SYMBOLIZES	SYNCARPIES	SYNERGISMS	SYNTONISE
SYLLABLED	SYMBOLIZING	SYNCARPS	SYNERGIST	SYNTONISED
SYLLABLES	SYMBOLLED	SYNCARPY	SYNERGISTS	SYNTONISES
SYLLABLING	SYMBOLLING	SYNCED	SYNERGY	SYNTONISING
SYLLABUB	SYMBOLOGIES	SYNCH	SYNES	SYNTONIZE
SYLLABUBS	SYMBOLOGY	SYNCHED	SYNESES	SYNTONIZED
SYLLABUS	SYMBOLS	SYNCHING	SYNESIS	SYNTONIZES
SYLLABUSES	SYMITAR	SYNCHRONIES	SYNGAMIC	SYNTONIZING
SYLLEPSES	SYMITARE	SYNCHRONY	SYNGAMIES	SYNTONOUS

SYNTONY
SYPE
SYPED
SYPES
SYPHILIS
SYPHILISE
SYPHILISED
SYPHILISES
SYPHILISING
SYPHILIZE
SYPHILIZED
SYPHILIZES
SYPHILIZING
SYPHILOID

SYPHILOMA
SYPHILOMAS
SYPHON
SYPHONED
SYPHONING
SYPHONS
SYPING
SYREN
SYRENS
SYRINGA
SYRINGAS
SYRINGE
SYRINGEAL
SYRINGED

SYRINGES
SYRINGING
SYRINX
SYRINXES
SYRLYE
SYRPHID
SYRPHIDS
SYRTES
SYRTIS
SYRUP
SYRUPED
SYRUPING
SYRUPS
SYRUPY

SYSSITIA
SYSTALTIC
SYSTEM
SYSTEMED
SYSTEMIC
SYSTEMISE
SYSTEMISED
SYSTEMISES
SYSTEMISING
SYSTEMIZE
SYSTEMIZED
SYSTEMIZES
SYSTEMIZING
SYSTEMS

SYSTOLE
SYSTOLES
SYSTOLIC
SYSTYLE
SYSTYLES
SYTHE
SYTHES
SYVER
SYVERS
SYZYGIAL
SYZYGIES
SYZYGY

T

TA	TABOGGANING	TACHOGRAMS	TADPOLES	TAIGAS
TAAL	TABOGGANS	TACHYLITE	TADS	TAIGLE
TAALS	TABOO	TACHYLITES	TADVANCE	TAIGLED
TAB	TABOOED	TACHYLYTE	TAE	TAIGLES
TABANID	TABOOING	TACHYLYTES	TAED	TAIGLING
TABANIDS	TABOOS	TACHYON	TAEDIUM	TAIL
TABARD	TABOR	TACHYONS	TAEDIUMS	TAILARD
TABARDS	TABORED	TACIT	TAEING	TAILARDS
TABARET	TABORER	TACITLY	TAEL	TAILBACK
TABARETS	TABORERS	TACITNESS	TAELS	TAILBACKS
TABASHEER	TABORET	TACITNESSES	TAENIA	TAILED
TABASHEERS	TABORETS	TACITURN	TAENIAE	TAILING
TABASHIR	TABORIN	TACK	TAENIAS	TAILINGS
TABASHIRS	TABORING	TACKED	TAENIASES	TAILLESS
TABBED	TABORINS	TACKER	TAENIASIS	TAILLEUR
TABBIED	TABORS	TACKERS	TAENIATE	TAILLEURS
TABBIES	TABOUR	TACKET	TAENIOID	TAILLIE
TABBINET	TABOURED	TACKETS	TAES	TAILLIES
TABBINETS	TABOURET	TACKETY	TAFFEREL	TAILOR
TABBING	TABOURETS	TACKIER	TAFFERELS	TAILORED
TABBOULEH	TABOURIN	TACKIEST	TAFFETA	TAILORESS
TABBOULEHS	TABOURING	TACKINESS	TAFFETAS	TAILORESSES
TABBY	TABOURINS	TACKING	TAFFETASES	TAILORING
TABBYHOOD	TABOURS	TACKINGS	TAFFETIES	TAILORINGS
TABBYHOODS	TABRERE	TACKLE	TAFFETY	TAILORS
TABBYING	TABRERES	TACKLED	TAFFIES	TAILPIECE
TABEFIED	TABRET	TACKLER	TAFFRAIL	TAILPIECES
TABEFIES	TABRETS	TACKLERS	TAFFRAILS	TAILPLANE
TABEFY	TABS	TACKLES	TAFFY	TAILPLANES
TABEFYING	TABU	TACKLING	TAFIA	TAILRACE
TABELLION	TABUED	TACKLINGS	TAFIAS	TAILRACES
TABELLIONS	TABUING	TACKS	TAG	TAILS
TABERDAR	TABULA	TACKSMAN	TAGETES	TAILSKID
TABERDARS	TABULAE	TACKSMEN	TAGGED	TAILSKIDS
TABES	TABULAR	TACKY	TAGGER	TAILYE
TABESCENT	TABULARLY	TACO	TAGGERS	TAILYES
TABETIC	TABULATE	TACONITE	TAGGING	TAILZIE
TABID	TABULATED	TACONITES	TAGHAIRM	TAILZIES
TABINET	TABULATES	TACOS	TAGHAIRMS	TAINT
TABINETS	TABULATING	TACT	TAGLIONI	TAINTED
TABLA	TABULATOR	TACTFUL	TAGLIONIS	TAINTING
TABLAS	TABULATORS	TACTFULLY	TAGMEME	TAINTLESS
TABLATURE	TABUN	TACTIC	TAGMEMES	TAINTS
TABLATURES	TABUNS	TACTICAL	TAGMEMIC	TAINTURE
TABLE	TABUS	TACTICIAN	TAGMEMICS	TAINTURES
TABLEAU	TACAHOUT	TACTICIANS	TAGRAG	TAIPAN
TABLEAUX	TACAHOUTS	TACTICITIES	TAGRAGS	TAIPANS
TABLED	TACAMAHAC	TACTICITY	TAGS	TAIRA
TABLEFUL	TACAMAHACS	TACTICS	TAGUAN	TAIRAS
TABLEFULS	TACE	TACTILE	TAGUANS	TAIS
TABLELAND	TACES	TACTILIST	TAHA	TAISCH
TABLELANDS	TACET	TACTILISTS	TAHAS	TAISCHES
TABLES	TACH	TACTILITIES	TAHINA	TAISH
TABLET	TACHE	TACTILITY	TAHINAS	TAISHES
TABLETED	TACHES	TACTION	TAHINI	TAIT
TABLETING	TACHISM	TACTIONS	TAHINIS	TAITS
TABLETS	TACHISME	TACTISM	TAHR	TAIVER
TABLEWISE	TACHISMES	TACTISMS	TAHRS	TAIVERED
TABLING	TACHISMS	TACTLESS	TAHSIL	TAIVERING
TABLINGS	TACHIST	TACTS	TAHSILDAR	TAIVERS
TABLOID	TACHISTE	TACTUAL	TAHSILDARS	TAIVERT
TABLOIDS	TACHISTES	TACTUALLY	TAHSILS	TAJ
TABOGGAN	TACHISTS	TAD	TAI	TAJES
TABOGGANED	TACHOGRAM	TADPOLE	TAIGA	TAK

TAKA	TALIPES	TALUK	TAMMIES	TANGLES
TAKABLE	TALIPOT	TALUKDAR	TAMMY	TANGLIER
TAKAHE	TALIPOTS	TALUKDARS	TAMP	TANGLIEST
TAKAHEA	TALISMAN	TALUKS	TAMPED	TANGLING
TAKAHEAS	TALISMANS	TALUS	TAMPER	TANGLINGS
TAKAHES	TALK	TALUSES	TAMPERED	TANGLY
TAKAMAKA	TALKABLE	TALWEG	TAMPERER	TANGO
TAKAMAKAS	TALKATHON	TALWEGS	TAMPERERS	TANGOED
TAKAS	TALKATHONS	TAM	TAMPERING	TANGOING
TAKE	TALKATIVE	TAMABLE	TAMPERINGS	TANGOIST
TAKEABLE	TALKED	TAMAL	TAMPERS	TANGOISTS
TAKEN	TALKER	TAMALE	TAMPING	TANGOS
TAKEOVER	TALKERS	TAMALES	TAMPINGS	TANGRAM
TAKEOVERS	TALKFEST	TAMALS	TAMPION	TANGRAMS
TAKER	TALKFESTS	TAMANDUA	TAMPIONS	TANGS
TAKERS	TALKIE	TAMANDUAS	TAMPON	TANGUN
TAKES	TALKIES	TAMANOIR	TAMPONADE	TANGUNS
TAKIN	TALKING	TAMANOIRS	TAMPONADES	TANGY
TAKING	TALKINGS	TAMANU	TAMPONAGE	TANIST
TAKINGLY	TALKS	TAMANUS	TAMPONAGES	TANISTRIES
TAKINGS	TALL	TAMARA	TAMPONED	TANISTRY
TAKINS	TALLAGE	TAMARACK	TAMPONING	TANISTS
TAKS	TALLAGED	TAMARACKS	TAMPONS	TANK
TAKY	TALLAGES	TAMARAS	TAMPS	TANKA
TALA	TALLAGING	TAMARI	TAMS	TANKAGE
TALAK	TALLAT	TAMARILLO	TAN	TANKAGES
TALAKS	TALLATS	TAMARILLOS	TANA	TANKARD
TALANT	TALLBOY	TAMARIN	TANADAR	TANKARDS
TALANTS	TALLBOYS	TAMARIND	TANADARS	TANKAS
TALAPOIN	TALLENT	TAMARINDS	TANAGER	TANKED
TALAPOINS	TALLENTS	TAMARINS	TANAGERS	TANKER
TALAQ	TALLER	TAMARIS	TANAGRA	TANKERS
TALAQS	TALLEST	TAMARISK	TANAGRAS	TANKFUL
TALAR	TALLET	TAMARISKS	TANAGRINE	TANKFULS
TALARIA	TALLETS	TAMASHA	TANAISTE	TANKIA
TALARS	TALLIABLE	TAMASHAS	TANAISTES	TANKIAS
TALAS	TALLIATE	TAMBER	TANAS	TANKING
TALAUNT	TALLIATED	TAMBERS	TANDEM	TANKINGS
TALAUNTS	TALLIATES	TAMBOUR	TANDEMS	TANKS
TALAYOT	TALLIATING	TAMBOURA	TANDOORI	TANLING
TALAYOTS	TALLIED	TAMBOURAS	TANDOORIS	TANLINGS
TALBOT	TALLIER	TAMBOURED	TANE	TANNA
TALBOTS	TALLIERS	TAMBOURIN	TANG	TANNABLE
TALBOTYPE	TALLIES	TAMBOURING	TANGA	TANNAGE
TALBOTYPES	TALLITH	TAMBOURINS	TANGAS	TANNAGES
TALC	TALLITHS	TAMBOURS	TANGED	TANNAH
TALCKY	TALLNESS	TAMBURA	TANGELO	TANNAHS
TALCOSE	TALLNESSES	TAMBURAS	TANGELOS	TANNAS
TALCOUS	TALLOT	TAMBURIN	TANGENCIES	TANNATE
TALCS	TALLOTS	TAMBURINS	TANGENCY	TANNATES
TALCUM	TALLOW	TAME	TANGENT	TANNED
TALCUMS	TALLOWED	TAMEABLE	TANGENTS	TANNER
TALE	TALLOWING	TAMED	TANGERINE	TANNERIES
TALEFUL	TALLOWISH	TAMELESS	TANGERINES	TANNERS
TALEGALLA	TALLOWS	TAMELY	TANGHIN	TANNERY
TALEGALLAS	TALLOWY	TAMENESS	TANGHININ	TANNEST
TALENT	TALLY	TAMENESSES	TANGHININS	TANNIC
TALENTED	TALLYING	TAMER	TANGHINS	TANNIN
TALENTS	TALLYMAN	TAMERS	TANGIBLE	TANNING
TALES	TALLYMEN	TAMES	TANGIBLES	TANNINGS
TALESMAN	TALLYSHOP	TAMEST	TANGIBLY	TANNINS
TALESMEN	TALLYSHOPS	TAMIN	TANGIE	TANREC
TALI	TALMA	TAMINE	TANGIER	TANRECS
TALION	TALMAS	TAMINES	TANGIES	TANS
TALIONIC	TALON	TAMING	TANGIEST	TANSIES
TALIONS	TALONED	TAMINGS	TANGING	TANSY
TALIPAT	TALONS	TAMINS	TANGLE	TANTALATE
TALIPATS	TALPA	TAMIS	TANGLED	TANTALATES
TALIPED	TALPAE	TAMISE	TANGLER	TANTALIC
TALIPEDS	TALPAS	TAMISES	TANGLERS	TANTALISE

TANTALISED	TAPETI	TARBOOSH	TARRAS	TARTLETS
TANTALISES	TAPETIS	TARBOOSHES	TARRASES	TARTLY
TANTALISING	TAPETS	TARBOUSH	TARRE	TARTNESS
TANTALISINGS	TAPETUM	TARBOUSHES	TARRED	TARTNESSES
TANTALISM	TAPEWORM	TARBUSH	TARRES	TARTRATE
TANTALISMS	TAPEWORMS	TARBUSHES	TARRIANCE	TARTRATES
TANTALITE	TAPING	TARCEL	TARRIANCES	TARTS
TANTALITES	TAPIOCA	TARCELS	TARRIED	TARTY
TANTALIZE	TAPIOCAS	TARDIED	TARRIER	TARWEED
TANTALIZED	TAPIR	TARDIER	TARRIERS	TARWEEDS
TANTALIZES	TAPIROID	TARDIES	TARRIES	TARWHINE
TANTALIZING	TAPIRS	TARDIEST	TARRIEST	TARWHINES
TANTALIZINGS	TAPIS	TARDILY	TARRINESS	TASAR
TANTALUM	TAPISES	TARDINESS	TARRINESSES	TASARS
TANTALUMS	TAPIST	TARDINESSES	TARRING	TASH
TANTALUS	TAPISTS	TARDIVE	TARRINGS	TASHED
TANTALUSES	TAPLASH	TARDY	TARROCK	TASHES
TANTARA	TAPLASHES	TARDYING	TARROCKS	TASHING
TANTARARA	TAPPA	TARE	TARROW	TASIMETER
TANTARARAS	TAPPAS	TARED	TARROWED	TASIMETERS
TANTARAS	TAPPED	TARES	TARROWING	TASK
TANTI	TAPPER	TARGE	TARROWS	TASKED
TANTIVIES	TAPPERS	TARGED	TARRY	TASKER
TANTIVY	TAPPET	TARGES	TARRYING	TASKERS
TANTO	TAPPETS	TARGET	TARS	TASKING
TANTONIES	TAPPICE	TARGETED	TARSAL	TASKINGS
TANTONY	TAPPICED	TARGETEER	TARSALGIA	TASKS
TANTRA	TAPPICES	TARGETEERS	TARSALGIAS	TASLET
TANTRAS	TAPPICING	TARGETING	TARSALS	TASLETS
TANTRIC	TAPPING	TARGETS	TARSEL	TASS
TANTRUM	TAPPINGS	TARGING	TARSELS	TASSE
TANTRUMS	TAPPIT	TARIFF	TARSI	TASSEL
TANYARD	TAPROOM	TARIFFED	TARSIA	TASSELL
TANYARDS	TAPROOMS	TARIFFING	TARSIAS	TASSELLED
TAOISEACH	TAPROOT	TARIFFS	TARSIER	TASSELLING
TAOISEACHS	TAPROOTS	TARING	TARSIERS	TASSELLINGS
TAP	TAPS	TARLATAN	TARSIOID	TASSELLS
TAPA	TAPSMAN	TARLATANS	TARSUS	TASSELLY
TAPACOLO	TAPSMEN	TARMAC	TART	TASSELS
TAPACOLOS	TAPSTER	TARMACKED	TARTAN	TASSES
TAPACULO	TAPSTERS	TARMACKING	TARTANA	TASSET
TAPACULOS	TAPSTRIES	TARMACS	TARTANAS	TASSETS
TAPADERA	TAPSTRY	TARN	TARTANE	TASSIE
TAPADERAS	TAPU	TARNAL	TARTANED	TASSIES
TAPADERO	TAPUS	TARNATION	TARTANES	TASSWAGE
TAPADEROS	TAR	TARNISH	TARTANS	TASTABLE
TAPAS	TARA	TARNISHED	TARTAR	TASTE
TAPE	TARAKIHI	TARNISHER	TARTARE	TASTED
TAPED	TARAKIHIS	TARNISHERS	TARTARES	TASTEFUL
TAPELESS	TARAND	TARNISHES	TARTARIC	TASTELESS
TAPELINE	TARANDS	TARNISHING	TARTARISE	TASTER
TAPELINES	TARANTARA	TARNS	TARTARISED	TASTERS
TAPEN	TARANTARAED	TARO	TARTARISES	TASTES
TAPER	TARANTARAING	TAROC	TARTARISING	TASTEVIN
TAPERED	TARANTARAS	TAROCS	TARTARIZE	TASTEVINS
TAPERER	TARANTAS	TAROK	TARTARIZED	TASTIER
TAPERERS	TARANTASES	TAROKS	TARTARIZES	TASTIEST
TAPERING	TARANTASS	TAROS	TARTARIZING	TASTILY
TAPERINGS	TARANTASSES	TAROT	TARTARLY	TASTING
TAPERNESS	TARANTISM	TAROTS	TARTARS	TASTINGS
TAPERS	TARANTISMS	TARP	TARTER	TASTY
TAPERWISE	TARANTULA	TARPAN	TARTEST	TAT
TAPES	TARANTULAS	TARPANS	TARTIER	TATAMI
TAPESTRIED	TARAS	TARPAULIN	TARTIEST	TATAMIS
TAPESTRIES	TARAXACUM	TARPAULINS	TARTINE	TATE
TAPESTRY	TARAXACUMS	TARPON	TARTINES	TATER
TAPESTRYING	TARBOGGIN	TARPONS	TARTINESS	TATERS
TAPET	TARBOGGINED	TARPS	TARTINESSES	TATES
TAPETA	TARBOGGINING	TARRAGON	TARTISH	TATH
TAPETAL	TARBOGGINS	TARRAGONS	TARTLET	TATHED

TATHING	TAUS	TAXAMETER	TEAED	TEAZELED
TATHS	TAUT	TAXAMETERS	TEAGLE	TEAZELING
TATIE	TAUTED	TAXATION	TEAGLED	TEAZELLED
TATIES	TAUTEN	TAXATIONS	TEAGLES	TEAZELLING
TATLER	TAUTENED	TAXATIVE	TEAGLING	TEAZELS
TATLERS	TAUTENING	TAXED	TEAING	TEAZES
TATOU	TAUTENS	TAXER	TEAK	TEAZING
TATOUS	TAUTER	TAXERS	TEAKS	TEAZLE
TATS	TAUTEST	TAXES	TEAL	TEAZLED
TATT	TAUTING	TAXI	TEALS	TEAZLES
TATTED	TAUTIT	TAXIARCH	TEAM	TEAZLING
TATTER	TAUTLY	TAXIARCHS	TEAMED	TEBBAD
TATTERED	TAUTNESS	TAXICAB	TEAMER	TEBBADS
TATTERING	TAUTNESSES	TAXICABS	TEAMERS	TECH
TATTERS	TAUTOG	TAXIDERMIES	TEAMING	TECHIER
TATTERY	TAUTOGS	TAXIDERMY	TEAMINGS	TECHIEST
TATTIE	TAUTOLOGIES	TAXIED	TEAMS	TECHNIC
TATTIER	TAUTOLOGY	TAXIES	TEAMSTER	TECHNICAL
TATTIES	TAUTOMER	TAXIMAN	TEAMSTERS	TECHNICS
TATTIEST	TAUTOMERS	TAXIMEN	TEAMWISE	TECHNIQUE
TATTILY	TAUTONYM	TAXIMETER	TEAMWORK	TECHNIQUES
TATTINESS	TAUTONYMS	TAXIMETERS	TEAMWORKS	TECHS
TATTINESSES	TAUTS	TAXING	TEAPOT	TECHY
TATTING	TAVER	TAXINGS	TEAPOTS	TECKEL
TATTINGS	TAVERED	TAXIS	TEAPOY	TECKELS
TATTLE	TAVERING	TAXIWAY	TEAPOYS	TECTIFORM
TATTLED	TAVERN	TAXIWAYS	TEAR	TECTONIC
TATTLER	TAVERNA	TAXMAN	TEARAWAY	TECTONICS
TATTLERS	TAVERNAS	TAXMEN	TEARAWAYS	TECTORIAL
TATTLES	TAVERNER	TAXON	TEARER	TECTRICES
TATTLING	TAVERNERS	TAXONOMER	TEARERS	TECTRIX
TATTLINGS	TAVERNS	TAXONOMERS	TEARFUL	TED
TATTOO	TAVERS	TAXONOMIC	TEARFULLY	TEDDED
TATTOOED	TAVERT	TAXONOMIES	TEARIER	TEDDER
TATTOOER	TAW	TAXONOMY	TEARIEST	TEDDERS
TATTOOERS	TAWDRIER	TAXOR	TEARING	TEDDIES
TATTOOING	TAWDRIES	TAXORS	TEARLESS	TEDDING
TATTOOIST	TAWDRIEST	TAXYING	TEARS	TEDDY
TATTOOISTS	TAWDRILY	TAYBERRIES	TEARY	TEDESCA
TATTOOS	TAWDRY	TAYBERRY	TEAS	TEDESCHE
TATTOW	TAWED	TAYRA	TEASE	TEDESCHI
TATTOWED	TAWER	TAYRAS	TEASED	TEDESCO
TATTOWING	TAWERIES	TAZZA	TEASEL	TEDIOSITIES
TATTOWS	TAWERS	TAZZAS	TEASELED	TEDIOSITY
TATTS	TAWERY	TAZZE	TEASELER	TEDIOUS
TATTY	TAWIE	TCHICK	TEASELERS	TEDIOUSLY
TATU	TAWING	TCHICKED	TEASELING	TEDISOME
TATUED	TAWINGS	TCHICKING	TEASELINGS	TEDIUM
TATUING	TAWNEY	TCHICKS	TEASELLED	TEDIUMS
TATUS	TAWNEYS	TE	TEASELLER	TEDS
TAU	TAWNIER	TEA	TEASELLERS	TEDY
TAUBE	TAWNIES	TEABERRIES	TEASELLING	TEE
TAUBES	TAWNIEST	TEABERRY	TEASELLINGS	TEED
TAUGHT	TAWNINESS	TEACH	TEASELS	TEEHEE
TAULD	TAWNINESSES	TEACHABLE	TEASER	TEEHEED
TAUNT	TAWNY	TEACHER	TEASERS	TEEHEEING
TAUNTED	TAWPIE	TEACHERS	TEASES	TEEHEES
TAUNTER	TAWPIES	TEACHES	TEASING	TEEING
TAUNTERS	TAWS	TEACHIE	TEASINGLY	TEEL
TAUNTING	TAWSE	TEACHING	TEASINGS	TEELS
TAUNTINGS	TAWSES	TEACHINGS	TEASPOON	TEEM
TAUNTS	TAWT	TEACHLESS	TEASPOONS	TEEMED
TAUPE	TAWTED	TEACUP	TEAT	TEEMER
TAUPES	TAWTIE	TEACUPFUL	TEATED	TEEMERS
TAUPIE	TAWTING	TEACUPFULS	TEATIME	TEEMFUL
TAUPIES	TAWTS	TEACUPS	TEATIMES	TEEMING
TAUREAN	TAX	TEAD	TEATS	TEEMLESS
TAURIC	TAXA	TEADE	TEAZE	TEEMS
TAURIFORM	TAXABLE	TEADES	TEAZED	TEEN
TAURINE	TAXABLY	TEADS	TEAZEL	TEENAGE

TEENAGED	TEHEES	TELEPHEMES	TELLURIAN	TEMPO
TEENAGER	TEHR	TELEPHONE	TELLURIANS	TEMPORAL
TEENAGERS	TEHRS	TELEPHONED	TELLURIC	TEMPORALS
TEEND	TEIL	TELEPHONES	TELLURIDE	TEMPORARIES
TEENDED	TEILS	TELEPHONIES	TELLURIDES	TEMPORARY
TEENDING	TEIND	TELEPHONING	TELLURION	TEMPORE
TEENDS	TEINDED	TELEPHONY	TELLURIONS	TEMPORISE
TEENE	TEINDING	TELERGIC	TELLURISE	TEMPORISED
TEENED	TEINDS	TELERGIES	TELLURISED	TEMPORISES
TEENES	TEKNONYMIES	TELERGY	TELLURISES	TEMPORISING
TEENIER	TEKNONYMY	TELESALE	TELLURISING	TEMPORISINGS
TEENIEST	TEKTITE	TELESALES	TELLURITE	TEMPORIZE
TEENING	TEKTITES	TELESCOPE	TELLURITES	TEMPORIZED
TEENS	TEL	TELESCOPED	TELLURIUM	TEMPORIZES
TEENSIER	TELA	TELESCOPES	TELLURIUMS	TEMPORIZING
TEENSIEST	TELAE	TELESCOPIES	TELLURIZE	TEMPORIZINGS
TEENSY	TELAMON	TELESCOPING	TELLURIZED	TEMPOS
TEENTIER	TELAMONES	TELESCOPY	TELLURIZES	TEMPS
TEENTIEST	TELARY	TELESEME	TELLURIZING	TEMPT
TEENTSIER	TELD	TELESEMES	TELLUROUS	TEMPTABLE
TEENTSIEST	TELECAST	TELESES	TELLY	TEMPTED
TEENTSY	TELECASTED	TELESIS	TELOPHASE	TEMPTER
TEENTY	TELECASTING	TELESM	TELOPHASES	TEMPTERS
TEENY	TELECASTS	TELESMS	TELOS	TEMPTING
TEEPEE	TELECHIR	TELESTIC	TELOSES	TEMPTINGS
TEEPEES	TELECHIRS	TELESTICH	TELPHER	TEMPTRESS
TEER	TELECINE	TELESTICHS	TELPHERS	TEMPTRESSES
TEERED	TELECINES	TELETEX	TELS	TEMPTS
TEERING	TELECOM	TELETEXES	TELSON	TEMPURA
TEERS	TELECOMS	TELETEXT	TELSONS	TEMPURAS
TEES	TELEDU	TELETEXTS	TELT	TEMS
TEETER	TELEDUS	TELETHON	TEMBLOR	TEMSE
TEETERED	TELEFILM	TELETHONS	TEMBLORES	TEMSED
TEETERING	TELEFILMS	TELETRON	TEME	TEMSES
TEETERS	TELEGA	TELETRONS	TEMED	TEMSING
TEETH	TELEGAS	TELEVIEW	TEMENOS	TEMULENCE
TEETHE	TELEGENIC	TELEVIEWED	TEMENOSES	TEMULENCES
TEETHED	TELEGONIES	TELEVIEWING	TEMERITIES	TEMULENCIES
TEETHES	TELEGONY	TELEVIEWS	TEMERITY	TEMULENCY
TEETHING	TELEGRAM	TELEVISE	TEMEROUS	TEMULENT
TEETHINGS	TELEGRAMS	TELEVISED	TEMES	TEN
TEETOTAL	TELEGRAPH	TELEVISES	TEMP	TENABLE
TEETOTALS	TELEGRAPHED	TELEVISING	TEMPED	TENACE
TEETOTUM	TELEGRAPHING	TELEVISOR	TEMPER	TENACES
TEETOTUMS	TELEGRAPHS	TELEVISORS	TEMPERA	TENACIOUS
TEF	TELEMARK	TELEX	TEMPERAS	TENACITIES
TEFF	TELEMARKED	TELEXED	TEMPERATE	TENACITY
TEFFS	TELEMARKING	TELEXES	TEMPERATED	TENACULUM
TEFS	TELEMARKS	TELEXING	TEMPERATES	TENACULUMS
TEG	TELEMETER	TELIC	TEMPERATING	TENAIL
TEGG	TELEMETERED	TELL	TEMPERED	TENAILLE
TEGGS	TELEMETERING	TELLABLE	TEMPERER	TENAILLES
TEGMEN	TELEMETERS	TELLAR	TEMPERERS	TENAILLON
TEGMENTAL	TELEMETRIES	TELLARED	TEMPERING	TENAILLONS
TEGMENTUM	TELEMETRY	TELLARING	TEMPERINGS	TENAILS
TEGMENTUMS	TELEOLOGIES	TELLARS	TEMPERS	TENANCIES
TEGMINA	TELEOLOGY	TELLER	TEMPEST	TENANCY
TEGS	TELEONOMIES	TELLERED	TEMPESTED	TENANT
TEGUEXIN	TELEONOMY	TELLERING	TEMPESTING	TENANTED
TEGUEXINS	TELEOSAUR	TELLERS	TEMPESTS	TENANTING
TEGULA	TELEOSAURS	TELLIES	TEMPI	TENANTRIES
TEGULAE	TELEOST	TELLING	TEMPING	TENANTRY
TEGULAR	TELEOSTS	TELLINGLY	TEMPLAR	TENANTS
TEGULARLY	TELEPATH	TELLINGS	TEMPLATE	TENCH
TEGULATED	TELEPATHED	TELLS	TEMPLATES	TENCHES
TEGUMENT	TELEPATHIES	TELLTALE	TEMPLE	TEND
TEGUMENTS	TELEPATHING	TELLTALES	TEMPLED	TENDANCE
TEHEE	TELEPATHS	TELLURAL	TEMPLES	TENDANCES
TEHEED	TELEPATHY	TELLURATE	TEMPLET	TENDED
TEHEEING	TELEPHEME	TELLURATES	TEMPLETS	TENDENCE

TENDENCES	TENONS	TENTORIAL	TERBIC	TERMITES
TENDENCIES	TENOR	TENTORIUM	TERBIUM	TERMLESS
TENDENCY	TENORIST	TENTORIUMS	TERBIUMS	TERMLIES
TENDENZ	TENORISTS	TENTS	TERCE	TERMLY
TENDENZEN	TENORITE	TENTWISE	TERCEL	TERMOR
TENDER	TENORITES	TENTY	TERCELET	TERMORS
TENDERED	TENOROON	TENUE	TERCELETS	TERMS
TENDERER	TENOROONS	TENUES	TERCELS	TERN
TENDERERS	TENORS	TENUIOUS	TERCES	TERNAL
TENDEREST	TENOTOMIES	TENUIS	TERCET	TERNARIES
TENDERING	TENOTOMY	TENUITIES	TERCETS	TERNARY
TENDERINGS	TENOUR	TENUITY	TERCIO	TERNATE
TENDERISE	TENOURS	TENUOUS	TERCIOS	TERNATELY
TENDERISED	TENPENCE	TENUOUSLY	TEREBENE	TERNE
TENDERISES	TENPENCES	TENURABLE	TEREBENES	TERNED
TENDERISING	TENPENNY	TENURE	TEREBINTH	TERNES
TENDERIZE	TENPINS	TENURES	TEREBINTHS	TERNING
TENDERIZED	TENREC	TENURIAL	TEREBRA	TERNION
TENDERIZES	TENRECS	TENUTO	TEREBRAE	TERNIONS
TENDERIZING	TENS	TENZON	TEREBRANT	TERNS
TENDERLY	TENSE	TENZONS	TEREBRANTS	TERPENE
TENDERS	TENSED	TEOCALLI	TEREBRAS	TERPENES
TENDING	TENSELY	TEOCALLIS	TEREBRATE	TERPENOID
TENDINOUS	TENSENESS	TEOSINTE	TEREBRATED	TERPENOIDS
TENDON	TENSENESSES	TEOSINTES	TEREBRATES	TERPINEOL
TENDONS	TENSER	TEPAL	TEREBRATING	TERPINEOLS
TENDRE	TENSES	TEPALS	TEREDINES	TERRA
TENDRES	TENSEST	TEPEE	TEREDO	TERRACE
TENDRIL	TENSIBLE	TEPEES	TEREDOS	TERRACED
TENDRILS	TENSILE	TEPEFIED	TEREFA	TERRACES
TENDRON	TENSILITIES	TEPEFIES	TEREFAH	TERRACING
TENDRONS	TENSILITY	TEPEFY	TEREK	TERRACINGS
TENDS	TENSING	TEPEFYING	TEREKS	TERRAE
TENE	TENSION	TEPHIGRAM	TERETE	TERRAIN
TENEBRAE	TENSIONS	TEPHIGRAMS	TERF	TERRAINS
TENEBRIO	TENSITIES	TEPHRA	TERFE	TERRAMARA
TENEBRIOS	TENSITY	TEPHRAS	TERFES	TERRAMARE
TENEBRISM	TENSIVE	TEPHRITE	TERFS	TERRANE
TENEBRISMS	TENSON	TEPHRITES	TERGAL	TERRANES
TENEBRIST	TENSONS	TEPHRITIC	TERGITE	TERRAPIN
TENEBRISTS	TENSOR	TEPHROITE	TERGITES	TERRAPINS
TENEBRITIES	TENSORS	TEPHROITES	TERGUM	TERRARIA
TENEBRITY	TENT	TEPID	TERGUMS	TERRARIUM
TENEBROSE	TENTACLE	TEPIDER	TERIYAKI	TERRARIUMS
TENEBROUS	TENTACLED	TEPIDEST	TERIYAKIS	TERRAS
TENEMENT	TENTACLES	TEPIDITIES	TERM	TERRASES
TENEMENTS	TENTACULA	TEPIDITY	TERMAGANT	TERRAZZO
TENENDUM	TENTAGE	TEPIDLY	TERMAGANTS	TERRAZZOS
TENENDUMS	TENTAGES	TEPIDNESS	TERMED	TERREEN
TENES	TENTATION	TEPIDNESSES	TERMER	TERREENS
TENESMUS	TENTATIONS	TEQUILA	TERMERS	TERRELLA
TENESMUSES	TENTATIVE	TEQUILAS	TERMINAL	TERRELLAS
TENET	TENTED	TEQUILLA	TERMINALS	TERRENE
TENETS	TENTER	TEQUILLAS	TERMINATE	TERRENELY
TENFOLD	TENTERED	TERAI	TERMINATED	TERRENES
TENIA	TENTERING	TERAIS	TERMINATES	TERRET
TENIAE	TENTERS	TERAKIHI	TERMINATING	TERRETS
TENIAS	TENTFUL	TERAKIHIS	TERMINER	TERRIBLE
TENIOID	TENTFULS	TERAPH	TERMINERS	TERRIBLES
TENNÉ	TENTH	TERAPHIM	TERMING	TERRIBLY
TENNER	TENTHLY	TERAPHIMS	TERMINI	TERRICOLE
TENNERS	TENTHS	TERAS	TERMINISM	TERRICOLES
TENNÉS	TENTIE	TERATA	TERMINISMS	TERRIER
TENNIS	TENTIER	TERATISM	TERMINIST	TERRIERS
TENNISES	TENTIEST	TERATISMS	TERMINISTS	TERRIES
TENON	TENTIGO	TERATOGEN	TERMINUS	TERRIFIC
TENONED	TENTIGOS	TERATOGENS	TERMINUSES	TERRIFIED
TENONER	TENTING	TERATOID	TERMITARIES	TERRIFIES
TENONERS	TENTINGS	TERATOMA	TERMITARY	TERRIFY
TENONING	TENTORIA	TERATOMATA	TERMITE	TERRIFYING

TERRINE
TERRINES
TERRIT
TERRITORIES
TERRITORY
TERRITS
TERROR
TERRORISE
TERRORISED
TERRORISES
TERRORISING
TERRORISM
TERRORISMS
TERRORIST
TERRORISTS
TERRORIZE
TERRORIZED
TERRORIZES
TERRORIZING
TERRORS
TERRY
TERSE
TERSELY
TERSENESS
TERSENESSES
TERSER
TERSEST
TERSION
TERSIONS
TERTIA
TERTIAL
TERTIALS
TERTIAN
TERTIANS
TERTIARIES
TERTIARY
TERTIAS
TERTIUS
TERTIUSES
TERTS
TERVALENT
TERZETTA
TERZETTAS
TERZETTI
TERZETTO
TERZETTOS
TES
TESLA
TESLAS
TESSELLA
TESSELLAE
TESSELLAR
TESSERA
TESSERACT
TESSERACTS
TESSERAE
TESSERAL
TESSITURA
TESSITURAS
TEST
TESTA
TESTABLE
TESTACIES
TESTACY
TESTAMENT
TESTAMENTS
TESTAMUR
TESTAMURS
TESTAS
TESTATE

TESTATION
TESTATIONS
TESTATOR
TESTATORS
TESTATRIX
TESTATRIXES
TESTATUM
TESTATUMS
TESTE
TESTED
TESTEE
TESTEES
TESTER
TESTERN
TESTERNED
TESTERNING
TESTERNS
TESTERS
TESTES
TESTICLE
TESTICLES
TESTIER
TESTIEST
TESTIFIED
TESTIFIER
TESTIFIERS
TESTIFIES
TESTIFY
TESTIFYING
TESTILY
TESTIMONIED
TESTIMONIES
TESTIMONY
TESTIMONYING
TESTINESS
TESTINESSES
TESTING
TESTINGS
TESTIS
TESTON
TESTONS
TESTOON
TESTOONS
TESTRIL
TESTRILL
TESTRILLS
TESTRILS
TESTS
TESTUDINES
TESTUDO
TESTUDOS
TESTY
TETANAL
TETANIC
TETANIES
TETANISE
TETANISED
TETANISES
TETANISING
TETANIZE
TETANIZED
TETANIZES
TETANIZING
TETANOID
TETANUS
TETANUSES
TETANY
TETCHIER
TETCHIEST
TETCHILY

TETCHY
TÊTE
TÊTES
TETHER
TETHERED
TETHERING
TETHERS
TETRA
TETRACID
TETRACT
TETRACTS
TETRAD
TETRADIC
TETRADITE
TETRADITES
TETRADS
TETRAGON
TETRAGONS
TETRAGRAM
TETRAGRAMS
TETRALOGIES
TETRALOGY
TETRAPLA
TETRAPLAS
TETRAPOD
TETRAPODIES
TETRAPODS
TETRAPODY
TETRARCH
TETRARCHIES
TETRARCHS
TETRARCHY
TETRAS
TETRAXON
TETRAXONS
TETRODE
TETRODES
TETRONAL
TETRONALS
TETROXIDE
TETROXIDES
TETRYL
TETRYLS
TETTER
TETTERED
TETTERING
TETTEROUS
TETTERS
TETTIX
TETTIXES
TEUCH
TEUCHAT
TEUCHATS
TEUCHER
TEUCHEST
TEUCHTER
TEUCHTERS
TEUGH
TEUGHER
TEUGHEST
TEW
TEWART
TEWARTS
TEWED
TEWEL
TEWELS
TEWHIT
TEWHITS
TEWING
TEWIT

TEWITS
TEWS
TEXAS
TEXASES
TEXT
TEXTBOOK
TEXTBOOKS
TEXTILE
TEXTILES
TEXTORIAL
TEXTS
TEXTUAL
TEXTUALLY
TEXTUARIES
TEXTUARY
TEXTURAL
TEXTURE
TEXTURED
TEXTURES
TEXTURING
TEXTURISE
TEXTURISED
TEXTURISES
TEXTURISING
TEXTURIZE
TEXTURIZED
TEXTURIZES
TEXTURIZING
THACK
THACKS
THAE
THAGI
THAGIS
THAIM
THAIRM
THAIRMS
THALAMI
THALAMIC
THALAMUS
THALASSIC
THALER
THALERS
THALIAN
THALLI
THALLIC
THALLINE
THALLIUM
THALLIUMS
THALLOID
THALLOUS
THALLUS
THALLUSES
THALWEG
THALWEGS
THAN
THANA
THANADAR
THANADARS
THANAGE
THANAGES
THANAH
THANAHS
THANAS
THANATISM
THANATISMS
THANATIST
THANATISTS
THANATOID
THANE
THANEDOM

THANEDOMS
THANEHOOD
THANEHOODS
THANES
THANESHIP
THANESHIPS
THANK
THANKED
THANKEE
THANKER
THANKERS
THANKFUL
THANKING
THANKINGS
THANKLESS
THANKS
THANNA
THANNAH
THANNAHS
THANNAS
THAR
THARS
THAT
THATAWAY
THATCH
THATCHED
THATCHER
THATCHERS
THATCHES
THATCHING
THATCHINGS
THATCHT
THATNESS
THATNESSES
THAUMATIN
THAUMATINS
THAW
THAWED
THAWER
THAWERS
THAWIER
THAWIEST
THAWING
THAWINGS
THAWLESS
THAWS
THAWY
THE
THEACEOUS
THEANDRIC
THEARCHIC
THEARCHIES
THEARCHY
THEATER
THEATERS
THEATRAL
THEATRE
THEATRES
THEATRIC
THEATRICS
THEAVE
THEAVES
THEBAINE
THEBAINES
THECA
THECAE
THECAL
THECATE
THECODONT
THECODONTS

THEE	THEOMANCIES	THEREOUT	THIAZIDE	THINGHOODS
THEED	THEOMANCY	THERES	THIAZIDES	THINGIES
THEEING	THEOMANIA	THERETO	THIBET	THINGNESS
THEEK	THEOMANIAS	THEREUNTO	THIBETS	THINGNESSES
THEEKED	THEONOMIES	THEREUPON	THIBLE	THINGS
THEEKING	THEONOMY	THEREWITH	THIBLES	THINGUMMIES
THEEKS	THEOPATHIES	THERIAC	THICK	THINGUMMY
THEES	THEOPATHY	THERIACA	THICKED	THINGY
THEFT	THEOPHAGIES	THERIACAL	THICKEN	THINK
THEFTBOOT	THEOPHAGY	THERIACAS	THICKENED	THINKABLE
THEFTBOOTS	THEOPHANIES	THERIACS	THICKENER	THINKER
THEFTBOTE	THEOPHANY	THERM	THICKENERS	THINKERS
THEFTBOTES	THEORBIST	THERMAE	THICKENING	THINKING
THEFTS	THEORBISTS	THERMAL	THICKENINGS	THINKINGS
THEFTUOUS	THEORBO	THERMALLY	THICKENS	THINKS
THEGITHER	THEORBOS	THERMALS	THICKER	THINLY
THEGN	THEOREM	THERMIC	THICKEST	THINNED
THEGNS	THEOREMS	THERMICAL	THICKET	THINNER
THEIC	THEORETIC	THERMION	THICKETED	THINNERS
THEICS	THEORETICS	THERMIONS	THICKETS	THINNESS
THEINE	THEORIC	THERMITE	THICKETY	THINNESSES
THEINES	THEORICS	THERMITES	THICKHEAD	THINNEST
THEIR	THEORIES	THERMOS	THICKHEADS	THINNING
THEIRS	THEORIQUE	THERMOSES	THICKING	THINNINGS
THEISM	THEORIQUES	THERMOTIC	THICKISH	THINNISH
THEISMS	THEORISE	THERMOTICS	THICKLY	THINS
THEIST	THEORISED	THERMS	THICKNESS	THIOL
THEISTIC	THEORISER	THEROID	THICKNESSES	THIOLS
THEISTS	THEORISERS	THEROLOGIES	THICKO	THIOUREA
THELEMENT	THEORISES	THEROLOGY	THICKOES	THIOUREAS
THELEMENTS	THEORISING	THEROPOD	THICKOS	THIR
THELF	THEORIST	THEROPODS	THICKS	THIRAM
THELVES	THEORISTS	THESAURUS	THICKSET	THIRAMS
THELYTOKIES	THEORIZE	THESAURUSES	THICKSETS	THIRD
THELYTOKY	THEORIZED	THESE	THICKSKIN	THIRDED
THEM	THEORIZER	THESES	THICKSKINS	THIRDING
THEMA	THEORIZERS	THESIS	THICKY	THIRDINGS
THEMATA	THEORIZES	THESPIAN	THIEF	THIRDLY
THEMATIC	THEORIZING	THESPIANS	THIEVE	THIRDS
THEME	THEORY	THETA	THIEVED	THIRDSMAN
THEMED	THEOSOPH	THETAS	THIEVERIES	THIRDSMEN
THEMES	THEOSOPHIES	THETCH	THIEVERY	THIRL
THEMING	THEOSOPHS	THETCHED	THIEVES	THIRLAGE
THEN	THEOSOPHY	THETCHES	THIEVING	THIRLAGES
THENABOUT	THEOTOKOS	THETCHING	THIEVINGS	THIRLED
THENABOUTS	THEOW	THETE	THIEVISH	THIRLING
THENAR	THEOWS	THETES	THIG	THIRLS
THENARS	THERALITE	THETHER	THIGGER	THIRST
THENCE	THERALITES	THETIC	THIGGERS	THIRSTED
THENS	THERAPIES	THETICAL	THIGGING	THIRSTER
THEOCRACIES	THERAPIST	THEURGIC	THIGGINGS	THIRSTERS
THEOCRACY	THERAPISTS	THEURGIES	THIGGIT	THIRSTFUL
THEOCRASIES	THERAPSID	THEURGIST	THIGH	THIRSTIER
THEOCRASY	THERAPSIDS	THEURGISTS	THIGHS	THIRSTIEST
THEOCRAT	THERAPY	THEURGY	THIGS	THIRSTILY
THEOCRATS	THERBLIG	THEW	THILK	THIRSTING
THEODICIES	THERBLIGS	THEWED	THILL	THIRSTS
THEODICY	THERE	THEWES	THILLER	THIRSTY
THEOGONIC	THEREAT	THEWIER	THILLERS	THIRTEEN
THEOGONIES	THEREAWAY	THEWIEST	THILLS	THIRTEENS
THEOGONY	THEREBY	THEWLESS	THIMBLE	THIRTIES
THEOLOGER	THEREFOR	THEWS	THIMBLED	THIRTIETH
THEOLOGERS	THEREFORE	THEWY	THIMBLES	THIRTIETHS
THEOLOGIC	THEREFROM	THEY	THIMBLING	THIRTY
THEOLOGIES	THEREIN	THIAMIN	THIN	THIRTYISH
THEOLOGUE	THEREINTO	THIAMINE	THINE	THIS
THEOLOGUES	THERENESS	THIAMINES	THING	THISNESS
THEOLOGY	THERENESSES	THIAMINS	THINGAMIES	THISNESSES
THEOMACHIES	THEREOF	THIASUS	THINGAMY	THISTLE
THEOMACHY	THEREON	THIASUSES	THINGHOOD	THISTLES

THISTLY	THOWELS	THREEPS	THRIVES	THRUMMERS
THITHER	THOWL	THREES	THRIVING	THRUMMING
THIVEL	THOWLESS	THREESOME	THRIVINGS	THRUMMINGS
THIVELS	THOWLS	THREESOMES	THRO	THRUMMY
THLIPSES	THRAE	THRENE	THROAT	THRUMS
THLIPSIS	THRALDOM	THRENES	THROATED	THRUSH
THLIPSISES	THRALDOMS	THRENETIC	THROATIER	THRUSHES
THO	THRALL	THRENODE	THROATIEST	THRUST
THOFT	THRALLDOM	THRENODES	THROATILY	THRUSTED
THOFTS	THRALLDOMS	THRENODIC	THROATS	THRUSTER
THOLE	THRALLED	THRENODIES	THROATY	THRUSTERS
THOLED	THRALLING	THRENODY	THROB	THRUSTING
THOLES	THRALLS	THRENOS	THROBBED	THRUSTINGS
THOLI	THRANG	THRENOSES	THROBBING	THRUSTS
THOLING	THRANGED	THREONINE	THROBBINGS	THRUTCH
THOLOBATE	THRANGING	THREONINES	THROBLESS	THRUTCHED
THOLOBATES	THRANGS	THRESH	THROBS	THRUTCHES
THOLOI	THRAPPLE	THRESHED	THROE	THRUTCHING
THOLOS	THRAPPLED	THRESHEL	THROED	THRUWAY
THOLUS	THRAPPLES	THRESHELS	THROEING	THRUWAYS
THON	THRAPPLING	THRESHER	THROES	THRYMSA
THONDER	THRASH	THRESHERS	THROMBI	THRYMSAS
THONG	THRASHED	THRESHES	THROMBIN	THUD
THONGED	THRASHER	THRESHING	THROMBINS	THUDDED
THONGS	THRASHERS	THRESHINGS	THROMBOSE	THUDDING
THORACES	THRASHES	THRESHOLD	THROMBOSED	THUDS
THORACIC	THRASHING	THRESHOLDS	THROMBOSES	THUG
THORAX	THRASHINGS	THRETTIES	THROMBOSING	THUGGEE
THORAXES	THRASONIC	THRETTY	THROMBUS	THUGGEES
THORITE	THRAVE	THREW	THRONE	THUGGERIES
THORITES	THRAVES	THRICE	THRONED	THUGGERY
THORIUM	THRAW	THRID	THRONES	THUGGISM
THORIUMS	THRAWARD	THRIDACE	THRONG	THUGGISMS
THORN	THRAWART	THRIDACES	THRONGED	THUGS
THORNBACK	THRAWING	THRIDDED	THRONGFUL	THUJA
THORNBACKS	THRAWN	THRIDDING	THRONGING	THUJAS
THORNED	THRAWS	THRIDS	THRONGINGS	THULIA
THORNIER	THREAD	THRIFT	THRONGS	THULIAS
THORNIEST	THREADED	THRIFTIER	THRONING	THULITE
THORNING	THREADEN	THRIFTIEST	THROPPLE	THULITES
THORNLESS	THREADER	THRIFTILY	THROPPLED	THULIUM
THORNS	THREADERS	THRIFTS	THROPPLES	THULIUMS
THORNSET	THREADIER	THRIFTY	THROPPLING	THUMB
THORNTREE	THREADIEST	THRILL	THROSTLE	THUMBED
THORNTREES	THREADING	THRILLANT	THROSTLES	THUMBIER
THORNY	THREADS	THRILLED	THROTTLE	THUMBIEST
THORON	THREADY	THRILLER	THROTTLED	THUMBING
THORONS	THREAP	THRILLERS	THROTTLER	THUMBKINS
THOROUGH	THREAPING	THRILLING	THROTTLERS	THUMBLESS
THOROUGHER	THREAPIT	THRILLS	THROTTLES	THUMBLING
THOROUGHEST	THREAPS	THRILLY	THROTTLING	THUMBLINGS
THOROUGHS	THREAT	THRIMSA	THROTTLINGS	THUMBNAIL
THORP	THREATED	THRIMSAS	THROUGH	THUMBNAILS
THORPE	THREATEN	THRIP	THROUGHLY	THUMBPOT
THORPES	THREATENED	THRIPS	THROVE	THUMBPOTS
THORPS	THREATENING	THRIPSES	THROW	THUMBS
THOSE	THREATENINGS	THRISSEL	THROWE	THUMBY
THOTHER	THREATENS	THRISSELS	THROWER	THUMP
THOTHERS	THREATFUL	THRIST	THROWERS	THUMPED
THOU	THREATING	THRISTED	THROWES	THUMPER
THOUGH	THREATS	THRISTING	THROWING	THUMPERS
THOUGHT	THREAVE	THRISTLE	THROWINGS	THUMPING
THOUGHTED	THREAVES	THRISTLES	THROWN	THUMPS
THOUGHTEN	THREE	THRISTS	THROWS	THUNDER
THOUGHTS	THREEFOLD	THRISTY	THROWSTER	THUNDERED
THOUING	THREENESS	THRIVE	THROWSTERS	THUNDERER
THOUS	THREENESSES	THRIVED	THRU	THUNDERERS
THOUSAND	THREEP	THRIVEN	THRUM	THUNDERING
THOUSANDS	THREEPING	THRIVER	THRUMMED	THUNDERINGS
THOWEL	THREEPIT	THRIVERS	THRUMMER	THUNDERS

THUNDERY	THYRSUS	TIDDY	TIGGING	TILTED
THUNDROUS	THYSELF	TIDE	TIGHT	TILTER
THURIBLE	TI	TIDED	TIGHTEN	TILTERS
THURIBLES	TIAR	TIDELESS	TIGHTENED	TILTH
THURIFER	TIARA	TIDEMARK	TIGHTENER	TILTHS
THURIFERS	TIARAED	TIDEMARKS	TIGHTENERS	TILTING
THURIFIED	TIARAS	TIDEMILL	TIGHTENING	TILTINGS
THURIFIES	TIARS	TIDEMILLS	TIGHTENS	TILTS
THURIFY	TIBIA	TIDES	TIGHTER	TIMARIOT
THURIFYING	TIBIAE	TIDIED	TIGHTEST	TIMARIOTS
THUS	TIBIAL	TIDIER	TIGHTISH	TIMBAL
THUSES	TIBIAS	TIDIES	TIGHTLY	TIMBALE
THUSNESS	TIC	TIDIEST	TIGHTNESS	TIMBALES
THUSNESSES	TICAL	TIDILY	TIGHTNESSES	TIMBALS
THUSWISE	TICALS	TIDINESS	TIGHTS	TIMBER
THWACK	TICCA	TIDINESSES	TIGHTWAD	TIMBERED
THWACKED	TICE	TIDING	TIGHTWADS	TIMBERING
THWACKER	TICED	TIDINGS	TIGLON	TIMBERINGS
THWACKERS	TICES	TIDIVATE	TIGLONS	TIMBERS
THWACKING	TICH	TIDIVATED	TIGON	TIMBÓ
THWACKINGS	TICHES	TIDIVATES	TIGONS	TIMBÓS
THWACKS	TICHIER	TIDIVATING	TIGRESS	TIMBRE
THWAITE	TICHIEST	TIDS	TIGRESSES	TIMBREL
THWAITES	TICHY	TIDY	TIGRINE	TIMBRELS
THWART	TICING	TIDYING	TIGRISH	TIMBRES
THWARTED	TICK	TIE	TIGROID	TIME
THWARTER	TICKED	TIED	TIGS	TIMED
THWARTERS	TICKEN	TIELESS	TIKA	TIMELESS
THWARTING	TICKENS	TIER	TIKAS	TIMELIER
THWARTINGS	TICKER	TIERCE	TIKE	TIMELIEST
THWARTLY	TICKERS	TIERCÉ	TIKES	TIMELY
THWARTS	TICKET	TIERCEL	TIKI	TIMENOGUY
THY	TICKETED	TIERCELET	TIKIS	TIMENOGUYS
THYINE	TICKETING	TIERCELETS	TIL	TIMEOUS
THYLACINE	TICKETS	TIERCELS	TILAPIA	TIMEOUSLY
THYLACINES	TICKEY	TIERCERON	TILAPIAS	TIMEPIECE
THYLOSE	TICKEYS	TIERCERONS	TILBURIES	TIMEPIECES
THYLOSES	TICKIES	TIERCES	TILBURY	TIMER
THYLOSIS	TICKING	TIERED	TILDE	TIMERS
THYME	TICKINGS	TIERING	TILDES	TIMES
THYMES	TICKLE	TIERS	TILE	TIMESCALE
THYMIDINE	TICKLED	TIES	TILED	TIMESCALES
THYMIDINES	TICKLER	TIETAC	TILEFISH	TIMETABLE
THYMIER	TICKLERS	TIETACK	TILEFISHES	TIMETABLED
THYMIEST	TICKLES	TIETACKS	TILER	TIMETABLES
THYMINE	TICKLIER	TIETACS	TILERIES	TIMETABLING
THYMINES	TICKLIEST	TIFF	TILERS	TIMID
THYMOCYTE	TICKLING	TIFFANIES	TILERY	TIMIDER
THYMOCYTES	TICKLINGS	TIFFANY	TILES	TIMIDEST
THYMOL	TICKLISH	TIFFED	TILING	TIMIDITIES
THYMOLS	TICKLY	TIFFIN	TILINGS	TIMIDITY
THYMUS	TICKS	TIFFING	TILL	TIMIDLY
THYMUSES	TICKY	TIFFINGS	TILLABLE	TIMIDNESS
THYMY	TICS	TIFFINS	TILLAGE	TIMIDNESSES
THYRATRON	TID	TIFFS	TILLAGES	TIMING
THYRATRONS	TIDAL	TIFT	TILLED	TIMINGS
THYREOID	TIDBIT	TIFTED	TILLER	TIMIST
THYREOIDS	TIDBITS	TIFTING	TILLERED	TIMISTS
THYRISTOR	TIDDIES	TIFTS	TILLERS	TIMOCRACIES
THYRISTORS	TIDDLE	TIG	TILLIER	TIMOCRACY
THYROID	TIDDLED	TIGE	TILLIEST	TIMON
THYROIDS	TIDDLER	TIGER	TILLING	TIMONEER
THYROXIN	TIDDLERS	TIGERISH	TILLINGS	TIMONEERS
THYROXINE	TIDDLES	TIGERISM	TILLITE	TIMONS
THYROXINES	TIDDLEY	TIGERISMS	TILLITES	TIMOROUS
THYROXINS	TIDDLIER	TIGERLY	TILLS	TIMORSOME
THYRSE	TIDDLIES	TIGERS	TILLY	TIMOTHIES
THYRSES	TIDDLIEST	TIGERY	TILS	TIMOTHY
THYRSI	TIDDLING	TIGES	TILT	TIMOUS
THYRSOID	TIDDLY	TIGGED	TILTABLE	TIMOUSLY

TIMPANI	TINKERED	TIPPERS	TIRRIVIE	TITRATE
TIMPANIST	TINKERING	TIPPET	TIRRIVIES	TITRATED
TIMPANISTS	TINKERINGS	TIPPETS	TIRRS	TITRATES
TIMPANO	TINKERS	TIPPIER	TIS	TITRATING
TIMPS	TINKING	TIPPIEST	TISANE	TITRATION
TIN	TINKLE	TIPPING	TISANES	TITRATIONS
TINAJA	TINKLED	TIPPINGS	TISICK	TITRE
TINAJAS	TINKLER	TIPPLE	TISICKS	TITRES
TINAMOU	TINKLERS	TIPPLED	TISSUE	TITS
TINAMOUS	TINKLES	TIPPLER	TISSUED	TITTED
TINCAL	TINKLIER	TIPPLERS	TISSUES	TITTER
TINCALS	TINKLIEST	TIPPLES	TISSUING	TITTERED
TINCHEL	TINKLING	TIPPLING	TISWAS	TITTERER
TINCHELS	TINKLINGS	TIPPY	TISWASES	TITTERERS
TINCT	TINKLY	TIPS	TIT	TITTERING
TINCTED	TINKS	TIPSIER	TITAN	TITTERINGS
TINCTING	TINMAN	TIPSIEST	TITANATE	TITTERS
TINCTS	TINMEN	TIPSIFIED	TITANATES	TITTIES
TINCTURE	TINNED	TIPSIFIES	TITANIC	TITTING
TINCTURED	TINNER	TIPSIFY	TITANITE	TITTIVATE
TINCTURES	TINNERS	TIPSIFYING	TITANITES	TITTIVATED
TINCTURING	TINNIE	TIPSILY	TITANIUM	TITTIVATES
TIND	TINNIER	TIPSINESS	TITANIUMS	TITTIVATING
TINDAL	TINNIES	TIPSINESSES	TITANOUS	TITTLE
TINDALS	TINNIEST	TIPSTAFF	TITANS	TITTLEBAT
TINDED	TINNING	TIPSTAFFS	TITBIT	TITTLEBATS
TINDER	TINNINGS	TIPSTAVES	TITBITS	TITTLED
TINDERS	TINNITUS	TIPSTER	TITCH	TITTLES
TINDERY	TINNITUSES	TIPSTERS	TITCHES	TITTLING
TINDING	TINNY	TIPSY	TITE	TITTUP
TINDS	TINPOT	TIPT	TITELY	TITTUPED
TINE	TINPOTS	TIPTOE	TITER	TITTUPING
TINEA	TINS	TIPTOED	TITERS	TITTUPS
TINEAS	TINSEL	TIPTOEING	TITFER	TITTUPY
TINED	TINSELLED	TIPTOES	TITFERS	TITTY
TINEID	TINSELLING	TIPTOP	TITHABLE	TITUBANCIES
TINEIDS	TINSELLY	TIPTOPS	TITHE	TITUBANCY
TINES	TINSELRIES	TIPULA	TITHED	TITUBANT
TINFOIL	TINSELRY	TIPULAS	TITHER	TITUBATE
TINFOILS	TINSELS	TIRADE	TITHERS	TITUBATED
TINFUL	TINSEY	TIRADES	TITHES	TITUBATES
TINFULS	TINSEYS	TIRASSE	TITHING	TITUBATING
TING	TINSMITH	TIRASSES	TITHINGS	TITULAR
TINGE	TINSMITHS	TIRE	TITI	TITULARIES
TINGED	TINSNIPS	TIRED	TITIAN	TITULARLY
TINGES	TINSTONE	TIREDER	TITIANS	TITULARS
TINGING	TINSTONES	TIREDEST	TITILLATE	TITULARY
TINGLE	TINT	TIREDNESS	TITILLATED	TITULE
TINGLED	TINTED	TIREDNESSES	TITILLATES	TITULED
TINGLER	TINTER	TIRELESS	TITILLATING	TITULES
TINGLERS	TINTERS	TIRELING	TITIS	TITULING
TINGLES	TINTIER	TIRELINGS	TITIVATE	TITUP
TINGLIER	TINTIEST	TIRES	TITIVATED	TITUPED
TINGLIEST	TINTINESS	TIRESOME	TITIVATES	TITUPING
TINGLING	TINTINESSES	TIRING	TITIVATING	TITUPPED
TINGLINGS	TINTING	TIRINGS	TITLARK	TITUPPING
TINGLISH	TINTINGS	TIRL	TITLARKS	TITUPS
TINGLY	TINTLESS	TIRLED	TITLE	TITUPY
TINGS	TINTS	TIRLING	TITLED	TIZWAS
TINGUAITE	TINTY	TIRLS	TITLELESS	TIZWASES
TINGUAITES	TINTYPE	TIRO	TITLER	TIZZ
TINHORN	TINTYPES	TIROES	TITLERS	TIZZES
TINHORNS	TINWARE	TIROS	TITLES	TIZZIES
TINIER	TINWARES	TIRR	TITLING	TIZZY
TINIEST	TINY	TIRRED	TITLINGS	TMESES
TININESS	TIP	TIRRING	TITMICE	TMESIS
TINING	TIPI	TIRRIT	TITMOSE	TO
TINK	TIPIS	TIRRITS	TITMOUSE	TOAD
TINKED	TIPPED	TIRRIVEE	TITOKI	TOADFISH
TINKER	TIPPER	TIRRIVEES	TITOKIS	TOADFISHES

TOADFLAX	TODDLERS	TOILFUL	TOLLMAN	TOMIUMS
TOADFLAXES	TODDLES	TOILINET	TOLLMEN	TOMMIED
TOADGRASS	TODDLING	TOILINETS	TOLLS	TOMMIES
TOADGRASSES	TODDY	TOILING	TOLSEL	TOMMY
TOADIED	TODIES	TOILINGS	TOLSELS	TOMMYING
TOADIES	TODS	TOILLESS	TOLSEY	TOMOGRAM
TOADRUSH	TODY	TOILS	TOLSEYS	TOMOGRAMS
TOADRUSHES	TOE	TOILSOME	TOLT	TOMOGRAPH
TOADS	TOECAP	TOISE	TOLTER	TOMOGRAPHS
TOADSTOOL	TOECAPS	TOISEACH	TOLTERED	TOMORROW
TOADSTOOLS	TOECLIP	TOISEACHS	TOLTERING	TOMORROWS
TOADY	TOECLIPS	TOISECH	TOLTERS	TOMPION
TOADYING	TOED	TOISECHS	TOLTS	TOMPIONS
TOADYISH	TOEING	TOISES	TOLU	TOMPON
TOADYISM	TOENAIL	TOISON	TOLUATE	TOMPONS
TOADYISMS	TOENAILS	TOISONS	TOLUATES	TOMS
TOAST	TOES	TOKAMAK	TOLUENE	TOMTIT
TOASTED	TOFF	TOKAMAKS	TOLUENES	TOMTITS
TOASTER	TOFFEE	TOKE	TOLUIC	TON
TOASTERS	TOFFEES	TOKED	TOLUIDINE	TONAL
TOASTIE	TOFFIER	TOKEN	TOLUIDINES	TONALITE
TOASTIES	TOFFIES	TOKENED	TOLUOL	TONALITES
TOASTING	TOFFIEST	TOKENING	TOLUOLS	TONALITIES
TOASTINGS	TOFFISH	TOKENISM	TOLUS	TONALITY
TOASTS	TOFFS	TOKENISMS	TOLZEY	TONANT
TOASTY	TOFFY	TOKENS	TOLZEYS	TONDI
TOAZE	TOFORE	TOKES	TOM	TONDINI
TOAZED	TOFT	TOKING	TOMAHAWK	TONDINO
TOAZES	TOFTS	TOKO	TOMAHAWKED	TONDINOS
TOAZING	TOFU	TOKOLOGIES	TOMAHAWKING	TONDO
TOBACCO	TOFUS	TOKOLOGY	TOMAHAWKS	TONDOS
TOBACCOES	TOG	TOKOLOSHE	TOMALLEY	TONE
TOBACCOS	TOGA	TOKOLOSHES	TOMALLEYS	TONED
TOBIES	TOGAED	TOKOS	TOMAN	TONELESS
TOBOGGAN	TOGAS	TOLA	TOMANS	TONEME
TOBOGGANED	TOGATE	TOLAS	TOMATO	TONEMES
TOBOGGANING	TOGATED	TOLBOOTH	TOMATOES	TONEMIC
TOBOGGANINGS	TOGE	TOLBOOTHS	TOMB	TONES
TOBOGGANS	TOGED	TOLD	TOMBAC	TONETIC
TOBOGGIN	TOGES	TOLE	TOMBACS	TONEY
TOBOGGINED	TOGETHER	TOLED	TOMBAK	TONG
TOBOGGINING	TOGGED	TOLERABLE	TOMBAKS	TONGA
TOBOGGINS	TOGGERIES	TOLERABLY	TOMBED	TONGAS
TOBRAKE	TOGGERY	TOLERANCE	TOMBIC	TONGS
TOBY	TOGGING	TOLERANCES	TOMBING	TONGUE
TOCCATA	TOGGLE	TOLERANT	TOMBLESS	TONGUED
TOCCATAS	TOGGLED	TOLERATE	TOMBOC	TONGUELET
TOCCATINA	TOGGLES	TOLERATED	TOMBOCS	TONGUELETS
TOCCATINAS	TOGGLING	TOLERATES	TOMBOLA	TONGUES
TOCHER	TOGS	TOLERATING	TOMBOLAS	TONGUING
TOCHERED	TOGUE	TOLERATOR	TOMBOLO	TONGUINGS
TOCHERING	TOGUES	TOLERATORS	TOMBOLOS	TONIC
TOCHERS	TOHEROA	TOLES	TOMBOY	TONICITIES
TOCO	TOHEROAS	TOLING	TOMBOYISH	TONICITY
TOCOLOGIES	TOHO	TOLINGS	TOMBOYS	TONICS
TOCOLOGY	TOHOS	TOLL	TOMBS	TONIER
TOCOS	TOIL	TOLLABLE	TOMBSTONE	TONIES
TOCSIN	TOILE	TOLLAGE	TOMBSTONES	TONIEST
TOCSINS	TOILED	TOLLAGES	TOME	TONIGHT
TOD	TOILER	TOLLBOOTH	TOMENTOSE	TONIGHTS
TODAY	TOILERS	TOLLBOOTHS	TOMENTOUS	TONING
TODAYS	TOILES	TOLLDISH	TOMENTUM	TONISH
TODDE	TOILET	TOLLDISHES	TOMENTUMS	TONISHLY
TODDED	TOILETED	TOLLED	TOMES	TONITE
TODDES	TOILETING	TOLLER	TOMFOOL	TONITES
TODDIES	TOILETRIES	TOLLERS	TOMFOOLED	TONK
TODDING	TOILETRY	TOLLGATE	TOMFOOLING	TONKED
TODDLE	TOILETS	TOLLGATES	TOMFOOLS	TONKER
TODDLED	TOILETTE	TOLLING	TOMIAL	TONKERS
TODDLER	TOILETTES	TOLLINGS	TOMIUM	TONKING

TONKS
TONLET
TONLETS
TONNAG
TONNAGE
TONNAGES
TONNAGS
TONNE
TONNEAU
TONNEAUS
TONNELL
TONNELLS
TONNES
TONNISH
TONNISHLY
TONOMETER
TONOMETERS
TONOMETRIES
TONOMETRY
TONS
TONSIL
TONSILLAR
TONSILS
TONSOR
TONSORIAL
TONSORS
TONSURE
TONSURED
TONSURES
TONTINE
TONTINER
TONTINERS
TONTINES
TONUS
TONUSES
TONY
TOO
TOOART
TOOARTS
TOOK
TOOL
TOOLBAG
TOOLBAGS
TOOLBOX
TOOLBOXES
TOOLED
TOOLER
TOOLERS
TOOLHOUSE
TOOLHOUSES
TOOLING
TOOLINGS
TOOLKIT
TOOLKITS
TOOLMAKER
TOOLMAKERS
TOOLMAN
TOOLMEN
TOOLROOM
TOOLROOMS
TOOLS
TOOM
TOOMED
TOOMER
TOOMEST
TOOMING
TOOMS
TOON
TOONS
TOORIE

TOORIES
TOOT
TOOTED
TOOTER
TOOTERS
TOOTH
TOOTHACHE
TOOTHACHES
TOOTHCOMB
TOOTHCOMBS
TOOTHED
TOOTHFUL
TOOTHFULS
TOOTHIER
TOOTHIEST
TOOTHING
TOOTHLESS
TOOTHPICK
TOOTHPICKS
TOOTHS
TOOTHSOME
TOOTHWASH
TOOTHWASHES
TOOTHWORT
TOOTHWORTS
TOOTHY
TOOTING
TOOTLE
TOOTLED
TOOTLES
TOOTLING
TOOTS
TOOTSIE
TOOTSIES
TOOTSY
TOP
TOPARCH
TOPARCHIES
TOPARCHS
TOPARCHY
TOPAZ
TOPAZES
TOPAZINE
TOPCOAT
TOPCOATS
TOPE
TOPECTOMIES
TOPECTOMY
TOPED
TOPEE
TOPEES
TOPEK
TOPEKS
TOPER
TOPERS
TOPES
TOPFULL
TOPHI
TOPHUS
TOPI
TOPIARIAN
TOPIARIES
TOPIARIST
TOPIARISTS
TOPIARY
TOPIC
TOPICAL
TOPICALLY
TOPICS
TOPING

TOPIS
TOPKNOT
TOPKNOTS
TOPLESS
TOPLOFTY
TOPMAKER
TOPMAKERS
TOPMAKING
TOPMAKINGS
TOPMAN
TOPMAST
TOPMASTS
TOPMEN
TOPMINNOW
TOPMINNOWS
TOPMOST
TOPOI
TOPOLOGIC
TOPOLOGIES
TOPOLOGY
TOPONYM
TOPONYMAL
TOPONYMIC
TOPONYMICS
TOPONYMIES
TOPONYMS
TOPONYMY
TOPOS
TOPPED
TOPPER
TOPPERS
TOPPING
TOPPINGLY
TOPPINGS
TOPPLE
TOPPLED
TOPPLES
TOPPLING
TOPS
TOPSAIL
TOPSAILS
TOPSIDE
TOPSIDES
TOPSMAN
TOPSMEN
TOPSPIN
TOPSPINS
TOQUE
TOQUES
TOR
TORAN
TORANA
TORANAS
TORANS
TORBANITE
TORBANITES
TORC
TORCH
TORCHED
TORCHER
TORCHÈRE
TORCHÈRES
TORCHERS
TORCHES
TORCHING
TORCHON
TORCHONS
TORCS
TORCULAR
TORCULARS

TORDION
TORDIONS
TORE
TOREADOR
TOREADORS
TORERO
TOREROS
TORES
TOREUTIC
TOREUTICS
TORGOCH
TORGOCHS
TORI
TORIC
TORII
TORIIS
TORMENT
TORMENTED
TORMENTIL
TORMENTILS
TORMENTING
TORMENTINGS
TORMENTOR
TORMENTORS
TORMENTS
TORMENTUM
TORMENTUMS
TORMINA
TORMINAL
TORMINOUS
TORN
TORNADE
TORNADES
TORNADIC
TORNADO
TORNADOES
TOROID
TOROIDAL
TOROIDS
TORPEDO
TORPEDOED
TORPEDOER
TORPEDOERS
TORPEDOES
TORPEDOING
TORPEDOS
TORPEFIED
TORPEFIES
TORPEFY
TORPEFYING
TORPID
TORPIDITIES
TORPIDITY
TORPIDLY
TORPIDS
TORPITUDE
TORPITUDES
TORPOR
TORPORS
TORQUATE
TORQUATED
TORQUE
TORQUED
TORQUES
TORR
TORREFIED
TORREFIES
TORREFY
TORREFYING
TORRENT

TORRENTS
TORRET
TORRETS
TORRID
TORRIDER
TORRIDEST
TORRIDITIES
TORRIDITY
TORRS
TORS
TORSADE
TORSADES
TORSE
TORSEL
TORSELS
TORSES
TORSION
TORSIONAL
TORSIONS
TORSIVE
TORSK
TORSKS
TORSO
TORSOS
TORT
TORTE
TORTEN
TORTES
TORTILE
TORTILITIES
TORTILITY
TORTILLA
TORTILLAS
TORTIOUS
TORTIVE
TORTOISE
TORTOISES
TORTRICES
TORTRICID
TORTRICIDS
TORTRIX
TORTS
TORTUOUS
TORTURE
TORTURED
TORTURER
TORTURERS
TORTURES
TORTURING
TORTURINGS
TORTUROUS
TORUFFLED
TORULA
TORULAS
TORULIN
TORULINS
TORULOSE
TORULOSES
TORULOSIS
TORULUS
TORULUSES
TORUS
TOSE
TOSED
TOSES
TOSH
TOSHACH
TOSHACHS
TOSHED
TOSHERS

TOSHES	TOTTIE	TOURNEYED	TOWMONDS	TOXOCARAS
TOSHIER	TOTTIER	TOURNEYER	TOWMONS	TOXOID
TOSHIEST	TOTTIES	TOURNEYERS	TOWMONT	TOXOIDS
TOSHING	TOTTIEST	TOURNEYING	TOWMONTS	TOXOPHILIES
TOSHY	TOTTING	TOURNEYS	TOWN	TOXOPHILY
TOSING	TOTTINGS	TOURNURE	TOWNEE	TOY
TOSS	TOTTY	TOURNURES	TOWNEES	TOYED
TOSSED	TOUCAN	TOURS	TOWNHOUSE	TOYER
TOSSEN	TOUCANET	TOUSE	TOWNHOUSES	TOYERS
TOSSER	TOUCANETS	TOUSED	TOWNIE	TOYING
TOSSERS	TOUCANS	TOUSER	TOWNIER	TOYINGS
TOSSES	TOUCH	TOUSERS	TOWNIES	TOYISH
TOSSIER	TOUCHABLE	TOUSES	TOWNIEST	TOYISHLY
TOSSIEST	TOUCHÉ	TOUSING	TOWNISH	TOYLESOME
TOSSILY	TOUCHED	TOUSINGS	TOWNLAND	TOYLSOM
TOSSING	TOUCHER	TOUSLE	TOWNLANDS	TOYMAN
TOSSINGS	TOUCHERS	TOUSLED	TOWNLING	TOYMEN
TOSSPOT	TOUCHES	TOUSLES	TOWNLINGS	TOYS
TOSSPOTS	TOUCHIER	TOUSLING	TOWNLY	TOYSHOP
TOSSY	TOUCHIEST	TOUSTIE	TOWNS	TOYSHOPS
TOST	TOUCHILY	TOUSY	TOWNSCAPE	TOYSOME
TOT	TOUCHING	TOUT	TOWNSCAPED	TOYWOMAN
TOTAL	TOUCHINGS	TOUTED	TOWNSCAPES	TOYWOMEN
TOTALISE	TOUCHLESS	TOUTER	TOWNSCAPING	TOZE
TOTALISED	TOUCHWOOD	TOUTERS	TOWNSCAPINGS	TOZED
TOTALISER	TOUCHWOODS	TOUTIE	TOWNSFOLK	TOZES
TOTALISERS	TOUCHY	TOUTIER	TOWNSFOLKS	TOZIE
TOTALISES	TOUGH	TOUTIEST	TOWNSHIP	TOZIES
TOTALISING	TOUGHEN	TOUTING	TOWNSHIPS	TOZING
TOTALITIES	TOUGHENED	TOUTS	TOWNSKIP	TRABEATE
TOTALITY	TOUGHENER	TOUZE	TOWNSKIPS	TRABEATED
TOTALIZE	TOUGHENERS	TOUZED	TOWNSMAN	TRABECULA
TOTALIZED	TOUGHENING	TOUZES	TOWNSMEN	TRABECULAE
TOTALIZER	TOUGHENINGS	TOUZING	TOWNY	TRACE
TOTALIZERS	TOUGHENS	TOUZLE	TOWPATH	TRACEABLE
TOTALIZES	TOUGHER	TOUZLED	TOWPATHS	TRACEABLY
TOTALIZING	TOUGHEST	TOUZLES	TOWROPE	TRACED
TOTALLED	TOUGHIE	TOUZLING	TOWROPES	TRACELESS
TOTALLING	TOUGHIES	TOVARISH	TOWS	TRACER
TOTALLY	TOUGHISH	TOVARISHES	TOWSE	TRACERIED
TOTALS	TOUGHLY	TOW	TOWSED	TRACERIES
TOTARA	TOUGHNESS	TOWAGE	TOWSER	TRACERS
TOTARAS	TOUGHNESSES	TOWAGES	TOWSERS	TRACERY
TOTE	TOUGHS	TOWARD	TOWSES	TRACES
TOTED	TOUK	TOWARDLY	TOWSING	TRACHEA
TOTEM	TOUKED	TOWARDS	TOWSY	TRACHEAE
TOTEMIC	TOUKING	TOWBAR	TOWT	TRACHEAL
TOTEMISM	TOUKS	TOWBARS	TOWTED	TRACHEARiES
TOTEMISMS	TOUN	TOWED	TOWTING	TRACHEARY
TOTEMIST	TOUNS	TOWEL	TOWTS	TRACHEATE
TOTEMISTS	TOUPEE	TOWELLED	TOWY	TRACHEID
TOTEMS	TOUPEES	TOWELLING	TOWZE	TRACHEIDE
TOTES	TOUPET	TOWELLINGS	TOWZED	TRACHEIDES
TOTHER	TOUPETS	TOWELS	TOWZES	TRACHEIDS
TOTHERS	TOUR	TOWER	TOWZING	TRACHITIS
TOTIENT	TOURACO	TOWERED	TOXAEMIA	TRACHITISES
TOTIENTS	TOURACOS	TOWERIER	TOXAEMIAS	TRACHOMA
TOTING	TOURED	TOWERIEST	TOXAEMIC	TRACHOMAS
TOTITIVE	TOURER	TOWERING	TOXAPHENE	TRACHYTE
TOTITIVES	TOURERS	TOWERLESS	TOXAPHENES	TRACHYTES
TOTS	TOURING	TOWERS	TOXIC	TRACHYTIC
TOTTED	TOURINGS	TOWERY	TOXICAL	TRACING
TOTTER	TOURISM	TOWHEE	TOXICALLY	TRACINGS
TOTTERED	TOURISMS	TOWHEES	TOXICANT	TRACK
TOTTERER	TOURIST	TOWING	TOXICANTS	TRACKAGE
TOTTERERS	TOURISTIC	TOWINGS	TOXICITIES	TRACKAGES
TOTTERING	TOURISTS	TOWLINE	TOXICITY	TRACKED
TOTTERINGS	TOURISTY	TOWLINES	TOXIN	TRACKER
TOTTERS	TOURNEDOS	TOWMON	TOXINS	TRACKERS
TOTTERY	TOURNEY	TOWMOND	TOXOCARA	TRACKING

TRACKINGS	TRAGI	TRAMPLINGS	TRANSFUSES	TRANSUMPTS
TRACKLESS	TRAGIC	TRAMPOLIN	TRANSFUSING	TRANSVEST
TRACKMAN	TRAGICAL	TRAMPOLINS	TRANSHIP	TRANSVESTED
TRACKMEN	TRAGOPAN	TRAMPS	TRANSHIPPED	TRANSVESTING
TRACKROAD	TRAGOPANS	TRAMS	TRANSHIPPING	TRANSVESTS
TRACKROADS	TRAGULE	TRAMWAY	TRANSHIPPINGS	TRANT
TRACKS	TRAGULES	TRAMWAYS	TRANSHIPS	TRANTED
TRACKWAY	TRAGULINE	TRANCE	TRANSHUME	TRANTER
TRACKWAYS	TRAGUS	TRANCED	TRANSHUMED	TRANTERS
TRACT	TRAHISON	TRANCEDLY	TRANSHUMES	TRANTING
TRACTABLE	TRAHISONS	TRANCES	TRANSHUMING	TRANTS
TRACTATE	TRAIK	TRANCHE	TRANSIENT	TRAP
TRACTATES	TRAIKED	TRANCHES	TRANSIENTS	TRAPAN
TRACTATOR	TRAIKING	TRANCHET	TRANSIRE	TRAPANNED
TRACTATORS	TRAIKIT	TRANCHETS	TRANSIRES	TRAPANNING
TRACTED	TRAIKS	TRANCING	TRANSIT	TRAPANS
TRACTILE	TRAIL	TRANECT	TRANSITS	TRAPE
TRACTING	TRAILED	TRANECTS	TRANSITTED	TRAPED
TRACTION	TRAILER	TRANGAM	TRANSITTING	TRAPES
TRACTIONS	TRAILERED	TRANGAMS	TRANSLATE	TRAPESED
TRACTIVE	TRAILERING	TRANGLE	TRANSLATED	TRAPESES
TRACTOR	TRAILERS	TRANGLES	TRANSLATES	TRAPESING
TRACTORS	TRAILING	TRANKUM	TRANSLATING	TRAPESINGS
TRACTRIX	TRAILS	TRANKUMS	TRANSMEW	TRAPEZE
TRACTRIXES	TRAIN	TRANNIE	TRANSMEWED	TRAPEZED
TRACTS	TRAINABLE	TRANNIES	TRANSMEWING	TRAPEZES
TRACTUS	TRAINED	TRANNY	TRANSMEWS	TRAPEZIA
TRACTUSES	TRAINEE	TRANQUIL	TRANSMIT	TRAPEZIAL
TRAD	TRAINEES	TRANQUILLER	TRANSMITS	TRAPEZING
TRADABLE	TRAINER	TRANQUILLEST	TRANSMITTED	TRAPEZIUM
TRADE	TRAINERS	TRANSACT	TRANSMITTING	TRAPEZIUMS
TRADEABLE	TRAINING	TRANSACTED	TRANSMOVE	TRAPEZIUS
TRADED	TRAININGS	TRANSACTING	TRANSMOVED	TRAPEZIUSES
TRADEFUL	TRAINS	TRANSACTS	TRANSMOVES	TRAPEZOID
TRADELESS	TRAIPSE	TRANSAXLE	TRANSMOVING	TRAPEZOIDS
TRADEMARK	TRAIPSED	TRANSAXLES	TRANSMUTE	TRAPING
TRADEMARKS	TRAIPSES	TRANSCEND	TRANSMUTED	TRAPPEAN
TRADENAME	TRAIPSING	TRANSCENDED	TRANSMUTES	TRAPPED
TRADENAMES	TRAIPSINGS	TRANSCENDING	TRANSMUTING	TRAPPER
TRADER	TRAIT	TRANSCENDS	TRANSOM	TRAPPERS
TRADERS	TRAITOR	TRANSE	TRANSOMS	TRAPPIER
TRADES	TRAITORLY	TRANSECT	TRANSONIC	TRAPPIEST
TRADESMAN	TRAITORS	TRANSECTED	TRANSONICS	TRAPPING
TRADESMEN	TRAITRESS	TRANSECTING	TRANSPIRE	TRAPPINGS
TRADING	TRAITRESSES	TRANSECTS	TRANSPIRED	TRAPPY
TRADINGS	TRAITS	TRANSENNA	TRANSPIRES	TRAPS
TRADITION	TRAJECT	TRANSENNAS	TRANSPIRING	TRAPUNTO
TRADITIONS	TRAJECTED	TRANSEPT	TRANSPORT	TRAPUNTOS
TRADITIVE	TRAJECTING	TRANSEPTS	TRANSPORTED	TRASH
TRADITOR	TRAJECTS	TRANSES	TRANSPORTING	TRASHED
TRADITORS	TRAM	TRANSFARD	TRANSPORTINGS	TRASHERIES
TRADS	TRAMMEL	TRANSFECT	TRANSPORTS	TRASHERY
TRADUCE	TRAMMELLED	TRANSFECTED	TRANSPOSE	TRASHES
TRADUCED	TRAMMELLING	TRANSFECTING	TRANSPOSED	TRASHIER
TRADUCER	TRAMMELS	TRANSFECTS	TRANSPOSES	TRASHIEST
TRADUCERS	TRAMP	TRANSFER	TRANSPOSING	TRASHILY
TRADUCES	TRAMPED	TRANSFERRED	TRANSPOSINGS	TRASHING
TRADUCING	TRAMPER	TRANSFERRING	TRANSSHIP	TRASHTRIE
TRADUCINGS	TRAMPERS	TRANSFERS	TRANSSHIPPED	TRASHTRIES
TRAFFIC	TRAMPET	TRANSFIX	TRANSSHIPPING	TRASHY
TRAFFICKED	TRAMPETS	TRANSFIXED	TRANSSHIPS	TRASS
TRAFFICKING	TRAMPETTE	TRANSFIXES	TRANSUDE	TRASSES
TRAFFICKINGS	TRAMPETTES	TRANSFIXING	TRANSUDED	TRATTORIA
TRAFFICS	TRAMPING	TRANSFORM	TRANSUDES	TRATTORIAS
TRAGEDIAN	TRAMPLE	TRANSFORMED	TRANSUDING	TRATTORIE
TRAGEDIANS	TRAMPLED	TRANSFORMING	TRANSUME	TRAUCHLE
TRAGEDIES	TRAMPLER	TRANSFORMINGS	TRANSUMED	TRAUCHLED
TRAGEDY	TRAMPLERS	TRANSFORMS	TRANSUMES	TRAUCHLES
TRAGELAPH	TRAMPLES	TRANSFUSE	TRANSUMING	TRAUCHLING
TRAGELAPHS	TRAMPLING	TRANSFUSED	TRANSUMPT	TRAUMA

TRAUMAS	TREADLER	TREFOIL	TRENCHES	TRIABLE
TRAUMATA	TREADLERS	TREFOILED	TRENCHING	TRIACID
TRAUMATIC	TREADLES	TREFOILS	TREND	TRIACT
TRAVAIL	TREADLING	TREGETOUR	TRENDED	TRIACTINE
TRAVAILED	TREADLINGS	TREGETOURS	TRENDIER	TRIAD
TRAVAILING	TREADMILL	TREHALA	TRENDIES	TRIADIC
TRAVAILS	TREADMILLS	TREHALAS	TRENDIEST	TRIADIST
TRAVE	TREADS	TREILLAGE	TRENDING	TRIADISTS
TRAVEL	TREAGUE	TREILLAGES	TRENDS	TRIADS
TRAVELLED	TREAGUES	TREILLE	TRENDY	TRIAGE
TRAVELLER	TREASON	TREILLES	TRENISE	TRIAGES
TRAVELLERS	TREASONS	TREK	TRENISES	TRIAL
TRAVELLING	TREASURE	TREKKED	TRENTAL	TRIALISM
TRAVELLINGS	TREASURED	TREKKER	TRENTALS	TRIALISMS
TRAVELS	TREASURER	TREKKERS	TREPAN	TRIALIST
TRAVERSAL	TREASURERS	TREKKING	TREPANG	TRIALISTS
TRAVERSALS	TREASURES	TREKS	TREPANGS	TRIALITIES
TRAVERSE	TREASURIES	TREKSHUIT	TREPANNED	TRIALITY
TRAVERSED	TREASURING	TREKSHUITS	TREPANNER	TRIALLIST
TRAVERSER	TREASURY	TRELLIS	TREPANNERS	TRIALLISTS
TRAVERSERS	TREAT	TRELLISED	TREPANNING	TRIALOGUE
TRAVERSES	TREATABLE	TRELLISES	TREPANNINGS	TRIALOGUES
TRAVERSING	TREATED	TRELLISING	TREPANS	TRIALS
TRAVERSINGS	TREATER	TREMA	TREPHINE	TRIANGLE
TRAVERTIN	TREATERS	TREMAS	TREPHINED	TRIANGLED
TRAVES	TREATIES	TREMATIC	TREPHINES	TRIANGLES
TRAVESTIED	TREATING	TREMATODE	TREPHINING	TRIAPSAL
TRAVESTIES	TREATINGS	TREMATODES	TREPID	TRIARCH
TRAVESTY	TREATISE	TREMATOID	TREPIDANT	TRIARCHIES
TRAVESTYING	TREATISES	TREMATOIDS	TREPIDER	TRIARCHS
TRAVIS	TREATMENT	TREMBLANT	TREPIDEST	TRIARCHY
TRAVISES	TREATMENTS	TREMBLE	TREPONEMA	TRIATHLON
TRAVOIS	TREATS	TREMBLED	TREPONEMAS	TRIATHLONS
TRAWL	TREATY	TREMBLER	TREPONEMATA	TRIATIC
TRAWLED	TREBLE	TREMBLERS	TRESPASS	TRIATICS
TRAWLER	TREBLED	TREMBLES	TRESPASSED	TRIATOMIC
TRAWLERS	TREBLES	TREMBLIER	TRESPASSES	TRIAXIAL
TRAWLING	TREBLING	TREMBLIEST	TRESPASSING	TRIAXIALS
TRAWLINGS	TREBLY	TREMBLING	TRESS	TRIAXON
TRAWLS	TREBUCHET	TREMBLINGS	TRESSED	TRIAXONS
TRAY	TREBUCHETS	TREMBLY	TRESSEL	TRIBADE
TRAYBIT	TRECENTO	TRÉMIE	TRESSELS	TRIBADES
TRAYBITS	TRECENTOS	TREMIE	TRESSES	TRIBADIC
TRAYFUL	TRECK	TRÉMIES	TRESSIER	TRIBADIES
TRAYFULS	TRECKED	TREMIES	TRESSIEST	TRIBADISM
TRAYNE	TRECKING	TREMOLANT	TRESSING	TRIBADISMS
TRAYNED	TRECKS	TREMOLANTS	TRESSURE	TRIBADY
TRAYNES	TREDDLE	TREMOLITE	TRESSURED	TRIBAL
TRAYNING	TREDDLED	TREMOLITES	TRESSURES	TRIBALISM
TRAYS	TREDDLES	TREMOLO	TRESSY	TRIBALISMS
TREACHER	TREDDLING	TREMOLOS	TRESTLE	TRIBALIST
TREACHERIES	TREDILLE	TREMOR	TRESTLES	TRIBALISTS
TREACHERS	TREDILLES	TREMORS	TRET	TRIBALLY
TREACHERY	TREDRILLE	TREMULANT	TRETS	TRIBASIC
TREACHOUR	TREDRILLES	TREMULANTS	TREVALLIES	TRIBBLE
TREACHOURS	TREE	TREMULATE	TREVALLY	TRIBBLES
TREACLE	TREED	TREMULATED	TREVIS	TRIBE
TREACLED	TREEING	TREMULATES	TREVISES	TRIBELESS
TREACLES	TREELESS	TREMULATING	TREVISS	TRIBES
TREACLIER	TREEN	TREMULOUS	TREVISSES	TRIBESMAN
TREACLIEST	TREENAIL	TRENAIL	TREW	TRIBESMEN
TREACLING	TREENAILS	TRENAILS	TREWS	TRIBLET
TREACLY	TREENS	TRENCH	TREWSMAN	TRIBLETS
TREAD	TREES	TRENCHAND	TREWSMEN	TRIBOLOGIES
TREADER	TREESHIP	TRENCHANT	TREY	TRIBOLOGY
TREADERS	TREESHIPS	TRENCHARD	TREYBIT	TRIBRACH
TREADING	TREETOP	TRENCHARDS	TREYBITS	TRIBRACHS
TREADINGS	TREETOPS	TRENCHED	TREYS	TRIBUNAL
TREADLE	TREF	TRENCHER	TREZ	TRIBUNALS
TREADLED	TREFA	TRENCHERS	TREZES	TRIBUNATE

TRIBUNATES	TRICORN	TRIGAMY	TRIMARAN	TRIPEMAN
TRIBUNE	TRICORNE	TRIGGED	TRIMARANS	TRIPEMEN
TRIBUNES	TRICORNES	TRIGGER	TRIMER	TRIPERIES
TRIBUTARIES	TRICORNS	TRIGGERED	TRIMERIC	TRIPERY
TRIBUTARY	TRICOT	TRIGGERING	TRIMEROUS	TRIPES
TRIBUTE	TRICOTS	TRIGGERS	TRIMERS	TRIPEWIFE
TRIBUTER	TRICROTIC	TRIGGEST	TRIMESTER	TRIPEWIVES
TRIBUTERS	TRICUSPID	TRIGGING	TRIMESTERS	TRIPHONE
TRIBUTES	TRICYCLE	TRIGLOT	TRIMETER	TRIPHONES
TRICAR	TRICYCLED	TRIGLOTS	TRIMETERS	TRIPITAKA
TRICARS	TRICYCLER	TRIGLY	TRIMETHYL	TRIPLANE
TRICE	TRICYCLERS	TRIGLYPH	TRIMETRIC	TRIPLANES
TRICED	TRICYCLES	TRIGLYPHS	TRIMLY	TRIPLE
TRICEPS	TRICYCLIC	TRIGNESS	TRIMMED	TRIPLED
TRICEPSES	TRICYCLING	TRIGNESSES	TRIMMER	TRIPLES
TRICERION	TRICYCLINGS	TRIGON	TRIMMERS	TRIPLET
TRICERIONS	TRIDACNA	TRIGONAL	TRIMMEST	TRIPLETS
TRICES	TRIDACNAS	TRIGONIC	TRIMMING	TRIPLEX
TRICHINA	TRIDACTYL	TRIGONOUS	TRIMMINGS	TRIPLEXES
TRICHINAE	TRIDARN	TRIGONS	TRIMNESS	TRIPLIED
TRICHINAS	TRIDARNS	TRIGRAM	TRIMNESSES	TRIPLIES
TRICHITE	TRIDE	TRIGRAMS	TRIMS	TRIPLING
TRICHITES	TRIDENT	TRIGRAPH	TRIN	TRIPLINGS
TRICHITIC	TRIDENTAL	TRIGRAPHS	TRINAL	TRIPLOID
TRICHOID	TRIDENTED	TRIGS	TRINARY	TRIPLOIDIES
TRICHOME	TRIDENTS	TRIGYNIAN	TRINDLE	TRIPLOIDY
TRICHOMES	TRIDUAN	TRIGYNOUS	TRINDLED	TRIPLY
TRICHORD	TRIDUUM	TRIHEDRAL	TRINDLES	TRIPLYING
TRICHORDS	TRIDUUMS	TRIHEDRALS	TRINDLING	TRIPOD
TRICHOSES	TRIDYMITE	TRIHEDRON	TRINE	TRIPODAL
TRICHOSIS	TRIDYMITES	TRIHEDRONS	TRINED	TRIPODIES
TRICHROIC	TRIE	TRIHYBRID	TRINES	TRIPODS
TRICHROME	TRIECIOUS	TRIHYBRIDS	TRINGLE	TRIPODY
TRICING	TRIED	TRIHYDRIC	TRINGLES	TRIPOLI
TRICK	TRIENNIAL	TRIKE	TRINING	TRIPOLIS
TRICKED	TRIER	TRIKED	TRINITIES	TRIPOS
TRICKER	TRIERARCH	TRIKES	TRINITRIN	TRIPOSES
TRICKERIES	TRIERARCHS	TRIKING	TRINITRINS	TRIPPANT
TRICKERS	TRIERS	TRILBIES	TRINITY	TRIPPED
TRICKERY	TRIES	TRILBY	TRINKET	TRIPPER
TRICKIER	TRIETERIC	TRILBYS	TRINKETED	TRIPPERS
TRICKIEST	TRIETHYL	TRILD	TRINKETER	TRIPPERY
TRICKILY	TRIFACIAL	TRILEMMA	TRINKETERS	TRIPPET
TRICKING	TRIFECTA	TRILEMMAS	TRINKETING	TRIPPETS
TRICKINGS	TRIFECTAS	TRILINEAR	TRINKETINGS	TRIPPING
TRICKISH	TRIFFID	TRILITH	TRINKETRIES	TRIPPINGS
TRICKLE	TRIFFIDS	TRILITHIC	TRINKETRY	TRIPPLE
TRICKLED	TRIFFIDY	TRILITHON	TRINKETS	TRIPPLED
TRICKLES	TRIFID	TRILITHONS	TRINKUM	TRIPPLER
TRICKLESS	TRIFLE	TRILITHS	TRINKUMS	TRIPPLERS
TRICKLET	TRIFLED	TRILL	TRINOMIAL	TRIPPLES
TRICKLETS	TRIFLER	TRILLED	TRINOMIALS	TRIPPLING
TRICKLIER	TRIFLERS	TRILLING	TRINS	TRIPS
TRICKLIEST	TRIFLES	TRILLINGS	TRIO	TRIPSES
TRICKLING	TRIFLING	TRILLION	TRIODE	TRIPSIS
TRICKLINGS	TRIFOCAL	TRILLIONS	TRIODES	TRIPTANE
TRICKLY	TRIFOCALS	TRILLIUM	TRIOLET	TRIPTANES
TRICKS	TRIFOLIES	TRILLIUMS	TRIOLETS	TRIPTOTE
TRICKSIER	TRIFOLIUM	TRILLO	TRIONES	TRIPTOTES
TRICKSIEST	TRIFOLIUMS	TRILLOES	TRIONYM	TRIPTYCH
TRICKSOME	TRIFOLY	TRILLS	TRIONYMAL	TRIPTYCHS
TRICKSTER	TRIFORIA	TRILOBATE	TRIONYMS	TRIPTYQUE
TRICKSTERS	TRIFORIUM	TRILOBE	TRIOR	TRIPTYQUES
TRICKSY	TRIFORM	TRILOBED	TRIORS	TRIPUDIUM
TRICKY	TRIFORMED	TRILOBES	TRIOS	TRIPUDIUMS
TRICLINIC	TRIG	TRILOBITE	TRIOXIDE	TRIQUETRA
TRICOLOR	TRIGAMIES	TRILOBITES	TRIOXIDES	TRIQUETRAS
TRICOLORS	TRIGAMIST	TRILOGIES	TRIP	TRIRADIAL
TRICOLOUR	TRIGAMISTS	TRILOGY	TRIPE	TRIREME
TRICOLOURS	TRIGAMOUS	TRIM	TRIPEDAL	TRIREMES

TRISAGION	TRIUMPHERS	TROG	TROPED	TROUPING
TRISAGIONS	TRIUMPHING	TROGGED	TROPES	TROUSE
TRISECT	TRIUMPHINGS	TROGGING	TROPHESIES	TROUSERED
TRISECTED	TRIUMPHS	TROGGS	TROPHESY	TROUSERS
TRISECTING	TRIUMVIR	TROGGSES	TROPHI	TROUSES
TRISECTOR	TRIUMVIRI	TROGON	TROPHIC	TROUSSEAU
TRISECTORS	TRIUMVIRIES	TROGONS	TROPHIED	TROUSSEAUS
TRISECTS	TRIUMVIRS	TROGS	TROPHIES	TROUSSEAUX
TRISEME	TRIUMVIRY	TROIKA	TROPHY	TROUT
TRISEMES	TRIUNE	TROIKAS	TROPHYING	TROUTER
TRISEMIC	TRIUNES	TROILISM	TROPIC	TROUTERS
TRISHAW	TRIUNITIES	TROILISMS	TROPICAL	TROUTFUL
TRISHAWS	TRIUNITY	TROILIST	TROPICS	TROUTIER
TRISKELE	TRIVALENT	TROILISTS	TROPING	TROUTIEST
TRISKELES	TRIVALVE	TROILITE	TROPISM	TROUTING
TRISKELIA	TRIVALVED	TROILITES	TROPISMS	TROUTINGS
TRISMUS	TRIVALVES	TROKE	TROPIST	TROUTLESS
TRISMUSES	TRIVET	TROKED	TROPISTIC	TROUTLET
TRISOME	TRIVETS	TROKES	TROPISTS	TROUTLETS
TRISOMES	TRIVIA	TROKING	TROPOLOGIES	TROUTLING
TRISOMIC	TRIVIAL	TROLL	TROPOLOGY	TROUTLINGS
TRISOMIES	TRIVIALLY	TROLLED	TROPPO	TROUTS
TRISOMY	TRIVIUM	TROLLER	TROSSERS	TROUTY
TRIST	TRIVIUMS	TROLLERS	TROT	TROUVÈRE
TRISTE	TRIZONAL	TROLLEY	TROTH	TROUVÈRES
TRISTFUL	TRIZONE	TROLLEYS	TROTHED	TROUVEUR
TRISTICH	TRIZONES	TROLLIES	TROTHFUL	TROUVEURS
TRISTICHS	TROAD	TROLLING	TROTHING	TROVER
TRISUL	TROADE	TROLLINGS	TROTHLESS	TROVERS
TRISULA	TROADES	TROLLOP	TROTHS	TROW
TRISULAS	TROADS	TROLLOPED	TROTLINE	TROWED
TRISULS	TROAT	TROLLOPEE	TROTLINES	TROWEL
TRITE	TROATED	TROLLOPEES	TROTS	TROWELLED
TRITELY	TROATING	TROLLOPING	TROTTED	TROWELLER
TRITENESS	TROATS	TROLLOPS	TROTTER	TROWELLERS
TRITENESSES	TROCAR	TROLLOPY	TROTTERS	TROWELLING
TRITER	TROCARS	TROLLS	TROTTING	TROWELS
TRITES	TROCHAIC	TROLLY	TROTTINGS	TROWING
TRITEST	TROCHAL	TROMBONE	TROTTOIR	TROWS
TRITHEISM	TROCHE	TROMBONES	TROTTOIRS	TROWSERS
TRITHEISMS	TROCHEE	TROMINO	TROTYL	TROY
TRITHEIST	TROCHEES	TROMINOES	TROTYLS	TROYS
TRITHEISTS	TROCHES	TROMINOS	TROUBLE	TRUANCIES
TRITIATE	TROCHI	TROMMEL	TROUBLED	TRUANCY
TRITIATED	TROCHILIC	TROMMELS	TROUBLER	TRUANT
TRITIATES	TROCHILUS	TROMP	TROUBLERS	TRUANTED
TRITIATING	TROCHILUSES	TROMPE	TROUBLES	TRUANTING
TRITICAL	TROCHISK	TROMPES	TROUBLING	TRUANTRIES
TRITICALE	TROCHISKS	TROMPS	TROUBLINGS	TRUANTRY
TRITICALES	TROCHITE	TRON	TROUBLOUS	TRUANTS
TRITICISM	TROCHITES	TRONA	TROUGH	TRUCAGE
TRITICISMS	TROCHLEA	TRONAS	TROUGHS	TRUCAGES
TRITIDE	TROCHLEAR	TRONC	TROULE	TRUCE
TRITIDES	TROCHLEAS	TRONCS	TROULED	TRUCELESS
TRITIUM	TROCHOID	TRONE	TROULES	TRUCES
TRITIUMS	TROCHOIDS	TRONES	TROULING	TRUCHMAN
TRITON	TROCHUS	TRONS	TROUNCE	TRUCHMANS
TRITONE	TROCHUSES	TROOLIE	TROUNCED	TRUCHMEN
TRITONES	TROCK	TROOLIES	TROUNCER	TRUCIAL
TRITONIA	TROCKED	TROOP	TROUNCERS	TRUCK
TRITONIAS	TROCKING	TROOPED	TROUNCES	TRUCKAGE
TRITONS	TROCKS	TROOPER	TROUNCING	TRUCKAGES
TRITURATE	TROD	TROOPERS	TROUNCINGS	TRUCKED
TRITURATED	TRODDEN	TROOPIAL	TROUPE	TRUCKER
TRITURATES	TRODE	TROOPIALS	TROUPED	TRUCKERS
TRITURATING	TRODES	TROOPING	TROUPER	TRUCKING
TRIUMPH	TRODS	TROOPS	TROUPERS	TRUCKINGS
TRIUMPHAL	TROELIE	TROPARIA	TROUPES	TRUCKLE
TRIUMPHED	TROELIES	TROPARION	TROUPIAL	TRUCKLED
TRIUMPHER	TROELY	TROPE	TROUPIALS	TRUCKLER

TRUCKLERS	TRUNDLES	TSADDIQS	TUBERCLED	TUG
TRUCKLES	TRUNDLING	TSAMBA	TUBERCLES	TUGGED
TRUCKLING	TRUNK	TSAMBAS	TUBERCULE	TUGGER
TRUCKLINGS	TRUNKED	TSAR	TUBERCULES	TUGGERS
TRUCKMAN	TRUNKFISH	TSARDOM	TUBEROSE	TUGGING
TRUCKMEN	TRUNKFISHES	TSARDOMS	TUBEROUS	TUGGINGLY
TRUCKS	TRUNKFUL	TSAREVICH	TUBERS	TUGGINGS
TRUCULENT	TRUNKFULS	TSAREVICHES	TUBES	TUGRIK
TRUDGE	TRUNKING	TSAREVNA	TUBFAST	TUGRIKS
TRUDGED	TRUNKINGS	TSAREVNAS	TUBFASTS	TUGS
TRUDGEN	TRUNKS	TSARINA	TUBFISH	TUI
TRUDGENS	TRUNNION	TSARINAS	TUBFISHES	TUILLE
TRUDGEON	TRUNNIONS	TSARISM	TUBFUL	TUILLES
TRUDGEONS	TRUQUAGE	TSARISMS	TUBFULS	TUILLETTE
TRUDGER	TRUQUAGES	TSARIST	TUBICOLAR	TUILLETTES
TRUDGERS	TRUQUEUR	TSARISTS	TUBICOLE	TUILYIE
TRUDGES	TRUQUEURS	TSARITSA	TUBICOLES	TUILYIED
TRUDGING	TRUSS	TSARITSAS	TUBIFORM	TUILYIEING
TRUDGINGS	TRUSSED	TSARS	TUBING	TUILYIES
TRUE	TRUSSER	TSESSEBE	TUBINGS	TUILZIE
TRUED	TRUSSERS	TSESSEBES	TUBS	TUILZIED
TRUEING	TRUSSES	TSETSE	TUBULAR	TUILZIEING
TRUEMAN	TRUSSING	TSETSES	TUBULATE	TUILZIES
TRUEMEN	TRUSSINGS	TSIGANE	TUBULATED	TUIS
TRUENESS	TRUST	TSIGANES	TUBULATES	TUISM
TRUENESSES	TRUSTED	TSOTSI	TUBULATING	TUISMS
TRUEPENNIES	TRUSTEE	TSOTSIS	TUBULE	TUITION
TRUEPENNY	TRUSTEES	TSUBA	TUBULES	TUITIONAL
TRUER	TRUSTER	TSUBAS	TUBULOUS	TUITIONS
TRUES	TRUSTERS	TSUNAMI	TUCHUN	TULAREMIA
TRUEST	TRUSTFUL	TSUNAMIS	TUCHUNS	TULAREMIAS
TRUFFLE	TRUSTIER	TUAN	TUCK	TULAREMIC
TRUFFLED	TRUSTIES	TUANS	TUCKAHOE	TULBAN
TRUFFLES	TRUSTIEST	TUART	TUCKAHOES	TULBANS
TRUG	TRUSTILY	TUARTS	TUCKED	TULCHAN
TRUGS	TRUSTING	TUATARA	TUCKER	TULCHANS
TRUING	TRUSTLESS	TUATARAS	TUCKERBAG	TULE
TRUISM	TRUSTS	TUATERA	TUCKERBAGS	TULES
TRUISMS	TRUSTY	TUATERAS	TUCKERBOX	TULIP
TRUISTIC	TRUTH	TUATH	TUCKERBOXES	TULIPANT
TRULL	TRUTHFUL	TUATHS	TUCKERED	TULIPANTS
TRULLS	TRUTHLESS	TUB	TUCKERING	TULIPS
TRULY	TRUTHLIKE	TUBA	TUCKERS	TULLE
TRUMEAU	TRUTHS	TUBAE	TUCKET	TULLES
TRUMEAUX	TRUTHY	TUBAGE	TUCKETS	TULWAR
TRUMP	TRY	TUBAGES	TUCKING	TULWARS
TRUMPED	TRYE	TUBAL	TUCKS	TUM
TRUMPERIES	TRYER	TUBAR	TUCOTUCO	TUMBLE
TRUMPERY	TRYERS	TUBAS	TUCOTUCOS	TUMBLED
TRUMPET	TRYING	TUBATE	TUCUTUCO	TUMBLER
TRUMPETED	TRYINGLY	TUBBED	TUCUTUCOS	TUMBLERS
TRUMPETER	TRYINGS	TUBBER	TUFA	TUMBLES
TRUMPETERS	TRYP	TUBBERS	TUFACEOUS	TUMBLING
TRUMPETING	TRYPS	TUBBIER	TUFAS	TUMBLINGS
TRUMPETINGS	TRYPSIN	TUBBIEST	TUFF	TUMBREL
TRUMPETS	TRYPSINS	TUBBINESS	TUFFE	TUMBRELS
TRUMPING	TRYPTIC	TUBBINESSES	TUFFES	TUMBRIL
TRUMPINGS	TRYSAIL	TUBBING	TUFFET	TUMBRILS
TRUMPS	TRYSAILS	TUBBINGS	TUFFETS	TUMEFIED
TRUNCAL	TRYST	TUBBISH	TUFFS	TUMEFIES
TRUNCATE	TRYSTED	TUBBY	TUFT	TUMEFY
TRUNCATED	TRYSTER	TUBE	TUFTED	TUMEFYING
TRUNCATES	TRYSTERS	TUBECTOMIES	TUFTER	TUMESCE
TRUNCATING	TRYSTING	TUBECTOMY	TUFTERS	TUMESCED
TRUNCHEON	TRYSTS	TUBED	TUFTIER	TUMESCENT
TRUNCHEONED	TSADDIK	TUBEFUL	TUFTIEST	TUMESCES
TRUNCHEONING	TSADDIKIM	TUBEFULS	TUFTING	TUMESCING
TRUNCHEONS	TSADDIKS	TUBELESS	TUFTINGS	TUMID
TRUNDLE	TSADDIQ	TUBER	TUFTS	TUMIDITIES
TRUNDLED	TSADDIQIM	TUBERCLE	TUFTY	TUMIDITY

TUMIDLY	TUNNAGE	TURBOPROPS	TURNDUNS	TUSKIEST
TUMIDNESS	TUNNAGES	TURBOS	TURNED	TUSKING
TUMIDNESSES	TUNNED	TURBOT	TURNER	TUSKLESS
TUMMIES	TUNNEL	TURBOTS	TURNERIES	TUSKS
TUMMY	TUNNELLED	TURBULENT	TURNERS	TUSKY
TUMOR	TUNNELLER	TURCOPOLE	TURNERY	TUSSAH
TUMOROUS	TUNNELLERS	TURCOPOLES	TURNING	TUSSAHS
TUMORS	TUNNELLING	TURD	TURNINGS	TUSSAL
TUMOUR	TUNNELLINGS	TURDINE	TURNIP	TUSSEH
TUMOURS	TUNNELS	TURDION	TURNIPED	TUSSEHS
TUMP	TUNNIES	TURDIONS	TURNIPING	TUSSER
TUMPED	TUNNING	TURDOID	TURNIPS	TUSSERS
TUMPHIES	TUNNINGS	TURDS	TURNKEY	TUSSIS
TUMPHY	TUNNY	TUREEN	TURNKEYS	TUSSISES
TUMPING	TUNS	TUREENS	TURNOFF	TUSSIVE
TUMPS	TUNY	TURF	TURNOFFS	TUSSLE
TUMPY	TUP	TURFED	TURNOVER	TUSSLED
TUMS	TUPEK	TURFEN	TURNOVERS	TUSSLES
TUMULAR	TUPEKS	TURFIER	TURNPIKE	TUSSLING
TUMULARY	TUPELO	TURFIEST	TURNPIKES	TUSSOCK
TUMULI	TUPELOS	TURFINESS	TURNROUND	TUSSOCKS
TUMULT	TUPIK	TURFINESSES	TURNROUNDS	TUSSOCKY
TUMULTED	TUPIKS	TURFING	TURNS	TUSSORE
TUMULTING	TUPPED	TURFINGS	TURNSKIN	TUSSORES
TUMULTS	TUPPENCE	TURFITE	TURNSKINS	TUT
TUMULUS	TUPPENCES	TURFITES	TURNSOLE	TUTANIA
TUN	TUPPENNIES	TURFMAN	TURNSOLES	TUTANIAS
TUNA	TUPPENNY	TURFMEN	TURNSPIT	TUTEE
TUNABLE	TUPPING	TURFS	TURNSPITS	TUTEES
TUNABLY	TUPS	TURFY	TURNSTILE	TUTELAGE
TUNAS	TUPTOWING	TURGENT	TURNSTILES	TUTELAGES
TUNBELLIES	TUQUE	TURGENTLY	TURNSTONE	TUTELAR
TUNBELLY	TUQUES	TURGID	TURNSTONES	TUTELARIES
TUND	TURACIN	TURGIDITIES	TURNTABLE	TUTELARS
TUNDED	TURACINS	TURGIDITY	TURNTABLES	TUTELARY
TUNDING	TURACO	TURGIDLY	TURPETH	TUTENAG
TUNDRA	TURACOS	TURGOR	TURPETHS	TUTENAGS
TUNDRAS	TURBAN	TURGORS	TURPITUDE	TUTIORISM
TUNDS	TURBAND	TURION	TURPITUDES	TUTIORIST
TUNDUN	TURBANDS	TURIONS	TURPS	TUTIORISTS
TUNDUNS	TURBANED	TURKEY	TURQUOISE	TUTMAN
TUNE	TURBANS	TURKEYS	TURQUOISES	TUTMEN
TUNEABLE	TURBANT	TURKIES	TURRET	TUTOR
TUNED	TURBANTS	TURKIESES	TURRETED	TUTORAGE
TUNEFUL	TURBARIES	TURKIS	TURRETS	TUTORAGES
TUNEFULLY	TURBARY	TURKISES	TURRIBANT	TUTORED
TUNELESS	TURBID	TURLOUGH	TURRIBANTS	TUTORESS
TUNER	TURBIDITE	TURLOUGHS	TURTLE	TUTORESSES
TUNERS	TURBIDITES	TURM	TURTLED	TUTORIAL
TUNES	TURBIDITIES	TURME	TURTLER	TUTORIALS
TUNESMITH	TURBIDITY	TURMERIC	TURTLERS	TUTORING
TUNESMITHS	TURBIDLY	TURMERICS	TURTLES	TUTORINGS
TUNGSTATE	TURBINAL	TURMES	TURTLING	TUTORISE
TUNGSTATES	TURBINALS	TURMOIL	TURTLINGS	TUTORISED
TUNGSTEN	TURBINATE	TURMOILED	TURVES	TUTORISES
TUNGSTENS	TURBINE	TURMOILING	TUSCHE	TUTORISING
TUNIC	TURBINED	TURMOILS	TUSCHES	TUTORISM
TUNICATE	TURBINES	TURMS	TUSH	TUTORISMS
TUNICATED	TURBIT	TURN	TUSHED	TUTORIZE
TUNICATES	TURBITH	TURNABOUT	TUSHERIES	TUTORIZED
TUNICIN	TURBITHS	TURNABOUTS	TUSHERY	TUTORIZES
TUNICINS	TURBITS	TURNAGAIN	TUSHES	TUTORIZING
TUNICKED	TURBO	TURNAGAINS	TUSHING	TUTORS
TUNICLE	TURBOCAR	TURNBACK	TUSK	TUTORSHIP
TUNICLES	TURBOCARS	TURNBACKS	TUSKAR	TUTORSHIPS
TUNICS	TURBOFAN	TURNCOAT	TUSKARS	TUTRESS
TUNIER	TURBOFANS	TURNCOATS	TUSKED	TUTRESSES
TUNIEST	TURBOND	TURNCOCK	TUSKER	TUTRIX
TUNING	TURBONDS	TURNCOCKS	TUSKERS	TUTRIXES
TUNINGS	TURBOPROP	TURNDUN	TUSKIER	TUTS

TUTSAN	TWATTLINGS	TWIDDLING	TWINSHIP	TWOPENCE
TUTSANS	TWAY	TWIDDLINGS	TWINSHIPS	TWOPENCES
TUTTED	TWAYS	TWIDDLY	TWINTER	TWOPENNIES
TUTTI	TWEAK	TWIER	TWINTERS	TWOPENNY
TUTTIES	TWEAKED	TWIERS	TWINY	TWOS
TUTTING	TWEAKING	TWIFOLD	TWIRE	TWOSEATER
TUTTIS	TWEAKS	TWIFORKED	TWIRED	TWOSEATERS
TUTTY	TWEE	TWIFORMED	TWIRES	TWOSOME
TUTU	TWEED	TWIG	TWIRING	TWOSOMES
TUTUS	TWEEDIER	TWIGGED	TWIRL	TWOSTROKE
TUTWORK	TWEEDIEST	TWIGGEN	TWIRLED	TWYER
TUTWORKER	TWEEDLE	TWIGGER	TWIRLER	TWYERE
TUTWORKERS	TWEEDLED	TWIGGERS	TWIRLERS	TWYERES
TUTWORKS	TWEEDLES	TWIGGIER	TWIRLIER	TWYERS
TUXEDO	TWEEDLING	TWIGGIEST	TWIRLIEST	TWYFOLD
TUXEDOES	TWEEDS	TWIGGING	TWIRLING	TWYFORKED
TUXEDOS	TWEEDY	TWIGGY	TWIRLS	TWYFORMED
TUYÈRE	TWEEL	TWIGHT	TWIRLY	TYCHISM
TUYÈRES	TWEELED	TWIGHTED	TWIRP	TYCHISMS
TUZZ	TWEELING	TWIGHTING	TWIRPS	TYCOON
TUZZES	TWEELS	TWIGHTS	TWISCAR	TYCOONATE
TWA	TWEELY	TWIGS	TWISCARS	TYCOONATES
TWADDLE	TWEENESS	TWIGSOME	TWIST	TYCOONERIES
TWADDLED	TWEENESSES	TWILIGHT	TWISTABLE	TYCOONERY
TWADDLER	TWEENIES	TWILIGHTED	TWISTED	TYCOONS
TWADDLERS	TWEENY	TWILIGHTING	TWISTER	TYDE
TWADDLES	TWEER	TWILIGHTS	TWISTERS	TYE
TWADDLING	TWEERED	TWILIT	TWISTIER	TYED
TWADDLINGS	TWEERING	TWILL	TWISTIEST	TYEING
TWADDLY	TWEERS	TWILLED	TWISTING	TYES
TWAE	TWEEST	TWILLIES	TWISTINGS	TYG
TWAES	TWEET	TWILLING	TWISTS	TYGS
TWAFALD	TWEETED	TWILLS	TWISTY	TYING
TWAIN	TWEETER	TWILLY	TWIT	TYKE
TWAINS	TWEETERS	TWILT	TWITCH	TYKES
TWAITE	TWEETING	TWILTED	TWITCHED	TYKISH
TWAITES	TWEETS	TWILTING	TWITCHER	TYLECTOMIES
TWAL	TWEEZE	TWILTS	TWITCHERS	TYLECTOMY
TWALHOURS	TWEEZED	TWIN	TWITCHES	TYLER
TWALPENNIES	TWEEZERS	TWINE	TWITCHIER	TYLERS
TWALPENNY	TWEEZES	TWINED	TWITCHIEST	TYLOPOD
TWALS	TWEEZING	TWINER	TWITCHING	TYLOPODS
TWANG	TWELFTH	TWINERS	TWITCHINGS	TYLOSES
TWANGED	TWELFTHLY	TWINES	TWITCHY	TYLOSIS
TWANGIER	TWELFTHS	TWINGE	TWITE	TYLOTE
TWANGIEST	TWELVE	TWINGED	TWITES	TYLOTES
TWANGING	TWELVEMO	TWINGES	TWITS	TYMBAL
TWANGINGS	TWELVEMOS	TWINGING	TWITTED	TYMBALS
TWANGLE	TWELVES	TWINIER	TWITTEN	TYMP
TWANGLED	TWENTIES	TWINIEST	TWITTENS	TYMPAN
TWANGLES	TWENTIETH	TWINING	TWITTER	TYMPANA
TWANGLING	TWENTIETHS	TWININGLY	TWITTERED	TYMPANAL
TWANGLINGS	TWENTY	TWININGS	TWITTERER	TYMPANI
TWANGS	TWENTYISH	TWINK	TWITTERERS	TYMPANIC
TWANGY	TWERP	TWINKED	TWITTERING	TYMPANICS
TWANK	TWERPS	TWINKING	TWITTERINGS	TYMPANIES
TWANKAY	TWIBILL	TWINKLE	TWITTERS	TYMPANIST
TWANKAYS	TWIBILLS	TWINKLED	TWITTERY	TYMPANISTS
TWANKS	TWICE	TWINKLER	TWITTING	TYMPANO
TWAS	TWICER	TWINKLERS	TWITTINGS	TYMPANS
TWASOME	TWICERS	TWINKLES	TWIZZLE	TYMPANUM
TWASOMES	TWICHILD	TWINKLING	TWIZZLED	TYMPANY
TWAT	TWICHILDREN	TWINKLINGS	TWIZZLES	TYMPS
TWATS	TWIDDLE	TWINKS	TWIZZLING	TYND
TWATTLE	TWIDDLED	TWINLING	TWO	TYNDE
TWATTLED	TWIDDLER	TWINLINGS	TWOER	TYNE
TWATTLER	TWIDDLERS	TWINNED	TWOERS	TYNED
TWATTLERS	TWIDDLES	TWINNING	TWOFOLD	TYNES
TWATTLES	TWIDDLIER	TWINNINGS	TWONESS	TYNING
TWATTLING	TWIDDLIEST	TWINS	TWONESSES	TYPAL

TYPE
TYPECAST
TYPECASTING
TYPECASTS
TYPED
TYPES
TYPEWRITE
TYPEWRITES
TYPEWRITING
TYPEWRITINGS
TYPEWRITTEN
TYPEWROTE
TYPHLITIC
TYPHLITIS
TYPHLITISES
TYPHOID
TYPHOIDAL
TYPHOIDS
TYPHON
TYPHONIAN
TYPHONIC

TYPHONS
TYPHOON
TYPHOONS
TYPHOUS
TYPHUS
TYPHUSES
TYPIC
TYPICAL
TYPICALLY
TYPIFIED
TYPIFIER
TYPIFIERS
TYPIFIES
TYPIFY
TYPIFYING
TYPING
TYPINGS
TYPIST
TYPISTS
TYPO
TYPOLOGIES

TYPOLOGY
TYPOMANIA
TYPOMANIAS
TYPOS
TYPTO
TYPTOED
TYPTOING
TYPTOS
TYRAMINE
TYRAMINES
TYRAN
TYRANNE
TYRANNED
TYRANNES
TYRANNESS
TYRANNESSES
TYRANNIC
TYRANNIES
TYRANNING
TYRANNIS
TYRANNISE

TYRANNISED
TYRANNISES
TYRANNISING
TYRANNIZE
TYRANNIZED
TYRANNIZES
TYRANNIZING
TYRANNOUS
TYRANNY
TYRANS
TYRANT
TYRANTED
TYRANTING
TYRANTS
TYRE
TYRED
TYRELESS
TYRES
TYRO·
TYROES
TYRONES

TYROSINE
TYROSINES
TYSTIE
TYSTIES
TYTE
TYTHE
TYTHED
TYTHES
TYTHING
TZADDIK
TZADDIKIM
TZADDIKS
TZADDIQ
TZADDIQIM
TZADDIQS
TZAR
TZARS
TZIGANIES
TZIGANY
TZIMMES

U

UAKARI	UITLANDERS	ULTION	UMBRETTE	UNANCHORED
UAKARIS	UKASE	ULTIONS	UMBRETTES	UNANCHORING
UBEROUS	UKASES	ULTRA	UMBRIERE	UNANCHORS
UBERTIES	UKELELE	ULTRAISM	UMBRIERES	UNANELED
UBERTY	UKELELES	ULTRAISMS	UMBRIL	UNANIMITIES
UBIETIES	UKULELE	ULTRAIST	UMBRILS	UNANIMITY
UBIETY	UKULELES	ULTRAISTS	UMBROSE	UNANIMOUS
UBIQUE	ULCER	ULTRARED	UMBROUS	UNANXIOUS
UBIQUITIES	ULCERATE	ULTRAS	UMIAK	UNAPPAREL
UBIQUITY	ULCERATED	ULULANT	UMIAKS	UNAPPARELLED
UDAL	ULCERATES	ULULATE	UMLAUT	UNAPPARELLING
UDALLER	ULCERATING	ULULATED	UMLAUTED	UNAPPARELS
UDALLERS	ULCERED	ULULATES	UMLAUTING	UNAPPLIED
UDALS	ULCERING	ULULATING	UMLAUTS	UNAPT
UDDER	ULCEROUS	ULULATION	UMPH	UNAPTLY
UDDERED	ULCERS	ULULATIONS	UMPIRAGE	UNAPTNESS
UDDERFUL	ULE	ULYIE	UMPIRAGES	UNAPTNESSES
UDDERLESS	ULEMA	ULYIES	UMPIRE	UNARGUED
UDDERS	ULEMAS	ULZIE	UMPIRED	UNARISEN
UDO	ULES	ULZIES	UMPIRES	UNARM
UDOMETER	ULEX	UM	UMPIRING	UNARMED
UDOMETERS	ULEXES	UMBEL	UMPTEEN	UNARMING
UDOMETRIC	ULICHON	UMBELLAR	UMPTEENTH	UNARMS
UDOS	ULICHONS	UMBELLATE	UMPTIETH	UNARTFUL
UDS	ULICON	UMBELLULE	UMPTY	UNASHAMED
UEY	ULICONS	UMBELLULES	UMQUHILE	UNASKED
UEYS	ULIGINOUS	UMBELS	UMWHILE	UNASSAYED
UFO	ULIKON	UMBER	UN	UNASSUMED
UFOLOGIES	ULIKONS	UMBERED	UNABASHED	UNASSURED
UFOLOGIST	ULITIS	UMBERING	UNABATED	UNATONED
UFOLOGISTS	ULITISES	UMBERS	UNABLE	UNATTIRED
UFOLOGY	ULLAGE	UMBERY	UNACCUSED	UNAU
UFOS	ULLAGED	UMBILICAL	UNACHING	UNAUS
UG	ULLAGES	UMBILICI	UNACTABLE	UNAVENGED
UGGED	ULLAGING	UMBILICUS	UNACTED	UNAVOIDED
UGGING	ULLING	UMBILICUSES	UNACTIVE	UNAVOWED
UGH	ULLINGS	UMBLES	UNADAPTED	UNAWARE
UGHS	ULMACEOUS	UMBO	UNADMIRED	UNAWARES
UGLI	ULMIN	UMBONAL	UNADOPTED	UNAWED
UGLIED	ULMINS	UMBONATE	UNADORED	UNBACKED
UGLIER	ULNA	UMBONES	UNADORNED	UNBAFFLED
UGLIES	ULNAE	UMBOS	UNADVISED	UNBAG
UGLIEST	ULNAR	UMBRA	UNAFRAID	UNBAGGED
UGLIFIED	ULNARE	UMBRAE	UNAIDABLE	UNBAGGING
UGLIFIES	ULNARIA	UMBRAGE	UNAIDED	UNBAGS
UGLIFY	ULOSES	UMBRAGED	UNAIMED	UNBAITED
UGLIFYING	ULOSIS	UMBRAGES	UNAIRED	UNBAKED
UGLILY	ULOTRICHIES	UMBRAGING	UNAKING	UNBALANCE
UGLINESS	ULOTRICHY	UMBRAL	UNALIGNED	UNBALANCED
UGLINESSES	ULSTER	UMBRAS	UNALIKE	UNBALANCES
UGLIS	ULSTERED	UMBRATED	UNALIST	UNBALANCING
UGLY	ULSTERS	UMBRATIC	UNALISTS	UNBANDED
UGLYING	ULTERIOR	UMBRATILE	UNALIVE	UNBANKED
UGS	ULTIMA	UMBRE	UNALLAYED	UNBAPTISE
UGSOME	ULTIMACIES	UMBREL	UNALLIED	UNBAPTISED
UHLAN	ULTIMACY	UMBRELLA	UNALLOYED	UNBAPTISES
UHLANS	ULTIMAS	UMBRELLAS	UNALTERED	UNBAPTISING
UHURU	ULTIMATA	UMBRELLO	UNAMAZED	UNBAPTIZE
UHURUS	ULTIMATE	UMBRELLOES	UNAMENDED	UNBAPTIZED
UINTAHITE	ULTIMATES	UMBRELLOS	UNAMERCED	UNBAPTIZES
UINTAHITES	ULTIMATUM	UMBRELS	UNAMIABLE	UNBAPTIZING
UINTAITE	ULTIMO	UMBRERE	UNAMUSED	UNBAR
UINTAITES		UMBRERES	UNAMUSING	UNBARBED
UITLANDER		UMBRES	UNANCHOR	UNBARE

UNBARED	UNBIASSED	UNBOWED	UNCANDOUR	UNCHOSEN
UNBARES	UNBIASSING	UNBOX	UNCANDOURS	UNCHRISOM
UNBARING	UNBID	UNBOXED	UNCANNIER	UNCHURCH
UNBARK	UNBIDDEN	UNBOXES	UNCANNIEST	UNCHURCHED
UNBARKED	UNBIND	UNBOXING	UNCANNILY	UNCHURCHES
UNBARKING	UNBINDING	UNBRACE	UNCANNY	UNCHURCHING
UNBARKS	UNBINDINGS	UNBRACED	UNCANONIC	UNCI
UNBARRED	UNBINDS	UNBRACES	UNCAP	UNCIAL
UNBARRING	UNBISHOP	UNBRACING	UNCAPABLE	UNCIALS
UNBARS	UNBISHOPED	UNBRAIDED	UNCAPE	UNCIFORM
UNBASHFUL	UNBISHOPING	UNBRASTE	UNCAPED	UNCINATE
UNBATED	UNBISHOPS	UNBRED	UNCAPES	UNCINATED
UNBATHED	UNBITT	UNBREECH	UNCAPING	UNCINI
UNBE	UNBITTED	UNBREECHED	UNCAPPED	UNCINUS
UNBEAR	UNBITTING	UNBREECHES	UNCAPPING	UNCIPHER
UNBEARDED	UNBITTS	UNBREECHING	UNCAPS	UNCIPHERED
UNBEARING	UNBLAMED	UNBRIDGED	UNCAREFUL	UNCIPHERING
UNBEARS	UNBLENDED	UNBRIDLE	UNCARING	UNCIPHERS
UNBEATEN	UNBLENT	UNBRIDLED	UNCART	UNCIVIL
UNBED	UNBLESS	UNBRIDLES	UNCARTED	UNCIVILLY
UNBEDDED	UNBLESSED	UNBRIDLING	UNCARTING	UNCLAD
UNBEDDING	UNBLESSES	UNBRIZZED	UNCARTS	UNCLAIMED
UNBEDS	UNBLESSING	UNBROKE	UNCASE	UNCLASP
UNBEEN	UNBLEST	UNBROKEN	UNCASED	UNCLASPED
UNBEGET	UNBLIND	UNBRUISED	UNCASES	UNCLASPING
UNBEGETS	UNBLINDED	UNBRUSED	UNCASHED	UNCLASPS
UNBEGETTING	UNBLINDING	UNBRUSHED	UNCASING	UNCLASSED
UNBEGGED	UNBLINDS	UNBUCKLE	UNCATE	UNCLE
UNBEGOT	UNBLOCK	UNBUCKLED	UNCAUGHT	UNCLEAN
UNBEGOTTEN	UNBLOCKED	UNBUCKLES	UNCAUSED	UNCLEANED
UNBEGUILE	UNBLOCKING	UNBUCKLING	UNCE	UNCLEANER
UNBEGUILED	UNBLOCKS	UNBUDDED	UNCEASING	UNCLEANEST
UNBEGUILES	UNBLOODED	UNBUILD	UNCERTAIN	UNCLEANLY
UNBEGUILING	UNBLOODY	UNBUILDING	UNCES	UNCLEAR
UNBEGUN	UNBLOTTED	UNBUILDS	UNCESSANT	UNCLEARED
UNBEING	UNBLOWED	UNBUILT	UNCHAIN	UNCLEARER
UNBEINGS	UNBLOWN	UNBUNDLE	UNCHAINED	UNCLEAREST
UNBEKNOWN	UNBLUNTED	UNBUNDLED	UNCHAINING	UNCLEARLY
UNBELIEF	UNBODIED	UNBUNDLES	UNCHAINS	UNCLED
UNBELIEFS	UNBODING	UNBUNDLING	UNCHANCIER	UNCLENCH
UNBELIEVE	UNBOLT	UNBUNDLINGS	UNCHANCIEST	UNCLENCHED
UNBELIEVED	UNBOLTED	UNBURDEN	UNCHANCY	UNCLENCHES
UNBELIEVES	UNBOLTING	UNBURDENED	UNCHANGED	UNCLENCHING
UNBELIEVING	UNBOLTS	UNBURDENING	UNCHARGE	UNCLES
UNBELOVED	UNBONE	UNBURDENS	UNCHARGED	UNCLESHIP
UNBELT	UNBONED	UNBURIED	UNCHARGES	UNCLESHIPS
UNBELTED	UNBONES	UNBURIES	UNCHARGING	UNCLEW
UNBELTING	UNBONING	UNBURNED	UNCHARITIES	UNCLEWED
UNBELTS	UNBONNET	UNBURNT	UNCHARITY	UNCLEWING
UNBEND	UNBONNETED	UNBURROW	UNCHARM	UNCLEWS
UNBENDED	UNBONNETING	UNBURROWED	UNCHARMED	UNCLING
UNBENDING	UNBONNETS	UNBURROWING	UNCHARMING	UNCLIPPED
UNBENDS	UNBOOKED	UNBURROWS	UNCHARMS	UNCLIPT
UNBENIGN	UNBOOKISH	UNBURTHEN	UNCHARNEL	UNCLOAK
UNBENT	UNBOOT	UNBURTHENED	UNCHARNELED	UNCLOAKED
UNBEREFT	UNBOOTED	UNBURTHENING	UNCHARNELLING	UNCLOAKING
UNBERUFEN	UNBOOTING	UNBURTHENS	UNCHARNELS	UNCLOAKS
UNBESEEM	UNBOOTS	UNBURY	UNCHARTED	UNCLOG
UNBESEEMED	UNBORE	UNBURYING	UNCHARY	UNCLOGGED
UNBESEEMING	UNBORN	UNBUSY	UNCHASTE	UNCLOGGING
UNBESEEMS	UNBORNE	UNBUTTON	UNCHECK	UNCLOGS
UNBESPEAK	UNBOSOM	UNBUTTONED	UNCHECKED	UNCLOSE
UNBESPEAKING	UNBOSOMED	UNBUTTONING	UNCHECKING	UNCLOSED
UNBESPEAKS	UNBOSOMER	UNBUTTONS	UNCHECKS	UNCLOSES
UNBESPOKE	UNBOSOMERS	UNCAGE	UNCHEERED	UNCLOSING
UNBESPOKEN	UNBOSOMING	UNCAGED	UNCHEWED	UNCLOTHE
UNBIAS	UNBOSOMS	UNCAGES	UNCHILD	UNCLOTHED
UNBIASED	UNBOUGHT	UNCAGING	UNCHILDED	UNCLOTHES
UNBIASES	UNBOUND	UNCALLED	UNCHILDING	UNCLOTHING
UNBIASING	UNBOUNDED	UNCANDID	UNCHILDS	UNCLOUD

UNCLOUDED	UNCOUTHLY	UNDAZZLED	UNDERCARD	UNDERGONE
UNCLOUDING	UNCOVER	UNDAZZLES	UNDERCARDS	UNDERGOWN
UNCLOUDS	UNCOVERED	UNDAZZLING	UNDERCART	UNDERGOWNS
UNCLOUDY	UNCOVERING	UNDE	UNDERCARTS	UNDERGRAD
UNCLOVEN	UNCOVERS	UNDÉ	UNDERCAST	UNDERGRADS
UNCLUTCH	UNCOWL	UNDEAD	UNDERCASTS	UNDERHAND
UNCLUTCHED	UNCOWLED	UNDEAF	UNDERCLAD	UNDERHANDS
UNCLUTCHES	UNCOWLING	UNDEAFED	UNDERCLAY	UNDERHUNG
UNCLUTCHING	UNCOWLS	UNDEAFING	UNDERCLAYS	UNDERKEEP
UNCO	UNCOYNED	UNDEAFS	UNDERCLUB	UNDERKEEPING
UNCOCK	UNCRATE	UNDEALT	UNDERCLUBBED	UNDERKEEPS
UNCOCKED	UNCRATED	UNDEAR	UNDERCLUBBING	UNDERKEPT
UNCOCKING	UNCRATES	UNDEBASED	UNDERCLUBS	UNDERKING
UNCOCKS	UNCRATING	UNDECAYED	UNDERCOAT	UNDERKINGS
UNCOIL	UNCREATE	UNDECEIVE	UNDERCOATS	UNDERLAID
UNCOILED	UNCREATED	UNDECEIVED	UNDERCOOK	UNDERLAIN
UNCOILING	UNCREATES	UNDECEIVES	UNDERCOOKS	UNDERLAP
UNCOILS	UNCREATING	UNDECEIVING	UNDERCOOL	UNDERLAPPED
UNCOINED	UNCROPPED	UNDECENT	UNDERCOOLED	UNDERLAPPING
UNCOLT	UNCROSS	UNDECIDED	UNDERCOOLING	UNDERLAPS
UNCOLTED	UNCROSSED	UNDECIMAL	UNDERCOOLS	UNDERLAY
UNCOLTING	UNCROSSES	UNDECK	UNDERCUT	UNDERLAYING
UNCOLTS	UNCROSSING	UNDECKED	UNDERCUTS	UNDERLAYS
UNCOMBED	UNCROWDED	UNDECKING	UNDERCUTTING	UNDERLET
UNCOMBINE	UNCROWN	UNDECKS	UNDERDECK	UNDERLETS
UNCOMBINED	UNCROWNED	UNDEE	UNDERDECKS	UNDERLETTING
UNCOMBINES	UNCROWNING	UNDÉE	UNDERDID	UNDERLETTINGS
UNCOMBINING	UNCROWNS	UNDEEDED	UNDERDO	UNDERLIE
UNCOMELY	UNCRUDDED	UNDEFACED	UNDERDOER	UNDERLIES
UNCOMMON	UNCRUMPLE	UNDEFIDE	UNDERDOERS	UNDERLINE
UNCOMMONER	UNCRUMPLED	UNDEFIED	UNDERDOES	UNDERLINED
UNCOMMONEST	UNCRUMPLES	UNDEFILED	UNDERDOG	UNDERLINES
UNCONCERN	UNCRUMPLING	UNDEFINED	UNDERDOGS	UNDERLING
UNCONCERNS	UNCTION	UNDEIFIED	UNDERDOING	UNDERLINGS
UNCONFINE	UNCTIONS	UNDEIFIES	UNDERDONE	UNDERLINING
UNCONFINED	UNCTUOUS	UNDEIFY	UNDERDRAW	UNDERLIP
UNCONFINES	UNCULLED	UNDEIFYING	UNDERDRAWING	UNDERLIPS
UNCONFINING	UNCURABLE	UNDELAYED	UNDERDRAWINGS	UNDERLYING
UNCONFORM	UNCURBED	UNDELIGHT	UNDERDRAWN	UNDERMAN
UNCONGEAL	UNCURDLED	UNDELIGHTS	UNDERDRAWS	UNDERMANNED
UNCONGEALED	UNCURED	UNDELUDED	UNDERDREW	UNDERMANNING
UNCONGEALING	UNCURIOUS	UNDER	UNDERFED	UNDERMANS
UNCONGEALS	UNCURL	UNDERACT	UNDERFEED	UNDERMEN
UNCOOKED	UNCURLED	UNDERACTED	UNDERFEEDING	UNDERMINE
UNCOOL	UNCURLING	UNDERACTING	UNDERFEEDS	UNDERMINED
UNCOPE	UNCURLS	UNDERACTS	UNDERFELT	UNDERMINES
UNCOPED	UNCURRENT	UNDERARM	UNDERFELTS	UNDERMINING
UNCOPES	UNCURSE	UNDERBEAR	UNDERFIRE	UNDERMININGS
UNCOPING	UNCURSED	UNDERBEARING	UNDERFIRED	UNDERMOST
UNCORD	UNCURSES	UNDERBEARINGS	UNDERFIRES	UNDERN
UNCORDED	UNCURSING	UNDERBEARS	UNDERFIRING	UNDERNOTE
UNCORDIAL	UNCURTAIN	UNDERBID	UNDERFLOW	UNDERNOTED
UNCORDING	UNCURTAINED	UNDERBIDDING	UNDERFLOWS	UNDERNOTES
UNCORDS	UNCURTAINING	UNDERBIDS	UNDERFONG	UNDERNOTING
UNCORK	UNCURTAINS	UNDERBIT	UNDERFONGED	UNDERNS
UNCORKED	UNCUS	UNDERBITE	UNDERFONGING	UNDERPAID
UNCORKING	UNCUT	UNDERBITES	UNDERFONGS	UNDERPASS
UNCORKS	UNDAM	UNDERBITING	UNDERFOOT	UNDERPASSES
UNCORRUPT	UNDAMAGED	UNDERBITTEN	UNDERFOOTED	UNDERPAY
UNCOS	UNDAMMED	UNDERBORE	UNDERFOOTING	UNDERPAYING
UNCOSTLY	UNDAMMING	UNDERBORNE	UNDERFOOTS	UNDERPAYS
UNCOUNTED	UNDAMNED	UNDERBOUGHT	UNDERFUR	UNDERPEEP
UNCOUPLE	UNDAMPED	UNDERBRED	UNDERFURS	UNDERPEEPED
UNCOUPLED	UNDAMS	UNDERBUSH	UNDERGIRD	UNDERPEEPING
UNCOUPLES	UNDASHED	UNDERBUSHED	UNDERGIRDED	UNDERPEEPS
UNCOUPLING	UNDATE	UNDERBUSHES	UNDERGIRDING	UNDERPIN
UNCOURTLY	UNDATED	UNDERBUSHING	UNDERGIRDS	UNDERPINNED
UNCOUTH	UNDAUNTED	UNDERBUY	UNDERGO	UNDERPINNING
UNCOUTHER	UNDAWNING	UNDERBUYING	UNDERGOES	UNDERPINNINGS
UNCOUTHEST	UNDAZZLE	UNDERBUYS	UNDERGOING	UNDERPINS

UNDERPLAY
UNDERPLAYED
UNDERPLAYING
UNDERPLAYS
UNDERPLOT
UNDERPLOTS
UNDERPROP
UNDERPROPPED
UNDERPROPPING
UNDERPROPS
UNDERRAN
UNDERRATE
UNDERRATED
UNDERRATES
UNDERRATING
UNDERRUN
UNDERRUNNING
UNDERRUNNINGS
UNDERRUNS
UNDERSAID
UNDERSAY
UNDERSAYE
UNDERSAYES
UNDERSAYING
UNDERSAYS
UNDERSEA
UNDERSEAL
UNDERSEALED
UNDERSEALING
UNDERSEALINGS
UNDERSEALS
UNDERSELF
UNDERSELL
UNDERSELLING
UNDERSELLS
UNDERSELVES
UNDERSET
UNDERSETS
UNDERSETTING
UNDERSHOT
UNDERSIDE
UNDERSIDES
UNDERSIGN
UNDERSIGNED
UNDERSIGNING
UNDERSIGNS
UNDERSKIES
UNDERSKY
UNDERSOIL
UNDERSOILS
UNDERSOLD
UNDERSONG
UNDERSONGS
UNDERTAKE
UNDERTAKEN
UNDERTAKES
UNDERTAKING
UNDERTAKINGS
UNDERTANE
UNDERTIME
UNDERTIMES
UNDERTINT
UNDERTINTS
UNDERTONE
UNDERTONES
UNDERTOOK
UNDERTOW
UNDERTOWS
UNDERUSE
UNDERUSED

UNDERUSES
UNDERUSING
UNDERVEST
UNDERVESTS
UNDERWAY
UNDERWEAR
UNDERWEARS
UNDERWENT
UNDERWING
UNDERWINGS
UNDERWIT
UNDERWITS
UNDERWOOD
UNDERWOODS
UNDERWORK
UNDERWORKED
UNDERWORKING
UNDERWORKS
UNDESERT
UNDESERTS
UNDESERVE
UNDESERVED
UNDESERVES
UNDESERVING
UNDESIRED
UNDEVOUT
UNDID
UNDIES
UNDIGHT
UNDIGHTING
UNDIGHTS
UNDIGNIFIED
UNDIGNIFIES
UNDIGNIFY
UNDIGNIFYING
UNDILUTED
UNDIMMED
UNDINE
UNDINES
UNDINISM
UNDINISMS
UNDINTED
UNDIPPED
UNDIVIDED
UNDIVINE
UNDO
UNDOCK
UNDOCKED
UNDOCKING
UNDOCKS
UNDOER
UNDOERS
UNDOES
UNDOING
UNDOINGS
UNDONE
UNDOOMED
UNDOUBLE
UNDOUBLED
UNDOUBLES
UNDOUBLING
UNDOUBTED
UNDRAINED
UNDRAPED
UNDRAW
UNDRAWING
UNDRAWN
UNDRAWS
UNDREADED
UNDREAMED

UNDREAMT
UNDRESS
UNDRESSED
UNDRESSES
UNDRESSING
UNDRESSINGS
UNDREST
UNDREW
UNDRIED
UNDRILLED
UNDRIVEN
UNDROSSY
UNDROWNED
UNDRUNK
UNDUBBED
UNDUE
UNDUG
UNDULANCIES
UNDULANCY
UNDULANT
UNDULATE
UNDULATED
UNDULATES
UNDULATING
UNDULLED
UNDULOSE
UNDULOUS
UNDULY
UNDUTEOUS
UNDUTIFUL
UNDYED
UNDYING
UNDYINGLY
UNEARED
UNEARNED
UNEARTH
UNEARTHED
UNEARTHING
UNEARTHLIER
UNEARTHLIEST
UNEARTHLY
UNEARTHS
UNEASE
UNEASES
UNEASIER
UNEASIEST
UNEASILY
UNEASY
UNEATABLE
UNEATEN
UNEATH
UNEATHES
UNEDGE
UNEDGED
UNEDGES
UNEDGING
UNEDITED
UNEFFACED
UNELATED
UNELECTED
UNEMPTIED
UNENDING
UNENDOWED
UNENGAGED
UNENTERED
UNENVIED
UNENVIOUS
UNENVYING
UNEQUABLE
UNEQUAL

UNEQUALLY
UNEQUALS
UNERRING
UNESPIED
UNESSAYED
UNESSENCE
UNESSENCED
UNESSENCES
UNESSENCING
UNETH
UNETHICAL
UNEVEN
UNEVENER
UNEVENEST
UNEVENLY
UNEXALTED
UNEXCITED
UNEXPIRED
UNEXPOSED
UNEXTINCT
UNEYED
UNFABLED
UNFACT
UNFACTS
UNFADABLE
UNFADED
UNFADING
UNFAILING
UNFAIR
UNFAIRED
UNFAIRER
UNFAIREST
UNFAIRING
UNFAIRLY
UNFAIRS
UNFAITH
UNFAITHS
UNFALLEN
UNFAMED
UNFANNED
UNFASTEN
UNFASTENED
UNFASTENING
UNFASTENS
UNFAULTY
UNFAZED
UNFEARED
UNFEARFUL
UNFEARING
UNFED
UNFEED
UNFEELING
UNFEIGNED
UNFELLED
UNFELT
UNFENCED
UNFETTER
UNFETTERED
UNFETTERING
UNFETTERS
UNFEUDAL
UNFEUED
UNFIGURED
UNFILDE
UNFILED
UNFILIAL
UNFILLED
UNFILMED
UNFINE
UNFIRED

UNFIRM
UNFISHED
UNFIT
UNFITLY
UNFITNESS
UNFITNESSES
UNFITS
UNFITTED
UNFITTER
UNFITTEST
UNFITTING
UNFIX
UNFIXED
UNFIXES
UNFIXING
UNFIXITIES
UNFIXITY
UNFLAWED
UNFLEDGED
UNFLESH
UNFLESHED
UNFLESHES
UNFLESHING
UNFLESHLY
UNFLOORED
UNFLUSH
UNFLUSHED
UNFLUSHES
UNFLUSHING
UNFOCUSED
UNFOLD
UNFOLDED
UNFOLDER
UNFOLDERS
UNFOLDING
UNFOLDINGS
UNFOLDS
UNFOOL
UNFOOLED
UNFOOLING
UNFOOLS
UNFOOTED
UNFORBID
UNFORCED
UNFORGED
UNFORGOT
UNFORM
UNFORMAL
UNFORMED
UNFORMING
UNFORMS
UNFORTUNE
UNFORTUNES
UNFOUGHT
UNFOUND
UNFOUNDED
UNFRAMED
UNFRANKED
UNFRAUGHT
UNFRAUGHTED
UNFRAUGHTING
UNFRAUGHTS
UNFREE
UNFREEMAN
UNFREEMEN
UNFREEZE
UNFREEZES
UNFREEZING
UNFRETTED
UNFRIEND

UNFRIENDS	UNGLUES	UNHANDING	UNHELED	UNHUSKING
UNFROCK	UNGLUING	UNHANDLED	UNHELES	UNHUSKS
UNFROCKED	UNGOD	UNHANDS	UNHELING	UNI
UNFROCKING	UNGODDED	UNHANDY	UNHELM	UNIAXIAL
UNFROCKS	UNGODDING	UNHANG	UNHELMED	UNICITIES
UNFROZE	UNGODLIER	UNHANGED	UNHELMING	UNICITY
UNFROZEN	UNGODLIEST	UNHANGING	UNHELMS	UNICOLOR
UNFUELLED	UNGODLIKE	UNHANGS	UNHELPED	UNICOLOUR
UNFUMED	UNGODLILY	UNHAPPIED	UNHELPFUL	UNICORN
UNFUNDED	UNGODLY	UNHAPPIER	UNHEPPEN	UNICORNS
UNFUNNY	UNGODS	UNHAPPIES	UNHEROIC	UNICYCLE
UNFURL	UNGORD	UNHAPPIEST	UNHERST	UNICYCLES
UNFURLED	UNGORED	UNHAPPILY	UNHEWN	UNIDEAL
UNFURLING	UNGORGED	UNHAPPY	UNHIDDEN	UNIFIABLE
UNFURLS	UNGOT	UNHAPPYING	UNHINGE	UNIFIC
UNFURNISH	UNGOTTEN	UNHARBOUR	UNHINGED	UNIFIED
UNFURNISHED	UNGOWN	UNHARBOURED	UNHINGES	UNIFIER
UNFURNISHES	UNGOWNED	UNHARBOURING	UNHINGING	UNIFIERS
UNFURNISHING	UNGOWNING	UNHARBOURS	UNHIP	UNIFIES
UNFURRED	UNGOWNS	UNHARDY	UNHIRED	UNIFILAR
UNGAIN	UNGRACED	UNHARMED	UNHITCH	UNIFORM
UNGAINFUL	UNGRADED	UNHARMFUL	UNHITCHED	UNIFORMED
UNGAINLIER	UNGRASSED	UNHARMING	UNHITCHES	UNIFORMING
UNGAINLIEST	UNGRAVELY	UNHARNESS	UNHITCHING	UNIFORMLY
UNGAINLY	UNGRAZED	UNHARNESSED	UNHIVE	UNIFORMS
UNGALLANT	UNGROOMED	UNHARNESSES	UNHIVED	UNIFY
UNGALLED	UNGROUND	UNHARNESSING	UNHIVES	UNIFYING
UNGARBLED	UNGROWN	UNHASP	UNHIVING	UNIFYINGS
UNGAUGED	UNGRUDGED	UNHASPED	UNHOARD	UNILLUMED
UNGAZED	UNGUAL	UNHASPING	UNHOARDED	UNILOBAR
UNGEAR	UNGUARD	UNHASPS	UNHOARDING	UNILOBED
UNGEARED	UNGUARDED	UNHASTING	UNHOARDS	UNIMBUED
UNGEARING	UNGUARDING	UNHASTY	UNHOLIER	UNIMPEDED
UNGEARS	UNGUARDS	UNHAT	UNHOLIEST	UNIMPOSED
UNGENIAL	UNGUENT	UNHATCHED	UNHOLILY	UNINCITED
UNGENTEEL	UNGUENTS	UNHATS	UNHOLPEN	UNINDEXED
UNGENTLE	UNGUES	UNHATTED	UNHOLY	UNINJURED
UNGENTLY	UNGUESSED	UNHATTING	UNHOMELY	UNINSURED
UNGENUINE	UNGUIDED	UNHATTINGS	UNHONEST	UNINURED
UNGERMANE	UNGUIFORM	UNHAUNTED	UNHOOD	UNINVITED
UNGET	UNGUILTY	UNHEAD	UNHOODED	UNION
UNGETS	UNGUIS	UNHEADED	UNHOODING	UNIONISE
UNGETTING	UNGULA	UNHEADING	UNHOODS	UNIONISED
UNGHOSTLY	UNGULAE	UNHEADS	UNHOOK	UNIONISES
UNGIFTED	UNGULATE	UNHEAL	UNHOOKED	UNIONISING
UNGILD	UNGULATES	UNHEALED	UNHOOKING	UNIONISM
UNGILDED	UNGULED	UNHEALING	UNHOOKS	UNIONISMS
UNGILDING	UNGUM	UNHEALS	UNHOOP	UNIONIST
UNGILDS	UNGUMMED	UNHEALTH	UNHOOPED	UNIONISTS
UNGILT	UNGUMMING	UNHEALTHIER	UNHOOPING	UNIONIZE
UNGIRD	UNGUMS	UNHEALTHIEST	UNHOOPS	UNIONIZED
UNGIRDED	UNGYVE	UNHEALTHS	UNHOPED	UNIONIZES
UNGIRDING	UNGYVED	UNHEALTHY	UNHOPEFUL	UNIONIZING
UNGIRDS	UNGYVES	UNHEARD	UNHORSE	UNIONS
UNGIRT	UNGYVING	UNHEARSE	UNHORSED	UNIPAROUS
UNGIRTH	UNHABLE	UNHEARSED	UNHORSES	UNIPED
UNGIRTHED	UNHACKED	UNHEARSES	UNHORSING	UNIPEDS
UNGIRTHING	UNHAILED	UNHEARSING	UNHOUSE	UNIPLANAR
UNGIRTHS	UNHAIR	UNHEART	UNHOUSED	UNIPOD
UNGIVING	UNHAIRED	UNHEARTED	UNHOUSES	UNIPODS
UNGLAD	UNHAIRING	UNHEARTING	UNHOUSING	UNIPOLAR
UNGLAZED	UNHAIRS	UNHEARTS	UNHUMAN	UNIQUE
UNGLOSSED	UNHALLOW	UNHEATED	UNHUMBLED	UNIQUELY
UNGLOVE	UNHALLOWED	UNHEDGED	UNHUNG	UNIQUER
UNGLOVED	UNHALLOWING	UNHEEDED	UNHUNTED	UNIQUES
UNGLOVES	UNHALLOWS	UNHEEDFUL	UNHURRIED	UNIQUEST
UNGLOVING	UNHALSED	UNHEEDILY	UNHURT	UNIRONED
UNGLUE	UNHAND	UNHEEDING	UNHURTFUL	UNIS
UNGLUED	UNHANDED	UNHEEDY	UNHUSK	UNISERIAL
UNGLUEING	UNHANDILY	UNHELE	UNHUSKED	UNISEX

UNISEXUAL	UNKINDLED	UNLEASED	UNLORD	UNMEWING
UNISON	UNKINDLIER	UNLEASH	UNLORDED	UNMEWS
UNISONAL	UNKINDLIEST	UNLEASHED	UNLORDING	UNMILKED
UNISONANT	UNKINDLY	UNLEASHES	UNLORDLY	UNMILLED
UNISONOUS	UNKING	UNLEASHING	UNLORDS	UNMINDED
UNISONS	UNKINGED	UNLED	UNLOSABLE	UNMINDFUL
UNIT	UNKINGING	UNLESS	UNLOST	UNMINGLED
UNITAL	UNKINGLIER	UNLET	UNLOVABLE	UNMIRY
UNITARIAN	UNKINGLIEST	UNLICH	UNLOVE	UNMISSED
UNITARIANS	UNKINGLY	UNLICKED	UNLOVED	UNMIXED
UNITARY	UNKINGS	UNLID	UNLOVELY	UNMIXEDLY
UNITE	UNKISS	UNLIDDED	UNLOVES	UNMOANED
UNITED	UNKISSED	UNLIDDING	UNLOVING	UNMODISH
UNITEDLY	UNKISSES	UNLIDS	UNLUCKIER	UNMONEYED
UNITER	UNKISSING	UNLIGHTED	UNLUCKIEST	UNMONIED
UNITERS	UNKNELLED	UNLIKABLE	UNLUCKILY	UNMOOR
UNITES	UNKNIGHT	UNLIKE	UNLUCKY	UNMOORED
UNITIES	UNKNIGHTED	UNLIKELIER	UNMADE	UNMOORING
UNITING	UNKNIGHTING	UNLIKELIEST	UNMAILED	UNMOORS
UNITINGS	UNKNIGHTS	UNLIKELY	UNMAIMED	UNMORAL
UNITION	UNKNIT	UNLIKES	UNMAKABLE	UNMOTIVED
UNITIONS	UNKNITS	UNLIMBER	UNMAKE	UNMOULD
UNITISE	UNKNITTED	UNLIMBERED	UNMAKES	UNMOULDED
UNITISED	UNKNITTING	UNLIMBERING	UNMAKING	UNMOULDING
UNITISES	UNKNOT	UNLIMBERS	UNMAKINGS	UNMOULDS
UNITISING	UNKNOTS	UNLIME	UNMAN	UNMOUNT
UNITIVE	UNKNOTTED	UNLIMED	UNMANACLE	UNMOUNTED
UNITIVELY	UNKNOTTING	UNLIMES	UNMANACLED	UNMOUNTING
UNITIZE	UNKNOWING	UNLIMING	UNMANACLES	UNMOUNTS
UNITIZED	UNKNOWN	UNLIMITED	UNMANACLING	UNMOURNED
UNITIZES	UNKNOWNS	UNLINE	UNMANAGED	UNMOVABLE
UNITIZING	UNLACE	UNLINEAL	UNMANLIER	UNMOVABLY
UNITS	UNLACED	UNLINED	UNMANLIEST	UNMOVED
UNITY	UNLACES	UNLINES	UNMANLIKE	UNMOVEDLY
UNIVALENT	UNLACING	UNLINING	UNMANLY	UNMOVING
UNIVALENTS	UNLADE	UNLINK	UNMANNED	UNMOWN
UNIVALVE	UNLADED	UNLINKED	UNMANNING	UNMUFFLE
UNIVALVES	UNLADEN	UNLINKING	UNMANS	UNMUFFLED
U'IIVERSAL	UNLADES	UNLINKS	UNMANTLE	UNMUFFLES
UNIVERSALS	UNLADING	UNLISTED	UNMANTLED	UNMUFFLING
UNIVERSE	UNLADINGS	UNLIT	UNMANTLES	UNMUSICAL
UNIVERSES	UNLAID	UNLIVABLE	UNMANTLING	UNMUZZLE
UNIVOCAL	UNLASH	UNLIVE	UNMANURED	UNMUZZLED
UNIVOCALS	UNLASHED	UNLIVED	UNMARD	UNMUZZLES
UNJADED	UNLASHES	UNLIVELY	UNMARKED	UNMUZZLING
UNJEALOUS	UNLASHING	UNLIVES	UNMARRED	UNMUZZLINGS
UNJOINT	UNLAST	UNLIVING	UNMARRIED	UNNAIL
UNJOINTED	UNLASTE	UNLOAD	UNMARRIES	UNNAILED
UNJOINTING	UNLATCH	UNLOADED	UNMARRY	UNNAILING
UNJOINTS	UNLATCHED	UNLOADER	UNMARRYING	UNNAILS
UNJOYFUL	UNLATCHES	UNLOADERS	UNMASK	UNNAMABLE
UNJOYOUS	UNLATCHING	UNLOADING	UNMASKED	UNNAMED
UNJUST	UNLAW	UNLOADINGS	UNMASKER	UNNANELD
UNJUSTER	UNLAWED	UNLOADS	UNMASKERS	UNNATIVE
UNJUSTEST	UNLAWFUL	UNLOCATED	UNMASKING	UNNATURAL
UNJUSTLY	UNLAWING	UNLOCK	UNMASKS	UNNEATH
UNKED	UNLAWS	UNLOCKED	UNMATCHED	UNNEEDED
UNKEMPT	UNLAY	UNLOCKING	UNMATED	UNNEEDFUL
UNKENNED	UNLAYING	UNLOCKS	UNMATURED	UNNERVE
UNKENNEL	UNLAYS	UNLOGICAL	UNMEANING	UNNERVED
UNKENNELLED	UNLEAD	UNLOOKED	UNMEANT	UNNERVES
UNKENNELLING	UNLEADED	UNLOOSE	UNMEEK	UNNERVING
UNKENNELS	UNLEADING	UNLOOSED	UNMEET	UNNEST
UNKENT	UNLEADS	UNLOOSEN	UNMEETLY	UNNESTED
UNKEPT	UNLEAL	UNLOOSENED	UNMELTED	UNNESTING
UNKET	UNLEARN	UNLOOSENING	UNMERITED	UNNESTS
UNKID	UNLEARNED	UNLOOSENS	UNMET	UNNETHES
UNKIND	UNLEARNING	UNLOOSES	UNMETED	UNNETTED
UNKINDER	UNLEARNS	UNLOOSING	UNMEW	UNNOBLE
UNKINDEST	UNLEARNT	UNLOPPED	UNMEWED	UNNOBLED

UNNOBLES	UNPEOPLES	UNPOISONED	UNPULLED	UNREBUKED
UNNOBLING	UNPEOPLING	UNPOISONING	UNPURGED	UNRECKED
UNNOTED	UNPERCH	UNPOISONS	UNPURSE	UNRED
UNNOTICED	UNPERCHED	UNPOLICED	UNPURSED	UNREDREST
UNOBEYED	UNPERCHES	UNPOLISH	UNPURSES	UNREDUCED
UNOBVIOUS	UNPERCHING	UNPOLISHED	UNPURSING	UNREEL
UNOFFERED	UNPERFECT	UNPOLISHES	UNPURSUED	UNREELED
UNOFTEN	UNPERPLEX	UNPOLISHING	UNQUALIFIED	UNREELING
UNOILED	UNPERPLEXED	UNPOLITE	UNQUALIFIES	UNREELS
UNOPENED	UNPERPLEXES	UNPOLITIC	UNQUALIFY	UNREEVE
UNOPPOSED	UNPERPLEXING	UNPOLLED	UNQUALIFYING	UNREEVED
UNORDER	UNPERSON	UNPOPE	UNQUEEN	UNREEVES
UNORDERED	UNPERSONED	UNPOPED	UNQUEENED	UNREEVING
UNORDERING	UNPERSONING	UNPOPES	UNQUEENING	UNREFINED
UNORDERLY	UNPERSONS	UNPOPING	UNQUEENLIER	UNREFUTED
UNORDERS	UNPERVERT	UNPOPULAR	UNQUEENLIEST	UNREIN
UNOWED	UNPERVERTED	UNPOSED	UNQUEENLY	UNREINED
UNOWNED	UNPERVERTING	UNPOSTED	UNQUEENS	UNREINING
UNPACK	UNPERVERTS	UNPOTABLE	UNQUELLED	UNREINS
UNPACKED	UNPICK	UNPRAISE	UNQUIET	UNRELATED
UNPACKER	UNPICKED	UNPRAISED	UNQUIETED	UNRELAXED
UNPACKERS	UNPICKING	UNPRAISES	UNQUIETING	UNREMOVED
UNPACKING	UNPICKS	UNPRAISING	UNQUIETLY	UNRENEWED
UNPACKINGS	UNPIERCED	UNPRAY	UNQUIETS	UNRENT
UNPACKS	UNPILOTED	UNPRAYED	UNQUOTE	UNREPAID
UNPAGED	UNPIN	UNPRAYING	UNQUOTED	UNREPAIR
UNPAID	UNPINKED	UNPRAYS	UNQUOTES	UNREPAIRS
UNPAINED	UNPINKT	UNPREACH	UNQUOTING	UNRESERVE
UNPAINFUL	UNPINNED	UNPREACHED	UNRACED	UNRESERVES
UNPAINT	UNPINNING	UNPREACHES	UNRACKED	UNREST
UNPAINTED	UNPINS	UNPREACHING	UNRAISED	UNRESTFUL
UNPAINTING	UNPITIED	UNPRECISE	UNRAKE	UNRESTING
UNPAINTS	UNPITIFUL	UNPREDICT	UNRAKED	UNRESTS
UNPAIRED	UNPITYING	UNPREDICTED	UNRAKES	UNREVISED
UNPALSIED	UNPLACE	UNPREDICTING	UNRAKING	UNREVOKED
UNPANEL	UNPLACED	UNPREDICTS	UNRATED	UNRHYMED
UNPANELLED	UNPLACES	UNPREPARE	UNRAVEL	UNRIBBED
UNPANELLING	UNPLACING	UNPREPARED	UNRAVELLED	UNRID
UNPANELS	UNPLAGUED	UNPREPARES	UNRAVELLING	UNRIDABLE
UNPANGED	UNPLAINED	UNPREPARING	UNRAVELLINGS	UNRIDDEN
UNPANNEL	UNPLAIT	UNPRESSED	UNRAVELS	UNRIDDLE
UNPANNELLED	UNPLAITED	UNPRETTY	UNRAZORED	UNRIDDLED
UNPANNELLING	UNPLAITING	UNPRICED	UNREACHED	UNRIDDLER
UNPANNELS	UNPLAITS	UNPRIEST	UNREAD	UNRIDDLERS
UNPAPER	UNPLANKED	UNPRIESTED	UNREADIER	UNRIDDLES
UNPAPERED	UNPLANNED	UNPRIESTING	UNREADIEST	UNRIDDLING
UNPAPERING	UNPLANTED	UNPRIESTS	UNREADILY	UNRIFLED
UNPAPERS	UNPLEASED	UNPRIMED	UNREADY	UNRIG
UNPARED	UNPLEATED	UNPRINTED	UNREAL	UNRIGGED
UNPARTIAL	UNPLEDGED	UNPRISON	UNREALISE	UNRIGGING
UNPATHED	UNPLIABLE	UNPRISONED	UNREALISED	UNRIGHT
UNPAVED	UNPLIABLY	UNPRISONING	UNREALISES	UNRIGHTS
UNPAY	UNPLIANT	UNPRISONS	UNREALISING	UNRIGS
UNPAYABLE	UNPLUCKED	UNPRIZED	UNREALISM	UNRIMED
UNPAYING	UNPLUG	UNPROP	UNREALISMS	UNRINGED
UNPAYS	UNPLUGGED	UNPROPER	UNREALITIES	UNRIP
UNPEELED	UNPLUGGING	UNPROPPED	UNREALITY	UNRIPE
UNPEERED	UNPLUGS	UNPROPPING	UNREALIZE	UNRIPENED
UNPEG	UNPLUMB	UNPROPS	UNREALIZED	UNRIPER
UNPEGGED	UNPLUMBED	UNPROVED	UNREALIZES	UNRIPEST
UNPEGGING	UNPLUMBING	UNPROVEN	UNREALIZING	UNRIPPED
UNPEGS	UNPLUMBS	UNPROVIDE	UNREALLY	UNRIPPING
UNPEN	UNPLUME	UNPROVIDED	UNREAPED	UNRIPPINGS
UNPENNED	UNPLUMED	UNPROVIDES	UNREASON	UNRIPS
UNPENNIED	UNPLUMES	UNPROVIDING	UNREASONS	UNRISEN
UNPENNING	UNPLUMING	UNPROVOKE	UNREAVE	UNRIVEN
UNPENS	UNPOETIC	UNPROVOKED	UNREAVED	UNRIVET
UNPENT	UNPOINTED	UNPROVOKES	UNREAVES	UNRIVETED
UNPEOPLE	UNPOISED	UNPROVOKING	UNREAVING	UNRIVETING
UNPEOPLED	UNPOISON	UNPRUNED	UNREBATED	UNRIVETS

UNROBE
UNROBED
UNROBES
UNROBING
UNROLL
UNROLLED
UNROLLING
UNROLLS
UNROOF
UNROOFED
UNROOFING
UNROOFS
UNROOST
UNROOSTED
UNROOSTING
UNROOSTS
UNROOT
UNROOTED
UNROOTING
UNROOTS
UNROPE
UNROPED
UNROPES
UNROPING
UNROSINED
UNROTTED
UNROTTEN
UNROUGED
UNROUGH
UNROUND
UNROUNDED
UNROUNDING
UNROUNDS
UNROUSED
UNROYAL
UNROYALLY
UNRUBBED
UNRUDE
UNRUFFE
UNRUFFLE
UNRUFFLED
UNRUFFLES
UNRUFFLING
UNRULE
UNRULED
UNRULES
UNRULIER
UNRULIEST
UNRULY
UNRUMPLED
UNS
UNSADDLE
UNSADDLED
UNSADDLES
UNSADDLING
UNSAFE
UNSAFELY
UNSAFER
UNSAFEST
UNSAFETIES
UNSAFETY
UNSAID
UNSAILED
UNSAINED
UNSAINT
UNSAINTED
UNSAINTING
UNSAINTLIER
UNSAINTLIEST
UNSAINTLY

UNSAINTS
UNSALABLE
UNSALTED
UNSALUTED
UNSAPPED
UNSASHED
UNSATABLE
UNSATED
UNSATIATE
UNSATING
UNSAVED
UNSAVOURY
UNSAY
UNSAYABLE
UNSAYING
UNSAYS
UNSCALE
UNSCALED
UNSCALES
UNSCALING
UNSCANNED
UNSCARRED
UNSCATHED
UNSCENTED
UNSCOURED
UNSCREW
UNSCREWED
UNSCREWING
UNSCREWS
UNSCYTHED
UNSEAL
UNSEALED
UNSEALING
UNSEALS
UNSEAM
UNSEAMED
UNSEAMING
UNSEAMS
UNSEASON
UNSEASONED
UNSEASONING
UNSEASONS
UNSEAT
UNSEATED
UNSEATING
UNSEATS
UNSECRET
UNSECULAR
UNSECURED
UNSEDUCED
UNSEEABLE
UNSEEDED
UNSEEING
UNSEEL
UNSEELED
UNSEELING
UNSEELS
UNSEEMING
UNSEEMINGS
UNSEEMLIER
UNSEEMLIEST
UNSEEMLY
UNSEEN
UNSEENS
UNSEIZED
UNSELDOM
UNSELF
UNSELFED
UNSELFING
UNSELFISH

UNSELFS
UNSELVES
UNSENSE
UNSENSED
UNSENSES
UNSENSING
UNSENT
UNSERIOUS
UNSET
UNSETS
UNSETTING
UNSETTLE
UNSETTLED
UNSETTLES
UNSETTLING
UNSEVERED
UNSEW
UNSEWED
UNSEWING
UNSEWN
UNSEWS
UNSEX
UNSEXED
UNSEXES
UNSEXING
UNSEXIST
UNSEXUAL
UNSHACKLE
UNSHACKLED
UNSHACKLES
UNSHACKLING
UNSHADED
UNSHADOW
UNSHADOWED
UNSHADOWING
UNSHADOWS
UNSHAKED
UNSHAKEN
UNSHALE
UNSHALED
UNSHALES
UNSHALING
UNSHAMED
UNSHAPE
UNSHAPED
UNSHAPELIER
UNSHAPELIEST
UNSHAPELY
UNSHAPEN
UNSHAPES
UNSHAPING
UNSHARED
UNSHAVED
UNSHAVEN
UNSHEATHE
UNSHEATHED
UNSHEATHES
UNSHEATHING
UNSHED
UNSHELL
UNSHELLED
UNSHELLING
UNSHELLS
UNSHENT
UNSHEWN
UNSHIP
UNSHIPPED
UNSHIPPING
UNSHIPS
UNSHOCKED

UNSHOD
UNSHOE
UNSHOED
UNSHOEING
UNSHOES
UNSHOOT
UNSHOOTED
UNSHOOTING
UNSHOOTS
UNSHORN
UNSHOT
UNSHOUT
UNSHOUTED
UNSHOUTING
UNSHOUTS
UNSHOWN
UNSHRIVED
UNSHRIVEN
UNSHROUD
UNSHROUDED
UNSHROUDING
UNSHROUDS
UNSHRUBD
UNSHUNNED
UNSHUT
UNSHUTS
UNSHUTTER
UNSHUTTERED
UNSHUTTERING
UNSHUTTERS
UNSHUTTING
UNSICKER
UNSICKLED
UNSIFTED
UNSIGHING
UNSIGHT
UNSIGHTED
UNSIGHTLIER
UNSIGHTLIEST
UNSIGHTLY
UNSIGNED
UNSINEW
UNSINEWED
UNSINEWING
UNSINEWS
UNSISTING
UNSIZABLE
UNSIZED
UNSKILFUL
UNSKILLED
UNSKIMMED
UNSKINNED
UNSLAIN
UNSLAKED
UNSLING
UNSLINGING
UNSLINGS
UNSLUICE
UNSLUICED
UNSLUICES
UNSLUICING
UNSLUNG
UNSMART
UNSMILING
UNSMITTEN
UNSMOOTH
UNSMOOTHED
UNSMOOTHING
UNSMOOTHS
UNSMOTE

UNSNAP
UNSNAPPED
UNSNAPPING
UNSNAPS
UNSNARL
UNSNARLED
UNSNARLING
UNSNARLS
UNSNECK
UNSNECKED
UNSNECKING
UNSNECKS
UNSNUFFED
UNSOAPED
UNSOCIAL
UNSOCKET
UNSOCKETED
UNSOCKETING
UNSOCKETS
UNSOD
UNSODDEN
UNSOFT
UNSOILED
UNSOLACED
UNSOLD
UNSOLDER
UNSOLDERED
UNSOLDERING
UNSOLDERS
UNSOLEMN
UNSOLID
UNSOLIDLY
UNSOLVED
UNSONSY
UNSOOTE
UNSORTED
UNSOUGHT
UNSOUL
UNSOULED
UNSOULING
UNSOULS
UNSOUND
UNSOUNDED
UNSOUNDER
UNSOUNDEST
UNSOUNDLY
UNSOURCED
UNSOURED
UNSOWN
UNSPAR
UNSPARED
UNSPARING
UNSPARRED
UNSPARRING
UNSPARS
UNSPEAK
UNSPEAKING
UNSPEAKS
UNSPED
UNSPELL
UNSPELLED
UNSPELLING
UNSPELLS
UNSPENT
UNSPHERE
UNSPHERED
UNSPHERES
UNSPHERING
UNSPIDE
UNSPIED

UNSPILLED	UNSTOWS	UNTAMABLE	UNTHRONES	UNTRUSSER
UNSPILT	UNSTRAP	UNTAMABLY	UNTHRONING	UNTRUSSERS
UNSPOILED	UNSTRAPPED	UNTAME	UNTIDIED	UNTRUSSES
UNSPOILT	UNSTRAPPING	UNTAMED	UNTIDIER	UNTRUSSING
UNSPOKE	UNSTRAPS	UNTAMES	UNTIDIES	UNTRUSSINGS
UNSPOKEN	UNSTRING	UNTAMING	UNTIDIEST	UNTRUST
UNSPOTTED	UNSTRINGED	UNTANGLE	UNTIDILY	UNTRUSTS
UNSPRUNG	UNSTRINGING	UNTANGLED	UNTIDY	UNTRUSTY
UNSPUN	UNSTRINGS	UNTANGLES	UNTIDYING	UNTRUTH
UNSQUARED	UNSTRIP	UNTANGLING	UNTIE	UNTRUTHS
UNSTABLE	UNSTRIPED	UNTANNED	UNTIED	UNTUCK
UNSTABLER	UNSTRIPPED	UNTAPPED	UNTIES	UNTUCKED
UNSTABLEST	UNSTRIPPING	UNTARRED	UNTIL	UNTUCKING
UNSTACK	UNSTRIPS	UNTASTED	UNTILE	UNTUCKS
UNSTACKED	UNSTRUCK	UNTAUGHT	UNTILED	UNTUMBLED
UNSTACKING	UNSTRUNG	UNTAX	UNTILES	UNTUNABLE
UNSTACKS	UNSTUCK	UNTAXED	UNTILING	UNTUNABLY
UNSTAID	UNSTUDIED	UNTAXES	UNTILLED	UNTUNE
UNSTAINED	UNSTUFFED	UNTAXING	UNTIMELIER	UNTUNED
UNSTAMPED	UNSTUFFY	UNTEACH	UNTIMELIEST	UNTUNEFUL
UNSTARCH	UNSTUFT	UNTEACHES	UNTIMELY	UNTUNES
UNSTARCHED	UNSUBDUED	UNTEACHING	UNTIMEOUS	UNTUNING
UNSTARCHES	UNSUBJECT	UNTEAM	UNTIN	UNTURBID
UNSTARCHING	UNSUBTLE	UNTEAMED	UNTINGED	UNTURF
UNSTATE	UNSUCCESS	UNTEAMING	UNTINNED	UNTURFED
UNSTATED	UNSUCCESSES	UNTEAMS	UNTINNING	UNTURFING
UNSTATES	UNSUCKED	UNTEMPER	UNTINS	UNTURFS
UNSTATING	UNSUIT	UNTEMPERED	UNTIRABLE	UNTURN
UNSTAYED	UNSUITED	UNTEMPERING	UNTIRED	UNTURNED
UNSTAYING	UNSUITING	UNTEMPERS	UNTIRING	UNTURNING
UNSTEADIED	UNSUITS	UNTEMPTED	UNTITLED	UNTURNS
UNSTEADIER	UNSULLIED	UNTENABLE	UNTO	UNTUTORED
UNSTEADIES	UNSUMMED	UNTENANT	UNTOILING	UNTWINE
UNSTEADIEST	UNSUNG	UNTENANTED	UNTOLD	UNTWINED
UNSTEADY	UNSUNNED	UNTENANTING	UNTOMB	UNTWINES
UNSTEADYING	UNSUNNY	UNTENANTS	UNTOMBED	UNTWINING
UNSTEEL	UNSUPPLE	UNTENDED	UNTOMBING	UNTWIST
UNSTEELED	UNSURE	UNTENDER	UNTOMBS	UNTWISTED
UNSTEELING	UNSURED	UNTENT	UNTONED	UNTWISTING
UNSTEELS	UNSURER	UNTENTED	UNTORN	UNTWISTINGS
UNSTEP	UNSUREST	UNTENTING	UNTOUCHED	UNTWISTS
UNSTEPPED	UNSUSPECT	UNTENTS	UNTOWARD	UNTYING
UNSTEPPING	UNSWADDLE	UNTENTY	UNTRACE	UNTYINGS
UNSTEPS	UNSWADDLED	UNTESTED	UNTRACED	UNTYPABLE
UNSTERILE	UNSWADDLES	UNTETHER	UNTRACES	UNTYPICAL
UNSTICK	UNSWADDLING	UNTETHERED	UNTRACING	UNURGED
UNSTICKING	UNSWATHE	UNTETHERING	UNTRACKED	UNUSABLE
UNSTICKS	UNSWATHED	UNTETHERS	UNTRADED	UNUSABLY
UNSTIFLED	UNSWATHES	UNTHANKED	UNTRAINED	UNUSED
UNSTILLED	UNSWATHING	UNTHATCH	UNTREAD	UNUSEFUL
UNSTINTED	UNSWAYED	UNTHATCHED	UNTREADING	UNUSHERED
UNSTITCH	UNSWEAR	UNTHATCHES	UNTREADS	UNUSUAL
UNSTITCHED	UNSWEARING	UNTHATCHING	UNTREATED	UNUSUALLY
UNSTITCHES	UNSWEARINGS	UNTHAW	UNTRESSED	UNUTTERED
UNSTITCHING	UNSWEARS	UNTHAWED	UNTRIDE	UNVAIL
UNSTOCK	UNSWEET	UNTHAWING	UNTRIED	UNVAILE
UNSTOCKED	UNSWEPT	UNTHAWS	UNTRIM	UNVAILED
UNSTOCKING	UNSWORE	UNTHINK	UNTRIMMED	UNVAILES
UNSTOCKS	UNSWORN	UNTHINKING	UNTRIMMING	UNVAILING
UNSTOP	UNTACK	UNTHINKS	UNTRIMS	UNVAILS
UNSTOPPED	UNTACKED	UNTHOUGHT	UNTROD	UNVALUED
UNSTOPPER	UNTACKING	UNTHREAD	UNTRODDEN	UNVARIED
UNSTOPPERED	UNTACKLE	UNTHREADED	UNTRUE	UNVARYING
UNSTOPPERING	UNTACKLED	UNTHREADING	UNTRUER	UNVEIL
UNSTOPPERS	UNTACKLES	UNTHREADS	UNTRUEST	UNVEILED
UNSTOPPING	UNTACKLING	UNTHRIFT	UNTRUISM	UNVEILER
UNSTOPS	UNTACKS	UNTHRIFTS	UNTRUISMS	UNVEILERS
UNSTOW	UNTAILED	UNTHRIFTY	UNTRULY	UNVEILING
UNSTOWED	UNTAINTED	UNTHRONE	UNTRUSS	UNVEILINGS
UNSTOWING	UNTAKEN	UNTHRONED	UNTRUSSED	UNVEILS

UNVENTED	UNWEENED	UNWOODED	UPBOIL	UPCURLING
UNVERSED	UNWEETING	UNWOOED	UPBOILED	UPCURLS
UNVEXED	UNWEIGHED	UNWORDED	UPBOILING	UPCURVED
UNVIABLE	UNWELCOME	UNWORK	UPBOILS	UPDATE
UNVIEWED	UNWELDY	UNWORKED	UPBORE	UPDATED
UNVIRTUE	UNWELL	UNWORKING	UPBORNE	UPDATES
UNVIRTUES	UNWEPT	UNWORKS	UPBOUND	UPDATING
UNVISITED	UNWET	UNWORLDLIER	UPBOUNDEN	UPDRAG
UNVISOR	UNWETTED	UNWORLDLIEST	UPBRAID	UPDRAGGED
UNVISORED	UNWHIPPED	UNWORLDLY	UPBRAIDED	UPDRAGGING
UNVISORING	UNWHIPT	UNWORMED	UPBRAIDER	UPDRAGS
UNVISORS	UNWIELDIER	UNWORN	UPBRAIDERS	UPDRAW
UNVITAL	UNWIELDIEST	UNWORRIED	UPBRAIDING	UPDRAWING
UNVIZARD	UNWIELDY	UNWORTH	UPBRAIDINGS	UPDRAWN
UNVIZARDED	UNWIFELIER	UNWORTHIER	UPBRAIDS	UPDRAWS
UNVIZARDING	UNWIFELIEST	UNWORTHIEST	UPBRAST	UPDREW
UNVIZARDS	UNWIFELY	UNWORTHS	UPBRAY	UPFILL
UNVOCAL	UNWIGGED	UNWORTHY	UPBRAYED	UPFILLED
UNVOICE	UNWILFUL	UNWOUND	UPBRAYING	UPFILLING
UNVOICED	UNWILL	UNWOUNDED	UPBRAYS	UPFILLINGS
UNVOICES	UNWILLED	UNWOVEN	UPBREAK	UPFILLS
UNVOICING	UNWILLING	UNWRAP	UPBREAKING	UPFLOW
UNVOICINGS	UNWILLS	UNWRAPPED	UPBREAKS	UPFLOWED
UNVULGAR	UNWIND	UNWRAPPING	UPBRING	UPFLOWING
UNWAGED	UNWINDING	UNWRAPS	UPBRINGING	UPFLOWS
UNWAKED	UNWINDINGS	UNWREAKED	UPBRINGINGS	UPFLUNG
UNWAKENED	UNWINDS	UNWREATHE	UPBRINGS	UPFOLLOW
UNWALLED	UNWINGED	UNWREATHED	UPBROKE	UPFOLLOWED
UNWANTED	UNWINKING	UNWREATHES	UPBROKEN	UPFOLLOWING
UNWARDED	UNWIPED	UNWREATHING	UPBROUGHT	UPFOLLOWS
UNWARE	UNWIRE	UNWRINKLE	UPBUILD	UPFRONT
UNWARELY	UNWIRED	UNWRINKLED	UPBUILDING	UPFURL
UNWARES	UNWIRES	UNWRINKLES	UPBUILDINGS	UPFURLED
UNWARIE	UNWIRING	UNWRINKLING	UPBUILDS	UPFURLING
UNWARIER	UNWISDOM	UNWRITE	UPBUILT	UPFURLS
UNWARIEST	UNWISDOMS	UNWRITES	UPBURNING	UPGANG
UNWARILY	UNWISE	UNWRITING	UPBURST	UPGANGS
UNWARLIKE	UNWISELY	UNWRITTEN	UPBURSTING	UPGATHER
UNWARMED	UNWISER	UNWROTE	UPBURSTS	UPGATHERED
UNWARNED	UNWISEST	UNWROUGHT	UPBY	UPGATHERING
UNWARPED	UNWISH	UNWRUNG	UPBYE	UPGATHERS
UNWARY	UNWISHED	UNYEANED	UPCAST	UPGAZE
UNWASHED	UNWISHES	UNYOKE	UPCASTING	UPGAZED
UNWASHEN	UNWISHFUL	UNYOKED	UPCASTS	UPGAZES
UNWASTED	UNWISHING	UNYOKES	UPCATCH	UPGAZING
UNWASTING	UNWIST	UNYOKING	UPCATCHES	UPGO
UNWATCHED	UNWIT	UNZEALOUS	UPCATCHING	UPGOES
UNWATER	UNWITCH	UNZIP	UPCAUGHT	UPGOING
UNWATERED	UNWITCHED	UNZIPPED	UPCHEARD	UPGOINGS
UNWATERING	UNWITCHES	UNZIPPING	UPCHEER	UPGONE
UNWATERS	UNWITCHING	UNZIPS	UPCHEERED	UPGRADE
UNWATERY	UNWITS	UNZONED	UPCHEERING	UPGRADED
UNWAYED	UNWITTED	UP	UPCHEERS	UPGRADES
UNWEAL	UNWITTILY	UPADAISY	UPCLIMB	UPGRADING
UNWEALS	UNWITTING	UPAITHRIC	UPCLIMBED	UPGREW
UNWEANED	UNWITTY	UPAS	UPCLIMBING	UPGROW
UNWEAPON	UNWIVE	UPASES	UPCLIMBS	UPGROWING
UNWEAPONED	UNWIVED	UPBEAR	UPCLOSE	UPGROWINGS
UNWEAPONING	UNWIVES	UPBEARING	UPCLOSED	UPGROWN
UNWEAPONS	UNWIVING	UPBEARS	UPCLOSES	UPGROWS
UNWEARIED	UNWOMAN	UPBEAT	UPCLOSING	UPGROWTH
UNWEARY	UNWOMANED	UPBEATS	UPCOAST	UPGROWTHS
UNWEAVE	UNWOMANING	UPBIND	UPCOIL	UPGUSH
UNWEAVED	UNWOMANLIER	UPBINDING	UPCOILED	UPGUSHED
UNWEAVES	UNWOMANLIEST	UPBINDS	UPCOILING	UPGUSHES
UNWEAVING	UNWOMANLY	UPBLEW	UPCOILS	UPGUSHING
UNWEBBED	UNWOMANS	UPBLOW	UPCOME	UPHAND
UNWED	UNWON	UPBLOWING	UPCOMES	UPHANG
UNWEDDED	UNWONT	UPBLOWN	UPCURL	UPHANGING
UNWEEDED	UNWONTED	UPBLOWS	UPCURLED	UPHANGS

UPHAUD
UPHAUDED
UPHAUDING
UPHAUDS
UPHEAP
UPHEAPED
UPHEAPING
UPHEAPINGS
UPHEAPS
UPHEAVAL
UPHEAVALS
UPHEAVE
UPHEAVED
UPHEAVES
UPHEAVING
UPHELD
UPHILD
UPHILL
UPHILLS
UPHOARD
UPHOARDED
UPHOARDING
UPHOARDS
UPHOIST
UPHOISTED
UPHOISTING
UPHOISTS
UPHOLD
UPHOLDER
UPHOLDERS
UPHOLDING
UPHOLDINGS
UPHOLDS
UPHOLSTER
UPHOLSTERED
UPHOLSTERING
UPHOLSTERS
UPHOORD
UPHOORDED
UPHOORDING
UPHOORDS
UPHROE
UPHROES
UPHUNG
UPHURL
UPHURLED
UPHURLING
UPHURLS
UPJET
UPJETS
UPJETTED
UPJETTING
UPKEEP
UPKEEPS
UPKNIT
UPKNITS
UPKNITTED
UPKNITTING
UPLAID
UPLAND
UPLANDER
UPLANDERS
UPLANDISH
UPLANDS
UPLAY
UPLAYING
UPLAYS
UPLEAD
UPLEADING
UPLEADS

UPLEAN
UPLEANED
UPLEANING
UPLEANS
UPLEANT
UPLEAP
UPLEAPED
UPLEAPING
UPLEAPS
UPLEAPT
UPLED
UPLIFT
UPLIFTED
UPLIFTER
UPLIFTERS
UPLIFTING
UPLIFTINGS
UPLIFTS
UPLIGHTED
UPLIGHTER
UPLIGHTERS
UPLOCK
UPLOCKED
UPLOCKING
UPLOCKS
UPLOOK
UPLOOKED
UPLOOKING
UPLOOKS
UPLYING
UPMAKE
UPMAKER
UPMAKERS
UPMAKES
UPMAKING
UPMAKINGS
UPMOST
UPON
UPPED
UPPER
UPPERMOST
UPPERS
UPPILED
UPPING
UPPINGS
UPPISH
UPPISHLY
UPPITY
UPRAISE
UPRAISED
UPRAISES
UPRAISING
UPRAN
UPRATE
UPRATED
UPRATES
UPRATING
UPREAR
UPREARED
UPREARING
UPREARS
UPREST
UPRESTS
UPRIGHT
UPRIGHTED
UPRIGHTING
UPRIGHTLY
UPRIGHTS
UPRISAL
UPRISALS

UPRISE
UPRISEN
UPRISES
UPRISING
UPRISINGS
UPRIST
UPRISTS
UPRIVER
UPROAR
UPROARED
UPROARING
UPROARS
UPROLL
UPROLLED
UPROLLING
UPROLLS
UPROOT
UPROOTAL
UPROOTALS
UPROOTED
UPROOTER
UPROOTERS
UPROOTING
UPROOTINGS
UPROOTS
UPROSE
UPROUSE
UPROUSED
UPROUSES
UPROUSING
UPRUN
UPRUNNING
UPRUNS
UPRUSH
UPRUSHED
UPRUSHES
UPRUSHING
UPRYST
UPS
UPSEE
UPSEES
UPSEND
UPSENDING
UPSENDS
UPSENT
UPSET
UPSETS
UPSETTER
UPSETTERS
UPSETTING
UPSETTINGS
UPSEY
UPSEYS
UPSHOOT
UPSHOOTING
UPSHOOTS
UPSHOT
UPSHOTS
UPSIDE
UPSIDES
UPSIES
UPSILON
UPSILONS
UPSITTING
UPSITTINGS
UPSPAKE
UPSPEAK
UPSPEAKING
UPSPEAKS
UPSPEAR

UPSPEARED
UPSPEARING
UPSPEARS
UPSPOKE
UPSPOKEN
UPSPRANG
UPSPRING
UPSPRINGING
UPSPRINGS
UPSPRUNG
UPSTAGE
UPSTAGED
UPSTAGES
UPSTAGING
UPSTAIR
UPSTAIRS
UPSTAND
UPSTANDING
UPSTANDS
UPSTARE
UPSTARED
UPSTARES
UPSTARING
UPSTART
UPSTARTED
UPSTARTING
UPSTARTS
UPSTATE
UPSTAY
UPSTAYED
UPSTAYING
UPSTAYS
UPSTOOD
UPSTREAM
UPSTREAMED
UPSTREAMING
UPSTREAMS
UPSTROKE
UPSTROKES
UPSURGE
UPSURGED
UPSURGES
UPSURGING
UPSWARM
UPSWARMED
UPSWARMING
UPSWARMS
UPSWAY
UPSWAYED
UPSWAYING
UPSWAYS
UPSWEEP
UPSWEEPS
UPSWELL
UPSWELLED
UPSWELLING
UPSWELLS
UPSWEPT
UPSWING
UPSWINGS
UPSY
UPTAK
UPTAKE
UPTAKEN
UPTAKES
UPTAKING
UPTAKS
UPTEAR
UPTEARING
UPTEARS

UPTHREW
UPTHROW
UPTHROWING
UPTHROWN
UPTHROWS
UPTHRUST
UPTHRUSTED
UPTHRUSTING
UPTHRUSTS
UPTHUNDER
UPTHUNDERED
UPTHUNDERING
UPTHUNDERS
UPTIE
UPTIED
UPTIES
UPTIGHT
UPTIGHTER
UPTIGHTEST
UPTILT
UPTILTED
UPTILTING
UPTILTS
UPTOOK
UPTORE
UPTORN
UPTOWN
UPTOWNS
UPTRAIN
UPTRAINED
UPTRAINING
UPTRAINS
UPTREND
UPTRENDS
UPTRILLED
UPTURN
UPTURNED
UPTURNING
UPTURNINGS
UPTURNS
UPTYING
UPVALUE
UPVALUED
UPVALUES
UPVALUING
UPWAFT
UPWAFTED
UPWAFTING
UPWAFTS
UPWARD
UPWARDLY
UPWARDS
UPWELL
UPWELLED
UPWELLING
UPWELLINGS
UPWELLS
UPWENT
UPWHIRL
UPWHIRLED
UPWHIRLING
UPWHIRLS
UPWIND
UPWINDING
UPWINDS
UPWOUND
UPWROUGHT
UR
URACHUS
URACHUSES

URACIL
URACILS
URAEMIA
URAEMIAS
URAEMIC
URAEUS
URAEUSES
URALI
URALIS
URALITE
URALITES
URALITIC
URALITISE
URALITISED
URALITISES
URALITISING
URALITIZE
URALITIZED
URALITIZES
URALITIZING
URANIAN
URANIC
URANIDE
URANIDES
URANIN
URANINITE
URANINITES
URANINS
URANISCUS
URANISCUSES
URANISM
URANISMS
URANITE
URANITES
URANITIC
URANIUM
URANIUMS
URANOLOGIES
URANOLOGY
URANOUS
URANYL
URANYLS
URAO
URAOS
URARI
URARIS
URATE
URATES
URBAN
URBANE
URBANELY
URBANER
URBANEST
URBANISE
URBANISED
URBANISES
URBANISING
URBANITE
URBANITES
URBANITIES
URBANITY
URBANIZE
URBANIZED
URBANIZES
URBANIZING
URCEOLATE
URCEOLI
URCEOLUS
URCEOLUSES
URCHIN

URCHINS
URD
URDÉ
URDEE
URDÉE
URDS
URDY
URE
UREA
UREAL
UREAS
UREDIA
UREDINE
UREDINES
UREDINIA
UREDINIAL
UREDINIUM
UREDINOUS
UREDIUM
UREDO
UREIDE
UREIDES
UREMIA
UREMIAS
UREMIC
URENA
URENAS
URENT
URES
URESES
URESIS
URETER
URETERAL
URETERIC
URETERS
URETHAN
URETHANE
URETHANES
URETHANS
URETHRA
URETHRAE
URETHRAL
URETHRAS
URETIC
URGE
URGED
URGENCE
URGENCES
URGENCIES
URGENCY
URGENT
URGENTLY
URGER
URGERS
URGES
URGING
URGINGS
URIAL
URIALS
URIC
URICASE
URICASES
URIDINE
URIDINES
URINAL
URINALS
URINANT
URINARIES
URINARY
URINATE

URINATED
URINATES
URINATING
URINATION
URINATIONS
URINATIVE
URINATOR
URINATORS
URINE
URINED
URINES
URINING
URINOLOGIES
URINOLOGY
URINOUS
URITE
URITES
URMAN
URMANS
URN
URNAL
URNED
URNFIELD
URNFIELDS
URNFUL
URNFULS
URNING
URNINGS
URNS
UROCHORD
UROCHORDS
UROCHROME
UROCHROMES
URODELAN
URODELANS
URODELE
URODELES
URODELOUS
UROGRAPHIES
UROGRAPHY
UROKINASE
UROKINASES
UROLAGNIA
UROLAGNIAS
UROLITH
UROLITHS
UROLOGIC
UROLOGIES
UROLOGIST
UROLOGISTS
UROLOGY
UROMERE
UROMERES
UROPOD
UROPODS
UROPYGIAL
UROPYGIUM
UROPYGIUMS
UROSCOPIES
UROSCOPY
UROSES
UROSIS
UROSOME
UROSOMES
UROSTEGE
UROSTEGES
UROSTYLE
UROSTYLES
URSINE
URSON

URSONS
URTICA
URTICANT
URTICARIA
URTICARIAS
URTICAS
URTICATE
URTICATED
URTICATES
URTICATING
URUBU
URUBUS
URUS
URUSES
URVA
URVAS
US
USABLE
USAGE
USAGER
USAGERS
USAGES
USANCE
USANCES
USE
USED
USEFUL
USEFULLY
USELESS
USELESSLY
USER
USERS
USES
USHER
USHERED
USHERESS
USHERESSES
USHERETTE
USHERETTES
USHERING
USHERINGS
USHERS
USHERSHIP
USHERSHIPS
USING
USNEA
USNEAS
USTION
USTIONS
USUAL
USUALLY
USUALNESS
USUALNESSES
USUALS
USUCAPION
USUCAPIONS
USUCAPT
USUCAPTED
USUCAPTING
USUCAPTS
USUFRUCT
USUFRUCTED
USUFRUCTING
USUFRUCTS
USURE
USURED
USURER
USURERS
USURES
USURESS

USURESSES
USURIES
USURING
USURIOUS
USUROUS
USURP
USURPED
USURPEDLY
USURPER
USURPERS
USURPING
USURPS
USURY
USWARD
USWARDS
UT
UTAS
UTASES
UTE
UTENSIL
UTENSILS
UTERI
UTERINE
UTERITIS
UTERITISES
UTEROTOMIES
UTEROTOMY
UTERUS
UTES
UTILE
UTILISE
UTILISED
UTILISER
UTILISERS
UTILISES
UTILISING
UTILITIES
UTILITY
UTILIZE
UTILIZED
UTILIZER
UTILIZERS
UTILIZES
UTILIZING
UTIS
UTISES
UTMOST
UTMOSTS
UTOPIA
UTOPIAN
UTOPIANS
UTOPIAS
UTOPIAST
UTOPIASTS
UTOPISM
UTOPISMS
UTOPIST
UTOPISTS
UTRICLE
UTRICLES
UTRICULAR
UTRICULI
UTRICULUS
UTS
UTTER
UTTERABLE
UTTERANCE
UTTERANCES
UTTERED
UTTERER

UTTERERS
UTTEREST
UTTERING
UTTERINGS
UTTERLESS
UTTERLY
UTTERMOST

UTTERNESS
UTTERNESSES
UTTERS
UTU
UTUS
UVA
UVAROVITE

UVAROVITES
UVAS
UVEA
UVEAL
UVEAS
UVEITIS
UVEITISES

UVULA
UVULAE
UVULAR
UVULARLY
UVULAS
UVULITIS
UVULITISES

UXORIAL
UXORICIDE
UXORICIDES
UXORIOUS

V

VAC
VACANCE
VACANCES
VACANCIES
VACANCY
VACANT
VACANTLY
VACATE
VACATED
VACATES
VACATING
VACATION
VACATIONED
VACATIONING
VACATIONS
VACATUR
VACATURS
VACCINAL
VACCINATE
VACCINATED
VACCINATES
VACCINATING
VACCINE
VACCINES
VACCINIA
VACCINIAL
VACCINIAS
VACCINIUM
VACCINIUMS
VACHERIN
VACHERINS
VACILLANT
VACILLATE
VACILLATED
VACILLATES
VACILLATING
VACKED
VACKING
VACS
VACUA
VACUATE
VACUATED
VACUATES
VACUATING
VACUATION
VACUATIONS
VACUIST
VACUISTS
VACUITIES
VACUITY
VACUOLAR
VACUOLATE
VACUOLE
VACUOLES
VACUOUS
VACUOUSLY
VACUUM
VACUUMED
VACUUMING
VACUUMS
VADE
VADED
VADES
VADING

VAE
VAES
VAGABOND
VAGABONDED
VAGABONDING
VAGABONDS
VAGAL
VAGARIES
VAGARIOUS
VAGARISH
VAGARY
VAGI
VAGILE
VAGILITIES
VAGILITY
VAGINA
VAGINAE
VAGINAL
VAGINALLY
VAGINANT
VAGINAS
VAGINATE
VAGINATED
VAGINITIS
VAGINITISES
VAGINULA
VAGINULAE
VAGINULE
VAGINULES
VAGITUS
VAGITUSES
VAGRANCIES
VAGRANCY
VAGRANT
VAGRANTS
VAGROM
VAGROMS
VAGUE
VAGUED
VAGUELY
VAGUENESS
VAGUENESSES
VAGUER
VAGUES
VAGUEST
VAGUING
VAGUS
VAHINE
VAHINES
VAIL
VAILED
VAILING
VAILS
VAIN
VAINER
VAINESSE
VAINESSES
VAINEST
VAINGLORIED
VAINGLORIES
VAINGLORY
VAINGLORYING
VAINLY
VAINNESS

VAINNESSES
VAIR
VAIRÉ
VAIRS
VAIRY
VAIVODE
VAIVODES
VAKASS
VAKASSES
VAKEEL
VAKEELS
VAKIL
VAKILS
VALANCE
VALANCED
VALANCES
VALE
VALENCE
VALENCES
VALENCIES
VALENCY
VALENTINE
VALENTINES
VALERIAN
VALERIANS
VALES
VALET
VALETA
VALETAS
VALETE
VALETED
VALETES
VALETING
VALETINGS
VALETS
VALGOUS
VALGUS
VALGUSES
VALI
VALIANCE
VALIANCES
VALIANCIES
VALIANCY
VALIANT
VALIANTLY
VALIANTS
VALID
VALIDATE
VALIDATED
VALIDATES
VALIDATING
VALIDER
VALIDEST
VALIDITIES
VALIDITY
VALIDLY
VALIDNESS
VALIDNESSES
VALINE
VALINES
VALIS
VALISE
VALISES
VALLAR

VALLARY
VALLECULA
VALLECULAE
VALLEY
VALLEYS
VALLONIA
VALLONIAS
VALLUM
VALLUMS
VALONEA
VALONEAS
VALONIA
VALONIAS
VALORISE
VALORISED
VALORISES
VALORISING
VALORIZE
VALORIZED
VALORIZES
VALORIZING
VALOROUS
VALOUR
VALOURS
VALSE
VALSED
VALSES
VALSING
VALUABLE
VALUABLES
VALUABLY
VALUATE
VALUATED
VALUATES
VALUATING
VALUATION
VALUATIONS
VALUATOR
VALUATORS
VALUE
VALUED
VALUELESS
VALUER
VALUERS
VALUES
VALUING
VALUTA
VALUTAS
VALVAL
VALVAR
VALVASSOR
VALVASSORS
VALVATE
VALVE
VALVED
VALVELESS
VALVELET
VALVELETS
VALVES
VALVING
VALVULA
VALVULAE
VALVULAR
VALVULE

VALVULES
VAMBRACE
VAMBRACED
VAMBRACES
VAMOOSE
VAMOOSED
VAMOOSES
VAMOOSING
VAMOSE
VAMOSED
VAMOSES
VAMOSING
VAMP
VAMPED
VAMPER
VAMPERS
VAMPING
VAMPINGS
VAMPIRE
VAMPIRED
VAMPIRES
VAMPIRIC
VAMPIRING
VAMPIRISE
VAMPIRISED
VAMPIRISES
VAMPIRISING
VAMPIRISM
VAMPIRISMS
VAMPIRIZE
VAMPIRIZED
VAMPIRIZES
VAMPIRIZING
VAMPISH
VAMPLATE
VAMPLATES
VAMPS
VAN
VANADATE
VANADATES
VANADIC
VANADIUM
VANADIUMS
VANADOUS
VANDAL
VANDALISE
VANDALISED
VANDALISES
VANDALISING
VANDALISM
VANDALISMS
VANDALIZE
VANDALIZED
VANDALIZES
VANDALIZING
VANDALS
VANDYKE
VANDYKED
VANDYKES
VANDYKING
VANE
VANED
VANELESS
VANES

VANESSA
VANESSAS
VANG
VANGS
VANGUARD
VANGUARDS
VANILLA
VANILLAS
VANILLIN
VANILLINS
VANISH
VANISHED
VANISHER
VANISHERS
VANISHES
VANISHING
VANISHINGS
VANITAS
VANITASES
VANITIES
VANITORIES
VANITORY
VANITY
VANNED
VANNER
VANNERS
VANNING
VANNINGS
VANQUISH
VANQUISHED
VANQUISHES
VANQUISHING
VANS
VANT
VANTAGE
VANTAGED
VANTAGES
VANTAGING
VANTBRACE
VANTBRACES
VANTS
VANWARD
VAPID
VAPIDER
VAPIDEST
VAPIDITIES
VAPIDITY
VAPIDLY
VAPIDNESS
VAPIDNESSES
VAPOR
VAPORABLE
VAPORED
VAPORETTI
VAPORETTO
VAPORETTOS
VAPORIFIC
VAPORING
VAPORISE
VAPORISED
VAPORISER
VAPORISERS
VAPORISES
VAPORISING
VAPORIZE
VAPORIZED
VAPORIZER
VAPORIZERS
VAPORIZES
VAPORIZING

VAPOROUS
VAPORS
VAPOUR
VAPOURED
VAPOURER
VAPOURERS
VAPOURING
VAPOURINGS
VAPOURISH
VAPOURS
VAPOURY
VAPULATE
VAPULATED
VAPULATES
VAPULATING
VAQUERO
VAQUEROS
VARA
VARACTOR
VARACTORS
VARAN
VARANS
VARAS
VARDIES
VARDY
VARE
VAREC
VARECH
VARECHS
VARECS
VARES
VAREUSE
VAREUSES
VARGUEÑO
VARGUEÑOS
VARIABLE
VARIABLES
VARIABLY
VARIANCE
VARIANCES
VARIANT
VARIANTS
VARIATE
VARIATED
VARIATES
VARIATING
VARIATION
VARIATIONS
VARIATIVE
VARICELLA
VARICELLAS
VARICES
VARICOSE
VARIED
VARIEDLY
VARIEGATE
VARIEGATED
VARIEGATES
VARIEGATING
VARIER
VARIERS
VARIES
VARIETAL
VARIETIES
VARIETY
VARIFORM
VARIOLA
VARIOLAR
VARIOLAS
VARIOLATE

VARIOLATED
VARIOLATES
VARIOLATING
VARIOLE
VARIOLES
VARIOLITE
VARIOLITES
VARIOLOID
VARIOLOUS
VARIORUM
VARIORUMS
VARIOUS
VARIOUSLY
VARISCITE
VARISCITES
VARISTOR
VARISTORS
VARIX
VARLET
VARLETESS
VARLETESSES
VARLETRIES
VARLETRY
VARLETS
VARLETTO
VARLETTOS
VARMENT
VARMENTS
VARMINT
VARMINTS
VARNA
VARNAS
VARNISH
VARNISHED
VARNISHER
VARNISHERS
VARNISHES
VARNISHING
VARNISHINGS
VARROA
VARROAS
VARSAL
VARSITIES
VARSITY
VARTABED
VARTABEDS
VARUS
VARUSES
VARVE
VARVED
VARVEL
VARVELLED
VARVELS
VARVES
VARY
VARYING
VARYINGS
VAS
VASA
VASAL
VASCULA
VASCULAR
VASCULUM
VASCULUMS
VASE
VASECTOMIES
VASECTOMY
VASES
VASIFORM
VASOMOTOR

VASSAIL
VASSAILS
VASSAL
VASSALAGE
VASSALAGES
VASSALED
VASSALESS
VASSALESSES
VASSALING
VASSALRIES
VASSALRY
VASSALS
VAST
VASTER
VASTEST
VASTIDITIES
VASTIDITY
VASTIER
VASTIEST
VASTITIES
VASTITUDE
VASTITUDES
VASTITY
VASTLY
VASTNESS
VASTNESSES
VASTS
VASTY
VAT
VATFUL
VATFULS
VATIC
VATICIDE
VATICIDES
VATICINAL
VATMAN
VATMEN
VATS
VATTED
VATTING
VAU
VAUDOO
VAUDOOS
VAUDOUX
VAULT
VAULTAGE
VAULTAGES
VAULTED
VAULTER
VAULTERS
VAULTING
VAULTINGS
VAULTS
VAULTY
VAUNCE
VAUNCED
VAUNCES
VAUNCING
VAUNT
VAUNTAGE
VAUNTAGES
VAUNTED
VAUNTER
VAUNTERIES
VAUNTERS
VAUNTERY
VAUNTFUL
VAUNTING
VAUNTINGS
VAUNTS

VAURIEN
VAURIENS
VAUS
VAUT
VAUTE
VAUTED
VAUTES
VAUTING
VAUTS
VAVASORIES
VAVASORY
VAVASOUR
VAVASOURS
VAWARD
VAWARDS
VAWTE
VAWTED
VAWTES
VAWTING
VEAL
VEALE
VEALES
VEALIER
VEALIEST
VEALS
VEALY
VECTOR
VECTORED
VECTORIAL
VECTORING
VECTORINGS
VECTORS
VEDALIA
VEDALIAS
VEDETTE
VEDETTES
VEDUTA
VEDUTE
VEDUTISTA
VEDUTISTI
VEE
VEENA
VEENAS
VEER
VEERED
VEERIES
VEERING
VEERINGLY
VEERINGS
VEERS
VEERY
VEES
VEG
VEGA
VEGAN
VEGANIC
VEGANISM
VEGANISMS
VEGANS
VEGAS
VEGETABLE
VEGETABLES
VEGETABLY
VEGETAL
VEGETALS
VEGETANT
VEGETATE
VEGETATED
VEGETATES
VEGETATING

VEGETATINGS	VELDTS	VENDED	VENIN	VENTURIS
VEGETE	VELE	VENDEE	VENINS	VENTUROUS
VEGETIVE	VELES	VENDEES	VENIRE	VENUE
VEGETIVES	VELETA	VENDER	VENIREMAN	VENUES
VEGGIE	VELETAS	VENDERS	VENIREMEN	VENULE
VEGGIES	VELIGER	VENDETTA	VENIRES	VENULES
VEGIE	VELIGERS	VENDETTAS	VENISON	VENUS
VEGIES	VELL	VENDEUSE	VENISONS	VENUSES
VEHEMENCE	VELLEITIES	VENDEUSES	VENITE	VENVILLE
VEHEMENCES	VELLEITY	VENDIBLE	VENITES	VENVILLES
VEHEMENCIES	VELLENAGE	VENDIBLES	VENNEL	VERACIOUS
VEHEMENCY	VELLENAGES	VENDIBLY	VENNELS	VERACITIES
VEHEMENT	VELLET	VENDING	VENOM	VERACITY
VEHICLE	VELLETS	VENDIS	VENOMED	VERANDA
VEHICLES	VELLICATE	VENDISES	VENOMING	VERANDAH
VEHICULAR	VELLICATED	VENDISS	VENOMOUS	VERANDAHS
VEHM	VELLICATES	VENDISSES	VENOMS	VERANDAS
VEHME	VELLICATING	VENDITION	VENOSE	VERATRIN
VEHMIC	VELLON	VENDITIONS	VENOSITY	VERATRINE
VEHMIQUE	VELLONS	VENDOR	VENOUS	VERATRINES
VEIL	VELLS	VENDORS	VENT	VERATRINS
VEILED	VELLUM	VENDS	VENTAGE	VERATRUM
VEILIER	VELLUMS	VENDUE	VENTAGES	VERATRUMS
VEILIEST	VELOCE	VENDUES	VENTAIL	VERB
VEILING	VELOCITIES	VENEER	VENTAILE	VERBAL
VEILINGS	VELOCITY	VENEERED	VENTAILES	VERBALISE
VEILLESS	VELODROME	VENEERER	VENTAILS	VERBALISED
VEILLEUSE	VELODROMES	VENEERERS	VENTANA	VERBALISES
VEILLEUSES	VELOUR	VENEERING	VENTANAS	VERBALISING
VEILS	VELOURS	VENEERINGS	VENTAYLE	VERBALISM
VEILY	VELOUTÉ	VENEERS	VENTAYLES	VERBALISMS
VEIN	VELOUTÉS	VENEFIC	VENTED	VERBALIST
VEINED	VELOUTINE	VENEFICAL	VENTER	VERBALISTS
VEINIER	VELOUTINES	VENERABLE	VENTERS	VERBALITIES
VEINIEST	VELSKOEN	VENERABLY	VENTIDUCT	VERBALITY
VEINING	VELSKOENS	VENERATE	VENTIDUCTS	VERBALIZE
VEININGS	VELUM	VENERATED	VENTIFACT	VERBALIZED
VEINLET	VELURE	VENERATES	VENTIFACTS	VERBALIZES
VEINLETS	VELURED	VENERATING	VENTIGE	VERBALIZING
VEINOUS	VELURES	VENERATOR	VENTIGES	VERBALLED
VEINS	VELURING	VENERATORS	VENTIL	VERBALLING
VEINSTONE	VELVERET	VENEREAL	VENTILATE	VERBALLY
VEINSTONES	VELVERETS	VENEREAN	VENTILATED	VERBALS
VEINSTUFF	VELVET	VENEREANS	VENTILATES	VERBARIAN
VEINSTUFFS	VELVETED	VENEREOUS	VENTILATING	VERBARIANS
VEINY	VELVETEEN	VENERER	VENTILS	VERBATIM
VELA	VELVETEENS	VENERERS	VENTING	VERBENA
VELAMEN	VELVETING	VENERIES	VENTINGS	VERBENAS
VELAMINA	VELVETINGS	VENERY	VENTOSE	VERBERATE
VELAR	VELVETS	VENEWE	VENTOSITIES	VERBERATED
VELARIA	VELVETY	VENEWES	VENTOSITY	VERBERATES
VELARIC	VENA	VENEY	VENTRAL	VERBERATING
VELARISE	VENAE	VENEYS	VENTRALLY	VERBIAGE
VELARISED	VENAL	VENGE	VENTRALS	VERBIAGES
VELARISES	VENALITIES	VENGEABLE	VENTRE	VERBICIDE
VELARISING	VENALITY	VENGEABLY	VENTRED	VERBICIDES
VELARIUM	VENALLY	VENGEANCE	VENTRES	VERBLESS
VELARIZE	VENATIC	VENGEANCES	VENTRICLE	VERBOSE
VELARIZED	VENATICAL	VENGED	VENTRICLES	VERBOSELY
VELARIZES	VENATION	VENGEFUL	VENTRING	VERBOSER
VELARIZING	VENATIONS	VENGEMENT	VENTROUS	VERBOSEST
VELARS	VENATOR	VENGEMENTS	VENTS	VERBOSITIES
VELATE	VENATORS	VENGER	VENTURE	VERBOSITY
VELATED	VEND	VENGERS	VENTURED	VERBS
VELATURA	VENDACE	VENGES	VENTURER	VERDANCIES
VELD	VENDACES	VENGING	VENTURERS	VERDANCY
VELDS	VENDAGE	VENIAL	VENTURES	VERDANT
VELDSKOEN	VENDAGES	VENIALITIES	VENTURI	VERDANTLY
VELDSKOENS	VENDANGE	VENIALITY	VENTURING	VERDELHO
VELDT	VENDANGES	VENIALLY	VENTURINGS	VERDELHOS

VERDERER
VERDERERS
VERDEROR
VERDERORS
VERDET
VERDETS
VERDICT
VERDICTS
VERDIGRIS
VERDIGRISED
VERDIGRISES
VERDIGRISING
VERDIT
VERDITER
VERDITERS
VERDITS
VERDOY
VERDURE
VERDURED
VERDURES
VERDUROUS
VERECUND
VERGE
VERGED
VERGENCIES
VERGENCY
VERGER
VERGERS
VERGES
VERGING
VERGLAS
VERGLASES
VERIDICAL
VERIER
VERIEST
VERIFIED
VERIFIER
VERIFIERS
VERIFIES
VERIFY
VERIFYING
VERILY
VERISM
VERISMO
VERISMOS
VERISMS
VERIST
VERISTIC
VERISTS
VERITABLE
VERITABLY
VERITIES
VERITY
VERJUICE
VERJUICED
VERJUICES
VERKRAMP
VERLIG
VERLIGTE
VERLIGTES
VERMEIL
VERMEILED
VERMEILING
VERMEILLE
VERMEILLES
VERMEILS
VERMELL
VERMELLS
VERMES
VERMIAN

VERMICIDE
VERMICIDES
VERMICULE
VERMICULES
VERMIFORM
VERMIFUGE
VERMIFUGES
VERMIL
VERMILIES
VERMILION
VERMILIONED
VERMILIONING
VERMILIONS
VERMILS
VERMILY
VERMIN
VERMINATE
VERMINATED
VERMINATES
VERMINATING
VERMINED
VERMINOUS
VERMINS
VERMINY
VERMIS
VERMISES
VERMOUTH
VERMOUTHS
VERNAL
VERNALISE
VERNALISED
VERNALISES
VERNALISING
VERNALITIES
VERNALITY
VERNALIZE
VERNALIZED
VERNALIZES
VERNALIZING
VERNALLY
VERNANT
VERNATION
VERNATIONS
VERNICLE
VERNICLES
VERNIER
VERNIERS
VERONICA
VERONICAS
VÉRONIQUE
VERQUERE
VERQUERES
VERQUIRE
VERQUIRES
VERREL
VERRELS
VERREY
VERRUCA
VERRUCAE
VERRUCAS
VERRUCOSE
VERRUCOUS
VERRUGA
VERRUGAS
VERRY
VERS
VERSAL
VERSALS
VERSANT
VERSANTS

VERSATILE
VERSE
VERSED
VERSELET
VERSELETS
VERSER
VERSERS
VERSES
VERSET
VERSETS
VERSICLE
VERSICLES
VERSIFIED
VERSIFIER
VERSIFIERS
VERSIFIES
VERSIFORM
VERSIFY
VERSIFYING
VERSIN
VERSINE
VERSINES
VERSING
VERSINGS
VERSINS
VERSION
VERSIONAL
VERSIONER
VERSIONERS
VERSIONS
VERSO
VERSOS
VERST
VERSTS
VERSUS
VERSUTE
VERT
VERTEBRA
VERTEBRAE
VERTEBRAL
VERTED
VERTEX
VERTICAL
VERTICALS
VERTICES
VERTICIL
VERTICILS
VERTICITIES
VERTICITY
VERTIGINES
VERTIGO
VERTIGOES
VERTIGOS
VERTING
VERTIPORT
VERTIPORTS
VERTS
VERTU
VERTUE
VERTUES
VERTUOUS
VERTUS
VERVAIN
VERVAINS
VERVE
VERVEL
VERVELLED
VERVELS
VERVEN
VERVENS

VERVES
VERVET
VERVETS
VERY
VESICA
VESICAE
VESICAL
VESICANT
VESICANTS
VESICATE
VESICATED
VESICATES
VESICATING
VESICLE
VESICLES
VESICULA
VESICULAE
VESICULAR
VESPA
VESPAS
VESPER
VESPERAL
VESPERS
VESPIARIES
VESPIARY
VESPINE
VESPOID
VESSAIL
VESSAILS
VESSEL
VESSELS
VEST
VESTA
VESTAL
VESTALS
VESTAS
VESTED
VESTIARIES
VESTIARY
VESTIBULE
VESTIBULED
VESTIBULES
VESTIBULING
VESTIGE
VESTIGES
VESTIGIA
VESTIGIAL
VESTIGIUM
VESTIMENT
VESTIMENTS
VESTING
VESTINGS
VESTITURE
VESTITURES
VESTMENT
VESTMENTS
VESTRAL
VESTRIES
VESTRY
VESTRYMAN
VESTRYMEN
VESTS
VESTURAL
VESTURE
VESTURED
VESTURER
VESTURERS
VESTURES
VESTURING
VESUVIAN

VESUVIANS
VET
VETCH
VETCHES
VETCHIER
VETCHIEST
VETCHLING
VETCHLINGS
VETCHY
VETERAN
VETERANS
VETIVER
VETIVERS
VETKOEK
VETKOEKS
VETO
VETOED
VETOES
VETOING
VETS
VETTED
VETTING
VETTURA
VETTURAS
VETTURINI
VETTURINO
VEX
VEXATION
VEXATIONS
VEXATIOUS
VEXATORY
VEXED
VEXEDLY
VEXEDNESS
VEXEDNESSES
VEXER
VEXERS
VEXES
VEXILLA
VEXILLARIES
VEXILLARY
VEXILLUM
VEXING
VEXINGLY
VEXINGS
VEZIR
VEZIRS
VIA
VIABILITIES
VIABILITY
VIABLE
VIADUCT
VIADUCTS
VIAL
VIALFUL
VIALFULS
VIALLED
VIALS
VIAMETER
VIAMETERS
VIAND
VIANDS
VIAS
VIATICA
VIATICALS
VIATICUM
VIATICUMS
VIATOR
VIATORIAL
VIATORS

VIBE	VICINITY	VIED	VILDNESSES	VIMS
VIBES	VICIOSITIES	VIELLE	VILE	VIN
VIBEX	VICIOSITY	VIELLES	VILELY	VINA
VIBICES	VICIOUS	VIER	VILENESS	VINACEOUS
VIBIST	VICIOUSLY	VIERS	VILENESSES	VINAL
VIBISTS	VICOMTE	VIES	VILER	VINAS
VIBRACULA	VICOMTES	VIEW	VILEST	VINASSE
VIBRAHARP	VICTIM	VIEWABLE	VILIACO	VINASSES
VIBRAHARPS	VICTIMISE	VIEWDATA	VILIACOES	VINCA
VIBRANCIES	VICTIMISED	VIEWDATAS	VILIACOS	VINCAS
VIBRANCY	VICTIMISES	VIEWED	VILIAGO	VINCIBLE
VIBRANT	VICTIMISING	VIEWER	VILIAGOES	VINCULA
VIBRATE	VICTIMIZE	VIEWERS	VILIAGOS	VINCULUM
VIBRATED	VICTIMIZED	VIEWIER	VILIFIED	VINDALOO
VIBRATES	VICTIMIZES	VIEWIEST	VILIFIER	VINDALOOS
VIBRATILE	VICTIMIZING	VIEWINESS	VILIFIERS	VINDEMIAL
VIBRATING	VICTIMS	VIEWINESSES	VILIFIES	VINDICATE
VIBRATION	VICTOR	VIEWING	VILIFY	VINDICATED
VIBRATIONS	VICTORESS	VIEWINGS	VILIFYING	VINDICATES
VIBRATIVE	VICTORESSES	VIEWLESS	VILIPEND	VINDICATING
VIBRATO	VICTORIA	VIEWLY	VILIPENDED	VINE
VIBRATOR	VICTORIAS	VIEWPHONE	VILIPENDING	VINED
VIBRATORS	VICTORIES	VIEWPHONES	VILIPENDS	VINEGAR
VIBRATORY	VICTORINE	VIEWPOINT	VILL	VINEGARED
VIBRATOS	VICTORINES	VIEWPOINTS	VILLA	VINEGARING
VIBRIO	VICTORS	VIEWS	VILLADOM	VINEGARS
VIBRIOS	VICTORY	VIEWY	VILLADOMS	VINEGARY
VIBRIOSES	VICTRESS	VIFDA	VILLAGE	VINER
VIBRIOSIS	VICTRESSES	VIFDAS	VILLAGER	VINERIES
VIBRISSA	VICTRIX	VIGESIMAL	VILLAGERIES	VINERS
VIBRISSAE	VICTRIXES	VIGIA	VILLAGERS	VINERY
VIBRONIC	VICTUAL	VIGIAS	VILLAGERY	VINES
VIBS	VICTUALLED	VIGIL	VILLAGES	VINEW
VIBURNUM	VICTUALLING	VIGILANCE	VILLAGIO	VINEWED
VIBURNUMS	VICTUALS	VIGILANCES	VILLAGIOS	VINEWING
VICAR	VICUÑA	VIGILANT	VILLAGREE	VINEWS
VICARAGE	VICUÑAS	VIGILANTE	VILLAGREES	VINEYARD
VICARAGES	VIDAME	VIGILANTES	VILLAIN	VINEYARDS
VICARATE	VIDAMES	VIGILS	VILLAINIES	VINIER
VICARATES	VIDE	VIGNERON	VILLAINS	VINIEST
VICARESS	VIDELICET	VIGNERONS	VILLAINY	VINING
VICARESSES	VIDENDA	VIGNETTE	VILLAN	VINO
VICARIAL	VIDENDUM	VIGNETTED	VILLANAGE	VINOLENT
VICARIATE	VIDEO	VIGNETTER	VILLANAGES	VINOLOGIES
VICARIATES	VIDEODISC	VIGNETTERS	VILLANIES	VINOLOGY
VICARIES	VIDEODISCS	VIGNETTES	VILLANOUS	VINOS
VICARIOUS	VIDEOED	VIGNETTING	VILLANS	VINOSITIES
VICARS	VIDEOFIT	VIGOR	VILLANY	VINOSITY
VICARSHIP	VIDEOFITS	VIGORISH	VILLAR	VINOUS
VICARSHIPS	VIDEOGRAM	VIGORISHES	VILLAS	VINS
VICARY	VIDEOGRAMS	VIGORO	VILLATIC	VINT
VICE	VIDEOING	VIGOROS	VILLEIN	VINTAGE
VICED	VIDEOS	VIGOROUS	VILLEINS	VINTAGED
VICENARY	VIDEOTAPE	VIGORS	VILLENAGE	VINTAGER
VICENNIAL	VIDEOTAPES	VIGOUR	VILLENAGES	VINTAGERS
VICEREINE	VIDEOTEX	VIGOURS	VILLI	VINTAGES
VICEREINES	VIDEOTEXES	VIHARA	VILLIAGO	VINTAGING
VICEROY	VIDEOTEXT	VIHARAS	VILLIAGOES	VINTAGINGS
VICEROYS	VIDEOTEXTS	VIHUELA	VILLIAGOS	VINTED
VICES	VIDETTE	VIHUELAS	VILLIFORM	VINTING
VICESIMAL	VIDETTES	VIKING	VILLOSE	VINTNER
VICIATE	VIDIMUS	VIKINGISM	VILLOSITIES	VINTNERS
VICIATED	VIDIMUSES	VIKINGISMS	VILLOSITY	VINTRIES
VICIATES	VIDUAGE	VIKINGS	VILLOUS	VINTRY
VICIATING	VIDUAGES	VILAYET	VILLS	VINTS
VICINAGE	VIDUAL	VILAYETS	VILLUS	VINY
VICINAGES	VIDUITIES	VILD	VIM	VINYL
VICINAL	VIDUITY	VILDE	VIMANA	VINYLS
VICING	VIDUOUS	VILDLY	VIMANAS	VIOL
VICINITIES	VIE	VILDNESS	VIMINEOUS	VIOLA

VIOLABLE	VIRGINAL	VISAED	VISITATOR	VITALIZES
VIOLABLY	VIRGINALLED	VISAGE	VISITATORS	VITALIZING
VIOLAS	VIRGINALLING	VISAGED	VISITE	VITALLY
VIOLATE	VIRGINALS	VISAGES	VISITED	VITALS
VIOLATED	VIRGINING	VISAGIST	VISITEE	VITAMIN
VIOLATES	VIRGINITIES	VISAGISTE	VISITEES	VITAMINE
VIOLATING	VIRGINITY	VISAGISTES	VISITER	VITAMINES
VIOLATION	VIRGINIUM	VISAGISTS	VISITERS	VITAMINS
VIOLATIONS	VIRGINIUMS	VISAING	VISITES	VITASCOPE
VIOLATIVE	VIRGINLY	VISAS	VISITING	VITASCOPES
VIOLATOR	VIRGINS	VISCACHA	VISITINGS	VITATIVE
VIOLATORS	VIRGULATE	VISCACHAS	VISITOR	VITE
VIOLD	VIRGULE	VISCERA	VISITORS	VITELLARY
VIOLENCE	VIRGULES	VISCERAL	VISITRESS	VITELLI
VIOLENCES	VIRICIDAL	VISCERATE	VISITRESSES	VITELLIN
VIOLENT	VIRICIDE	VISCERATED	VISITS	VITELLINE
VIOLENTED	VIRICIDES	VISCERATES	VISIVE	VITELLINES
VIOLENTING	VIRID	VISCERATING	VISNE	VITELLINS
VIOLENTLY	VIRIDIAN	VISCID	VISNES	VITELLUS
VIOLENTS	VIRIDIANS	VISCIDITIES	VISNOMIE	VITEX
VIOLER	VIRIDITE	VISCIDITY	VISNOMIES	VITEXES
VIOLERS	VIRIDITES	VISCIN	VISNOMY	VITIABLE
VIOLET	VIRIDITIES	VISCINS	VISON	VITIATE
VIOLETS	VIRIDITY	VISCOSE	VISONS	VITIATED
VIOLIN	VIRILE	VISCOSES	VISOR	VITIATES
VIOLINIST	VIRILISED	VISCOSITIES	VISORED	VITIATING
VIOLINISTS	VIRILISM	VISCOSITY	VISORING	VITIATION
VIOLINS	VIRILISMS	VISCOUNT	VISORS	VITIATIONS
VIOLIST	VIRILITIES	VISCOUNTIES	VISTA	VITIATOR
VIOLISTS	VIRILITY	VISCOUNTS	VISTAED	VITIATORS
VIOLONE	VIRILIZED	VISCOUNTY	VISTAING	VITICETA
VIOLONES	VIRION	VISCOUS	VISTAL	VITICETUM
VIOLS	VIRIONS	VISCUM	VISTALESS	VITICETUMS
VIPER	VIRL	VISCUMS	VISTAS	VITICIDE
VIPERINE	VIRLS	VISCUS	VISTO	VITICIDES
VIPERISH	VIROGENE	VISE	VISTOS	VITILIGO
VIPEROUS	VIROGENES	VISÉ	VISUAL	VITILIGOS
VIPERS	VIROID	VISED	VISUALISE	VITIOSITIES
VIRAEMIA	VIROIDS	VISÉED	VISUALISED	VITIOSITY
VIRAEMIAS	VIROLOGIES	VISÉING	VISUALISES	VITRAGE
VIRAEMIC	VIROLOGY	VISES	VISUALISING	VITRAGES
VIRAGO	VIROSE	VISÉS	VISUALIST	VITRAIL
VIRAGOES	VIROSES	VISIBLE	VISUALISTS	VITRAIN
VIRAGOISH	VIROSIS	VISIBLES	VISUALITIES	VITRAINS
VIRAGOS	VIROUS	VISIBLY	VISUALITY	VITRAUX
VIRAL	VIRTU	VISIE	VISUALIZE	VITREOUS
VIRANDA	VIRTUAL	VISIED	VISUALIZED	VITREUM
VIRANDAS	VIRTUALLY	VISIEING	VISUALIZES	VITREUMS
VIRANDO	VIRTUE	VISIER	VISUALIZING	VITRIC
VIRANDOS	VIRTUES	VISIERS	VISUALLY	VITRICS
VIRELAY	VIRTUOSA	VISIES	VISUALS	VITRIFIED
VIRELAYS	VIRTUOSE	VISILE	VITA	VITRIFIES
VIREMENT	VIRTUOSI	VISILES	VITAE	VITRIFORM
VIREMENTS	VIRTUOSIC	VISING	VITAL	VITRIFY
VIRENT	VIRTUOSO	VISION	VITALISE	VITRIFYING
VIREO	VIRTUOSOS	VISIONAL	VITALISED	VITRINE
VIREOS	VIRTUOUS	VISIONARIES	VITALISER	VITRINES
VIRES	VIRTUS	VISIONARY	VITALISERS	VITRIOL
VIRESCENT	VIRUCIDAL	VISIONED	VITALISES	VITRIOLIC
VIRETOT	VIRUCIDE	VISIONER	VITALISING	VITRIOLS
VIRETOTS	VIRUCIDES	VISIONERS	VITALISM	VITTA
VIRGA	VIRULENCE	VISIONING	VITALISMS	VITTAE
VIRGAS	VIRULENCES	VISIONINGS	VITALIST	VITTATE
VIRGATE	VIRULENCIES	VISIONIST	VITALISTS	VITTLE
VIRGATES	VIRULENCY	VISIONISTS	VITALITIES	VITTLES
VIRGE	VIRULENT	VISIONS	VITALITY	VITULAR
VIRGER	VIRUS	VISIT	VITALIZE	VITULINE
VIRGERS	VIRUSES	VISITABLE	VITALIZED	VIVA
VIRGES	VIS	VISITANT	VITALIZER	VIVACE
VIRGIN	VISA	VISITANTS	VITALIZERS	VIVACIOUS

VIVACITIES	VIZIRATES	VOGUES	VOLED	VOLUTE
VIVACITY	VIZIRIAL	VOGUEY	VOLENS	VOLUTED
VIVAED	VIZIRS	VOGUING	VOLERIES	VOLUTES
VIVAING	VIZIRSHIP	VOGUISH	VOLERY	VOLUTIN
VIVAMENTE	VIZIRSHIPS	VOICE	VOLES	VOLUTINS
VIVANDIER	VIZOR	VOICED	VOLET	VOLUTION
VIVANDIERS	VIZORED	VOICEFUL	VOLETS	VOLUTIONS
VIVARIA	VIZORING	VOICELESS	VOLING	VOLUTOID
VIVARIES	VIZORS	VOICER	VOLITANT	VOLVA
VIVARIUM	VIZSLA	VOICERS	VOLITATE	VOLVAS
VIVARIUMS	VIZSLAS	VOICES	VOLITATED	VOLVATE
VIVARY	VIZY	VOICING	VOLITATES	VOLVE
VIVAS	VIZZIE	VOICINGS	VOLITATING	VOLVED
VIVAT	VIZZIED	VOID	VOLITIENT	VOLVES
VIVDA	VIZZIES	VOIDABLE	VOLITION	VOLVING
VIVDAS	VIZZYING	VOIDANCE	VOLITIONS	VOLVULUS
VIVE	VLEI	VOIDANCES	VOLITIVE	VOLVULUSES
VIVELY	VLEIS	VOIDED	VOLITIVES	VOMER
VIVENCIES	VLIES	VOIDEE	VOLKSRAAD	VOMERINE
VIVENCY	VLY	VOIDEES	VOLKSRAADS	VOMERS
VIVER	VOAR	VOIDER	VOLLEY	VOMICA
VIVERRINE	VOARS	VOIDERS	VOLLEYED	VOMICAS
VIVERS	VOCABLE	VOIDING	VOLLEYING	VOMIT
VIVES	VOCABLES	VOIDINGS	VOLLEYS	VOMITED
VIVESES	VOCABULAR	VOIDNESS	VOLOST	VOMITING
VIVIANITE	VOCAL	VOIDNESSES	VOLOSTS	VOMITINGS
VIVIANITES	VOCALIC	VOIDS	VOLPINO	VOMITIVE
VIVID	VOCALION	VOILÀ	VOLPINOS	VOMITIVES
VIVIDER	VOCALIONS	VOILE	VOLPLANE	VOMITO
VIVIDEST	VOCALISE	VOILES	VOLPLANED	VOMITORIES
VIVIDITIES	VOCALISED	VOISINAGE	VOLPLANES	VOMITORY
VIVIDITY	VOCALISER	VOISINAGES	VOLPLANING	VOMITOS
VIVIDLY	VOCALISERS	VOITURE	VOLS	VOMITS
VIVIDNESS	VOCALISES	VOITURES	VOLT	VOODOO
VIVIDNESSES	VOCALISING	VOITURIER	VOLTA	VOODOOED
VIVIFIC	VOCALISM	VOITURIERS	VOLTAGE	VOODOOING
VIVIFIED	VOCALISMS	VOIVODE	VOLTAGES	VOODOOISM
VIVIFIER	VOCALIST	VOIVODES	VOLTAIC	VOODOOISMS
VIVIFIERS	VOCALISTS	VOL	VOLTAISM	VOODOOIST
VIVIFIES	VOCALITIES	VOLA	VOLTAISMS	VOODOOISTS
VIVIFY	VOCALITY	VOLABLE	VOLTE	VOODOOS
VIVIFYING	VOCALIZE	VOLAE	VOLTES	VOR
VIVIPARIES	VOCALIZED	VOLAGE	VOLTIGEUR	VORACIOUS
VIVIPARY	VOCALIZER	VOLAGEOUS	VOLTIGEURS	VORACITIES
VIVISECT	VOCALIZERS	VOLANT	VOLTINISM	VORACITY
VIVISECTED	VOCALIZES	VOLANTE	VOLTINISMS	VORAGO
VIVISECTING	VOCALIZING	VOLANTES	VOLTMETER	VORAGOES
VIVISECTS	VOCALLY	VOLAR	VOLTMETERS	VORANT
VIVO	VOCALNESS	VOLARIES	VOLTS	VORPAL
VIVRES	VOCALNESSES	VOLARY	VOLUBIL	VORTEX
VIXEN	VOCALS	VOLATIC	VOLUBLE	VORTEXES
VIXENISH	VOCATION	VOLATILE	VOLUBLY	VORTICAL
VIXENLY	VOCATIONS	VOLATILES	VOLUCRINE	VORTICES
VIXENS	VOCATIVE	VOLCANIAN	VOLUME	VORTICISM
VIZAMENT	VOCATIVES	VOLCANIC	VOLUMED	VORTICISMS
VIZAMENTS	VOCES	VOLCANISE	VOLUMES	VORTICIST
VIZARD	VOCODER	VOLCANISED	VOLUMETER	VORTICISTS
VIZARDED	VOCODERS	VOLCANISES	VOLUMETERS	VORTICITIES
VIZARDING	VOCULAR	VOLCANISING	VOLUMINAL	VORTICITY
VIZARDS	VOCULE	VOLCANISM	VOLUMING	VORTICOSE
VIZCACHA	VOCULES	VOLCANISMS	VOLUMIST	VOTARESS
VIZCACHAS	VODKA	VOLCANIST	VOLUMISTS	VOTARESSES
VIZIER	VODKAS	VOLCANISTS	VOLUNTARIES	VOTARIES
VIZIERATE	VOE	VOLCANIZE	VOLUNTARY	VOTARIST
VIZIERATES	VOES	VOLCANIZED	VOLUNTEER	VOTARISTS
VIZIERIAL	VOGIE	VOLCANIZES	VOLUNTEERED	VOTARY
VIZIERS	VOGIER	VOLCANIZING	VOLUNTEERING	VOTE
VIZIES	VOGIEST	VOLCANO	VOLUNTEERS	VOTED
VIZIR	VOGUE	VOLCANOES	VÖLUSPA	VOTEEN
VIZIRATE	VOGUED	VOLE	VÖLUSPAS	VOTEENS

VOTELESS
VOTER
VOTERS
VOTES
VOTING
VOTIVE
VOUCH
VOUCHED
VOUCHEE
VOUCHEES
VOUCHER
VOUCHERS
VOUCHES
VOUCHING
VOUCHSAFE
VOUCHSAFED
VOUCHSAFES
VOUCHSAFING
VOUDOU
VOUDOUED
VOUDOUING
VOUDOUS
VOUGE
VOUGES
VOULGE
VOULGES
VOULU
VOUSSOIR
VOUSSOIRED
VOUSSOIRING
VOUSSOIRS
VOUTSAFE
VOUTSAFED
VOUTSAFES

VOUTSAFING
VOW
VOWED
VOWEL
VOWELISE
VOWELISED
VOWELISES
VOWELISING
VOWELIZE
VOWELIZED
VOWELIZES
VOWELIZING
VOWELLED
VOWELLESS
VOWELLING
VOWELLY
VOWELS
VOWESS
VOWESSES
VOWING
VOWS
VOX
VOYAGE
VOYAGED
VOYAGER
VOYAGERS
VOYAGES
VOYAGEUR
VOYAGEURS
VOYAGING
VOYEUR
VOYEURISM
VOYEURISMS
VOYEURS

VRAIC
VRAICKER
VRAICKERS
VRAICKING
VRAICKINGS
VRAICS
VRIL
VRILS
VROOM
VROOMED
VROOMING
VROOMS
VROUW
VROUWS
VUG
VUGGY
VUGS
VULCAN
VULCANIAN
VULCANIC
VULCANISE
VULCANISED
VULCANISES
VULCANISING
VULCANISM
VULCANISMS
VULCANIST
VULCANISTS
VULCANITE
VULCANITES
VULCANIZE
VULCANIZED
VULCANIZES
VULCANIZING

VULCANS
VULGAR
VULGARER
VULGAREST
VULGARIAN
VULGARIANS
VULGARISE
VULGARISED
VULGARISES
VULGARISING
VULGARISM
VULGARISMS
VULGARITIES
VULGARITY
VULGARIZE
VULGARIZED
VULGARIZES
VULGARIZING
VULGARLY
VULGARS
VULGATE
VULGATES
VULGO
VULGUS
VULGUSES
VULN
VULNED
VULNERARIES
VULNERARY
VULNERATE
VULNERATED
VULNERATES
VULNERATING
VULNING

VULNS
VULPICIDE
VULPICIDES
VULPINE
VULPINISM
VULPINISMS
VULPINITE
VULPINITES
VULSELLA
VULSELLAE
VULSELLUM
VULTURE
VULTURES
VULTURINE
VULTURISH
VULTURISM
VULTURISMS
VULTURN
VULTURNS
VULTUROUS
VULVA
VULVAL
VULVAR
VULVAS
VULVATE
VULVIFORM
VULVITIS
VULVITISES
VUM
VUMMED
VUMMING
VUMS
VYING
VYINGLY

W

WABAIN	WAEFUL	WAGON	WAISTS	WALIES
WABAINS	WAENESS	WAGONAGE	WAIT	WALIEST
WABBLE	WAENESSES	WAGONAGES	WAITE	WALING
WABBLED	WAESOME	WAGONED	WAITED	WALIS
WABBLER	WAESUCKS	WAGONER	WAITER	WALISE
WABBLERS	WAFER	WAGONERS	WAITERAGE	WALISES
WABBLES	WAFERED	WAGONETTE	WAITERAGES	WALK
WABBLING	WAFERING	WAGONETTES	WAITERING	WALKABLE
WABBLY	WAFERS	WAGONFUL	WAITERINGS	WALKABOUT
WABOOM	WAFERY	WAGONFULS	WAITERS	WALKABOUTS
WABOOMS	WAFF	WAGONING	WAITES	WALKED
WABSTER	WAFFED	WAGONS	WAITING	WALKER
WABSTERS	WAFFING	WAGS	WAITINGLY	WALKERS
WACKE	WAFFLE	WAGTAIL	WAITINGS	WALKING
WACKES	WAFFLED	WAGTAILS	WAITRESS	WALKINGS
WACKIER	WAFFLES	WAHINE	WAITRESSES	WALKS
WACKIEST	WAFFLING	WAHINES	WAITS	WALKWAY
WACKINESS	WAFFS	WAHOO	WAIVE	WALKWAYS
WACKINESSES	WAFT	WAHOOS	WAIVED	WALL
WACKY	WAFTAGE	WAID	WAIVER	WALLA
WAD	WAFTAGES	WAIDE	WAIVERS	WALLABA
WADD	WAFTED	WAIF	WAIVES	WALLABAS
WADDED	WAFTER	WAIFED	WAIVING	WALLABIES
WADDIE	WAFTERS	WAIFING	WAIVODE	WALLABY
WADDIED	WAFTING	WAIFS	WAIVODES	WALLAH
WADDIES	WAFTINGS	WAIFT	WAIWODE	WALLAHS
WADDING	WAFTS	WAIFTS	WAIWODES	WALLAROO
WADDINGS	WAFTURE	WAIL	WAKE	WALLAROOS
WADDLE	WAFTURES	WAILED	WAKED	WALLAS
WADDLED	WAG	WAILER	WAKEFUL	WALLED
WADDLES	WAGE	WAILERS	WAKEFULLY	WALLER
WADDLING	WAGED	WAILFUL	WAKELESS	WALLERS
WADDS	WAGELESS	WAILING	WAKEMAN	WALLET
WADDY	WAGENBOOM	WAILINGLY	WAKEMEN	WALLETS
WADDYING	WAGENBOOMS	WAILINGS	WAKEN	WALLFISH
WADE	WAGER	WAILS	WAKENED	WALLFISHES
WADED	WAGERED	WAIN	WAKENER	WALLIER
WADER	WAGERER	WAINAGE	WAKENERS	WALLIES
WADERS	WAGERERS	WAINAGES	WAKENING	WALLIEST
WADES	WAGERING	WAINED	WAKENINGS	WALLING
WADI	WAGERS	WAINING	WAKENS	WALLINGS
WADIES	WAGES	WAINS	WAKER	WALLOP
WADING	WAGGED	WAINSCOT	WAKERIFE	WALLOPED
WADINGS	WAGGERIES	WAINSCOTED	WAKERS	WALLOPER
WADIS	WAGGERY	WAINSCOTING	WAKES	WALLOPERS
WADMAAL	WAGGING	WAINSCOTINGS	WAKIKI	WALLOPING
WADMAALS	WAGGISH	WAINSCOTS	WAKIKIS	WALLOPINGS
WADMAL	WAGGISHLY	WAINSCOTTED	WAKING	WALLOPS
WADMALS	WAGGLE	WAINSCOTTING	WAKINGS	WALLOW
WADMOL	WAGGLED	WAINSCOTTINGS	WALD	WALLOWED
WADMOLL	WAGGLES	WAIST	WALDFLUTE	WALLOWER
WADMOLLS	WAGGLING	WAISTBAND	WALDFLUTES	WALLOWERS
WADMOLS	WAGGLY	WAISTBANDS	WALDGRAVE	WALLOWING
WADS	WAGGON	WAISTBELT	WALDGRAVES	WALLOWINGS
WADSET	WAGGONED	WAISTBELTS	WALDHORN	WALLOWS
WADSETS	WAGGONER	WAISTBOAT	WALDHORNS	WALLPAPER
WADSETT	WAGGONERS	WAISTBOATS	WALDS	WALLPAPERS
WADSETTED	WAGGONING	WAISTCOAT	WALE	WALLS
WADSETTER	WAGGONS	WAISTCOATS	WALED	WALLSEND
WADSETTERS	WAGHALTER	WAISTED	WALER	WALLSENDS
WADSETTING	WAGHALTERS	WAISTER	WALERS	WALLWORT
WADSETTS	WAGING	WAISTERS	WALES	WALLWORTS
WADY	WAGMOIRE	WAISTLINE	WALI	WALLY
WAE	WAGMOIRES	WAISTLINES	WALIER	WALLYDRAG

WALLYDRAGS	WANGLINGS	WAPINSHAW	WARHEADS	WARRANDS
WALNUT	WANGS	WAPINSHAWS	WARIER	WARRANED
WALNUTS	WANGUN	WAPITI	WARIEST	WARRANING
WALRUS	WANGUNS	WAPITIS	WARILY	WARRANS
WALRUSES	WANHOPE	WAPPED	WARIMENT	WARRANT
WALTY	WANHOPES	WAPPEND	WARIMENTS	WARRANTED
WALTZ	WANIER	WAPPER	WARINESS	WARRANTEE
WALTZED	WANIEST	WAPPERED	WARINESSES	WARRANTEES
WALTZER	WANIGAN	WAPPERING	WARING	WARRANTER
WALTZERS	WANIGANS	WAPPERS	WARISON	WARRANTERS
WALTZES	WANING	WAPPING	WARISONS	WARRANTIES
WALTZING	WANINGS	WAPS	WARK	WARRANTING
WALTZINGS	WANK	WAR	WARKS	WARRANTINGS
WALY	WANKED	WARATAH	WARLIKE	WARRANTOR
WAMBLE	WANKER	WARATAHS	WARLING	WARRANTORS
WAMBLED	WANKERS	WARBLE	WARLINGS	WARRANTS
WAMBLES	WANKING	WARBLED	WARLOCK	WARRANTY
WAMBLIER	WANKLE	WARBLER	WARLOCKRIES	WARRAY
WAMBLIEST	WANKS	WARBLERS	WARLOCKRY	WARRAYED
WAMBLING	WANLE	WARBLES	WARLOCKS	WARRAYING
WAMBLINGS	WANLY	WARBLING	WARLORD	WARRAYS
WAMBLY	WANNED	WARBLINGS	WARLORDS	WARRE
WAME	WANNEL	WARBY	WARM	WARRED
WAMED	WANNER	WARD	WARMAN	WARREN
WAMEFUL	WANNESS	WARDED	WARMBLOOD	WARRENER
WAMEFULS	WANNESSES	WARDEN	WARMBLOODS	WARRENERS
WAMES	WANNEST	WARDENED	WARMED	WARRENS
WAMMUS	WANNING	WARDENING	WARMEN	WARREY
WAMMUSES	WANNISH	WARDENRIES	WARMER	WARREYED
WAMPEE	WANS	WARDENRY	WARMERS	WARREYING
WAMPEES	WANT	WARDENS	WARMEST	WARREYS
WAMPISH	WANTAGE	WARDER	WARMING	WARRIGAL
WAMPISHED	WANTAGES	WARDERED	WARMINGS	WARRIGALS
WAMPISHES	WANTED	WARDERING	WARMLY	WARRING
WAMPISHING	WANTER	WARDERS	WARMNESS	WARRIOR
WAMPUM	WANTERS	WARDING	WARMNESSES	WARRIORS
WAMPUMS	WANTHILL	WARDINGS	WARMONGER	WARRISON
WAMPUS	WANTHILLS	WARDOG	WARMONGERS	WARRISONS
WAMPUSES	WANTIES	WARDOGS	WARMS	WARS
WAMUS	WANTING	WARDRESS	WARMTH	WARSHIP
WAMUSES	WANTINGS	WARDRESSES	WARMTHS	WARSHIPS
WAN	WANTON	WARDROBE	WARN	WARSLE
WANCHANCY	WANTONED	WARDROBER	WARNED	WARSLED
WAND	WANTONER	WARDROBERS	WARNER	WARSLES
WANDER	WANTONEST	WARDROBES	WARNERS	WARSLING
WANDERED	WANTONING	WARDROP	WARNING	WARST
WANDERER	WANTONISE	WARDROPS	WARNINGLY	WARSTED
WANDERERS	WANTONISED	WARDS	WARNINGS	WARSTING
WANDERING	WANTONISES	WARDSHIP	WARNS	WARSTS
WANDERINGS	WANTONISING	WARDSHIPS	WARP	WART
WANDEROO	WANTONIZE	WARE	WARPATH	WARTED
WANDEROOS	WANTONIZED	WARED	WARPATHS	WARTIER
WANDERS	WANTONIZES	WAREHOUSE	WARPED	WARTIEST
WANDLE	WANTONIZING	WAREHOUSED	WARPER	WARTIME
WANDOO	WANTONLY	WAREHOUSES	WARPERS	WARTIMES
WANDOOS	WANTONS	WAREHOUSING	WARPING	WARTLESS
WANDS	WANTS	WAREHOUSINGS	WARPINGS	WARTS
WANE	WANTY	WARELESS	WARPLANE	WARTWEED
WANED	WANWORDY	WARES	WARPLANES	WARTWEEDS
WANES	WANWORTH	WARFARE	WARPS	WARTWORT
WANEY	WANY	WARFARED	WARRAGAL	WARTWORTS
WANG	WANZE	WARFARER	WARRAGALS	WARTY
WANGAN	WANZED	WARFARERS	WARRAGLE	WARWOLF
WANGANS	WANZES	WARFARES	WARRAGLES	WARWOLVES
WANGLE	WANZING	WARFARIN	WARRAGUL	WARY
WANGLED	WAP	WARFARING	WARRAGULS	WAS
WANGLER	WAPENSHAW	WARFARINGS	WARRAN	WASE
WANGLERS	WAPENSHAWS	WARFARINS	WARRAND	WASES
WANGLES	WAPENTAKE	WARHABLE	WARRANDED	WASH
WANGLING	WAPENTAKES	WARHEAD	WARRANDING	WASHABLE

WASHED	WASTRELS	WATTMETERS	WAVEYS	WAYMENTS
WASHEN	WASTRIES	WATTS	WAVIER	WAYS
WASHER	WASTRY	WAUCHT	WAVIES	WAYSIDE
WASHERED	WASTS	WAUCHTED	WAVIEST	WAYSIDES
WASHERIES	WAT	WAUCHTING	WAVINESS	WAYWARD
WASHERING	WATCH	WAUCHTS	WAVINESSES	WAYWARDLY
WASHERMAN	WATCHABLE	WAUFF	WAVING	WAYWISER
WASHERMEN	WATCHCASE	WAUFFED	WAVINGS	WAYWISERS
WASHERS	WATCHCASES	WAUFFING	WAVY	WAYWORN
WASHERY	WATCHED	WAUFFS	WAW	WAYZGOOSE
WASHES	WATCHER	WAUGH	WAWE	WAYZGOOSES
WASHIER	WATCHERS	WAUGHED	WAWES	WAZIR
WASHIEST	WATCHES	WAUGHING	WAWL	WAZIRS
WASHINESS	WATCHET	WAUGHS	WAWLED	WE
WASHINESSES	WATCHETS	WAUGHT	WAWLING	WEAK
WASHING	WATCHFUL	WAUGHTED	WAWLINGS	WEAKEN
WASHINGS	WATCHING	WAUGHTING	WAWLS	WEAKENED
WASHLAND	WATCHMAN	WAUGHTS	WAWS	WEAKENER
WASHLANDS	WATCHMEN	WAUK	WAX	WEAKENERS
WASHROOM	WATCHWORD	WAUKED	WAXBERRIES	WEAKENING
WASHROOMS	WATCHWORDS	WAUKING	WAXBERRY	WEAKENS
WASHY	WATE	WAUKRIFE	WAXBILL	WEAKER
WASP	WATER	WAUKS	WAXBILLS	WEAKEST
WASPIE	WATERAGE	WAUL	WAXED	WEAKFISH
WASPIER	WATERAGES	WAULED	WAXEN	WEAKFISHES
WASPIES	WATERED	WAULING	WAXER	WEAKLIER
WASPIEST	WATERER	WAULINGS	WAXERS	WEAKLIEST
WASPISH	WATERERS	WAULK	WAXES	WEAKLING
WASPISHLY	WATERFALL	WAULKED	WAXIER	WEAKLINGS
WASPS	WATERFALLS	WAULKING	WAXIEST	WEAKLY
WASPY	WATERIER	WAULKS	WAXINESS	WEAKNESS
WASSAIL	WATERIEST	WAULS	WAXINESSES	WEAKNESSES
WASSAILED	WATERING	WAUR	WAXING	WEAL
WASSAILER	WATERINGS	WAURST	WAXINGS	WEALD
WASSAILERS	WATERISH	WAURSTED	WAXWING	WEALDS
WASSAILING	WATERLESS	WAURSTING	WAXWINGS	WEALS
WASSAILINGS	WATERLILIES	WAURSTS	WAXWORK	WEALSMAN
WASSAILRIES	WATERLILY	WAVE	WAXWORKER	WEALSMEN
WASSAILRY	WATERLOG	WAVEBAND	WAXWORKERS	WEALTH
WASSAILS	WATERLOGGED	WAVEBANDS	WAXWORKS	WEALTHIER
WASSERMAN	WATERLOGGING	WAVED	WAXY	WEALTHIEST
WASSERMEN	WATERLOGS	WAVEFORM	WAY	WEALTHILY
WAST	WATERMAN	WAVEFORMS	WAYBREAD	WEALTHS
WASTAGE	WATERMARK	WAVEFRONT	WAYBREADS	WEALTHY
WASTAGES	WATERMARKED	WAVEFRONTS	WAYED	WEAMB
WASTE	WATERMARKING	WAVEGUIDE	WAYFARE	WEAMBS
WASTED	WATERMARKS	WAVEGUIDES	WAYFARED	WEAN
WASTEFUL	WATERMEN	WAVELESS	WAYFARER	WEANED
WASTEFULL	WATERS	WAVELET	WAYFARERS	WEANEL
WASTEL	WATERSHED	WAVELETS	WAYFARES	WEANELS
WASTELAND	WATERSHEDS	WAVELIKE	WAYFARING	WEANER
WASTELANDS	WATERSIDE	WAVELLITE	WAYFARINGS	WEANERS
WASTELS	WATERSIDES	WAVELLITES	WAYGONE	WEANING
WASTENESS	WATERWAY	WAVEMETER	WAYGOOSE	WEANLING
WASTENESSES	WATERWAYS	WAVEMETERS	WAYGOOSES	WEANLINGS
WASTER	WATERWORK	WAVER	WAYING	WEANS
WASTERED	WATERWORKS	WAVERED	WAYLAID	WEAPON
WASTERFUL	WATERY	WAVERER	WAYLAY	WEAPONED
WASTERIES	WATS	WAVERERS	WAYLAYER	WEAPONRIES
WASTERIFE	WATT	WAVERING	WAYLAYERS	WEAPONRY
WASTERIFES	WATTAGE	WAVERINGS	WAYLAYING	WEAPONS
WASTERING	WATTAGES	WAVEROUS	WAYLAYS	WEAR
WASTERS	WATTER	WAVERS	WAYLESS	WEARABLE
WASTERY	WATTEST	WAVERY	WAYMARK	WEARED
WASTES	WATTLE	WAVES	WAYMARKED	WEARER
WASTING	WATTLED	WAVESHAPE	WAYMARKING	WEARERS
WASTINGS	WATTLES	WAVESHAPES	WAYMARKS	WEARIED
WASTNESS	WATTLING	WAVESON	WAYMENT	WEARIER
WASTNESSES	WATTLINGS	WAVESONS	WAYMENTED	WEARIES
WASTREL	WATTMETER	WAVEY	WAYMENTING	WEARIEST

WEARIFUL	WEDGE	WEET	WEIZES	WELTERING
WEARILESS	WEDGED	WEETE	WEIZING	WELTERS
WEARILY	WEDGES	WEETEN	WEKA	WELTING
WEARINESS	WEDGEWISE	WEETING	WEKAS	WELTS
WEARINESSES	WEDGIE	WEETINGLY	WELAWAY	WEM
WEARING	WEDGIES	WEETLESS	WELCH	WEMB
WEARINGS	WEDGING	WEEVER	WELCHED	WEMBS
WEARISH	WEDGINGS	WEEVERS	WELCHER	WEMS
WEARISOME	WEDLOCK	WEEVIL	WELCHERS	WEN
WEARS	WEDLOCKS	WEEVILED	WELCHES	WENCH
WEARY	WEDS	WEEVILLED	WELCHING	WENCHED
WEARYING	WEE	WEEVILLY	WELCOME	WENCHER
WEASAND	WEED	WEEVILS	WELCOMED	WENCHERS
WEASANDS	WEEDED	WEEVILY	WELCOMER	WENCHES
WEASEL	WEEDER	WEFT	WELCOMERS	WENCHING
WEASELED	WEEDERIES	WEFTAGE	WELCOMES	WEND
WEASELER	WEEDERS	WEFTAGES	WELCOMING	WENDED
WEASELERS	WEEDERY	WEFTE	WELD	WENDIGO
WEASELING	WEEDICIDE	WEFTED	WELDABLE	WENDIGOS
WEASELLED	WEEDICIDES	WEFTES	WELDED	WENDING
WEASELLER	WEEDIER	WEFTING	WELDER	WENDS
WEASELLERS	WEEDIEST	WEFTS	WELDERS	WENNIER
WEASELLING	WEEDINESS	WEID	WELDING	WENNIEST
WEASELLY	WEEDINESSES	WEIDS	WELDINGS	WENNISH
WEASELS	WEEDING	WEIGELA	WELDLESS	WENNY
WEATHER	WEEDINGS	WEIGELAS	WELDMENT	WENS
WEATHERED	WEEDLESS	WEIGH	WELDMENTS	WENT
WEATHERING	WEEDS	WEIGHABLE	WELDMESH™	WENTS
WEATHERINGS	WEEDY	WEIGHAGE	WELDMESH™	WEPT
WEATHERLY	WEEING	WEIGHAGES	WELDMESHES™	WERE
WEATHERS	WEEK	WEIGHED	WELDMESHES™	WEREGILD
WEAVE	WEEKDAY	WEIGHER	WELDOR	WEREGILDS
WEAVED	WEEKDAYS	WEIGHERS	WELDORS	WEREWOLF
WEAVER	WEEKE	WEIGHING	WELDS	WEREWOLVES
WEAVERS	WEEKEND	WEIGHINGS	WELFARE	WERGILD
WEAVES	WEEKENDS	WEIGHS	WELFARES	WERGILDS
WEAVING	WEEKES	WEIGHT	WELFARISM	WERNERITE
WEAVINGS	WEEKLIES	WEIGHTED	WELFARISMS	WERNERITES
WEAZAND	WEEKLY	WEIGHTIER	WELFARIST	WERSH
WEAZANDS	WEEKNIGHT	WEIGHTIEST	WELFARISTS	WERSHER
WEAZEN	WEEKNIGHTS	WEIGHTILY	WELK	WERSHEST
WEAZENED	WEEKS	WEIGHTING	WELKE	WERT
WEAZENING	WEEL	WEIGHTINGS	WELKED	WERWOLF
WEAZENS	WEELS	WEIGHTS	WELKES	WERWOLVES
WEB	WEEM	WEIGHTY	WELKIN	WESAND
WEBBED	WEEMS	WEIL	WELKING	WESANDS
WEBBIER	WEEN	WEILS	WELKINS	WEST
WEBBIEST	WEENED	WEIR	WELKS	WESTBOUND
WEBBING	WEENIER	WEIRD	WELKT	WESTED
WEBBINGS	WEENIEST	WEIRDED	WELL	WESTER
WEBBY	WEENING	WEIRDER	WELLADAY	WESTERED
WEBER	WEENS	WEIRDEST	WELLANEAR	WESTERING
WEBERS	WEENY	WEIRDIE	WELLAWAY	WESTERINGS
WEBS	WEEP	WEIRDIES	WELLED	WESTERLIES
WEBSTER	WEEPER	WEIRDING	WELLIE	WESTERLY
WEBSTERS	WEEPERS	WEIRDLY	WELLIES	WESTERN
WEBWHEEL	WEEPHOLE	WEIRDNESS	WELLING	WESTERNER
WEBWHEELS	WEEPHOLES	WEIRDNESSES	WELLINGS	WESTERNERS
WEBWORM	WEEPIE	WEIRDO	WELLS	WESTERNS
WEBWORMS	WEEPIER	WEIRDOS	WELLY	WESTERS
WECHT	WEEPIES	WEIRDS	WELSH	WESTING
WECHTS	WEEPIEST	WEIRED	WELSHED	WESTINGS
WED	WEEPING	WEIRING	WELSHER	WESTLIN
WEDDED	WEEPINGLY	WEIRS	WELSHERS	WESTMOST
WEDDING	WEEPINGS	WEISE	WELSHES	WESTS
WEDDINGS	WEEPS	WEISED	WELSHING	WESTWARD
WEDELN	WEEPY	WEISES	WELT	WESTWARDS
WEDELNED	WEER	WEISING	WELTED	WET
WEDELNING	WEES	WEIZE	WELTER	WETBACK
WEDELNS	WEEST	WEIZED	WELTERED	WETBACKS

WETHER	WHANGS	WHEELWORK	WHEREON	WHIFFLES
WETHERS	WHAP	WHEELWORKS	WHEREOUT	WHIFFLING
WETLAND	WHAPPED	WHEELY	WHERES	WHIFFLINGS
WETLANDS	WHAPPING	WHEEN	WHERESO	WHIFFS
WETLY	WHAPS	WHEENGE	WHERETO	WHIFFY
WETNESS	WHARE	WHEENGED	WHEREUNTO	WHIFT
WETNESSES	WHARES	WHEENGES	WHEREUPON	WHIFTS
WETS	WHARF	WHEENGING	WHEREVER	WHIG
WETTED	WHARFAGE	WHEENS	WHEREWITH	WHIGGED
WETTER	WHARFAGES	WHEEPLE	WHERRET	WHIGGING
WETTEST	WHARFED	WHEEPLED	WHERRETED	WHIGS
WETTING	WHARFING	WHEEPLES	WHERRETING	WHILE
WETTISH	WHARFINGS	WHEEPLING	WHERRETS	WHILED
WEX	WHARFS	WHEESHT	WHERRIES	WHILES
WEXE	WHARVE	WHEESHTED	WHERRY	WHILING
WEXED	WHARVES	WHEESHTING	WHERRYMAN	WHILK
WEXES	WHAT	WHEESHTS	WHERRYMEN	WHILLIED
WEXING	WHATEN	WHEEZE	WHET	WHILLIES
WEY	WHATEVER	WHEEZED	WHETHER	WHILLY
WEYARD	WHATNA	WHEEZES	WHETS	WHILLYING
WEYS	WHATNESS	WHEEZIER	WHETSTONE	WHILLYWHA
WEYWARD	WHATNESSES	WHEEZIEST	WHETSTONES	WHILLYWHAED
WEZAND	WHATNOT	WHEEZILY	WHETTED	WHILLYWHAING
WEZANDS	WHATNOTS	WHEEZING	WHETTER	WHILLYWHAS
WHACK	WHATS	WHEEZINGS	WHETTERS	WHILOM
WHACKED	WHATSIS	WHEEZLE	WHETTING	WHILST
WHACKER	WHATSIT	WHEEZLED	WHEUGH	WHIM
WHACKERS	WHATSITS	WHEEZLES	WHEUGHED	WHIMBREL
WHACKIER	WHATSO	WHEEZLING	WHEUGHING	WHIMBRELS
WHACKIEST	WHATTEN	WHEEZY	WHEUGHS	WHIMMED
WHACKING	WHAUP	WHEFT	WHEW	WHIMMIER
WHACKINGS	WHAUPS	WHEFTS	WHEWED	WHIMMIEST
WHACKO	WHAUR	WHELK	WHEWING	WHIMMING
WHACKOES	WHAURS	WHELKED	WHEWS	WHIMMY
WHACKOS	WHEAL	WHELKIER	WHEY	WHIMPER
WHACKS	WHEALS	WHELKIEST	WHEYEY	WHIMPERED
WHACKY	WHEAR	WHELKS	WHEYISH	WHIMPERER
WHAISLE	WHEARE	WHELKY	WHEYS	WHIMPERERS
WHAISLED	WHEAT	WHELM	WHICH	WHIMPERING
WHAISLES	WHEATEAR	WHELMED	WHICHEVER	WHIMPERINGS
WHAISLING	WHEATEARS	WHELMING	WHICKER	WHIMPERS
WHAIZLE	WHEATEN	WHELMS	WHICKERED	WHIMPLE
WHAIZLED	WHEATS	WHELP	WHICKERING	WHIMPLED
WHAIZLES	WHEE	WHELPED	WHICKERS	WHIMPLES
WHAIZLING	WHEECH	WHELPING	WHID	WHIMPLING
WHALE	WHEECHED	WHELPS	WHIDAH	WHIMS
WHALEBONE	WHEECHING	WHEMMLE	WHIDAHS	WHIMSEY
WHALEBONES	WHEECHS	WHEMMLED	WHIDDED	WHIMSEYS
WHALED	WHEEDLE	WHEMMLES	WHIDDER	WHIMSICAL
WHALER	WHEEDLED	WHEMMLING	WHIDDERED	WHIMSIES
WHALERIES	WHEEDLER	WHEN	WHIDDERING	WHIMSILY
WHALERS	WHEEDLERS	WHENAS	WHIDDERS	WHIMSY
WHALERY	WHEEDLES	WHENCE	WHIDDING	WHIN
WHALES	WHEEDLING	WHENCES	WHIDS	WHINCHAT
WHALING	WHEEDLINGS	WHENCEVER	WHIFF	WHINCHATS
WHALINGS	WHEEL	WHENEVER	WHIFFED	WHINE
WHALLY	WHEELBASE	WHENS	WHIFFER	WHINED
WHAM	WHEELBASES	WHERE	WHIFFERS	WHINER
WHAMMED	WHEELED	WHEREAS	WHIFFET	WHINERS
WHAMMING	WHEELER	WHEREAT	WHIFFETS	WHINES
WHAMPLE	WHEELERS	WHEREBY	WHIFFIER	WHINGE
WHAMPLES	WHEELIE	WHEREFOR	WHIFFIEST	WHINGED
WHAMS	WHEELIER	WHEREFORE	WHIFFING	WHINGEING
WHANG	WHEELIES	WHEREFORES	WHIFFINGS	WHINGEINGS
WHANGAM	WHEELIEST	WHEREFROM	WHIFFLE	WHINGER
WHANGAMS	WHEELING	WHEREIN	WHIFFLED	WHINGERS
WHANGED	WHEELINGS	WHEREINTO	WHIFFLER	WHINGES
WHANGEE	WHEELMAN	WHERENESS	WHIFFLERIES	WHINIARD
WHANGEES	WHEELMEN	WHERENESSES	WHIFFLERS	WHINIARDS
WHANGING	WHEELS	WHEREOF	WHIFFLERY	WHINIER

WHINIEST	WHIRRED	WHITED	WHIZZED	WHORESONS
WHININESS	WHIRRET	WHITEFISH	WHIZZER	WHORING
WHININESSES	WHIRRETED	WHITEFISHES	WHIZZERS	WHORISH
WHINING	WHIRRETING	WHITEHEAD	WHIZZES	WHORISHLY
WHININGLY	WHIRRETS	WHITEHEADS	WHIZZING	WHORL
WHININGS	WHIRRIED	WHITELY	WHIZZINGS	WHORLED
WHINNIED	WHIRRIES	WHITEN	WHO	WHORLS
WHINNIES	WHIRRING	WHITENED	WHOA	WHORT
WHINNY	WHIRRINGS	WHITENER	WHODUNNIT	WHORTS
WHINNYING	WHIRRS	WHITENERS	WHODUNNITS	WHOSE
WHINS	WHIRRY	WHITENESS	WHOEVER	WHOSEVER
WHINSTONE	WHIRRYING	WHITENESSES	WHOLE	WHOSO
WHINSTONES	WHIRS	WHITENING	WHOLEFOOD	WHOSOEVER
WHINY	WHIRTLE	WHITENINGS	WHOLEFOODS	WHOT
WHINYARD	WHIRTLES	WHITENS	WHOLEMEAL	WHOW
WHINYARDS	WHISH	WHITER	WHOLEMEALS	WHUMMLE
WHIP	WHISHED	WHITES	WHOLENESS	WHUMMLED
WHIPBIRD	WHISHES	WHITEST	WHOLENESSES	WHUMMLES
WHIPBIRDS	WHISHING	WHITEWALL	WHOLES	WHUMMLING
WHIPCAT	WHISHT	WHITEWALLS	WHOLESALE	WHUNSTANE
WHIPCATS	WHISHTED	WHITEWARE	WHOLESALES	WHUNSTANES
WHIPCORD	WHISHTING	WHITEWARES	WHOLESOME	WHY
WHIPCORDS	WHISHTS	WHITEWASH	WHOLESOMER	WHYDAH
WHIPCORDY	WHISK	WHITEWASHED	WHOLESOMEST	WHYDAHS
WHIPJACK	WHISKED	WHITEWASHES	WHOLISM	WHYEVER
WHIPJACKS	WHISKER	WHITEWASHING	WHOLISMS	WICK
WHIPLASH	WHISKERED	WHITEWING	WHOLISTIC	WICKED
WHIPLASHED	WHISKERS	WHITEWINGS	WHOLLY	WICKEDER
WHIPLASHES	WHISKERY	WHITEWOOD	WHOM	WICKEDEST
WHIPLASHING	WHISKET	WHITEWOODS	WHOMBLE	WICKEDLY
WHIPLIKE	WHISKETS	WHITEY	WHOMBLED	WICKEN
WHIPPED	WHISKEY	WHITEYS	WHOMBLES	WICKENS
WHIPPER	WHISKEYS	WHITHER	WHOMBLING	WICKER
WHIPPERS	WHISKIES	WHITHERED	WHOMEVER	WICKERED
WHIPPET	WHISKING	WHITHERING	WHOMMLE	WICKERS
WHIPPETS	WHISKS	WHITHERS	WHOMMLED	WICKET
WHIPPIER	WHISKY	WHITIER	WHOMMLES	WICKETS
WHIPPIEST	WHISPER	WHITIEST	WHOMMLING	WICKIES
WHIPPING	WHISPERED	WHITING	WHOOBUB	WICKING
WHIPPINGS	WHISPERER	WHITINGS	WHOOBUBS	WICKS
WHIPPY	WHISPERERS	WHITISH	WHOOP	WICKY
WHIPS	WHISPERING	WHITLING	WHOOPED	WIDDIES
WHIPSTAFF	WHISPERINGS	WHITLINGS	WHOOPEE	WIDDLE
WHIPSTAFFS	WHISPERS	WHITLOW	WHOOPEES	WIDDLED
WHIPSTALL	WHISPERY	WHITLOWS	WHOOPER	WIDDLES
WHIPSTALLED	WHISS	WHITRET	WHOOPERS	WIDDLING
WHIPSTALLING	WHISSED	WHITRETS	WHOOPING	WIDDY
WHIPSTALLS	WHISSES	WHITS	WHOOPINGS	WIDE
WHIPSTER	WHISSING	WHITSTER	WHOOPS	WIDELY
WHIPSTERS	WHIST	WHITSTERS	WHOOSH	WIDEN
WHIPT	WHISTED	WHITTAW	WHOOSHED	WIDENED
WHIPWORM	WHISTING	WHITTAWER	WHOOSHES	WIDENER
WHIPWORMS	WHISTLE	WHITTAWERS	WHOOSHING	WIDENERS
WHIR	WHISTLED	WHITTAWS	WHOOT	WIDENESS
WHIRL	WHISTLER	WHITTER	WHOOTED	WIDENESSES
WHIRLBAT	WHISTLERS	WHITTERED	WHOOTING	WIDENING
WHIRLBATS	WHISTLES	WHITTERING	WHOOTS	WIDENS
WHIRLED	WHISTLING	WHITTERS	WHOP	WIDER
WHIRLER	WHISTLINGS	WHITTLE	WHOPPED	WIDES
WHIRLERS	WHISTS	WHITTLED	WHOPPER	WIDEST
WHIRLIGIG	WHIT	WHITTLER	WHOPPERS	WIDGEON
WHIRLIGIGS	WHITE	WHITTLERS	WHOPPING	WIDGEONS
WHIRLING	WHITEBAIT	WHITTLES	WHOPPINGS	WIDGET
WHIRLINGS	WHITEBAITS	WHITTLING	WHOPS	WIDGETS
WHIRLPOOL	WHITEBASS	WHITTLINGS	WHORE	WIDISH
WHIRLPOOLS	WHITEBASSES	WHITTRET	WHORED	WIDOW
WHIRLS	WHITEBEAM	WHITTRETS	WHOREDOM	WIDOWED
WHIRLWIND	WHITEBEAMS	WHITY	WHOREDOMS	WIDOWER
WHIRLWINDS	WHITECAP	WHIZ	WHORES	WIDOWERS
WHIRR	WHITECAPS	WHIZZ	WHORESON	WIDOWHOOD

WIDOWHOODS	WILDFIRE	WIMPIER	WINDOWING	WINN
WIDOWING	WILDFIRES	WIMPIEST	WINDOWINGS	WINNA
WIDOWS	WILDGRAVE	WIMPISH	WINDOWS	WINNABLE
WIDTH	WILDGRAVES	WIMPLE	WINDPIPE	WINNER
WIDTHS	WILDING	WIMPLED	WINDPIPES	WINNERS
WIDTHWAYS	WILDINGS	WIMPLES	WINDRING	WINNING
WIDTHWISE	WILDISH	WIMPLING	WINDROSE	WINNINGLY
WIEL	WILDLIFE	WIMPS	WINDROSES	WINNINGS
WIELD	WILDLY	WIMPY	WINDROW	WINNLE
WIELDABLE	WILDNESS	WIN	WINDROWED	WINNLES
WIELDED	WILDNESSES	WINCE	WINDROWING	WINNOCK
WIELDER	WILDOAT	WINCED	WINDROWS	WINNOCKS
WIELDERS	WILDOATS	WINCER	WINDS	WINNOW
WIELDIER	WILDS	WINCERS	WINDSES	WINNOWED
WIELDIEST	WILE	WINCES	WINDSHIP	WINNOWER
WIELDING	WILED	WINCEY	WINDSHIPS	WINNOWERS
WIELDLESS	WILEFUL	WINCEYS	WINDSTORM	WINNOWING
WIELDS	WILES	WINCH	WINDSTORMS	WINNOWINGS
WIELDY	WILFUL	WINCHED	WINDSURF	WINNOWS
WIELS	WILFULLY	WINCHES	WINDSURFED	WINNS
WIFE	WILI	WINCHING	WINDSURFS	WINO
WIFEHOOD	WILIER	WINCHMAN	WINDSWEPT	WINOS
WIFEHOODS	WILIEST	WINCHMEN	WINDTHROW	WINS
WIFELESS	WILILY	WINCING	WINDTHROWS	WINSEY
WIFELIER	WILINESS	WINCINGS	WINDWARD	WINSEYS
WIFELIEST	WILINESSES	WINCOPIPE	WINDWARDS	WINSOME
WIFELY	WILING	WINCOPIPES	WINDY	WINSOMELY
WIG	WILIS	WIND	WINE	WINSOMER
WIGAN	WILL	WINDAC	WINED	WINSOMEST
WIGANS	WILLABLE	WINDACS	WINERIES	WINTER
WIGEON	WILLED	WINDAGE	WINERY	WINTERED
WIGEONS	WILLEMITE	WINDAGES	WINES	WINTERIER
WIGGED	WILLEMITES	WINDAS	WINEY	WINTERIEST
WIGGERIES	WILLERS	WINDASES	WING	WINTERING
WIGGERY	WILLET	WINDBLOW	WINGBEAT	WINTERISE
WIGGING	WILLETS	WINDBLOWS	WINGBEATS	WINTERISED
WIGGINGS	WILLEY	WINDBURN	WINGDING	WINTERISES
WIGGLE	WILLEYED	WINDBURNS	WINGDINGS	WINTERISING
WIGGLED	WILLEYING	WINDED	WINGE	WINTERIZE
WIGGLER	WILLEYS	WINDER	WINGED	WINTERIZED
WIGGLERS	WILLIE	WINDERS	WINGEDLY	WINTERIZES
WIGGLES	WILLIED	WINDFALL	WINGEING	WINTERIZING
WIGGLIER	WILLIES	WINDFALLS	WINGER	WINTERLY
WIGGLIEST	WILLING	WINDIER	WINGERS	WINTERS
WIGGLING	WILLINGLY	WINDIEST	WINGES	WINTERY
WIGGLY	WILLIWAW	WINDIGO	WINGIER	WINTLE
WIGHT	WILLIWAWS	WINDIGOS	WINGIEST	WINTLED
WIGHTED	WILLOW	WINDILY	WINGING	WINTLES
WIGHTING	WILLOWED	WINDINESS	WINGLESS	WINTLING
WIGHTLY	WILLOWING	WINDINESSES	WINGLET	WINTRIER
WIGHTS	WILLOWISH	WINDING	WINGLETS	WINTRIEST
WIGLESS	WILLOWS	WINDINGLY	WINGS	WINTRY
WIGS	WILLOWY	WINDINGS	WINGSPAN	WINY
WIGWAG	WILLS	WINDLASS	WINGSPANS	WINZE
WIGWAGGED	WILLY	WINDLASSED	WINGY	WINZES
WIGWAGGING	WILLYARD	WINDLASSES	WINIER	WIPE
WIGWAGS	WILLYART	WINDLASSING	WINIEST	WIPED
WIGWAM	WILLYING	WINDLE	WINING	WIPEOUT
WIGWAMS	WILT	WINDLES	WINK	WIPEOUTS
WILCO	WILTED	WINDLESS	WINKED	WIPER
WILD	WILTING	WINDMILL	WINKER	WIPERS
WILDCAT	WILTS	WINDMILLED	WINKERS	WIPES
WILDCATS	WILY	WINDMILLING	WINKING	WIPING
WILDCATTED	WIMBLE	WINDMILLS	WINKINGLY	WIPINGS
WILDCATTING	WIMBLED	WINDOCK	WINKINGS	WIRE
WILDER	WIMBLES	WINDOCKS	WINKLE	WIRED
WILDERED	WIMBLING	WINDORE	WINKLER	WIREDRAW
WILDERING	WIMBREL	WINDORES	WINKLERS	WIREDRAWING
WILDERS	WIMBRELS	WINDOW	WINKLES	WIREDRAWINGS
WILDEST	WIMP	WINDOWED	WINKS	WIREDRAWN

WIREDRAWS
WIREDREW
WIRELESS
WIRELESSED
WIRELESSES
WIRELESSING
WIREPHOTO
WIREPHOTOS
WIRER
WIRERS
WIRES
WIRETAP
WIRETAPPED
WIRETAPPING
WIRETAPS
WIREWORK
WIREWORKS
WIREWOVE
WIRIER
WIRIEST
WIRILY
WIRINESS
WIRINESSES
WIRING
WIRINGS
WIRRICOW
WIRRICOWS
WIRY
WIS
WISARD
WISARDS
WISDOM
WISDOMS
WISE
WISEACRE
WISEACRES
WISECRACK
WISECRACKED
WISECRACKING
WISECRACKS
WISED
WISELING
WISELINGS
WISELY
WISENESS
WISENESSES
WISENT
WISENTS
WISER
WISES
WISEST
WISH
WISHBONE
WISHBONES
WISHED
WISHER
WISHERS
WISHES
WISHFUL
WISHFULLY
WISHING
WISHINGS
WISING
WISKET
WISKETS
WISP
WISPED
WISPIER
WISPIEST
WISPING

WISPS
WISPY
WIST
WISTARIA
WISTARIAS
WISTED
WISTERIA
WISTERIAS
WISTFUL
WISTFULLY
WISTING
WISTITI
WISTITIS
WISTLY
WISTS
WIT
WITAN
WITCH
WITCHED
WITCHEN
WITCHENS
WITCHERIES
WITCHERY
WITCHES
WITCHETTIES
WITCHETTY
WITCHING
WITCHINGS
WITCHKNOT
WITCHKNOTS
WITE
WITED
WITELESS
WITES
WITGAT
WITGATS
WITH
WITHAL
WITHDRAW
WITHDRAWING
WITHDRAWN
WITHDRAWS
WITHDREW
WITHE
WITHED
WITHER
WITHERED
WITHERING
WITHERINGS
WITHERITE
WITHERITES
WITHERS
WITHES
WITHHAULT
WITHHELD
WITHHOLD
WITHHOLDING
WITHHOLDS
WITHIER
WITHIES
WITHIEST
WITHIN
WITHING
WITHOUT
WITHOUTEN
WITHS
WITHSTAND
WITHSTANDING
WITHSTANDS
WITHSTOOD

WITHWIND
WITHWINDS
WITHY
WITHYWIND
WITHYWINDS
WITING
WITLESS
WITLESSLY
WITLING
WITLINGS
WITLOOF
WITLOOFS
WITNESS
WITNESSED
WITNESSER
WITNESSERS
WITNESSES
WITNESSING
WITS
WITTED
WITTER
WITTERED
WITTERING
WITTERS
WITTICISM
WITTICISMS
WITTIER
WITTIEST
WITTILY
WITTINESS
WITTINESSES
WITTING
WITTINGLY
WITTINGS
WITTOL
WITTOLLY
WITTOLS
WITTY
WITWALL
WITWALLS
WITWANTON
WITWANTONED
WITWANTONING
WITWANTONS
WIVE
WIVED
WIVEHOOD
WIVEHOODS
WIVERN
WIVERNS
WIVES
WIVING
WIZARD
WIZARDLY
WIZARDRIES
WIZARDRY
WIZARDS
WIZEN
WIZENED
WIZENING
WIZENS
WIZIER
WIZIERS
WO
WOAD
WOADED
WOADS
WOBBEGONG
WOBBEGONGS
WOBBLE

WOBBLED
WOBBLER
WOBBLERS
WOBBLES
WOBBLIER
WOBBLIES
WOBBLIEST
WOBBLING
WOBBLINGS
WOBBLY
WOBEGONE
WOCK
WOCKS
WODGE
WODGES
WOE
WOEBEGONE
WOEFUL
WOEFULLER
WOEFULLEST
WOEFULLY
WOEFULNESS
WOEFULNESSES
WOES
WOESOME
WOFUL
WOFULLY
WOFULNESS
WOFULNESSES
WOG
WOGGLE
WOGGLES
WOGS
WOIWODE
WOIWODES
WOK
WOKE
WOKEN
WOKS
WOLD
WOLDS
WOLF
WOLFED
WOLFER
WOLFERS
WOLFING
WOLFINGS
WOLFISH
WOLFISHLY
WOLFKIN
WOLFKINS
WOLFLING
WOLFLINGS
WOLFRAM
WOLFRAMS
WOLFS
WOLFSBANE
WOLFSBANES
WOLLIES
WOLLY
WOLVE
WOLVED
WOLVER
WOLVERENE
WOLVERENES
WOLVERINE
WOLVERINES
WOLVERS
WOLVES
WOLVING

WOLVINGS
WOLVISH
WOLVISHLY
WOMAN
WOMANED
WOMANHOOD
WOMANING
WOMANISE
WOMANISED
WOMANISER
WOMANISERS
WOMANISES
WOMANISH
WOMANISING
WOMANIZE
WOMANIZED
WOMANIZER
WOMANIZERS
WOMANIZES
WOMANIZING
WOMANKIND
WOMANLIER
WOMANLIEST
WOMANLY
WOMANS
WOMB
WOMBAT
WOMBATS
WOMBED
WOMBING
WOMBS
WOMBY
WOMEN
WOMENFOLK
WOMENFOLKS
WOMENKIND
WOMERA
WOMERAS
WON
WONDER
WONDERED
WONDERER
WONDERERS
WONDERFUL
WONDERING
WONDERINGS
WONDEROUS
WONDERS
WONDRED
WONDROUS
WONGA
WONGAS
WONING
WONINGS
WONKIER
WONKIEST
WONKY
WONNED
WONNING
WONS
WONT
WONTED
WONTING
WONTLESS
WONTS
WOO
WOOBUT
WOOBUTS
WOOD
WOODBIND

WOODBINDS
WOODBINE
WOODBINES
WOODBLOCK
WOODBLOCKS
WOODCHIP
WOODCHIPS
WOODCHUCK
WOODCHUCKS
WOODCOCK
WOODCOCKS
WOODCRAFT
WOODCRAFTS
WOODCUT
WOODCUTS
WOODED
WOODEN
WOODENER
WOODENEST
WOODENLY
WOODHOUSE
WOODHOUSES
WOODIE
WOODIER
WOODIES
WOODIEST
WOODINESS
WOODINESSES
WOODING
WOODLAND
WOODLANDS
WOODLESS
WOODLICE
WOODLOUSE
WOODMAN
WOODMEN
WOODMICE
WOODMOUSE
WOODNESS
WOODNESSES
WOODRUFF
WOODRUFFS
WOODS
WOODSHED
WOODSHEDDED
WOODSHEDDING
WOODSHEDS
WOODSIER
WOODSIEST
WOODSMAN
WOODSMEN
WOODSY
WOODWALE
WOODWALES
WOODWARD
WOODWARDS
WOODWIND
WOODWINDS
WOODWORK
WOODWORKS
WOODWOSE
WOODWOSES
WOODY
WOOED
WOOER
WOOERS
WOOF
WOOFED
WOOFER
WOOFERS
WOOFIER
WOOFIEST
WOOFS
WOOFY
WOOING
WOOINGLY
WOOINGS
WOOL
WOOLD
WOOLDED
WOOLDER
WOOLDERS
WOOLDING
WOOLDINGS
WOOLDS
WOOLFAT
WOOLFATS
WOOLFELL
WOOLFELLS
WOOLLED
WOOLLEN
WOOLLENS
WOOLLIER
WOOLLIES
WOOLLIEST
WOOLLY
WOOLMAN
WOOLMEN
WOOLS
WOOLSACK
WOOLSACKS
WOOLSEY
WOOLSEYS
WOOLWARD
WOOLWORK
WOOLWORKS
WOOMERA
WOOMERANG
WOOMERANGS
WOOMERAS
WOON
WOONED
WOONING
WOONS
WOORALI
WOORALIS
WOORARA
WOORARAS
WOOS
WOOSEL
WOOSELL
WOOSELLS
WOOSELS
WOOSH
WOOSHED
WOOSHES
WOOSHING
WOOT
WOOTZ
WOOTZES
WOOZIER
WOOZIEST
WOOZILY
WOOZINESS
WOOZINESSES
WOOZY
WOP
WOPPED
WOPPING
WOPS
WORCESTER
WORCESTERS
WORD
WORDAGE
WORDAGES
WORDBOOK
WORDBOOKS
WORDBOUND
WORDED
WORDIER
WORDIEST
WORDILY
WORDINESS
WORDINESSES
WORDING
WORDINGS
WORDISH
WORDLESS
WORDS
WORDSMITH
WORDSMITHS
WORDY
WORE
WORE WORN
WORK
WORKABLE
WORKADAY
WORKBOAT
WORKBOATS
WORKBOOK
WORKBOOKS
WORKED
WORKER
WORKERIST
WORKERISTS
WORKERS
WORKFOLK
WORKFOLKS
WORKFORCE
WORKFORCES
WORKFUL
WORKHORSE
WORKHORSES
WORKHOUSE
WORKHOUSES
WORKING
WORKINGS
WORKLESS
WORKLOAD
WORKLOADS
WORKMAN
WORKMANLY
WORKMEN
WORKPIECE
WORKPIECES
WORKPLACE
WORKPLACES
WORKROOM
WORKROOMS
WORKS
WORKSHOP
WORKSHOPS
WORKSOME
WORKTOP
WORKTOPS
WORKWEAR
WORKWEARS
WORLD
WORLDED
WORLDLIER
WORLDLIEST
WORLDLING
WORLDLINGS
WORLDLY
WORLDS
WORLDWIDE
WORM
WORMED
WORMER
WORMERIES
WORMERS
WORMERY
WORMIER
WORMIEST
WORMING
WORMS
WORMWOOD
WORMWOODS
WORMY
WORN
WORRAL
WORRALS
WORREL
WORRELS
WORRICOW
WORRICOWS
WORRIED
WORRIER
WORRIERS
WORRIES
WORRIMENT
WORRIMENTS
WORRISOME
WORRIT
WORRITED
WORRITING
WORRITS
WORRY
WORRYCOW
WORRYCOWS
WORRYGUTS
WORRYING
WORRYINGS
WORRYWART
WORRYWARTS
WORSE
WORSED
WORSEN
WORSENED
WORSENESS
WORSENESSES
WORSENING
WORSENS
WORSER
WORSES
WORSHIP
WORSHIPPED
WORSHIPPING
WORSHIPS
WORSING
WORST
WORSTED
WORSTEDS
WORSTING
WORSTS
WORT
WORTH
WORTHED
WORTHFUL
WORTHIED
WORTHIER
WORTHIES
WORTHIEST
WORTHILY
WORTHING
WORTHLESS
WORTHS
WORTHY
WORTHYING
WORTLE
WORTLES
WORTS
WOS
WOSBIRD
WOSBIRDS
WOST
WOT
WOTCHER
WOTS
WOTTED
WOTTEST
WOTTETH
WOTTING
WOUBIT
WOUBITS
WOULD
WOULDS
WOULDST
WOUND
WOUNDABLE
WOUNDED
WOUNDER
WOUNDERS
WOUNDILY
WOUNDING
WOUNDINGS
WOUNDLESS
WOUNDS
WOUNDWORT
WOUNDWORTS
WOUNDY
WOURALI
WOURALIS
WOVE
WOVEN
WOW
WOWED
WOWEE
WOWF
WOWFER
WOWFEST
WOWING
WOWS
WOWSER
WOWSERS
WOX
WOXEN
WRACK
WRACKED
WRACKFUL
WRACKING
WRACKS
WRAITH
WRAITHS
WRANGLE
WRANGLED
WRANGLER
WRANGLERS
WRANGLES
WRANGLING

WRANGLINGS	WREAKLESS	WRETHE	WRITABLE	WRYEST
WRAP	WREAKS	WRETHED	WRITATIVE	WRYING
WRAPOVER	WREATH	WRETHES	WRITE	WRYLY
WRAPOVERS	WREATHE	WRETHING	WRITER	WRYNECK
WRAPPAGE	WREATHED	WRICK	WRITERESS	WRYNECKS
WRAPPAGES	WREATHEN	WRICKED	WRITERESSES	WRYNESS
WRAPPED	WREATHER	WRICKING	WRITERLY	WRYNESSES
WRAPPER	WREATHERS	WRICKS	WRITERS	WRYTHEN
WRAPPERS	WREATHES	WRIED	WRITES	WUD
WRAPPING	WREATHIER	WRIER	WRITHE	WUDDED
WRAPPINGS	WREATHIEST	WRIES	WRITHED	WUDDING
WRAPROUND	WREATHING	WRIEST	WRITHEN	WUDS
WRAPROUNDS	WREATHS	WRIGGLE	WRITHES	WULFENITE
WRAPS	WREATHY	WRIGGLED	WRITHING	WULFENITES
WRAPT	WRECK	WRIGGLER	WRITHINGS	WULL
WRASSE	WRECKAGE	WRIGGLERS	WRITHLED	WULLED
WRASSES	WRECKAGES	WRIGGLES	WRITING	WULLING
WRAST	WRECKED	WRIGGLIER	WRITINGS	WULLS
WRASTED	WRECKER	WRIGGLIEST	WRITS	WUNNER
WRASTING	WRECKERS	WRIGGLING	WRITTEN	WUNNERS
WRASTS	WRECKFISH	WRIGGLINGS	WRIZLED	WURLEY
WRATE	WRECKFISHES	WRIGGLY	WROATH	WURLEYS
WRATH	WRECKFUL	WRIGHT	WROATHS	WURLIES
WRATHED	WRECKING	WRIGHTS	WROKE	WURST
WRATHFUL	WRECKINGS	WRING	WROKEN	WURSTS
WRATHIER	WRECKS	WRINGED	WRONG	WURTZITE
WRATHIEST	WREN	WRINGER	WRONGED	WURTZITES
WRATHILY	WRENCH	WRINGERS	WRONGER	WUSHU
WRATHING	WRENCHED	WRINGING	WRONGERS	WUSHUS
WRATHLESS	WRENCHES	WRINGINGS	WRONGEST	WUTHER
WRATHS	WRENCHING	WRINGS	WRONGFUL	WUTHERED
WRATHY	WRENCHINGS	WRINKLE	WRONGING	WUTHERING
WRAWL	WRENS	WRINKLED	WRONGLY	WUTHERS
WRAWLED	WREST	WRINKLES	WRONGNESS	WUZZLE
WRAWLING	WRESTED	WRINKLIER	WRONGNESSES	WUZZLED
WRAWLS	WRESTER	WRINKLIES	WRONGOUS	WUZZLES
WRAXLE	WRESTERS	WRINKLIEST	WRONGS	WUZZLING
WRAXLED	WRESTING	WRINKLING	WROOT	WYANDOTTE
WRAXLES	WRESTLE	WRINKLY	WROOTED	WYANDOTTES
WRAXLING	WRESTLED	WRIST	WROOTING	WYE
WRAXLINGS	WRESTLER	WRISTBAND	WROOTS	WYES
WREAK	WRESTLERS	WRISTBANDS	WROTE	WYND
WREAKE	WRESTLES	WRISTIER	WROTH	WYNDS
WREAKED	WRESTLING	WRISTIEST	WROUGHT	WYTE
WREAKER	WRESTLINGS	WRISTLET	WRUNG	WYTED
WREAKERS	WRESTS	WRISTLETS	WRY	WYTES
WREAKES	WRETCH	WRISTS	WRYBILL	WYTING
WREAKFUL	WRETCHED	WRISTY	WRYBILLS	WYVERN
WREAKING	WRETCHES	WRIT	WRYER	WYVERNS

X

XANTHATE	XENOLITHS	XERASIAS	XOANON	XYLOMAS
XANTHATES	XENOMANIA	XERIC	XOANONS	XYLOMETER
XANTHEIN	XENOMANIAS	XEROCHASIES	XYLEM	XYLOMETERS
XANTHEINS	XENOMENIA	XEROCHASY	XYLEMS	XYLONIC
XANTHENE	XENOMENIAS	XERODERMA	XYLENE	XYLONITE
XANTHENES	XENON	XERODERMAS	XYLENES	XYLONITES
XANTHIC	XENONS	XEROMA	XYLENOL	XYLOPHAGE
XANTHIN	XENOPHILE	XEROMAS	XYLENOLS	XYLOPHAGES
XANTHINE	XENOPHILES	XEROMORPH	XYLIC	XYLOPHONE
XANTHINES	XENOPHOBE	XEROMORPHS	XYLITOL	XYLOPHONES
XANTHINS	XENOPHOBES	XEROPHAGIES	XYLITOLS	XYLORIMBA
XANTHOMA	XENOPHOBIES	XEROPHAGY	XYLOCARP	XYLORIMBAS
XANTHOMAS	XENOPHOBY	XEROPHILIES	XYLOCARPS	XYLOSE
XANTHOUS	XENOPHYA	XEROPHILY	XYLOGEN	XYLOSES
XEBEC	XENOPHYAS	XEROPHYTE	XYLOGENS	XYLYL
XEBECS	XENOTIME	XEROPHYTES	XYLOGRAPH	XYLYLS
XENIA	XENOTIMES	XEROSES	XYLOGRAPHS	XYST
XENIAL	XENURINE	XEROSIS	XYLOID	XYSTER
XENIAS	XERAFIN	XEROSTOMA	XYLOIDIN	XYSTERS
XENIUM	XERAFINS	XEROSTOMAS	XYLOIDINE	XYSTI
XENOCRYST	XERANSES	XEROTES	XYLOIDINES	XYSTOI
XENOCRYSTS	XERANSIS	XEROTESES	XYLOIDINS	XYSTOS
XENOGAMIES	XERANTIC	XEROTIC	XYLOL	XYSTOSES
XENOGAMY	XERAPHIM	XI	XYLOLOGIES	XYSTS
XENOGRAFT	XERAPHIMS	XIPHOID	XYLOLOGY	XYSTUS
XENOGRAFTS	XERARCH	XIPHOIDAL	XYLOLS	XYSTUSES
XENOLITH	XERASIA	XIS	XYLOMA	

Y

YABBER
YABBERED
YABBERING
YABBERS
YABBIE
YABBIES
YABBY
YACCA
YACCAS
YACHT
YACHTED
YACHTER
YACHTERS
YACHTING
YACHTINGS
YACHTS
YACHTSMAN
YACHTSMEN
YACK
YACKED
YACKER
YACKERS
YACKING
YACKS
YAFF
YAFFED
YAFFING
YAFFLE
YAFFLES
YAFFS
YAGER
YAGERS
YAGGER
YAGGERS
YAH
YAHOO
YAHOOS
YAK
YAKHDAN
YAKHDANS
YAKKA
YAKKAS
YAKKED
YAKKER
YAKKERS
YAKKING
YAKS
YAKUZA
YALD
YALE
YALES
YAM
YAMEN
YAMENS
YAMMER
YAMMERED
YAMMERING
YAMMERINGS
YAMMERS
YAMS
YAMULKA
YAMULKAS
YANG
YANGS

YANK
YANKED
YANKER
YANKERS
YANKIE
YANKIES
YANKING
YANKS
YAOURT
YAOURTS
YAP
YAPOCK
YAPOCKS
YAPOK
YAPOKS
YAPON
YAPONS
YAPP
YAPPED
YAPPER
YAPPERS
YAPPING
YAPPS
YAPS
YAPSTER
YAPSTERS
YARD
YARDAGE
YARDAGES
YARDANG
YARDANGS
YARDED
YARDING
YARDLAND
YARDLANDS
YARDMAN
YARDMEN
YARDS
YARDSTICK
YARDSTICKS
YARDWAND
YARDWANDS
YARE
YARELY
YARER
YAREST
YARFA
YARFAS
YARMULKA
YARMULKAS
YARMULKE
YARMULKES
YARN
YARNED
YARNING
YARNS
YARPHA
YARPHAS
YARR
YARROW
YARROWS
YARRS
YARTA
YARTAS

YARTO
YARTOS
YASHMAK
YASHMAKS
YATAGAN
YATAGANS
YATAGHAN
YATAGHANS
YATE
YATES
YATTER
YATTERED
YATTERING
YATTERINGS
YATTERS
YAUD
YAUDS
YAULD
YAUP
YAUPON
YAUPONS
YAW
YAWED
YAWEY
YAWING
YAWL
YAWLED
YAWLING
YAWLS
YAWN
YAWNED
YAWNIER
YAWNIEST
YAWNING
YAWNINGLY
YAWNINGS
YAWNS
YAWNY
YAWP
YAWPED
YAWPER
YAWPERS
YAWPING
YAWPS
YAWS
YAWY
YBET
YBLENT
YBORE
YBOUND
YBOUNDEN
YBRENT
YCLAD
YCLED
YCLEEPE
YCLEPED
YCLEPT
YCOND
YDRAD
YDRED
YE
YEA
YEAD
YEADING

YEADS
YEAH
YEALDON
YEALDONS
YEALM
YEALMED
YEALMING
YEALMS
YEAN
YEANED
YEANING
YEANLING
YEANLINGS
YEANS
YEAR
YEARD
YEARDED
YEARDING
YEARDS
YEARLIES
YEARLING
YEARLINGS
YEARLONG
YEARLY
YEARN
YEARNED
YEARNING
YEARNINGS
YEARNS
YEARS
YEAS
YEAST
YEASTED
YEASTIER
YEASTIEST
YEASTING
YEASTS
YEASTY
YEDE
YEDES
YEED
YEEDS
YEGG
YEGGMAN
YEGGMEN
YEGGS
YELD
YELDRING
YELDRINGS
YELDROCK
YELDROCKS
YELK
YELKS
YELL
YELLED
YELLING
YELLINGS
YELLOCH
YELLOCHED
YELLOCHING
YELLOCHS
YELLOW
YELLOWED
YELLOWER

YELLOWEST
YELLOWING
YELLOWISH
YELLOWS
YELLOWY
YELLS
YELM
YELMED
YELMING
YELMS
YELP
YELPED
YELPER
YELPERS
YELPING
YELPINGS
YELPS
YELT
YELTS
YEN
YENNED
YENNING
YENS
YENTA
YENTAS
YEOMAN
YEOMANLY
YEOMANRIES
YEOMANRY
YEOMEN
YEP
YEPS
YERBA
YERBAS
YERD
YERDED
YERDING
YERDS
YERK
YERKED
YERKING
YERKS
YERSINIA
YERSINIAE
YERSINIAS
YES
YESES
YESHIVA
YESHIVAH
YESHIVAHS
YESHIVAS
YESHIVATH
YESHIVOTH
YESK
YESKED
YESKING
YESKS
YESSES
YEST
YESTER
YESTERDAY
YESTERDAYS
YESTEREVE
YESTEREVES

YESTERN	YLKE	YOJANS	YOUNGSTER	YU
YESTREEN	YMOLT	YOK	YOUNGSTERS	YUAN
YESTS	YMOLTEN	YOKE	YOUNGTH	YUCA
YESTY	YMPE	YOKED	YOUNGTHLY	YUCAS
YET	YMPES	YOKEL	YOUNGTHS	YUCCA
YETI	YMPING	YOKELISH	YOUNKER	YUCCAS
YETIS	YMPT	YOKELS	YOUNKERS	YUCK
YETT	YNAMBU	YOKES	YOUR	YUCKED
YETTS	YNAMBUS	YOKING	YOURN	YUCKER
YEUK	YO	YOKINGS	YOURS	YUCKERS
YEUKED	YOB	YOKKED	YOURSELF	YUCKIER
YEUKING	YOBBISH	YOKKING	YOURSELVES	YUCKIEST
YEUKS	YOBBISHLY	YOKS	YOURT	YUCKING
YEVE	YOBBO	YOKUL	YOURTS	YUCKS
YEVEN	YOBBOES	YOLD	YOUTH	YUCKY
YEVES	YOBBOS	YOLDRING	YOUTHFUL	YUFT
YEVING	YOBS	YOLDRINGS	YOUTHHEAD	YUFTS
YEW	YOCK	YOLK	YOUTHHEADS	YUG
YEWEN	YOCKED	YOLKED	YOUTHHOOD	YUGA
YEWS	YOCKING	YOLKIER	YOUTHHOODS	YUGAS
YEX	YOCKS	YOLKIEST	YOUTHIER	YUGS
YEXED	YOD	YOLKS	YOUTHIEST	YUK
YEXES	YODE	YOLKY	YOUTHLY	YUKE
YEXING	YODEL	YOMP	YOUTHS	YUKED
YFERE	YODELLED	YOMPED	YOUTHSOME	YUKES
YGLAUNST	YODELLER	YOMPING	YOUTHY	YUKIER
YGO	YODELLERS	YOMPS	YOW	YUKIEST
YGOE	YODELLING	YON	YOWE	YUKING
YIBBLES	YODELS	YOND	YOWES	YUKKIER
YIELD	YODLE	YONDER	YOWIE	YUKKIEST
YIELDABLE	YODLED	YONGTHLY	YOWIES	YUKKY
YIELDED	YODLER	YONI	YOWL	YUKS
YIELDER	YODLERS	YONIS	YOWLED	YUKY
YIELDERS	YODLES	YONKER	YOWLEY	YULAN
YIELDING	YODLING	YONKERS	YOWLEYS	YULANS
YIELDINGS	YOGA	YONKS	YOWLING	YULE
YIELDS	YOGAS	YONT	YOWLINGS	YULES
YIKKER	YOGH	YOOP	YOWLS	YULETIDE
YIKKERED	YOGHOURT	YOOPS	YOWS	YULETIDES
YIKKERING	YOGHOURTS	YOPPER	YPIGHT	YUMMIER
YIKKERS	YOGHS	YOPPERS	YPLAST	YUMMIEST
YILL	YOGHURT	YORE	YPLIGHT	YUMMY
YILLS	YOGHURTS	YORES	YPSILOID	YUMP
YIN	YOGI	YORK	YPSILON	YUMPIE
YINCE	YOGIC	YORKED	YPSILONS	YUMPIES
YINS	YOGIN	YORKER	YRAPT	YUMPS
YIP	YOGINI	YORKERS	YRAVISHED	YUNX
YIPPED	YOGINIS	YORKIE	YRENT	YUNXES
YIPPEE	YOGINS	YORKIES	YRIVD	YUP
YIPPIES	YOGIS	YORKING	YSAME	YUPON
YIPPING	YOGISM	YORKS	YSHEND	YUPONS
YIPPY	YOGISMS	YOS	YSHENDING	YUPPIE
YIPS	YOGURT	YOU	YSHENDS	YUPPIES
YIRD	YOGURTS	YOUK	YSHENT	YUPPY
YIRDED	YOHIMBINE	YOUKED	YSLAKED	YUPS
YIRDING	YOHIMBINES	YOUKING	YTOST	YURT
YIRDS	YOICK	YOUKS	YTTERBIA	YURTS
YIRK	YOICKED	YOUNG	YTTERBIAS	YUS
YIRKED	YOICKING	YOUNGER	YTTERBIUM	YWIS
YIRKING	YOICKS	YOUNGEST	YTTERBIUMS	YWRAKE
YIRKS	YOICKSED	YOUNGISH	YTTRIA	YWROKE
YITE	YOICKSES	YOUNGLING	YTTRIAS	YWROKEN
YITES	YOICKSING	YOUNGLINGS	YTTRIC	
YLEM	YOJAN	YOUNGLY	YTTRIOUS	
YLEMS	YOJANA	YOUNGNESS	YTTRIUM	
YLIKE	YOJANAS	YOUNGNESSES	YTTRIUMS	

Z

ZABAIONE	ZANYISMS	ZEBRASSES	ZERO	ZILLIONTHS
ZABAIONES	ZANZE	ZEBRINE	ZEROED	ZIMB
ZABETA	ZANZES	ZEBRINNIES	ZEROING	ZIMBI
ZABETAS	ZAP	ZEBRINNY	ZEROS	ZIMBIS
ZABRA	ZAPATEADO	ZEBROID	ZEROTH	ZIMBS
ZABRAS	ZAPATEADOS	ZEBRULA	ZERUMBET	ZIMMER
ZABTIEH	ZAPOTILLA	ZEBRULAS	ZERUMBETS	ZIMMERS
ZABTIEHS	ZAPOTILLAS	ZEBRULE	ZEST	ZIMOCCA
ZACK	ZAPPED	ZEBRULES	ZESTFUL	ZIMOCCAS
ZACKS	ZAPPIER	ZEBU	ZESTFULLY	ZINC
ZADDIK	ZAPPIEST	ZEBUB	ZESTIER	ZINCED
ZADDIKIM	ZAPPING	ZEBUBS	ZESTIEST	ZINCIER
ZADDIKS	ZAPPY	ZEBUS	ZESTS	ZINCIEST
ZAFFER	ZAPS	ZECCHINE	ZESTY	ZINCIFIED
ZAFFERS	ZAPTIAH	ZECCHINES	ZETA	ZINCIFIES
ZAFFRE	ZAPTIAHS	ZECCHINI	ZETAS	ZINCIFY
ZAFFRES	ZAPTIEH	ZECCHINO	ZETETIC	ZINCIFYING
ZAG	ZAPTIEHS	ZECCHINOS	ZETETICS	ZINCING
ZAGGED	ZARAPE	ZED	ZEUGMA	ZINCITE
ZAGGING	ZARAPES	ZEDOARIES	ZEUGMAS	ZINCITES
ZAGS	ZARATITE	ZEDOARY	ZEUGMATIC	ZINCKED
ZAIRE	ZARATITES	ZEDS	ZEUXITE	ZINCKIER
ZAKUSKA	ZAREBA	ZEE	ZEUXITES	ZINCKIEST
ZAKUSKI	ZAREBAS	ZEES	ZEZE	ZINCKIFIED
ZAMAN	ZAREEBA	ZEIN	ZEZES	ZINCKIFIES
ZAMANG	ZAREEBAS	ZEINS	ZHO	ZINCKIFY
ZAMANGS	ZARF	ZEITGEIST	ZHOMO	ZINCKIFYING
ZAMANS	ZARFS	ZEITGEISTS	ZHOMOS	ZINCKING
ZAMARRA	ZARIBA	ZEK	ZHOS	ZINCKY
ZAMARRAS	ZARIBAS	ZEKS	ZIBELINE	ZINCO
ZAMARRO	ZARNEC	ZEL	ZIBELINES	ZINCODE
ZAMARROS	ZARNECS	ZELANT	ZIBELLINE	ZINCODES
ZAMBO	ZARNICH	ZELANTS	ZIBELLINES	ZINCOID
ZAMBOMBA	ZARNICHS	ZELOSO	ZIBET	ZINCOS
ZAMBOMBAS	ZARZUELA	ZELOTYPIA	ZIBETS	ZINCOUS
ZAMBOORAK	ZARZUELAS	ZELOTYPIAS	ZIFF	ZINCS
ZAMBOORAKS	ZASTRUGA	ZELS	ZIFFIUS	ZINCY
ZAMBOS	ZASTRUGI	ZEMINDAR	ZIFFIUSES	Z:NEB
ZAMIA	ZATI	ZEMINDARI	ZIFFS	ZINEBS
ZAMIAS	ZATIS	ZEMINDARIES	ZIG	ZINFANDEL
ZAMINDAR	ZAX	ZEMINDARIS	ZIGAN	ZINFANDELS
ZAMINDARI	ZAXES	ZEMINDARS	ZIGANKA	ZING
ZAMINDARIS	ZEA	ZEMINDARY	ZIGANKAS	ZINGED
ZAMINDARS	ZEAL	ZEMSTVO	ZIGANS	ZINGEL
ZAMOUSE	ZEALANT	ZEMSTVOS	ZIGGED	ZINGELS
ZAMOUSES	ZEALANTS	ZENANA	ZIGGING	ZINGIBER
ZAMPOGNA	ZEALFUL	ZENANAS	ZIGGURAT	ZINGIBERS
ZAMPOGNAS	ZEALLESS	ZENDIK	ZIGGURATS	ZINGIER
ZANDER	ZEALOT	ZENDIKS	ZIGS	ZINGIEST
ZANDERS	ZEALOTISM	ZENITH	ZIGZAG	ZINGING
ZANELLA	ZEALOTISMS	ZENITHAL	ZIGZAGGED	ZINGS
ZANELLAS	ZEALOTRIES	ZENITHS	ZIGZAGGING	ZINGY
ZANIED	ZEALOTRY	ZEOLITE	ZIGZAGGY	ZINKE
ZANIER	ZEALOTS	ZEOLITES	ZIGZAGS	ZINKED
ZANIES	ZEALOUS	ZEOLITIC	ZIKKURAT	ZINKENITE
ZANIEST	ZEALOUSLY	ZEPHYR	ZIKKURATS	ZINKENITES
ZANJA	ZEALS	ZEPHYRS	ZILA	ZINKES
ZANJAS	ZEAS	ZEPPELIN	ZILAS	ZINKIER
ZANJERO	ZEBEC	ZEPPELINS	ZILCH	ZINKIEST
ZANJEROS	ZEBECK	ZERDA	ZILCHES	ZINKIFIED
ZANTE	ZEBECKS	ZERDAS	ZILLAH	ZINKIFIES
ZANTES	ZEBECS	ZEREBA	ZILLAHS	ZINKIFY
ZANY	ZEBRA	ZEREBAS	ZILLION	ZINKIFYING
ZANYING	ZEBRAS	ZERIBA	ZILLIONS	ZINKING
ZANYISM	ZEBRASS	ZERIBAS	ZILLIONTH	ZINKY

ZINNIA
ZINNIAS
ZIP
ZIPPED
ZIPPER
ZIPPERED
ZIPPERS
ZIPPIER
ZIPPIEST
ZIPPING
ZIPPY
ZIPS
ZIPTOP
ZIRCALLOY
ZIRCALLOYS
ZIRCON
ZIRCONIA
ZIRCONIAS
ZIRCONIC
ZIRCONIUM
ZIRCONIUMS
ZIRCONS
ZIT
ZITHER
ZITHERN
ZITHERNS
ZITHERS
ZITS
ZIZ
ZIZEL
ZIZELS
ZIZZ
ZIZZED
ZIZZES
ZIZZING
ZLOTY
ZLOTYS
ZO
ZOA
ZOARIUM
ZOARIUMS
ZOBO
ZOBOS
ZOBU
ZOBUS
ZOCCO
ZOCCOLO
ZOCCOLOS
ZOCCOS
ZODIAC
ZODIACAL
ZODIACS
ZOEA
ZOEAE
ZOEAL
ZOEAS
ZOECHROME
ZOECHROMES
ZOEFORM
ZOETIC
ZOETROPE
ZOETROPES
ZOETROPIC
ZOIATRIA
ZOIATRIAS
ZOIATRICS
ZOIC
ZOISITE
ZOISITES
ZOISM
ZOISMS

ZOIST
ZOISTS
ZOMBI
ZOMBIE
ZOMBIES
ZOMBIISM
ZOMBIISMS
ZOMBIS
ZOMBORUK
ZOMBORUKS
ZONA
ZONAE
ZONAL
ZONARY
ZONATE
ZONATED
ZONATION
ZONATIONS
ZONDA
ZONDAS
ZONE
ZONED
ZONELESS
ZONES
ZONING
ZONINGS
ZONKED
ZONOID
ZONULA
ZONULAR
ZONULAS
ZONULE
ZONULES
ZONULET
ZONULETS
ZOO
ZOOBIOTIC
ZOOBLAST
ZOOBLASTS
ZOOCHORE
ZOOCHORES
ZOOCHORIES
ZOOCHORY
ZOOCYTIA
ZOOCYTIUM
ZOOEA
ZOOEAE
ZOOEAL
ZOOEAS
ZOOECIA
ZOOECIUM
ZOOGAMETE
ZOOGAMETES
ZOOGAMIES
ZOOGAMOUS
ZOOGAMY
ZOOGENIC
ZOOGENIES
ZOOGENOUS
ZOOGENY
ZOOGLOEA
ZOOGLOEAS
ZOOGLOEIC
ZOOGONIES
ZOOGONOUS
ZOOGONY
ZOOGRAFT
ZOOGRAFTS
ZOOGRAPHIES
ZOOGRAPHY
ZOOID

ZOOIDAL
ZOOIDS
ZOOKS
ZOOLATER
ZOOLATERS
ZOOLATRIA
ZOOLATRIAS
ZOOLATRIES
ZOOLATRY
ZOOLITE
ZOOLITES
ZOOLITH
ZOOLITHIC
ZOOLITHS
ZOOLITIC
ZOOLOGIES
ZOOLOGIST
ZOOLOGISTS
ZOOLOGY
ZOOM
ZOOMANCIES
ZOOMANCY
ZOOMANTIC
ZOOMED
ZOOMETRIC
ZOOMETRIES
ZOOMETRY
ZOOMING
ZOOMORPH
ZOOMORPHIES
ZOOMORPHS
ZOOMORPHY
ZOOMS
ZOON
ZOONAL
ZOONIC
ZOONITE
ZOONITES
ZOONITIC
ZOONOMIA
ZOONOMIAS
ZOONOMIC
ZOONOMIES
ZOONOMIST
ZOONOMISTS
ZOONOMY
ZOONOSES
ZOONOSIS
ZOONOTIC
ZOONS
ZOOPATHIES
ZOOPATHY
ZOOPERAL
ZOOPERIES
ZOOPERIST
ZOOPERISTS
ZOOPERY
ZOOPHAGAN
ZOOPHAGANS
ZOOPHILE
ZOOPHILES
ZOOPHILIA
ZOOPHILIAS
ZOOPHILIES
ZOOPHILY
ZOOPHOBIA
ZOOPHOBIAS
ZOOPHORIC
ZOOPHORUS
ZOOPHORUSES
ZOOPHYTE

ZOOPHYTES
ZOOPHYTIC
ZOOPLASTIES
ZOOPLASTY
ZOOS
ZOOSCOPIC
ZOOSCOPIES
ZOOSCOPY
ZOOSPERM
ZOOSPERMS
ZOOSPORE
ZOOSPORES
ZOOSPORIC
ZOOTAXIES
ZOOTAXY
ZOOTECHNIES
ZOOTECHNY
ZOOTHECIA
ZOOTHEISM
ZOOTHEISMS
ZOOTHOME
ZOOTHOMES
ZOOTOMIC
ZOOTOMIES
ZOOTOMIST
ZOOTOMISTS
ZOOTOMY
ZOOTOXIN
ZOOTOXINS
ZOOTROPE
ZOOTROPES
ZOOTROPHIES
ZOOTROPHY
ZOOTYPE
ZOOTYPES
ZOOTYPIC
ZOOZOO
ZOOZOOS
ZOPILOTE
ZOPILOTES
ZOPPO
ZORGITE
ZORGITES
ZORIL
ZORILLE
ZORILLES
ZORILLO
ZORILLOS
ZORILS
ZORINO
ZORINOS
ZORRO
ZORROS
ZOS
ZOSTER
ZOSTERS
ZOUNDS
ZOUNDSES
ZOWIE
ZUCCHETTO
ZUCCHETTOS
ZUCCHINI
ZUCCHINIS
ZUCHETTA
ZUCHETTAS
ZUCHETTO
ZUCHETTOS
ZUFFOLI
ZUFFOLO
ZUFOLI
ZUFOLO

ZUGZWANG
ZUGZWANGS
ZULU
ZULUS
ZUMBOORUK
ZUMBOORUKS
ZUPA
ZUPAN
ZUPANS
ZUPAS
ZURF
ZURFS
ZUZ
ZUZES
ZYGAENID
ZYGAENINE
ZYGAENOID
ZYGAL
ZYGANTRA
ZYGANTRUM
ZYGANTRUMS
ZYGODONT
ZYGOMA
ZYGOMAS
ZYGOMATIC
ZYGON
ZYGONS
ZYGOPHYTE
ZYGOPHYTES
ZYGOSE
ZYGOSES
ZYGOSIS
ZYGOSPERM
ZYGOSPERMS
ZYGOSPORE
ZYGOSPORES
ZYGOTE
ZYGOTES
ZYGOTIC
ZYLONITE
ZYLONITES
ZYMASE
ZYMASES
ZYME
ZYMES
ZYMIC
ZYMITE
ZYMITES
ZYMOGEN
ZYMOGENIC
ZYMOGENS
ZYMOID
ZYMOLITIC
ZYMOLOGIC
ZYMOLOGIES
ZYMOLOGY
ZYMOLYSES
ZYMOLYSIS
ZYMOME
ZYMOMES
ZYMOMETER
ZYMOMETERS
ZYMOSES
ZYMOSIS
ZYMOTIC
ZYMURGIES
ZYMURGY
ZYTHUM
ZYTHUMS